PROCEEDINGS OF THE FORTY-NINTH COLLOQUIUM ON THE LAW OF OUTER SPACE

INTERNATIONAL INSTITUTE OF SPACE LAW

2–6 OCTOBER 2006
VALENCIA, SPAIN

AIAA
The World's Forum for Aerospace Leadership

Published and Distributed by
AMERICAN INSTITUTE OF AERONAUTICS AND ASTRONAUTICS

Editor:
Corinne M. Contant Jorgenson
Washington, D.C., USA

ISBN-13: 978-1-56347-877-2
ISBN-10: 1-56347-877-3

Printed in the U.S.A.

IISL BOARD OF DIRECTORS 2006-2007

INTRODUCTION

BY

N. JASENTULIYANA

PRESIDENT

Once again, this year was a busy year for the members of the Institute. Considering the multidisciplinary nature of issues arising from the exploration and use of outer space, the Institute's programs must afford opportunities to analyze national and international legal matters in the total context of space science, technology as well as social sciences by rallying the specialists in various disciplines relating to space activities.

With this in view, multiple events were organized, during the year under review, to provide such interdisciplinary interaction among scholars and practitioners. The Plenary Session organized by the Institute in Valencia on the subject of 'Enabling the Frontier: Regulatory Challenges to the Utilization of Space', with a panel consisting of scientists, managers and lawyers, attracted a large number of scientists and engineers attending the International Astronautical Congress and was a resounding success.

Similarly, the Institute had the honor to co-organize with the Institute of Air and Space Law at McGill University, an 'International Interdisciplinary Workshop on Policy and Law Relating to Outer Space Resources: The Example of the Moon, Mars and Other Celestial Bodies', in honor of our Honorary Director Dr. Eilene Galloway to commemorate her one hundredth birthday. It was held in Montreal in June, and a group of leading space scientists, engineers, managers, lawyers and academics examined every facet of the subject and produced an extensive report. Later, on 11th December, the Institute co-organized with the National Center for Remote Sensing, Air & Space Law at the University of Mississippi School of Law, a one day interdisciplinary meeting, the Eilene M. Galloway Symposium on Critical Issues in Space Law, at the Cosmos Club in Washington DC and attended by a group of invited high level space scientists, lawyers and astronauts.

Two other opportunities for a broad-scale discussion of space issues were provided by the fourth in the Institute's series of regional conferences held in Bangkok in August on the subject of 'Asian cooperation in space activities: a common approach to legal matters'. The other was the IISL/ECSL Symposium organized in Vienna for the benefit of members of the Legal Sub-Committee of the United Nations COPUOS on the subject of 'Legal Aspects of Disaster Management and the Contribution of the Law of Outer Space'.

As for other significant aspects of the Institute's work, it is gratifying that younger members are taking an active part in the work of the Institute as evinced by the large number of papers presented by young authors in Valencia as was the case in other recent Colloquia. The Institute encouraged this trend with the award of the Diederiks-Verschoor Medal and Prize for the best paper presented by a young author at the annual Colloquia.

Another manifestation of the interest of the young is the enthusiastic participation of large number of university students in the Manfred Lachs Space Law Moot Court Competition. This year, the number of universities participating in the competition at regional level increased significantly.

In recognition of the desirability of strengthening the important role played by the younger members of the Institute and students, proposals are being considered for enhancing the presentation of papers and discussion by young authors at the annual Colloquia, including the possibility of arranging for a special session for the presentation and discussion of such papers. This proposal is also considered in the context of enabling at the same time to raise the level of papers and discussions at the other sessions of the Colloquia. Thus, the Institute continues to explore innovative ways of increasing its effectiveness. Specific proposals are being formulated and will be considered soon.

In the mean time, continuing activities of the Institute have proceeded in a most satisfactory manner. The annual Colloquium held in Valencia attracted a good number of scholars who presented papers and conducted a spirited discussion of current and important space law issues. The Manfred Lachs Space Law Moot Court Regional Competitions in North America, Europe and Asia Pacific regions continued to be successfully conducted, as was the finals of the competition held in Valencia judged by three judges of the International Court of Justice. The Institute is grateful to the judges for their generous support, which makes the competition uniquely prestigious. The annual IISL dinner in Valencia was held at an elegant location with an historic ambiance and with the judges of the World Court and other high ranking IAC and local officials in attendance.

Cooperation with the United Nations continued with the holding of the annual symposium organized by IISL with ECSL during the Legal Sub-Committee of COPUOS and the preparation of two reports (one, on the work of the Institute and the other, comprising part of the "Highlights in Space" publication of the UN). Several IISL members attended the annual meetings of COPUOS and its subsidiary bodies as well as the workshops conducted by the United Nations for the benefit of participants from developing countries.

The Institute continued close cooperation with IAA particularly in the work of the IAA/IISL joint legal/scientific Roundtable on Nuclear Power Systems in Space. held in Valencia. The Institute also continued its close collaboration with IAF.

Finally, I wish to place on record my grateful appreciation of the support given by members of the Institute without which a voluntary organization such as the Institute cannot thrive. Foremost among them, is of course, our dedicated and highly competent Secretary, Ms. Tanja Masson-Zwaan, who spared no effort in seeing that multifaceted tasks are carried out in due time. Her continuing friendly and efficient cooperation with the Board and members at large, is vital to the success of the work of the Institute. Our Treasurer Dr. Frans von der Dunk has carried out his tasks in a very professional manner and this year, he undertook the additional burden of carrying out the arduous task of establishing the Institute as an association in the Netherlands, a task that he successfully completed, for all of which, the Institute is most grateful to him.

The Local Organizing Committee members overseeing the arrangements for IISL activities in Valencia led by Ms. Esther Enjuto should be congratulated and thanked for the outstanding arrangements they made for the Valencia Colloquium, the Moot Court and the Annual Dinner.

I am grateful to Dr. Sylvia Ospina and Dr. Ingo Baumann for assisting the Institute in preparing the Institute's contribution to the report on Highlights in Space that were submitted to the United Nations; to Dr. Andrei Terekhov, Chairman of the committee which prepared the report on the Status of International Space Treaties; to Dr. Corinne Contant-Jorgenson and AIAA staff who assisted in the preparation of the manuscript of the Institute's annual Proceedings published by AIAA; to Prof. Ram Jakhu for organizing the Workshop in Montreal and Prof. Paul Dempsey for his strong support for the meeting; to Dr. Stephen Doyle for preparing the final report of the Montreal Workshop and conducting the task force charged to help in its preparation; Prof. Joanne Gabrynowicz for organizing the one day meeting held in Washington DC and Ms. Marcia Smith for her support for this event; to Prof. Nipant Chitasombat for organizing the IISL Regional Conference in Bangkok, Thailand; to Mr. Chris Stott for organizing the IISL Plenary in Valencia; to Mr. Ricky Lee, Dr. Skip Smith and Mr. Alberto Marchini for organizing the regional rounds of the Moot Court; the judges of the semifinals and the written briefs of the Moot Court and the team that prepared the case; to the members of the nominating committee and members of the jury which selected the best paper presented at the Valencia Colloquium; as well as to the other members of the Institute who assisted its work in numerous other ways. Without their commitment the work of the Institute would not be carried out with success and therefore their support is gratefully acknowledged.

I look forward to another successful year in which new orientations and activities that are already under consideration would be introduced to enhance the continuing work of the Institute.

GENERAL INFORMATION

I. Background

The International Institute of Space Law (IISL) was founded by the International Astronautical Federation (IAF) in 1960. The IISL replaced the Permanent Committee on Space Law which the IAF had created in 1958 under the chairmanship of Andrew G. Haley. Since 1958, the IISL has held annual colloquia on space law in many nations. The IISL presently has elected individual and institutional members from over 40 countries, who are distinguished for their contributions to space law development. While a component of the IAF, the IISL is authorized to function autonomously in accordance with its Statutes.

The purposes and objectives of the Institute include the cooperation with appropriate international organizations and national institutions in the field of space law, the carrying out of tasks for fostering the social science aspects of astronautics, space travel and exploration, the organization of meetings and colloquia on juridical and sociological aspects of the space sciences, and the publication of proceedings, reports and other publications. Each year, the Institute publishes a report of the Standing Committee on the Status of International Agreements Relating to Activities in Outer Space, headed by Dr. A. Terekhov.

The financial resources of the Institute are derived from membership dues, research grants, remuneration received from the sale of its publications, and donations received from individuals, associations, institutions, foundations, and other organizations with interests in the development of law governing space activities.

II. IISL and the United Nations

IISL members have been appointed by the International Astronautical Federation as Official Observers to annual sessions of the United Nations (UN) Committee on the Peaceful Uses of Outer Space and its Legal Subcommittee. In addition, the IISL has, like in past years, prepared a report on legal developments under contract with the UN, to be published in the annual Highlights in Space Report, and provides yearly reports on its activities to the Legal Subcommittee.
On 26 and 27 March 2007 the IISL and ECSL will again co-organize a symposium for the delegates and staff of the Legal Subcommittee session. The symposium, which for the first time will cover two half days, will deal with *Space Law Capacity Building*.

III. 49th IISL Colloquium

The 49th IISL Colloquium was held from 2-6 October 2006 in Valencia, Spain. Around 70 papers had been accepted for 5 sessions. About 15 papers were withdrawn, and 6 were summarized by others. The colloquium was well attended and discussion was good. Most papers and presentations had been uploaded to the central system. The following sessions were held:

1. Legal aspects of space transportation and launching;
2. Legal aspects of disaster management;
3. International cooperation in space activities, with special focus on remote sensing;
4. Space law at times of armed conflict;
5. Other legal matters, including the relationship between government and private sector in space activities.

A Scientific/Legal Roundtable was held in Valencia on "Nuclear Power Systems in space – the new reality".
IISL also organised a Plenary Session on the topic 'Enabling the Frontier: Regulatory Challenges to the Utilization of Space'. Finally. Lastly, a late breaking news (LBN) event on the new definition of planets was initiated by IISL.

Manfred Lachs Space Law Moot Court Competition

The 15th Manfred Lachs Space Law Moot Court Competition was held during the Valencia IISL Colloquium. The *Case concerning the Sale and Operation of Certain Commercial Remote Sensing Satellites (Galatea v Thalassa: Proteus Intervening)* was written by Ricky Lee.

Preliminaries were held at regional level in Europe (6 teams), North America (10 teams) and in the Asia Pacific region (40 teams). The Finals were judged by three Judges of the International Court of Justice, Judge Abdul Koroma, Judge Peter Tomka and Judge Bernardo Sepúlveda.

The local organising committee, the Generalitat Valenciana - Conselleria de Justicia, Interior y Administraciones Públicas, the Facultad de Derecho, Universitat de València, the Universidad Nacional de Educación a Distancia (UNED) in Valencia, the University CEU-Cardenal Herrera, and Colegio Notarial de Valencia kindly sponsored the 2006 World Finals and IISL Dinner. In addition, McGill IASL, ESA/ ECSL and JAXA sponsored the winners of the regional rounds, and DLR published the Brochure of the moot court.

The results of the world finals were as follows:

- **Winner**: University of Auckland, New Zealand (James Townshend and Jonathan Orpin; Coach: Mr. Isaac Hikaka)
- **Runner-up:** Institute of Air and Space Law, McGill University (IASL), Montreal, Canada (Michael Taylor, Susan Trepczynski and Andrew Williams; Coach: Prof. Ram Jakhu)
- **2nd Runner-up**: Catholic University, Leuven, Belgium (Emmanuel De Groof, Gareth Price and Batist Paklons; Coach: Dr. Walter Thiebaut)
- **Eilene M. Galloway Award** for Best Written Brief: Institute of Air and Space Law, McGill University
- **Sterns and Tennen Award** for Best Oralist: Mr Andrew Williams (Institute of Air and Space Law, McGill University)

A report on the competition, the case and the finalists' briefs are published in this volume. The competition will be held for the 16th time in Hyderabad, India, in September 2007.

IV. Awards

A Lifetime Achievement Award was presented to Dr. Lubos Perek (Czech Republic), and a Distinguished Service Award was presented to Mr. Leslie Tennen (USA).
The Dr. I.H.Ph. Diederiks-Verschoor Award and Prize were given for the 6th time in Valencia, to Dr. Yun Zhao from City University in Hong Kong, for his paper "Protection of Intellectual Property Rights in Outer Space", published in these Proceedings. This Award honours the best paper presented at an IISL Colloquium by an author not older than 40 years and who has not published more than five papers in the Proceedings of IISL Colloquia. A total of 4 papers had been submitted. The Award consists of a medal and a money prize of 500 Euros.

V. Publications

• *Proceedings IISL Colloqiuia*: The Fukuoka Proceedings have been published by the AIAA. The publication contract with AIAA has been renewed up to and including the publication of the proceedings of the 2010 Colloquium.

• *Proceedings India Conference:* ISRO has published the Proceedings of the conference held in Bangalore in June 2005.

• *Summary Report of the McGill Workshop:* The McGill Institute of Air and Space Law has published a summary report of the "IASL-IISL International and Interdisciplinary Workshop on Policy and Law Relating to Outer Space Resources: the Example of the Moon, Mars and Other Celestial Bodies", held in June 2006 in Montreal. McGill will also publish the proceedings of the Workshop.

• *Proceedings of the Bangkok regional space law conference*: The McGill Institute of Air and Space Law will publish the proceedings of this IISL regional conference, held in August 2006 in Bangkok, Thailand.

• *History of the IISL:* the book "Origins of International Space Law and the International Institute of Space Law of the International Astronautical Federation" (Univelt, 2002, see http://univelt.com/univeltpubs/index.html for details) can be purchased at the special price of USD 25. Contact the Secretary.

• *Standing Committee on the Status of International Agreements Relating to Activities in Outer Space*, Dr. Terekhov's report is as usual included in these Proceedings.

• *UN Contract for IISL contribution to Highlights in Space Report:* the report has been prepared by Dr. Sylvia Ospina and Dr. Ingo Baumann.

VI. Registering the IISL

The General Assembly in Valencia adopted by consensus a proposal for amendment of the Statutes, necessary to comply with Dutch law in order to register the Institute in the Netherlands. After registration, a new committee will look at the Bye-Laws and other issues that may need updating.

VII. The Eilene Galloway Symposium on Critical Issues in Space Law

On December 11, 2006, this event was organised by the National Center for Remote Sensing, Air, and Space Law at the University of Mississippi School of Law, the Journal of Space Law, and the IISL, at the Cosmos Club in Washington DC.

Speakers were Dr. Jonathan F. Galloway, Dr. Stephen Doyle, Dr. George Robinson, Dr. Rusty Schweickart and Ms. Corinne Jorgenson, and a Panel Discussion was moderated by Prof. Joanne Irene Gabrynowicz. Mrs Galloway was unable to attend in pertson, but a special video message by her was broadcast for the participants.

The Center will host "The 2nd Eilene M. Galloway Symposium on Critical Issues in Space Law" on December 10, 2007 at the Cosmos Club.

VIII. 50th IISL Colloquium

The 50th IISL Colloquium on the Law of Outer Space will be held from 24 to 28 September 2007 in Hyderabad, India. The theme is: Touching Humanity: Space for Improving Quality of Life. The Colloquium will have the following session-topics:

1. *The Impact of Outer Space Law on Regional Policies*

This session will focus on outer space policy and the legal implication on national law in Europe, Asia and America. Particularly, it will look into regional coordination as well as current and future programs and legislations.

2. *Legal Issues of Private Spaceflight and Space Tourism*

Since the X-Prize was won in October 2004, plans for private spaceflight bringing tourists into outer space have rapidly grown. The session solicits papers addressing the many legal aspects of these developments, as well as the broader contexts of private spaceflight in the service of public manned missions.

3. *New Legal Developments in the Protection of the Space Environment*

This session will combine views on space debris and planetary protection. In the field of space debris mitigation, the UN is in the course of adopting guidelines and national space legislation and licensing regimes provide new means for establishing innovative regulation. In the field of planetary protection, the recent plans for space exploration have to be checked with existing and to-be-developed regulations. The session aims at providing new ideas for legal but also ethical approaches.

4. *Legal Aspects of Satellite Navigation*

Legal aspects of satellite navigation including air traffic services applications, are becoming ever more important with

GALILEO shortly coming online, GPS being planned for modernization and Russia's efforts to bring GLONASS back to full operational status. Moreover, these developments take place in a broader context such as satellite communications and remote sensing (including geographical information systems). This session intends to address the legal issues involved both at the global and national levels.

5. *40th Anniversary of the Outer Space Treaty, and other legal matters*

In this session, authors are invited to write papers focusing on the 40th Anniversary of the Outer Space Treaty, not only looking back but also discussing its values for the future of space activity. They may also address any other matters relating to the law of outer space, with special emphasis on recent developments.

In Hyderabad, the IISL will celebrate its 50th Colloquium, as well as the 40th anniversary of the Outer Space Treaty and the 50th of the International Geophysical Year (IGY). IISL may organise a one day event prior to the IAC. Ideas are to be finalised.

A *Scientific/Legal Roundtable* will be held in Hyderabad on "Google Earth et al. – Pros and cons of easier access to satellite images".

IISL has also proposed a *Plenary Session* which has been accepted. It will address "New Space Industry Actors in the Global Market Place; Policy and Regulatory Aspects".

Manfred Lachs Space Law Moot Court Competition

The world finals of the 16th Manfred Lachs Space Law Moot Court Competition will be held during the 2007 Colloquium in Hyderabad. The *Case Concerning International Liability (Emeralda v Mazonia)* was written by Jean-François Mayence and David Sagar. Three Judges of the International Court of Justice will be invited to judge the Finals. Regional rounds will be held in the Asia Pacific, Europe, and North America, and details about each round and the case are on www.spacemoot.org

IX. 51st IISL Colloquium

The 51st Colloquium on the law of outer space will be held during the IAF Congress in Glasgow, Scotland, from 29 September – 3 October 2008. The session topics for this colloquium will be decided in Spring 2007.

X. Elections 2006

Board of Directors:
Dr. von der Dunk, Prof. Galloway, Prof. Kopal, Prof. Kosuge, Ms. Masson-Zwaan, Prof. Monserrat, Mr. Murthi, Dr. Ospina, Prof. Gabrynowicz, and Prof. Kapustin were (re-)elected. Prof. Kopal and Prof. Galloway were (re-) elected Vice-President. Ms. Masson-Zwaan was re-elected Secretary, and Dr. von der Dunk was re-elected Treasurer. Ms. Marcia Smith and Dr. Terekhov had announced that they would not stand for re-election.

Members: The following 2 institutional and 22 individual members were elected throughout 2006:

INSTITUTIONAL:

MacDonald, Dettwiler and Associates, Ltd
Ms. Indra Heed
13800 Commerce Parkway
Richmond, BC,
V6V 2J3 CANADA
T 1-604 278 3411
F 1-604 231 2759
E iheed@mdacorporation.com

Devas Multimedia America, Inc.
Mr. Ramachandran Viswanathan
CEO & President
One Metro Center,
700 12th Street, NW, Suite 700
Washington, DC 20005. USA
T 1-202-536-3240
E rv@devasmedia.com

INDIVIDUAL:

Dr. iur. Ingo BAUMANN
Contract Management
German Aerospace Centre DLR
Linder Höhe
51147 Cologne, GERMANY
T 49-2203 601 2908
F 49-2203 601 2893
E ingo.baumann@dlr.de

Prof. Dr. Christian BRÜNNER
University of Graz, Institute for Austrian, European & Comparative Public Law, Political Sciences & Public Administration
Universitätsstrasse 15 C/3, A-8010 Graz, AUSTRIA
T 43 316 380 3388
F 43 316 380 9450/
E christian.bruenner@uni-graz.at

Dr. Maria BUZDUGAN
McGill University, IASL
3661 Peel street
Montreal Quebec H3A 1X1 CANADA
T 1-514 3985093
F 1-514 398 8197
E Maria.Buzdugan@mcgill.ca

Ms Macha EJOVA
Analyst Space & Communications
Euroconsult
163, Bld Lefebvre 75015 Paris, FRANCE
ejova@euroconsult-ec.com/ ejovama@voila.fr

Dr. Annette FROEHLICH
Angerstrasse 14
D86179 Augsburg, GERMANY
T 49 221 470 2988
E annette.froehlich@web.de

Mr. Isaac HIKAKA
PO Box 2026, Shortland Street
Auckland, NEW ZEALAND
T 64 9912 7116 / 64 2121 69532
F 64-9912 7109
E isaac.hikaka@lsl.co.nz

Mr William N. HULSEY
Principal, Hulsey Intellectual Property Lawyers P.C.
1250 S. Capital of Texas Highway, Bldg 3, S. 610
Austin, Texas 78746, USA
T 1-512 795 1295
F 1-512 795 1295
E bill.hulsey@hulseyiplaw.com

Corinne JORGENSON
President , Advancing Space Consulting Group
10509 Center Street, Suite 100
Fairfax, VA 22030, USA
T 1-703-655-3813
F 1-703-352-2998
E cmj@advancingspace.com

Ms Yukiko KODACHI
3-15-7 Kamitakada Nakano-ku
Tokyo, 164-0002 JAPAN
T 3-3386 8459
F 3-3386 8459
E kodachov@nifty.com

Ms. Donna LAWLER
Corporate Counsel
SingTel Optus Pty Limited
Level 29 101 Miller Street,
North Sydney NSW 2022, AUSTRALIA
T (612) 9342 9361
F (612) 9342 7667
E Donna.Lawler@optus.com.au

Mr. Philip MEEK
Associate General Counsel, USAF
6319 Falling Brook Drive
Burke, Virginia 22015, USA
T 1-703 697 4370
F 1-703 695 0889
E philip.meek@pentagon.af.mil

Mr Muhamed MUSTAQUE
M.K. Associates
Power House Extension road, Cochin-18
Kerala , PIN 682018 INDIA
T 91-9447197815
F 91-4842397815
E mushiamm@hotmail.com / mushiamm@yahoo.com

Ms Julia NEUMANN
Schaafenstrasse 27-29
D50676 Cologne, GERMANY
T 49 221 5800668
E jneuman4@uni-koeln.de

Ms. Zeldine O'BRIEN
134 Broadmeadows
Swords, County Dublin, IRELAND
T 44-1-840 3514
E zeldineobrien@gmail.com

Ms. Isabel PESSOA-LOPES
Consultant, Space Risks
Flat 3, "Redholme", The Hermitage
Richmond, Surrey TW10 6SH, UNITED KINGDOM
T 44-20 894 84 862
E ipl@spacerisks.com

Mr. Ray PURDY
Faculty of Laws, University College London
Bentham House, Endsleigh Gardens
London WC1H 0EG, UNITED KINGDOM
T 44-207 679 4554
F 44-207 679 1440
E raymond.purdy@ucl.ac.uk

Prof. Sang-Myon RHEE
Professor of Law, College of Law,
Seoul National University
Gwanag-gu, Seoul 151-743, SOUTH KOREA
T 82-2 880 7561
F 82-2 871 7408
E smrhee@snu.ac.kr

Prof. Eligar SADEH
Professor of Space Studies
Department of Space Studies, Univ. of North Dakota
Clifford Hall Room 532
4149 University Ave. Stop 9008
Grand Forks, ND 58202-9008 USA
T 1-701-777-3462
F 1-701-777-3711
E sadeh@space.edu

Ms Amanda SHAFER
Associate
Shearman & Sterling LLP
801 Pennsylvania Ave., N.W.
Washington, D.C. 20004, USA
T 1-202 508 8105
amanda.shafer@shearman.com

Ms. Justine WHITE
University of Witswatersrand
PO Box 1044
Gallo Manor, 2052, SOUTH AFRICA
T 27-11 656 9122
F 27-11 656 9106
E whitej@law.wits.ac.za

Prof.. Haifeng ZHAO
Professor and Dean,
Harbin Institute of Technology, School of Law
92 West Dazhi Street
P.O. Box 235, Harbin, 150001, P.R. CHINA
T 86- 451 86402419
F 86- 451 86402419
E zhaohaifeng-c@yahoo.com.cn

Ms. Ilaria ZILIOLI
Contracts Officer
ESA, 8-10, rue Mario Nikis
75015 Paris, FRANCE
T +33.1.53697179
E ilaria.zilioli@esa.int

TRIBUTE TO DR. EILENE MARIE GALLOWAY-SLACK

Dr. Eilene Marie Galloway-Slack was born in Kansas City, Missouri, on May 4, 1906. She married George Galloway in 1924 and has two sons, David and Jonathan, six grandchildren, and five great-grandchildren.

Dr. Galloway graduated from Swarthmore College in 1928 and holds honorary doctorates from Swarthmore and Lake Forest College.

She was working as a senior specialist in international relations of of what is now known as the Congressional Research Service at the Library of Congress. Among her many functions, she worked with Senate Majority Leader Lyndon B. Johnson and Chairman Richard Russell of the Senate Armed Services Committee. She also took part in drafting the National Aeronautics and Space Act of 1958, which established NASA and has remained an enduring framework for U.S. civil space policy. Dr. Galloway acted as a consultant to NASA and the State Department on policy and law, regarding the exploration and utilization of outer space.

At the occasion of her 100th birthday, Hon. Bart Cordon mentioned rightly during a session of the House of Representatives that, throughout her professional career, Dr. Galloway has been an influential force in the development and analysis of domestic and international space policy and law.

She is an Honorary Fellow of the American Institute of Aeronautics and Astronautics. Also, she received the Lifetime Achievement Award from the International Academy of Astronautics and the International Institute of Space Law and numerous other awards.

The International Institute of Space Law was very happy to have Eilene Galloway as Vice President from 1967 to1979. After that she was elected Honorary Director. Even now, the Institute continues to consult her for advice. She has lived her life of distinguished service to the United States and to the space community and she has been an inspiration to us all—and above all, a reliable friend.

INTERNATIONAL INSTITUTE OF SPACE LAW
FORTY-NINTH COLLOQUIUM ON THE LAW OF OUTER SPACE

Valencia, Spain, 2–6 October 2006

The futuristic Palacio de Congresos, where the meetings were held.

Judges P. Tomka, A. Koroma, and B. Sepúlveda of the International Court of Justice with the finalists from McGill University (Canada) and the University of Auckland (New Zealand); the latter won the Manfred Lachs Trophy, while the former won the awards for Best Brief and Best Oralist.

First session, with Chairmen Dr. Peter van Fenema (Netherlands) and Dr. Alvaro Azcárraga (Sener, Spain), Rapporteur Petra Vorwig (USA), and Speaker Gen. Michael Wholley (NASA General Counsel, USA).

Dr. Leslie Tennen (USA) with the IISL Distinguished Services Award, and Dr. Lubos Perek (Czech Republic) with the IISL Lifetime Achievement Award.

Dr. Zhao Yun (Hong Kong) won the Isabella H.Ph. Diederiks-Verschoor Award for best paper by a young author; the award consists of a medal and a prize.

Semifinals between the regional winners from Europe (University of Leuven, Belgium) and Asia Pacific [University of Auckland (New Zealand)], with the judges, Dr. Olivier Ribbelink (Netherlands), Prof. Steven Freeland (Australia), and Ms. Marcia Smith (USA).

Dr. Rosa Maria Ramirez de Arrellano (Mexico), Prof. Elisabeth Back Impallomeni (Italy), and Mr. and Mrs. Casal (Switzerland).

Guests at the IISL Annual Dinner at the Masia del Siglo XIX, outside Valencia.

IASL - IISL INTERNATIONAL AND INTERDISCIPLINARY WORKSHOP
ON POLICY AND LAW RELATING TO OUTER SPACE RESOURCES: THE EXAMPLE OF THE MOON, MARS & OTHER CELESTIAL BODIES

McGill Institute of Air and Space Law, Montreal, Canada, 28–30 June 2006

Mr. Howard Baker, Dr. Leslie Tennen, IISL Honorary Director Dr. Steven Doyle, IISL Board Member Dr. Patricia Sterns, IISL President Nandasiri Jasentuliyana, Secretary Tanja Masson-Zwaan, and Treasurer Dr. Frans von der Dunk.

IISL Board Member Prof. Ram Jakhu with Dr. Leslie Tennen and Board Member Dr. Patricia Sterns.

Former classmates at McGill IASL, Prof. Paul Larsen, Dr. Jasentuliyana, and Dr. Steven Doyle, with their professor, Prof. Ivan Vlasic (2nd from left).

IISL SPACE LAW CONFERENCE 2006
ASIAN COOPERATION IN SPACE ACTIVITIES: A COMMON APPROACH TO LEGAL MATTERS

Bangkok, Thailand, 1–4 August 2006

Left to right: Speaker Dr. Visoot Tuvayanond (Thailand); Session Chairs Prof. V. Kopal (Czech Republic) and Prof. Elisabeth Back Impallomeni (Italy); Commentators Prof. Robert C. Beckman (Singapore) and Prof. Cheng Cia-jui (Taiwan ROC); and Rapporteur Dr. Maria Buzdugan (McGill IASL).

HRH Princess Maha Chakri Sirindhorn of Thailand, who opened the conference, welcomed by Prof. Nipant Chitasombat (Thailand), Tanja Masson-Zwaan (IISL Secretary), Prof. V. Kopal (IISL Vice-President), and Prof. Sompong Sucharitkul (Thailand).

Dr. I.B.R. Supancana (Indonesia) and Mr. K.R.S. Murthi (India).

Prof. V.S. Mani (India) and Prof. S.M. Rhee (Rep. of Korea).

Group photo of speakers and participants.

Prof. Sergio Marchisio (Italy), IISL Secretary Tanja Masson-Zwaan, and Ms. Debarupa Banerjee (India).

THE EILENE M. GALLOWAY SYMPOSIUM ON CRITICAL ISSUES IN SPACE LAW

Washington, D.C., December 2006

(Photos courtesy of The National Center for Remote Sensing, Air, and Space Law of the University of Mississippi School of Law.)

Dr. George Robinson, Dr. Rusty Schweickart, Prof. Joanne Gabrynowicz, Prof. Jonathan Galloway, and Dr. Maria Buzdugan.

Dr. Amanda L. Moore, Ms. Corinne Jorgenson, and Mr. Jason Steptoe, NASA HQ.

Mrs. Eilene Galloway receiving a visit from Prof. Joanne Gabrynowicz, her son Prof. Jonathan Galloway, and Tanja Masson-Zwaan on the occasion of the event held at the Cosmos Club.

Dr. Stephen Doyle with the Summary Report of the Montreal Workshop held in June 2006, which was at the basis of the Cosmos Club event. In the background, a video is playing containing a message from Dr. Eilene Galloway, who had initiated the Montreal Workshop.

Galloway Symposium participants.

TABLE OF CONTENTS

Session 2A:
THE MOON, PROPERTY RIGHTS AND LEGAL ISSUES

Session 3:
COOPERATION IN SPACE ACTIVITIES, WITH SPECIAL FOCUS ON REMOTE SENSING

Session 4: SPACE LAW AT TIMES OF ARMED CONFLICT

Session 5: OTHER LEGAL MATTERS, INCLUDING THE RELATIONSHIP BETWEEN GOVERNMENT AND PRIVATE SECTOR IN SPACE ACTIVITIES

SESSION REPORTS

LATE BREAKING NEWS SESSION: PLANET DEFINITION VALENCIA, SPAIN

IISL-ECSL SPACE LAW SYMPOSIUM 2006 HELD ON THE OCCASION OF THE 45TH SESSION OF THE LEGAL SUBCOMMITTEE OF UNCOPUOS, VIENNA, AUSTRIA

THE EILENE M. GALLOWAY SYMPOSIUM ON CRITICAL ISSUES IN SPACE LAW WASHINGTON, D.C., DECEMBER 2006

ADDENDA

Session 1:
LEGAL ASPECTS OF SPACE TRANSPORTATION AND LAUNCHING

Chairmen: Alvaro Azcarraga
Peter van Fenema

Rapporteur: Petra Vorwig

International Institute of Space Law
49th Colloquium on Law of Outer Space
Valencia, Spain
October 3, 2006

Paper: IAC-06-E6.1.01

THE U.S. "VISION FOR SPACE EXPLORATION" LEGAL ISSUES PRESENTED BY INNOVATIVE COMMERCIAL INITIATIVES

Michael C. Wholley
General Counsel
National Aeronautics and Space Administration
United States of America
(Michael.C.Wholley@NASA.gov)

Abstract

As part of the U.S. Vision for Space Exploration, NASA is forging significant partnerships with the developing commercial space sector. With the recent success of the Ansari X-Prize and other ongoing private space efforts, the potential for the commercial space sector to engage new markets, especially those involving human spaceflight, is stronger than ever. NASA is pursuing collaborations that will help expand the commercial space sector while simultaneously supporting NASA's mission and the Vision for Space Exploration. By working with established commercial launch service providers and encouraging development of the emerging entrepreneurial launch sector, NASA, consistent with its mandate under the National Aeronautics and Space Act, seeks to accelerate the growth of the commercial space industry.

In summarizing these initiatives and discussing the innovative statutory and contractual legal arrangements necessary for their success, the paper focuses primarily upon the most ambitious of them: a US$500 million "Commercial Orbital Transportation Services" (COTS) project for development and demonstration of technologies to deliver cargo – and at a later stage, humans – to low earth orbit, as well as on-orbit rendezvous and docking capabilities. The paper highlights the unique features of the COTS Demonstrations agreements. It also explains the legal and regulatory requirements to ensure COTS demonstrations are conducted consistent with U.S. international obligations under the Outer Space Treaty and Liability Convention.

Introduction

On January 14, 2004, President Bush set a new course for the U.S. space program and gave NASA "a new focus and vision for future exploration." He stated: "We will build new ships to carry man forward into the universe, to gain a new foothold on the moon, and to prepare for new journeys to worlds beyond our own."

Two important elements of this "Vision for Space Exploration" (VSE) bear highlighting. The first is the mandate to NASA to pursue opportunities for international participation in exploration activities. The second is to "pursue commercial opportunities for providing transportation and other services supporting the international space station and exploration missions beyond low earth orbit."[1]

In announcing the VSE, the President also chartered a national commission of business, academic, and government leaders to recommend specific measures for implementing the VSE.[2] One significant recommendation by the Commission was that NASA "aggressively use its contractual authority to reach broadly into the commercial and nonprofit communities to bring the best ideas, technologies and management tools into the accomplishment of exploration goals."[3] The Commission's report further recommended that "Congress increase the potential for commercial opportunities related to the national space exploration vision by providing incentives for entrepreneurial investment in space, by creating significant monetary prizes for the accomplishment of space missions and/or technology developments and by assuring appropriate property rights for those who seek to develop space resources and infrastructure."[4]

In implementing the VSE, NASA has moved aggressively to act on these recommendations:

Prizes

NASA has utilized legal authority from Congress to establish a "Centennial Challenges" program that is conducting prize competitions (or Challenges) that support the VSE and ongoing NASA programs. Specifically, the Centennial Challenges program conducts prize competitions to stimulate innovation in basic and applied research, technology development, and prototype demonstration that have potential application to NASA space and aeronautical activities.

By making awards based on actual achievements instead of proposals, Centennial Challenges encourages novel and lower-cost solutions to engineering ob-

[1] "A Renewed Spirit of Discovery: The Vision for Space Exploration," http://www.whitehouse.gov/space/renewed_spirit.html

[2] Executive Order 13326, President's Commission on Implementation of United States Space Exploration Policy, 27 January 2004.

[3] *A Journey to Inspire, Innovate, and Discover*, Report of the President's Commission on Implementation of United States Space Exploration Policy, Recommendation 5-1, p. 32 (June 2004).

[4] Recommendation 5-2, *Id.*, at p. 33.

stacles in civil space and aeronautics from sources of innovation in industry, academia, and the public. Currently, NASA has announced seven prize competitions for a total combined purse value of US$13.9 million. Team registration has already begun for six of these contests and the rules for the remaining one will soon be made final. Three of the Centennial Challenges competitions, the Beam Power Challenge, the Tether Challenge, and the Lunar Lander Challenge, will be conducted at this year's "X-Prize Cup" event to be held in Las Cruces, New Mexico on October 20-21.[5]

Venture Capital

NASA's Red Planet Capital project (also known as the "Enterprise Engine") has engaged a venture capital fund to provide NASA earlier and broader exposure to emerging technologies and to leverage external venture capital in the development of products with a likelihood of supporting NASA's future mission needs.

NASA recently entered into an agreement with Red Planet Capital, Inc. (RPC), a non-profit corporation, under which RPC will become a Limited Partner in a strategic investment fund called Red Planet Capital Partners, L.P. RPC will invest in the fund, monitor fund operations and receive fund distributions.

The fund will be operated by a team of three experienced venture capital fund managers. It will invest in emerging, privately-held companies developing innovative technologies with potential for both government and commercial applications. NASA will provide strategic direction and technical input for investments to RPC and the fund managers.

Commercial Orbital Transportation Services Demonstrations

In January 2006, NASA released an announcement concerning a "Commercial Orbital Transportation Services (COTS) Demonstrations" project, seeking proposals from U.S. companies for development and operation of an end-to-end space transportation system of services. The project will culminate with a crew/cargo transportation mission to and from a low earth orbit "test bed," such as the International Space Station. NASA will make available US$500 million for this effort over the next five years. These sums, however, will fund only a portion of the total anticipated investment needed to achieve mission objectives. Thus, to supplement this financial support, the companies receiving funding for COTS Demonstrations will need to obtain significant additional private funding and contribute substantial resources of their own.

Twenty companies responded to the COTS announcement. NASA entered into further negotiations with six of these companies. This past August, the agency selected two start-up space companies to receive funding for COTS Demonstrations:

- Space Exploration Technologies Corp. (SpaceX), El Segundo, California
- Rocketplane Kistler Limited, Inc. (RpK), Oklahoma City, Oklahoma.

[5] The X-Prize Foundation is conducting the Lunar Lander competition and the Spaceward Foundation is conducting the Beam Power and Tether competitions, all pursuant to Space Act agreements.

Each of the above commercial initiatives raises novel and sometimes complex legal and policy issues. This paper, however, will focus upon the largest and most ambitious of the initiatives: the COTS project. It examines how these issues are addressed in a unique NASA legal instrument used for funding COTS demonstrations: "funded" Space Act Agreements. It also explains the legal and regulatory requirements to ensure the COTS Demonstrations will be conducted in accordance with U.S. international obligations under the Outer Space Treaty[6] and Liability Convention.[7]

Overview of the COTS Demonstrations Program

NASA has established a "Commercial Crew/Cargo Program Office" within its Exploration Systems Mission Directorate. The major objectives of the Commercial Crew/Cargo Program are to:

- Implement U.S. space exploration policy with an investment to stimulate commercial enterprise in space;
- Facilitate demonstration by U.S. commercial providers of cargo and crew space transportation capabilities, with the goal of achieving reliable, cost effective access to low Earth orbit; and
- Create a market environment in which commercial space transportation services are available to Government and private sector customers.

COTS is the initial development and demonstration phase of the Commercial Crew/Cargo Program. NASA's agreements with SpaceX and RpK for COTS are for the purposes of developing and demonstrating the vehicles, systems and operations needed to re-supply and return cargo from a space facility, with the International Space Station providing the representative requirements for such a facility. Crew transport is included as a potential future option in each of the COTS Demonstrations agreements. If the options were to be funded, it would represent the first time NASA utilized non-government vehicles for human space flight.[8]

COTS represents a significant opportunity for U.S. commercial providers because of the likely needs for: (1) logistics support during International Space Station assembly, (2) cargo and crew transport during the time between Shuttle retirement in 2010 and the availability of NASA's Crew Exploration Vehicle (CEV) , and (3) the ongoing need for ISS transport capability even after the CEV becomes operational.

The goal is for successful flight demonstrations in the 2008-2010 timeframe.

---

6 Treaty on Principles Governing the Activities of States in the Exploration and Use of Outer Space, Including the Moon and Other Celestial Bodies, 27 January 1967 (entered into force 10 October 1967).

7 Convention on International Liability for Damage Caused by Space Objects, 29 March 1972 (entered into force 1 September 1972).

8 Legal and policy issues associated with human space flight by private entities are beyond the scope of this paper. For information on U.S. Government oversight of human space flight activities, *see*: Federal Aviation Administration (FAA), Human Space Flight Requirements for Crew and Space Flight Participants; Proposed Rule, 249 Federal Register 77262 (29 December 2005).

During the first phase of this technology demonstration initiative, NASA intends to provide capital and assistance similar to an investor, to help provide the financial stimulation necessary to ensure the success of this venture.

"Funded" Space Act Agreements

As mentioned above, NASA's agreements with SpaceX and RpK were concluded as "funded" Space Act Agreements. NASA's organic statute, the National Aeronautics and Space Act of 1958 (Space Act),[9] grants NASA broad discretion in the performance of its functions. Specifically, the Space Act authorizes the NASA Administrator "to enter into and perform such contracts, leases, cooperative agreements, *or other transactions* as may be necessary in the conduct of its work and on such terms as it may deem appropriate..." (Emphasis added.)

Under this "other transactions" authority of the Space Act, NASA is able to enter into agreements in furtherance of its mission with reduced administrative burdens and greater flexibility in negotiating terms. In the great majority of activities conducted under Space Act agreements, NASA does not provide funding to the other party. Instead, each party contributes resources (personnel, facilities, etc.) to the effort, or NASA performs reimbursable work for the other party. For example, all such agreements between NASA and its international partners or with other foreign entities are based upon Space Act authority.)

In contrast, a "funded" Space Act agreement, such as COTS, is used by NASA to transfer funds to another party to accomplish the goals of the agreement. These agreements involve funded R&D collaborations (usually jointly-funded) with individual companies or consortia to advance NASA's mission-related projects, to enhance U.S. industry's global competitiveness, or to commercialize aerospace technology. In addition to funding, NASA may provide services, facilities, equipment, information, intellectual property, or personnel to support the collaboration.

COTS Demonstrations Agreements

The provisions of funded Space Act agreements are unique to the particular entity and activity being funded. The COTS Demonstrations agreements, in particular, are designed to minimize NASA requirements and oversight of the commercial ventures. Indeed, certain provisions differ significantly from legal provisions found in a standard NASA procurement contract. For example:

- Government cost accounting standards do not apply, and the Government has limited audit rights. Payments will be made based on meeting negotiated milestones. When a milestone is met, the participant receives the negotiated payment for that milestone.

- Maximum retention of intellectual property rights by participant(s) allowed by law and regulations.

- The space transportation systems developed with assistance from the COTS program will be owned by the companies that develop them, not by NASA. NASA will have a limited

9 42 U.S.C. § 2451 *et seq.*

negotiated right to repurchase COTS property at a reduced cost.

- NASA has more limited rights to terminate the agreements. This is in contrast to the typical "termination for convenience" clauses found in U.S. Government procurement contracts.

Other noteworthy features of the agreements include the following:

- Foreign participation is permitted to the maximum extent allowed by law and policy, including participation as commercial partners, investors or subcontractors.

- Launch activities are subject to Federal Aviation Administration (FAA) licensing, including risk allocation requirements.

- NASA Centers may provide participants with technical support on a reimbursable basis (e.g., wind tunnel testing).

Once it has been demonstrated that a commercial entity or entities can provide an orbital transportation service, NASA plans to acquire the service under standard contracting procedures (i.e., via requests for proposals from any company, including non-participants in the COTS program). The provider will also be able, of course, to offer these new services to non-NASA customers. The intent is to help spread development costs, thereby reducing costs to government customers and further stimulating the commercial space industry.

The following sections examine some of the above features in greater detail:

Foreign Participation in COTS

As stated above, the COTS Demonstrations project is structured to enable foreign participation to the maximum extent allowed by U.S. law and policy.[10] To receive NASA funding, SpaceX and RpK were required to demonstrate that U.S. nationals have more than a 50 percent ownership interest.[11]

---

[10] Specifically, U.S. Space Transportation Policy, Guideline IV.5(b) (6 January 2005):

> The use of foreign components or technologies, and the participation of foreign governments and entities, in current and future U.S. space transportation systems is permitted consistent with U.S. law and regulations, as well as nonproliferation, national security, and foreign policy goals and commitments and U.S. obligations under the Strategic Arms Reduction Treaty, Intermediate Nuclear Forces Treaty, and the Missile Technology Control Regime. Such use or participation will not be permitted where it could result in critical national security or civil space launches being jeopardized by delays or disruptions in receipt of foreign-produced systems, components, technology, or expertise.

[11] U.S. Law also permits funding of a subsidiary of a foreign company, provided the Secretary of Transportation finds (A) a substantial commitment to the United States market through long-term investments in the United States, (B) significant contributions to employment in the United Sates, and (C) the country or countries in which the foreign company is incorporated or organized, and, if appropriate, in which it principally conducts its business, affords reciprocal treatment to companies comparable to that afforded to the foreign company's subsidiary in the United States. This would include the ability to participate in government sponsored research, absence of barriers with respect to local investment opportunities, and protection of intellectual property rights.

In addition, Guideline V.1(b) of the Space Transportation Policy provides, in relevant part, that: "United States Government payloads shall be launched on space launch vehicles manufactured in the United States, unless exempted by the Director of the Office of Science and Tech-

In addition, the participants must comply with all U.S. export control laws and regulations. Specifically:

(a) the International Traffic in Arms Regulations (ITAR)[12] and the Export Administration Regulations (EAR).[13] In the absence of available license exemptions or exceptions, participants will be responsible for obtaining the appropriate licenses or other approvals, if required, for exports of hardware, technical data, and software, or for the provision of technical assistance;

(b) obtaining export licenses, if required, before utilizing foreign persons in the performance of the agreement, including instances where COTS efforts are to be performed on-site at NASA Centers, where the foreign person will have access to export-controlled technical data or software;

(c) all regulatory record keeping requirements associated with the use of licenses and any applicable exemptions or exceptions; and

(d) ensuring that the above provisions are made applicable to their subcontractors.

Intellectual Property

As mentioned earlier, the COTS Demonstrations agreements emphasize that participants will retain the maximum rights to intellectual property allowed by law and regulations. Specifically:

- NASA will not obtain rights in a participant's "background" intellectual property (data and inventions developed at private expense that existed or were made prior to, or outside of, the participant's agreement with NASA).

- NASA may request a participant's technical data (engineering, software, etc.) arising from work under a COTS agreement with NASA. Such data will be used only to evaluate a participant's performance under a COTS agreement.

- For any inventions made by participants in performance of work under a COTS agreement, NASA is required by law – the National Aeronautics and Space Act of 1958 – to take title to such inventions. However, upon petition by a participant, NASA will grant an advance waiver of title to such inventions to the participant. NASA will retain only a "government purpose" license to use inventions for which it has waived rights, but will refrain from any NASA use for a period specified in the COTS agreement.

- A participant's proprietary data, both pre-existing proprietary data and data arising from work conducted under this agreement which a participant considers proprietary, will be appropriately marked by the participant and protected by NASA.

---

nology Policy, in consultation with the Assistant to the President for National Security Affairs."

[12] 22 Code of Federal Regulations (CFR) Parts 120 through 130.

[13] 15 CFR Parts 730 through 799.

Authorization and Supervision of COTS Demonstrations Launches: FAA Licensing

Article 6 of the Outer Space Treaty requires that launching states authorize and supervise space launches by their nongovernmental entities. The U.S. fulfills this responsibility through the Commercial Space Launch Act (CSLA),[14] which requires that U.S. companies obtain licenses issued by the Secretary of Transportation through the Federal Aviation Administration (FAA). Because COTS Demonstrations launch activities will be conducted by Space X and RpK and not by NASA, the launches will therefore be subject to CSLA requirements.

The scope and content of State responsibility for authorizing and supervising launches conducted from its territory or facilities, or by its nationals, has been a subject of extensive discussion within the Legal Subcommittee of the United Nations Committee on the Peaceful Uses of Outer Space (UN/COPUOS) in recent years. That discussion culminated in a U.N. General Assembly resolution urging that

> States conducting space activities, in fulfilling their international obligations under the United Nations treaties on outer space, ...as well as other relevant international agreements, consider enacting and implementing national laws authorizing and providing for continuing supervision of the activities in outer space of non-governmental entities under their jurisdiction. [15]

While there is as yet no formal international consensus regarding the required contents of national space laws regulating commercial space activities, discussions in UN/COPUOS and other fora suggest that such statutes should include, at a minimum, certain common elements or "building blocks." These include:

- *Authorization* (licensing and regulation), including application to activities with regard to territory and persons (legal/natural); observance of treaty principles (e.g., avoidance of harmful planetary contamination); sharing the financial risk of liability between government and non-governmental actors; fulfillment of the obligation concerning cooperation and mutual assistance;

- *Supervision*, including periodic reporting by licensees or collected by the public authority concerning the terms of the authorization; sanctions for violating license conditions, including revocation or suspension);

- *Registration* of space objects; and

- *Indemnification*, including implementation of a right of recourse if the (launching) State has paid indemnification to another State under Art. VII of the Outer Space Treaty and the Liability Convention. Indemnification should apply even if the damage has been caused solely by a non-governmental entity, limited to a cer-

[14] 49 U.S.C. 70101 *et seq.*

[15] U.N. General Assembly, Res. 59/115, Application of the concept of the "launching State," 10 December 2004.

tain fixed sum, to the insured sum, or to the policy period, beyond which the State will guarantee payment (or, alternatively, provide State payment for all claims).[16]

NASA and FAA supervision of COTS Demonstrations encompasses all of these elements. Briefly stated, applicable FAA launch and reentry licenses will govern the launch and return of COTS vehicles; the International Space Station agreements, applied contractually through the Space Act agreements with SpaceX and RpK, will cover the rendezvous and docking activities of the vehicles within the operational control zone of the ISS.

Termination

NASA may terminate a COTS agreement if a participant fails to perform, but may terminate unilaterally only under limited circumstances: (a) upon a declaration of war by the Congress of the United States; (b) upon a declaration of a national emergency by the President of the United States; or (c) upon a NASA determination, in writing, that NASA is required to terminate the demonstrations for reasons beyond its control. Reasons beyond NASA's control include, but are not limited to, acts of God or of the public enemy, acts of the U.S. Government other than NASA, in either its sovereign or contractual capacity (to include failure of Congress to appropriate sufficient funding), and for other specified emergency circumstances. NASA's liability for damages due to unilateral termination is limited to the next milestone payment under the agreement.

In the event of termination of a COTS agreement due to failure by a participant to perform, NASA may immediately exercise any government-purpose license to inventions arising under the COTS agreement, and will have the right to use and disclose for governmental purposes any technical data produced by a participant under the agreement. The participant and NASA will negotiate rights in data in the event of termination for any other reason.

Risk Allocation / Liability

Finally, in light of the considerable interest in liability arrangements for private commercial launch activities, I will conclude by outlining the liability arrangements applicable to COTS Demonstrations. These include extensive provisions governing third party liability as well as inter-party liability.

Liability between parties directly involved in launch activities is addressed through "cross-waivers" between the launch companies and U.S. Government agencies (and their related entities). Under a cross-waiver arrangement, each party agrees not to bring claims against the other or the other's related entities (e.g., contractors, subcontractors, users, customers or investors) for any harm to its property or employees. This means that each party reciprocally agrees to accept the risk of its own participation in the activity. Each party is thereby relieved of concern that other parties involved in the activity may bring claims against it.

---

[16] *See:* Schrogl and Gerhard, "Findings of the Project 2001 Workshop – Need and Prospects for National Space Legislation, 29 January 2004 (in *Project 2001 Plus: Global And European Challenges For Air And Space Law At The Edge Of The 21st Century* (http://www.uni-koeln.de/jur-fak/instluft/projectplus/presentations.html)

Cross waiver provisions are important elements of NASA's agreements with SpaceX and RpK for activities under those agreements as well as for FAA-licensed launch activities. For a cross-waiver to apply, both the entity causing damage and the entity sustaining damage must be involved in activities under the agreement. Each party then requires its own related entities to agree to waive claims against similar entities that may be legally related to any other party. This is referred to as the requirement to "flow down" the cross-waiver.

Third party liability is also addressed through FAA licensing. The FAA provides limited, conditional government indemnification for third-party claims arising from activities conducted under the license. FAA cross-waivers effectively require a private launch participant to assume responsibility for its employees' losses and property damage, as these claims are excluded from third party coverage.[17] The FAA also requires the COTS licensee/participant to obtain a specified amount of third party liability insurance and property insurance for government property used in a licensed activity.

For COTS activities not subject to the provisions of an FAA license or permit, the Space Act agreements between NASA and the COTS participants provide the risk allocation scheme. As the participants will be demonstrating rendezvous, proximity operations, docking or berthing, or other activities that are related to, or which could affect the ISS, the cross-waiver provision required for ISS activities will apply.[18]

NASA is not authorized to, and will not, indemnify a COTS participant for any claims or damages of any kind. Thus, COTS participants will need to consider obtaining appropriate insurance coverage, in addition to FAA requirements. Such insurance coverage could include coverage for damage caused by anyone to the participant's property (such as its launcher and any other flight hardware) and for third-party damages not subject to FAA requirements.

Moreover, the COTS Demonstrations agreements provide that each party is responsible for damages to third parties arising from that party's own negligence.

Conclusion

The COTS Demonstrations project represent a significant NASA investment in commercial space, offering the prospect of more efficient, and less expensive, means of access to LEO. The potential reward is great, but so is the risk: the funded Space Act agreements will place much of the risk and liabilities associated with developing a new program on industry rather than NASA. At the same time, the initiative will remove as many barriers to commercial development of space as allowable, to encourage maximum participation and innovation. Participants will be able to retain rights to their work, and once their technologies are successfully demonstrated, the opportunity to provide commercial launch services to NASA, other federal agencies and private entities. If successful, COTS Demonstrations may also enable ISS

[17] Commercial Space Transportation Financial Responsibility Requirements for Licensed Launch Activities, 14 CFR Chapter III Part 440, Sec. 440.5(b(2).

[18] *See:* Cross-Waiver of Liability, 14 CFR Part 1266, currently being revised by NASA.

commercial servicing while NASA is undergoing the transition from the Space Shuttle to the Orion Crew Exploration Vehicle.

As the legal and policy issues surrounding the COTS Demonstrations are further identified and addressed, their resolution will have significant influence on future NASA efforts to encourage commercial space ventures to further NASA's mission and the Vision for Space Exploration.

IAC-06-E.6.1.03

REGULATORY ASPECTS FOR LAUNCH ACTIVITIES IN A FUTURE SPACE TRAFFIC MANAGEMENT REGIME

Kai-Uwe Schrogl
European Space Policy Institute, Austria
kai-uwe.schrogl@espi.or.at

Corinne Contant Jorgenson
Advancing Space Consulting Group, United States
cmj@advancingspace.com

Petr Lala
Czech Republic
petr@lala-web.cz

Space traffic already takes place. It seems, however, minuscule with regard to the dimension of near-Earth outer space. Around 13.000 man-made objects larger than about 10 cm are currently tracked out of which only 650 are operational spacecraft. On the surface, the management of space traffic does not appear to be a pressing problem. Investigated further, this judgement has to be challenged. A high level or even growing number of launches from more and more launch sites and space ports, the entering of non-governmental entities, the positioning of satellite constellations, an increase in space debris and the advent of reusable launch vehicles supports this judgement.

Considering this scenario, conceptualizing space traffic management will turn out to become a relevant task during the next two decades. Space traffic management will, however, limit the freedom of use of outer space. Therefore an international consensus on internationally binding regulations will only be achieved, if States identify a certain urgency and expect a specific as well as collective benefit from this.

I. Definition of Space Traffic Management

The dimension of this task can be assessed, when the following definition of space traffic management is taken as a starting point:

> Space traffic management means the set of technical and regulatory provisions for promoting safe access into outer space, operations in outer space and return from outer space to Earth free from physical or radio-frequency interference.

Since an authoritative definition of space traffic management does not yet exist, this definition has been set up for the purpose of this study. Through this definition, the purpose of space traffic management becomes clear: it is to provide appropriate means so that space activities can be conducted without harmful interference. By that it supports the universal freedom to use outer space as laid down in the Outer Space Treaty of 1967. It should also be clear that for this purpose of achieving a common good, actors have to follow specific rules, which is also in their self-interest.

II. Dimensions and Phases of Space Traffic

Space traffic touches two dimensions: the scientific and technical area, and the regulatory field that are analyzed in this study. Then, those two dimensions of space traffic are applied to analyzing the three phases of space traffic: the launch phase, the in-orbit operation phase, and the re-entry phase. Below are the findings.

III. Findings

The Current Legal and Regulatory Framework

- The general principles of space law provide for a basis and rationale to establish a space traffic management regime.
- There exist some singular rules in international space law as well as in international telecommunication law, which constitute elements for a space traffic management system (especially for the GEO through the ITU). They are, however neither complete nor are they harmonized. ITU rules, aiming at the avoidance of radio-frequency interference are far more advanced than rules, aiming at the avoidance of physical interference.
- In this context, the IADC space debris mitigation guidelines of 2002 (non-binding soft law) encompass elements of space traffic management (use of disposal orbits, notification in case of controlled re-entry; but so far no provisions on the environment, i.e. avoidance of polluting the atmosphere/troposphere).

- Space law is, however, lacking numerous provisions, which are essential for a comprehensive traffic management regime (i.e. pre-launch notification). Of particular importance is a legal recognition of a difference between space objects considered as valuable assets by their owners, and space debris which have no value at all.
- A space traffic management regime has to touch also the question of harmonizing national space legislation (mostly to be established) and its consequential licensing standards and procedures, since they provide the building blocks for assuring technical safety.
- In the context of arms control/disarmament negotiations notification practices (prior to launch) are currently discussed, thus surpassing the status of civilian space law and negotiations in UNCOPUOS.
- The implementation of a comprehensive space traffic management regime would require additional regulation (with regard to information and the execution of space missions), which would further limit the freedom of use of outer space; in order to achieve a consensus on this, States have to perceive a certain urgency and have to expect a specific as well as collective benefit (as they receive from existing regulation).
- There are interfering factors, in particular military doctrines, which might hinder the establishment and working of a space traffic management regime.

The Launch Phase

- There is a rise in the number of launch vehicles (today 18).
- There is also a rise in the number of launch centers (today 11).
- The prospects for the inauguration of full/partly RLV are still open. In any case, by 2020 they would still be limited to supporting missions below 1000 km.
- Human space flight might only change dramatically beyond 2020.
- Safety certifications should be introduced.
- A clarification of the term "space object" is needed.
- The question of delimitation of air space and outer space should be revisited.
- The concept of the "launching State" has to be clarified.
- A pre-launch notification is necessary.
- Obligatory information in cases of damage is relevant.
- An international level playing field for transport services should be aimed for with a balance of public and private/economic interest.

The In-Orbit Operation Phase

- Maneuvering and in-orbit collision avoidance (with regard to other operational space objects as well as with regard to space debris) is growing in number and importance.

- Maneuvering in the GEO is intensely applied but with little consideration of possible collisions.
- Reliable collision probabilities can be estimated only when reliable information exists, which currently is not guaranteed.
- There is no prioritization with regard to maneuvers.
- There is no prioritization of certain space activities, no "right-of-way-rules", nor is any kind of utilization of space ruled out (except it is against the peaceful uses).
- There is no traffic separation ("one-way-traffic").
- There are no "zoning" rules (restriction of certain activities in certain areas).
- There are no communication rules (advance notification and communication if orbits of other operators are passed).
- The ITU system of nominal orbital positions finds application only to satellites in the GEO.
- Private/commercial actors have started (i.e. through SUIRG and ITU) coordinating against radio-frequency interference.

<u>The Re-Entry Phase</u>

- Intentional (RLVs as well as active debris mitigation) and un-intentional de-orbiting (natural debris mitigation through decay) is now more frequent but care should be taken that large debris structures will be de-orbited in fragments.
- Responsibilities and liabilities for damages caused by space objects or its components ensue not only from international space law but also from the general provisions of national (tort) civil and administrative law.
- The generally shared wish to reduce space debris raises the question, whether regulation should also set a standard under which conditions a re-entry activity is in general legitimate and under which conditions it is not.
- Notification of, and coordination with, local and downrange air traffic, maritime authorities, and local government officials are already considered a best practice in coordinating launch activities.
- Space Law and Air Law have to solve the open issue of passage of space objects through airspace (the Chicago Convention does not apply to space objects in air space).
- The question is posed to introduce certain internationally recognized descent corridors and possibly even impact areas which are not frequently used by other traffic and which might be dedicated to space traffic.

IV. Conclusion

In the following, a model is provided on how a comprehensive space traffic management regime for 2020 could look like. There could be drafting of an international inter-governmental agreement building on and not replacing the existing treaties. It would include provisions for liability and the basic principle that States are the primary actors but that provisions of the agreement are applicable for private activities as well through national licensing regimes (certain issues will be clarified in the agreement).

This international inter-governmental agreement would comprise a legal text, which cannot be changed easily and technical annexes, which can be adapted more easily (modeled from ICAO or IMO) and contain three parts: the first one would relate to securing the information needs, the second one would focus on the notification system and the third part would concentrate on traffic management. Regarding traffic management, the agreement would:

- Clarify "space objects", including legal distinction between valuable objects and valueless space debris
- Clarify "fault" in case of damage caused in outer space
- Set delimitation for the launch phase and clarifying the concept of the "launching State"
- Provide traffic management rules based on the use of the database for the purpose of collision avoidance, including:
  - Safety provisions for launches
  - Zoning (selection of orbits)
  - Right of way rules for in-orbit phase
  - Prioritization with regard to maneuver
  - Specific provisions for GEO (in harmonization with ITU rules)
  - Specific rules for LEO satellite constellations
  - Debris mitigation mechanisms
  - Safety provisions for re-entries
  - Environment provisions (pollution of the atmosphere/troposphere, etc.)
- Clarify "space objects", including legal distinction between valuable objects and valueless space debris
- Give a framework and main features for national licensing regimes, which implement the provisions of the agreement
- Set out an enforcement mechanism (e.g. renouncement of access to information) and dispute settlement
- Clarify institutionalized interlinks with ICAO and ITU

SPACE FOR TOURISM?

Legal Aspects of Private Spaceflight for Tourist Purposes

Frans G. von der Dunk
International Institute of Air and Space Law, Leiden - The Netherlands
F.G.vonderDunk@law.leidenuniv.nl

Abstract

It is barely five years ago since the first space tourist proper, Mr. Dennis Tito, made his much-publicised 20 million-dollar flight to the ISS. And now, purportedly thousands of prospective customers are lining up with such nascent companies as Sir Richard Branson's Virgin Galactic, for a 200,000-dollar, few-minute flight into the nearest part of outer space. In other words: it looks like space tourism is here to stay.

This obviously raises a number of key legal issues, stretching from proper application of such international space treaties as the Liability and Registration Conventions to national legal issues pertaining to liabilities, licensing and certification, and civil and criminal jurisdiction and control.

The present paper seeks to offer an overview of some of these, the most salient legal issues as they are on the table right now, keeping in mind the need to maintain a fair balance between the interests of private enterprise and of the public at large – nationally as well as internationally – respectively.

1. Introduction

Over the span of just a handful of years, space tourism (for the moment to be defined as "flights into outer space of humans for their own pleasure and excitement") has been transformed from a notion being little more than science fiction to an impending commercial business. If the flight of Mr. Tito in 2001 could still be considered an exotic multi-millionaire's stunt, already three years later the X-prize changed such perceptions dramatically. Twice within a few weeks in that October of 2004 did a privately-financed craft, using relatively simple but rather revolutionary technology, reach an altitude of over 100 km, the unofficial boundary of outer space. The technology has immediately been picked up by Virgin Galactic, which about half a year ago already had some 43,000 bookings and down-payments to the tune of 13 million US$ for trips to be offered as of 2008.[1]

While the US government has reacted by enunciating a specific Act to deal with this latest development,[2] this Act was only a temporary one.[3] Moreover, it is clear that space tourism will also generate substantial legal issues beyond the borders and jurisdiction of the United States – already in the case of Virgin Galactic it should be noted that this concerns a UK company.

The present paper offers a summary overview of some of the most salient legal issues as they play out both at an international and at a national level.

2. International level

2.1. Introductory remark

Starting at the international level – as should be the case, bearing in mind the fundamentally international character of outer space as an area[4] – it is immediate obvious that spaceflights for pure pleasure purposes were never as such envisaged by the drafters of the key space treaties.

2.2. The Outer Space Treaty

The Outer Space Treaty was essentially focused on two reasons for conducting any, including manned, spaceflight: military/political ones (where it tried to minimise the risks of space becoming a battleground) and scientific ones (where it tried to establish and protect the freedom to investigate, explore and even use outer space).[5] With a view to space tourism, the major conclusion too be drawn from the Outer Space Treaty therefore is: as long as no specific rules prohibit or condition (certain forms of) space tourism, the freedom of use of outer space as point of departure allows space tourism as part of such use, even if nowhere specifically mentioned.

The only more directly relevant reference to the current issue is offered by Article V, which had been drafted to ensure that astronauts (and cosmonauts and taikonauts) would be treated in conformity with certain standards – as mainly expressed by the concept of "envoys of mankind". That concept had never been defined any further, although it was generally considered not to equate in law with an 'envoy' in the terrestrial, diplomatic sense of the word. Formally, no diplomatic immunities were offered to an astronaut stranded in a foreign country. Under Article V, the duties of the 'receiving state' had been 'limited' to assistance as well as prompt and safe return to his 'sending' state; they did not provide for any formal entitlement of the astronaut to immunity from jurisdiction. To be sure, the astronaut's presence within a foreign jurisdiction was essentially of an emergency and – as a consequence – supposedly rather temporary character. In view of that fact of life, it was simply not very likely the astronaut would even get the chance to undertake any deliberate action in violation of domestic laws potentially triggering the receiving state's jurisdiction and, thus, the question of any immunities.

The relevant provisions were, of course, drafted keeping in mind humans going into space as 'professionals', that is trained and paid by their respective governments (or exceptionally by an intergovernmental organisation, read ESA) to go into outer space. Hence, it was precisely the fundamental non-professional nature of space tourists which raised the issue in many minds of whether they should be considered astronauts and hence enjoy the status of the relevant provisions.

The 'follow-up' treaties to the Outer Space Treaty equally proceeded on that basis, although in view of the more explicit and concrete character of most of their articles the question whether individual articles would impose relevant conditions on space tourist activities became much more acute.

2.3. The Rescue Agreement

This firstly concerned the Rescue Agreement[6], which elaborated Article V of the Outer Space Treaty. The Rescue Agreement followed the latter's exclusive focus on professional astronauts and even seemed to elaborate it, by referring throughout to "personnel of a spacecraft" as enjoying the rights of being assisted and safely and promptly returned as spelled out by the Agreement.[7] Not entering into the discussion here of the extent to which the "personnel of a spacecraft" of the Rescue Agreement would equate with the "astronauts" of Article V of the Outer Space Treaty, it remains obvious that as such space tourists would seem to fall outside of that category.

Apparently, there is considerable hesitation to accept this conclusion outright, as it may seem to deny space tourists the benefits of Articles 1 through 4 in particular of the Rescue Agreement, and efforts are made to stretch the concepts of 'personnel of a spacecraft' and 'astronaut' so as to include, after all, any human being in outer space including space tourists. This would be a fallacy, however, inasmuch as general humanitarian duties to assist human beings in distress do not depend on those Articles; they derive – apart from moral and ethical considerations – from customary and in many cases also codified general international law. It is not necessary for those general humanitarian purposes to interpret these Articles as extending to space tourists as well.

On the contrary, should space tourists be allowed to enjoy in particular the rights to safe and prompt return provided for by Article 4 without any *caveat* as to the possibility of those tourists somehow infringing national laws? That would seem to be a proposition which many, in particular non-space-faring, states would not particularly agree with – but at any rate, sufficient doubts may be cast on the validity of the claim that space tourists should enjoy the same international legal protection as personnel or astronauts under the current treaties without further ado, to warrant an effort to somehow clarify the matter on the international plane.

With regard to the flight crew, however, things would seem to lie less clear. Both their reasons for going into outer space (professional and being paid to do a job) and the types of their activities there (guiding the vehicle safely in and out of outer space, and in the case of orbital tourism, even guiding it around in outer space) are much closer to those of the 500 or so human beings that have so far entered into outer space. The only major difference, certainly from a legal perspective, is that the latter are in the service of governments or an intergovernmental organisation, the former in the service of private commercial companies.

In this case, therefore, it would make sense to equate space tourist vehicle crew, certainly the flight deck crew but possibly also any service e crew on board, to "personnel of a spacecraft", hence endowing them with the rights enunciated by the Rescue Agreement.

2.4. The Liability Convention

Another example of outer space treaty-law potentially relevant for the present situation would concern the Liability Convention,[8] since the obvious risk exists that through the doings of a space tourist damage falling within its scope might result. As a matter of fact, however, for the Liability Convention itself it does not make any distinction whether the ultimate cause of damage would be a tourist or not – the state or states qualifying under the well-known criteria as "launching State" of the object which caused the damage will be liable.[9]

As a consequence, just like with respect to any other private space activity for which a particular state may be held liable on the international level, that state simply has to ensure that the relevant tourist activity is subjected to its jurisdiction and a license including proper arrangements regarding third party liabilities and insurance therefor. In other words: it becomes a matter of national (space) law and any applicable licensing system part thereof.

The only issue on which space tourism, even if *de facto* and for the time being, might be special concerns sub-orbital tourism and the craft used therefore. As is well-known, the application of the

Liability Convention's regime hinges on the damage being caused by a 'space object'.[10] While a space object has not been defined any further by the treaties, it is generally perceived as something which was at least *intended* to be launched into outer space.

As has been discussed abundantly elsewhere, there is no clear legal delimitation of outer space as of yet. This fact opens the door to a discussion as to whether flights going up vertically to an altitude of at most 120 km – as Virgin Galactic is currently planning to do with its SpaceShipTwo vehicles being built – and then immediately returning would qualify SpaceShipTwo craft as space objects so as to trigger the application of the Liability Convention in case of damage. As will be seen, this actually transposes the issue to the level of national law.

2.5. The Registration Convention

Similar considerations as regards the Liability Convention apply to Article VIII of the Outer Space Treaty and the Registration Convention[11] as its elaboration, since the definition of a 'space object' through the determination of the 'launching State' underlies any retention of jurisdiction by the state of registry over that space object and its personnel while in outer space. In other words: if a craft carrying space tourists (or anything else for that matter) into the outer edge of outer space and back would qualify as a 'space object', jurisdiction of the state of registry could be applied through the workings of Article VIII of the Outer Space Treaty and Article II(2) of the Registration Convention.

The difference is not really relevant, however, as otherwise basically the same amount of jurisdiction could be exercised under air law over the craft if it would be defined as an aircraft,[12] or even in the absence of such registration the craft at issue would be subject to the jurisdiction of the state that *could* have registered it – and might prefer other legal instruments to make the exercise of any jurisdiction effective.

It is furthermore with respect to such space objects – again not defined any further by the Convention itself – that the duty of the state of registry arises under the Registration Convention to establish a national registry and then inform the United Nations Secretary-General, read the Office for Outer Space Affairs about such registered space object on at least a handful of parameters offered by the Convention.[13]

3. National law issues

3.1. Introductory remarks

As is the case on many other issues where international space law is not sufficiently elaborated, as soon as a practical need arises for certain states to deal in legal terms with an issue, attention automatically should be directed towards national legal actions and developments – and space tourism, obviously is no exception.

As has been discussed in many instances elsewhere, the fundamental basis for the role of national law and jurisdiction *vis-à-vis* space activities fundamentally derives from three parameters at the international level, which warrant being briefly reiterated here.

Firstly, there is the international responsibility of a state under Article VI of the Outer Space Treaty for "national activities in outer space", and the related obligation to exercise "authorization and continuing supervision" over private entities involved therein. Secondly, the international liability for damage by space objects also if ultimately caused by private actors, which results for (launching) states as a consequence of Article VII of the Outer Space Treaty and the whole of the Liability Convention, represents at least a strong stimulus for those states to try and exercise jurisdiction over those actors, in order *inter alia* to deal with reimbursement and insurance. And thirdly, Article VIII of the Outer Space Treaty as further elaborated by the Registration Convention, as mentioned, offers to states a specific, space-oriented tool to exercise some measure of jurisdiction over a space object – for example for any of the above reasons – as a consequence of registering the space object in question.

In addition, however, to these major international legal parameters for national legislative action, national law, once it starts to deal with space tourism, also inserts some further parameters in this case largely stemming from the experience in aviation.

From this perspective, it may be concluded that three major issues need to be dealt with: the craft, the crew, and the passengers.

As for the craft, the above discussion already to some extent indicates the need under international law to determine whether the craft used for space tourism – certainly as long as suborbital and of the SpaceShipTwo-mode – constitutes an aircraft or a space object, or possibly even both. This issue in addition however also has some distinct national law-aspects, as will be seen.

As for the crew and the passengers, in respect of both the international aspects have also been addressed above. Here, national laws play an even more important role than on the issue of the craft, and from the experience of aviation, it is clear that the distinction between crew and craft is much more perfected.

3.2. The United States

In the absence of any authoritative guidance on the international level, the United States, as the one country so far actually having had to deal with space tourism, by means of the Commercial Space Launch Amendments Act of 2004 had to deal with the three issues referred to.

With regard to the craft, the US authorities decided for SpaceShipOne to consider it as an experimental aircraft, as it did with respect to its carrier aircraft White Knight.[14] By contrast, SpaceShipTwo, it is the US authorities' intention, will be registered as a spacecraft, even as the carrier is a more or less normal aircraft and SpaceShipTwo, like SpaceShipOne, in its return phase will operate as a glider and will be registered with the Federal Aviation Administration with a code usually reserved for aircraft.[15] It remains to be seen, of course, to what extent this precedent will be followed by other examples, read other countries, with a view to the possible formation of a rule of customary law, but it is obvious that this US example would tend to be followed unless solid reasons would tell against that.

At the national level, however, the issue of the craft has another, more down-to-earth aspects as well: that of certification. Though even in aviation there is little harmonisation as to the contents and detailed procedures for certification of craft – basically, all is left to national authorities in that context – at least the *principle* of certification is well established at the international level, leading to an enormous amount of certification regulation and activity at the national level.[16] And, it should be added, in Europe also at the regional international level, in the context of the Joint Aviation Authorities (JAA)[17] and the newly established European Aviation Safety Agency (EASA)[18].

In this respect it is noteworthy that, purportedly without any obligation to do so, Virgin Galactic with regard to its SpaceShipTwo craft is looking for Part 25 certification for aircraft in the United States, without however intending to go through all the testing normally required for that purpose.[19]

The Commercial Space Launch Amendments Act itself remains silent on the issue, but it is likely that in the process of updating and amending or replacing it this issue will be taken on board prominently.

When it comes to the issue of the crew, the Act is quite specific and defines it as "any employee of a licensee or transferee, or of a contractor or subcontractor of a licensee or transferee, who performs activities in the course of that employment directly relating to the launch, reentry, or other operation of or in a launch vehicle or reentry vehicle that carries human beings".[20] The tourists themselves are clearly distinguished therefrom, as anyone on board not being a member of the crew, by means of the term "space flight participants".[21]

As to the latter, Mr. Whitehorn, CEO of Virgin Galactic, at his keynote speech addressing the ECSL Practitioners' Forum in Paris on March 17, 2006, stated that "individual medical risks [of passengers] now would constitute the highest ones, not those of equipment or vehicle failure".[22] Hence, Virgin Galactic was developing a policy for its SpaceShipTwo operations which would fundamentally exclude only passengers with cardiac or coronary weaknesses, as well as those under sixteen years of age.

This might still raise some issues regarding potential (passenger) liability, which may ultimately lead to the establishment of a national regime on passenger liability or even an international convention trying to harmonise such national regimes along the lines of the Warsaw system in air transport.[23]

For the time being, this problem has been pushed forward in that, for operations of this nature under the Commercial Space Launch Amendments Act, the obligation to clearly inform passengers of the dangers inherent in a relevant flight was the sole relevant requirement on this issue for obtaining a license under the Act, effectively excluding him from claiming any liability as a third party.[24]

This would leave intact, barring further provisions to the contrary, the application of the existing US regime for dealing with third party liability including international claims under the Liability Convention. This regime, essentially operating through a licensing process, is well-known.

In short, it amounts to a licensing obligation for launches conducted from US territory and/or by US persons or legal entities abroad, and under circumstances also by non-US companies if a controlling interest would be in US hands.[25] Included in any license then is the obligation for the licensee to either insure himself or show "financial responsibility" up to an amount which is the lowest of the three following: (1) the maximum probable loss as calculated by the licensing authority; (2) the maximum liability insurance available on the world market at reasonable cost as determined by the licensing authority; and (3) the amount of US $ 500,000,000.[26]

3.3. The United Kingdom

As briefly discussed, so far only the United States has, to any appreciable extent, drafted legislation dealing with space tourism. That leaves the question open, to what extent other states would, if not from their own national legal perspective at least from the international legal perspective, be involved in space tourism, and whether whatever law is currently in place, would suffice for the moment to deal with it.

The first state coming to mind is obviously United Kingdom, in view of the fact that Virgin Galactic, the company closest to realizing sub-orbital tourist flights, is still a UK company, even as the technology is owned by a (presumably American) joint daughter company of Virgin Galactic and Scaled Composites, and the operations, for the time being, will be conducted from US soil, in the state of New Mexico.

Virgin Galactic flights, to the extent constituting "activities in outer space" with reference to Article VI of the Outer Space Treaty, would certainly trigger UK responsibility as a state. It could even be argued that the United Kingdom, by allowing Virgin Galactic flights to go ahead, would come to qualify as a state that "procures" the launch, the notion of 'procuring a launch' never having been authoritatively defined. This, of course, might entail liability for the United Kingdom – in this case next to the United States, qualifying as a launch state already by reason of the launch taking place from New Mexico.[27]

The United Kingdom has, indeed, a national space law[28] in place, which provides in this regard for a license obligation for any body "incorporated under the law of any part of the United Kingdom" if it undertakes the launch or procurement of the launch of a space object, or operates it, "whether carried on in the United Kingdom or elsewhere".[29]

By way of exceptions, if "arrangements have been made between the United Kingdom and another country to secure compliance with the international obligations of the United Kingdom", a license is not required, and in addition the UK Secretary of State may waive the license obligation "if he is satisfied that the requirement [of obtaining a license] is not necessary to secure compliance with the international obligations of the United Kingdom".[30]

Part of the license obligation finally concerns the obligation to indemnify the UK government in respect of any international liability claims which the latter had to submit to, in principle comprehensively but in practice likely limited to the amount of obligatory insurance coverage.[31]

Thus, it seems, the United Kingdom at least in theory seems well equipped with the national legal means to exercise control over any space tourism operations in respect of which it may be held responsible or liable on the international level.

3.4. United Arab Emirates & Singapore

In regard of other states, it may be pointed out that their possible involvement in space tourist operations seems to be considerably further away, since the plans concerned are in considerably less advanced stages as compared to those of Virgin Galactic.

The plans coming closest as of yet concern those of Space Adventures, which is involved in projects leading to spaceports adapted for space tourist flights in the United Arab Emirates/Dubai and/or Singapore. Space Adventures itself being a US company, it will be subject to the aforementioned US legislation, so it is essentially the other states mentioned which warrant a brief look at this point.

If, indeed, such spaceport projects will turn into successful take-off sites for space tourist flights, the mere fact that the territory of the United Arab Emirates respectively Singapore might be used for such launches would entail possible liability for those two state as launching state – presuming of course, in the light of the discussion above, the craft in question would qualify as a 'space object'.

Neither of these two states have any specific national space law in place as of yet, and it remains doubtful whether any existing general piece of law on, for example, the licensing of private activities, and/or reimbursement obligations *vis-à-vis* the government would be effective to deal with the matter.

3.5. The Russian Federation

Furthermore, another company Rocketplane plans to offer space trips seem to consider the option of using Russian aircraft as the lower stage carrier for the craft which is to enter into outer space. In that case, not only Russian aviation law on registration and certification of aircraft may come into play, but in view of the inherently resulting character of the carrier aircraft as the "launch vehicle" also space law-consequences result (once more, of course, assuming that the upper stage craft could be considered a 'space object'). Such a character, namely, would qualify Russia (also) as a launching state in the context of the Liability Convention.[32]

That brings into the picture the national space law which Russia has enacted over a decade ago.[33] The Law of the Russian Federation on Space Activities provides for a licensing obligation for all "organizations and citizens of the Russian Federation or (...) foreign organizations and citizens under the [territorial] jurisdiction of the Russian Federation".[34] This licensing obligation *ratione materiae* applies to space activities, including "preparation for launching and launching of space objects, as well as control over space flights".[35]

In other words: a non-Russian company like Rocketplane does not as such fall within the licensing obligation provided for by the Law of the Russian Federation on Space Activities, even though such launches may entail liability of Russia under the prevailing international liability regime.

The way out here for Russia may be provided by another clause in the Law of the Russian Federation on Space Activities, which deals with registration: Article 17(2) namely explicitly provides that the jurisdiction of Russia applies also to Russian-registered space objects. This, of course, presumes a choice on the part of the Russian government to consider an aircraft carrier for an upper stage space tourist vehicle to be the launch vehicle of a space object in the sense of the Liability Convention – in order to cater for any potential liability claims at the international level: the circle is completed here...

Moreover, it certainly requires a Russian law somehow obliging Russian aircraft used for the purpose of launching space objects, by whomsoever wherever, to be registered as such. In sum, in this case it could be deemed rather doubtful whether the Russian authorities have the proper legal tools at hand to deal with the matter.

Once the licensing obligation is made to apply, however, the Law of the Russian Federation on Space Activities does provide for a reimbursement obligation of the licensee in case of international third party damage claims to be honored by the Russian government, as well as for the likelihood that such obligation would be without limit.[36] Furthermore, insurance against such an event for the licensee is mandatory, although the maximum amount of obligatory cover is to be determined by future legislation, which very likely therefore will mean such an amount will be limited.[37]

4. Concluding remarks

It is clear that within the scope of the present paper it has not been possible even summarily to deal with all important legal issues – which in itself testifies that space tourism is a rather interesting new phenomenon in space law if it is, indeed, to stay. This in turn raised the overarching question: is (there) space for tourism also in a legal sense?

The current, summary overview seems to answer this question largely in the affirmative: space tourism certainly is not prohibited by any of the relevant treaties, at least as long as the specific relevant rules and obligations contained therein are complied with.

Here, however, the first major issues arise. On a number of counts, too little clarity exists as to the precise *impact* of international space law on this new phenomenon. In turn, this gives rise to the fact of life that those states which find themselves confronted with relevant space tourist activities will of necessity find their own particular way in dealing with, for example, certification of craft or liability of operators. In addition, specific national idiosyncrasies may also creep in.

This is not to say that there is, necessarily, a need right now for any international convention – history has shown, that such efforts are too often ill-fated and/or extraordinarily slow if there is no general consensus on their desirability or need. For the time being, moreover, it will be most interesting to closely follow national US law developments, since the United States at this moment is the only state more or less immediately confronted with space tourist operations.

Yet, if we accept the fundamental premise that space tourism can contribute to the overall benefits mankind would draw from space and space activities (for instance by making access to space much cheaper and safer) these are important issues for further analysis in the forthcoming years – and not just by American lawyers, since from the one end US legal developments may have a profound impact on any international legal developments, and from the other end such developments should not lead to any unnecessary conflict with the established body of international space law either. In that sense, there is not only space for tourism, but also space for further discussion.

Endnotes

1. See ECSL 33 – Special Edition, Report on the 2006 ECSL Practitioners' Forum, p. 2.

2. Commercial Space Launch Amendments Act of 2004, Public Law 108-492, 108th Congress, 23 December 2004, 49 U.S.C.; 118 Stat. 3974.

3. Cf. Sec. 2(b), Commercial Space Launch Amendments Act, sub (14), referring to a period of eight years.

4. Cf. already Art. II, Treaty on Principles Governing the Activities of States in the Exploration and Use of Outer Space, including the Moon and Other Celestial Bodies (hereafter Outer Space Treaty), London/Moscow/ Washington, done 27 January 1967,

entered into force 10 October 1967; 610 UNTS 205; TIAS 6347; 18 UST 2410; UKTS 1968 No. 10; Cmnd. 3198; ATS 1967 No. 24; 6 ILM 386 (1967).

5. Cf. e.g. Artt. III, IV, resp. Art. I, Outer Space Treaty.

6. Agreement on the Rescue of Astronauts, the Return of Astronauts and the Return of Objects Launched into Outer Space (hereafter Rescue Agreement), London/Moscow/ Washington, done 22 April 1968, entered into force 3 December 1968; 672 UNTS 119; TIAS 6599; 19 UST 7570; UKTS 1969 No. 56; Cmnd. 3786; ATS 1986 No. 8; 7 ILM 151 (1968).

7. Artt. 1-4, Rescue Agreement.

8. Convention on International Liability for Damage Caused by Space Objects (hereafter Liability Convention), London/Moscow/Washington, done 29 March 1972, entered into force 1 September 1972; 961 UNTS 187; TIAS 7762; 24 UST 2389; UKTS 1974 No. 16; Cmnd. 5068; ATS 1975 No. 5; 10 ILM 965 (1971).

9. See Artt. I(c), II, III, IV & V, Liability Convention.

10. See Artt. II, III, Liability Convention.

11. See in particular Artt. I(b), (c), II(2), Convention on Registration of Objects Launched into Outer Space (hereafter Registration Convention), New York, done 14 January 1975, entered into force 15 September 1976; 1023 UNTS 15; TIAS 8480; 28 UST 695; UKTS 1978 No. 70; Cmnd. 6256; ATS 1986 No. 5; 14 ILM 43 (1975).

12. Based on Art. 17, Convention on International Civil Aviation (hereafter Chicago Convention), Chicago, done 7 December 1944, entered into force 4 April 1947; 15 UNTS 296; TIAS 1591; Cmd. 6614; UKTS 1953 No. 8; ATS 1957 No. 5; ICAO Doc. 7300, as this determines the nationality of aircraft based on their registration.

13. See Artt. II(1), IV(1), Registration Convention.

14. See ECSL 33 – Special Edition, Report on the 2006 ECSL Practitioners' Forum, p. 2.

15. See ECSL 33 – Special Edition, Report on the 2006 ECSL Practitioners' Forum, p. 3.

16. Most prominently, Article 31, Chicago Convention, provides that "Every aircraft engaged in international navigation shall be provided with a certificate of airworthiness issued or rendered valid by the State in which it is registered."

17. The JAA is based on a *sui generis* set of legal documents known as the JAA Arrangements, signed in Cyprus in 1990 by (at the time) ten states.

18. EASA was established by means of Regulation of the European Parliament and of the Council on common rules in the field of civil aviation and establishing a European Aviation Safety Agency, No. 1592/2002/EC, of 15 July 2002; OJ L 240/1 (2002).

19. See ECSL 33 – Special Edition, Report on the 2006 ECSL Practitioners' Forum, p. 3.

20. Sec. 2(b), Commercial Space Launch Amendments Act, sub (2).

21. See Sec. 2(b), Commercial Space Launch Amendments Act, sub (17).

22. See ECSL 33 – Special Edition, Report on the 2006 ECSL Practitioners' Forum, p. 3.

23. The Warsaw system consists of a great number of partly overlapping international treaties, ranging from the 1929 Warsaw Convention (Convention for the Unification of Certain Rules Relating to International Transportation by Air, Warsaw, done 12 October 1929, entered into force 13 February 1933; 137 LNTS 11; USTS 876; UKTS 1933 No. 11; ATS 1963 No. 18) to the 1999 Montreal Convention (Convention for the Unification of Certain Rules for International Carriage by Air, Montreal, done 28 May 1999, entered into force 4 November 2003; ICAO Doc. 9740; 48 ZLW 326 (1999)).

24. See Sec. 2(c)(13), Commercial Space Launch Amendments Act.

25. See Sec. 70104, Commercial Space Transportation – Commercial Space Launch Activities, 49 U.S.C. 70101 (1994).

26. See Sec. 70112, Commercial Space Transportation – Commercial Space Launch Activities, 49 U.S.C. 70101 (1994).

27. See Art. VII, Outer Space Treaty; Art. I(c)(i), Liability Convention.

28. Outer Space Act, 18 July 1986, 1986 Chapter 38; National Space Legislation of the World, Vol. I (2001), at 293; Space Law – Basic Legal Documents, E.I; 36 Zeitschrift für Luft- und Weltraumrecht (1987), at 12.

29. Secc. 1, 2(1), 3, Outer Space Act.

30. See Sec. 3(2)(b), resp. (3), Outer Space Act.

31. See Secc. 5(2)(f), 10(1), Outer Space Act.

32. Art. I(d), Liability Convention, includes the "launch vehicle" in the definition of "space object".

33. Law of the Russian Federation on Space Activities, No. 5663-1, 20 August 1993, effective 6 October 1993; National Space Legislation of the World, Vol. I (2001), at 101.

34. Art. 9(2), Law of the Russian Federation on Space Activities.

35. Art. 9(2), Law of the Russian Federation on Space Activities.

36. See Art. 30(1) & (2), Law of the Russian Federation on Space Activities.

37. See Art. 25(1), Law of the Russian Federation on Space Activities.

Space Tourism: Regulatory Framework of Private Initiatives and Projects with a Special Interest on RLV Regulations (IAC-06-E6.1.08)

Axelle Cartier, LL.M. (adv.)
Leiden University / Campus The Hague, the Netherlands
axellecartier@hetnet.nl

Ioana Cristoiu, LL.M. (adv.)
Hitter Law Offices, Brussels, Belgium
ioana_cristoiu@yahoo.fr

ABSTRACT

The airline experience has shown us that it is not just technology that provides safety but the maturity that comes from a high level of flight activity.
Entrepreneur Burt Rutan before the U.S. Congress on 20 April 2005.
Independent market research data compiled over the last several years shows that commercial space travel has the potential to be a billion-dollar industry in the next 20 years and the success of RLV (Reusable Launch Vehicles) projects has contributed to this observation. In April 2005, SpaceShipOne designer Burt Rutan as one of several entrepreneurs in the emerging commercial space market reported before the House Subcommittee on Space and Aeronautics in the attempt of the Congress to define what role the government should or should not play in supporting entrepreneurial space progress. Public interest has to be served by creating a clear legal, regulatory safety regime and certification for commercial human spaceflight carried on by private companies.

I. INTRODUCTION: SPACE BUSINESS AND COMPLEXITY

The structure of space industry evolves rapidly due to the technological and commercial progress and strategies. Space faring nations increasingly recognized the potential of outer space whose commercial prospects lead to significant participation by the private sector.[1]
Due to its complex structure and from a strict legal point of view, space business is particularly difficult to regulate.

[1] S. Freeland, *Up, Up and...Back: The Emergence of Space Tourism and its Impact on the International Law of Outer Space*, Chicago Journal of International Law, vol. 6 No.1, Summer 2005 at p.5.

Satellites or others space objects are at the same time "space assets", commercial items, money providers and actors of international public space law. The *corpus iuris specialis* is in the meantime more than forty years old. Its conventions were drafted during the cold war period and influenced by the fierce competition between the two only space faring nations of the time, the U.S. and the former USSR.

Any other space business venture involves an extraordinarily high amount of money along with a remarkably high level of technology requirement. If, in the early years, governments were the only actors involved in outer space activities, the commercialization of outer space increasingly influences the typical customers profile and the current needs of the space business industry. The problems the satellite industry has been recently facing due to the privatization and the commercialization is an illustration thereof. With the development of yet dynamic projects involving space tourism, other major issues, questions and problems come to the fore. Existing international space law will need to keep pace with technological and commercial progress. With the commercial development of the space tourism industry, hence of Reusable Launch Vehicle (RLV) technologies, there is a crucial need for uniform, clear national and international regulations.

A space business venture involves the participation of a significant amount of actors, as well as it requires several and various licenses and authorizations. The financing of the space sector evolved considerably. As an illustration, satellite financing was twenty years ago rather straight forward: *Governments were using their treasury, the few private groups involved in the satellite " business" had enough cash treasury, while the few private groups owned to rely on pure equity financing. The banks involved were providing loans only when the corporate treasures preferred to leave the cash untouched. For example, the European Investment Bank would occasionally finance Eutelsat, as is convenient between governments.*[2]
That situation changed in the late 1980s. First and as a consequence of the cyclical downturn that affected satellites markets, there was a lack of new financial backers and the satellite community started to search for other sources of financing, such as commercial sources. Second, the profiles of the customers interested in space financing constantly evolve due to an actual trend towards the commercialization of space.

Typical customers, such as governmental or intergovernmental agencies, and large multinationals with a long credit history and capable of guaranteeing the entirety of their assets are not anymore the only ones looking for financial resources. Start-up companies with no real credit history and no assets to offer as collateral other than a satellite are the new generation of clientele. Raising the necessary capital for any space activity is extraordinarily difficult, also based on the amounts required and the many risks involved.
In the example of the satellite industry: *Such satellites will be typically commercial communication satellites each of which with an estimated value of 75-100 million U.S. dollars. It is anticipated that more than 1,000 satellites for commercial telecommunications will be launched over the next decade and generating well over 500 billion U.S. dollars in revenues. Clearly, this represents a unique opportunity for asset-based financing.*[3]

The success of the RLVs and the hopes raised in this technology are another key step on a further and continuously growing commercialization and privatization of space business. SpaceShipOne and SpaceShipTwo are entirely privately funded projects by a very successful space entrepreneur, Sir Richard Branson. Smaller companies involved in the space sector or wishing to do so, do not have such an asset(s). These figures do not allow to

[2] S. Chenard, *Financing satellites: easier said than done*, Air & Space Law Europe, vol.1, issue 1,1999, p. 29-32

[3] Martin J. Stanford & Alexandre de Fontmichel, *Vue d'ensemble de l' avant-projet de Protocole sur les questions spécifiques aux matériels d'équipement spatial et son examen par le COPOUS*, Uniform Law Review (2001-1), p.61-77.

acknowledge the existence of an open access to space commercialization. The access is made rather restrictive.

The authors of this paper will accordingly address the issue of whether the Draft Protocol to the Convention on International Interests in Mobile Equipment on Matters specific to Space Assets[4] [hereinafter Space Protocol] could contribute to change this situation. The development and sustainability of RLV technology is the cornerstone of the development of a viable commercial space tourism industry. In order to understand how critical this path is, it is first necessary to introduce the concept of RLV as well as the evolution of their regulation.

II. REUSABLE LAUNCH VEHICLES: AN INTRODUCTION

A- Key Feature for Space Tourism

A RLV, a Reusable space vehicle or a reusable launch system can be defined as a launch vehicle capable of launching into space more than once, in contrast with expendable launch vehicles (ELVs) or systems where the launch vehicle is discarded after the launching.

An expendable launch vehicle is made up of one or more rocket stages. After each stage has burned its compliment of propellant, it is expended (jettisoned from the vehicle) and left to crash back to Earth. As an example, the entire Saturn V rocket was expended while sending humans to the Moon. The U.S. Space Shuttle, which transports astronauts to Low Earth Orbit and back, is reusable.

The vehicle charged with a payload or with humans is released to space from a shuttle or launched on top of an expendable and then operates in space. At the end of the mission the RLV will de-orbit, return to Earth and can be used again for other similar missions.

As space vehicle designed to perform multiple missions and being re-used, RLVs dramatically reduce the cost of access to low orbit, a quality desirable for various types of missions, including human trips to and from space. Moreover, RLV construction costs could be amortized over multiple launches, reducing the financial charge not only for governments but also at the same time opening access to space to private commercial users.

However, the technical challenges of designing a system to fly to orbit and return are phenomenal. RLV technology development is thus an extremely challenging enterprise, "not only technologically and operationally but as well in terms of performance requirements, market developments and costs.*"* [5]

A number of government research projects, most notably in the United States the X-33, X-34, X-37 and X-38, were initiated to develop and test new RLV technologies to reduce the risk of developing a next generation of RLVs. At the same time, a number of entrepreneurial companies have developed their own RLV concepts in an effort to reduce launch costs and undercut established launch vehicle providers.

Historically, payloads have been government and commercial communications satellites, such as satellites, remote observation satellites as well as many other types of unique spacecraft.

[4] UNIDROIT draft Space Protocol www.unidroit.org

[5] 2004, U.S. Commercial Space Transportation Developments and Concepts: Vehicles, Technologies and Spaceports, FAA/AST.

In terms of RLVs, there are no true orbital launch systems in use at present. The Space Shuttle is the first and remains actually the only operational partially reusable launch vehicle. The orbiter, which includes the main engines, and two solid rocket boosters, are reused after several months of refitting work for each launch. The external fuel drop tank is discarded.
The former Soviet Union developed Energia-Buran, a partially reusable launch vehicle similar to the U.S. Space Shuttle, which however only flew once in 1988. The Shuttle Buran program was eventually abandoned in 1993.

In terms of other planned orbital initiatives, one can find the PlanetSpace Silver Dart, a partly reusable spaceplane, based on hypersonic glider design, SpaceX Falcon 1, announced as partially reusable, but the maiden flight on March 24, 2006 failed; SpaceX Falcon 5/Falcon 9, announced as fully reusable whose maiden flight is scheduled for the first quarter of 2008; Skylon, an airbreathing SSTO spaceplane, the Kistler Aerospace K-1, Hopper (proposed reusable European launch system) and the RLV/Avatar, a proposed reusable Indian launch system for small payloads. The Excalibur Almaz initiative, whose holding is headquartered on the Isle of Man, is by far the most ambitious.[6]

If orbital RLVs are supposed to be a vector for a high reliable space access by providing low costs, reusability, however implies weight penalties such as reentry shielding and possibly a stronger structure to survive multiple uses, and given the lack of experience with these vehicles, the actual costs and reliability are yet to be seen. These entrepreneurs are well aware of the latter, as commercial risk reduction is a key to the success of such ventures.

[6] Excalibur Almaz Ltd.

B- RLVs Regulations in the United States: a Brief Genesis

The RLV regulations were subject to hesitations, uncertainty and lacked uniformed system of legislation. Private space entrepreneurs, such as Burt Rutan addressed virulent critics to the FAA and on the AST applicable regulations.
Gary C. Hudson, in his testimony before the House Subcommittee on Space and Aeronautics in November 2003, reproached the AST to have grown increasingly bureaucratic and not up to challenge of the RLVs technological development. He established a comparison between the U.S. regulatory system to the one established for commercial launches in the Russia Federation: *There are no launch licenses, no environmental impact statements, no two-year process costing hundreds of thousands of money. Provide your insurance certificate, submit proper notifications and you are good to go. Bureaucrats from the former Soviet Empire are more sensible than we are.*[7] He went as far as suggesting the closing of the AST, as in his opinion, no third parties were really at seriously high risk from space launch activities. He further invited the withdrawal of the United States from the 1972 UN Liability Convention.
According to Burt Rutan declarations in 2003 and to the documents provided by Scales Composites at the rollout, SpaceShipOne was conducting the flight tests under experimental license to avoid the burden of the regulatory costs.

[7] Available from www.house.gov/science/hearings/space03/nov5/hudson.pdf Accessed on 30 July 2006.

Developers of RLVs have been concerned with the potentially high cost of the regulatory paperwork. "To go from an experimental vehicle to a certified vehicle is typically a ten times increase in price, on the rough order of magnitude" as put by X-Prize chairman Peter Diamandis during the Space Access 2003 conference in Scottsdale, Arizona. Dan DeLong, chief engineer for XCOR Aerospace, estimated certification costs up to 100 times as much as development. *It's tough raising the money to build the vehicle [...] but if you have to certify it before you're allowed to make money with it, it will be 100 times harder and it just won't happen.*[8]

However, according to FAA officials and industry executives, the regulatory issues, while significant, may not be as big an obstacle as some entrepreneurs fear. Although the various issues and obstacles regarding RLV licensing may create an antagonistic relationship between the companies and the government, the FAA and the industry representatives made it clear that the two sides get along quite well with each other. The AST wants to be proactive and anticipate industry needs in order to reduce regulatory risks.

While against regulations imposing perfect safety that would stop everyone to fly, Jeff Greason, president of XCOR Aerospace declared: *I don't think it's bad in a free society to have a situation where certain minimum requirements have to be imposed on people before they can launch something with destructive potential that can kill people. The mere presence of a federal agency requiring you to demonstrate a certain level of public safety is not bad. The details can be quibbled over, but we need something, because if we don't have something someone is going to go out and kill 100 people with a rocket.*[9]

As to RLVs, until the U.S. Space Act of 2004, there was no express statutory jurisdiction for the licensing and safety regulation of private human space flight. Moreover, until very recently, only ELVs and certain types of ballistic missiles were available for private sector use.

After President Bush presented its " Vision for exploration" in January 2004, the United States issued during the same year a new National Space Transportation Policy recognizing commercial human space flight: *To exploit space to the fullest extent [...] requires a fundamental transformation in U.S. space transportation, capabilities and infrastructure. In that regard, the United States Government must capitalize on the entrepreneurial spirit of the U.S. private sector, which offers new approaches and technology innovation in U.S. space transportation, options for enhancing space exploration activities and opportunities to open next commercial markets, including public space travel.*[10]

The 1984 Commercial Space Launch Act [hereinafter the CSLA] is the principal legislation governing the licensing and the regulation of commercial space transportation. The law was drafted

[8] Jeff Foust, *RLV regulation: licensing vs. Certification* Monday, April 28, 2003. Available from www.thespacereview.com/article/18/1

[9] *Ibid.*

[10] Vision for Exploration for Space and a New National Space Transportation Policy the 21st of December 2004 establishing Guidelines and Actions to ensure Nation's Ability to maintain Access and Use of Space. Available from www.ostp.gov/html/Space/TransFactSheet2005.pdf Accessed 12 June 2006.

especially for the commercial ELVs and established the Department of Transportation (DOT) as the lead branch authority to oversee and coordinate space launch activities in the U.S.

In 1990, a license needed to be issued on the reentry of a vehicle, COMET, a vehicle developed in conjunction with NASA Center for the Commercial Development of Space, for the purpose of returning experimental payloads from space to Earth. The DOT delivered for the first time a licensing reentry, however in order to avoid exceeding its bounds of authority, the license was issued by focusing exclusively on public health and safety issues.

Consequently at that time there was no clear and identifiable statutory authority for the licensing of payloads, as DOT was considered as the licensing authority exclusively for ELVs.

In 1998, nevertheless, the Congress amended the CSLA to explicitly grant authority to the FAA to license the return of vehicles from space to Earth and extend the DOT licensing authority to reentry vehicle operators.

In 2000 the FAA's Office of Commercial Space Transportation (AST) issued final rules defining the licensing process for RLV missions, including RLV missions with on-board crew and reentry of a reentry vehicle. On-orbit operations were excluded from the scope of the FAA license.

Despite the Congress enactment of legislation extending licensing authority and indemnification for reentry flights and the above regulations of the FAA, it was not clear what the FAA approach was to hybrid regulations for hybrid concepts combining both airframe and rocket characteristic and technology. Should they be regulated as civil aircraft (FAA civil aviation, AVS Aviation Safety) or as launch vehicles subject to licensing standards established by AST, or under both regimes? Another issue is whether they were considered as "suborbital rocket" under the provisions of the CSLA?

According to the HR 3752 bill, AST was the primary and central entity regulating "all commercial space flight authority, including authority to regulate commercial human space flight."[11] Due to the fact that the CSLA did not define the term "suborbital rocket" the classification of hybrid vehicles remained open to interpretation. In fact there was no need for such definition until the advent of the private sector RLV technology development. One important issue was therefore to clearly avoid two separate regulatory regimes.

The experimental permits now issued by the FAA were previously absent from the regulatory landscape for licensing rockets. These permits were called for by the HR 3752 to allow for RLV research and development similar to experimental airworthiness certificate issued in the aviation area. By issuing the experimental permits the intention was to grant more quickly and with fewer requirements than licenses.

The Committee Report instructed AST to work closely with the applicants on a case-by-case basis to determine what modification may be made to suborbital rocket without changing the vehicle design

[11] Commercial Space Launch Amendments Act of 2004. Available from http://thomas.loc.gov/cgi bin/query/D?c108:1:./temp/~c108CuqpzE::Library of congress THOMAS Accessed on 12 June 2006. *See also,* the detailed article of T.R. Hughes and E. Rosenberg, *Space Travel Law (and politics): The Evolution of the Commercial Space Launch Amendments Act of 2004*, Journal of Space Law, 2005, vol.31 (page 3-79).

to an extent that would invalidate the permit.

Thanks to the efforts of the U.S. Congress, the FAA accordingly issued the first-ever RLV mission license to Scaled Composites on April 1, 2004. Because of the hybrid nature, the FAA also required Scaled Composites to obtain an Experimental Airworthiness Certificate (EAC) under 14 CFR parts 21 and 91. Some of the tests flights needed an RLV mission license and others because of their short duration engine burn times, were to be conducted solely under the EAC. Twenty days after the FAA issued another mission license to XCOR Aerospace Inc., a multiple RLV suborbital mission based exclusively on plans and blueprints, as the Sphinx vehicle had not yet been constructed. The HR 3752 was a general framework for the 2004 Space Act.

Under the above Space Act The FAA is required to issue the experimental permits in order to allow for RLV research and development. It is a more rapid regulatory procedure with fewer requirements; shorter review period and involving a different approach to public risk analysis than the one employed by the FAA in issuing launch licenses. The experimental permits however are issued only under restrictive conditions such as the R&D testing for new design concepts, equipment or operating techniques. Consequently, once an operator obtains a license to operate the vehicle, the latter can no longer be operated under an experimental permit.

One major difference, however, is that the definition of suborbital rockets is much broader, allowing a wider range of vehicles to be defined as such: a *vehicle, rocket-propelled in whole or in part, intended for flight on a suborbital trajectory, and the trust of which is greater than its lift for the majority of the rocker-powered portion of its ascent.*[12]

Jurisdiction for orbital operations remains undefined under the current regime.

Suborbital flights are at present the major issue to be dealt with under the current legislation. SpaceShipOne launched successfully a new era making human suborbital flight possible. Ambitious similar initiatives are being developed, however none of them did materialize so far. As vehicle technologies develop, RLVs may provide point-to-point delivery and transportation services on a suborbital and orbital basis. It is not clear what will be the applicable law. It is to be expected that the issues will depend on different national legislations. One can thus wonder how the standardization, so necessary to ensure the development of commercial suborbital or orbital flights, will be achieved.

C- Existing Projects and Private Initiatives

The 1990s saw increasing interest in the development of new reusable vehicles. The military Strategic Defense Initiative program "Brilliant Pebbles" required low cost, rapid turnaround space launch.[13] From this requirement came the McDonnell Douglas Delta Clipper VTVL SSTO. From a commercial point of view, large satellite constellations such as Iridium were proposed which also had low cost space access demands. The nineties

[12] 49 U.S.C. § 70102(19) (2000 & Supp. 2005).

[13] Available from http://www.missilethreat.com/systems/bp_usa.html Accessed on 18 June 2006.

hence encouraged the development of a private launch industry, including partially reusable vehicle players, such as Kistler, and reusable vehicle players such as Rotary Rocket.
The end of that decade saw the implosion of the satellite constellation market with the bankruptcy of Iridium and the nascent private launch industry collapsed. The "Brilliant Pebbles" program was abandoned due to the collapse of the former Soviet Union. The EELV program replaced the old expendable launchers evolved from ballistic missiles.

From the eve of the 21st century, rising costs lead to cancellation of both the X-33 and the X-34 program. Then followed the dramatic event of the Space Shuttle Columbia disaster that lead to the suspension of the Shuttle program until the summer of 2005.

With the Ansari X-Prize competition, inspired by the aviation competitions made hundred years before, a new entrepreneurial era in space was launched. Among many private competitors that disputed the Ansari X-Prize, Scaled Composites won with the reusable SpaceShipOne ten million dollars prize, by reaching 100 kilometers in altitude twice in a two week period with the equivalent of three people on board, with no more than ten percent of the non-fuel weight of the spacecraft replaced between flights. While SpaceShipOne is suborbital like the X-15, the private sector hopes it can be eventually developed for reusable orbital vehicles.

On 17 December 2003, Scaled Composites, formerly the Rutan Aircraft Factory announced SpaceShipOne's first supersonic flight, the first flight of its kind by a privately funded aircraft. SpaceShipOne successfully made this flight, reaching 68000 feet and 930mph (Mach 1.2). The craft was brought aloft by the White Knight carrier aircraft. On the same day, Paul Allen, one of the founders of Microsoft, confirmed publicly the rumors that he was the angel investor behind the SpaceShipOne venture. On 1 April 2004, the U.S. Department of Transportation issued the company the world's first license for a suborbital manned rocket flight. The license was approved by the Federal Aviation Administration's Office of Commercial Space Transportation (AST). Scaled Composites Model 316 SpaceShipOne completed the first privately funded human spaceflight on June 21, 2004.

SpaceShipTwo is a suborbital vehicle currently under development by The Spaceship Company, a joint venture between Scaled Composites and Sir Richard Branson's Virgin Group of the U.K. The Virgin Galactic space line plans to operate a fleet of five of these craft in passenger-carrying private spaceflight service starting in 2008. The SpaceShipTwo craft is based on a technology developed for SpaceShipOne as part of the Scaled Composites Tier One program, funded by Paul Allen. Both SpaceShipTwo and its new carrier aircraft, Eve (or White Knight Two), will be twice the size of the first generation spacecraft and mothership that won the Ansari X-Prize. In August 2005, the president of Virgin Galactic stated that if the upcoming suborbital service with SpaceShipTwo is successful, the follow-up SpaceShipThree will be an orbital craft.[14]
Virgin Galactic remains convinced, nearly 18 months after the SpaceShipOne flight,

[14] Presentation of Mr. Whitehorn, President of Virgin Galactic, to European Centre for Space Law/ESA, yearly Practionners forum, Paris, 17 March 2006.

that space tourism will be a healthy and sustainable business.[15] Financially supported by Sir Richard Branson and the Virgin Group, Virgin Galactic is investing between $200 million and $240 million to build five SpaceShipTwo vehicles, with a first flight planned in 2008 or 2009 — a year or two later than originally planned. Passengers will be paying $200,000 each to make the flight, and will be permitted to leave their seats to experience weightlessness. The entire flight is expected to last about two hours.

The Virgin Galactic business plan calls for 50,000 passengers to be flown in the company's first 10 years of operations. With that revenue stream, the company is assured of an average 25 percent annual return on invested capital. Mr. Whitehorn declared the FAA could have killed all hopes for Virgin Galactic if it had insisted on full certification of SpaceShipTwo as an aircraft, which would have cost a billion dollars under the estimation of Virgin Galactic.[16]

III- UNIDROIT DRAFT PROTOCOL AS FINANCING MODEL LEGISLATION? AN ILLUSTRATION

ARCA (Aeronautics and Cosmonautics Romanian Association)[17] is a non-governmental organization promoting aerospace projects as well as other space-related activities. Officially registered in 1999, ARCA was founded by a group of Romanian students with no funds and no support but with passion and a strong will to change the limited space activities landscape in Romania.

The work for participation to the X-Prize Competition on the first rocket, Demonstrator 1, started in 2001. The results were positive and the vehicle was presented in August 2002. Soon after that, ARCA joined the X-Prize Competition in September 2002. The space suborbital vehicle ORIZONT, in competition at the X-Prize, developed by ARCA took 8 years to be created, built and being operational due to the cruel lacks of funds. ARCA actually developed projects in partnership with other international private or governmental organizations involved in the space business launch. The public projects of ARCA are financed mainly from donations and sponsorships.

The example of ARCA is one of the many illustrations of projects and initiatives that due to lack of financial support, took a huge amount of time to develop. In most cases, projects were abandoned. A developing country space operator or company would not be able to carry out a whole space commercial project technically or financially. Quite to the opposite, the SpaceShipOne and SpaceShipTwo initiatives were from the start supported by wealthy companies and successful entrepreneurs.

Moreover, space activities and respectively RLVs launches involve a high level of risks: market, schedule, regulatory and liability, export controls, technical risks, strategic risks and management risks.

Insurance is required and insurance premiums are prohibitive. Some states or companies will accordingly always be in the position to have access to space independently of the market changes and customer demands, while others will not.

Given the existence of the UNIDROIT Convention and its draft Space Protocol, it becomes interesting to assess if such a model protocol could be a way of developing and securing space commercial activities, including commercials business

---

[15] *Ibid.*

[16] *Ibid.*

[17] Available from www.arcaspace.ro Accessed on 14 July 2006.

plans based on RLVs transportation. The protocol could hence become a financial instrument that by addressing private law issues, would secure space business transactions.

As an illustration of the above, Dr. Fleissing, World Bank economist is of the opinion that "*the acute credit problems of many developing countries is a direct consequence of their security interest law. Their laws do not provide for the creation of secured interests in movable property; such interests cannot be perfected or enforced. Potential borrowers that own movable property, such as cars, airplanes or space assets can rarely borrow. Lenders in developing countries largely prefer real estate as a guarantee for their money.*"[18]

Similarly: "*If there were a line of credit, companies from developing countries could contract the specialized services of companies from developed countries. Developed countries would benefit directly through commercialization of components and satellites, this increasing jobs, profits and subsequent tax revenues.*" [19]

The main problem of a security interest in mobile equipment is the lack of recognition, priority or enforcement in one State. The space sector, due to its many specificities, cannot in a very efficient way be the object of a traditional security interest. Compared to other infrastructure projects, space business is for the most part, based on the credit worthiness of the borrower.

The main purpose of the Convention on International Interests in Mobile Equipment (CIME) is to facilitate the financing of the acquisition and use of mobile equipment. The instrument provides for an international regime for the enforcement, registration and protection of international interest in mobile equipment of particular financial significance such as airframes, aircraft engines and helicopters, railway rolling stock and space assets.

The Space Protocol is not only applicable to satellites, first items to be subject to a growing commercialization and privatization, but through its broad definition of space objects / space assets, it is relevant as well to the Reusable Launch Vehicles. Its draft Article I(2)(g), Definition of Space Assets, reads as follows: (i) Any identifiable asset that is intended to be launched and placed or that is in space; (ii) Any identified asset assembled or manufactured in space; (iii) Any identifiable launch vehicle that is expendable or can be reused to transport persons or goods to and from space; and, (iv) Any separately identifiable component forming a part of an asset referred to in the preceding sub-paragraphs or attached to or contained within such an asset.

Unfortunately, due to the fragmented space community encompassing individual satellite manufacturing companies, satellite operators, banks, insurance companies, regional intergovernmental organizations like the European Space Agency, national space agencies and space lawyers, the Protocol is currently still under consideration and no substantial advances have been accomplished from 2004.

It nevertheless remains that the draft Space Protocol remains a very interesting tool for the private sector to secure their investments. Space assets are not defined in any of the five space law treaties. It is

---

[18] Heywood Flessing, *Secured Transactions: The Power of Collateral*, Fin. & Dev., June 1996, p. 44

[19] Alvaro Fabricio dos Santos, *Developing countries and the UNIDROIT Protocol on Space Property*, Proceedings of the 45th Colloquium on the Law of Outer Space, IISL/IAF, Texas USA (2002), p. 23-32

also a very innovative financial instrument, as the security rights apply to the moveable thing itself. Moreover, the security rights also apply to the economic benefits (creditor rights) devolving from the use thereof. The draft Space Protocol is thus benefiting countries with different levels of economic and technological development that can take part in space activities by reducing the financial risk arising from these activities.

It is possible that the efficiency of such a protocol will be assessed on a short-term. Indeed, some nations that are not developing nations are considering adopting part of the model protocol in their legislation, such as, for example, the Isle of Man in the U.K.

CONCLUDING REMARKS

In any business venture, there is always a risk if an activity is pursued without a commercial perspective. Commercial risk reduction is hence critical. The approach of the draft UNIDROIT Space Protocol takes into account the importance of private activities in the future development of outer space activities, and the need to facilitate the establishment of adequate financing mechanisms. The new U.S. Space Policy guidelines include the development of international and commercial participation stressing the pursuance of commercial contributions and opportunities for providing space transportation to NASA.

The entrepreneurial risks in the space sector are many: technological, economic as well as institutional, legal and regulatory.

The Organization for Economic Co-Operation and Development (OECD),[20] encourages private sector participation in space applications. The OECD recommendations are divided into pillars. It is interesting to note, in terms of the need for standardization of the regulatory framework, the recommendations in the fifth pillar: *Recommendation 5.1* – Develop national space laws when none exists, or complement existing ones; *Recommendation 5.2* – Make existing space laws and regulations more business-friendly; *Recommendation 5.3* – Adapt international space laws to business needs; *Recommendation 5.4* *Special Focus* – Review the application of general laws and their impacts on the development of space applications.

The OECD also foresees the possibility that suborbital space tourism may be a critical path for commercial viability of orbital flights. If commercial success follows progressive technical mastery of suborbital flights, one may expect the initialization of a virtuous circle with a) more activities and accumulation of experience and, b) development of systems that fly faster and higher. Along this virtuous circle, the systems developed and operated for space tourism may converge with orbital space planes and RLV systems by 2030 and add into the operation of commercial RLV the experience accumulated with tourism to develop orbital space tourism.[21]

Space Entrepreneurship needs to be fostered as it creates opportunities.

In other words, space commerce needs...commerce.

---

[20] OECD, Space 2030: Exploring the Future of Space Applications, OECD, 2004, ISBN 92-64-02032-2.

[21] *Ibid*, at 147.

IAC-06-E6.1.09

COMMERCIAL SPACEPORT DEVELOPMENT: THE ROLE OF DOMESTIC AND INTERNATIONAL SPACE LAW AND REGULATIONS

Kenneth M. Weidaw III, Esq.
Weidaw, Peck & Associates, L.L.P.
Pittsburgh, Pennsylvania, U.S.A.
Member IISL, AIAA
kenneth_weidaw@yahoo.com

ABSTRACT

Competition for commercial space launch business has continued to increase over the last decade. In expanding its services, the commercial launch industry is now preparing to accommodate tourists as they explore low earth orbit. Given the launch business growth, traditional government controlled spaceports are increasingly unable to offer timely and cost-effective launch services prompting private and municipal alliances to develop private spaceports. Domestic and international space law and regulations play a significant role in controlling growth through each nation's licensing powers.

We are now witnessing the early stages of commercial spaceport development in the United States and in other nations. The purpose of this paper is to summarize the recent development of commercial spaceports, the reasons for their creation and the manner in which they are being formed. Space law pertinent to their development and growth, including national licensing regimes, will be outlined. As local and international spaceports continue to evolve, creative solutions will have to be developed to regulate launch traffic between spaceports, to low earth orbit stations, communications satellites, solar energy platforms and the nearby planets. International space laws can and should play an important role. However, it is argued the extant international and domestic space and aerospace laws and regulations are inadequate. A general convention must be convened to address the predictable legal liability, space traffic, launch trajectory and recovery issues that will develop as nations create spaceports and launches proliferate.

INTRODUCTION
SPACEPORTS - BACKGROUND

The term "spaceport" brings to mind a futuristic facility at which spacecraft are launched, sheltered, and maintained for travel to distant cities on planet Earth and to planets and celestial bodies in our solar system. The term came into prominence during the 1950s in various movies and science fiction books. Although functionally distinct, one also thinks of the modern airports as a companion facility. Indeed, we will see that the operations of modern international airports as well as the legal and regulatory regimes that govern them have set the international tenor for future development of the spaceport.

The FAA in its February 2005 report, entitled, *Suborbital Reusable Launch Vehicles and Emerging Markets*, page i, advises: "Suborbital launch activity has long been overlooked by the commercial market which for many years focused exclusively on launching satellites. Recently, however, there has been a resurgence of interest in commercial suborbital spaceflight, stimulated by the emergence of new markets, notably space tourism and new vehicles developed by entrepreneurs. With the successful claiming of the Ansari X-Prize [won in October 2004 by Mojave Aerospace Ventures – a $10 million dollar award offered to the builders of the first privately-developed reusable suborbital vehicle capable of carrying three people to 100 kilometers (62 miles) altitude twice within two weeks], high public interest in space travel, and new vehicles under construction, entrepreneurial ventures are pushing a new industry forward at a rapid pace."

As suborbital launch vehicles are developed to travel to 100 kilometers, they will serve more than tourists. They will serve the commercial, civil and military or remote sensing markets as well. Additionally, suborbital vehicles can also serve as the first stage of an orbital launch system, carrying an expendable upper stage that could carry small spacecraft into orbit at potentially lower costs than existing expendable launch vehicles.[1] The FAA report notes that: "Should some or all of these initial suborbital markets prove viable, the impetus will be present to develop more capable reusable suborbital vehicles that can fly higher, longer distances downrange, including high speed critical cargo/packages and eventually, high speed passenger transportation."[2]

"Spaceport" is not yet a recognized term by the United States Federal Aviation Administration (FAA) despite its use in numerous reports; instead, the term "launch site operator" is used in its regulations. Furthermore, the term "spaceport" does not appear in any of the international space law treaties and conventions; instead, some of the treaties and conventions use the term "station." Therefore, one may surmise that when the Outer Space Treaty of 1967, Article XII, makes reference to "All stations, installations, equipment and space vehicles…" it relates to the future spaceports that will be constructed on the Moon, Mars and other planets. Now, with the advent of commercial space transportation, "spaceport" has come into prominence especially in relation to the private, commercial launching of spacecraft to service the International Space Station (ISS) and for taking

---

[1] *Id.* at 1
[2] *Id.* at 2

tourists into suborbital and orbital space. Considering that the United States Department of Transportation issued its first commercial launch operator's license in 1987 and the first commercial launch occurred in 1989, the term "spaceport" has a short history.

Launch facilities throughout the world are overwhelmingly government owned, operated and controlled for use by the military and non-governmental commercial interests. Worldwide, there now exist 26 launch facilities, both government and commercial.[3] Some of the existing launch sites will become the future spaceports upon which businesses and travelers rely to transport goods and personnel to remote destinations. The newest launch facilities are currently located within the United States and are being established to serve commercial interests only. We will hereafter call them – "commercial spaceports." Given the global interest in establishing new spaceports, international coordination and regulation of future space vehicle launches will prove a challenge.

Spaceports vary with respect to the types of commercial space operations that can be supported. The types of vehicle operations that can be accommodated at a given spaceport are determined by such factors as:

a. Destination/mission objectives (e.g. launching into low earth orbit, medium earth orbit or geosynchronous earth orbit and the preferred trajectory).
b. Ability of the spaceport to accommodate the vehicle operational, performance and support requirements.
c. Spaceport scheduling assurance and range turn-around time (e.g. time needed to process successive operations).
d. Environmental constraints (e.g. noise abatement, hazard concerns).
e. Economics (e.g. launch costs)
f. Weather trends (i.e. the probability that weather patterns/trends will present a risk to the launch window).
g. Traffic Flow Patterns (i.e. the constraints that must be dealt with in use of the National Aerospace System such as conflicting use flight paths)[4]

SCOPE OF PAPER

The commercial spaceports of primary concern in this paper are non-military launch facilities funded with state grants, controlled by a governmental authority that may be jointly operated with one or more private companies for the primary purpose of launching commercial payloads and tourists. Such spaceports are currently located primarily in the United States. However, other nations are now planning to develop their own commercial spaceports.

COMMERCIAL SPACEPORTS IN THE UNITED STATES

As private, commercial space interests evolve, launch facility operators do not want to compete with the military for use of the government-operated facilities with their expensive personnel and facilities infrastructure; instead, they

[3] FAA/AST Launch Information, Vehicles &Sites: Launch Sites, http://ast.faa.gov/linfo_vsite/maps/as.cfm

[4] FAA website, *Commercial Space Transportation Concept of Operations In the National Airspace System*, FAA, Version 2.0, May 11, 2001, page 4, www.faa.gov

want flexible flight schedules and minimum range fees. Presently, there are eleven licensed and operational federal and commercial spaceports in the United States. There exist as of September 22, 2006, merely six commercial spaceports licensed by the FAA to conduct launch activities. To handle the increasing number of commercial launches in the 1990s, commercial spaceports were organized in the United States: (1) the California Spaceport is co-located at Vandenberg Air Force Base (licensed in1996); (2) the Florida Spaceport is co-located at Cape Canaveral Air Force Station (licensed in 1997); and (3) the Virginia Spaceport Center is co-located at Wallops Flight Facility on Wallops Island (licensed in 1997). More recently, spaceports have been established and licensed at: (4) the Kodiak Launch Complex on Kodiak Island, Alaska (licensed in 1998); (5) the East Kern Airport District – for the Mojave Airport, in California (licensed in 2004); and (6) the Oklahoma Space Industry Development Authority spaceport at the Clinton-Sherman Industrial Airpark located in Burns Flat, Oklahoma (licensed in 2006).

Other states within the United States have proposed spaceports that are now in the various stages of development. New Mexico , Cecil Field near Jacksonville, Florida and Texas – Gulf Coast Regional Spaceport at Brazoria County are currently in pre-application consultation with the FAA and have begun the NEPA process; none have yet submitted a launch license application to the FAA. Legislation has recently been passed in Wisconsin for construction of a spaceport in Sheboygan, Wisconsin. The state of Alabama wants to construct a spaceport on the Gulf of Mexico. Texas currently has three proposed sites for spaceports; the sites are in Brazos, Pecos and Willacy Counties. Montana enacted legislation creating a spaceport authority to create a spaceport in Great Falls, Montana, but has not pursued its development or licensing. Utah, Nevada, South Dakota, Washington and New Jersey are each engaged in development activity that may eventually lead to the creation of spaceports.

Outside of the United States, commercial spaceports have been proposed for the United Arab Emirates, outside Dubai; Singapore and Scotland. Other nations that have emerged as major providers of suborbital launch services include, Australia, Norway, Japan, Brazil and India.[5] The future will undoubtedly see other nations develop commercial spaceports in anticipation of future international air and orbital travel as well as to serve commercial customers. When a lunar colony is established later in the 21st century, additional travel needs will be serviced through the multitude of both governmental-controlled and commercial spaceports.

CREATING THE COMMERCIAL SPACEPORT

Within the United States, certain states that enacted legislation to establish state spaceport authorities have created their definition of a "spaceport." Although similar, the definitions are different in each of the states. For example, Chapter 13 of the Utah Spaceport Authority Act defines a spaceport as follows:

[5] FAA website, *Suborbital Reusable Launch Vehicles and Emerging Markets*, February 2005, page 9, www.faa.gov

"Spaceport means an area of land or water which is used, or is made available for, the landing and takeoff of spacecraft, including any appurtenant areas which are used, or intended for use, for spaceport buildings, other spaceport facilities or rights-of-way, together with all spaceport buildings and facilities located thereon, … including, parking, dining, recreational, and hotel facilities."[6] A recent definition from the state of New Mexico defines spaceport to mean "…an installation and related facilities used for the launching, landing, recovery, servicing and monitoring of vehicles capable of entering or returning from space."[7] One of the early commercial spaceports in the United States, the California Spaceport, co-located on Vandenberg Air Force Base in California, defines spaceport to mean: an entity designated by the California Spaceport Authority for the operation of launch sites or reentry sites such as a city, county, special district …whose application requires a written notice of intent to apply for a federal launch site operator's license, a copy of the "perfected application" submitted to the Department of Transportation and written notice of acceptance of the license.[8]

Given the desirability of having a spaceport located within its state, the listed state governments have enacted legislation creating spaceport authorities that will receive funds from the state to construct and operate the facility. Some of the more recent spaceport authorities, such as the New Mexico and Mojave spaceports, have secured the active involvement of certain commercial space flight companies that are involved in the development of suborbital and orbital space vehicles for commercial and tourist uses. To insure future launch business, the newest spaceports, both in the United States and internationally, will seek the involvement and monetary support - in a business alliance - of commercial launch companies and supporting service companies to participate in the continued growth of the spaceport. The spaceport authorities must construct support facilities for the launch vehicles, supporting personnel, cargo storage areas and accommodations for future passengers. One recognizes similarities in the commercial development of international airport properties and the surrounding areas and the future commercial spaceports. The lessons learned in the growth of airports over the last fifty years will, in some instances, apply to the future development of the spaceport. However, given the hazards of launching space vehicles and having them reenter the spaceport from distant locations, spaceports will continue to be located in geographically remote areas with climates appropriate for continuous use throughout the year. We may find that the commercial airports of today will provide continuous passenger services to the spaceports where passengers will be accommodated until their launch departure date.

SPACEPORT LICENSING REGIME IN THE UNITED STATES

The FAA Office of the Associate Administrator for Commercial Space Transportation (FAA/AST) licenses and

---

6 Utah Spaceport Authority Act, Section 3. Section 72-13-102(2)

7 New Mexico Statutes Annotated 1978, 9-15-43 F.

8 California Space Enterprise Development Act, Chapter 627 of the 2003 Statutes, Section 13999.1 (p) and Section 13999.3(a)-(c)

regulates United States commercial space launch and reentry activity, as well as non-federal launch and reentry sites, as authorized by Executive Order 12465 and Title 49, United States Code, Subtitle IX, Sections 70101-70119. The FAA/AST is directed to encourage, facilitate, and promote commercial space launches and reentries.[9]

AST issues launch licenses for commercial launches or orbital and suborbital rockets, and licenses the operations of non-federal launch sites or "spaceports."

AST issues two types of launch and reentry licenses: (a) a launch or reentry specific license – issued for one or more launches or reentries having the same operational parameters; and (b) a launch or reentry operator license – issued to a launch site operator that conducts launches and reentries from one site within a range of operating parameters. A spaceport operator seeks the second of the two licenses permitting multiple launches from the site. The operator's license remains in effect for two to five years from the issuance date.[10]

The key components of the licensing process for a spaceport operator are the following:

a. Pre-application Consultation: Consultation with the FAA precedes the filing of an application;

b. Policy Review and Approval: The license application is received by FAA and reviewed to determine whether there are any issues affecting United States national security or foreign policy interests or international obligations of the United States;

c. Safety Review and Approval: The purpose of the safety review is to determine whether the spaceport can safely conduct its proposed operation;

d. Environmental Review: It ensures that the proposed spaceport activities pose no unacceptable danger to the natural environment; and

e. Compliance Monitoring: Making certain that the spaceport is operating within the regulations and terms of its license.[11]

Commercial spaceport personnel such as launch safety specialists and commercial space transportation vehicle personnel, including mission planning, mechanics, and vehicle operators (on-board pilots), receive FAA approved training, authorization and medical qualification similar to aircraft pilots.[12] Spaceport security and passenger safety will also be a significant and continuing concerns of the international spaceport community and the FAA, not unlike those currently experienced by air travelers in the year 2006.

Given the decreased commercial satellite launches over the last few years, the FAA expends considerable time with state governments and their economic

[9] FAA website, http://ast.faa.gov/aboutast/

[10] FAA website, http://ast.faa.gov/lrra/about_lrra.htm, page 1 of 4

[11] FAA website, *Id.* at page 2 of 4, and page 3 of 4

[12] FAA website, *Commercial Space Transportation Concept of Operations In The National Airspace System*, Version 2.0, May 11, 2001, page 8, www.faa.gov

development bodies in the pre-application consultation stage. No state wishes to expend taxpayer funds on a spaceport that cannot attract imminent launch business. Until we see a substantial upturn in launch business, many of the states that have expressed an interest in establishing a commercial spaceport (listed above) will likely not pursue the license past the first stage.

SPACEPORTS – SPACE AND AIR TRAFFIC MANAGEMENT

The growth of commercial spaceports will demand a newer, more sophisticated and integrated planet-wide space and air traffic management system. Such a system does not now exist. International space law has not yet considered space traffic management.

In the United States, the FAA recognizes the critical need to develop a space and air traffic management system. "Changes in the magnitude and complexity of space operations will place new demands on the NAS [National Airspace System] as vehicles in route to and from earth orbit and beyond transition through airspace that is currently the near exclusive domain of aviation traffic."[13] It is expected that the increased frequency of commercial launches and reentries, from a broad range of locations, in the United States will contribute substantially to competition for airspace amongst NAS users.[14] Space and aviation operations must be seamlessly integrated in order to continue to provide efficient service to all NAS users.

[13] *Id.* at 1

[14] *Id.* at 1

The FAA proposes to phase in the new, integrated traffic management system; the system serves traffic transitioning to and from space by providing reserved and released airspace (calling them "Flexible Spaceways") that allows space vehicles to transition through the NAS.[15] The FAA plan deals with the vertical assent to orbit and horizontal transition through the NAS to an airborne point where a vertical, high-acceleration assent is initiated. For flights operating above the NAS, the mission profile includes: (1) the vehicle's target point for insertion into space and (2) its reentry point into international airspace.[16]

Establishing an international regulatory body to provide for a safe, reliable, and efficient space and air traffic management system is the coming challenge. Some noted legal scholars recommend that we examine the institutional model established by the 1944 Chicago Convention and the charter of the International Civil Aviation Organization (ICAO).[17] "There are many reasons for the success of the ICAO system. One of them has been the ability to delimitate the matters falling under its competence and the matters belonging to the domestic jurisdiction of each State. It surely will be one of the most arduous issues to cope with in shaping the Space Traffic Management System."[18] Closely related

[15] *Id.*at 4

[16] *Id.* at 8, 16

[17] Convention on International Civil Aviation, December 7, 1944, 15UNTS 295; ICAO Doc. 7300/6 and Filho, J., "Space Traffic Management: Comparative Institutional Aspects," *Proceedings of the Forty-Fifth Colloquium on the Law of Outer Space*, 491 (2002)

[18] Filho, J., *id.* at 492

to the ICAO is another international regulatory body, the International Telecommunications Union (ITU) which deals with orbital satellite telecommunications regulation. The two bodies are considered already to engage in some forms of space traffic management.[19]

The literature dealing with proposed space traffic management systems are concerned with three phases of space traffic: (1) the launch phase – deals with expendable and reusable launch vehicles from government and commercial spaceports. Space debris mitigation is a significant concern, especially for expendable launch systems; keeping track of debris and providing sufficient warning to orbiting or transitioning space vehicles will prove critical to the safety of the vehicle and its passengers. Pre-launch notification must also be one of the many concerns to be addressed by concerned nations. (2) The in-orbit phase – requires the creation of a comprehensive collision-warning system. On-time status information regarding the movements of multiple space vehicles in a variety of orbits will be critical to a safe and reliable traffic management system just as it is for the current international air traffic system. (3) The reentry phase – notification of reentry will be required. It concerns primarily reusable space vehicles but will also include deorbiting space debris, satellites and other space objects.[20]

[19] Contant, C., Lala, P., Schrogl, K-U, "Status of the IAA Study Group on "Traffic Management Rules for Space Operations," *Proceedings of the Forty-Sixth Colloquium on the Law of Outer Space*, 300 (2003)

[20] *Id.* at 300-301; See, Perek, L., "Early Concepts for Space Traffic," *Proceedings of the Forty-Fifth Colloquium on the Law of Outer Space*, 496-503 (2002)

An integrated space and air traffic management system must deal not only with the concerns of the National Airspace System over the United States but also the air space over all other nations on Earth, including, satellites in orbit, space debris, and the increasing number of spacefaring nations utilizing commercial spaceports.

CONCLUSION

There exists an urgent need for the spacefaring nations to convene a general convention, similar to the 1944 Chicago Convention, to address and plan a future integrated space and air traffic management system. Given the time it takes to convene such a convention and successfully complete its business, commercial spaceports will continue to evolve worldwide as well as new and improved space vehicles to transport cargo and passengers within the current airspace system. Without the benefit of an international regulatory body to control air and space traffic, spacefaring nations may regulate the airspace above their respective nations in an uncoordinated manner. The detriment to future launch providers and their customers will become apparent within twenty years unless action is taken now. Some legal scholars have recommended that the United Nations, through its Committee on the Peaceful Uses of Outer Space (COPUOS), assume the burden of forging an international space traffic management system considering the difficulty in calling a general convention; work has begun to have the Committee study the project. With many nations now engaging in launch activity, it is imperative that coordinated action be taken. Commercial space launches into suborbital and orbital space will continue to increase over the coming years. With no national or international body capable of taking on the task of coordinating and controlling integrated space and air traffic, problems will undoubtedly occur in disrupting the regular flow of aviation traffic between airports and spaceports. Such unsafe conditions will not long be tolerated by commercial aviation and space launch providers. We have the luxury of time to prepare for the future; let us not ponder the matter too long.

IAC-06-E6.1.10

ADVERTISING OF PRIVATE COMMERCIAL SPACE SERVICES IN THE EUROPEAN COMMUNITY

Miss Zeldine Niamh O'Brien L.L.B.*
University of Dublin, Trinity College, Ireland
zeldineobrien@gmail.com

Abstract

There is much potential for European Union law to apply through its Member States' national laws to space contracts and space activities. This is particularly valuable for potential space consumers within Member States that do not have any specific domestic space law binding within the States. This paper will examine the impact of Council Directive 84/450/EEC of the 10th September 1984 as amended to include comparative advertising by Directive 97/55/EC of the 6th October 1997 on the private commercial space tourism market in the European Community. The purpose of the directive, as amended, is to provide a minimum level of protection to consumers from any advertising which in any way, including its presentation, deceives or is likely to deceive the persons to whom it is addressed or whom it reaches and which, by reason of its deceptive nature, is likely to affect their economic behaviour or which, for those reasons, injures or is likely to injure a competitor and to lay down the conditions where comparative advertising is permitted.

INTRODUCTION

Although, international law is stated in the Outer Space Treaty to apply to outer space and national law will apply to space objects and any personnel aboard that are on a state's national registry (and therefore subject to their jurisdiction in accordance with Art. VIII of that Treaty), there is also great potential for the application of European Union law to apply, through its Member States' national laws, to space contracts and space activities. This is particularly valuable for potential space consumers within Member States that do not have any specific domestic space law binding within them (for example, Ireland). In this regard, Community measures in relation to consumer protection[1] that have the potential to apply to the space tourism market are of particular interest as these measures were not drafted in the light of the needs of the emergent private commercial space industry. Such measures also provide a contrasting approach to existing specific national space law dealing with the industry such as the Commercial Space Launch Amendments Act 2004. The European Union, as one of the world's great economic blocks with a population of 459.5m[2], is an ideal target market for the services sector, including private commercial space tourism services.[3] Critical to that sector is the role of advertising which is defined here as 'the process of persuasion, using the paid media in which purchasers of goods, services and ideas are sought.'[4] It enables the market to expand by allowing producers and service-providers access to consumers and by increasing consumer awareness of particular goods and services, both of which are of much importance for the space tourism industry at its current phase of development. This paper will examine the impact of EU advertising law on the content of advertising for the space tourism industry. It will also assess the

---

alternate approach to existing specific national space law dealing with the industry, such as the Commercial Space Launch Amendments Act 2004, in illustrating the protection given to pre-contractual space consumers'/space flight participants' knowledge.

THE FREEDOM TO PROVIDE SPACE SERVICES

Art. 49 (ex. Art.59) of the Treaty establishing the European Community provides for a prohibition on restrictions on the freedom to provide services in respect of nationals of Member States who are established in a State of the Community other than that of the person for whom the services are intended.[5] Measures may be extended to apply to nationals of third countries who provide services and who are established in the Community. Both Art.49 and Art.50 have direct effect.[6] It is clear from the parameters provided in Art.50 (ex. Art.60) regarding 'services' that both advertising[7] and private space services fall within its scope as activities of a commercial character provided for remuneration within the meaning of Art.50 (ex Art.60)[8] (provided the remuneration does not come from the public purse of a Member State)[9]. The recreational element to space tourism does not affect the construction of the activity as economic;[10] nor does the remuneration have to come from the recipient of the service.[11] However, Art.51 (ex Art.61), excludes transport services from the chapter as it is dealt with in Title V (ex IV).

Under Art.71 of Title V (ex Art.75) the Community is empowered to lay down common rules applicable to international transport to or from the territory of a Member State or passing across the territory of one or more Member States, the conditions under which non-resident carriers may operate transport within a Member State, measures to improve safety and any other appropriate provisions. It is possible therefore that either the services or the transport provisions may be relied on in respect of space tourism/ hospitality, with the choice depending on its interpretation either as a service or as a form of transport. Given the current state of development of space tourism and the ruling in *Cowan*, where a tourist was found to be the recipient of a service,[12] it is submitted to be viewed more as the former than the latter. However, there has been no determination by the ECJ on the matter.

ADVERTISING AND THE E.U.

While advertising is highly subjective, it is important that consumers receive correct, accurate and objective information regarding goods and services. This is vital where a new service enters into the market, especially one that is attendant with high risk. It will be essential for the private space tourism sector when the industry develops and the market expands. Advertising has a direct effect on the establishment and the functioning of the common market by causing, *inter alia*, distortions in competition. The increase of cross-frontier advertising also increases the desirability of harmonisation as discrepancies may disrupt intra-Community trade.[13] The second programme of the EEC for a consumer protection and information strategy provided for appropriate action to be taken in the field of misleading advertising.[14] Council Directive 84/450/EEC of 10 September 1984 relating to the approximation of the laws, regulations and administrative provisions of the Member States concerning misleading advertising[15] was subsequently passed.

Directive 84/450 notes that advertising "affects the economic welfare of consumers" whether it induces a contract or not. The purpose of the Directive is "to protect consumers, persons carrying on a trade or business or practising a craft or profession and the interests of the public in general against misleading advertising and the unfair consequences thereof" (Art.1).[16] Recipients of space services, such as space tourists, would constitute such consumers and would therefore have their economic welfare expressly protected in a way that does not occur within national space laws, such as the Commercial Space Launch Amendments Act 2004(CSLAA). While the latter Act safeguards the physical safety of space flight participants, their economic welfare is only indirectly protected insofar as the Act provides for extensive pre-disclosure of space flight risks prior to the receipt of any compensation. Furthermore, the requirement for a waiver, applicable, under the Commercial Space Launch Act 1984,[17] to space flight participants arguably protects the economic welfare of the emerging private commercial space flight industry more than that of individual consumers.

APPLICATION OF DIRECTIVE 84/450 TO SPACE SERVICES

Directive 84/450 applies to advertising of space service providers operating within the Community. It establishes conditions for determining whether an advertisement is misleading. In doing so, it ensures a minimal level of protection for the consumer's right to information, even if that information is not impartial, at the inducement stage, rather than prior to the exchange of consideration. This requirement for the provision of information is also safeguarded by the CSLAA but not at the inducement stage. Art.2 defines advertising as "the making of a representation in any form in connection with a trade, business, craft or profession in order to promote the supply of goods or *services*, including immovable property, rights and obligations". All three constituents must be present for the announcement to constitute an advertisement.[18] Misleading advertising is defined as "any advertising which in any way, including its presentation, deceives or is likely to deceive the persons to whom it is addressed or whom it reaches and which, by reason of its deceptive nature, is likely to affect their economic behaviour or which, for those reasons, injures or is likely to injure a competitor." It is clear that the advertising of private commercial space services within the Community will fall within the scope of the directive.

In determining whether advertising is misleading, the directive requires that account be taken of all its features noting in particular any information concerning:

> "(a) the characteristics of goods or services, such as their availability, nature, execution, composition, method and date of manufacture or provision, fitness for purpose, uses, quantity, specification, geographical or commercial origin or the results to be expected from their use, or the results and material features of tests or checks carried out on the goods or services;
> (b) the price or the manner in which the price is calculated, and the conditions on which the goods are supplied or the services provided;
> (c) the nature, attributes and rights of the advertiser, such as his identity and assets, his qualifications and ownership of industrial, commercial or intellectual property rights or his awards and distinctions". (Art.4)

Condition (a), with its requirement to take account the results and material features of tests and checks on the service in assessing whether an advertisement is misleading, is of particular benefit in protecting the interests of space consumers by restricting misleading claims regarding the safety of the space activity in question. Where a space service provider has included certain claims regarding the tests conducted on their space vehicle and its general safety features etc., they may be required by the courts of Member States to provide factual evidence to support the accuracy of those claims.

IMPLEMENTATION OF THE DIRECTIVE

The Directive leaves a degree of flexibility to Member States in the level of protection afforded to the consumer, which may be above that set out by the measure itself. However, as the ECJ noted, it "should be remembered, however, that that power must be exercised in a way that is consistent with the fundamental principle of the free movement of goods, as expressed in the prohibition contained in Art.28 EC on quantitative restrictions on imports and any measures having equivalent effect between Member States."[19]

The definition of misleading advertising is not uniform throughout the Community. In England, advertising is misleading 'if it conveys a false impression to an average reasonable viewer of the advertisement… there must be a reasonable probability of confusion being caused by the advertisement, and not just an abstract risk'.[20] Furthermore, "both literal and implied meanings must be considered; all persons likely to see the advertisement must be taken into consideration, including persons of low intelligence or limited means."[21] In Belgium omissions of essential characteristics will also amount to misleading advertising.[22] In France, pictoral representations may amount to misleading statements.[23] In Greece, false statements that misled can result in imprisonment for up to six months, a fine or both.[24] In Ireland, persons are forbidden from publishing advertisements which are likely to mislead and cause loss, damage or injury to members of the public to a material degree.[25] However, Spanish law only prohibits advertising that causes an error resulting in economic action or omission or that may or does damage a competitor. Ohly points out two additional questions, first whether the deception is to be determined as a purely factual matter or as a normative one[26] and second, the actual number of consumers who need to be deceived for the advertisement to be construed as misleading, both of which have received varied responses before the national courts and the ECJ.[27] Advertisers of space services should refer in each case to national law to ensure full compliance with any additional requirements.

COMPARATIVE ADVERTISING

Directive 97/55/EC of 6 October 1997, as amended by Directive 84/450/EEC[28] to include comparative advertising,[29] was borne out of a need to create a uniform provisions governing the form and content of comparative advertising in the interest of the internal market and the consumer's right to information. The Directive also protects the economic welfare of space consumers in assisting them in choosing amongst competitors. This protection is, of course, only advantageous where there are multiply space service providers operating within the market. Art.2 inserts a new Art.2a into Directive 84/450 which provides a definition of comparative advertising, *viz*, "any advertising which explicitly or by implication identifies a competitor or goods or services offered by a competitor."[30] Thus where space service providers resort to comparative advertising, as a weapon against their competitor the provisions of the directive, as incorporated into national law, will be engaged. Art.3a of the amended Directive provides exhaustively[31] the cumulative conditions[32] under which a comparative advertisement is permitted:

(a) it is not misleading according to Arts 2 (2), 3 and 7 (1);
(b) it compares goods or services meeting the same needs or intended for the same purpose;
(c) it objectively compares one or more material, relevant, verifiable and

representative features of those goods and services, which may include price;

(d) it does not create confusion in the market place between the advertiser and a competitor or between the advertiser's trade marks, trade names, other distinguishing marks, goods or services and those of a competitor;

(e) it does not discredit or denigrate the trade marks, trade names, other distinguishing marks, goods, services, activities, or circumstances of a competitor;

(f) for products with designation of origin, it relates in each case to products with the same designation;

(g) it does not take unfair advantage of the reputation of a trade mark, trade name or other distinguishing marks of a competitor or of the designation of origin of competing products;

(h) it does not present goods or services as imitations or replicas of goods or services bearing a protected trade mark or trade name."

The conditions above have a number of consequences. Condition (b) only requires that the service meet the same need, rather than being identical, so space hospitality advertising comparing different space vehicles will meet the condition because of their reasonable interchangeability. According to the ECJ's case law, it may be legitimate to use a competitor's registered trade mark where necessary to inform the public of the intended purpose of the service offered.[33] Under the Directive, the use of another's trade mark in comparative advertising will not infringe the Trade Marks Directive[34] as long as it is not unfair, does not denigrate the competitor's services, nor cause confusion.[35] Denigration, in this context, varies between claiming a competitor's service inferior[36] to depictions as 'generally unsatisfactory'.[37] Ohly suggests that a better approach to condition (e) is 'to apply it in situations in which an otherwise acceptable comparison is expressed in a manner that is denigrating, though not so exaggerated as to make the advertisement lacking in objectivity or misleading'.[38] In addition, as Kelly observes, the condition at (c) "ensures that the test is essentially an objective one. A statement will only be verifiable if the advertiser can provide the respective information upon request."[39] The ECJ has held that these conditions must be interpreted in the sense most favourable to such advertisements.[40] Any such advertising must "indicate in a clear and unequivocal way the date on which the offer ends or, where appropriate, that the special offer is subject to the availability of the goods and services, and, where the special offer has not yet begun, the date of the start of the period during which the special price or other specific conditions shall apply." Price comparisons have been found not to constitute misleading advertising as they are 'extremely useful to enable the consumer to make his choice in the full knowledge of the facts'[41] nor can they *per se* entail the discrediting or denigration of a competitor's trade mark.[42] The comparator has economic freedom in selecting which prices to compare.[43] A "failure to mention a better known brand name in a comparative advertisement would be contrary to the Directive if the omission significantly [affected] a consumer's choice." However, selecting the most favourable comparisons to be drawn is not contrary to the Directive as consumers reasonably expect this. Puffery is permitted.[44] In assessing if an advertisement violates the terms of the directive, the court will take account of its overall presentation and the target consumer group. In the case of a specific group of consumers with specialist knowledge, the probability of violating the directive is lower. For space tourism providers, this means that the expansion of the target consumer group beyond the limited numbers of the pioneer stage of development will affect the nature of their comparative advertising insofar as a determination may be made as to whether it infringes the directive or not. It may also be possible for space service competitors to raise other challenges against comparative advertisements based in copyright law or in tort, for example, malicious falsehood[45] or passing off.[46]

The amended Directive does not preclude voluntary controls on misleading or comparative advertising through the use of self-regulatory codes (Art.5) nor does it prevent Member States from taking measures that provides more extensive measures of protection for consumers in the case of misleading advertising (Art.7). However, while the Directive sets out only a minimum standard, "stricter national provisions on protection against misleading advertising cannot be applied to comparative advertising as regards the form and content of the comparison."[47] Therefore, any national measure regulating the form and content of comparative advertising will be assessed in light of the Directive and not Art.28.[48] Many Member States have such additional self-regulation in advertising. Member States may maintain bans on comparative advertising in the case of certain vulnerable categories of consumers or for the advertising of professional groups, although no current limitations exist for space consumers.

Actions Against Misleading and Comparative Advertisers

Member States must ensure that adequate and effective means exist for the control of misleading advertising or unpermitted comparative advertising, including legal provisions "under which persons or organizations regarded under national law as having a legitimate interest in prohibiting misleading advertising" may take legal action or bring the matter before a competent administrative authority. The Court /administrative body is empowered under the directive to order the cessation of, or to institute appropriate legal proceedings for an order for the cessation of, misleading advertising, or to order the prohibition of, or to institute appropriate legal proceedings for an order for the prohibition of the publication of an advertisement where this had not yet occurred but is imminent without proof of actual loss or damage or of intention or negligence on the part of the advertiser. Actions for an injunction may also be brought by qualified entities, such as consumer organisations, as provided for by Directive 98/27/EEC.[49] The measures taken may also amount to unfair commercial practices under Directive 2002/65/EC which includes misleading and comparative advertising as such.[50]

Other Directives[51]

The directive on the coordination of certain provisions laid down by law, regulation, or administrative action in Member States concerning the pursuit of television broadcasting activities[52] as amended is also of interest for space tourism operators. Television advertising is defined as 'any form of announcement broadcast whether in return for payment or for similar consideration or broadcast for self-promotional purposes by a public or private undertaking in connection with a trade, business, craft or profession in order to promote the supply of goods' and therefore will encompass the advertisement of space services. It must be 'readily recognizable' as such and kept separate from other parts of the programme service. Art.10 prohibits both surreptitious and subliminal advertising.[53] Art. 12 provides that television advertising must not prejudice respect for human dignity, include any discrimination on the grounds of race, sex or nationality, be offensive to religious or political beliefs or encourage behaviour prejudicial to health or to safety or the protection of the environment. It must no cause physical detriment to minors. (Art.16). The Directive does not prohibit a Member State from taking general measures in the interest of consumer protection from misleading advertising as long as the retransmission of advertisements from another Member State is not prohibited and no secondary control applies to such advertisements.[54]

The Distance Contracts directive[55] also has a bearing on advertising where done through the telephone and facsimile machines. Art. 10(1) prohibits the use of automatic calling systems without human intervention without the prior consent of the consumer. Where space service providers resort to direct mail advertising that leads to a contract, this will also be regulated by the Distance Contracts directive. Consumers under such contracts are given a seven-day cooling-off period with a right of withdrawal. This right to withdraw as well as the identity of the supplier, the main characteristics of the service and the cost (inc. taxes) should be provided in a clear and comprehensible manner but this is not applicable where the contract is for a service to be supplied only once and invoiced by the operator through distance communication. The consumer is entitled to know the geographical address of the supplier and has a non-waiveable right of cancellation. Those consumers that do not wish to receive direct mail advertising must be removed from the mailing list under Art.8 of Directive 9/46/EC.

The Package Holidays Directive[56] also prohibits misleading advertising and requires that the price be clearly disclosed. Additional details relating to the package holiday such as the transportation, accommodation and visa and passport requirements must be provided.

Other National Laws

In addition to the Community laws, Member States have their own national laws governing advertising that impose additional limitations.[57] France also imposes 'an absolute obligation of truthfulness for advertising of every kind'.[58] The law on the discounts that may be advertised with any service or product also varies among States. In England, the Trade Descriptions Act 1968 prohibits any person in the course of their trade or business from making a statement which s/he knows to be false, or recklessly make a statement which he knows to be false, including statements concerning the examination, approval or evaluation of any services, accommodation or facilities.[59] Germany, Austria, Belgium and Italy have fairly strict regimes. Cold-calling is also another area without uniformity with outright bans operating in Germany to countries with no specific legislation (Spain). The law on promotional gifts also varies among states. Germany restricts promotional gifts[60]; in France, this is banned unless identical to the service sold or if low value.[61] Promotional gifts are permitted in Ireland[62] and subject to only a few limitations in the Netherlands. Again, as above, reference should be made to the law in which the advertisement is made in order to ensure compliance.

Challenging National Advertising Legislation

National legislation that restricts or prohibits certain forms of advertising may limit the volume of imports by affecting the marketing opportunities for the imported service and amount to a measure equivalent to a quantitative restriction thus contravening Art.28 (ex.30) of the Treaty of Rome.[63] However, while art 28 is applicable to commercial communications, it is also limited by the *Keck* proviso[64] which permits certain selling arrangements provided they apply to all relevant traders within the national area and affect them all equally in law and in fact.[65] This approach was adopted by the ECJ in the advertising field.[66] If the measure taken is not discriminatory, the national court will be left to decide if the measure is necessary in order to meet the overriding requirement of general public importance or one of the Art.36 aims and the test of proportionality.

Restrictions on advertising in national law may also be challenged directly by space service providers as a restriction on the freedom to provide services within the Community as prohibited in Art.49 (ex.59) of the Treaty as occurred in *Bond van Advereerders v The Netherlands*[67] where the ECJ held that the Kableregeling in question discriminated against broadcasters established in other Member States by prohibiting them from advertising on their station intended for the Dutch public. Most restrictions imposed on the basis of residence have been held by the ECJ to operate contrary to Art.49.[68] However, it is essential that there is some inter-state element; the ECJ have held that "the provisions of the Treaty on the freedom to provide services cannot be applied to activities whose relevant elements are confined to a single Member State."[69] But where the prospective consumer moves between Member States before the completion of the contract, the matter will cease to be solely internal[70]. The focus is arguably 'on the mobility and availability of the service in question rather than emphasising the person.'[71] Art.49 covers both discriminatory and non-discriminatory restrictions in the same fashion as the free movement of goods under Art.28 following the *Cassis de Dijon* jurisprudence because "[t]here might be a variety of restrictions in different Member States, none of them intrinsically justified, which collectively might wholly frustrate the aims of [Art.49] and render impossible the attainment of a single market in services."[72]

Where a challenge is made to a discriminatory restriction, Member States may be able to justify the restriction within the exemptions provided in Art.49, as amended by the Treaty of Amsterdam, *viz* public policy, security or health. Economic aims do not constitute grounds of public policy.[73] In addition, such restrictions may also be objectively justified by reference to certain 'imperative requirements'. The ECJ set down the requirements in *Van Binbergen*[74]. First, the restriction in national law must pursue a legitimate public interest which is not at variance with the objectives of the Community, a determination of which is to be made by the national court.[75] Public interest objectives include the protection of workers[76], consumers[77], intellectual property[78] and fair trading. Second, the restriction must be equally applicable to all persons on undertakings operating within the particular Member State and be applied without discrimination.[79] Third, the measure must be proportionate to its aim, i.e. it must be an appropriate means of attaining the aim and no less restrictive measure must be available. If the restriction duplicates a condition in the Member State where the provider of the service is established, thus imposing a double burden, it will not be found to meet the test of proportionality.[80] Finally, the restriction must respect fundamental rights, particularly freedom of expression as embodied in Art.10(1) of the European Convention on Human Rights[81] and Art.19 of the UN International Covenant on Civil and Political Rights.[82] Where these conditions are satisfied, the restriction will be upheld.

The approach to non-discriminatory restrictions may be seen in *Alpine Investments*[83] where a Dutch measure prohibiting unsolicited commercial calls was found to constitute a restriction although it was a general measure that did not seek to provide an advantage to the national market. It was not analogous to measures taken in *Keck*. The provision affected not only offers made by the provider of services to the addresses established in the Netherlands or those who moved there to receive services but also offers made to potential recipients in another Member State directly affecting access to the market and hindering intra-Community trade.[84]

Where a national measure relates to both the free movement of goods under Art.28 and freedom to provide services under Art.49, the Court will, in principle, "examine it in relation to one only of those two fundamental freedoms if it appears that, in the circumstances of the case, one of them is entirely secondary in relation to the other and may be considered together with it."[85] In the event that the dissemination of advertising is not an end in itself, but a secondary element in relation to the sale, the free movement of goods aspect will prevail over the freedom to provide services aspect. The question should not be viewed in the abstract but in the context of the case[86]

CONCLUSION

Community advertising law provides protection to consumers by safeguarding their economic welfare and their right to information at the inducement stage. In doing so, advertising law may be seen to protect the interests of space consumers in addition to the protections provided by national space law measures. Space service providers should be aware that their advertisement policies, whether through broadcasting or direct mail, will attract the provisions of a number of directives as incorporated into domestic law as well as additional national measures, such as self-regulating codes. Advertisements should not be misleading. Comparative advertisements are permitted provided they do not create confusion in the market place between the brand names of the advertiser and those of a competitor, discredit or denigrate the brands of a competitor nor take unfair advantage of the reputation of a competitor's brand. The protection afforded in the regulation of comparative commercial space service advertising safeguards the free economic choice of the space consumer, regardless of whether a contract is entered into or not. Courts of Member States are empowered to order the cessation of publication of any advertisement breaching the law. Service providers may challenge unduly restrictive laws under the Treaty of Rome as a restriction on the freedom to provide services under Art.49. Such challenges extend to both discriminatory and non-discriminatory measures, by analogy to the case law on the free movement of goods.

---

* My thanks to Dr. Gernot Biehler for his comments and advice on an earlier draft. All errors and omissions are my own.

[1] K.P.E. Lasok, *Law and Institutions of the European Union*, 7th ed., (Butterworths, London, 2001), ch.34 p.800 et seq; Kendall, V., *EC Consumer Law*, (Wiley Chancery, London , 1994); Weatherill, S. "Consumer Policy" in Craig, P. and De Búrca, G., *The Evolution of EU Law*, (OUP,1999) at pp. 693-720, Weatherill, S., *EC Consumer Law and Policy*, (Longman, London, 1997), Quinn, A., "Consumer Policy – No Longer the EC Cinderella," (1990) 18 *ILT* 171and *Green Paper on European Union Consumer Protection*, Brussels, 2.10.2001, COM (2001) final.

[2] On 1st January 2005. Excludes DOMs. Schäfer, Gunter (ed.), *Key Figures on Europe: Statistical Pocketbook 2006*, Eurostat, Luxembourg, 2006, p.39.

[3] On the E.U. and tourism in general, see Bovagnet, F-C., *Statistics in Focus*, 18/2006 and Dimitrakopoulou, C., *Statistics in Focus*, 19/2006, Eurostat, 2006.

[4] Campbell of Alloway and Yaqub, Zahd (eds) , *The European Handbook on Advertising Law*, Cavendish Publishing Ltd., London, 1999, p.1.

[5] See generally Craig, Paul and De Búrca, Gráinne, *EU Law: Text, Cases and Materials*, 3rd ed., OUP, 2003, pp. 800-824, Crown, Giles, *Advertising Law and Regulation*, Butterworths, London, 1998, ch.12 and C-299/89 *Stichting Collectieve Antennevoorziening Gouda and Others v Commissariet voor de Media* [1991] 1 ECR 4007.

[6] C-33/74 *Van Binsbergen v. Bestuur van de Bedrijfsvereniging voor de Metaalnijverheid* [1974] ECR 1299, para. 26.

[7] C-52/79 *Procurer du Roi v. Marc JVC Debauvèe and Others* [1980] ECR 833; C-155/73 *Re Giuseppe Saachi* [1974] 1 ECR 409.

[8] See C-159/90 *SPUC v. Grogan* [1991] ECR I-4685.

[9] C-263/86 *Belgium v. Humbel* [1988] ECR 5365 para.18 but see C-186/87 *Cowan v. Le Trésor Public* [1989] ECR 195 and C-45/93 *Commission v. Spain* [1994] ECR I-911.

[10] C-275/92 *HM Customs and Excise v. Schindler* [1994] ECR 1039, paras 33-4.

[11] C- 352/85 *Bond van Adverteerders v. The Netherlands* [1988] ECR 2085.

[12] C-186/87 *Cowan v. Le Trésor Public* [1989] ECR 195.
[13] See generally, K. Mortelmans, "Minimum Harmonization and Consumer Law," [1988] *ECLJ* 2.
[14] OJ No C 133, 3. 6. 1981, p. 1.
[15] OJ No L 250, 19.9.1984, p.17.
[16] Kendall, *supra*, ch.7.
[17] The Commercial Space Launch Act 1984 (US), s.70112(b).
[18] *Dunnes Stores v Mandate* [1996] 1 ILRM 384; [1996] E.L.R. 56 (Irish Supreme Court applying the definition of advertising in Council Directive 84/450/EEC as incorporated into Irish law by the European Communities (Misleading Advertising) Regulations 1988 (SI No. 134 of 1988)).
[19] Para.34 Case C-71/02 *Herbert Karner Industrie-Auktionen GmbH v Troostwijk GmbH.* [2004] ECR I-3025. See also Case C-23/99 *Commission v France* [2000] ECR I-7653, paragraph 33).
[20] Crown, Giles, *op cit*, p.2.
[21] Ibid.
[22] Art.23 of the Trade Practices Act.
[23] Cass. Crim. De Mars 4, 1976, Bull. Crim. 199.
[24] Peri Athemitou Antagonismou, Art.3.
[25] Sale of Goods and Supply of Services Act 1980 (IR) s.8.
[26] Olivier, Peter, *Free Movement of Goods in the European Community*, 4th ed., (Sweet and Maxwell, London, 2003), para. 8.146. See Case C-220/98 *Estée Lauder Cosmetics GmbH & Co. OHG v Lancaster Group GmbH* [2000] ECR I-0117.
[27] Ohly, Ansgar and Spence, Michael, *The Law of Comparative Advertising: Directive 97/55/EC in the United Kingdom and Germany*, Hart Publishing, Oxford, 2000, pp. 61-65.
[28] See Ohly, *supra.*
[29]On the implementation, see generally, *Report from the Commission to the European Parliament on Consumer Complaints in Respect of Distance Selling and Comparative Advertising*, Brussels 10.3.2000, COM (2000)127 final, p.28 *et seq*.
[30] Case C-112/99 *Toshiba Europe* [2001] ECR I-7945, paragraphs 30 and 31. See Kelly, Gerard, "Comparative Advertising – Bringing the Advertising War into the Enemy Camp," (2005) 12(10) *Commercial Law Practitioner* 281; Carey, "Comparative Advertising – European Harmonisation" [2000] *Ent. L.R.* 21.
[31] See Case C-44/01 *Pippig Augenoptik GmbH and Co. KG v Hartlauer Handelsgesellschaft mbh.* [2004] E.T.M.R. (5) 65; [2003] ECR I-3095, para. 44.
[32] Recital 11 of the Directive; Spink and Petty, "Comparative Advertising in the European Union" [1998] 47 *I.C.L.Q.* 855 at p.858.
[33] Case C-63/97 *BMW* [1999] ECR I-905, paras 58-60.
[34] Council Directive 89/104/EEC to approximate the laws of the Member States relating to trade marks [1989] O.J. L40/1. See Case C-44/01 *Pippig Augenoptik GmbH and Co. KG v Hartlauer Handelsgesellschaft mbh.* [2004] E.T.M.R. (5) 65; [2003] ECR I-3095, paras 49-51.
[35] Recital 15 of the Directive. See Ohly, pp.52-55.
[36] By analogy to *Testpreis-Angebot* BGH GRUR 1998, 824.
[37] U.K. Radio Authority's Advertising and Sponsorship Code RAC 9. See Ohly, pp.80-81.
[38] Ohly, p.81.
[39] Kelly, *op cit.*
[40] Case C-112/99 *Toshiba Europe GmbH v Katun Germany GmbH.* [2002] F.S.R. 39, para.38.
[41] C-126/91 *Scutzverband gegen Unwesen in de Wirtschaft eV v. Yves Rocher GmbH* [1991] 3 ECR I-2361 of 18.5.93.
[42] Case C-44/01 *Pippig Augenoptik GmbH and Co. KG v Hartlauer Handelsgesellschaft mbh.* [2004] E.T.M.R. (5) 65, [2003] ECR I-3095.
[43] *Id.*, para 49.
[44] *Erven Warnink BV v J. Townend and Sons (Hull) Ltd.* [1979] A.C. 731.
[45] See *Vodafone Group PLC v Orange Personal Communications Services Ltd.* [1997] FSR 34 where Jacob J. observed that to succeed Vodafone had to show: '(1) the word complained of where false (2) they were published maliciously; and (3) they were calculated to cause the plaintiff pecuniary damage.'
[46] See Kelly, *op cit.*
[47] Case C-44/01 *Pippig Augenoptik GmbH and Co. KG v Hartlauer Handelsgesellschaft mbh.* [2004] E.T.M.R. (5) 65; [2003] ECR I-3095, para.44.
[48] Case C-150/88 *Parfümerie-Fabrik 4711* [1989] ECR 3891, paragraph 28, Case C-37/92 *Vanacker and Lesage* [1993] ECR I-4947, paragraph 9, and Case C-324/99 *DaimlerChrysler* [2001] ECR I-9897, paragraph 32.
[49] OJ No.L166, 11.6.1998, p.51.
[50] See generally, Reilly, N., "The Unfair Commercial Practices Directive and the Average Consumer" (2005) 12 (5) *Commercial Law Practitioner* 125.
[51] Schotthöfer, Peter and Maxeiner, James R., "European Union", in Maxeiner and Schotthöfer, *op cit*, p. 557 *et seq.*
[52] Directive 89/552/EEC as amended. See Crown, Giles), *supra*, p.108 *et seq.*
[53] Surreptitious advertising as defined in Art.1(c).
[54] *Konsumentombudsmannen v De Agostini (Svenska) Forlag AB* [1997] All ER (EC) 697.
[55] Directive 97/7/EC as amended by Directive 2002/65/EC [1997] OJ L144/19.
[56] Directive 90/314/EEC on package travel, package holidays and package tours (OJ L 158 of June 23rd 1990, pp. 59-64). See Saggeron A., *Travel Law and Litigation*, 2nd ed. (CLT Professional Publishing, 2000), ch. 1 and Buttimore J, *Holiday Law in Ireland*, 1992.

[57]For example: Austria: Gesetz gegen den unlauteren Wettbewerb BGBI 1988 No.422; Zugabengetsetz BGBI 1971 II No.196; Gesetz über Preisnachläss; (Rabattgesetz) RGBI 1933 I 1011; Mediengesetz Belgium: Wet betreffende de handelspraktijken en de voorlichting en bescherming van de consument, Luxembourg: Law of November 27, 1986 on Unfair Competition, Denmark: Marketing Practices Act, Finland: Kuluttajansuojalaki; Laki sopimattomasta menettelystä elinkeinotoiminnassa, France: Art.121.1 CdC, Germany: Gesetz gegen den unläuteren Wettbewerb, Greece: Peri Athemitou Antagonismou 146/1914, the Netherlands: Gedragsregelen voor het Reclamewezen, Portugal: Lei de Defensa do Consumidor Law 29/81 of August 21, 1981.

[58] Art. L. 121.1 CdC.

[59] S.14.

[60] Zugabeverordnung.

[61] Decree Law (Ordonnance) of December 18, 1986.

[62] Code of Advertising Standards for Ireland, para. B (8).

[63] C-286/81 *Re Oosthoek's Uitgeversmaatschappij* [1982] 4 ECR 4575 of 15.12.1982.

[64] Reich, 'The November Revolution of the European Court of Justice: *Keck* , Meng and Audi Revisited' (1994) 31 *CMLRev* 459, Maduro, " *Keck* : The End? The Beginning of the End? Or just the End of the Beginning?" (1994) 3 *IJEL* 30; Travers, Noel J., "The Keck Legacy," (1995) 13 *ILT* 39.

[65] C-267 and 268/91 *Re Keck and Mithouard* [1993] 7 ECR I-6097 of 24.11.93; [1995] 1 CMLR 101; Case C-292/92 *Hünermund and Others* [1993] ECR I-6787, paragraphs 21 and 22; Joined Cases C-401/92 and C-402/92 *Tankstation 't Heukske and Boermans* [1994] I-2199, paragraphs 12 to 14.

[66] *Konsumentombudsmannen v De Agostini (Svenska) Forlag AB* [1997] All ER (EC) 697; C-71/02 *Herbert Karner Industrie-Auktionen GmbH v Troostwijk GmbH.* [2004] ECR I-3025 C-320/93 *Lucien Ortscheit GmbH v Eurim-Pharm Arzneimittel GmbH* [1994] ECR I-5243. C-152/78 Commission v France [1980] ECR 2299.

[67] C-352/85 [1988] 2 ECR 2085 ; [1989] 3 CMLR 147.

[68] C-350/96 *Clean Car Autoservice v Landeshauptmann von Wien* [1998] ECR I-2521; C- 224/97 *Ciola v. Land Vorarlberg* [1999] ECR I-2517.

[69] C-52/79 *Procureur du Roi v. Debauvée* [1980] ECR 833, para. 9.

[70] C-15/78 *Société Générale Alsacienne de Banque S.A. v. Koestler* [1978] ECR 1971.

[71] Craig and De Búrca, p.805.

[72] C-76/90 *Säger v. Dennemeyer* [1991] ECR I-4221 per Advocate General Jacobs.

[73] Case 352/85 *Bond van Adverteerders* [1988] ECR 2085 para 34.

[74] C-33/74 *Van Binsbergen v. Bestuur van de Bedrijfsvereniging voor de Metaalnijverheid* [1974] ECR 1299.

[75] C-49/98 *Finalarte Sociedade Construçao Civil v. Urlaubs- und Lohnausgleichskasse der Bauwirtschaft* [2001] ECR I-7831.

[76] C-279/80 *Re Alfred John Webb* [1981] ECR 3305; C-62-63/81 *Seco SA and Desquenne and Giral SA v Etablissement d'Assurance contre la Viellesse et l'Invalidité* [1982] 1 ECR 223.

[77] C-220/83 *Commission v France* [1986] 4 ECR 3663.

[78] C-6/9 SA *Compagnie Gènèrale pour la Diffusion de la Tèlèvision Coditel and Others* [1980] ECR 881.

[79] C- 279/80 *Criminal Proceedings against Webb* [1981] ECR 3305, para.17. See also C-110-111/78 *Ministère Public v. Van Wesemael* [1979] ECR 35

[80] C- 279/80 *Criminal Proceedings against Webb* [1981] ECR 3305.

[81] *Groppera Radio AG and Others v. Switzerland Series* A No. 173 of 28.3.10 (ECtHR); C-260/89 *Elleniki Radiophonia Tilèorassi AE v. Dimotiki Etaireia Pliroforissis and Sotiros Kouvelas* [1991] ECR I-2925; C-71/02 *Herbert Karner Industrie-Auktionen GmbH v Troostwijk GmbH.* [2004] ECR I-3025, para.48-52.

[82] C-4/73 *Nold KG v. Baustoffgroßhandlung v Commission* [1974] 1 ECR 491; [1974] 2 CMLR 338..

[83] C-384/93 [1995] ECR I-1141.See also Hilson, C., "Discrimination in Community Free Movement Law" (1999) 24 *European Law Review* 445.

[84] C-384/93 *Alpine Investments BV v Minister van Financiën* [1995] ECR I-1141, paras 36-38.

[85] C-71/02 *Herbert Karner Industrie-Auktionen GmbH v Troostwijk GmbH.* [2004] ECR I-3025, para.46; Case C-275/92 *Schindler* [1994] ECR I-1039, paragraph 22; and Case C-390/99 *Canal Satélite Digital* [2002] ECR I-607, paragraph 31.

[86] C-71/02 *Herbert Karner Industrie-Auktionen GmbH v Troostwijk GmbH.* [2004] ECR I-3025, see the Advocate General's opinion para. 91-93.

MINIMIZING REGULATION OF SPACE TOURISM TO STIMULATE COMMERCIAL, PRIVATE LAUNCH CAPABILITIES

Rachel A. Yates, Esq.
Holland & Hart LLP, USA
ryates@hollandhart.com

ABSTRACT

The development of commercial, private launch capabilities to provide tourism opportunities is in a nascent stage. Until the design and engineering of launch, orbital, and reentry vehicles are validated, regulation of the industry must be flexible, liberal, and practical. The United States Federal Aviation Administration appropriately followed this approach in the promulgation of draft regulations on human space flight. Specifically, the agency weighed several competing interests and policies to avoid artificial or rigid barriers that might stifle innovation unnecessarily. To stimulate space tourism and the development of reliable spacecraft, the final version of these regulations should impose the least restrictive requirements that encourage safety, in recognition of the competence of space flight participants and crew to understand and accept the risks inherent in space travel.

FULL TEXT

RECENT DEVELOPMENTS IN PRIVATE SPACE TRAVEL SPUR LEGAL CHANGES

Space travel has long been the fodder for futuristic science fiction. A scan of top news stories, however, reveals that the future is at hand. Entrepreneurs who can pay the twenty-million dollar (US) fee are training for flights to the International Space Station, brokered by Space Adventures under an agreement with the Russian Federal Space Agency.[i] For an additional fifteen million dollars (US), the space tourist may be able to take a 90-minute spacewalk or extravehicular activity.[ii]

The European Space Agency announced in the summer 2006 an initiative called "The Survey of European Privately-funded Vehicles for Commercial Human Spaceflight" as part of its General Studies Programme.[iii] The initiative is designed to fund the development and study of technologies for the next-generation launchers.

In July 2006, Bigelow Aerospace launched Genesis 1, an inflatable spacecraft designed as the first in a series of habitats.[iv] To stimulate development of transportation alternatives to the habitats, Bigelow Aerospace has created America's Space Prize, a fifty-million dollar (US) inducement to an American company which can dock with the Bigelow space habitat, remain on station for at least six months, carry a crew of no fewer than five people, and perform two consecutive, safe, and successful orbital missions within a sixty-day period. The test missions must be completed by January 10, 2010, when Bigelow hopes to have a fully-habitable module on orbit.[v]

Given the increased activity by well-funded, non-governmental ventures to provide opportunities for human space travel, the United States (US) Congress recognized the need for additional oversight and regulation. Under the 1972 Convention on International Liability for Damage Caused by Space Objects (Liability Convention),[vi] the US government bears responsibility as a launching state for activities conducted on its territory or by its citizens which launch or procure a launch. The Commercial Space Launch Activities Act of 1994, as significantly amended in 1998 (CSLA),[vii] constituted the first comprehensive legislation to regulate US launch and reentry activities. By delegation from the US Secretary of Transportation, the Federal Aviation Administration (FAA) became the agency authorized to oversee, license, and regulate launches, reentries, and the operation of launch and reentry sites carried out by US citizens or from US territory.[viii] Historically, the FAA licensed only operators of expendable launch vehicles which did not carry crew or passengers.[ix] Its regulation of the industry addressed primarily the safety of the uninvolved public.

That changed in 2004, when the FAA issued two reusable launch vehicle (RLV) licenses for missions involving an on-board pilot: one for Scaled Composites and one for XCOR Aerospace, both of which were competing for the ten million dollar (US) Ansari X Prize.[x] Later that year, the US Congress adopted amendments to the CSLA to specifically address the regulation of private industry engaged in human space transportation for hire.[xi]

Policy of CSLA and Scope of Authority Delegated to FAA to Regulate Human Space Flight.

The US Congress gave general guidance to the FAA, but also imposed specific limitations on the FAA's authority to regulate human space flight. As is common in (US) statutes affecting the space industry, the CSLA first enumerates the policy reasons for the amendments, which are primarily safety-driven:

- the goal of safely opening space to the American people and their private commercial , scientific, and cultural enterprises should guide Federal space investments, policies, and regulations;
- private industry has begun to develop commercial launch vehicles capable of carrying human beings into space, and greater private investment in these efforts will stimulate the Nation's commercial space transportation industry as a whole;
- space transportation is inherently risky, and the future of the commercial human space flight industry will depend on its ability to continually improve its safety performance;
- a critical area of responsibility for the Department of Transportation is to regulate the operations and safety of the emerging commercial human space flight industry;
- the public interest is served by creating a clear legal, regulatory, and safety regime for commercial human space flight; and
- the regulatory standards governing human space flight must evolve as the industry matures so that regulations neither stifle technology development nor expose crew or space flight participants to avoidable risks as the public comes to expect greater safety for crew and space flight participants.[xii]

In the context of these policy pronouncements, the FAA was mandated to "encourage, facilitate, and promote the continuous improvement of the safety of launch vehicles designed to carry humans, and...promulgate regulations to carry out this subsection."[xiii] For instance, the amendments require that, as a condition to receiving a permit or license, the operator must ensure that its crew has training and satisfies medical standards; that the crew has been informed that the US government has not certified the launch vehicle as safe for carrying humans; and that the operator has complied with all laws applying to crews.[xiv] This delegation appears to give the FAA a good degree of leeway on how it can impose regulations in the name of safety.

As pertains to space flight participants, however, the delegation of authority was limited almost exclusively to regulating the flow of information. Under the CSLA, to obtain a license or permit, the operator must certify that it has informed the space flight participants of the risks of launch and reentry, including the safety record of the vehicle type; that the US government has not certified the launch vehicle as safe for carrying humans; that the space flight participant has provided written, informed consent to participate; and that the operator has complied with FAA regulations. The CLSA limited the FAA's initial control over qualifications for space flight participants, authorizing only "appropriate medical examinations" until 2007.[xv] After that date, the FAA was authorized to issue additional regulations setting reasonable medical and training requirements for space flight participants.[xvi]

Similarly, the amendments restrict how the FAA can regulate the design or operation of the launch vehicle. Until 2012, the FAA may only restrict or prohibit design features that have resulted in a serious or fatal injury to crew or space flight participants during a licensed or commercial human space flight or contributed to an unplanned event that posed a high risk of causing a serious or fatal injury.[xvii]

Finally, the CLSA required the FAA to issue proposed regulations within one year of the amendments' adoption and a final rule within six months thereafter.[xviii] It required the issuance of guidelines or advisory circulars as soon as practicable until the regulations could be finalized.[xix]

<u>FAA Issued Guidance Documents and Solicited Comments on Proposed Regulations</u>.

The FAA's Civil Aerospace Medical Institute had previously issued its Guidance for Medical Screening of Commercial Aerospace Passengers in 2003.[xx] This guidance memorandum was designed to identify individuals who have medical conditions that might result in an in-flight medical emergency or death or otherwise compromise the health and safety of occupants.

In February 2005, the FAA issued a related set of draft guidelines for commercial, suborbital RLV operations: one for crew and one for space flight participants.[xxi] Where practical, the guidelines attempted to draw on aviation experience to craft recommendations for crew training and qualifications. For instance, the Crew Guidelines recommended that a pilot possess an FAA pilot certificate, hold ratings to operate aircraft with similar characteristics, and possess an FAA 2nd-class medical certificate.[xxii] The Crew Guidelines similarly offered a set of recommendations for environmental controls, fire detection, and human factors that might implicate safe operation of the spacecraft.[xxiii]

Consistent with the mandate of the CSLA, the focus of the Participant Guidelines was on disclosing sufficient information about risks, so that the space flight participant could make an informed judgment about whether to participate.[xxiv] The guidelines also suggested that the participant provide a medical history and, if needed, a physical examination to a physician knowledgeable in aerospace medicine.[xxv] Finally, they identified safety training and security measures that should be undertaken by the operator.[xxvi]

After taking comments on these guidelines from industry and other interested parties, the FAA issued a formal Notice of Proposed Rulemaking for human space flight requirements, setting out proposed regulations to address these areas.[xxvii] The Proposed Rules incorporated many of the industry comments received on the guidelines. The official comment period on the Proposed Rules closed on February 27, 2006, though some comments trickled in after that date.[xxviii] As of the writing of this article, the final rule had not been published but was expected this Fall..

HUMAN SPACEFLIGHT REGULATIONS BALANCE COMPETING INTERESTS AND POLICIES TO ENCOURAGE HUMAN SPACE FLIGHT.

In any effort to write statutory or regulatory law in a new field, the drafters must be sensitive to the competing interests and policies affected by the law. The FAA draft regulations successfully balance these interests in compliance with the agency's statutory authority.

The comments solicited on the guidelines and Proposed Rules demonstrate a wide range of interests. The remainder of this paper address the conflicts posed by those comments and the compromise achieved in the FAA regulations.

Specificity v. Flexibility in Design and Operational Requirements.

One competing tension in the regulation of human space flight is the desire to impose specific requirements to improve safety, while allowing the operators flexibility in the design and operation of their spacecraft. That is, should the regulations tightly control design and operation to prevent accidents, or should they be liberal enough to allow accidents to occur so long as the lessons learned from those accidents are used to develop safety requirements in the future?

The US Congress largely resolved this tension in favor of giving operators flexibility to creatively design and operate their spacecraft, subject to only narrow requirements for protection of the crew and space flight participants. This policy determination is most evident by the statutory limit on the FAA's authority to regulate design and operations before 2012. By only prohibiting design features that pose a high risk of, or have resulted in, a serious or fatal injury to crew or space flight participants, the US Congress has made the policy decision that the potential loss of human life is an acknowledged risk that does not outweigh the benefits of developing our space flight capabilities. Rather, for the next six years, US operators may explore new technologies, learning as they go but not repeating mistakes that risk human life or health.[xxix]

The draft regulations balance these competing interests by imposing only limited controls on cabin conditions, including environmental and life support systems, smoke detection, fire suppression, and security.[xxx] They allow the operator to choose the best method for achieving these general safety requirements, employing active or passive systems, on board or remote operations, or open-loop or closed-loop systems. Inherent in this regulatory approach is an acknowledgement that mandating accepted aviation safety technologies in an untested micro-gravity environment or during the stresses of launch and reentry could actually increase risk. Systems that have not been validated under relevant conditions might fail, as might novel or complex systems designed to overcome the unique conditions of suborbital or orbital flight.[xxxi]

For the same reasons, the regulations do not attempt to dictate whether the spacecraft must launch or land in a particular configuration or whether launch and reentry are pilot-controlled or done by remote operations. While uniformity in the application of the law is desirable, the FAA readily agreed that these design and operations decisions must be made by the operator based on the evolution of technology; they cannot be driven by inflexible regulations that attempt to anticipate the technological advances to a diverse family of RLVs and, thereby, stifle the innovation needed to move the industry forward.

<u>Duty of Government to Protect Space Flight Participants and Crew v. Duty of Government to Respect Individual Right to Choose</u>.

Some comments on the Proposed Rules strongly spoke out on the government's legal or moral obligation to protect citizens from physical harm. From this view, the government should dictate specific requirements for crew and space flight participant training. The government should require the operator to provide gap insurance to the space flight participant. The FAA should carefully examine the content of any disclosures to ensure they are both comprehensive yet understandable, and a government representative should be present when the consent form is signed to judge the mental competence of the space flight participant.[xxxii]

To balance this view, other comments suggested the government should acknowledge the capacity of space flight participants and crew to understand risks and make informed decisions. Individuals should consult with their own advisors (physicians, attorneys, insurers) to protect their interests. In this view, giving more information to the space flight participant only increases the risk that none of it will be read.[xxxiii]

To balance these views, the proposed regulations focus on making sure the crew and space flight participants are sufficiently trained so as not to create additional perils, but only trained as needed for their particular roles. As proposed, crew training requirements give the operators flexibility to determine the best training methods. Crew training devices must "realistically represent the vehicle's configuration and mission" or the operator must advise the crew members of the differences.[xxxiv] The training must be updated to reflect lessons learned and to ensure that crew qualifications are current.[xxxv] Rather than apply a one-size-fits-all approach to training, the FAA believes that it can more appropriately account for the diversity in vehicles by adding terms and conditions specific to the vehicle in the license or permit.[xxxvi] While this creates initial uncertainty about the regulatory process, it appears to be the only practical means for achieving the goal of encouraging adequate training of crew members.

The regulations are largely silent on training and medical requirements for space flight participants. The space flight participant must be trained to respond to emergency situations and must not be able to jeopardize the safety of the flight crew or the public.[xxxvii] However, the rider does not need to possess the same medical certifications as the flight crew.[xxxviii] Rather, the FAA relies on the space flight participant's self-interest in obtaining medical advice, until a demonstrable need arises to mandate medical examinations through regulation.[xxxix] As one of the commenters noted in a very practical way: "FAA should not set an artificially high barrier to space flight on medical grounds. Tolerance should not be interpreted to mean absence of symptoms; it should be interpreted to mean absence of permanent injury. If the space flight participant passes out because he or she forgot to execute his or her straining maneuver, no harm will be done."[xl]

Apart from training, the draft regulation ensure that the crew and space flight participants are adequately informed of the mission risks, but are not overwhelmed with data. The operator must present information "in a manner that is understandable to the space flight participant."[xli] In particular, the regulations require the operator disclose to the space flight participant the known hazards and risks that could result in a serious injury, death, disability, or total partial loss of physical or mental function; the fact that participation may result in a serious injury, death, disability, or total partial loss of physical or mental function; and the safety record of all crewed vehicles. The safety record must include statistics about death or injury to people on the flights, the number of catastrophic failures, the number of vehicle flights, the number of safety-related anomalies or failure, and any corrective actions taken to resolve them.

In turn, the space flight participant must sign an informed consent acknowledging that the participant understands the risks and that his or her presence on board the vehicle is voluntary. While the informed consent provides evidence of the participant's knowledge and state of mind, it may be insufficient to protect the operator from liability in many jurisdictions. For protection of the operator, a contractual waiver and release should accompany any informed consent. Waivers and releases are not otherwise mandated by the regulations except for reciprocal waivers vis-à-vis the government.[xlii]

Companies and others offering comments on the Proposed Rules almost universally agreed on one point related to these disclosures: if a safety record of all crewed vehicles must be maintained and disclosed to the space flight participant, then the FAA should maintain it.[xliii] Failing to satisfy disclosure obligations can nullify an informed consent, and so the operators wanted to put the onus of determining the content of that disclosure on the government. This is especially appropriate because an operator typically would not have access to the data from other operators or governments with which to complete a full safety record. Conversely, out of concern that operators would not provide a complete disclosure reflecting safety problems, others wanted to have an independent body maintain the safety record and apply uniform standards.

The disclosure of this safety record raises other concerns as well. Some of the information regarding mishaps and, particularly, corrective actions is likely to be proprietary. The operators objected to disclosure of proprietary information that could benefit their competitors. At another level, disclosure of some information to non-US citizens could violate export control requirements, particularly the International Traffic in Arms Regulations (ITAR)[xliv], unless an export license or technical assistance agreement were obtained.

<u>Creating Meaningful Safety, Training, and Disclosure Requirements v. Containing the Cost of Regulatory Compliance.</u>

In a nascent industry expected to have enormous research and development, verification, and operational expenses, the cost of regulatory compliance must be manageable. In connection with its Proposed Rules, the FAA evaluated the monetary impact on affected companies of regulatory compliance.[xlv] The study concluded that the cost of compliance to operators would range from one million nine-hundred thousand dollars (US) to three million eight-hundred thousand dollars (US) over a ten-year period.[xlvi] This estimated cost was based on a range of missions over the same time period between 5,000 and 10,000, and it excluded costs that were consistent with current and expected practice (such as crew training, environmental and life support systems, etc.).[xlvii] Spread over each mission, it was believed that the cost of the mission increased by less than three hundred dollars (US), which was deemed an insignificant increase.[xlviii]

Not all operators agreed with this analysis. Although compared against total revenues or total expenses, the increased cost of compliance might be small, a comparison against expected profit might tell a very different story.[xlix]

At this stage of industry development, however, the FAA has taken conscious steps to minimize the regulatory requirements. Moreover, the regulations spell out when an operator can use alternate means of compliance, mitigating the cost of regulatory requirements when cheaper but equally appropriate alternatives are available.[l]

Regulating Safety Through Government Agencies v. Self-Regulation by the Affected Industry.

In its purest sense, the regulation of conduct can be strictly imposed by a government agency or it can develop, formally or informally, by the industry itself. Where an industry self-regulates successfully, the government can take a more laissez-faire approach. Because this segment of the launch industry is in a formative stage, reliance on self-regulation may be risky.

The FAA regulations nonetheless recognize that operators have an incentive to operate safely. Doing so minimizes the cost associated with operational failures. Logically, an operator with a better safety record is more likely to attract space flight participants. Operators likewise have an incentive to apply pressure on other companies to follow safety protocols because safe operations may lower industry costs, such as insurance, and enhance the overall market demand for the services offered.

The comments to the Proposed Rules reflect a secondary incentive to self-regulate: the promotion of businesses which provide safety services or products. These comments encouraged both training of flight crew and participants and verification of spacecraft design and operation, and proposed the formation of a Blue Ribbon Panel or standards-setting body to oversee these efforts.[li] Other comments noted the existence of training facilities or services available to ensure regulatory compliance.[lii]

It may be premature to expect the private launch industry to self-regulate human spaceflight for hire. Each potential operator is facing more immediate challenges in the research, development, and verification of its spacecraft that override the long-term need to develop and conform to standards that would be applicable to every type of spacecraft in each operational phase of flight. At this stage, it is sufficient that the FAA regulations not prohibit the formation of industry standards and best practices. Because the current regulations implicitly tolerate more restrictive self-regulation on an industry-wide basis, the industry maintains appropriate flexibility to set its own governing bodies and standards in years to come.

SUMMARY

The draft FAA regulations represent a solid, initial attempt to regulate an evolving industry. They accord adequate flexibility to individual operators in the design and operation of the spacecraft and in the training of crew and participants, without sacrificing safety unnecessarily. In recognition of the inherent risks of human space flight, the regulations are designed to give crew and space flight participants sufficient information to make informed decisions about whether to take part in a mission. This approach balances competing interests while stimulating the development of the next-generation launch and reentry vehicles necessary to sustain our human spaceflight program.

---

[i] "First Woman Tourist? U.S. Entrepreneur Determined to Reach Orbit," by Tariq Malik, *Space News*, Aug. 14, 2006, at 12.

[ii] http://www.spaceadventures.com/flight/spacewalk/details (Aug. 30, 2006).

[iii] http://www.esa.int/SPECIALS/GSP/SEM2YABUQPE_0.html (July 20, 2006).

[iv] "Space News: 10 Who Made a Difference in Space," *Space News*, Aug. 28, 2006, at 9.

[v] http://www.bigelowaerospace.com/multiverse/space_prize.php (Aug. 30, 2006); "Space News: 10 Who Made a Difference in Space," *Space News*, Aug. 28, 2006, at 9.

[vi] *Convention on International Liability for Damage Caused by Space Objects*, Mar. 29, 1972, 961 UNTS 187, at Art. I(c).
[vii] 49 U.S.C. § 70101 *et seq.* (1994).
[viii] 49 U.S.C. §§ 70104, 70105; US Federal Aviation Administration, Commercial Space Transportation Delegations of Authority, N1100.240 (Nov. 21, 1995).
[ix] On August 25, 2006, the FAA promulgated its most recent amendments to regulations of expendable launch vehicles. *See* 71 Fed. Reg. 50508 (Aug. 25, 2006).
[x] *Human Space Flight Requirements for Crew and Space Flight Participants*, 70 Fed. Reg. 77262 (2005) (notice of proposed rulemaking) (proposed Dec. 29, 2005).
[xi] *Commercial Space Launch Amendments Act of 2004*, 118 Stat. 3974 (Dec. 23, 2004).
[xii] *Id.* at Sec.2(b).
[xiii] *Id.* at Sec. 2(c).
[xiv] *Id.* at Sec. 2(d).
[xv] *Id.* at Sec. 2(d)
[xvi] *Id.*
[xvii] *Id.* at Sec. 2(d)(14).
[xviii] *Id.* at Sec. 2(d)(25).
[xix] *Id.*
[xx] *Guidance for Medical Screening of Commercial Aerospace Passengers*, FAA (Mar. 31, 2003).
[xxi] *Draft Guidelines for Commercial Suborbital Resuable Launch Vehicle Operations with Flight Crew*, ver. 1.0, FAA Office of Commercial Space Transportation (Feb. 11, 2005) (hereinafter "Crew Guidelines"); *Draft Guidelines for Commercial Suborbital Resuable Launch Vehicle Operations with Flight Space Flight Participants*, ver. 1.0, FAA Office of Commercial Space Transportation (Feb. 11, 2005) (hereinafter "Participant Guidelines").
[xxii] Crew Guidelines at § 6.
[xxiii] Crew Guidelines at §§ 10-12.
[xxiv] Participant Guidelines at §§ 6-7.
[xxv] Participant Guidelines at § 8.
[xxvi] Participant Guidelines at §§ 10-11.
[xxvii] *Human Space Flight Requirements for Crew and Space Flight Participants*, 70 Fed. Reg. 77262 (2005) (notice of proposed rulemaking) (proposed Dec. 29, 2005) (hereinafter "Proposed Rule").
[xxviii] http://dms.dot.gov/search/searchResults Simple.cfm?numberValue=23449&searchType=docket (Aug. 31, 2006).
[xxix] 14 C.F.R. §460.7
[xxx] 14 C.F.R. §§ 460.11, 460.13, 460.53.
[xxxi] Comments of Predesa, LLC, Feb. 27, 2006, http://dms.dot.gov/search/searchResults Simple.cfm?numberValue=23449&searchType=docket (Aug. 31, 2006), at 9.
[xxxii] Comments of James Michael Snead, Feb. 20, 2006, http://dms.dot.gov/search/ searchResults Simple.cfm?numberValue=23449&searchType=docket (Aug. 31, 2006).
[xxxiii] Comments of XCOR Aerospace on Review of James Michael Snead's Comments, Mar. 1, 2006, http://dms.dot.gov/search/searchResults Simple.cfm?numberValue=23449&searchType=docket (Aug. 31, 2006).
[xxxiv] 14 C.F.R. § 460.7.
[xxxv] *Id.*
[xxxvi] Proposed Rule at 77265.
[xxxvii] 14 C.F.R. §§ 460.51, 460.53.
[xxxviii] Proposed Rule at 77264 n.2 ("The FAA has decided against prescribing specific medical requirements for space flight participants at this time.").
[xxxix] Proposed Rule at 77271.
[xl] XCOR Aerospace Review of Guidance for Medical Screening of Commercial Aerospace Passengers, May 30, 2005, http://dms.dot.gov/ search/searchResults Simple.cfm?numberValue =23449&searchType=docket (Aug. 31, 2006).
[xli] 14 C.F.R. § 460.45(a).
[xlii] Appendix E to 14 C.F.R. Part 440.
[xliii] http://dms.dot.gov/search/searchResults Simple.cfm?numberValue=23449&searchType=docket (Aug. 31, 2006).
[xliv] 22 C.F.R. Parts 120-130.
[xlv] *Draft Regulatory Evaluation, Draft Regulatory Flexibility Analysis, International Trade Impact Assessment, and Unfunded Mandates Assessment*, Office of Aviation Policy and Plans, Operations Regulatory Analysis Branch, FAA (June 10, 2005).
[xlvi] *Id.* at 9.
[xlvii] *Id.* at 9, 32.
[xlviii] *Id.* at 11.
[xlix] Comments of Spaceport Associates, Feb. 25, 2005, http://dms.dot.gov/search/ searchResults Simple.cfm?numberValue=23449&searchType=docket (Aug. 31, 2006).
[l] *See, e.g.*, 14 C.F.R. § 460.5.
[li] Comments of Dii Aerospace Laboratories, Feb. 27, 2006, at 9; and Joint Comments of the International Ass'n of Space Entrepreneurs and the Institute for Space Policy and Law, Feb. 27, 2006, at 10-11, http://dms.dot.gov/search/ searchResults Simple.cfm?numberValue=23449 &searchType=docket (Aug. 31, 2006).

[lii] *E.g.*, "Wyle Creates Unit for Space Tourism Business," *Space News*, Aug. 7, 2006, at 9; Rocket Academy Spaceflight Training, http://x-rocket.com/rocket-academy.htm (Aug. 29, 2006); Comments of Aerospace Medical Ass'n, Feb. 1, 2006, http://dms.dot.gov/search/searchResults Simple.cfm?numberValue=23449&searchType=docket (Aug. 31, 2006).

IAC-06-E.6.1.13

UNITED STATES SPACE LAW: COMMERCIAL SPACE LAUNCHES AND FACILITES*

by
Paul Stephen Dempsey**

INTRODUCTION

Stephen Hawking observed, "It is important for the human race to spread out into space for the survival of the species. Life on Earth is at the ever-increasing risk of being wiped out by a disaster, such as sudden global warming, nuclear war, a genetically engineered virus or other dangers we have not yet thought of." There are three major catalysts for space exploration and development: (1) scientific discovery, pursued predominantly by governmental institutions such as NASA; (2) military development, pursued by defense ministries and their contractors; and (3) commercial development.

President Ronald Reagan encouraged "domestic commercial exploration of space capabilities, technology, and systems for national economic benefit", though such activities must be consistent with "national security concerns, treaties, and international agreements."[1]

The US aerospace and aeronautics industry are viewed as significant contributors to US international prestige, influence, competitiveness, and economic well-being.[2] Private sector commercial activities are seen as having the potential to contribute both to the strength of the US economy and the US space program.[3] Congress has decreed that NASA "seek and encourage, to the maximum extent possible, the fullest

---

** Tomlinson Professor of Global Governance in Air & Space Law, and Director of the Institute of Air & Space Law, McGill University. A.B.J. (1972), J.D. (1975), University of Georgia; LL.M. (1978) George Washington University; D.C.L. (1986), McGill University.

[1] Ronald Reagan, National Space Policy, National Security Decision Directive No. 42 (July 4, 1982).

> The United States Government will provide a climate conducive to expanded private sector investment and involvement in civil space activities, with due regard to public safety and national security. Private sector space activities will be authorized and supervised or regulated by the government to the extent required by treaty and national security. Id.

[2] National Aeronautics and Space Administration Authorization Act of 1993 §§ 101(11), 501, Pub. L. 102-588, 106 Stat. 5107 (Nov. 4, 1992).

[3] National Aeronautics and Space Administration Authorization Act of 1991, § 101(14), Pub. L. 101-611, (Nov. 16, 1990).

commercial use of space."[4] Space transportation services (including launch services)[5] must be acquired from commercial providers whenever they are required.[6] Private sector transportation systems are to be encouraged.[7] The private commercial launch industry should be facilitated and promoted, and therefore launch services should be purchased from the private sector to the fullest extent possible.[8]

With promulgation of the Commercial Space Launch Amendments Act of 2004[9], the US Congress established a strong policy in favor of promoting commercial launches, reentry, and launch sites with stable and minimal regulatory oversight applied fairly and expeditiously, so as to enable the US to retain its competitive position internationally, and contribute to the national defense and economic well being of the nation.[10] Congress encouraged creation of a strong space transportation infrastructure with robust private sector participation.[11] The US government is instructed to encourage and facilitate a domestic commercial space transportation industry and its industrial base, including "launch systems, infrastructure and workforce, necessary to meet ongoing . . . security and civil requirements."[12]

Space transportation accounted for $7 billion of the $105 billion US commercial space industry in 2002. A "commercial launch" may carry a variety of payloads (civil, commercial, scientific, or military); it is deemed commercial if the payload owner commercially procured the launch.[13]

The Commercial Space Launch Act of 1984 [CSLA][14] authorized the U.S. Department of Transportation (which subdelegated such authority to the Federal Aviation Administration [FAA])[15] to license the launch of a launch vehicles, reentry of a reentry vehicles, as well as the operation of a launch or reentry site.[16] CSLA gave the FAA authority to:

- regulate the commercial space transportation industry, to the extent necessary, to ensure compliance with international obligations of the

[4] National Aeronautics and Space Act of 1958 § 102(c), Pub. L. 85-568 (as amended through Pub. L. 106-391, 114 Stat. 1577 (Oct. 30, 2000).
[5] Commercial Space Launch Act § 3, Pub. L. 98-575, 98 Stat. 3055 (Oct. 30, 1984). Commercial Space Launch Act Amendments of 1988, Pub. L. 100-657 (Nov. 15, 1988). 49 U.S.C. § 70101 (2003).
[6] Commercial Space Act of 1998 § 201, Pub. L. 105-303, 112 Stat. 2843 (Oct. 28, 1998). The general rule is subject to numerous exceptions, however.
[7] National Aeronautics and Space Administration Authorization Act of 1989 § 101(16)(C), Pub. L. 100-685, 102 Stat. 4083 (Nov. 17, 1988).
[8] Launch Services Purchases Act of 1990, 42 U.S.C. § 2465b (2003).
[9] Pub. L. 108-492.
[10] 49 U.S.C. § 70101(a)(5), (6).
[11] 49 U.S.C. § 70101(a)(8).
[12] U.S. Space Transportation Policy (Jan. 6, 2005), reprinted in Space Law IV.B.1. 25(P. Dempsey, ed. Feb. 2006).
[13] US Dep't of Commerce, Trends in Space Commercialization, republished in Paul Stephen Dempsey, Space Law IV.B.United States.6-2 (2004).
[14] 49 U.S.C. Subtitle IX, §§ 70101-70119 (2004); 14 CFR Parts 400-450 (2004).
[15] 64 Fed. Reg. 19,586 (Aug. 19, 1999).
[16] Chapter 701 of Title 49 of the United States Code confers upon the U.S. Secretary of Transportation authority to issue launch vehicle and site certificates and permits and regulate their operations. This authority, in turn, has been delegated by the Secretary to the Federal Aviation Administration [FAA].

United States and to protect the public health and safety, safety of property, and national security and foreign policy interest of the United States;

- encourage, facilitate, and promote commercial space launches and re-entries by the private sector;
- recommend appropriate changes in Federal statutes, treaties, regulations, policies, plans, and procedures; and
- facilitate the strengthening and expansion of the United States space transportation infrastructure.

This legislation was significantly amended by the Commercial Space Launch Amendments Act of 2004,[17] which sought to reduce regulatory barriers to space launches so as to encourage the commercial development of space.[18] It directs the Secretary of Transportation to "encourage, facilitate, and promote commercial space launches and reentry by the private sector".[19] One source describes this legislation as "the most significant piece of domestic space law, and its passage shows, for the first time, assertive steps by the government to promote public space travel."[20]

A U.S. citizen must obtain FAA authorization to launch, reenter or operate a launch or reentry site anywhere in the world.[21] Any person seeking to conduct commercial space transportation in the U.S. must also obtain FAA authorization.[22] Such licenses are issued by the FAA's Associate Administrator for Commercial Space Transportation [AST], who prescribes the terms and conditions for conducting authorized activity by the vehicle or site operator. Regulatory review of a launch application focuses on public health and safety, safety of property, and U.S. national security and foreign policy concerns and obligations.[23] U.S. government space activities (such as those by NASA and the Defense Department), however, are not subject to FAA jurisdiction.

The first licensed commercial suborbital launch occurred on March 29, 1989. Since then, more than 100 launches have

[17] Pub. L. 108-492.

[18] See Recent Development, Commercialization of Space: Commercial Space Launch Amendments Act of 2004, 17 Harv. J. Law & Tech. 619 (2004).

[19] 49 U.S.C. § 70103 (b)(1).

[20] Spencer Bromberg, Public Space Travel – 2005: A Legal Odyssey into the Current Regulaotry Environment for United States Space Adventurers Pioneering the Final Frontier, 70 J. Air L. & Com. 639, 569 (2005).

[21] 49 U.S.C. § 70104(a)(2).

[22] 49 U.S.C. § 70104(a)(1).. However, "amateur rocket activities" are not licensed by the FAA, although an Experimental Airworthiness Certificate may be required. Such launch activities conducted at private sites must satisfy the following characteristics: -Powered by a motor(s) having a total impulse of 200,000 pound-seconds or less; -Total burning or operating time of less than 15 seconds; and -A ballistic coefficient- *i.e.*, gross weight in pounds divided by frontal area of rocket vehicle-less than 12 pounds per square inch.

[23] 68 Fed. Reg. 59977 (Oct. 20, 2003). The CLSA gave the FAA jurisdiction to regulate commercial space activities, "only to the extent necessary to ensure compliance with international obligations of the United States and to protect the public health and safety, safety of property, and national security and foreign policy interest of the United States, . . . encourage, facilitate, and promote commercial space launches by the private sector, recommend appropriate changes in Federal statutes, treaties, regulations, policies, plans, and procedures, and facilitate the strengthening and expansion of the United States space transportation infrastructure."

been authorized. [24] But by 2002, the US was responsible for only 14% of space launches worldwide, compared with 18% for Europe, and 61% for Russia.[25]

Interest in suborbital flights increased significantly after the Ansari X-Prize foundation offered a $10 million reward to the first private vehicle that can carry a crew of three at an altitude of 100 kilometers, and can replicate the feat within two weeks.[26] In the 19th century, various prizes were awarded to the first airship flight (won by Alberto Santos-Dumont in 1901), or fly an airplane in a circle and land it intact (won by Henry Farman in 1906), or fly an aircraft across the Atlantic Ocean (by Charles Lindbergh in 1927).[27]

In June 2004, Space Ship One inaugurated private-sector launches of passengers into space. In October 2004, it concluded a second successful launch, thereby winning the $10 million X-Prize. Richard Branson's company, Virgin Gallactic, then contracted with its builders to develop a fleet of commercial sub-orbital and launch vehicles.[28] Several thousand people have signed up to pay for a $275,000 flight, scheduled to commence in 2008. Meanwhile, a $30 million prize was established for the first sub-orbital passenger flight.[29]

Clearly, there is a market for taking people into space, initially as tourists enjoying the novelty of the experience. As technology permits, space transportation likely will eclipse space tourism as a commercial market. Moreover, as other commercial sectors grow, such as space mining, transportation will be essential to shuttle technicians and workers to mining sites.

LAUNCH AND RE-ENTRY LICENSES

Under authority delegated by the Secretary of Transportation, licensing of commercial space launch and reentry is regulated by the FAA's Associate Administrator for Commercial Space Transportation. Final rules were promulgated for launches of expendable launch vehicles [ELVs] from non-federal launch sites in August 2006.[30] They are lengthy and comprehensive.[31] The FAA conducts a safety review to determine whether the applicant can launch a vehicle and its payload without jeopardizing public health, safety or property.[32] Under certain circumstances, license requirements may be waived.[33]

Unless the launch and reentry is exempt from regulation,[34] the applicant may

[24] 71 Fed. Reg. 27772 (May 12, 2006).
[25] Frank Mooring, Jr., Losing Thrust, Aviation Week & Space Tech. 28 (June 9, 2003).
[26] http://apo.faa.gov/foreca03/CHAP9-04.pdf (visited May 17, 2004).
[27] Bill Gunston, Aviation: The First 100 Years 10 (2002).
[28] John Lewis & Christopher Lewis, A Proposed International Legal Regime for the Era of Private Commercial Utilization of Space, 37 Geo. Wash. Int'l L. Rev. 745 (2005).
[29] Steven Freeland, Up, Up and . . . Back: The Emergence of Space Tourism and Its Impact on the International Law of Outer Space, 6 Chi. J. Int'l L. 1 (2005).
[30] 71 Fed. Reg. 50,508 (Aug. 25, 2006).
[31] The Federal Register publication announcing them consists of more than 200 pages.
[32] 14 CFR §§ 415.31, 415.103(a).
[33] The waiver provisions were added by the Commercial Space Act of 1998, Pub. L. 105-303. 49 U.S.C. § 70105(b)(3). The denial of a waiver may be appealed under 14 CFR § 404.5.
[34] An exemption applies if the vehicle is launched from a private site and the rocket: (1) has (a) motor(s) with a total impulse of 200,000

apply for: (1) a launch- or reentry-specific license; or (2) a launch or reentry operator license.[35] The FAA has 180 days to process a license application.[36] The licensing process consists of several steps:

- Pre-application consultation;
- Policy review and approval;
- Safety review and approval;
- Payload review and determination;
- Financial responsibility determination;
- Environmental review; and
- Compliance monitoring.[37]

Pre-Application Consultation

An applicant for a license must consult with the FAA before submitting an application.[38] The applicant must provide information regarding the launch vehicle, the proposed mission and the launch site. This enables the applicant to become familiar with the FAA's expectations, and gives the AST the opportunity to become acquainted with the applicant's proposal.

Policy Review

The statute requires that a license be issued, "Consistent with the public health and safety, safety of property, and national security and foreign policy interests of the United States . . . ."[39] Policy review requires that the application be assessed for consistency with these goals, and any international obligations of the United States. The FAA engages in interagency review with the U.S. Department of Defense, Department of State, and NASA to assess the security, foreign policy or international obligations.

Safety Review

In order to protect the crew and any space flight participants, the FAA is authorized to issue regulations governing the design or operation of a launch vehicle.[40] Though initial regulations must be limited to design features or operating practices that have resulted in a serious or fatal injury or contributed to an unplanned event, the FAA may promulgate more expansive regulations after an eight year developmental period (in 2012).[41]

The FAA conducts a safety review in order to determine whether the applicant is capable of launching without jeopardizing public health and safety, and the safety of property.[42] A flight safety analysis determines where a launch vehicle may and may not fly, and monitors and controls the risk to the public.[43] In assessing the flight safety, the FAA reviews the proposed trajectory, malfunction turn, debris, flight safety limits, straight-up time, time

---

pound-seconds or less; (2) and a total burning time of less than 15 seconds; and (3) has a ballistic content of less than 12 pounds per square inch. 14 CFR § 400.2.

35 http://ast.faa.gov/lrra/about_lrra.htm (visited August 1, 2006).

36 49 U.S.C. § 70105(a).

37 http://ast.faa.gov/lrra/ (visited August 1, 2006).

38 14 CFR § 415.105.

39 49 U.S.C. § 70105(a).

40 49 U.S.C. § 70105(c).

41 49 U.S.C. § 79195(c)(2)(C).

42 14 CFR § 415.31. See 14 CFR Part 417 Subpart C.

43 Licensing and Safety Requirements for Launch – Part II, 71 Fed. Reg. 50,508 (Aug. 25, 2006). 14 CFR § 417.107(f).

delay, flight hazard, probability of failure, debris risk, toxic release, collision avoidance, overflight gate, and hold and resume gate.[44] The FAA also assesses the flight safety system (i.e., the system that provides control during flight to prevent a hazard from reaching a populated or other protected area during a launch vehicle failure).[45] Typically, a flight safety system includes a flight termination system and a command control system.[46]

For orbital and suborbital expendable launch vehicles, the applicant must also file a comprehensive safety review document,[47] that reveals:

- Launch vehicle description;
- Payload description;
- Launch site description;[48]
- Launch operator organization;[49]
- Launch personnel certification program;[50]
- Flight safety analysis;[51]
- Ground safety analysis;[52]
- Launch plans;[53]
- Launch schedule;[54]
- Computing systems and software;[55]
- Unique safety policies and practices;[56]
- Flight safety system design and operational data;[57]
- Flight safety system test data;[58]
- Flight safety system crew data;[59] and
- Safety at the end of the launch.[60]

The FAA conducts a qualitative and quantitative risk analysis of the application to discern whether it satisfies the safety obligations.[61] The risk analysis evaluates vehicle reliability, casualty areas, the probability of a crash, the populations at risk, and the potential consequences.[62] The qualitative analysis focuses on the reliability of the critical safety systems, the hazards potentially posed by the hardware, the risks posed to persons or property near the launch site or along the flight path, and to satellites and other orbital spacecraft. The quantitative analysis focuses on the applicant's launch safety practices and procedures, and the qualifications of key individuals.[63] The licensee must demonstrate that the risk of its launch falls below specified risk criteria.[64]

---

[44] Licensing and Safety Requirements for Launch – Part II, 71 Fed. Reg. 50,508 (Aug. 25, 2006). 14 CFR §§ 417.105, 417.205 – 417.233.
[45] 14 CFR Part 417 Subpart D.
[46] Licensing and Safety Requirements for Launch – Part II, 71 Fed. Reg. 50,508 (Aug. 25, 2006).
[47] 14 CFR § 415.107.
[48] 14 CFR § 415.109.
[49] 14 CFR § 415.111.
[50] 14 CFR § 415.113.
[51] 14 CFR § 415.115.
[52] 14 CFR § 415.117.
[53] 14 CFR § 415.119.
[54] 14 CFR § 415.121.
[55] 14 CFR § 415.123.
[56] 14 CFR § 415.125.
[57] 14 CFR § 415.127.
[58] 14 CFR § 415.129.
[59] 14 CFR § 415.131.
[60] 14 CFR § 415.133.
[61] "Acceptable flight risk through orbital insertion for an orbital launch vehicle, and through impact for a suborbital launch vehicle, is measured in terms of the expected average number of casualties ([c] c) to the collective members of the public exposed to debris hazards from any one launch." 14 CFR § 415.35.
[62] 71 Fed. Reg. 16251 (Mar. 31, 2006).
[63] http://ast.faa.gov/lrra/about_lrra.htm (visited August 1, 2006).
[64] 71 Fed. Reg. 16251 (Mar. 31, 2006).

The applicant must document the systems safety organization and identify safety personnel.[65] No license or permit holder may launch or reenter crew unless the crew has been trained and satisfied medical standards as specified in the license or permit.[66]

Payload Review

Unless the payload is exempt, the FAA determines whether the payload owner or operator has obtained the necessary licenses, authorizations and permits. Payloads regulated by the U.S. Federal Communications Commission, the National Oceanic and Atmospheric and Oceanic Administration, or owned or operated by the U.S. government are exempt.[67] Congress forbade payloads that result in obtrusive space advertising[68] in the National Aeronautics and Space Administration Authorization Act of 2000.[69]

Financial Responsibility Review

Applicants must demonstrate adequate financial responsibility in an amount sufficient to compensate an injured party for personal or property injury for the maximum probable loss.[70] Limits are prescribed by the FAA.[71] Most applicants ordinarily satisfy these requirements by purchasing liability insurance.[72]

Environmental Review

The FAA is required to engage in an environmental evaluation, for a launch and reentry is considered a major federal action significantly affecting the quality of the human environment under the National Environmental Policy Act.[73]

Compliance Monitoring

The FAA provides oversight to determine whether a licensed applicant is complying with its obligations under the law and rules and regulations promulgated thereunder. A licensee is obliged to permit the FAA to position an observer at the launch or reentry site.[74] The FAA may suspend immediately the operation of a launch site or the reentry of a vehicle if it concludes such action is necessary to protect the public health and safety, property, the national security, or a foreign policy interest of the United States.[75]

SAFETY APPROVALS

In August 2006, the FAA promulgated regulations establishing procedures for obtaining a safety approval for a safety

[65] 71 Fed. Reg. 16251 (Mar. 31, 2006).

[66] 49 U.S.C. § 70105(b)(4).

[67] http://ast.faa.gov/lrra/about_lrra.htm (visited August 1, 2006).

[68] Obtrusive space advertising is defined as "advertising in space that is capable of being recognized by a human being on the surface of the Earth without the aid of a telescope or other technological device." 49 U.S.C. § 70102.

[69] Pub. L. 106-391 (Oct. 30, 2000). The FAA reviews payloads to ensure that they will not result in obtrusive space advertising under 14 CFR § 415.51. 41 Fed. Reg. 51,968 (Aug. 31, 2006).

[70] 49 U.S.C. § 70112(a).

[71] 49 U.S.C. § 70112(a)(2). 14 CFR § 417.21.

[72] See 49 U.S.C. § 70112. Certain third party liability claims above the insurance coverage, but below $1.5 billion (adjusted for inflation) also may be paid by the U.S. government. 49 U.S.C. § 70113.

[73] 42 U.S.C. § 4321 et seq.

[74] 49 U.S.C. § 70106(a).

[75] 49 U.S.C. § 70108(a).

element.[76] Once issued, the holder could offer the approved safety element to launch and reentry operators. This allows different operators of approved equipment, components, parts, personnel or services[77] on different launch or reentry vehicles, thereby streamlining the process of reviewing and issuing licenses. An approved safety element can be used by different launch and reentry vehicle operators within the specified scope without having to go through a regulatory examination of the element's fitness and suitability for a particular launch or reentry. Applicants may include manufacturers or designers of a launch or reentry vehicle or component thereof, the designer or developer of a safety system or process, or personnel who perform critical safety functions in launch or reentry.[78] Applications are assessed based on performance-based criteria established by: (1) the FAA or other federal regulations; (2) government-developed or adopted standards; (3) industry consensus standards; or (4) applicant developed criteria, in that order.[79] Approvals are valid for five years, and are renewable.[80]

EXPERIMENTAL PERMITS

The Commercial Space Launch Amendments Act of 2004 established an experimental permit regime for the development of reusable suborbital rockets. Congress intended that, "At a minimum, permits should be granted more quickly and with fewer requirements than licenses."[81] The experimental permit regime is intended to reduce the regulatory burdens upon developers of reusable suborbital rockets.

The FAA has reduced the number of requirements imposed upon permit vis-à-vis license applications, consonant with the special airworthiness certificates the FAA issues on special airworthiness certificates granted to experimental aircraft. [82] The applicant must submit; (1) a program description (a description of the purpose for which the rocket will be operated, its dimensions, weight, thrust profiles, payloads, propellants, hazardous materials and systems); (2) a flight test plan (estimated number of flights, important flight-safety events, and maximum altitude); and (3) operational safety documentation.[83] If the applicant satisfies the applicable statutory and regulatory requirements, experimental permits should be issued within 120 days of receipt of a completed application.[84] Eligibility for an experimental permit depends upon whether the suborbital rocket is flown for one of the following purposes:

- Research and development to test new design concepts, equipment or operating techniques;

---

[76] Safety Approvals, 71 Fed. Reg. 46,847 (Aug. 15, 2006).

[77] Safety elements eligible for approval are launch vehicles, reentry vehicles, safety systems, processes, services or any identified component thereof, as well as qualified and trained personnel performing a process or function involving licenses launch activities or vehicles. 14 CFR § 414.3.

[78] 14 CFR § 414.5.

[79] 14 CFR § 414.19.

[80] 14 CFR § 414.21(d).

[81] H. Rep. 108.429 § VII.

[82] 71 Fed. Reg. 16251 (Mar. 31, 2006).

[83] 71 Fed. Reg. 16251 (Mar. 31, 2006).

[84] 49 U.S.C. § 70105a(a). 71 Fed. Reg. 15251 (Mar. 27, 2006).

- Showing compliance with requirements as apart of the process for obtaining a license;
- Crew training before obtaining a launch or reentry license using the design for which the permit would be issued.[85]
- No one may operate a reusable suborbital rocket under an experimental permit for the carriage of property or person for hire.[86]

LAUNCH SITES

Since 1996, AST has issued site operator licenses to several US spaceports including California Spaceport at Vandenberg Air Force Base, Spaceport Florida at Cape Canaveral Air Force Station, the Virginia Space Flight Center at Wallops Island, and Kodiak Launch Complex on Kodiak Island, Alaska. These sites augment the launch capacity of the NASA and US Air Force facilities (particularly those at Cape Canaveral and Vandenberg Air Force Bases).[87] The first launch from a licensed, non-federal facility was at Spaceport Florida of NASA's Lunar Prospector aboard a Lockheed Martin Athena 2 on January 6, 1998.[88]

Most FAA-licensed launches have been from U.S. Air Force launch sites.[89] The FAA performs a Launch Site Safety Assessment [LSSA] to determine whether a federal launch range meets applicable safety requirements.[90] If the launch operator has contracted with a federal launch site for provision of the flight safety system, the FAA will accept that system as used or approved on the federal launch range. The FAA treats a federal launch range as that of the launch operators.[91]

For launches from a non-federal site, compliance with the requirements of the flight safety system is assessed through the licensing process.[92] The FAA conducts a ground safety analysis, consisting of an identification of each potential hazard, causes, and controls the launch operator must establish to prevent the hazard from affecting the public.[93]

CONCLUSION

US policies have evolved over time. The competition between the US and USSR for dominance of space has evolved into cooperation between the US and Russia in the International Space Station, though even in the post-Cold War era, defensive (and even offensive) applications of space garnish significant public investment. The US set out to be the leader in space research, science and technology, and undoubtedly accomplished that goal. Public

[85] 49 U.S.C. § 70105a(d). 71 Fed. Reg. 16251 (Mar. 31, 2006).

[86] 49 U.S.C. § 70105a(h).

[87] US Dep't of Commerce, Trends in Space Commercialization, republished in Paul Stephen Dempsey, Space Law IV.B.United States.6-2 (2004).

[88] http://ast.faa.gov/aboutast/ (visited May 17, 2004).

[89] Safety Approvals, 71 Fed. Reg. 46,847 (Aug. 15, 2006).

[90] Licensing and Safety Requirements for Launch – Part II, 71 Fed. Reg. 50,508 (Aug. 25, 2006).

[91] See 14 CFR § 417.13.

[92] Licensing and Safety Requirements for Launch – Part II, 71 Fed. Reg. 50,508 (Aug. 25, 2006).

[93] Licensing and Safety Requirements for Launch – Part II, 71 Fed. Reg. 50,508 (Aug. 25, 2006). 14 CFR § 415.117. 14 CFR §§ 417.109 - 113

development of space activity is being replaced, albeit slowly, with privatization and commercial development.

No nation has accomplished as much space as has the US. As the European Space Agency, and as nations such as China fulfill their ambitions in space, we shall see if the US continues its insatiable thirst for triumph.

As the global economy grows, so too will commercial activities in space. As is the case with multinational corporations in other trade sectors, the ability of any individual nation to regulate them will be circumscribed. Moreover, a fragmented patchwork of national laws governing such issues as safety, security, environmental harm, and liability, in the long term, will impede the ability of space commerce to reach its full potential. An international body—the International Civil Aviation Organization [ICAO]—promulgates standards and recommended practices [SARPs] in many of these areas for commercial aviation, facilitating international harmonization of law and enhancing the development of commercial aviation.

The day may come when the world community realizes that an international body is needed to address common issues in the commercial development of space.[94] Progressive domestic laws in industrial nations addressing labor, taxation and the environment have already driven mining and manufacturing industries off-shore. Stringent safety regulations and export restrictions could do the same for space. Hence harmonization of law can create a "level playing field" globally, alleviate uncertainty, and thereby facilitate private investment. Global harmonization of Space Law could come in the form of creation of a new international organization, or by amending the Chicago Convention of 1944[95] to include space within ICAO's jurisdiction.[96]

[94] Jurgen Cloppenburg, The Future Regulation of Global Mobile Personnel Communications by Satellite: A Farewell to Lex Americana?, XXV Annals of Air & Space L. 83, 134-37 (2000).

[95] Convention on International Civil Aviation, 61 Stat. 1180 (1944).

[96] ICAO's membership of 189 nations comprises virtually the entire world community. It also possesses both quasi-legislative and quasi-judicial authority, and has more than a half century of experience in addressing safety international commercial aviation.

Session 2:
LEGAL ASPECTS OF DISASTER MANAGEMENT

Chairmen: Sergio Marchisio
Juan Faraminan Gilbert

Rapporteur: Sylvia Ospina

IAC-06-E6.2.2

"SOS"— Is Anyone Getting This Message?[1]

SYLVIA OSPINA, JD, LL.M.
S. Ospina & Associates-Consultants
Coral Gables, Florida
sospina@bellsouth.net

Since December 2004, we have witnessed a series of devastating natural disasters, with huge losses of life and homes, as well as the displacement of millions of people. Hundreds of organizations of all kinds have endeavored to provide a variety of rescue and relief services to the victims of these calamities. But most of them seem to face the same problem: lack of communication amongst themselves, leading to, or resulting in less than well-coordinated and effective relief efforts.

One reason for the lack of coordinated efforts is that terrestrial means of communication, whether telephone lines or accessible roads, are usually the first to be knocked out of service. Another reason is that the different agencies, whether governmental, non-governmental, international, national, local, public or private institutions, each has its own communications policies and systems, utilizing different radio frequencies. These systems often are not compatible with each other, thus delaying notification amongst the users, and consequently, delaying relief efforts as well.

At the end of the day, communications will either "make" or "break" disaster relief efforts, and satellite communications have proven that they are the best, if not essential, means to convey information in times of disaster, since they do not rely entirely on the terrestrial infrastructure. Even so, much remains to be done to improve communications at all levels, even amongst users of satellite systems.

The International Telecommunication Union (ITU) as well as national entities involved in radio frequency management are striving to improve on this situation, by studying the possibility of ensuring that certain frequencies bands are available on a regional basis for emergency communications. If they succeed in setting apart frequencies to be used by most, if not all the entities involved in emergency response and relief efforts, in future these efforts will be more productive and efficient.

Greater coordination amongst national and international agencies is needed, as well as greater cooperation between the technical people and policy makers. This paper will examine some of the efforts that are being made to make better use of the radio frequency spectrum and in particular, of satellite systems, to improve rescue and relief efforts on a global basis.

Many natural (and man-made) disasters[1] have greatly affected our lives in the past few years. Are there more of them, or are they reported more frequently, thanks to the globalization of television and news programs? The same media that bring us the bad news are the ones that are used to facilitate emergency assistance, humanitarian aide to the victims of these tragedies. The focus of this paper will be on natural disasters, those that occur without direct human intervention (such as wars), even though the results may be the same: displacement of people, contamination of arable land, destruction of the infrastructure.

Several "leitmotifs" recur when referring to natural disasters: lack of adequate

International Telecommunications /Space Law Consultant.

forecasting, and therefore, lack of planning for them; lack of equipment, both minimal and back-up, and lack of coordination amongst the entities providing relief or recovery efforts after the event. Another "leitmotif" is the need for adequate means of communication, prior to, during, and after the disaster occurs.

Terrestrial means of communication, whether telephone lines or accessible roads, are usually the first to be knocked out of service, making local communications, and access to the victims difficult, if not impossible. While the provision of physical aide may be hindered, having more wireless communications available would improve the rescue and relief efforts; at least, they could be better coordinated. This will be elaborated upon later.

Another "leitmotif" are the regulatory/policy[2] hurdles faced by the emergency / relief entities, whether governmental or non-governmental, international or national. Regulatory barriers seem to exist at all levels; they tend to impede adequate assessments of the damages sustained, and thus affect subsequent recovery efforts. They may have a significant impact on local recovery efforts, from the deployment of manpower, to delivery of medical supplies, and other essential goods, such as wireless means of communication.

In examining some of the legal /regulatory aspects of disaster relief efforts, these seem to fall into two general categories: one, those that apply to man-made disasters, such as wars, and are subject to international humanitarian laws.[3] The other, are regulations that may apply in times of natural disasters, but involve different treaties and laws. Two recent efforts at simplifying international satellite-based communications for disaster relief and rescue efforts are the Charter on Space and Disaster,[4] and the Tampere Convention.[5] These will be elaborated upon later.

Further, there seem to be four levels of regulations / legislation related to relief / rescue efforts: local, regional, national, and international. The local regulations are applicable within a particular community, such as city ordinances. Regional regulations may apply either within an administrative or a geographic sector.[6] National regulations, however, may supercede regional ones, and international laws, in turn, may be supercede national legislation. A brief examination of the local and international levels follows.[7]

Local Level

It's said that "charity (or in this instance, communications) begins at home," but at the local level, channels of communication usually are the first to be disrupted, and the local authorities are unsure of what course of action to take. Even where people are trained to provide emergency assistance, local policies (and politics) and regulations may cause unwanted interference in rescue /relief efforts, further exacerbating the crisis situation.[8] This was quite evident during the relief efforts following Hurricane Katrina, as noted by the Independent Panel on Hurricane Katrina in its report to the Federal Communications Commission (FCC).[9]

In August of 2005, Hurricane Katrina caused the worst natural disaster in the United States' recent history. Thousands were left homeless and without adequate medical care; thousands more people were displaced, with few means of knowing where they were after the hurricane and evacuation. Even now, families are looking for relatives that disappeared during or after the storm, and the Gulf coast is barely beginning to recuperate.[10]

One of the points emphasized or recommended by the Independent Panel is the need for better coordination of efforts at the local level, as well as loosening up and waiving some of the requirements to authorize people to act. Thus, at the very basic, local level, regulatory barriers were deemed to have made a bad situation worse. If the lack of coordination and preparedness caused such chaos in the world's most developed country, are these problems compounded in developing countries, where the infrastructure and resources are scarcer?

The Katrina report recommends paying greater attention to the resources available locally, prior to having to use them; the local level is the "last mile" or "first mile," and usually the weakest link. However, this is where satellites, both for communications, and earth observation, can play an important role.

Earth-observation / remote-sensing satellites can provide images and data from before, during, and after the disaster, which can be used to assess the extent of the damage, as well give some indication as to the type of assistance that is required immediately. The following section will present an overview of recent major international legislative and cooperative efforts that have had a significant positive impact in disaster relief and mitigation endeavors.

International Disaster Mitigation Endeavors

I. The Charter to Achieve Coordinated Use of Space in the Event of Natural and Technological Disasters emerged from UNISPACE III, held in Vienna, Austria, in July, 1999, as an initiative of several space agencies, and was adopted in November 2000.[11] The Charter "aims at providing a unified system of data acquisition and delivery to those affected by natural or man-made disasters through Authorized Users. Each member agency has committed resources to support the provisions of the Charter and to help mitigate the effects of disasters on human life and property."[12]

The purpose of the Charter is to provide data and information resulting from the exploitation of space facilities, in anticipation of a disaster, in the organization of emergency assistance or reconstruction or operations subsequent to a natural disaster.[13] This objective reflects the intent of Principle XI of the UN Principles Related to Remote Sensing from Outer Space, which states: *Remote sensing shall promote the protection of mankind from disasters. To this end, States participating in remote sensing activities that have identified processed data and analysed information in their possession that may be useful to States affected by natural disasters, or likely to be affected by impending natural disasters, shall transmit such data and information to States concerned as promptly as possible.*[14]

Charter members cooperate on a voluntary basis, providing data collected by their earth observation /remote sensing satellites, making the data and processed information available to affected, or potentially affected States as soon as possible, allegedly at no cost to them, or at least "without exchange of funds between them."[15] It has been pointed out, however, that responding to Charter activations is expensive, but the cost is usually borne at the agency level, without any significant impact on the national budget.[16]

The Charter encourages the widest possible accession of national or international space systems operators, primarily those of earth observation /remote sensing spacecraft, to the Charter,[17] and to date, the Charter has been of benefit in more than 80 instances to countries in all regions of the world that have suffered from floods, hurricanes, earthquakes, forest fires, and other natural disasters.[18] The numerous activations or interventions of the Charter members, attest to its usefulness, and to the value of remote-sensing images and other data in times of disasters.

While the achievements of the Disasters Charter members have been significant, the Charter itself has a few drawbacks. One of them is that becoming -and remaining a member- is on a voluntary basis, and it seems that the member has no legal obligation to provide data or processed information even if doing so would be beneficial to a State affected by a disaster. Since it is a "charter", it has no force of law; there is no legal obligation for the Parties that have adopted it to comply with its purpose or intention. However, it would be pointless to join the Charter without being willing to share data and information; thus, the goodwill of the participating agency is assumed.

Another drawback is the fact that, should the data or information that is shared be erroneous, the Charter member(s) incur(s) no liability. Art.V, 5.4 states that "*no legal action will be taken against the parties in the event of bodily injury or financial loss arising from the execution or non-execution of activities, services or supplies arising out of the Charter.*"[19] Thus, despite members' best efforts, should they provide erroneous data or information that may further worsen the disaster, they are under no legal duty to mitigate the consequences of their error. Further, despite any "Good Samaritan" principle, the agencies are not obliged to provide assistance; they do so on a voluntary basis only.[20]

However, could liability still be incurred by the State that has given the space agency its legal personality? The Charter members are juridical persons of a State that has launched or procured the launch of an object to outer space, and as such, the State in which it is organized could be held liable under Art. VII of the Outer Space Treaty, which states: *"Each State Party to the Treaty which launches or procures the launching of an object into outer space...is internationally liable for damage to another State Party to the Treaty or to its natural or juridical persons by such object or its component parts on the Earth."* [21] While it could be argued that remote-sensing data are not a component part of a space object, the data can be collected only by using one of the space object's components, i.e., transponders or other equipment on board the spacecraft.

The Disasters Charter and the Remote Sensing Principles have similar limitations; namely, they are not legally binding. Some authorities maintain that, in order for UN R/S Principle XI[22] (and the Charter) to be meaningful, what is needed is an international system based on an enforceable international public policy to monitor potential natural disasters, as well as taking measures to prevent them, or at least reduce the chances of their occurring, and to mitigate their harmful consequences.[23] Another author stresses the need to have an unambiguous legal regime regarding remote-sensing and disasters, "clearly stipulating the...rights and obligations of sensed States and sensing States, data providers, and data recipients," and their consequent liability.[24] Yet another author recommends that international obligations should be identified, policy and procedures clarified, with the aim of establishing a working [legal?] framework.[25]

While the Disasters Charter is a good starting point in the use of remotely sensed data and information to prevent and mitigate disasters, its usefulness is limited at present by its being a voluntary effort on the part of some space agencies and associated bodies, and not having a clear legal mandate. (Notably absent from its membership roster is the US NASA, the Chinese Space Agency, and the Brazilian Space Agency (SBA), especially since China and Brazil have a cooperative program on earth observation, the CBERS.)[26]

The Charter will become more useful as more agencies become members, and more countries and corporations develop earth observation capabilities, as well as the capacity to analyze the data. Further, having a more formal legal status than a voluntary association would likely add to the Charter's and its members' credibility.

Greater cooperation between the operators of earth observation / remote sensing satellites and the telecommunication satellite operators is also needed. Without the latter, the data and information garnered cannot reach the intended recipient(s) in a timely manner. The following section will look at the some of the telecommunications sector's disaster relief and mitigation efforts.

II. The Tampere Convention and the International Telecommunication Union (ITU)

Telecommunications play a crucial role in all emergencies, ranging from local calls to the fire brigade, to providing satellite data and images of disasters, as well as facilitating international post-disaster relief efforts.

The ITU Constitution has always accorded absolute priority to emergency life-saving communications, and has recognized the vital role played by telecommunications in deploying resources essential to reducing loss of life, human suffering and physical damage caused by disasters.[27] After many years of adopting Resolutions and holding conferences on Disaster Communications, the ITU, together with other United Nations agencies, determined that an International Convention on Disaster Communications was needed, to facilitate the deployment of emergency communication systems, thus facilitating disaster mitigation and relief efforts.

Removal of regulatory barriers and strengthening cooperation among States were endorsed at the first World Telecommunications Development Conference, held in Argentina in 1994. Following the Second World Telecommunications Development Conference (WTDC-98), held in Malta in 1998, the ITU's Development Sector was given the task of ensuring that attention be given to emergency telecommunications as an element of telecom development. One specific result was the drafting of a Handbook on Disaster Communications.[28]

The 1991 Tampere Declaration on Disaster Communication called for a convention to facilitate reliable telecom systems for disaster mitigation, and finally it became part of the

Tampere Convention on the Provision of Telecommunication Resources for Disaster Mitigation and Relief Operations. It was adopted in 1998, and entered into force 8 January 2005, upon ratification by 30 States. Unlike the Disasters Charter, the Tampere Convention has many international legal underpinnings, and is enforceable law.

Coordination of operations under the terms of this convention is assigned to the United Nations Emergency Relief Coordinator, through the UN Office for the Coordination of Humanitarian Affairs (OCHA), but the Coordinator's responsibilities are limited to coordinating activities of an international nature.[29] A State Party requiring telecommunications for disaster mitigation may request assistance from any other State Party, either directly, or through the operational coordinator. The State requesting the assistance shall specify the scope and type of assistance required, and the State(s) to which the request is directed shall determine whether it will provide the assistance requested, and shall specify the terms and conditions, restrictions and cost related to such assistance.[30] (The Disasters Charter states that data and information shall be provided without exchange of funds between members.)

Art.4.5, recognizing the importance of national telecommunications law and policy, states that no telecoms assistance shall be provided without the prior consent of the requesting State Party. Intergovernmental and non-governmental agencies are not considered "requesting Parties", and may not request telecoms assistance under this Convention. In other words, the local chapters of international relief organizations, such as the Red Cross/Red Crescent, must ask the State to make the request for telecoms relief; they cannot request it on their own.

On the one hand, Art. 4.8 is quite emphatic on the issue of national sovereign rights: "Nothing in this convention shall interfere with the right of a State Party, under its national law, to direct, control, coordinate and supervise telecommunications assistance provided under this Convention within its territory."

On the other hand, the requesting State is urged to grant certain privileges and immunities to persons and organizations (other than those domiciled within its territory) that have accepted the request for telecoms assistance, in order for them to perform their functions.[31]

Among the immunities recommended are immunity from arrest and other legal processes in regard to acts or omissions specifically and directly related to the provision of telecoms assistance, although nationals of the requesting Party are not granted these immunities. (The Disasters Charter also states that its members shall not be held liable for losses or injury due to their non/performance under the Charter.)[32]

Another immunity sought is exemption from taxation, duties, and other charges for telecoms equipment brought into or purchased in the territory for the purpose of providing telecoms assistance. Further, the Convention urges the expedited issue of licenses, or even exemption from licensing of telecoms equipment brought into the requesting Party's territory. Ownership of the equipment remains with the Party responding to the request, and will be returned to that Party.[33]

The Convention also emphasizes that the persons entering the requesting Party's territory have a duty to respect national laws and regulations, and have the duty not to interfere in the domestic affairs of the territory they enter. In other words, while providers of telecoms emergency assistance may enjoy certain privileges and immunities, they need to bear in mind that they are guests of the requesting State, and not above its laws.

One difference between the Disasters Charter and the Tampere Convention relates to payment or reimbursement of costs and fees for the provision of telecoms assistance. Whereas remote sensing data and information are supposed to be provided at no cost, telecoms assistance is provided with the expectation of being remunerated therefor. Article 7 states that these fees will be set forth in writing, as well as the currency in which they will be paid. In determining the cost of services, however, several factors should be kept in consideration, such as the nature of the disaster, the territory in which it occurred, the State's capacity to prepare and respond to the disaster.[34]

Despite the fact that telecoms have become so essential at all times, but especially during a crisis or disaster, several hurdles remain which hinder rescue and relief efforts in a timely manner. Article 9 of the Tampere Convention addresses these regulatory barriers, urging States Parties to lift these restrictions, or at least reduce them. This Article is the core of the Convention.

Art. 9 of the Convention refers to certain practices, which the ITU Handbook on Disaster Communications regards as the "regulatory paranoia" prevalent among some ITU Administrations. The underlying fear is that communications, and not only telecoms equipment, may fall into the wrong hands, or cause harmful interference.[35]

Regulatory barriers include, but are not limited to regulations restricting the import or export of telecommunications equipment; the use of the radio frequency spectrum and of certain telecoms equipment; restrictions related to the movement of personnel operating the telecoms equipment; delays in granting licenses or permissions, which impede the rapid deployment of telecom resources for disaster relief operations, and may even defeat the purpose of obtaining the license.

The Convention urges the adoption of several means to reducing regulatory barriers, such as revising existing national regulations (and streamlining the license application procedures); exemption from, or granting temporary waivers of the regulations for specific telecom resources (those that are being provided in response to a disaster).

Another recommendation is recognition of type-approval of telecom equipment and/or operating licenses. Acceptance of foreign type-approval also is one of the recommendations made in the Global Mobile Personal Communication Systems Memorandum of Understanding (GMPCS MOU) drafted by the ITU in the 1990s, to facilitate the deployment of the mobile personal satellite communications systems, such as Iridium and Globalstar. These systems, together with Inmarsat and Thuraya, have provided a variety of emergency telecommunication services around the world, including during and after the Hurricane Katrina disaster.[36]

The Tampere Convention requests each State to notify the UN operational coordinator of the measures that it has taken to reduce or remove regulatory barriers, pursuant to the Convention.[37] However, "nothing in this Article [9] shall permit the violation or abrogation of obligations and responsibilities imposed by national law, international law, or multi- or bilateral agreements," including customs and export controls.[38]

Despite the United Nations and the ITU's urging for its speedy adoption, it took 7 years for the Tampere Convention to come into force. Only 30 States have ratified it, even though natural disasters have struck all regions in the last few years. Countries that have been the most affected recently by tsunamis, earthquakes, hurricanes and floods, including Afghanistan, China, Cuba, Indonesia, Malaysia, Mexico and Thailand, have not signed the Tampere Convention, although they benefited from emergency telecommunications assistance, *post facto*. However, had early warning equipment been available, some of the damage caused by these disasters may have been avoided, or at least reduced.[39] The lack of planning for disasters seems to prevail in most countries, although some are making efforts to be better prepared for future emergencies and natural catastrophes.[40]

The ITU, and the UN's Secretary-General, Kofi Annan, have emphasized the importance of reliable telecoms links in disaster reduction, and encouraged partnerships among inter/national development programs and the private sector to take appropriate preventive and planning measures to cope with future disasters.[41] But it seems that many States remain unpersuaded. Are there means to induce the ITU Administrations that have not acceded to the Tampere Convention, to do so? Could these States be held liable under some international humanitarian law for not signing this Convention, especially if, by not subscribing to it and not seeking emergency assistance, they worsen the crisis in their territory? Do States not have some responsibility to protect their citizens, to provide emergency (and on-going) rescue and relief to them, or at least to mitigate the damages caused by natural disasters in their territory?

Conclusion and Recommendations

Numerous international organizations, NGOs, and national entities have expended much energy and countless hours in mitigating potential disasters, providing post-facto emergency assistance, and in rebuilding efforts. The recommendations, resolutions, and even international conventions that have emerged from their experience and efforts all stress the crucial role played by telecommunications operators and service providers in times of emergencies or disasters, and the need to have trained telecoms personnel, beginning at the local level.

Both the Disasters Charter[42] and the ITU-D Handbook on Disaster Communications[43] as well as the Katrina Report[44] point to this need, and make specific recommendations to improve disaster communications and relief efforts. Emergency (and basic) telecom equipment providers could be very instrumental, since they usually provide some training to service providers on the use of their equipment which, in turn, could train the end users. Further, new technologies and equipment are more widely available, which can facilitate emergency communications efforts locally.

At the international level, the ITU and other UN agencies are providing training as well as satellite imagery, for post-disaster telecoms network planning in several countries.[45] These efforts are in addition to their cooperation within the framework of the World Summit on the Information Society (WSIS),[46] one of whose aims is to diminish the "digital divide," the gap between the telecom "haves" and the "have-nots."[47]

One proposal that emerged from the 2003 WSIS was the creation of a "digital solidarity fund" to help the less developed countries / regions acquire the necessary equipment to bridge the "digital divide," thereby facilitating their joining the information society. These funds could be used to acquire equipment for basic as well as emergency telecommunications, thus reducing what seems to be a "disaster divide;" i.e., the lack of basic telecoms, let alone back-up equipment for use in emergency situations.[48]

The UN's and ITU's efforts also entail cooperation with the private sector, particularly now that the major international satellite service providers and operators are mostly private corporations.[49] The intergovernmental part of INTELSAT, now called "ITSO", and its counterpart at INMARSAT (IMSO) play a key role in enforcing the public service obligations undertaken by their new private owners, to provide services in thin routes and underserved regions. Intelsat and Inmarsat and other private satellite operators have provided emergency telecommunications during and after the recent tsunami, hurricanes and earthquakes, but at cost, without necessarily giving any special discounts to the afflicted territory. (The Tampere Convention states that the cost of the emergency telecoms shall be put in writing, and agreed to prior to services being provided.)[50]

Specific recommendations that have been made by those involved in emergency telecommunications and disaster relief efforts include having solar powered emergency equipment available; more satellite telephones (Globalstar, Iridium, Inmarsat, Thuraya), and radios. It would also be helpful to have these systems operators' willingness to provide low-cost communications for authorities and even the victims' families. (Could they be considered as tax-deductible charitable contributions?)

While much of the emergency telecom and relief efforts are provided by international organizations based in developed countries, the developing countries can also provide lessons on the use of rudimentary equipment that is available to them, and that does not require specialized training to operate. Hand-held radios, simple battery-powered generators, solar energy are available worldwide, and can be used when the infrastructure is damaged. Even hand-cranked radios and telephones are available, and useful in all countries.

Of great importance, regardless of the territory concerned, is the designation of one agency as head coordinator of communications (as recommended in the Katrina Report and ITU-D Handbook, and established in the Tampere Convention). In this respect, the Amateur Radio operators can play a significant role, since they provide services at the local level as well as at the international level, and are familiar with a variety of telecoms equipment and radio frequency usage. At the community level, it would be helpful to designate a few individuals as focal points for relief or emergency communications and operations.

Another initiative that merits greater attention is allocating and allotting certain radio frequencies on a worldwide and regional basis for emergency telecommunications. Several ITU Members are working on this issue, albeit for implementation at the national level.

Perhaps one of the most important recommendations made in the Tampere Convention, the ITU-D Handbook and the Katrina Report is the need to relax, reduce, or waive some of the national regulatory requirements, all while respecting national sovereignty over telecommunications. Perhaps special licenses could be devised and granted *a priori* to certain organizations or individuals (and type-approval for their essential equipment), that would be registered as emergency telecom providers / operators. If and when their services were required, they would be licensed, and ready to provide services, without having to wait for official decisions.

In this respect, some of the European Union/ European Commission initiatives could serve as guidelines; namely, reform of spectrum management, and easing of licensing requirements, as well as achieving greater harmonization in the provision of services.[51] These issues, however, are not new; they have been discussed and proposed not only in Europe, but also at the WSIS[52] and in the Global Mobil Personal Communications Services/ Systems Memorandum of Understanding (GMPCS MOU).[53] Perhaps the recommendations to reduce regulatory barriers would be accepted more readily by States if they acknowledged that fast telecoms response are crucial in times of disasters. The law should not be an impediment in providing emergency humanitarian aide.

In times of emergencies, mankind tends to unite or bond in ways that do not usually occur, perhaps because what affects our brother humans on one side of the globe affects us all, thanks to the immediacy of global communications. And so, we need to acknowledge that satellite imagery and communications have become an essential component of all these rescue and relief and other humanitarian endeavors, at all levels.

---

[1] The American Heritage Dictionary of the English Language defines 'disaster' as 'an occurrence inflicting widespread destruction and distress; a grave misfortune; an evil influence of a celestial body, or "ill-starred", from the Italian disastro, and French désastre.'

[2] The distinction between policies and regulations is sometimes blurred, particularly when personal decision-making power or authority is involved. Thus, rather than violate "policies", and take action, an agency's policy may be interpreted as a regulation, and result in lack of action.

[3] The International Red Cross / Red Crescent Societies (ICRC) play a significant role in times of war, and in enforcing the observance of the Geneva Convention and other treaties related to man-made disasters or casualties. The aide these organizations provide at times of natural disasters, such as earthquakes or floods is significant, but different rules and regulations apply. For the Principles and Rules that the ICRC applies in response to humanitarian assistance and protection, see www.icrc.org.

[4] Charter on Cooperation to Achieve the Coordinated Use of Space Facilities in the Event of Natural or Technological Disasters [Cited hereinafter as the Disasters Charter.] For the full text, see www.disasterscharter.org.

[5] Tampere Convention on the Provision of Telecommunications Resources for Disaster Mitigation and Relief Operations, adopted by the Intergovernmental Conference on Emergency Communications (ICET-98), entered into force 8 January 2005. [Cited hereinafter as the Tampere Convention.] For the full text see www.reliefweb.int/telecoms/tampere/icet98-e.htm.

[6] The International Telecommunication Union (ITU), for purposes of allocating use of the radio frequency spectrum (RFS), has delimited the world in three regions: Region 1 encompasses Europe and Africa; Region 2, the Americas; Region 3, the rest of the world.

[7] Regional and national regulations are so varied that they deserve a more in-depth analysis than can be provided in this paper.

[8] See note 2, supra, and notes related to the Tampere Convention, infra.

[9] Federal Communications Commission (FCC), Independent Panel Reviewing the Impact of Hurricane Katrina on Communications Networks. One result of this report was the Notice of Proposed Rulemaking, EB Docket No. 06-119, 71 Fed. Reg. 38564, July 7, 2006, aimed at addressing and implementing the recommendations of the

Independent Panel. [Cited hereinafter as the Katrina Report.]

[10] The casualties incurred as a result of this and other hurricanes seem minimal when compared to a recent headline: "Chinese storms leave 15 million homeless". AP (Associated Press), 25 Aug. 2006.

[11] The space agencies participating in the Charter are the European Space Agency (ESA), the French Centre national d'études spatiales (CNES), the Canadian Space Agency (CSA); Argentina's Comisión Nacional de Actividades Espaciales (CONAE); the Indian Space Research Organisation (ISRO); Japan's Aerospace Exploration Agency (JAXA), the US National Oceanic and Atmospheric Administration (NOAA); Centre National des Techniques Spatiales of Algeria; the Nigerian National Space Research and Development entity; Turkey's Tübitak-BILTEN, the UK's BNSC and Surrey Satellite Technology Ltd.

[12] Main web page, Disasters Charter, supra, note 4.

[13] Art. II, "Purpose of the Charter." Disasters Charter, supra, note 4.

[14] Principles Related to Remote Sensing from Outer Space; UN Resolution 411/65, adopted 3 December 1986. [Cited hereinafter as the UN R/S Principles.]

[15] Art. III, 3.1, Disasters Charter, supra note 4.

[16] Gabrynowycz, Joanne. Contribution to the IISL/ECSL symposium on 'Legal Aspects of Disaster Management and the Contribution of the Law of Outer Space,' held during the 45th Session of the UN COPUS Legal Subcommittee, Vienna, Austria, 3 April 2006.

[17] Art.VI – Accession, Disasters Charter, note 4.

[18] "Recent Activations", www.disasterscharter.org. (Accessed 10 July /06.)

[19] Art. 5.4 –Associated Bodies, Disasters Charter, supra, note 4.. The 1972 Liability Convention is unlikely to be applicable, since liability is limited to damage caused by a space object to aircraft in flight and to the surface of the Earth.

[20] Ito, Atsuyo provides a good discussion on the applicability of the "Good Samaritan" principle to remote-sensing activities and the Disasters Charter. See "Legal Aspects of the International Charter on Space and Major Disasters." Proceedings of the 47th Colloquium on the Law of Outer Space, Vancouver, Canada (2004), pp.233-41.

[21] Art.VII, Treaty on Principles Governing the Activities of States in the Exploration and Use of Outer Space, including the Moon and other Celestial Bodies. Entered into force Oct. 1967. [Cited as the Outer Space Treaty hereinafter.]

[22] UN R/S Principles, supra, note 14.

[23] Jose Monserrat Filho, Vice President, Brazilian Society of Aerospace Law, in response to this author's query. Dr. Monserrat is one of Brazil's Delegates to the UN COPUOS. On 15 June 2006, COPUOS approved a new agenda item proposed by the Brazilian delegation, "International Cooperation in the Promotion of the Use of Geospatial data for Sustainable Development." This item includes a 3-year work plan, which promises to have a positive impact in the use of remote sensing data for sustainable development.

[24] Ito, supra, note 20.

[25] International Law and Disasters. Contribution of the Japanese delegate to the IISL/ECSL symposium on "Legal Aspects of Disaster Management and the Contribution of the Law of Outer Space," held during the 45th Session of the UN COPUS Legal Subcommittee, Vienna, Austria, 3 April 2006.

[26] According to a recent press report, Brazil will join the US NOAA and other space agencies to create a "planetary big brother," the Global Earth Observation System of Systems (GEOSS), whose objective will be to track natural disasters before they occur, and attempt to mitigate them. GEOSS plans to compile data from satellites, buoys, and other monitoring systems; to coordinate and centralize the location of the data collected, so that they will be useful. Brazil will be represented by its National Space Research Institute, the Instituto Nacional de Pesquisas Espaciais (INPE) in this endeavor. "Folha de S. Paulo", 26 Aug, 06. (This press item does not mention the Chinese-Brazilian earth observation satellite program, CBERS.)

[27] Preamble, Tampere Convention, supra, note 5. The introduction to this Convention includes references to the numerous UN and ITU Resolutions on which it is based.

[28] ITU-D Handbook on Disaster Communications, Chapter 3, "The International Regulatory Framework." In Sept. 2000 the International Amateur Radio Union (IARU) issued a two-part Handbook on Disaster Communications for the ITU's Telecom Development Sector (ITU-D), to provide training to persons and organizations involved in disaster relief operations and communications. According to IARU, amateur radio operators play a key role at the local—and international—level in times of natural disasters. The Handbook drafters rightfully urge its wide dissemination among all Administrations, telecoms users and operators, not only those in developing countries. It is available at www.itu.int\ ITU-D\SG-D\SGO2\100\167VE.DOC. [Cited as the ITU-D Handbook hereinafter.]

[29] Art. 2, Tampere Convention, supra, note 5.

[30] Art. 4.1-4.3, ibid.

[31] Art.5,, ibid. "Privileges, Immunities, and Facilities."

[32] Art.V, 5.4, Disasters Charter, supra, note 4.

[33] Art.5, 5.2-5.5, Tampere Convention, supra, note 5.

[34] In regard to fees and cost of telecoms service, bilateral agreements between Administrations and service providers, as well as the World Trade Organization's Annex on Telecommunications should be kept in mind. Now that many, if not most telecommunications operators and service providers are private companies, and no longer State-run monopolies, the issue of paying for services takes on a different meaning. Even during Hurricane Katrina, telecoms services provided by the Red Cross and other agencies were not exactly free. Globalstar, Iridium, Inmarsat, and other satellite operators and service providers charged for their services and the equipment they supplied, ranging from satellite antennas to personal hand-held satellite telephones.

[35] Chapter 1, ITU-D Handbook, supra, note 28.

[36] "Télécommunications sans frontières (TSFI), an organization based in France, has provided emergency telecom satellite services to many countries, in cooperation with the UNDP, UNICEF, under the terms of the Tampere Convention. TSFI is a member of the UN's Working Group on Emergency Telecommunications (WGET), which was responsible for developing and drafting the Tampere Convention; it is also a partner in the European Community's Humanitarian Office (ECHO). See www tsfi.org for some of TSFI's telecom partners and projects in which they have been involved.

[37] Art. 9.5, Tampere Convention, supra, note 5.

[38] Art. 9.7, ibid.

[39] A recent US government report concluded that 5 years after the 9/11 attacks and months after Hurricane Katrina, most cities and states are unprepared for these types of catastrophes. Major failures include plans to take care of the elderly and others who are unable to help themselves; lack of early warning to the citizens, and failure to designate a clear chain of command. (AP wire service, 6/16/06.)

[40] An interesting example worth emulating is a disaster communication network set up in one state in India, which has been operating since March 2000. The network is based on VSAT and VHF networks, and has built-in redundancies. In addition to being used for disaster management, the network serves for general government administration and rural development. For a fuller account, see N.K. Chhibber, "Maharashtra's Communication Network for Disaster Management." ITU copyright 2005. http:// www.itu.int/ITU-D/pdf/fg7/mah001.html.

[41] Excerpt from the Intergovernmental Conference on Emergency Communications (ICET-98), Tampere, Finland, as cited by Zavazava, Cosmas in his article, "[ITU's] Role in Disaster Reduction Through Emergency Telecommunications. ITU, Geneva, 2005. Dr. Zavazava is the ITU's Focal Point for Emergency Telecommunications.

[42] Disasters Charter, supra, note 4.

[43] ITU-D Handbook, supra, note 28.

[44] Katrina Report, supra, note 9.

[45] See ITU Newsroom, in particular the ITU-D, or BDT Newslog, (http://itu,int/ITU-D/CDS/newslog), which centralizes news activities related to the ITU-D, including emergency telecommunications.

[46] The World Summit on the Information Society (WSIS) was first convened in Geneva in 2003, and met again in Tunisia in 2005.

[47] Since its establishment in 1989, the ITU's Development Bureau (ITU-D) has served as a means of channeling UNDP and other funds for telecom development, particularly in the less developed regions of the world. It also serves as a focal point for emergency telecommunications. (See note 41, supra.) The UN's Office for Outer Space Affairs (OOSA) has also been instrumental in the use of space technology in disaster management. See www.oosa.unvienna.org/SAP/stdm.

[48] Prior to Phase Two of the WSIS in Tunisia (Nov. 2005), a Special Session on Telecoms for Disaster Relief was held in February 2005 in Geneva. It included an overview of ITU work in Telecoms for Disaster Relief, highlighted the key elements of the Tampere Convention, and presumably addressed the "disaster divide" issue.

[49] INMARSAT and INTELSAT were privatized under terms and conditions specified in the "Open-market Reorganization for the Betterment of International Telecommunications Act, or the ORBIT Act." Public Law 108-180, 17 March 2000. Their intergovernmental components (IMSO and ITSO respectively) are relatively small and less influential than in the past.

[50] Art.4, Tampere Convention, supra, note 5.

[51] See Gerald Oberst, *European Communications Rules in Play*; VIA SATELLITE, Sept. 2006, p. 14.

[52] WSIS, supra, note 46.

[53] The GMPCS MOU, drafted in the 1990s, could be a useful model and tool to facilitate the importation, type approval, and use of mobile equipment in times of emergency or disaster, if the country involved has incorporated the GMPCS recommendations in its legislation. Otherwise, the GMPCS MOU is not legally binding.

HURRICANES AND REMOTE SENSING

By

Carl Q. Christol
Distinguished Emeritus Professor of International Law and Political Science
University of Southern California
Los Angeles, CA 90089-0044
Member: IISL, IAA, AIAA

Abstract

Students of the Earth's natural environment are calling attention, with increasing urgency, to particularly unusual and dangerous weather and climate conditions. Informed opinions have indicated concerns respecting permanent changes. The experts have relied on data and analyzed information obtained via remote sensing to describe past events and to make predictions and recommendations for future action. Killer hurricanes have been selected to demonstrate the scientific basis for concerns and as a rallying point for national and international responses.

Important measures will be necessary to preserve and protect the world's ecosystems against continued threats and to allow for an acceptable quality of life for the world's inhabitants. To reach these goals there will have to be very careful planning, the execution of meaningful plans, and jointly shared international accountability since exceedingly large costs will be entailed.

1. Introduction

The international lawyers, who in 1986 drafted the Principles Relating to Remote Sensing of the Earth from Outer Space, demonstrated a practical awareness of the capabilities of remote sensing and the general conditions of the Earth's natural environment.

Principle I spoke generally of the need to improve "natural resources management, land use, and the protection of the environment." Principle X recited that "Remote sensing shall promote the protection of the Earth's natural environment." Principle XI stated that "Remote sensing shall promote the protection of mankind from natural disasters." Those who forged these principles, while recognizing the utility of ensuring that remote sensing would serve environmental needs and that there was a linkage between such needs and the prospect of international disaster, had no way of knowing how quickly and gravely the Earth's natural environment would deteriorate. Although predictions by respected scientists were being published, doubts were being voiced. It was not until the 1972 United Nations Conference on the Human Environment that widespread international recognition was given to the seriousness of the environmental crisis.

By the time the Remote Sensing Principles were adopted the space-resource countries had perfected sophisticated means for obtaining raw data. At that time and in the following years the world's scientific community was almost entirely in agreement that, owing in large part to large volumes of greenhouse gases that the world's temperature, including the Ocean--and very noticeably the South Atlantic—was rising and that changes in climate could produce dire consequences.

Traditional concerns over the atmosphere and climate relating to public safety, agriculture, business operations, fishing, mining, transportation, and other pursuits, had produced studies of the weather, and weather forecasting, including predictions respecting precipitation and wind levels, and hours of sunshine or darkness. With the evolution of sensing procedures and expertise in the interpreting of raw data, national measuring and reporting institutions were greatly enlarged, international cooperation was substantially increased, and international intergovernmental weather organization began to multiply. The results of their investigations were widely distributed.

The concerns of environmentalists, expressed over 30 years ago, have materialized. During the ensuing years there have been substantial changes to the Earth's atmosphere, air quality, and climate. Not the least of the scientific factors under constant study has been the hurricane cycle affecting the Western Hemisphere including the East Coast of the United States, the Gulf Area, much of Eastern Mexico, and the Caribbean islands. In the Orient in those areas prone to typhoons comparable concerns and studies have attracted the attention of countries and international organizations.

2. A Bit of History.

Hurricanes, which are produced by heightened sea-surface temperatures, when the surface reaches 80 degrees F, have been observed in the above areas for many years. Such temperatures are reached in the South Atlantic in August and September. A storm in the Lesser Antilles in 1780 resulted in 22,000 deaths. The Galveston, Texas, hurricane in 1900 caused 12,000 deaths and resulted in the destruction of the city.

The U. S. Weather Service uses the Saffir-Simpson model to classify hurricanes with category 5 being the most serious. Of the five classes number 3 requires winds of 110-130 miles per hour and storm surges of 9-12 feet; class 4 winds of 131-155 mph and surges to 13-18 feet; class 5 winds of over 155 mph and surges exceeding 18 feet. Comparative figures reveal that the average number of hurricanes and average size impacting the South Atlantic Coast of the United States had increased in 1970-1974 over 1955 and that since 1974 even more increases have been recorded.

Heavy precipitation accompanies hurricanes. When Katrina, a class 5 hurricane, came ashore in the New

Orleans area of Louisiana on August 29, 2005, following heavily publicized warnings by the U. S. Weather Service, precipitation rapidly reached 8-10 inches along much of the hurricane's path. As it moved inland and became a tropical storm rainfall was measured between 2-4 inches across much of the Gulf Coast and into the Ohio Valley. Katrina also produced quantities of hail with widespread damage in Georgia. The storm produced levee breaks. Portions of New Orleans were covered with 20 feet of water. Mobile, Alabama, was submerged, while Biloxi and Gulfport, Mississippi, were very heavily flooded. Katrina produced power outages, and destroyed or damaged oil wells and oil-refining facilities. As Katrina receded it was estimated that 95% of these facilities were non-operational. Damages were estimated at over $100B with more than 1,300 deaths and enormous social costs. Normalcy cannot be expected for many years.

3. Governmental Activities

To provide warnings of impending hurricanes so that lives might be saved and property damages and social costs might be minimized governments acting alone and collectively have taken measures designed to promote their self-interests. In the United States the national government, though a large number of departments, agencies, and offices, has been the guiding force. International agreements have been entered into with foreign governments and international intergovernmental organizations. Since weather and climate are of universal concern international cooperation has become the means to secure the needs of humanity.

In the United States satellites have been the principal means used to identify hurricanes, although these have been supplemented by aircraft, maritime buoys, maritime vessels, radar, and visual observations. The collection and integration of the data acquired from these resources is very complex. The large number of government agencies engaged in such activities has resulted in calls for consolidation. The early dissemination of suitable warnings has become a major challenge. Comparisons have been made of the accuracy of forecasts. Records indicate that this has improved over time

The National Hurricane Center (NHC) working with the National Weather Service (NWS), agencies of the National Oceanic and Atmospheric Administration (NOAA), provides public advisories on an hourly basis on storms in the Atlantic and Pacific Oceans. NOAA operates Geostationary Operational Satellites (GOES). These satellites hover at 22,300 mile above the equator. Remaining on a fixed position the GOES has a full-disc view of the Earth. They are critical to monitoring rapid changes in weather conditions. GOES measure sea-surface temperatures on a one-half hourly basis. This allows for short-range warnings of impending hurricane conditions.

NOAA also operates Polar Orbiting Environmental Satellites (POES). These satellites make a nearly polar orbit 14.1 times a day. They have been designed to provide data for long-range weather and climate forecasting. The POES system is augmented by Very High Resolution Radiometers (AVHRR) and by TIROS Operational Vertical Sounders (TOVS).

PEOS facilitates the gathering of ocean data including weather analysis and forecasting, climate research and prediction, global sea surface temperatures, atmospheric sounding of temperature and humidity, and ocean dynamics research, as well as studies of land-based conditions.

The number of U. S. governmental entities having an interest in Earth observation has been identified by the subcommittee of the National Science and Technology Council of the larger committee on Environmental and Natural Resources. Included in this inventory are 15 member agencies, 3 White House Offices, 10 departments, and a host of other governmental offices. Among these bodies is NASA and the Department of Defense (DOD). NASA through its Earth Observing System (EOS) engages in global climate change research . The DOD Defense Meteorological Satellite Program (DMSP) focuses on supplying weather and environmental information and support to military operations.

NASA has conducted extensive studies on atmospheric radiation since such radiation has substantial effects on climate change. Studies reported in July, 2006, revealed that there had been significant increases in the number of heavy rain storms between 1991 and 2004 as compared with storms bringing moderate amounts of precipitation. There was an increase in the number of category 3-5 hurricanes during this period. The NASA Goddard Space Flight Center also called attention to various types of aerosols differently affecting cloud cover, which could enhance or reduce sunshine, which in turn would have an influence of the surface temperatures of the ocean. The Goddard Institute of Space Studies using historic records for comparative purposes reported in 2006 that the five hottest years on record occurred since 1998, with the record being established for the hottest in 2005. These temperatures have produced rapid melting of the Greenland and Antarctic ice sheets with progressive threats to coastal areas
and to hurricane formation.

With so many offices being involved in a common project it has become necessary to achieve coordination and cooperation. This can produce additional supervisory bodies. For example, there is National-Polar Orbiting Operational Environmental Satellite System (NPOESS) designed to integrate existing polar-orbiting satellite systems under a single national program. This has allowed for the combination of NOAA's POES and the DOD DMSP. This has resulted in increasing the timeliness and accuracy of forecasting severe weather changes.

4. International Organizations and International Cooperation

A European Organization for the Exploitation of Meterological Satellites (EUMETSAT), now consisting of 20 countries, was established on May 24, 1983. Created by treaty it became operational on June 19, 1986. Using eighth generation METEOSAT satellites EUMETSAT serves world needs by supplying information on global weather, environmental, and climate changes. It engages in studies of the atmosphere, the environment, natural hazards and disasters occurring on Earth, snow and ice conditions, and establishes formats and standards. Its survey of clouds includes their wind motion, cloud and sea-surface temperatures, and upper tropospheric humidity.

NOAA maintains close contact with EUMETSAT. Cooperation has benefited through their involvement in the Initial Joint Polar Orbiting Operational Satellite System (IJPS). Coordinated efforts have improved operational meterological and environmental forecasting and world-wide climate monitoring services. Dissemination of data and analyzed information has been made to the World Meterological Organization (WMO), the UN Environmental Program (UNEP), and the Intergovernmental Oceanographic Commission (IOC), and other related programs. Principal beneficiaries have been those less-developed countries located in tropical storm areas.

In July, 2006, EUMETSAT's plan to launch a METEOSAT was interrupted when a failure occurred in the SOYEZ/ST launcher. It was to have been equipped with instruments furnished by the European Space Agency (ESA), the French Space Agency (CNES), and NOAA.

5. Conclusion

Satellites have been very effective in capturing data allowing for an effective assessment of weather and climate conditions in general and of hurricanes in particular. Disasterous as prior hurricanes have been their increase in number and their growing size, coupled with the planet's increase in temperature, has raised the question of whether the global warming trend can be reversed. Unfortunately, green house emissions show no sign of abating in the United States, which has rejected the Kyoto Protocol, and are now growing at an alarming rate in India, China, and the developing countries. Observers of this larger picture have speculated that if reduction efforts are not soon adopted on a world wide-basis that a worst scenario case of very substantial, if not unrivaled proportions, will befall the human race. At this time serious thought has been given to adaptation strategies, but it may be possible that prospects for such a course of action may be too little and too late. Experience with hurricanes will have to be taken into account in determining what will have to be done in the future.

Suggested Readings

K. Choo, "Feeling the Heat: The Growing Debate Over Climate Change Takes on Legal Overtones," ABA Journal, July, 2006, p. 29.

E. J. Gaines, "Home No More [New Orleans Portfolio after Katrina]," 210 National Geographic, No. 2, August, 2006, p. 42.

JOHN HOUGHTON, GLOBAL WARMING; THE COMPLETE BRIEFING (2004).

E. LINDEN, THE WINDS OF CHANGE; CLIMATE, WEATHER AND THE DESTRUCTION OF CIVILIZATIONS (2006).

L. Nardon, "GEOS and Its US and European Components; Challenges and Impact," 22 Space Policy, No. 2, May, 2006, p. 149.

R. A. Williamson and J. C. Baker, "Current US Remote Sensing Policies: Opportunities and Challenges," 20 Space Policy, No. 2, 2004, p. 109.

Session 2A:
THE MOON, PROPERTY RIGHTS AND LEGAL ISSUES

Chairmen: Sergio Marchisio
Juan Faraminan Gilbert

Rapporteur: Sylvia Ospina

IAC-06-E6.2.A.01

UPDATING OF LUNAR TREATY

Milan Pospisil
Verifik, PO Box 5, 281 63 Kostelec, Czech Republic,
milan.pospisil@c-box.cz

ABSTRACT

This paper specifies why and how the respective principles and treaties governing activities of people on the moon should be modified / amended and stresses the need to do that as soon as possible due to the expected development of industrial space activities.

INTRODUCTION

The extension of international law to outer space is typically done in three steps: identification of problems related to legal aspects, formulation of corresponding legal principles and incorporating such principles in general multilateral treaties [1]. This paper deals predominantly with the first two steps.

PROBLEM

Among the most pressing problems of our civilization is shortage of energy sources, their uneven distribution and pollution of environment caused by their exploitation.

One of the ways how to ease this situation was proposed by Dr. Glaser in Science in the year 1968 under the name of Space Power Satellite, the SPS [2]: To collect solar radiation above atmosphere of the earth, transmit it to ground and insert as electricity into the power grid. See the Fig. 1.

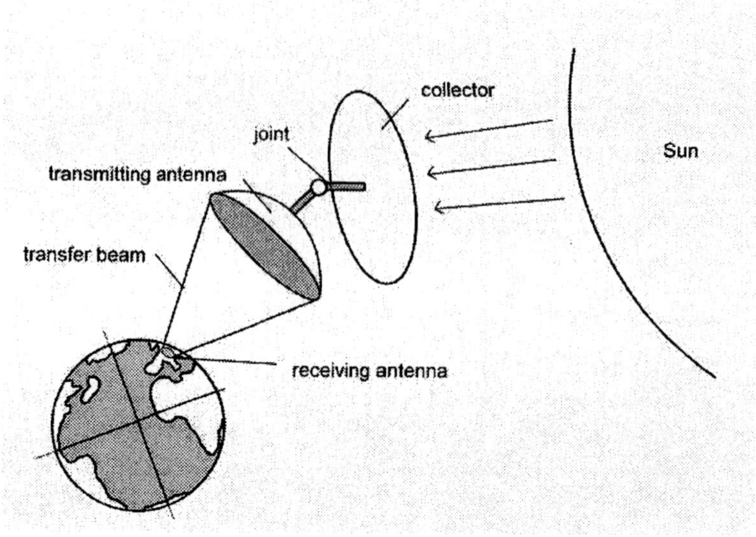

Fig. 1 Sketch of the solar power satellite

Energy of solar radiation is received by the collector, converted into electricity, led through the rotating and swinging joint to adjust to different motions of the sun and earth, sent as microwave beam by the transmitting antenna to earth and there converted and put into the utilities power grid.

The sun is compared to our needs an infinite source both in magnitude and time, the transmitting beam can be directed to anywhere on the earth, there would be no smoke or wastes resulting from the SPS operation, and even most of the waste heat would be left in space.

In spite of that Glaser's promising idea had not been implemented in the past almost 40 years. There were two main obstacles: money and pollution related to the construction.

NASA contracted studies of feasibility of Glaser's project in the seventies [3]. Some assumptions were set, like that the transmitting beam had to be in the microwave region, and all parts had to be manufactured on earth and transported to orbit from there.

Final evaluation in the year 1980 stated: Costs and pollution caused by mining, manufacture, space transport, irradiation by the microwave beam, dimensions of the receiving antennas of the system of 60 SPS stations of 5 GW_{el} each would be too high.

In the subsequent years some enthusiasts tried to solve difficulties. Miller and Akin [4] published a study showing that initial capital costs of space manufacture would be higher but operational lower than those of terrestrial production [4]. An example of their thinking is in the Fig. 2. Not only in their paper the moon was the centre of construction activity, see e.g. works of groups of which the driving force was prof. H. H. Koelle [5-7] and many others like [8-10].

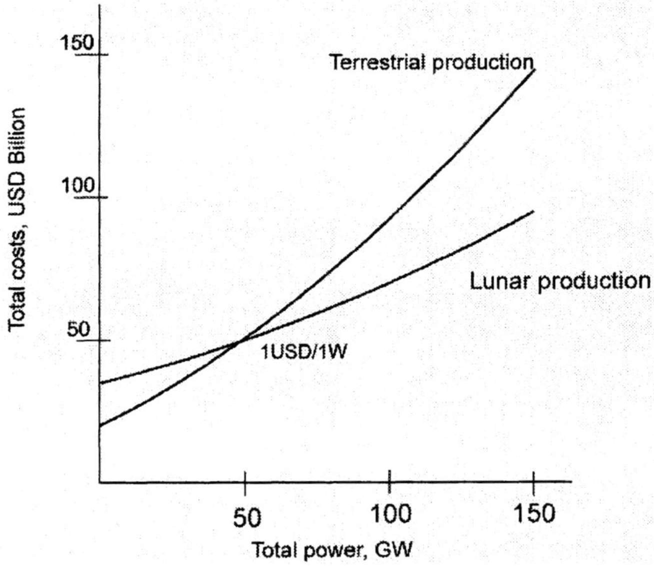

Fig. 2 Costs

The capital costs (investment) of manufacture on the moon are higher but the operational costs are lower than those on earth. At some amount of installed capacity becomes the "lunar" electricity cheaper.

Let's go the moon then.

THE MOON

The moon is a rocky airless sphere of radius of 1700 km and surface area of 36 millions km^2 (approximately area of Africa, 7 % of area of the earth). Volume of the moon is approximately 2 % of volume of the earth, density 60 % of average density of earth, so the mass of the moon is roughly 1 % mass of the earth, [11].

The moon circles the earth in distance of 380 000 km once in approximately 27 terrestrial days. It also rotates round its axis. Interesting is that period of this rotation is the same; the lunar day lasts 27 terrestrial days. From which results that the moon faces earth all the time with the same face. An observer residing on the near side of the moon sees ceaselessly the surface of the earth. Fortunately for him he can observe various parts of it, because the period of rotation of the earth is different and the plane of the moon travel round the earth is tilted towards the plane in which rotates the earth. On the other hand an inhabitant of the other side of the moon has nice opportunity to see the whole universe round us. Without limitations of atmosphere, lights of cities, dust and pollen of flowers and trees, which so readily cover lenses and mirrors of terrestrial astronomers.

Being rocky moon offers also many valuable materials – like 42 % of oxygen, 21 % silicon, 13 % iron, and others like calcium, aluminum, magnesium etc. [12].

These can be easily transported into space, because due to smaller mass of the moon its gravitation force is 0,166 of the earth, roughly 6 times lower. To this corresponds also the energy needed to raise a body into space and from it resulting costs, Fig. 3.

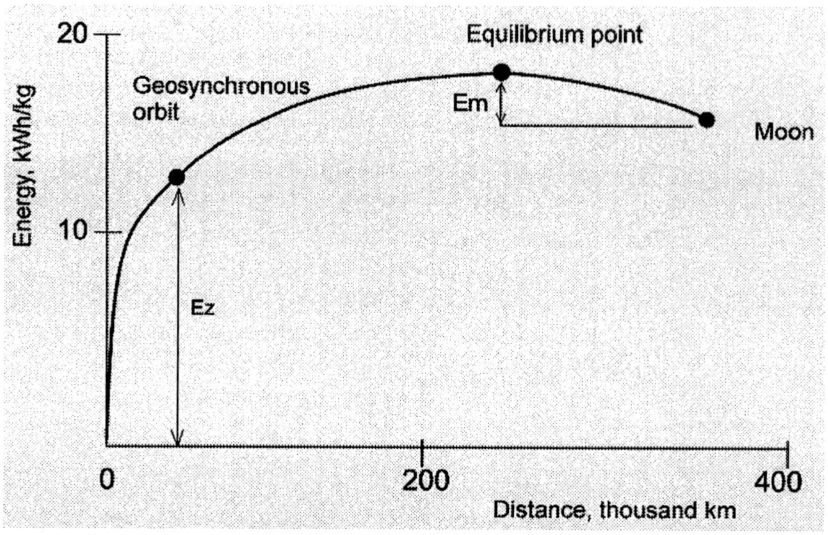

Fig. 3 Gravitational well

On vertical axis is energy (costs) needed to transport load from one place in space to other, on horizontal axis is the distance (time needed for transport) of the selected points. The earth is the "zero" point.

Small but some gravity of the moon is other advantage in comparison to work in a complete weightlessness of an orbit of earth or a place in open space. There is no danger that your spanner or friend starts flowing away for ever into the infinite universe.

The perfect vacuum which governs on the moon is favorable for special types of production. It is not only much better than can be achieved on surface of the earth, but capacity of its "vacuum pumps" is unlimited. Sensitive parts of space stations can be produced there and transported to place of destination without need to be protected against damaging influence of the terrestrial atmosphere.

It would be fair to list also some disadvantages of stay on the moon. There is no air there, so people have to wear pressurized suits and live in well tighten and sheltered quarters. Long day and night result in big differences in temperatures. No atmosphere also means no protection against meteorites and radiation. And nonexistence of greenery gives the surrounding rather sad look.

To summarize: Building of big space structures, like collectors of solar energy of space power satellites can be made feasible by using of space resources, especially of the moon. This is going to be very costly enterprise, not quite corresponding in its time scale to the election campaigns of politicians. But the pressures of need one day will prevail and after that will result an avalanche of trips, constructions, use and misuse of the moon. To prevent the last reasonable rules, laws and mechanisms for enforcing of the laws must be defined. The sooner the better.

PRINCIPLES

We have just defined what is needed: rules how to use the moon reasonably. Something like highway code for human activities there. Next we can start to define the principles. The basic intentions are to allow development of industry on the near side of the moon only, to reserve the other side, the far side, for science.

What is covered by the principles agreed up to now?

The UN General Assembly adopted the basic legal principles governing the activities of states in the exploration and use of outer space in the year 1963, [13], they were further refined in the Treaty on Principles ... in 1967, [14].
This Treaty says except others (in the following the "state" means "The State Party to this Treaty"):

Article:

I: No discrimination, free access to all areas.

IV: Use only for peaceful purposes, but military personnel can be used for scientific research. Any equipment necessary for peaceful exploration shall not be prohibited (anywhere).

VI: States are responsible for activities of non-governmental entities; their activities require authorization / continuous supervision of the state.

VIII: A state retains jurisdiction and ownership of objects launched into outer space.

IX: Exploration should avoid contamination (of the moon), adverse changes in the environment of the earth and harmful interference with space activities of other states.

XI: The Secretary General of the UN shall be informed of space activities.

XII: Right of inspection of space facilities of other states.

XV: Any state can propose amendments to this Treaty on Principles.

These Principles are general; they cover the whole outer space, including the moon and other celestial bodies. Because the moon of our earth is a unique natural source and its near and far side have different special advantages, we think that the principles on its exploitations should be defined in more detail.

TREATIES

On base of the above mentioned principles the UN member states adopted the Agreement Governing the Activities of States on the Moon and Other Celestial Bodies, which entered into force in 1984, [15].

This Agreement recognizes in its preamble that "... the moon, as the natural satellite of the earth, has an important role to play in the exploration of outer space.", and says in its Article

1. Provisions of this Agreement relating to the moon shall apply to other celestial bodies.
3. The moon shall be used exclusively for peaceful purposes; the use of military personnel for peaceful purposes shall not be prohibited.
4. Due regard shall be paid to the interests of present and future generations ...
5. States shall inform UN Secretary General of their activities.
6. No discrimination, right to collect on and remove from the moon samples for scientific purposes.
7. Paragraph 1: No disruption of lunar environment, no harmful affecting the environment of earth. Par. 2: Notification of placement of radio-active materials on moon. Par. 3: Designation of areas of special scientific interest for special protective arrangements.
8. Exploration and use of the moon anywhere on or bellow its surface.
9. Establishment of manned and unmanned stations on the moon (anywhere).
11. The moon is common heritage of mankind; no part of it shall become property of any state or other entity. The states will establish the international régime, including appropriate procedures to safeguard the orderly and safe development of the natural resources of the moon, the rational management of those resources, the expansion of opportunities in the use of those resources. Interests and needs of the developing countries and efforts of the countries, which have contributed to the exploration of the moon, shall be given special consideration.
12. States retain jurisdiction over their personnel, and ownership of their facilities and equipment.
14. States shall bear responsibility for their activities and have authority /right of supervision of non-governmental entities.
17. Any state can propose amendments to this Agreement.
18. Ten years after the entry into force of this Agreement (1984) review of it shall be included in the agenda of the General Assembly of UN.

This Agreement follows rather closely the Principles listed in the Treaty [14]. New is recognition of the unique status of the moon in preamble and its role in this Agreement, right to exclude parts of the moon only for scientific purposes which rather contradicts to do specified activities on the moon anywhere, like placement of radio-active materials in Art. 7, exploration in A.8, stations in the Article 9.

PROPOSED EXTENSION

Once we recognize importance of the moon for space industry and science, we should define "special lunar" principles and treaty, which would ensure reasonable development of the moon.

The corresponding principles should include:

First: Moon must never be used as a deposit site for any type of terrestrial wastes. Wastes created by lunar activities might be at the beginning transported back to earth, but as soon as possible they should be recycled on spot.

Second: Only the near side of the moon shall be used for industry. The far side has to be reserved for scientific purposes only. The system of telescopes for wide range of wavelengths (no limitation by the atmosphere, no dispersed light in the sky like at terrestrial observation facilities, etc. [16, 17]) will make possible discoveries undreamed of. They will allow also spotting of dangerous space bodies well in advance of collision.

Third: All industrial activities on the Moon must observe strict rules, prohibition of explosives probably one of them. They could create clouds of small particles of which time of settlement is unknown. Additionally, vibrations caused by explosions could influence scientific activities on the far side.

Fourth: Responsibilities and penalties have to be defined, enforcement of laws ensured.

To become the lunar enthusiast is useful to read the The Moon Book by geologist B.M. French, [18]. Despite being first printed in 1977, it still retains it flair. Some ideas and pictures in this paper were taken from the book Verifik 1 [19].

Lunar base plans of different nations and/or private companies can be speeded up by energy and environmental concerns significantly. Thus modification of the lunar legislature is as urgent as ever.

SUMMARY

Purpose of this paper was to draw attention to the fact that the moon of our earth is a unique natural resource, which can help to solve our energy problems and make possible advancement of science undreamed of. Unless it is spoiled during its development
To prevent that a special lunar treaty is suggested. Strict exclusion of the far side of the moon only for science should be one of its leading rules.

REFERENCES

1. UN Treaties and Principles on Outer Space, United Nations Office in Vienna, 1994
2. Glaser P.E.: Power from the Sun, Science 162, 1968, p. 857
3. DOE/NASA: Satelllite Power System, DOE/ER-0023, October 1978
4. Miller R.H., Akin D.A.: Logistic costs of solar power satellites, Space Solar Power Review 1, 1980, p. 191
5. Koelle at al.: Entwurf eines Projektplanes für die Errichtung einer Mondfabrik, Institut für Luft- und Ruaufahrt, Technische Universität Berlin, 1983
6. Apel U. at al: Comparison of alternative strategies of "Return-to-the-moon", Institut für Luft- und Raumfahrt, Technische Universität Berlin, 1985
7. Koelle H.H.: The case for an international lunar base, 1987, IAA Ad Hoc Committee
8. Space Research Associates: Solar power satellite built of lunar materials, Space Studies Institute, New Jersey, 1985
9. Woodcock G.R.: Economic potentials for extraterrestrial resources utilization, IAA-86-451
10. Waldron R.D.L Lunar manufacturing: A survey of products and processes, IAA-86-508
11. Valouch and Valouch: Pětimístné tabulky logaritmické, p. 135, Nakladatelství ČSAV, Praha 1953
12. SSI Update: Why use space resources, Space Studies Institute, New Jersey, 1986
13. Declaration of Legal Principles Governing the Activities of States in the Exploration and use of Outer Space, G.A.Res. 1962 (XVIII), [1], p. 37
14. Treaty on Principles Governing the Activities of States in the Exploration and Use of Outer Space, including the Moon and Other Celestial Bodies, entered into force on 10 October 1967, [1], p. 4
15. Agreement Governing the Activities of States on the Moon and other Celestial Bodies, entered into force on 11 July 1984 [1], p. 28
16. Duke M.B., Mendell W.W.: Science investigation at a lunar base, IAA-86-509
17. Snoddy at al.: Design considerations and strtegies for lunar-based observatories, IAF-93-Q.2.391
18. French B.M.: The moon book, Pinguin, New York, 1978
19. Pospec M.: Verifik 1, VERIFIK, Voderady, 2003, www.verfik.com

IAC-06-E.6.2.A.02

Author

C. Jimenez Monroy

TOWARDS A LEGAL FRAMEWORK FOR SUSTAINABLE DEVELOPMENT ON THE MOON: THE CASE OF IN-SITU RESOURCE UTILIZATION.

ABSTRACT

Many experts agree that In- Situ Resource Utilization (ISRU) is necessary to support the long term scientific missions on the Moon from economic and technological perspectives. This brings up a series of important questions: should we determine a limit for ISRU activities? What could be the legal justification for such a limitation? Which authority would be in charge?

ISRU on the Moon is the key to help with two main problems of long term missions: First, the reduction of the mass and cost of transportation with the production of propellant from natural resources on the Moon: Oxygen, Hydrogen (Atomic hydrogen). Secondly, ISRU provides the option of self-sufficiency and safety for missions with the production of elements required for life support systems to assure the daily crew needs (such as oxygen: 0.84 kg and water :2.28 kg per crew member).

The International Legal Framework for ISRU has two principal instruments: The Treaty on Principles Governing the Activities of States in the Exploration and Use of Outer Space, Including the Moon and other Celestial Bodies and the Agreement Governing the Activities of States on the Moon and Other Celestial Bodies. The latter is one of the most controversial of the United Nations Treaties because it deals with the exploitation of natural resources and some countries found its language deficient with vague concepts and "anti-developmental" approaches to space resources. – Spacefaring nations have not ratified the Moon Agreement-

The analysis of these two documents cover the following aspects: Freedom of Use and Exploration of Outer Space, Exploration of Outer Space for the benefit of all Mankind, Outer Space as Common Heritage of Mankind, sovereignty over Celestial Bodies, the duty to avoid harmful contamination of Celestial Bodies and to inform UN about the activities concerned with the exploration and use of the Moon.

A proposal for Sustainable Development (SD) on the Moon should include an analysis of the consequences of present actions and the effects on future public and environmental health. Such an analysis should be interdisciplinary, and focus on the environmental, economic and social concerns for the preservation of the environment and social well being.

SD considers the economy as a very important field of sustainability. Hence, SD is not against the lunar economy or the use of ISRU. This model invites the decision makers to consider not only the economy issues but also the environmental and social aspects to design a suitable model for long term use of ISRU by considering the Moon environment – geologically dead, airless, lifeless- and the rights of the future generations, as a subject of law recognized by Space Law and Environmental Law.

The proposal for SD of ISRU on the Moon identifies the necessary guidelines for the International Regime on the Moon.

1. INTRODUCTION

Specific policy and regulation for ISRU on the Moon shall consider space exploration targets. The limit of ISRU activities and its guidelines for the different scenarios could improve the efficiency in the use of space resources. Decision maker's shall consider a cost-effectiveness analysis, taking into account the environmental and health costs (astronauts and the Moon) of technological options.

The present document implies a basic knowledge of basic concepts to understand the legal approach to space exploration, for that reason the first part deals with the explanation of necessary concepts with regard to space exploration.

The second part is the analysis of SD and how can be applied this model to IRSU on the Moon.

The third part of this paper is the legal regime of ISRU and planetary protection.

The last part handles the conclusions and specific recommendations to implement SD for ISRU on the Moon.

1.1 In- Situ Resource Utilization ("ISRU")

This term has been defined as "living of the land" (ESA, 2001).

The National Aeronautics and Space Administration (NASA) through the Study on Capability Road Maps which was develop according with NASA's objectives, set that ISRU is "...harness and utilize space resources to create products and services which enable and significantly reduce the mass cost and risk of near term and long term exploration".

To explore the Solar System, any product from indigenous materials that significantly reduces mass, cost and risk should be considered, such as oxygen, hydrogen and water. The high upload mass requirements and today's launch capability means that ISRU is a prerequisite for missions beyond the Moon to produce indigenous propellants –methane, oxygen and carbon monoxide-.

1.1.1 Advantages of ISRU for space exploration.

- Allows sustainable human presence beyond Low Earth Orbit for long term missions.
- Reduce the cost of space missions.
- Reduce risk to face emergencies during the mission as a part of interrelationships among lunar base subsystems, such as transportation.
- Assist in further human exploration and create self-sustaining and adaptable colonies on the Moon and beyond, such as Mars.

1.1.2 Main areas of space exploration to apply ISRU

As we can see from the advantages described above, it is possible to identify two main areas, which would benefit from ISRU:

1. Life support- ISRU life support consumables directly needed are water, oxygen and nitrogen.
The crew aspects of exploration must be to a large extent and self-sufficient, and shall include the follow elements:
A) Life support consumables (oxygen, water, food) must be recycled.
B) Biohazards and chemical contamination must be controlled.
C) Life support consumables (oxygen, water, food) must be recycled.
D) Biohazards and chemical contamination must be controlled.

2. Propellant production. The preferred propellants are cryogenic oxygen and cryogenic methanes in the ratio (ESA, 2001). ISRU helps with the production of propellants and reactants for fuels cells. These are the basic elements needed to ensure the safe return to Earth with the provision of fuel for the crew vehicle to ensure the possibility of fast return to Earth when something goes wrong.

In particular, oxygen, which is considerably heavier than hydrogen, is costly to transport from Earth to the point of use in space. However, in the Moon oxygen is much more abundant than hydrogen in lunar rocks.

1.2 Moon principal characteristics.

Three principal characteristics of the Moon (Wikipedia, 2006):

- The Moon's crust is blanketed of dusty outer rock layer called regolight. The regoligh is the result of rocks shattered by billions of year impacts. The crust ranges from 60 km on the near side to 100 km on the far side. The regolight varies from 3 to 5 m in the maria to 10 to 20 m in the highlands.
- Moon has been geologically dead for around three billion years, and has no atmosphere shape its surface. Any changes to its features have been made by outside forces, mainly the impact of meteors (Tumilson, 2005).
- Clementine orbiter also indicate that there maybe long-frozen deposits of ice under the shadows of some polar craters. The presence of usable quantities of water on the Moon would be an important factor in rendering lunar habitation cost-effective, since transporting water (or hydrogen and oxygen) from Earth would be very expensive.

1.2.1 Natural resources on the Moon

- Oxygen. A current assumption is that oxygen would be the most valuable product (Burt, 1989). The Lunar regolight has been studied since the Apollo missions. Available information demonstrates that the process to produce oxygen on the Moon would need a specific technique because without a lunar atmosphere, oxygen has to be produced from oxygen-rich minerals. More than 20, mostly non-terrestrial, physico-chemical processes have been identified to produce oxygen from the solid lunar regolight, all requiring the build-up of an extensive chemical factory.

Demand for huge amounts of energy to be able of recover the oxygen from ilmenite has led NASA's dreamers to think about the option of a nuclear power project for the oxygen plant. However, it will be very difficult to justify building a large nuclear power plan on the Moon for the oxygen extraction (Herkenhoff, 1989).

- Hydrogen. Important element of water or reactants on the Sabatier process, if not indigenously available, inevitably has to be recycled and (re) supplied from Earth. If cryogenic hydrogen is carried, the extremely long mission duration imposes special constraints in order to minimize the hydrogen boil-off.
  Finding concentrations of water at the lunar poles or extracting the dispersed solar wind derived hydrogen in the lunar regolight would gently improve the economics of the transportation system.

1.3 Sustainable Development

Sustainable Development tries to improve human's productivity without damaging or undermining society or the environment. This development proposes a progressive socio-economic advance without growing beyond the ecological carrying capacity for natural resource regeneration and waste absorption.

Moreover, this model of development takes into account for any decision the possible consequences of the currently actions on future public and environmental health through previous interdisciplinary analysis of environmental, economic and social concerns for the preservation of the environment, social well-being and security of the entire world.

The follow model resumes SD on three dimensions and shows the continuous interaction among the different elements: environmental (conservations), economic (growth) and social (equity) dimensions (Flint, 2004).

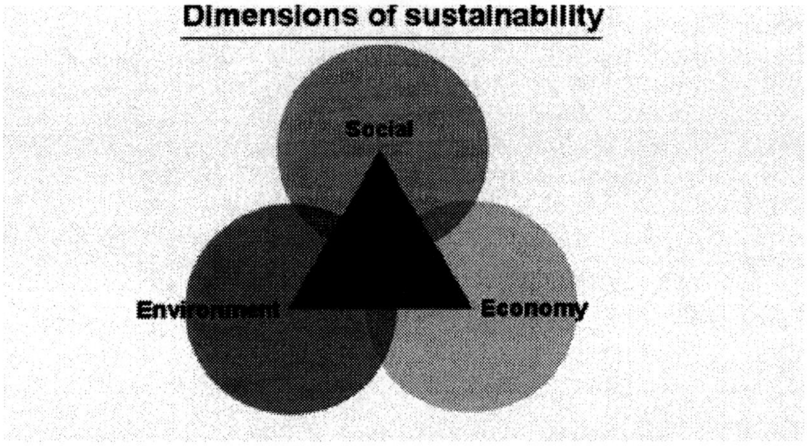

1.3.1 Sustainable development on the Moon

Economy. The analysis of cost-benefit considering environment and economic issues in the management of ISRU on the Moon shall include this information in the final decision:

- The study of the special environmental and developmental characteristics of the Moon, producing profiles and inventories of environmental resources.
- The development of techniques for determining and monitoring the carrying capacity of the Moon under different development assumption and resource constraints.
- The preparation of medium-and long-term plans for sustainable development. The integration of environmental consideration with economic and sector planning and policies.
- The adoption of Moon area management techniques, such as planning and environmental impact assessments, using Geographical Information Systems (GIS).
- The implementation of sustainable development plans.
- Bases on precautionary and anticipatory approaches, the design and implementation of rational response strategies to address the environmental, social and economic impacts of environmental change, and the preparation of appropriate contingency plans.

  Precautionary strategies are related with air pollution, water pollution, waste management and natural resource management.

Environment. The main concern in planetary protection policy is how to protect the extraterrestrial life against contamination and back-contamination. Otherwise, there were almost no interest in the preservation of the existing lifeless surfaces of extraterrestrial bodies as the Moon, although some planetary transformation plans were made public a long time ago (Almar, 2002).

Moon environment are practically unchanged since ages and damage caused by any human intervention would be irreversible, this is a problem for ISRU, but can be justify for survival reasons in a limited way to control the human disturbance activities and contamination.

From the scientific point of view, a limited, well-defined initiative has to be done to select scientific investigation areas and objects of highest priority on different celestial bodies.

The last, sentence is according with the suggestion of Tennen (2002), who provides two approaches on planetary protection policy:

1. The creation of the category of target bodies which are of interest for biological or chemical evolution, but which are considered to present only a remote chance that contamination could jeopardize future exploration.
2. The establishment of "special regions" where it is believed water may be present.

An option to incorporate planetary environment in space activities is through the Environmental Impact Assessment for Space Activities which could be included for the decision maker's. This is probably the best example of one approach that integrates economic, social and environmental considerations (Viikary, 2002).

Social. From this point the view the problem is the different levels of development among the countries on the use of outer space. However, the astronauts as envoys of humankind can be considered as subjects who represent equity benefits of space activities as a right of all humankind on the basis of common heritage.

2. LEGAL REGIME

ISRU on the Moon has two main international instruments to consider. First, the Treaty on Principles governing the Activities of States in the Exploration and Use of Outer Space, including the Moon and Other Celestial Bodies called the Outer Space Treaty (United nations, 1967). The second main international instrument is the Agreement governing the Activities of States on the Moon and Other Celestial Bodies, also known as the Moon Agreement (United Nations, 1979).

The Moon Agreement has not been ratified by any of the main spacefaring nations for that reason most of the countries consider is not effective under international law (Oosterlinck, 1996). The importance of this document is because it was the first legal attempt to deal with exploitation of natural resources on the Moon, which is directly related with ISRU.

For many years the Moon Agreement has been object of revision by the Legal subcommittee of the Commission of Peaceful Uses of Outer Space. Most of the space faring Nations argues a deficient language, vague concepts and anti-developmental approaches to space resources (Harris, 1996). Some countries talk about four instead of five Treaties of the United Nations for Outer Space.

However, some authors consider that the Moon Agreement is not needed for further development of lunar resources, because the Outer space Treaty provides the legal framework for the use of lunar resources (Schmitt, 1998).

I agree that the main principles to use space resources are provided by the Outer Space Treaty, hence the specific practice of ISRU has a recognized international framework. For that reason, although most of the countries have not ratified the Moon Agreement, it doesn't mean countries have not limits or any regulation to follow in the use of space resources.

2.1 Common Heritage of Mankind

The Moon Agreement dealt for the first time with the exploitation of natural resources. Article 11.1 refers to the Moon and its natural resources as "Common Heritage of Mankind" (Schmitt, 1998).

The concept of Common Heritage of Mankind as used in the Outer Space Treaty is considered as unique and its interpretation and independent of the concept defined by the wording in the Treaty of the High Seas as res communis (Oosterlinck, 1996). The Law of the Sea expands on the Common Heritage of Mankind doctrine and goes further to mandate an International Seabed Authority. Now the Law of the Sea may serve as a model for Space Law (Clayton, 1999).

Apart from this understanding, Oosterlinck believes that as far as the exploitation of mineral resources is concerned, the similarity is striking between space law and the law of the High Seas and Antarctica.

The interstellar space would be similar to the sea and the celestial bodies to res nullius (Oosterlinck, 1996).

The Moon Agreement incorporates the Common Heritage of Mankind principle, and for this reason the spacefaring nations are reluctant to ratify it because there are resources on the Moon that may have significant economic value sometime in the future and nations would eventually be pressured by their firms to withhold signing away valuable rights (Hertzfeld, 2005).

An extension of the benefits to all mankind principle is the Common Heritage of Mankind. The idea is that all nations should benefit from the knowledge and technology and profits generated by using resources in outer space. This provision is advocated by nations that do not currently have the ability to access these resources on their own, but with the idea of Mankind richer nations would share the benefits with all the other nations. This is a controversial point because commercial interests do not support this since it means the sharing of proprietary technology as well as reducing potential profits (Hertzfeld, 2005).

2.2 International Regime of outer space

Article 11.7 of the Moon Agreement states the international regime for the Moon. Concentrating on an international order in the freedom of the use of Outer Space for the benefit of all countries, States party to the Agreement shall assume to establish an international regime including the appropriate procedures to govern the exploitation of the natural resources of the Moon.

According to this article, the main purposes of the international regime to be established shall include:

- The orderly and safe development of the natural resources of the Moon
- The rational management of those resources
- The expansion of opportunities in the use of those resources
- An equitable sharing by all States party in the benefits derived from those resources

Considering these key issues, all activities with respect to the natural resources of the Moon shall be in accordance with the purposes adopted in the international regime.

Schmitt considers that the international regime would complicate private commercial efforts and give other countries political control over the permissibility, timing and management of all private commercial activities (Schmitt, 1998).

States, Mankind, Future Generations as Subjects of Space Law and the Future of Enterprises. Other legal topics related with ISRU that must be addressed concern the present increase of interest of private companies in space activities. One of the topics is the definition of subjects of Space Law.

Currently, States are responsible for their national space activities. According to Article VI of the Outer Space Treaty, States Party to the Treaty are internationally responsible for their national activities in outer space, including on the Moon and Mars. Such activities are historically carried on by governmental agencies or by non-governmental entities. At the beginning of the Space Era only States were interested in space projects, but now there are many space companies that are interested to invest and develop space projects.

Intergovernmental Organizations can also be subjects of Space Law but not private commercial companies, which have become the new players to support the commercialization of space activities in specific areas.

Article 4 of the Moon Agreement stated that the exploration of the Moon and other celestial bodies shall be considered as a province of all "Mankind", so we can consider Mankind as a subject of Space Law. The problem with the concept of Mankind as a subject of International Space Law is that Mankind does not have any authority to represent and defend its interests in Outer Space.

Moreover, this Article also refers to the future generations as new a subject of law, that are not well defined but the term is commonly used in the environmental law related with sustainable development issues. This article deals with issues that have to be considered to generalize the legal framework of space exploration and for ISRU. Such subjects as the sustainable exploitation of the Moon resources and other celestial bodies as Mars, mean the long term planning has to be sure that future generations will have the opportunity to use the resources from other celestial bodies for its development.

2.3 International Law and outer space

The extension of international law to outer space has been gradual and evolutionary, commencing with the study of questions relating to legal aspects, and then proceeding to the formulations of a legal nature.

Article III of the Outer Space Treaty specifies that the activities in the exploration and use of the Moon and other celestial bodies shall go on in accordance with international law, including the Charter of the United Nations. Moreover, Article II of the Moon Agreement indicates that all activities on the Moon shall be carried out in accordance with international law.

When no direct references exist in the UN Treaties it is possible to check International Law to find references applicable to the subject; for instance, the protection of the Common Heritage of Humankind: such a concept was not foreseen in the 1967, until it was included into the Moon Agreement in 1979. However, this concept was defined before in the UN agreement on the Law of the Seas in 1982, and signed by the US in 1995, under the rules of the treaty. These proceedings would also be applicable to space law (Harris, 1996).

2.4 Protection of Interplanetary Environment

Planetary environments change very little over time, and therefore any damage caused by human interaction would be irreversible. Almar classifies the activities on celestial bodies linking the consequences as follows:

• Research: In Situ Research produces some kind of pollution.

• Industrial activity: mining in particular, destroys smaller bodies. If mankind decides to mine the Moon or colonize Mars, the environmental impact will increase by at least an order of magnitude.
• Colonization and terraforming: the result is a large-scale transformation of the environment to accommodate human life.
• Free for all: whoever gets there first should have the right to do whatever they want with the materials they find (Almar, 1999).

At present, in accordance with the UN Treaties, the protection of the environment of the Moon and Mars and other celestial bodies is a duty of all the States involved in the space exploration activities.

Therefore, the next regulations shall be followed:
Article IX of the Outer Space Treaty declares that States shall conduct exploration of the Moon and the other celestial bodies in such a manner so as to avoid their harmful contamination and also adverse changes in the environment of the Earth, resulting from the introduction of extraterrestrial matter and when necessary, adopt appropriate measures for this purpose.

With this respect, the phrase "harmful contamination" is not clear and it can be open to interpretation and argument in the context of the Treaty, that it means harmful to humans rather than harmful to the environment. Some space activities will not immediately be harmful to humans, but it could prove extremely harmful to science.

Article IX of the Outer Space Treaty is well intentioned, but avoids the definitions of "harmful" (Williamson, 1997). The Outer Space Treaty provides insufficient protection for the space environment. in particular for the protection of the planetary bodies from the creation of further debris, which will undoubtedly accompany future development exploitation.

Article 7.1 of the Moon Agreement states that in the exploration and use of the Moon, States party shall take measures to prevent disruption of the existing environment, whether by introducing adverse changes in that environment, by its harmful contamination through the introduction of extraenvironmental matter or otherwise.

In Article 7.3 of the Moon Agreement, it is suggested that consideration be given to the designation of areas of special scientific interest, or international scientific preserves, which, it states, would require agreement in consultation with the competent bodies of the UN. This is not an end in itself because of the need for further consultation, but suitably extended to include other celestial bodies, would make a useful addition to Outer Space Treaty (Williamson, 1997).

Finally, regarding extraterrestrial exploration missions, the Committee of Space Research (COSPAR) has established Planetary Protection recommendations in order to protect the environment of celestial bodies from biological contamination by terrestrial microorganisms. According to these recommendations, projects involved in planetary exploration programs include in their development plans specifications for biological cleanliness.

COSPAR recommendations includes sterilization, biocleanings and planetary landers integration in sterile environment in order to ensure Mars environment protection (Debus et al, 1997).

3. CONCLUSIONS

Sustainable Development for ISRU on the Moon:

1. Policies, plans, and activities that improve equality of access and quality of life for all. This point is specially controversial because as we know space activities are carry out only for space fairing nations, not all the countries are participating as an actors in space activities so it is hard to imagine an scenario where all the countries has access to the ISRU as the SD states.
2. Recognizes the limits and boundaries beyond which the Moon environment behavior might change in unanticipated ways.
3. Challenges us to look to the future, and to fully asses and understand the implications of the decisions made today on the lives and livelihoods of future generations and the natural environment of the Moon.

Goals that lead to sustainability:

- Provide safe and equal access to Moon resources
- Measure and protect against environmental degradation on the Moon
- Reduce discharges of pollutants into surface and ground
- Prevent human health risk due to spread of waste diseases, water contamination and hostile e actions.
- Prevent physical modifications from land use / cover changes or disturbances with Moon surface that cause risks to humans, natural systems. The important point here is that it is not possible to refer on the Moon property rights to protect and justify the exploitation.
- Encourage a holistic approach to evaluating all Moon resources issues that is participatory, equitable and socioeconomically sensitive.
- Develop appropriate Moon resources policies; institutional arrangements and structures; financial systems; and legal and regulatory authorities to achieve integrated Moon Resources Management.

For a long term and in ideal scenario, Sustainable Development can be designed with more precision if the follow information would be collected:

A. Strategic → Possible decision: Intensive exploration for mineral resources→ Information required: current reserves of resources, rate of consumption (present and future), projected need of resources.
B. Tactical → Possible decision: develop exploration → Information required: Potential reserves, probable reserves and in-shelf deposits, economics of exploration.
C. Technical → Possible decision: detailed estimates of reserves → Information required: structural data, lithological data, geochemical data, geophysical data, borehole data.

Sustainable Development on the Moon proposal.
It is necessary to develop an international legal framework in order to establish rules for environmental protection of Planets, such as the Moon. The technical and specific rules

could be included on the base of ISO standards format but for space activities. Moreover, it is necessary to set the Authority in charge for monitoring and enforcement the rules for space activities according with planetary protection, and provide the legal options to appeal by the Countries.

ISRU is necessary for space exploration, but also is absolutely necessary have a clear rules for ISRU in order to prevent situations such as the environmental problems on the Earth and the Space Debris on outer space.

References

Almár, I. (2002) Protection of the Lifeless Environment In The Solar System. Proceeding of The Forty-Fifth Colloquium On The Law of Outer Space, International Institute of Space Law of the International Astronautical Federation, Houston, USA, pp. 438, 440.

Berger Brian, Griffin Takes NASA Back to the Future in Exploration, December 19, 2005, volume 16, ISSUE 50, p.10

Bull, W.R., and Spottiswood, DJ., "Expanding Our Horizons- Mining the Moon, " Thw mines Maganize, June 1982, pp 7-9

Burt, D.M., "Mining the Moon" American Scientist, V 77, Nov-Dec 1989, pp.574-579
Cockell S. Charles. (2005) Planetary Protection-A microbial ethics approach. Space Policy, Elsevier Ltd., 287-292, available online at www.sciencedirect.com, p. 290.

European Space Agency (2001) "Technologies for exploration. Aurora Programme Proposal: Annex: D". (SP-1254) November 2001, Netherlands

Fasán, E. Planetary Protection-Some Legal Questions. Proceeding of The Forty-Fifth Colloquium On The Law of Outer Space, International Institute of Space Law of the International Astronautical Federation, Houston, USA, p. 452.

Flint, Warren (2004) The Sustainable Development of Water Resources Update the Sustainable Development of Water Resources.

Harris, P. R. (1996). Living and Working in Space: Human Behavior, Culture and Organization. Second Edition,John Wiley & Sons.

Hertzfeld, H. R. & Von der Dunk, F. G. (2005). Issues in Space Law: Bringing Space Law into the Commercial World: Property Rights without Sovereignty. Chicago Journal of International Law, USA.

Oosterlinck, R. (1996). Tangible and Intangible Property in Outer Space. IISL Proceedings

Tennen, L.I. (2002) Evolution of the Planetary Protection Policy: Conflict of Science and Jurisprudence. Proceeding of The Forty-Fifth Colloquium On The Law of Outer Space, International Institute of Space Law of the International Astronautical Federation, Houston, USA, p. 472.

Tumlinson, Rick (2005) Return to the Moon. The Moon, Apogee Books, Canada.

United Nations (1967). Outer Space Treaty. Retrieved November 22, 2005 from http://www.oosa.unvienna.org/SpaceLaw/outerspt.html

United Nations (1979). Moon Agreement. Retrieved November 22, 2005 from http://www.oosa.unvienna.org/SpaceLaw/Moon.html

Viikari, L.E. (2002) Environmental Impact Assesment and Space Activities. Proceeding of The Forty-Fifth Colloquium On The Law of Outer Space, International Institute of Space Law of the International Astronautical Federation, Houston, USA, p. 479.

Williamson Mark. (2002) Protection of the Space Environment: The First Small Steps. Proceeding of The Forty-Fifth Colloquium On The Law of Outer Space, International Institute of Space Law of the International Astronautical Federation, Houston, USA, p. 459.

Wikipedia contributors, 'Moon', Wikipedia, The Free Encyclopedia, 9 March 2006, 17:25 UTC, <http://en.wikipedia.org/w/index.php?title=Moon&oldid=42993059> [accessed 9 March 2006]

IAC-06-E6.2.A.03

FLY ME TO THE MOON: LEGAL AND POLITICAL CONSIDERATIONS OF SPACE EXPLORATION INITIATIVES *

*Dr. Ulrike M. Bohlmann, European Space Agency, Paris, France***
*Dr. Larry F. Martinez, California State University, Long Beach, CA, USA****

Abstract

The recent announcements by the United States, the European Space Agency, the People's Republic of China and others of their respective space exploration programmes indicate a resurgent interest in large-scale space exploration on the part of a growing number of nations, organizations and commercial enterprises. The authors of this paper examine elements of the legal and political backgrounds of the announced exploration initiatives. After a short introduction, the authors sketch the current status of international law applicable to these initiatives, including issues of non-appropriation, planetary protection, the use of nuclear power sources, and international cooperation. This account of the status quo of international law is followed by an analysis of the political impulses driving space exploration initiatives. Based on these findings the authors develop prospects for the further development of international law.

I. Introduction

For the purposes of this paper, we define "space exploration initiatives" as high-risk, complex techno-scientific programmes undertaken by national and international entities to extend human infrastructure into the solar system and beyond. A wide range of other space-based activities are primarily earth-focused, including communication, navigation, environmental, or military reconnaissance missions, and are therefore not "explorations" outward from the more immediate earth-space environment. Space exploration is about leaving the earth.

** The views expressed are purely personal and do not necessarily reflect those of the European Space Agency or of any other entity with which the author may be affiliated.

*** The views expressed are purely personal and do not necessarily reflect those of the California State University or any other entity with which the author may be affiliated.

While the initial stages of such efforts are generally robotic information-gathering projects, the longer-term goals include transporting human beings to explore and exploit celestial bodies.[2]

Since the turn of the millennium, a significant mutation has altered the seemingly inexorable evolutionary trend toward a commercialized civilian international space sector.[3] While the commercial-civilian sector continues to diversify both in terms of space systems (navigation, Internet, reconnaissance), system operators (hybrid international consortia of commercial launch and network providers), and user communities (military, civilian and commercial, including tourism), they are not alone on the launch pad. Governments have rediscovered the solar system and are implementing massive strategies to move human infrastructure to the moon and Mars by the mid-21st Century.

For not only are the long-standing space powers (United States, European Space Agency), but also the governments of China, Japan, India, and others, implementing a growing number of space exploration initiatives. This paper asks 'why?' and examines the implications of this resurgence in governmental space exploration initiatives for the evolution and structure of the international space legal regime, which up to now has been adapting successfully to a diminishing role of governmental entities amid a plethora of hybrid commercial-civilian space systems.

The last time a human walked on the moon was in December 1972, since then, no space explorers have ventured more than 1000 km from the earth's surface. Money has also been locked into earth orbit, particularly in the International Space Station (ISS), "the world's largest public works project." In fact, one could argue that more money has been spent showing the exploration of outer space from 1972 to 2006, than was spent on actual space exploration probes, whether manned or robotic.[4] To successfully get human beings to Mars and back will cost trillions of dollars. Consequently, the resurgence of governmental space exploration initiatives represent not only a massive increase in space sector funding, but also a re-emergence of governments as major players in the commercial-civilian space sector.

Who are the major players going to be?

> <u>United States</u>: On January 14, 2004, three months following the first successful Chinese orbital mission, U.S. President George W. Bush announced a major U.S. space exploration initiative, which includes milestone dates for returning humans to the moon and eventual missions to Mars.[5] Calling for "human and robotic missions to the moon, Mars and beyond," the presidential announcement set in motion a presidential commission to outline the vision's goals and implementation, and a major space

---

2 See, Frank Morring, Jr., "Configuration Concepts: Early lunar habitat work focuses on dust, storage, and crew privacy," *Aviation Week and Space Technology*, July 24, 2006, pp. 56-8. For details of the different initiatives see Objectif Mars - La Conquête Spatiale depuis ses origins, *Air & Cosmos Hors-Série*, June 2006.

3 Although the governmental military space platforms constitute the largest near-earth space presence, they are major users of commercial space services.

4 According to conservative estimations, the six *Star Wars* movies *alone* have earned more than \$3.4 billion in worldwide revenues, http://www.supershadow.com/starwars/boxoffice.html, which is more than the most expensive space exploration project to date: the joint US-ESA Cassini-Huygens mission currently orbiting Saturn after landing the ESA Huygens probe on Titan in January 2005 will end up costing \$3.26 billion, http://saturn.jpl.nasa.gov/faq/mission.cfm.

5 The text can be found at: http://www.whitehouse.gov/space/renewed_spirit.html.

architecture study describing the plan's operational strategy.[6]

European Space Agency: The European Space Agency (ESA) in 2001 announced its Aurora Programme, designed "to create, and then implement, a European long-term plan for the robotic and human exploration of the solar system, with Mars, the Moon and the asteroids, [and] to search for life beyond the Earth."[7]

China: On October 15, 2003, China succeeded its first manned orbital mission[8] In February 2004, China announced its program to explore the moon and to land human beings there sometime after 2017, with *taikonauts* walking on Mars in the 2040-2060 timeframe.[9]

Japan: In 2005, the Japanese Aerospace Exploration Agency (JAXA) released its long-term vision plan, which articulated plans for manned spaceflight and lunar landings in the 2025 timeframe.[10] Japan reaffirmed its ambitions as major space exploring nation in November 2005 as its Hayabusa spacecraft made a soft landing on the asteroid Itokawa.[11]

India: The Indian Space Research Organization (ISRO) announced in 2004 its Chandrayaan I lunar reconnaissance and surface impacter mission, due to be launched in 2007-2008 timeframe.[12]

Other Space-faring Nations: Following time-tested footsteps of the space-faring pioneers, countries with significant ballistic missile capabilities find that they also can launch scientific satellites into earth orbit or beyond. Both Israel and Brazil have satellite and/or launcher capabilities.[13]

- The Politics of Space Law

There are several explanations for the rather sudden resurgence in governments' interest in mounting massive space exploration initiatives. Conventional political analysis would point to the traditional nation-state motives of military prowess and national prestige.[14] Both factors are certainly operating here, but are deficient in their explanatory power. While military motives were central to early space exploration programs using dual-use launching and orbital payload technologies, military space programs are now well established with their own R&D establishments and operating networks.[15] If a military lunar presence had been perceived as advantageous to the U.S. or Soviet military services, there would have been a much more assertive lunar program by either during the 1970s while both countries were pursuing moon programs.

The prestige factor appears to have more explanatory power. The ubiquitous World

6 See, *Report of the President's Commission on Implementation of United States Space Exploration Policy* (June 4, 2004), and, NASA's *Exploration Systems Architecture Study: Final Report*, November 2005.

7 ESA, http://www.esa.int/SPECIALS/Aurora/ESA9LZPV16D_0.html

8 From Wikipedia :http://en.wikipedia.org/wiki/Chinese_space_program

9 *Ibid.*

10 See, http://www.jaxa.jp/about/vision_missions/long_term/jaxa_vision_e.pdf

11 http://en.wikipedia.org/wiki/Hayabusa

12 See, http://en.wikipedia.org/wiki/Chandrayaan

13 See, http://www.globalsecurity.org/space/worldindex.html

14 See, Isabelle Sourbès-Verger, "L'espace dans le monde", in: Géoéconomie, no. 20, "Géoéconomie de l'espace", hiver 2002, pp. 49-63, for a typology of the space powers according to their traditional motives.

15 See, Roger Handberg, *Seeking New World Vistas: the Militarization of Space*, (Westport: Praeger Publishers, 2000).

Wide Web facilitates global distribution of space-based images that exert a tightening grip on humankind's increasingly planetary consciousness. Issues such as global warming[16] and possible collisions with comets or asteroids propel both public and private entities to feed the public's growing appetite for knowledge about the earth-space environment, creating also in the process a growing constituency for "outer" space exploration, generating thereby also the scientific, economic and political rewards for those who survive the unforgiving realities of passage into space and its exploration. Inevitably, such highly visible ventures must pass through rigorous legal environments as well. However, prestige advantages for space-faring states is increasingly diluted by the commercialization of space ventures; company logos on the sides of Russian boosters, wealthy tourists tumbling in the zero-G of the International Space Station, or Virgin Galactic selling tickets for spacerides.[17] Immediate political advantages for politicians stemming from space exploration projects spanning decades in planning and years in execution are also diffuse.

We argue that a third factor that combines political and legal motivations deserves analytic scrutiny. In short, space is too important to entrust its development and governance to the profit motives of the commercial space sector. But having gone past the point of no return on the commercialization road, there still exists one space sector where commercial entities fear to tread – high risk, complex techno-scientific development programs requiring decades to accomplish.

Both political and legal motivations are fuelling the reappearance of space exploration initiatives, often with inherently contradictory impulses. While they feed from intense scientific and technological collaborations among the world's research and development communities, space exploration initiatives also operate as factors of political, economic, and military competition[18] in the global arenas of international politics.[19] Thus two impulses shape the development and implementation of the "rules of the road" for space exploration: the largely consensual collaborations among scientists to share information in their common quest to explore new frontiers of knowledge, and the more competitive, largely political, impulses of the space-faring powers to leverage space exploration for an enhanced governmental presence on the high ground of space with concomitant global power and prestige advantages. Finally, our argument points to the key role played by international space law in codifying the commonality of interests between the open and consensual culture of the scientific community operating the space exploration initiatives, with the new-found consensus among space-faring powers that effective governance, i.e, that governmental interests are represented in the space legal regime requires their visible presence.

- The Law of Space Politics

Thus, the "legal reflex" of space-faring nations to reduce uncertainty of high-risk exploration endeavours through "rules of the road" conventions is constantly being tested by risk-accepting commercial and political entrepreneurs pursuing their "political (and economic) impulses" for space exploration. Distilled out of the anarchy of a globalizing and commercia-

[16] See, Al Gore, "An Inconvenient Truth," documentary film, 2006, http://en.wikipedia.org/wiki/An_inconvenient_truth.

[17] http://www.virgingalactic.com/en/news.asp

[18] See, Gabriele Garibaldi, "Guerra nello spazio. Full Spectrum Dominance vs. Shashoujian e i rischi della corsa all'armamento dello spazio tra Stati Uniti e Cina", Lulu, http://www.lulu.com/content/339923, 2006.

[19] See, Cornelia Riess, "International Cooperation Patterns and Trends of Future Space Regulations," in Benkö and Schrogl, *Essential Air and Space Law*, Utrecht: Eleven International Publishing, Inc., 2005, pp. 175-190.

lizing international system, international space law is becoming a "witches' brew" of customary and codified rules that can only partially reconcile the seemingly intractable tension between legal order and market power.[20]

This tension between the legal and political impulses shaping the international regime for outer space activities, in general, and space exploration initiatives, in particular, is evolving in response to three systemic changes:

> (1) Growing number and diversity of space-faring nations and entities;
>
> (2) ownership and regulatory liberalization of space high technology sectors; and,
>
> (3) increasing military utility of space assets.[21]

All three factors are accelerating the breadth and depth of space exploration initiatives into new and unexpected directions, with concomitant pressures to steer adaptations in the space legal regime to meet these new requirements.[22]

While outside the purview of this paper, one can nonetheless observe how the space exploration regime is evolving in a manner closely corresponding to other transnational commons regimes dominated by the scientific and/or technological imperatives, Antarctica being a very visible example.[23] The evolution of international law governing space exploration provides a scintillating example of the key role played by the scientific community where its ability to legitimize and implement the legal "rules of the road" actually performs an important political function.

The scientific community, which gives an important impulse for the development and operation of space exploration programmes, plays also a central role in developing the legal "rules of the road" for these exploration activities, and, consequently is steering the evolution of the entire space legal regime into a third phase of its evolution.[24]

This paper's examination of the resurgence of governments into space exploration initiatives and its effect on the evolving international space legal regime will proceed in three steps. Part Two of the paper outlines the legal *status quo*. Part Three explores the political impulse for space exploration and how it forces the legal regime to conform to new realities. Part Four synthesizes the two aspects and gives an outlook on the potential evolution of the international law for outer space.

---

20 See, "Report of the Project 2001 Working Group Report on Privatisation," *Project 2001 – Legal Framework for the Commercial Use of Outer Space*, University of Cologne, 2002, pp. 405-529.

21 Riess accurately points out that three trends are shaping future collaborations: (1) space globalization (2) the growing macro economic significance of space, and, (3) the military-security role played by the space sector. *Ibid*, pp. 177-8.

22 See, *Project 2001: Legal Framework for the Commercial Use of Outer Space*, University of Cologne, 2002.

23 See, Larry Martinez, "International Law and the Antarctic: Future for an International Commons Regime," in K. Tatsuzawa (ed.), *The Law of International Relations*, (Chuogakuin University Press, Japan, 1997), pp. 585-622.

24 See, Marietta Benkö and Kai-Uwe Schrogl in their introduction to Space Law: Current Problems and Perspectives for Future Regulations, Utrecht: Eleven International Publishing, Inc., 2005, who recall that after a first phase during the 1960s and 1970s which saw the elaboration of the fundamental international space law conventions, and a second phase with the adoption of special legal regimes in form of General Assembly resolutions, the development of space law has entered its third phase characterized by a growing diversification, which goes hand-in-hand with a new flexibility in law.

II. The legal *status quo*

In order to detect and evaluate systemic change, one must establish a starting point, or *status quo*. It is important to observe during this discussion the underlying tension between those early space-faring powers (i.e., the Soviet Union) recognizing only governmentally-sponsored and operated space systems, in contrast to the position of the United States in advocating a more porous international space regime that would also allow non-governmental space systems. The evolution of international space law over the past three decades has been, to a large degree, the gradual process of adaptation to the growing presence of non-governmental commercial entities operating in the space environment.[25] Consequently, the legal status quo can be divided into the first phase of space exploration law that emphasized legal principles and later legal agreements that addressed the specific concerns of the space scientific community with regard to the activities of non-governmental entities:

The starting point for depicting the legal status quo with regard to space exploration is Articles I, 2 and 3 of the 1967 Outer Space Treaty[26], which stipulates that

> *"Outer space, including the Moon and Other Celestial Bodies, shall be free for exploration and use by all States without discrimination of any kind, on a basis of equality and in accordance with international law, and there shall be free access to all areas of celestial bodies.*
>
> *There shall be freedom of scientific investigation in outer space, including the Moon and Other Celestial Bodies, and States shall facilitate and encourage international cooperation in such investigation."*

The fundamental freedom to explore outer space encounters numerous boundaries, which are not only those imposed by the classical international space law, but also increasingly those that at first glance cannot be counted among the traditional space law instruments.

The primary limit of the freedom to explore outer space is the ***principle of non-appropriation*** as enshrined in Article II of the Outer Space Treaty, which is the necessary corollary to the general freedom to use outer space, since the freedom to use outer space is only conceivable if territorial sovereignty is excluded. Any means of appropriation is prohibited by the Outer Space Treaty. The principle of non-appropriation confirms that all nations are vested with equal rights and enjoy an equal access to space resources, regardless of their current degree of technological development.[27]

Apart from legal prohibitions about assertions of national sovereignty or appropriations of the space "commons," international space law has increasingly focused on the scientific "rules of the road" governing how exploration may proceed. Foremost is the ***protection of the space environment***. In this context, regulations exist on quite different levels and with different degrees of intensity. The provisions contained in the classical *corpus iuris spatialis*, above all Articles IX and XI

---

25 See, Wayne White, "The Outer Space Treaty," *Space Exploration and Humanity: A Historical Encyclopedia*, unpublished monograph, January 23, 2006.

26 The Outer Space Treaty, 610 UNTS 205, was adopted by the UN General Assembly in its resolution 2222 (XXI). It was opened for signature on 27 January 1967 and entered into force on 10 October 1967. As of 1 January 2005, it received 99 ratifications and 27 signatures. Thus, it can be regarded as having universal legal value.

27 For a more detailed analysis of the principle of non-appropriation see, Ulrike M. Bohlmann, Legal Aspects of Space Exploration Initiatives, in: Benkö and Schrogl, *Essential Air and Space Law*, Utrecht: Eleven International Publishing, Inc., 2005, pp. 215-240, under 2.

of the Outer Space Treaty, remain ambiguous and leave any "appropriate measures" to be adopted by the States Parties to avoid the harmful contamination of celestial bodies and also adverse changes in the environment of the Earth at the sole discretion of the respective Party to the Treaty. The Moon Agreement[28], especially its Articles 7 and 4 elaborates a bit more on the principles regarding the protection of the extra-terrestrial environment by addressing the well-known issues of forward and backward contamination as well as the principle of intergenerational equity, and reflects thereby the fact that at the time it was written, in the late 1970s, environmental considerations had become a global concern. However, the language of the Moon Agreement remains as anodyne and unspecific as that of the Outer Space Treaty.

Based on the policy statement, that

> *"Although the existence of life elsewhere in the solar system may be unlikely, the conduct of scientific investigations of possible extra-terrestrial life forms, precursors, and remnants must not be jeopardized. In addition, the Earth must be protected from the potential hazard posed by extraterrestrial matter carried by a spacecraft returning from another planet."*

COSPAR (Committee on Space Research)[29] has elaborated a detailed Planetary Protection Policy[30]. In addition to providing specific guidelines, shortly summarised below, the policy recommends that COSPAR members provide information to COSPAR within a reasonable time not to exceed six months after launch about the procedures and computations used for planetary protection for each flight and again within one year after the end of a solar-system exploration mission about the areas of the target(s) which may have been subject to contamination. Five different categories for target body/mission type combinations and respective suggested ranges of requirements are established along the degrees of the interest they represent for the understanding of the process of chemical evolution or the origin of life. Implementation guidelines and category specifications for select solar system bodies, such as Mars or Europa, are spelt out in the appendix to the Policy. The COSPAR Planetary Protection Policy is a very consistent and highly developed system of recommendations by an independent and international body of scientists with a high reputation in the field. Although COSPAR is a non-government organisation lacking an institutionalised authority, it is nonetheless the continuous policy of many actors in the space field to comply with COSPAR's recommendations and even to mould their national planetary protection policies according to the COSPAR standards[31]. However, the price to pay for the specificity and wealth of

---

28 Agreement Governing the Activities of States on the Moon and Other Celestial Bodies, Opened for signature on 18 December 1979 and entered into force on 11 July 1984, 1364 UNTS 3. However, since the Moon Agreement, has received only twelve ratifications and four additional signatures, as of 1 January 2006, its force and value are rather limited; no customary value can be attributed to its regulations and it is only binding upon its States Parties.

29 COSPAR, the Committee on Space Research, was established in October 1958 by the International Council of Scientific Unions, ICSU, to continue the co-operative programmes of rocket and satellite research undertaken during the International Geophysical Year (1957 – 1958). Its objectives are to promote on an international level scientific research in space, with emphasis on the exchange of results, information and opinions, and to provide a forum, open to all scientists, for the discussion of problems that may affect scientific space research.

30 The text of this policy can be downloaded at: <http://www.cosparhq.org/scistr/PPPPolicy.htm>.

31 One of the most prominent examples is the NASA Planetary Protection Policy, see: <http://planetaryprotection.nasa.gov/pp/index.htm>.

detail of these guidelines is their lack of legal force; they constitute a mere moral kind of obligation.

The elements of general international environmental law, which need to be mentioned in this paper, are Principle 21 of the Stockholm Declaration[32], Principle 15 of the Rio Declaration[33] and the Convention on Biological Diversity[34].

According to Principle 21 of the Stockholm Declaration:

> *"States have, in accordance with the Charter of the United Nations and the principles of international law, [...] the responsibility to ensure that activities within their jurisdiction or control do not cause damage to the environment of other States or of areas beyond the limits of national jurisdiction."*

Thus, the environment of outer space as one of the areas beyond the limits of national jurisdiction is protected by this principle. The United Nations General Assembly Resolution 2996 (XXVII) 1972 asserts that Principle 21 [and 22] of the Stockholm Declaration 'lay down the basic rules governing the matter'.[35] Principle 2 of Rio Declaration and Article 3 of the Convention on Biological Diversity repeat the Principle, so that – although the Stockholm Declaration has no legally binding character – at least Principle 21 may be regarded as reflecting customary international law. Principle 15 of the Rio Declaration elaborates further on the so-called precautionary approach[36] but is significantly weakened by the reference to the respective States' capabilities. The essence of the precautionary approach as contained in Principle 15 of the Rio Declaration is best described by P. Birnie and A. Boyle[37]: in performing their obligations of environmental protection states cannot rely on scientific uncertainty to justify a lack of action when there is enough evidence to establish the possibility of a risk of serious harm, even if there is as yet no proof of harm.

Article 8 (h) of the Convention on Biological Diversity provides that

> *"Each Contracting Party shall, as far as possible and as appropriate prevent the introduction of, control or eradicate those alien species which threaten ecosystems, habitats or species".*

According to Article 4 of the Convention, its provisions apply, in relation to each Contracting Party, regardless of where the effects of activities occur, when carried out under the jurisdiction or control of a Contracting Party, within the area of its national jurisdiction or beyond the limits of national jurisdiction. Thus, it is also applicable to outer space activities carried on by Contracting Parties[38]. Accordingly, the issues of forward and backward

---

32 Declaration of the United Nations Conference on the Human Environment, adopted in Stockholm on 16 June 1972, 11 ILM 1416.

33 Declaration of the United Nations Conference on Environment and Development, adopted in Rio de Janeiro on 12 August 1992, 31 ILM 874.

34 31 ILM 818 (1992), opened to signature on 22 May 1992 and entered into force on 29 December 1993.

35 112 States voted in favour of this resolution, none opposed, the then Eastern Bloc States abstained on Res. 2996, but have supported subsequent treaties recognising the normative character of Principle 21.

36 The Principle reads: "In order to protect the environment, the precautionary approach shall be widely applied by States according to their capabilities. Where there are threats of serious or irreversible damage, lack of full scientific certainty shall not be used as a reason for postponing cost-effective measures to prevent environmental degradation."

37 International Law and the Environment, 2nd ed. Oxford 2002, pp. 120.

38 With the exception of the United States of America, all space-faring nations are Party to the Convention.

contamination are dealt with by the Convention; the potentially harmful introduction of species that are foreign to a given environment, be it terrestrial or extraterrestrial, is to be prevented, or at least controlled or eradicated. This obligation is, however, limited to "as far as possible and as appropriate".

For a number of technical reasons, nuclear power sources, ***NPS***, constitute the only viable option for power supply for most exploration missions, a fact that is already recognised in the preamble of the "Principles Relevant to the Use of Nuclear Power Sources in Outer Space"[39]. According to Principle 3, individuals, populations, and the biosphere are to be protected against radiological hazards and the contamination of outer space is to be avoided.[40] Principle 4 stipulates that a launching State has to ensure that a thorough and comprehensive safety assessment is conducted. The results of this assessment shall be made publicly available prior to each launch. Furthermore, the Principles contain provisions as to the notification in case of re-entry of satellites with nuclear power sources on board, Principle 5.[41] Principle 9 concretises Article VII of the Outer Space Treaty and the Liability Convention: it affirms that international liability fully applies to cases where a space object carries a nuclear power source.[42] The Principles Relevant to the Use of Nuclear Power Sources in Outer Space are currently under review.[43]

---

39 They were adopted unanimously by the UN General Assembly in its Resolution 47/68 of 14 December 1992 thereby obtaining universal acceptance, even though they do not create binding commitments under public international law. For a general overview of international law regarding nuclear energy, see: *M. Elbaradei, E. Nwogugu, J. Rames*: International law and nuclear energy: overview of the legal framework, available at: http://ecolu-info.unige.ch/colloques/Chernobyl/pages/Opelz.html, where the authors also sketch the picture of a mix of legally binding rules and agreements on the one hand and advisory standards and regulations on the other hand. The authors describe the evolution of non-binding standards to binding commitments.

40 Sections 2 and 3 of Principle 3 establish specific rules for the use of nuclear reactors on the one hand and radioisotope generators on the other hand. Principle 3 Section 2 thus allows - with some further restrictions as to the fuel to be used, the design, and the construction of the reactor - the operation of nuclear reactors on interplanetary missions, in sufficiently high orbits and in low-Earth orbits, if the reactor is stored in a sufficiently high orbit after the operational part of the mission. Principle 3 Section 3 allows the use of radioisotope generators – under certain technical and design conditions - for interplanetary missions and other missions leaving the gravity field of the Earth. They may also be used in Earth orbit if, after the conclusion of the operational part of their mission, they are stored in a high orbit. In any case, ultimate disposal is necessary.

41 These provisions complete the stipulations of the Convention on Early Notification of a Nuclear Accident, ENNA, which entered into force on 27 October 1986. Very detailed on the relationship between the NPS Principles and the Convention, see *M. Benkö*, Nuklearenergie im Weltraum, in: *K.-H. Böckstiegel* (ed.) Handbuch des Weltraumrechts, Köln, Berlin, Bonn, München 1991, pp. 457, 475. Other authors are of opinion that the NPS Principles are in conflict with the ENNA Convention, see *A. D. Terekhov*, The 1986 IAEA Conventions on Nuclear Accidents and the Considerations of the Use of Nuclear Power Sources in Outer Space in the Legal Subcommitteee of COPUOS, in: IISL, Proceedings of the 30th Colloquium on the Law of Outer Space, 10 - 17 Oct 1987, Brighton, United Kingdom, pp. 403; *G. M. Danilenko*, Outer Space and the Multilateral Treaty-Making Process, available at: http://www.Law.Berkeley.edu/journals/btlj/articles/vol4/Danilenko/HTML/text.html.

42 Concerning compensation, it provides that such compensation shall be determined in accordance with international law and the principles of justice and equity, in order to provide such reparation in respect of damages to restore the person, natural or juridical, State or international organization on whose behalf a claim is presented to the condition which would have existed if the damage had not occurred. Compensation includes reimbursement of the duly substantiated expenses for search, recovery and clean-up operations.

43 The Scientific and Technical Subcommittee of the UN COPUOS is working on the development of goals and recommendations for the safety of NPS applications in outer space.

Due to the huge ambitions connected with space exploration initiatives, ***international cooperation*** will be a key issue in their implementation. Article I, 1 of the Outer Space Treaty, declaring the exploration and use of outer space, as the 'province of all mankind' that shall be carried out for the benefit and in the interest of all countries has been condensed as inducing the change in the orientation of public international law from a law of mere co-existence to a law aiming at cooperation.[44] This formulation rightly highlights a notion of solidarity, which embraces: a prohibition of monopolisation of products resulting from space activities for national purposes; the striving for the establishment of equal possibilities to use outer space, and the postulate to implement space activities by means of cooperation wherever possible[45]. However, most authors in contemporary space law agree that this provision does not constitute the basis for specific claims regarding participation but is to be understood as a programmatic principle. To complete this cursory overview, we also need to mention the *Declaration on International Cooperation in the Exploration and Use of Outer Space for the Benefit and in the Interest of All States, taking into Particular Account the Needs of Developing Countries*[46], which underlines in its second operational paragraph the freedom of the States to cooperate and to determine all aspects of such cooperation as well as the requirement to organise cooperation in an equitable manner and emphasises in its third operational paragraph that international cooperation shall take place on a basis that is acceptable for all Parties concerned.

This cursory synopsis of the legal status quo with regard to public international law addressing space exploration initiatives[47] illustrates that existing rules and regulations reflect a compromise between opposite and conflicting positions. They attempt to strike a balance between the general freedom to explore and use outer space by the current space powers, and, the wish to guarantee those same freedoms to States not yet capable to exercise these legal freedoms, as well as to ensure the benefits of such activities to future generations.

As the space sector diversifies, so too does the legal regime designed to govern its access and use. The mélange of binding Treaties and Agreements with deliberately imprecise and vague language on the one hand and detailed and very specific non-binding standards and guidelines, creates important discretionary prerogatives to the policy- and lawmakers around the globe to respond to different political impulses driving space exploration initiatives or deriving from them. Most crucially, the shift in emphasis to science-based "rules of the road" indicates that states are unwilling to abandon regulation of outer space

---

44 *S. Hobe*, Die rechtlichen Rahmenbedingungen der wirtschaftlichen Nutzung des Weltraums, Berlin 1992, pp. 112.

45 It is interesting to note that here again, the Moon Agreement goes some steps further and shows a higher degree of concretisation, see the last but one sentence of its Article 6.2 *"States Parties shall have regard to the desirability of making a portion of such samples available to other interested States Parties and the international scientific community for scientific investigation."* Article 5 of the Moon Agreement aims at securing a flow of mutual information and suitable coordination of simultaneously planned activities.

46 Adopted by the UN General Assembly on 13 December 1996, UN Doc. A/RES/51/122, available at: http://www.oosa.unvienna.org/SpaceLaw/gares/index.html. See also on the foregoing developments: *S. Hobe,* Common Heritage of Mankind - an outdated Concept in International Space Law ?, in: IISL, Proceedings of the 41st Colloquium on the Law of Outer Space, 28 Sept. - 02 Oct 1998, Melbourne, Australia, pp. 271, 278.

47 A more comprehensive analysis can be found by Ulrike M. Bohlmann, Legal Aspects of Space Exploration Initiatives, in: Benkö and Schrogl, *Essential Air and Space Law*, Utrecht: Eleven International Publishing, Inc., 2005, pp. 215-240

completely to marketplace mechanisms. Stirring the pot as well, are growing numbers of statutes emanating from sub-national legislatures that address space activities[48].

It is precisely here, in this mélange, that the evolution of the international legal regime is taking place, largely in response to political impulses among space powers confronting an increasingly diverse, and most importantly, commercialized, space sector.

III. The Political Impulse

In Part I, we reviewed the factors that may explain the recent resurgence in governmental space exploration initiatives. In Part II, we examined the relevant aspects of space law governing space exploration initiatives, and how it has evolved to take into account the changed cast of actors and their activities in the space environment. In Part III, our attention turns to a more theoretical scrutiny of how the motives for space exploration have evolved and adapted to the increasing commercialization of the space environment.

To explain the resurgence of space exploration requires investigations into the motives and decision-making calculi of states.[49] These coalesce into three broad theoretical approaches for explaining and predicting state behavior and changes in the international system in general, and the formation and maintenance of legal regimes in particular.

Axiomatic to ***Realist theories*** of international politics is that States are motivated to undertake actions perceived as promoting their national interests of survival and power maximization.[50] The first era of space exploration corresponds closely to the realist view of superpower competition conducted as a "space race" using or adapting dual-use military launch vehicles and spacecraft. Just as Sputnik in 1957 invoked the credibility crisis for the U.S. strategic doctrine of massive retaliation, the Soviet Union's problems to develop a manned moon exploration capability with the United States also mirrored the country's military limitations in space-based technologies, manifesting itself in the 1980s with the single flight of the Soviet *Buran* re-usable space shuttle in 1988.[51]

The ***Liberalism theories*** of the international system pose positive-sum outcomes in contrast to the realists' zero-sum gamesmanship. By the late-1960s, communications satellites were creating massive new broadcast and telecommunications markets as globalizing business and entertainment sectors sought real-time connectivity between continents. Hybrid intergovernmental and commercial consortia such as INTELSAT, INMARSAT, EUTELSAT, ARABSAT, and even INTERSPUTNIK demonstrated the benefits of collaboration and the positive network effects of ubiquitous satellite connectivity on a worldwide basis. Just as the vast majority of communications satellites were owned and operated by governmental monopolists, space exploration, too, was almost

48 For example, Virgin Galactic has formed a consortium with the U.S. state of New Mexico, while the California legislature in 2003 passed the "Space Enterprise Development Act (Assembly Bill 1532) which tasked the California Spaceport Authority to facilitate commercial, scientific and technology development in California, See, http://www.californiaspaceauthority.org/html/spaceport-authority.html#topofpageanchor.

49 Increasingly, the motives and actions of intergovernmental organizations must be taken into account as well. See, Paul Diehl (ed.), *Politics of International Organizations:Patterns and Insights* , (Chicago: Dorsey Press, 1989).

50 See, John Mearsheimer, *The Tragedy of Great Power Politics*, (New York: W.W. Norton & Company, 2001).

51 http://en.wikipedia.org/wiki/Shuttle_Buran (August 14, 2006).

exclusively a governmental activity, albeit with growing international collaborations, as seen for example in the establishment of the European Space Agency in 1975, and multi-national experiments developed for the Galileo and Cassini-Huygens spacecraft to Jupiter and Saturn, respectively.

With the advent of the globalizing information age in the late 1980s, a third group of international relations theories focused on how the international system is a "construct" of political, economic and military "discourse" between states. The ***Constructivist theories*** explain the international system's structure and functioning as a manifestation of states' perceptions of the opportunities and challenges inherent in the system's anarchic nature.[52] The growing diversification of formerly governmental space activities to include intergovernmental, governmental-military, governmental-civilian, and commercial sponsoring entities, coincided also with the emergence of a commercialized information economy and society, where decentralized Internet network architectures are replacing centrally-controlled governmental network monopolists. In space, just as in cyberspace, traditional governmental monopolistic roles are being supplanted by deployments of commercial space technologies, including space tourism to the International Space Station (ISS), and in cyberspace with emergence of the "blogosphere" as a user-controlled news networks.

As part of the World Wide Web, commercializing space activities have become an almost transparent discourse between spacecraft (including astronauts) and Internet-connected viewers, in much the same way exploration of the earth's systems - environmental, political, economic, military, and most importantly, cultural - are also evolving to direct discourse between users on the global information grid, with diminishing roles for governments and media organizations. Just as Russian launchers carry commercial logos into earth orbit, space exploration provides immense publicity and prestige benefits to those entities creating worldwide space experiences for millions of Internet users. As a result, images of space-related explorations have gained vast worldwide audiences with near-real time imaging of bouncing Mars rovers or crashing comet probes flashing simultaneously on millions of computer screens. Monitoring of the earth from space or from earth to space is now possible in ways that underline the challenge these activities pose to traditional tenets of international legal supervision, required under the Outer Space Treaty.

The table below summarizes the three theoretical approaches with their primary focus for space exploration:

Theoretical Approach	National Interest Paradigm	Space Exploration	Actor
Realism	Zero-Sum; Relative Advantage	Military Competition	Governments
Liberalism	Positive-Sum; Absolute Advantage	International Cooperation	Multilateral Governmental Organizations
Constructivism	Self-Defined	Prestige/Profit	Commercial-Governmental Partnerships

The international law of space exploration is the result of states pursuing ***national interests***[53] in the anarchic international system. Analyzing these interests provides

[52] See, Alexander Wendt, "Anarchy is what states make of it: the social construction of power politics" in *International Organization*, vol. 46, no. 2, 1992.

[53] Indeed, the very concept of national interest requires careful redefinition, according to Professor Joseph Nye of Harvard University: "Can one define interests conventionally in the information age? The "national interest" is a slippery concept, used to describe as well as prescribe foreign policy. Hence the considerable debate about it. Some scholars have even regretted the waning of the very idea of a "national" interest today", see: Joseph Nye, "Redefining the National Interest," *Foreign Affairs*, July-August 1999, pp. 22-35.

important clues about the structure and function of international law. The aggregation of these interests with respect to actions of states in the exploration of space constitutes the "political impulse." To paraphrase Professor Joseph Nye of Harvard University, who points out, that in the post-Cold War era, these interests can be categorized into three groupings according to the respective threat they correspond to:

> A-List Threats: These threaten the survival of States.
>
> B-List Threats: Conflicts that may negatively affect the national interests of States, but do not threaten their survival.
>
> C-List Threats: Issues that indirectly affect a State's security, but do not directly threaten a state's national interests.

Space has migrated from its original A-List priority to a C-List interest, largely due to the growing commercialization and diversification of space exploration initiatives away from their original military dual-use applications. Or to put it even more bluntly, states increasingly find themselves *nolens volens* in a C-List, constructivist international system, where - to a certain extent - they abandon control in a globalizing and commercializing marketplace of technologies and actors. Although ranked lower in terms of the threat posed to national survival or long term national interests, C-List issues are, in many respects, more visible as they represent important cultural and prestige elements that play a leading role in post-modern international politics.[54]

Divorced from its previous dependency on military motives, States in the 21st Century undertake space exploration initiatives increasingly for the intrinsic boost to their scientific and technological sectors[55], and, predominately for the prestige and visibility such ventures provide to their sponsors. Beagle II was slated to unwrap itself on the surface of Mars on Christmas Day, just as Pathfinder bounced to fame on July 4th, or NEAR rendezvoused with *Eros* on Valentine's Day. Within the constructivist analytical framework, such actions by States create their own political reality, closely corresponding to the parameters of "soft power" argued by Joseph Nye to be the currency of the global agora.

---

54 For example, the United States is arguing for continuing the classification of Pluto as a planet at the 2006 International Astronomical Union meeting in Prague, ostensibly because it is the only "planet" discovered by an American, See, Matt Stearns, "Pluto's Predicament: Solar System's ninth planet faces demotion at astronomical conference in Prague," McClatchy News Service, published in Santa Barbara *News-Press*, August 12, 2006, B-5. NASA said Pluto's downgrade would not affect its $700 million *New Horizons* spacecraft mission, which this year began its 9-1/2 year journey to the oddball object to unearth (*sic*) more of its secrets. ... But mission head Alan Stern said he was "embarrassed" by Pluto's undoing and predicted that the vote would not end the debate. William J. Kole, "International Astronomical Union reclassifies Pluto as dwarf-planet," Santa Barbara *News-Press*, August 25, 2006, A-1.

55 President Bush announced his vision for space exploration as intending to rally the US behind an ambitious technological challenge, and in the process strengthen the US economy and national security. While the vision "to explore space and extend human presence across the solar system" declares discovery to be the goal of the space exploration program, there are also some benefits sought on Earth. The advancement of US scientific, security, and economic interests through a robust space exploration programme are explicitly mentioned. The text can be found at: http://www.whitehouse.gov/space/renewed_spirit.html. Europe's strategy for space, which was endorsed by the European Union Council of Research and the ESA Council in 2001 calls for Europe to explore the solar system and the Universe, stimulate new technology, and inspire the young people of Europe to take a greater interest in science and technology. The text is available at: http://europa.eu.int/eur-lex/pri/en/oj/dat/2000/c_371/c_37120001223en 00020003.pdf.

Being 'high-risk, complex techno-scientific programmes undertaken by national and international entities to extend human infrastructure into the solar system and beyond,' space exploration initiatives are exclusively the bailiwick of the state, which alone among the other space sector actors, has the capacity to conduct such activities.

IV. Synthesis and Outlook

Why the sudden surge in space exploration initiatives? Our proto-theory would posit that space powers gradually abandoning their quasi-hegemonic control over other space sectors may perceive highly visible and prestigious space exploration initiatives as a means for re-asserting their national interest prerogatives.[56] Their hegemonic role in the space exploration sector also acts to legitimize their rule-making on an almost exclusive basis, emphasizing the role of science as the primary motive. By way of illustration, Europe and the United States can look back on a long history of cooperative governmental space ventures that have benefited both, directly as prescribed by the outer space treaties, and exemplified by the successful joint Cassini-Huygens mission to explore the Saturnian system. Closer to Earth, Europe and the United States have, however, experienced some complications to deploy and operate satellite navigation systems, where commercial entities and multiple user communities project their interests into an intergovernmental dialogue about a space technology with far-reaching military, economic and political effects. In other words, governments have been abandoning parts of their ability to shape the discourse over some space activities for the sake of an increasingly diversified and commercialized space sector. Such a development has not occurred in the context of space exploration.

Where does this perception lead us with regard to the future development of the law applicable to space exploration initiatives? *The resurgence of the space-faring powers into the space exploration sector will have the effect of demarcating the space exploration regime as an increasingly distinct legal-political arena.* This allows the space-faring powers to regain their decision-making roles partly abandoned as growing numbers of other nations follow their own political impulses into the near earth-space environment with concomitant demands for expansion of decision-making mechanisms and fora. Curiously, the shift of the political impulse from hard to soft power also creates an opportunity for the development of a scientifically-based legal regime, as opposed to the earlier military-political-economic treaties. What we witness today is the tendency of States to voluntarily accept non-binding international standards and guidelines as a basis for their own national policy and legislation. The NASA Planetary Protection Policy based on the COSPAR model may be cited as a prominent example.

In sum, the evolution of space exploration law towards a scientific focus reflects the shift of space-faring powers back into space exploration. This shift is motivated by numerous factors, among which the more obvious ones are the quest for scientific knowledge, the advancement of technology, the stimulation of the economy and, not to be neglected: the prestige factor. In the process, governments may also re-assert their role as the major actors in the space arena.

---

56 As an example, one may look at the resistance posed by NASA to the use of the International Space Station by its Russian partners as a visiting hotel by fee-paying space tourists ferried up by Russian spacecraft, each paying \$20 million for the privilege. Some of the arguments pointed out that hosting *pauschal* tourists on a taxpayer-funded public works project muddies the discourse when seeking budget authority in front of the U.S. Congress. See, CNN LIVE TODAY: U.S. and Russian Officials Feuding Over Space Tourist, Aired April 27, 2001 - 13:21 ET, http://transcripts.cnn.com/TRANSCRIPTS/0104/27/lt.03.html .

IAC-O6-E6.2.A.04

2006 STATUS REPORT ON THE UNIDROIT SPACE PROTOCOL

By Paul B. Larsen©

I. Introduction

In the immediate post-Sputnik I (1957) era, space commerce was conducted by and regulated by governments. Private activities in outer space did not exist, except in science fiction. In the 1980s the nature of the space industry began to change rapidly due to developments in the regulatory environment, technologies, commercial strategies, and consumer demands. Private space commerce developed significantly. Government deregulation and enactment of the WTO Agreement on Basic Telecommunications[1] boosted private enterprise in space commerce. The increase in launch capacity, the number of transponders per satellite, the size and volume of satellites, and the decreasing costs for manufacturing, launching and operating satellites stimulated the entire space industry. The demands for space services keep growing as the services become stronger and more reliable. Consumers indicate increasing requirements for international telephony, broadcast, and mobile satellite services. Consequently, there is an increasing demand for private and public satellite infrastructure and satellite service companies. Privately operated satellite networks utilize existing contractual laws but may require new private international laws specially designed for private contracts on space assets [2]

II. Private Commercial Space Transactions

A. Private Contracts Subject to National Law of Contracts

In the absence of international laws, international trade of space assets is subject to domestic laws.[3] Many of the contracts for construction of satellites, launches and for satellite services take place in the United States or in European countries. They are subject to U.S. laws or European laws, either because an effective 'choice of law' clause is entered into the contract, or application of U.S or European laws are required by the state laws governing conflict of laws

The relevant U.S. national law on contracts is the U.S. Uniform

*)The author teaches space law at Georgetown University Law Center. Copyright retained.

[1] Agreement on Basic Telecommunications, Feb. 5 1998, See discussion in Larsen, Future Protocol on Security Interests in Space Assets, 67 J. Air. L .& Com. 1097 – 1100.

[2] Larsen and Heilbock, UNIDROIT Project on Security Interests: How the Project affects Space Objects, 64 J. Air L. & Com. 3-5.

[3] Examples of choice of law treaties are the Convention on the International Recognition of Rights in Aircraft, 310 UNTS 152, and the UNIDROIT Convention on International Financial Leasing, Unidroit@Unidroit.org

Commercial Code (UCC).[4] The UCC is not U.S. federal law. It is state law, establishing virtual uniformity of law in all the States of the United States. Space equipment sold in the United States is subject to the UCC. It is only natural that the manufacturers, financiers, and borrowers, located in the United States, where the property (the res) is also located, will feel most comfortable being subject to U.S. law with which they are familiar. Even when non-U.S. parties are involved they may feel most secure choosing U.S. laws in their contracts. Thus the UCC governs many international contracts for sale of space equipment.

U.S laws may govern not only the contract to purchase space assets but also the financing of that contract, because space assets may be purchased subject to secured interests in the assets. [5] The UCC governs agreements on security interests in space assets. The UCC section 9-103(3) provides that:

> The law (including the conflict of laws rules) of the jurisdiction in which the debtor is located governs the perfection and the effect of perfection or non-perfection of the security interest. If, however, the debtor is located in a jurisdiction which is not a part of the United States, and which does not provide for perfection of the security interest by filing or recording in that jurisdiction, the law of the jurisdiction in the United States in which the debtor has its major executive office in the United States governs the perfection and the effect of perfection or no-perfection of the security interests through filing.

The UCC, Section 9-203, states three situations in which a security interest attaches to space equipment: (1) when the debtor enters into a security agreement with the creditor and their agreement describes the collateral; (2) when the loan has been issued for value; and (3) when the debtor has rights in the collateral. The holder of the security interest may then file the security interest in a state registry in order to obtain the protection added by the filing. The major idea of the registry is "that a good faith effort at filing would be successful and that a good faith search would reveal the presence of the secured creditor's claim."[6] Under UCC Section 9-312(5) secured creditors' claims to priority in collateral are based on the time of filing. First priority is given to the person who files first.

The laws of the European Continental countries on security interests originate in Roman law. The creditor retains title to the chattel until the debt is paid in full. Thus the debtor cannot transfer ownership to third parties until the debt is paid. Continental European laws tend to respect legal rights derived from the law of the original situs of mobile property if those legal rights can be

[4] See UCC text, The Portable UCC, American Bar Association (ABA). All subsequent UCC references are to this text.

[5] This issue is relevant to later discussion of a possible space protocol to the Cape Town Convention on International Interests in Mobile Equipment, Unidroit@unidroit.org, see Draft Uniform Space Protocol, Section III, below. Note that space equipment is classified as "mobile equipment" under the UCC

[6] White and Summers, Uniform Commercial Code, at 797 (1972).

accommodated within the municipal law of the new situs. Thus, if legal rights cannot be accommodated under the municipal law of the new situs, the Continental approach may result in failure to recognize legal rights in space equipment, causing financial losses for the financiers. Uncertainty as to the legal rights of the financier of the secured interest causes uncertainty and impedes trade in space assets [7] In order to create certainty, the parties to a contract may include a choice of law clause in their contracts. That choice may be U.S. national law if that results in greater certainty. Contracts law governing private contracts on space assets include contracts on financing of those assets. Financing contracts have become an area of possible new uniform international law designed specially for financing of space assets.

III The 2001 Cape Town Convention and Its Draft Space Protocol: [8]

A. The Space Industry Working Group and UNIDROIT

A space industry working group established under the aegis of the International Institute for the Unification of Private Law (UNIDROIT) undertook the preparatory work on a treaty instrument on space asset financing, This working group has met regularly since 1997. Represented on the working group are manufacturers, financiers, insurers, and satellite operators, as well as space lawyers from representative countries. The purpose is to involve experts with practical experience in financing space assets. The space industry working group is chaired by a U.S. space finance expert. This working group drafted a space protocol which initially was transmitted to UNIDROIT in 2002. UNIDROIT then convened a committee of experts representing governments because only government representatives can finally negotiate treaties; however, the government representatives work closely with the space industry working group. The objective is to create a special space asset protocol to the 2001 Convention on International Interests in Mobile Equipment (known as the Cape Town Convention). The Convention itself came into force on April 1, 2004.[9] This Convention is designed to have three separate protocols, one for aviation, [10] which is in force and became operational on March 1, 2006. Other protocols for rail and space assets are planned.[11]

The Cape Town Convention's purpose is to secure financing of high value equipment such as aircraft, railroad and space assets that move easily and frequently from one national territory to another or move into non-sovereign territory (outer space, in the case of space assets). Convenient financing requires ability of financiers to quickly seize security assets.. The Convention helps to remove creditors' feeling of

[7] Larsen & Heilbock, supra n. 2, at 10-20.

[8] International Institute for the Unification of Private Law (UNIDROIT), International Interests in Mobile Equipment – Study LXXII, http://www.unidroit.org/english/workprogramme/study072/main.htm

[9] Id. Convention on International Interests in Mobile Equipment (Cape Town Convention), ___UNTS____, 118 Stat. 1095 (2004))

[10] Id,

[11] Id, A final diplomatic conference on the rail protocol is scheduled to be held in Luxemburg, 12 – 23 February, 2007; afterwards only the space protocol remains to be finalized..

uncertainty about the legal status of their secured interests when the secured assets are moved into foreign territory. Recovery of satellites in outer space is particularly intriguing. Lessors have similar difficulties recovering leased objects. The assets are outside the state and enforcement becomes complicated. The national laws on secured interests vary. Financiers and satellite operators may face the uncertainty of law of foreign countries that cannot be identified beforehand. Some state laws do not favor non-possessory security arrangements,[12] An international uniform regime would establish certainty and predictability which encourages international financing. The Cape Town Convention creates an international uniform regime linked to an international registry of filed assets.

In brief, under the Cape Town Convention, secured interest in mobile equipment, known as 'international interests' are registered in an international registry which supercedes national registries, such as the U.S. Uniform Commercial Code (UCC) state registries. The international registry becomes *the* authoritative, comprehensive registry. [13]

Aviation, rail, and space assets each have separate international registries. Certain formal familiar conditions are mandatory (registrations must be in writing, the asset must be possessed by the obligor, it must be identified and secured), in order. to qualify as an international interest. To come within the scope of the Convention, debtors must be located in a contracting state at the time of contracting. In case of default the creditor may take possession, or sell the assets, or grant a lease, or collect income from the assets. The international interests are filed electronically in the international registry. Parties may register secured interests as well as assignments of interests, subordination of interests, extensions and discharges. A Supervisory Authority is designated to supervise the Registrar, prepare regulations for operation of the registry, receive complaints, audit the registry and make regular reports. The Supervisory Authority may be an international organization. For example, ICAO is the Supervisory Authority for the Aviation Protocol. The Registrar may be a contractor specially created to operate the registry. Both the Supervisory Authority and the Registrar enjoy immunity, but the Registrar may be liable for negligent acts and may therefore acquire insurance for its protection. Access to the electronic registry is open to the public. Any party to a financing agreement may register a financial interest. The filing of a financial interest establishes priority over later filings and over unfiled interests. International interests may be assigned. Parties may select a forum to have exclusive jurisdiction over disputes arising under the Convention.[14]

Each Protocol to the Cape Town Convention may modify the basic framework of the Convention to suit its own special financing needs, whether it is an aviation, rail or space asset. Financing of the three kinds of assets have developed differently and thus it

[12] Roberts, Carruth, Stuber, and Sundahl, International Secured Transactions and Insolvency, 40 International Lawyer, at 389.

[13] http://www.unidroit.ort/english/implementat/i-2001-convention.pdf

[14] Id.

became necessary to structure separate legal regimes. The success of this structural separation is evidenced in the practical experience with the Aviation Protocol. The aviation registry began to operate on March 1, 2006. Parties to aviation equipment transactions experienced initial problems, but they have now adjusted to the new registration system. At the time of writing (2006) only a few aviation states have ratified the Aviation Protocol, but the United States, a major aircraft manufacturing state, is a party. Therefore approximately 90% of the existing filings have originated in the United States. Other aviation states, the European Union states, Russia, China, India and others are reportedly preparing to ratify. It is significant that several states with developing economies have joined. They are particularly reliant on asset-based financing because they do not have other assets to use as security. The U.S. Export-Import Bank has reduced transactional fees on its loans for aircraft equipment which benefits developing economies. It is reported that in the first three months "[T]he registry recorded 2,500 registration sessions in which 8,200 financial interests in individual aircraft and engines were chronicled. Some 11,000 searches of the registry were conducted," New filings in the registry are reported to have been completed within two days. [15]

The experience of the first three months of operation under the Aviation Protocol shows that the Cape Town treaty systems work as intended. However, practical experience shows that the regime is not perfect. For example, parties discovered that they could not file fractional aircraft ownerships. It is now too late to change the Aviation Protocol which is a treaty instrument. Such shortcomings must now be remedied by private contracts. The financiers, manufacturers, and lawyers involved in financing aviation equipment transactions are now familiar with the Aviation Protocol and recommend it to their customers. Furthermore, the U.S. Federal Aviation Administration has identified all aircraft and helicopter equipment in the U.S. national registry that is eligible for filing under the Aviation Protocol regime in order to facilitate filings with the new registry. [16]

The success of the Aviation Protocol shows international acceptance of the basic concept of the Cape Town Convention. That reflects favorably on using this proven legal system for international financing of other subjects such as financing of space assets. Another positive factor is at work regarding space asset financing. There is considerable overlap of parties involved in aviation and space equipment financing. Among these parties there existed a feeling that the Aviation Protocol would succeed best on its own merits without being weighed down by association with a space protocol. However, there is no longer a feeling that the space protocol should be delayed just to further the Aviation Protocol, because the Aviation Protocol regime is now effectively launched. Finally, there has been some concern that the users would object to paying the registration fee. However, experience with the Aviation Protocol now shows that parties to a financing agreement find the benefits of the registry outweigh the expense of using it.

[15] OTT, Protecting Assets, Aviation Week & Space Technology, July 17, 2006, at 170.

[16] Id.

B. Critical Issues in the Space Protocol

The draft space protocol is in a fluid state in which the stakeholders can adjust the treaty legal regime to suit their needs. This adjustment process takes place in the space industry working group and is subject to negotiations in the UNIDROIT government committee. Because the protocol will have to be adopted as a treaty by the states, states can still shape it for maximum compatibility with their national financing laws. For example, the U.S. seeks to shape the space protocol to be as much like its Uniform Commercial Code as possible. Continental users prefer the regime to be as much as possible like the European laws on security interests. The space industry working group has yet to determine a number of critical issues. Also, the protocol must be compatible with existing international laws, in particular the existing space law treaties. [17]

1. Two Registries: The Registration Convention's Registry and the Space Protocol's Registry

The Convention on Registration of Objects Launched into Outer Space (Registration Convention) is a public law treaty. Its purpose is to avoid collisions among satellites in outer space, retrieve space objects, identify space objects, establish jurisdiction over space objects, and promote safety. The launching state must register space objects in its national registry and in the international registry maintained by the U.N. Office of Outer Space Affairs (OOSA).[18] States mainly ratify the Registration Convention because they have satellites. States which do not have satellites have no significant reason to ratify. Thus, many states would not become parties to the Registration Convention

Registry of security interests under the space protocol will be organized to serve different purposes than registration under the Registration Convention. First, individual companies rather than states would register their financial interests in space assets. Secondly, the space protocol would regulate relationships between creditors and debtors rather than relationships between states. Third, the scope of the Space Protocol would be broader than the scope of the Registration Convention because the definition of space *assets* is broader than the definition of space *objects*. There are no clauses in either of the two treaties requiring membership in the other treaty. There is no linkage between the two treaties. On the other hand there is no legal obstacle for contracting parties to agree to register under the Registration Convention at the same time or prior to registration of financial interests in assets under the space protocol. Coexistence and independent

[17] Treaty on Principles Governing the Activities of States in the Exploration and Use of Outer Space, Including the Moon and Other Celestial Bodies, 610 U.N.T.S. 205 (Outer Space Treaty).
Agreement on Rescue of Astronauts, the Return of Astronauts and the Return of Objects Launched into Outer Space, 672 U.N.T.S. 1119 (Rescue Convention).
Convention on International Liability for Damage Caused by Space Objects, 961 U.N.T.S. 18 (Liability Convention).
Convention on Registration of Objects Launched Into Outer Space, 1023 U.N.T.S. 15 (Registration Convention).
Agreement Governing Activities of States on the Moon and Other Celestial Bodies, 1363 U.N.T.S. 21 (1979 Moon Agreement).

[18] http://www.unoosa.org

functioning of the two registries is not a cause of concern. The Space Protocol respects the primacy of the Registration Convention whenever it applies.[19]

2. Space Protocol's Definition of Space Asset

The reason for the draft space Protocol's broad definition of space asset is that the private parties to a commercial space transaction prefer that the entire financing transaction, from the very beginning of the manufacturing process to deployment in outer space should become subject to one comprehensive financing agreement in order to avoid conflicts between financiers of separate financing agreements. The result will be easier, more comprehensive and simpler financing of entire outer space projects. However, space assets are so broadly defined that its exact boundaries may be difficult to ascertain. The space industry working continues to work on realistic criteria for identification of space assets and in order to simplify the definition. and thus make registry of space assets more manageable

3. Protocol's Definitions of Debtors ' Rights and Related Rights

The space industry working group is still working on the definition of transfer from debtors to creditors of so-called 'related rights.' These are the valuable permits, licenses, authorizations, concessions issued by government authorities to the debtor to manufacture, launch, and operate the space asset including rights to use radio frequencies and orbital slots. The draft space protocol would include within its scope security interests in related rights along with security interests in rights defined as space assets. Permitting separate registrations of security interests in debtors rights and related rights would complicate the registry established by the space protocol.. The space industry working group is considering further simplification of the process of registry of debtors' rights and related rights..

4. Liability of States Parties to the Liability Convention for Launching Space Objects after Title to the Space Object Has Been Defaulted to a Financier in a Non-launching State..

The Convention on International Liability for Damage Caused by Space Objects[20] is an agreement among states: Only states have rights under the Liability Convention. Individual companies and individuals that have been damaged can only present claims through the contracting states on a government-to-government basis. For example, the Canadian government presented claim for damages to the then-USSR for damages caused by the disintegration of the Cosmos 954 reconnaissance satellite over Northern Canada. The launching state is liable for damages under the Liability Convention. Suppose a financier from a non-launching state obtains possession of a satellite upon default of the debtor from a launching state that is liable for damages while the satellite is in possession of the financier? The launching state still remains liable under the Liability Convention. The financier's state and the launching state can, on a bilateral basis, negotiate transfer of liability to the financier's

[19] See discussion of primacy below in Section III (B)(1)(c), Formal Recognition of the Primacy of the International Space Law Treaties.

[20] Supra n.17.

state. Such bilateral agreements are not uncommon among states. [21] For that purpose, states will need to know when a financier obtains ownership of satellites. Registration of secured assets under the draft space protocol is subject to the public law provisions of the Liability Convention and related bilateral agreements concluded with the launching state. The draft space protocol respects the primacy of the Liability Convention.[22]

5. Formal Recognition of the Primacy of the International Space Law Treaties over the Space Protocol.

At the December 2003 UNIDROIT Governmental Experts meeting there was significant discussion of the basic operating principle that the existing space law treaties have primacy over the space protocol. The industry working group explained that the principle was implied in the protocol. Several Governmental delegates, asked that this acknowledgement also be inserted into the text of the Protocol. Consequently, the U.S. Delegation proposed the following language:[23]

"The Convention as applied to space assets does not affect State Party rights and obligations under the existing United Nations Outer Space Treaties or instruments of the International Telecommunications Union."

This language is a clear statement of the primacy of the international space treaties and the ITU instrument. It reflects the view of the industry working group that the space financing contracts registered under the Space Protocol are subject to existing public space law.

6 Safeguarding private satellite services that may be vital to national interest.

Satellite services are sometimes essential to national public safety and social order. For example the individual members of the International Telecommunications Union may suspend international telecommunication service of their national operators after due notice to ITU.[24] Furthermore, under the ITU Rules, states may require that emergency communications services continue to function to preserve the safety of life. States may also insert conditions to safeguard continuing services in the operating permit. Such conditions are imposed by public law, and financiers conclude financing agreements subject to these safeguards. This issue is of concern to several governments representative in the UNIDROIT committee of government experts. A proposal was made that a contracting state should be able to make a treaty reservation limiting transfer of space assets used for safety of life of life functions such as global navigation satellite systems, rescue and similar operations. [25] Financiers, who need to know the risks involved in a security

[21] For example U.S. - China memorandum of agreement on liability for satellite launches.. Dec.17, 1988, TIAS.

[22] See discussion of primacy below in Section III (B)(1)(c). Formal Recognition of the Primacy of the International Space Law Treaties

[23] Draft Protocol on Matters Specific to Space Assets, Art. XXI bis, Relationship with the United Nations Outer Space Treaties and Instruments of the International Telecommunication Union, www.unidroit.org

[24] ITU Constitution, Art. 35.

[25] See UNIDROIT 2004 study LXXIIJ – Doc. 13 rev., Art XVI. This proposal is bracketed and subject to further discussion.

interest, want such a limitation from remedies for default to be as narrow as possible. The governments want to protect basic safety services derived from satellites. Thus this is another critical issue in need of resolution.

.

7.Is the operator's operating permit a legitimate space asset, if the owner's property rights cannot be transferred to a financier holding a security interest?

The operator's permit is often difficult to obtain. The Government issuing the license may by law have to conduct an examination of the operator to determine whether grant of the license is in the public interest. Subsequent transfer of the license requires another examination of whether a transfer is in the public interest. In fact the Government may disapprove any transfer of the operating permit. On the other hand the permit has value because it may be exclusive. For example only one operator can occupy an orbital slot. Another person will not be able to obtain an identical permit. The holder of a permit may expect income from its exclusivity and thus a bank may decide to finance the activity for which the operator is permitted. The bank will consider the permit to have value for. financing purposes. The operator may go bankrupt, but then the bank may be able to seize control of the operating permit (that is if the Government agrees).[26]

C. Conclusion

The space industry working group has drafted a space protocol establishing a legal framework for registry of secured interests in space assets. The basic idea for the legal system establishing an international registry and legal protection of secured assets on file in the registry has proved successful in aviation and will soon be tested in the rail mode. A window of opportunity now exists for extending this concept to space assets. Other international mobile assets such as automobiles and ships were left out of the 2001 Cape Town Convention on International Interests in Mobile Equipment. The question now is whether space asset financing should occur under a variety of state laws, or whether the field of space financing is best served by a private international law regime for private space commerce?

[26] Id.

IAC-06-E.6.2.A.05

Author
J. Pearce

Application of Free Trade Zone Concepts to Space Development

Introduction

We will here suggest a framework for considering a way to use market organization, subject to regularized codes of conduct, to serve historical and current objectives for space development rather than depending entirely upon the more political forms of allocation mechanism presumed to be necessary four to five decades ago. We believe such an approach may, in some circumstances, better serve the widely agreed objectives of peaceful development of off-earth venues, efficiently tapping global resources for such development, and efficiently spreading benefits globally.

The vehicle we choose for this paper is the 'free trade zone', or free economic zone, concept employed in over 120 nations today. In essence, an FTZ involves an area which uses a commercial code suited to purpose, has minimal regulation and taxes, is open to all reputable entities, allows for the free flow of capital, materials, and individuals, draws upon common infrastructure necessary to conduct economical operations, and is subject to efficient, non-partisan oversight.

We will draw on historical precedents, abstract key features of the FTZ system, assess restraints on its use by existing international treaties, visualize how the concept might be implemented by various illustrative actors on the world and off-world stages, and discuss briefly such scenarios for off earth development might be pursued.

In addressing 'space development' as the area for application of free trade zone concepts, we address a range of possible loci. One can imagine artifacts like a space station, existing mass concentrations like the Moon and asteroids, or assemblages of physical embodiments of economic activity. However, as an aid to giving shape to thought by applying it to an identifiable existing object, the authors have focused on Earth's Moon. [1]

We start by reviewing historical precedents for free trade zone operation, identifying characteristics of historical experiments of this sort, and then defining a set of concepts which can be said to derive from or at least be consistent with various assays in free city, free trade zone, and free economic zone organization. The concepts will be abstracted from an historical welter of organizational experiments. Thus any given historical experiment may not embody all the concepts, and not all of the experiments to date will combine the concepts in any single unique configuration.

1. Historical Precedents

The Hanseatic League is often taken as an example of 'free' trade not organized by or subject to the control of nation states of the modern sort.

Over a period of about five hundred years, merchants in a group of cities concentrated in the Baltic Sea area organized trade routes, ports, and trading centers, with activities extending from the British Isles into Russia. Early on the City Council of Lubeck provided a rule determining function, with Lubeck law governing transactions and appeals made to the Lubeck city council. But the league

[1] One point about terminology merits mention at the inception of this piece: the term “free trade zone” and many of the historical precedents of such zones on Earth implies some kind of exclusive control over a certain “zone.” For example, one might imagine the attempt to declare a certain physical zone of the surface of the Moon to be accessible to only to those who accepted the principles of the FTZ. The layout might be something like a shopping mall, with the zone users having access to life support, transport, medical facilities, and communications infrastructure. We do not intend to suggest that international law would allow a FTZ authority to claim exclusive control or jurisdiction over areas of territory beyond the immediate vicinity of facilities with ongoing activities. We envision a scenario in which a moon base operator might administer the base in the model of a shopping mall on earth, allowing others access the essential facilities of the base (e.g., life support, transportation, communications and medical care) on contractual terms. The “zone” in this example would include the base and a limited safety zone beyond the base itself. Beyond this, one can imagine a system of agents interacting voluntarily across physical expanses, but let us not go that far at this time.

embodied an alliance structure, and consensual mechanisms were used in the operation of the assemblage. The Hanseatic League has been characterized as a network of alliances. These alliances involved up to 170 participating local entities, often characterized as cities.

The League often negotiated terms by which trading posts could operate in the territory of local political organizations, seeking freedom from tolls and access to local markets. Often League trading centers operated as enclaves within the surrounding economic and political structure. Activities within the enclaves used the commercial protocols customary to League participants, not necessarily those of the surrounding populations. The League actively sought monopoly arrangements for its participants. And it embodied some collective security arrangements.

The trade nexi of Singapore and Hong Kong may be precedents of a sort, if one recognizes suitable qualifications. Both were creations of a sovereign state, Great Britain, and both were governed as colonies. The trade activities of both were oriented to an organizing center external to themselves, and thus were not as free as a serve-all-comers entity might arguably be. But both were specialized trade centers with a significant degree of local organization, both were designed to integrate into a global trade complex, both over time came to incorporate human and capital components other than that of the metropolitan power which created them, both over time came to have a significant degree of political autonomy (before Hong Kong was swallowed by China), and both came to facilitate commercial transactions over a much broader range than those of the political entity which created them. Both also demonstrated a characteristic similar to elements of the Hanseatic League which preceded them and the 'modern' free trade zone experiments which succeeded them, integral to their competitive advantages – the creation of a sophisticated local infrastructure closely and parsimoniously adapted economically and efficiently to support the trade by which they made their living.

A global proliferation of a formula for local free trade zones began in 1951 with the creation of an entity in Puerto Rico designed to attract manufacturers to export from there. At present there may be about 3,000 entities or locations having a claim to be a free trade zone, spread over about 120 countries.

Free trade zone entities demonstrate both considerable differentiation and substantial commonalities. Among the features commonly found, in varying degrees, are the following

- **Freedom from taxes, including real estate and income taxes, and customs duties;**
- **Invitations to participation to entities from all over the globe, with few visible exclusions;**
- **The ability to create local entities in the zone;**
- **Liberal repatriation of capital and profits to the owners of zone participants;**
- **A defined, usually geographically contiguous location;**
- **An administrative authority specifically designated for the zone, with a rule set configured for zone activity;**
- **Prompt decisions on applications for zone participation, with relatively simple requirements;**
- **Licenses for activity in the zone, rather than perpetual title to defined premises there;**
- **Organizational arrangements tailored to facilitate movement of materiel, labor and capital into and out of the zone;**
- **Facilities which could be characterized as infrastructure – water, sewer, telecommunications, etc.; and**
- **The close availability of factors of production – such as labor and material resources -- and market opportunities.**

The differentiations include variations in the degree and format of the elements described above, and specializations in products and activities. For

example, Dubai has projects for an airport free trade zone (not just a gift shop), an automobile FTZ, an internet city and a financial center city.

FTZs can be quite small. For example, one of us (Frazier) has participated in setting up telecom centers designed to be portals to Earth's cyberspace. Not a lot of geography is required for this purpose.

FTZs can be quite ingenious in creating value. For example, a successful FTZ can enhance the value of the real estate around it, thus offering market inducement both to participants and to the hosting country.

2. Key Concepts

What might we say are the key concepts to be abstracted from this experience to be applied to space development, such as development of the Moon?

A zone entity might

- In concept at least, be organized by any entity on Earth, not merely a sovereign nation, capable of organizing the logistics of operations ,
- Be open to Earth-wide participation
- Be sustained by resources mobilized Earth-globally, and value exchanges feeding into the global earth exchange network, and
- Have a zone-specific governance entity (though that entity might itself have relationships with broader entities on Earth), with zone specific and zone adapted rule sets.

Implicit in such a structure is the set of conventions supporting voluntary, peaceful mutualistic exchanges – otherwise known as trade – on earth. These conventions, which include contracts, modern financial intermediation systems, consortia, insurance, etc., are widely known and practiced.

Such a zone entity might use administrative techniques widely used by FTZ entities on Earth – renewable licenses, simplified registrations, etc. It might very well also use a device common in homesteading and mineral rights situations in the United States – forfeiture of any license not exercised in a reasonable time.

We have selected concepts which seem to us to accord with some of the underlying drivers of world opinion concerning the development of space – that space development draw upon and reward as many earth venues as possible, that it not become a locus of competing sovereign claims, and that it be peaceful.

We have suggested that a space development FTZ might be organized by 'any entity', not only by a sovereign state. This apparently radical suggestion may

not seem so radical when one considers that such an entity could be a sovereign, a coalition of sovereigns (including the coalition known as the United Nations), a coalition of 'private sector' entities, a coalition of both private and public sector entities, etc.

Under the 1967 space treaty, some sovereign must take responsibility for at least some elements of such an undertaking. But this responsibility could be syndicated, and backed up by both public and private organizations. (Many a sovereign has been bankrolled by private purses.)

In suggesting a somewhat fluid organizational field, not tightly constrained by sovereignty traditions, we have in effect suggested opening the organizational field globally, and thus perhaps improving the competition for viable development constructs. If one can get organizing entities across a global framework, one could have competition for launch vehicles, for safety standards, for development concepts, for capital, and the like.

3. Constraints of International Treaties

Our approach here is perhaps the classic 'western' -- or more particularly frontier, tradition – that what is not clearly forbidden is, or may be made, legal. This approach has the communal merit, paradoxically, of preserving a field of possibilities for mutually beneficial activity.

This approach is not inconsistent with the perspectives of the basic treaty governing outer space matters – the 'Multilateral Treaty on Principles Governing the Activities of States In The Exploration and Use of Outer Space, Including the Moon and Other Celestial Objects' of 1967. As suggested by Christol, quoted in Reynolds and Merges, in their "Outer Space, Problems of Law and Policy' (pp.81,82), "The negotiators were not laboring under the assumption that the Principles Treaty was a definitive statement of the emerging international law of

outer space. Rather, they acknowledged without exception that they were at the threshold of the law, and much of the book remained to be opened." Or, one might more accurately say, shaped.

We would take the treaty to be just what it says it is – an indication of guidelines which the subscribing states proposed to follow as among themselves, in working out rule sets in and for space. The first and third guiding principles articulated in the treaty include in them the advice that 'States Parties' will carry out 'exploration and use' of space bodies 'in accord with international law'. In other words, the principles articulated were to be inserted in an envelope, or fabric, of international law.

Our proposal draws upon a rich grounding of public and private international law. We seek to use well understood principles to put in place serviceable legal structures. We proceed in the general conceptual framework of constructing rule sets for space development, in effect conducting legal engineering.

Let us start by recognizing extant statements of principles obviously relevant to establishing free trade zones, as on Earth's Moon.

Article II states that outer space is 'not subject to national appropriation.' This was clearly directed at the practice of nation states of planting flags, and otherwise asserting exclusive control over territories on Earth.

Article II provides that the state signatories are to be governed by international law. This implies but not states that non-state parties will be governed by the complex of customs, precedents, practices and legal formats which have evolved to deal with transnational situations on Earth.

Article IV states that the Moon and other bodies are to be used exclusively for peaceful purposes.

The treaty seeks to make subscribing states responsible to each other in a field of space related activities. These responsibilities may lead to substantial control over non-state entities by state entities.

Article VI states that state parties to the treaty will be responsible to each other for their 'national activities' , except that the activities of an international organization is to the joint responsibility of the organization and such states as are its participants. In express terms, this responsibility is to extend only to 'national activities', however that may be defined.[2] To the extent that a 'national activity' involved non-state parties, a subscribing state would be required to respond to other states for the effects upon them of that entity's activities.

Article VI also states that non-state entities are to be authorized and supervised by subscribing state parties.

Article VII provides that state parties are to be responsible to other state parties and their juridical persons for damages caused by the launch of any object from its territory or facility.

Article IX contains a sort of mediation mechanism to deal with 'interference' between activities of either state parties or 'their nationals'. That mechanism is 'appropriate consultations' between state parties, before such an activity proceeds.

The 1976 Convention of Registration of Objects Launched into Outer Space provides that a State which launches or procures the launching of a space object, or a State from whose territory the object is launched, will register the object on a registry of space objects. The registering state maintains 'jurisdiction and control' of the object.

---

[2] A broad reading of this provision might in effect say that any activity of any national citizen would incur state party responsibility. But with intermixed nationalities on a space locus, with transnational entities engaged, and with complex interactions, such a system could be unworkable. This provision might be interpreted in a more limited fashion in a series of events, leading to a commonly understood framework, or be modified by a new convention, as will be discussed later.

4. A Changed World -- 'Globalization', and the Development of Other Concepts, Since 1967

In the four decades since the drafting of this 1967 statement of 'principles' to be followed by nation states, the world has evolved in the direction of greater reliance upon market forces -- acting upon both sovereign and non sovereign entities -- to organize economic activities, greater use of international non-governmental entities both for economic activities and a range of other activities characterized by a wide variety of labels, and greater use of international coordinating mechanisms, such as the World Trade Organization, the International Monetary Fund, the International Atomic Energy Agency, etc. While nation states continue to execute a level of coordination and organization, they have to some degree become subsumed in a global network which has one-level-up, or even more than one level up, coordination. In that global network, a host of actors assume substantial roles not supervised in detail by nation states. What these actors can do is still conditioned by nation states, in a variety of ways. But what nation states can do is in significant practical effect also conditioned by these various actors, and the complex of forces which animate them.

The surge of global economic activity has resulted in more 'development' in poorer venues of the earth being accomplished by market mediated transactions, as among 'private' entities, including private funding sources, than by direct state-to-state activity. 'Outsourcing' of activity from high income, high cost venues to lower income, lower cost venues regularly spreads significant wealth around the globe. Transactions of this sort are flexible and relatively efficient. One could expect this pattern of activity to be operative in efforts of entities on Earth to invest in and gain income from activities off earth.

At the same time, the nature of 'law' has lost some of its aura of abstract grandeur, and often is now seen as embodiments of 'rule sets'. Such 'rule sets' can be seen as experimental, adjusted to purpose, arranged in levels of hierarchy, and evaluated in terms of productive yield. 'Rule sets' can be parsed and constructed in

broader analytic contexts than traditional legal analysis. Today, we are more prone to think in terms such as coding efficiency and evolutionary underpinnings for human-evolved and human-engineered rule sets.

5. Some General Observations Preliminary to Case Analysis

Now let us try to place free trade zones in the contexts of international law, the objectives and principles of the 1967 multilateral treaty, and this emerging set of global financial, industrial, cultural, and informational networks.

'International law', generically and broadly speaking, offers a substantial toolkit for organizing entities such as free trade zones. It allows localization of rule sets, choices of law, dispute settling mechanisms, etc. The terms of the charters of such entities can be drafted drawing upon concepts and mechanisms widely used and well understood.

As to the 1967 treaty 'principles', a central observation is that the free trade zone or free economic zone concept seems well adapted to concerns of the treaty signatories which were central to the treaty effort, and which are apt to have a long life. In particular, the concept is well adapted to making benefits of activity in the space locus available to and spread among worldwide venues. Capital and labor can be organized globally. The fruits of activity in the economic zones can be introduced into and disseminated in a globally interconnected web of trade and technology. The economic investments and economic benefits could be marshaled, largely, by economic, or market, forces rather than detailed allocation mechanisms of nation states or multilateral political bodies.

It appears that the responsibilities for damage to nation states and their nationals from launch procedures would have to be localized in one or more nation states, in many cases, but as indicated before such liabilities could be syndicated and reinsured.

The Outer Space Treaty's objective of peaceful use is consistent with a regime of voluntary economic arrangements organized to serve mutual advantage by the transacting entities. It would also be encouraged by the strong desire of entities investing substantial sums to seek and maintain stable and peaceful conditions, at the space locus, and in loci supporting it. The prohibition of nation state appropriation of space territory can also be seen as a factor facilitating free economic zone activities.[3]

A potential detriment to the freedom of FTZ activities is the requirement that one or more state entities authorize' and 'supervise' the activity of non-governmental entities. However, the scope and nature of authorization and supervision are not defined. FTZ zones on earth are in effect authorized and supervised, at some level, by state entities. Also, consortia are contemplated, and this is another mechanism permitting delegation of authority, supervision, and operations.

The Article VI requirement that a nation state be responsible to other nation states and their nationals for 'national activities' could inhibit FTZ formation. An FTZ could indeed be organized as an explicitly national activity. But an FTZ drawing upon international capital, technology and labor, though formally chartered in one or more national venues, might well in substance not be a 'national activity'. And in the event an FTZ were deemed a national activity, its mere existence as a platform for voluntary economic transactions would not necessarily entail liability for breaches of contracts or torts by entities using the zone. Further, as noted above, responsibility could be syndicated and/or insured. And voluntary assumptions of risk could be employed.

---

[3] One might make a case that national sovereignties might provide stable environments for economic activity in space venues. This could be of value if a 'free and fair field' for economic activity could not otherwise be established. But effective prohibition on nation state armed contests for territory could serve to reduce economic instability in an hostile and unforgiving environment.

The provision of the 1967 treaty calling for consultation between nation states before launching an activity by a State or a national of a state which would interfere with the activities of another state or its nationals is not necessarily an impediment to FTZ establishment. If the 'interference' term were limited to physical disruption or obstruction, rather than, say, economic competition, the grounds for invoking this term could be narrow and avoidable in most foreseeable circumstances. The question whether the FTZ activity were really that of a state or one of its nationals would still exist. And the procedure called for – consultation – is not necessarily very restrictive.

6. Application of Concepts to Hypothetical Situations

With these preliminary observation in hand, let us try to imagine some of the legal issues which could arise, and be provided for, as to different forms of 'Free Trade Zone' off the earth, such as on the Moon. Let us imagine the following kinds of sponsoring/creating entities:

- **a national state;**
- **a consortium of national states;**
- **a private sector consortium which is chartered in one or more national states;**
- **the United Nations; and**
- **An entity created for the purpose pursuant to a new international agreement, as a follow-on to the Outer Space Treaty of 1967.**

Following is a chart which sets out for comparisons some of the key features of the patterns operation and responsibilities which might be involved in these different arrangements.

Sponsor	Act of Launch	Objects Launched	Zone Operator	FTZ Users	Parties Contracting with FTZ Users
Single Nation	Launching nation (same or other nation) has responsibility to others: could syndicate or insure responsibility	Would be put on registry of country launching or procuring launch. 'Jurisdiction and control' implications follow registration. Some play for contractual arrangements as to use and responsibility.	Nation could be operator, or delegate to special authority. Could hire service from bidders. Scope for contractual allocation of responsibilities.	Could be from all portions of Earth. Might or might not get involved in launching objects. Scope for contractual allocation of responsibilities.	Could be from all portions of Earth. Less likely to get involved with launching objects. Scope for contractual allocation of responsibilities.
Coalition of Nations	Same: somewhat more likely to use several national sites.	Same.	As above, multilateral agreement on operator obviously needed.	As above.	As above.
Private Sector Entity	Same: likely to use several national sites over time	Same, but transnational entity and mix of many co-located objects on separate registries highlights awkwardness of disparate national object controls.	Could be Zone operator, or delegate operation. Could hire from bidders, etc.	As above.	As above.
United Nations	Similar to private sector case.	Similar to private sector case.	Special purpose operator entity would seem obvious solution.	As above.	As above.
New Convention Entity	Launch responsibility to be identified	Probably revised registration provisions. Contractual allocation of responsibility for placement and use probably recognized.	Probably considerable latitude for designation; responsibilities probably contractually allocated: tort responsibilities could be recognized.	Responsibilities probably contractually allocated. Tort responsibilities could be recognized.	Responsibilities probably contractually allocated. Tort responsibilities could be recognized.

One can see considerable similarities as between these various scenarios.

For example, the FTZ Operating Entity could have any composition determined by the Sponsoring Nation, coalition of nations, private sector entity, or United Nations vehicle. If under the current OST one or more Sponsoring Nations were involved, it or they would be responsible to others for the actions of the Operating Entity. But his would not preclude the Operating Entity itself from making contracts and assuming responsibilities. Nor would it preclude the Operating Entity from putting limitation of liability and assumption of risk clauses in its contracts.

As to objects lifted to the space site, a registry nation might delegate control and use of the object. A long term lease concept comes to mind. This might be convenient if the object were put in place for an user of the FTZ. The Zone Operator, or a Zone user, might have a contract specifying the terms of use, delegation of authorization and control, or a cession of control. The delegation or cession of control could be to a Sponsoring Nation or a Zone Operator, or to a user of the FTZ. [4]

Users of the FTZ could contract with the Operating Entity. They could use Operating Entity infrastructure, and objects, both lifted and locally made. If they put objects in the FTZ, then under current treaty provisions they may need to arrange launch, and may need an arrangement as to use of object with the nation on whose registry the object is launched. The Zone user might fabricate objects, owned by it, if a contract with the Operating Entity were to allow for this. Zone users could make contracts with Earth entities – e.g. suppliers and customers.

We have included in the chart a scenario for a regime created by a modification of or follow on to the 1967 statement of principles. Any such follow on

[4] The 1967 Outer Space treaty and the 1976 follow-on appear to contemplate things like space capsules or stations. The regime contemplated does not seem well suited to things like plug-in elements on a stationary facility on, say, the Moon. This might be managed by the contractual techniques suggested above, or by treaty amendment, discussed below.

protocol might be considered as a refinement of the OST rather than an abnegation of it. We think that examination of the various scenarios depicted will reveal awkwardness in attempting detailed control by many nations of operations in a space venue, like the Moon, where many actors from many venues on Earth could be combined and permuted in a flexible, contract mediated regime.

Such a multinational crystallization of a new framework could take many forms, obviously. A central issue to be addressed, we have suggested, would be dispersed, fractional national control of what would be transnational/translunar activity an hierarchical level up from the nation state. This issue would include the control of property brought to and used in an FTZ. The particular constraints embodied in the 1967 OST and the 1976 object registration treaty would, in our opinion, probably be lifted or substantially modified.

In effect, we are addressing the emergence of a new organizational form above the national level. In using the Free Trade Zone concept, we are suggesting an investment and trading format in which participants can generate rule sets adapted to the needs of the collective enterprise, and in which markets would be relied upon to draw upon and distribute resources rather than politically mediated allocations. If this were the object of an exercise to create a new treaty format, then the question of liabilities for launch might remain to be dealt with by treaty, and the delegation of rule sets could be provided for in the treaty, drawing on the principles of public and private international law.

Central issues to be addressed prior to launching an effort to modify the 1967 and 1976 treaties would be whether

*** One could achieve the objective of market mediated transactions in space development, using the minimal adequate global rule set to facilitate them, instead of activity on national foundations with politically allocated investments, gains and losses, assuming that this objective would have economic and social benefits worth pursuing, and whether**

*** This goal could be more readily achieved by means of a global effort to achieve a new nationally based treaty foundation, or by means of ad hoc interpretations of the existing framework.**

7. Some Additional General Considerations, and Concluding Remarks

The reader will note that up to this point we have not explicitly discussed 'property rights' in space venues. As a prior footnote sets out, we do not assume the absolute necessity of an FTZ entity making a territorial claim on a specified portion, or all, of an existing concentration of matter outside the boundaries of Earth, in all cases. Another presenter at this conference will discuss the property rights issue, and we look forward with great interest to her presentation.

We have assumed that rights to property other than the most basic sense of rights to a specified area of matter based on sovereign grant, could be created by contract and facilitated by access to arbitration and other tribunals. The parties to an FTZ operation could specify the laws applicable to their undertakings, and the means of adjudication of disputes.

As to States, and other entities undertaking 'national activities', the 1967 OST requires that any such entity is obliged to undertake consultations with any other State party with respect to actual or potential interference with 'the activities' of a state or 'national activity' in space. And, of course, the treaty calls for conduct in accord with 'international law'.

One can imagine an entity not denominated as a State, and not engaged in a 'national activity', undertaking trespass – to use an common law concept, which surely must have analogues -- upon another such entity, or engaging in violence which would be deemed criminal in most or all Earth venues. If and to the extent both actors were tethered to Earth, actions could be brought in Earth venues for

such actions. We do not claim inexorable and perfect justice would result, of course. If the aggressive actor had no ties to earth, directly or indirectly, we could obviously have a problem in achieving regularized remedy.

We find interesting the implications of this discussion for the concepts of 'contracts with no governing law', or 'self regulatory contracts', and a 'new lex mercatoria'. In effect, we are indeed suggesting that contracts and a law merchant could be 'resident', or operative, as to a site where there is no territorial sovereign, and where there is no single territorial state which embraces all parties to transactions.

This situation is not new to Earth, or Earth entities. Functional economic regimes have been repeatedly created from the 'ground' (albeit in our present context one would read 'space') up by concord among the participating entities.[5] In recent centuries the rise of effectively organized nation states has to a considerable degree superseded such systems. But as this has proceeded, a layer of global economic and, to a degree, political integration has developed, above the nation state level.[6]

Now we imagine a leap outward. This may be done solely by nation state entities, acting individually. But we have suggested that it need not be so, and there are possible great advantages from global organization using market forces and non-state entities rather than detailed political mediation by a given nation or among nation states to mobilize capital and spread benefits.

---

[5] In such regimes, the major sanction has been exclusion from the participating group. Imagine exclusion on the Moon, or from the supply routes to it,

[6] One of the interesting issues which arises is the question of a transnational antitrust regime affecting space venues, where supply lines will be long and local 'market power' could be great. At least, this is interesting to one of the authors, with an antitrust law background. There could be a clear 'essential facilities' problem in a moon venue, for example, where the controller of the infrastructure could control competition with it in one or more particulars associated with it or with its commercial or national partners/sponsors. The best remedy for this would be competition among FTZs. However, such competition could presumably be slow evolving and limited. There would remain competition among the moon venue, other space venues, and the earth venue for particular economic activities.

We recognize that the structure of issues which this paper suggests may be added to or otherwise modified. Also, we expect that ingenious minds around the world can recombine and permute the conceptual elements we mention here, and others, in ways we have not attempted in this brief initial exploration. We hope we have made a contribution to an ongoing conversation in which fertile minds can construct new possibilities.

Acknowledgements

We would like to recognize indebtedness to Brad Blair, for encouraging an exploration of current legal issues in space law, and an encouraging response to this topic suggestion; Wayne White, for his many instructive articles on space law issues, which he generously has shared with us; and Berin Szoka, who has contributed a great deal through sharing of research materials, contacts, insights, and editing suggestions.

Authors typically disclaim any responsibility on the part of others for the authors' work product. Such a disclaimer is particularly appropriate in this case, where we have ventured so far from any one person's tether. Our benefactors have done the best they could for us: we must take responsibility for what we have done with the information they have provided us.

Mark Frazier

Laurence Latourette

Jack Pearce

IAC-06-E6.2.A.06

PROTECTION OF INTELLECTUAL PROPERTY RIGHTS IN OUTER SPACE

Dr. Yun ZHAO

City University of Hong Kong

E-mail: lwzhao@cityu.edu.hk

ABSTRACT

The commercialization of outer space is developing into a new stage. Intellectual property rights are based on a strict territorial approach, which is incompatible with the rules regarding space activities. This paper aims at examining the issue of patent protection in outer space and proposing a viable regime for the protection of the so-called "space patent". It is believed that such an international framework will promote the development of space activities and respond primarily to the need of patent protection by the States and private entities.

1. INTRODUCTION

Intellectual property rights are based on a "strict territorial" approach. However, the concept of territorial sovereignty does not exist in rules regarding space activities.

As clearly defined in the Outer Space Treaty, outer space is not subject to national appropriation and free use shall be carried out for the benefits and interests of all countries.[1] Reconciling these two different approaches proves to be a difficult task. Nevertheless, providing protection for intellectual property rights arising out of space activities is vital to the sustainable development of outer space. With no appropriate intellectual property regime in place, interests and enthusiasm of private entities in space activities will wane, which will be devastating to space development.[2]

This paper aims at examining the issue of patent protection in outer space, comparing the international Patent legal framework for space-related activities and proposing a viable regime for the protection of the so-called "space patent". Detailed analysis will be made in Part 2 to the application of current concept of patent to inventions from space activities. Part 3 will be devoted to the discussion on the US and ESA regimes for use, transfer and ownership of patents.

Part 4 will analyze relevant provisions in the 1998 Intergovernmental Agreement (IGA). Part 5 elaborates on the establishment of a special regime and the improvements to be made in view of the special nature of space patents. This paper concludes that space patents are special in many different ways and that a special regime for space patents will be meaningful in many aspects.

2. SUBSTANTIAL REQUIREMENTS FOR PATENT PROTECTION

Three substantial requirements should be satisfied for an invention to enjoy patent protection: novelty, inventive step and industrial application. The third element is easy to satisfy as long as the invention can be made or used in any kind of industry actually or constructively.[3]

The first two elements are closely related. It involves two-step analysis. Firstly, what is considered as "novel" compared with the prior state of art? Second, what is the degree of inventiveness to satisfy patentability?

Novelty is determined in reference to existing knowledge at the invention. The Patent Ordinance of Hong Kong adopted the term "state of the art" to determine the degree of novelty.[4] This ordinance further defines the time factor in determining admissible state of the art: before the deemed date of filing of an application for a standard patent for the invention or, if priority was claimed, before the date of priority; or before the date of filing of an application for a short-term patent for the invention or, if priority was claimed, before the date of priority.[5]

The provisions above are important to patent protection in outer space. Scientific staff normally station in the ISS for some period of time. Before formal application for the Patent protection is submitted, the invention could have been used in the ISS or known by other staff stationed in the ISS. In this situation, it is important to make sure that the present rules will not cause problem to the interpreting the term of "novelty".

Then, to what extent will the above situation be exempted from normal rules? With no clear rules in place, we may rely on the strict confidentiality rules in the ISS Crew Code of Conduct.[6] According to this Code, each Cooperating Agency, or the data owner or provider shall give instruction to their astronauts for the marking of data generated onboard the ISS and consequently trigger the application of the protective measures;[7] any disclosure by the crewmembers without prior written approval will be considered as violation of the confidential requirement; the crewmembers are required to mark and protect as long as the confidential requirement remain in place; such requirement may last till after the return phase and when the mission is finished.[8] Based on the above strict rules, we can see that the novelty requirement will not be easily compromised by acts of any disclosure without prior approval.

The Patent Ordinance requires that to qualify for a patent an invention must involve an inventive step.[9] The requirement of non-obviousness or inventiveness, forming one of the important bases for patent application, is particularly relevant for space products or inventions. Outer space provides a zero-gravity and ultra-vacuum environment not available on Earth. For example, the purity level may be sufficient to justify the inventiveness requirement.

If not, the process of production or invention in the unique environment itself could possibly provide another justification for inventiveness. It has been suggested that the process reactions in outer space are not the same and that the resulting product is patentable. [10] By emphasizing and patenting the process, protection will automatically extend to the product of such process. However, it is important to note that "even though product-by-process claims are limited by and defined by the process, determination of patentability is based on the product itself" and if "the product in the product-by-process claim is the same as or obvious from a product of the prior art, the claim is unpatentable even though the prior product was made by a different process."[11] A recent decision from the U.S. Court of Appeals for the Federal Circuit (CAFC) again states, "Regardless of how broadly or narrowly one construes a product-by-process claim, it is clear that such claims are always to a product, not a process." [12] The above observation is especially meaningful to the potential product-by-process claim for products arising out of scientific experiments in outer space. By identifying at least one novel feature of the product, relevant parties may submit product-by-process claim upon returning to the Earth and successfully obtain patent protection.

3. USE, TRANSFER AND OWNERSHIP OF PATENTS

3.1. Present Regimes Concerning Ownership of Patents

With private entities increasingly active in space activities, a proper framework to identify the ownership of a certain patent becomes more and more important. Based on the 1958 regime, patent will be the property of the US if any private entities enter into contract with NASA. [13] This will no doubt discourage private parties from participating in space activities. The US has taken the initiative to formulate a structure for the creation, use, transfer and ownership and protection of patent with relation to the ISS as an ISS intellectual property reference guide.[14]

NASA makes allocation of the ISS resources available to a commercial user through two forms of agreements: Space Act Agreement and Cooperative Research and Development Agreement (CRADA). The two forms are quite similar, but the first form is more flexible, thus, the second form is not routinely used by NASA. [15] The form of Space Act Agreement is especially meaningful for the commercialization of outer space. Previously, under the 1958 National

Aeronautics and Space Act (Space Act), NASA may enter into and perform contracts, leases, cooperative agreements, or other transactions as may be necessary to conduct its work;[16] the owner of the inventions arising out of the above contracts or agreements shall be the United States government.[17] The form of Space Act agreement does not fall under any specific category defined in the above Space Act, but is considered as other transactions.[18] Under this categorization, Space Act Agreement aims to procure property or services for the direct benefit of NASA with little or no involvement of NASA and NASA can accordingly tailor the allocation of intellectual property rights according to the nature of the particular agreement and contributions of the parties.[19]

With this new arrangement, NASA can further elaborate on the detailed ways of allocation. Space Act Agreements are further divided into non-reimbursable and reimbursable agreements based on whether NASA received payment for the goods or services it provides. No matter which type of agreement it belongs to, title to inventions will remain with the respective investing parties. In view of the fact that NASA is reimbursed under reimbursable agreements, NASA will grant an exclusive, royalty-free, irrevocable license to the other party.[20] No exchange of patents is required under non-reimbursable agreements, but NASA may consider granting to the participant an exclusive or partially exclusive commercial license.[21]

European Space Agency (ESA), as one of the most important international organizations on space activities, does not have specific regulations on the above issue. Relevant rules and guidelines can only be found in the General Provisions on Intellectual Property Right: the General Clauses and Conditions for ESA Contracts (General Provision)[22] and the Resolution on the Rules concerning Information, Data and Intellectual Property (ESA Resolution) adopted by the ESA Council on December 19th, 2001[23]. Both documents adopt similar position as defined by NASA, though the elaboration has been much simpler. Under the General Provision, "the contractor shall be the owner of any invention made in the course of or resulting from the work undertaken for the purpose of the contract and shall be entitled to protect such invention by patent or other form of industrial property right in accordance with the applicable laws."[24] Similarly, the ESA Resolution takes it as the general principle that the ownership of information, data and intellectual property developed under a contract with ESA will remain with the contract whoever has developed them.[25]

<u>3.2. Joint Invention</u>

For joint inventions on Earth, there is so far no clear answer to the application of rights and obligations. Usually, in agreements related to joint invention on Earth, the resolution of the issue depends on the definition of joint invention and any provisions relating to invention where the owner is only one of the cooperating parties.[26]

Scientific experiments in outer space normally require the involvement and collaboration of the inventive endeavors of two or more parties. Thus, the question arises as to who can be considered as an inventor. Inventors should be those making contribution to the inventive idea and to the final result.[27] Normally, crew members or astronauts merely follow instructions in performing experiments and thus, cannot be considered as inventor(s). But it is of course possible that a crew member or astronaut conceives of a patentable invention while working on the experiment. In this situation, inventorship can be confirmed based on the above standard of contribution to the inventive idea and the final result. This situation is, however, quite rare; no crew member or astronaut has become an inventor so far.[28]

The second issue relates to the rights of each co-inventor. In the US, each co-inventor named on a patent application owns that patent. In the absence of any agreement, each co-inventor owns 100 per cent of the patent, regardless of the share of contribution of each inventor.[29] NASA offers general principles on joint inventions arising out of Space Act Agreements: NASA and the other party will identify and report the invention to each other and cooperate in obtaining patent protection; the two sides will consult with possible support and advice from the US Government, and agree on the title of ownership, protection and license conditions.[30]

4. THE IGA PROVISIONS CONCERNING INTELLECTUAL PROPERTY

Article 21 of the IGA touches on several important aspects. First of all, it clearly provides a territorial approach based on the ownership/registry of elements for the issue of jurisdiction: an invention taking place in or on a Space Station flight element shall be deemed to have occurred in the territory of the Partner State of that element's registry.[31] Such a conclusion results from the application of the principles of jurisdiction and control of the state of registry over the individual flight element.[32]

However, the above assumption does not impact the ownership of the invention, nor does it preclude the right to file a patent application in multiple States.[33] The IGA further provides that, "in respect of an invention made in or on any Space Station flight element by a person who is not its national or resident, a Partner State shall not apply its laws concerning secrecy of inventions so as to prevent the filing of a patent application in any other Partner

State that provides for the protection of the secrecy of patent applications contacting information that is classified or other protected for national security purposes."[34] Accordingly, the territorial provision in the IGA simply supports the place where the invention takes place.

The territorial approach in the IGA is especially meaningful in dealing with the issue of utilizing a patent in outer space, but it does not clearly speak out under which law patent utilization or infringement activities will governed. Under normal situation, once the utilization of a patent occurs in a US space element, then it will be treated in the same way as any other such activities within the US territory. That means, any patent utilization or infringement activities will be solely governed by national law of the Partner State of that space element's registry. This understanding is also in line with the normal national rules on intellectual property protection whose application extends to anywhere within its jurisdiction. However, it can be argued that the activities will be governed by the law of the State which grants the patent. This argument can be deduced from relevant provisions in the IGA. According to Article 21 (4), if the infringement occurs in or on an ESA-registered element, it is not possible to recover in more than one European Partner State for the same infringement of the same intellectual property; in case of multiple actions are brought for the infringement of the same right in different European Partner States, a court may grant a temporary stay of proceeding in order to wait for the outcome of an earlier-filed action; furthermore, satisfaction for recovery of damages in one of the actions shall prevent further recovery in any pending or future action based on the same act of infringement.[35]

5. A SPECIAL SPACE PATENT REGIME

With States drastically relaxing their monopoly over space exploration and activities, private entities are increasingly interested in space investment and research.[36] As discussed above, the three requirements of patentability need to be further elaborated to accommodate the special outer space environment. While the IGA provides guidelines for intellectual property protection at international level, national laws have a final say in detailed application process. Patent protection in outer space environment is not well coordinated against international background. Conflicts can arise when two patents from two nations cover essentially the same invention out of scientific experiments in outer space. Considering the exorbitant expenses involved in space activities, the lacking in a coordinated patent regime specially designed for the environment of outer space will in the end let many potential interested private entities down and drive them away from this field.

Accordingly, it is important to consider creating a special international legal regime for patents arising out of space activities.[37]

Two important treaties exist at the moment dealing with patent application: Paris Convention and Patent Cooperation Treaty. Now the question is whether we should have a separate treaty to define the new type of patent. The author takes the view that it is not necessary to add to the patent field a new treaty. All patents are the same in essence. As discussed above, the difference lies in the evaluation stage: how to apply the existing requirements. The purpose of creating a regime for this type of patents basically serves to facilitate patent application and easy reference, while keeping in mind the fact that outer space is a special environment to carry out scientific experiments. Accordingly, the present coordination work needs to focus on the procedural aspects. The author proposes to set up a new category named 'space patent' under the framework of the Patent Cooperation Treaty. A special patent office (say, Space Patent Office) could be established for the purpose of space patent application.[38]

5.1. Space Patents

The first question is what kind of invention can be registered as 'space patent'. Or we may say, what subject matter will be dealt with by the 'space patent office'. No doubt, space patent office shall deal with patent related to space activities. Five categories of inventions have been identified to be related to space activities: (a) inventions made on earth for space applications; (b) inventions made on earth for terrestrial applications as a result of space activities (including telecommunications); (c) inventions made in outer space for terrestrial applications; (d) inventions made in outer space for spatial applications; (e) inventions patented on earth for spatial applications used in outer space.[39] Some scholar has been able to re-categorize space patents into two: space-activity inventions resulting from job done on earth (including categories (a), (b) and (e)); space-related inventions made in outer space (including categories (c) and (d)).[40] The author would single out category (e) for discussion due to its special legal status as mentioned below.

5.2. Space Patent Cooperation

Space-activity inventions resulting from job done on earth do not distinguish much from other inventions on earth. The only difference is the original purpose of the activities. Thus, the existing patent regime does not need for major change for those inventions, but we do need to note that considerations on public policy and national security will play an important role in the application process due to its sensitiveness to national interests. The problems exist with other two types of space patents, which will be discussed below.

5.2.1. Extension of Patent Protection in Outer Space

As mentioned above, intellectual property law is territorial in nature. No protection will be provided outside national boundaries, and of course not to the non-sovereignty area of outer space. Then, the problem arises as to whether inventions patented on earth enjoy protection when applied in outer space (referring to categories (c), (d) and (e)). The IGA resolved the issue in a restricted sense: for purposes of intellectual property law, national jurisdiction shall extend to a specific part or a flight component of the ISS itself.

However, outer space is much broader; so how about the protection of intellectual property in other parts of outer space? Little national legislation has touched on the point. International agreements on patent protection (namely, the Paris Convention, the Patent Cooperation Treaty and the WTO Agreement on the Trade-related Intellectual Property Rights (TRIPs)) have also been very ambiguous, lacking ostensible wording on the issue. The only possibility for patent protection in outer space is to extract some words or provisions in the international agreements and give them a broad explanation. For example, we may interpret the term "vessel" in the Paris Convention [41] to include a space object or rely on the simple statement in the TRIPs that patents shall be available and patent rights enjoyable without discrimination as to the place of invention[42]. But all these efforts are marginal and do not form a strong legal basis for patent protection in outer space.

The actual legal vacuum and uncertainty of the legal status constitutes one of the most important concerns for those potential private entities. It is important to clarify the issue by noting that relevant national laws will be extended to outer space and that inventions patented on earth will be protected while using in outer space. While the States can make explicit national rules on the issue of extension, it would be more efficient and effective to make such rules in an international agreement like the IGA.

A further question to be resolved concerns the applicable law. By referring to the Outer Space Treaty, jurisdiction and control over a specific space object lies on the State of registry. [43] The act of registration has accordingly resolved the issue of jurisdiction. With regard to patent protection in outer space, we can similarly rely on the connecting factor of the State patenting the invention. The national law of the State which has patented an invention will continue to apply to the use or infringement of the patent in outer space.

5.2.2. Cooperation on Priority of Claims

Following the same model in the Patent Cooperation Treaty, a centralized 'international application' procedure will be set up for the granting of various space patents at national or regional level. A declaration may be attached in the application claiming the priority of one or more earlier applications filed in or for any State. This will be done through a single operation which calls for the designation of targeted States. As discussed above, a space patent office will be established to examine applications and issue space patents. An 'international search' system will also be created to facilitate the application examination process. The rules in the existing Patent Cooperation Treaty on the priority of claims will continue to apply.[44] However, we need to reconsider the issue of the priority period concerning space patent in categories (c) and (d).

Two main patent systems exist currently: first-to-invent and first-to-file.[45] Under the two systems, the awarding of patent will be based on the two different factors: the activity of developing an invention and the act of filing an application. During the WTO Uruguay Round negotiations, the TRIPs was reached, trying to unify the intellectual property regime, particularly with respect to patents. One of the most achievements was the adoption of the "first to file" system.[46] The act of filing becomes a vital point. However, as mentioned above, scientific staff will normally station in the ISS for several months. The act of filing will start only after their return to the earth and showing of the product or invention. The priority period of six months may not be sufficient for the purpose of protection in this situation. It is thus necessary to consider a longer priority period for space patent in categories (c) and (d).

6. CONCLUSION

The present legal regime for outer space does not provide clear guidelines on property rights. From the first sight, the territorial nature of Patent law and the non-territorial nature of space law are difficult to reconcile. However, we should note that intellectual property has attracted a significant amount of interest on an international scale and international conventions have been adopted ensuring minimum rights and providing certain measures for enforcement of those rights by the Contracting Members.[47] Accordingly, barriers between these two areas of law are not insurmountable.

This paper has analyzed the application of the existing patent conception to space activities and necessary accommodations need to be made for protection of space patents. The paper proposes to set up a special regime for space protection within the current regime created by the Patent Cooperation Treaty. Further conceptual clarification is made to the extended application of patent protection on earth to outer space. Such an international framework will in the end promote the development of space activities and respond primarily to the need of intellectual property protection by the States and private entities.

---

[1] Outer Space Treaty, 1967, Article 2.

[2] Anna Maria Balsano, Intellectual Property within Public International Research Organizations: The Example of the European Space Agency, *The Proceedings of the 36th Colloquium on the Law of Outer Space*, IISL 3 (1993).

[3] Office of Technology Licensing, University of Florida, Invention and Inventorship to Potential Investors, available at <http://www.rgp.ufl.edu/otl/inventorship.html> (last visited May 10, 2006).

[4] Patent Ordinance (Cap. 514), s. 94 (1).

[5] Patent Ordinance (Cap. 514), s. 94 (2).

[6] ESA Council Information Document: The ISS Crew Code of Conduct, ESA/C (2000)14, February 29, 2000.

[7] Andre Farand, Astronauts' Behavior onboard the International Space Station: Regulatory Framework, available at <http://portal.unesco.org/shs/en/file_download.php/785db0eec4e0cdfc43e1923624154cccFarand.pdf> (last visited May 11, 2006).

[8] The ISS Crew Code of Conduct, Section V.

[9] Patent Ordinance (Cap. 514), s. 96.

[10] Sa'id Mosteshar (Ed.), Research and Invention in Outer Space: Liability and Intellectual Property Rights 193 (Martinus Nijhoff Publishers: Dordrecht, 1995).

[11] The Manual of Patent Examining Procedure of the U.S. Patent and Trademark Office, s. 2113, quoting *In Re Thorpe*, 777 F.2d 695, 698, 227 USPQ 964, 966 (Fed.Cir. 1985).

[12] *SmithKline Beecham Corp. v. Apotex Corp.*, Fed. Cir., No. 04-1522, decided February 24, 2006.

[13] Section 305 (a) 1-2 of the 1958 National Aeronautics and Space Act, P.L. 85-569, as amended.

[14] Intellectual Property and the International Space Station: Creation, Use, Transfer, and Ownership and Protection, prepared by the Office of the General Counsel, National Aeronautics and Space Administration, September 1999, available at <http://www.hq.nasa.gov/ogc/iss/index.html> (last visited April 29, 2006).

[15] For a brief outline of some of the significant differences between CRADAs and Space Act Agreements, see *id.*

[16] Space Act, section 203 (c) 5.

[17] *Id.* Section 305 (a).

[18] 42 U.S.C. section 2473 (c) (5) and (6).

[19] Part II: Relationship of Intellectual Property Provisions in the ISS Agreements to NASA's Agreement Authority and Policies, in Intellectual Property and the International Space Station: Creation, Use, Transfer, Ownership and Protection, available at <http://www.hq.nasa.gov/ogc/iss/main.html> (last visited May 3, 2006).

[20] Space Act Agreement, Annex I sample clause 1.2.e.e. II-III.

[21] Space Act Agreement, Annex I sample clause 1.2.d.d.

[22] ESA/C/290, rev. 5.

[23] ESA/C/CLV?Res.4 (Final).

[24] General Provision, Clause 37.

[25] ESA Resolution, Chapter II: Rules

concerning Information, Data and Intellectual Property, section I.

[26] O. Vorobieva, Intellectual Property Rights with Respect to Inventions Created in Space, in Sa'id Mosteshar (Ed.), *Research and Invention in Outer Space: Liability and Intellectual Property Rights* 181-187 (Martinus Nijhoff Publishers: Dordrecht, 1995).

[27] Office of Technology Licensing, *supra* note 3.

[28] Marguerite B. Broadwell, ISS Commercial Development Manager, National Aeronautics and Space Administration, Intellectual Property and the Economic Development of the International Space Station, Presentation on the Space Technology and Applications International Forum (STAIF-2000), Albuquerque, NM, February 2000.

[29] Stephaniel Paul, Joint Ownership of Patents: A to Z, available at <http://wwe.legalzoom.com/articles/article_content/article14005.html> (last visited May 3, 2006).

[30] Space Act Agreement 3.5.10.2.

[31] IGA 1998, Article 21 (2).

[32] Leo B. Malagar & Marlo Apalisok Magdoza-Malagar, International law of Outer Space and the Protection of Intellectual Property Rights, 17 Boston University International Law Journal 363-364 (Fall 1999).

[33] ISS Legal Framework, available at <http://www.esa.int/esaHS/ESAH700VMOC_iss_0.html> (last visited on March 29, 2006).

[34] IGA 1998, Article 21 (3).

[35] IGA 1998, Article 21 (4) provides.

[36] Dan L. Burk, Protection of Trade Secrets in Outer Space Activity: A Study in Federal Pre-emption, 23 *Seton Hall Law Review* 563 (1993).

[37] Chukeat Noichim, The Protection of Intellectual Property Rights in Outer Space of the EU and Thailand, available at <http://www.thailawforum.com/articles/ipspacenoichim.html> (last visited May 15, 2006).

[38] Erickson & Fisher, Mars Society Steering Committee, Mars Foundation, Treasurer & Design Team, Space Patents: Intellectual Property in Outer Space, presentation at the 8th Mars Society Convention, August 12, 2005, available at <http://www.marshome.org/files2/SPACE-PATENTS-MS2005.ppt> (last visited May 11, 2006).

[39] European Space Agency, Intellectual Property Rights and Space Activities in Europe, ESA Publication Division: the Netherlands, 4-5 (1997).

[40] R. Oosterlinck, Intellectual Property and Space Activities, *The Proceedings of the 26th Colloquium on the Law of Outer Space*, IISL, October 10-15, 1983.

[41] Paris Convention, Article 5 ter.

[42] TRIPs, Article 27.

[43] Outer Space Treaty, Article 8.

[44] Patent Cooperation Treaty, Article 8.

[45] Alejandro Piera, Intellectual Property in Space Activities: An Analysis of the United States Patent Regime, 29 *Air & Space Law*, No. 1, 50-51 (February 2004).

[46] Patent Perspectives, available at <http://www.ladas.com/patents/patpers.html> (last visited on April 29, 2006).

[47] A.M. Balsano, ESA Legal Affairs, Paris, Intellectual Property Rights and Space Activities, available at <http://esapub.esrin.esa.it/ecsl/ecsl15/ecsl15ba.

htm> (last visited May 11, 2006).

By Any Other Means – Some Remarks to Interpretation of Article II Space Treaty

by Gyula Gál

IAC – 06-E.6.2.A.08

Péter Pázmány Catholic University
Budapest

I

To this day in six moon-landings only twelve astronauts touched the surface of the Moon. The last one 34 years ago. Next target is Mars – may be in some decades. Interplanetary travel is subject of science fiction.

Despite of realities, without human presence on the Moon and other celestial bodies clever business-men exploiting invincible human credulousness could establish a world-wide trade in outer space real estate.

The best-known space-broker is the company founded by Mr. Denis Hope. His website informs us that his "Lunar Embassy" is the only company in the world to be recognized to possess a legal basis for selling and registering extraterrestrial properties. A declaration of ownership was filed with the American government 26 years ago, to ensure legal basis for the sale of such properties within the confirms of our solar system. Mr. Hope also sent notice of his claim to the Russian government and the United Nations. (1) They did not protest – this silence proves that the Lunar Embassy deeds are valid. (Qui tacet, negat!)

Mr. Hope alleges that 2,524.728 people are already proud owners on the Moon – two former U.S. presidents and 40 NASA employees among them – 945.344 are Mars-owners. (2)

It is a satisfaction to know that Moon Embassy has never and will never sell a past or planned NASA landing site on any celestial body, and the moon Europa of Jupiter will be reserved as a heavenly national park. (3)

The website cautions against copy cat companies, "highly irresponsible pretenders", offering unauthorized products. One of them even calls themselves "consulate" to copy the Lunar Embassy.

A German pensioner Martin Jürgens protested against the activity of Mr. Hope alleging, that the Moon was donated to one of his ancestors by Frederic II (the Great). (4) An Italian woman claimed that Lunar Embassy sold two plots which she purchased from a company named "Celestial Garden". She sued for fraud and petitioned the White House. (5)

Gregory Nemetz U.S. citizen in 2003 filed a claim against NASA and the State Department. The NEAR Shoemaker spacecraft in 2001 landed on asteroid 433 Eros. As owner of this celestial body he demanded a parking-storage fee. This case Nemetz vs. U.S. has been the first case in United States courts concerning real property rights in outer space.

As a matter of fact, the business activity of the Lunar Embassy basically has nothing to do with space law. Mr. Hope and others do not own the Moon by a simple declaration of ownership Not even by registration of their claim anywhere. No legal systems of regulation of real property permit acquisition of property based upon nothing more than a claim of ownership. (6)

All civilized private law systems accept the roman law principles of property rights: possession needs both the intention (animus) and physical apprehension of a thing (corpus). (7)

Mr. Hope as previously other persons, science-fiction fan clubs who isolated without internet made the same, is no owner by mere declaration of ownership. Consequently he can not transfer ownership in accordance with the Roman law principle "nemo plus juris transferre potest, quam ipse habet." (8)

II

Absurd though it may appear, the Outer Space business of Mr. Hope as a catalyst contributed to discussions on real property right in the theory of space law. Namely to analysis of treaty law concerning possibility or prohibition of claim to property on real estates on the Moon and other celestial bodies.

The principle of non-appropriation as a fundamental rule of space law stated in Article II of the Space Treaty reads:

> Outer space including the Moon and other celestial bodies, is not subject to national appropriation by claim of sovereignty, by means of use or occupation, or by any other means

Article XI al. 2 of the Moon Agreement for the Moon and other celestial bodies within the solar system repeats it literally, adding in al. 3:

> Neither the surface nor the subsurface of the Moon, nor any part thereof or natural resources in place shall become property of any state, international intergovernmental organization, national organization or non-governmental entity or of any natural person.

The Outer Space Treaty in Article II contrary to national appropriation does not refer to the acquisition of private property on any part of the surface of the Moon . The Moon Agreement excludes it expressis verbis. This difference could be interpreted in the way, that a contrario: the principle of Article II of the Space Treaty concerns only non-private appropriation.

The Space Treaty till today has been ratified by 97 the Moon Agreement only by 11 states, all being parties to the Space Treaty. In later case, due to this interpretation the parties to the Moon Agreement would be at least for the celestial bodies of the solar system in an unequal legal situation, being bound by a broader prohibition than other parties to the Space Treaty.

The grammatical interpretation of Article II applying earth-bound legal terminology based mainly on Roman law principles may rise certain doubts. Legal notions linked to the tangible earth should be analyzed, in context with extraterrestrial conditions allowing rather per analogiam application of traditional legal terms.

"Appropriation" itself does not belong to the traditional international law terminology. It is connected with civil law "proprietas" being the result of appropriation.

"Claim of sovereignty" is undoubtedly an act of a subject of international law, an unilateral state act. Article II designates the effective implementation of claim of sovereignty occupation, as means of national appropriation.

"Occupation" in the international law terminology consists in establishing sovereignty over a territory not under the authority of any other state. Act of a state extending sovereign rights to a terra nullius. This international law occupation goes back again to the Roman law notion of acquisition of property (res nullius cedit occupanti). In this sense a non-national entity may be a "first person to appropriate an unappropriated thing". (9)

Article II prohibits *national* appropriation by use. From the viewpoint of the question whether this prohibition extends also to acquisition of real property by private entities can not be meaningless that the Space Treaty considered private space activities too. According to Article VI states parties to the treaty shall be responsible for national activities carried on by governmental agencies or by non-governmental entities.

Such activity may be a certain kind of *use* carried on by private entities prohibited by Article II as means of national appropriation. (10) In the debates of Space Treaty the relationship between use and appropriation was noted by the Belgian delegation suggesting Article II. It was their view that use of any kind does not produce a condition of titles to property in private law. (11) Though concerning "use of outer space" in Article I and use in this context there was no unanimity, this interpretation was not rejected.

Article II does not contain a taxative, itemized enumeration of means of national appropriation. It is exemplificative referring to denominated possible kinds of appropriation adding the words "by any other means".

The meaning of this additional words is disputed in space law theory. The analysis of the travaux préparatoire in the excellent paper of *R. J. Lee–F. K. Eylward* demonstrates that the formulation of Article II was focused on states and not on natural or juridical persons. Nevertheless several participating states affirmed the application of Article II to property rights. They had the opinion that "appropriation" included both the establishment of sovereignty and creating private law property. No state has positively stated that Article II does not extend to prohibit property rights on celestial bodies. (12)

Exclusion of appropriation by civil law claims as "other means" is accepted by majority of Authors. To quote some views:

The mere fact that Article II does not prohibit "private appropriation" does not give private entities authority to immovable real property (*W. N. White*). (13) If states cannot appropriate the extraterrestrial realms, than a fortiori neither can their nationals (*V. Pop*). (14) Article II prohibits also acquisition of private law property. It is clarified and completed by Article XI of the Moon Agreement (*A. Bueckling*). (15) The assertion of claims of ownership of areas of space including the Moon and other celestial bodies is contrary to the non-appropriation principle of Article II of the Outer Space Treaty (*P. M. Sterns–L. I. Tennen*). (16)

Some authors refer to a not meaningless aspect of excluding private appropriation. When Article II. would have application only to governmental entities it may be possible for states to circumvent the prohibitions contained in the Treaty singly by "privatizing" contravening activities (*R. V. Lee–F. K. Eylward*). (17) From establishing private property in a roundabout way exclusive rights of states could be derived (*W. Heymer*). (18)

The teleological and systematic interpretation supports these views. Purpose of Article II is to exclude any exclusive claims to outer space or parts thereof. Article I par. 1 states that outer space shall be free for exploration and use by all states without discrimination of any kind. Property involve exclusive right to possess and use something – in this case a certain part of the Moon or other celestial bodies, excluding others. Reading together the two provisions can be concluded, that private appropriation of any part of celestial bodies would be an "other means" in the sense of Article II and contrary to Article I of the Space Treaty.

III

The "Lunar Embassy" alleges to have legal right to sell real property on the Moon based on registration of its claim in conformity with local (national) rules of procedures. This argument – if correct – would mean applying national jurisdiction to a celestial body. This follows more evidently from the allegation, that the claim has been footed also on the so called Homestead Act legislated by the Congress in 1862. This act at that time intended to stimulate the post-civil war westward movement giving to settlers public land for a nominal fee. (19) The Act is current, but the available land is restricted to Alaska and Territories (possessions of the United States) and by no means to the Moon and other celestial bodies.

In the Case U.S. vs. Nemitz the General Counsel of NASA refusing the claim of appropriation of an asteroid stated: it is unlike an individual's claim for seabed minerals, which was considered and debated by the U.S. Congress that subsequently enacted a statute The Deep Seabed Hard Mineral Resource Act expressly authorizing such claims. *There is no similar statute related in outer space.* This motivation raises the logical question: could the U.S. Congress in this way enact a statute authorizing U.S. citizens to appropriate an asteroid? (20) By no means. Article II excludes national appropriation. It includes the exclusion of application of national legislations. Hence no national laws on private ownership of immovable property or related issues could ever apply to the Moon and other celestial bodies.

In a background paper on "Extraterrestrial Property and Space Law: Facts and Fiction" circulated by the Moon Embassy we find the following pretentious statement: "On the Moon itself or on any other planets apart from the Earth, apart from the laws of the Head Cheese (Mr. Hope) currently no law exists". (21)

What really does not exist on the Moon is a Civil Code of Outer Space with rules of acquisition of real property, transfer of property etc. *W. N. White Jr.* author of excellent studies on this subject presented a remarkable Draft for a multilateral treaty regarding jurisdiction and real property rights in Outer Space. (22)

According to this uniform civil law regulation to be accepted by the parties to the multilateral treaty: "Private non-governmental owners who or which inhabit, maintain and/or operate a space facility for a period of at least one year shall be entitled to formal recognition and registration of certain rights designated "real property rights". Among them the right to exclude natural persons and legal entities from the space facility and its related safety zone, the exclusive right to appropriate resources in the same place, the right to sell real property rights to other natural persons or legal entities.

The treaty would admit acquisition of real property for private entities and states as well – excluding sovereign rights of owner states stating that real property rights which states confer pursuant to this treaty shall not provide the basis for any claims of territorial sovereignty in outer space and on celestial bodies.

The proposal provides creating a civil law order on the Moon and other celestial bodies named by the author "regime of limited property rights in the absence of territorial sovereignty", (23) or of functional property rights. (24)

A treaty of this kind accepting real property on celestial bodies, nevertheless, would be for parties to the Outer Space Treaty which do not adhere, inter alios acta. They could insist on the prohibitions of Article II. The limited property rights suggested would be based upon the jurisdiction conferred by Article VIII and not territorial sovereignty prohibited by Article II. As the author admits, the result is a new form of quasi property rights which are in reality a delegation of jurisdictional authority to their national citizens. (25) According to this conception states are free to enact property laws without seeking the approval of other states. Article VIII, however, is about jurisdiction of the state of registry over the objects and over any personnel thereof launched into outer space creating no property rights on the landing place of the space objects.

Enacting property laws for celestial bodies?

In his commentary to the case Nemitz vs. U.S. W. White states that the Outer Space Treaty is not self-executing under U.S. law and the case illustrates the need for governments to legally address the issue of property rights in their national legislation. S. T. should be implemented by national space legislation on property rights. (26)

I share the opinion of authors who refuge this interpretation of S. T. Article II is self-executing not needing national legislative actions to be operative. (27) National space acts do not implement space treaties in the sense of adding anything to the legal regime created by international space law. They intend e.g. to make rules of authorization and continuous supervision, or for domestic consequences of liability for national space activities.

May I quote as a conclusion ILA Resolution 1/2002: "What is by no means permitted is any kind of national appropriation of areas of the Moon and other celestial bodies. Any claims to private property on the Moon and other celestial bodies undermine this clear prohibition of self-executing character. States are therefore even under a legal obligation to prevent the coming into existence of such private claims to property in order to avoid their international legal responsibility." (28)

Footnotes

1.) http://archives.cnn.com/2000/tech/space/11/20/lunar.land
The Hungarian agency of L. A. sold Moon plots "cheepest real estate in the Universe" for abt. USD 8–180!
2.) http://www.lunarembassy.com/lunar/shops.lasso
Lunar Embassy World Headquarters website informed us that Mr. Hope on 19th May 2006 has survived a plan crash "much to the great delight of over 2 million lunar property owners".
3.) http://www.lunarembassy.com/ls/lespacelaw.e.shtml
4.) Mr. Hope in a CNN interview 20th November 2000: "he sent me a long letter in German which roughly translated said I should cease and send him all money I had made".
5.) *W. N. White*: Interpreting Article II of the Outer Space Treaty. Proceedings IISL Coll. 2004, p. 171
6.) *W. N. White*: Nemitz vs. U.S. The First Real Estate Property Case in the United States Courts. Proceedings IISL Coll. 2004, p. 342
Witty comparison of *V. Pop*: Masai tribesmen claim they own all the cows by divine command. If a claim alone would entail ownership, this would entitle the Masai to universal cattle ownership. In: Extraterrestrial Real Estate: Debunking the Myth. Proceedings IISL Coll. 2004, p. 335
7.) *Th. Collettsanders*: The Institutes of Justinian. London etc. 1948, p. 131
8.) In Hungarian Civil Code § 117 "... property can be acquired from its owner."
9.) *J. A. C. Thomas*: Textbook of Roman Law. Amsterdam etc. 1976, p. 93
10.) *M. A. Dauses*: Das Weltraumrecht im Rechtsgefüge. Beiträge zum Luft- und Weltraumrecht. Festschrift zu Ehren von Alex Meyer. Köln etc. p. 293 "Acquisition of exclusive territorial rights by uses". H. B. Bittlinger: Hoheitsgewalt und Kontrolle im Weltraum. Köln etc. 1988, p. 136
11.) *C. Q. Christol*: The Modern International Law of Outer Space. New York etc. 1982, p. 40
12.) *R. J. Lee–F. K. Eylward*: Article II of the Outer Space Treaty and Human Presence on Celestial Bodies. Proceedings IISL Coll. 2005, pp. 95–96
13.) *W. N. White*: Implications of a Proposal for Real Property Rights in Outer Space. Proceedings IISL Coll. 1999, p. 371
14.) *V. Pop*: Extraterrestrial Real Estate: Debunking the Myth. Proceedings IISL Coll. 2004, p. 336
15.) *A. Bueckling*: Der Weltraumvertrag. Köln etc. 1980, p. 61
16.) *P. M. Sterns–L. I. Tennen*: Private Enterprise and the Resources of Outer Space. Proceedings IISL Coll. 2005, p. 247
17.) Note 13, p. 96
18.) *W. Heymer*: Rechtsfragen der Nutzung des Weltraums und der Himmelskörper durch Privatunternehmen. Festschrift A. Meyer p. 376
19.) *M. Martin–L. Gerber*: Dictionary of American History. Totowa–New Jersey 1981, pp. 292–293
20.) Cit. in *W. N. White* Note 6, p. 340
21.) http://www.lunarembassy.com/ls/lespacelaw.e.shtml
22.) *W. N. White*: Proposal for a Multilateral Treaty Regarding Jurisdiction and Real Property Rights in Outer Space. Proceedings IISL Coll. 2000, pp. 245-253
23.) Note 13, p. 371
24.) Idem: Real Property Rights in Outer Space. Proceedings IISL Coll. 1997, p. 381
25.) Note 5, p. 176
26.) Note 6, p. 349
27.) Note 16, p. 249
28.) ILA Res. 1/2002 with Regard to the Common Heritage of Mankind Principle in the Moon Agreement by Professor Dr. Stephan Hobe. Proceedings IISL Coll. 2005, p. 536

Session 3:
COOPERATION IN SPACE ACTIVITIES, WITH SPECIAL FOCUS ON REMOTE SENSING

Chairmen: Joanne Gabrynowicz
José Monserrat Filho

Rapporteur: Martha Mejia-Kaiser

IAC-06-E6.3.1

EUROPEAN TRANSFORMATION COUNTRIES ON THEIR PATH TO ESA

Mahulena Hofmann
Professor of European Law and Transformation Studies, Faculty of Law, University of Giessen, Germany; (on leave from Max Planck Institute for Comparative Public Law and International Law, Heidelberg, Germany)
mhofmann@mpil.de

ABSTRACT

ESA established legal relations with transformation countries in the 1900s by signing Framework Agreements with the Czech Republic, Hungary, Poland and Romania. In 2001, a new agreement opening up opportunities for their closer participation in ESA programs has been defined: The pertinent European Cooperating State Agreement was signed by Hungary in April 2003, followed by the Czech Republic in November 2003 and by Romania in February 2006. These bilateral agreements constitute the legal basis for developing Plans for European Cooperation State Charter (PECS). Their main objective is to associate the transformation countries with ESA programs and activities and to prepare them in the most efficient manner for their accession to the ESA Convention or their status of ESA Associate Members. During this process, several legal problems must be solved.

I. INTRODUCTION

It is generally known that, before 1989, the majority of the space research in the former Eastern Bloc countries was organized in the framework of the *Intercosmos* program initiated by the USSR. This was an asymmetrical international structure with the USSR supplying in general the budget and launching sites, and other Member States participating in various optional programs but being without any substantial influence on its decision-making processes. The program run on the basis of a temporary Agreement on Cooperation of Working Groups signed in 1968, accompanied in 1976[1] by a more general Agreement on Cooperation in the Exploration and Use of Outer Space for Peaceful Purposes.

After 1989, the situation changed. Space research ceased to play its strategic role in Eastern and Central European countries; the *Intercosmos* program and most of the national space programs were dissolved. Remaining national research sites and institutions scattered throughout the territories of these countries suffered severe financial shortages. In the changed political situation, they started to search for potential partners in the "traditional" European structures, most significantly in ESA and the European Communities.

This mutual cooperation has evolved on a corresponding legal framework which has been developed during the years. It must be seen, however, that the next significant steps in this development are now being faced by the Parties of the respective legal instruments: On the one hand, this will be the enlargement of the European Union by Bulgaria and Romania and by their space structures, most probably on 1 January 2007, and, on the other hand, ESA will have to evaluate and decide upon the question of granting the status of Associate Members or Member States to

Hungary and the Czech Republic in 2008 and Romania in 2011 at the latest: According to Article 15.1 of the respective European Cooperating State Agreements binding at present these States with ESA, the question of granting the status of Associate Members or Member States of the Agency has to be examined at the latest one year before the expiry of these Agreements. This means, that, as of today, there remain at least two years for formulating a respective ESA policy; some issues can be, however, explored in advance.

II. THE LEGAL FRAMEWORK OF THE RELATION OF THE TRANSFORMATION COUNTRIES WITH ESA

The first step of the mutual treaty relations of the Hungary, Romania, Poland, and the Czech Republic, respectively, with ESA were Framework Agreements concluded in the 1990s.[2] They established the basis for cooperation as defined in Article XIV of the ESA Convention.[3] As one result of this development, the Czech Republic and Hungary have been participating in one of ESA's optional programs, PRODEX, since 1998.

In 1999, a new process started redefining the participation in the European space program of these four European countries. ESA´s policy was that a cooperating status was better suited for the needs and industrial and financial capacities of these countries than other forms of mutual cooperation foreseen in Article XIV of the ESA Convention – namely Associate Membership.[4] Hence, the Framework Agreements with the Czech Republic[5], Hungary[6] and Romania[7] were substituted by new agreements - the European Cooperating State Agreements (ECSAs) in 2003 (with Romania in 2006). The precondition for concluding these agreements was that the candidates must had already signed a Framework Agreement and they must be European. Poland has not decided to become being bound by such an ECS yet.

The ECSAs are bilateral agreements between Non-member States and ESA[8] and allow the partner countries to participate indirectly in all ESA procurements and activities. According to their preambles, they should lead to a "possible accession to the ESA Convention".[9]

Only in 2001, ESA accepted the policy of the PECS program - the Plan for European Cooperating States (PECS). The objective of this policy is to create more favorable conditions for such European Cooperation States (ECS) for wider cooperation without their full financial participation and without exposing them to the "threat of possible economic losses in the already established, highly competitive ESA-system".[10] The aim of the PECS is to support the creation and strengthening of the respective domestic capacity employable in European space research, to improve the understanding of the Agency's organization and rules applicable in competition environment, as well as to develop the infrastructure required for full participation in Agency programs. The overall objective of the PECS is to associate the countries in question with the Agency's programs and activities and to prepare them in the most efficient manner for possible future accession to the ESA Convention. These plans are concluded for a time period of five years.

The benefits of all rights granted by the Plan can be enjoyed only after the signing of an additional instrument, the PECS Charter defining the terms and conditions of the financial contributions of the participating States to the Plan. This PECS Charter was signed by the representatives of Hungary in 2003 and of the Czech Republic in 2004. It is expected that Romania will sign a similar instrument in 2007.

The implementation of the PECS program showed, however, some difficulties: The idea to create an autonomous structure of Cooperating States with its own institutional mechanism was only slowly followed by the ECS States. With presently only two "full" members of this system - Hungary and the Czech Republic - it was and is obviously impossible to design any decision-making procedure based on majority votes. Only the recent accession of Romania to the ECS opened the perspective of Romania joining the PECS program and, thereby, making its structures meaningful. It is also not quite clear whether Poland which was in fact bound by a Framework Agreement of 1994 would be ready to join the PECS system or whether it awaits the next opportunity to apply directly for an associate or full membership.

III. The Perspective of a Membership in ESA

The ESA Convention introduced a flexible framework which enables to adapt the form of association of States to its structure in accordance to mutual needs.

a) Full Membership (Article XXII of the ESA Convention)

According to Article XXII of the ESA Convention, any State may accede thereto, subsequent to a pertinent decision of the ESA Council taken by the unanimous vote of all Member States. A State that wishes to accede to this Convention shall notify the Director General, who shall inform the Member States of this request at least three months before it is submitted to the Council for decision. Further obligations connected with adhering to ESA are of financial nature: The newcomers are expected to pay an "entrance fee" which relates to the current value of the assets of the Agency and shall be fixed by the ESA Council by a two-thirds majority of Member States (Article XIII para 4 of the ESA Convention).

As a consequence of full membership, Member States have to participate in the ESA activities and shall contribute to its fixed common costs (Article I.3 of the ESA Convention). Representatives of the Member States are present in the Council and take part in its decision processes (Article XI of the ESA Convention).

From the point of view of the former ECSs, the full membership as defined in the Preamble of the ECS Agreements remains to be the final goal. As the first one of the former *Intercosmos* States, Hungary notified its intention to apply for full membership this year. It is no secret, however, that this perspective meets some reservations in some of the current Member States, especially the powerful ones: On the one hand, also they are convinced that this enlargement would constitute an important step, from the political point of view, by strengthening ESA´s weight on the international playground. Moreover, they are no more strategic reasons why to keep the transformation states out: Several former *Intercosmos* States - the Czech Republic, Hungary, and Poland - as well as Baltic States, Slovakia, and Slovenia are, since 1 May 2004[11], Member States of the European Union and, as such, share the Union's space activities e.g. in the Galileo program with Bulgaria and

Romania very probably joining in 2007.[12] The hesitation stems, however, from the misgivings as to the consequences of such a development in light of one of ESA's main principles (one state, one vote) that gives to "smaller" States the same powers in the decision making processes as to the "big" ones and from the fear of overloading and slowing down the whole ESA decision-making procedure. The second group of reservations concerns the industrial and financial capacities of transformation States to cope with the present and future programs of ESA.

b) Participation in ESA Programs (Article XIV.2 of the ESA Convention)
As an alternative to full membership, cooperation on the basis of Article XIV.2 of the ESA Convention might be theoretically considered. Such a decision has to be taken unanimously by the ESA Council; participating States do contribute only to the activities of the programs concerned but shall have the right to vote in the Council when it examines matters dealing with the program concerned.[13] As to the knowledge of this author, this option has not been suggested to the ECSs and, thus, does not seem, at present, to play any serious role in the discussion on the future of the transformation States.

c) Associate Membership (Article XIV.3 of the ESA Convention)
This form of association of Non-member States with ESA has been introduced in 1971 as a better option than the observer status known and applied by ESA's predecessor, the ESRO. Also in this case, the ESA Council decides unanimously about granting this status, the only precondition being the participation of the State in "at least studies on future programs" as defined in Article V.1 a.i. of the ESA Convention. The details of mutual rights and obligations have been defined in General Guidelines of Associate Membership approved by ESA Council in 1985.[14] In principle, Associated States are obliged to participate in the general budget of the ESA; however, they have only an observation status in the ESA Council – which means that they are not allowed to vote and the policy of industrial return shall not be applied to them. Because of the wide range of possibilities for participation in the ESA activities and the support of the present ESA members for this form of association, this option might play an important role in the discussions on ESA enlargement strategies.

d) Other Forms of Cooperation according to Article XIV.1 of the ESA Convention
The full or associate memberships are not the only possibilities of cooperation of Non-member States with ESA structures. Article XIV.1 of the ESA Convention allows for a whole range of forms, e.g. the presently applicable cooperation agreements with transformation countries (Partnership Agreements, ECSs). As a substitute for a full membership, the prolongation of the PECS program is discussed as an alternative among ESA members; the full membership should follow at the point in time when the potential newcomers would be prepared to bear their financial and industrial burdens and to fulfill all their duties. The difficulties connected with the implementation of the PECS program until now do not give, however, any substantial reason for hoping that this perspective could be really fruitful.

e) Status of Observer (Rule Nr. 23.1 of the ESA Rules of Procedure)
Rule Nr. 23.1 of the ESA Rules of Procedure[15] contains an old instrument

of the former ESRO, the possibility of granting a status of observer to a Non-member State. As other forms of cooperation, also this decision must be taken unanimously by the members of the ESA Council. It entitles the Non-member State to be represented in the Council; there are no financial or industrial obligation connected with this status. The Member States are rather reluctant to this form of cooperation considering it as being very passive from the position of the States concerned and as not bringing any positive results for ESA as such.

IV. National Space Legislation as a Precondition of ESA membership?

The ESA Convention defines the formal precondition for the membership in this international organization (notification to the Director General, unanimous vote of all Member States, "entrance fee"). After accessing the ESA, the Member States are expected to fulfill their obligations under the Convention, to participate in the mandatory activities referred to in Article V.1 a of the ESA Convention and to contribute to the fixed common costs of the Agency the scale being based on the average national income of each Member State and adopted by the Council as a rule by two-thirds majority of all Member States (Article XIII para 1 of the ESA Convention). In case Member States cease to fulfill their obligations, they shall cease to be member of the Agency on a decision of the Council taken by a two-thirds majority of all Member States (Article XVIII of the ESA Convention).

From the perspective of international law, States Parties to international obligations must fulfill them in good faith. Concerning the form and methods of their implementation, neither general international law nor the ESA Convention prescribes by which measures under national law States have to adopt in order to fulfill this obligation of implementation. Thus, from the perspective of accessing ESA, the drafting and adoption of national space law is not necessary. This conclusion can be illustrated by the practice of the present members States: Out of 17 ESA members, only four - Belgium, Norway, Sweden and the United Kingdom - have approved such legislation until now.

The question remains, however, whether the adoption of national space legislation would facilitate accession to ESA and would foster the fulfillment of the obligations of a Member State.

The former practice of those States which have adopted such national space legislation shows that it consists, as a rule, of the following "building blocs":[16] the authorization of space activities including the activities of non-governmental entities in accordance with Art. VI para 2 OST, the continuing supervision of space activities including those of non-governmental entities (Art. VI par 2 OST), the registration of space objects (Article II para 1 of the Registration Convention), as well as the issue of indemnification.

As already mentioned, none of these blocs must be obligatorily regulated by national legislation from the perspective of international law. From the perspective of national law, the majority of legal orders of transformation countries even guarantee the implementation of their international obligations by means of their constitutional order, giving international law precedence before national statutory regulations. The only question which remains to be answered is, thus, whether adoption of such national "space" legislation would enhance the implementation of international obligations.

The criterion of "enhancing" does not belong to the strict legal argumentation but can be assessed from the point of view of the expected efficiency of the considered legislation.[17] In general, it can hardly be denied that creating procedures for the authorization and supervision of space activities would bring certain transparency into these mechanisms and would, thus, also enable entities from other Member States to assess more easily their rights and obligations. Also the establishment of a national registry of space objects could clarify several questions - e.g. the procedure of getting the appropriate information - which might be of interest for entities interested in space activities. Third, the national legislation could establish the statutory framework of an institution responsible for the national implementation of the ESA Convention. This step would give this institution a firm legal basis which could not be changed by a mere administrative measure. All these preconditions seem to be, however, meaningful only in case of a certain intensity of expected space activities. In view of the not exactly central character of these activities in some transformation countries, the efficiency of such national legislation could be rather low. In this regard, the experiences of ESA Member States should be studied thoroughly.

V. AN EXAMPLE: THE CZECH REPUBLIC

The Czech (former Czechoslovak) space research was part of the program *Intercosmos*. The central body for organizing its activities was a *Czechoslovak Commission for the Exploration and Peaceful Exploitation of Outer Space* which was dissolved after *Intercosmos's* dissolution in 1991. After 1991, the absence of any State involvement in space activities and of any coordination center and meaningful state support led to the breakdown of scientific and production teams and usually to their disappearance.[18] In this situation, official relations with ESA were seen as a way out of this situation. The pertinent initiative of a group of experts found support at the Ministry of Education which became the national institution charged with the implementation of this new cooperation.

In 1996, the Framework Agreement between the Government of the Czech Republic and ESA concerning Cooperation in the Exploration and Use of Outer Space for Peaceful Purposes was signed, approved by the Czech Parliament and ratified by the President of the Republic.[19] According to its Article 9, the Agreement entered into force on 5 November 1998. The aim of the Agreement was to establish a framework for mutual cooperation (Article 1). Mutual obligations were of only general character: The Parties obliged "to keep themselves informed" and they defined areas offering a "potential" for cooperation. Moreover, ESA declared itself "favorably disposed towards making available... hardware no longer required for its programs" (Article 2). For the execution of the obligations of this Agreement, each Party was expected to "normally meet its own costs". The most important developments took place on the institutional level: ESA was given the status of a legal person established in the Czech Republic (Article 6) and for disputes concerning the interpretation or application of the Agreement arbitration tribunals were envisaged (Article 8). According to Article 3, the Parties obliged themselves to designate a point of contact which was tasked to coordinate actions relating to the implementation of this Agreement.

As a direct consequence of the 1996 Agreement, a coordination structure able to respond to the needs of the Agreement started to be established in the Czech Republic. The Ministry of Education, entrusted with the implementation of the Agreement, established a Council for the Cooperation with ESA in 1997, later renamed as Czech Board for Space Activities (CBSA), composed of members from all various areas of space activities. The Council serves as an advisory organ of the Ministry, as well as a coordinating organ in the sphere of space activities.

The executive part of the activites of the Board for Space Activities and the nucleus of the institutional framework of the contacts with ESA is the Czech Space Office (CSO), a non-profit association established in November 2003. Its main bodies are the Management Board, the Supervisory Board and the Managing Director. The main acitvities of the Czech Space Office are to serve as an information and advisory centre in space activities including international cooperation, a contact point for communication with ESA, as well as a contact point between the Czech professional institutions and experts and for foreign organisations interested in space activities in the Czech Republic.[20]

The work of CSO includes gathering and storing information about Czech space projects as well as information on foreign space programs relevant to the development of Czech space activities. It covers the management of databases of Czech institutions, both academia and industry, and data on space projects carried out in the Czech Republic, as well as their status and results. Last but not least, CSO serves as information point for the general public.[21] CSO also represents the Czech Republic in the High-level Space Policy Group jointly chaired by EC and ESA. In March 2004, a CSO representation has been opened in Germany.

From the present perspective, the dynamics of the institutional framework of the Czech space activities are corresponding to the intensity of the mutual relations and the number of common projects. A restructuring of the CSO from its present status of a non-profit association under Czech law into a new State institution is not excluded in the future but seems to be premature at this point.

In 2003, the Framework Agreement was replaced by the European Cooperating State Agreement (ECSA) which was - similarly to the procedure of adopting the Framework Agreement - approved by the Czech Parliament and ratified by the President of the Republic. Among the substantive obligations resulting from this Agreement are the entitlement of the Czech Republic to be "associated with implementation of the Agency programs ...with the exception of the Agency's basic Technology Research Program" (Article 2) and to have an access to the Agency facilities on a cost-reimbursable basis (Article 3). On the other side, the Czech Republic is obliged to support the European transportation systems (Article 3), to contribute financially to the ESA activities (Article 7) and to "discuss the convergence and complementarity of Czech industries" with the industries of the ESA member States" (Article 8). Concerning institutional arrangements, the Ministry of Education was declared an authority "responsible for the implementation of the Agreement" (Article 10).

According to its Article 13, the Czech Republic accepted the terms and conditions of the attached appendices, the most significant being the Plan for European Cooperating States (PECS) (Appendix 1). This Plan defined its purpose as to "associate the Czech Republic with Agency programs and to prepare it in the most efficient manner for possible accession" to the ESA Convention. It was intended to intensify the mechanisms of mutual cooperation by defining its areas, the amount of financial contribution of the Czech Republic (Art. II.4), as well as establishing a new institutional mechanism, the "PECS Committee" expected to monitor and control its implementation (Article II.1).

According to Article 14 of the ECS Agreement, the Agreement entered into force on the date of notification by the Czech Republic to the Agency of its approval by the adequate national organs (19 November 2004). The "enjoyment of the benefits and rights from the Agreement" was conditioned by the signing, by the Czech Republic, of a Charter of a Plan for European Cooperation States which defined the terms and conditions of the financial contribution of the Czech Republic to the PECS. This Charter had to be signed "at the latest one year after the signature" of the Agreement. In case "the said subscription had not occurred within the above time limit, the present Agreement would have been automatically terminated". The PECS Charter was signed by the representatives of the Czech Republic exactly in this term, namely on 24 November 2004.[22]

The ECS Agreement has been concluded for a period of five years starting from the date of signature of the PECS Charter (Article 15), which means until 24 November 2009. One year before the expiry of this Agreement, i.e. in November 2008, the Parties shall review the results of its implementation and shall examine ways and means of continuing or further developing such cooperation, in particular the possibility of the Czech Republic being granted the status of Associate Member or Member State of the Agency.

The results of this review can be hardly predicted. From the present point of view, it can be only repeated that until the accession of Romania to the PECS-system there was no possibility to establish its mechanism in practice which was expected to be based principally on the participation of at least three countries: According to Article 3.12 of the Appendix II of the ECS Agreement, the rules of procedure of the PECS Committee should be implemented and become fully applicable when at least three ECS have joined the PECS Committee. The next matter which will have to be considered, will be the readiness of the present members to approve the accession of the Czech Republic as a new Member State: As already mentioned before, according to Article XXII of the ESA Convention, a unanimous vote of all members will be necessary for this step which means that each of the present Member States can negatively affect the accession procedure even by its abstention in the Council.

Some changes have to be done also in the Czech Republic itself: First, it is generally recognized that all natural and legal persons, institutions and entities active in space research have to familiarize themselves more thoroughly with the aims and purposes of their involvement in ESA. Second, there is a strong necessity to improve the knowledge and understanding of all existing ESA mechanisms by those who are active in the Czech space initiatives, especially practical matters like how to fill a form for an ESA project.

Additional improvements are also called for as concerns the communication between the ESA organs and their Czech partners. Notwithstanding the plentitude of quite detailed legal regulations on the modalities of any ESA representation on the territory of the Cooperation States (e.g. Article 9 ESC Agreement), ESA has not yet established any such representation in the Czech Republic and, at least to the best of the knowledge available, no such plans have so far been disclosed.

Generally considered as a very positive step in the mutual relations is the invitation of the representatives of the Czech Republic to take part in a session of one of the ESA Councils - the Council on Earth Observation in May this year. This decision had to be taken by the Committee for International Relations – IRC, although it seems that, as yet, the general procedures for such decisions have not been clearly established.

In this situation, the CSO considers – while being aware of the difficulties connected with this status in the past - granting the status of observer (in ESA) to the Czech Republic in accordance with Rule 23 of the ESA Council Rules of Procedure as a provisional and additional solution connected with its present ECS status. In this transitory period in which the strategies of the Parties have not crystallized yet, it seems to be a solution which would enable the representatives of the Czech Republic to fast acquaint themselves with the ESA mechanisms and to prepare for the full membership in the future. In despite of the fact that so far no Non-member State has been granted this status *stricto sensu*, it is seen by the CSO as an optimal reflection of the state of the present formal and factual relations between ESA and the Czech Republic.

The question of elaborating national space legislation starts to be discussed in Czech Republic but its adoption seems to be premature in this point. According to Article 10 of the Constitution of the Czech Republic[23], promulgated international agreements, the ratification of which has been approved by the Parliament and which are binding on the Czech Republic, shall constitute a part of the legal order; should an international agreement make provision contrary to a statutory law, the international agreement shall be applied. All space treaties and ESA-Agreements were – in general - approved in this procedure; thus, their rules precede any conflicting national norms. As a consequence, the Czech Republic is e.g. obliged to authorize and supervise the space activities of its subjects, including non-state entities, to keep a register of space objects and is responsible for space activities of the entities under her control. If ratified by the national parliament and published in the respective national official collection of laws, also the ESA Convention would become part of the Czech national legal order and have applicatory precedence over domestic legal rules.

It is not excluded, however, that despite of this fact national space legislation will be adopted in the future. This step seems to be necessary at the latest if the Czech Space Agency should be given a form of a new State agency; this step could not be approved on another than a statutory basis. More probably, the competencies of the Agency, its relation to other State organs as well as mechanisms of its decision procedure would have to be defined in this statute. Moreover, the statute could also provide for the regulation of other issues such as the institutionalization of the space register or the procedure of licensing space activities.

VI. Conclusion

According to Article 15.1 of the ECS Agreement with the Czech Republic and fully in line with the ECSAs concluded with Hungary and Romania, the question of granting these States the status of Associate Members or Member States of the Agency has to be examined at the latest one year before the expiry of these Agreements. One of the possibilities envisaged in the Agreements would be the prolongation of the ECSAs by mutual agreement of its Parties (Article 15.2 of the ECSAs). This scenario seems to be, however, rather improbable: The implementation of the present PECS program faces difficulties connected with the hesitation of the transformation States to join its mechanisms and, thus, with the failing possibility to bring its institutional framework into effect.

The general conditions for accessing ESA are defined in Article XXII of the ESA Convention and the additional condition – the payment of an "entrance fee" - in Article XIII para 4 of the ESA Convention. For approval of the accession, a unanimous vote of the present members is necessary. Not the formal legal preconditions but this unanimity requirement might constitute a considerable obstacle for the accession of the transformation countries to ESA. In this situation, other forms of formal relationship with the ESA, such as Associate Membership or an observer status, might be taken into consideration.

From the perspective of international law and, as such, the ESA Convention, no elaboration of national space law is necessary for the implementation of the various forms of cooperation with Member- or Non-member States. The States have to guarantee the implementation of its rules and its appendices; the form of their implementation remains a matter of the domestic legal order.

This principle is applicable also as concerns the legal relations between ESA and the Czech Republic: At the time being, the national framework for these relations seems to be sufficient. In case the Czech Republic would, in the future, become either an Associate Member or full member of ESA, it is not excluded that the present structure of the national coordination of space activities will have to be modified and that the Czech Space Office will be rebuilt into a new State institution. In this case, the adoption of a statute regulating its position and competencies would be not only feasible but necessary.

The enlargement of ESA is not only a legal process, but is at first a process based on a political decision. The present Member States can by no means be forced to accept the newcomers – their decision is based only on their free will. However, accepting the transformation States with their *Intercosmos* know-how would terminate the anomaly of the cold-war period in the area of space activities as has already been done by the European Union.

---

[1] July 13, 1976.

[2] Agreement between the Government of Hungary and the European Space Agency Concerning Cooperation in the Exploration and Use of Outer Space for Peaceful Purposes of 1991, Romania of 1992, Poland of 1994 and the Czech Republic of 1996.

[3] CSE/CS(73)19, rev. 7.

[4] *C. Baudin*, Cooperation and International Agrements, Article XIV of the ESA Convention, Air & Space Law 23 (1998) 1, 8 -15.

[5] Nr. 111/2005 Coll. of International Treaties of the Czech Republic.

[6] ESA and Hungary sign European Cooperating State Agreement, http://www.spaceref.com/calendar.htmp?pid=2087.

[7] Romania becomes third ESA European Cooperating State, http://www.esa.int/esaCP/SEMI2HMVGJE_index_0.html.

[8] ESA stimulates scientific and industrial relations with four East European Countries, 4 October 2001, http://www.esa.int/esaCP/ASAMPTNW9SC.

[9] See e.g. the Preamble of the European Cooperating State Agreement between the Government of the Czech Republic and the European Space Agency, Nr. 111/2005 Coll. of the Czech Republic.

[10] Czech Republic signed plan for European Cooperation State (PECS) Agreement with ESA, http://www.czechspace.cz/CSO/PECSe/pecs.htm.

[11] Treaty Concerning the Accession of the Czech Republic, the Republic of Estonia, the Republic of Cyprus, the Republic of Latvia, the Republic of Lithuania, the Republic of Hungary, the Republic of Malta, the Republic of Poland, the Republic of Slovenia and the Slovak Republic to the European Union,
L 157/11, 21.6.2005.

[12] Treaty Concerning the Accession of Bulgaria and Romania to the European Union signed on 25 April 2005, http://www.consilium.europa.eu/cms3_fo/showPage.asp?id=963&lang=de&mode=g.

[13] See also *S. Hobe*, Financial contributions of participating states to optional programmes of the European Space Agency (ESA), Zeitschrift für Luft- und Weltraumrecht, 52 (2003) 3, 297-313.

[14] 23 October 1985.

[15] ESA/C(79)69.

[16] *M. Gerhard*, Analysing the Presentations and Discussions: Potential Building Blocs of a National Space Legislation, in: Need and Prospects for National Space Legislation, Proceedings of the Project 2001 – Workshop on National Space Legislation, 2001, 181 ff.

[17] More on this question see *V. Kopal*, International and National Space Law, izeilenabstand ibidem, 187.

[18] S. *J. Kolář*, Organizační podmínky kosmických aktivit v České republice, Československý časopis pro fyziku, 4 (2002), 3.

[19] Nr. 307/1998 Coll.

[20] The Hungarian Space Board consists of members delegated by ministries and government offices. It is responsible for policy issues, working under the supervision of the Minister of Transport and Communication. The Scientific Council for Space Research consists of experts ensuring the scientific background for the Board and the Space Office. The Hungarian Space Office is an operative body which coordinates activities of institutions taking part in space research, permitting the participation in international institutions. In: *G. Gál*, Elements of Space Law in the Hungarian Legal System, Journal of Space Law 23 (1998) 1, 61-65.
The Polish Space Office was created by the Decision of the President of the Polish Academy of Sciences (Decision Nr. 19/2001) on 12th October 2001. Its task is to ensure required assistance to the Inter-Ministerial Consultation and Coordination Board for Space Affairs, an advisory board to the Prime Minister. The Polish Space Office is located in the Space Research Centre of the Polish Academy of Sciences; the SRC provides necessary equipment and facilities. The Polish Space Office supports all space-related activities in Poland and serves as a contact point for foreign institutions interested in cooperation with the Polish space sector. It promotes and supports the implementation and use of space technologies in Poland. It also promotes Polish space activities abroad. The Director of the Space Research Centre supervises the activities of PSO. http://www.kosmos.gov.pl/PSO/AboutPSO.htm.
The Romanian Space Agency (ROSA) which was established in 1991, by the Government Decision no. 923/ 20 Nov 1995, is an independent public institution. The mission of the Agency is to coordinate the national space research and applications programs; to promote space development; to be the Government representative in the international space cooperation; and to develop specific project oriented research. ROSA is authorized to establish research and development centers oriented on specific objectives of the Romanian Space Program.
http://portal.rosa.ro/index.php?item_id=1.

[21] Http://www.czechspace.cz/CSO/cso.htm.

[22] Nr. 112/2005 Coll. of International Treaties.

[23] Constitutional Act No. 1/1993 Coll., as amended.

IAC-06-E6.3.02

EUMETSAT INTERNATIONAL COOPERATION ACTIVITIES

Werner Balogh
EUMETSAT, Germany
werner.balogh@eumetsat.int
Piero Valabrega
EUMETSAT, Germany
piero.valabrega@eumetsat.int

ABSTRACT

Since its foundation in 1986, the European Organisation for the Exploitation of Meteorological Satellites (EUMETSAT) has been involved in international cooperation activities, ranging from the interaction with its Member States and Cooperating States to the negotiation and conclusion of agreements with European and other international organisations and with non-Member States in the fields of satellite meteorology cooperation and the exchange of remote sensing satellite data. EUMETSAT is also making major contributions to a number of coordinated global Earth Observation initiatives. This paper presents a summary overview of these activities. Its main purpose is to give a general idea about the practical conduct of a wide range of international cooperation activities in an organisation which stands synonymous for the operational use of satellite-based Earth Observation applications.

INTRODUCTION

The European Organisation for the Exploitation of Meteorological Satellites (EUMETSAT) is an intergovernmental organisation. Its legal basis is laid out in the EUMETSAT Convention which entered into force on 19 June 1986, and was subsequently amended on 5 June 1991 [1]. Its privileges and immunities are defined in a protocol registered with the Secretary General of the United Nations in accordance with Article 102 of the Charter of the United Nations [2]. EUMETSAT has its Headquarters in Darmstadt, as stated in the Headquarters Agreement signed with the Federal Republic of Germany on 7 June 1989 and replaced by a new Agreement signed on 18 June 2002 [3].

EUMETSAT's objectives are the establishment, maintenance and exploitation of European systems of operational meteorological satellites, which provide essential information to the national meteorological services in its Member States and contribute to the operational monitoring of the climate and the detection of global climate changes. These objectives are implemented through a series of mandatory and optional programmes.

Fig.1 depicts the EUMETSAT internal organisation structure. The supreme body of the organisation is the EUMETSAT Council, supported by a number of Delegated Bodies, where Member States representatives prepare the decisional work of Council and follow up on its implementation.

The EUMETSAT Secretariat is structured into three Departments: Programme Development, Operations and Administration. The Office of the

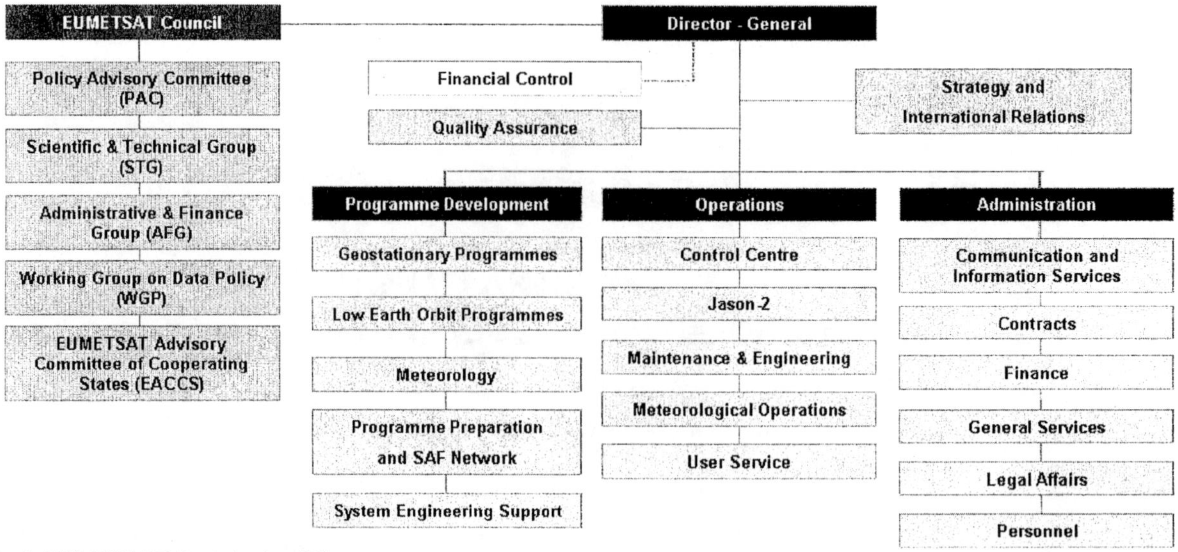

Fig. 1: EUMETSAT Organisational Structure

Director-General is comprised of two Divisions, Quality Assurance and Strategy and International Relations. The Director-General is appointed by EUMETSAT Member States and is the legal representative of EUMETSAT.

The long-term EUMETSAT Strategy, including the international relations component, is defined in a strategy document, which is periodically revised and updated by the EUMETSAT Council. The time horizon of the present version of the Strategy stretches to 2030 [4]. The responsibility for a coherent implementation of the international relations political and strategic components and their overall consistency with the EUMETSAT Strategy guidelines and targets rests with the Strategy and International Relations Division, which is coordinating EUMETSAT international relations activities. The responsibility for the legal elements of international relations rests with the Legal Affairs Division.

International negotiations are led by the Strategy and International Relations Division in cooperation with the Legal Affairs Division and involve other relevant Departments as necessary in accordance with the subject matter under discussion.

EUMETSAT's international relations activities are conducted on the basis of the Organisation's objectives set out in the Convention and as mandated by Council. They involve cooperation with EUMETSAT Members, with intergovernmental organisations, and with institutions of non-Member States. The following chapters describe these activities in detail.

EUMETSAT MEMBERS

EUMETSAT presently encompasses 20 Member States and 10 Cooperating States. Each Member State has one vote in the Council. The organisation is funded through membership contributions calculated on a scale proportional to the gross national income of the concerned Member State.

The current Cooperating States (Bulgaria, Czech Republic, Hungary, Iceland, Latvia, Lithuania, Poland, Romania, Serbia&Montenegro*, Slovenia) have signed cooperation agreements with EUMETSAT and contribute at a level of 50% of the full membership fee. They have un-restricted access to EUMETSAT data and services and are expected to become full members within a fixed period of time, usually within five years from the entry into force of the Cooperating State agreement.

The 16 founding Member States (Belgium, Denmark, Finland, France, Germany, Greece, Italy, Ireland, The Netherlands, Norway, Portugal, Spain, Sweden, Switzerland, Turkey, United Kingdom) were joined by Austria and Luxembourg through the conclusion of accession agreements, respectively in 1993 and 2001. The transition of two former Cooperating States, the Slovak Republic and Croatia, to full Member States was achieved in 2006.

Several bilateral agreements on satellite data relay, cooperation on satellite instruments on EUMETSAT missions, the establishment and

* Pending Ratification

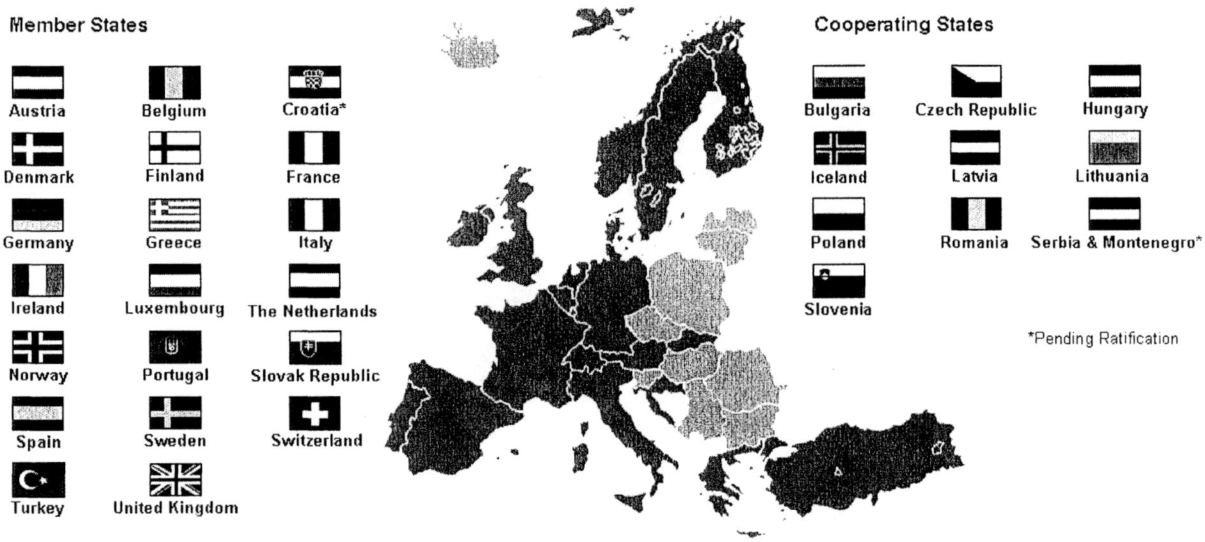

Fig. 2: EUMETSAT Member States and Cooperating States

operation of meteorological data distribution and uplink stations, EUMETCast, and the development of Satellite Application Facilities (SAFs) have been signed with EUMETSAT Member States and Cooperating States and are implemented through the National Meteorological Services (NMSs) and other relevant State entities. The EUMETSAT Member States and Cooperating States are shown in Fig.2.

INTERGOVERNMENTAL ORGANISATIONS

EUMETSAT has an extensive network of international relations based on cooperation agreements with several intergovernmental organisations.

ESA

There is a long-standing history of cooperation and partnership between EUMETSAT and the European Space Agency (ESA). In the 1970s, ESA conceptualised and developed the first generation of Meteosat satellites, and was the driving force behind the formation of EUMETSAT: Following EUMETSAT's foundation in 1986, ESA transferred to it, by a set of agreements, the complete responsibility for the Meteosat First Generation Operational Programme.

Today the European Space Agency (ESA) is acting as the development and procurement agency for the mission space segment of EUMETSAT mandatory programmes, including Meteosat Second Generation, the EUMETSAT Polar System (EPS), and the planned Meteosat Third Generation and Post-EPS programmes. The ground segment development and procurement is coordinated by EUMETSAT, whose Members typically provide 80% of the mission development cost and the total cost of mission operations.

EUMETSAT is cooperating with ESA on the development of future operational satellite missions in the Global Monitoring for Environment and Security (GMES) initiative. These satellites, called the GMES Sentinels, are planned for launch in the 2010-2020 time-frame. EUMETSAT is focusing in particular on the Sentinel-3 (ocean and global land monitoring), Sentinel-4 (GEO atmospheric composition mission) and Sentinel-5 (LEO atmospheric composition mission) missions.

ECMWF

Through an Exchange of Letters signed on 18 May 1988[†], EUMETSAT established a fruitful long-term relationship with the European Centre for Medium-range Weather Forecasts (ECMWF) located in Reading, United Kingdom [5]. ECMWF is routinely and on a daily basis integrating millions of data points collected by EUMETSAT satellites for data assimilation. The use of space-derived data has enabled successive, considerable improvements in the accuracy and numerical modelling of weather forecasts.

† "Exchange of Letters between EUMETSAT and ECMWF Working Relationship between the two Organisations"

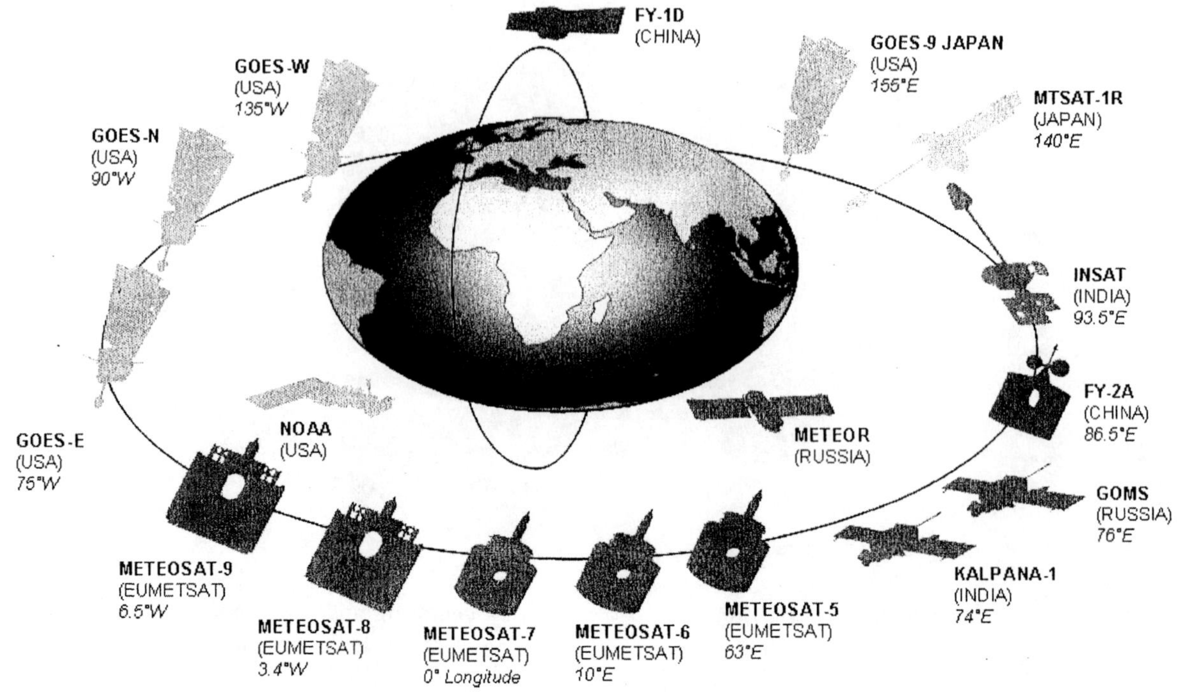

Fig. 3: Global Observing System of the World Meteorological Organisation

WMO

The EUMETSAT Convention commits the organisation to carry out its mission in accordance with the recommendations of the World Meteorological Organization (WMO). An Exchange of Letters signed on 1 September 1988 sets out the working relationship between the two organisations‡.

The WMO is a Specialized Agency of the United Nations, responsible for coordinating Members States activities related to the Earth's atmosphere, including the atmosphere's interaction with oceans and water resources and its effects on the climate [6].

For this purpose, WMO has established the concept of the WMO Global Observing System (GOS) as a component of the World Weather Watch (WWW), a planet-wide ground-, in-situ and space based observations network of the atmosphere and ocean surface [7]. The WMO GOS objectives are to improve and optimize the global observations system and to facilitate the standardisation of observing techniques and practices.

EUMETSAT is contributing its operational geostationary satellite missions to the GOS, whose capabilities will be further enhanced with the addition of the EUMETSAT Polar System satellites (see Fig.3).

To meet the information requirements of all WMO programmes, affiliated international organisations and initiatives, as well as those of other relevant users, the WMO has established the concept of an integrated information system, the WMO Information System (WIS). The WIS includes provisions for data collection, exchange, dissemination, archiving and retrieval.

One element of the WIS, implemented by the WMO Member States and Member State organisations, is the Integrated Global Data Dissemination Service (IGDDS), a circulation scheme of space-based observation data and products.

EUMETCast, EUMETSAT's Broadcast System for Environmental Data, is the EUMETSAT contribution to the IGDDS. It is a multi-service dissemination system based on standard Digital Video Broadcast (DVB) technology, using commercial telecommunication geostationary satellites to multicast files (data and products) to a wide user community.

‡ "Exchange of Letters between EUMETSAT and WMO Working Relationship between the two Organisations"

European Commission

In the late 1990's, the European Commission (EC), the executive body of the European Union (EU), began to take a growing interest in space activities [8]. Following the publication of a Green Paper and White Paper in 2003, the European Union and ESA Member States embarked on the definition of a European Space Policy, a process that is still on-going. The European Space Policy will be based on a European Space Programme.

On 25 January 2006, the EC and EUMETSAT concluded an Exchange of Letters, setting out the basis to establish a working relationship between the two parties in the implementation of the European Space Policy[§].

This agreement represents the initial step towards a formal framework agreement that shall set out a long-term framework for cooperation between the two organisations.

GMES

The Global Monitoring for Environment and Security (GMES) is a joint initiative of the European Commission and the European Space Agency [9]. GMES was launched in 1998 and EUMETSAT has been an active contributor to GMES-related activities since then. GMES is a concerted effort to establish an operational European capacity for the timely provision of quality ground-, air-, and space-based data, information and knowledge in support of a wide range of European policy areas for the benefit of European citizens.

To implement the provisions set out in the Exchange of Letters, EUMETSAT is closely working with the European Commission's newly established GMES Bureau and with the Implementation Groups of the three GMES Fast-track Services (Marine Core Service, Land Monitoring Core Service, Information Service in Response to Crises, Disasters and Emergencies) which constitute the initial set of GMES Pilot Services. EUMETSAT has also coordinated the ground-work for establishing a future GMES Atmosphere Service.

[§] "Cooperation between EUMETSAT and EC - Exchange of Letters"

PUMA/AMESD

Since 1996 EUMETSAT has been contributing to sustainable development in Africa with the Preparation for the Use of MSG in Africa (PUMA) initiative to set up a network of EUMETCast receiving stations across the continent, enabling African users to receive data from Meteosat Second Generation satellites. PUMA has led to the successful installation of at least one EUMETCast station in each of 53 African countries, together with the provision of extensive training efforts targeting the staff of the African National Meteorological Services.

This programme will be succeeded by the African Monitoring of the Environment for Sustainable Development (AMESD) project. It will utilise the infrastructure established by the PUMA initiative to improve environmental management policies at national and sub-regional level in Africa. PUMA and AMESD are fully funded and supported by the European Commission development cooperation policy. EUMETSAT contributes as an in-kind donor.

In this context of cooperation on satellite meteorology with the countries and institutions situated within the footprint of its geostationary satellites, EUMETSAT has also concluded various agreements with the African Centre for Meteorological Application for Development (ACMAD) and the Centre Regional AGRHYMET, both located in Niamey, Nigeria.

CGMS

A major portion of the WMO GOS is based on the global network of meteorological satellites coordinated by the Coordination Group for Meteorological Satellites (CGMS), founded in 1972 under the name Coordination of Geostationary Meteorological Satellites.

CGMS provides a forum for the exchange of technical and operational information on geostationary and polar-orbiting meteorological satellite systems and the coordination of initiatives in these areas. Among other tasks, CGMS is also considering contingency plans for assuring operational continuity and reliability, as well as a complete global coverage.

EUMETSAT joined CGMS in 1987 and is acting as its Secretariat, especially in the context of its annual meetings [10].

CEOS

The Committee on Earth Observation Satellites (CEOS) was established in 1994 as a coordinating mechanism for civil Earth Observation missions, comprising 25 Members and 20 Associates [11].

EUMETSAT is a Member of CEOS and represented in the CEOS Secretariat and in the Working Group on Education, Training, and Capacity Building (WG-Edu).

Through CEOS EUMETSAT is also contributing to the Integrated Global Observing Strategy (IGOS) Partnership Process and to the Global Climate Observing System (GCOS) [12], [13].

CEOS is in the process of re-defining its role as the organisation coordinating the space-based components of the Global Earth Observations System of Systems (GEOSS).

GEO/GEOSS

The Group on Earth Observations (GEO) was formally established in February 2005, following a series of ministerial-level meetings [14]. As of September 2006 it is comprised of 65 member countries and 43 participating organizations, including EUMETSAT.

GEO aspires to establish a Global Earth Observation System of Systems (GEOSS) based on a 10-year implementation plan, covering nine societal benefit areas (Disasters, Health, Energy, Climate, Water, Weather, Ecosystems, Agriculture, Biodiversity) and five transverse areas (User Engagement, Architecture, Data Management, Capacity Building, Outreach).

EUMETSAT is closely following the activities in the GEOSS initiative and is represented in the four GEOSS committees (Architecture and Data Committee, User Interface Committee, Capacity Building Committee, Science and Technology Committee) and in the Working Group on Tsunami Activities.

EUMETSAT is contributing – either directly or through WMO, CEOS, the European GEO High-Level Working Group, and via its contributions to the European GMES initiative – to several of the tasks identified in the 2006 GEO Work Plan and will continue to do so in the framework of the future multi-year work plans.

The current focus of EUMETSAT activities in GEOSS is the GEONETCast data disseminations system based on EUMETSAT's EUMETCast environmental data dissemination scheme [15].

Furthermore EUMETSAT is also contributing to the Virtual Constellations, based on the "CEOS constellation concept" aiming at providing guidance for the planning phase of missions considered by space agencies and related organisations, ensuring better coordination of sensors, data continuity and availability, and addressing the nine societal benefit areas of GEO.

UN COPUOS

EUMETSAT is occasionally participating as an observer in the meetings of the United Nations Committee on the Peaceful Uses of Outer Space (UNCOPUOS) and its Legal and Scientific and Technical Subcommittees.

On 25 May 1998 the organisation submitted a declaration of acceptance of the Convention on Registration of Objects Launched into Outer Space ("Registration Convention") followed by the acceptance of the Convention on International Liability for Damage Caused by Space Objects ("Liability Convention") on 29 September 2005 and the Agreement on the Rescue of Astronauts, the Return of Astronauts and the Return of Objects Launched into Outer Space ("Rescue Agreement") on 19 December 2005.

It should be noted that a number of EUMETSAT Member States and Cooperating States are not member States of UNCOPUOS.

COSPAS-SARSAT

Instruments of the international COSPAS-SARSAT international search-and-rescue system are carried on board of the MSG satellites, and will be part of the instruments provided by NOAA to fly on the EPS MetOp-A and B satellites. Concerning the instrument on the MSG satellites, an exchange of letters has been signed with COSPAS-SARSAT on 28 June 2001.

NON-MEMBER STATES

EUMETSAT has concluded agreements with various organisations and institutions in non-Member States.

United States of America

The National Oceanic and Atmospheric Administration (NOAA) is a major cooperation partner for EUMETSAT. The two organisations will be operating together a European-US satellite system flying in complementary orbits, called the Initial Joint Polar-Orbiting Operational Satellite System (IJPS). The IJPS Agreement was signed in 1998.

The European contribution to IJPS system is the EUMETSAT Polar System., whose Metop satellites will provide the mid-morning orbit coverage.

EUMETSAT and NOAA will operate and control their respective polar orbiting satellites and ground segments; however, data collected by all the satellites will be shared and exchanged between the two organisations. It is expected that this cooperation framework will continue with the Post-EPS missions through the establishment of a Joint Polar System (JPS).

EUMETSAT and NOAA also cooperate as the operational agencies of the Jason-2 satellite, the space segment of the Ocean Surface Topography Mission (OSTM). Jason-2 is developed by the National Aeronautics and Space Administration (NASA) and the Centre National d'Etudes Spatiales (CNES) as a successor to the Jason-1 and TOPEX/Poseidon satellites. To this extent, a quadripartite Memorandum of Understanding between NASA, NOAA, CNES and EUMETSAT for Cooperation in the Ocean Surface Topography Mission has been signed on 7 April 2006.

China, India, Russia

Agreements have been signed with the China Meteorological Administration (CMA) on cooperation in the field of meteorological satellites and satellite meteorology, the Russian Federal Service for Hydrometeorology and Environmental Monitoring (ROSHYDROMET) on cooperation and exchange of images from geostationary meteorological satellites in support of weather analysis and forecasting, and the Indian Space Research Organisation (ISRO) on cooperation and exchange of images from geostationary meteorological satellites in support of weather analysis and forecasting and other areas.

Cooperation agreements with meteorological services in other space-faring non-Member States are under consideration or are being negotiated.

SUMMARY AND CONCLUSIONS

The data and products acquired and disseminated by EUMETSAT satellites enable more accurate daily weather forecasting, provide support to industry, such as the aviation and maritime transport sector; assist human forecasters in diagnosing and monitoring the development of hazardous weather systems and contribute to global climate and climate change monitoring.

The wide range of EUMETSAT's international cooperation activities serve the purpose to make relevant data, products and services readily available to all potential users and user organizations around the globe. Through this EUMETSAT contributes to sustainable development of Planet Earth.

Not least to its long history, the world-wide meteorological community is being considered a mature and well-organised user community of data collected by Earth Observation satellites. International cooperation activities in space-based meteorology therefore appear to provide a particularly successful and useful example for cooperation in other disciplines that may benefit from the use of Earth Observation data.

REFERENCES

[1] Convention for the Establishment of a European Organisation for the Exploitation of Meteorological Satellites (EUMETSAT) as amended by the EUMETSAT Council in Resolution EUM/C/Res. XXXVI of 5 June 1991, and subsequently accepted by all EUMETSAT Member States, EUMETSAT Basic Documents, Vol.1, April 2005

[2] Headquarters Agreement between the Government of the Federal Republic of Germany and the European Organisation for the Exploitation of Meteorological Satellites (EUMETSAT), EUMETSAT Basic Documents, Vol.1, April 2005

[3] Protocol on the Privileges and Immunities of the European Organisation for the Exploitation of Meteorological Satellites (EUMETSAT) as amended in accordance with notification of the Depository of the Protocol on Privileges and Immunities dated 12 January 2004, EUMETSAT Basic Documents, Vol.1, April 2005

[4] EUMETSAT Strategy: 2030, EUM.05, Version 1, 1 October 2005, www.eumetsat.int/groups/cps/documents/document/pdf_br_eum05_en.pdf

[5] ECMWF Homepage, www.ecmwf.int

[6] WMO Homepage, www.wmo.int

[7] Global Observing System Homepage, www.wmo.ch/web/www/OSY/GOS.html

[8] European Space Policy, ec.europa.eu/enterprise/space

[9] GMES Homepage, www.gmes.info

[10] CGMS Documents, Calibration Publications and Meeting Reports are available at www.eumetsat.int/Home/Main/Publications/CGMS_Publications

[11] CEOS Homepage, www.ceos.org

[12] IGOS Partnership, www.igospartners.org

[13] Global Climate Observing System Homepage, www.wmo.ch/web/gcos/

[14] Group on Earth Observations Homepage, www.earthobservations.org

[15] GEONETCast - The EUMETCast Contribution - Delivering operational services to users, E.01, Version 2, 2°September 2006,

Disclaimer: The views expressed in this paper are purely those of the authors and do not necessarily reflect the position of EUMETSAT.

IAC-06-E6.3.03

THE COOPERATION BETWEEN ESA AND EU REGARDING THE EARTH OBSERVATION

Mª del Carmen Muñoz Rodríguez*
Juan Manuel de Faramiñán Gilbert**

ABSTRACT[1]

Even if the 2004 Project of the Treaty establishing a Constitution for Europe has not already come into force, nowadays, the European Union (EU) considers that space activities are "strategic for their construction of Europe" and they will "serve the interests of the EU, its Member States and its citizens". Therefore, the EU and the European Space Agency (ESA) are defining a European Space Policy, and a European Space Program, in which Galileo and Global Monitoring for Environment and Security (GMES) are the currently most advanced projects. Giving the particular strategic importance of the Earth observation, the purpose of this paper is to analyse the strategy set out for GMES, whose objective is to provide, on a sustained basis, reliable ad timely services related to environmental and security services in support of public policy makers' needs. This initiative offers another opportunity to create a closer cooperation between the ESA and the EU, as the 2003 Framework Agreement established. Then, it is necessary to examine which role ESA and EU can/must play and which legal/institutional tools are provided to develop and to implement the GMES.

I. INTRODUCTION

The European cooperation in the space activities began in the 1960s under the ESRO/ELDO framework, and, after, under the ESA framework. Nowadays, the space activities are considered under another European vision, and are required by a new global actor: "Space is a tool to serve the interest of the EU, its Member States and its citizens: strategic influence, scientific progress, economic growth in the knowledge economy and security"[2]. Therefore, the EU, in closer cooperation with the ESA aims to develop a coherent and progressive European Space Policy ESP) and, consecutively, a European Space Program (ESPr).

The 2003 White Paper[3] sets down the legal/institutional tools and the two phases-calendar needed to implement the ESP: the phase 1 (2004-2007) will consist of implementing the 2003 Framework Agreement between the European Community (EC) and ESA[4], and the phase 2 (2007-onwards) will consist of implementing the 2004 Treaty establishing a Constitution for Europe (the Draft Constitutional Treaty)[5].

*Mª del Carmen Muñoz Rodríguez, Assistant Lecturer of Public International Law, University of Jaén (Spain), mcrodri@ujaen.es
**Juan Manuel de Faramiñán Gilbert, Professor of Public International Law, University of Jaén (Spain) jmfarami@ujaen.es

The Draft Constitutional Treaty does not specify the model of the common legal and political structure for the relationship between the ESA and the EU. It just stresses the obligation to carry out this relationship, as it happens in the current EU Treaties, when they emphasize the interest of the relationship between the EC and United Nations or the Counsel of Europe[6].

Even if the Draft Constitutional Treaty has not already come into force[7], the ESA and the EC work jointly to identify and encourage the most effective sharing of tasks and responsibilities for determining and continuously delivering the benefits of space to the European citizens[8]. Fortunately, the 2003 Framework Agreement designs the basic legal/institutional tools and to implement the cooperation between ESA and EC, in the due respect of the international agreements related to ESA[9] and EC[10].

The art. 3 of the 2003 Framework Agreement outlines the specific fields of the cooperation between EC and ESA, including the Earth observation. Therefore, giving that now when the command of information has important geo-strategic implications, Europe needs to have available a capacity which allows it to implement and monitor the environmental and security policies in a reliable and timely manner. This own capacity will be based in a comprehensive Earth observation system, that is, the GMES programme.

II. THE JUSTIFICATION OF GMES: ITS STRATEGIC AND ECONOMIC DIMENSION.

At the present time, GMES is viewed as the second EU flagship of space policy, after the Galileo programme. Since the Gothenburg European Council in 2001, where the Chiefs of States and Governments expressed their political mandate, all the European Institutions have already supported it[11], because it meets strategic and economic objectives.

Concerning the strategic justification, the need for reliable and timely information about the natural and manmade catastrophes all over the world or about security issues has been underlined in the recent past years. The double-side dimension of the benefits of the GMES, inside and outside Europe, will sustain not only the EU's civil security needs but also the potential of the European Security and Defence Police. Likewise, GMES will become the main contribution to the EU international commitments, for instance, the global climate observing system[12], and to the global 10-Year Implementation Plan for a Global Earth Observation System of Systems (GEOSS).

Regarding the economic justification, GMES will stimulate the economic growth by facilitating the creation of innovative added value services. That is, the European industrial sector should expand its service offer and develop the innovative observing communications and information technologies that will be required within a dynamic GMES capacity[13].

In particular, the GMES will provide the geospatial information necessary to implement the following EU policy and legislation:

1. The environmental policy, within EU territory and globally[14].
2. The Common Foreign and Security Policy, including the European Defence Policy[15].
3. Other internal / external policies as agriculture[16], fisheries[17], regional development, transport, external relation, development aid[18], humanitarian assistance, and, lately, the increasing focused justice and home affairs cooperation, as the surveillance and management of external borders.

III. THE IMPLEMENTATION OF GMES.

The European Commission has set out a strategy for delivering GMES, beginning with the pilot phase of the three first operational GMES services by 2008, delivering a document, which discusses about the main axes involved in the above strategy[19].

The users

The goal of the current development phase is to build a strong user base for GMES information services; the European Commission is one key issue, however it still has to identify its own needs.

The pilot operational services

The complex nature of GMES requires the integration of data from space-based and in-situ (airborne, water-based and ground-based) earth observation capacities into user-driven operational application services. This capacity has to be introduced gradually, depending of the maturity of the services, the response by the users' community and the long-term sustainability of demand and supply. Anyway, the services will be funded by the combination of Community, national and regional resources. The implementation of these services has to solve different challenges: the harmonisation and the standardisation of data structures and interfaces; the policy barriers to data sharing; the design of quality assurance mechanisms, the fusion of data from different sources at different levels, and, finally, the cost effective and sustainable services.

To meet the 2008 compromise, the operational services have to receive fast track treatment, according to the validation process that the European Commission has established. So far, the three services proposed are the following: emergency response, land monitoring and marine services[20].

Funding

At the beginning, GMES obviously depends on public funding, via the 6th and the 7th Framework Programme (FP). In the last case, it is envisaged that GMES will be allocated a substantial majority of funding available for Space under the 7th FP for Research, Technological Development and Demonstration activities, in particular, the thematic priorities such as "Environment" or "Information Society Technologies".

In the future, where services become integral to the implementation of public policies, they should be supported by the relevant institutional users and, in some areas, they may also attract private sector customers, making possible some public-private partnerships.

Building on existing capacities

GMES will use the existing European and national capacities to the maximum extent. This is why EC, ESA, EUMETSAT and the Member States, and even the international partners, have to map then and to ensure their interoperability. Notwithstanding, as a matter or urgency, it has to be pointed out that the majority of the GMES-like services rely on observations from a number of satellites that have exceeded, or will do, their nominal end-of-life[21].

Impact assessment

In line with the overall European Commission Policy, GMES will require justification based on a solid impact assessment, -more that the one related to 7th FP -, before substantial funds are committed. GMES is being studied, in two phases, by independent consultants (whose methodology is supervised by a team of experts named by the Member States). The study identifies a range of strategic benefits, some *non-quantifiable*, and some susceptible to generate *quantifiable* benefits for the period 2005-2030.

Governance

The 2003 Framework Agreement between EC and ESA provides for a "common basis and appropriate operational arrangements for an efficient and mutually beneficial cooperation between the Parties with regard to space activities", but "in accordance with their respective tasks and responsibilities and fully respecting their institutional settings"[22]. This can be considered the appropriate first step, in order to create a joint strategy and programmes for two independent international organizations; however, it results insufficient to create a common structure. According to this and to the effective division of competencies between EC and its Member States:

1. EC will define the priorities and requirements; aggregate the political will and user demand; and ensues the availability and continuity of the service.
2. ESA will support and define the technical specifications of the space component, implement the space component -coordinating the European centres of excellence-, and advise the EU on future space component requirements.
3. Members States may strengthen internal coordination of related data collection and management activities and federate national demand; contribute to the implementation of the spatial data infrastructures and in-situ components; and support the implementation of the space component.

Therefore, the European Commission will manage (either directly or through externalisation) the development of GMES services supported through 7th FP. ESA will manage the development of the space infrastructures identified for support under the 7th FP, in accordance with the rules of the programme.

In setting up its organisational frame, GMES will fully take into account the experience gained through the Galileo process.

IV. CONCLUSION

This new European vision of space, reflected in the 2003 Framework Agreement and in the 2004 Draft Constitutional Treaty, deems and need a big effort of politicians, jurists and economists in order to find the appropriate answer to these new political, legal and economic challenges related to space activities. The benefits of the Earth observation through the GMES programme, give the European citizens a special opportunity to improve their standard of life, and the European market an unique occasion to enhanced their commercial potential.

Nevertheless, the complexity nature of the EU/EC and ESA as international organisations (applicable also to their mutual relations) and the increasing difficulties to approve their respective budgets, should receive a comprehensive and integrated answer through a well-established legal framework, implemented by a specific legislation by EU/EC, ESA and their Member States.

Notwithstanding, in the absence of a political and legal general basis, the particular joint action of EU, ESA, its Member States, in collaboration with the international partners, can give rise to a fruitful experience that can make easier to achieve two objectives. The first objective would be to legitimize the ESP and the ESPr, including Galileo or GMES initiatives, vis-à-vis the public opinion. The second one would be to approve the 2004 Draft Constitutional Treaty, or whichever substitute option, because it can be showed as a one of the key points in favour of the adoption of that legal instrument (evidently, it would be maintained as a competence shared between the EU and the Member States).

---

[1] This paper has been prepared in the framework of the Research Project "Convergences and divergences among the outer space law and particular sea spaces law", Spanish Ministry of Science and Education, SEJ2004-06116.

[2] Communication from the Commission to the Council and the European Parliament "*European Space Policy - Preliminary Elements*", COM (2005) 208 final, 23.5.2005, p. 4.

[3] Communication from the Commission to the Council and the European Parliament *White Paper "Space: a new frontier for an expanding Union. An action plan for implementing the European Space Policy"*, COM (2003) 673 final, 11.11.2003, p. 37.

[4] Framework Agreement between the European Community and the European Space Agency, done at Brussels on the 25th of November in 2003, OJ, L261, of 6.8.2004, p. 63-68.

[5] The article III-255 of the Treaty states that: "the Union shall draw up a European space policy...;...European laws or framework laws shall establish the necessary measures, which may take the form of a European space programme;...[and] the Union shall establish any appropriate relations with the European Space Agency".

[6] It is a *minimum,* but this mention is legally and politically very important (the

first Draft of the Constitutional Treaty did not mention even the ESA).

[7] See the current debate in http://europa.eu/

[8] See the large list of documents in http://europe.eu.int/comm/space/off_docs_en.htm. The EISC members (European Interparliamentary Space Conference) call upon the national governments and the European Council to work in the spirit of the relevant articles in the 2004 Draft Treaty (8th EISC Conclusions, Brussels, 12-14 June 2006), www.belspo.be/belspo/eisc/

[9] The ESA is a European intergovernmental organization, committed to carry out their science and applications activities for exclusively peaceful purposes (art. II of the ESA Convention). The historical perspective of ESA shows us that the national and the European policy logics are clearly interrelated, because if there is a harmony of national policy logics among all the governments, it is easier to define the European policy logics. Regarding to the finance, this logics appears on every occasion that the European logic is fragile. Finally, some new and innovative rules and procedures are created when the logic of commerce begins to have influence in national governments (the principle of fair return or the rule of the optional participation). *Vid.* Suzuki, K.: *Policy Logics and Institutions of European Space Collaboration*, Ashgate, 2003, p. 209-212.

[10] The EU is the most important sophisticated European structure, which has two different frameworks: the European Communities, and the Cooperation policies (Common Foreign and Security Policy and Justice and Home Affairs). The first one establishes a method of integration, based on the transfer of the exercise of sovereignty rights to the EC, on the respect of the *acquis communitaire*, and on the existence of a unique budget system with its own resources. The second one seems to be closer to the model of intergovernmental organization. The current basic set-up of the EU do not refer to outer space, nevertheless, this dimension can be found implicit in the European Treaties: research, industrial development, transport networks, telecommunications, agriculture and fisheries, environment, health services, development aid, regional development and security. The Council of the EU approved the 2003 Framework Agreement having regard the art. 170 of the EC Treaty, in conjunction with art. 300. See Faramiñán Gilbert, J.M. and Muñoz Rodríguez, M.C.: "European Space Policy: a Common Future for EU and ESA?", *Proceedings of the 47th Colloquium on Outer Space,* AAIA, 2005.

[11] Council Resolutions 2001/C 350/02 (13.11.2001). Communication from the Commission to the Council and the European Parliament "*Global Monitoring for Environment and Security (GMES): Establishing GMES capacity by 2008 – Action Plan 2004-2008",* COM (2004), 65 final, 1.2.2004. B-5-0045/2004 European Parliament Resolution on the action plan for implementing the European Space Policy.

[12] G8 Recommendation, July 2005. Thus, the EU has included it in the dialogue with their international partners (USA, Russia, China and India) and even in their development strategy (as Africa, through the creation of an African observatory and the implementation of the African Monitoring of the Environment for sustainable Development -AMESD-); *vid. "EU Strategy form Africa"*, COM (2005) 489 final, 12.10.2005.

[13] The European Commission has selected the GMES as one of the quick start projects in its final report to the European Council *"European initiative for growth: investing in networks and knowledge for growth and jobs"*, COM (2003) 609 final/2, 1.11.2003.

[14] The 6th Environmental Action Plan (2004-2010) addresses: climate change, nature and biodiversity, environment and health, natural resources and waste; as

well as natural hazards, e.g. forest fires, floods, tsunami response).

[15] For instance, the imagery acquisition for specific instruments, as the Rapid Reaction Mechanism.

[16] For instance, the area acreages checks and agri-environmental measures.

[17] For instance, the vessels monitoring and detection.

[18] For instance, water, vegetation and food security monitoring activities.

[19] Communication *"Global Monitoring for Environment and Security(GMES): from concept to reality", vid. supra* note n. 11.

[20] Further pilot services will be introduced, using the same validation process, for instance, the atmospheric monitoring, the crisis prevention or the external border surveillance, to which some Member States have emphasised the importance the attach, such as Spain.

[21] In this sense, the ESA Director General has proposed to secure an initial budget to cover the first phases of the future structure of GMES (space and ground segment).

[22] Art. 1, para. 2 of the 2003 Framework Agreement.

IAC-06-E6.3.04

MONITORING GREENHOUSE GASES FROM SPACE AND THE KYOTO PROTOCOL

Masami Onoda
Research Fellow, Japan Society for the Promotion of Science;
PhD. Candidate, Graduate School of Global Environmental Studies, Kyoto University
Kyoto, Japan
masami.naito@gakushikai.jp

ABSTRACT

As the 1997 Protocol to the Framework Convention on Climate Change has become an increasingly significant political agenda, space agencies have initiated satellite programs to respond to the international demands for scientific information. Satellite Earth observation can improve the observation gaps of current carbon observation networks needed as the basis for scientific understanding as required by the UNFCCC and its Kyoto Protocol, a response by Parties to the general and loose obligation to cooperate in systematic observation. For the reporting and reviewing procedures, however, satellite data is not directly applicable at the present stage, since it is difficult to identify anthropogenic emissions or land use changes. Thus, there seems to be little it can do for "compliance monitoring" in the field of climate change. To pursue this kind of a role by satellite Earth observation in the future, it is necessary to alter the present procedures through intensive interaction between policy, science and technology. Further, there is a possibility that satellite data may provide options for the next steps, by providing means to "validate" or "verify" the state of accomplishment of the treaty objectives and to assess the workability of the treaty regime, in the arena of scientific research as the basis for future decision-making.

1. Introduction

International framework based on treaty often constitutes a rationale to promote a national or international activity related to its implementation. On one hand, this could be understood as a positive effect of the treaty, but on the other hand, it could be dangerous to rely on such rationale without careful determination of the specific treaty objectives and obligations in relation to the individual implementation efforts. Correct understanding of the treaty obligations in relation to the surrounding implementation efforts is essential for effective management of such projects and achievement of treaty objectives.

In this regard, the adoption and enter into force of the Protocol to the Framework

Convention on Climate Change (Kyoto Protocol) [1] has accelerated the race between the U.S. and Japan to be the first to launch a greenhouse gases measuring mission. Japan is developing the Greenhouse gases Observing SATellite (GOSAT) [2] and the U.S. is developing the Orbiting Carbon Observatory (OCO)[3]. While these two major space-faring countries are confronted over their policies towards the Protocol, the fact that they have both initiated satellite programs with the aim to observing greenhouse gases from space is highly interesting. GOSAT mission is linked to the "implementation" of the Kyoto Protocol[4], while OCO is mainly scientific.

Some point out, in relation to the Kyoto Protocol, that satellite Earth observation may permit closer monitoring of information that is self-reported by parties and supply information for adjudicating disputes, a Global Earth Observation System of Systems[5] figuring prominently as a means of "monitoring compliance" [6]. Would this prospect still stand, when we look into specific technologies and the role they can play in the present international framework? What are the specific obligations of the Kyoto Protocol that greenhouse gases observation by satellite is relevant to? What are the significances and obstacles of satellite observation in the process of implementation of the Kyoto Protocol? What can we expect as possible developments in this area, in the near future?

To answer these questions, this paper will attempt to provide a case study as to the legal and policy aspects of greenhouse gases monitoring by satellites in relation to the Kyoto Protocol. There are technical limits to the information from satellites as well as programmatic obstacles that prevent the efforts from providing certain information. By considering such limits in light of the specific supervisory techniques required by the legal framework, it should be possible to provide an initial analysis of the legal status of satellite Earth observation in the framework of the Protocol.

The paper will consider existing studies on Kyoto Protocol requirements and possible satellite observation technologies to establish a comprehensive understanding of the issue. Then the significance of the planned two greenhouse gases observing satellites will be examined, in light of their relation to the climate change regime. Through such considerations, we will try to identify, if any, specific obligations to which satellite greenhouse gases monitoring relates to, and the range of compliance or cooperation issues concerned. Based on such considerations, the paper will discuss the potential of satellite observation in international cooperation.

2. The Role of Satellite Observation in Greenhouse Gases Monitoring

"Satellite Earth observation" encompasses a variety of observations performed from space, in parameters observed, technology involved and application. Historically, space-faring nations have launched various Earth observation satellites for land observation, resources monitoring, disaster monitoring, and environmental monitoring. We can start from examining how these existing satellite data have been, or could be applied to international cooperation in the field of climate change.

2.1 Land Observation

A cross-disciplinary study on existing satellite data identifies the following areas where remote sensing[7] technology (land observation) could be applied to the requirements of the Kyoto Protocol (The greenhouse gases considered relevant in the context of remote sensing are CO_2 and CH_4) [8]:

Relevant Provisions in Kyoto Protocol	Corresponding Remote Sensing Technology
Provision of systematic observations of relevant land cover (Articles 5 and 10)	Presently provided at a global level by coarse and medium resolution sensors including NOAA, Landsat, SPOT, Terra, and ADEOS-II sensors
Support to the establishment of a 1990 carbon stock baseline (Article 3)	Historical Landsat, SPOT and JERS-1 SAR
Detection and spatial quantification of change in land cover (Articles 3 and 12)	A the local or regional level, finer resolution data such as Landsat and SPOT required. Space-borne SAR is useful in areas of persistent cloud cover.
Quantification of above-ground vegetation biomass stocks and associated changes therein (Articles 3 and 12)	Airborne LIDAR, polarimetric SAR and VHF band radar for biomass estimation.
Mapping and monitoring of certain sources of anthropogenic CH4 (Articles 3, 5 and 10)	Space-borne SAR and optical data.

Table 1: Kyoto Protocol Requirements and Corresponding Remote Sensing Measurements[9]

The study concludes that, as the Kyoto Protocol requires quantification of afforestation, reforestation and deforestation (ARD)[10], revegetation and land use management[11], and to establish a baseline of carbon stocks for 1990[12], existing and historical remote sensing data could play an important role in supporting the establishment these information.

2.2 Carbon Cycle

On a broader issue of global carbon cycle observation, the report[13] of the Integrated Global Observing Strategy[14] Carbon Theme sets forth a strategy to realize a coordinated system of integrated global carbon cycle observations. The objectives are to provide the long-term observations required to improve understanding of the present state and future behavior of the global carbon cycle, particularly the factors that control the global atmospheric CO_2 level; and to monitor and assess the effectiveness of carbon sequestration and/or emission reduction activities on global atmospheric CO_2 levels, including attribution of sources and sinks by region and sector[15]. It identifies the global observation required, corresponding existing space instruments and potential new missions[16]. Among groundbased observations at monitoring stations, aircraft, ship and other observation networks, satellite observation provides parameters relevant to terrestrial carbon (land cover, land cover changes induced by land use practices, vegetation phenology and bio physical properties, fires, radiation); ocean carbon (surface winds, sea surface temperature, ocean color). Space-based measurement of atmospheric CO_2 using existing long-wave infrared measurements on NOAA[17] satellites and retrieval of CO_2 by short-wave infrared signal from an Envisat[18] sensor are identified as existing possibilities, though these satellite instruments are not launched with the measurement of atmospheric CO_2 concentration as their focus. As the next generation atmospheric CO_2 observation, the report identifies the Orbiting Carbon Observatory (OCO), and the Greenhouse Gases Observing SATellite (GOSAT), using measurements of reflected sunlight in the short-wave infrared or thermal infrared to provide global, high-precision measurements of CO_2. This new development will be discussed in the following.

2.3 Atmospheric Greenhouse Gases Observation

The Greenhouse gases Observing SATellite (GOSAT), planned for launch in August 2008, will monitor CO_2 globally from orbit. It is a joint project of the Japan Aerospace Exploration Agency (JAXA) and the Ministry of Environment (MOE), and the National Institute for Environmental Studies (NIES). It is a satellite to monitor CO_2 and CH_4 globally from orbit, and aims to contribute to the international efforts to prevent global warming, such as the Kyoto Protocol[19].
The mission targets are (i) to observe CO_2 and CH_4 column density at 100-1000km spatial scale, with 1% relative accuracy for CO_2 and 2% for CH_4, during the Kyoto Protocol's first commitment period; and (ii) to reduce sub-continental scale CO_2 annual flux estimation errors by half[20].

This challenging mission certainly has many technical issues to overcome, but scientifically, there would be an important value of global repetitive data collected over a continuing period. Currently, the profile of greenhouse gas concentration is mapped by some 300 ground and airborne observations, while GOSAT will be capable of providing 56,000 observation points. Such measurement by satellite is expected to significantly enhance the current observation network capability.

Another mission to observe atmospheric greenhouse gas from space is the Orbiting Carbon Observatory (OCO) [21] , a mission of the Earth System Science Pathfinder Project (ESSP) of the National Aeronautics and Space Administration, designed to make precise, time-dependent global measurements of atmospheric CO_2. Using a space-based platform, OCO will collect a far greater number of high resolution measurements which in turn will provide the distribution of CO_2 over the entire globe. OCO will acquire the space-based data needed to identify CO_2 sources and sinks and quantify their variability over the seasonal cycle. The Approach is to: Collect spectra of CO_2 and O_2 absorption in reflected sunlight; Use these data to resolve variations in the column averaged CO_2 dry air mole fraction over the sunlit hemisphere, and to validate measurements to ensure its accuracies of 1-2 ppm (0.3-0.5%) on regional scales at monthly intervals[22]. These measurements will be combined with data from the ground-based network to provide scientists with the information that they will need to better understand the processes that regulate atmospheric CO_2 and its role in the carbon cycle. This enhanced understanding is essential to improve predictions of future atmospheric CO_2 increases and their impact on the climate. This information could help policy makers and business leaders make better decisions to ensure climate stability and, at the same time, retain our quality of life.

The OCO and GOSAT share the same objective of space-based column measurements of greenhouse gases, which will complement the existing surface measurement network. GOSAT measures CO_2, CH_4, O_2, O_3 and H_2O, while OCO measures CO_2 and O_2. GOSAT is a medium size satellite with total mass of 1750kg, carrying two sensors, while OCO is a much smaller satellite of 440kg mass, dedicated to a single spectrometer. Both are in the sun-synchronous orbit, GOSAT's revisit time being 3 days and OCO 16 days. Both satellites are planned for launch in August – September 2008. With such similar missions, the OCO highlights its contribution to climate change research, and GOSAT emphasizes its contribution to international efforts such as the Kyoto Protocol.

3. Relative Obligations in the UNFCCC and Kyoto Protocol

3.1 Kyoto Protocol's Monitoring Procedures

There is a growing need to enhance information for environmental treaties. Provisions for the gathering and dissemination of information appear with great regularity in major multilateral agreements[23]. The modern international agreements build a system of regulation based on "supervisory techniques" [24] to ensure implementation of and compliance to the international obligations. Such supervisory techniques are designed to gather information on the general situation of the field and to create a continuing flow of information on parties' performance of treaty obligations. Most treaty regimes rely on self-reporting by parties, rather than creating a centralized data gathering organization, as a means to ensure this data flow. Incidence of reporting requirements are so high that they seem to be included almost pro forma in many agreements, with little concern about cost or implementing capacity[25].

The Kyoto Protocol also adopts a methodology of information gathering, primarily by way of self-reporting. It is recognized that its effectiveness will depend upon two critical factors: whether Parties follow the Protocol's rulebook and comply with their commitments; and whether the emissions data used to assess compliance is reliable[26]. The Kyoto Protocol and Marrakesh Accords[27] adopted by the first meeting of the

Parties to the Kyoto Protocol (COP/MOP1), include a set of monitoring and compliance procedures to enforce the Protocol's rules, address and compliance problems and avoid any error in calculating emissions data and accounting for transactions under the three Kyoto mechanisms. In the following, such rules will be examined in detail.

The Protocol's monitoring procedures are based on existing reporting and review procedures under the 1992 United Nations Framework Convention on Climate Change (UNFCCC)[28]. Articles 5,7 and 8 of the Kyoto Protocol address reporting and review of information by Parties listed in Annex I of the UNFCCC (Annex I Parties) [29] under the Protocol, as well as national systems and methodologies for the preparation of greenhouse gas inventories.

1) Article 5 commits Annex I Parties to having in place, no later than 2007, national systems for the estimation of greenhouse gas emissions by sources and removals by sinks[30]. Article 7 requires Annex I Parties to submit annual greenhouse gas inventories, as well as national communications, at regular intervals, both including supplementary information to demonstrate compliance with the Protocol.
2) Article 8 establishes that expert review teams will review the inventories, and national communications submitted by Annex I Parties.
3) Article 10 calls for cooperation of the Parties in research and to promote systematic observation systems and development of data archives.

For the purpose of the discussion of this paper, we will examine specifically two methodologies of the Kyoto Protocol monitoring procedures: reporting and review (1 and 2 above), and systematic observation (3 above).

3.2 Reporting and Review

While environmental treaties require constant information to ensure the treaty implementation as well as for further decision-making, the question is how to collect such constant and reliable data. Particularly, with the sensitivity to sovereignty in the international arena, international treaty regimes often rely on self-reporting by the parties[31], the UNFCCC and Kyoto Protocol not being an exception. In this process, reporting is coupled with review, which may lead to appropriate action taken by the Conference of Parties.

The UNFCCC requires that all Parties shall develop, periodically update, publish and make available national inventories of anthropogenic emissions by sources and removals by sinks of all greenhouse gases; and communicate information related to implementation.

The Kyoto Protocol provides that each Annex I Party shall incorporate in its annual inventory of anthropogenic emissions by sources and removals by sinks of greenhouse gases the necessary supplementary information for the purposes of ensuring compliance.[32]

Thus, the information to be reported by Parties under these provisions is quite comprehensive and widespread. It includes not only a "national inventory" of anthropogenic emissions by sources and removals by sinks of all greenhouse gases, but also general description of steps taken or envisaged by the Party to implement the Convention, and any other information that the Party considers relevant to the achievement of the objective of the Convention[33], together with information on anthropogenic greenhouse gas emissions by sources and removals by sinks from land use, land-use change and forestry activities under Article 3. 3 of the Kyoto Protocol, and other supplementary information according to Kyoto Protocol Article 7.1. As they will be more detailed, these annual inventories will supersede those currently required under UNFCCC.

The Kyoto Protocol also requires in the "communications" to be included a detailed description of the policies and measures, and specific estimate of the effects that such policies and measures will have on anthropogenic emissions by its sources and removals by its sinks of greenhouse gasses, together with supplementary information according to Kyoto Protocol Article 7.2. These will be merged with national communications submitted under UNFCCC.

The comprehensiveness and detail of requirements for information under the UNFCCC and Kyoto Protocol indicates the understanding of the significance of reporting requirements, which needs to be matched by the seriousness of purpose and adequacy of resources to implement them[34].

The UNFCCC requires that the information communicated by the Parties shall be reviewed by the Conference of the Parties. The Conference of the Parties shall take appropriate action, which may include adoption of amendments to the required commitments[35]. The Kyoto Protocol specifically requires that the submitted information shall be reviewed by expert review teams, as part of the annual compilation and accounting of emissions inventories and assigned amounts, and of the review of communications. The review process is to provide a thorough and comprehensive technical assessment of all aspects of the implementation by a Party. The expert review teams are to prepare a report to the Conference of Parties, assessing the implementation of the commitments of the Party and identifying any potential problems in, and factors influencing, the fulfillment of commitments[36].

The annual inventory review will be conducted as a desk or centralized review and in addition, each Annex I Party will be subject to at least one in-country visit during the commitment period. If any problems are found, the expert review team may recommend adjusting the data to make sure that emissions during any year of the commitment period are not underestimated. If there is disagreement between a Party and the expert review team about the data adjustment that should be made, the Compliance Committee may intervene. Aside from recommending data adjustments, the expert review team has the mandate to raise any apparent implementation problems with the Compliance Committee. Once the expert review team is satisfied with a Party's annual inventory, the compilation and accounting database will be updated with a record of the Party's emissions for that year[37].

Each national communication submitted under the Protocol will be subject to an in-depth review by an expert review team as well, performed as an in-country visit. The expert review team will prepare a report on its review, including any identified potential implementation problems[38].

3.3 Systematic Observation

The term "systematic observations" [39] first appears in a multilateral treaty in the 1985 Vienna Convention for the Protection of the Ozone Layer (Vienna Convention) [40]. In the Vienna Convention, Parties have agreed to undertake, "in accordance with the means at their disposal and their capabilities" to "Co-operate by means of systematic observations, research and information exchange"[41]. This includes satellite observations and research using satellite data, instrument development and the establishment of an operational observing system integrated with groundbased systems.[42]

The UNFCCC provides that all Parties shall "Promote and cooperate in scientific, technological, technical, socio-economic and other research, systematic observation and development of data archives ..."[43] It also requires that Parties shall support and further develop international and intergovernmental programs and networks or organizations, taking into account the need to minimize duplication of effort[44].

The Kyoto Protocol[45] requires that "Parties shall cooperate in scientific and technical research and promote the maintenance and the development of systematic observation systems and development of data archives... and promote the development and strengthening of endogenous capacities and capabilities to participate in international and intergovernmental efforts, programs and networks on research an systematic observation, taking into account Article 5 of the Convention".

The Convention's Subsidiary Body for Scientific and Technological Advice (SBSTA) [46] has discussed regularly the item of Systematic Observation. The Conference of Parties (COP) has adopted reporting guidelines[47] on global climate observing systems and invited Parties to provide detailed reports on systematic observation as part of their national communications (on a voluntary basis, in the case of non-Annex I Parties[48]). COP 9 (Milan, December 2003) adopted a decision on global observing systems for climate[49]. This decision calls for the preparation of an implementation plan for global climate observations to be coordinated by GCOS in collaboration with the Group on Earth Observations (GEO)[50]. The implementation plan was submitted to and endorsed by COP 10 (Buenos Aires, December, 2004)[51]. SBSTA 22 (Bonn, May 2005) welcomed the endorsement of the 10-year Implementation Plan at the third Earth Observation Summit in February 2005 which establishes the Global Earth Observation System of Systems (GEOSS) as an important development in systematic observation to contribute to the enhancement of climate change research[52].

The above considerations on monitoring procedures of the Kyoto Protocol, and the UNFCCC which provides the basis for it, indicates that the specific flow of information is designed in two ways. One flow starts with the Parties' self-reporting, going through a review process and providing feedback to Conference of Parties for their decisions on further measures to be taken. According to such decisions, Parties will provide future reports, thus consisting a continuing flow of information. This is a procedure of monitoring of national performances.

The other monitoring procedure is that of international cooperation. Article 4 of the UNFCCC provides that the Parties are committed to "promote and cooperate" in systematic observation to "further the understanding and to reduce or eliminate the remaining uncertainties regarding the causes, effects, magnitude and timing of climate change". In Article 3.3. , it should be understood that systematic observation is intended to provide general information to support Parties' decisions to take precautionary policies and measures to deal with climate change in a cost-effective manner. The Kyoto Protocol essentially repeats the commitments of UNFCCC for systematic observation. Parties are to communicate their activities on systematic observation in their national communications.

4. Present Role, Potential and Implications

The OCO mission is focused on science, which is understandable from the background of U.S. climate change policy[53]. The GOSAT mission, on the other hand, has a certain political focus. In the Long Term Plan of Space Development[54] issued by Space Activities Commission in September 2003, it is stated that Japan shall develop, operate and advance, in cooperation with related institutions, a satellite observation system to observe the global distribution of greenhouse gas concentration, in order to *clarify* the stabilization concentration of CO_2 and other greenhouse gases, and to *verify* the reduction status of greenhouse gases by combination with in-situ data and models etc. For this, the Plan says that Japan shall develop a sensor that will observe the global distribution of greenhouse gas concentration, and by its operation, establish the effectiveness of greenhouse gas observation method by a satellite observation system. It also states that further, so as to enable continuing *monitoring*, Japan will establish a technology basis by which national emissions and removals can be *estimated*[55].

The Mid-Term Plan[56] of JAXA states that GOSAT will be developed with the aim to contribute to administration including *verification* of the statues of greenhouse gases reduction in the first commitment period (2008-2012) of the Kyoto Protocol, in preparation for global observation of concentration distribution at sub-continental level (relative accuracy approximately 1%).

The Ministry of Environment (MOE) has decided, as some countries did not ratify the Kyoto Protocol to UNFCCC saying that the scientific understanding is not enough, to promote greenhouse gas observation for *validating* national emission inventories and to *understand* the carbon cycle, and to *predict* the future climate including feedback process[57]. It is the belief of the Ministry of Environment and NIES that parallel efforts to reduce the greenhouse gas emission and to *understand* the carbon cycle are very urgent targets of science and technology[58].

In these usages of terms in the political rationale of the GOSAT satellite mission, there seems to be a mixture of focus in "validating (verifying)" "understanding (clarifying, estimating)" and "predicting". Though Kyoto Protocol is silent about "verification" or "validation", this could be understood as part of the review process. "Understanding" and "predicting" are part of the information that is the basis for decisions of Parties, which would be an effort of research and systematic observation.

The role satellite Earth observation can play in the Kyoto Protocol procedures is, however, still limited at the present stage. There are two reasons for this: firstly, most satellite programs are not designed nor operated particularly for use in an international treaty framework. They are aimed to collect data primarily for scientific purposes, or in some cases, operational purposes such as meteorology, which limits their capacity in continuity and adequacy in relation to a specific objective such as that of the Kyoto Protocol. Secondly, the methodology of the Kyoto Protocol is to ensure that "their aggregate anthropogenic carbon dioxide equivalent emissions of the greenhouse gases… do not exceed their assigned amount". As discussed in the previous sections of this paper, Parties are to demonstrate and promote compliance to this obligation by submitting and communicating information on their performances as to the treaty obligations. The measurements by Earth observation satellites in themselves do not coincide with such requirements of the Protocol, as it does not provide, for example, "land use" data, but "land cover" data, nor does it distinguish between "human induced" deforestation and otherwise. Such information is only acquired by in-situ information. What can be said at most seems to be that remote sensing would be able to support quantification of the observations required in the Kyoto Protocol procedures.

The estimation guidelines for establishing national inventories are based on calculations of CO_2 equivalence of anthropogenic emissions using global warming potentials as accepted by Intergovernmental Panel on Climate Change[59] and agreed upon by the Conference of Parties. On the other hand, satellite data is not capable of distinguishing between natural or anthropogenic emissions. Even for a satellite mission such as GOSAT that is developed with a certain political focus, this requirement is not easily matched. The first of the GOSAT series is expected to achieve sub-continental estimation of CO2 emissions and removals. National-level estimation is only planned to be achieved by the follow-on missions of GOSAT.

Therefore, it is not realistic to expect satellite data to be able to contribute directly in the reporting and review process of national inventories, or to replace such data in this process in the Kyoto Protocol, as long as the calculating guidelines remain to be based on human-induced CO_2 emissions.

Thus, the role at present and in the foreseeable future of greenhouse gases observations by satellite is, in the context of implementation of Kyoto Protocol obligations, that they can provide an integral part of systematic observation on greenhouse gases (CO_2 and CH_4). This would enhance the quality of information and understanding on the long-term and general status of climate change, thus reducing the uncertainty of the scientific basis of the treaty.

5. Conclusion

Scientifically, satellite Earth observation can improve the observation gaps of current carbon observation networks needed as the basis for scientific understanding as required by the UNFCCC and its Kyoto Protocol. Thus, satellite observation is a response by Parties to the general and loose obligation to cooperate in systematic observation. For the reporting and reviewing procedures, however, satellite data is not directly applicable at the present stage, since it is difficult to distinguish anthropogenic emissions or land use changes induced by human activities from the net value using satellite data. As the UNFCCC and Kyoto Protocol build upon the rights and obligations of States, it is certainly difficult to combine the process with scientific data acquired from space.

Therefore, if we understand "compliance" as the degree of implementation by a Party of obligations of the Kyoto Protocol, that is, in essence, the commitment to reduce anthropogenic emissions of greenhouse gases, there seems to be little that satellite Earth observation can do for "compliance monitoring" in the field of climate change at the present stage. To pursue this kind of a role by satellite Earth observation in the future, it is necessary to alter the present procedures through intensive interaction between policy, science and technology.

However, it is possible only from space to acquire continuous, repetitive and independent data with global coverage by a centralized and standardized system. The role of these upcoming satellites would be to offer systematic observation, enhancing understanding of the present and future situation of greenhouse gases. Further, there is a possibility that satellite data may provide options for the next steps, by providing means to "validate" or "verify" the state of accomplishment of the treaty objectives and to assess the workability of the treaty regime. This would be in the arena of scientific research as the basis for future decision-making.

---

1 Kyoto Protocol to the Framework Convention on Climate Change, Dec. 10, 1997, 37 I.L.M. 22 [hereinafter Kyoto Protocol].

2 Greenhouse Gases Observing Satellite (GOSAT) , *Homepage, at* http://www.jaxa.jp/missions/projects/sat/eos/gosat/index_e.html (last visited Sept. 11, 2005).

3 Orbiting Carbon Observatory, *Homepage, at* http://oco.jpl.nasa.gov/ (last visited Sept. 11, 2005).

4 Japan Aerospace Exploration Agency (JAXA), Plan to Achieve the Mid-term Goal of the Japan Aerospace Exploration Agency, at 11, *available (only in Japanese) at* http://www.jaxa.jp/missions/plan/pdf/mid-term_plan.pdf (last visited Sept. 20, 2006) ; National Institute for Environmental Studies (NIES) Center for Global Environmental Research, GOSAT *brochure, available at* http://www-cger.nies.go.jp/cger-e/e_pub/e_pamph/pamph_index-e.html (last visited Sept. 14, 2006).

5 See generally, Group on Earth Observations, *Homepage, at* http://earthobservations.org/ (last visited Sept. 11, 2005).

6 Molly K Macouley, *Is the Vision of Earth Observation Summit Realizable?*, 21 SPACE POLICY, 29-39 (2005).

7 In this paper, the meaning of "remote sensing" is almost equivalent to "Earth observation". The former could have a broader meaning of detection from a distance regardless the object to be sensed, while the latter focuses on the object of observation, which is the Earth.

8 Ake Rosenqvist, Anthony Milne, Richard Lucas, Marc Imhoff, & Craig Doson, *A Review of Remote Sensing Technology in Support of the Kyoto Protocol,* 6 ENVIRONMENTAL SCIENCE & POLICY 441-455 (2003).

9 Generated by the Author based on Rosenqvist, *supra* note 8.

10 Kyoto Protocol, *supra* note 1, Art 3.3.

11 *Id.* Art. 3.4.

12 *Id.* Art. 3.1.

13 IGOS, Carbon Theme Report (2004), *available at* http://www.igospartners.org/Carbon.htm (last visited Sept 29, 2006).

14 Integrated Global Observing Strategy Partnership (IGOS), *Homepage*, http://www.igospartners.org/ (last visited Sept 29, 2006).

15 *Id.*, at 6.

16 *Id.*, at 40-43.

17 See NOAA Satellite and Information Service, at http://www.nesdis.noaa.gov/satellites.html (last visited Oct. 1, 2006).

18 See European Space Agency, *Envisat at* http://envisat.esa.int/ (last visited Oct. 1, 2006).

19 Akihiko Kaze, Tomoyuki Urabe, Hiroshi Suto, Yukitaka Kaneko, & Takashi Hamazaki, *The instrumentation and the BBM test results of Thermal And Near Infrared Sensor for carbon Observation (TANSO) on GOSAT*, 6297-20, presented at the International Society for Optical Engineering, San Diego (2006) at 1.

20 Akihiko Kuze, Kayoko Kondo, Yutaka Kaneko & Takashi Hamazaki, *Greenhouse Gases Observation from the GOSAT Satellite*, A14C-03, presented at the American Geophysical Union Fall Meeting, San Francisco (2005) at 3.

21 *Supra* note 3.

22 David Crisp, *The NASA Orbiting Carbon Observatory*, presented at the 3rd GOSAT Symposium, Tokyo (2006).

23 ABRAM CHAYES & ANTONIA HANDLER CHAYES, THE NEW SOVEREIGNTY 172 (Cambridge: Harvard University Press, 1995).

24 PATRICIA BIRNIE & ALAN BOYLE, INTERNATIONAL LAW & THE ENVIRONMENT 206-211 (2d ed., 2002).

25 CHAYES, *supra* note 5, at 154.

26 *Methodological Issues, Reporting and Review under the Kyoto Protocol, at* http://unfccc.int/national_reports/accounting_reporting_and_review_under_the_kyoto_protocol/items/1029.php (last visited Sept. 14, 2005).

27 Conference of the Parties, Marrakesh, Oct. 29-Nov. 10, 2001, Report of the Conference of the Parties on its Seventh Session, Addendum, Part II: Action Taken by the Conference of Parties, Volume II, at FCCC/CP/2001/13/Add.2 (Jan. 21, 2002).

28 United Nations Framework Convention on Climate Change, May 9, 1992, 1771 U.N.T.S. 107 [hereinafter UNFCCC].

29 *Id.*, at Annex I; Annex I countries include the industrialized countries that were members of the OECD (Organisation for Economic Co-operation and Development) in 1992, plus countries with economies in transition (the EIT Parties), including the Russian Federation, the Baltic States, and several Central and Eastern European States.

30 Kyoto Protocol, *supra* note 1, at art 5.1.

31 CHAYES, *supra* note 23, at 154.

32 Kyoto Protocol, *supra* note 1, at art 7. 1.

33 UNFCCC, *supra* note 28.

34 CHAYES, *supra* note 23 at 173.

35 UNFCCC, *supra* note 28, at art 4.1. (d).

36 Kyoto Protocol, *supra* note 1, at art 8.1.

37 UNFCCC *Homepage, Reporting and Review, at* http://unfccc.int/national_reports/accounting_reporting_and_review_under_the_kyoto_protocol/items/1113.php (last visited Sept. 18, 2006)

38 *Id.*

39 See Masami Onoda, *Satellite Earth Observation As Systematic Observation in Multilateral Environmental Treaties*, 31 Journal of Space Law 339-411 (2005).

40 Vienna Convention for the Protection of the Ozone Layer, Mar. 22, 1985, T.I.A.S. No. 11,097, 1513 U.N.T.S. 293 [hereinafter Vienna Convention].

41 *Id.*, at art. 2.

42 *Id.*, at Annex I.

43 *Id.*, at art. 4.1. (g).

44 *Id.*, at art. 5.

45 Kyoto Protocol, *supra* note 1, at art 10 (d).

46 See UNFCCC, *Homepage, Systematic Observation, at* http://unfccc.int/methods_and_science/research_and_systematic_observation/items/3462txt.php (last visited Sept. 11, 2005).

47 Conference of the Parties, Bonn, F.R.G., Oct. 25-Nov. 5, 1999, *Review of the Implementation of Commitments and of other Provisions of the Convention: UNFCCC guidelines on reporting and review*, FCCC/CP/1999/7 (Feb. 16, 2000).

48 UNFCCC, *supra* note 28, at Annex I.

49 Conference of the Parties, Milan, Italy, Dec. 1-12, 2003, *Report of the Conference of the Parties on its Ninth Session, Addendum*, at 20-22, FCCC/CP/2003/6/Add1, 11/CP.9 (Apr. 22, 2004).

50 *Supra* note 5.

51 Confernece of the Parties, Buenos Aires, Arg., Dec. 6-18, 2004, *Report of the Conference of the Parties on its Tenth Session, Addendum*, at 2, FCCC/CP/2004/-/Add1, -/CP.10 (Apr. 22, 2004).

52 Subsidiary Body for Scientific and Technological Advice , Bonn, Germany, May 19-27, 2005, *Report of the Subsidiary Body for Scientific and Technological Advice on its twenty-second session*, at 14, FCCC/SBSTA/2005/4 (Jul. 29, 2005).

53 See U.S. Climate Change Policy, Fact Sheet Released by the White House, Washington DC, Nov. 19, 2004.

54 Space Activities Commission, Long Term Plan of Space Development, *available (only in Japanese) at* http://www.mext.go.jp/b_menu/shingi/uchuu/keikaku/03090101.htm (last visited Sept. 14, 2006).

55 *Id.* at 10.

56 JAXA, *supra* note 4.

57 NIES, *supra* note 4 at 2.

58 *Id.*, at 3.

59 Intergovernmental Panel on Climate Change, *Revised 1996 Guidelines for National Greenhouse Gas Inventories*, *available at* http://www.ipcc-nggip.iges.or.jp/public/gl/invs1.htm (last visited Sept. 30, 2006).

IAC-06-E6.3.05

GLOBAL SPATIAL DATA INFRASTRUCTURE: ISSUES FOR SPACE LAW AND INTERNATIONAL COOPERATION

Satya Sagar Priyatham Singamsetty
International Institute of Air and Space Law, Leiden, Netherlands
email: sagar_nalsar@yahoo.co.uk

Debarupa Banerjee
NALSAR University of Law, Hyderabad, India
email: deba_rupa@yahoo.com

ABSTRACT

The recent concept of a global spatial data infrastructure (GSDI) and its potential realization has captured the imagination and attention of policy makers, administrators, academia, industry and affiliated professions the world over. GSDI is essentially a movement towards widespread sharing of geographic information on a global level which bases itself on the concept of international cooperation through a borderless information flow- smooth, continuous, and most importantly, non discriminatory. From a humble beginning in 1996, as the dream of a small group of visionaries, GSDI has undergone tremendous expansion in terms of sheer concept alone. Though it aims to further global coordination, facilitation and cooperation among national and regional data producers/providers and users, GSDI actually ends up creating a plethora of legal and policy concerns instead. Using remote sensing and GIS as examples, this paper examines the various legal and policy issues which surround GSDI- public-private dichotomy, sovereignty, privacy, copyright and liability in particular. As a solution, international consensus through development of contextual understanding in a multilateral framework is suggested to make global spatial data infrastructure a reality.

1. INTRODUCTION

As we enter the twenty-first century, the concept of a global spatial data infrastructure and its potential realization has captured the imagination and attention of policy makers, administrators, academia, industry and affiliated professions the world over.

The Global Spatial Data Infrastructure (GSDI) began in 1996 as the dream of a small group of visionaries. In its initial stages it was a forum for those concerned with global spatial data to get together and discuss topics of interest, and try to come to agreement on activities that would help achieve their common aims. Now it has undergone tremendous expansion in terms of sheer concept alone. Making local geographic datasets available internationally and establishing a common inter-operability framework over shared data interchange protocols are important components of this concept.[i] It is essentially a widespread sharing of geographic information on a global level which bases itself on the concept of international cooperation through a borderless information flow- smooth, continuous, and most importantly, non discriminatory. The importance and relevance of global spatial data infrastructure cannot be overlooked when we consider its immense potential in addressing global environmental and health challenges, in supporting international telecommunication, commerce, and human development, and in stimulating economic growth and productivity.[ii] The benefits of global coordination, facilitation and cooperation among national and regional data producers/providers to create a unified data infrastructure is, needless to say, a huge step forward for international cooperation in space activities.

The spatial data and processing capabilities supplied by technologies like remote sensing and geographic information systems (GIS) constitute a significant component of GSDI. Therefore, for the purposes of this paper, the various aspects of GSDI will be examined in the context of geographic information (GI), remote sensing and geographic information systems (GIS). Geographic information systems (GI) used interchangeably with the term 'spatial data', is any information that can be geographically referenced, i.e., describing a location or any information that can be linked to a location.[iii] To put it simply, when the information or data is referenced to the objects or the events that are geographic features on earth, then the information is geographic information.[iv] GI has to be further understood in the various technologies which employ it. Of them all, remote sensing and GIS are the most significant. GI consists of both remote sensing and non-remote sensing data. Remote sensing is a technology that collects data relating to the earth's surface without contacting with it, through a sensor mounted in a satellite or high-flying aircraft.[v] To just go by the layperson's definition- it is only a fancy way of referring to observation from space. In the broadest possible terms, geographic information systems (GIS) are tools in the form of computer software programs that allow for the processing of spatial data into information, generally information tied explicitly to, and used to make decisions about, some portion of the earth.[vi] This working definition is, however, neither comprehensive nor particularly precise as it represents a technology which envisages the integration of many subject areas.[vii]

With the advent of high resolution satellites in commercial domain, the Internet revolution and the convergence of GIS and space based remote sensing has improved access to detailed information to both civilian and government users.[viii] As a result, the need for development of a harmonized legal regime balancing national sovereignty, protection of privacy, liability and security concerns with public good and commercial objectives is increasingly being felt. In particular, GIS tools which enable combining of spatially referenced data such as socio-economic data and even personal data are subject to various legal regimes that govern different elements of generation and use of GIS databases, products and software. These have wide ranging legal and policy ramifications.

Hence, when we say that GSDI supports ready global access to geographic information we have to remember that it is really not that simple. As of now, the ideals have a long way to go before they can match up against the practical realities. The worldwide exchange and sharing of spatial data is all set to open another Pandora's Box. This paper will attempt to investigate the possible legal, policy and allied economic impediments to the adoption of global spatial data infrastructure. Using remote sensing and GIS as examples, this paper will examine the working of GSDI which, though it aims to further global coordination, facilitation and cooperation among national and regional data producers/providers and users, actually ends up creating a plethora of legal and policy concerns instead. As a solution, international consensus through development of contextual understanding in a multilateral framework is suggested to make global spatial data infrastructure a reality.

2. THE INCREASINGLY HYBRID PUBLIC-PRIVATE ENVIRONMENT[ix]

Any discussion on the possibility of GSDI has to be made in the background of the public-private dichotomous environment that is the space industry. But this dichotomy has not been a recent phenomenon. It is the result of a long drawn process. Initially space always demonstrated a state-led character, witness to the immediate political and military goals it was assigned from the end of the 1950s in the U.S.A and U.S.S.R.[x] Because the development and exploitation of space programs, calls for national capabilities and investment beyond the norm, there has been a gradual shift towards commercialization of such space programs.

This is where space activity seems to be caught in a double bind. It is in the national interest and general public good to ensure that data are collected, archived and disseminated on an open and non-discriminatory basis. But more and more, the pressure to privatize is drawing decision makers away from this public good argument towards that of commercial market viability.[xi]

These moves toward commercialization and the integration of government space systems are premised on a patchwork of international and domestic legal regimes.[xii] The clarity of space law is particularly challenged by the expanding context of a hybrid public-private, international commercial space segment environment.[xiii] There have been a lot of controversies surrounding different national philosophies regarding the necessity or desirability of public-private separation, direct and indirect subsidies, and trade practices in the aerospace industry.[xiv] The problem can be best illustrated taking the example of remote sensing, which is at the forefront of all space applications. Leading remote sensing nations, including France, Canada, India and Japan, operate remote sensing systems based on mixed public-private institutions and principles. Other leading remote sensing nations have commercial technology applications that are clearly emerging from a government-funded, military heritage. Post-Cold War national budgets have created pressure to forge public-private partnerships even in nations historically committed to the separation of these sectors.[xv]

Remote sensing activities provide critical national technology capability and also ensure infrastructure for telecommunication, television broadcasting, meteorology, resource survey and management, and disaster management support. In addition to enabling applications that were previously impossible or impractical by other means, satellite-derived geospatial information products promise both time and cost savings over older or more conventional methods.[xvi] In fact, the particular activities recognized in the U.N. Principles on Remote Sensing- "improving natural resources management, land use and the protection of the environment"[xvii]- are increasingly identified among the potential markets for private and government space-based systems and have become the economic rationale for aggressive, commercial-like cost recovery policies for some public systems.[xviii]

With the rapid emergence of the private sector, technological advances in imaging satellites and GIS, GI will be disseminated openly and supplied to the international market. Global accessibility to remote sensing technologies and data has, however, broad international security implications. Given that much of today's remote sensing technology also has a heritage of supporting military reconnaissance and defense planning, and given the importance that space-based information products prove during war times, it is important to consider the security impacts that expanding access to Earth imaging technology will bring.[xix] Security is just one of the many concerns. Issues of state sovereignty, privacy, intellectual property rights and liability are the other ghosts GSDI has to battle with if its full potential is to be attained.

Thus, the inter-relationship of public and private functions in space activities is a space law subject that has far reaching legal and policy consequences on the way GSDI can be put into practice.

2.1 Sovereignty and Rights of the Sensed State

Sovereignty is the key characteristic of any state and cannot be compromised in any situation whatsoever. This right becomes all the more important in the context of GSDI. With the possibility of GSDI, with the potential for worldwide dissemination of high quality remote sensing imageries which can provide a lot of details regarding land surface and oceans, the sovereignty concerns of states is being seen by many as under direct challenge.[xx] Envisaging such a situation, Principle IV of the U.N. Principles on Remote Sensing lays down, *inter alia* that remote sensing activities "shall be conducted on the basis of respect for the principle of full and permanent sovereignty of all states and peoples over their own wealth and natural resources, with due regard to the rights and interests, in accordance with international law, of other states and entities under their jurisdiction. Such activities shall not be conducted in a manner detrimental to the legitimate rights and interests of the sensed state."

The rights of sensed states should be seen in the light of the sovereignty of states over their natural resources. It is a well established rule of international law that every state is free to manage and utilize the natural resources within its jurisdiction and to pursue its own environmental and developmental policies.[xxi] This right is, however, neither unlimited nor unguided. It is a right which is to be exercised within the limits set by international law.

Rao and Murthi have pointed out how access to data about their territories can be problematic for governments and lead to possible infringement of privacy. As data availability will be purely driven by market considerations, the affordability for assessing such data will be another major issue for a large number of states. As there are concerns about governments losing some degree of control over information about their territory, there could be tensions, particularly when a state considers that entities abroad have exploited information about its territory even as it had no fair and affordable access to the same- due to commercially driven policies. There are real threats to the rights to privacy- due to possibilities of industrial espionage, and potential use of imagery by anti-social groups. Commercial corporations from one country could gather information on exploitable natural resources in another country without the knowledge of its government and could possibly gain strategic advantages in negotiations. The consequences of these are far reaching.

2.2 Privacy

The ability of public and private entities to obtain and manipulate vast amounts of information about people, their property, and their activities creates the potential for exploitation and further intrusion into traditionally private matters. In this regard, GSDI, through the medium of GIS, has a serious potential for exploitative and invasive uses by the government and private users. In "providing instant access to vast amounts of data, (a GIS) provides the opportunity to abuse, to misinform, and to invade the privacy of individuals on a greater scale than ever before."[xxii] Digital files can be "transferred, accessed, and combined in ways unforeseen by the provider and without the consent of the individuals affected."[xxiii] As a result, the "unanticipated uses of data may compromise individual rights or privacy or cause injury."[xxiv]

Beyond general privacy concerns, GIS can be misused in making policy itself. Maps and charts based on electronic databases can be manipulated quickly and more readily than maps on paper or microfilm. As one expert has repeatedly emphasized, "a single map is but one of an indefinitely large number of maps that might be produced from the same set of data."[xxv] Due to advances in low-cost computer graphics, "inadvertent yet serious cartographic lies can appear respectable and accurate."[xxvi] As a result, a profusion of slick but deceptive charts, exhibits, and photographs can been thrust upon cartographically challenged policymakers and the general population.

Also, an uncomfortable political dimension to GSDI is the degree to which those controlling the system can influence what the system produces.[xxvii] Political groups can search databases to target individuals based on their wealth, profession, residential location, tax payments, and even their racial background.[xxviii] There may be legitimate government uses of this type of information, but it can also be used for improper political or personal goals. Drawing voting or zoning districts to maximize one's own political and economic stature (or to minimize opponents') is one example.[xxix]

The final angle to this entire privacy issue stems from the fact that governments engaged in selling spatial data sets to the private sector have found that cadastral data (that is, the household level data that tie ownership information to the location and physical attributes of the land) are more in demand than any other layer of information. Having this kind of information allows businesses to conveniently aggregate information through computer cross matching. When local jurisdictions fail to have cadastral data available or readily accessible in digital form, businesses have found their own survey methods to generate "simulated" spatial datasets they use and market. The practice of collecting data about customers and profiling those draws attention to the very thin line between data collection for permissible commercial goals and impermissible intrusion into personal privacy.[xxx] This is something GSDI has to contend with as all this is going to herald a new social and technological era in which conflicts relating to privacy no longer affect single individuals but the entire community as a whole.

2.3 Copyright and Data Protection

Of the several areas of law that affect access to and use of geographic information, copyright is perhaps the most important. Protecting at least minimally creative and expressive aspects of the intellectual content of art, music, and literature, regardless of the effort or skill (or lack thereof) that went into their creation, is probably the major feature of copyright.[xxxi]

In general, copyright protection for spatial databases raises a series of emerging, unresolved theoretical questions. Resolving rights in spatial databases implicates the theoretical shortcomings of copyright law both as applied to geographic representations and to computer representations.[xxxii] The first problem crops up over the issue of idea-expression dichotomy itself. Copyright protects expression but not the underlying ideas, which can be and should be used without compensation to the spatial databases.[xxxiii] That copyright protects only expression, not facts was expressed in the 1986 Berne Convention[xxxiv]. The expression protected must be the product of intellectual creativity and not merely labour, time, or money invested. Facts, algorithms, physical truths, and ideas exist for use by everyone. These may be extracted and used freely.[xxxv]

Regardless of the nation, copyright subsists usually in compilations of geographic facts if there is some creative "authorship" in the "selection, coordination, or arrangement" of the compilation. There is a modicum of creativity in the selection, arrangement and coordination of almost any geographic data set. Thus, in the U.S. for example, wholesale copying of a competitor's geographic data set without permission is typically illegal under existing copyright law because, in the process of copying a data set, one is inevitably copying the creative elements of the work as well.[xxxvi]

Professor Raskind has pointed out, with specific reference to maps, that many interpretive problems of copyright derive from our failure to define originality in terms of the specific authorship criteria relevant to the variety of works that are in principle copyright protected.[xxxvii] He would seek originality in the special skills applicable to the type of work in question. In the case of maps, these would be skills in displaying spatial and quantitative relationships through scale, color, symbols, and overall design, including skills in compiling new maps from existing maps.[xxxviii]

Then, of course, we have the entire remote sensing angle to copyright. Now that commercial remote sensing programmes are operational in most of the space-faring nations, the continued existence of the technology depends upon how well the private sector can market satellite data. An understanding of the application of intellectual property rights to remote sensing data requires an understanding of the difference between enhanced and unenhanced data. Unenhanced data, or raw data, is obtained directly from the satellite, and primarily consists of digital information or photographs. Enhanced data, in contrast, is the result of human or electronic analysis of the raw data.[xxxix]

Copyright protection is unavailable to unenhanced data because the very nature of a copyright is to give exclusive rights to the copyright owner. The policy of nondiscriminatory access would be undermined by private operators attempting to exact royalties or licensing fees from users of raw data. Because of the value addition in enhanced data, intellectual property rights in enhanced data are necessary to increase the number of data enhancement firms and thereby increase the market for raw data.[xl]

Even a small data enhancement firm must invest significant capital in software, equipment, and trained personnel before it can begin operation. Copyright laws will protect this investment and, by making processed data more valuable, will provide an incentive for firms to enter the market. Without the economic rents created by copyright, it is unlikely that enough firms will produce sufficient enhanced data to make commercialization worthwhile. This is because the data enhancement industry will constitute the market for raw data necessary to realise a profit.

Competition from foreign remote sensing systems provides another reason why legal protection of enhanced data is necessary. Many countries operate commercial remote sensing systems, and some of these, such as the French SPOT system and the European Space Agency's ERS-1 (both commercialised systems), compete with U.S.A.'s Landsat for international as well as domestic data markets. A significant feature of international intellectual property rights is that these rights shall protect competition among all entities producing enhanced data worldwide. Without copyright protection, an individual or entity could pirate enhanced data produced by someone else and legitimately pass it off as its own. There would be no mechanism to prevent such an entity from distorting the data to obtain financial or political benefits. Therefore, the nature of a commercial remote sensing programme mandates copyright protection for enhanced data. Such copyright protection will benefit producers of enhanced data worldwide due to the existence of multilateral copyright agreements.[xli]

A host of international instruments and conventions related to remote sensing like the Outer Space Treaty (1967), Principles Relating to Remote Sensing of Earth from Space (1986), The Berne Convention (1971), the Universal Copyright Convention (1971), the Rome Convention (1961), the Phonogram Convention (1971) and the Satellite Convention (1974) do make references to the copyrightable aspects of remote sensing but are not adequate in the real sense of the word.[xlii]

On the whole, there is currently no adequate and efficient protection of remote sensing data in international law. In the wake of the various copyright conventions, one may think that there is a need for such a specific convention, which may be a necessary step if the trend towards the proposed borderless information flow is to materialize. There are observers who clearly state that the Berne Convention itself is an "inadequate mechanism" for new technologies,[xliii] including remote sensing imagery.

Issues of copyright thus become a major cause of concern for GSDI.

2.4 Liability[xliv]

The importance of liability is crucial to every use of global technology and GIS is no exception. Considering the fact that the GIS is essentially a database centric technology, liability comes in the manner it is used. When an action or decision is taken based upon the information and analysis in a GIS, the liability exposure of those involved with the development of GIS software and databases, or with provision of information based upon analysis in a GIS, can be important. To elaborate, use of GIS data and software inevitably results in some action or decision. If errors or shortcomings have resulted in inappropriate actions or decisions and parties are harmed, the issue of liability arises for dataset and software producers as well as for all other parties involved in handling geographic information. As a general proposition, legal liability for damages is a harm-based concept. For instance, those who have been specifically hired to provide data for a database or those who are offering data for sale to others are responsible for some level of competence in the performance of the service or for some level of fitness in the product offered. If others are damaged by mistakes that a producer should not have made or by inadequacies that should not have been allowed, the courts have reasoned that producers should bear some responsibility for the damages. But for their mistake or defective product, the damages would not have occurred. In commercial settings, liability exposure often may be reduced through appropriate communications, contracts, and business practices. However, liability exposure may never be eliminated completely; under current legal principles, it can be merely minimized.

Nor is its elimination desirable. Modern societies generally support the proposition that individuals and businesses should take responsibility for their actions if those actions have unjustifiably caused harm to others.

Those who have been hired specifically to provide spatial data for a database or those who are offering data for sale to others are responsible for some level of competence in the performance of the service or for some level of fitness in the product offered.[xlv]

There is the obvious formulation that liability exposure may have a substantial impact on whether businesses and others will be willing to share GIS data and whether they will be willing to offer GIS data for sale in a networked electronic marketplace.[xlvi]

However, it is also inevitable that errors and blunders will be contained in any practical database. Thus, the law holds that those in the information chain should be liable only for those damages they had a duty to prevent. Legislation affecting liability for spatial datasets and software typically might be found in statutes addressing such issues as tort law, contract law, intellectual property rights, privacy rights, anti-trust issues, and access rights. The liability in data, products, and services related to computerized geographic information systems is complicated by legal theory uncertainties surrounding liability for maps. This is compounded by the complexities and uncertainties in liability for information system products and services generally. Liability in GIS is further confused by the wide array of current and potential applications of geographic information technologies. Each application requires integration of information specific to the application and often will involve different attributes, analytical methods, spatial features, and accuracy requirements. The specific software and end users will also vary depending on the application to which the technology is being applied.[xlvii]

Another way of addressing the issue of liability is in relation to the public good aspect of geographic information. Pricing and financing information is a special kind of commodity: its use is non exclusive, the quantity is difficult to measure, and it has the character of a public good.[xlviii] Further, it is questionable if all users should be charged the same price. Therefore it is difficult to set a fair price, and the market does not really play. This issue then boils down to the question whether the spatial data infrastructure is considered a public utility that can be used by anybody regardless of his financial means, or a profit centre which has to recover its cost. In each case, the nature and quantum of liability attached would be different.[xlix]

Thus, the complexity of the legal questions surrounding geographic information system liability combined with the diversity of problems to which geographic information technologies are being applied has tended to create diffuse, changing, and often undefined liability concerns for all parties who would be involved in geographic information production and use.

3. CONCLUSION

The goal of global spatial data infrastructure is to promote sharing and communication of geospatial knowledge across national boundaries. Its growth and proliferation will likely be a natural market-driven growth, based on the principle of international cooperation for information exchange at a global level. Incorporating the efforts of governments and non-governmental spatial data providers and users into a flexible and extensible system can be done only once the specific hurdles in building a spatial data infrastructure as described in this paper are overcome. It can be foreseen that GSDI will increasingly become a part of the governmental and managerial landscape in the coming years. Legal and public policy issues associated with GSDI have slowly but steadily been rising and therefore they need to be given greater attention by policy makers. Liability, privacy, and public access are but a few of the many legal and policy concerns surrounding GSDI. Law and policymakers should be prepared to address these and other issues as the benefits and uses of GSDI become more apparent.

The only way out is to find a common platform so that the diverse issues related to GSDI can be tackled in a single forum at the international level. Perhaps the best way of doing this would be to mobilize international consensus through development of contextual understanding in a multilateral framework. This will be highly useful to make global spatial data infrastructure a workable reality.

ACKNOWLEDGEMENTS

The authors would like to express their sincere thanks to Mr. K.R. Sridhara Murthi, Ms. T.S. Shoba, and Mr. Mukund Rao for their valuable inputs which have greatly influenced and improved this paper. Our thanks also to Mr. V. Gopalakrishnan for his kind help and support.

Notes

[i] Zaslavsky, Ilya et al., *XML-based Spatial Data Mediation Infrastructure for Global Interoperability* at http://www.sdsc.edu/~gupta/publications/gsdi_iz.html (last visited June 17, 2006).

[ii] Zaslavsky, ibid.

[iii] "Spatial Information Related Terms" at http://www.anzlic.org.au/glossary_terms.html (last visited May 4, 2006)

[iv] Juppenlatz, Morris and Tian, Xiaofeng, *Geographic Information Systems and Remote Sensing,* Mcgraw-Hill Book Co., 1996 at 3.

[v] Juppenlatz, ibid. at 12.

[vi] Demers, Michael N., *Fundamentals of Geographic Information Systems*, John Wiley & Sons, 2000 at 7.

[vii] Demers, ibid.

[viii] Sridhara Murthi, K.R. and Rao, Mukund, "Establishing Spatial Data Infrastructures- Some Legal Perspectives", *Global Spatial Data Infrastructure, 7th International Conference, February 2-6, 2004, Bangalore, India.*

[ix] Term proposed by Gabrynowicz, Joanne Irene, " Space Law: Its Cold War Origins and Challenges in the Era of Globalization", *37 Suffolk U. L. Rev.* 1041 (2004).The terms 'dichotomous' and 'hybrid' can coexist in the context of the space industry as any activity that is not public may be either private or partly public (hybrid). The dichotomy remains, in any case.

[x] Pasco, Xavier, "A New Role for a New Millennium? The Changing Nature of Space Activities," *Space Policy* 19 (2003) 15.
[xi] Pasco, ibid.
[xii] See a summary of framework conditions of United States and five other nations in Harr, Michael and Kohli, Rajiv, *Commercial Utilization of Space- An International Comparison of Framework Conditions*, 1990 at 69-71; as quoted in Gabrynowicz, supra n. 9.
[xiii] Gabrynowicz, ibid.
[xiv] Gabrynowicz, ibid.
[xv] See Commercial Space Act of 1998, Pub. L. No. 105-303, § 102, 112 Stat. 2843, 2846-2851 (1998). Programs include Earth Observations Commercial Applications Program and the data buy program at NASA Stennis Space Center.
[xvi] Tahu, George J. et al., "Expanding Global Access to Civilian and Commercial Remote Sensing Data: Implications and Policy Issues", *Space Policy* 14 (1998) 179.
[xvii] Principle I(a), G.A. Res. 41/65, U.N. GAOR, 41st Sess., 95th Plenary Meeting at 2, U.N. Doc A/RES/41/65 (1986) (hereinafter U.N. Principles on Remote Sensing).
[xviii] Gabrynowicz, supra n. 9.
[xix] Tahu, supra n. 16 at 179- 180.
[xx] Rao, Mukund K. and Sridhara Murthi, K.R., "Remote Sensing Images and GI Information: Policy and Legal Perspectives", *Proceedings of the ISRO- IISL Space Law Conference*, June 26-29, 2005, Bangalore, India at 5-14.
[xxi] Jayaraj, C. and Dayal, Gaurab, "Commentary paper on Remote Sensing Images and GI Information: Policy and Legal Perspectives", *Proceedings of the ISRO- IISL Space Law Conference*, June 26-29, 2005, Bangalore, India at 5-42.
[xxii] Aronoff, Stan, "Geographic Information Systems: A Management Perspective", (1993) at 284; as quoted in Makar, Scott D. and Makar Jr., Michael R., "Geographic Information Systems: Legal and Policy Implications", *69-NOV Fla. B.J.* 44 (1995).
[xxiii] Aronoff, ibid.
[xxiv] Aronoff, ibid. at 277.
[xxv] Monmonier, Mark, "How to Lie with Maps", (1991) at 2; as quoted in Makar, Scott D. and Makar Jr., Michael R., "Geographic Information Systems: Legal and Policy Implications", *69-NOV Fla. B.J.* 44 (1995).
[xxvi] Monmonier, ibid.
[xxvii] Aronoff, supra n. 22 at 285.
[xxviii] The use of geographic data, such as racial demographics associated with zip codes, can yield erroneous results. See Monmonier, Mark, "Zip Codes, Data Compatibility, and Environmental Racism", *2 GIS LAW 4 (Spring 1994)*.
[xxix] Monmonier, ibid.
[xxx] Rao and Murthi, supra n. 20 at 5-20.
[xxxi] Karjala, Dennis S., "Copyright and Misappropriation", *17 U. Dayton L. Rev.* 885 (1992). The vast majority of copyright- protected works fall into this category.
[xxxii] Holland, W.S., "Copyright, Licensing and Cost Recovery for Geographic and Land Information Systems Data: A Legal, Economic and Policy Analysis", (1994) at http://www.spatial.maine.edu/tempe/holland.html (last visited May 22, 2006).
[xxxiii] Rao and Murthi, supra n. 20 at 5-20.
[xxxiv] U.S. Treaty Doc. 99-27, KAV 2245.
[xxxv] Onsrud, Harlan J., "Geographic Information: Legal Issues" at http://www.spatial.maine.edu/~onsrud/pubs/GILegalIssues.html (last visited May 22, 2006).
[xxxvi] Onsrud, ibid.
[xxxvii] Raskind, Leo J., "The Continuing Process of Refining and Adapting Copyright Principles", *14 COLUM.-VLA J.L. & ARTS* 127, 134 (1990); as quoted in Karjala, supra n. 31.
[xxxviii] Raskind, ibid. at 136-37, 149.
[xxxix] Section primarily constructed with the help of West, J. Richard, "Copyright Protection for Data Obtained by Remote Sensing: How the Data Enhancement Industry will ensure Access for Developing Countries", *11 Nw. J. Int'l L. & Bus.* 403 (1990).
[xl] West, ibid.

[xli] West, ibid.

[xlii] See Feder, Harry, "The Sky's The Limit? Evaluating the International Law of Remote Sensing", *23 N.Y.U. J. Int'l L. & Pol.* 599 (1991). See also Salin, Patrick A., "Proprietary Aspects of Commercial Remote-Sensing Imagery", *13 Nw. J. Int'l L. & Bus.* 349 (1992).

[xliii] Motyka, Carol A., "Effects of U.S. Adherence to the Berne Convention", *16 Rutgers Computer & Tech. L. J.* 195, 212 (1990).

[xliv] Constructed primarily with the help of Onsrud, Harlan J., "Liability in the Use of Geographic Information Systems and Geographic Datasets" at http://www.spatial.maine.edu/~onsrud/pubs/liability40.pdf (last visited June 22, 2006).

[xlv] Rao and Murthi, supra n. 20 at 5-21.

[xlvi] Rao and Murthi, ibid.

[xlvii] Onsrud, supra n. 44.

[xlviii] Bitter, Peter and Shrestha, Basanta, "Regional Geographic Information Infrastructure in the Hindu Kush Himalayan Region" at http://www.gisdevelopment.net/application/nrm/mountain/moung0001.htm (last visited August 26, 2006).

[xlix] Bitter, ibid.

IAC-06-E6.3.06

THE IMPORTANCE OF INTERNATIONAL COOPERATION IN BUILDING NATIONAL SPACE DATA INFRASTRUCTURE IN ALL COUNTRIES

José Monserrat Filho
Brazilian Association of Air and Space Law (SBDA)
Brazilian Society for the Advancement of Science (SBPC)
E-mail: monserrat@alternex.com.br

How to imagine the advancement of all mankind,
without the national development of each country?

Abstract

The use of geospatial data and geoprocessing technology is critical for surveying and monitoring natural resources (land, water, mine), environmental changes, meteorology, hydrology, and natural, geological disasters; in creating and updating national topographic map system for territorial planning and management; in supporting economic development and administration; in researching, applying and creating new technologies for Earth observation; in implementing programmes, projects, scientific research and technology exchange with different countries, international organizations and private enterprises.

This kind of information and its benefits are today an indispensable part of a country's strategic infrastructure for national sustainable development, just as networks for transportation, healthcare, education, telecommunication and water supply systems.

Hence it is essential that each country, irrespective of its degree of economic or scientific development, have an appropriate infrastructure and human resources specialized in the knowledge and the application of modern techniques for geospatial data acquisition and processing, culture management and to reach a high level of public awareness of its usefulness in all areas of national life.

States conducting remote sensing and geographic information system programmes are called upon to make special efforts to cooperate with other States in building their national space data infrastructure, in the modes considered most effective and appropriate by the countries concerned.

The aim is that all countries should be, as soon as possible, adequately equipped to capture, analyze and apply the geospatial data indispensable for the national sustainable development, as well as for the prevention and mitigation of natural disasters.

The paper hereby proposes that this concrete objective become an integral item underlying the principle of internacional space cooperation. It would be, no doubt about it, for the benefit and in the interest of all countries.

1. Space Law and cooperation for national sustainable development

At the beginning, the International Space Law used to make references to cooperation, but not to cooperation for national development. The 1967 Outer Space Treaty utilizes the word "cooperation" twice in the Preamble and in five articles[1]. However, the major concern is "promoting international cooperation and understanding" in the interest of "maintaining international peace and security", as it is clear in its Article II.

The world lived then the hardest Cold War times. There were only two space powers: the United States and the Soviet Union. And they were deeply envolved in a mass destruction arms race. Their central legal and political objectives were to regulate – within the United Nations Charter system, convenient for both – and reduce as much as possible the potential conflicting issues between them in outer space, as well as to establish the principle of free exploration and use of the new environment and its principle of non-appropriation. It included the free use of satellite surveillance and intercontinental balistic missiles, which fly through outer space. The non-appropriation principle, in turn, was thought to prevent the outer space acquisition or ocupation by one of the rival powers.

Not by chance the American Professor Nathan C. Goldman[2] rightly notes: "The history of International Space Law, therefore, cannot be understood apart from its origins in the Cold War. Indeed, the development of the International Law of outer space is inextricably linked to this context of international politics and policy."

The matter at issue is that Article III of the Outer Space Treaty determines that space activities shall be carried out "in accordance with international law, including the Charter of United Nations", and the Charter establishes as one of the purposes of United Nations the promotion of "economic and social progress and development."

Its Article 55 is very clear in this sense: "With a view to the creation of conditions of stability and well-being which are necessary for peaceful and friendly relations among nations based on respect for the principle of equal rights and self-determination of peoples, the United Nations shall promote: (a) higher standards of living, full employment, and conditions of economic and social progress and development; (b) solutions of international economic, social, health, and related problems; and international cultural and educational cooperation; and (c) universal respect for, and observance of, human rights and fundamental freedoms for all without distinction as to race, sex, language, or religion."

And Article 56 completes: "All Members pledge themselves to take joint and separate action in cooperation with the Organization for the achievement of the purposes set forth in Article 55."

By relating Article III of Outer Space Treaty to Articles 55 and 56 of the United Nations, one comes logically to the conclusion that the exploration and use of outer space by all States shall be carried out aiming at the economic and social progress and development of each nation.

This disposition could be included in Article I of Outer Space Treaty, the so-called "common benefit clause". According to it, "the exploration and use of outer space, including the Moon and celestial bodies, shall be carried out for the benefit and in the interests of all countries, irrespective of their degree of economic or scientific development, and shall be the province of all mankind." It would be entirely proper to add, after "irrespective of their degree of economic or scientific development," a more material reference, for instance: "with a view to promote conditions of their economic and social progress and development" (...).

Thus, Article I, § 1, could be read this way: "The exploration and use of outer space, including the Moon and celestial bodies, shall be carried out for the benefit and in the interests of all countries, irrespective of their degree of economic or scientific development, with a view to promote conditions of their economic and social progress and development, and shall be the province of all mankind."

Of course, it is possible to give such an interpretation to the real wording of Article I, § 1, but would it reach a consensus?

However, the mentioned connection is not new. It was explicitly recognized for the first time in the 1979 Moon Agreeement[3]. Its Article 4, § 1, says: "The exploration and use of the Moon shall be the province of all mankind and shall be carried out for the benefit and in the interests of all countries, irrespective of their degree of economic or scientific development. Due regard shall be paid to the interests of present and future generations as well as to the need to promote higher standards of living and conditions of economic and social progress and development in accordance with the Charter of the United Nations."

The same reference is made by the Resolution on the Principles Governing the Use by States of Artificial Earth Satellites for International Direct Television Broadcasting[4], approved by the UN General Assembly in 1982. Its Article D, § 6, says that "special consideration should be given to the needs of the developing countries in the use of international direct television broadcasting by satellite for the purpose of accelerating their national development."

However, there is not any mention to national development in the Resolution on the Principles Relating to Remote Sensing of the Earth from Outer Space[5], adopted by the UN General Assembly in 1986. At that time, the States did not realize yet how indispensable remote sensing activities will become for their national development. That is one of the reasons why this UN Resolution must be updated.

Nevertheless, according to its Principle I, the sensing of the Earth's surface from space is made "for the purpose of improving natural resources management, land use and protection of the environment." It could be interpreted as meaning "natural resources management, land use and protection of the environment for national development", but a further guarantee would be provided should that very wording be included to the Resolution it self. After all, obviously, there are kinds of natural resources management, land use and protection of the environment that can be seen as not corresponding to national development by a State. And all States have the sovereign right to define their own ways and programs of national development, since they are not harmful to the international community as a whole.

Depending on the interpretation, two other Principles reinforce the idea of national development, although this concept is not directly mentioned. The Principle II says that "remote sensing activities shall be carried out... taking into particular consideration the needs of the developing countries." And Principle IV affirms that "such activities shall not be conducted in a manner detrimental to the legitimate rights and interests of the sensed State." In the first case, we can argue that for a developing country, logically, no need is no a more crucial than its national development. In the second case, we can surely consider that the national development is, without any doubt about it, a legitimate right, as well as one of the major interests of any State, even more a developing State, including the sensed ones.

A step ahead in the process of recognition of the exploration and use of outer space as indispensable requirement for national development is the Declaration on International Cooperation in the Exploration and Use of Outer Space for the benefit and in the Interest of All States Taking into Particular Account the Needs of Developing Countries[6] – known as the "Space Benefit Declaration" –, adopted by the UN General Assembly in 1996.

Specially significant in this connection is the § 5 of the Declaration, which says:

"International cooperation, while taking into particular account the needs of developing countries, should aim, *inter alia*, at the following goals, considering their need for technical assistance and rational and efficient allocation of financial and technical resources:

(a) Promoting the development of space science and technology and of its applications;

(b) Fostering the development of relevant and appropriate space capabilities in interested States;

(c) Facilitating the exchange of expertise and technology among States on a mutually acceptable basis."

Needless to say that all these activities are essential for national development by and large. It is unthinkable in the contemporary world to develop a country without consistent programs in the most important fields of science, technology, innovation – including the space one – and its respective facilities and human capabilities. Unfounded is also to realize an isolated national development which could dispense with international cooperation and refuse to exchange expertise and technology with other countries.

The 1996 UN Declaration is in a good way. Yet it can be improved still more in vital aspects. To affirm that "States are free to determine all aspects of their participation in international cooperation", as it is said in the § 2, happens to be obviously insuffIcent in such a interdependent world we all live today. It is necessary to establish, at last, that States have the duty to seek to cooperate with other countries on an equitable and mutually acceptable basis, as a kind of legitimate pressure put by international community of nations in order to stimulate as much as possible the national development in a large number of countries. Sustainable development for all Peoples is the basis of peace, justice, long life, as well as social, cultural and political advancement for the present and future generations on Earth, on the Moon, on Mars and elsewhere mankind could reach.

In this sense, the 1996 UN Declaration can serve as a platform to create new and more detailed resolution, relating for instance to the "relevant and appropriate space capabilities in interested States" – more precisely the capabilities to capture, process, analyze and intensively use geospatial data for their national development, which is the subject of the present paper.

This proposal has the support of some more general international documents, approved in the framework of United Nations in the last twenty years.

In 1986, the UN General Assembly adopted a Resolution with the Declaration on the Right to Development[7], prepared on the basis and as a derivative of the purposes and principles of the Charter of United Nations. Its article 1, § 1, defines the right to development as "an inalienable human right by virtue of which every human person and all peoples are entitled to participate in, contribute to, and enjoy economic, social, cultural and political development, in which all human rights and fundamental freedoms can be fully realized." The Article 3, § 1, in its turn, says that "States have the primary responsibility for the creation of national and international conditions favourable to the realization of the right to development," meanwhile the § 3 affirms that "States have the duty to cooperate with each other in ensuring development and eliminating obstacles to development." It is also relevant to quote also the § 1 of Article 4: "States have the duty to take steps, individually and collectively, to formulate international development policies with a view to facilitating the full realization of the right to development." And the § 2: "Sustained action is required to promote more rapid development of developing countries. As a complement to the efforts of developing countries, effective international cooperation is essential in providing these countries with appropriate means and facilities to foster their comprehensive development." These recommendations are fully valid for all space activities too.

It is appropriate to remember the Principle 9 of the Rio Declaration on Environment and Development[8], proclaimed by the UN Conference on Environment and Development, held at Rio de Janeiro in 1992, which proclaims: "States should cooperate to strengthen endogenous capacity-building for sustainable development by improving scientific understanding through exchanges of scientific and technological knowledge, and by enhancing the development, adaptation, diffusion and transfer of technologies, including new and innovative technologies". A genuine national development lies above all upon endogenous capacity building for strategic iniciatives and decisions, even recognising the necessity of internacional cooperation to construct this capacity.

The Space Millennium: Vienna Declaration on Space and Human Development[9], adopted by the Third UN Conference on the Exploration and Peaceful Uses of Outer Space (UNISPACE III), held in July 1999, recommended a set of actions in order "to protect the Earth's environment and managing its resources, as well as to use space applications for human security, development and welfare."

At last two of them deserve to be highlighted here:

"To improve knowledge-sharing by giving more importance to the promotion of universal access to space-based communication services and by devising effective policies, infrastructure, standards and applications development projects;" and

"To assist States, especially developing countries, in applying the results of space research with a view to promoting the sustainable development of all peoples."

Following this sequence, the UN Member States have taken a remarkable decision in the § 12 ot the United Nations Millennium Declaration[10], adopted by the UN General Assembly in 2000: "We resolve (...) to create an environment – at the national and global levels alike – which is conducive to development and to the elimination of poverty." This constructive environment, of course, should include cooperative actions aiming at building the geospatial data infrastructure so needed to every nation.

Finally, it is equally worthywhile mentioning the Resolution on international cooperation in the peaceful uses of outer space, adopted by the UN General Assembly in 2005[11]. The point of the present paper is in harmony with this resolution, as it:

"Emphasizes the need to increase the benefits of space technology and its applications and to contribute to an orderly growth of space activities favourable to sustained economic growth and sustainable development in all countries, including mitigation of the consequences of disasters, in particular in the developing countries;

"Urges the Committee [on the Peaceful Uses of Outer Space] to expand the scope of international cooperation relating to the social, economic, ethical and human dimension in space science and technological applications;

"Requests the Committee [on the Peaceful Uses of Outer Space] to identify and consider new areas and mechanisms of international cooperation in the peaceful uses of outer space to strengthen multilateralism, in accordance with the preamble to the present resolution, and to submit a report to the General Assembly at its Sixtieth Session, including its views on which subjects should be studied in the future."

The main thesis of this paper seems to fit entirely in these recomendations, as it attempts to show how high is the importance of international cooperation in building geo-spatial data infrastructure in all countries for their national sustainable development, as well as for the prevention and mitigation of natural disasters.

These documents for their most part take up an International Space Law not passive, nor static, nor distant from and unaware of the existing situation, but, on the contrary, a dynamic, enterprising, active and even creative Space Law. It is an old aspiration of International Law, not always turned into reality. Wolfgang Friedmann[12] used to consider International Law as "an agent of progress and evolution." Oscar Schachter[13] wrote that "International Law is more than a given body of rules and obligations. It involves purposive activities undertaken by governments, directed to a variety of social ends." And Rein Müllerson[14] noted that "the only form of the existence of International Law is its functioning" and that "there are currently four major areas where the role of International Law in contributing to progress in international society and beyond is crucial: protection of the natural environment; limitation of violence both whithin and across national borders; promotion of democracy and human rights; facilitating economic growth and stability."

2. Space data infrastructure for national development

To the effect of this paper, national space data infrastructure is defined as a joint of specialists, equipments and facilities that permit a country to capture, process, analyze and apply satellite data from its own satellite or from one of any other country.

Each country must have its national space data infrastructure, because it needs geo-spatial information to identify and overcome – in a most efficient manner – its territorial and climate specific difficulties for national development, as well as for prevention and mitigation as much as possible of natural disasters. Today geospatial data is crucial for all countries, whether big or small ones, to face all their natural resources problems and challenges.

The use of geospatial information and geoprocessing technology is absolutly indispensable to: natural resources (land, water, minerals) management, including the research and development of new technologies to that end; monitoring and surveying environmental changes; meteorology; hydrology; prevention and mitigation of natural disasters; creating and updating national topographic map systems for territorial planning and management; supporting economic development; guiding the formulation and implementation of public policies; implementing programs, projects, scientific research and technology transfer activities both at national level and among different countries, international organizations and private enterprises.

National geospatial infrastructure is, therefore, a primary necessity for all nations. As technological advances in geospatial data collection and application must benefit all countries, irrespective of their degree of economic or scientific development, it is essential to foster, in each country, the establishment of an appropriate national infrastructure and the training of human resources specialized in the application of modern techniques of geo-spatial data acquisition and processing. It is basic as well to disseminate a higher level of public awareness of the usefulness of geoinformation in fundamental areas of national life.

In our days, national sustainable development depends on a number of factors, such as the availability of an adequate human and technical infrastructure that enables appropriate use of geospatial information, as well as high quality data collection and the establishment of suitable organization and management practices. There is a need to do a better job of managing information and science, to provide decision-makers with a solid understanding of global, regional and local environmental challenges upon which to base policy decisions. Environmental administration and protection are, clearly, knowledge-intensive activities, which demand a high degree of scientific and technological expertise.

Rational allocation of resources, both in public and private-oriented activities, as well as sound environmental management decisions, should be based on accurate information about natural resources, atmospheric conditions, and also about anthropogenic elements that threaten life support systems on Earth.

The competence to use maps and geospatial data should be recognized as an integral part of a nation's infrastructure, just as a network of transportation, healthcare, education, telecommunication and water supply systems.

"In order do implement sustainable social and economic development it is necessary to apply advanced sciences and technologies. Out of a number of high technologies, remote sensing, especially satellite remote sensing, has become an effective and powerful tool to promote the sustainable development owing to its unique advantages," Professor Zhu Yilin[15], former Secretary of Science and Technology Commission of Chinese Academy of Space Technology (CAST), stressed. And concluded: "Satellite remote sensing has become an indispensable technological support in the formulation of the policies for environmental protection and resources exploitation and utilization. It has been widely used in a variety of fields of sustainable social and economic development." According to Professor Zhu Yilin, for China the satellite remote sensing is specially useful in the following fields: Investigation and monitoring of land resources; crop output estimation and fine agriculture; forest survey and monitoring; geologic investigation of mineral, oil and gas; monitoring, prevention and control of desertification; survey and utilization of water resources; and disasters prevention and relief. To face all these tasks, China has today 500 units and over ten thousand scientists and technicians who are directly involved in research, tests or production related to the application of satellite remote sensing.

International cooperation is essential to capacity building for the development of a national geospatial data infrastructure in all interested countries. States carrying out geo-spatial activities have the opportunity to play a promiment role in the promotion of international cooperation efforts in order to develop national geospatial infrastructure in all interested countries. Such action, in line with the already refered to 1996 UN Declaration, should be conducted in the modes that are considered most effective and appropriate by the States concerned, including, *inter alia*, governmental and non-governmental; commercial and non-commercial; global, multilateral, regional or bilateral; and international cooperation among States at all levels of development.

It is symptomatic that the Convention of The Asia-Pacific Cooperation Organization (APSCO)[16], signed up to now by nine countries (Bangladesh, China, Indonesia, Iran, Mongolia Pakistan, Peru, Thailand and Turkey) has begun its Preamble "recognizing the importance in peaceful exploitation of space technology for promoting sustainable economic and social development in Asia-Pacific Region for the common prosperity of the region."

Earth observation satellites have been increasingly providing essential data in support of projects for sustainable development. That is certainly why South African Science and Technology Minister Mosibudi Mangena has announced last July 31 the launch of a domestically built Earth observation satellite – named Sumbandilasat – next December, saying that "space assets like satellites are no longer matter of prestige for any country, but have become essential tools." The construction of the satellite costs US$ 3.8 million. The spacecraft will carry on an optical sensor capable of distinguishing objects with a diameter of 6.25 meters and is expected to operate for three years in a near-polar low Earth orbit at an altitude of 500 kilometers[17].

Another good news in this sense is that the Inter-American Development Bank (IDB) announced last September 6 a US$50 million loan to Argentina to finance a program to develop a satellite system and applications based on Earth observation (PROSAT)[18]. It is the first multilateral financing for development of an Earth observation satellite program. Managed by the National Commission for Space Activities (CONAE) as an initiative of Argentina's Science and Technology Policy and the National Development Strategy, PROSAT is expected to help increase long-term productivity and economic sustainability. As commented by the IDB project team leader, "productivity growth, necessary for long-term economic and social development, is largely determined by the level of scientific development and innovation." He also added: "One interesting aspect of remote sensing is that it can allow for a less costly and more rapid means of data collection over wide geographic areas than field observation." Three high impact strategic applications were selected for implementation through PROSAT: Soil humidity maps for improving agricultural productivity, to help optimize timing of decisions to sow and apply fertilizers in wheat, maize, and sunflower crops; Plant and ground cover humidity maps for the reduction of crop losses through more precise prediction of plagues that affect major crops; and hydrology models and risk maps for early warning and better management of floods in the Plata, Salado and Bermejo river basins. The program will also foster private sector participation for the development of value added services based on satellite images, as well as research and development efforts in the national and international academic community to support the development of new applications. At the same time, the program is expected to strengthen Argentina's existing science and technology capacity, positioning the country in a technological niche, and establishing meaningful collaboration with the country's industrial base and with suppliers of services and products that are necessary for the design, construction, and operation of the satellites and their applications. The loan is for a 20-year term, with a seven-year grace period at a variable interest rate. Local counterpart financing will total $100 million, concluded the IDB information.

3. New item on agenda of the COPUOS

All these ideas have inspired the proposal "International Cooperation in Promoting the Use of Geospatial Data for Sustainable Development"[19], presented by the Brazilian Delegation to the Committee on the Peaceful Uses of Outer Space (COPUOS), in its plenary session last June. The proposal was approved and will be implemented along the next three years, beginning with the 2007 session.

The adopted text of the proposal reads as follows:

"The capacity to use geospatial information is critical to a range of activities having a direct impact on national development. Environmental monitoring, natural resources management, meteorology, prevention and mitigation of natural disasters, the creation of national topographic map systems for territorial planning are but a few examples of how geospatial data has come to play an indispensable role in the promotion of national sustainable development.

International cooperation has a prominent role to play in the promotion of such capacity. The experience of countries which have emerged in the last two decades as effective users of geospatial data makes a compelling case for expanding international cooperation in that field. Notwithstanding, in the whole globe a larger part still lacks the human, technological and institutional capacity to benefit from the use of geospatial data.

The international community should consider ways and means to foster the dissemination of such capacity, with a view to achieving its true universalization.

To that end, a proposal is submitted to the Committee on the Peaceful Uses of Outer Space to consider, during its next three sessions, a new agenda item entitled "International Cooperation in Promoting the Use of Geospatial Data for Sustainable Development".

The main purpose of this proposal is to foster international cooperation in the establishment of the national spatial data infrastructure necessary to capture, process, analyze and apply geospatial data, as an important tool for the achievement of national sustainable development.

While discussing this issue, the Committee might wish to focus on and draw lessons from activities already undertaken in that regard by countries, regional and/or multilateral organizations and arrangements. By acknowledging and building upon these past and present experiences, the Committee would be in a better position to propose more widespread and integrated recommendations to attain the goal of universalizing that capacity.

Also, recent experiences in developing countries have suggested that these countries wield a considerable market for services and products related to the use of geospatial data. That market remains, nevertheless, largely untapped, due to gaps in terms of awareness and capacity building. International cooperation in building up national capacity to use geospatial data can thus be expected to have a significant impact on the activities of companies developing and operating space-based applications, increasing the demand for their services and products.

But a concerted international effort to create capacity, at national level, to use geospatial data, would bear effects that would not be limited to the private sphere. Much has been discussed and done about the creation of Earth observation systems, both at the regional and global levels. The positive impact that the establishment of such systems would have on the human capacity to understand and deal with a range of global challenges has been extensively acknowledged. This is undoubtedly a most welcome endeavour, one to which the international community should continue to give its support.

A growing recognition has emerged, though, that the effectiveness of Earth observation systems in dealing with such global problems depends also on a consistent effort to integrate user communities at the country level into these systems, overcoming human, technological and institutional gaps hampering that goal. The implementation of regional or international Earth observation systems have, thus, a national dimension of its own, one which should elicit the recognition and the attention of COPUOS.

As a last point, the Committee might also wish to take stock of the activities undertaken within the UN system that are directly related to this important topic and consider ways to highlight the links existing amongst those activities and the means to give them a stronger international recognition.

A possible multi-year working plan for the discussions to be held under that new agenda item would be:

2007

- Presentations by Member States and Observers, regional/international organizations and informal coordination groups on their respective activities related to geospatial information for sustainable development. These could include UN Regional Centers for Space Science and Technology Education, GEO, CEOS, UNESCO, FAO, etc.

2008

- Expert presentations on experiences in the establishment of appropriate national infrastructure for geospatial data collection, processing and application, including human resource training, technical infrastructure and financial requirements, and institutional arrangements.

- Expert presentations on national capacity building activities and their impact on the international market for Earth observation services and applications.

2009

- Evaluation of the activities undertaken within the UN system that are directly related to the use of geospatial information for sustainable development and consideration of ways to highlight the links existing amongst those activities and the means to give them stronger international recognition.

- Drafting of a report containing recommendations on ways and means to foster international cooperation with a view to building up a national infrastructure to use geospatial data.

Conclusions

If satellite data are today a *conditio sine qua non* for national development, every country must have the required capacity to work with these data. Crucial in this capacity is a competent national infrastructure – hardware, software and specialized human resources. It can be built on the basis of the own efforts of each country and necessarily with a great international cooperation. Adopting such a constructive approach as a kind of common understanding and a practical line of actions, the community of nations will be able to actively contribute to create and strengthen a material and modern science and technology foundation indispensable for a true national development of all countries or at last the overwhelming majority of them. This way, the economic, social and cultural situation in a lot of developing States may be improved considerably in a not so long period of time, probably helping change some of the most backward aspects of the present world. Moreover, it is a valuable opportunity for International Space Policy and Law to play a proactive role in solving fundamenal issues of our own Planet.

Notes and references

(1) The word "cooperation" appears twice in the Preamble of Treaty on Principles Governing the Activities of States in the Exploration and Use of Outer Space, including the Moon and Other Celestial Bodies: "Desiring to contribute to broad international cooperation in the scientific as well as legal aspects of the exploration and use of outer space fot peaceful purposes."; and "Believing that such cooperation will contribute to the development of mutual understanding and to the strengthening of friendly relations between States and peoples."; and in the following articles: Article I, § 1: "The exploration and use of outer space, including the Moon and celestial bodies, shall be carried out for the benefit and in the interests of all countries, irrespective of their degree of economic and scientific development..."; Article III: "States to the Treaty shall carry out on activities in the exploration and use of outer space, including the Moon and other celestial bodies, in accordance with international law, including the Charter of the United Nations, in the interest of maintaining international peace and security and promoting international cooperation and understanding."; Article IX: "In the exploration and use of outer space, including the Moon and other celestial bodies, States Parties to the Treaty shall be guided by the principle of cooperation and mutual assistance and shall conduct all their activities in outer space, including the Moon and other celestial bodies, with due regard to the corresponding interests of all other States Parties to the Treaty."; Article X: "In order to promote international cooperation in the exploration and use of outer space, including the Moon and other celestial bodies, in conformity with the purposes of this Treaty,

the States Parties to the Treaty shall consider on a basis of equality any requests by other States Parties to the Treaty to be afforded an opportunity to observe the flight of space objects launched by those States."; Article XI: "In order to promote international cooperation in the peaceful exploration and use of outer space, States Parties to the Treaty, conducting activities in outer space, including the Moon and other celestial bodies, agree to inform the Secretary-General of the United Nations as well as the public and the international scientific community, to the greatest extent feasible and practicable, of the nature, conduct, locations and results of such actitivies..." See the text of the Outer Space Treaty at <http://www.unoosa.org/oosa/en/SpaceLaw/treaties.html>

(2) Goldman, Nathan C., *Space Law*, in *Space Politics and Policy – An Evolutionary Perspective*, edited by Eligar Sadeh, The Netherlands: Kluwer Academic Publishers, 2002, pp. 163-180.

(3) See <http://www.unoosa.org/oosa/en/SpaceLaw/treaties.html>

(4) See <http://www.unoosa.org/oosa/en/SpaceLaw/treaties.html>

(5) See <http://www.unoosa.org/oosa/en/SpaceLaw/treaties.html>

(6) See <http://www.unoosa.org/oosa/en/SpaceLaw/treaties.html>

(7) See <http://www.unhchr.ch/html/menu3/b/74.htm>

(8) See <http://www.un.org/esa/sustdev/documents/agenda21/index.htm >

(9) See <http://www.unoosa.org/pdf/reports/unispace/viennadeclE.pdf >

(10) Resolution 55/2 of September 8, 2000.

(11) Resolution 59/116 on international cooperation in the peaceful uses of outer space, adopted by the UN General Assembly on January 25, 2005.

(12)Friedmann, Wolfgang, *Mudança da Estrutura do Direito Internacional* (*The Changing Structure of International Law*, 1964), Rio de Janeiro: Freitas Bastos, 1971, p. 50.

(13) Schachter, Oscar, *International Law in Theory and Practice*, The Netherlands: Martinus Nijhoff Publishers, 1991, p. 10.

(14) Müllerson, Rein, *Ordering Anarchy – International Law in International Society*, The Netherlands: Martinus Nijhoff Publishers, 2000. p. 48 and p. 79.

(15) Asia-Pacific Space Outlook, N° 2 (Serial n° 9), June 2006.

(16) See <www.apmcsta.org>

(17) *Space News*, August 7, 2006.

(18) Press release from Inter-American Development Bank (IDB), September 6, 2006.

(19) See <http://www.unoosa.org/pdf/gadocs/A_61_20E.pdf>

IAC-06-E6.3.07

AN ANALYSIS OF ISSUES ARISING FROM THE COMMERCIALIZATION OF REMOTE SENSING ACTIVITIES

Ketan Mukhija
NALSAR, University of Law, Hyderabad, India.
ketanmukhija@gmail.com
Yugank Goyal
SV National Institute of Technology, Surat, India.
yugankgoyal@gmail.com

ABSTRACT

The pursuit of space technology in remote sensing has expanded itself from the confinements of the government bodies to private players in recent years, not only because of the large amount of capital necessary to fund space programmes but also due to the ever widening scope of its applications. Therefore, the commercialization calls for a certain protection of commercial interests in order to provide incentives for further developments in that direction. This paper, thereby, shall attempt to demonstrate that copyright protection of enhanced remote sensing data is vital and will serve the divergent needs of both industrialized and developing nations. The paper will carve an argument in favour of a space IPR regime, wherein rules can be improved while concepts can balance various competing interests, thereby establishing perspective of such efforts to forge international space cooperation among various legal and economic systems. The paper discusses the existing legal mechanisms and their limitations in remote sensing market, with a comparative assessment of copyright provisions in various space-faring nations. Further, the paper elaborates on the Indian IPR perspectives and proves that that legal provisions in India are not yet specific enough to provide protection to its highly active remote sensing programme. Finally the paper concludes that protection of commercial remote sensing end-products is not adequately achieved through available legal international instruments, and argues that an international cooperation is essential in making an effort to this end.

FULL TEXT

INTRODUCTION

Space activities today have come a long way from the days of being reconnaissance tools they were originally meant to be. Today they are all set to take the world by storm. One of the fundamental aspects of space activities is remote sensing* - sensing of the earth's surface from space.

Remote sensing is the use of satellite imagery from space for applications on

* The term 'remote sensing' refers to a variety of information-gathering activities undertaken from space such as satellite photography, infrared, laser, and radar imaging, and the gathering of electronic intelligence. (Reynolds, 1992).

Earth. The government first used remote sensing for land management, environmental monitoring, and urban planning.[*] Remote sensing technology has led from advanced applications involving meteorology, hydrology, cartography, and reconnaissance, to more consumer-oriented applications such as insurance claims adjustment, marketing, real estate, and farming. Remote sensing sales and services alone are expected to grow to a $2 billion market by the next century.

The imagery yielded by remote sensing satellites has traditionally been of great strategic importance, as they have the potential to be used in military and intelligence activities. Until a decade ago, high resolution satellite imagery was purely the domain of the most powerful and technologically advanced nations in the world. However, rapid developments in remote sensing technology have now put previously privileged information within easy reach of every person with access to the Internet. Now that commercial remote sensing programmes are operational in most of the space-faring nations, the continued existence of the technology depends upon how well the private sector can market satellite data. We thus need to assess the importance of strong copyright regime in the area of remote sensing.

THE COMMERCIALIZATION OF SPACE ACTIVITIES

The unlimited applications of remote sensing make it an extremely valuable tool with the potential of solving many of the problems which face humankind as it enters the twenty-first century. Although a predominant role was played by states during the initial stages of remote sensing, recent remote sensing activities within a commercial framework undertaken by various countries show particular interest in the protection of intellectual property rights resulting from remote sensing activities. This is because of the large amount of capital necessary to fund space programmes and partly due to the exploratory nature of these programmes. States exercised virtual monopoly over space activities in those early stages. The participation of private enterprises in these activities was limited to that of industrial partners as manufacturers of rockets or satellites for exclusive government use and under a government license. Gradually, these private companies showed a strong interest and increased participation in space ventures. At present, the private sector is a primary actor in commercial remote sensing activities (Leo et. al., 1999).

Commercialization in this sense means that remote sensing data would be available to the public under ordinary rules of supply and demand, with profit as an end for the private operator. The commercialization of remote sensing data must be considered as an irreversible, though only a recent characteristic, of space activities throughout the world. It appears to be a logical consequence of the Open Skies Policy adopted by the US. This position enables states to widely disseminate data obtained by satellites except data of military relevance.[t]

---

[*] See Jonathan Ball, Satellite Remote Sensing, at (visited Jan. 22, 1997) <http://www.doc.gov/oasc/rmtsens.html>.

[t] Nan Ball, et al., Space Manufacturing and Processing (visited Jan. 22, 1997) <http://www.doc.gov/oasc/spcmfg.html> (quoting

Many developments are taking place in most countries, which at the same time raise a number of questions both nationally and internationally. This is because commercialization calls for a certain protection of commercial interests in order to provide incentives for further developments in that direction. Remote sensing from space is not an exception. It is obvious, therefore, that countries which have developed a remote sensing capability and which have free market economies are determined to protect IPR resulting from remote sensing activities. In fact, as the United States entered the process of commercializing its remote sensing capability via a phased transition to the private sector, these commercial institutions were offered a certain degree of protection of their business interests through the insurance of proprietary rights connected with data acquired from remote sensing activities.

National regulation remains central when international implications have to be examined because international space law does not provide for the protection of private rights and even less for the protection of intellectual property rights in particular.

REQUIREMENTS FOR AN *IPR* REGIME IN SPACE

Now that commercial remote sensing programmes are operational in most of the space-faring nations, the continued existence of the technology depends upon how well the private sector can market satellite data. An understanding of the application of intellectual property rights to remote sensing data requires an understanding of the difference between enhanced and unenhanced data. Unenhanced data, or raw data, is obtained directly from the satellite, and primarily consists of digital information or photographs. Enhanced data, in contrast, is the result of human or electronic analysis of the raw data.

Copyright protection is unavailable to unenhanced data because the very nature of a copyright is to give exclusive rights to the copyright owner. The policy of non-discriminatory access would be undermined by private operators attempting to exact royalties or licensing fees from users of raw data. Because of the value addition in enhanced data, intellectual property rights in enhanced data are necessary to increase the number of data enhancement firms and thereby increase the market for raw data (Richard, 1990).

The full potential of remote sensing could not be reached with a governmentally owned and operated remote sensing programme. Commercialisation was thus necessary for the further development of this technology. Now that commercialisation is in place, marketing of such data needs to be maximised. For this purpose, intellectual property rights in enhanced data are necessary to increase the number of data enhancement firms and thereby increase the market for raw data.

International copyright protection for enhanced data is necessary to induce firms to enter the data enhancement industry. Even a small data enhancement firm must invest significant capital in software, equipment, and trained personnel before it can begin operation. Copyright laws will protect this

---

Mark Holderman, NASA engineer at the Johnson Space Center in Houston, Texas)

investment and, by making processed data more valuable, will provide an incentive for firms to enter the market. Without the economic rents created by copyright, it is unlikely that enough firms will produce sufficient enhanced data to make commercialisation worthwhile. This is because the data enhancement industry will constitute the market for raw data necessary to realise a profit.

Competition from foreign remote sensing systems provides another reason why legal protection of enhanced data is necessary. Many countries operate commercial remote sensing systems, and some of these, such as the French SPOT system and the European Space Agency's ERS-1 (both commercialised systems), compete with U.S.A.'s LANDSAT for international as well as domestic data markets. A significant feature of international intellectual property rights is that these rights shall protect competition among all entities producing enhanced data worldwide. Without copyright protection, an individual or entity could pirate enhanced data produced by someone else and legitimately pass it off as its own. There would be no mechanism to prevent such an entity from distorting the data to obtain financial or political benefits. Therefore, the nature of a commercial remote sensing programme mandates copyright protection for enhanced data. Such copyright protection will benefit producers of enhanced data worldwide due to the existence of multilateral copyright agreements (Richard, 1990).

Although representatives from developing nations have expressed concern regarding the legal protection of processed data, it is conceivable that in the near future their views will change. This will occur upon the realisation that the benefits of copyright (widespread availability and low prices for unenhanced data) will outweigh the disadvantages (decreased availability of processed data). As developing nations become capable of processing data themselves, they may also accept copyright due to the fact that it will protect their own processed data from theft and misappropriation by entities which might use the information to exploit the developing nations' resources. These considerations, combined with the protection of international space agreements, clearly demonstrate that copyright protection of enhanced remote sensing data will serve the divergent needs of both industrialised and developing nations (Richard, 1990).

OVERVIEW AND LIMITATIONS OF EXISTING SPACE LAWS WITH RESPECT TO REMOTE SENSING

The limited applicability of copyright to remote sensing data and the differing needs of developed and developing nations combine to create possibilities of potential abuses of intellectual property rights. A number of international agreements try to negative such possibilities by attempting to both define and limit the rights and duties of producers and consumers of remote sensing data, but fail in their efforts.

The Outer Space Treaty (1967)

The 1967 Outer Space Treaty codified certain basic principles of space law first articulated by the UNCOPUOS in the General Assembly Resolution of 1962, the "Declaration of Legal Principles Governing the Activities of States in the

Exploration and Use of Outer Space".[*] Several of these principles have significance for remote sensing activities.

Article I of the Treaty establishes the right of all states to explore and use outer space, the moon, and celestial bodies for the benefit and in the interests of all countries, without discrimination and regardless of the stage of development of any country. Article II prohibits the appropriation of outer space, in the name of sovereignty, by any country. Today, there is widespread agreement that the twin principles of freedom and non-appropriation have acquired the status of customary international law.[t] The international law regarding the acquisition of remote sensing information incorporates the Article I principle of non-discriminatory access to space.

Remote sensing as defined by the Principles is legal under Article IV which prohibits military activity in space. Article VI of the 1967 Treaty requires states that are parties to the Treaty to "bear international responsibility for national activities in outer space ... whether such activities are carried on by governmental agencies or by non-governmental entities, and for assuring that national activities are carried out in conformity with the provisions set forth in the present Treaty" thus recognising that commercial entities as well as governments are covered by the treaty's provisions. However, Article VIII of the 1967 Outer Space Treaty provides for the retention of jurisdiction and control by the State of Registry over its space objects and personnel while in outer space. Thus, such a State is offered the possibility of extending its national law to space activities performed in outer space. Therefore, it will depend solely on the action of the individual state whether it will act to protect the intellectual property interests of its nationals and others in relation to space activities (Twibell, 1997). This in itself can create numerous problems since the private law systems, including private international law of the different countries are far from equal. The Principles, anyhow, endorse the promotion of international cooperation and assistance (Feder, 1991).

Principles Relating to Remote Sensing of Earth from Space (1986)

The United Nations addressed remote sensing when it adopted a resolution entitled Principles Relating to Remote Sensing of Earth from Outer Space.[:t] It took seventeen years to develop the Principles, finally passed by the General Assembly in 1986. The Principles resulted from a process of compromise necessary to remedy the differences between the position of the developing world and that of the space powers, particularly the United States (Christol, 1988). The major stumbling block to agreement was the divergence in opinion on the extent to which sovereignty principles should give a state an inherent right to control sensed data of its territory in a manner similar to rights regarding control of natural resources

[*] G.A.Res.1962, 18 GAOR (Supp. No. 15) at 15, U.N. Doc. A/5515 (Dec 13, 1963).

[t] Dept. For Disarmament Affairs, "The Implications of Establishing an International Satellite Monitoring Agency" at 52, U.N. Doc. A/AC.206/14 (Disarmament Study Series No. 9 1983); as quoted in infra n. vii

[:t] G.A. Res. 41/65 Annex, "Principles Relating to Remote Sensing of the Earth from Outer Space", (Principle I(b)), U.N. Doc. A/41/751 (1986).

located in a sovereign territory. The developing nations wanted to require prior consent before any nation's territory could be sensed, whereas the space powers wanted an 'open skies' rule under which consent would not be required (Feder, 1991). By recognising each country's sovereignty over its own wealth and resources (Principle IV), this agreement attempts to prevent an entity from using information about a sensed state to exploit the state's resources. The Principles encourage states conducting remote sensing to provide data sharing, opportunities for participation, and technical assistance to other states (Principles V-VIII). They also require states gaining information about environmental damage or natural disasters to inform any nation which might be in danger (Principles IX-X.). Like the Outer Space Treaty, the Principles apply to non- governmental entities as well (Principle XIV).

It is apparent that the principles represent a contractarian approach to remote sensing activities. Many commentators view the Principles as having no significant limiting effect on remote sensing activities, thus failing to circumscribe present practice in any important way (Hayward, 1990; Myers, 1987). At best, the resolution is "an attempt to apply modest legal safeguards to the conduct of remote sensing which some states feel, if left unregulated, might adversely affect their national interests."(Hayward, 1990; Myers, 1987). At worst, the debate surrounding the Principles resulted in little more than a reaffirmation of the broad ideals embodied in the major space treaties (De Saussure, 1989).

<u>The Berne Convention (1971)</u>

The Berne Convention is believed to provide the protection necessary to meet the needs of a commercial remote sensing industry. This agreement consists of two principal components. The first is the main body of the agreement which details and defines the functions and operation of international copyright protection for protected works. The second component of the Berne Convention is the appendix, which provides special mechanisms for developing nations to gain access to copyrighted material. This section is especially relevant to remote sensing data which may significantly benefit developing countries.

Remote sensing imagery is part of the general scope of Article 2 of the Berne Convention. At a minimum, the Convention covers the first imagery product after the bits transmitted by the satellite have been converted into a readable photograph, which raises the question of the protection of raw data. In order to help copyright protection be effective, the Berne Convention provides that works must be "fixed in some material form,"[*] and national laws may not renege on their obligation to participate in such protection. Only news information is not covered by these

[*] Excerpts from Art. 2, Berne Convention (1971): "... (2) It shall, however, be a matter for legislation in the countries of the Union to prescribe that works in general or any specified categories of works shall not be protected unless they have been fixed in some material form...". Convention for the Protection of Literary and Artistic Works, Sept. 9, 1886, 12 MARTENS NOUVEAU RECUEIL (ser. 2) 173, revised Nov. 13, 1908, 1 L.N.T.S. 218; June 2, 1928, 123 L.N.T.S. 233; June 26, 1948, 331 L.N.T.S. 217; July 14, 1967, 828 U.N.T.S. 221; July 24, 1971 at 227; as quoted in infra n. xxiii.

provisions.[*] The extent to which automatic protection is afforded to the author is determined by the Convention in association with the country where protection is sought. The amount of protection which is granted to a foreign work is based on the principle of national treatment which essentially states that the protection afforded in country A to works created in country B, (both countries A and B being parties to the convention), is as ample as that provided by country A to works created on its territory. In a parallel manner, for countries which are not members of those conventions and which are not deemed to be granting national treatment in the meaning of the Berne Convention, one may expect the worse in terms of copyright infringement. However, a specific reference could be made in the bilateral agreement to local legislation with the effect of extending protection to data received by the local ground station. This amounts to a de facto national treatment.

Finally, authors have the right to authorize "the reproduction of their works,"[t] but this should not harm their own interest. Quite obviously, the 38 articles and the appendix of the Berne Convention are mostly geared towards works of the everyday life: remote sensing imagery cannot be protected on the basis of the provisions of this Convention (Salin, 1992).

The Universal Copyright Convention (1971)

The UCC contains some complementary points. The visual aspect of the copyright is taken care of with the appearance of the (C) special logo with the name of the beneficiary.[:t] Therefore, end-product imagery may affix a visible indication of the copyright, its owner and the date of first use on each imagery item. Under UCC regulation, the duration of the copyright equals the author's lifetime plus an extra twenty-five years. This duration is shorter than that provided under the Berne Convention which provides that the protection lasts for fifty years after the author's death. The other provisions of the UCC do not differ substantially from those of the Berne Convention and are mostly devoted to standard works of a literary or artistic nature. It is generally recognised that the Berne Convention

---

[*] Excerpts from Art. 2, Berne Convention (1971): "... (6) The works mentioned in this Article shall enjoy protection in all countries of the Union. This protection shall operate for the benefit of the author and his successors in title. ... (8) The protection of this Convention shall not apply to news of the day or to miscellaneous facts having the character of mere items of press information." Convention for the Protection of Literary and Artistic Works, at 227; as quoted in infra n. xxiii.

[t] Excerpts from Art. 9, Berne Convention: "(1) Authors of literary and artistic works protected by this Convention shall have the exclusive right of authorizing the reproduction of these works, in any manner or form ...
(2) ... provided that such reproduction does not conflict with a normal exploitation of the work and does not unreasonably prejudice the legitimate interests of the author ...." Convention for the Protection of Literary and Artistic Works, 63 U.K.T.S. at 31 (1990); as quoted in infra n. xxiii.

[:t] Excerpts from Art. III of the Universal Copyright Convention: "1.... [F]rom the time of the first publication all the copies of the work published with the authority of the author or other copyright proprietor [must] bear the symbol (C) accompanied by the name of the copyright proprietor and the year of first publication placed in such a manner and location as to give reasonable notice of claim of copyright ...". July 24, 1971, 6 U.S.T. 2731, 2734, 216 U.N.T.S. 133, 136; as quoted in Salin (1992).

provides a higher standard of copyright protection than the UCC (Stewart, 1983). As a matter of fact, the UCC itself provides that if a nation is a member of both conventions, the terms of the Berne Convention will govern, and if a nation is a member of the Berne Convention, it cannot withdraw and become only a member of the UCC. If it tries to do so, it will lose both memberships (Article 2).

ASSESSMENT OF THE LAWS

In fact, the core of the copyright recognition problem for remote sensing imagery lies around the nature of raw data. WIPO identifies four conditions which must be fulfilled so that a work may be eligible for protection (Murphy et al., 1988): 1) The work must be unique and original, not the copy of some other work. Beyond any doubt, remote sensing raw data is unique and original. 2) The work must be presented on some material support. In that respect, remote sensing looks like a live television report. In practice, it seems that the protection of such a transmission is not challengeable, but the difficulty arises from the fact that there is no simultaneous public broadcasting. It must then be paralleled to a television report which is recorded in advance for future public broadcast. 3) The work must be authored by somebody. In this vein, a provision of the Berne Convention provides for a collective authorship*, which may be what remote sensing imagery is about, since authorship derives from the work of an observation machine. 4) The work must be creative, which supposes the particular intervention of a human being.

On the whole, obviously, there is currently no adequate and efficient protection of remote sensing data in international law. In the wake of the various copyright conventions, one may think that there is a need for a specific convention, which may be a necessary step if the trend towards the commercialisation of remote sensing is to be maintained in order to let private organisations be attracted by substantial profits to be made from the use of raw data. There are observers who clearly state that the Berne Convention itself is an "inadequate mechanism" for new technologies (Motyka, 1990), including remote sensing imagery.

COMPARATIVE ASSESSMENT OF THE ACTUAL COPYRIGHT PROVISIONS IN VARIOUS COUNTRIES

We have the LANDSAT, SPOT, MOS-1, ERS-1 AND RADARSAT programmes in the countries of the United States of America, France, Japan, European Union and Canada respectively. Even though these copyright provisions were created at approximately the same period, in the late 1980s, it is possible to distinguish provisions which aim at protecting the satellite operator from uncontrolled dissemination of data through the intermediary of the contract partner (i.e. the agency in charge of the foreign local ground-station), and from possible external abuses beyond the will of the foreign local partner. It is also of interest to analyse how these copyright provisions are translated in the market at the client level through a plain sales contract (Salin, 1992). All these

* Excerpt from Article 7b from the Berne Convention: "The provisions of the preceding Article (Art. 7: "Term of Protection") shall also apply in the case of a work of joint authorship ..."; as quoted in Salin.

contracts are recent in their making, having been signed by the five space agencies of the five countries which have already been named, with their foreign partners between 1989 and 1991. There are three broad heads of copyright provisions in the contracts where the first one holds a paramount importance.

General Restrictions to Raw Data Ownership Transfer

General restrictions are the first line of protection that all satellite operators have set with their partner. However, important differences already appear at this minimal stage. In the case of LANDSAT, EOSAT does not mention the word "copyright" but asks for the station to "design and implement a data protection plan" to be submitted and approved by EOSAT.[*] In other words, protection is a matter to be designed on a case by case basis and one way of doing so is to ask the other partner to submit his/her own views and ask him/her to implement those views with tangible measures. In the case of the Japanese satellite MOS-1, NASDA only faintly mentions a copyright. It specifies that "intellectual property rights ... are and will remain the property of NASDA," adding that the local agency "will refrain from registering or attempting to register any intellectual or industrial property rights, including, without limitation, copyright or patent rights."[t] A restriction could hardly be more general and vague. NASDA also recognizes that the local agency may have property rights on "analyzed information ... depending on the level of processing, analysis or interpretation which has been applied" (Article 8.2). No more precision is provided for in this respect. For the European satellite ERS-1, ESA explicitly asserts that the contract partner "acknowledges the copyright of ESA ... under the terms of this agreement and under the legislation and conventions concerning copyright." Details are then provided regarding how to let the "(C) ESA, year" logo appear on all ERS-1 data, as well as the "ERS-1-R" trademark logo, irrespective of its degree of analysis or its form (Arts. 11.1, 11.2). The local authority may also add its own (C) logo depending on its own contribution to the analysed information. The effectiveness of such a clause is doubtful because the conventions this agreement refers to are not specific enough with regard to the specific situations of remote sensing raw data. For RADARSAT, CSA simply says that "all copyright and ownership rights for SAR data will be vested or reserved solely in or to CSA, the other party having rights of use as described in this MoU to the extent permitted by the laws of the Parties."[:t] This restriction is general, very much like the NASDA one, and it specifically refers to the laws of the other party. The SPOT contract is by far the most complete of the five agreements. The CNES copyright is asserted right away and it is specified that a clear mention of that copyright, with the "(C), CNES, year" logo must appear on all data and derivative works and products. The "SPOT-R-year"

[*] Landsat Data Downlink Agreement, Art. IV, Sec. D., signed by EOSAT; as quoted in Salin.

[t] Arrangement Between NASDA and a Foreign Partner for the Direct Reception and Distribution of MOS-1 Data, Art. 8.1; as quoted in Salin.

[:t] Memorandum of Understanding Concerning the Radarsat Project, Art. 12.4, signed by CSA. See also International Memorandum of Understanding, Art. 12.4, signed by CSA with NASA and NOAA which co-manage the Radarsat project; as quoted in Salin.

trademark logo must also be affixed to all pertinent documents. Interestingly, such copyright and trademark may co-appear with the one of the local authority in charge of the supervision of the contract, in case derivative works are developed by such authority.[*]

PROBLEMS WITH AN EXHAUSTIVE *IPR* STRATEGY IMPLEMENTATION

Another aspect of IPR in space activities refers to inventions and trademarks, including data and products. It should be observed that the US, Canada, and the Philippines are the only countries in the world which apply a first-to-invent system, the rest of the world applying the first-to-file system to prove first inventorship, resulting in the right to protection.

In fact, the policy of the US towards commercialization of a range of space activities has been focused recently on this issue. The policy of the NASA was to encourage the commercialization of technology developed through its financial resources. Efforts are now being undertaken to guarantee more proprietary rights protection for private aerospace industries as manifested through a number of joint agreements. Likewise, Section 305 of the NASA Act provides that although title to such invention rests with the government, NASA includes a broad waiver policy. It retains only a non-exclusive royalty free license for government use and the right to use it if the contractor does not develop the invention.

The International Space Station raises relatively new issues regarding the protection of industrial property among the state and non-state participants. Nevertheless, these issues were addressed in various provisions of IGA on the Space Station. Article 16 provides for a cross-waiver of liability and Article 3(d)(4) provides that intellectual property claims do not fall within the scope of application of the Agreement. Article 21 deals explicitly with intellectual property. It defines intellectual property in its first paragraph by reference to the terminology used in Article 2 of the Convention Establishing the World Intellectual Property Organization.[t]

Because intellectual property rights are generally based on territoriality, their application to situations in outer space may cause problems, because outer space can not be the subject of national appropriation. Hence, paragraph 2 of Article 21 applies the fiction of territoriality over activities taking place in or on a specific space station element, the space segment where the invention was developed. Moreover, inventions in any space segment of any ESA Member State are deemed to have occurred within the territory of any European Partner State. Therefore, the territoriality concept can be applied by the state concerned, while in relation to ESA registered elements, the regulation facilitates the application of each individual nation's law on intellectual property. Such a conclusion results from the application of the principles of jurisdiction and control of the state of registry over the individual flight element.

[*] Agreement Regarding the Reception and Distribution of SPOT Data, Arts. 11, 12, 14, signed by SPOT IMAGE; as quoted in Salin.

[t] See Nathan C. Goldman, American Space Law: International & Domestic 25 (1996)

National laws on patents differ from state to state, in that the law may be based either on filing or the fact of invention itself. In the space law context, this problem is partially answered through Article 21 of the IGA with respect to inventions made by non-nationals or non-residents by restricting the application of national laws concerning secrecy of invention. This prevents the filing of a patent application. If patent protection exists in more than one European partner state, Article 21 prohibits, through paragraph 4, recovery in more than one of those states for the same rights in such invention for infringement, which occurs in or on an ESA registered element. In paragraph 5, the European partner states are prohibited from refusing the recognition of a license in relation to patents if that patent is enforceable under the laws of any European partner state. This likewise also bars recovery for infringement in any European partner state.

INDIAN PERSPECTIVE

The growth of Indian space programme during the past four decades has been phenomenal.[*] The success, which India has achieved in the application of remote sensing, and perhaps, surpasses the efforts of even the most advanced countries. Today India has become a leader in satellite based remote sensing providing services on an end-to-end base with a series of state-of-art satellites, the necessary data reception and processing facilities and the commensurate launch capability.[t]

During the last two decades increasing emphasis on reducing governmental budgets worldwide has forced the world's space faring nations to reassess their civil space programs. Developing countries like India are hard pressed to allocate funds for space activities. Therefore the need for privatization of space activities deserves the maximum attention in countries like India, which need these activities even more than their richer counterparts for their national development. The space application sector witnessed tremendous developments with the active involvement of the private sector. There is a huge market to be tapped in India in the field of cable and satellite television. Recognizing the privatization and commercialization of space activities many developed nations have drafted National Space Laws for various complex facets of space activities, including a core licensing system for Private Space Activities. Thus, it is abundantly clear that even countries, which are lagging far behind India in technological advancement, have some sort of Space Law for their country, which places them ahead of India in attracting cross border investments. It is

[*] India entered the Nineties with the launch of more ASLV and PSLV launchers. With the launch of IRS-IB and INSAT 2A & 2B, the Indian space programme becomes fully operational through its own communication and remote-sensing satellites. The INSAT series satellites, with the capabilities to provide communications, meteorological and disaster management systems, have proved unique, as other countries have separate spacecraft for each of these functions.[*] The IRS satellites have helped in the extensive mapping of our natural resources, and the voluminous data generated through these are used in a variety of fields. Even the developed countries – including the US—have started acquiring the IRS data.

[t] Department of Space, Govt. of India, Annual report, 1994-95, pp/42-43, India

therefore imperative for India also to have specialized Space Legislation so as to emerge as a global destination in attracting foreign investment. India has demonstrated indigenously developed technology in space programmes, just as it has showcased matchless expertise in software. However it is disheartening to note that because of lack of an adequate legal framework India is losing many opportunities in the field of investment in space technology.

To fulfil International commitments and domestic regulations of space activities, every nation state should draft a space legislation that would bring or achieve the necessary coherence between Space law, international agreements, and domestic legislations. As far as India is concerned, until now it does not have any comprehensive or specific law dealing with space activities/conflicts, unlike other countries i.e. USA, Canada, France, Germany and Australia. However, with the rapid development of activities in space and its commercialization, there is a growing need for enacting domestic space legislation. As this area involves huge amounts and high risks of public and private funds, in all probability there would be growing litigation or conflicts that cannot be solved by the existing system. Therefore, the proposed legislation should provide for Creation of National Space Agency, Licensing, and Certification of space activities, Economic Conditions of Space Activities, A Provision on Space Infrastructure, Space Safety and Space Liability, Space Insurance, International Cooperation and Protection of Intellectual Property Rights in Outer Space. This draft legislation should be a convergence of divergent regulations in order to bring a comprehensive and harmonious space legislation that would be beneficial for India.

To now examine the types of IPR in the context of Indian remote sensing activities- we have copyright and trade secrecy. As we examine them within the framework of the domestic legislation, we can try and analyse whether they can be extended to remote sensing activities as well.

Copyright

The Copyright Act, 1957 now stands amended by the Copyright (Amendment) Act of 1994. Copyright is important in the Indian context as they have a very strong and active remote sensing programme in place.

According to the earlier definition of "literary work" contained in Section 2(o), a literary work included computer programmes and compilations. The Copyright (Amendment) Act, 1994 now defines a literary work to specifically include a computer database within its ambit. On account of the doctrine of "independent creation" the data collected by one agency even if identical to that owned by another would not infringe copyright. There would be no infringement or violation of copyright unless there is copying of data. For copyright to subsist in a literary work, it must be original although originality simply means that the work has not been copied from elsewhere. The copyright which would so subsist includes the exclusive right to do several acts (called restricted acts) which include the right to reproduce the work in any material form, to publish the work or to communicate the work by broadcast. Under Section 17 of the Copyright Act, the first owner of a literary work is the author of the work unless of course one of the provisions to the said section is attracted.

In the case of a satellite collecting data, there are two possibilities. Under the Copyright Act, 1957, it was difficult to establish who the author was as the data collected by a machine did not involve human intervention like the creation of other literary works. For this reason, the definition of author in relation to literary works which are computer generated has now been changed and under Section 2(d) (vi), "author" means the person who caused the work to be created. Consequently, the owner of the satellite would be the author. The second possibility arises in the case of public undertakings- the proviso to Section 17 in the form of (dd) states that in the case of a work made or first published by or under the direction or control of any public undertaking in the absence of an agreement to the contrary, the first owner of the copyright therein would be the public undertaking. Since satellites in India are all government owned and controlled, the data collected by them would be a literary work made or first published under the direction or control of a public undertaking such as ISRO. Consequently, ISRO would be the first owner of the copyright in the data so collected.

According to the ISRO viewpoint, remote sensing data is protected by copyright law and normally belongs to the satellite owners. This is an international practice which ISRO respects. The data collected by a U.S. satellite over India, for example, by the Landsat satellite is passed on to India under an agreement which specifies the fees for data access and for payment of royalties for the data distributed to users on a commercial basis. The principles for distribution provide for non discriminatory access to users. The copyright however remains with the U.S.

Trade Secrecy

Apart from copyright, data is also protected under the law of trade secrecy. Indian courts protect confidential know-how irrespective of contract.[*] One weakness of the trade secrecy law is its difficulty in restraining third parties with whom there was neither any privacy of contract nor disclosure made. In recent years, courts in England and other jurisdictions have accepted that innocent defendants can also be restrained. In Wheatley v. Bell[t], the court rejected the idea that an innocent defendant can be likened to a bonafide purchaser for value without notice and granted the injunction against all the defendants. Although there has been no Indian case which has extended the principle in a similar way, it is likely that this would be the approach even of the Indian courts.

Normally, in commercial transactions involving breach of confidentiality only

[*] Although it is recommended to have a confidentiality clause in an agreement, even in the absence thereof, if

a) the know-how is confidential or secret, that is, not in the public domain so to preserve the confidentiality of a technology there must be a clear intention to restrict the access of the document, and

b) it is disclosed in circumstances which gave rise to an obligation of confidence, and

c) there is actual or anticipated violation, misuse or disclosure of the said information,

the same can be restrained. These principles were reiterated by the Delhi High Court in John Richard Brady v. Chemicals Process Equipment Pvt. Ltd (AIR 1987 Delhi 372).

[t] 1984 FSF 16 at p. 22.

civil remedies are available, such as, injunctions, damages, rendition of accounts etc. However, space research being predominantly government controlled, most secrets would come within the ambit of the Indian Official Secrets Act, 1923. Section 3 of the Act lays down parameters for spying which broadly includes obtaining, collecting, publishing or communicating, recording any document or information which is likely to affect the sovereignty, integrity and security of India. This is the only legislation they have which could be applied to secrets in space technologies. However in the light of the Freedom of Information Act passed recently, even its importance has dwindled immensely.

It is clear from the preceding discussion that legal provisions in India are not yet specific enough to provide protection to its highly active remote sensing programme. Legally suitable clauses for data privacy rights are included in the agreements with buyers/partners. While they do have a Remote Sensing Data Policy in place[*], it is interesting to note that the Remote Sensing Data Policy does not address the IPR issues, as it is intended for different purpose- to assess the user's requirement, the end use, justifications etc. As regards the IPR policy, it is addressed in the agreement to be signed for obtaining remote sensing data from NRSA, Hyderabad.[t]

[*] See Statement in the Lok Sabha by Vasundhara Raje, Minister of State in the Department of Atomic Energy and Department of Space, on Wednesday August 8, 2001, regarding "Remote Sensing Data Policy".

[t] See Section 4 of NRSA Product Purchase Agreement available online at http//: www.nrsa.gov.in (last visited November 4, 2005): "The customer acknowledges the copyrightable character of satellite data under the legislation and conventions concerning copyrights. Accordingly, the customer acknowledges the NRSA ownership (including ownership of copyright and intellectual property rights) of satellite data."

CONCLUSION

The problem of protecting intellectual and industrial property rights in outer space endeavours will partially be addressed through the efforts of space countries towards international cooperation. The construction and full operation of the International Space Station is a step towards this end. Efforts towards international space cooperation are nothing new to the space countries. Their experience with INTELSAT, INMARSAT, EUTELSAT and ESA may become a solid foundation in the future endeavours. From this experience, rules can be improved while concepts can balance various competing interests. The perspective of such efforts to forge international space cooperation is the establishment of uniform IPR protection laws among national law systems.

The active presence of the WIPO would certainly make such effort less difficult. The presence of the WIPO assures that there would be representation of the various views and opinions of the world community not only in IPR protection but also in international space law as well. It is hoped that the presence of underdeveloped states in this international effort could stimulate and coordinate a rather relevant and developmental legal regime of IPR protection resulting from outer space endeavours.

While the importance of remote sensing cannot be disputed, the protection of commercial remote sensing end-products is not adequately achieved through available legal international instruments.

Protection clauses which are included in specific contracts between satellite operators or commercial managers on the one hand and either foreign ground stations or commercial and industrial final clients on the other hand are, at best, 'ad hoc' clauses which attempt to chart legitimate uses of such imagery and establish, in the most elaborate cases, conditions for a potential pursuit of the offender by both the satellite operators, the image distributors, and the foreign ground station managing agency. In the Indian context as well, there is a need for the drafting of a convention on remote sensing which would, among other things, provide for the conditions of the exercise of a specific copyright in reference to satellite imagery. The legal provisions at best support a stretch-fit exercise, stretching the available legal provisions to fit the required level of protection. India should make all efforts to capitalise on its capabilities, tying the loose ends. Other anticipated developments like the use of such information by news media organizations and possible conflicts between proprietary aspects of satellite imagery and issues of personal freedom also illustrate the need for a new international convention as a matter of urgency.

REFERENCES

Glenn H. Reynolds, International Space Law: Into the Twenty-First Century, 25 V and. J. Transnat'l L. 225, 230 (1992).

Malagar, Leo B. & Magdoza-Malagar, Marlo Apalisok, "International Law of Outer Space and the Protection of Intellectual Property Rights", 17 B.U. Int'l L.J. 311(1999) at http//: international.westlaw.com (last visited Oct 19, 2005).

West, J. Richard, "Copyright Protection for Data Obtained by Remote Sensing: How the Data Enhancement Industry will ensure Access for Developing Countries", 11 Nw. J. Int'l L. & Bus. 403 (1990) at http//: international.westlaw.com (last visited Oct 17, 2005).

Feder, Harry, "The Sky's The Limit? Evaluating the International Law of Remote Sensing", 23 N.Y.U. J. Int'l L. & Pol. 599 (1991) at http//: international.westlaw.com (last visited Oct 17, 2005).

Twibell, Ty S., "Space Law: Legal Restraints on Commercialization and Development of Outer Space", 65 UMKC L. Rev. 589 (1997) at http//: international.westlaw.com (last visited Oct 17, 2005).

Christol, Remote Sensing and International Space Law, 16 J.Space L. 21, 37-38 (1988); as quoted in Feder (1991).

See Myers, "United Nations Activity on Remote Sensing: Legal and Political Implications", Proceedings of the Thirtieth Colloquium on the Law of Outer Space 361 (1987); as quoted in Hayward, Cynthia M., "Remote Sensing: Terrestrial Laws for Celestial Activities", 8 B.U. Int'l L.J. 157 (1990) at http//: international.westlaw.com (last visited Oct 17, 2005)

See DeSaussure, "Remote Sensing Satellite Regulation by National and International Law", 15 Rutgers Computer & Tech. L.J. 356 (1989).

Salin, Patrick A., "Proprietary Aspects of Commercial Remote-Sensing Imagery", 13 Nw. J. Int'l L. & Bus. 349 (1992) at http//: international.westlaw.com (last visited Oct 19, 2005).

Stewart, Stephen M., "International Copyright and Neighbouring Rights", 7-8 (1983); as quoted in Salin (1992.

Murphy, Marie F. & Oosterlinck, Rene, "Protection des Données et des Inventions dans L'Espace" published in Droit de L'espace 279 (Jacqueline Dutheil de la Rochere ed., 1988); as quoted in Salin.

Murphy, Marie F. & Oosterlinck, Rene, "Protection des Données et des Inventions dans L'Espace" published in Droit de L'espace 279 (Jacqueline Dutheil de la Rochere ed., 1988); as quoted in Salin.

Motyka, Carol A., "Effects of U.S. Adherence to the Berne Convention", 16 Rutgers Computer & Tech. L. J. 195, 212 (1990); as quoted in Salin.

LIST OF ACRONYMS

CNES	Centre National d'Etudes Spatiales
CSA	Canadian Space Agency
EOSAT	Earth Observation Satellite
ERS	Earth Remote-Sensing Satellite
ESA	European Space Agency
EUTELSAT	European Telecommunication Satellite
IGA	International Government Agreement
INMARSAT	International Marine/Maritime Satellite
INTELSAT	International Satellite
IPR	Intellectual Property Rights
ISRO	Indian Space Research Organisation
LANDSAT	Land Remote-Sensing Satellite
MOS	Marine/Maritime Observation Satellite
NASA	National Aeronautical and Space Agency
NASDA	National Aeronautic and Space Development Agency
NRSA	National Remote Sensing Agency
RADARSAT	Radar Satellite
SPOT	Systeme Pour Observation de la Terre
UCC	Universal Copyright Convention
UNCOPUOS	United Nations Committee On the Peaceful Uses of Outer Space
WIPO	World Intellectual Property Organization

IAC-06-E6.3.08.

REMOTE SENSING DATA: SOME CRITICAL COMMENTS ON THE CURRENT STATE OF REGULATION AND REFLECTIONS ON REFORM

Prof. Dr. Lesley Jane Smith, LL.M.
University of Lueneburg,
21335 Lueneburg
Faculty II, Business, Law and Behavioural Sciences,
Email: ljsmith@barkhof.uni-bremen.de

C. Doldirina, LL.M Eur.,
University of Bremen,
Email: kdoldyrina@yahoo.com

ABSTRACT

This paper provides an overview of the current international and national regulation in relation to remote sensing data, with a view to analysing its effectiveness in the face of modern demands for (more) information.

In a preliminary review, the international legal instruments and national laws relevant to the subject will be analysed. Thereafter, the national legislation of some major space-faring nations will be examined as a means of establishing differences in the regulation and handling of remote sensing data, alongside its effects on information policy. The final part of the paper focuses on whether there is a need for a revised approach to the international legal regulation of remote sensing data and control of its use. This latter point is important in the face of publicly or privately enforceable restrictions on access to essential information. The article thereafter highlights the most important issues to be addressed by any such proposal for reform.

INTRODUCTION

The commercial remote sensing data[1] market is evolving and expanding[2] its services, which today range from online mapping, forestry, agricultural and geological studies[3], to the support for news-making, shipping, real estate and other activities[4].

Because of the nature of market players and the characteristics of space-related activities (e.g. dual use of "space" products and services, leading to export control), including its commercial development, regulations for RS data acquisition, processing and distribution have and continue to be introduced in different countries. Among the issues to be considered in adopting such regulations include the imposition of government limitations on the availability of images from high resolution systems, the options for industry self-regulation, suitability of copyright legislation, pricing, equity and competition with government programs.[5]

The immediate interest of this paper is to explore the varying approaches to the status of RS data, itself crucial to data circulation and protection, as well as to the development of value-adding activities.

Current research shows that RS data, as part of other commercial applications for space exploitation, has become an expensive commodity subject to great demand[6]. The

[1] Hereinafter RS data.

[2] See e.g. Satellite Industry Association, *State of the Satellite Industry Report*, prepared by Futron Corporation, June 2006 available at http://www.futron.com/pdf/SIA_2005_Indicators.pdf, last visited 17.08.2006.

[3] Cited e.g. in Gabriela Seiz et al., *Earth Observation Market Development: Benefits to Industry*, ESA Bulletin 125, February 2006, available at http://www.esa.int/esapub/bulletin/bulletin125/bul125d_seiz.pdf, last visited 17.08.2006.

[4] Lawrens W. Fritz, *High Resolution Commercial Remote Sensing Satellites and Spatial Information Systems,* available at http://www.isprs.org/publications/highlights/highlights0402/fritz.html, last visited 17.08.2006.

[5] Lawrens W. Fritz, *ibid.*

[6] See eg Joanne Irene Gabrynowicz, J.D., Space Law: Its Cold War Origins and Challenges in the New Era

particular remote sensing activities protected by space law[7] are increasingly identified among the potential markets for private and government space-based systems.[8] RS data from commercial sensors offer the geospatial information communities in the public and private sectors important new sources of timely and accurate spatial information that can augment data provided by public-sector remote sensing systems.[9]

Certain national laws have a degree of similarity in their regulatory content that could provide a conceivable approach to a comprehensive international regulation. Pursuing an international approach to trans-border remote sensing activities appears only logical, since they cannot be effectively regulated by national law alone.

A new regulatory mechanism could clarify and establish the status of RS data, unify the types of RS data and determine equal conditions of distribution and restriction on use. This in turn would help create a common policy towards the "public-private" interests' dichotomy in space.

After analysing the international legal instruments and national laws on remote sensing in a preliminary review, the national legislation of some major space-faring nations will be examined as a means of establishing differences in regulation and handling of RS data, and its effects on information policy. The final part of the paper focuses on whether there is a need for a revised approach to the international legal regulation of RS data and control of its use. The article concludes by highlighting the most important issues to be addressed in any future reform.

of Globalization, *37 Suffolk U. L. Rev. 1041*, at 1055-1057.

[7] See U.N. Principles on Remote Sensing U.N. Doc A/RES/41/65 (1986); hereinafter Principles.

[8] See Commercialisation of European Meteorological Operational System and of World Meteorological Organisation, WMO Res. 40, 1995.

[9] R. J. Birk, T. Stanley, G. I. Snyder, T. A. Hennig, M. M. Fladeland and F. Policelli, Government Programs for Research and Operational Uses of Commercial Remote Sensing Data, *Remote Sensing of Environment*, 88 (2003), at 3-16.

1. OVERVIEW OF NATIONAL AND INTERNATIONAL LEGISLATION

a. International instruments

The Treaty on Principles Governing the Activities of States in the Exploration and Use of Outer Space, including the Moon and Other Celestial Bodies[10] is the main treaty governing all "national space activities" carried out or supervised by states (Art. VI). Remote sensing activities by their very nature fall within the ambit of the Treaty and international space law. The only 'problem' is that the detailed regulation (supervisory framework) for national space activities carried out by non-governmental (private) entities falls squarely within the sole jurisdiction of states (Art. VI para. 2). Apart from this short provision, the OST does not contain any norms that are directly applicable to private actors within the space (and remote sensing) industry. Regulation of commercial space activities did not appear on the agenda at the time the Treaty was drafted and adopted.[11]

The UN Principles Relating to Remote Sensing of the Earth from Outer Space constitute a particular international set of rules. Although the Principles are not a binding international treaty, many space law researchers agree that the document has become a codification of the customary law that has emerged.[12] Its fifteen principles set out the basis for the remote sensing activities around the world. The Principles regulate in general the cooperation (relationship) among sensing and sensed states.

The definition of remote sensing laid down in the Principles does not, however, adequately respond to the current state of affairs: the conditions of access to the RS data are fairly vague and the specific obligations of the private

[10] January 27, 1967, 610 *UNTS* 205, hereinafter OST.

[11] ILA Space Law Committee Report 2004, *Remote Sensing Earth Observation Satellites*, available at http://www.ila-hq.org/pdf/Space%20Law/Space%20Law%20Report%202004.pdf. Hereinafter ILA Report 2004, last visited 17.08.2006.

[12] ILA Toronto Conference (2006) Space Law, Second Report, *Legal Aspects of the Privatisation and Commercialisation of Space Activities: Remote Sensing and National Space Legislation*, at 5, available at http://www.ila-hq.org/pdf/Space%20Law/Report%202006.pdf, last visited 17.08.2006. Hereinafter ILA Report 2006.

remote sensing companies in data exchange transactions are not laid down.[13] All this makes the application of the Principles somewhat difficult.

There are a number of bi- and multilateral agreements that regulate various aspects (largely technical) of remote sensing,[14] but which are not designed to fill the gaps within the Principles. For instance, EUMETSAT / and the US National Oceanic and Atmospheric Administration (NOAA) Agreement on Joint Transition Activities regarding Polar-Orbiting Operational Environmental Satellite Systems[15] and other EUMETSAT agreements do not contain any precise reference to the status of RS data. This is subject to states' and organisations' remote sensing policies.

It is debatable whether a RS data exchange agreement can be seen as a public international law mechanism, or whether it should be seen as a transaction of a nature closer to private law, be it concluded between states, or states and international organisations. These agreements lay down data exchange mechanisms between the parties and therefore are very close to licence agreements set by private companies.

Another example is the Agreement Concerning Operation of Commercial Remote Sensing Satellite Systems between Canada and the USA[16] aims at adopting legislation in Canada similar to that of the USA as a means of avoiding inconsistencies in cooperation between these countries and at the private remote sensing activities level.

b. National regulations

i. Special laws and other legislative acts

A *lex specialis* regulating remote sensing activities is a rare occurrence among the regulations on space activities in existence in different national legal systems.

The USA has the most extensive space law legislation, Canada and Russia have general provisions with regard to space activities, as well as some provisions explicitly or implicitly addressing remote sensing activities: licensing conditions for remote sensing activities, (some) restrictions on the supply of data dependent on resolution quality and e.g. matters of national security / fulfilment of international obligations. Europe has no comparable EU-level legislation. Some cases of national legislation, mostly general in character, fall outside the scope of the current regulatory analysis.[17]

Canada adopted an Act governing the operation of remote sensing systems in November 2005.[18] This legislation is designed to promote the development of the commercial remote sensing industry in Canada, whilst providing the government with the power to curb satellite operations to protect national security, a process referred to in the industry as 'shutter control'. The legislation also fulfils Canada's obligations under the Agreement with the U.S. Concerning Operation of Commercial Remote Sensing Satellite Systems.

The USA has for the time being provided the most detailed regulation, be it of the space activities on the whole or of remote sensing activities in particular. The relevant legislation includes: US Land Remote Sensing Policy Act,[19] Department of Commerce / NOAA Interim Final Rule on the Licensing of Private Land Remote-Sensing Space Systems.[20]

The Russian Federation has a Law on Space Activities,[21] as well as the Rules on the Licensing of Space Activities.[22] Private remote sensing activities are explicitly included within the activities under the scope of that regulation. The draft law on commercial space activities was rejected by the Russian Federation President in late 1999, leading to abandonment of any subsequent discussion of the matter in Parliament.

One point worth mentioning is that the US American and Canadian legislation meet on

[13] See ILA Report 2004, above fn. 11; ILA Report 2006, above fn. 12.

[14] See ILA Report 2004, at 4, above fn. 11.

[15] State Dept. N0. 03-82, 2003 WL 22137190.

[16] See U.S. Department of State fact sheet from June 16, 2000, available at www.licensing.noaa.gov/rsat2 factsheet.htm, last visited 17.08.2006.

[17] Information from the UN COPUOS web-site, at www.unoosa.org/oosa/en/SpaceLaw/index.html, last visited 17.08.2006.

[18] From 25.11.2005, S.C. 2005, c. 45.

[19] Title II and V.

[20] 15 CFR 960, April 25, 2006, hereinafter NOAA Rules.

[21] Federal Law No 5663-1, from August 20, 1993, as amended.

[22] Rules No. 403 from June 30, 2006, hereinafter Russian Rules.

many points (by dint of their co-operation), whereas the Russian acts differ greatly in content. The differences relate to e.g. licensing conditions[23] and terms thereof,[24] and provisions regarding protection of the RS data. What makes them similar is that none of the acts (sufficiently) regulates the status of the RS data. The questions of ownership and protection remain unaddressed. The NOAA Rules in § 960.12 lay down data policy for remote sensing space systems that regulate access modes to unenhanced data (only), depending on the financing of a remote sensing system. Furthermore, conditions of sharing unenhanced data with sensed states are provided in § 960.11 (10), while § 960.11 (13) regulates the requirement to submit a Data Protection Plan (that encompasses tasking, operations, processing, archiving and dissemination). Taking into account the NOAA commentary on the Rules that "*actual licences may differ in certain terms and respects*",[25] it is not clear whether the licensees' data dissemination plans will be identical or indeed differ substantially. The Russian Rules contain very general provisions with regard to data protection, stating that the information has to be protected from unauthorised access. As a result a remote sensing company must obtain a special licence allowing it access and work with the documents that are state secrets: RS data, especially of high resolution, falls within the definition of state secret.

ii. Space policies

Many countries (as well as some international organisations) choose to establish official policies with regard to space exploration in general and remote sensing in particular. Those documents do not create legal rights and remedies, rather setting only objectives for the development of a certain sphere. The majority of these states have only overall space policies that address, *inter alia*, (commercial) remote sensing.

The EU has adopted the White Paper on Space Policy,[26] subsequent to its predecessor Green Paper.[27] Both documents address the issues that have to be encompassed by a future common space policy document. The White Paper notes that the efficient use of spatial data is possible only where co-ordinated data policies exist.[28] Licensing is mentioned as a target for future drafts. Despite these assertions, several Member States (e.g. Italy, France) do not have any written space policies whatsoever.

The Russian Federation has a general National Space Policy Concept from 1996 (although never published); the National Remote Sensing System Development Concept is currently being drafted.[29]

Two countries that adhere to operative policy documents dealing specifically with remote sensing are the U.S. and India. US Commercial Remote Sensing Policy does not refer to the status of RS data:[30] conditions for dissemination in its Part II provide only the goal of timely and responsive regulation of the licensing operations; Part VI regulates export control mechanisms.

The Indian Remote Sensing Data Policy[31] sets its goal in better management of RS data acquisition and distribution, proclaiming that the Government of India (through its national remote sensing agency) is "the sole and exclusive owner of all data collected/received from IRS (Indian Remote Sensing Satellites)". Governments are furthermore in control of imaging tasks and distribution, rendering a licence a pre-requisite to data acquisition and / or distribution. The Indian policy makes data

[23] Cf. No.4 (e) (*) Russian Rules – receiving and/or processing of the information from the remote sensing satellites (here and further authors' own translation), § 960 (a) – operation of a remote sensing system.

[24] Cf. No.8 Russian Rules (5 years), § 960.9 NOAA Rules (operational lifespan of the system).

[25] See at www.licensing.noaa.gov/eolicense.htm, last visited 17.08.2006.

[26] COM (2003) 673, available at http://ec.europa.eu/comm/space/whitepaper/pdf/spwhpap_en.pdf, last visited 17.08.2006.

[27] COM (2003) 17 final January 21, 2003, available at http://ec.europa.eu/comm/space/whitepaper/greenpaper/greenpaper_en.html, last visited 17.08.2006.

[28] White Paper, at 16, above fn. 26.

[29] Information from www.gisa.ru.

[30] Presidential Directive from April 25, 2003, available at http://crsp.usgs.gov/pdfs/factsheet.pdf.

[31] ISRO:EOS:POLICY-01:2001, available at http://www.isro.org/Announcement-opportunity/rdsp.pdf, last visited 17.08.2006.

distribution further dependent on the quality of resolution.

The European Space Agency (ESA) has its own data dissemination policy.[32] The rules relate to contractual matters mostly: modes and conditions of licensing, issues of IP rights and copyright. Therefore, their provisions will be analysed in a separate section below on private regulation of remote sensing.

iii. Relevant norms of (private) law

The rules of law with the greatest impact on the handling of RS data, particularly by private actors, are those of intellectual property (IP) and copyright law in particular. This body of law flanks any enquiry as to data ownership and status: whether raw data is copyrightable, whether the deployment of computer programmes provides enough creativity to render the processed data copyrightable and finally, whether archiving can create database protection rights (at least for European producers).

Intellectual property laws are claimed to be applicable in relation to RS data. Some national space laws,[33] as well as both national[34] and corporate[35] data policies operate with copyright terminology or refer to existing national and international intellectual property (copyright) regimes. It is, however, questionable whether the IP laws are applicable to RS data and whether the latter is copyrightable and subject to legal protection.

The number of contracting parties to the Berne Convention for the Protection of Literary and Artistic Works[36] is a first indication of the support by a majority of legal systems for copyright protection in "literary and artistic works" in terms of Article 2 Berne Convention. This embodies the "creator doctrine"[37] by which copyright protection requires a degree of skill and novelty. For a work to be eligible for protection, an author must demonstrate creative effort. Ideas, processes, methods of operation, including data, do not fall within the ambit of copyright protection.[38] RS data is generated automatically, i.e. by using special computer programmes. It is thereafter subjected to processing. It contains factual information (the look of the earth surface, the depth of oceans etc.). Consequently, it is not generally eligible for copyright protection at all.

A solution to the lack of protection for databases was found at European Union level through its introduction in the Database Directive.[39] The Directive grants the database-maker a new *sui generis* right against unauthorised extraction or re-utilisation of the substantial parts of the database, as a means of protecting substantial investment in creating a database (namely, in obtaining, verifying or presenting the contents of a database).[40] The protection is granted to only those databases created within the Common Market, or if created outside, then under special conditions (through bi- or multilateral agreements).[41] Such protection is particularly suited to RS data which is (electronically) archived after being received by the ground stations.

The first decisions of the European Court of Justice (ECJ) relating to the interpretation of the Directive have, however, raised doubts as to the scope of interested parties and protective mechanisms involved *vis à vis* the organisations

[32] E.g. Earth Explorer Data Policy, December 18, 2003 EEXP-MMAN-EOPG-PD-03-0001, available at http://www.knmi.nl/~meulenvd/esa/Envisat/ESA_PB-EO_2002_79,REV_3.pdf, last visited 17.08.2006; Envisat Data Policy, August 23, 2000, available at http://www.knmi.nl/~meulenvd/esa/Envisat/envisat-data.pdf, last visited 17.08.2006.

[33] E.g. Russian Law Regarding Space Activities.

[34] E.g. Indian Space Policy.

[35] E.g. SPOT general licence, Eurimage licensing conditions, ESA ENVISAT Data Policy.

[36] Paris Act of July 24, 1971, as amended on September 28, 1979 1161 *UNTS* 3; 169 states parties, information from www.wipo.org, last visited 17.08.2006.

[37] L. Guibault, B.P Hugenholtz, *Study on the Conditions Applicable to Contracts Relating to Intellectual Property in the European Union*, Final Report, Institute for Information Law, Amsterdam, May 2002, at 24, available at http://www.ivir.nl/publications/other/final-report2002.pdf, last visited 17.08.2006.

[38] Articles 2, 5 WIPO Copyright Treaty (WCT) December 20, 1996, 36 *ILM* 65.

[39] Directive 96/9/EC of the European Parliament and of the Council of 11 March 1996 on the legal protection of databases, OJ 1996 L 77, at 20-28, hereinafter the Directive.

[40] Article 7 Directive.

[41] Article 11 Directive.

/ companies generating the satellite data.[42] The ECJ ruling from 2005 states that protection is only granted to those database makers that substantially invested in creation of databases by checking, verification or updating the database, but not to those who have invested in creating the database contents itself.[43] On July 13, 2005, the English Court of Appeal, sitting on the originator case, again confirmed the ECJ view, stating that the database right cannot be derived from the mere creation of a database.[44] Given the influence of a preliminary ruling on domestic courts when deciding similar cases, it is highly questionable whether the *creators* of the RS databases will be able to protect the contents of those databases under the Database Directive.

Interestingly, the recent evaluation report on the Directive itself states that the economic impact of the *sui generis* right on database production is unproven. One of the harshest criticisms against the Directive is that the scope of the protection is unclear: it does not stimulate the growth of the areas supposed and is perceived as locking up information.[45]

2. Operative Level: The Industry

a. Key players

In the opinion of the authors, the commercial remote sensing market does exist, because RS data is traded in: "it does not much matter who is buying or from where their funding ultimately derives".[46] It is true that such projects as French SPOT, Canadian RADARSAT, Indian IRS, European ERS-1, 2, Japanese JERS-1 were developed and carried out by governments, but each created a private company for the operation of the project's data gathering and distribution system.[47] Their products (as well as of US companies) are available to anyone on a commercial basis. It is precisely this combination of government-furnished space imagery with that supplied by private corporations which have relegated earth observations into a new range of opportunities with wide commercial implications.[48]

The ownership and operation of remote sensing satellites by the private sector has long been encouraged by many governments (in some cases, with only marginal success).[49] Even if there are only a few private companies actually operating private remote sensing satellite systems, the value-adding firms "play an important role in converting raw imagery data into the products desired by customers",[50] and their number and revenues gained are growing.[51] This growth is largely driven by evolving business opportunities through new and continuing military and intelligence imagery contracts, including expanding civil and commercial imagery markets, such as e.g. online mapping services.[52]

---

[42] Cases C-203/02 *British Horseracing Board Ltd and others v. William Hill Organisation Ltd*; see also Case C-46/02 *Fixtures Marketing Ltd v Oy Veikkaus Ab*, Case C-338/02 *Fixtures Marketing Ltd v Svenska Spel AB,* Case C-444/02 *Fixtures Marketing Ltd v. Organismos prognostikon agonon podosfairou AE (OPAP)*, ECJ Decisions of November 9, 2004, OJ C 6, 08.01.2005, at 4, 10.

[43] Case C-203/02 Decision, para. 31.

[44] Case No. A3/2001/0632 [2005] EWCA Civ 863.

[45] *First Evaluation of Directive 96/9/EC on the Legal Protection of Databases*, Working Paper, 12 December 2005, available at http://ec.europa.eu/internal_market/copyright/docs/databases/evaluation_report_en.pdf, last visited 17.08.2006.

[46] *The State of Commercial Remote Sensing Market*, available at http://www.eomonline.com/Common/Archives/2004augsep/04augsep_Conversation.tml, last visited 17.08.2006.

[47] *The Commercialisation of Remote Sensing*, available at http://rst.gsfc.nasa.gov/AppA/Part1_25.html, last visited 17.08.2006.

[48] Id.

[49] L. W. Fritz, above fn. 4.

[50] K. M. O'Connell, J. C. Baker, B. Lachman, S. Berner, D. Frelinger, K. E. Gavin, U.S. Commercial Remote Sensing Satellite Industry: An Analysis of Risks, RAND Monograph Report, 2001, at xi.

[51] The global commercial satellite industry generated some $88.8 billion in revenue in 2005, an increase of 7.4 percent over 2004 revenues – see *Commercial Satellite Industry Continues To Grow,* Report of the Satellite Industry Association available at http://www.sia.org/PDF/06142006PRStateofSatelliteIndustryReport.pdf, last visited 17.08.2006; see also Gabriela Seiz et al., above fn. 3.

[52] Satellite Industry Association, *State of the Satellite Industry Report*, June 2006, available at

Global competition in remote sensing "is here and will continue evolving" among purely commercial actors, hybrid companies (e.g. public-private partnerships) and even among governments that themselves choose to sell or license RS data generated under state-run programmes.[53] This is especially true for the European market, where the concentration between private earth observation companies and profit-bearing military contracts is lower than among its US counterparts.[54]

Described in simple terms, the satellite industry creates and manages remote sensing data in the following way: firstly, data is generated; secondly, data is archived and undergoes first-step processing; thirdly (or sometimes in parallel to the second phase), value-adding activities follow; the final stage is the marketing of satellite-produced data (satellite imagery, weather data etc.).

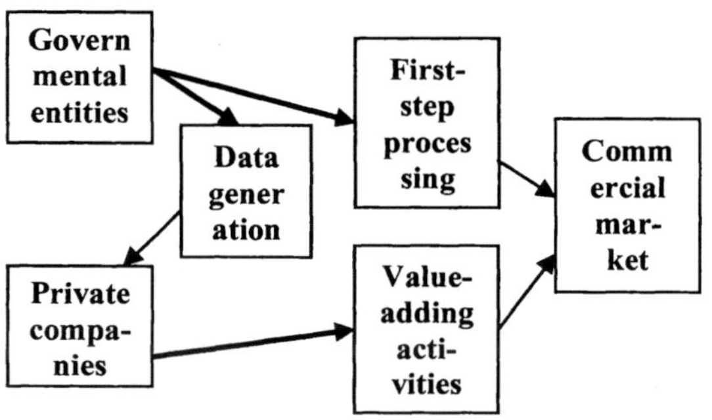

The whole process, from generating data until its marketing stage, can indeed be carried out by the same entity (a satellite operating company, e.g. OrbImage, ESA). The value-adding companies are not, however, necessarily concomitant with those who operate satellites.

The following digital mapping activities of the famous web-portals may serve as an example. Yahoo and Microsoft's Virtual Earth and Windows Local programmes are using both commercial and government imagery of GeoEye and Information Integration and Imaging LLC. Google Maps obtains imagery from Digital Globe. It is worth noting that neither the mapping engine companies nor the satellite imagery providers disclose how their contracts operate.[55]

This brings us to the question of data-acquisition. How do value-adding companies access the (raw / processed) data? What kind of rights do they obtain under the licence agreements with the satellite operating companies? These questions are addressed in the subsection below.

b. <u>Private regulations: licences, market practices</u>

The particular constellation of the market players, as well as uncertainties with regard to the regulation of the remote sensing activities described above have forced governmental agencies, international organisations alongside privately operated companies to develop their own data policies and licensing conditions as to the acquisition and distribution of RS data.

Data distribution methods can be divided into two basic types: selection and appointment of distributors for a certain area (or product), and licensing of the data directly to the end-user. The first option can be used by the data-generator companies or state actors; the second by both the data-generator companies and distributing entities. Licensing schemes of both types are briefly presented below.

i. <u>International organisations</u>

ESA

The first major issue regulated by the data policies of ESA[56] is the ownership of RS data: ESA maintains the ownership of all primary data and over ESA-derived products on behalf of the Member States. The mechanisms of protection are provided by virtue of database rules, copyright laws and other forms of intellectual property rights.

The distribution modes (as well as prices) depend further on the category of use. Category-1 Use includes research and application development use in support of the mission

http://www.futron.com/pdf/SIA_2005_Indicators.pdf, last visited 17.08.2006.

[53] Kevin O'Connell, *Commercial Applications of Payloads and Services: Remote Sensing*, in TOWARDS FUSION OF AIR AND SPACE, D.J. Johnson and A.E. Levite (eds.) RAND 2003, at 32.

[54] Gabriela Seiz et al., above fn. 3.

[55] *Internet Mapping Portal Competition Benefits Satellite Imagery Businesses*, available at http://www.space.com/spacenews/businessmonday_060424.html, last visited 17.08.2006.

[56] E.g. Earth Explorer Data Policy, Envisat Exploitation Policy.

objective, Category-2 Use encompasses all other uses. ESA is solely responsible for the distribution of data under Category-1 Use, and services for Category-2 Use are delivered to the users by the "distributing entities". (ESA will grant *non-exclusive licences* to selected distributing entities for the distribution of ENVISAT data over *well identified areas* for a period of 3 years). Data distribution in accordance with the UN Remote Sensing Principles is therefore ensured.

The data for Category-1 Uses has to be used exclusively within the project and solely for these purposes; it may not be distributed. Data are provided under these conditions at the cost of reproduction.

Two consortia (EMMA and SARCOM) are responsible for the distribution of data for Category-2 Uses. They hold agreements with ESA since 2000. The consortia enjoy full freedom of price-setting in accordance with market developments and own business plans. Data distribution by third parties (who obtained data from a distributing entity), without separate agreement by the latter, is prohibited. The distributing entities are required to guarantee access of value-added operators and service providers to the data, as well as the right to sell products and services to users.[57]

The end user thus enjoys copyright over his own interpretation of the ESA processed data.

EUMETSAT

EUMETSAT holds full ownership and all intellectual property and utilisation rights to its satellites and data.[58] The National Meteorological Services are Exclusive Licence Agents of EUMETSAT data with respect to their national territories.[59] They are also responsible for commercial data distribution.

The images based on Meteosat data are shared between Meteosat and the service provider generating the images, and all other value added services are owned by the generating service provider alone.[60]

[57] Part 6.6 Envisat Data Policy Summary.

[58] Preamble of the Resolution EUM/C/98/Res. IV, *EUMETSAT Principles on Data Policy.* 1-3 July 1998 (hereinafter EUMETSAT Resolution).

[59] Para. II EUMETSAT Resolution.

[60] Part 3 Annex I of Resolution EUM/C/04/Res. V, Implementing Rules for Meteosat Data and Products, 2-3 December, 2004.

ii. Private companies

ORBIMAGE operates 5 types of end-user licences, all for internal use. All contents are property of OrbImage; re-use and re-sale of copyrighted materials for any purpose is strictly prohibited.[61]

Under the licensing conditions *of MDA Geospatial Service Inc.*[62] the licensee has to accept MDA's copyright over the data provided. The licensee's rights depend on the type of product / data licensed (geospatial products and services, satellite imagery), as well as the type of licence itself (single site, multi-work station, and agency-wide licences grant only internal use of the data). Integrator and unlimited licences grant further dissemination rights with regard to the licensed data.[63]

EURIMAGE holds the copyright and other intellectual property rights over its products, the products moreover being trade secrets of EurImage the user thereby agrees to maintain this status. The licences granted by EurImage are non-transferable licences for internal uses of its products. Under such licences the right of sub-licensing is expressly prohibited.[64]

Spot Image's products and imagery are protected by IP, copyright and database laws; CNES is the owner of the imagery data. The products remain property of Spot Image and are provided to the end-user on a confidential basis. The licence is limited and non-exclusive, permitting only internal use of the data products and value-added products developed by the end-user which contain licensed imagery.[65]

[61] ORBIMAGE information on licensing, available at http://www.orbimage.com/docs/Catalog-FINAL-Dec28-2004.pdf, last visited 17.08.2006.

[62] The new name for the distribution entity for RADARSAT 1-2 data. Hereinafter MDA.

[63] See e.g. MDA's licensing terms for EarthSat GeoCover Project, available at http://www.mdafederal.com/geocover/licensing, last visited 17.08.2006.

[64] EURIMAGE Standard Terms and Conditions of Licence, available at http://www.eurimage.com/products/docs/standard_terms.pdf, last visited 17.08.2006.

[65] Non-Exclusive Licence to Use Spot Satellite Products between Spot Image and the End-User, available at http://cstars.rsmas.miami.edu/ndas/SPOT-EULA-0305.pdf, last visited 17.08.2006.

Space Imaging retains all copyright and ownership in all of its images and grants non-exclusive licences to use them. The products are provided on a confidential basis, as they contain valuable assets and proprietary information. The user is expressly prohibited from selling, licensing, transferring or disclosing products licensed. The licences relating to data from different satellites (e.g. Landsat, IKONOS, RSD, RADARSAT) contain minor differences.[66]

The only distribution agreement that the authors could access is the *Data Licence and Distribution Agreement* between Radarsat International and OrbImage[67] from 1999, which is still in force for the distribution of RADARSAT-1 data.[68] According to this agreement, OrbImage became a non-exclusive distributor of RADARSAT-1 data, data products and associated services on USA territory.[69] All copyright is vested in the Canadian Space Agency,[70] from which (under the agreement with Natural Resources Canada) Radarsat International has received an exclusive, unrestricted, worldwide licence for the distribution of RADARSAT data.[71] The terms of the end-user licence were also provided by Radarsat International, together with a prohibition on OrbImage to alter them on its own.[72] Interestingly, OrbImage has no right to archive or reproduce data provided by Radarsat International,[73] thereby putting a stop to the creation of any databases whatsoever.

c. Loopholes in existing regulations and their impact on the commercial market in remote sensing

The main problem surrounding the regulating of generation and dissemination of RS data by private actors is that the status of the RS data is unclear. This is particularly evident in relation to raw data which, as a "reflection of facts", and not even a picture. It constitutes a mere combination of signals transmitted to the ground station and subjected to a combination of mathematic formulae, thereafter to be encoded by a computer programme[74] in order to become readable, at least for professionals.

This uncertainty has lead to e.g. the US licensing regulation, which sets forth a condition for the licensee to develop a Data Protection Plan that provides information on how the licensee will protect data and information from tasking through to dissemination[75].

The status of the processed data is far from clear: moreover, the processing occurs with the help of a computer programme. It is highly debateable whether the images (other types of processed data) are subject to any copyright protection whatsoever.

It is equally debateable whether the database right now available within the European market – by virtue of the Database Directive – is a suitable tool for protection of collections of RS data. ESA claims that this type of protection is the best that can be secured (principally because the raw RS data is not copyrightable).[76] But the ECJ interpretation of the Directive's scope raises fundamental questions as to whether the creator of a database (in the sense of creator of the database content, i.e. those entities operating remote sensing satellites) is in fact protected by the database right.[77]

This uncertainty is in part supported by the licence clauses of the European and other RS data providers (e.g. SPOT Image) that refer in their licences to the fact that the data / products are protected under copyright, including the database right, and which are in addition

[66] Space Imaging Licensing, available at http://www.spaceimaging.com/aboutus/Licensing1.htm, last visited 17.08.2006.

[67] Available at http://sec.edgar-online.com/1999/11/15/16/0000950133-99-003634/Section29.asp, hereinafter Agreement, last visited 17.08.2006.

[68] The authors have no immediate information as to whether the agreement itself has since been altered.

[69] Article 2 2.1 Agreement.

[70] Article 9 9.1 Agreement.

[71] Preamble, Agreement.

[72] Article 9 9.2, Exhibit A Agreement.

[73] Article 3 3.2 Agreement.

[74] For technical peculiarities see G. Raber, J. Tullis, J.Jensen, *Remote Sensing Data Acquisition and Initial Processing*, available at http://www.eomonline.com/EOM_Jul05/article.php?Article=department3, last visited 17.08.2006.

[75] 15 CFR Part 960 Licensing of Private Land Remote-Sensing Space Systems, Section 960.11(b)(13).

[76] See ESA press-release at http://www.esa.int./SPECIALS/Intellectual_Property_Rights/SEM1101A90E_0.html, last visited 17.08.2006.

[77] See above fn. 42 and accompanied text.

provided to the end-user on a confidential basis.[78]

The conditions of RS data dissemination differ substantially, depending on the aim of use (commercial – non-commercial) and the user (e.g. government of the sensed state – state suffering a disaster – researcher – commercial user). The data in these cases is provided under different conditions of use within a different time-framework. The licences grant different rights with regard to the alteration of images and their possible uses.

None of this decries the remaining issue of national security on the commercial market scene. The USA, for instance, empowers the government with the right to exercise the "shutter control", in terms of which any company licensed under the US laws to engage in commercial remote sensing activities can, when national security is at stake, be prohibited from selling RS data to anyone other than US government for a certain period of time.[79] Canada last year enacted the same provisions, and Germany is working on a similar draft.[80] There is a clash between ownership of the data from (privately owned) satellites (in the case of US private remote sensing companies) and decisions as to the use of data, subject to government control.

3. PROPOSALS FOR REGULATING THE REMOTE SENSING DATA MARKET

a. Areas in need of legislative response

The foregoing has demonstrated several ongoing issues of private law stemming from remote sensing activities, particularly when of a commercial nature.

One of the most fundamental issues addressed is the status of RS data. There is a lack of consensus on a general concept of the protection this type of data can *per se* enjoy. The current situation allows data owners to claim all possible kinds of protection for their data – from copyright to classified information – where this may not always be the case.

The process of generating data from its initial stage through to the final stage of (commercial) distribution may often be divided between different entities (be they of public or private nature). As a result, the information licensing schemes require to be very precise, clear and respect principles of equality. There is a need to specify the scope of rights enjoyed by all those participating in the data process. A unified approach towards the content of licence agreements would create a first point of entry.

Reliance on national policies (which are not always contained in written form) cannot constitute a basis for transparent modes of distribution. Nor is reliance on the data policies of separate organisations or private companies in itself sufficient. There is a need for those states engaging in remote sensing activities to confer with private company licensees in a process of consultation culminating in adoption of codes, containing normative rules to regulate the licensing process (both licensing of the remote sensing activities and data distribution).

b. Possible regulatory instruments

i. International level

It comes as no surprise, therefore, that a reform of the Principles or their transformation within a convention is currently being discussed at international level. The need for reform is recognised both by the COPUOS and the Space Law Committee of the International Law Association. ILA Space Law Committee members do not support the adoption of a binding international convention: the "political climate" is not currently suitable.[81] As a purely public international law instrument, even the updated Principles would not serve as an appropriate regulatory mechanism for commercial transactions relating to RS data. In this sense, it would nevertheless be useful for the COPUOS to reshape the definition of remote sensing used by the Principles to make this more precise and clear.

When contemplating other alternatives, a draft model convention under the aegis of UNIDROIT, mirroring the draft protocol on

[78] See e.g. SPOT Standard Licence, Non-Exclusive Licence to Use SPOT Satellite Products between SPOT Image and the End-User, above fn. 55.

[79] See U.S. Commercial Remote Sensing Policy.

[80] M. Gerhard, B. Schmidt-Tedd, *Regulatory Framework for the Distribution of Remote Sensing Satellite Data: Germany's Draft Legislation on Safeguarding Security Interests*, International Aeronautical Congress, 2005.

[81] ILA Report 2006, at 10-11, above fn. 12.

matters specific to space assets within the Convention on International Interests in Mobile Equipment seems equally feasible. In this case, it should include a provision regulating issues surrounding intangible assets.

Taking this prototype solution one step further, UNIDROIT could be encouraged to work on a draft model law that encompasses at least the licensing issues.[82] Given that few states have adopted a *lex specialis* relating to commercial remote sensing activities, the model law could be of great assistance to those nations currently in the process of shaping their remote sensing policies or drafting corresponding legislative acts. Adherence by national legislators to the provisions drafted by UNIDROIT experts would result in a degree of harmonisation between current approaches to licensing remote sensing activities and remote sensing data, without the constraints posed by the "hard-law" of an international convention.

ii. European level

The issues still unsolved at European level go beyond the task of harmonising the substantive law of the legal status of information and information products. The law is in a precarious state since the Database Directive and recent rulings on its exact parameters. These include matters of competition law in relation to licensing issues. Whether or not licensing of remote sensing falls within the exclusive, as opposed to joint or attributed competence of the EU and/or Member States requires to be assessed. Harmonisation in this field is not necessarily concomitant with the principle of subsidiarity.[83]

A further issue remains that of regional regulation within the sphere of commercial remote sensing. Given the international spectrum of the remote sensing market, such an approach is unlikely to be sufficient.

CONCLUSION

The foregoing discussion serves to highlight the deficiencies, uncertainties and loopholes in relation to the current regulation of remote sensing, and its commercial side in particular. It has examined examples of international and national rules in force in this area. If commercial space activities are to be increased and its key players encouraged to adopt a clear line towards value operated services, the legal parameters for such activities should be set on a clear new footing.[84]

The paper proposes a concerted approach to regulating ownership of informational and information property rights in the face of commercial growth within this area. Security issues aside, a consolidated and coherent approach from within the international community would be seen to lend credibility to what continue to constitute important issues of rights of ownership, exploitation and access. The international community has a variety of regulatory tools available at its fingers, be they hard or soft law. Given the advantages of model laws on national governments as prototypes and legislative guidelines, a new UNIDROIT model law might proffer a timely benchmark for legal progress in what is otherwise an inconsistently regulated market that sways between serving public and private interests. It would also prove a response to a legal challenge that currently remains unanswered.

If only by way of conclusion, we refer to this challenge: *'Whereas remote sensing technology has rapidly evolved, law-making has come to a halt'.*[85]

This summarises and emphasises what is at stake and what can be done to regulate important informational, albeit at times sensitive, issues of national and international concern.

[82] E.g. see UNIDROIT Model Franchise Disclosure Law, Rome, International Institute for the Unification of Private Law (UNIDROIT), 2004.

[83] L. Guibault, B.P Hugenholtz, at 153, above fn. 37.

[84] Proceedings of the Canadian Standing Committee on Foreign Affairs and International Trade, February 3, 2005, at 9, 12, available at http://www.parl.gc.ca/infocomdoc/38/1/FAAE/Meetings/Evidence/FAAEEV21-E.PDF, last visited 17.08.2006.

[85] Dr. José Monserrat Filho, Introductory Report, in Report 2004, at 9, above fn. 11.

IAC-06-E6.3.9

The Registration Convention Thirty Years On

Professor Dr. Maureen Williams
Chair - ILA Space Law Committee (HQ, London)
National Council for Scientific and Technical Research (Conicet, Argentina)

Part I

The subject is gradually gaining momentum as a result of the growing involvement of private entities and developing countries in space activities. This is particularly so in the field of remote sensing as a good number of these countries have become, nowadays, both "sensed" and "sensing" states. The underlying question may, therefore, be stated as follows: is it advisable to introduce amendments to the text of the 1975 Convention on the Registration of Objects launched into Outer Space? Or, alternatively, should it be kept in its present reading and the gaps covered with some kind of separate international instrument, such as a UNGA Resolution? The political climate in the international arena seems to be indicating the latter course of action.

The Registration Convention became effective in 1976 but has not done too well since. It has, indeed, gone downhill in light of the figures provided by a recent Copuos document on Registration Statistics for 1957-2004 [1]. Over the last thirty years, streamlined by impressive technological advances, it appears unrealistic not to include further requirements for the registration of space objects on the international level. Just as important is the need to achieve a reasonable degree of uniformity for national registries.

In recent times some national administrative regulations, both in industrialised and developing countries, are becoming rather strict on this point. In fact, the position of developing countries, which day by day become further involved in space activities, is that the conditions laid out in Article IV of the 1975 Convention do not meet the necessary requisites to establish the link between damage caused by a space object to persons or property, or to the environment, and the space object involved.

This question is surfacing with increased frequency in many circles.. It was brought up a few times on the occasion of the UN/Brazil Workshop on Space Law (21-25 November 2004, ST/SPACE/28-OOSA) -where the shortcomings of this Convention were addressed by participants- and further pursued in June 2005 in Cologne during the International Symposium on Project 2001 Plus. In Argentina a Research Project is underway in the framework of the National Council for Scientific Research (Conicet / University of Buenos Aires) [2] in consultation with the national space agency of this country (CONAE), with special reference to registration issues.

On the international front, the Space Law Committee of the International Law Association, in its Report for the 72nd Conference (Toronto 2006), includes an analysis of the matter which shows that the links between remote sensing, national space legislation and registration issues get stronger by the day.

On the governmental level a special Working Group on the topic began its task in 2005 in the framework of the Legal Subcommittee of Copuos, presently under the chairmanship of Kai-Uwe Schrogl, and submitted its first report in April 2006 [3].

These and other equally topical questions relating, for example, to the somewhat dated requirement of a modest "five-state-ratification" for space treaties to enter into force should be further explored.

Part II

At this point in time it is reasonable to assume that, following the adoption of the Moon Agreement in 1979, the "United Nations Space Treaties era" is over, at least for the immediate future. Only Principles -intended to serve as guidelines - have been adopted by the UN since. However, some of these Principles, such as the UN Principles on Remote Sensing (1986), are reflecting to a great extent the general practice of states in today's world context [4].

At the most one may think of outlining some kind of binding separate protocol to give a more precise meaning to the requirements laid down for the registration of space objects in the 1975 Registration Convention, and adding more details to be provided in connection with the space object. This course of action appears ideal from and entirely theoretical and legal point of view.

Yet, at this stage, experience shows that the "five-state-ratification formula", a number which sufficed for a space treaty to be effective, is now outdated. It has led, more often than not, to contradiction resulting from the interpretation of treaties which –even though in force- have gained only a timid support from the international community. The Registration Convention and the Moon Agreement are glaring examples thereof.

Even though UNGA Resolutions -for clarifying purposes, in this case- appear a more realistic course of action in the present political context for the updating of the Space Treaties, should we happen to go back to the treaty-adoption days, new mechanisms should be devised for the entry into force of international space treaties. Briefly, a proper equilibrium should be sought between, on the one hand, the advantages of having binding rules on a topic which is strongly influenced by technological advancement and, on the other, the necessity of getting the greater possible support from the international community concerning new binding rules.

Part III

The changing scenarios of state practice in the field of remote sensing are a clear illustration thereof. Day by day, stricter requirements become essential for the registration of space objects both at the national and international levels. This is indeed the way opinion is moving today in most circles, both private and governmental. For these reasons, the ideas suggested by the UN Working Group on Registration appear sensible and should be supported. To the new requirements suggested by that Group, namely:

- Information relevant to mass of the space object.
- Information concerning the owner and operator of the space object.
- Information concerning a change of owner or state of registry.
- Information concerning the use of nuclear power sources on board.
- Information concerning the presence of astronauts on board.
- Information in the case of the non-functioning of a space object.
- Date of decay of the space object based on GMT/UTC.
- Information concerning a military satellite provided this does not affect strategic information.
- Date of entry into a national registry.
- Designation of the national authority for registration.
- Any change of the mission or of the fundamental parameters of the orbits shall also be furnished to the UN Secretary-General,

the following addition is hereby suggested:

- Details on measures adopted concerning the protection of the environment from the activity of the space object in question.

It is currently known that the use of Earth Observation Satellites (EOS) and its many implications is permanently growing, predominantly in a private context [5]. This situation prompts support for doctrines holding, on the grounds of Article VI of the 1967 Space Treaty, that states are under the ***obligation*** [6] to authorise and supervise the activities of non-state actors carrying out activities in outer space. In like manner, a time limit should be established for states parties to register state objects given the lenient provision of the Registration Convention in this regard. At the moment anything between 24-72 hours appears reasonable.

As observed at the outset, in the present international scenes a number of sensed states have become sensing states as well. This situation is likely to ease the provision proclaimed in Principle XII of the UN Principles on Remote Sensing on the highly controversial "right of access", on the part of sensed states, to information obtained about their territory.

Research carried out in recent times and different regions is revealing that, in general, state practice is consistent with most of the UN Principles, whether by devise or, simply, by coincidence. Yet, it is also true that some of the Principles are in need of interpretation in this dynamic international context [7].

Voices were raised in many a forum pointing to the need of adjustment of certain articles of the Registration Convention [8], the strength of which is in decline in spite of the recent ratifications of Italy and Brazil [9]. This claim for further precision comes from both industrialised and developing countries and is aiming at having more official details for every object launched into outer space.

Both in industrialised and developing countries the use of Earth Observation Satellites is constantly growing and, as observed initially, entails a need for new law to be created on the international level.

As far as national registries are concerned, every effort should be made to preserve a reasonable uniformity which, in this field, should focus on specific requirements, inter alia:

- In case of joint launches, the text of the relevant agreements.
- Details relating to insurance.
- Details on measures adopted relating to the protection of the environment from the activity of the space object in question [10].

This, in turn, calls for national space legislation within the states parties to the Registration Convention. In some cases, interesting specific provisions may be found on the administrative level. A few examples, taken at random, will follow as illustration thereof.

The Report of the ILA Space Law Committee to the Toronto Conference (2006) addressed this question in the context of a questionnaire circulated to members in early 2005. In Sweden, for example, the Swedish National Space Board is entrusted with the authorisation and supervision of space activities and the keeping of the national registry for space objects. The national requisites for the registration of space objects are similarly entrusted to this body where Sweden is acting as launching state pursuant to the Registration Convention. Likewise, in the USA there exists a national registry and national space legislation on registration. In the Czech Republic a national registry was established on the administrative level in the framework of the Institute of Atmospheric Physics, Academy of Sciences. This country, as a party to the Registration Convention, has recorded the launching of all its space objects –as well as its predecessor, Czechoslovakia- with the Secretary-General of the UN. France, so far, does not have a national registry. On this point Kerrest points out the importance of drawing a clear line between registration and licensing, the latter being a much wider concept than the former. For instance, under Article I of the Registration Convention, a state may be liable as a launching state and still not be the state of registration. Moreover, in his view, insurance topics should be linked to licensing procedures and not to registration [11].

Brazil - as noted earlier - has recently become a party to the Registration Convention. So far this country has no domestic law on registration but, in the new circumstances, this should follow shortly. As to the national registry, the Brazilian Space Agency would appear the most likely body to be in charge thereof [12]. The United Kingdom has set up a national registry of space objects of which this country is the launching state pursuant to the terms of the Registration Convention. The UK Outer Space Act (1986), in section 7, provides that the government shall maintain a register of space objects containing "the details it deems necessary for compliance with its international obligations". Furthermore, the UK has set up a Supplementary Registry of Space Objects in respect of which the UK has granted a license under the 1986 Act. Good examples thereof are the Inmarsat satellites which had not been licensed by the British government prior to the transfer, in 1999, to a UK private company. This procedure is also applicable in cases of transfer of ownership in orbit. In Argentina the registry is maintained by the national space agency (CONAE) which operates within the framework of the Ministry for Foreign Affairs. Registration is mandatory and entails the responsibility of this country, which has jurisdiction and control over the space objects registered with CONAE. There are a large number of mandatory details to be provided for entries in this registry which go far beyond those laid down by the Registration Convention, as follows:

1. In case of joint launches with other countries, the full text of the pertinent agreements.
2. The name of the space object.
3. The date and place of launching, date envisaged for recovery or loss of contact or disintegration of the space object and date of termination of the mission or lifespan of the space object.
4. Basic orbital parameters.
5. General functions established for the object.
6. Name and address of the proprietors and/or operators of the space object.
7. Companies responsible for its construction.
8. Insurance modalities.
10. Location and characteristics of telemetry, command and control station of the satellite.
11. Frequency and power of transmission of the space station on board.
12. Details relating to the mass of the space object.
13. Lifespan.
14. Measures concerning contamination.
15. Date of registration.

Part IV

A first general conclusion is, therefore, that the changing scenario of state practice in the field of remote sensing, and its ever-growing implications, call for stricter requirements in the registration of space objects both on the international and national fronts. The conditions laid down in the 1975 Registration Convention are today insufficient to determine the link between damage caused by a space object to persons or property, or to the environment, and the space object in question. Concerning national registries, a reasonable uniformity should be maintained by the states parties to the Registration Convention.

A second general conclusion is that, if and when the era of binding space law instruments is back, the "five-state-ratification" formula should be revised with a view to adopting mechanisms more consistent with the present time.

Part V

Hereunder, some specific conclusions on the topic.

1. In line with the first general conclusion, the changes and additions suggested in this paper should be made by means of a UNGA Resolution or separate international instrument keeping the text of the 1975 UN Registration Convention intact.
2. On the national level it is suggested that more specific requirements be introduced for the registration of space objects, including further details than those proposed to supplement the provisions laid down by the UN Registration Convention.
3. To this end, national space legislation should be enacted by the states parties which, pursuant to Article VI of the 1967 Space Treaty, are under the obligation of authorising and supervising space activities within their jurisdiction or control.
4. On both fronts -international and domestic- it is essential that details should be provided on the measures adopted to avoid contamination resulting from the operation of the space object.
5. In the present international context it is imperative to establish a clear time-limit -in the region of 24-72 hours following the launch- for the registration of space objects. This is, of course, without prejudice to certain cases, such as GEO satellites, some of which may take many months to reach final orbital position –particularly

when using electric propulsion- and, therefore, final details will not be certain for some time. This also applies to space objects purchased in orbit.

6. Once again - and both on the international and domestic fronts - international cooperation plays a major role in the pursuance of the objectives outlined.

Notes

[1] Doc. A/AC.105/C.2/2005/CRP.10, 14 April 2005, 44th Session of the LSC.
[2] "Proyecto PIP/Conicet 5718" (2005-2006), Consejo Nacional de Investigaciones Cientificas y Tecnicas, Conicet/Universidad de Buenos Aires, Argentina, conducted by the present author.
[3] Doc. A/AC.105/871.
[4] See, in this respect, the Report of the Space Law Committee of the International Law Association (ILA) to its 72nd Conference (Toronto, June 2006), on the ILA website: www.ila-hq.org. The reports submitted to this Conference, working sessions and resolutions adopted will be published shortly, in book format, in London.
[5] This is nowadays not so much the case in the USA. See Toronto ILA Report 2006, note 2 supra.
[6] Italics added by the present author.
[7] See the ILA Toronto Report, note 4 supra.
[8] See, *inter alia*, the proceedings of the UN/Brazil Workshop on "Disseminating and Developing International and National Space Law: the Latin and Caribbean Perspective (Rio de Janeiro, 21-25 November 2004, published in 2005 by the Office for Outer Space Affairs, Vienna, ST/SPACE28, the Cologne Symposium which marked the end of Project 2001 Plus (8-10 June 2005, published by Carl Heymanns Verlag, Berlin, in 2005)) and the Report of the ILA Space Law Committee to the Toronto Conference 2006.
[9] Italy became a party to the Registration Convention on 8 December 2005 and Brazil on 20 February 2006.
[10] Requirements of the kind have been adopted, *inter alia*, by Argentina and the United Kingdom for the registration of space object in their national registries.
[11] See answers to the Questionnaire circulated by the Chair and Rapporteur of the ILA Space Law Committee to members, *inter alia*, Hedman (Sweden), Gabrynowicz (USA), Kopal (Czech Republic) and Kerrest (France), op. cit. in note 4 *supra*.
[12] Ibid. Answers from Monserrat Filho (Brazil), Sagar (UK) and, on the Argentine national system, comments from the present author.

London, 15 September 2006

IAC-06 –E6.3.10

PUBLIC AND PRIVATE INTEREST IN REMOTE SENSING ACTIVITIES: THE NEED FOR AN EFFECTIVE LEGAL ENVIRONMENT

Dr. Marianna Morelli
CORILA
Consortium for Coordination of Research Activities Concerning the Venice Lagoon System
Venezia, Italy, morelli@corila.it - marianna_morelli@yahoo.it

ABSTRACT

Space technology provides mankind with the potential tools for economic, social and cultural development. Earth observation systems are powerful tools to guarantee an information control on many key indicators that are closely related to many interdependent and trans-boundary issues such as industrial policies, economic strategies, environmental protection agreements and local development plans. Today, remote sensing is an important instrument to recognize major environmental changes, water and soil quality and to manage natural resources. During the last decades, however, the practice of remote sensing has largely changed, private interests have been stimulated disregarding the public interests.

This paper aims to analyse the international legal framework of remote sensing. International space law does not cover many of organizational and legal issues emerging from the new practices of remote sensing. The need for the widest availability of data to all interested users, the growing expansion of remote sensing commercial services, the international and scientific cooperation and the emerging of the private operators of satellite systems must be duly considered in a proper regulating environment. The paper takes into consideration the aspect of the open access to data combining the obligations of space law with the need of environmental law while the private interest in data control is introduced by the national data policies. The emerging approach of cooperation represents, in this context, a new way to find a real synergy between public and private interests.

INTRODUCTION

"In the middle of the 20th century we saw our planet from space for the first time"[1]. It was the view of the Earth, dominated by a pattern of clouds, oceans, greenery and soils, that inspired the world to see the environment as a whole, and to move forward to protect it. Since then, the collection of data and images acquired by remote sensing satellites has offered information on the Earth's system. Earth observation from space has permitted to point out and to understand phenomena such as the greenhouse effect and the global warming, the global climate change and the loss of biodiversity, the deforestation and the desertification of land in arid regions and various other environmental features. Space technologies also represent valuable tools for disaster prevention and management.

Data have been used in the past, and will be used in the future, to address issues of social and economic importance in areas such as the land use management, the management of renewable and non-renewable resources, global health and agricultural and fishery management[2].

During the last decades, however, the practice of remote sensing has largely changed: the number of states active as remote sensing actors has increased. The technical possibilities of sensing specified areas have greatly advanced and consequently opened an unlimited commercial access to raw data and analysed information.

Even if satellite remote sensing activities are far from being a business attractive as telecommunications, the private interests have been strongly stimulated disregarding the public interests involved in these specific space activities.

The balance between public and private interests constitutes today the central political and legal question of current space activities.

This paper will analyse how this relation is regulated under the existing remote sensing regime, not only on the basis of the 1986 UN Principles, but also taking into account the new approach to cooperation in remote sensing activities and the information required under the rules of international environmental law.

The focus of the paper is to analyse one of the most prominent issues connected to the public and private interests in the recent remote sensing activities: the access to data and the legal protection of these data.

1. DATA ACCESS AND PRIVATE CONTROL

Article 19 of the 1948 UN Universal Declaration of Human Rights affirms the everyone's "right to seek, receive and impart information and ideas through any media and regardless of frontiers". This principle, ascertaining the freedom of flow of information, is frequently invoked in order to refute any restrictive effect of State sovereignty and to promote the unlimited dissemination of information and non-discriminatory access to it[3].

If the freedom of use of satellites for acquiring remote sensing data from anywhere in the world is generally recognized, and the interest of State to protect data concerning their own territory is decreasing, today the main focus of the debate concerns the distribution of remote sensing imagery acquired with the use of satellites.

In the absence of a uniform and clear international legislation covering Earth observation in all its aspects, the problem can be analysed from two different points of view:

1. the respect of the widest availability of data to all interested users in conformity of the Resolution 41/65, approved in the United Nation framework in 1986, and in view of the international environmental legal regime, which promotes the open access to environmental information for the benefit of all citizens.

2. the respect of ownership over the remote sensing data pertaining to private rather than to public international law, involving principles such as privacy, intellectual property rights, and standards.

1.1 PUBLIC INTEREST AND DATA ACCESS: THE INTERNATIONAL SPACE LAW

Article 1 of the Outer Space Treaty of 1967 introduces to the international space regime the idea of global public interest in space activities. It states that "the exploration and use of Outer Space, including the Moon and other celestial bodies, shall be carried out for the benefit and in the interests of all countries, irrespective of their degree of economic or scientific development, and shall be the province of all mankind"[4].

Furthermore, the Outer Space Treaty calls for international cooperation establishing that all space activities fall under general norms of international law, including the Charter of the United Nations, and shall be carried out in the interest of maintaining international peace and security and promoting international cooperation and understanding[5].

The same concepts are announced in principles II and III of the UN Resolution relating to the Sensing of the Earth from Outer Space.

The significance of the Remote Sensing Principles, adopted by consensus by the General Assembly in its resolution 41/65 of 3 December 1986[6], was the attempt to

coordinate two antipodal concepts: the freedom of actions of the sensing State, on the one part, and the sovereignty over the natural resources of the sensed State, on the other, as well as the legitimate rights and interests of any State and its entities.
The compromise of the two interests has been achieved by Principle XII, which provides the sensed State with a right of access to primary and processed data relating to the territory under its jurisdiction, on a "non-discriminatory basis" and on "reasonable cost terms"[7]. The sensed State shall also have access to the available analysed information, concerning the territory under its jurisdiction, in the possession of any State participating in remote sensing activities.
In this way the right of the sensing State to acquire satellite imagery without the consent of the sensed State and, at the same time the interest of the sensed State in having non-discriminatory access to satellite imagery of its territory, have been fully recognized[8].
Principle XII does not exclude the commercialisation of the data, access to data should be assured on a non discriminatory basis and on reasonable cost terms, taking particularly into account the needs and interests of the developing countries.
This principle of access right to data and information, on an equal and equity basis, applies both to the protection of the "Earth's natural environment" and to the protection of "mankind from natural disasters".
Principle X[9] indicates that remote sensing promotes the protection of the Earth's natural environment. For this purpose, States participating in remote sensing activities that have identified information in their possession that is capable of averting any phenomenon harmful to the Earth's environment have the obligation to disclose such information to the State concerned.
In the same way, Principle XI[10] establishes the role of remote sensing in the protection of mankind from natural disasters. For this purpose, States that have identified processed data and analysed information in their possession that may be useful to States affected by natural disasters, or likely to be affected by impending natural disasters, have the obligation to transmit such data and information to the State concerned as promptly as possible.
Since the adoption of the 1986 UN Remote Sensing Principles, the practice of the States and the international community has changed. In the beginning of space activities, States constituted the primary category of players. As a consequence, the legal regime dealing with remote sensing activities is a public legal regime, providing for rights and obligations of States. Nowadays, with the tendency towards the privatisation of data retrieval, raw data processing, data analyses and data sales, it may become more difficult to guarantee reliable access to data, especially by developing countries.
Even if Principle XII provides that the sensed State can have access to data and information on a "non discriminatory access and at reasonable cost terms" there is no clear interpretation which could possibly make it an effective right[11]. The pricing policies are of crucial importance, especially with regard of environmental information and the interests of the less developed countries.
Therefore, the privatisation of activities implies the necessity to protect data rights, where the State has to provide non-discriminatory access, at no cost, for certain environmental and disaster applications, as provided in Principles X and XI.
The balance between commercial activities and non-discriminatory access in the pricing policy is quite open and is often left to the discretion of national legislation.

However, as mentioned in the last paragraph, the Resolution 41/65 seems to give a special status to the data and information concerning environmental harm and the protection of humankind from natural disasters.
The first tool put in place to cope with disaster prevention and mitigation was the International Charter on Space and Major Disasters. The purpose of the Charter, announced at the UNISPACE III in 1999, is to support, by means of space assets and the associated information and services, the organization of emergency assistance or subsequent operations[12].

Concluded in October 2000, among the main national and international space agencies and institutions of public nature, such as the European Space Agency, the French Space Agency (CNES), the Indian Space Research Organisation (ISRO), the Canadian Space Agency (CSA), and the US's NOAA, the Charter offers a unified and co-ordinated system of space data acquisition and data delivery to those countries affected by disasters. In other words, it provides timely and critical data at no cost.

In this sense, the Charter gives full implementation of the UN Principle XI and recalls the Principle 18 of the UN Declaration on environment and development adopted at Rio de Janeiro in 1992, where it is established that "States shall immediately notify other States of any natural disasters or other emergencies that are likely to produce sudden harmful effects on the environment of other States. Every effort shall be made by the international community to help States so afflicted"[13].

1.2 PUBLIC INTEREST AND DATA ACCESS: THE IMPACT OF THE INTERNATIONAL ENVIRONMENTAL LAW

The increasing awareness towards environmental issues has led to an expanding need for global observations. In this context, the capability of satellites has been perceived as a great opportunity to monitor Earth's system and its processes. Remote sensing technologies, enabling the detection of alterations of the environment status (atmosphere, oceans, biodiversity and other parameters) with extreme accuracy, at different times of the year and in different points of the Earth, constitute an essential tool in order to obtain a systematic observation of our planet.

If we look at State practice, in recent years international environmental treaties have frequently envisaged the use of remote sensing to supervise the compliance with obligations embodied in their text.

The proliferation of multilateral environmental agreements has led to an increased need for a larger availability of spatial data for the scientific community as well as for the public decision makers. Most of these agreements require continuous monitoring of a number of different parameters concerning the land surface, the oceans and the atmosphere.

In order to make some examples, we recall the Convention on Wetlands, signed in Ramsar - Iran in 1971 (commonly referred as Ramsar Convention)[14], which provides the framework for national action and international cooperation for the conservation and wise use of wetlands and their resources.

This objective requires that each contracting party has access to information in order to better understand wetland areas, their processes and their significance in the global environment, to efficiently manage wetland areas and promote their conservation and protection. In order to prevent any changes in ecological character brought by human interference, art.3 of the Ramsar Convention establishes that all the national and international bodies involved in the implementation of the Convention shall arrange to be informed at the earliest possible time about any detrimental changes[15]. Earth observation images can be useful to inform at the early possible time of any changes and represent a viable tool to provide detailed and continuous wide areas views of individual wetlands to aid national and local conservation efforts.

The same interest in the distribution of information in a timely manner is also mentioned in the Convention on Biological Diversity[16], where article 17 requires that all contracting Parties exchange and share information relevant to the conservation and sustainable use of biological diversity, taking particularly into account the special needs of developing countries[17]. Information gathered by remote sensing, according to the Convention on Biological Diversity, contributes to the development and implementation of plans or other management strategies finalised to rehabilitate and restore degraded ecosystems and promote the recovery of threatened species. Data should be used to "develop, where necessary, guidelines for the selection, establishment and management of protected areas"[18].

In the same way, within the context of the United Nations Framework Convention on Climate Change (UNFCC)[19], many articles recognise the importance of establishing systematic observation and data archives, in order to understand the climate change phenomenon in all its complexity. Countries' information requirements under the UNFCC can be divided into two categories: national inventories and global climate observations. The first category covers the information needs related to land use, land use changes and forests. Art. 4.1 establishes that all parties have to publish yearly national inventories of anthropogenic emissions by sources and removals by sinks of all greenhouse gases[20].

The second category covers the need for global climate change observation systems in order to improve climate forecasts and impact of climate change[21].

Earth observation can be used for the two categories of information, providing a number of measurements, including concentration of atmospheric trace gases, rise in sea level, the extent and evolution of sea ice cover and the dynamics of the atmosphere and oceans.

The Kyoto Protocol, which contains specific binding commitments to limit or reduce greenhouse gas emissions in the atmosphere, identifies a number of areas where the support of remote sensing is essential, such as the detection and spatial quantification of change in land cover, the quantification of above – ground vegetation, biomass stocks and associated changes therein, the systematic observation of relevant land cover, the mapping and monitoring of anthropogenic sources[22].

In conclusion, the World Summit on Sustainable Development adopted the Johannesburg Declaration in September 2002, which identifies a series of environmental and development issues for the coming century. The Plan of Implementation[23] indicates satellite Earth observation as a crucial information source for a number of disciplines relevant to sustainable development.

This short excursus stresses the global public interest in access to environmental information and in a large exchange of data and information between public authorities, the scientific community, intergovernmental organizations and non-governmental entities.

In this way, access to information is not only reinforced by remote sensing law by means of principles X and XI of the Remote Sensing Resolution, but also by the environmental law and through several other Conventions such as the Aahrus Convention of 1998[24] on access to information, public participation in decision-making and access to justice in environment matters. The Convention, which represents a new kind of environment agreement, calls for an open access to the environment information for the benefit of citizens. It links environmental rights with human rights, having particular attention to the interaction between public and private authorities.

All these provisions regarding the collection and sharing of information on the global environment underline the international common interest in protecting by international cooperation the different ecosystems. Satellite observation, monitoring the large areas without regard to territorial borders of State, represents, in the frame of monitoring for environment a very powerful tool.

1.3 PRIVATE CONTROL AND NATIONAL DATA POLICIES

Having analysed the international rights and obligations contained in the international space law and environmental treaties, it is clear that there are still many issues to be solved. If the international public law recognises the public interest in the widest availability of data and in a large cooperation among countries to exchange information, the problem of data policies and the legal framework under which they are carried out still remains open[25].

The lack of a clear provision in international law necessitates the development of national Earth observation data policies.

Data policies differ among countries and regions depending on many economic, social and political factors. These policies, based on the concept of ownership, copyright, licence and managing issues such as access, pricing, and privacy rights, offer the best chance for the economic development in the use of outer space benefits. Therefore they include many implications for the relationship between the public sector and the emerging private sector.

In fact, the common aim of any data policy is the promotion of the data market in accordance with commercial criteria. The intention is to be able to invest in remote sensing activities and generate a possible stream of revenues with the control over data entitlements. The main question today is how to guarantee public interest and, at the same time, find incentives for the development of a market for remote sensing products.

By now the balance of these interests depends upon the discretion of the sensing state. Depending on the socio-political and legal system of certain States, there is a clear contrast between the developed and developing countries, as the latter are almost exclusively sensed States.

In Europe many space systems are developed within the framework of the European Space Agency, which has established a policy in the distribution of data resulting from these activities.

We would like to outline the ERS (European Remote Sensing Satellite) missions. The original objectives established for ERS-1 were both scientific and economic, allowing a versatile use of their capabilities, including the commercial potentials. The ESA data policy for ERS–1 and 2[26], as well as for the ENVISAT (advanced polar-orbiting Earth observation satellite) mission, aims to stimulate a balanced development of science, public and commercial applications, consistent with the mission objectives. This purpose defines the ESA approach regarding access to data and pricing of data. ESA implements differential access to data classifying different user's categories in accordance with the use of the data[27]:

1. the scientific users category for research, including research on long term issues of the Earth system. In this category ESA promotes non discriminatory access to data for global environmental studies

2. the economic users category for commercial and operational applications with reference to the promotion of the remote sensing sector and to the meeting of returns on investments covering the costs of programmes development and operations. The data policy concerning these data is based on the respect of ownership.

The consequence of this idea of ownership is the act of licensing the use or the reproduction of the data. ESA retains full ownership of rights to data and while access is open for the first category, the licences to use data for the second category prohibit the redistribution of data.[28]

In the same way, SPOT Image, the first company set up in France in order to distribute data coming from Spot satellites, bases its data policy on the concept of copyright. The copyright belongs to the CNES, the Centre National d'Etudes Spatiales, while Spot Images has a licence for the distribution of data.

In addition, the protection of data in Europe is also foreseen in the EU Directive on the Protection of Electronic Databases of 11 March 1996[29], which is of relevance also for Remote Sensing data. The directive provides that space data can be defined as the collection of independent data arranged in a systematic or methodical way and individually accessible by electronic or other means. The directive introduces two different rights to protect: the copyright of the database and "sui generis" rights in order to prevent extraction and/or reutilization of the whole or of a substantial part of the content of that database[30].

2.2 EMERGING NEW FORMS OF INTERNATIONAL COOPERATION

As we have seen in the previous paragraphs, space based Earth observation technology, first carried out as individual national programs, has developed into a worldwide harmonized effort in monitoring the global environment.

One of the first examples of international cooperation in space activities is the Committee on Earth Observation Satellites (CEOS), created in 1984, on the initiative of the US Government. The Committee has become the major forum for the exchange of information and the harmonization of space programmes[31].

During the time the efforts to harmonize the individual national Earth observation projects into a global multilateral system of systems have greatly increased[32]. The aim of this new model of cooperation is to integrate different available data and information (i.e. remote sensing sources, in situ measurement networks and socio-economic data sources).

This is, for example, the case of the Global Climate Observing System, sponsored by the World Meteorological Organization (WMO), the United Nations Educational Scientific and Cultural Organization (UNESCO) and its Intergovernmental Oceanographic Commission (IOC), the United Nations Environment Programme (UNEP) and the International Council for Science (ICSU).

The Scientific Community is also developing a plan for the Global Ocean Observing System (GCOS) and the Global Terrestrial Observing System (GTOS).

Furthermore the third Earth Observation Summit, held in Brussels in 2005, starting the creation of a Global Earth Observation System of Systems (GEOSS). The purpose of GEOSS is to achieve comprehensive, coordinated and sustained observations of the Earth system, in order to improve the monitoring of the state of the Earth, increase the understanding of Earth processes, and enhance the forecasting of future changes of the Earth system[33].

At European level, the contribution to the Global Earth Observation System of Systems is constituted by the Global Monitoring for Environment and Security, GMES. The programme is a joint ESA/EU initiative, launched in 1998 with the "Baveno Manifesto", and adopted by the European Council in 2001. The common objective is to develop and bring into operational service a European independent capacity for the global monitoring of environment and security. GMES has to support European policies and strategies in the fields of environment, transport, agriculture, development and foreign policy.

By now GMES has reached a rather advanced stage. The Fourth GMES Forum, held again in Baveno in November 2003, marked the end of the GMES Initial Period and the beginning of the implementation phase. The last Communication of the European Commission to the Council and the European Parliament of 10 November 2005, "GMES From Concept to Reality", defines three candidate services for fast track introduction: land monitoring, marine services and emergence responses.

At the moment, the main challenge of GMES is to develop a real market for GMES services in Europe. This objective requires a great effort in order to find a balance between "non discriminatory access", economic viability and the necessary incentives for private services providers to invest in the development of such capability[34].

The discussion occurred in the GMES Forum held in Graz on 19- 20 of April 2006, has shown that "the long-term sustainability of GMES service development can only be achieved through a user-driven approach"[35].

In this stage of GMES development, the involvement of the regional dimension can represent a fundamental gear in order to collect users' requirements and consequently define public and private interest in the use of services. In fact most European regional governments deal with a number of issues in areas linked to the environment, emergency and security, agricultural and fishery management, air quality monitoring, integrated management of coastal areas as well the economic development and the

promotion of innovation system. In these different priority areas they could represent the public interest having also the equal interest in the economic growth increasing the value of their industries.
In line with these reflections, the European Union is promoting a strong involvement of Regions at both ends of the space chain, from infrastructures and technology development to applications[36].

CONCLUSIONS

The need for the widest availability of data to all interested users, the growing expansion of remote sensing commercial services, the effects of the international and scientific cooperation, as well as the emergence of the first private operators of remote sensing satellites represent today the main changes in the field of remote sensing activities and they pose a series of legal and institutional questions.
How to balance public and private interests? How to guarantee non discriminatory access at reasonable cost and at the same time to find incentive in order to develop adequate rules for remote sensing market? How the new approaches to cooperation provide solutions for the main legal issues in the field of Remote Sensing?
The key questions are those of access and consequently of private control.
The perspective, proposed in this paper, takes into consideration the aspect of the open access to the data combining the obligations of space law with the need of environmental law and human rights while the private interest in data control is introduced by the national data policies that are different among countries.
The emerging approach of cooperation represents, in this context, a new way to find a real and efficient synergy between public and private interests. These new forms of relations and institutions take into consideration first of all the public interest connected to the remote sensing activities, almost in the field of environmental protection, and have the same interest to actively stimulate private participation and commercial distribution.
The European objective to involve Regions in the GMES organizational structure aims to consider the final users needs in the realization of GMES services, following a subsidiarity principle.
Even though many questions still remain open, a new perspective is emerging that looks upon space law from a different point of view, taking into consideration the environmental treaties, the scientific community and the economic development.

References

[1] Brundtland Report, "Our Common Future: The World Commission on Environment and Development", Oxford, 1987, p.18.

[2] Report of the Third United Nations Conference on the Exploration and Peaceful Uses of Outer Space, Vienna, 19 – 30 July 1999, A/Conf.184/6, United Nations, pp. 23-24.

[3] Back - Impallomeni E., "Legal Protection through Agreements, Contracts of Scientific Information and Data", Proceedings of the International Conference: Satellite Remote Sensing in Aid of Development, Legal Considerations, CRETEAN (Centre Régional de Télédétection des Etats de l'Afrique du Nord), Tunis, 26-27 September 2002, p. 58.

[4] Treaty on Principles Governing the Activities of States in the Exploration and Use of Outer Space, Including the Moon and Other Celestial Bodies, 610 UNTS 205, 27 January 1967.

[5] Ibidem, Art. III.

[6] Principles Relating to Remote Sensing to the Earth from Outer Space, UNGA Resolution 41/65, 3 December 1986.

[7] Ibidem, Principle XII: "As soon as the primary data concerning the territory under its jurisdiction are produced, the sensed State shall have access to them on a non discriminatory basis and on a reasonable cost terms. The sensed State shall also have access to the available analysed information concerning the territory under its jurisdiction in the possession of any State participating in remote sensing activities on the same basis and terms, taking particularly into account the needs and interest of the developing countries."

[8] Jakhu R., "International Law Governing the Acquisition and Dissemination of Satellite Imagery", Journal of Space Law, Volume 29, 2003, pp.65-91.

[9] Principle X of UNGA Resolution 41/65 December 1986: "Remote Sensing shall promote the protection of the Earth's natural environment. To this end, States participating in remote sensing activities that have identified information in their possession that is capable of averting any phenomenon harmful to the Hearth's natural environment shall disclose such information to States concerned."

[10] Principle XI of UNGA Resolution 41/65 December 1986: "Remote sensing shall promote the protection of mankind from natural disasters. To this end, States participating in remote sensing activities that have identified processed data and analysed information in their possession that may be useful to States affected by natural disasters, or likely to be affected by impeding natural disasters, shall transmit such data and information to States concerned as promptly as possible."

[11] Jakhu R., "International Law Governing the Acquisition and Dissemination of Satellite Imagery", op.cit., p.88.

[12] Béquignon M.J., "The International Charter 'Space and Major Disasters'", in Proceedings of the International Conference: Satellite Remote Sensing in Aid of Development, Legal Considerations, CRETEAN (Centre Régional de Télédétection des Etats de l'Afrique du Nord), Tunis, 26-27 September 2002, p.62.

[13] Rio Declaration on Environment and Development, Rio de Janeiro, 19 June 1992, 31 ILM 874 (1992).

[14] Convention on Wetlands of International Importance especially as Waterfowl Habitat, Ramsar - Iran, 2 February 1971, 996 UNTS 245.

[15] Ibidem, Art.3.2: "each contracting party shall arrange to be informed at the earliest possible time if the ecological character of any wetland in its territory and included in the List has changed, is changing or is likely to change as the result of technological developments, pollution or other human interference. Information on such changes shall be passed without delay to the organization or government responsible for the continuing bureau duties specified in Article 8."

[16] United Nations Convention on Biological Diversity, Rio de Janeiro, 5 June 1992, 1760 UNTS 79.

[17] Ibidem, Art. 17: "Contracting Parties shall facilitate that exchange of information, from all publicly available sources, relevant to the conservation and sustainable use of biological diversity, taking into account the special needs of the developing countries".

[18] Ibidem, Art. 8: "Each Contracting Party shall, as far as possible and as appropriate: (a) Establish a system of protected areas or areas where special measures need to be taken to conserve biological diversity; (b) Develop, where necessary, guidelines for the selection, establishment and management of protected areas or areas where special measures need to be taken to conserve biological diversity;"

[19] United Nations Framework Convention on Climate Change, New York, May 1992, 1771 UNTS 107.

[20] Ibidem, Art. 4.1(a): "All parties (...) shall develop, periodically update, publish and make available to the Conference of Parties (...) national inventories of anthropogenic emissions by sources and removals by sinks of all greenhouse gases not controlled by Montreal Protocol, using comparable methodologies to be agreed upon by the Conference of the Parties".

[21] Ibidem, Art. 4.1 (g) and (h): "All parties(...)shall: g) promote and cooperate in scientific, technological, technical, socio-economic and other research, systematic observation and development of data archives related to the climate system and intended to further the understanding and to reduce or eliminate the remaining uncertainties regarding the causes, effects, magnitude and timing of climate change and the economic and social consequences of various response

strategies; h) Promote and cooperate in the full, open and prompt exchange of relevant scientific, technological, technical, socio-economic and legal information related to the climate system and climate change, and to the economic and social consequences of various response strategies;"

[22] Kyoto Protocol to the Framework Convention on Climate Change, 10 December 1997, 37 ILM 22.

[23] Report of the World Summit on Sustainable Development, Plan of Implementation of the World Summit on Sustainable Development, UN Doc. A/Conf. 199/20 (2002), available at http://www.Johannesburgsummit.org/html/documents/summit_docs.html

[24] Convention on Access to Information, Public Participation in Decision Making and Access to Justice in Environmental Matters, Aahrus 25 June 1998, EMut 998,48.

[25] Dunk von der F. "Private Enterprise and Public Interest in the European 'Spacescape' – towards Harmonized National Space Legislation for Private Space Activities in Europe", Leiden, 1998, pp.12-13.
Monserrat Filho J., "Why and How to Define 'Global Public Interest'", Proceedings of the 43rd Colloquium on the Law of Outer Space of IISL, Rio De Janeiro, 2000, pp. 22-33.

[26] The first European Remote Sensing Satellite (ERS-1), launched on 17 July 1991, was ESA's first Earth observation satellite. ERS-2 wich overlapped with ERS-1 was launched in 1995 with an additional sensor for atmospheric ozone research. ERS data used with complementary geospatial data have stimulated European companies to initiate commercial applications, serving particularly the marine, agricultural and oil and gas industries in home markets and overseas. SP -1228 "ERS Further Achievements", ESA Publications, The Netherlands, 1998, p. V.

[27] SP -1228 "ERS Further Achievements", ESA Publications, The Netherlands, 1998, p. 1-5.

[28] Ferrazzani M., "ESA Rules and Practices", Project 2001 Working Group on Remote Sensing: Legal Framework for Commercial Remote Sensing Activities, Proceedings of Project 2001 – Workshop on Legal Remote Sensing issues, Toulouse, October 1998, p. 43.

[29] Directive 96/9/EC of the European Parliament and of the Council of 11 March 1996 on the Legal Protection of Databases.

[30] Dufresne L., "Protection of Space Data Products under the European Directive on the Legal Protection of Databases", Proceedings of the 44th Colloquium on the Law of Outer Space of IISL, Toulouse, 2001, p.265.

[31] Ferrazzani M., "Alternative Approaches to International Space Cooperation", 110th ESA Bulletin, May 2002, p.77.

[32] Onoda M., "Satellite Earth Observation as "Systematic Observation" in Multilateral Environment Treaties", Journal of Space Law, Volume 31, Number 2, 2005, pp.339-411.

[33] The Global Earth Observation System of Systems (GEOSS) 10 - Years Implementation Plan, Brussels adopted the 16 February 2005, p. 1.

[34] Marchisio S., "Legal aspects of disaster management: European efforts including GMES", IISL and ECSL Space Law Symposium 2006: Legal Aspects of Disaster Management and the Contribution of the Law of Outer Space, Vienna, 3 April 2006, http://www.unoosa.org/oosa/en/COPUOS/Legal/2006/symposium.html

[35] Report from the Presidency to the Council, "A Market for GMES in Europe and its Regions – the Graz Dialogue 19 20 April 2006, Graz, Austria", presented in Brussels on 15 May 2006.

[36] Ibidem p.7, the roadmap designed by the European Presidency mentions a future European Region's Conference on GMES Use.

IAC-06-E.6.3.12

57th International Astronautical Congress 2006

Mr. Bruce Mann

DRAFTING LEGISLATION TO REGULATE COMMERCIAL REMOTE SENSING SATELLITES: A HOW-TO GUIDE FROM CANADA

Government of Canada
(Canada)
bruce.mann@international.gc.ca

Abstract

When the Canadian Space Agency (CSA) and MacDonald, Dettwiler and Associates Ltd. (MDA) proposed a jointly funded, but commercially operated RADARSAT-2 remote sensing satellite, the Government of Canada announced that it would regulate commercial remote sensing systems operated from Canada, in order to address Canadian security, defence and foreign policy issues that were bound to arise with increasingly higher performance satellites. The announcement included a 20 point *Canadian Access Control Policy* that, among other things, reserved the government's right to review and approve satellite systems, invoke shutter control over any satellite, and obtain priority access to satellite data.

A year later, the June 16, 2000 *Agreement Between the Government of Canada and the Government of the United States of America Concerning the Operation of Remote Sensing Satellite Systems*, referring specifically to the RARARSAT-2 project, called on Canada to enact the *Access Control Policy* into law, and at the same time ensure that Canadian commercial satellites would be controlled in a "comparable manner" to United States systems. The lawyers in the Department of Justice knew that a challenging legislative drafting task lay ahead of them.

Canada's *Remote Sensing Space Systems Act* is examined from the perspective of its drafters, explaining why it is written as it is. The *Act* reflects concerns about national security, defence, environmental protection, public safety and foreign policy interests, including the desirability of sensed states being able to obtain data about their own territory as set out in the U.N. *Principles Relating to Remote Sensing of the Earth from Outer Space.* The final product, which became law on November 25, 2005, meets Canada's needs by incorporating all aspects of the *Canadian Access Control Policy*, and at the same time meeting the comparability commitment in the *Canada-US Agreement.* This latter consideration is very important to the success of RADARSAT-2 because of the high degree of international cooperation involved, notably in obtaining US export permits for certain components of the satellite. Unexpected difficulties and pleasant surprises arising from the export control regime are described.

This paper can serve as a "how to" guide for jurists from like-minded countries contemplating the regulation of commercial remote sensing satellite systems.

Introduction

Since the launch of RADARSAT in 1995 the Canadian Space Agency (CSA) has managed the synthetic aperture radar satellite as a governmental operation. The CSA has sold data and imagery worldwide–looking very much like a commercial undertaking–without the guidance or control of any Canadian remote sensing satellite legislation.

However, shortly after the Canadian Space Agency's announcement in February 1998, that they had awarded a contract to MacDonald, Dettwiler and Associated (MDA) to construct and manage RADARSAT-2, government lawyers in Ottawa started dreaming of new laws to restrict, regulate, supervise, audit and police the Canadian remote sensing industry. Or at least that is how it must have seemed to MDA.

Canada's Remote Sensing Space Systems Act was passed by Parliament in November 2005, and will come into force soon, in anticipation of the launch of RADARSAT-2 which is scheduled for March 2007. The purpose of this paper is to explain why it was necessary to enact legislation governing the operation of commercial remote sensing satellites and why we drafted the Canadian legislation as we did. Particular attention will be given to issues which generated a great deal of discussion during the Parliamentary process: the right of sensed states to obtain data about their own territory, and the government's right of shutter control and priority access to satellite services.

The Act is available from the web site of the Department of Justice, Canada, under the heading "Laws."

Canada's interest in regulating commercial satellites

Five factors of a national character were instrumental in the Government of Canada's decision to enact legislation regulating the operation of commercial remote sensing satellite systems:

–national security, –the defence of Canada, –the safety of Canadian Forces, –Canada's conduct of international relations and –Canada's international obligations.

There was no real debate that remote sensing satellite legislation, with its underpinnings in international affairs, national security, and international commerce, was constitutionally a matter within the jurisdiction of Canada's federal Parliament to legislate, even though satellite control in theory could be carried out entirely within or from a single province of Canada.

Three other factors, for which the Government of Canada has responsibility at a national level, were also involved in the decision to legislate:

–the environment, –public health and –the safety of persons and property.

All of these factors are recited throughout the Act as matters to guide the government in the issuing of licences and the regulation of remote sensing satellite systems.

Another fundamental driver of Canadian legislation was the issue of liability for damage caused by Canadian space activity, even when carried out by non-governmental entities. Under the United Nations Outer Space Treaty and the Liability Convention, Canada is liable to other states or persons in other states for injury or loss caused by satellites if the launch was carried out in Canada, or was procured elsewhere by Canada or by a Canadian person. As a matter of risk management, it is up to Canada to regulate its own nationals and any other persons whose activities could incur liability on the part of Canada.

Canada–United States Treaty sets parameters for legislation

International Treaties do not have the force of domestic law within Canada. It is necessary for Canada to enact legislation implementing such treaties. The June 16, 2000 Agreement between the Government of Canada and the Government of the United States of America concerning the Operation of Commercial remote Sensing Satellite Systems was signed with the RADARSAT-2 satellite in mind, and in fact referred to the satellite in the text. A very clear expectation was established in the Agreement that legislation would be put in place, and that it would follow certain lines as set out in the first three clauses of the Agreement:

"1. The parties agree to ensure that such commercial remote sensing satellite systems will be controlled by each Part in a comparable manner in order to protect and serve shared national security and foreign policy interests".

This clause committed Canada to enacting legislation similar in principle to the United States Land remote Sensing Policy Act and related rules including the capability for the government to obtain exclusive access to satellite services in critical situations.

"2. Canada agrees to keep in place, until its provisions are enacted into law, the Canadian national access control policy announced on 9 June 1999, set forth in Annex I hereto, concerning such commercial remote sensing satellite systems owned, operated or registered in Canada".

The access control policy, which had been developed by a Canadian government interdepartmental team, was the cornerstone for the government's drafting instructions for the Remote Sensing Space Systems Act. It included the most fundamental and controversial elements of the legislation that followed:

–Canada's right to review and set limits on data access, system architecture, system performance and foreign ownership of remote sensing satellite systems.

–Shutter control—the interruption of normal commercial service where the availability of data could be detrimental to Canada's national security and foreign affairs interests.

–Priority access where data would be beneficial to national security and foreign affairs interests.

The access control policy also listed 17 obligations on the satellite operator ranging from the requirement to maintain positive control of the satellite from Canada at all times to the requirement to make data available to sensed states in accordance with the United Nations Principles Related to Remote Sensing of the Earth from Space. Obligation 4, "Obtain export or import permits(s) pursuant to applicable to laws" presumably was included because four critical modules in RADARSAT-2 incorporate technology for which an export permit was required under the United States International Trafficking in Arms Regulations (ITAR), even though the launch was expected to be from Vandenberg, California. An export permit was required for the assembly of the spacecraft in Europe and Canada.

We incorporated all the elements of the policy in the legislation, (except for item 4, which did not require legislation) substantively or in the form of enabling provisions giving the government the authority to enact regulations.

Although the ITAR requirement for United States export permits was not mentioned in the Canadian legislation, it had a significant impact on the RADARSAT program. Without going into details, employees of the CSA were scrutinized as to their place of birth, and other citizenship in the case of dual nationals. Under ITAR policy rules, contact with or exposure of sensitive technology requiring an export permit to a person who is a national of a proscribed country constitutes a "deemed export" of the technology to the proscribed country. As a result, the CSA was required to keep certain employees away from sensitive technology or meetings where technology was discussed, on the basis of their place of birth, even if the employees were Canadian citizens with high level security clearances.

Ironically, the ITAR rules facilitated the RADARSAT-2 launch plans in 2005 when, for technical reasons, it became necessary to use a Soyuz launch vehicle from Baikonur, Kazakhstan. A tripartite agreement exists between the United States, Russia and Kazakhstan, which enables the launch of United States spacecraft from Baikonur under the supervision of United States Defense Technology Security Administration (DTSA) personnel, and exempts spacecraft from customs inspections in Russia and Kazakhstan. Because RADARSAT-2 contains technology requiring United States export permits, RADARSAT-2 qualifies as a United States Spacecraft under the Baikonur launch agreement, and can be launched without Canada having to negotiate a separate agreement with Russia and Kazakhstan.

3. Canada agrees to implement controls pursuant to this Agreement, set forth in Annex II hereto, which is protected as commercially confidential, with regard to the operator of RADARSAT-2.

This clause in the Agreement obliges Canada to put in place restrictions on performance characteristics of the satellite and the remote sensing space system, ultimately resulting in limits to the resolution of imagery from satellite data. The House of Commons Standing Committee on Foreign Affairs and International Trade examined Annex II in camera to confirm that it did indeed contain only technical parameters, and not secret priority access rights in favour of the United States as suggested by one Committee witness.

Performance limits are not part of the legislation, but the legislation does specifically authorize the Minister of Foreign Affairs to set conditions for a licence which will include approved performance limits. This information is considered commercial confidential because its disclosure could give an unfair advantage to competitors from other jurisdictions if they knew the actual performance limits of RADARSAT-2 or the limits that the Government of Canada intends to impose. Presumably the satellite operator will seek amendment of the performance limits as international competitors offer higher resolution imagery and it becomes pointless for Canada to maintain more stringent restrictions for security purposes.

Act applies to public and private sector

Section 4 of the Act states "This Act binds Her Majesty in right of Canada or a province," formal Canadian statutory language directing that government departments and agencies at all levels in Canada are subject to the legislation. Even the Canadian Space Agency, which has operated the original RADARSAT satellite for eleven years, will be subject to the licensing regime of the Act.

The reason we used this approach in the legislation was because of the difficulty and uncertainty in attempting to confine the application of the legislation to commercial satellites. What did we mean by commercial? Does the term imply non-governmental, for-profit ownership of the satellite? Or is the nature of the use of the satellite the appropriate criterion? RADARSAT-2, destined to be the first satellite to be licensed in Canada, has been described all along as a commercial satellite, but the fact that it is more than 75

This definition is broad in scope and includes satellites with optical, thermal infra-red, and other types of sensors–not just synthetic aperture radar satellites such as RADARSAT and RADARSAT-2. Even weather satellites come within the purview of the Act. However, individual satellites, or classes of satellites, or specific uses of satellites can be exempted from the licensing requirement of the Act, as will be discussed later.

Act applies to operations carried on outside Canada

Persons carrying on remote sensing space system activities (including satellite control, and data gathering, treatment and delivery) within Canada or from Canada, of course are subject to the Act—just as they are to other Canadian legislation. To protect Canada's national interests, and risk manage potential liability, the requirement for a Canadian satellite licence also applies to the following categories of persons in respect of their activities outside Canada:

(a) Canadian citizens;

(b) Permanent residents. These are people who have legal status entitling them to remain in Canada and generally enjoy most of the rights and responsibilities of Canadian citizens;

(c) Canadian corporations. This includes companies with a Canadian charter, i.e. actually incorporated in Canada, as well as companies that have converted their corporate citizenship from another country to federal or provincial jurisdiction within Canada;

(d) Specified persons tied to Canada. The federal government can enact regulations defining classes of persons (individuals, corporations, partnerships, etc.) who have a connection to Canada related to remote sensing space systems that warrants bringing them within the ambit of the legislation. An example might be foreign persons who procure the launch of a satellite from Canada. We made this provision open-ended so that the government could deal relatively quickly with unexpected situations. Federal regulations can be enacted in an abbreviated time frame, if necessary. Unlike statutes, they are not dependant on Parliament being in session.

Exemptions from the Act

The foregoing broad-reaching provisions were drafted ex abundante cautela. We considered this necessary to promote Canada's national interests to the maximum extent possible, and to protect Canada from liability. To avoid inappropriate application of the Act, the Minister of Foreign Affairs is authorized to exempt any persons, satellite systems, or data, on an individual or class basis, from any or all aspects of the licensing regime, so long as the Minister is satisfied that none of Canada's national interests will be compromised. For example, if Canadians are involved in the operation of a satellite system licensed by a foreign country, it would be appropriate to clarify by Ministerial order that the system is exempt from the Act, or at least is exempt insofar as those Canadians are concerned.

Where the Department of National Defence or the Canadian Space Agency operates a remote sensing satellite system, the government may issue a Cabinet order modifying or adapting any provisions of the Act for that application. We drafted this provision as a compromise, instead of completely exempting either of these federal government entities from the Act. This will ensure that any commercial operations carried out by either entity (most notably the CSA) will remain subject to the same international data distribution controls set by the Minister of Foreign Affairs for normal commercial operators. Yet for their own governmental or military uses of remote sensing satellites, they can be exempt from the Act. To further maintain their independence from the Minister of Foreign Affairs, neither National Defence nor the CSA have to apply to Foreign Affairs for an exemption order. The special order modifying or adapting the Act for their purposes is issued by the federal Cabinet.

It is anticipated that as soon as the remote sensing

legislation comes into force, an order will be issued either by the Minister of Foreign Affairs or the federal Cabinet exempting the CSA from any licensing requirements for the original RADARSAT satellite.

Time limits and representations

A criticism that was raised on several occasions during and after the legislative process is that the Act does not contain time limits, such as the time within which the Minister of Foreign Affairs should issue a licence after an application is filed.

A satellite licence is extremely complex. The application process involves the submission and consideration of information ranging from technical details of the proposed satellite system and its capabilities, to financial and other corporate information about the licensee and potential system participants, and details of prospective sales agreements. Establishing customer access profiles (CAPs), an intricate series of conditions for the distribution of data and remote sensing products, involves considerable dialogue about who is to receive data, about which sensed territories, at what resolution, and after what time delay. Throughout the application process the applicant will have the opportunity to make representations about all aspects of the requested licence. It did not make sense to set a time limit for the complex, variable application process.

Because of the interactive nature of the application process, we did not provide in the Act the right to make representations after a licence application is refused. However, in order to give a rejected applicant the opportunity to challenge a refusal to grant a licence, the Minister is required to provide reasons to the applicant for the refusal, which can be made the subject of judicial review.

Another feature in the legislation designed to relieve some of the time pressure in an initial licence application is the authority to grant a provisional approval of a licence application, which is binding on the Minister of Foreign Affairs so long as the material facts on which the approval was based remain substantially unchanged. This provision in the legislation was inspired by a request from MDA for the Minister of Foreign Affairs to issue a latter approving the terms of a contract that MDA was negotiating with a data customer for RADARSAT-2 services.

The only time limit binding on the government is when a satellite licence is suspended. The Minister of Foreign Affairs must decide within 90 days whether the licence is to be cancelled, otherwise the suspension will end and the licence is restored. In other situations, such as an application for a licence or for a change in licence conditions, with national security issues at play, it would not make sense to issue a license by default if the government failed to reach a decision within a time limit.

This being said, the Act authorizes the government to make regulations respecting the issuance, amendment and renewal of licences, which could include time limits for the government to respond. Alternatively, the Minister has authority to establish policies and guidelines which could include time frames for government action. Under Canadian law, if government action is not forthcoming, an affected person has recourse to the Federal Court of Canada for prerogative relief in the nature of mandamus, compelling the relevant government official to do his or her job.

Mandatory licence conditions

Although the Minister of Foreign Affairs can set out conditions of any kind in a licence, mandatory conditions were included in paragraphs 8(4)(a) to (g) of the Act to inform satellite operators and data customers of certain fundamental obligations:

(a) The licensee must keep control of the system. This refers to functional control by the person who operates the system. There are a number of exceptions, perhaps better referred to as clarifications, elsewhere in the Act which permit others to control a satellite of a system, so long as the licensee maintains overriding control. Also, the Minister may specifically approve someone else taking control of a satellite, or approve a complete transfer of the licence to someone else.

(b) It is up to the licensee to ensure that only persons specifically authorized in the licence perform certain controlled activities. In the normal operation of a remote sensing space system, the Act does not call on the government to directly regulate the activities of anyone but the licensee.

(c) This mandatory licence condition derives from Principle XII of United Nations Resolution 41/65, adopted on December 3, 1986, Principles Relating to Remote Sensing of the Earth from Outer Space, which gives sensed states access to certain data concerning their territory.

Principle XII

As soon as the primary data and the processed data concerning the territory under its jurisdiction are produced, the sensed State shall have access to them on a non-discriminatory basis and on reasonable cost terms. The sensed State shall also have access to the available analysed information concerning the territory under its jurisdiction in the possession of any State participating in remote sensing activities on the same basis and terms, taking particularly into account the needs and interests of the developing countries.

The sensed state's right is expressed in the legislation in terms of a mandatory licence condition obliging the licensee to make raw data and remote sensing products available to the government of the sensed state. This right of access in not unrestricted, as limitations on the rights of sensed states are inherent in the definition of "remote sensing" used by the UN:

Principle I

For the purposes of these principles with respect to remote sensing activities:

(a) The term "remote sensing" means the sensing of the Earth's surface from space by making use of the properties of electromagnetic waves emitted, reflected or diffracted by the sensed objects, for the purpose of improving natural resources management, land use and the protection of the environment. [emphasis supplied]

There is no obligation to provide sensed states with data for purposes other than improving natural resources management, land use, and protection of the environment. In practical terms, this means that sensed states will not automatically be entitled to receive sensitive, high quality information gathered by sensing states for security purposes or which raises security concerns. Customer access profiles established and maintained by the Minister pursuant to the licence, along with other licence conditions, may limit the nature and timeliness of information that the licensee is required to provide to sensed states.

This interpretation of the UN principles is certainly subject to debate. Some would argue that the sensed state's right of access need not be mentioned at all, since the UN resolution is not binding, and probably never will be. Nevertheless, the Parliament of Canada approved paragraph 8(4)(c) of the Act based on the foregoing interpretation of the UN principles.

The underlying theme of UN Principle XII, as it has been incorporated in paragraph 8(4)(c) of the Act, is to prevent discrimination against the government of a sensed state as a purchaser of raw data or remote sensing products from the licensee for management of natural resources, land use and protection of the environment. For example, the licensee cannot provide such data or products to someone else on an exclusive basis, nor can it restrict access to such information about the sensed state to the highest bidder. The licensee is obliged to offer the raw data or remote sensing products (subject to the limitations discussed above) in a timely manner at reasonable rates. This obligation does not extend to enhanced data or value-added products, which the licensee may sell on a competitive basis to whomever the licensee chooses.

The licensee is not obliged to store data indefinitely for the possible use by the sensed state. The obligation to provide data or remote sensing products exists only so long as they have not been disposed of.

(d) The condition requiring the licensee to keep control of raw data and remote sensing products until they are disposed of has two facets to it. The "sale" of data to customers cannot be an outright transfer of all proprietary rights to the customer. It is standard industry practice to maintain such control by entering into system participant agreements and end-user licence without conveying intellectual property rights associated with the data. The other facet to condition (d) is the requirement to honour the terms of the system disposal plan (see section 9), which will spell out the circumstances in which the licensee may dispose of data and products. The plan could call for the destruction of data, the government's right to acquire all interests in the data or the right to convey all interests in data to other persons approved by the Minister.

(e) The condition that raw data from the system may be communicated only to authorized persons is fundamental to the security of the system. Normally raw data will be communicated only to system participants, since the communication of raw data is a controlled activity, but this provision recognizes that there can be exceptions–where the government of a sensed state is entitled to receive raw data in accordance with condition (c) discussed above, or where the Minister, in the licence, expressly authorizes such communication to other persons.

(f) This condition is somewhat unusual. Under paragraphs 8(6)(b) and 8(7)(b) of the Act the Minister of Foreign Affairs can require that the communication of raw data or remote sensing products be done under a legally enforceable agreement respecting their security and non-disclosure. It is up to the licensee to police the agreement and "encourage" system participants and other persons who receive data to handle it appropriately. This encouragement could be accomplished through legal action for breach of the agreement or other means, such as cutting off the supply of data or products to customers who do not comply. The Minister, in turn, can require the licensee to enforce the agreement by means of administrative monetary penalties, by suspending the licence, or by taking other more serious corrective measures if the licensee violates this condition.

(g) Paying fees has been set as a condition of a licence so that failure to pay can be dealt with as a breach of condition.

Conditions set by the Minister

Two kinds of conditions that are almost certain to be set are described in subsection 8(5): conditions relating to cryptography and information assurance; and conditions naming system participants and the controlled activities the licensees may allow them to perform.

Customer access profiles (CAPs) are authorized by this clause, as well as by clauses 8(6) and 8(7) which follow. CAPs are detailed sets of conditions on the dissemination of raw data and remote sensing products, including rules for the communication of raw data and remote sensing products among the licensee, system participants and their customers. They very likely will include a proscribed entity list, naming entities that are prohibited from receiving raw data or remote sensing products under various circumstances.

Shutter control

By analogy to restrictions on time and place of exposures taken by a conventional camera, orders for the interruption or restriction of land sensing operations of a remote sensing satellite are popularly called "shutter control" orders. In the context of a synthetic aperture radar satellite, such as RADARSAT 2, a shutter control order could entail any combination of a complete cessation of sensing activities over certain territories or at certain times, attenuated sensing performance, delays in downloading data from the satellite, restrictions on the resolution of remote sensing products, and delays or outright bans on the provision of certain data products.

No one objected to the concept of shutter control, accepting the premise that for matters of national security, the state must be able to prevent the collection of data inimical to national interests. Complex criteria for the exercise of shutter control could delay or prevent its implementation, and for this reason were rejected. Instead, three safeguards against the misuse of shutter control were adopted: (1) An order can be made only by the Minister of Foreign Affairs or the Minister of National Defence. No delegation of authority is permitted. (2) A potential injury test, appropriate for each Minister's portfolio, must be met for the Minister to make a shutter control order. (3) The licensee has the opportunity, after the fact, to make representations about the order, which may be helpful to the licensee to persuade the Minister that other measures can be taken in lieu of continuing or repeating shutter control.

Up to date fine tuning of the Customer Access Profiles (licence conditions setting out the parameters for distribution of data about sensed territories) will reduce or eliminate the need to invoke shutter control. The experience in the United States has been that despite having exclusive access authority for over 20 years, the government has never had to use its shutter control power over commercial satellites.

Priority Access Priority access refers to the government's right to jump the queue for the provision of services from a remote sensing space system in urgent circumstances.

The tests that the Minister of Foreign Affairs, the Minister of National Defence, or the Minister of Public Safety must meet in order to justify a priority access order are geared to their respective portfolios, on the grounds that they are desirable for the listed purposes. For this reason academics, industry officials and Parliamentarians all expressed concern during Committee hearings about abuse of this exceptional power, to the detriment of remote sensing satellite operators who would not only lose revenue from displaced customer service, but would not be compensated by the government for the expropriation of services. The fact that the government is immune to claims for damages resulting from shutter control orders or priority access orders only heightened this concern.

Ultimately, Parliament was satisfied that mitigating factors in the Act minimized potential loss to operators, and enacted these elements of the legislation without amendment. The mitigating factors were as follows:

Ministers can delegate the power to issue priority access orders only to their respective deputy ministers or certain agency heads, namely, the Chief of the Defence Staff, the Commissioner of the Royal Canadian Mounted Police (RCMP - Canada's federal police force) or the Director of the Canadian Security Intelligence Service. No further delegation is permitted. RCMP orders are confined to the investigation of offences arising from threats to the security of Canada. The RCMP cannot use priority access orders for their other domestic policing responsibilities.

The licensee has the opportunity, after the fact, to make representations about the order. This may assist the licensee in working out a level of priority for the order that will meet the relevant Minister's requirements while minimizing the interference with other commercial business. It is anticipated that government needs, even on an urgent basis, will be met through the licensee's commercial priority service ordering process and, as in the United States, a statutory order for priority access will never be necessary.

No liability for government intervention

The "No Liability" provision in the Act gives the government immunity from claims for financial losses for actions taken in good faith, but does not prevent the government from providing compensation on a voluntary basis, under normal ex gratia prerogative authority. In the case of priority access orders, the Act specifically authorizes the Minister who made the order to pay the satellite system licensee an amount determined in accordance with government regulations for the service. Draft regulations have been prepared and discussed with MDA, which will ensure that satellite operators receive the same level of compensation they have received over the previous year for commercial services on a priority basis, or an otherwise agreed upon level of compensation.

The single greatest advocacy task for the Department of Justice in the course of development of the Act was to convince sceptics that the permissive language of the Act ("A Minister may pay a licensee an amount determined in accordance with the regulations...") did not give the Minister an unfettered discretion to refuse to pay compensation. There is ample jurisprudence in Canada to the effect that such permissive language in a statute actually creates an obligation to act where all the required conditions for action have been met.

Powers of Inspection and Audit

The powers of inspectors in the Remote Sensing Space Systems Act are typical of those found in other Canadian statutes, and respect the right to be secure from unreasonable search and seizure under the Canadian Charter of Rights and Freedoms. For example, a judicial warrant is required before an inspector can enter a private dwelling without the consent of the occupant.

While the Act specifically claims jurisdiction over Canadians and certain other classes of persons outside of Canada in respect of the prohibition on operating a remote sensing space system without a licence, no extra-territorial claim is made about the powers of inspectors outside Canada.

This does not necessarily mean that inspectors are prohibited from entering the premises of system participants and other persons in foreign jurisdictions. The authorities in other countries may be prepared to allow, or even assist, inspectors to enter premises in their jurisdiction under mutual legal assistance agreements between Canada and foreign countries. Also, a licensee may enter into agreements with system participants or end users in foreign jurisdictions in which those persons specifically agree to let the licensee, or persons designated by the licensee (including Canadian government inspectors), enter their premises to conduct inspections and perform audits.

Rather than require inspectors to cart away boxes of documents, tapes and data storage devices, which could harm the affected person's capacity to carry on business, the Act gives inspectors the slightly more intrusive, but less disruptive, powers to examine things on site, test equipment, use equipment to generate records, and make copies of records to take away for examination.

Both the obligation to assist inspectors and the prohibition against obstructing inspectors or providing false information to them are offences under the Act. We are doubtful that someone could be prosecuted in Canada for an obstruction that took place outside Canada. However, it is possible that the offence of providing false information could be prosecuted in Canada if it could be shown that the person in question knew and intended that the false information would be taken back to Canada by the inspector.

These questions are largely academic because the enforcement of the Act weighs mainly on the licensee, with the expectation that the licensee will facilitate investigations and provide information as requested.

Requests for Information

For the most part, monitoring compliance with the Act will be a matter of reviewing records of data collection, treatment and transmission. The Minister can request any person to provide pertinent information or documents. There is no reason to expect non-compliance, but if a request is refused or ignored it can be the basis for an order by a superior court or the Federal Court of Canada for an order requiring production of the information or documents. A judge may order a person to produce information or documents if satisfied that they are necessary under the regulatory scheme, and the public interest in having the information or documents outweighs other interests, including the person's right to privacy.

The advantage of a judicial order is that it can be enforced through the court system by means of access to the person's premises and the possibility of penal sanctions for contempt of court.

Foreign countries may not be willing to enforce a Canadian Minister's request for information or to give Canadian inspectors the right to operate in their jurisdiction. However, at the judicial level, most courts of superior jurisdiction in the world honour the custom of letters rogatory, or mutual legal assistance conventions, under which they will exercise their own inherent jurisdiction to compel persons within their territory to appear, produce documents, and answer questions, at the request of a judge in another jurisdiction.

Administrative Monetary Penalties

Except for a few very serious contraventions of the Act, for which heavy fines and prison sentences may be imposed, the Act regulates conduct through administrative monetary penalties (AMPs) for violations, with the option of entering into voluntary compliance agreements and terminating the violation proceedings. The emphasis is on correcting conduct at the earliest possible opportunity.

For the most part the violation provisions are directed at licensees, including employees of licensees, for breaches of licence conditions. Licensees are expected to make sure that their system participants and customers follow the rules.

Violation proceedings begin with the issuing of a notice of violation. The recipient may pay the fine set out in the notice, ending the matter. Alternatively, the person may exercise the right to make representations about the violation to the enforcement officer, who will decide whether the person committed the violation. During the course of the representations, the enforcement officer may enter into a compliance agreement with the person, ending the proceedings without a violation record–so long as the person abides by the compliance agreement.

If a penalty is imposed, the person has the right of appeal to the Minister. As with any Ministerial decision, the Minister's disposition of the appeal is subject to judicial review.

We considered another novel system where licensees would be immune from prosecution for violations that they identified, admitted, and corrected before being detected by regulators. However, we did not consider this appropriate in an environment where the regulator learns of improprieties so long after the fact. Such a system might lead licensees to deliberately flout the rules and capitalize on data sales, with the knowledge that they could admit to and correct their misconduct before government auditors would notice it. The AMPs system strikes an appropriate balance between self-regulation and liability for misconduct.

Consistent with the principle of adjusting conduct at the earliest opportunity, rather than penalizing parties for breach after the fact, the Act contains a special injunction authority, enabling the Minister, with the assistance of a Court, to take steps to prevent someone from operating a remote sensing space system unlawfully. The proposed or purported transfer of ownership of a remote sensing satellite system, without having notified the Minister, could be grounds for an injunction against the licensee or former licensee, or the person intending to acquire the system, blocking the transfer.

The injunction power is the only way to deal with persons who are not, and never have been, licensees, before they commence an unlawful operation.. The Court can order them to take any measure that a licensee could be ordered to take under the Act.

Session 4:
SPACE LAW AT TIMES OF ARMED CONFLICT

Chairmen: Ram Jakhu
Jonathan Galloway

Rapporteur: Kelly Gable

IISL 49TH COLLOQUIUM ON LAW OF OUTER SPACE, VALENCIA, SPAIN, 2-6 OCTOBER 2006

IAC-06-E6.4.01 : The Question of Legitimacy of Threat or Use of Force in and from Outer Space: A Reflection on the Sanctity and Legal Binding Force of the Charter of the United Nations and the 1967 Outer Space Treaty

Maurice N. Andem, Faculty of Law, University of Lapland. Rovaniemi, Finland

ABSTRACT

The theme of the 57th International Astronautical Congress is "BRINGING SPACE CLOSER TO PEOPLE" and the theme of this session of the IISL Colloquium is "Space Law at Times of Armed Conflict".

This paper will be devoted to the examination and analysis of the relevant provisions of the UN Charter and the 1967 Outer Space Treaty on Principles Governing the Activities of States in the Exploration and Use of Outer Space, including the Moon and Other Celestial Bodies, with the view to demonstrating the legal binding force of their provisions on all States.

I. Introduction

The beginning of the 21st century has witnessed and is witnessing the intensification of the development, testing and deployment new weapon systems into outer space. This process has been gaining momentum from day to day, particularly after the sad and horrifying event in New York on 11 September 2001, in which almost 3000 people were killed. It should be pointed out that the death of those innocent souls following the terrorist attack of the New York World Trade Centre was an attack on all human beings. As a matter of fact, war in general, no matter its nature, is terrorism in itself and a crime against humanity.[1]

---

[1] Alex P. Schmid and Albert J. Jongman in their book **POLITICAL TERRORISM,**

A NEW GUIDE TO ACTORS, AUTHORS, CONCEPTS, DATA BASES, THEORIES AND LITERATURE, North-Holland publishing Company, Amsterdam (1988), at page 28 state that: "Terrorism is an anxiety-inspiring method of repeated violent action, employed by (semi-)clandestine individual, group, or state actors, for idiosyncratic, criminal, or political reasons, whereby– in contrast to assassination–the direct targets of violence are not the main targets. The immediate human victims of violence are generally chosen randomly (targets of opportunity) or selectively (representative or symbolic targets) from a target population, and serve as message generators. Threat- and violence-based communication processes between terrorist (organization), (imperiled) victims, and main targets are used to manipulate the main target (audience(s)), turning it into a target of terror, a target of demands, or a target of attention, depending on whether intimidation, coercion, or propaganda is primarily sought:"

Since its establishment 61 years ago, the United Nations, pursuant to the provisions of its Charter, has done a lot in promoting peace, security, disarmament and co-operation among States and peoples of the world. Since the beginning of the space era in 1957, it has done a lot in the establishment, progressive development and codification of space law.[2] The topic of this session deals with matters relating to peaceful uses of outer space. Thus, in order to avoid repetition of what I had already contributed on the same subject matter, I would like to proceed directly on the topic of my paper.[3]

II. Space Law at Times of Armed Conflict

Before commencing on my paper, I would like to make a brief observation on the sources of space law. In contemporary international law relations between states, international treaties are the primary and the most important source of international law and all its branches, including space law. It is the most effective form of expressing the concurrent and compromising wills (consent) of the subjects of international law (states) in the course of their co-operative efforts and mutual relations. Article 38 of Statute of the International Court of Justice (ICJ) stipulates sources of contemporary international law.

It stipulates in paragraph 1 that: "The Court whose function is to decide in accordance with international law such disputes as submitted to it, shall apply:
(a) International conventions, whether general or particular, establishing rules expressly

---

[2] For more details, see, for example, Lachs, Manfred, **THE LAW OF OUTER SPACE**, Sijthoff, Leiden (1972); Jenks, C. Wilfred, **SPACE LAW**, Steven & Sons, London (1965).

[3] For more information, see, for example, Andem, Maurice N., "Implementation of the 1967 Outer Space Treaty in the New Millennium: A Brief Reflection on the Implication of Proposed Missile Defence System", in the **PROCEEDINGS OF THE FORTY-THIRD COLLOQUIUM ON THE LAW OF OUTER SPACE**, 2 October -6 October 2000, Rio De Janeiro, Brazil, AIAA (2001), pp.275-291; **INTERNATIONAL LEGAL PROBLEMS IN THE PEACEFUL EXPLORATION AND USE OF OUTER SPACE**, University of Lapland Publications in Law, Rovaniemi (1992), pp. 12-121,185-234.

recognized by the contesting states;
(b) international custom, as evidence of a general practice acceped as law;
(c) the general principles of law recognized by civilized nations;
(d) subject to the provisions of Article 59, judicial decisions and the teachings of the most highly qualified publicists of various nations, as subsidiary means for the determination of rules of law".

It should be noted that conventions have the same meaning as treaties. According to **BLACK'S LAW DICTIONARY Fifth Edition,** a treaty is defined as: "A compact made between two or more independent nations with a view to the public welfare."

The public welfare of the international community of states and peoples of the world was deep in the hearts and thoughts of the Founding Fathers of the United Nations (UN). A gloss over the various documents pertaining to the deliberations in the Teheran, Yalta and Potsdam Conferences will strengthen this conviction in the mind of any researcher or inquirer.[4] For example, in the communique on the Crimea Conference of 11 February 1945, the Heads of Government of the Soviet Union, the United States and Great Britain declared:

Our meeting here in Crimea has reaffirmed our common determination to maintain and strengthen in the peace to come that unity of purpose and of action which has made victory possible and certain for the United Nations in the war. We believe that this is a sacred obligation which our Governments owe to our peoples and to all the peoples of the world. Only with continuing and growing co-operation and understanding among our three countries and among all the peace-loving nations can the highest aspiration of humanity be realised - a secure and lasting peace which will, in the words of Atlantic Charter, "afford assurance, that all the men in all lands may live out their lives in freedom from fear and want".
Victory in this war and the establishment of the proposed international organisation will provide the greatest opportunity in all history to create in the years to come the essential conditions of such a peace.[5]

It should be borne in mind that the above declaration has further been elaborated and consolidated particularly in the provisions of the Preamble, Articles 1 and 2 of the UN Charter. The primacy and mandatory legal binding character of the provisions of the UN Charter are further consolidated in the provisions of Article 103. It stipulates as follows:

In the event of a conflict between the obligations of the Members of the United Nations under the present Charter and their obligations under any other international agreement, obligations under the present Charter shall prevail.

Thus the UN Charter is the primary and fundamental source of contemporary international law, including all its branches, and in this sense, the primary and the most important source of

---

[4] For more details, see, **THE TEHERAN-YALTA & POTSDAM CONFERENCES DOCUMENTS**, Progress Publishers, Moscow (1969).

[5] Ibid., pp. 139-140

space law or the law of outer space. It is construed that every treaty, including national legislation of states, pertaining to any sphere of activities of states in the exploration and peaceful uses of outer space, including the moon and other celestial bodies, must be in conformity with the UN Charter, as expressed in the provisions relating to the purposes and principles (Articles 1 and 2). Article III of the 1967 Outer Space Treaty (OST), that is, the Treaty on Principles Governing the Activities of States in the Exploration and Use of Outer Space, including the Moon and Other Celestial Bodies, provides that:

States Parties to the Treaty shall carry on activities in the exploration and use of outer space, including the moon and other celestial bodies, in accordance with international law, including the Charter of the United Nations, in the interest of maintaining international peace and security and in promoting international co-operation and understanding.

Consequently, following the process of privatization and commercialization of outer space activities, it is mandatory that states should ensure that their nationals must, through their outer space national laws, observe and comply with the provisions of all the outer space treaties.

Moreover, it should be emphasized that 1967 Outer Space Treaty was the first legal instrument adopted by the UN General Assembly under the auspices of the UN Committee on the Peaceful Uses of Outer Space (UNCOPUOS), pursuant to the provisions of Article 13 of the UN Charter. Besides the UN Charter, it is primary and fundamental source of this new branch of contemporary international law - space law or the law of outer space. It laid the legal foundation for the progressive development and codification of space law during the Cold War era. Thanks to the indefatigable efforts of UNCOPUOS, four other international legal instruments which are also sources of space law have been adopted by the UN General Assembly. They are as follows:[6]

1.1968 Agreement on the Rescue of Astronauts, the Return of Astronauts and the Return of Objects Launched into Outer Space (Rescue Agreement;
2. 1972 Convention on International Liability for Damage Caused by Space Objects;
3. 1975 Convention on Registration of Objects Launched into Outer Space; and
4. 1979 Agreement Governing Activities of States on the Moon and Other Celestial Bodies.

Bearing the foregoing observation in mind, I would like to commence my reflection on the topic of my paper. Since the UN Charter is mentioned in the provisions of the Article III of the 1967 Outer Space Treaty, in order to avoid repetition, I would discuss the relevant provisions together when reflecting on the provisions of the 1967 Space Treaty.

The 1967 Outer Space Treaty (1967 OST)

The 1967 OST is the **Magna Carta** and cornerstone of contemporary space law or international law of outer space. It establishes the legal status and regime governing all

[6] For more detail, see, **A/AC.105/572/Rev.1 UNITED NATIONS TREATIES AND PRINCIPLES ON OUTER SPACE**, United Nations, New York (1996).

activities of states in the exploration and use of outer space, the moon and other celestial bodies.It consists of 17 articles.[7] I would like concentrate more on the provisions of Articles I, II, III and IV.[8]

According to paragraph 1 of Article I, exploration and use of outer space, the moon and other celestial bodies shall be carried out for the benefit and in the interests of all countries, irrespective of their degree of economic or scientific development, and shall be the province of mankind. Paragraph 2 provides that outer space, the moon and other celestial bodies shall be free for exploration and use by all states without discrimination of any kind, on a basis of equality and in accordance with international law, and there shall be free access to all areas of celestial bodies. Paragraph 3 also provides that there shall be freedom of scientific investigation in outer space, the moon and other celestial bodies and states are to facilitate and encourage international co-operation in such investigation. However, it should be pointed out that this freedom is not absolute.

Article II consolidates the legal status of outer space, the moon and other celestial as enshrined in the provisions of Article I above. According to its provisions, national appropriation by claim of sovereignty, by means of use or occupation, or by any other means is strictly prohibited.

---

[7] Ibid., pp. 4-9.

[8] See footnote 3 above.

It is sad to observe that more scientific investigations, tests, experiments, etc., for military purposes, have been taking place in the new domain which is considered in space law, as the province of all mankind, common heritage of mankind and a zone of peace and international co-operation.[9] It should be emphasized that all military activities in outer space, the moon and other celestial bodies are contrary to the letter and spirit of the provisions of Articles I, II, III and IV of 1967 OST, including the UN Charter.

Pursuant to the provisions of Article III, States Parties to 1967 OST shall carry on activities in the exploration and use of outer space, including the moon and other celestial bodies, in accordance with international law, including the UN Charter, in the interest of maintaining international peace and security and promoting international co-operation.

As mentioned earlier, the UN Charter is the principal and fundamental source of contemporary international law, including space law. Furthermore, it could be seen that the provisions of the Preamble and Article 1 and 2 of the UN Charter have been consolidated in the provision of Article III of the 1967 OST.

Article IV of 1967 OST is very important in strengthening and consolidating the legal status of outer space, the moon and other celestial bodies. It stipulates:

States Parties to the Treaty undertake not to place in orbit around the earth any objects carrying nuclear weapons or any other kinds of weapons of mass destruction, install such weapons on the celestial bodies, or station such weapons in outer space in any other manner.

The moon and other celestial bodies shall be used by States Parties to the Treaty exclusively for peaceful purposes. The establishment of military bases, installations and fortifications, the testing of any type of weapons and the conduct of military manoeuvres on the celestial bodies shall be forbidden. The use of military personnel for scientific research or for any other peaceful purposes shall not be prohibited. The use of any equipment or facility neccessary for peaceful exploration of the moon and other celestial bodies shall also not be prohibited.
As could be seen from the foregoing provisions of Article IV, the legal regime of neutralization and demilitarization has been established in the new domain - outer space, the moon and other celestial bodies..

It should be borne in mind that the prevention of an arms race into outer space and its maintenance for peaceful purposes have been one of the most important challenges confronting the United Nations from the very beginning of outer space/ nuclear era.. Thus the topic of this session is a direct challenge to the legal binding force of provisions of the UN Charter, the 1967 OST (Articles I, II, III and IV),and other international legal instruments on

---

[9] For more detail, see, **AW&ST., October 24, 2005**, pp. 47-55.

disarmament and arms control.

Thus, at this juncture, it will be useful for me to examine some relevant provisions of the UN Charter.

The UN Charter

It would be recalled that in the last paragraph of the Preamble of the 1967 OST the States Parties expressed their conviction that the Treaty will further the purposes and principles of the UN Charter. Therefore, it is construed that all activities in outer space **must be carried out** in accordance with the purposes and principles as embodied in the provisions of CHAPTER I, Articles 1 and 2 of the UN Charter. This must be taken into consideration in the interpretation of the provisions of the 1967 OST.

According to Article 1, the following are the Purposes of the United Nations:

1. To maintain international peace and security, and to this end: to take effective collective measures for the prevention and removal of threats to the peace, and for suppression of acts of aggression or other breaches of the peace, and to bring about by peaceful means, and in conformity with the principles of justice and international law, adjustment or settlement of international disputes or situations which might lead to a breach of the peace;

2. To develop friendly relations among nations based on respect for the principle of equal rights and self-determination of peoples, and to take other appropriate measures to strengthen universal peace;

3. To achieve international co-operation in solving international problems of an economic, social, cultural or humanitarian character, and in promoting and encouraging respect for human rights and for fundamental freedoms for all without distinction as to race, sex, language, or religion; and

4. To be a centre for harmonizing the actions of nations in the attainment of these common ends.

Since the beginning of the space/nuclear era, the United Nations, with the co-operation of its members, has done a lot in implementation and realization of the provisions of the above Article 1 of the Charter. It has been and will continue to be the centre of bringing space closer to the peoples of the world through the peaceful uses of space applications techniques in fields, such as, communications, remote sensing, meteorology, navigation, disaster management, education and training, monitoring of arms control agreements, etc.

Article 2 of the UN Charter provides mandatory principles to guide Members in the implementation and realization of the purposes of the UN. It is divided into seven (7) paragraphs. They have further been elaborated in the UN General Assembly **DECLARATION on Principles of International Law concerning Friendly Relations and Co-operation among States in Accordance with the Charter of the United Nations** of 24 October 1970 (resolution 2625(XXV)). Considering the limitation in space and time, it will not possible for me to make a detailed examination and analysis of these principles in this paper.

According to Article 2 (1), all states are sovereign and equal. This means that all sovereign states have equal rights and obligations under contemporary international law, irrespective of their degree of socio-economic, political, technological or scientific development. It further means that no state has any right whatsoever to meddle or intervene in the internal affairs of any other state. According the **1970 UNGA Declaration on Principles concerning Friendly Relations and Co-operation** the principle of sovereign equality contain the following six (6) elements:

(i). States are judicially equal;
(ii). Each State enjoys the rights inherent in full sovereignty;
(iii). Each State has the duty to respect the personality of other States;
(iv). The territorial integrity and political independence of the State are inviolable;
(v). Each State has the right freely to choose and develop its political, social, economic and cultural systems;
(vi). Each State has the duty to comply fully and in good faith with its international obligations and live in peace with other States.

Pursuant to the provisions of the above elements, all invasions and interventions are gross violation of the principle of sovereign equality. Presently, Iraq can serve as a very good example of the violation. No state is above the law.

Article 2 (2) provides that all members of the UN shall in good faith fulfil obligations assumed by them under the provisions of the Charter. They are further obliged to fulfil in good faith their obligations under the generally recognized principles and rules of contemporary international law.

This principle is very important in the implementation and realization of the purposes and other principles enshrined in the provisions of the UN Charter, including other international treaties, conventions, agreements etc. Commenting on this principle, Professor Bing Cheng correctly pointed out that: "Treaties of every kind when made by the competent authority, are as obligatory upon nations as private contracts are binding upon individuals ...and to be kept with most scrupulous good faith."[10] Furthermore, Professor P. S. Atiyah in this respect also submitted that: "The sanctity of contractual obligations is merely an expression of the principle that once a contract is freely and voluntarily entered into, it should be held sacred, and should be enforced by the Courts if it is broken. No doubt this very sanctity was an outcome of freedom of contract, for the reason why contracts were held sacred was the fact that the parties entered into them of their own choice and volition, and settled the terms by mutual agreement."[11]

---

[10] CHENG BIN, GENERAL PRINCIPLES OF LAW as applied by INTERNATIONAL COURTS AND TRIBUNALS, Cambridge Grotius Publications Ltd. (1987), p.112.

[11] Atiyah, P. S., An Introduction TO THE LAW OF CONTRACT, Third Edition, Clarendon Press, Oxford (1981), p. 12.

Therefore, taking into consideration the above observation, it is submitted that the interpretation of the provisions of the UN Charter, the 1967 OST and other international treaties, conventions, etc., must be in good faith.

Article 2 (3) provides that states shall settle their international disputes by peaceful means in such a manner that international peace and security, and justice, are not endangered. This is a very important and necessary principle in making this world more safer and harmonious. Stability, progress, co-operation, mutual respect and understanding will never be attained through the use of force or threat. Chapter VI of the UN Charter embodies provisions on pacific or peaceful settlement of disputes (Articles 33-38).

Article 33 (1), for example, embodies provisions concerning pacific means of settling disputes. It stipulates: "The parties to any dispute, the continuance of which is likely to endanger the maintenance of international peace and security, shall, first of all, seek a solution by negotiation, enquiry, mediation, conciliation, arbitration, judicial settlement, resort to regional agencies or arrangements, or other peaceful means of their own choice." The Security Council shall, when it deems necessary, call upon the parties to settle their disputes by such means. It should be pointed out that these pacific means of settling are embodied in the private laws of all countries. They have pre-eminence above the use of force in resolving all types disputes under municipal or international law.

According the principle established under Article 2 (4), states shall refrain in their international relations from the threat or use of force against the territorial integrity or political independence of any state, or in any other manner inconsistent with the Purposes of the UN.

Chapter VII of the UN Charter embodies provisions pertaining to **Actions with Respect to Threats to the Peace, Breaches of the Peace., and Acts of Aggression (Articles 39-51)**.

Pursuant to the provisions of Articles 24-26 of the UN Charter, the Security Council is primarily responsible for the maintenance of international peace and security. We have already noticed the role of the Security Council in the process of pacific settlement of disputes Let´s briefly reflect on some the provisions of Chapter VII because of their relevance to the topic of this session.

According to Article 39, the Security Council shall determine the existence of any threat to the peace, breach of the peace, or act of aggression and shall make recommendations, or decide what measures shall be taken in accordance with Articles 41 and 42, to maintain or restore international peace and security.

It is very sad and disheartening to point out that some powerful states, as recent events have shown, have been obstructing the Security Council in performing the duties enshrined in the provisions of Articles 40-50. In most cases they use the provisions of Article 51 to undermine the legal binding force of the principle enshrined in Article 2 (4) of the UN Charter. This article contains the notion of self-defence. A lot has already been written by many authorities and experts in international law.[12]

At this juncture, it should be borne in mind that most the events which have resulted to the use of force in the so-called self-defence has occurred here on earth. The provisions contained in the UN Charter, if strictly complied with by all states, big or small, will eliminate war here on earth.

Conclusion

In the foregoing pages I have tried to reflect on the provisions of the UN Charter and the 1967 Treaty Governing the Activities of States in the Exploration and Use of Outer Space, including the Moon and Other Celestial Bodies. These legal instruments as we have pointed out are the primary and fundamental sources of space law and **must be** complied by all states, including their nationals, in the exploration and use of outer space the moon and other celestial bodies.

Taking into considerations the provisions of Article IV of the 1967 OST snd the principle enshrined in Article 2(4) of the UN Charter, outer space **cannot be used in any form or manner** in times of armed conflict. I consider it to be a serious crime against humankind. In this respect, I would like to submit that all objects launched into outer space must register in accordance with the provisions of the 1975 Registration Convention. It is the right of the states and peoples of the world to know what is hovering over their heads.

In the **UN Millennium Declaration** of 8 September 2000 the Heads of State and Government declared that they will spare no effort to free their peoples from the scourge of war, whether within or between states, which has claimed more than 5 million lives in the past decade. They also expressed their intention to seek to eliminate the dangers posed by weapons of mass destruction.

There is so fear, violence, hatred, bitterness, intolerance and war in the world today. We need

---

[12] For example, see, Schachter, Oscar, **International Law in Theory and Practice**, Kluwer Law International, The Hague (1995), pp.135-183; Henkin. Louis, **International Law: Politics and Values**, Kluwer Law International, The Hague (1995), pp. 121-124, esp.; Cheng, Bin, op. cit., pp. 69-102

one another as members the same human family. We should therefore use space science and technology for the well-being, progress and development of the human race, and not for its destruction.

IAC-06-E.6.4.03

CONTEMPORARY DOCTRINE OF SELF-DEFENSE IN OUTER SPACE LAW

Professor S. Bhatt
Formerly Professor of Space Law, and
Honorary Professor of International Law
School of International Studies
Jawaharlal Nehru University, New Delhi – 110067
Adviser, United Nations (ICAO)
Commentator to UNISPACE III Conference, Vienna, July 1999
Post-Doctoral Fulbright Fellow, School of Law, Dallas,
Texas, USA 1969-70

Abstract

This paper analyses the contemporary law on self-defense contained in the UN Charter Article 51, as also in air and space law from the Chicago Convention of 1944 and the Outer Space Treaty of 1967. It takes into account the events of global terrorism ever since 9/11, 2001 attack in New York and its impact on global security and self-defense.

CHAPTER VII OF UN CHARTER

Chapter VII of the UN Charter contains Articles 39 to 54 relating to threats to the peace, breaches of the peace, and acts of aggression. Article 39 provides that the Security Council shall determine the existence of any threat to the peace etc. and make recommendations in accordance with Articles 41 and 42 to restore peace and security. Article 41 provides for measures not involving the use of armed force and involves interruption of[1] economic relations. Article 42 is called for when Article 41 does not help and the use of air, sea, or land forces is necessary by the members of the United Nations. However, Article 51 of the Charter says that nothing in the present Charter shall impair the inherent rights of individual or collective self-defense if an armed attack occurs against a member of the UN, until Security Council has taken measures for maintaining peace and security.

The Charter provisions for self-defense were drafted in 1945; much before space exploration began in 1957. Even during 1945-57, there were varying interpretations of the use of force in self-defense. To safeguard national security, scholars and nations debated whether a pre-emptive strike is a legal course of self-defense when a war or an armed conflict is imminent, and a country cannot wait for an armed attack to occur first. In the case of nuclear weapons, some countries have adopted "No First Use" doctrine while some say that a pre-emptive strike is necessary for self-defense. A massive retaliation by a second counter strike in self-defense can deter a potential aggressor. The USA relied on the latter doctrine against former USSR during the Cold War period. The threshold was crossed when both super powers had massive weapons stockpile.

Use of Force In Air Law

Modern air law is based on the Chicago Convention of 1944. The objectives of ICAO are to ensure safe, economic and orderly movement of global aviation. The sovereignty over air space rests with the superjacent State. The Convention was amended to include Article 3 bis to avoid the use of force against a civil aircraft after a civil aircraft was shot down by former USSR forces when it strayed by mistake into its territory. Today, however, this doctrine of no use of force against a civil aircraft is open to new ideas and action. As we know civil aircrafts were hijacked and used in 9/11 attack in New York. The US was forced to use military aircraft to intercept civil aircraft to safeguard its security against terrorist attacks. The terrorists originated from Afghanistan. Thus US has redrawn its self-defense doctrine to use force which includes a pre-emptive strike where there is a threat to US security from terrorism. India has made a similar pronouncement, as France and some other countries have. The use of force against civil aircraft is now a subject involving the security interests of States for self-defense.

Space Law And Self-Defense

Space law is a part of international law and the UN Charter. Space is geographically an earth-space arena, as Professor Myres McDougal and Professor Ivan Vlasic described in their treatise on Law And Public Order In Space published in 1963. The Outer Space Treaty is the Charter for outer space law. It does not permit militarisation of outer space, nor the orbiting of nuclear weapons in the orbit of earth. It does permit the use of military craft and personnel for the scientific exploration and uses of outer space. The doctrine of self-defense in armed conflict becomes urgent for examination of scholars and nation States.

Major Goals of Space Exploration

It may be recalled that space exploration has given many substantial benefits to the world society. The UNISPACE III Conference by the UN in July 1999 was a landmark occasion and a great step to harvest the economic and scientific uses for the developing and the developed countries. The conference promoted international cooperation which has become a grand norm of space law for States. In the abovementioned UN Conference many States and international organizations have come forth with the major goals of space exploration.

The International Society for Photogrammetry and Remote Sensing has 167 member societies and organizations for advancement of knowledge, research, development and education in photogrammetry, remote sensing and spatial information sciences, to help well-being of humanity and sustainability of environment. The International Organization of Space Communication has been working since 1971 to develop world communication.

The European Space Agency has following major goals as stated in the Conference of observation and analysis of earth systems of atmosphere, oceans, land and their complex interactions; Global Navigation Satellite System; Global Information Infrastructure; basic space sciences, and international cooperation. The UNITAR has major goal to monitor environments for decision-making of Agenda 21. The Economic and Social Commission for Asia and Pacific has emphasis on Space Application and Sustainable Development (See UNISPACE III A/CONF. 184/AB/IGO/4). India has taken a lead in this region to bring application of space to the people at large. The INTELSAT has promoted the use of frequency spectrum and geostationary orbit. It has helped in deregulation and globalisation of economies and services (A/CONF.184/AB/IGO/5). The IMO has benefited much by observation of satellite data. The FAO uses space exploration in environmental monitoring, and global information and early warning system for emergency affecting growth of crops. This is done by remote-sensing, or the use of new technology for rapid growth of food-cultivation and new seeds (A/CONF.184/AB/IGO/7). Indeed a perspective of subjects discussed in the present 57 IAF on "Bringing Space Closer to People" provides a glimpse of new knowledge for mankind. It includes the use of nuclear power systems in space, social benefits of space spin-off, space tourism, for which many spaceports are coming up as in Dubai etc., space and global security, policies for new era in space, new commercial opportunities in space, legal aspect of space transportation (we seem to be very close to the era of aerospace transport of passengers and cargo world over), and expansion of knowledge for world society. Professor Stephen Hawking has in his book 'A Brief History of Time' stated that 21st century scholars view all knowledge in one perspective. Besides, the growth of a biologist view of the world was provided by the UNESCO Conference in 1971 on the 10th death anniversary of Einstein and biologist Chardin. The above Conference under Julian Huxley also made a case for the integration of all knowledge for the human benefit that Einstein and Justice Holmes have been recommending.

New Global Evolution

Thus the world society today is in a new period of integration and evolution. There have been some major ideas and changes introduced in the structure of world society that include the space exploration since 1957, the environment revolution since 1972 Stockholm Declaration, the de-regulation and globalization in air law since the De-regulation Act of USA in 1978 and the integration of global economy by WTO that has produced an interdependent world society. The major concerns of States is for welfare economics for which Professor Amartaya Sen, the Noble Laureate has invited world attention.

Clash of Civilizations And Armed Action In Space: The Shape of Things

The 9/11 event of 2001 in New York has produced global changes indeed. Professor Samuel Huntington from Harvard has brought forth a book earlier on 'The Clash of Civilizations And the Remaking of World Order' in 1996. Armed conflict in space law is to be seen in the totality of global order which according to Huntington is experiencing in recent period a clash of civilizations based on a conflict of cultures. In fact outer space law is closely watching the political dialogue on the clash of cultures. President George Bush of USA has to a very large extent responded to this world challenge after terrorists' attacks in New York. At home, he has announced the home guard movement for national security. Externally, he has made the pre-emptive strike a national policy against a foreign country that trains terrorists against USA. He has declared that global freedom and democracy are important parameters for peaceful world order. He has also sought international cooperation with India, China, former USSR, EU and countries in Asia, Africa and in the Middle East. President Bush has achieved a large measure of success in creating international cooperation to fight and control global terrorism which is number one threat to world peace. Thus the comity of nations through the UN and by individual efforts of States are controlling global terrorism. Thus self-defense in outer space is based on new cooperation among States against global terrorism. Outer space is being used to monitor terrorist training camps. US is using air power to control terrorism in Afghanistan and Iraq. Major powers are engaged to control the spread of nuclear weapons to countries especially in the Middle East where terrorism has created armed conflicts. It is therefore in the interest of Collective Self-defense of States that space law should promote international cooperation for control of global terrorism. Then alone will follow freely many scientific and social benefits to mankind by space applications.

It is seen, however, that the use of force for self-defense has to be based on the doctrine of proportional use of force and not on massive weapons for destruction. Professor Myres McDougal from Yale Law School has strongly recommended the doctrine of proportional use of force for self-defense. The use of nuclear weapons from outer space, or from any source, is not permitted under international law. These weapons are against all laws of war and are a threat to the survival of mankind. Hence their proliferation in the hands of terrorists, States who cannot handle them with responsibility, has to be stopped. Articles 41 and 42 of UN Charter can be applied to stop States to produce such weapons of mass destruction. This has become the collective responsibility of all States. The US and other allied States are pursuing above legal measures to secure a peaceful world. These are measures for collective self-defense as provided under the UN Charter.

India has moved on to control terrorism on the cultural front as well. Even USA and other major powers have agreed to avoid a clash of civilizations and promote a multi-cultural heritage of world society. India is a multi-cultural country. Many other countries have now major pockets of composite culture. Unity in diversity is a global doctrine.

Global federalism helps to ensure diversity of cultures. Professor Huntington also feels that a war will not result because of a clash of cultures. The problems of world society, he says, are due to global corruption, inadequate governance, lack of moral standards, and resulting terrorism. In any case, we cannot afford a global war based on a clash of civilizations. The world has moved so much for a single civilization based on the attractions of a variety of cultures. We are living in a unified world order based on the rule of law. No religion doubts this thesis. Nevertheless, States need vigilance and cooperation to weed out the virus of terrorism. India is experimenting a new life-style based on the combination of ideas of West and East. A stable world order is likely to rest on freedom, democracy, cultural tolerance and multi-cultural global civilizations. Eminent anthropologist, Margaret Mead has said that all of mankind belong to one species, called Homo Sapiens, and the diversity of cultures helps promote unity of mankind. The world is increasingly realizing this thesis for common survival of mankind. The environmenting problems of this planet further call upon all States and peoples to live in harmony and peace. This concept of unity in diversity of mankind has been forged by space law and space benefits. That is why the IAF has this theme for the 57th Conference in Spain in 2006 – Bringing Space closer to people.

Selected References

1. Space Benefits for Humanity in the Twenty-first Century, UNISPACE III A/CONF./BP/13, United Nations 1999. Compilation of papers and background papers.

2. Workshop for Space Law in 21st Century, 20-24 July 1999, Vienna, UNISPACE III.

3. National Paper of India UNISPACE III A/CONF.184/NP/35.

4. Myres McDougal, Harold Lasswell and Ivan Vlasic, Law and Public Order in Space, 1963, New Haven, Conn., USA.

5. S. Bhatt, Legal Controls of Outer Space: Law, Freedom and Responsibility, S. Chand, New Delhi, 1974, Foreword by Professor Quincy Wright.

6. S. Bhatt, Environment Protection and Sustainable Development, APH Publishing, New Delhi, 2004.

7. S. Bhatt and Akhtar Majid, Environmental Management and Federalism: The Indian Experience, Uppal Publishing, New Delhi, 2002.

8. V.S. Mani, S. Bhatt and V.B. Reddy, Recent Trends in Space Law and Policy, JNU, Lancers, New Delhi, 1997.

9. A.G. Haley, Space Law and Government, New York, 1963.

10. Manfred Lachs, The Law of Outer Space, Leiden, 1972.

11. N.M. Matte, Aerospace Law, London, 1969.

12. Tanja Masson-Zwan, Space Law: Views of the Future, Martinus Nijhoff, 1992.

13. N. Jesentuliyana and Lee R.S.K., eds., Manual on Space Law Vol. III, Oceana Publications, 1981.

14. Diederiks-Verschoar I.H. Ph., An Introduction to Space Law, Deventer: Kluwer, 1993.

15. Samuel P. Huntington, The Clash of Civilizations and the Re-making of World Order, Penguin Books, 1996.

16. Stephen W. Hawking, A Brief History of Time, London, 1988.

17. S. Bhatt, ed., Kashmiri Pandits: A Cultural Heritage, Lancers Book, 1994, pp. 631.

18. Amartaya Sen (Noble Laureate), Argumentative Indian: Writings on Indian history, culture and identity, Penguin Books, London, 2005.

19. S. Bhatt, "An Ecological Approach to Aerospace Law", Annals of Air Space Law, McGill University, Canada, vol. 4(1979), pp. 85-96.

20. S. Bhatt, "The Contributions of Aerospace Law to Evolution of Man and Global Society", Annals of Air and Space Law, McGill University, Canada, vol. 5, 1980, pp. 309-23.

21. S. Bhatt, International Aviation and Outer Space Law and Relations: Reflections on Future Trends, New Delhi, 1996.

22. Carl Q. Christal, The Modern International Law on Outer Space, New York, 1982.

23. V.B. Reddy, ed., Recent Trends in Air and Space Law, proceedings of a national seminar, NALSAR, Hyderabad, India, in press with Uppal Publishing House, New Delhi to be released soon.

IAC-06-E6.4.4

MILITARY APPLICATIONS AND SPACE LAW

by Gabriella Catalano Sgrosso*
University of Rome, Italy

ABSTRACT

The conflicts which recently took place (The Gulf War, the War in Kosovo and in Iraq) show how space has been used to a much further extent than before, for military operations purposes, as preparation and planning, as well as execution. These operations have the peculiar feature of being able to guarantee a continuous exchange of data and information between weapon devices, due to state-of-the-art technology, as: satellite-driven smart weapons to strike military targets, AWACS (Airborne Warning Control System) and JSTARS (Joint Surveillance and Targeting Radar System) systems. Technological progress changes human perception of space and distance, so it subsequently modifies the relationship between war and space.

This paper aims at analyzing the effects of technological progress on the relationship between war and Space within the legal context of European Union's and United Nations' current regulations.

The first part of the paper analyzes Space militarization and its limits, set by States for prevention reasons, to safeguard Outer Space, seen as development and knowledge resource.

The second part analyzes States' security and defense concepts, one of which is the Strategic Defense Initiative –SDI - or Space Shield, and another one is the Russian Defense Initiative – SSDP. On the other hand, stressing the two Powers' commitment to limit offensive weapons' development and use in Outer Space, is essential.

These agreements on weapon limitation include weapon control, as SALT I and II, the Limited Test Ban Treaty, the Non Proliferation Treaty and START I and II for nuclear weapon reduction.

The third part of the paper focuses on the European Union's concern on the growing militarization of Space, which leads to the drafting of the "Green Paper"; through this project, the European Commission and the European Space Agency put up questions on Europe's future space power and develop an action plan, the "White Paper". The realization of GALILEO, Europe's current effort, planned for civil purposes, is already embedded in problems regarding its possible use for military and security reasons. The EU – ESA environment and security monitoring project, the Global Monitoring for Environment and Security (GMES), is under examination.

States are currently considering using remote sensing satellites for both civil and military purposes, (dual use); remote sensing satellites provide high quality services and relevant economic benefits. On the matter, European HELIOS satellite and Cosmo Sky-Med project must be mentioned. They strengthen even further the legality of military remote sensing satellites, which are also used to monitor military agreements' compliance.

The research will be carried out on the basis of the current space regulations, which up to date set the total demilitarization of the Moon and of other celestial bodies, while the demilitarization of Outer Space is set only partially; but we must keep in mind that banning any use of Outer Space for dangerous and offensive purposes, as well as for any purpose which could be harmful for resources and Patrimony of Mankind, is the basic principle of the current space regulations.

---

*Professor of International Law and Space Law, Faculty of Economics, University of Rome, Italy, Director IISL.

1.1 The military importance of outer space

Outer space has become an environment where new weapons are being tested and where there is growing military presence.

Hence the potential danger for outer space to turn into the battlefield of the future.

Most space activities are carried out by the superpowers, and regard projects for military purposes; this results from the strong political, ideological and military rivalry between the major world powers, typical of the post-war period.

Outer space has therefore started to play a leading role in the global balance of powers; its influence is so strong that it could even take control over a war fought on the Earth's surface.

If, instead, a war should begin in outer space, the latter should be the "theater" of war and international conflicts, and the war itself should not be a localized phenomenon, but it would certainly cause repercussions on the terrestrial surface.

At present times, almost all sectors regarding planning and execution of the Great Powers' political-strategic plans depend on systems placed in outer space: all the different aspects of conflicts, from identification of targets to execution of Special Forces' secret operations, depend on the abovementioned space devices and communication.

Potential enemy targets are constantly monitored, weapons detected, missiles counted and identified by reconnaissance satellites.

New technologies, thanks to some, perhaps deliberately left open, lacuna in the regulations, are radically changing all countries' concept of defense, by introducing the idea of a space defense system, having great offensive and destructive potential.

So it seems we are definitely moving away from the principle of freedom of outer space, despite all the efforts made to stop the arms race and legitimize the demilitarization process.

Article 4 of this Treaty is the only one that specifically regulates the issue regarding the "militarization" of outer space and celestial bodies, resuming the contents of the UN Resolution 1884[1] between the United States and USSR. The resolution calls upon States to refrain from placing nuclear weapons or any other kinds of weapons of mass destruction in outer space; the US and USSR accepted the resolution and its principles, and encouraged other countries to do the same.

Reading article 4, we notice how important the principle of "peaceful use" of space activities is; as clear as it may seem though, it has often been a topic of debate, since, up to day, no clear definition of the term can be found in the agreement itself. In the last ten years, the technological development of new weapons has pointed out how uncertain and ambiguous the meaning of the term "peaceful" is.

On the matter, there are two opposite doctrines[2]: the first one, which is the prevailing opinion in the western world, considers the term "peaceful" as "non aggressive"[3]; thus, all military actions carried out on the Moon and other Celestial Bodies must be considered peaceful until proven aggressive[4].

On the other hand, the second doctrine, which is most common in Socialist countries, inclines to a stricter interpretation of the term, and considers "peaceful" as "non military"; so, even the mere use of surveillance satellites placed in orbit by military personnel or for military purposes, must be considered illegal[5]..

The problem thickens if we read the abovementioned article 4 very carefully: it explicitly states the principle of "exclusive use for peaceful purposes" with regard to the Moon and the other "Celestial Bodies" only. In fact, outer space as a separate entity is not explicitly mentioned.

Despite this omission, the existence of an only partial "demilitarization" has been granted with regard to outer space, compared to the total one stated for the Moon and other Celestial Bodies; this partial demilitarization, though, only concerns the ban on placing nuclear weapons or any other kinds of weapons of mass destruction in orbit, as stated in article 4[6].

This partial ban on nuclear weapons can be deduced not only from the abovementioned principles, which are stated in the Preamble to the Treaty as well as in the abovementioned articles of the Treaty itself, but also from the interpretation of the latter.

The fact that these regulations specify which kind of devices have been willfully banned, leads to the opinion that all other devices not explicitly prohibited are to be considered permitted[7].

The United States, as well as other western countries such as France and Canada, have always been great supporters of the use of outer space for non aggressive military activities; on the other hand, the Soviet Union and the other Socialist States opted for the strict interpretation until the '60s, when 'Remote Sensing' satellites made observing the Earth possible, which led Socialist countries to approach the American version[8].

Many authors have tried to broaden the scope of article 4, mainly referring to the Charter of the United Nations[9], which was already mentioned in article 3 of the Treaty. The fact that the abovementioned article 3 also refers to international law seems to strengthen this interpretation. Article 39 of the Charter only prohibits those activities which may constitute a threat to peace or an act of aggression, and, at the same time, it allows military operations which are necessary to exercise the right of self-defense[10]. So what makes single uses of outer space legitimate or not is the peaceful or aggressive nature of the use itself, and not whether it is military or not.

Another issue which supports the western interpretation of this article, is the dual use[11] of civil satellites, which may also be used for military purposes, in certain cases of international tension.

Unfortunately, despite all these efforts made to interpret the "Treaty on principles", its provisions are still insufficient to prohibit certain behaviors.

The vagueness of this provision must be considered in light of the ways it was interpreted in the different political-social contexts; but banning all military activity doesn't seem very convincing.

1.2 Legitimacy of military activities in outer space and limitations deriving from the main Treaties

Treaties, bilateral and multilateral agreements play a very important role in the creation of rules concerning space law, as they are effective means of international collaboration.

The evolution of space law is diametrically opposed to the evolution of space technology: in fact, the first military satellite programs were carried out for surveillance purposes, to transport missile seeker systems, and for military communications and navigation purposes.

CORONA satellites were launched back in 1959, in total secrecy[12]; it was then, in this atmosphere of tension, that arose the need to regulate the exploitation of outer space, considered as heritage of mankind.

The "Treaty on Principles" was signed at London, Moscow and Washington, on January 27, 1967 and entered into force October 10, 1967.

In general, the Treaty states the same principles already outlined in the General Assembly Resolutions, explicitly referring to Resolutions 1884 and 1962 in its Preamble.

The provisions that place specific limitations on military activities in outer space and on Celestial Bodies are the following:

article 4, which binds all State Parties to undertake "not to place in orbit around the earth any objects carrying nuclear weapons or any other kinds of weapons of mass destruction[13], install such weapons on celestial bodies or station such weapons in outer space in any other manner".

It also states that the Moon and other Celestial Bodies shall be used exclusively for "peaceful purposes", and that "the establishment of military bases, installations, and fortifications, the testing of any type of weapons and the conduct of military maneuvers" shall be forbidden.

On the other hand, "the use of military personnel for scientific research and for any other peaceful purposes shall non be prohibited", nor the "use of any equipment or facility necessary for peaceful exploration of the Moon and other Celestial Bodies".

Article 12 states that "all stations, installations, equipment and space vehicles on the Moon and other Celestial Bodies shall be open to representatives of other States Parties to the treaty on a basis of reciprocity".

The 1963 "Moscow Treaty"[14] owes its existence to the Geneva Conference on Disarmament[15]; this Treaty introduced the issue of demilitarization of outer space and regulated it for the first time, by erecting barriers to the development of armaments in outer space.

The historical context of the Moscow Treaty was quite complex and characterized by a strong tension between States; the atomic bombings of Hiroshima and Nagasaki in 1945 and the nuclear testing carried out in the 50s awakened public opinion to the growing nuclear threat.

The Treaty was first signed by the nuclear forces, and by the other countries[16] immediately after; by the end of 1973, it had already reached 106 ratifications. The only dissenting countries carrying out space activities were China, which opposed the nuclear monopoly of the three countries organizers of the Treaty, and France, which still conducts nuclear tests and follows the armament policy.

For what concerns demilitarization, the most important part of the Treaty is article 1, which bans all nuclear weapon test explosions, at any place under the jurisdiction or control of the States Parties[17]. Moreover, each of the States Parties to the Treaty undertakes to refrain from participating in any way in the abovementioned nuclear testing[18].

It is important to recall how the Treaty does not include any provisions on weapon disposition control, due to the fact that the States thought they could count on using artificial satellites and new technologies for this purpose.

Although the "Treaty on the non-proliferation of nuclear weapons"[19], signed at London, Moscow and Washington in 1968, doesn't include any provision which explicitly refers to outer space, there is no doubt as to its validity on the matter; article 6[20] states that each of the States Parties undertakes to cooperate and to reach an agreement so as to pursue nuclear disarmament.

The 1979 Moon Agreement[21] broadened the scope of the ban on military use of celestial bodies; this treaty aimed at clearing up any problems left unsolved by the Treaty on Principles. The connection between article 4 of the abovementioned Treaty and article 3 of the 1979 Agreement is clear, since it reasserts the principle of exclusive use of the Moon and other Celestial bodies for peaceful purposes, confirming that placing in orbit nuclear weapons or any other kinds of weapons of mass destruction or establishing military bases on the Moon is forbidden, and prohibiting the testing of any type of weapons and the conduct of military maneuvers on the Moon, allowing for the use of military personnel and equipment for scientific research only. The innovations introduced by the Agreement are the following:

- the areas included in the ban, such as the Moon's orbit, routes to the Moon, the Moon itself and other Celestial Bodies
- any threat or use of force or any other hostile act is forbidden: on the Moon, or using the Moon to harm the Earth, spacecrafts, personnel of spacecrafts or other manmade space objects.

Unfortunately, the principle that states the use of the Moon and other Celestial Bodies exclusively for peaceful purposes is effective only for those countries that have ratified the Agreement, which are very few, and none of which is a nuclear force.

This agreement represents a model for international cooperation; it doesn't simply reaffirm and apply rules already stated in the Treaty on principles and in previous acts regarding activities on the Moon, but it introduces innovations of great importance. Article 11.1 provides that the Moon and its natural resources be considered as Common Heritage of Mankind, reaffirming the principle of Common Heritage of Mankind for the exploitation of depletable resources, that must be managed through international agreements.

The main problem is that the States involved in space activities still lack will to create an international regime to regulate the exploitation of the Moon's resources, and assure that all the benefits deriving from these resources be equally dispersed between all States. Perhaps this can represent a further reason why many States have not ratified this Treaty.

2. Main satellite projects for defense purposes

2.1 Remote Sensing satellites

The military use of outer space for peaceful purposes has recently been growing; it has been investing in new development sectors including: surveillance systems, state-of-the-art traditional space weapons, anti-satellite satellites and long-range missile control, guiding and aiming.

After launching the first scientific satellites (such as Sputnik, Explorer, Vanguard, etc.), the United States started launching satellites for military purposes in 1959[22]; the first ones were the **Corona "spy" satellites[23], which took photographs** of the most strategically relevant targets and then transmitted data to Earth, for elaboration and analysis, by means of a film-return capsule, which was retrieved in mid-air by an aircraft before hitting the ground. But the film-return capsule of the second Corona satellite was retrieved by the Soviets in the Barents sea; this gave them the opportunity to start carrying out their own surveillance activity: Zenit "spy" satellite, which flew under the guise of a research vehicle[24], was launched in orbit in 1962.

Very soon both sides started to feel threatened by the fact that this space race, which had military origins, could become offensive in nature, due to the fact that one of the two States could achieve such a high technological progress to be able to overwhelm the other.

All these events led to the signature of the 1967 Treaty on Outer Space by the United States and the Soviet Union; this treaty also aimed at limiting the militarization of outer space: it allowed all states to carry out operations for reconnaissance and surveillance purposes.

Satellites used for these purposes fall within the "spy" satellite category, and have the following aims:

- surveillance, in all weather and light conditions, of specific activities on the Earth surface, which may constitute a threat for allied countries and for national or international security;
- reducing the efficaciousness of the enemy's concealment and identifying its command, control and communications centers;
- alarming own national civil and military command centers so as to timely react;
- verifying that all Treaties drawn up between States be observed.

These instruments transmit photographs and TV images via radio, are capable of detecting ballistic missiles, during night or day, by means of sensors, and of spotting concealed military objectives.

They can also see through clouds and vary own orbital height to perform closer observation; they have such a high resolution that people can be seen clearly and military objectives can be distinguished from civil ones.

Earth Observation satellites also have great political and strategic importance, since they have often been used during international crises for security and defense purposes, allowing to control the current state of the disarmament process[25].

Military activity for remote sensing purposes cannot be considered espionage.

According to the law of war, gathering information is considered obtaining of military secrets with the aid of members of the enemy armed forces. Reconnaissance, on the other hand, although carried out in the same way, aims at civil or military objectives of great interest.

Espionage in peacetime, instead, means secretly acquiring a foreign country's political, military or economical secrets [26].

International Law lacks any positive provision providing the definition of espionage[27]; nonetheless, it is certain that military reconnaissance flights cannot be considered peacetime espionage, as they lack of "secrecy", taking place in the airspace, and thus being observable[28]. National regulations confirm this point of view, since they consider intelligence activity as indictable: in the Italian Criminal Code[29] the definition of the term "espionage" includes all those crimes concerning violation of the secrecy of information, especially with regard to state security; the German Criminal

Code instead does not stress the "secrecy of attaining" information, but the "secrecy of the information attained".

Therefore, in principle, according to the Italian and German regulations, the use of reconnaissance satellites is to be considered legitimate, as they are information collection instruments.

The military sector is a special client: from a commercial point of view, it demands and pays for complex services. Structures used for military purposes, though, become strategic targets during wartime[30], which can be attacked and neutralized by the enemy forces; all infrastructures connected to the gathering, interpretation and distribution of data for military purposes, also become military targets.

An important aspect of remote sensing satellites which has recently arisen regards an eventual dual use of these satellites, which means a combined use, for both civil and military purposes.

In many space applications, as telecommunications, GPS and remote sensing, satellites are often used in a combined way, especially with regard to those activities where technology development has been financed by the Department of Defense[31].

After the end of the Cold War, military satellites started to be used, to some extent, for civil purposes also; at the same time, the military started to attain data from commercial operators, instead of developing their own expensive systems.

HELIOS satellite is a project developed by France, in collaboration with Italy and Spain[32]; it was launched to replace the SAMRO satellite, launched at the beginning of the 80s, and it's based on the experience achieved through the SPOT civil satellite. HELIOS and SPOT use the same platform and magnetic recorders, capable of storing hundreds of images.

This project regards the construction of two satellites: at first, only one of the two was launched in orbit, since the second was held in reserve, in case of difficulties with the first satellite, HELIOS 1 A[33].

HELIOS 2 A satellite instead, was launched on the 18th of December 2004; this is a strong symbol of European defense cooperation.

The program developed by three countries (France, Spain and Belgium) is a political-military instrument of crisis management, since it allows to use high-resolution images and infrared rays, to see clearly during night and day.

HELIOS 1 A is still operating, while HELIOS 1 B was taken out of service in October 2004. HELIOS 2 B is scheduled for launch in March 2008, but it could be launched earlier in case of malfunctioning of H. 2 A.

Success achieved by the HELIOS programs, developed through a cooperation between European countries, is an important step forward in European space policy, which might help Europe face the United States and China, which are investing more an more in the field.

Italy will not participate in the development of Helios 2, since it decided to focus on another project in cooperation with France. The Intergovernmental Agreement[34] between the governments of Italy and France was signed on January 29, 2001 in Turin; it aims at cooperating on the development of an Earth observation capacity which uses optical sensors and radars to develop the dual use system.

The Preamble to the agreement[35] defines the meaning of the term "dual use" as a satellite observation system for military and civil (meaning both institutional and commercial) purposes, based on French and Italian small satellite programs, respectively **PLEIADES** and **COSMO-SkyMed**[36]; it is composed of an optical component including two satellites and the relevant ground functions, managed by France; a radar component including four satellites and the relevant ground functions, managed by Italy; and a user ground segment, jointly developed by the two countries[37].

The Department of Defense and ASI assume responsibility, towards the French partners and potential domestic and foreign users, respectively, for military, institutional and commercial needs.

Since the dual system may be used by different categories of users, as public, institutional, private and commercial users, it must respect certain obligations, related to the needs of the Department of Defense. The Ministry of Defense's demands are considered top priority, more important than those of any other subject, apart from requests made by countries dealing with a crisis, particularly in "Very Urgent Cases"[38].

The success of this collaboration depends on timely and complete exchange of the information necessary for dual system cooperation[39].

2.2 Telecommunications satellites: SICRAL, the first Italian satellite system for military telecommunications.

Space communications systems are considered a mainstay of worldwide policy of peace.

After some pioneering activities carried out in the 60s, it is only at the end of the 70s that the Defense Administration focuses its attention again on the exploitation of outer space for national security and defense purposes.

In particular, the feasibility study for a classified communications satellite is undertaken thanks to the Air Force; this satellite is to be used for tactical communications by the Department of Defense, and as an alternative to traditional connection systems, in case of natural catastrophes and disasters.

The commitment of the Department of Defense in this sector leads to the Italian Classified Communications and Alarm System (SICRAL-Sistema Italiano di Comunicazioni Riservate ed Allarmi)[40], the first device that is totally planned, developed, and managed by the Defense Administration.

This project is developed together with another one, which uses satellite systems: the HELIOS project, a remote sensing optical satellite, designed by France in collaboration with Italy and Spain; the growing participation in these programs is a sign of the increased interest in the potential of outer space use for national defense and security purposes[41].

The system has been placed in geostationary orbit[42], and is made up of a satellite, a management and control center and sea-based and air-based ground terminals; therefore it provides a wide-area coverage of the Earth's surface, as well as voice, video and data transmission on national territory, and the possibility to connect to forces engaged in operations abroad[43].

The fall of the Berlin wall changes the geo-strategic situation, and the current military needs which now demand for communications systems other than traditional ones; the latter aimed at supporting operational forces mostly on national territory, but the current needs regard dynamic systems, characterized by flexibility, integration between forces, timely reaction and transmission, mobility and interoperability[44]. From an operational point of view, SICRAL is a "force multiplier"[45], a telecommunications system capable of supporting the Armed Forces in any part of the world where there is a crisis or tension or war which requests intervention and peace maintenance operations.

2.3 Anti-satellite satellites and anti-missile missile systems

In 1957 the presence of an innovative soviet vehicle in outer space causes the so-called "Sputnik shock" within US political and military bodies, a widespread sense of uncertainty for a threat believed to be insurmountable[46].

Only three years after the launch of the first artificial earth satellite, both the United States and the Soviet Union had already developed the first armament projects regarding weapons specifically aimed at neutralizing the enemy's satellites, to be placed on the terrestrial surface or in outer space.

The term "anti-satellite"[47] means any device capable of putting out of action or shooting down a vehicle in earth orbit.

Regulations are not very helpful in this case: there is no ban regarding anti-satellite satellites in article 4 of the "Treaty on principles", it only prohibits nuclear weapons and weapons of mass destruction in earth orbit; therefore, some experts believe it should be revised and this prohibition introduced.

The general principle of the UN Charter, which prohibits the "recourse to force" doesn't apply either, since the destruction of a military satellite by an anti-satellite system does not constitute attack against the territorial integrity or the political independence of a State.

The idea that was becoming widespread within the two superpowers is that neither one could ever be capable of protecting own population, as according to the principle known as Mutual Assured Destruction (MAD): the development of these defense systems results in the fact that any nuclear conflict is avoidable only if the enemy's nuclear weapon capabilities be such that a mutual destruction is certain. **The ABM Treaty**[48] prohibits the deployment of nationwide defense systems against ballistic missiles, but allows, to a certain extent, the development and testing of fixed land-based radars, interceptor missiles and launchers.

It explicitly prohibits the development, testing, and deployment of sea-based, air-based, space-based, and mobile land-based ABM systems and ABM components.

Keeping this research's cost and strategic repercussions into account, US and USSR signed the Strategic Arms Limitation Treaties **(SALT I and II)**.

The Strategic Arms Reduction Treaty **(START I)** was signed on July 31st 1991 between the US and the USSR and the **START II** on January 1993 between US and Russia. In the **SORT** Treaty, stipulated on May 2002, US and Russia agreed to a unilateral reduction.

2.4 The "American National Missilistic Defense" initiative and the Soviet Strategic Initiative

The previous statements on the benefits for mankind deriving from the exploitation of outer space for peaceful purposes become of minor importance after the statement of US President Reagan of the 4th of July 1982: on that occasion, he declares that the attention shall be focused on new action lines[49]. The Strategic Defense Initiative (SDI) is nothing more than a four-layer defense system, capable of hitting enemy missiles in all phases of their trajectory[50]: the first layer regards the boost phase, when a missile is launched, it should be detected by surveillance satellites and destroyed by laser-guided weapons placed in outer space; the second one is the "post-boost" phase, which occurs after the missile has exhausted its boost phase, when it takes up its ballistic trajectory and starts releasing multiple warheads. During the last two phases, missile warheads are intercepted during their trajectory and brought back within earth's atmosphere by defense detection devices.

Despite all researches and studies carried out on all possible defense systems and weapons, SDI has never gone beyond the phase regarding the selection of weapons to use in the different defense layers.

The US Strategic Defense Initiative, also known as "Space Shield" or "Star Wars", has often been subject of political debate at both national and international level, due to the potential repercussions it could cause on worldwide balance between the State and to its effects on European security.

During the first stages of the Cold War, only the United States and the Soviet Union held ballistic missiles; at the end of this period, though, new countries approached this defense policy position, such as France, the UK, Germany, Bulgaria, Poland, Hungary, China etc.[51].

Many of these countries, though, are politically unstable, therefore the risk that these devices could actually be used or acquired by terrorists arises.

On the matter, some technologically advanced countries are developing anti-ballistic defense systems, such as the Arrow System, designed by Israel, S300/400 by Russia and MEADS, jointly developed by West Europe and the US.

But, apart from advanced countries, most of the other countries do not have the money to invest in these defense systems nor the technological know-how necessary to develop them.

Consequently, the world will be divided into two separate groups: one consisting of those countries who have developed a missile defense system and one of those who haven't.

On July 23rd 1999, US President Bill Clinton shakes the international community by announcing the **1999 "National Missile Defense Act" (NMD)**, making it in the policy of the US to deploy, as soon as is technologically possible, a national missile defense system, capable of defending the US territory against ballistic missile attack, whether accidental or deliberate.

Russian President Putin immediately opposes the NMD, claiming that it would constitute a violation of the Treaty on the Limitation of ABM systems, of the interim agreement and of the Protocol on the Limitation of Offensive Strategic Arms.

The NMD testing constitutes a serious infringement of the provisions of the treaties signed between the US and the USSR-Russia in the period going from 1972 to 1997.

On the other hand, the Soviet Union too on developed both active and passive defense measures, to prevent enemy attacks against the Soviet territory.

Soviet developments in the field of active Defense included air and ballistic missile Defense, similarly to the project presented by the United States.

The Soviet Strategic Defense Program (SSDP) included both active and passive defense measures; it provides continuous updating of the ABM system surrounding Moscow, adjustment of the Krasnoyarsk radar for ballistic missile detection and tracking, investments in technology research in the field of laser, kinetic energy and subatomic particle beam weapons, as well as the strengthening of passive defense, which consists of bunkers and physical protection of government members.

These defense measures provide immunity to the country, denying the enemy forces which have survived the first attack, any chance of destroying national targets.

This shows how important global defense is for Moscow, as it's a deep-rooted concept within Soviet doctrine and strategy.

In case of nuclear conflict, the offensive forces' task is to destroy, or cause damage to the enemy's command, control and communications system and to destroy or neutralize the largest possible quantity of the enemy's nuclear weapons.

On the other hand, defense forces have to intercept and destroy the enemy's weapon systems, before they hit their targets, and to protect the Party, the State, military forces and industries.

Therefore the Soviet defense system, apart from having been developed before the American one, also reflects and anticipates the defense model[52] announced by Reagan; nonetheless, the Kremlin never stopped opposing the militarization of outer space.

2.5 Effects of the "Strategic Defense Initiative" on international law.

According to US President Reagan's concept, the Strategic Defense Initiative would have allowed to change the essence of the philosophy of discouragement, previously based on offensive weapons, to defensive weapons; this way it would achieve higher credibility and develop a less dangerous strategic asset than before[53].

Article III of the ABM Treaty states that every party undertakes not to deploy ABM systems or their components except that within two geographical areas: an area surrounding the country's national capital, for government protection purposes; and an intercontinental ballistic missile (ICBM) launch site, so as to grant the survival and retaliatory capacity of the country in case of attack.

The ABM systems deployment areas shall have a radius of maximum 150 km, and may hold no more than one hundred ABM interceptor missiles and one hundred ABM launchers.

The Treaty provides that each Party undertakes not to deploy, outside its national territory, ABM systems (article IX), and that each Party shall use national technical means of verification at its disposal, as surveillance satellites and radars (art. XII).

The Treaty explicitly bars ABM defense systems capable of protecting the entire national territory of both State Parties to the agreement.

Only few days after Reagan's speech, the Soviet Union started declaring that SDI constitutes a violation to the SALT agreements, and, in particular, to the ABM Treaty provisions that prohibit the development, testing, and deployment of space-based ABM systems and ABM components.
The United States responds to the charges by confirming that SDI is totally compatible with ABM obligations[54] on one side, and by referring to the principle of international law sanctioned by the 1969 Vienna Convention on the Law of Treaties on the other[55]. The US accuses the Soviet Union of having infringed the abovementioned Treaties by constructing a new huge radar station in Krasnoyarsk, oriented towards inland regions and by developing a mobile ABM system.
Moreover, the US tries to legitimize the SDI program by insisting on the fact that it be for advanced technology research purposes, and by referring to article VII of the ABM treaty, which explicitly allows for modernization of ABM systems; according to a literal interpretation of the Treaty, though, this faculty should regard only the systems listed in article III[56].
Finally, December 13, 2001, under the Bush administration, the US decided to withdraw from the ABM Treaty. This strategy has often been criticized, since it could lead to a new arms race, involving not only Russia.
China is developing new types of missiles, the Dong Feng 31 and the Dong Feng 41, so as to achieve a credible minimum deterrence. The situation in Asia will become particularly alarming, due to Asian countries like India and Pakistan having nuclear weapons, and other countries which are about to pursue the nuclear option. There is an actual risk of nuclear proliferation, which is a source of instability that will further destabilize one of the most turbulent regions of the world.

An eventual realization of SDI would call into question especially the Outer Space Treaty, which tried to limit military activity in outer space, and to direct the use of this environment for peaceful purposes only. This treaty might not apply in case of laser weapons aiming at the Earth, or of anti-satellite arms since the treaty doesn't consider these types of weapons, which therefore are not prohibited.
Since it is impossible for chemical or laser Earth-based weapons to destroy these missiles, due to their speed, it seems necessary to use X or gamma rays, powered by nuclear explosions generating high-intensity roentgen ray beams; this clearly clashes with the provisions of the "Treaty on principles"[57], which explicitly prohibits to place any nuclear weapons in outer space.

3. Evolution of European Defense policy and the EU Commission's White Paper

The EU has recently realized how important outer space is, and is developing the space applications necessary to achieve its policy goals, such as the GALILEO project (a satellite-navigation and positioning system) and the GMES initiative (for surveillance, environment protection and security purposes).
The GALILEO system, essentially developed for civil, commercial use, will eventually be used for military defense purposes also. Surveillance services, mapping of the Earth's surface and telecommunications security will be necessary, since the European need for security is growing, also with regard to the broader concept of Defense.
The growing challenges in the field of security, and the dual use of space devices, allow us to reflect upon Europe's role in the space sector; on the matter, special attention must be paid to the quick development of the **Common Foreign and Security Policy (CFSP)** and the **European Security and Defense Policy (ESDP)**.
The green paper, prepared by the EU Commission in cooperation with ESA, aims at raising the most important issues and at identifying medium and long term options; comments made by interested parties help

develop an action plan, outlined in the White Paper.
The Green Paper defines the Common Foreign and Security Policy (CFSP) as the policy aiming at providing the EU with the capacity to act and decide autonomously, in sight of a global crisis management approach, including conflict prevention by civil and military means[58].
In the European military space sector there are five telecommunications satellite and three observation satellite programs, each based on own technology, which makes it difficult to achieve interoperability between them[59].
On the other side, technologies for civil and military purposes have many characteristics in common, therefore the European policy aims at combining all means and at developing a wholly European defense and security satellite system.
Obviously the security sector and military users have special needs; therefore it seems necessary to draw up protocols so as to meet the different needs, satisfied by multiple-use technologies.
The European Security and Defense Policy (ESDP) needs a priority access to space systems and services, due to their strategic capabilities and to the decision-making autonomy they provide.
Currently most information used by EU comes from satellites managed at national, bilateral or intergovernmental levels; it is therefore crucial to grant EU long-term access to strategic information, by supporting space infrastructures.
Space services contribute to increase security for citizens, by allowing to efficaciously verify that border and coast restrictions on illegal border-crossers and illicit trade be met; they also favor conflict prevention by keeping potential threats under control, and by identifying humanitarian crises when still in the initial stages.
No member State shall ever have the necessary means to satisfy all space capabilities by itself; therefore, this goal must be achieved through cooperation at EU level, for what regards telecommunications and observation satellites, satellite navigation and positioning, global monitoring and signal intelligence[60].
For what concerns monitoring the Earth, most observations will be carried out by GMES services, with benefit for treaty compliance control, border surveillance, surveillance of sites and installations in critical situations, forecasting and monitoring of eventual EU crisis.
For what concerns signal intelligence, timely alarm and space surveillance, instead, Europe will have to develop tools capable of monitoring electromagnetic activities, of timely detecting missile proliferation activities as well as a space surveillance system, capable of providing the EU with an autonomous capability to detect and identify space objects[61].
The **Global Monitoring for Environment and Security (GMES)** is a joint initiative of the EU Commission and of the European Space Agency[62].
The GMES concept was initiated in 1998 by the EU Commission and a group of Space Agencies, with the aim of integrating institutional, scientific and industrial structures so as to assure consistency in information and to respond to policymakers' growing demands in an independent and reliable way, with regard to new international challenges, which go from environmental monitoring to crisis management, from peace-keeping operations to humanitarian and development aids.
For what concerns the space segment, there are several national or bilateral projects and systems that are currently active, such as: the Italian Cosmo-SkyMed initiative; the UK-German "Infoterra/TerraSar" project, aimed at developing next-generation Earth observation radar satellites; the French Earth observation program called Pleiades; the military observation satellite system called Helios II; and the Spanish Ishtar program. It has been suggested that some of the abovementioned initiatives be developed as part of the Earth Watch program.
At the beginning, the action plan on GMES focused on priorities requesting high-quality information, in particular with regard to climate changes and public health risks, to

grant a more responsible use of natural resources and a better management of territorial assets. On the matter, GMES services meet environmental priorities set by the Sixth environmental action program of the EU on climate change, nature and biodiversity, environment, health and quality of life, natural resources and waste.

Organizations participating in this initiative are the following: Eumetsat, the European Environment Agency, the European Space Agency together with national space agencies, the WEU Satellite Center, Environmental Ministries and Agencies of member States, Eurostat, research organizations, telecommunications and space (EUROSPACE) industries, value-added sectors (EARSC), and civil society organizations, such as NGOs and partnerships with other regions of the world.

GMES means Global Monitoring for Environment and Security: the term "security" appears due to the fact that environmental deterioration and a non-sustainable use of vital resources may lead to potential conflicts. GMES can therefore become an information collection instrument for conflict prevention purposes, in line with the so-called "Petersberg missions", outlined by the European Security and Defense Policy. The Amsterdam Treaty also considers the European need to develop own Earth observation systems to analyze and evaluate potential international crisis situations.

At this stage, the political relevance still regards the capability of providing early warning before embarking upon military intervention. A "serious request ..." was also made "...aiming at providing the EU with strategic knowledge (intelligence) in the future"[63].

The integration of the former WEU Satellite Center into EU is something to keep into account with regard to the GMES initiative's developments.

The GMES Forum was created to support the involvement of the stakeholder community, especially end-users, in the identification of future operational services. The Forum aims at considering current or planned initiatives to rally users and/or suppliers around the different priority applications. The Forum has been a major element of the GMES Initial Period since it formed the platform where a broad range of users, suppliers, and service providers have met.

The initial period (2001-2003) of the program is now over and GMES has currently reached its stage of development and implementation, which will end in 2008. It will be necessary to achieve a core capacity, i.e. the initial set of services and the supporting components needed to deliver these services on an operational basis.

Conclusions

Even though the military aspect of space activities has been known since the beginning of space applications, the use of space systems for military purposes has only recently become widespread.

The US Defense is reorganizing its space structures to favor commercial use also, by developing a new integrated approach between national security and profit; Europe is about to do the same.

This integration involves investments, scientific and technology research and industrial applications, so as to call into question the peaceful use of outer space "carried out for the benefit and in the interest of all countries, irrespective of their degree of economic or scientific development", monopolized by the richest nations.

The issue on how to establish solid legal guarantees for safeguarding peace and security in outer space appears now more relevant than ever: current concerns are more or less those of the past, only now they are more urgent and realistic than before[64].

Analyzing the conflicts which recently took place, we notice how, nowadays, the US and allied countries have to face a totally different situation compared to the Cold War: the enemy is unknown, and the political and military pressure is very high.

The arms race in outer space is currently taking place; this could affect the global strategic balance, cause the militarization on the Earth to increase, hinder the disarmament process and wipe out mutual trust between countries.

The military use of outer space is destined to increase in the future, with the development of new technologies and the increase of operational needs, which will eventually regard outer space also.

It is hard to say how the use of outer space will expand, but what is certain is that it will depend on how conflicts evolve, since conflicts have always been and will always be a part of human history.

The most direct way to safeguard the use of outer space for peaceful purposes is to strengthen multilateral agreements and treaties, through a peaceful and general use of outer space.

This can be achieved by suggesting the development of new treaties, or by updating and revising existing ones, especially now that drawing the line between military space activities, scientific research and commercial applications seems impossible; it is also necessary to grant free circulation of data between non-military users[65].

The analysis carried out shows how militarization constitutes a risk which regards political, institutional, ideological and strategic aspects, as well as local conflicts: only an integrated approach shall keep us on the right track, and allow us to achieve important results in the future.

NOTES

[1] Resolution 1884 of 17 October 1963, also known as the "no bombs in orbit resolution"

[2] CATALANO SGROSSO, "Demilitarisation of Outer Space", Proc. 35th Colloquium on the Law of Outer Space", 1992

[3] BALLARINO-BUSTI, "Diritto aeronautico e spaziale", Milan, 1988. Cf. the stance of US Senator Albert Gore in UN-Doc A/C.1-PV 1289

[4] VINCINEU, "Aspects juridiques de la militarisation de l'espace extra-atmosphèrique », Colloque international sur la militarisation de l'espace extra-atmosphèrique, Bruxelles, 1988, p.44 ; ZWAAN, « The (il)legality of the military use of Outer Space », ibidem, p.303 ; LAKSHMAN, »Prohibition of weaponisation of Outer Space », Proc. 28th Colloquium, on the Law of Outer Space 1985; MENTER, "Peaceful uses of Outer Space and national security", Proc. 25th Colloquium on the Law of Outer Space , 1982

[5] CHRISTOL, "Arms control and disarmament in Space; the rough road to Vienna 1984", Space Policy, 1985; GORBIEL, "Some observations in the juridical essence of the 1967 Treaty's article 4°", Proc.25th Colloquium on the Law of Outer Space, 1982; GAL, "Activities on orbit and celestial bodies: two notions of peaceful purposes?", Proc. 28th Colloquium on the Law of Outer Space, 1985

[6] Article 4, second paragraph of the Treaty on principles: "the moon and other celestial bodies shall be used by all States Parties to the treaty exclusively for peaceful purposes".

[7] CATALANO SGROSSO, "Demilitarisation of Outer Space", Proc.35th Colloquium on the Law of Outer Space, 1992; BALLARINO, "Demilitarizzazione dello Spazio", in "Diritto dello Spazio: recenti sviluppi e prospettive" by Catalano Sgrosso, Rome 13-14 March 1992; GOROVE, "Study in Space Law: its Challenge and Prospects", 1997

[8] GAL, "Military Space Activity in the Light of General International Law", in Proc. 44th Colloquium on the Law of Outer Space 2001; MONSERRAT FILHO, "Total militarization of Space Law: the future of the article 4 of the Outer Space Treaty", Proc.40th Colloquium of Outer Space, 1997.

[9] UN Charter, S. Francisco 26 June 1945.

[10] GOROVE, "Development in Space Law" The Netherlands, Martinus Publishers, 1991. The UN Charter supports this opinion, since it doesn't consider general military activity as illicit, prohibiting only threats to the peace and acts of aggression.

[11] Dual use of satellites = use of the satellite for both military and civil purposes; peaceful purposes = non aggressive activity

[12] PEEBLES , "The Corona project: America's first spy satellites", 1997

[13] The treaty doesn't contain any clear definition of the terms "nuclear weapons" and "weapons of mass destruction" , not even in the article itself.

[14] The Moscow Treaty, signed on August 5, 1963, which is the treaty banning nuclear weapon tests in the atmosphere, in outer space and under water (NTB), entered into force on the 1st of October 1963. By January 1st 2004 it had been ratified by 124 countries and signed by 10. In United Nations Treaties and Principles on Outer Space.

[15] United Nations and Disarmament 1945-1970, UN Department of Political and Security Council Affairs, 1970. The Conference was held for the first time on the 31st of October 1958, with the participation of the US, the USSR and the UK, which aimed at achieving general and total prohibition of nuclear testing.

[16] Italy ratified the Treaty with the law number 1147 of October 12, 1964

[17] The treaty prohibits nuclear explosions in the atmosphere, beyond its limits, including outer space and under water, including territorial waters or high seas, or in any other environment, if they can cause radioactive debris to be present outside the territorial limits of the State under whose jurisdiction or control the explosions were conducted.

[18] "Each of the Parties to this Treaty undertakes furthermore to refrain from causing, encouraging, or in any way participating in, the carrying out of any

nuclear weapon test explosion, or any other nuclear explosion, anywhere which would take place in any of the environments described, or have the effect referred to, in paragraph 1 of this Article".

[19] The Treaty on the non proliferation of nuclear weapons, signed on the 1st of July 1968, entered into force March 5, 1970, and ratified by Italy on April 24, 1975 by law number 131.

[20] Article 6: "Each of the Parties to the Treaty undertakes to pursue negotiations in good faith on effective measures relating to cessation of the nuclear arms race at an early date and to nuclear disarmament, and on a treaty on general and complete disarmament under strict and effective international control."

[21] Known as the "Moon Treaty", signed on the 18th of December 1979, entered into force July 11, 1984. By January 1st 2004 the treaty had been ratified by 11 countries and signed by 5 countries; "United Nations Treaties and Principles on Outer Space", United Nations publications, 2000.

[22] CHRISTOL, "Gathering and dissemination of space-based data in time of armed conflict", Proc. 47th Colloquium on the Law of Outer Space, 2004.

[23] Corona "spy" satellites' real purpose was conducting photographic reconnaissance, but they were publicly included in the NASA "Discoverer" program, which was a cover project.

[24] The Cosmos satellite program, for scientific purposes only, was the cover for the Zenit satellite.

[25] CATALANO SGROSSO, "Aspetti giuridici del telerilevamento", "Diritto dello Spazio: recenti sviluppi e prospettive", by CATALANO SGROSSO, Rome, March 13-14, 1992, p.152.

[26] This definition omits to specify "on this country's territory", which was included in the 4th Aja Convention.

[27] KISS gives a non accurate definition of espionage: "the action of an individual attempting to acquire foreign State secrets, to be used by own country". « Repertoire de la Pratique Francaise en Matière de Droit International », Paris, 1969, Vol.5° p. 94.

[28] HEILBRONNER, "Der Schutz der Luftgrenze in Frieden", Koln, 1972.

[29] Criminal Code, article 256: "any person who acquires confidential information, which must remain confidential, in the interest of state security or anyway in the State's domestic and international political interest, commits information crime, as in obtaining of information regarding State security".

[30] BOURBONNIERE, "Radarsat-2 regulatory issues and international law perspectives on commercial remote sensing and military operations", 44° Colloquium on the Law of Outer Space, 2001, p. 258.

[31] LEE, "Military use of commercial remote sensing data", Proc.44th Colloquium on the Law of Outer Space, 2001.

[32] HELIOS 1 A is a project developed by France (79%), Italy (14%) and Spain (7%).

[33] HELIOS 1 A was launched in helio-synchronous orbit on July 5th, 1995; Helios 1 B in December 1999.

[34] G.U. N°25, 31st of January 2004

[35] Convention for the COSMO-SkyMed program between ASI and SGD/DNA, point 8.

[36] Point 8

[37] Preamble to the Convention, point 9.

[38] article V, paragraph 1 of the agreement

[39] article IX, paragraph 1.

[40] The system operates in the UHF, SHF and EHF/ka bands. It has been active since May 2001, and was launched from Kouros (French Guinea) on February 8, using an Ariane rocket.

[41] BUONGIORNO, "L'importanza militare dello Spazio: difesa e politica spaziale nazionale", RIVISTA MILITARE, N°7/1990

[42] Geostationary orbit = circular orbit having a radius of 36000 km

[43] FRANCESCO IANNUZZELLI, "Satellite SICRAL, Italia in guerra anche dallo Spazio", http://www.peacelink.it/tematiche/disarmo.

[44] NAZZARENO CARDINALI, "Le telecomunicazioni militari nello Spazio", www.adnkronos.com.

[45] GIORGIO RAINO', "Il ruolo dello Spazio nelle strategie militari", RIVISTA MILITARE, n° 2/2002

[46] FEDERICO ZAMPARELLI, "Diritto internazionale e attività militari nello Spazio extra-atmosferico", Rome 1998, p. 163.

[47] Anti-satellite, known as ASAT, Anti-Satellite System

[48] Anti Ballistic Missile (ABM) Treaty, signed between the US and the USSR on the 26th of May 1972, entered into force on the 3rd of October 1972.

[49] This initiative, instead, was presented by US President Reagan during a speech on the 23rd of March 1983. New York Times, March 24, 1983, p. 20.

[50] PRINCE, "SDI: Gamble, Salvation or what?" Defense attaché n° 2, 1987, p. 18

[51] HASHIMOTO, "Missile Defense and International Law", .."In 2002, there are already 46 countries which hold ballistic missiles", 45°Colloquium on the Law of Outer Space, 2002, p. 149.

[52] ZAMPARELLI, "Diritto internazionale e attività militari nello Spazio extra-atmosferico", Rome, 1998, p. 238.

[53] BARTOLUCCI, "Scudo Spaziale: proposta di una strategia antinucleare", Informazioni Difesa, 1984, p. 21.

[54] TITO BALLARINO, "Demilitarizzazione dello Spazio", "Diritto dello Spazio: recenti sviluppi e prospettive", by CATALANO SGROSSO, Rome, March 13-14, 1992, "Also US President Reagan, in his 1983 speech, had declared that SDI was compatible with their obligations".

[55] Article 60, 1st, *inadimplenti non est adimplendum.* .

[56] Article III: "a deployment area having a radius of 150 km, with 100 launchers, and 2 large radars"

[57] CATALANO SGROSSO, "Demilitarisation of Outer Space" in Proc. 35th Colloquium on the Law of Outer Space", 1992, p.330.

[58] Green Paper, May 30th, 2003, p. 24

[59] EUROPEAN COMMUNITIES, "Research for a secure Europe- report of the group of personalities in the field of security research", in www.europa.eu.int, Luxemburg 2004.

[60] V. MONTUORO, "La politica d'intelligence nell'Europa comunitaria", in Informazioni della Difesa 4/2004, p. 26.

[61] A. POLITI, "Perché è necessaria un'intelligence policy europea?", in www.sisde.it, 10 January 1998.

[62] White Paper, EU Commission, Brussels, November 11, 2003, p. 17

[63] (Statement to the EU General Affairs Council, 20.XI.2000)

[64] MONSERRAT FILHO, "Acts of aggression in Outer Space", 44th Colloquium on the Law of Outer Space, 2001, p. 365.

[65] J. W. HEATH, "The vanishing horizon: will the asymmetric battlefield make space-based weapons a reality?", Proc.45th Colloquium on the Law of Outer Space, 2002, p 206.

IAC-06-E6.4.07

THE AMBIT OF THE LAW OF NEUTRALITY AND SPACE SECURITY

Author

Michel Bourbonnière*[*], Department of Justice, Canada
Michel.bourbonniere@pwgsc.gc.ca

ABSTRACT

Superiority within both the air and space medium is presently considered within American military doctrine, to be the crucial first step in the success of any military operation. Although the law of armed conflict structures the legal relationship between belligerents and the civilian population, it is the law of neutrality that structures the legal relationship between belligerent States and non-belligerent States. The importance of the law of neutrality was elaborated upon by the ICJ in its advisory opinion on the legitimacy of nuclear weapons. Space control and the means and methods through which space control can be achieved remain constrained within the legal boundaries established by the international community through both the law of war and the law of neutrality. This paper will examine the origins and effects of the law of neutrality and its application to the US doctrine of space control. The paper will argue that neutral rights and duties in space are a corollary of the theory of space control promoted by US military doctrine. The paper presents two arguments. First, the law of neutrality confers on neutral states protection from belligerent acts such as those either expressed or implied by the doctrine of space control. Second, the international community is presently at a diplomatic stalemate on the question of the weaponization of space. The Conference on Disarmament (CD) is unable to break the diplomatic stalemate, handicapping the UN discussions on the Prevention of an Arms Race in Outer Space (PAROS). The international community has also frequently expressed concern over the weaponization of space. Given the improbability of the development of an effective legal regime to resolve conflicting national priorities concerning the weaponization of space, the law of neutrality remains, if only by default, a primary normative structure in the regulation of the practical effects of space control.

---

* Legal Counsel, Department of Justice, PWGSC, Canada; Prof. of Law, at Royal Military College of Canada, Kingston, Ontario, and at the International Institute of Humanitarian Law, San Remo, Italy; Fellow of the Centre for Hemispheric Defense Studies, National Defense University, Washington, D.C.

The author would like to thank Lt. Col. Andrew Williams USAF for his comments in the preparation of this text. The views, opinions and conclusions expressed in this article are those of the author alone and should not be construed as those of Canada, other individuals, or institutions.

FULL TEXT

Superiority within both the air and space medium are presently considered within American military doctrine to be the crucial first step in the success of any military operation.[1] Space superiority is defined as "the degree of dominance in space of one force over another that permits the conduct of operations by the former and its related land, sea, air, space and special operations forces at a given time and place without prohibitive interference by the opposing forces".[2] United States Air Force (USAF) doctrine adds to this definition by including "the degree of control necessary to employ, maneuver, and engage space forces while denying the same capability to an adversary".[3] The result of space superiority is space control, which in turn is defined by the Department of Defense as "the combat, combat support, and combat service support operations to ensure freedom of action in space for the United States and its allies, and when directed, deny any adversary freedom of action in space".[4] This space control "mission" is achieved through the use of counter-space operations.[5] It is important to note that even though counter-space operations target space assets and capabilities, such operations are not limited to occurring within the space environment and may be conducted anywhere within a multidimensional battle-space.[6] In fact counter-space operations are defined as being "those offensive and defensive operations conducted by air, land, sea, space, special operations and information forces with the objective of gaining and maintaining control of activities conducted in or through the space environment".[7] Offensive counter-space measures aim to preclude an opposing belligerent force from exploiting space to their advantage. The means and methods through which offensive counter-space measures work[8] include both "hard kill" and "soft kill" means and methods.[9] Hard Kill weapons are those, which are designed to physically destroy, either completely, or partially the targeted space assets, thus rendering them useless. Soft kill weapons can be equally effective in precluding the use of a space asset but may simply disable the space asset or alter its function without serious physical impact upon the space asset. Examples of hard kill technology that can operate within the space environment are Directed Energy Weapons (DEW[10]) or Kinetic Energy Weapons (KEW[11]). Examples of soft kill means and methods that can also operate within the space environment include KEW weapons that impair without physically destroying the satellite or that simply change the satellite's orbit, Electro Magnetic Pulse weapons (EMP) that degrade the electronic circuitry of a satellite, lasers which temporarily interfere with a satellite sensor (dazzling), high-powered microwave attacks (HPM) and Electronic Warfare Weapons. It is important to note that satellites are not the only targets of offensive counter-space operations, which may target all aspects of a space asset's architecture such as communication links,[12] including up-links and down-links, ground stations, launch facilities, Command, Control, Communication, computer, Intelligence, Surveillance and Reconnaissance (C4ISR) Systems and

---

1 *Counter-space Operations, Air Force Doctrine Doc.* 2-2.1, 2 Aug. 2004, at 1. (hereinafter: *AFDD* 2-2.1).

2 *Ibid.*, 55.

3 *Id.*

4 U.S. Department of Defense, Joint Chiefs of Staff, Joint Doctrine for Space Operations, *Joint Publication* 3-14 Aug. 9, 2002, at GL-6, available at: www.dtic.mil/doctrine/jpoperationsseriespubs.html (hereinafter: *J.P.* 3-14).

5 For an interesting analysis concerning Rules of Engagement applicable to space military operations *see* R.L. Simerall, "A Space Strategy Imperative: Linking Policy, Force, and Rules of Engagement", 39 *Naval L. Rev.*, 117 (1990). For a detailed analysis on the physics of counterspace operations *see* D. Wright, L. Grego & L. Gronlund, *The Physics of Space Security, A Reference Manual*, published by the American Academy of Arts and Sciences (AAAS), available at: http://www.amacad.org/publications/rulesSpace.aspx (hereinafter: *Physics of Space Security*).

6

7 *AFDD* 2-2.1 *supra* note 1, at 51.

8 "U.S. Air Force counterspace operations are the ways and means by which the Air Force achieves and maintains space superiority"; *id.*

9 *AFDD* 2-2.1 (*supra* note 1) lists five such means *Ibid.*, 31.

10 *See* B. Preston *et. al., Space Weapons Earth Wars Project Air Force* (Rand 2002); *see also* Maj. Gen. (Ret.) D.L. Lamberson *et. al.*, "Whither High-Energy Lasers?", *Air & Space Power J.* (Spring 2004), available at: www.airpower.maxwell.af.mil/airchronicles/apj04/;

.

11 For a description of the technology *see*: http://www.rand.org/pubs/monograph_reports/MR1209/MR1209.appb.pdf;

12 In Sept. 2004 the USAF "fielded its first dedicated OCS capability, the Counter Communications System.. *See* Herbert *supra* note 4, at 5. According to Maj. Ge

even third party providers.[13] Defensive counter-space operations include Camouflage, Concealment and Deception (CC&D), system hardening or shielding, dispersal of space systems, maneuvering and redundancy.[14] From an operational perspective space control comprises four mission areas, these are: surveillance of space, negation, prevention and protection.[15]

I. THE LEGAL MATRIX GOVERNING THE RECOURSE TO THE USE OF FORCE

International law governs the use of force by States. The use of force in space is not an exception to this rule. In fact the primary international treaty governing the activities of States in outer space clearly refers to the international collective security structure within Article III of the 1967 Outer Space Treaty (OST). [16]
The normative deference within OST Article III to international law, the UN Charter[17] and to international peace and security textually launches the law governing both the recourse to force and the law governing the means and methods of the use of force by States into outer space. National security law is thus conventionally present in space.

II. LAW GOVERNING THE USE OF FORCE

The use of force by States is judged twice, firstly, the decision concerning the recourse to force is legally constrained by, customary international law, the UN Charter and the collective security system of the United Nations. This body of law is referred to as *jus ad bellum*. It is comprised mainly of the right to individual and collective self-defense as established in Article 51 of the UN Charter and in customary international law. The United Nations Security Council also has a crucial role to play in determining the legality of the use of force, as its primary function concerns the maintenance of international peace and security.[18]
Secondly, the use of force requires legitimate use of the means and methods as established within a body of law commonly referred to as *jus in bello*. This body of law is composed of customary international law as well as various instruments and is also generally referred to as International Humanitarian Law (IHL), or Law of Armed Conflict (LOAC) and is principally, but not exclusively comprised of the 1907 Hague Conventions, the four 1949 Geneva Conventions and the two 1977 Additional Protocols.[19] Although the applicability of the main space treaties (OST, the 1968 Rescue Agreement,[20] the 1972 Liability Convention,[21] and the 1975 Registration Convention[22]) during an international armed conflict remains a debatable issue, conversely, the applicability of the IHL, or LOAC during an international armed conflict is indisputable.

Furthermore, although IHL structures the legal relationship between warring belligerents and between belligerents and the civilian population, the law of neutrality complements this body of law by structuring the legal relationship between belligerent and non-belligerent States. The importance of the law of neutrality was elaborated upon by the ICJ.[23]

Thus space control and the means and methods through which space control can be achieved remain constrained within the legal boundaries established by the

13 *AFDD* 2-2.1 *supra* note 1, at 33-34.

14 *Ibid*., at 25-26.,

15 M. Perdomo, "United States National Space Security Policy and the Strategic Issues for DOD Space Control", *US Army War College* 3 (18 Mar. 2005), available at: http://www.strategicstudiesinstitute.army.mil/pdffiles/ksil8.pdf

16 Treaty on the Principles Governing the Activities of States in the Exploration and Use of Outer Space, Including the Moon and Other Celestial Bodies, 1967, 720 *U.N.T.S.* 843 (hereinafter: OST).

17 *Can. T.S.* 1945, No. 7.

18 *See* UN Charter, *supra* note 17, Ch. VII, Arts. 39-51.

19

1949, *ibid*., 135; Geneva Convention Relative to the Protection of Civilian Persons in time of War 1949, 75 *ibid*., 287; Protocol Additional to the Geneva Conventions of 12 August 1949, and Relating to the Protection of Victims of International Armed Conflicts (Protocol I), 1977, 1125 *U.N.T.S.* 3; Protocol Additional to the Geneva Conventions of 12 August 1949, and Relating to the Protection of Victims of Non-International Armed Conflicts (Protocol II), 1977, 1125 *U.N.T.S.* 609.

20 Agreement on the Rescue of Astronauts, the Return of Astronauts, and the Return of Objects Launched Into Outer Space, 1968, *T.I.A.S.* 6599 (hereinafter: Rescue Agreement).

21 Convention on the International Liability for Damage Caused by Space Objects, 1972, NO. *U.N.T.S.* 187 (hereinafter: Liability Convention).

22 Convention on Registration of Objects Launched Into Outer Space, 1975, 1023 *U.N.T.S.* 15 (hereinafter: Registration Convention).

23 *Ibid*., para. 89.

international community through IHL or LOAC and the laws of neutrality, irrespective of the jus ad bellum issues.

III. EFFECT OF NEUTRALITY

The laws of neutrality have a limiting effect on armed conflicts. This effect is multi-dimensional for both belligerents and neutrals. First, neutrality limits the geographical scope of an armed conflict. Consequently, belligerents may not exercise belligerent rights within the territory of neutral States, which includes vessels, aircraft, and space assets listed on their registry.[24] Second, and as a corollary to the first premise, neutrality helps to reduce the number of States, which participate in a conflict. The limitation of the number of participants in a conflict is a direct consequence of the duty of belligerents to respect the sovereign rights of States that decide not to participate in an armed conflict. The scope of the duty to respect the sovereign rights of a State applies to both respect for the territorial integrity of the neutral State and to the exercise of the sovereign rights of the neutral States within international spaces. The standard of the duty to respect the sovereign rights of neutral States is high. As Justice Fleischhauer stated in his separate opinion in the *Nuclear Weapons Case*: "...the respect for the neutrality of States not participating in an armed conflict is a key element of orderly relations between States".[25]

24 "The territory of neutral Powers is inviolable": Art. 1, Hague Convention (V) Respecting the Rights and Duties of Neutral Powers and Persons in Case of War on Land (hereinafter: Hague Convention V), repr. in *Documents on the Laws of War* 87 (A. Roberts & R. Geulff eds., 3rd ed., 2000). In the *Nuclear Weapons Case* (*supra* note 25), Shahabuddeen J., within his Dissenting Opinion correctly points out that the term "inviolable" is not defined within the Hague Convention V and argues for a broad interpretation of the concept, not limiting the concept to belligerent acts occurring physically within the territory of a State but including "trail Smelter type of situation" where a State "suffers substantial physical effects of acts of war carried out elsewhere". Shahabuddeen J. then completes his argumentation proffering: "The 1907 Hague principle that the territory of a neutral State is inviolable would lose much of its meaning if in such a case it was not considered to be breached"; *ibid.*, sec. 4, at 10. Neutral territory includes all national waters and airspace, *i.e.*, land, internal waters, territorial seas, and archipelagic waters as well as the airspace above them; *see* M.N. Schmitt & J. Ashley III, "The Law of the Sea and Naval Operations", 42 *Air Force L. Rev.* 119, at 139 (1997).

25 *Nuclear Weapons Case*, *supra* note 25, Separate Opinion of Fleischhauer J., para. 2.

A. History of Neutrality

The concept of neutrality can easily be traced to antiquity.[26] International normative instruments on neutrality are, however, relatively more recent. The principal instruments dealing with neutrality and war were drafted at the onset of the 20th century. These are the 1907 Hague Convention V Respecting the Rights and Duties of Neutral Powers in Case of War on Land[27] and the 1907 Hague Convention No. XIII Concerning the Rights and Duties of Neutral Powers in Naval War.[28] From these treaties one can deduce a legalistic concept of neutrality, namely "the legal position of states which do not actively participate in a given armed conflict".[29] Furthermore, as Oppenheim wrote: "Neutrality may be defined as the attitude of impartiality adopted by third States towards belligerents and recognized by belligerents, such attitude creating rights and duties

26 *See* P. Constantineau, *La Doctrine classique de la Politique Etrangere* (1998); R.A. Bauslaugh, *The Concept of Neutrality in Classical Greece* (1991); D.J. Bederman, *International Law in Antiquity* (2001). Some publicists argue that the legal concept of neutrality emerged later in the middle Ages. For an interesting discussion on this polemic *see* G. Politakis, *Modern Aspects of the Laws of Naval Warfare and Maritime Neutrality* 348 (1999).

27 *Supra* note 27. According to Roberts & Guelff (*supra* note 27), at the time of its adoption Hague V was considered to be declaratory of customary international law. The "general participation" Article is now obsolete.

28 Repr. in *Documents on the Laws of War, supra* note 27, at 127 (hereinafter: Hague Convention No. XIII). According to Roberts & Guelff, *ibid.*, at the time of its adoption Hague XIII was considered to be declaratory of customary international law. The "general participation" Art. 28 is consequently obsolete. The Hague Conventions are considered to represent customary international law, even jus cogens Nuclear Weapons Case (supra note 25).

29 According to Roberts & Guelff, *supra* note 27, this legalistic form of neutrality is to be "distinguished from other uses of the term, for example to describe the permanent status of a State neutralised by special treaty. In this latter case, particular duties arise in peace as well as in war, and the state may have a treaty obligation to remain neutral"; *ibid.*, 85. The *San Remo Manual on International Law Applicable to Armed Conflicts at Sea* (L. Doswald-Beck ed., 1995) defines "neutral" as "any State not party to the conflict" (at 13). For thorough discussion on the origins of neutrality *see Neutrality Changing Concepts and Practices* (A.T. Leonhard ed., 1988).

between the impartial States and the belligerents".[30] Neutrality is thus a reciprocal concept engendering both duties and rights on the part of both belligerents and neutral States.

B. *Juridical Status of Neutrality*

It has been argued that the neutrality of States exists merely by virtue of not participating in a war. Once a state of war was declared, neutrality need not be declared: [31]

The question of whether neutrality can still exist within an international system of collective security has been the subject of discussion by publicists since the days of the League of Nations.[32] They generally agree that collective security as structured within the UN Charter precludes States from establishing the juridical status of neutrality *vis-à-vis* an international armed conflict. The concept of neutrality is thus seen as antithetical to the premise of collective security. The argument is based on the application of Articles 2(5), 25 and 39 of the UN Charter. Publicists also generally agree that modern conflicts do not necessarily fit within the security paradigms established within Articles 2(5) 25 and 39 of the UN Charter. Indeed conflicts may arise where the UN does not take a position on determining the identity of the aggressor. An example of such a conflict is the Iran-Iraq War. Another example of silence of the Security Council on the legitimacy of the use of force by States was the NATO intervention in Kosovo. Contextually speaking, in conflicts where public actors decide to use force in a manner, which is outside the strict paradigms of the UN collective security system, the law of neutrality is revived and is once again pertinent to international legal order. Within this context, the argument advanced by Oppenheim[33] remains valid and in accordance with the customary international law of neutrality where any State that does not take part in the armed conflict automatically benefits from neutrality *vis-à-vis* the belligerent States and must respect the rights and exercise duties related to this status. Furthermore, and *a fortiori,* Articles 39 and 25 of the UN Charter have never been applied concurrently. Thus Security Council decisions to use force have been drafted in a manner, which leaves States the option to not participate in a conflict and to remain neutral.[34] In addition treaties subsequent to the UN charter have recognized the existence of neutrality within armed conflicts. As commentators have pointed out, the Geneva Conventions of 1949 quickly signaled the survival of neutrality despite the UN Charter, by specifically restricting the rights of neutral States.[35] Historically, neutrality was contingent upon a declaration of war being issued by belligerent States in accordance with the third Hague Convention of 1907.[36] Article 2(4) of the UN Charter has rendered the legal requirement for a declaration of war inoperative. Within the UN Charter security system there are aggressor States and those that use force for individual or collective self-defense. International armed conflicts now occur in a wide variety of contexts that are often very difficult to categorize. Practically speaking, neutrality is more correctly described as being contingent on the occurrence of a state of generalized hostilities.[37]

C. *Raison d'Être of Neutrality*

Although laws concerning neutrality have a humane effect by limiting armed conflict, their *raison d'être* is contingent upon historically variable paradigms. In antiquity, neutrality was primarily concerned with the security of city-States. The development of maritime neutrality as seen in the *Consolado Del Mare*, published in 1494, the French marine ordinances of 1543 and 1584, or the Rule of 1756,[38] represented the concerns of a

---

30 L. Oppenheim 2 *International Law* 653 (7th ed., by H. Lauterpacht, 1963).

31 *Ibid.*, 653-54.

32 *See* F. Deak, "Neutrality Revisited", in T*ransnational Law in a Changing Society – Essays in Honor of Philip C. Jessup* 137-54 (W. Friedman, L. Henkin, & O. Lissitzyn eds., 1972); *see also* L. Henkin, "Force, Intervention, and Neutrality in Contemporary International Law", 57 *Am. Soc'y Int'l L. Proc.* 147 (1963).

33 Oppenheim, *supra* note 33.

34 On this point *see* P.M. Norton, "Between the Ideology and the Reality: The Shadow of the Law of Neutrality", 17 *Harv. Int'l L. J.* 249 (1976).

35 *Ibid.*, at 254; Deak, *supra* note 35, at 144.

36 For an interesting comment on the topic of the effects and requirements of a formal declaration of war *see* "Effects of a Formal Declaration of War: U.S. Defense Department Statement", in 5 *I.L.M.* 791 (1966). For an interesting pre-Charter analysis *see* C. Eagleton, "Form and Function of the Declaration of War", 32 *A.J.I.L.* 19 (1938); F.R. Black, "The Declaration of War", 61 *Am. L. R.* 410 (1927).

37 This position is cogently argued by G.C. Petrochilos, "The Relevance of the Concept of War and Armed Conflict to the Law of Neutrality", 31 *Vand. J. Transnat'l L.* 575 (1998).

38 Politakis, *supra* note 29, at 352-57.

different era primarily motivated by commercial interests and the desire of States to protect them.[39] In studying the history and *raison d'être* of the laws of neutrality one commentator astutely pointed out the pragmatic origins of neutrality, stating that "laws of neutrality probably had their sources in the practical ability of non-participants in a war to insist on certain rights and on the corresponding practical ability of belligerents to impose some duties".[40] Other publicists have linked the development of neutrality with the development of international trade[41].

The same logic should now be applied to space military activities for two reasons. First, in a manner similar to the high seas, space is widely used by public and private entities for civil, commercial and military operations. Simply put, within our information-based society and global economy, space assets are an important link in the information, commercial and security pipelines. This makes the application of the law of neutrality in space necessary for the maintenance of the global public order.

IV. SPACE CONTROL AND NEUTRALITY

It can cogently be argued that neutrality rights and duties in space are a corollary of the theory of space control promoted by US military doctrine. There are two reasons for this. First, the law of neutrality confers on neutral States protection from belligerent acts such as those either expressed or implied by the doctrine of space control.[42] Second, the international community is presently at a diplomatic stalemate on the question of the weaponization of space. The Conference on Disarmament (CD) is unable to break the diplomatic stalemate, handicapping the UN discussions on the Prevention of an Arms Race in Outer Space (PAROS). Further, the international community has frequently expressed concern over the weaponization of space.[43] Given the improbability of the development of an effective legal regime to resolve conflicting national priorities concerning the weaponization of space, the law of neutrality remains, if only by default, a primary norm in the regulation of the practical effects of space control. The importance of neutrality in space is implicitly recognized in US military doctrine, which advocates targeting neutral commercial space assets, should these be inadvertently used in an international armed conflict. It is argued that the use of neutral commercial space assets indirectly in support of an adversary's military activities renders these assets legitimate military objectives, subject to attack even preemptively.[44] This is a serious warning to neutral States to develop the legal and technical capacity to maintain the neutrality of their space assets during an international armed conflict.

Although not expressly stated within AFDD 2-2.1,[45] a belligerent must respect the neutrality of a non-belligerent in space. The international legal order obliges a State, which exercises space control as advocated within the said doctrine to respect the right of neutral States to access space and the ensuing freedom of navigation in space. This is an important factor in space control, restraining both the targeting process and possible collateral damage that could result from attacking military objectives in space. During the exercise of space control, the question that needs to be asked is, does the weapon or its effects respect the sovereign rights of neutrals in outer space?

The risk of damaging or destroying neutral space assets requires a definition of a neutral satellite. The law concerning maritime neutrality can perhaps help in establishing such a definition. The San Remo Manual on International Law Applicable to Armed Conflicts at Sea[46] defines a neutral ship as any ship from a nation not party to a conflict. Nonetheless, the nationality of ships differs from the "nationality" of satellites. The determination of the neutral status of a satellite in international law is problematical. First, there is no text in international legal instruments that defines a neutral satellite. Secondly the normative structure within the

---

39 E. David argues: "Le fondement de la neutralite est cependant beaucoup moin humanitaire que commercial et ce n'est pas par hazard si, datan de l'antiquite, l'institition ne se developpe qu'au XIX siecle..."; *Principes de Droit des Conflits Armés* 17 (1999).

40 H.J. Taubenfeld, "International Actions and Neutrality", 57 *A.J.I.L.* 377 (1953).

41 *Documents on the Laws of War*, *supra* note 27, at 85.

42 The applicability of the law of neutrality is practically omitted from *AFDD* 2-2.1 *supra* note 1.

43 For a such expression of concern on the importance of preventing an arms race in space *see*: UN G.A. Res. 58/37, 17 Dec. 2003, adopted by a recorded vote of 113 in favour to 3 against (Federated States of Micronesia, Israel, United States), with 56 abstentions, online: United Nations.

44 *AFDD* 2-2.1, *supra* note 1, at 31.

45 *Supra* note 1.

46 *Supra* note 32.

major space law instruments compound the difficulty by dissociating the concepts of a State's "jurisdiction and control" of a satellite (Article VIII OST) from the State's international liability for national activities in outer space (Article VI OST)

Evidence of jurisdiction and control is established through the Registration Convention, which limits registration to Launching States. [47] Pursuant to Article III of the Registration Convention, the UN Secretary General maintains a register, which indicates, amongst various data the name of the launching State or States and the general function of the space object. Neither the OST nor the Registration Convention provides a mechanism, which allows for the transfer of the jurisdiction and control of a satellite to a non-launching State[48]. Considering that the ownership of a satellite can be transferred while in space, a satellite can conceivably be under the theoretical "jurisdiction and control" of a state while being owned and operated by nationals of a different state. State practice on this issue varies.[49] This discrepancy significantly increases the difficulty in determining the legal status of a targeted satellite as being an asset of either a belligerent or neutral state. This normative dilemma could result in the space treaties becoming irrelevant in the determination of the legal status of a satellite during an international armed conflict. The U.N.G.A. recently expressed its concern over current diverging State practices regarding on orbit transfer of ownership of space objects, recommending the enactment and implementation of national laws providing continuing supervision of space activities.[50] A harmonization of state practice on this issue would increase space security. Furthermore, a protocol to the Registration Convention could address this issue and further strengthen the impact of the Registration Convention on space security.

A. *Practical Applications*

The 1907 Hague Convention No. V[51] establishes in Article 8 that a Neutral Power is not called upon to forbid or restrict the use on behalf of the belligerents of Telegraph or Telephone cables or wireless telegraphy apparatus belonging to companies or private individuals. Although not originally intended to apply to space assets, the interpretation of the norm can evolve to become applicable to satellite telecommunications. Thus the use of a neutral telecommunication satellite by a belligerent would not necessarily be a violation of the duties of a neutral State. Article 40 of the 1923 Hague Rules also states "Belligerent military aircraft are forbidden to enter the Jurisdiction of a neutral state".[52] Although strictly speaking this paradigm cannot easily be transposed to apply to space assets and their applications, from a space law conceptual perspective the use of the word "jurisdiction" is nonetheless very interesting. Considering that sovereign territory in outer space does not exist but that States have "jurisdiction and control" over their space assets, by transposing the Hague Rules paradigm involving the use of the term "jurisdiction", interference with the national jurisdiction of States in Outer Space could be determined to be a violation of neutral rights.

The international trade of space related services during an armed conflict remain subject to the laws of neutrality. According to Article 7 of Hague Convention No. V[53] a neutral State is not obliged to prevent the export on behalf of belligerent of arms munitions or anything that can be of use to an army. The Hague Convention No. XIII[54] reaffirms this principle within its Article 7. Nonetheless Article 6 of Hague XIII prohibits the supply of war material of any kind in any manner, directly or indirectly, by a neutral State to a belligerent. The supply by a neutral state of earth imaging data to a belligerent, either raw or processed, would then be a violation of neutrality. However the export of data to a belligerent by a private company operating an Earth imaging satellite, which has no government ownership, would fall under Article 7 of Hague XIII and would not necessarily entail a State's violation of its neutral duties. The exception to this rule would be the presence of a UNSC resolution calling for an embargo of such commercial transactions. The sale by a purely private company of earth imaging data either raw or processed and/or the information

47 *Supra* note 24, there can be more than one Launching State.

48 U.N.Docs. ST/SG/SER.E/333 and 334, (Apr. 3, 1998).

49 Bin Cheng, *Space Objects and Their Various Connecting Factors, in* OUTLOOK ON SPACE LAW OVER THE NEXT 30 YEARS 214 (Gabriel Lafferranderie & Daphné Crowther eds., 1997)

50 G.A. Res. 59/115, ¶ 3, U.N. GAOR, 59th Sess., U.N. Doc. A/RES/59/115 (2005)

51 *Supra* note 27.

52 *Documents on the Laws of War*, *supra* note 27, at 139..

53 *Supra* note 27, at 85.

54 *Supra* note 31.

contained therein to a belligerent does however raise other important IHL issues such as that of being a mercenary as defined in additional Protocol II Article 47 or the direct participation in hostilities by civilians with their ensuing consequences. Nonetheless, the trade of Earth imaging data is also closely related to the draft 1923 Hague Rules (First Part) that establish in Article 6.1 that the transmission from a neutral vessel or aircraft, while on the high seas, of any military information intended for a Belligerent's immediate use is to be considered a hostile act. In applying this rule to space based earth imaging it can be cogently argued that the transmission of earth imaging data and/or of the information resulting from the processed data, which has either tactical or strategic value, in real time to a belligerent, is a hostile act. In these circumstances the "neutral" or private space asset violating these norms would then be liable to capture or attack as a legitimate military objective. The acquisition and use of space imagery and space communications is an issue of concern to US military planners and current American policy is to deny enemy access to these.[55]

Neutrality laws also have an impact on the international trade in launch services. Using the Alabama Claims Arbitration[56] logic as codified in Article 8 of Hague XIII, it can be argued that a State must use due diligence to prevent the launch of a satellite from its territory when it has reasonable grounds to believe that the satellite is intended for military use in a conflict within which it is neutral. Similarly a neutral state is bound to employ the means at its disposal to prevent the fitting or arming of a satellite within its territory which it has reason to believe is intended for hostile operation against a belligerent with which it is at peace.

The practical effects of the laws of neutrality upon belligerents is primarily that belligerents must not direct hostilities against a neutral State's space assets.[57] In transposing the paradigm of naval warfare into outer space, one can cogently argue and most would agree that unrestricted warfare against neutral space assets is unlawful.

B. Attacking a Neutral Satellite

The law of naval warfare allows, under certain conditions, belligerent acts against neutral vessels. On this point, the San Remo Manual points out that as a principle neutral vessels cannot be attacked, subject to certain exceptions such as carrying contraband.[58]

Contextually speaking,[59] the nature of space activity is considerably different from maritime trade. Nonetheless, in applying a similar rule to space assets, it can cogently be argued that a satellite of a neutral State cannot be attacked unless the satellite engages in a belligerent act or otherwise makes an effective contribution to the enemy's military action. Consequently, should a neutral space asset be used impermissibly by a belligerent, and should the neutral State be either unwilling or unable to stop the use of its asset, an attack upon the misused asset may be legally justified either under the doctrine of self-help or simply self-defense.[60] Although these two doctrines are very similar, an important difference exists in the conditions precedent to such attack. Under the doctrine of self-help, if time permits, a State should contact the neutral government allowing it time to react and correct the situation. Under the doctrine of self-defense, a State may react immediately to an imminent or ongoing attack originating from a neutral asset.[61]

V. OPERATIVE STANDARD OF SPACE NEUTRALITY

The international law standard applicable by belligerents towards neutral space assets and the latter's corresponding freedom of navigation in space is a primary factor that will determine the efficacy of neutral rights in space. In discussing the respect of neutral rights by belligerents, it is to be noted that in international humanitarian law the term "respect" has a very specific connotation amounting to a stringent duty of care upon belligerents. In fact, within the corpus of international

55 Perdomo, *supra* note 15, at 13.

56 Treaty Between Great Britain and the United States for the amicable settling of All Causes of Difference Between the Two Countries, signed at Washington, 8 May, 1871, Clive Parry (Ed.) The Consolidated Treaty Series (Oceana Publications, Inc, Dobbs Ferry, New York 1977), Vol. 143, p. 145.

57 Dinstein, *supra* note 51, at 99.

58 *San Remo Manual*, *supra* note 32, para. 67.

59 Container shipping presently severely restricts the ability to search ships on the high seas. *See* F.F. Megna, "Time for a Change: Maritime Neutrality in the War in Terror": http://atlas.usafa.af.mil/jscope/JSCOPE04/Megna04.html

60 Schmitt & Ashley, *supra note* 27, at 140.

61 *Ibid.*, at 141.

humanitarian law, the term "respect" is used to create legal protection for a category of individuals or objects, precluding a legitimate attack.[62] Consequently a duty of "respect" of neutral rights within a context of international humanitarian law terminology would presuppose a duty not to attack. It is perhaps more accurate to speak of a duty of "due regard" upon belligerents towards the neutral rights of space faring nations.[63] It has been cogently argued that the use of the standard of "due regard" in the law of naval military operations results from an "accommodation of interests or a balancing of rights and duties that can be summed up in the concept of reasonable use".[64] This argument can easily be transposed to space belligerent operations and to the rights of neutral States in space. Considering that a duty of due regard conventionally exists in outer space through Article IX of the OST a development of the law of space neutrality would strengthen the OST. Again, a Protocol could be added to the OST concerning this issue.

One of the primary difficulties in applying the law of neutrality to space military operations lies in the need to reconcile the law of neutrality and the right of self-defense as set out in Article 51 of the UN Charter. It is interesting to note that neither the UN Charter prohibiting the use of force primarily at Article 2(4) nor the Charter right of self defense is weapon specific.[65] These normative dispositions thus cannot be used to either justify or ban space weapons *per se*. Nonetheless, the argumentation which Justice Fleischhauer adroitly presented concerning the interface between the law of neutrality and the right of self defense in its application to nuclear weapons equally holds true when applied to space weapons. Justice Fleischhauer opined that these two principles were "in sharp contradiction to each other".[66] Although these two fundamental principles of the international legal system do not negate each other their coexistence remains problematic as a conflict of norms of equal standing or value.

The reasoning of the ICJ along with the Separate Opinion of Justice Fleischhauer posits that a violation of the law of neutrality could be breached should the survival of a State be contingent upon such actions.[67] An argument can be made that the threshold permitting the violation of neutral rights in outer space could be set at an equally high level as that established for the use of nuclear weapons on earth. It is to be noted that the ICJ did not limit the scope of its decision to the use of nuclear weapons on Earth. Consequently, the ICJ argument is easily applicable to nuclear space weapons. Nonetheless, considering the variety of the means and methods available to establish space control that may not involve the detonation of a nuclear weapon in space, a more nuanced and reasonable argumentation is perhaps one based on the principles of necessity and proportionality in the recourse to the use of force in space. Most publicists generally agree that an act of self-defense must be necessary and proportional.[68] The reasonableness and degree of violation of neutral rights in space would have to be proportional to the threat of the misuse of the neutral space asset faced by the State invoking the right. Such action should not be taken for a retaliatory or punitive purpose.[69] A space military operation that would affect the rights of neutral States within a geostationary orbit would require greater justification than the unintended consequences affecting a single

62 M.S. McDougal & W.T. Burke, *The Public Order of the Oceans* 51-52 (1962):

63 In applying this principle to naval warfare the *San Remo Manual (supra* note 32) states: "In carrying out operations in areas where neutral States enjoy sovereign rights, jurisdiction, or other rights under general international law, belligerents shall have due regard for the legitimate rights of those neutral States"; *ibid.*, para. 12.

64 J.A. Roach, "The Law of Naval Warfare at the Turn of Two Centuries", 94 *A.J.I.L.* 64, 68 (2000).

65 The ICJ stated in its Advisory Opinion in the *Nuclear Weapons Case* (*supra* note 25) in discussing Arts. 2(4), 42 and 51 of the UN Charter: "These provisions do not refer to specific weapons. *ibid.*, para. 39.

66 *Nuclear Weapons Case, supra* note 25, Separate Opinion of Fleischhauer J., para. 5.

67 *Id..*, para. 5.

1) 68

necessary promptly to secure the permissible purposes", in M.S. McDougal & F.P. Feliciano, *Law and Minimum Public World Order: The Legal Regulation of International Coercion* 217 (1961). In an excellent article Maj. E.S. Waldrop points out that the American SROE defines proportionality in the use of force as "reasonable in intensity, duration, and magnitude to the perceived or demonstrated threat based on all facts known to the commander at the time", in "Integration of Military and Civilian Space Assets: Legal and National Security Implications", 55 *Air Force L. Rev.* 219 (2004

Ibid., at 219-20.

69 Gray, *supra* note 67, at 106, points out the aim of such act must be limited to "halt and repel".

satellite of a neutral country within a different seldom used orbit.[70] Arguably, the creation of space debris resulting from the use of force in space weather as an act of self-defense or self-help, and its corresponding effects upon the rights of neutral States would necessarily be an important variable in determining whether such an act in outer space is proportionate. It is interesting to note that in 2004 the International Space Station and two classified US DOD satellites were forced to maneuver in order to avoid space debris.[71]

VI. THE AMBIT OF SPACE NEUTRALITY

The laws of naval neutrality were created in an effort to maintain international trade during wars. The laws of neutrality specifically addressed the problems caused by naval technology of the time. The challenge at hand is to establish a normative structure relating to both the freedom of neutral navigation in space and the acceptable space commercial activities of neutral States *vis-à-vis* belligerents. In space, current technology does not permit interception, and inspection of space assets. Space security concerns are different than those of naval security and are based on the use of the asset rather than the nature of the cargo it is carrying. Furthermore, space navigation differs considerably from naval navigation. Space assets are less capable of choosing their routes in a manner similar to ships at sea. Space navigation is predicated upon predictable orbital parameters or orbital coordinates. Some satellites, such as those in the crowded geostationary orbit must maintain a fixed position in orbit. Other satellites have more eccentric orbits or even polar sun-synchronous orbits such as Earth imaging satellites. Space weaponry and their corresponding effects differ considerably from naval weapons. The targeting and attack of a space asset can cause considerable havoc to the navigation of other satellites through either space debris or through the radiological effect of the weapon. Seen in this light, an additional cause of concern for neutral States is the effect of the weapon, and not just the targeting of a satellite. Consequently, the rule of due regard for neutral rights in space, becomes a rule affecting weapons and their use more than anything else. Space military operations thus have a distinct variable to factor into the calculus of targeting, namely the duty of due regard towards the rights of neutral States to freedom of use and navigation in outer space.

VII. INCIDENTS OF CONCERN

It is important to remember that the technological capacity to affect space assets is available on the open market. For example GPS jammers may be purchased for $38,000.00 and satellite "noisemakers" can be purchased for 7,500.00.[72] Modern weapon systems generally have a back up inertial guidance system in case of GPS signal jamming but will nonetheless have decreased accuracy from the jamming.[73] The international proliferation of space capable military technology is evidenced by the following occurrences. In 2005 the State of Libya was accused of jamming the broadcast of two satellites, namely Eutelsat's Hotbird[74] and Loral Skynet's Telsat 12. The effect of this jamming was the interruption of the signals from several TV and radio stations. The jamming signals had been identified as originating from Tripoli. There are several issues of concern here.[75] However, from the perspective of both the law of neutrality and the law of armed conflict, an issue of concern is the indirect effect of the Libyan actions, namely the disruption of US military communications in the Mediterranean. This incident demonstrated the possible unintended consequences of radio frequency jamming actions. Such

70 On this point it is important to note as T. Hitchins commented on *AFDD* 2-2.1 (*supra* note 1) that: the Counter-space Operations doctrine itself makes no mention of the dangers of space debris or the need to ensure against unintentional damage caused by its creation Available at: www.CDI.org

71 *See* Herbert, *supra* note 4, at 4. *see Physics of Space Security*, *supra* note 5, at 136.

72 According to Lt. Col. T. Freece, "GPS jamming is a verified adversary tactic"; *see* Herbert *supra* note 4, at 5. *see also*: http://www.f-16.net/f-16_armament_article9.html.

73 C.B. Puckett, "In This Era of Smart Weapons is a State Under an International Obligation to Use Precision-Guided Technology in Armed Conflict", 18 *Emory Int'l L. Rev.* 645, at 715 (2004).

74 *see:* http://www.washingtontimes.com/op-ed/20051215-092213-4859r.htm. and http://www.parliament.the-stationery-office.co.uk/pa/cm200506/cmhansrd/cm051208/text/51208w32.htm

75 According to the ITU Constitution, *supra* note 19, Art. 45, harmful interference with radio communications must be avoided and all States recognize the necessity of taking all practical steps to prevent harmful interference.

unintended consequences can be quite destabilizing, as space is increasingly considered a battleground.[76] Space is no longer considered by the US as a militarily benign environment. The importance of space dominance dictates that US military satellite operators should no longer assume that satellite failures are necessarily the result of equipment malfunction but rather the result of malicious acts of enemies.[77]

It is also reported that Iran in 2003 had succeeded in jamming the uplink to Telstar 12 from its embassy in Cuba.[78] That such an act could emanate from an embassy is an issue of serious legal concern.

A Chinese satellite was also the target of jamming activities in 2005.[79] More specifically on March 13 2005, six transponders on AsiaSat 3S satellite were jammed. Although the point of origin of the jamming remains unknown, the jamming signals could have originated from outside China. This incident also demonstrates that such act may be done not only by States but also by individuals or groups.

It must also be kept in mind that broadcasts of hate radio were an important part of the 1994 Genocide in Rwanda. A cogent argument can be made for a UN Chapter VII action in jamming such broadcasts.[80]

CONCLUSION

In observing the collective security system of the League of Nations, Professor Jessup had commented that a collective security system could benefit from the creation of an intermediate status between belligerents without retaining the classic status of neutrality.[81] Furthermore, Professor Lauterpacht's observation on the topic of neutrality during the era of the League of Nations still holds true today, namely that neutrality "has never been a doctrine with an immutably fixed content"[82] The observations of these two publicists might very well help to develop a contemporary concept of space neutrality embedded within a theory of space security. The concept of space security could encompass both space control and space neutrality creating a dynamic theoretical concept with a practical and justiciable regulatory effect upon international actors.

The law of neutrality remains an important normative corrolary to the doctrine of space control. Neutrality creates an active balance between the conflicting interests of the belligerents and those that wish to remain outside the conflict. As George P. Politakis has commented, "[n]eutrality is certainly not a static point of equilibrium; it is a dynamic power relation".[83] From this perspective, the law of neutrality unmasks the fundamental paradox that permeates the doctrine of space control. In justifying the US doctrine of space control, US military manuals stress, "US space systems are national property afforded the rights of passage through and operations in space without interference".[84] These documents then review the possible consequences that can result from interference with American space assets that is viewed as an infringement of the sovereign rights of the US justifying self-defense measures.[85] Yet neutral satellites also benefit from this same right of passage and operation in space without interference.

The development and clarification of space neutrality norms is a necessary corollary to a doctrine of space control. However for space neutrality to properly evolve, in a similar manner in which naval neutrality evolved, there must be an international synergy combining space policy and capacity to promote, enforce and protect neutral rights in space. The moment appears to be propitious for nations concerned about the weaponization of space to expand their space policy and space power to influence the development of the law of space neutrality and its impact upon space security. Space security can only be enhanced by the determination of clear norms helping belligerents identify neutral space assets and

---

76 According to Gen. L.W. Lord, commander of Air Force Space Command, "military leaders must think of space as a battleground. Indeed combat capabilities provided by advanced orbital systems increasingly are at risk"; *see* Herbert, *supra* note 1, at 1.

77 *See* Herbert, *supra* note 4, at 4-5.

78 http://www.washtimes.com/world/20030715-114937-2635r.htm

79 *See*: http://english.people.com.cn/200507/05/eng20050705_194131.html

80 A.C. Dale, "Countering Hate Messages that Led to Violence: The United Nations' Chapter VII Authority to use Radio Jamming to Halt Incendiary Broadcasts". Vol 11 Duke . Comp. 7 Int'l L. (2001) 109.

81 P.C. Jessup, "Should International Law Recognize an International Status Between Peace and War?", 58 *A.J.I.L.* 98 (1954).

82 Sir E. Lauterpacht, *International Law Being the Collected Papers of Hersch Lauterpacht* (Vol. 5, Disputes, War and Neutrality) 611 (2004).

83 Politakis, *supra* note 29, at 347.

84 Department of Defense Directive No. 3100.10 (July 9, 1999), Art. 4.1.

85 *Ibid.*, Art. 4.2, 4.2.1.

determining the corresponding rights and duties of neutral States.

IAC-06-E6.4.09

The Applicability of the *Jus in Bello* Rules of International Humanitarian Law to The Use of Outer Space

Steven Freeland[1]

Abstract

The Outer Space Treaty confirms that the principles of international law apply to the use and exploration of outer space. Given the development of technology, outer space is more frequently being used during the course of armed conflict, particularly through the use of sophisticated satellite technology, notwithstanding the 'peaceful purposes' provisions of that Treaty. Not only does this give rise to international law issues relating to the use of force, but it also requires an understanding of how and to what extent the international law principles of *jus in bello* – international humanitarian law – also apply to the conduct of these outer space activities. This paper examines a number of specific aspects of the *jus in bello* principles as they relate to the use of outer space. Although international humanitarian law does apply to activities in outer space, the principles may not be specific enough to provide appropriate regulation for the increasingly diverse ways in which outer space could be used during the course of armed conflict. There is therefore a growing need to reach a consensus on additional space law regulation directly applicable to the conduct of armed conflict which may involve the use of space technology.

Introduction

One of the fundamental principles in the *Treaty on Principles Governing the Activities of States in the Exploration and Use of Outer Space, including the Moon and Other Celestial Bodies* (*Outer Space Treaty*)[2] is that activities in the exploration and use of outer space shall be carried out 'in accordance with international law, including the Charter of the United Nations'.[3] One of the primary reasons for the inclusion of this provision was the concern among many States that outer space would become a new arena for international conflict. As Bin Cheng aptly put it, 'outer space brought with it a whole new ball game.'[4] Many of the fundamental principals that formed the basis of the *Outer Space Treaty* were concluded at a time when the world was in the midst of uncertainty and mistrust, largely as a result of the prevailing geopolitical environment of the Cold War. Almost as soon as Sputnik I was launched in October 1957, the international community was concerned about the use of outer space for military purposes, as well as the fear that it could perhaps ultimately be used as a theatre of war. In December 1958, the United Nations emphasised the need 'to avoid the extension of present national rivalries into this new field'.[5]

By 1961, the General Assembly had recommended that international law and the United Nations Charter should apply to 'outer space and celestial bodies'.[6] This was repeated in General Assembly Resolution 1962, which set out a number of important principles that were ultimately embodied in the *Outer Space Treaty.*[7] Specific reference to the United Nations Charter was important, given that the maintenance of international peace and security is the underlying principle of the system established under that instrument.[8] The prohibition on the use of force contained in Article 2(4) of the Charter represents a crucial element in the regulation of international relations and is equally applicable to the use of outer space.[9]

On the other hand, Article 51 of the Charter – which confirms the 'inherent right' of self-defence 'if an armed attack occurs'- is also applicable to the legal regulation of outer space.[10] Under the principles of public international law, this right of self-defence remains subject to express legal limitations – the requirements of necessity and proportionality.[11] In its Advisory Opinion in the *Legality of the Threat or Use of Nuclear Weapons*, the International Court of Justice observed: 'The submission of the exercise of the right of self-defence to the conditions of necessity and proportionality is a rule of customary international law'.[12] Moreover, even where the right of self-defence is lawfully exercised, the State acting in self-defence remains subject to the *jus in bello* principles described below.

The sentiments underlying the United Nations Charter were strengthened further by the restrictions imposed in relation to nuclear weapons and weapons of mass destruction by Article IV of the *Outer Space Treaty*, although, as has been well documented by leading commentators, this provision in and of itself does not represent a complete restriction on the placement of weapons in outer space.[13] Indeed, there have been, from time to time, proposals put forward to amend Article IV in order to enhance these restrictions, but this has not (yet) eventuated.[14]

The 'peaceful purposes' provision set out in Article IV of the *Outer Space Treaty* has been the subject of much analytical discussion as to its scope and meaning. While there is general agreement – but not complete unanimity – among space law commentators that this is directed against 'non-military' rather than merely 'non-aggressive' activities, the reality has, unfortunately, been different. It is undeniable that, in addition to the many commercial and scientific uses, outer space has and continues to be used for an expanding array of military activities. Unless concrete steps are taken to arrest this trend – which will require a significant shift in political will, particularly among the major powers of the world – it is likely that space will increasingly be utilised to further the military and strategic aims of specific countries, particularly as military and space technology continues to evolve and develop.

In this context, if one were to adopt a hard-line pragmatic (and non-legal) view of the current situation, one could suggest that the 'non-military v. non-aggressive' debate is a redundant argument, even though it represents an extremely important issue of interpretation of the strict principles set out in the *Outer Space Treaty*. Indeed, the focus of much discussion now centres (as it should) on issues involving the 'weaponisation' of space – witness the numerous United Nations General Assembly Resolutions on that issue.[15] In one sense, this assumes that the militarization of space is a given, as much as it pains international and space lawyers to admit this. Of course this is highly troubling and flies in the face of the principles of the *Outer Space Treaty*. Yet, it would be naive to ignore the realities – what must be done is, instead, to understand what legal principles currently apply to any military activities in space and what more needs to be done to provide, at least from a regulatory perspective, an appropriate framework to protect humankind from what could otherwise be unimaginable scenarios.

As mentioned above, the rules relating to the legal regulation of the use of force – *jus ad bellum* – apply to the use of outer space, by virtue of Article III of the *Outer Space Treaty*, as well as under customary international law.[16] Much has been written about the application of these principles, which are, of course, extremely important aspects of the use of outer space.[17] However, there are also many other areas of international law that are also highly relevant to the military uses of outer space. This paper looks at some of the specific principles of international humanitarian law – *jus in bello* – that are also applicable.

Jus in Bello – General Principles

The principles of *jus in bello* have emerged over time, as the international community has gradually agreed that there should be certain legal constraints applicable to the conduct of armed conflict. Wars have been with us since time immemorial and it has only been relatively recently that minimum international standards have been developed to regulate *how*, *with what* and *against whom* they could be fought – in effect the rules that have developed are 'intended to limit the terrible effects of war'.[18] Even though 'war' as a concept was declared illegal by the 1928 Pact of Paris,[19] it is evident that armed conflict still continues and has become more complex, particularly given the increasing role of non-State actors. Moreover, the scope for cataclysmic destruction and loss of life has also increased due to the development of sophisticated weaponry, which includes the use of space technology.

The 'laws and customs of war' had its origins in the customary practices of armies on the battlefield and has developed as an important branch of international law.[20] The application of these customary practices was not uniform, and it therefore became evident that more formalized standards were required. A major step forward in the development of the rules of war, which *inter alia* limit the method and means of conducting warfare and also provide for classes of protected persons and protected objects, came with the Brussels Conference of 1874 and, more significantly, The Hague Peace Conferences of 1899 and 1907, which gave rise to some important standard-setting Treaties that are still applicable today.[21] The 1899 Conference concluded that '[t]he right of belligerents to adopt means of injuring the enemy is not unlimited'.[22]

Further Treaties followed, specifying in greater detail the limits of what constituted acceptable behaviour in the context of armed conflict. As an example, those provisions of the Hague Conventions that applied the laws of war to restrict the use of poison or poisoned weapons and asphyxiating gases were further extended by the 1925 Geneva Protocol.[23]

The horrors of the Second World War demonstrated the inadequacy of the existing rules, particularly in relation to the treatment of civilians and non-combatants. The four 1949 Geneva Conventions were concluded to address these issues,[24] and these were strengthened by the Additional Protocols of 1977.[25] There have also been a growing number of other important Treaties that have added to the corpus of international humanitarian law and the rules regulating armed conflict, particularly in relation to restrictions on specific weapons and means of warfare. Among these are several Treaties that relate to the use of outer space, including those limiting the testing of nuclear and other weapons[26] as well as the 1977 Convention on the Prohibition of Military or Any Other Hostile Use of Environmental Modification Techniques (ENMOD),[27] which was the first instrument that dealt with deliberate destruction of the environment during warfare, although it also applies in time of peace.

International humanitarian law is now a well-developed area of international law, covering many aspects of terrestrial warfare. The importance of the obligations arising under international humanitarian law, particularly those contained in The Hague Conventions of 1899 and 1907 and the Geneva Conventions of 1949 and their Additional Protocols of 1977, has recently been reaffirmed by the United Nations Security Council in a landmark resolution relating to the protection of civilians in armed conflict.[28] In addition, the establishment of various national, regional and international mechanisms of justice to enforce these fundamental principles – culminating in the International Criminal Court, the world's first permanent court of its kind - clearly indicates that the international community is determined that those senior officials (both military and political) who breach these norms are to be brought to account.[29]

While there are many principles that have arisen through the evolution of the *jus in bello* principles, it is perhaps pertinent to briefly mention three specific concerns that form the basis of any decision to undertake an act of military engagement. They are the principles of distinction, military objective and proportionality. Each of these is relevant to a consideration of the applicability of the rules of war to the use of outer space.[30]

(a) the principle of distinction - deliberate attacks against civilians and non-combatants are prohibited.[31] In addition, those engaged in armed conflict must not use weapons that are incapable of distinguishing between combatants and non-combatants. These represent fundamental concepts in the conduct of military activities and illustrate the strong linkages between the scope of international humanitarian law and the development of formal legal principles for the human rights of the individual;[32]

(b) the principle of military objective – attacks not directed at a legitimate military target are prohibited. The important issue is the need to distinguish between civilian persons or objects and military objectives - comprising the elements of 'effective contribution to military action' and 'definite military advantage' specified in Article 52 of Additional Protocol I;[33]

(c) the principle of proportionality – even when attacking a legitimate military objective, the extent of military force used and any injury and damage to civilians and civilian property should not be disproportionate to any expected military advantage. This demands an assessment of any potential 'collateral damage' in the case of military action. However, it is often difficult to apply the proportionality principle in practice, given that different people ascribe differing relative 'values' to military advantage *vis-à-vis* civilian injury and damage.[34] One only need recall the Advisory Opinion in the *Legality of the Threat or Use of Nuclear Weapons*, where the International Court of Justice, could not say categorically that the threat or use of nuclear weapons would in every circumstance constitute a violation of international law,[35] while noting that the threat or use of a nuclear weapon should comply with the requirements of international law relating to armed conflict, in particular the principles of international humanitarian law.

The Relevance of *Jus in Bello* Principles to Outer Space

As mentioned above, it is clear that the principles of international humanitarian law, as an integral part of international law, are, in theory, to be regarded as applicable to the use and exploration of outer space. There is no specific 'territorial' limitation to the application of the *jus in bello* principles. The laws and customs of war apply both to the area where the hostilities actually take place, as well as the broader areas that are in some way affected by the hostilities. If, for example, direct military action takes place in one area, but the effects of that action impact on civilians elsewhere, that represents a relevant consideration in deciding whether such action is consistent with the rules of war – for example with the principle of proportionality. As a consequence, any military activity that takes place in outer space will be subject to the *jus in bello* in relation not only to the direct action, but also as to its effects elsewhere, including on Earth.

Having established that these principles can apply to outer space, it is necessary to determine whether this is just an issue of academic curiosity or whether the rules of war are 'relevant' to activities in outer space. The answer, unfortunately, appears to be self-evident. It seems that outer space may well become a region of war in the future. Just as States have been undertaking what might be termed 'passive' military activities in outer space since the advent of space technology, outer space is increasingly being used as part of active engagement in the conduct of armed conflict. Not only is the information gathered from outer space – through, for example, the use of remote satellite technology and communications satellites – used to plan military engagement on Earth, space assets are now used to direct military activity and represent an integral part of the military hardware of the major powers.

It was during the Gulf War in 1990 that the value of space assets to the conduct of war was first utilised to a significant degree – indeed, 'Operation Desert Storm' was regarded as 'the first space war'.[36] It was recognised that the use of space technology would create an 'integrated battle platform' to aid in the implementation of military strategies.[37] Following the attacks of 11 September 2001, the United States Administration issued a landmark policy paper in which it emphasised the need for '[i]nnovation within the armed forces [which] will rest on experimentation with new approaches to warfare, strengthening joint operations, exploiting U.S. intelligence advantages, and taking full advantage of science and technology'.[38] As an integral part of this policy, it was necessary to maintain technological supremacy so as to 'dominate the space dimension of military operations'.[39] This necessitates having 'the ability to defend the homeland, conduct information operations, ensure U.S. access to distant theaters, and protect critical U.S. infrastructure and assets in outer space.'[40]

Ballistic missiles play an increasingly important role in any sophisticated national security structure, and the development of defensive systems 'is both a result of and additional factor driving' a global arms race.[41] In 2001, a commission headed by current United States Secretary of Defense, Donald Rumsfeld, suggested that an 'attack on elements of U.S. space systems during a crisis or conflict should not be considered an improbable act.'[42] The Report went on to (in)famously warn of the possibility of a 'Space Pearl Harbor' – a surprise attack on the space assets of the United States.[43] The European Union has recently identified outer space as 'a key component for its European Defense and Security Policy'.[44] Even for smaller countries such as Australia, the political exigencies of a post-11 September world have significantly altered the landscape of national space policy, which now highlights the military and national security concerns associated with the use of outer space.[45]

In an effort to consolidate its policy of 'space control', the United States has pursued its national missile defence system (NMD), the development and testing of which led to its withdrawal in 2002 from the 1972 *Anti-Ballistic Missile Treaty*.[46] In addition to the advancement of its so-called 'defensive' military utilization of space, the United States has also vigorously pursued its stated goal of space technology superiority. Space technology played an increasingly important role in the military actions by NATO in Serbia and Kosovo in 1999 and by the 'Coalition of the Willing' forces in Afghanistan in 2001. During the invasion of Iraq in 2003, the United States used GPS satellite technology to a significant degree to guide and direct so-called 'smart bombs' to their assigned targets. As this paper is being written (July 2006), there are reports of the delivery of a multi-million dollar package of satellite and laser-guided bombs to Israel by the United States, at a time when hostilities in the Middle East are increasing significantly.[47]

In addition, the advent of China as a major space power – symbolised not only by that country, in 2003, becoming the third country to successfully send a man into space, but also by its ambitious plans for missions both to the Moon and Mars – have given rise to increasing concerns about the use of outer space for strategic purposes not necessarily in keeping with the underlying co-operative principles of the space Treaties. Outer space has in recent times been referred to as the

'Fourth Territory' (alongside land, sea and airspace) – a notion that clearly flies in the face of both the 'common heritage of mankind' and 'non-appropriation' principles that have guided the development of space law.

In this context, several commentators have gone even further and opined that space warfare is, in fact, inevitable and cannot be avoided.[48] If these suggestions turn out to reflect reality, the principles of the laws of war must be applied to any such actions. It is not clear how this should be done in practice and what are the consequences that follow. Given that an important group of space assets used for military purposes are 'dual-use' satellites – which also provide 'civilian' communications, remote sensing, and GPS services – one is drawn to the question of whether and in what circumstances such a satellite can now be regarded a legitimate target of war.

The answer to this question will depend upon a number of fundamental principles of international law. Clearly, the physical destruction of a satellite would constitute a use of force. Apart from a consideration of the principles in the space Treaties, one would have to determine whether such an action represented a legitimate (at law) use of force, with the only possible justification being Article 51 of the United Nations Charter. This issue would be determined by a consideration of the necessity and proportionality – as against the armed attack and threat of further attacks – of the act of self-defence. Even if the action did not violate these *jus ad bellum* principles, one would then need to consider the *jus in bello* principles raised earlier.

Let us assume, for the sake of example, that a combatant takes the view that a dual-use satellite - for example, a communications satellite – represents a legitimate military objective in accordance with the principles outlined above. Even if this were a correct assessment, the principle of proportionality would continue to apply, so that injury and damage to civilians and civilian property should not be disproportionate to any expected military advantage. Moreover, one could argue that, implicit in the principle of distinction is the obligation on the parties to a conflict to take 'all feasible precautions' to protect civilians from the effects of an attack.[49]

One can certainly envisage that the deliberate destruction of such a target, even if it does not result in any immediate civilian casualties, would have a devastating impact on a community, country or even region of the world. Millions of lives and livelihoods could, potentially, be affected, economies destroyed and essential services incapacitated. Obviously, some of the consequences of such an attack may be difficult to foresee, but such action would, one could argue, be regarded at least as reckless. However, there are uncertainties as to whether a 'recklessness' test is applicable in the determination of the proportionality principle.[50]

Indeed, given the unique nature of outer space, the principles under the *jus in bello* – developed as they were largely to regulate *terrestrial* warfare and armed conflict – are probably neither sufficiently specific nor entirely appropriate to military action in outer space. Even though every effort should be made to define the existing principles as clearly as possible, the looseness of some of the fundamental concepts, as well as the resistance they face from certain States[51] – means that more specific rules are required if they are to provide a comprehensive framework to protect outer space from becoming another theatre of warfare.

Concluding Remarks

All of this leads to some quite stark conclusions: firstly, there is an increasing likelihood that outer space will not only be used to facilitate armed conflict (as it already is) but will become a theatre of war. The tendency of the major militarised powers to rely ever increasingly on space technology may spiral a space weapons race, despite the best efforts of the international community. Even though the United States may currently be in a position to claim space superiority, it can only be a matter of time before other space-faring countries – perhaps China and India – will have developed equally sophisticated (and potentially devastating) space weapons technology.

Secondly, the development of such technology and the increasing range of military uses of outer space significantly heighten the dangers of a space war, as frightening as that prospect is. The proliferation of military space assets means that States regard themselves (and their 'opponents') as increasingly dependent upon outer space for the maintenance of their respective security interests. From a military and strategic viewpoint, the disabling or destruction of the space assets used by another country would provide very significant advantages. The fact that it has not happened in the past is no reason to assume that we will never see a space conflict.

Thirdly, it is clear that virtually all of the world's countries are also highly dependent on space technology to maintain and improve their livelihood and standard of living. The non-military uses of space – communications, earth observation, television broadcasting, internet services, navigation and GPS tracking – are vital aspects of any community's survival. At the same time, however, many of the satellites providing these services are now regarded as dual-use, in that they are also utilised for military and strategic purposes. This raises difficult questions about the 'status' of such assets under the rules of war – particularly as to whether they may actually be regarded as legitimate military objectives.

Fourthly, Article III of the *Outer Space Treaty*, which also reflects customary international law, specifies that rules of international law apply to the use and exploration of outer space. These rules include the *jus ad bellum* principles regulating the use of force as well as the *jus in bello* principles that reflect the laws and customs of war. Respect for both of these sets of principles is absolutely vital to the safety and security of humankind, as well as the interests of future generations. In terms of the principles of *jus in bello*, there are some fundamental rules that would apply, in theory, to military action in outer space. However, with the exception of those Treaties that seek to ban the use and testing of certain types of weapons, there are many uncertainties that arise when one seeks to apply these principles to a (at this stage hypothetical) space conflict. The consequences of a space war are potentially so enormous that one cannot be sure as to exactly how these rules - for example, the principle of proportionality - will apply.

Fifthly, if we are to avoid 'grey areas' in the law, it is necessary to develop specific and clear rules and standards that categorically sanction the weaponisation of space, as well as the engagement in any form of conflict in the region of space and against space assets. The *Outer Space Treaty*, as well as the other space Treaties and General Assembly Resolutions, do not currently provide stringent rules nor incentives to prevent an arms race in outer space, let alone conflict in space. This may, therefore, require additional space law regulation directly applicable to armed conflict involving the use of space technology. As part of these new rules, clear definitions need to be developed for concepts such as 'space weapons', 'peaceful purposes' and 'military uses'. Moreover, the fundamental issue of 'where space begins' should be definitively resolved so as to counter any arguments that outer space is, in fact, an area akin to the territory of a State for the purposes of national security.

Lastly and most significantly, in developing these new rules, we need to adhere strictly to the 'collective humanity' principles of space law in order to avoid the possibility of alternate scenarios too frightening to contemplate.

---

[1] Associate Professor of International Law, University of Western Sydney, Australia, Visiting Professor of International Law, University of Copenhagen, Denmark and Visiting Professional at the International Criminal Court, The Hague, The Netherlands. The views expressed in this paper are the author's alone. Email s.freeland@uws.edu.au.

[2] 610 U.N.T.S. 205.

[3] Article III, *Outer Space Treaty*. Article 2 of the *Agreement Governing the Activities of States on the Moon and other Celestial Bodies* (*Moon Agreement*), 1363 U.N.T.S. 3, extends these sentiments by referring to 'the Declaration on Principles of International Law concerning Friendly Relations and Co-operation among States in accordance with the Charter of the United Nations, adopted by the General Assembly on 25 October 1970'.

[4] Bin Cheng, 'The 1967 Outer Space Treaty: Thirtieth Anniversary' (1998) 23:4/5 *Air & Space Law* 157, 158.

[5] United Nations General Assembly Resolution 1348 (XIII), 13 December 1958, preambular paragraph 3.

[6] United Nations General Assembly Resolution 1721 (XVI), 20 December 1961, paragraph 1(a).

[7] United Nations General Assembly Resolution 1962 (XVIII), 13 December 1963, paragraph 4.

[8] 1 U.N.T.S. xvi (892 U.N.T.S. 119). The first 'Purpose' of the United Nations specified in Article 1(1) of the Charter begins with the words: 'To maintain international peace and security ...'

[9] Article 2(4) of the Charter provides: 'All Members shall refrain in their international relations from the threat or use of force against the territorial integrity or political independence of any state, or in any other manner inconsistent with the Purposes of the United Nations.'

[10] Article 51 of the Charter provides *inter alia*: 'Nothing in the present Charter shall impair the inherent right of individual or collective self-defence if an armed attack occurs ...'

[11] See *The Caroline Case* 29 B.F.S.P. 1137-1138; 30 B.F.S.P. 195-196, which also referred to a requirement of immediacy, although this was not mentioned in the recent decision of the International Court of Justice in *Oil Platforms* (*Merits*) (*Iran v. United States*) [2003] ICJ Rep. Judgment of 6 November 2003.

[12] [1996] 1 ICJ Rep. 245, para. 41.

[13] See, for example, Gyula Gál, '"Threat or Use of Force" - Observations to Article 2 of the U.N. Charter and Article III of the Outer Space Treaty' (1989) 17:1 *Journal of Space Law* 54, 57.

[14] See, for example, Vladimir Bogomolov, 'Prevention of an Arms Race in Outer Space: The Deliberations in the Conference on Disarmament in 1993' (1993) 21:2 *Journal of Space Law* 141, 141, where the author refers to a failed Venezuelan proposal to amend Article IV.

[15] Refer to the numerous United Nations General Assembly Resolutions, beginning with Resolution 36/97C, 9 December 1981 and culminating most recently with Resolution 59/65, 12 December 2004, which have been directed towards the 'Prevention of an arms race in outer space.' The political dimensions of this issue in the early 1980s were indicated by a split, along ideological grounds, on the main thrust of these resolutions: see Nandasiri Jasentuliyana, *International Space Law and the United Nations*, 1999, Kluwer Law, The Netherlands, 82.

[16] For a discussion on the customary international law status of specific provisions of the space treaties, see Ricky J Lee and Steven Freeland 'The Crystallisation of General Assembly Space Declarations into Customary International Law' (2003) 46 *Proceedings of the Colloquium on the Law of Outer Space* 122-130.

[17] See, for example, the papers presented in the session 'Legal Implications of Military Uses of Outer Space', (2002) 45 *Proceedings of the Colloquium on the Law of Outer Space* 134-277.

[18] Dissenting Opinion of Judge Koroma in *Legality of the Threat or Use of Nuclear Weapons* [1996] 1 ICJ Rep. 245.

[19] Article I of the *General Treaty for the Renunciation of War* (U.K.T.S. (1929) 29) provides: 'The High Contracting Parties solemnly declare in the names of their respective peoples that they condemn recourse to war for the solution of international controversies, and renounce it as an instrument of national policy in their relations with one another.'

[20] Jean-Marie Henckaerts and Louise Doswald-Beck, *Customary International Humanitarian Law – Volume 1: Rules*, 2005, Cambridge University Press, United Kingdom, xxv.

[21] The 1899 Hague Conventions were: Convention (I) for the Pacific Settlement of International Disputes and Convention (II) with

Respect to the Laws and Customs of War on Land. The 1907 Hague Conventions were Convention (II) for the Pacific Settlement of International Disputes, Convention (III) Relative to the Opening of Hostilities, Convention (IV) Respecting the Laws and Customs of War on Land, Convention (V) Respecting the Rights and Duties of Neutral Powers and Persons in Case of War on Land, Convention (VI) Relating to the Status of Enemy Merchant Ships at the Outbreak of Hostilities, Convention (VII) Relating to the Conversion of Merchant Ships into War-Ships, Convention (VIII) Relative to the Laying of Automatic Submarine Contact Mines, Convention (IX) Concerning Bombardment by Naval Forces in Time of War, Convention (X) for the Adaption to Maritime War of the Principles of the Geneva Convention, Convention (XI) Relative to Certain Restrictions with Regard to the Exercise of the Right of Capture in Naval War and Convention (XIII) Concerning the Rights and Duties of Neutral Powers in Naval War.

[22] 1899 Hague Convention II, [1907] Supp 1 *American Journal of International Law* 129.

[23] Protocol for the Prohibition of the Use in War of Asphyxiating, Poisonous or Other Gases, and of Bacteriological Methods of Warfare, xciv L.N.T.S (1929) 65-74.

[24] Geneva Convention for the Amelioration of the Condition of the Wounded and Sick in Armed Forces in the Field (75 U.N.T.S. 31), Geneva Convention for the Amelioration of the Condition of the Wounded, Sick and Shipwrecked Members of Armed Forces at Sea (75 U.N.T.S. 85), Geneva Convention Relative to the Treatment of Prisoners of War (75 U.N.T.S. 135) and Geneva Convention Relative to the Protection of Civilian Persons in Time of War (75 U.N.T.S. 287).

[25] Protocol I Additional to the Geneva Conventions of August 12, 1949, and relating to the Protection of Victims of International Armed Conflicts (Additional Protocol I), 16 I.L.M. 1391 (1977) and Protocol II Additional to the Geneva Conventions of 12 August 1949 and relating to the Protection of Victims of Non-International Armed Conflicts, adopted on 8 June 1977 by the Diplomatic Conference on the Reaffirmation and Development of International Humanitarian Law applicable in Armed Conflicts, 16 I.L.M. 1442 (1977).

[26] These include the 1963 Treaty Banning Nuclear Weapon Tests in the Atmosphere, in Outer Space and Under Water (480 U.N.T.S. 43), the 1996 Comprehensive Nuclear Test-Ban Treaty (not yet in force) and the 1972 Convention on the Prohibition of the Development, Production and Stockpiling of Bacteriological (Biological) and Toxin Weapons and on their Destruction (in force 26 March 1975).

[27] 16 I.L.M. 88 (1977).

[28] United Nations Security Council Resolution 1674 (2006), 28 April 2006, paragraph 6.

[29] For a description of the powers and operation of the International Criminal Court see, Steven Freeland, 'How Open Should the Door Be?: Declarations by non-States Parties under Article 12(3) of the Rome Statute of the International Criminal Court', forthcoming in (2006) 75:2 *Nordic Journal of International Law*.

[30] Many commentators combine issues of distinction and military objective into a broader principle known as 'discrimination'. This author prefers to differentiate between these two issues so as to emphasize the need to distinguish between civilians and combatants without reference to sometimes subjective considerations as to what constitutes a military target in the context of military advantage.

[31] Article 48 of Additional Protocol I provides *inter alia* that '[i]n order to ensure respect for and protection of the civilian population ... the Parties to a conflict shall at all times distinguish between the civilian population and combatants'

[32] In his Dissenting Opinion in *Legality of the Threat or Use of Nuclear Weapons*, Judge Koroma pointed out that 'both human rights law and international humanitarian law have as their *raison d'être* the protection of the individual as well as the worth and dignity of the human person, both during peacetime or in an armed conflict.' For a discussion of the links between international humanitarian law and international human rights law, see René Provost, *International Human Rights and Humanitarian Law*, 2002, Cambridge University Press, United Kingdom.

[33] Article 52 of Additional Protocol I provides *inter alia* that '[i]n so far as objects are concerned, military objectives are limited to those objects which by their nature, location, purpose or use make an effective contribution to military action and whose total or partial destruction, capture or neutralization, in the circumstances ruling at the time, offers a definite military advantage.'

[34] See, for example, W Fenrick, 'Prosecuting Violations of Combat Limitations' in *Protecting*

Civilians in 21st Century Warfare: Target Selection, Proportionality and Precautionary Measures in Law and Practice, 2001, Red Cross, Netherlands, 82-83.

[35] On this issue the Court was divided equally, with the casting vote of President Bedjaoui deciding the matter: see Article 55(2), Statute of the International Court of Justice.

[36] See Jackson N Maogoto, 'Weaponisation of Outer Space – From Playground to Battleground: Time to Raise Eyebrows', LLM thesis 2006 (copy with author), 46 and the references therein.

[37] Id, 35.

[38] The White House, 'The National Security of the United States of America', September 2002, 30, http://www.whitehouse.gov/nsc/nss.html (accessed 20 July 2006).

[39] See Sa'id Mosteshar, 'Militarization of Outer Space: Legality and Implications for the Future of Space Law' (2004) 47 *Proceedings of the Colloquium on the Law of Outer Space*, footnotes 1 and 2.

[40] See note 38 above.

[41] Regina Hagen and Jürgen Scheffran, 'International Space Law and Space Security – Expectations and Criteria for a Sustainable and Peaceful Use of Outer Space' in Marietta Benkö and Kai-Uwe Schrogl, *Space Law: Current Problems and Perspectives for Future Regulation*, 2005, Eleven International Publishing, The Netherlands, 273, 273.

[42] United States Department of Defense, *Report of the Commission to Assess United States National Security Space Management and Organization*, 11 January 2001, http://www.defenselink.mil/pubs/spaceintro.pdf (accessed 12 March 2006), p.8.

[43] Ibid.

[44] Hagen and Scheffran, note 41 above, 281-282.

[45] For a discussion of Australia's Space Policy, see Steven Freeland, 'Difficulties of Implementing National Space Legislation Exemplified by the Australian Approach' in Stephan Hobe, Bernhard Schmidt-Tedd and Kai-Uwe Schrogl (eds), *'Project 2001 Plus' - Global and European Challenges for Air and Space Law at the Edge of the 21st Century*, 2006, Carl Heymanns Verlag, Köln, 65-92.

[46] *Treaty on the Limitation of Anti-Ballistic Missile Systems (ABM Treaty)*, 26 May 1972, 23 U.S.T. 3435. Article V(1) of the *ABM Treaty* provided that '[e]ach Party undertakes not to develop, test or deploy ABM systems or components which are sea-based, air-based, space-based, or mobile land-based': see also Carl Q Christol, 'International Agreements of Unlimited Duration: The 1972 ABM Treaty', (2002) 45 *Proceedings of the Colloquium on the Law of Outer Space* 134.

[47] 'U.S. Speeds up Bomb Delivery for the Israelis', *The New York Times*, 21 July 2006, http://www.nytimes.com/ (accessed 23 July 2006).

[48] See, for example, Iole M De Angelis, 'Legal and Political Implications of Offensives Actions from and against the Space Segment' (2002) 45 *Proceedings of the Colloquium on the Law of Outer Space* 197.

[49] Henckaerts and Doswald-Beck, note 20 above, 70. There would also be adverse environmental consequences (including significant space debris) that may result from the destruction of a satellite. There are, of course, international environmental law principles that would also be applicable in these circumstances.

[50] For a discussion of the difficulties of applying the proportionality principle in the case of the 'high altitude bombing' during the NATO military action in Serbia and Kosovo in 1999, see Steven Freeland, 'The Bombing of Kosovo and the Milosevic Trial: Reflections on Some Legal Issues' (2002) *Australian International Law Journal* 150, 165-168.

[51] For example, a number of States have entered a reservation to Article 57(2)(a)(iii) of Additional Protocol I, which prohibits the launching of an attack where the incidental loss, injury or damage to civilians and/or civilian objects would be 'excessive in relation to the concrete and direct military advantage anticipated': see also Antonio Cassese, *International Law* (2nd ed), 2005, Oxford University Press, Great Britain, 417-420.

IAC-06-E6.4.11

Legal Status of Double-Uses Satellite Systems

Prof.Gennady P.Zhukov *

Russian People's Friendship University
Moscow, Russia E-mail:g-zhukov@ mtu-net.ru

Abstract.
The main task of this paper is to analyze and to discuss the present binding regime of the legal status of double-uses satellite systems. In particular to outline the urgent need to strength the regime of immunity of satellite systems due to the international terrorism threat. This may be obtained by turning of the appropriate bilateral agreements between the Russian Federation and the USA into multilateral Treaties. Such «immunity» would cover all operating space objects, irrespective of their military or civil designation. This approach is justified taking into consideration that military satellites enhanced international peace and security and had broad advantages as a counter-terrorism means.

1. Refrain from the Threat or Use of Force-jus cogens Principle of Modern International Law

In Outer Space as well as in any other province of mankind international law fixed in the Charter of the United Nations, including the principle which obliges all UN Members to refrain from the threat or use of force in their international relations (p.4 art.2 of the UN Charter).

Thus, according to the fundamental rules of international law, the States are obliged to abstain from any hostile operations when carrying out space activity, to settle their international conflicts and disputes by peaceful means. In particular, it means non-acceptance of any violent interference with the rightful activity of an automatic or manned space object of another country by demolishing or damaging such object, its capturing or displacing from orbit. It is necessary to take into account that the 1967 Outer Space Treaty reconfirmed the applicability of the United Nations General Assembly resolution 110(II)) to outer space passed in November 3 1947, which condemned propaganda designed or is likely to provoke or encourage any threat to the peace, breach of the peace or an act of aggression.

It is useful to remember that the 1979 Moon Agreement contains provisions prohibiting any threat or use of force or any other hostile act or threat of hostile act on the moon. It's likewise prohibited to use the moon in order to commit any such act or to engage in any such threat in relation to the earth, the moon, spacecraft, and personnel of spacecraft or man-made space objects.

2. Bilateral Legal Rules Securing Satellite Systems Immunity

In the time of "cold war" a positive step was made by conclusion of the bilateral Agreements securing satellite systems immunity between the Soviet Union and the United States.

The SALT-1 and SALT-2 Treaties are believed to provide for the immunity of satellites performing verification functions on an arms limitation and disarmament. Other satellites that enjoy immunity are those that perform communication functions directly sanctioned by the Nuclear Accident Agreement of 1971 and the subsequent Agreement on the Prevention of Nuclear War of 1973, as well as the «Hot Line» Treaties

. Russia as a successor of the former Soviet Union and the US strictly fulfils the obligation of these agreements. These agreements requires Parties to notify each other immediately about the signs of interference with their early warning systems or related communication facilities, including those in outer space, if such interference could create a risk of nuclear war; to notify in cases of unauthorized or unpredictable incident connected with a possible detonation of nuclear weapon; about detection of unidentified objects by their early warning systems; about missiles launched from the territory of one state in the direction of another.. All mentioned Agreements are of bilateral character (between the Russia and the USA), and in this connection the problem on the right of other countries to similar «inviolability» repeatedly arose After a series of consultations held between the Russia and the USA on May 30 1994 the Agreement on the end of targeting of strategic missiles against each other was signed that practically was realized during 1995. The American and Russian onboard missile computers with divided war heads were switched to the «zero» flight programs (tasks) put into memory of computers together with other real flight programs. In 1995 Great Britain and China also declared about the cease of targeting of the missiles at the territory of Russia and other nuclear powers. The shortcoming of such measure is that it is not subject to the control and can be quickly put on the reverse. Nevertheless, this Agreement has a great political value and is based on mutual confidence. According to the article 51 of the United Nations Charter, each state has the inherent right of individual or collective self-defence if an armed attack takes place against a Member of the United Nations until the Security Council has taken measures necessary to maintain international peace and security. Since the near-Earth outer space is not declared to be eliminated from an act of warfare in case of armed conflict between the States, according to the binding norms of international law including the United Nations Charter, it is necessary to recognize lawfulness of the use of outer space for a retaliatory strike against the State supporting international terrorism in the case of an armed attack on a satellite system as a lawful self-defence measure.

In the agenda of each session of the United Nations General Assembly we may find included the item: «International cooperation in peaceful use of outer space». It is necessary to remark, that the international cooperation on the peaceful use of outer space is out of harmony with the absence of the universal legal rules securing immunity of all Satellite Systems.

3. State Proposals on the Satellite Systems Immunity

From the moment of conclusion of the 1967 Outer Space Treaty the International Community try to reach the uniform understanding on the further measures to be undertaken on the ways of prevention of the use of force in outer space.

The Text of the Draft Treaty on the Prohibition of the Use of Force in Outer Space and from Space Against the Earth was put forward by the former Soviet Union in 1983. Among concrete aspects of securing the inviolable status of satellite systems first of all must be mentioned the proposals on complete prohibition of the Anti-Satellite weapons (ASAT). It is necessary to take into account that the express prohibition on carrying out of the ASAT tests is not provided by the agreements in force.

Under any conditions, the USA will enjoy superiority in space for at least the current decade and relatively few states could become an equal competitor of the USA on any level.. In this situation the vast majority of states would be unequal competitors, while a select number would be unequal adversaries able to develop some means to counter satellite threats.

The unilateral moratorium of the former Soviet Union on the development of the ASAT weapons has been declared in 1983. The Russia as a successor of the former USSR continues to observe this moratorium. The delegation of India to the CD has proposed in 1987 the conclusion of a multilateral agreement, which would transform the de facto moratorium observed by the USSR and the US on the development of ASAT weapons into a universally binding commitment covering both the dismantling of existing systems and the production of new ones The idea was supported by a number of developing countries and China. In 1989 Sweden made a proposal on the prohibition of the ASAT systems. The delegations of the Netherlands, Sri-Lanka, Great Britain and Pakistan also expressed the opinion in favour of an inhibitory action or limitation of the ASAT systems.

Attempting to put the problem out of deadlock, many States acted with idea of adoption of partial measures by ensuring «immunity» of the satellite systems. Among them were the Netherlands, Canada, Australia, Argentina, Poland, Hungary, Bulgaria, Germany, France, Great Britain, Japan, Indonesia, Pakistan, Sri-Lanka etc. The problem of inviolability of satellites, or their «immunity» has remained at the level of discussion in the 90s

.Practically speaking the discussions demonstrated that the need to consolidate the efforts against international terrorism, more positive result can be achieved in the field of the confidence-building measures (CBMs) and Space Traffic Management..

4. Transparency Measures

Such measures intended to obtain greater and predictability in prior notification of a space object launch, including prelaunch inspection procedures of satellites.

A number of countries attempted to attract attention to the necessity of taking measures on raising transparency and predictability in space activity and, in particular, on the problems of verification and control[1] In 1989 the French Government came back to its 1978 proposal for the establishment of an International Space Monitoring Agency (ISMA) by offering, in addition, the creation of an International Trajectography Centre (UNITRACE)[2] and Satellite Image Processing Agency (SIPA)[3] In 1993 a similar proposal was made by France with regard to the Centre of Notification about Start of Space Objects and Ballistic Missiles (CNSSOBM). In 1987 the USSR put forward the proposal on creation of an International Space Inspectorate (ISI)[4] to verify the non-deployment of weapons of any kind in outer space followed by the proposal of creation the International Space Monitoring Agency (ISMA)

In 1987 Canada proposed «the PAXSAT Concept»[5] as a verification measure.

5. Traffic Rules

This kind of measures would be used for the establishment of measures to increase the safety of space objects and predictability of space activity, including notification on change of a satellite orbit, rules concerning space debris and space manoeuvres.

.As was emphasized by world known space law experts the freedom of outer space use can only be guaranteed when all users respect this principle with regard to others as well.[6] The space debris pose a threat to all operational space systems {civil, military, double used} since objects in outer space can reach extremely high velocities. It's necessary to note the importance the effort of the COPUOS to develop a document on space debris mitigation using as a basis the technical content of the Interagency Space Debris Coordination Committee (IADC) space debris mitigation guidelines.[7]

6. The Double-Used Satellite Systems against International Terrorism.

At present-day situation the Double-Used Satellite Systems of various functions (early warning, communication, data acquisition, reconnaissance and navigation) were actively used and continue to be used with the purposes of raising efficiency of ground armed forces, especially in the fight against international terrorism and to protect the well-being peoples. In the United States one governmental agency, which has been increasingly engaged in the protection of individuals is the National Geospatial-Intelligence Agency (NGA)[8] At the same time such satellites are not a weapon in the literally sense of that word since they do not create by themselves the threats of armed attack in outer space or from outer space. The double-used satellite systems are not a combat force in itself irrespective of their space activity. They are completely different from such combat units as anti-satellite (ASAT), which are commonly referred to as space weapons based in space or on earth. We agree with the opinion of Dr. Benko that the term "weapon" is used without sufficient clarification since there is no indication as to the question of what could be a weapon in space[9]

Moreover, these satellite systems promote maintaining of stability in the international relations. For these reasons the reconnaissance and data acquisition satellites are effective means used for the verification of the observance by some States of non proliferation of nuclear and other weapons of mass destruction and non violation by them of the appropriate agreements. Such satellite systems must be under international protection as the national technical means of the verification and control. Similar protection is enjoyed by the early warning satellites. With the help of space communication facilities the more reliable operative connection of the statesmen is organized in the strained situations. By this way the probability of making the incorrect retaliatory decisions in critical political situations is reduced. At the same time it's necessary to take into consideration that the activities of the double-used satellite systems are tightly connected with ground armed forces of the States.

NOTES

---

[1] . Prevention of an Arms Race in Outer Space: A Guide to the discussions in the Conference on Desarmament.UNIDIR.NY 1991, p.117-128.

[2] Conference on Disarmaments CD/937, 1989 July 21

[3]. Conference on Disarmaments CD/OS/OW.59,1993 March 12

[4] Conference on Disarmaments CD/PV 428,1987 August 6

[5] Conference on Disarmaments CD/PV 410,1987,April 30

[6]Luboš Perek Ex Facto Sequitur Lex: Facts which Merit Reflection in Space Law in Particular with Regard to Registration and Space Debris Mitigation p.29-46 and Marietta Benkö The Problem of Space Debris A Valid Case Against the Use of Aggressive Military Systems in Outer Space? In essential air and space law SPACE LAW, current problems and perspectives for future regulation ed. by Marietta Benkö and Kai-Uwe Schrogl 2005 Eleven International Publishing p.155-174

[7] Dr.Lubos Perek Current Status of Mitigation Measures on Space Debris In: Bulletin of the European Centre for Space Law №32 May 2006 p.8-10

[8] Carl Q Christol Remote Sensing in the War Against Terrorism in: IISL Proceedings of 48Colloquium on the Law of. Outer Space 2005 p.471

[9] Marietta Benkö The Problem of Space Debris, op.cit, p.167

IAC-06-E6.4.12

INFORMATION WARFARE: THE LEGAL ASPECTS OF USING SATELLITES AND JAMMING TECHNOLOGIES IN PROPAGANDA BATTLES

Mark J. Sundahl*
Cleveland State University, Cleveland-Marshall College of Law
United States
mark.sundahl@law.csuohio.edu

ABSTRACT

This paper examines the right of states to broadcast propaganda by satellite in times of war. In exploring this issue, the author addresses the hypothetical question of whether a state may use DBS technology to broadcast a commercial news program, such as CNN, into an enemy state in wartime as part of a larger campaign to win the support of the civilian population. The author begins by establishing that that the consent of a receiving state is required prior to such broadcasts, whether in peacetime or in times of war. This requirement of "prior consent" is the only restriction of the broadcasting of such news programs since the programs do not rise to the level of illegal war propaganda nor would such broadcasts be prohibited by the international law demanding that outer space be used only for "peaceful purposes." This analysis concludes with the warning that the inviolability of the "prior consent" doctrine may be threatened by the recent adoption by the United States of a more relaxed theory of what measures may be taken under the right of self-defense. Finally, the author takes up the related question regarding the right of states to use jamming technologies to block illegal satellite transmissions.

I. INTRODUCTION

The fundamental question posed in this paper is whether a country has the right in times of war to use free-to-air direct broadcasting satellite (DBS) technology to broadcast commercial news programming, such as CNN, into an enemy state. A state may want to undertake such broadcasts during a defensive war as part of a larger campaign to win the support of the civilian population or at least counteract misinformation promulgated on the ground. The scenario of broadcasting commercial news programs was selected for this analysis because such programming constitutes a mild form of propaganda, as opposed to the more likely illegal forms of propaganda that

* Assistant Professor, Cleveland State University, Cleveland-Marshall College of Law. The author wishes to thank Cleveland-Marshall College of Law for supporting this research. This paper benefited from the able research assistance of Daniel Thiel.

incite sedition or racial hatred. The legalities of broadcasting news programs is less clear than in the case of more extreme war propaganda, and therefore raises more difficult and interesting questions.

II. "PRIOR CONSENT" AND OTHER RESTRICTIONS ON BROADCASTING PROPAGANDA

The legality of DBS broadcasts of commercial news programming hinges on the applicability of certain doctrines of international law including the "prior consent" doctrine, the prohibition of war propaganda, and the requirement that outer space be used for "peaceful purposes." As explained below, the right to broadcast commercial news is in fact limited only by the "prior consent" doctrine.

A. The "Prior Consent" Doctrine

The general rule governing television broadcasting using DBS technology is that the sending state must receive the consent of any receiving state before initiating transmission. This view is based on the fundamental principle of state sovereignty which has been broadly interpreted as granting states the right to control the flow of information across their borders. Although this rule is not recognized as settled law by all nations or scholars, evidence in the forms of international resolutions, declarations, regulations, and state practice almost certainly provides sufficient proof that customary international law requires prior consent.

The primary document supporting the "prior consent" doctrine is the *United Nations General Assembly Resolution on Principles Governing the Use by States of Artificial Earth Satellites for International Direct Television Broadcasting* (Resolution 37/92).[1] Paragraph 14 of Resolution 37/92 provides that "an international direct television broadcasting satellite service shall only be established *after the conditions set forth in Paragraph 13 . . . have been met.*"[2] Paragraph 13, in turn, requires a state intending to initiate DBS broadcasting into another state to "*notify* the proposed receiving State or States of such intention and . . . *promptly enter into consultation* with any of those States which so requests."[3]

The "prior consent" doctrine is expressed even more clearly in Article IX of the 1972 *UNESCO Declaration of Guiding Principles on the Use of Satellite Broadcasting for the Free Flow of Information, the Spread of Education and Cultural Exchange* which requires states to "*reach or promote prior agreements* concerning direct satellite broadcasting to the population of countries other than the country of origin of the transmission."[4]

In addition, the 1978 *UNESCO Declaration on Fundamental Principles Concerning the Contribution of the Mass Media to Strengthening Peace and International Understanding to the Promotion of Human Rights and to Countering Racialism, Apartheid and Incitement to War* (Mass Media

---

[1] Resolution on Principles Governing the Use by States of Artificial Earth Satellites for International Direct Television Broadcasting, G.A. Res. 37/92, U.N. Doc. A/37/646 (1982) [hereinafter, Resolution 37/92).

[2] *Id.* para. 14.

[3] *Id.* para. 13 (emphases added).

[4] UNESCO Declaration of Guiding Principles on the Use of Satellite Broadcasting for the Free Flow of Information, the Spread of Education and Cultural Exchange, art. IX, U.N. Doc. A/C.1/L. 605 (1972) (emphasis added).

Declaration) rejects the unlimited "free flow" approach by calling for a "wider and more balanced dissemination of information."[5] This language has been interpreted by some commentators as permitting international prohibitions on the broadcast of objectionable media.[6]

The regulations issued by the International Telecommunications Union (ITU) also embrace the "prior consent" doctrine by requiring states to "reduce, to the maximum extent practicable, the radiation over the territory of other countries *unless an agreement has been previously reached with such countries*."[7] In addition to this requirement for prior consent, the ITU regulations require that states be capable of immediately ceasing their broadcasts into other states if such states object to the transmission.[8]

The alternative to the "prior consent" approach is the "free flow" doctrine which asserts that a sending state need *not* acquire the consent of a receiving nation prior to broadcasting into that state. Proponents of the "free flow" doctrine point to certain documents which, they claim, indicate an inviolable right of peoples to send and receive information, whether by satellite broadcasts or other means. Proponents of the "free flow" doctrine rely primarily on Article 19 of the *Universal Declaration of Human Rights* which provides that all people have the right "to seek, receive, and impart information and ideas through any media and *regardless of frontiers*."[9] Article 19 of the *International Covenant on Civil and Political Rights* (ICCPR) contains virtually identical language asserting the right of all people to send and receive information across borders.[10]

Although the language of the *Declaration of Human Rights* and the ICCPR celebrating the fundamental right to information appears to give strong support to the "free flow" theory, the doctrine of "prior consent" wins out for two reasons.

First, although a reading of the above-mentioned documents may leave some ambiguity with respect to whether "prior consent" or "free flow" is the governing law, this ambiguity is resolved when state practice is taken into account.[11] The recognition of a

---

5 UNESCO Declaration on Fundamental Principles Concerning the Contribution of the Mass Media to Strengthening Peace and International Understanding to the Promotion of Human Rights and to Countering Racialism, Apartheid and Incitement to War, art. IX, UNESCO Gen. Conf. Res. 4/9.3/2, 20th Sess. (1978), reprinted in ANN. REV. U.N. AFF. 238-40 [hereinafter, Mass Media Declaration].

6 *See, e.g.*, Joel R. Paul, *Images from Abroad: Making Direct Broadcasting by Satellites Safe for Sovereignty*, 9 HASTINGS INT'L & COMP. L. R. 329, 340 (1986).

7 Final Acts of the World Administrative Radio Conference for Space Telecommunications, ITU, Radio Regulations No. 2674 (1971), 23 U.S.T. 1527, T.I.A.S. No. 7435 (1971).

8 *Id.* No. 470V.

9 Universal Declaration of Human Rights, art. 19, U.N. G.A. Res. 217A(III), U.N. Doc. A/811 (1948) (emphasis added). See also Recommendation 2 of the International Telecommunications Union which recommends that "Members of the Union facilitate the unrestricted transmission of news by telecommunication services." Recommendation 2 of the International Telecommunications Union, *Unrestricted Transmission of News and the Right to Communicate* (1994), available at http://www.itu.int/aboutitu/basic-texts/recommendations/recom02.html.

10 International Covenant on Civil and Political Rights, art. 19(2), G.A. Res. 2200A (XXI), 21 U.N. GAOR Supp. (No. 16) at 52, U.N. Doc. A/6316 (1966), 999 U.N.T.S. 171 (1976) [hereinafter, ICCPR].

11 Ambiguities are also present within the individual documents themselves. For example, the preamble to Resolution 37/92 invokes "the

customary international law requires evidence of the widespread and uniform practice of nations that engage in such practices out of a sense of legal obligation, or *opinio iuris.*[12] Although treaties, resolutions, and declarations are good source of evidence regarding customary international law, state practice can provide equally valid evidence.[13] And with respect to the issue of trans-border DBS broadcasting, state practice provides undeniable evidence that customary international law requires "prior consent." Virtually every country (and certainly all developed countries) regulate satellite transmissions into their country by way of rigorous licensing regimes.[14] Even the United States, which has been the strongest proponent of the "free flow" doctrine, regulates satellite transmissions through a rigorous licensing process administered by the Federal Communications Commission.[15] When divining a rule of customary international law, the *opinio iuris* of states carries great weight, and is most clearly expressed by a state's practices. The *opinio iuris* of the United States is undoubtedly that the "prior consent" doctrine governs DBS transmission. Otherwise, why would the United States adopt this approach in its domestic law in the form of license requirements? Once the weight of the United States is thrown behind the "prior consent" doctrine, there is little room left for arguing the "free flow" doctrine.

Second, application of the *lex specialis* rule of treaty interpretation demands that the more specific international law requiring "prior consent" for DBS television broadcasting trumps the more general rule permitting the "free flow" of information across borders. The *lex specialis* maxim states that "special provisions are ordinarily more effective than those that are general."[16] Under the rule of *lex specialis*, since the "prior consent" doctrine is a more specific rule that applies exclusively to satellite broadcasting, it should override the

right of everyone to seek, receive and impart information and ideas" which appears to support the "free flow" doctrine, despite the fact that the resolution takes a "prior consent" approach in its Article 19. Resolution 37/92, *supra* note 1, preamble. For a discussion of internal ambiguities contained in the Mass Media Declaration see Paul, *supra* note 5, at 359.

[12] See Jack L. Goldsmith & Eric A. Posner, *A Theory of Customary International Law*, 66 U. CHI. L. REV. 1113, 1116 (1999) (with citations).

[13] Evidence of customary international law can be found in treaties, international court decisions, domestic court decisions, domestic legislation, state action, and scholarship. See Mariana Mello, *Hagan v. Australia: A Sign of the Emerging Notion of Hate Speech in Customary International Law*, 28 LOY. L.A. INT'L & COMP. L. REV. 365, 368 (2006).

[14] *See* Paul, *supra* note 6, at 347 ("Even a cursory review of actual country practice . . . would indicate that countries do not in fact recognize an asserted right to impart and receive information across national borders.")

[15] For a detailed discussion of United States opposition to the "prior consent" doctrine (in contrast to its state practice) see DAVID I. FISHER, PRIOR CONSENT TO INTERNATIONAL DIRECT SATELLITE BROADCASTING 139 (1990).

[16] *See, e.g.*, Robert Howse & Petros C. Mavroidis, *Europe's Evolving Regulatory Strategy for GMOS – The Issue of Consistency With WTO Law: Of Kine and Brine*, 24 FORDHAM INT'L L.J. 317, 322 (2000) (quoting Grotius). Although the principle of *lex specialis* was not codified in the Vienna Convention on the Law of Treaties, it is widely recognized as a customary international law of treaty interpretation. *See* IAN SINCLAIR, THE VIENNA CONVENTION ON THE LAW OF TREATIES 96 (1984).

general pronouncements regarding the more generalized right to the "free flow" of information.

For the foregoing reasons, international law is likely to require the consent of a receiving state before a sending state can transmit DBS television signals. Of course, under Article 28 of the Statute of the *International Court of Justice*, this customary international law, once established, binds all nations.[17]

B. The Prohibition of War Propaganda

In addition to the requirement of "prior consent," DBS broadcastings could, depending on the content of the transmission, violate the international law prohibiting certain types of propaganda.

There is no international agreement on a definition of propaganda. The most liberal approach defines propaganda as any "systematic attempt through mass communication to influence thinking and behavior."[18] This definition of propaganda would capture even a fact-based news program, such as CNN, provided that it was broadcasted with the intent "to influence thinking and behavior." A more restrictive approach, as adopted by reference in the preamble of the Outer Space Treaty, is found in *United Nations General Assembly Resolution 110 (II)* which condemns "all forms of propaganda, in whatsoever country conducted, which is either designed or likely to provoke or encourage any threat to the peace, breach of the peace, or act of aggression."[19]

Only the latter, hostile type of propaganda is prohibited by international law. This prohibition arises under treaty law as well as international customary law. The 1936 *League of Nations Convention Concerning the Use of Broadcasting in the Cause of Peace* prohibits transmissions that "constitute an incitement either to war . . . or to acts likely to lead thereto."[20] Likewise, Article 20 of ICCPR prohibits "any propaganda for war."[21] Both documents contemplate the inflammatory propaganda that actively provokes war. The ICCPR, in particular, should be interpreted narrowly in light of its original purpose, namely, to prohibit the fascist war propaganda machine used by the Third Reich to promote German wars of aggression.[22] In addition to these explicit treaty prohibitions, it is widely recognized that customary international

---

[17] Statute of the International Court of Justice, art. 38, 59 Stat. 1055 (1945). *See also, e.g.*, Jordan J. Paust, *The Importance of Customary International Law During Armed Conflict*, 12 ILSA J. INT'L & COMP. L. 601, 602 (2006) (explaining that "when a customary norm comes into existence it is universally applicable.")

[18] LESLIE JOHN MARTIN, INTERNATIONAL PROPAGANDA: ITS LEGAL AND DIPLOMATIC CONTROL 12 (1958); *see also* Stephen T. Bayer, *The Legal Aspects of TV Marti in Relation to the Law of Direct Broadcasting Satellites*, 41 EMORY L.J. 541, 550 (1992).

[19] United Nations General Assembly Resolution 110(11)), 1947-48 U.N.Y.B. 93 (1947). The U.N. Committee on the Peaceful Uses of Outer Space (UNCOPUOS) has also defined propaganda as a hostile act intended to provoke war, incite sedition, interfere with the receiving state's internal affairs, slander the receiving state, or violate human rights. *See* U.N. GAOR Committee on the Peaceful Uses of Outer Space, 25th Sess., at 7, U.N. Doc. A/ AC.105/79 (1970).

[20] International Convention Concerning the Use of Broadcasting in the Cause of Peace, art. 2, Sept. 23, 1936, 186 L.N.T.S. 301.

[21] ICCPR, *supra* note 10, art. 20.

[22] *See* CENTRAL EUROPEAN AND EURASIAN LAW INITIATIVE, ICCPR LEGAL IMPLEMENTATION INDEX 140 (2003)

law prohibits war propaganda as well.[23] It can certainly be said that no country objects to such a prohibition.[24]

Since news programs such as CNN do not actively incite war, the DBS transmission of commercial news programs should not be affected by the prohibition against war propaganda.

C. The "Peaceful Purposes" Doctrine

Direct satellite broadcasts in time of war may also be affected by the restrictions on the military use of space contained in the *Treaty on Principles Governing the Activities of States in the Exploration and Use of Outer Space, Including the Moon and Other Celestial Bodies* (Outer Space Treaty) – which is often referred to as the *Magna Carta* of space law.[25] There are two ways to interpret the Outer Space Treaty with respect to the militarization of Earth orbits. One possible interpretation is that the military use of earth's orbit is permitted – with the sole limitation that no nation may place into orbit "any objects carrying nuclear weapons or any other kinds of weapons of mass destruction."[26] This interpretation is founded on a plain language reading of Article IV of the Outer Space Treaty which states that "[t]he Moon and other celestial bodies shall be used by all States Parties to the Treaty exclusively for peaceful purposes."[27] A plain reading of this provision suggests that the "peaceful purpose" requirement applies only to use of the Moon and celestial bodies – but does not apply to other regions of outer space, thus allowing for the militarization of the Earth orbits (with the exception of on-orbit weapons of mass destruction).[28]

An alternative interpretation of the Outer Space Treaty relies on a more expansive reading of the treaty and holds that the "peaceful purpose" doctrine applies to all of outer space, including Earth orbits. This interpretation relies both on customary international law as reflected in the practice of states (which is incorporated into the Outer Space Treaty via Article III which states that the use of outer space shall be carried out "in accordance with international law") and on the language of the preamble to the Outer Space Treaty which emphasizes the "use of outer space for peaceful purposes" in two places.[29] Commentators generally agree that customary international law requires that all of outer space, including earth orbits, be used only for "peaceful purposes."[30]

---

[23] *See* Elizabeth A. Downey, *A Historical Survey of the International Regulation of Propaganda*, in MICHIGAN YEARBOOK OF INTERNATIONAL LEGAL STUDIES: REGULATION OF TRANSNATIONAL COMMUNICATIONS 341 (1984); see also Bayer, *supra* note 18, at 549.

[24] *Id.*

[25] Treaty on Principles Governing the Activities of States in the Exploration and Use of Outer Space, including the Moon and Other Celestial Bodies, 18 U.S.T. 2410, 610 U.N.T.S. 205 (entered into force Oct. 10, 1967) [hereinafter, Outer Space Treaty].

[26] *Id.* art. IV.

[27] *Id.*

[28] *See* GENNADY ZHUKOV & YURI KOLOSOV, INTERNATIONAL SPACE LAW 53 (1984) (arguing that the Outer Space Treaty requires "total neutralization and demilitarization of celestial bodies and [only] partial demilitarization of outer space"); Michel Bourbonniere, *National-Security Law in Outer Space: The Interface of Exploration and Security*, 70 J. AIR L. & COM. 3, 16 (2005)

[29] Outer Space Treaty, *supra* note 25, preamble.

[30] *See, e.g.*, Bourbonniere, *supra* note 28, at 16; Richard A. Morgan, *Military Use of Commercial Communication Satellites: A New Look at the*

How does this "peaceful purposes" requirement affect the use of communications satellites in time of war? Before we answer this, further analysis should be given to the meaning of the phrase "peaceful purposes." There are three basic approaches to the interpretation of the "peaceful purposes" doctrine. Under the first approach, some commentators argue for the absolute demilitarization of outer space.[31] Pursuant to the second approach, the word "peaceful" is treated as equivalent to "non-aggressive," thus allowing the military to use communications satellites for non-tactical support of military operations, such as for communications, navigation, and weather monitoring.[32] The third approach also adopts the "non-aggressive" definition of "peaceful," but applies a broader interpretation which allows for the use of space assets, including satellites, for any action taken in accordance with the UN Charter, thus allowing full military use of space for purpose of self-defense or as ordered by the UN Security Council.[33]

Only under the first approach to the "peaceful purposes" doctrine might a state's DBS broadcasting of commercial news be restricted since this strict interpretation may be taken so far as to prohibit any use of space assets by the military, even if such use occurs in peacetime and is not related to a military strike.[34] However, this would require the broadcast to be characterized as a military operation, which may not be easily determined. Moreover, since this strict interpretation requiring the total demilitarization of space does not find wide support, it is unlikely to create a bar to DBS broadcasting of a news program. Under the second approach, the use of satellites to broadcast news, even if part of a broader campaign to achieve a military victory, is likely to be deemed permissible since it is more akin to a non-tactical support activity in light of the fact that it bears no relation to a military strike. Finally, under the third approach DBS news broadcasts would be permissible even if deemed to be part of a tactical military operation, provided that the broadcast was part of a military

---

Outer Space Treaty and "Peaceful Purposes", 60 J. AIR L. & COM. 237, 242 (1994) (explaining that "[s]upport for the conclusion that current international law requires all of outer space to be used for "peaceful purposes" is compelling.").

31 See, e.g., Ricky Lee, *Reconciling International Space Law with the Commercial Realities of the Twenty-First Century*, 4 SING. J. INT'L & COMP. L. 194, 214 (2000) ("[T]he United States would . . . not to undertake a new obligation involving the full demilitarisation of space. This interpretation is contrary to existing interpretations that are found in international law.")

32 *See, e.g.*, Robert L. Bridge, *International Law and Military Activities In Outer Space*, 13 AKRON L. REV. 649, 658 (1979). This interpretation of the "peaceful purposes" doctrine relies heavily on the language of the UN Charter which states as its overarching goal "international peace and security," but at the time allows for military action to "suppress acts of aggression." Charter of the United Nations, art. 1, 59 Stat. 1031, T.S. No. 993 (1945) [hereinafter, UN Charter].

33 This third approach reflects the principle stated in Resolution 3314 of the UN General Assembly which provides that "[a]ggression is the use of armed force by a State against the sovereignty, territorial integrity or political independence of another State, or in any other manner inconsistent with the Charter of the United Nations." United Nations General Assembly Resolution 3314 (XXIX): Definition of Aggression, art. I, G.A. Res. 3314, U.N. GAOR, 29th Sess., Supp. No. 31, U.N. Doc. A/9631 (Dec. 14, 1974). For a recent detailed discussion of various approaches to the "peaceful purposes" doctrine see Morgan, *supra* note 30.

34 *See, e.g.*, Lee, *supra* note 31, at 215.

campaign that was justified under the UN Charter.

D. Preliminary Conclusion: The "Prior Consent" Doctrine is the Only Restriction on the DBS Broadcasting of Commercial News Programs

In light of the foregoing, the DBS transmission of news programs should not be banned by either the prohibition against war propaganda or the "peaceful purposes" doctrine. Therefore, the "prior consent" doctrine is the only restriction on broadcasting commercial news programs, such as CNN, into an enemy state in time of war. This brings us to the final question addressed in this paper, namely, whether the right to self-defense can excuse a state from having to comply with the "prior consent" requirement in times of war.

III. "PRIOR CONSENT" IN TIMES OF WAR

Having established that the "prior consent" requirement applies to DBS satellite broadcasts of commercial news under our hypothetical scenario, the final question now presents itself: *can a state invoke the right of self-defense as a basis for refusing to comply with the "prior consent" doctrine in times of war?*[35]

The right of a state to act in self-defense is based on customary international law and is recognized in Article 51 of the UN Charter which states that "[n]othing in the present Charter shall impair the inherent right of individual or collective self-defence if an armed attack occurs."[36] Under customary international law, the right of self-defense permits a state to respond to an armed attack with "measures which are *proportional* to the armed attack and *necessary* to respond to it."[37] Therefore, a state would only be able to bypass the "prior consent" requirement if broadcasting into the enemy state was "necessary" for its defense. It is unlikely that a state could successfully make this argument in the context of the classical theory of self-defense which assumes that actions taken in self-defense are necessary in order to respond to an immediate threat. The broadcasting of a news program would not provide much protection against an immediate military threat. However, some nations have adopted a more liberal view which allows for anticipatory self-defense in the face of an imminent threat.[38] Moreover, in response to the growing threat of terrorism, the United States has further relaxed its understanding of the doctrine of self-defense to allow for military action to guard against a "continuing threat" even when no strike is known to be imminent.[39] It is under this "continuing threat" theory of self-defense that the "prior consent" requirement could, arguably, be set aside if DBS broadcasting of commercial news programs were deemed to be a necessary measure for the nullification

[35] It is assumed for purposes of the present discussion that the international law prohibiting broadcast without prior consent would continue in times of war. For further discussion regarding this issue see LaToya Tate, *The Status of the Outer Space Treaty at International Law During "War" and "Those Measures Short of War"*, 32 J. SPACE L. 177 (2006)

[36] UN Charter, *supra* note 32, art. 51.

[37] *Nicaragua v. United States of America*, 1986 I.C.J. 14 (emphasis added).

[38] *See, e.g.*, Howard A. Wachtel, *Targeting Osama Bin Laden: Examining the Legality of Assassination as a Tool of U.S. Foreign Policy*, 55 DUKE L.J. 677, 691-92 (2005).

[39] *Id.*

of a continuing terrorist threat. This argument of necessity could conceivably be based on the idea that force alone cannot defeat terrorism, but must be coupled with the free flow of information that can counteract misinformation and dispel the cultural misunderstandings that foster extremism.

IV. THE RIGHT TO JAM ILLEGAL SATELLITE TRANSMISSIONS

The question regarding the right of a state to broadcast satellite television is only part of a greater debate. The complementary issue is whether, and to what extent, a state has the right to jam satellite television transmissions.

As was true regarding the right to broadcast, there are two main schools of thought regarding jamming. Some argue that jamming violates the fundamental right of people to impart and receive information under Article 19 of the *Universal Declaration of Human Rights* and Article 19 of the ICCPR, both of which provide that all people have a fundamental right "to seek, receive, and impart information and ideas."[40] Others have argued that the right to jam unwanted signals goes hand-in-hand with a state's right to regulate the flow of telecommunications into its territory. It is argued that this right to use jamming technology is a necessary tool to assert state sovereignty and is complementary to the doctrine of "prior consent." Just as a state should not be subjected to media transmissions without its consent, so should a state have a right to jam a signal for which it has not given the required consent.

In support of the legality of jamming, proponents have argued that the general proclamations of the right to exchange information are trumped, under the rule of *lex specialis*, by more specific expressions of international law which have permitted states to maintain sovereign control over media transmissions. Such commentators have looked primarily to Article 19(2) of the *International Telecommunications Convention* (ITC) which allowed states to stop transmissions that endanger the "security of the State or are contrary to their laws, to public order or to decency."[41] Similarly, Article 20 of the ITC provided that a state may suspend "international telecommunications service" for an indefinite time (provided that the Secretary-General is notified).[42] However, the ITC has since been supplanted by the Constitution of the International Telecommunications Union (the "ITU Constitution") and the Convention of the International Telecommunications Union, which can be said to take a more liberal approach to the "free flow" of information.[43]

Even without a strong argument on the basis of *lex specialis*, state practice supports a customary international law allowing the jamming of unwanted signals. Although the majority of examples of state practice of signal jamming involve totalitarian states such as Soviet Russia, Cuba, Libya and Iran, there are also examples of western democracies engaging in jamming, at

---

[40] Universal Declaration of Human Rights, *supra* note 9, art. 19; ICCPR, *supra* note 10, art. 19.

[41] International Telecommunications Convention, art. 19(2), 32 U.S.T. 3821 [hereinafter ITC].

[42] *Id.* art. 20.

[43] Constitution of the International Telecommunications Union, available at http://www.itu.int/aboutitu/basic-texts/constitution.html [hereinafter ITU Constitution]; Convention of the International Telecommunication Union, available at http://www.ito.int/aboutitu/basic-texts/convention.html [hereinafter ITU Convention].

least in times of war.[44] Moreover, the practices of western states once again confirm that jamming is permissible as a customary international law in light of the pervasive licensing regimes that western countries administer. Unlicensed satellite broadcasts are not tolerated in any industrialized country. Therefore, it would be difficult to make the argument that such states do not support, at least to some extent, the principle that states have sovereign control over their media transmission in their territory.[45]

Pursuant to the foregoing, states likely have the right under international law to jam illegal transmissions. This right applies to the jamming of war propaganda without question, but it is also likely to apply to the jamming of any transmission made without the receiving state's consent. However, there are certainly limits to what form the jamming can take. If the purpose of the jamming is merely to enforce the doctrine of "prior consent" or block the transmission of war propaganda, then the jamming should be limited to what is necessary to jam the objectionable signals. Causing greater interference than necessary would likely violate Article 45 of the ITU Constitution which prohibits states from causing "harmful interference" to the telecommunications of other states.[46] Similarly, the jamming would likely be subject to the proportionality requirement applicable to actions taken in self-defense (although application of the proportionality requirement in the absence of an armed or imminent attack is uncertain). Therefore, the jamming should be of no greater magnitude than necessary to obstruct the illegal transmission. Disproportional jamming can cause harm to innocent third parties who use neighboring transponders, as was the case when U.S. commercial radio broadcasters suffered revenue loss due to interference caused by Cuban jamming of Radio Marti.[47]

V. CONCLUSION

Both treaty law and customary international law require that a sending

---

[44] *See* David Hencke & Owen Gibson, *Protest to Libya after Satellites Jammed*, THE GUARDIAN, Dec. 3, 2005, available at *http://www.guardian.co.uk/libya/story/0,,165691 4,00.html* (regarding Libya's jamming of two commercial satellites); Tom Carter, *Castro Regime Jamming U.S. Broadcasts into Iran*, THE WASHINGTON TIMES, July 16, 2003, available at *http://www.washingtontimes.com/functions/ print.php?StoryID=20030715-114937-2635r* (regarding Cuba's jamming of Telstar-12 transmission of Voice of America broadcasts in Farsi into Iran); Bayer, *supra* note 18, at 572 (describing how Cuba jammed TV Marti – broadcasted from an aerostat – within minutes of its launch in 1990); *see also* Adeno Addis, *The Thin State in Thick Globalism: Sovereignty in the Information Age*, 37 VAND. J. TRANSNAT'L L. 1, 30 (2004). The significance of jamming by Cuba and other countries with respect to the formation of customary international law may be weakened if it is shown that such practices are conducted in secret, which would indicate that such practices do not reflect the country's *opinio iuris*.

[45] *For further discussion regarding territorial sovereignty and media broadcasts see* OPPENHEIM'S INTERNATIONAL LAW 529 (1955). One question that presents itself here is whether an intermediate rule of customary international law can be formulated which only permits regulation of media transmissions in accordance with reasonable rules that are politically neutral.

[46] ITU Constitution, *supra* note 43, art. 45.

[47] *See* Bayer, *supra* note 18, at 570-71 & n. 191. The commercial broadcasters were compensated by the U.S. government pursuant to the Radio Broadcast to Cuba Act. *See Compensation of Expenses to Mitigate Cuban AM Interference Cuban Interference*, 97 F.C.C.2d 181 (1984).

state acquire the consent of a receiving state before using DBS broadcasting to transmit television programs, such as commercial news programs. The "prior consent" requirement is the only restriction under international law that is applicable to the broadcasting of such news programs since the programs do not rise to the level of illegal war propaganda nor would such broadcasts be prohibited by the international law demanding that outer space be used only for "peaceful purposes." Not restricted to peacetime, this requirement of "prior consent" continues in times of war. The only law of war that could threaten the integrity of the "prior consent" doctrine is a state's fundamental right to self-defense. However, it is unlikely that the right to self-defense could be invoked as an excuse for failing to comply with the "prior consent" requirement since the broadcasting of news media could never be necessary for self-defense against an immediate threat. However, the inviolability of the "prior consent" doctrine may be threatened by the recent adoption by the United States of a more relaxed theory of self-defense.

Finally, in the event that a state does broadcast into another state without first securing prior consent, the receiving state has the right to jam such broadcasts, with the sole proviso that any such jamming must be proportional so as to minimize unnecessary interference that might cause harm to innocent parties.

References Cited

1. Joel R. Paul, *Images from Abroad: Making Direct Broadcasting by Satellites Safe for Sovereignty*, 9 HASTINGS INT'L & COMP. L. R. 329 (1986)

2. Jack L. Goldsmith & Eric A. Posner, *A Theory of Customary International Law*, 66 U. CHI. L. REV. 1113 (1999)

3. Mariana Mello, *Hagan v. Australia: A Sign of the Emerging Notion of Hate Speech in Customary International Law*, 28 LOY. L.A. INT'L & COMP. L. REV. 365 (2006)

4. DAVID I. FISHER, PRIOR CONSENT TO INTERNATIONAL DIRECT SATELLITE BROADCASTING (1990)

5. Robert Howse & Petros C. Mavroidis, *Europe's Evolving Regulatory Strategy for GMOS – The Issue of Consistency With WTO Law: Of Kine and Brine*, 24 FORDHAM INT'L L.J. 317 (2000)

6. IAN SINCLAIR, THE VIENNA CONVENTION ON THE LAW OF TREATIES (1984)

7. Jordan J. Paust, *The Importance of Customary International Law During Armed Conflict*, 12 ILSA J. INT'L & COMP. L. 601 (2006)

8. LESLIE JOHN MARTIN, INTERNATIONAL PROPAGANDA: ITS LEGAL AND DIPLOMATIC CONTROL (1958)

9. Stephen T. Bayer, *The Legal Aspects of TV Marti in Relation to the Law of Direct Broadcasting Satellites*, 41 EMORY L.J. 541 (1992)

10. Elizabeth A. Downey, *A Historical Survey of the International Regulation of Propaganda*, in MICHIGAN YEARBOOK OF INTERNATIONAL LEGAL STUDIES: REGULATION OF TRANSNATIONAL COMMUNICATIONS (1984)

11. GENNADY ZHUKOV & YURI KOLOSOV, INTERNATIONAL SPACE LAW (1984)

12. Michel Bourbonniere, *National-Security Law in Outer Space: The Interface of Exploration and Security*, 70 J. AIR L. & COM. 3 (2005)

13. Richard A. Morgan, *Military Use of Commercial Communication Satellites: A New Look at the Outer Space Treaty and "Peaceful Purposes"*, 60 J. AIR L. & COM. 237 (1994)

14. Ricky Lee, *Reconciling International Space Law with the Commercial Realities of the Twenty-First Century*, 4 SING. J. INT'L & COMP. L. 194 (2000)

15. Robert L. Bridge, *International Law and Military Activities In Outer Space*, 13 AKRON L. REV. 649 (1979)

16. LaToya Tate, *The Status of the Outer Space Treaty at International Law During "War" and "Those Measures Short of War"*, 32 J. SPACE L. 177 (2006)

17. Howard A. Wachtel, *Targeting Osama Bin Laden: Examining the Legality of Assassination as a Tool of U.S. Foreign Policy*, 55 DUKE L.J. 677 (2005)

18. Adeno Addis, *The Thin State in Thick Globalism: Sovereignty in the Information Age*, 37 VAND. J. TRANSNAT'L L. 1 (2004)

19. OPPENHEIM'S INTERNATIONAL LAW (1955).

IAC-06- E6.4.13

GALILEO'S PUBLIC REGULATED SERVICE : FROM SECURITY TO MILITARY APPLICATIONS ?

Ms Amal RAKIBI

Researcher, PDH candidate,
Institute of Space and Telecommunications Law (IDEST), University Paris – Sud XI
amalrakibi@hotmail.com

ABSTRACT

Galileo is a satellite positioning and navigation system specifically for civil purposes. Galileo will provided five distinct service groups: the Open Service (OS), the Safety-of-Life Service (SoL), the Commercial Service (CS), the Search and Rescue Service (SAR) and the Public Regulated Service (PRS). The latter will have a highest level of security than the ones of OS, CS, SoL and SAR. PRS is required to be operational at all times and in all circusmstances, when other services may be jammed or spoofed. PRS will be an access-controlled and encrypted signal for governmental applications, controled by civil bodies, and used by identifed categories. The use of PRS will be allowed, by European Union and participating states. Member States will authorised, unanimously, users through the implementation of appropriate controlled access techniques. However, the purposes for which the governmental entities can use the PRS is not clear. Galileo's military use is never openly mentionned, in aid of the more consensual term of "security". All the more, it appears quite difficult that the European military forces make the deadlock on a new system which will reduce their dependence to the GPS.

FULL TEXT

BACKGROUND

Galileo is the first major programme to bring the European political institutions (EU) and the European space institutions (ESA) together. On the EU side, the European Council in June 1999, established the involvement of the European Community in Global Navigation Satellite Systems (GNSS) by the creation of the Galileo satellite navigation programme[1]. On the ESA side, the European Agency was formally involved in the process by the approval of GalileoSat program Declaration, at the ESA Council at the ministerial level, in May 1999. The regulation setting up the Galileo Joint Undertaking was adopted

[1] Council Resolution (EC) 1999/C 221/01, *The Involvement of Europe in a New Generation of Satellite Navigation Services – Galileo,* of 19 July 1999, Official Journal n° C 221/1, 3 August 1999; See also: WARINSKO (N.), TYTGAT (L.), "Le programme GALILEO, l'engagement de l'Europe dans une nouvelle génération de services de navigation par satellite", *Revue du Marché commun de l'Union européenne*, June 2000, n° 439, pp. 392-394.

on May 2002[2], following the Council decision of March 2002.

This initiative is the second step having towards satellite navigation technology, the first step having been the European Geostationary Navigation Overlay Service (EGNOS)[3]. Galileo is the most technically sophisticated and costly european space programme. The goal of this joint initiative is "to put in place the European contribution to a global multimodal navigation system under civilian control"[4]. Since Galileo is a civil system under civil control[5], does it prevent the military users to use it?

FROM A CIVIL SYSTEM TO A DUAL USE SYSTEM?

The need for a secured service

In contrast with the american GPS, a system completely controlled by the US Department of Defence, and the Russian Federation's military Glonass, Galileo is a satellite positioning and navigation system specifically for civil purposes. Galileo will provided five distinct service groups: the Open Service (OS), the Safety-of-Life Service (SoL), the Commercial Service (CS), the Search and Rescue Service (SAR) and the Public Regulated Service (PRS). The latter will have a highest level of security than the ones of OS, CS, SoL and SAR.

The European Commission reserves a particular attention to the regulated service. It reminds that "open signals are extremely sensitive to interference or to deliberate - potentially hostile - manipulation. The need for a PRS service is conditioned by the vulnerability of satellite navigation signals, the special features of the service and the very sensitive nature of the anticipated application"[6].

The PRS is required to be operational at all times and in all circusmstances, when other services may be jammed or spoofed. The regulated service will be separated from the other services, so it can be denied without affecting its operations[7]. This service will be an access-controlled and encrypted signal for governmental applications, controled by civil bodies, and used by identifed categories. It will be offered to a limited number of governmental and strategic civil users[8], at the EU level (such as Europol, the European Anti-Fraud Office (OLAF), civil protection services, safety services, peacekeeping forces, humanitarian response teams), as well as at the national level (i.e., police, fire, ambulance, customs or intelligence

[2] Council Regulation (EC) No 876/2002, *Setting up the Galileo Joint Undertaking*, Brussels, 21 May 2002, Official Journal n° L 138 of 28 May 2002, p. 001.

[3] ANDRIES (S.), "The European Initiative Galileo: A European Contribution to the Global Navigation Satellite System (GNSS)", *Yearbook of Air and Space Law*, vol. XXV, 2000, p. 48.

[4] European Commission, *Galileo definition Phase*, Initial results, Brussels, 7 June 2000, at. 26.

[5] Conclusions of the Council of the European Union, 2430th Council Meeting, Transport and Telecommunications, Brussels, 25-26 March 2002, 7282/02 (Presse 78), p. 20; Council Resolution (EC) 2001/C 157/01 on Galileo, of 5 april 2001 July 1999, Official Journal n° C 157, 30 may 2001, pp. 001-003.

[6] Communication from the Commission to the European Parliament and the Council, *State of progress of the Galileo Programme*, Section 3.2. "The need for a public regulated service (PRS)", Brussels, 24 september 2002, COM (2002) 518 final, p. 7.

[7] ESA/European Commission, *Galileo - The European Programme for Global Navigation Services*, 2003, p. 21; HOFMANN (M.), "Security Aspects of the Galileo Services", *I.I.S.L. Colloqiums*, n° 46, 2003, pp. 371-378.

[8] European Commission *The European Dependence on US-GPS and the Galileo Intitiative*, Technical Document, 8 February 2002, p. 4.

services responsible for national security). However, the purposes for which the governmental entities can use the PRS remains unclear.

The military use of the regulated service: a Taboo

If the Russian Glonass has generated only military applications, and the American GPS is official considered as a dual use system since 1996[9], Galileo remains exclusively a civil system. In the European official documents, the military dimension of Galileo is never openly mentionned, in aid of the more consensual term of "security".

By way of example, the Agreement between the US governement and the EU Member States on the promotion, provision and use of Galileo and GPS of June 2004, recalls "that the United States operates a satellite-based navigation system knows as the GPS, *a dual use system* that provides precision timing, navigation and position location signals for civil and military purposes", and "that the European Community is developing and plans to operate *a civil global satellite navigation, timing and positioning system*, Galileo"[10] (we underline). The Agreement also stipulates that the secured governmental services and signals are considered as "civil"[11].

If the defence applications of the PRS are officialy accepted, its military purposes remain uncertains. Therefore the borderline between homeland security (i.e. crisis management, law enforcement, intelligence services...) and military missions (i.e., guided weapons, soldiers...) tends to be more and more blurred[12].

Evaluation of the military benefits of Galileo

Recently, the European Parliament voted to ask the EU and the ESA Joint Undertaking on Galileo not to exclude the possibility for European armees to use Galileo in the context of peacekeeping operations. Galileo will provide the European governments and ESA member states with an extremely accurate satellite navigation system not subject to the operational control of the US army. This clearly has strategic advantages for the defence establishments of Europe.

Within a few years, the EU's dependence on satellite radionavigation will be as far reaching as in the US[13]. Galileo will allowed the European Member States to appear as credible actors: "if Europe truly wishes to be taken seriously as a partner by the US, while ensuring that it has access to capabilities critical for its economic development, it must demonstrate that is has both the will and the means to develop a presence in space. Galileo represents a litmus test for the EU in many different ways"[14].

---

[9] U.S. Presidential Decision Document of 29 March 1996 relating to the U.S. Global Positionning System Policy.

[10] Agreement between the US and the European Community, on the Promotion, Provision and Use of Galileo and GPS Satellite-Based Navigation Systems and Related Applications, 26 June 2004, Preamble.

[11] *Ibid.*, Article 2 "Definitions" (b), (d).

[12] BOU (J. F.), "Galileo on the way to a Dual-Use System", *in* Munich Satellite Navigation Summit, 2006 (not published).

[13] Communication from the Commission to the European Parliament and the Council, *State of progress of the Galileo Programme*, *op. cit.*, p. 7.

[14] BILDT (C.) *in Financial Times*, 31 December 2001; See also FERRAZZANI (M.), « Le projet européen Galileo, entreprise commerciale ou service public international », *in* S.F.D.I., *Le droit de l'espace et la privatisation des activités spatiales, Journée d'études*, Pedone, Paris, 2003, p. 74.

Without an autonomous European satellite navigation programme, Europe will in the next decades, lose its autonomy in defence[15], because every new weapon system and platform is incorporating satellite navigation technology. European defence industries will want to be able to sell precision guided weapons overseas without asking permission for the GPS Precise Positioning Service (PPS). All the more, it appears quite difficult that the European military forces make the deadlock on a new system which will reduce their dependence to the US.

LEGAL ASPECTS OF THE MILITARY USE OF GALILEO

From a legal point of view, nothing prohibits to a Member State of the EU or the ESA to use the PRS for military purposes. However, the process is extremely heavy.

The lack of an unanimous european will

On December 2004, the Council of the European Union recalls that because Galileo is a civil programme under civil control, any change to that principle would require examination in the framework of Title V of the Treaty on European Union, relating to a Common Foreign and Security Policy (CFSP), and particulary in accordance with the articles 17 and 23 of the Treaty[16]. In other words, it means that any decision on Galileo with defence, or military, implications would follow under the "Pilar II" procedure, and consequently shall be taken by the Council acting unanimously[17].

The problem is that participating states in the European global navigation system are not agree on its military use. Some EU Member States are neutral. Others, like the UK, a major Galileo financier, is adamant that Galileo remain non-military in every way possible, for political and strategic considerations. The British gouvernment recognises that, like any civil technology, Galileo can be used by the military for security purposes. But, it considers that, because the civil status of the PRS is clear, the development of specific military applications is ruled out unless the twenty five Members States agree at the unanimity[18].

The U.K. considers that adding dual use capacity for Galileo would not be justified, from a financial as well as from a strategic point of view. That is, the British gouvernment is concerned, in the one hand, by the fact that the PRS must not impact on the effectiveness of the GPS military codes, and on the other hand, by the needs to restrict the amount of overspends to the consequences of security. This economic argument was also underlines by the transport Council in 2004[19]. However, "studies have shown the impact of the cost of the governmental service on the design and equipment of the Galileo system as a whole in almost insignifiant as far as the space segment is concerned"[20].

[15] European Commission (EC) Directorate-General for Energy and Transport, *Galileo: An Imperative for Europe*, December 2001, position paper, p. 8.

[16] Conclusions of the Council of the European Union, 2629th Council Meeting, Transport, Telecommunications and Energy, *Intermodal Questions – Global Navigation Satellite System*, n° 6, Brussels, 9-10 December 2004, 15472/04 (Presse 345), p. 24.

[17] Article 23.1 of the Title V of the Treaty on European Union, Official Journal n° C 325 of 24 December 2004.

[18] DUTHIES (E.), "Galileo: a UK view of the PRS", *in* Munich Satellite Navigation Summit, 2005 (not published).

[19] Conclusions of the Council of the European Union, 2629th Council Meeting, *op. cit.*, p. 24.

[20] Communication from the Commission to the European Parliament and the Council, *Progress report on the Galileo research programme as at*

The overlay of signals

The PRS signal will be transmitted on two frequencies, distincts from those of the other Galileo services. Each frequency will occupied a wide bandwidth, providing a signal structure that is resistant to interference, not offered by the open access services.

Considering the limited space in the frequency spectrum allocated to satellite navigation, the overlay of frequency bands used by one of the two Galileo's PRS signal and one of the two GPS's Code M signal is unavoidable. However, such overlay is not only possible, it is also perfectly justifiable.

From a legal point of view, this overlay complies with the international law, as far as there is no harmful interference to either of the two systems[21]. From a technical point of view, it is the more preferable alternative in peacetime as well as in crisis, because it is the frequency spectrum which offers the best performance in terms of resistance and robustness, the best financial issues, and the best guarantee of continuity and integrity[22]. In addition, the European Community considers that, "it has the know-how to operate a secured signal, it believes that the complementary operation of the GPS and Galileo systems must depend on mutual trust and it has a prior claim on the right to use the signals"[23].

Also, because of the overlay of the Galileo's secured service signal and the GPS's one, the US efforts to jam Galileo signals without affecting the GPS's services will be greatly complicate. The US took the view that all civils signals, including the PRS can be used for hostil purposes. They therefore wished to have the option of jamming them without disrupting its own GPS's signals. However, in accordance with the provisions of the International Telecommunication Union regulations, if the European PRS and the American Code M use the same frequencies then it will be impossible to selectively jam one of the two signals without disrupting the other[24].

In reality, the existence of two highly gouvernmental services, will improve the robustness of the global system[25].

The access to the encrypted codes and data

The Member States Council invited the European Commission to develop a policy of access to the governmental service and to be implemented by the European GNSS Supervisory Authority in order to ensure that there are sufficiently robust controls over access to the governmental service[26]. The access and the use of the PRS should be open to the European Union and its Member States, on an optional basis.

---

the beginning of 2004, Brussels, 18 February 2004, COM (2004) 112 final, p. 17.

[21] International Telecommunication Union Radio Regulations, Article 0, Geneva : "All Stations, whatever their purpose, must be established and operated in such a manner as not to cause harmful interference to the radio services or communications of others Members".

[22] Communication from the Commission to the European Parliament and the Council, *State of progress of the Galileo Programme*, Brussels, 24 september 2002, COM (2002) 518 final, p. 9.

[23] *Ibid.*, p. 9.

[24] Energy and Transport, *Galileo: An Imperative for Europe*, December 2001, position paper, p. 9.

[25] BOU (J. F.), "Galileo on the way to a Dual-Use System", *op. cit.*

[26] Conclusions of the Council of the European Union, 2629th Council Meeting, *op. cit.*, p. 24.

The PRS, and more particulary its "military" use, could raise new political complications for Europe, because of the divergence of the Members States interests outside the bounds of the EU. Every european member has its one policy "overseas", for example Spain in Morocco or Greece and Cyprus in Turkey.

In addition, Galileo is not a purely European programme. It involved also international partners. Therefore, other participating states, such as China, could also be authorised to use the PRS by the EU Member States who are supposed to maintain the control of distribution of receivers suggested for this form of services[27]. The international dimension of Galileo would make the "militay' use of PRS more difficult, because of the divergence of the lack of a common EU international policy. Besides, the Agreement of June 2004 makes provision for a reciprocal visibility in the military data, between the US and the European Community[28].

CONCLUSION

The success of Galileo is closely linked to the exploration of all the possible applications, including the strategic purposes[29]. Even if Galileo is a civil system under civil control, the European navigation system would necessary have growing challenges in terms of security and defence, particulary in the context of the CFSP and the European Security and Defence Policy (ESDP)[30]. It seems indisputable, that without a "dual use" dimension, Galileo will not be fully justify. But the "dual use" dimension of Galileo will follow from its "military" applications and not only from its "security" purposes. The barriers for a dual use european system, seem to be in reality more political than legal.

[27] HOFMANN (M.), "Security Aspects of the Galileo Services", *op. cit.*, p. 372.

[28] Article 11 "National Security, Compatibility and Spectrum Use" of the Agreement between the US and the European Community, *op. cit.*

[29] Jacques Barrot, quoted *in Vers une nouvelle Europe spatiale,* Fondation Robert Schumann, 2005, p. 9.

[30] European Commission (EC), Green Paper on the European Space Policy, Brussels, 21 January 2003, COM (2003) 17 final, Foreword, p. 4.

Session 5:
OTHER LEGAL MATTERS, INCLUDING THE RELATIONSHIP BETWEEN GOVERNMENT AND PRIVATE SECTOR IN SPACE ACTIVITIES

Chairmen: Frans von der Dunk
Mª del Carmen Muñoz Rodriguez

Rapporteur: Ricky Lee

IAC-06-E6.5.01

INTERNATIONAL SPACE LAW IN ITS FIRST HALF CENTURY

Prof. Dr. Stephan Hobe, LL.M.
Board of Directors, International Institute of Space Law
Director, Institute of Air and Space Law, University of Cologne
Albertus-Magnus-Platz
D-50923 Cologne, Germany
stephan.hobe@uni-koeln.de

ABSTRACT

This paper will highlight three different phases of the past 50 years of the development of international space law. This development is characterised by a first hard law phase (1956-1979), a second UNGA Resolution soft law phase (1980-1992), and a third, current phase of reinterpretation of space law (1992 up to now). Furthermore, the paper will come to conclusions with regard to the method of law-making, the effectiveness of law-making, and the question of the existence of a tendency from hard to soft law.

With regard to the development of international space law, major conclusions will be that (a) public international law in the future will only be a frame for space activities filled in by more flexible special legal regimes, (b) a growing normative vagueness with regard to the major legal framework for outer space activities exists, (c) the legal regime for commercial activities on the Moon and other celestial bodies is still unclear, (d) the legal regime for touristic space activities is still growing, and could arguably combine air and space law approaches.

In conclusion, the paper will underline that in the second half century of development of international space law, a reorientation of international space law back to hard law would be very welcome. In view of the various challenges, only such strengthening of the international legal framework for space activities can preserve the authority of this international legal order. Public international law will remain the necessary frame for space activities also in the future. But, most likely, there will be more distinct legal rules for specific space activities. Furthermore, there could be a growing body of national space legislation. In sum, in view of the growing private space activities, the authority of the frame of public international law must be preserved.

INTRODUCTION

During the last half century, space legislation has achieved remarkable successes. Starting immediately after the launch of the first artificial satellite Sputnik I, within 20 years five international conventions have been adopted. But after this time and around the adoption of the fifth international agreement, the Moon Agreement in 1979, new developments took place in outer space legislation. The different phases of these developments shall be discussed in the perspective that it seems that in an increasing way the idea of concluding binding international agreements gets to be abandoned.

In the following paper, therefore, the attempt will be made to investigate reasons for the reluctance of the international community to adopt more binding international agreements. Moreover, the question for the prospects and the perspective of this development will be posed. It shall be asked whether we are heading towards relative normativity[1] with regard to the uses and the exploration of outer space. Furthermore, the consequences and the possible reasons of such possible relative normativity shall be earmarked. Finally, examples shall be given for a possible normative break-through that could enable the international community to come back to stronger normative standards characterised by hard law and clear definitions of key notions of outer space legislation.

I. THE ORIGINS OF SPACE FLIGHT AND EARLY WRITINGS ON SPACE LAW

Space flight belongs, of course, to the original dreams of mankind. Just take the example of Jules Verne[2] and you will discover how much inspiration mankind got by the pure idea of flying to the Moon or other celestial bodies. It was relatively early that the pioneers of space flight like the German Wernher von Braun and the Russian Konstantin Ziolkovsky[3] discovered the use of outer space as being necessary for defence purposes.[4] The German defence system during the Second World War was dependent on the concept of the V2 rocket that needed to use outer space. Interesting early writings on space law included such important authors like Dr. Vladimir Mandl, attorney-at-law in Pilsen, who published a short treatise of 48 pages in German entitled "Space law, a problem of space flight?"[5]. In this short treatise, Mandl described in a first part the public law and the public international law aspects of space flight. Mandl terminates this part with the Treaty of Paris of 13 October 1919 in which the states parties recognise the sovereignty over the airspace. He very foresightedly observes that the respect for the national sovereignty of the airspace would have a far-reaching consequence even for space flight. He, therefore, pleads for a transit right of space objects through the airspace. Mandl explicitly asks for an outer space law.[6] Moreover, he precisely asks the question how far the airspace would go[7]. He foresightedly thinks of the establishment of stations in outer space[8]. Finally, Mandl strongly pleads for international legal rules established in a space that does not, in his opinion, belong to any state[9]. This is again an observation that anticipates developments that later have been laid down in the Outer Space Treaty of 1967.

II. THE CRUCIAL FEATURES OF SPACE LAW-MAKING

Although, as we have seen, Vladimir Mandl foresaw many developments of the shape of international space law, space law making started only 20 years later.

1. The First Phase: Two Decades from1956 to 1979 of Space Law Making

And - viewed in a nutshell - space law-making at its initial phase was a tremendous success.[10] After the launch of the first artificial space satellite, the satellite Sputnik 1 on 4 October 1957, the United Nations started immediately to get concerned with these new activities all with a view to eventually implement legislation. Already in 1959, the Committee on the Peaceful Uses of Outer Space was established as an ad hoc Committee to the UN General Assembly.[11] This Committee concerned itself immediately with proposals for legislation. In 1963, the UN General Assembly passed Resolution 1962[12] which basically included all the important features of international space legislation. This was the starting point for the eventual making of the "Magna Charta" of outer space, the Outer Space Treaty of 1967.[13] In this Treaty, we have the non-appropriation principle in Art. II, the demilitarisation principle in Art. IV, the registration principle as embodied in Art. VIII, the principle of the preservation of jurisdiction and control in the same Article VIII, the general possibility of space activities being carried out by non-governmental entities in Art. VI, and the principle of liability in Art. VII as well as the non-contamination principle in Art. IX. These are the main principles of outer space legislation, somewhat overarched by the important principle that outer space and the celestial bodies are the common province of all mankind, as embodied in Art. I para. 1 of the Outer Space Treaty.[14]

Later on, the international community drafted more specific legislation on some principles for the exploration and use of outer space as contained in the Outer Space Treaty. First, in 1968, the Rescue Agreement was adopted which highlighted the importance of the rather non-contested duty of all states to support (help) astronauts in distress as contained in Art. V of the Outer Space Treaty.[15] A little more contested was the Convention on International Liability for Damage Caused by Space Objects[16] a more specific example of the general principle as contained in Art. VII of the Outer Space Treaty. Important refinements have taken place in that, for example, the differentiation in a strict liability provision as far as damage occurs to space objects and a fault-based liability if the damage occurs to other objects was only highlighted in the Liability Convention of 1972.[17] Moreover, this Convention contains several details, but, interestingly enough, does not very closely define such important notions as "launching state" or "space object".[18] The definition of "launching state" in Art. 1 c) of the Liability Convention contains of course elements of a definition. It provides for four different possibilities of a state being a launching state. This can be a state that launches itself, or procures the launch (for a private subject), or from whose territory a launch is made, or from whose facility a space object is launched. This has proven almost sufficient so far. However, with a view to registration, this is not sufficient any longer. On the other hand, the term "space object", although being of key importance for international space legislation, contains a virtual non-definition in Art. I d) of the Liability Convention. According to this provision, the term "space object" includes "component parts of a space object as well as its launch vehicle and parts thereof". It was clear that this "definition", which is contained as well in the Registration Convention, did not suffice as a definition.[19] It is interesting enough that so far, relatively few difficulties arose in spite of the non-definition.

As already mentioned, the registration principle of Art. VIII of the Outer Space Treaty that is further refined in the Registration Convention of 1975, contains a variety of different and interesting notions. The twofold obligation to provide for a national register as well as to provide information to the United Nations Secretary-General who, in an international register, includes also the information, is one of the key international obligations of this Convention.[20]

Finally, in 1979, the Agreement Governing the Activities of States on the Moon and other Celestial Bodies was adopted.[21] This Convention was a total failure. Although only five ratifications sufficed to bring it into force and these five ratifications were reached after a while (1984), this agreement received until now only 12 ratifications and is - one must clearly say this - although being ratified inter alia by Belgium and the Netherlands still a dead international agreement.[22] This is mostly so because of the rather unclear language as contained in Art. 11 of the Moon Agreement where the Moon and its resources as well as the resources of other celestial bodies are declared to be the common heritage of mankind.[23]

It is very interesting to observe that all of the five international agreements contain clauses that allow for the making of specific amendments after a certain period of time; this is e.g. the case in Art. XV of the Outer Space Treaty, Art. 8 of the Rescue Agreement and Art. XXV of the Liability Convention as well as Art. 9 of the Registration Convention. No such amendments have been made so far. Moreover, the Convention on the Registration of Objects Launched into Outer Space contains a review clause in its Art. XXVI that allows for such a review ten years after its entry into force; this would have been in 1985. Also the Moon Agreement contains in its Art. 18 such a review clause which would have become effective in 1989. It is thus indicative that of the five international agreements only the Outer Space Treaty with its almost 100 ratifications has found wide-spread support of the international community, the others being in the range of between 60 and only 12 ratifications. Interestingly enough, no amendments to international agreements and no request for a review of such agreements have been made so far.

2. A New Second Phase (1980 – 1992): UNGA Resolutions for a Softening of Legal Commitments?

Rather, in a next phase that started around 1980, a new method of international law-making for outer space activities was applied: the adoption of United Nations General Assembly resolutions. This was the case with regard to guidelines for the use of direct broadcasting satellites.[24] Here, the rather contested question of a signal overlap as well as the possibility of hindering incoming signals of other broadcasting entities from abroad was discussed by the international community. "Free flow of information" versus "prior consent" was the ideologically inspired question of these days[25] that, as one must clearly admit, in times of the globalised world of national telecommunications of today, does not play a vital role any longer. However, certain quota for national products still play a role if it comes, for example, to certain European states, e.g. France.

Moreover, in 1986, the United Nations General Assembly adopted a next resolution on the use of remote sensing satellites.[26] Here again, a similar question was at stake, namely that and in how far the sensed state could either deny the permission to the sensing state, or at least profit from the giving of a permission in that products of the sensing activities should be given to the sensed state. The principles do in fact signal a compromise. Some authors consider this greater part to be still valid customary international law, others contest such value.[27]

Finally, in 1992, the UN General Assembly adopted Guideline Principles on the Use of Nuclear Power Sources on Board of Space Objects.[28] Here, for safety reasons, certain requirements for the use of such sources were made and the resolution eventually adopted.

What is the effect of UN General Assembly resolutions? It is well known that these resolutions do not have a legally binding character. Rather, they are an indication of a certain state practice supported by *opinio juris*, but are, because of a lack of legislative power of the UN General Assembly, short of being hard public international law.[29] At least initially, the non-binding character of a resolution was deliberately chosen in order to soften the hardcore applications of the space-faring nations and of others. In other words: in order not to destroy the harmony, one could agree on something of legally non-binding character.[30]

3. After the End of the Cold War (after 1992 – 2005): A Phase of Reinterpretation of International Space Law?

Such developments went on through the1980ies until 1992. 1992, obviously, is indicative of a fundamental change of paradigm in international politics as well as in international (space) law. The end of the Cold War between the East and the West had of course important repercussions on the making of space law as well.[31] Moreover, very importantly, the one remaining super power felt more and more attempted to lose an interest in concerted UN space law-making.

a) What is characteristic for the new phase of space law-making that started a few years after the end of the Cold War around 1992? Interestingly enough, this new and third phase that lasts until today, for the last fifteen years or so is characterised by a re-definition of major notions of international space law in the form of UN General Assembly resolutions. So it is kind of a mix of the methods chosen in the first and in the second phase. This can be first exemplified by the 1996 Declaration on Space Benefits.[32] Since 1988, an almost rephrasing of Art. I para 1 of the Outer Space Treaty was on the agenda of the UN Committee on the Peaceful Uses of Outer Space. The Committee, at the request of developing countries, had given itself the task of making concrete recommendations of how states should fulfil their obligation to international cooperation in the sense of Art. I para. 1 of the Outer Space Treaty.[33] The Space Benefits Declaration is far from concretising such obligations.[34] It is more of the opposite: It highlights almost total freedom of states to choose the means and ways of implementing the cooperation obligation.[35] So, basically, nothing was specified in the Space Benefits Declaration.

b) Next, the rather unclear notion of "launching state" was subject to reconsideration by the Legal Subcommittee.[36] Here, a working group started with its work and come up with the interesting and new proposal declaring that with a view to the current difficulties of making progress in international space legislation, it was up to the member states to implement respective national space legislation where the problems of space objects should be dealt with.[37] This was insofar interesting and important as with this the new phenomenon of private space activities as a result of the growing commercialisation of space activities was taken into account. And indeed, after the year 2000, a number of important national space laws came into existence.[38] This all has to do with the important obligation as contained in the Outer Space Treaty that member states must authorise and continuously supervise private space activities (Art. VI OST). Up to now, 13 states have enacted national space legislation and another 8 are preparing it.[39] In other words: states started to discover that if one wanted to foster commercialisation and privatisation of space activities for the purpose of self-protection, some national space legislation was needed that e.g. allowed for the recourse against private actors. Thus, the more and more unclear international law is still accompanied by a growing body of national space law.

c) Finally, since 2005, the Outer Space Committee of the United Nations is concerned with the practice of states with regard to the registration of space objects.[40] Again, a key notion of international treaty law for outer space activities is going to be reconsidered, cautiously though as only an overview of current state practice is on the agenda of the Committee. But this overview shall be given also with a view to making more concrete and more effective the existing international legal obligations. Again, the final aim shall be the adoption of a UN General Assembly resolution that calls for an authoritative interpretation of key notions for international space legislation.

III. KEY ASPECTS OF INTERNATIONAL SPACE LEGISLATION RECONSIDERED

Besides other factors, two aspects of this new development deserve particular mentioning:

1. The consensus method as the basis of law-making

Relatively early after its coming into existence, the United Nations Committee on the Peaceful Uses of Outer Space agreed at adopting a consensus method to its decision-making.[41] Consensus is based on the fact that no formal vote is ever taken, but that informally, the search for consensus governs the entire negotiating process.[42] The chair person of the fora concerned with law-making must look for such consensus and basically any negotiating partner has the right to disagree with such statement of an achieved consensus. Therefore, basically each of the negotiating partners has a veto right. This, obviously, considerably prolongs the process for international law-making. It ensures on the other hand, that all the parties concerned can live with the result because they have consented to it. However, after some 40 years of applying this method, some critical remarks may be allowed.

In the opinion of the present author the consensus principle first of all leads basically to a considerable prolongation of the negotiating process. This is obvious, because instead of a vote always a search for consensus must take place. Moreover and maybe even more importantly, the search for consensus is in danger of causing a fatal dilution of the preciseness of the wording of international space legislation. The wording of "space object" or "launching state" or the timing for registration in terms of "as soon as practicable" are typical examples for the smallest denominator which can be a typical result as a consequence of a method that must always look for consensus in order to guarantee progress. It shall, however, not be negated that at least during the first twenty years, the consensus method was quite successful. But, as we have seen, there are also dark sides of this method in terms of the preciseness of key notions, especially in so-called package deals, that in the opinion of the present author might today overshadow the arguable merits of this method.

2. The importance of redefinitions

The more recent time has shown moreover, as demonstrated in the previous section, a tendency towards redefining international treaty law for outer space activities. This development started around the end of phase two. With regard to "space benefits" as a notion contained in Art. I para 1 of the Outer Space Treaty and later on "space object" as contained in the Registration and in the Liability Convention and now "registration" as contained in the Registration Convention by way of the UN General Assembly resolutions, new attempts to (re-)define key notions of outer space legislation are directly under way. Seen in a methodological perspective this is a doubtful undertaking. It very clearly pays tribute to the fact that the international space law community does not feel in a position to go ahead with space legislation by redrafting a treaty. Rather, the non-binding form of a UN General Assembly resolution is chosen in order to highlight the importance of certain key notions of international space legislation. From the point of view of the observance of the rule of law, this development can only be regretted. It may, of course, be that an interpretative note in the form of a UN General Assembly resolution is more than nothing, but the question is allowed why the method of amendments (or even of review) to the international agreements has not been taken so long. One of the reasons may be that some states feel more comfortable in having less binding agreements which means also less of an observance of the rule of law.[43]

IV. NEXT STEPS FOR GOING BACK TO STRONGER LEGAL COMMITMENTS

These rather sceptical observations do not lead to some kind of progress if they are not transformed into positive action. Therefore, four proposals in this regard shall be made:

1. Registration as a crucial principle

The international community has currently an opportunity to come back to the observance of strict international space law. The current process of reconsidering certain notions of the law as contained in the Registration Convention provides for such an opportunity. It is clear that some of the current problems with the Registration Convention are posed because there are a lot of private space activities. Take the example of transfer in orbit[44], or countries that negate their international legal obligation to register in cases of the launching by private companies from their territory or by international organisations.[45] Moreover, the information provided for by the Registration Convention is by far not sufficient in order to allow for a precise overview on the space object.[46] It is therefore in the interest of all mankind if important precisions to the Registration Convention are being identified through the working group currently under way and that the Committee makes a courageous step forward and comes up with some amendments to the

Registration Convention. The ILA Space Law Committee will provide concrete proposals for such amendments.[47] Obviously, the adoption of a UN General Assembly resolution on guidelines for the interpretation of the main principles of the Registration Convention are more than nothing and therefore would also be a first step into this direction with a view to a later development of such interpretative guidelines into an amendment to the Registration Convention.

2. Space Tourists as Astronauts?

The next step could be the Astronauts Convention of 1968. This Convention that will soon (in 2008) celebrate its 40th anniversary is still up to date as far as the traditional uses of outer space by astronauts are concerned. But it is rather doubtful whether it will suffice for modern undertakings like space tourism ventures. In that respect, it should urgently be reconsidered whether specific conditions for the flight of so-called "flight participants" – these are the non-professional astronauts that fly primarily for touristic purposes – should be worked out and added to the Astronauts Convention.[48] This would perhaps help a growing industry to grow further and would also shed some light upon the sometimes not undisputed question of the delimitation of airspace and outer space.[49] Again, either a UN General Assembly resolution in the form of interpretative guidelines to the Astronauts Convention or an explicit amendment to that Convention should be the order of the day.

3. Model Law for National Space Legislation

Moreover, the examples just given have clearly shown that national space legislation in times of a growing privatisation and commercialisation of space activities becomes more and more important.[50] And we have seen that the number of national space laws has grown, from just a few to already 13 of such laws, 8 more such laws being currently in preparation. It could therefore be worthwhile if the international community through the UN Committee on the Peaceful Uses of Outer Space would adopt a model law for national space legislation. Such model law would provide guidelines for domestic space law-drafting and thus stimulate the respective national processes and strengthen the rule of law.

4. Moon Agreement

The International Moon Agreement foresees a review 10 years after its coming into force (Art. 18). Such was the case in 1984 so that in 1994, the time limit was reached. Nothing has happened so far. But there is no clear understanding with regard to the limits of commercial exploitation of the Moon and other celestial bodies.[51] Such exploitation could become more and more feasible and it is rather unclear what apart from the rare provisions of the Outer Space Treaty its legal basis would be. The more recent debate on the selling of land on the Moon is an interesting demonstration of new developments.[52] Therefore, the UN Committee on the Peaceful Uses of Outer Space should take the initiative and look into the examples of the Law of the Sea Convention of 1982 and the Implementing Agreement of 1994.[53] It should start to creatively reconsider what the common heritage of mankind concept means in today's international legal environment with regard to the commercial exploitation of outer space and its resources as well as of the resources of celestial bodies. Here, the 2002 Resolution 1 of the International Law Association of the ILA Conference in New Delhi could be of some guidance.[54]

PERSPECTIVES

Without any doubt, the sharpening of key notions of international space law is needed. In times of the growing likelihood of future commercial exploitation of the Moon and other celestial bodies, a concrete and precise understanding of these key notions as anticipated already by Vladimir Mandl in 1932 is of great importance. What is also important in this respect is therefore that the international legal obligations of states and private entities are precisely phrased and have binding character. Therefore, a strong plea is made for the UN Committee on the Peaceful Uses of Outer Space and the UN General Assembly to come back to the first phase of international space law-making and to enrich such existing international agreements that are somewhat out of date by specific amendments accompanied by national space legislation. Such additions would bring the corpus iuris spatialis up to today's international needs and requirements.

---

[1] Expression from P. Weil, Towards Relative Normativity in International Law, AJIL 77 (1983), p. 413.

[2] J. Verne, De la terre à la lune, Paris 1865.

[3] K. Ziolkovsky, Investigations by means of propulsion space ships, Kaluga 1914.

[4] See also H. Oberth, Die Rakete zu den Planetenräumen, München 1923.

[5] V. Mandl, Das Weltraum-Recht – Ein Problem der Raumfahrt?, Pilsen 1932.

[6] Ibid. p. 22.

[7] Ibid. p. 31 seq.

[8] Ibid. p. 33.

[9] Ibid. p. 48.

[10] Examples of early writings on space law A. Meyer, Rechtliche Probleme des Weltraumfluges, in: ZL 1953, p. 37; N. Smirnov, La réglementation internationale des vols dans l'espace supra-atmosphérique, in: RGA 1957, 351; K.-H. Böhme, Lufthoheit und Weltraumflug, in: UL 1956, p. 184; W. Jenks, The common law of mankind, New York 1958, p. 394; Ph.C. Jessup/H.J.Taubenfeld, Controls for space and the Antarctic analogy, New York 1959, p. 193 et seq.; W.H. Prinz von Hannover, Luftrecht und Weltraum, Hannover 1953.

[11] UNGA Res. 1472 (XIV), 12 December 1959; see also K.-H. Böckstiegel, Grundlagen des Weltraumrechts, in: K.-H. Böckstiegel (ed.), Handbuch des Weltraumrechts, Köln et al. 1991, p. 1 et seq., p. 10 et. seq.

[12] UNGA Res, 1962 (XVIII), Definition of legal principles governing the activities of states in the exploration and use of outer space.

[13] U.N.T.S. Vol. 610, p. 205.

[14] See N. Jasentuliyana, Art. I of the Outer Space Treaty Revisited, in: Journal of Space Law 1989, p. 129-144.

[15] U.N.T.S. Vol. 672, p. 119.

[16] UNGA Res. 2777 (XXVI), Annex of 29 November 1991.

[17] UNGA Res. 3285 of 12 November 1974.

[18] See Art. 2 and 3 of the Liability Convention.

[19] Art. I lit (d) of the Liability Convention: The term "space object" includes component parts of a space object as well as its launch vehicle and parts thereof.

[20] See Art. II and IV para. 2 of the Registration Convention.

[21] UNGA Res. 34/38 Annex of 5 December 1979.

[22] Status: 1 January 2006; four states have signed; see for a comprehensive criticism on the Moon Agreement F. von der Dunk, Report on the Moon Agreement to the 70th Biannual Conference of the International Law Association in New Delhi 2002, London 2002, p. 201 et seq..

[23] See S. Hobe, Was bleibt vom gemeinsamen Erbe der Menschheit?, in: Liber Amicorum Jost Delbrück, Berlin 2005, p. 329, 338 et seq.

[24] UNGA Res. 37/92 Principles concerning the use by states of artificial earth satellites for direct television broadcasting of 10 December 1982.

[25] See on that problem J.A. Frowein, Das Problem des grenzüberschreitenden Informationsflusses und der „domaine réservé", in: Berichte der Deutschen Gesellschaft für Völkerrecht (BDVR) 1979, p. 1 et seq.; B. Simma, Grenzüberschreitender Informationsfluss und „domaine réservé", in: BDVR 1979, p. 39 et seq.

[26] UNGA Res. 41/65 of 3 December 1986.

[27] See Report of the ILA Space Law Committee of the Toronto Biannual Conference 2006, to be published in 2007.

[28] UNGA Res. 47/68 Principles relevant to the use of nuclear power sources in outer space of 14 December 1992.

[29] See S. Hobe/O. Kimminich, Einführung in das Völkerrecht, 8th ed., Tübingen et al. 2004, p. 196.

[30] Examples are the direct broadcasting satellite or the remote sensing principles where the prior consent / free flow of information policies were strictly opposed to one another.

[31] N. Matte, Space Policy and Programs Today and Tomorrow. The Vanishing Duopole, Montreal 1980.

[32] UNGA Res. 34/121 of 13 December 1996.

[33] The title of the Agenda Item was: „Consideration of the legal aspects related to the application of the principle that the exploration and utilisation of outer space should be carried out for the benefit and in the

interest of all states, taking into particular account the needs of the developing countries", of 1988.

[34] See for a critical appraisal M. Benkö/K.-U. Schrogl, The UN Committee on the Peaceful Uses of Outer Space: Adoption of a Declaration on "Space Benefits" and Other Recent Developments, in: ZLW 1997, p. 223.

[35] See id.

[36] See on this development K.-U. Schrogl/Ch. Davis, A new look at the concept of the „launching state", in: ZLW 2002, p. 358.; see also UNGA Res. 59/115, Application of the legal concept of the „launching state", of 10 December 2004.

[37] See the conclusion of the Working Group, in: Doc. A/AC.105/187 of 19 April 2002.

[38] See e.g. Belgium 2005, Korea 2006.

[39] See Norway, Sweden, United Kingdom, South Africa, Argentina, Russia, Ukraine, Australia, Hong Kong, Brazil, United States of America, Korea, Belgium; among the countries preparing national space legislation are The Netherlands, Germany and France.

[40] See Report of the Chairman of the Working Group on the Practice of States in International Organisations in Registering Space Objects, Doc. A/AC.105/871, p. 33.

[41] See inter alia E. Galloway, Consensus Decision-Making in U.N. COPUOS, in: Journal of Space Law 1979, p. 3 et seq.: N.M. Matte (ed.), Space Activities and Emerging International Law, Montreal 1984, p. 197 et seq.

[42] See for an analysis C. Christol, The modern international law of outer space, New York 1982, p. 18, 19.

[43] See the ILA Space Law Resolution of New Delhi 2002 that indicates that any international space law agreement has a need to be amended, Res. 1/2002, London 2002, p. 13 et seq.

[44] See on this problem M. Gerhard, Transfer of operation and control with respect to space objects – Problems of responsibility and liability of states, in: ZLW 2002, p. 571 et seq.; J. Hermida, Transfer of satellites in orbit – An international law approach, in: IISL Proceedings of the 46th Colloquium on the Law of Outer Space (2003), p. 189 et seq.

[45] See A. Kerrest, Remarks on the notion of launching state, in: IISL Proceedings of the 42nd Colloquium on the Law of Outer Space (1999), p. 308.

[46] These shortcomings are apparently mentioned in the Report of the Chairman of the Working Group on the State Practice of the Registration Convention, Doc. A/AC.105/871, p. 36.

[47] Considerations of the ILA Space Law Committee at its 72nd Biannual Conference in Toronto 2006, to be published.

[48] Concrete proposals will be made by S. Hobe, Challenge to the Astronaut Concept in the Era of Space Tourism, in: G. Lafferranderie (ed.), Agreement on the Rescue of Astronauts, the Return of Astronauts and the Return of Objects Launched into Outer Space 1968 – 2008. Lessons learned? Which Directions Now?, (shall be published in 2008).

[49] See on the delimitation discussion inter alia S. Hobe, Definition and Delimitation of Outer Space, in: ECSL 6th Summer Course on Space Law and Policy, Paris 1997, p. 49, 53 et seq.; see also S. Hobe/J. Cloppenburg, Towards a New Aerospace Convention? – Selected Legal Issues of "Space Tourism", in: IISL Colloquium on the Law of Outer Space, Vancouver 2004, p. 377, 378, 383.

[50] See S. Hobe/K.-U. Schrogl/B. Schmidt-Tedd (eds.), Project 2001 Plus, Workshop 2004 in Berlin, Köln et al. 2004.

[51] See for an attempt in this direction, S. Hobe, Adequacy of the Current Legal and Regulatory Framework Relating to the Extraction and Appropriation of Natural Resources, in: Proceedings of a Workshop held on 28-29 June 2006 in Montreal (to be published in Annals of Air and Space Law 2007).

[52] See in this particular direction, the Declaration of the Board of Directors of the International Institute of Space Law on claims to property rights regarding the Moon and other celectial bodies, http://www.iafastro-iisl.com/editional/20pages/statement_moon.htm (date of access: 15 August 2006).

[53] See J. Charney, Entry into Force of the 1982 Convention on the Law of the Sea, in: 35 Va.J.Int'l.L.1995, p. 381 et seq.; S. Hobe, Was bleibt vom gemeinsamen Erbe der Menschheit?, in: K. Dicke et al. (ed.) Weltinnenrecht, Liber Amicorum Jost Delbrück, Berlin 2005, p. 329, 338.

[54] The respective paragraph reads as follows: „Regarding the 1979 Moon Agreement: Considering further that the common heritage of mankind concept has developed today as also allowing the commercial uses of outer space for the benefit of mankind, and that certain adjustments are suggested to Art. 11 of this Agreement concerning the international regime to be set up for the exploitation of Moon resources, which will make it more realistic in today's international scenario."

IAC-06-E6.5.02.

Small States, Entrepreneurial States and Space

Francis Lyall
Emeritus Professor of Public Law,
University of Aberdeen, Scotland, UK.

Abstract

States are inherently equal having the same rights and duties irrespective of their size or power. But the development of space activities and particularly the involvement of private enterprise may produce problems. Some may not have the personnel, the knowledge or the abilities to meet their obligations in relation to space - particularly as to the duties of licensing and supervision prescribed by the Outer Space Treaty, 1967 and similar ITU obligations. Others may seek to establish themselves in the 'space business' by offering tax and other advantages. Private entrepreneurs may incorporate in states where constraints may be minimal. In such a case an important lacuna emerges in the legal regime applicable in outer space.

Should 'willingness and ability to fulfil international obligations' be resuscitated?

A. Introduction

The Convention on the Rights and Duties of States, Montevideo, 26 December 1933[1] is commonly held to articulate many principles of customary international law. Its Art. 4 states:

'States are juridically equal, enjoy the same rights, and have equal capacity in their exercise. The rights of each one do not depend upon the power which it possesses to assure its exercise, but upon the simple fact of its existence as a person under international law.'

Article VI of the Outer Space Treaty 1967[2] *inter alia* states:

'States Parties to the Treaty shall bear international responsibility for national activities in outer space, including the moon and other celestial bodies, whether such activities are carried on by governmental agencies or by non-governmental entities, and for assuring that national activities are carried out in conformity with the provisions set forth in the present Treaty. The activities of non-governmental entities in outer space, including the moon and other celestial bodies, shall require authorization and continuing supervision by the appropriate State Party to the Treaty.'

Article 1.2 of the Charter of the United Nations states a purpose of the UN as being:

'To develop friendly relations among nations based on respect for the principle of equal rights and self-determination of peoples, and to take other appropriate measures to strengthen universal peace.'

There may be a disjunction between these provisions. What is the relationship between the equality of the rights of states and their duties? What can be done when there is an imbalance? In particular what about the rights and duties of states in the realm of Space Law?

B. Small states

Over the years various individuals have tried to set up their own states, and to have them recognised by the community of nations.[3] These individual efforts have failed, but thanks to history there are a number of old small states in Europe.[4] However, following the Second World War the modern concept of 'self-determination' has led to the creation or emergence of many small states, some directly out of the former colonies, and some by later separation from the first generation of independence.[5] Many are economically disadvantaged. Indeed the category of 'least developed' countries (LDCs) has expanded from 25 in 1971 to 49 in 2006.[6]

When I was a student almost half a century ago, Iain MacGibbon introduced us to 'Recognition in International Law' and the mysteries of the 'Declaratory' and 'Constitutive' theories. He also went through the various grounds for the grant or withholding of recognition, and told us that test of 'willingness and ability' to fulfil international obligations was obsolete. In retrospect that was an interesting assertion.

The 'willingness and ability' of a state or government to fulfil international obligations did figure in a number of debates as to the entitlement of small states either to recognition itself, or as to membership of particular international organisations, including the United Nations itself.[7] Thus, although the Vatican was a member of Interim Intelsat,[8] and of the definitive INTELSAT Agreements,[9] it was not until 1983 that the US accredited an ambassador to the Vatican, thus granting recognition to the Vatican City state. The Vatican had formal existence as a state for Italy and many others since the Lateran Treaty of 1929, but the US reluctance to recognise was based at least in part on doubt whether the Vatican could fulfil the ordinary rights and duties of a state.[10] Other examples of the question being raised in connection with membership of international organisations are chronicled in Whiteman's *Digest*.[11]

But the matter is not obsolete. Whatever its application in actual practice, in substance 'willingness and ability to fulfil international obligations' re-surfaced in connection with the EU recognition of states which arose from the break-up of Yugoslavia.[12]

Of course, small states have on occasion made significant contributions to the work of organisations and in the development of International Law. The 1967 speech of Ambassador Parvo of Malta and the notion of the common heritage of mankind in relation to what was to become 'the Area' under Part XI of the UN Law of the Sea Convention of 1984 is a notable example.[13] There are others.[14] But sometimes the smaller or less wealthy states have difficulties in properly maintaining the full range of activity.[15] In the realm of Space Law are all the representatives sent to COPUOS as informed as they should be?[16]

It has also to be said that, as the Prime Minister of Barbados commented, the efforts of some small states seem sometimes to be seeking 'gratuitous international assistance' rather than properly exercising the rights and duties of independent states. Such he accurately described as 'impostors'.[17] Of course there is no reason to condemn the efforts of small states and the LDCs to re-shape at least some international institutions in order to improve their participation in the world. I think particularly of the creation of the Development Sector in the ITU. But on the other side of the scale there is the curious interest of certain small Pacific island states in the work of the International Whaling Commission which appears disproportionate to the benefit they might gain from the work of that organisation.[18]

A problem for some small states is simply that of finance. Some have done well by fostering business: Singapore is an excellent example. But others have found other sources of income. Many small states generate revenue through the issue of postage stamps eagerly collected by those who find pleasure in philately. Then there are the states which seem to consist largely of post-boxes for companies which are incorporated in them. Elements of the privatised side of INTELSAT and INMARSAT are incorporated in Bermuda. The Cayman Islands and the Channel Islands are well-known as shelters for companies whose actual business consists of activities far beyond their territorial confines, although in these cases the supervision of commercial dealings is considerable. Others seek a larger income through the exercise of the rights of a state to license activities by entrepreneurs. 'Flags of convenience' have caused immense problems down through the years, problems which have been alleviated, but not yet solved, by the 1984 UN Convention on the Law of the Sea,[19] and by the 1986 UN Convention on Conditions for the Registration of Ships.[20]

C. 'Entrepreneurial' states'

It is nothing new for states or state organs or departments to engage in commercial enterprise. In the past the doctrine of state immunity caused some problems, and still may. In the UK we have had famous cases including whether the Tass Agency could be sued, or was it protected as being an arm of the Soviet Government.[21] We have therefore taken steps to prevent the undue use of the doctrine to avoid the enforcement of contracts or penalties.[22]

It is the 'flags of convenience' example that particularly worries me.[23] In the arena of space business there is the example of Tongasat.[24] I remain convinced that, although the initial notification for registration of some thirty-six geostationary slots was reduced to six, the ITU really should have refused to register more than one, on the ground that a single orbital position was all that the telecommunication needs of Tonga could justify.[25] In that connection it may also be noted that there has been some international concern expressed as to the stability of Tonga,[26] and that is apart from the various cases in which some of those involved with Tongan system have been embroiled.[27] Then there is the news from Niue.

The Republic of Niue is the world's smallest state (www.niueisland.com) and is self-governing but in association with New Zealand.[28] It lies at 19 02 S, 169 52 W, east of Fiji, north-east of Tonga, south of Samoa and south-west of the Cook Islands with which it was once associated. Its land area of 260 sq km is about 1.5 times the area of

Washington DC. Its population was estimated for July 2006 as 2,166 by the CIA website, down from some 5200 in 1966 because of immigration to New Zealand. It offers the internet domain suffix .nu.[29] It licensed six banks operating in Australia which the Organisation for Economic Cooperation and Development (OECD) was trying to shut down, and the US applied trading sanctions in respect of Niue links to Latin-American tax-haven operations. Accordingly, in seeking other sources of revenue, in 2001 with the aid of US partners Niue was trying to emulate Tongasat, Niue to get 35% of the profit. Unlike Tongasat Niue seems to have had in contemplation launching its own geostationary satellite on US money, with 15% going to consultants, and the remaining 50% to the satellite builders.[30] I am not aware of progress in this project, but Niue appears to continue to decline, so the project may have deliquesced.[31]

As regards remote sensing and telecommunications, suffice it to say that many states have launched or procured the launching of their own satellites. That is good. But there may come a time when entrepreneurs may offer to finance services which some states are unable properly to supervise.

Another interesting development compromises the proposals to create private enterprise launch facilities in various places. Some of these are within the US, where, we must assume, suitable supervision will be exercised. Other plans have been announced in respect of Dubai and Singapore, to which the same applies. But somewhere in the archives, muddled by relocation on my retirement, I have notes of other possibilities where entrepreneurs have approached LDCs and similar states with proposals. In these last one attraction for entrepreneurs could be that the supervision of the 'launching state' might not be as rigorous as it might be elsewhere.[32]

So it seems that in various ways some states are seeking to establish themselves as suitable homes for space businesses. Advantages offered may be tax breaks or other concessions. While they can boost their incomes the question must be asked to what extent they are equipped to fulfil the duties and responsibilities properly to license, to scrutinise the applicants, to monitor compliance with licences and generally to fulfil 'due diligence' in all the duties which International Law now lays upon states in relation to space activities. Regrettably there is also the potential for corruption to be considered.

The matter of the corporate 'veil' may also be relevant. The beneficial (or real) ownership of an interest in a company or other entity engaged in space activities may be hidden. Bluntly, entrepreneurs engaged in a space activity may conceal themselves - their identity - behind a sequence of 'shell' companies in order to avoid the supervision which their real home state would/should be obliged to exercise by virtue of Art. VI of the Outer Space Treaty as well as any other liabilities connected thereto.[33] For our purposes the ratio in the *Barcelona Traction* case might therefore be unfortunate,[34] although it is useful that the ICJ is not bound by its precedents.[35] In such a circumstance other parties to a dispute may well and properly argue that the corporate veil may be lifted, as it may be within various national legal systems when it is considered that the purpose of the veil is the avoidance of legal liabilities. But that is a matter of court action. What can be done short of such to encourage states not to be deceived and less to be a willing participant in such manoeuvres?

One possible response to the problem is the education of the personnel who are or are to be responsible for compliance with the international obligations of the state and the implementation of appropriate domestic legislation. In this the efforts of the ITU must be acknowledged. The Report of the Council on the Activities of the Union 2002-2006 which is going to the Plenipotentiary Conference of the Union being held in Antalya, Turkey 6-24 November 2006, contains much information on relevant ITU programmes and efforts. The Development Sector has run many courses. In relation to those 'least developed countries' a Special Programme has been running since the 1990s in which six to twelve countries are selected for concentrated assistance for two years on a rotating basis.[36] More contentiously as to outcomes there was been the World Summit on the Information Society 2003-2005 (WSIS).[37] The UN Office for Outer Space Affairs has also been running Workshops with the intention of spreading information about Space Law.[38]

But all that assumes that states are willing to assign civil servants to the task, and that they have competent trainable persons. That may not always be the case.

Is a solution the contracting out of these functions? The operation of the International Registry for the Aviation Protocol to the Cape Town Convention on Mobile Assets has been contracted out to an Irish company.[39] But such a solution is not satisfactory for securing compliance with the international obligations concerned with space. More than the maintenance of records is required.

Another solution with greater potential would be for states which are interested in getting a foothold in the space business through licensing to combine together to provide a shared service of 'due process' and supervision by trained personnel. Of course the organisation that would be required would not meet the present requirements of the space treaties as it would not be a state. However, nominally one state might provide the 'official' status required, while acting as an agent for such an organisation.[40] And in the remote future, perhaps such responsibilities duties could be assigned to a world organisation – if we ever get such.

But the language of that last sentence reveals that such cooperation is unlikely. Can we hope to see such cooperation between states? History of conflict and jealousy indicate otherwise. And it would be better not to have such 'cooperation' were it merely a mask for incompetence and corruption.

But were the idea of cooperation to be considered, it might be boosted by the undertaking of the cooperative states to submit their activities to the supervision of another body. As far as some aspects of supervision are concerned, the Radiocommunication and Standardisation Sectors of the ITU might be thought suitable to exercise such a function. Of course that would require modification of the present ITU structure and powers, and seems unlikely under present conditions. Giving the ITU regulatory, dispositive or veto powers where it considers that 'due diligence' standards have not been met seems a remote possibility. But it might be a good development – a stage on the way towards making the ITU a more active agent in the safeguarding of the world public interest in such matters.[41] However, that would operate only for matters within the competence of the ITU. What about other 'activities' which require supervision by a licensing state? There something like the supervisory role of International Mobile Satellite Organisation (IMSO) in relation to INMARSAT could be used. States could be 'certified' as compliant with best practice. Of course IMSO's own membership is restricted to its members which are states formerly the members of pre-privatisation INMARSAT,[42] and its personnel is tiny. A new agency for those willing to be supervised would need to be constituted in order to have the expertise to monitor, sufficient independence to reassure, and standing such that its determinations could be enforced. But, short of a supervisory body for space with global competence, these steps could be useful.

What to do about the 'corporate veil'? I think that the corporate veil should be disregarded. We do that in relation to the financial links and routes of organised crime and in relation to terrorism. I see no reason why the 'veil' should not also be disregarded where entrepreneurs are in fact seeking to avoid the supervision which their 'home state' might well exercise, and to find a less rigorous 'home' for the licensing and supervision of their activities. What is the difference between such attempts and traditional crime? In space the highest standards should be required in the interests of all.

D. Conclusion

'Conclusion' is probably too confident a word to introduce the end of this paper. Suffice it to say that there are obligations laid on states at International Law in relation to their involvement in space activities. Some mechanisms are needed to ensure that they properly fulfil these obligations. The 'willingness' and the 'ability' of states to fulfil their international obligations in the space arena require to be tested, monitored and supervised. And mechanisms are needed to require compliance. Failure for whatever reason must be sanctioned. How?

NOTES

[1] Convention on the Rights and Duties of States, Montevideo, 26 December 1933, (1936) 165 LNTS 19; 49 Stat. 3097; UST 881; (1934) 28 AJIL Supp. 75.

[2] Treaty on Principles Governing the Activities of States in the Exploration and Use of Outer Space Including the Moon and Other Celestial Bodies, (1968) 610 UNTS 205; (1968) UKTS 10, Cmnd. 3519; 18 UST 2410, TIAS 6347; 6 ILM 386; 61 AJIL 644.

[3] See J.L. Erwin, 'Footnotes to History': www.buckyogi.com/ footnotes/index.htm for an extensive list with detail of some histories/stories.

[4] Monaco (1191?: 1861), Vatican (756?: 1929), Liechtenstein (1719?: 1806), Andorra (1278?), San Marino (301?).

[5] 'Declaration on the Granting of Independence to Colonial Countries and Peoples' UN GAOR 1514 (XIV). Cf. A. Cassese, *Self-determination of Peoples: a legal re-appraisal*, (Cambridge: Cambridge UP, 1995); K. Knop, *Diversity and Self-Determination in International Law* (Cambridge: Cambridge UP, 2002). The Wikipedia article 'Small Island Developing States' lists 51 such small states.

[6] ITU: Report of the Council on the Activities of the Union, 2002-2006, Plenipotentiary Conference, 2006, Doc. PP-06/20 paras 291/2.

[7] W.V. O'Brien and U.H. Goebel, 'US Recognition Policy towards the New

Nations' in W.V. O'Brien ed., *The New Nations in International Law and Diplomacy* (London: Stevens, 1965) 98-228 and J.E.S. Fawcett, 'The New States and the United Nations' at 229-52; T.C. Chen, *The International Law of Recognition* (London, Stevens, 1951) 124-30.

[8] Agreement Establishing Interim Arrangements for a Global Commercial Communications Satellite System, and Relative Special Agreement, 1964, (UK) Cmnd. 2436; (1964) 3 ILM 805-14.

[9] Agreement relating to the International Telecommunications Satellite Organisation (INTELSAT), 1220 UNTS 1220; 23 UST 3813, TIAS 7532; 1973 UKTS No. 80, Cmnd. 5610; 1973 ATS 6; (1971) 10 ILM 909. Operating Agreement relating to the International Telecommunications Satellite Organisation (INTELSAT) , 1220 UNTS 149; 23 UST 4091, TIAS 7532; 1973 UKTS No. 80, Cmnd. 5461; (1971) 10 ILM 946.

[10] S.W. Bettwy and M.K. Sheehan, 'United States Recognition Policy: The State of Vatican City' (1981) 11 *Cal. West I.L.J.* 1-31. Cf. T.J. Reese, 'Diplomatic Relations with Holy See' *America*, March 16, 1985 -: http://www.americamagazine.org/reese/america/a-wilson.htm, and 'Three Years Later: U.S. Relations with the Holy See' *America*, Jan. 17, 1987 - http://www.americamagazine.org/reese/america/a-us-vat.htm

[11] M.M. Whiteman, *Digest of International Law*, (Washington DC: USGPO, 1968) vol. 13, 206ff.

[12] European Community: Declaration on Yugoslavia and on the Guidelines on the Recognition of New States: (1992) 31 ILM 1485.

[13] UN GAOR 22nd Sess. First Ctee, 1515 Meeting, 1 Nov. 1967: http://www.un.org/Depts/los/convention_agreements/texts/pardo_ga1967.pdf: Convention on the Law of the Sea, Montego Bay, 1984, 1833 UNTS 3; (1999) UKTS 81, Cm. 4524.

[14] Cf. S. Waltz, 'Universalizing Human Rights: The Role of Small States in the Construction of the Universal Declaration of Human Rights' (2001) 23 *Hum. Rts. Q.* 44-72; A.M. Halvorssen, 'The UN General Assembly's Special Session on Small Island Developing States – Sustainable Development in a Nutshell' (2000) 11 *Colo. J. Int. L. & Policy* 113-26; T.N. Slade, 'The Making of International Law: The Role of Small States' (2003) 17 *Temple Int. & Comp. L.J.* 531-43.

[15] M. Mwagiru, 'Issues, Problems, and Prospects in Managing the Diplomatic Services in Small States; (2006) 30 *Fletcher F. World Aff.* 193-206. Whiteman (above n. 11) at 208 prints two notes by U Thant, (UN Sec. Gen. 1961-71) on the matter. Some 'micro-states' were having to restrict their membership of international organisations because of the burden of the attendant obligations. Small states could be a problem for the UN because of inability to meet all their legal obligations. Cf. J.E.S. Fawcett, 'The New States and the United Nations' in W.V. O'Brien, ed. (n. 7 above) 229-52.

[16] This query should not be construed as being directed only to small states. I understand that the representatives sent by major nations can be ignorant.

[17] Rt. Hon. O. Arthur 'Small States in a Changing World' (2000) 24 *Fletcher F. World Aff.* 3-14.

[18] See the effect of small states within the International Whaling Commission: the Solomon Islands, Nauru, Tuvalu, the Marshall Islands, Kiribati and Palau, voted for the Japan position within the IWC in June 2006, Cf. http://tvnz.co.nz/view/age/411749/755696. It seems that Japanese aid to the Pacific Islands is

set to increase to 430m USD over the next three years.

[19] Above, n.13.

[20] Final Act of the United Nations Conference on Conditions for Registration of Ships: (1987) 26 ILM 1229; Convention on Conditions for the Registration of Ships, (1987) 26 ILM 1232: www.admiraltylawguide.com/conven/registration1986.html; A/RES/39/213.

[21] *Krajina* v. *Tass Agency* [1949] 2 All ER 274 (CA); Cf. for the US, *Yessenin-Volpin* v. *Novosti Press Agency*, 433 F. Supp. 849 (1978).

[22] (UK) State Immunity Act, 1978. This Act arose from such cases as *The Philippine Admiral* [1977] AC 373 and *Trendtex Trading Corporation v Central Bank of Nigeria* [1977] QB 529 and was influenced by the European Convention on State Immunity of May 1972 (Cmnd. 5081). It was recently discussed in the House of Lords conjoined appeals *Jones and Mitchell* v. *Saudia (Kingdom of Saudi Arabia)* [2006] UKHL 26.

[23] F. Lyall, 'Expanding Global Communications Services' Sess. III, *Proceedings of the Workshop on Space Law in the Twenty-first Century*, UNISPACE III Technical Forum, 63-80 at 69-71.

[24] D. Riddick, 'Why does Tonga own Outer Space?' 19 *Air and Space Law*, 15-29; JC Thompson, 'Space for Rent: The International Telecommunications [sic] Union, Space Law, and Orbit/Spectrum Leasing', 1996 62 *J. Air Law and Comm.* 279-311 at 280-283 and 300-302. See also R. Freiden, 'Balancing Equity and Efficiency Issues in the Management of Shared Global Radiocommunication Resources', 2003 24 *U. Pa. Int'l. Econ. L.* 289-327 at307-8.

[25] A. Nöll, former ITU Legal Adviser disagrees: See his Commentary in the UNISPACE Workshop papers (n. 23) at 81-4.

[26] www.news.vu/en/news/RegionalNews/49.shtml : anomasimanews.com/AMN_No4.pdf (both 2005).

[27] E.g. *In re Rimsat Ltd* 193 BR 499; 196 BR 791; 208 BR 910; 223 BR 345; 224 BR 685; 229 BR 914; Matter of Rimsat Ltd. 98 F 3d 956; *In re Rimsat, Ltd., Debtor, Kauthar SDN BHD et al.* v *Tongasat et al.* 1999 230 B.R. 362; 212 F. 3d 1039; *Kauthar SDN BHD* v. *Sternberg* 1995 US Dist. Lexis 7845; (1998) 149 F. 3d 659. Cf. In the Matter of Loral Skynet Networks Services Inc., (2005) 20 FCC Rcd 11856; (2006) 21 FCC Rcd 1434.

[28] www.cia.gov/cia/publications/factbook/geos/ne.html

[29] www.nunames.nu. Niue also offers web-hosting services: http://203.97.34.63/niue11.htm

[30] http://news.bbc.co.uk/1/hi/business/1658301.stm ; www.cnn.com/2001/BUSINESS/asia/11/19/niue.satellite/index.html; www.spaceagepub.com/subscribers/LDarchive/LD20011116.html

[31] http://203.97.34.63/archives_pacific_stories.htm

[32] Guyana may be an example: see from 2002, http://www.spaceandtech.com/digest/sd2000-22/sd2000-22-004.shtml, http://www.spaceandtech.com/digest/sd2000-12/sd2000-12-004.shtml. And cf. Venezuela 2005 - http://www.nasaspaceflight.com/content/?cid=4076; http://www.findarticles.com/p/articles/mi_hb3118/is_200011/ai_n7860925

[33] I have to say that I am unsure whether the licensing requirements of the UK Outer Space Act 1986 would allow the UK authorities to intervene or to punish a failure to obtain a UK licence under such circumstances. See ss. 1-3 and 8-9 of the Act.

[34] *Barcelona Traction, Light and Power Co, Limited (New Application: 1962)* (Belgium v. Spain) (1962-1970) (Second Phase) 1970 ICJ 3.

[35] Art. 59, Statute of the International Court of Justice.

[36] ITU Council Report (n. 6) paras 291-3.

[37] *WSIS Outcome Documents* (Geneva: ITU 2005): www.itu.int/wsis/promotional/outcome.pdf

[38] E.g. the Workshops held at The Hague, 2002; Daejeon, Korea, 2003; Rio de Janiero, 2004; Abuja, 2005. For their Proceedings see http://www.unoosa.org/oosa/en/Space Law/workshops/index.html

[39] Aviareto, Shannon, Ireland., a joint-venture between SITA SC and the Irish Government: see www.aviareto.aero and www.sita.aero. Convention on International Interests in Mobile Equipment, Cape Town 2001: http://www.unidroit.org/english/conventions/mobile-equipment/main.htm; text at http://www.unidroit.org/english/conventions/mobile-equipment/mobile-equipment.pdf Cf. R. Goode, 'The Cape Town Convention on International Interests in Mobile Equipment: a Driving Force for International Asset-Based Financing' 2002 *Uniform L. Rev.* 4.

[40] In the EUTELSAT Assembly as was, a Party might represent others. In the INTELSAT Board of Governors, and the INMARSAT Council, one Board member might represent a number of Signatories.

[41] Cf. F. Lyall, 'The International Telecommunication Union: A World Communications Commission?' 1994 37 *Proc. IISL* 42-7; 'Expanding Global Communications Services' in *Proceedings of the Workshop in Space Law, UNISPACE III,* July 1999. (A.CONF-184/7) 63-80;'The Role of the World Interest in Space Telecommunication Activities', (2001) 44 *Proc IISL*.171-180; 'The International Telecommunication Union in the Twenty-First Century', in K-H Bocksteigel ed., *Project 2001, Legal Framework for the Commercial Use of Space.* (Cologne: Carl Heymanns Verlag). 259-281. 'The Role of the ITU', in *An Outlook on Outer Space Law in the Next Thirty Years*, G. Lafferanderie, ed. (Amsterdam: Nijhoff, 1996) 253-68. See also R.S. Jakhu, 'Safeguarding the Concept of Public Service and the Global Public Interest in Telecommunications", (2001) 5 *Sing. J. Int. & Comp. L.* 71.

[42] The revised INMARSAT Convention: www.imso.org/public/convclean1.pdf. See also Amendments to the Convention and Operating Agreements on the International Mobile Satellite Organisation 24 Oct 2001, 2001 UKTS 49, Cm. 5274; 02-57, 1998 UST LEXIS 213; Amended Convention of the International Mobile Satellite Organisation (IMSO (INMARSAT)) with Public Service Agreement (1999) XXIV *Annals of Air and Space Law* 477 – 506. In November 2006 the IMSO remit may be widened to allow the organisation to provide supervision of any provider of telecommunications services additional to INMARSAT: See Sec. 6 of F. Lyall, 'The Protection of the Public Interest in the Light of the Commercialisation and Privatisation of the Providers of International Satellite Telecommunications' (2004) 47 *Proc. IISL* 441-51.

IAC-06-E.6.5.04

The Future of Planetary Protection: Is there Reason for Optimism?

Patricia M. Sterns*
Leslie I. Tennen**
Law Offices of Sterns and Tennen***
Phoenix, Arizona, U.S.A.

Abstract

The search for extraterrestrial life has been a primary focus for interplanetary spacecraft. The integrity of scientific investigations for evidence of indigenous life is dependent upon the presence of a pristine extraterrestrial environment, free from Earth-based organic contaminants carried by the very spacecraft sent to conduct exploratory missions. Policies to protect planetary environments have been adopted by the international scientific and legal communities, however, the policies are not static, and can never be assumed to be adequate to the task. Recent discoveries that water may be more plentiful in the solar system than previously envisioned underscore the need for regular review and re-evaluation of the effectiveness of planetary protection policies. This paper examines recent developments in the evolution of planetary protection, and questions whether there is reason for optimism.

* Director IISL, Member IAA, ASIL, ABA, IBA, ILA, Senior Member AIAA

** Former Commissioner, Arizona Space Commission, Member IISL, IAA, IEAS

*** Member IAF

Introduction

Planetary Protection
All of the Planets All of the Time. . . .

This simple statement by NASA summarizes the essence of the policy of planetary protection: the pristine celestial environments must be protected from contamination by Earth based exploratory missions. This is a lofty goal in the abstract, but an absolutely essential goal in practice. The international scientific community, acting through COSPAR, has adopted specific policy guidelines and requirements, which have been modified in practice based largely on recommendations developed by the Space Studies Board of the National Research Council for NASA.[1]

---

1. *See, e.g., Outbound Spacecraft Basic Policy Relating to Lunar and Planetary Quarantine Control*, NASA Policy Directive 8020.7 (1967); *Outbound Planetary Biological and Organic Contamination Control*, NASA Policy Directive 8020.10A (1972); *Quarantine Provisions for Unmanned Extraterrestrial Missions*, NASA Hand Book 8020.12A (1976); *Biological Contamination Control for Outbound and Inbound Planetary Spacecraft*, NASA Management Instruction 8020.7A (1988), *Biological Contamination Control for Outbound and Inbound Planetary Spacecraft*, NASA Policy Directive 8020.7F (1999).

The planetary protection policy (PPP) developed by the scientific community is the implementation of the mandate contained in the Outer Space Treaty, which provides that:

> States Parties to the Treaty shall pursue studies of outer space, including the moon and other celestial bodies, and conduct exploration of them so as to avoid their harmful contamination. . . .[2]

The protection of celestial environments acts to enhance the scientific integrity of experiments conducted on celestial bodies, especially in relation to the search for the presence of extent or past life or the precursors thereof. The planetary protection policy also has important implications for the rights of all states to participate in the exploration of outer space, including the Moon and other celestial bodies.[3]

DEVELOPMENT OF THE PLANETARY PROTECTION POLICY

A. Trans-science and Risk Assessment

The application of the planetary protection policy necessarily involves an analysis of risks and probabilities. In basic terms, the risk that a spacecraft may cause forward contamination of a celestial body is dependent upon the initial microbial burden of the craft at launch, the ability of the organisms to survive launch, transit and deposition into an alien environment, and the receptivity of the alien environment to support and sustain the terran life forms.[4] The assessment of these risks

---

2. Treaty on Principles Governing the Activities of States in the Exploration and Use of Outer Space, Including the Moon and Other Celestial Bodies, *opened for signature* January 27, 1967, art. IX, 18 U.S.T. 2410, T.I.A.S. No. 6347, 610 U.N.T.S. 205, *text reproduced in* UNITED NATIONS TREATIES AND PRINCIPLES ON OUTER SPACE 3 (2002) [hereinafter referred to as the "Outer Space Treaty"]; see also Treaty on Principles Governing the Activities of States on the Moon and Other Celestial Bodies, art. 7, *entered into force* July 11, 1984, *text reprinted in* Report, Committee on Peaceful Uses of Outer Space, 34 U.N. GAOR Supp. (No. 20), U.N. Doc. A/RES/34/68 (1979); UNITED NATIONS TREATIES ON OUTER SPACE 27 (2002); *and* 18 I.L.M. 1434 (1979).

3. There are three basic interests which are sought to be safeguarded by the planetary protection policy: first, the prevention of contamination of pristine celestial environments by terrestrial sources, that is forward contamination; second, the prevention of the contamination of the Earth by the return of extraterrestrial materials, *i.e.* back contamination; and third, the prevention of interference with the activities of states in the peaceful exploration and use of outer space. All three of these interests are expressly mentioned in article IX of the Outer Space Treaty. *See* Tennen, *Evolution of the Planetary Protection Policy: Conflict of Science and Jurisprudence?*, PROCEEDINGS OF THE 45TH COLLOQUIUM ON THE LAW OF OUTER SPACE 466 (2003), and 34 ADV. S. RES. 2354 (2003).

4. The formula for determining the Probability of contamination (P(c)) is

$$P(c) = m(i)(o) \cdot P(vt) \cdot P(uv) \cdot P(a) \cdot P(sa) \cdot P(r) \cdot P(g)$$

where:

m(i)(o) = initial microbial burden at launch, after decontamination
P(vt) = probability of surviving space vacuum-temperature
P(uv) = probability of surviving ultra-violet space radiation
P(a) = probability of arriving at

is a function of determining and accumulating individual factors.

The outcome of the risk assessment can vary widely, based on the values assigned to the individual variables, and even the identification and definition of the particular factors can influence the ultimate quantification of the risk. Moreover, the analysis of the risk factors requires the placement of quantitative values to criteria which largely are unknown. As a result, there is an intrinsic and significant element of uncertainty, in which the issue of the assessment of risk contains a substantial grey area between scientific resolution and political choice.[5] Even when all available scientific data is considered, a residual level

> [of] uncertainty means that decisionmakers cannot determine policy on purely scientific grounds. At this point uncertainty itself becomes an aspect of the factual picture, and the question of what level of risk is acceptable in light of the uncertainty becomes a question of value, requiring political determination. . . . Failure to recognize the trans-scientific character of such questions too often lends 'scientific' credibility and authority as well as an air of 'factuality' to assertions or determinations that are at least as dependent on value choices as they are on 'scientific fact.'[6]

It is open to question whether the evolution of the planetary protection policy has adequately considered these ˜trans-scientific™elements, or whether political value choices have overshadowed scientific fact.

B. Planetary Quarantine Requirements

The inherent difficulties of assigning quantitative values to unknown qualitative factors can be seen in the evolution of the COSPAR planetary protection requirements. Following the lead of the International Astronautical Federation, and studies by competent international fora,[7] COSPAR adopted strict planetary quarantine requirements (PQR)

---

celestial body
P(sa) = probability of surviving atmospheric entry
P(r) = probability of release
P(g) = probability of growth

C.R. PHILLIPS, THE PLANETARY QUARANTINE PROGRAM: ORIGINS AND ACHIEVEMENTS 38 (1975), NASA Pub. No. SP-4902, U.S. GPO Stock No. 3300-00578.

5. Allen, *The Current Federal Regulatory Framework for Release of Genetically Altered Organisms into the Environment*, 42 FLORIDA L. REV. 531, 537 (1990), *citing* Weinberg, *Science and Trans-Science*, 10 MINERVA 209 (1972).

6. Allen, *supra* note 5, at 538-39, *citing* Yellin, *Science, Technology, and Administrative Government: Institutional Designs for Environmental Decisionmaking*, 92 YALE L.J. 1300 (1983).

7. Early studies were conducted by the *Ad Hoc* Committee on Contamination by Extraterrestrial Exploration (CETEX) of the National Academy of Sciences, and the COSPAR Consultive Group on Potentially Harmful Effects of Space Experiments. *See generally* Phillips, *supra* note 4, at 3; H.S. LAY & H.J. TAUBENFELD, THE LAW RELATING TO THE ACTIVITIES OF MAN IN SPACE, AN AMERICAN BAR FOUNDATION REPORT 189, n. 7 (1970); W.C. JENKS, SPACE LAW 34 (1965).

in 1964.[8] These initial COSPAR standards required that decontamination techniques were to be employed to reduce the probability of contamination of a celestial environment by a single viable terrestrial organism aboard any spacecraft intended for planetary landing or atmospheric penetration to less than 1×10^{-4}. COSPAR also set a probability limit for an accidental planetary impact by an unsterilized fly-by or orbiting spacecraft of 3×10^{-5} or less.

The COSPAR planetary quarantine requirements created bright line obligations for mission planners to ensure that interplanetary spacecraft, essentially, were sterilized. These planetary quarantine requirements were to apply to all missions for the initial period of planetary exploration of ten years.[9] Nations were allocated specific fractions of the overall probability limits, which were apportioned by the recipient state among the missions planned to be conducted under its jurisdiction.[10]

The PQR applied to interplanetary spacecraft through the Viking mission in 1976, including Mariner Mars in 1971; Pioneer to Jupiter; and Mariner to Venus and Mercury in 1973. In accordance with the PQR, the probability of contamination allocation for each of these missions, that is, the probability that a single viable organism would contaminate the celestial body subject of the mission, was as follows:[11]

Mariner Mars	7.1×10^{-5}
Pioneer Jupiter	6.4×10^{-5}
Mariner Venus	7×10^{-5}
Viking	1×10^{-4}

In 1969, COSPAR revised the planetary quarantine requirements, and stated:

> as the basic objective for planetary quarantine of Mars and other planets deemed important for the investigation of extraterrestrial life, or precursors or remnants thereof, a probability of no more than 1×10^{-3} that a planet will be contaminated during the period of biological exploration . . . ending in 1988.[12]

This decision by COSPAR made two significant alterations to the planetary quarantine requirements: first, it reduced the probability of contamination limit by a full order of magnitude; second, it limited the application of the quarantine requirements to ˜**Mars and**

---

8. COSPAR Res. 26, 20 COSPAR INFO. BULL. at Annex 4 (1964).

9. Report, Committee on the Peaceful Uses of Outer Space, at 13, U.N. Doc. A/5785 (November 13, 1964). *See* Committee on Planetary Biology and Chemical Evolution, Space Science Board, RECOMMENDATIONS ON QUARANTINE POLICY FOR MARS, JUPITER, SATURN, URANUS, NEPTUNE AND TITAN 27 (1978).

10. Sterns & Tennen, *Protection of Celestial Environments Through Planetary Quarantine Requirements*, in PROCEEDINGS OF THE 23RD COLLOQUIUM ON THE LAW OF OUTER SPACE 107 (1981).

11. NASA, Specification Sheets for U.S. Planetary Quarantine Program, Control No. 005 (1973) (prepared for COSPAR Meeting, Constanz, FRG, May, 1973).

12. COSPAR Decision No. 16, 50 COSPAR INFO. BULL. 15-16 (July, 1969), *quoted by* Stabekis, *History and Processing of Changes*, in REPORT, COSPAR/IAU WORKSHOP ON PLANETARY PROTECTION, Appendix C (2002).

other planets deemed important™ inhte search for extraterrestrial life.

The planetary protection policy was subject to continued re-examination as new data was obtained. However, criticisms to the policy grew within the scientific community. A primary criticism was that the assignment of numerical values to factors, such as the probability of growth, entailed inherent scientific uncertainty. Nevertheless, studies conducted by interplanetary spacecraft did not indicate the presence of extraterrestrial life or the ability of terran organisms to propagate. Thus, it was argued that the logic underlying the original policy was weakened, and that there were occasional inconsistencies in its application.[13]

C. Transformation of the PPP

In 1978, following studies by the Space Studies Board, the probability of growth factor was assigned a value sufficiently low so as to negate the necessity of engaging in any active decontamination techniques for most celestial bodies.[14] As a matter of policy, the assignment of negligible values to the probability of growth factors transformed the PQR from the norm to the exception.[15] In addition, active decontamination techniques were required only for certain mission type and target body combinations. The term PQR no longer was accurate to describe the circumstances, but was replaced with the phrase ˜planetary protection policy.™

In the early 1980's, the structure of planetary protection was transformed, such that planetary protection requirements could be imposed, depending upon the nature of the mission and the target body or bodies to be explored. Pursuant to this policy, missions to target bodies which were deemed not to be of biological interest in the search for life, including the Moon, did not require any planetary protection techniques to be utilized, nor was any specific documentation required. The classification of missions to other target bodies was to be determined on a case by case basis.[16]

In 1994, the planetary protection policy was revisited, particularly in relation to missions to Mars. The 1994 policy revisions tied the utilization of active planetary protection controls to whether the mission objectives included life-detection experiments. That is, craft landing on Mars which carried life detection instruments were subject to Viking level sterilization, but landing craft without such life detection instruments were subject to substantially less stringent decontamination techniques.[17]

---

13. DeVincenzi & Stabekis, *Revised Planetary Protection Policy for Solar System Exploration*, 4 Adv. Space Res. 291 (1984).

14. Space Science Board, Recommendations, *supra* note 9, at 27-28 (Appendix C).

15. *Id.* Nevertheless, the SSB continued to recommend that crafts intended for such celestial bodies employ clean room techniques. It justified such recommendation not on planetary protection considerations, but on the basis that the use of clean rooms would reduce the possibility of growth of organisms which might compromise the functioning of the spacecraft or its payload. *Id.* at 15-16.

16. COSPAR Internal Decision 7/84, *quoted by* Stabekis, *supra* note 12, Appendix C, at C-6.

17. *See* AN EXOBIOLOGICAL STRATEGY FOR MARS EXPLORATION 49 (1995), NASA Pub. No.

In 2002, the policy was subject to a comprehensive restatement, which was endorsed by COSPAR at the World Space Congress in Houston. This current statement of the planetary protection policy continues the application of active decontamination techniques based on the mission type and target body combination categories. The policy divides missions into 5 separate classifications of mission type/target body. In relation to bodies which are of "chemical evolution and/or origin of life interest or for which scientific opinion provides a significant chance of contamination which could jeopardize future biological experiments," notably Mars, three sub-classifications are made. These sub-classifications are based on the whether the landing craft is equipped with life detection experiments, or is intended to land in a "special region," where either terrestrial organisms are considered likely to propagate, or *in situ* evidence of extent life is considered to be possible.[18]

It is interesting to note that an Appendix to the current COSPAR policy states that as a numerical guideline, the probability of contamination should be no more than 1×10^{-3} for the initial period of exploration of not less than 50 years. However, no particular format is specified for calculating the probability of contamination. Nevertheless, the Appendix further establishes a probability of contamination for Europa flybys, orbiters and landing craft of 1×10^{-4}, and states that the "calculation of this probability of contamination should include a conservative estimate of poorly known parameters," the list of which is virtually identical to the factors designated in the original PQR P(c) formula.[19]

THE PLANETARY PROTECTION POLICY IN PRACTICE

A. Survey of Missions

The efficacy of the COSPAR policy can be tested by an examination of its application in practice. A brief review of missions, from a planetary protection perspective, will demonstrate whether the planetary protection policy has lived up to the goal of "all of the planets all of the time." With the exception of the Viking spacecraft, all of the mission listed below have been subject to the planetary protection policy which classifies and categorizes missions by mission type and target body, rather that the more strict planetary quarantine requirements.

The **Viking** mission to Mars soft landed twin spacecraft on the planet's surface in 1976. The landing craft were subject to cleaning to reduce the total surface bioburden to no more than 3×10^5 bacterial spores, with no more than 300 spores per square meter space, and a total bioburden for the craft of 5×10^5 spores. The craft were then subject to dry-heat sterilization of 111.7 degrees Celsius for 30 hours.[20]

SP-530; *see also* DeVincenzi, *Planetary Protection Issues and the Future Exploration of Mars*, in 12 ADV. S. RES., No. 4, 121 (1992); D.L. DEVINCENZI, H.P. KLEIN & J.R. BAGBY, JR., PLANETARY PROTECTION ISSUES AND FUTURE MARS MISSIONS, NASA Conf. Pub. 10086 (1991).

18. http://www.cosparhq.org/scistr/PPPolicy.htm

19. *Id.* at Appendix, *Implementation Guidelines and Category Specifications for Individual Target Bodies* (Version March 24, 2005).

20. http://planetaryprotection.nasa.gov/pp/missions/past/viking.htm

Mars Observer was launched in 1982, and was classified as a Category III mission. Contact was lost as the craft entered Martian orbit in 1983. NASA acknowledged that debris from the spacecraft "could have inadvertently impacted the surface of Mars, posing a risk of forward contamination."[21]

Mars Global Surveyor entered Martian orbit in 1997. The mission was classified as Category III, and according to NASA, the "orbit may be raised at the end of its mission to ensure against inadvertent entry into the planet's atmosphere."[22]

Mars Pathfinder was launched in late 1996, and carried a small rover named Sojourner. The mission was classified as Category IV-A. Pursuant to this classification, sterilization of the lander and the rover was not required.[23]

Mars Climate Orbiter was launched in 1998, and arrived at Mars in 1999. It was not intended to land on the planet, and was classified as Category III. Contact was lost with the spacecraft upon its arrival at Mars, and according to NASA "most likely inadvertently entered the atmosphere." If the craft did not burn up in the atmosphere, "the debris could pose the possibility of forward contamination."[24]

Mars Polar Lander was launched in 1999, consisting of a lander and two small probes, and was classified as Category IV-A. The spacecraft was assembled in a class 100,000 clean room, and subject to bioburden reduction techniques to meet requirements of "less than 300,000 spores at launch, with a surface distribution of no more than 300 culturable bacterial spores per square meter of surface area." Dry hear processes also were used for some, but not all, of the hardware. Contact was lost with the spacecraft upon arrival at Mars in December, 1999. According to NASA, no "unforeseen risk of contamination" was posed by the likely impact of the lander and probes on the planetary surface, and "fulfillment of planetary protection requirements for this mission was considered to be exemplary. . . ."[25]

Mars Odyssey entered orbit around the planet in late 2001. The spacecraft was classified as a Category III mission for planetary protection purposes, and its orbit may be raised to ensure against inadvertent entry into the Martian atmosphere.[26]

The Japanese **Nozomi, or Planet B** spacecraft, launched by the predecessor to JAXA, was intended to orbit Mars. Contact with the spacecraft was lost as it approached Mars in 2003, and it is believed to have entered solar orbit. The exact location of the craft is unknown.

JAXA has acknowledged the obligation to comply with the COSPAR policy, which

21. http://planetaryprotection.nasa.gov/pp/missions/past/mars_observer.htm

22. http://planetaryprotection.nasa.gov/pp/missions/current/mgs.htm

23. http://planetaryprotection.nasa.gov/pp/missions/past/pathfinder.htm

24. http://planetaryprotection.nasa.gov/pp/missions/past/climate_orbiter.htm

25. http://planetaryprotection.nasa.gov/pp/missions/past/polar_lander.htm

26. http://planetaryprotection.nasa.gov/pp/missions/current/marsodyssey.htm

would have classified the mission as Category III. According to the JAXA website,

> The international organization called "COSPAR" representing worldwide space science organs defines "Planetary Protection Policy" as special protective measure that provides for regulating a percentage possibility below one percent of falling upon Mars, within twenty years after the launch, for Mars orbiting satellites inadequately sterilized. On the other hand, from the standpoint of observing Mars, it is naturally better to get closer to Mars as much as possible, which means, therefore, the closest distance of 894km is marginally and most appropriately set for probe trajectory to take (sic).[27]

Mars Express was a mission conducted by the European Space Agency. Launched in 2003, the craft carried a lander, Beagle, intended to conduct exobiological and geochemical experiments. Contact with Beagle was lost on deployment into the Martian atmosphere. The mission was classified as Category IV-A pursuant to the COSPAR policy, which NASA says, like its own policy, "establishes strict sterilization requirements for Mars landers carrying instruments intended to search for evidence of biological activity."[28]

Mars Exploration Rovers Spirit and Opportunity landed on the planet in early 2004. The mission was classified as Category IV-A. According to NASA, "tests showed that the total spore count on both [rovers] was well below the allowable level." A primary mission objective was to search for evidence of water activity on Mars.[29]

B. Effectiveness of the Planetary Protection Policy

The Mariner Mars and Viking missions were subject to the rigorous PQR, which provided significant protection against forward contamination. However, by any objective standard, the revised planetary protection policy, based on classifications of mission type and target body combinations, has failed to prevent the contamination of Mars. Not less than three separate unsterilized rovers have landed on the surface of the red planet, together with associated mission hardware, and not less than four other unsterilized spacecraft have been lost while approaching the planet and may have impacted the surface. All seven of these unsterilized craft were in compliance with the applicable PPP classifications.

These missions each were classified either as Category III or IV-A, and under the more stringent requirements of the latter, a bioload burden at launch of 300,000 bacteriological spores still was deemed acceptable. Thus, each of the spacecraft can be expected to have carried a significant amount of contaminants to Mars. Moreover, the locations of the contaminated spacecraft are uncertain. While the location of the rovers can be known at the end of their respective missions, the

---

27. http://www.jaxa.jp/missions/projects/sat/exploration/nozomi/backnumber_e.html

28. http://planetaryprotection.nasa.gov/pp/missions/current/marsexpress.htm

29. http://planetaryprotection.nasa.gov/pp/missions/current/mer.htm

locations of the missing spacecraft are undetermined. Similarly, the extent of damage to the natural environment also is unknown. Significantly, these missing spacecraft even may have impacted areas that may qualify as "special regions."

The PPP based on mission type/target body classifications suffers from several inherent weaknesses. The PQR were criticized for the uncertainty in the required input parameters, especially the probability of growth factor. This is a valid criticism, and as noted above, focuses attention on the trans-scientific nature of planetary protection. Nevertheless, the probability of growth factor was subject to several downward revisions based on the absence of findings of indigenous life and indirect lines of reasoning. Thus, the PQR was transformed into the PPP as a result of the reduced P(g) values for several celestial target bodies. Nevertheless, there is a certain illogical circularity in criticizing a factor for its uncertainty, and then utilizing that same uncertain factor as the justification for a wholesale reduction in requirements.

A corollary to the foregoing weakness of the PPP is that it draws broad conclusions from limited information and extrapolation. The studies which have been conducted *in situ* in celestial environments have been limited in both scale and location. The data set is not well developed, and the experiments conducted to date have not yielded unambiguous, conclusive results. Reliance on limited *in situ* investigations to revise the PPP is premature, as the discovery of water on the Moon and other celestial bodies has demonstrated.

The PPP is directed toward considerations regarding life as we know it, and that is as it must be, as that is our frame of reference. Yet recent discoveries concerning extremeophiles are expanding the definition of life and our understanding of the extreme conditions in which life may not just exist, but may flourish. We must be prepared for an encounter with life as we do not know it, or may not even be able to recognize it.[30] Does red halophilic bacteria bear a sufficient resemblance to a blue footed booby that both would be instantly recognized as indigenous life forms by an alien observer?

We cannot answer, as any answer we give is filtered by the logic and experiences of homo sapiens, and thus may be very different than an answer from any alien we may encounter.[31] That, of course, is the point, we cannot know, but we must allow for the possibility. Perhaps we will know tomorrow, or the next day, or the day after that. In the meantime, we must not take readily avoidable chances of contaminating celestial environments.

This leads to another major weakness of the PPP, the division of celestial bodies into two categories: those which are of "chemical evolution and/or origin of life interest or for which scientific opinion provides a significant chance of contamination which could jeopardize future biological experiments," and all others. This distinction is unnecessarily restrictive and myopic. All celestial bodies are of interest for chemical evolution and/or origin of life issues,

---

30. Grinspoon, *The Case for Astrobiological Research of Venus*, SETI INSTITUTE EXPLORER Vol. 1, No. 1, at 4 (2004).

31. Sterns, *SETI and Space Law: Jurisprudential and Philosophical Considerations for Humankind in Relation to Extraterrestrial Life,* 46 ACTA ASTRONAUTICA 759, 761 (2000).

even those bodies which prove to be sterile. This is especially pertinent for celestial bodies which are thought to present environmental conditions which are conducive to life, as the building blocks of life are believed to be abundant throughout the universe. Thus, it is of crucial importance to understand why a sterile body is fundamentally different than Earth now or in past, such that life started here and holds on tenaciously, but failed to gain a toehold in a similar environment. The discovery of such a world would underscore the uniqueness of Earth and how precious is the gift of life.

C. New Optimism?

The COSPAR policy in relation to Mars recently was re-examined by the Space Studies Board. The SSB has recommended that the entire Martian planet be considered as a special region, and thus subject to Viking level sterilization, until designated areas can be exempted for less rigorous decontamination techniques based on further exploration and experimentation. This re-examination was conducted, according to the SSB, in light of current information regarding the science of Mars, the ability of extremeophiles to survive in conditions which have expanded the understanding of the tenacity of life, new technologies and life detection techniques, improvements in methods to decontaminate and sterilize spacecraft, and other factors.[32] Nevertheless, and while not stated by the SSB, perhaps the most significant factor mandating the re-examination is that the application of the COSPAR planetary protection policy has failed to achieve its essential purpose.[33]

CONCLUSION

The new SSB recommendations are an important development in the protection of the Martian environment. Perhaps they signal that the pendulum in planetary protection policies has reached its crest, and is now moving back in the direction of planetary quarantine. Nevertheless, the optimism engendered by this positive development is tempered by the further recommendation by the SSB that the new policy toward Mars is to be implemented over a lengthy ten year period.

---

32. Committee on Preventing the Forward Contamination of Mars, Space Studies Board, National Research Council, PREVENTING THE FORWARD CONTAMINATION OF MARS 2 (2006), http://www.nap.edu/catalog/11381.html.

33. Tennen, *Commentary on "Environmentally Sustainable" Space Exploration: Reconciling Challenges of Planetary Protection*, IASL – IISL INTERNATIONAL AND INTERDISCIPLINARY WORKSHOP ON POLICY AND LAW RELATING TO OUTER SPACE RESOURCES: THE EXAMPLE OF THE MOON, MARS & OTHER CELESTIAL BODIES (2006).

Paper IAC-06-E6.5.5

Mélanie VINCENT
University Paris XI (France)

For a Charter on Space as a Common Good

Apart from a handful of space experts, few are those on this planet who realize that a revolution, even more radical than that of aviation, is taking place above their heads. If we don't pay due attention to it, the "conquest of space" might end up as a colonization of space. The word "conquest" is seldom used nowadays—maybe out of political correctness (the term being too brutal) or because other words with mercantile, political or military connotations have superseded a noun which is now almost resounding with poetic overtones. Instead of "conquest," we now use terms like exploitation, domestication, privatization, marketing, militarization. (Words ending with '-tion' all come from verbs ending with '-ize' and expressing *action*, and, as we shall see, space law has indeed transformed itself and is now referred to as the law of space *activities*).

This change in vocabulary foreshadows the coming revolution. We are moving away from the founding document—the Outer Space Treaty that came into force in 1967 and which proposed a disinterested and pacifist vision of space exploration. The nineteen-sixties and nineteen-seventies were no doubt the era of space conquest and conquerors, but that era, with its scientific and military objectives, remained compatible with the humanist ideas of the founding treaty. Today, this humanist approach is jeopardized by marketing and its obsession with profit. Certain signs seem to show that the appropriation of space is not just—as one might think—a wild dream. Whereas the 1967 Treaty set rules for the *exploration* and the *use* of outer space, the "Agreement Governing the Activities of States on the Moon and Other Celestial Bodies" (1984), signed by very few states, refers to the notion of *exploitation.* A new stage was thus reached. The gold contained in asteroids, the magnesium, cobalt and uranium supposed to exist on Mars or the water and helium-3 present on the Moon have now become the new sources of wealth coveted by the great space powers of the globe. Although permitted by the freedom to explore and use outer space, this kind of greed may well tarnish the serene beginnings of man's venture into space. If emerging space powers set about challenging the supremacy of certain leading space powers, this could lead to new types of warfare. The goal of this paper is precisely to call for vigilance in order to preserve the resources and peace of the generations to come.

My purpose here will be (point 1) to bring to mind the humanist principles of space law, before examining (point 2) the problems posed for these principles by the space activities linked to technological progress. I will then venture to suggest a few proposals that might help us deal with the said problems.

I. The humanist principles of space law

The legal status of outer space is characterized by the absence of territorial sovereignty. The fact that no protest came from non-space states meant, prior to the framing of the 1967 space Treaty, that they refused to consider outer space as being part of their territories. Besides, the infinite vacuum that constitutes space did not lend itself to the exercise of prerogatives pertaining to state sovereignty. This principle of an absence of sovereignty was extended to celestial bodies by the 1967 Treaty, in spite of their quasi-territorial nature.

In order to avoid all temptation to extend the principle of state sovereignty to celestial bodies, artile 2 of the 1967 Outer Space treaty stipulates that "outer space, including the moon and other celestial bodies, is not subject to national appropriation by claim of sovereignty, by means of use or occupation, or by any other means." This principle of non-appropriation by states makes it impossible to consider outer space and celestial bodies either as *res nullius*—that is, as goods belonging to no-one but that may be appropriated by means of occupation (like game in internal law or ownerless territories in international law)—or as *res communis*—that is, as goods that come under the co-sovereignty of all existing states. But, above all, this principle entails the allotment of outer space and celestial bodies to humanity as a whole. That is why outer space and celestial bodies must be regarded as areas open to exploration and use by all members of the international community. This is where the principle of the free exploration and use of outer space and celestial bodies actually comes from. States having renounced all claims to outer space sovereignty, it seemed appropriate to grant them freedom of movement for spacecrafts in that sphere of human activity—freedom being one of the most powerful driving forces of all human action.

In order to avoid the legal gap resulting from the pure and simple non-appropriation principle, paragraph 1, article 11 of the Agreement on the Moon that came into force on July 11, 1984 stipulates that "the Moon and its natural resources are the common heritage of mankind," just as the treaty on principles governing the activities of states in the exploration and use of outer space, including the moon and other celestial bodies adopted in 1967, recognized space activities as part of "the common interest of all mankind." The necessity of filling the legal gap, combined with mankind's commonality of interests and benefits, inevitably leads to the notion of a common heritage of mankind, a notion that has more to do with law than with philosophy.

The customary origin of the founding principles contained in the Outer Space Treaty—principles of freedom like the right of free access, the right of free exploration of space, or the right to use space and celestial bodies—accounts for the particular strength of that principle. The freedom of space activities does not indeed follow from the contractual obligations stipulated in the Treaty. It in fact resulted from a principle born from, and based on, the practice of existing states even before the Treaty was achieved. That principle has a *universal value*, independent of the conventional system, which only gave it external expression. It also applies to the states that were not parties to the Outer Space Treaty of 1967. When in 1975 Colombia, together with other equatorial countries, claimed a right of sovereignty over the geostationary orbit segment located above their territories, the objection that was raised against them was grounded on the value of international custom. Article 2 of the 1967 Outer Space Treaty makes no mention of the countries that were parties to the treaty, which means that this principle applies to each and every country of the world, including the equatorial states that were signatories to the Bogota Declaration of 1976 but had not been parties to the 1967 Treaty. The said principle has also a *permanent value*, in that it would continue to apply to such states as might in future terminate the Treaty. A state that would withdraw from the Treaty could neither oppose the freedom of other nations to explore and use outer space, nor make any territorial claim in that field.

Non only does that principle establish a line of conduct for states involved in space acitivities, but it also gives them a subjective right of a public nature basically grounded on the absence of state sovereignty in outer space and on celestial bodies. This right, which can be exercised only by states having financial and technological capabilities, applies to all states without discrimination. In order to remedy this factual inequality, states must encourage international cooperation in the field of scientific research. It is through this kind of collaboration that the principle of freedom in space activities may eventually lead us to dedicate the exploration and use of space to the common interest of all.

The competence of states gets weaker in proportion as one moves from state territories into spaces that are of common interest. What counterbalances the renunciation by states of their right of sovereignty—I mean, the principle of free exploration and use of outer space, including the moon and other celestial bodies—presents a problem because it is incompatible with certain founding principles of space law. It is also clear that the notion of a common heritage of mankind is hardly reconcilable with the huge financial investments dedicated by certain states to the space adventure of our time: obviously more efforts and more thinking will be needed to square the circle.

II. The problems posed to these principles by space activities linked to technological progress

Technological progress opens new profit-making possibilities in space, and legal brain-teazers tend to multiply. By means of a few examples, I will mention some of these problems.

The lust for appropriation may come from the private sector. In 2006, the British multimillionnaire Richard Branson created—together with the American initiator of the first entirely private space flight in human history, Mojave Aerospace Ventures—a joint company called Virgin Galactic. The purpose of the founder of Virgin Music was to take "access to space out of the hands of the chosen few" and to render space tourism affordable for all, at least those who can pay 294,000 € for a two and a half hour escapade into space, including only five minutes in a state of weightlessness. His first tourist spacecraft, called *SpaceShip Two*, to be built in 2008, will be launched from a flying airplane. This makes one think of the "Sea Launch Company," which launches satellites from the high seas, or of "Pegasus" doing the same from flying aircrafts, without being subject to any national jurisdiction or control. Under which launch state control will this first tourist flight take place? When one knows that this private company is deeply shrouded in mystery, protected by scores of family trusts registered in the Channel Islands, and that the structure of Virgin Galactic resembles an amoeba, with a network of firms that keep popping up, vanishing or changing names, one has good reason to worry, should this venture succeed, about the appropriation of the orbit or about the determination of responsibilities in case of damage.

Since September 5, 2002, a website called "Luneimmo.com" has been offering anyone interested the possibility of acquiring property on the visible face of the moon. In 1980, an American, Dennis Hope, sent letters to the United Nations, the United States government and that of the former Soviet Union, informing them that he was officially claiming ownership of all planetary and lunar surfaces (apart from the Earth) inside our solar system. His claim was based on two legal texts. First, on the 1967 treaty on principles governing the activities of states in the exploration and use of outer space, including the moon and other celestial bodies: for him, the ban on the appropriation of celestial bodies as defined by article 2 of the 1967 Treaty applied to *states*, not to *individuals*—although paragraph 3 of article 11 of the 1979

Agreement Governing the Activities of States on the Moon and Other Celestial Bodies does stipulate that "neither the surface nor the subsurface of the moon, nor any part thereof or natural resources in place, shall become property . . . of any natural person. » The second text was the Homestead Act, adopted by the American Congress in 1862 during the conquest of the Wild West, an act thanks to which settlers could after a period of five years become the rightful owners of the 160 acres of land on which they had lived. For Dennis Hope's "Lunar Embassy," which now sells tracts of lunar land in France, space is the Far West of the XXI century, where whoever claims a plot of land as his own automatically becomes the owner.

In year 2000, a supermarket in Britanny called "Giant" decided to give each of its employees a plot of land on the moon. "One cannot appropriate a land that is not given by a state", explained Amel Kerrest, both law professor at the University of Western Britanny and head of the Institut de droit des espaces internationaux et des télécommunications (IDEIT). "Since, he went on to say, the moon and other celestial bodies cannot in any way be appropriated by a nation, these title deeds just mean nothing." Outer space being 'the common interest of all mankind', as are the Antarctic or the ocean floor, no entity whatsoever, whether a person or a nation, may claim to be a 'lunar' landowner.

And what shall we make of that American industrialist who'd like to become the first man in the world to own a celestial body? Suppose he launches a satellite, tows down an asteroid and bring it back on earth. International space law declares that no one may claim property on a celestial body. But if this industrialist manages to bring back an asteroid on earth, it won't be a celestial body any more, and therefore space law won't apply to the case.

These examples point to an unfortunate tendency of our time, that of turning everything into merchandise. The pseudo-privatization of the moon and other celestial bodies seems to conform to the same mercantile philosophy. "Everyone is led to think, Amel Kerrest comments, that the space cake is doomed to be shared and exploited, whereas it ought to be the property of all!" A position close to that of Philippe Achilleas, head of the Institut du droit de l'espace et des télécommunications (IDEST) : « This kind of appropriation is contrary to the very spirit of the treaties governing space law. The Moon is a common heritage of mankind that must be exploited for the benefit of all states."

The lust for appropriation may also come from states. On January 24, 2004, in a speech on the new strategic orientation of the American Space Agency, President Bush emphasized the establishment of "a permanent human presence in the solar system." In line with this, the development of an offensive technology enabling the United States to "control and dominate space," as is specified in a planning document entitled *United Space Command, Vision for 2020* (Washington, D.C., 2001), will give aerospace industry the means to exert a total domination over space and its resources. Another document issued in January 2003 by the Air Force Space Command under the title *Strategic Master Plan: 2006 and Beyond*, is even more explicit: "While our ultimate goals are to try to 'exploit' space . . . we cannot fully 'exploit' that medium until we first 'control' it." To this let us add the fact that the United States did not sign the Agreement governing the activities of states on the Moon—let alone the comment of former astronaut Harrison Schmitt, published in *Space News* (13-19 July 1998), according to whom "all ban on the appropriation of natural resources was a source of concern." Our last point here concerns the fact that aerospace industry provides important fundings to associations like United Societies in Space that have undertaken to revise the clauses of space law forbidding any individual, firm or country to claim property on all or part of a planetary object.

The United States, aware of the importance of *space dominance*, in particular for intelligence purposes, and strengthened by impressive budgets, is now the dominant force in space, not only from a financial and technological point of view, but also in the field of law. Their national space laws have become a reference in many areas, and this supremacy is a danger for the respect of the founding principles of space law.

After all is said and done, whether private or public, the attempts at appropriating space should be relentlessly condemned. The antinomy between the freedom of exploration and use of outer space, the liberty of private actors, placed under the responsibility of states since the 1967 Treaty, the principle of non appropriation of space and that of a common heritage and common interest of all mankind, must be clarified parallel to the advent of technological progress and social advances. A few possible solutions might be envisaged, for instance the drafting by all the states of the world of a non-binding document that could serve as a means to call to reason the ardent supporters of space hegemonism.

III. A few proposals to meet these problems

If those instances are still infrequent, if in the coming years only a few multimillionnaires can afford the luxury of an escapade in weightlessness, and if only this or that state has enough means to invest in the discovery of Mars, the fact is that technology is moving on at a rapid pace, as well as commercial activities and the desire of other countries to emerge as space powers. It is imperative for space law to follow this evolution because its highly generous principles for humanity run the risk of being more and more out of step with economic realities. On the other hand, fewer and fewer states ratify space law documents: 100 for the 1967 Treaty, 85 for the Agreement on the rescue of astronauts (the first humanitarian law in favor of astronauts that came into force in 1968), 80 signatories for the 1972 Convention on international responsibility, 40 signatories for the 1975 Convention on registration of objects launched into outer space, and finally only 9 signatories for the 1979 Agreement governing the activities of states on the Moon and other celestial bodies. Commitment does not seem to have been the main characteristic of the late twentieth century.

Another possible initiative would be the drafting of *Codes of Conduct* by the great space agencies so as to improve the reduction of space debris and thus save launch states from being financially responsible. The Centre national d'études spatiales (CNES) is the first space agency in Europe to have signed, in October 2002, a European Code of Conduct on space debris applicable to every new project of the French space agency.

These codes, which do not come under any national laws or international legislation, could be drawn up on a worldwide scale and go beyond the mere area of space debris. The United Nations General Assembly (UNGA) could ask space agencies to draw up a common code of conduct or at least devise some coordination of national codes with a view to eliciting more respect for the founding principles of space law. This would give those codes an international legitimacy and would clarify the appropriate conduct of space actors. The world code of conduct could be used by courts to characterize guilty conducts and apply to them the Convention on responsibility or any other law relating to responsibility.

Codes of conduct are not mandatory, even for the space agency that worked them out. They are only recommendations that the agency is supposed to take into account—recommendations which have even less the force of law against national third parties like private actors, and which have no legal impact on activities led by foreign companies or agencies controlled by foreign jurisdictions.

Nevertheless the 'common code of conduct' remains one of the best adapted solutions even though it is not a binding rule. As a coordination of various codes of conduct, the European code of conduct complements the principles discussed within the framework of the United Nations and that of the Committee on the Peaceful Uses of Outer Space (COPUOS). It defines the behavior to be observed in the last phase of life of orbital satellites. Even though the clauses contained in this code are only recommendations, for the last 8 years one third of the companies which operate geostationary satellites have complied with its principles, one third have applied them in part and one third ignored them, thus increasing the possibility of collisions and the risk for launch states to be viewed as responsible.

Finally, an even more universal solution would be an *Outer Space Charter*: a charter reminding all actors of the founding principles of space and the beneficial effects of space acitivities, and establishing flexible rules, whether in terms of remote sensing, health, environment or even defence. Scientists are expecting spectacular breakthroughs in the field of biotechnology as well as from research on renewable fuel and energy, or highly resistant metal alloys. Pharmaceutical companies are planning to launch into the International Space Station (ISS) very pure and precisely arranged protein crystals which might help produce new medications. Let us imagine that some Indian researcher, invited to conduct experiments in the Russian module, discovers a remedy against this or that disease. Should then the discovery be patented on a strictly commercial basis or should we provide for specific legal clauses giving free access to that discovery in order to help humanity as a whole?

In the field of intellectual property, rather than trying to apply traditional rules that are usually very protective and nationalist, it might prove more useful to take a different approach when the invention may be of help to all mankind. On this point, Maureen Williams, an expert on space law at the University of Buenos-Aires, had this remark: "Obviously countries and companies investing astronomical sums should be rewarded for their inventions. But should a formula with universal benefit . . . be licensed strictly on a commercial basis or should there be provisions to make it accessible?" Here Maureen Williams was referring to a major principle of space law embodied in the Outer Space Convention of 1967: "The exploration and use of outer space, including the Moon and other celestial bodies, shall be carried out for the benefit and in the interest of all countries, irrespective of their degree of economic or scientific development."

In the area of remote sensing, while the United Nations have adopted a set of principles in order to ensure equal access to remote sensing data, it might be desirable to reconcile the wishes of emerging nations—that keep demanding a legally binding agreement for the "detectors," who neither have to seek any previous authorization from the "detected" countries, nor to give them preferential access to data—and those of the states or firms of industrialized countries that see no need for that, preferring customary law and voluntary codes of conduct whose only use is to preserve the status quo.

The point, in fact, is to pragmatically organize, rather than impose, international cooperation. If we expect too much, nothing will be obtained from states. Instead of binding conventions, it would be preferable to propose instruments more flexible than the codes of conduct—a Charter, for instance, with declarations or resolutions that would not only aim at minimizing abuses, but would above all recall the beneficial effects of space activities. The principles of such a cooperation and of a more equitable access to data are already part of existing conventions. It would be useful to remind decision-makers of their existence and to facilitate their application by means of statements of principle that could later on open the way to regional or bilateral agreements.

During the drafting process of the 1967 Treaty on space, the United States tried to get other participants to adopt the principle of a "pacific use of outer space" that would ban the deployment of nuclear weapons and weapons of mass destruction in space, but would tolerate the deployment of satellites for military purposes; they thus wanted to protect an instrument of major interest to them, that is the observation systems aimed at a better knowledge of their potential opponents. An arms race carried out in space would have threatened those systems and put Americans at a disadvantage. Indeed, the Soviets did not need such systems to get information about the United States, a country that was more open than their own.

Another example, as far as the limitation of space debris is concerned, might be the fact that "the United States doesn't want anything resembling international regulations" while many other countries precisely ask for that. The author of this remark is Kai-Uwe Schrogl, a lawyer working for the German aerospace Center. Americans, he goes on to say, "would prefer to see regulations set in a non-governmental forum where they can do what they like. But they'll eventually be forced to go to the United Nations." Ironically, the United States is the only country having a national regulation on orbital debris, and the U.S. government is trying to reinforce these laws, whose implementation is costly. It is more expensive to build a satellite that does not drop its support rockets into space when launched than one that does so. As K.-U. Schrogl rightly predicted, "when cheaper, more polluting launchers developed by other countries begin to reduce America's competitive edge, we will find a U.S. administration favourable to international rules." Americans want to keep their advantage. It is in that direction that states should try to coax them into accepting new rules.

Conclusion:

If we don't want the next astronauts bound for Mars to be obliged to turn back right after landing because there is a sign saying "No entrance. Private property!", then the moment has come to put an end to the hegemonic and mercantile folly of men. Luckily, law exists, that helps deter and punish offenders. But parallel to that legal process, which is always a dozen years late compared to technological progress, we might and should add a citizen-oriented solution based on the founding principles of space law. The 1984 Agreement Governing the Activities of States on the Moon and Other Celestial Bodies advocates in paragraph 1 of its article 4 that "due regard shall be paid to the interests of present and future generations." It is incumbent on us to remind the world of this fundamental duty. Yes, the moment has come to educate our children otherwise than by telling them the story of the first dog sent into space or the first moon-landing in human history. The inclusion, in every schoolbook across the planet, of the basic principles contained in the founding space documents, together with the threat posed on these principles by the policy of space powers, would be a salutary measure and a sign of respect for the future inhabitants of planet Earth.

At a moment when a large part of mankind are beginning to enjoy the fruits of space activity, it is high time to remind them that the prerogatives of humanity must remain a common good. It is also high time we gave up those 'earthy' patterns of thought based on power, rivalry, so as to acquire a more universal and communal conception of our environment.

In his 1961 policy statement on satellite communications, President John F. Kennedy declared: "I invite all nations to participate in a communications satellite system in the interest of world peace and closer brotherhood among people of the world." It would be useful to adopt this wise invitation to continue the conquest of space in the interest of all mankind. Constraining the powerful by resorting to education and reason, instead of giving binding texts a more liberal turn, might be a new approach and a new motto.

IAC-06-E6.5.06

SATELLITE TELECOMMUNICATIONS AS A TOOL FOR BRIDGING THE DIGITAL DIVIDE – PUBLIC INTERNATIONAL LAW IMPLICATIONS

Julia Neumann
Institute of Air and Space Law
University of Cologne, Germany
julia.neumann@uni-koeln.de

ABSTRACT

The paper focuses on the international dimension of the digital divide, i.e. the discrepancy between developed and developing countries in their access to information technologies. It examines in how far public international law supports the reduction of the digital divide with regard to the use of satellite telecommunications. Against the background of a factual digital divide between nations, and considering that information technologies, including satellite, are major tools for participation in the global information society, the investigation leads to one major question: is there a right of states to (benefit from) satellite telecommunications? Focus in the examination of this question is on international telecommunications law, on space law, and on international economic law. Rules of customary international law are also being analysed.

I. INTRODUCTION

Telecommunications infrastructure and services are widely acknowledged as indispensable tools for the socio-economic and cultural development of a country, offering unprecedented opportunities for the betterment of quality of life for all.[1] However, many regions of the world still have only very limited telecommunications penetration.[2] This discrepancy is widely known as a facet of the 'digital divide', i.e. the gap between those who have access to the latest information technologies and those who do not.[3] Whereas a digital divide can not only be perceived between different countries (industrial nations/developing countries), but also between regions of a single country (urban/rural areas), focus of this paper will be on the international dimension of the divide. This international divide has caused serious concerns in developing countries and international institutions like the United Nations;[4] initiatives such as the recent World Summit on the Information Society (WSIS) give evidence of these concerns. Against the background that satellite telecommunications can help bridging the digital divide by supplying remote areas with telecommunications, I examine whether developing countries have any specific rights in public international law regarding the access to satellite telecommunications. The legal problems will be investigated in the context of the applicable multilateral rules of international telecommunications law, space law and international economic law. Recent developments such as WSIS 2003/2005 in Geneva and Tunis respectively will also be taken into account. Regional public international law (e.g. EC law) will not be considered.

II. THE INTERNATIONAL DIVIDE

The term "digital divide" was coined in the United States towards the end of the 1990s.[5] Already before the process of "digitization" had taken place, however, the problem of an international "divide" with respect to telecommunications access was perceived by the "McBride-Commission"[6] in 1980 and by the "Maitland-Commission"[7] in 1984. The latter observed that two-thirds of the world population had no access to telephone services, and Tokyo had more telephones than the whole of the African continent.[8] While this statement has been cited on several occasions also recently, it is clear that in times of mobile telecommunications this does not hold entirely true for our times. In Mid-2005, only eight national economies (with a population of less than 160 m. inhabitants or approx. 2.5% of the world's population) had a combined "teledensity"[9] (landlines and mobile) of less than one. The global teledensity figures around 50.[10] Even though the situation may thus have improved, there remains a significant disparity as between industrialised and developing countries with regard to telecommunications technologies. This conclusion can clearly be drawn from the UNDP Human Development Report of 2003, according to which developing countries possess 113 land lines per 1000 inhabitants, compared to 562 in high-income states. Even with regard to mobile phones there still are disparities: 134 users per 1000 inhabitants in developing countries compare to 710 users in high-income countries. Coming to speak of the internet use, the report counts 53 internet users per 1000 inhabitants in developing countries as opposed to 477 per 1000 inhabitants in high-income countries.[11] The findings of the ITU World Telecommunication/ICT Development Report 2006 underscore these results.[12]

III. SATELLITES AS A TOOL FOR BRIDGING THE DIGITAL DIVIDE

Obviously, the digital divide can be bridged by various technological means.[13] However, satellites offer some specific advantages making them extremely apt for bridging the digital divide. Major advantages of satellites are their broad geographical coverage as well as the avoidance of expensive terrestrial infrastructures, such as cable, and the practically unlimited number of transmission recipients, but also the possibility to build up global networks.[14] Regardless of some disadvantages to satellite communications,[15] satellite systems are the only means to connect all those states that are not linked to optical fibre networks to the international communications network ("lifeline connectivity"). To date, still almost two thirds of all states can only obtain international connections via the INTELSAT system.[16] As an integral part of the global "information highways", satellite communications complement the linking of distant regions through submarine cables,[17] and alongside optical fibre constitute the backbone of the information society.[18] Satellites are thus perfectly well suited for bridging the digital divide.

IV. WHY BRIDGE THE DIVIDE?

The lack of sufficient development in telecommunication facilities and the availability of efficient and cheap services in developing countries are due to various reasons, *inter alia* a lack of priority, since telecommunications were and often still are considered a luxury.[19] This may raise the question of why the international community should be concerned with the problem.

However, information and communications in modern society are neither a luxury nor a comfort, but a necessity.[20] Information and Communication Technology (ICT) can be used to promote economic growth[21] (in 2003, the global telecom market revenue was US$ 1.426 billion)[22]. Moreover, ICTs' role in promoting peace, security and stability, in enhancing democracy, social cohesion, good governance and the rule of law, at national, regional and international levels, has just recently been underscored by the ITU.[23] Accordingly, the need to address the international digital divide globally has also been recognised by international organisations and fora.[24] The final WSIS outcome documents emphasise the growing importance of ICTs as a development enabler, and as a tool for achieving the internationally agreed development goals and objectives, including the Millennium Development Goals (MDGs).[25] These considerations are expressions of the more general concept of "global public interest", which thus stands behind the idea of bridging the divide internationally.

It is clear that in the end, bridging the digital must serve the objective of providing high quality services to all people at an affordable price.[26] Insofar, the concept of digital divide is closely connected to the notions of "universal service" and "universal access". These are of a purely national nature, however, requiring regulatory initiatives of the respective nation states. Bridging the digital divide in a global perspective applies to another level though, in that it is concerned with the prerequisites for states that aim at universal service/access nationally: enabling states to acquire the necessary means to build up national telecommunications to cover their entire territory.

V. STATES' RIGHTS IN PUBLIC INTERNATIONAL LAW

It shall thus be asked whether public international law confers specific rights to states, i.e. developing countries, concerning satellite telecommunications.

Legal claims of developing countries in this respect might result from all sources of public international law. These are listed in Art. 38 para. 1 of the Statute of the International Court of Justice.[27] Focus of this paper will be especially on international agreements and rules of customary international law. Of particular interest are norms of international telecommunications law, of international economic law (esp. within the WTO), and of space law. It seems feasible to examine the legal rights according to the object of potential claims. Yet, it would go beyond the scope of this paper to examine all relevant provisions in detail. I will thus focus on the main aspects.

1. Access to the orbit/spectrum resource

The operation of telecommunication satellites necessitates availability of orbital positions and radio frequencies to communicate with Earth stations. Developing countries intending to build up their own satellite telecommunications system are thus dependent on access to the orbit/spectrum resource. In terms of orbital positions for telecommunications, the GEO is usually preferred since it offers many advantages.[28] Located at approx. 36.000 km above the equator[29] satellites revolve at the same rate as the Earth, so that they appear stationary viewed from the Earth.[30] For an almost complete global coverage three satellites are sufficient.[31] The GEO accordingly enables global coverage with only a few satellites, which with an average lifetime of 15 years have a considerably long life span. Due to the physical characteristics of radio waves, also only certain frequencies are suitable for communication via satellite.[32] In the following, I examine whether international agreements or rules of customary international law provide for rights to access certain positions in the GEO as the subject of the most heated discussion (and to use certain associated frequencies).

1.1 Art. 44 (2) ITU-Constitution

Developing countries that are members of the International Telecommunications Union (ITU)[33] might be able to claim access to the orbit/spectrum resource according to Art. 44 (2) of the ITU-Constitution[34]. Pursuant to this Article, "Member States shall bear in mind that radio frequencies and any associated orbits, including the geostationary orbit, are limited natural resources", which "must be used rationally, efficiently and economically [...] so that countries or groups of countries may have equitable access to those orbits and frequencies, taking into account the special needs of the developing countries and the geographical situation of particular countries."

First of all, it is important to note that the provision explicitly addresses member states that "shall bear in mind" the limited nature of the resources. That wording emphasises the fact that under general international law, particularly the principles of sovereignty and territorial jurisdiction, the regulation and control of national telecommunications belongs to the *domaine réservé* of states.[35] Therefore, in principle, each nation state is responsible for the assignment[36] of frequencies to certain users; the ITU itself is not in a position to assign the frequencies[37]. Accordingly, as a first result, it can be clearly stated that developing countries members to the ITU cannot claim to be assigned certain specific frequencies (and associated orbital positions) by the ITU.

However, Art. 44 (2) CS emphasises that the frequency/orbit spectrum is physically limited.[38] Consequently, states are necessarily restricted in their use of frequencies and associated orbital positions. Therefore, international coordination is necessary in order to avoid conflicts and enable the most efficient use of the resources in question.[39] The need of such cooperation is reinforced by the fact that frequencies inevitably extend beyond state boundaries.[40] International recognition of a nationally assigned frequency is thus vital for the use of such frequency free from harmful interference by other users. To this end, the ITU has the task, by virtue of Art. 1 (2) (a) CS, to "effect allocation of bands [...], the allotment of radiofrequencies and the registration of radiofrequency assignments and, for space services, of any associated orbital position in the geostationary orbit [...]". The ITU radio frequencies distribution process therefore encompasses the allocation[41] of radio frequencies to certain services,[42] and the allotment[43] of radio frequencies to different countries (*a priori* planning).[44]

For services that are allocated certain frequencies,[45] the basis for international recognition of a nationally assigned frequency is that of "first come, first served", meaning that the user that first notified ITU of the use of a specific frequency will be legally protected from interference. This may favour the technologically advanced countries and has thus been challenged by the developing

countries.[46] Therefore, the system of *a priori* planning, with WARC 1977's allotment plan for regions 1 and 3 (Europe, Asia, Australia), and with the WARC 1983's allotment plan for region 2 (America), indicated a certain trend towards an international administration of frequencies and orbital positions.[47] Nevertheless, to date "first come, first served" is still the dominant principle.[48]
The problem that becomes evident from the discussions on the two systems is that of a fair balance between "efficient and economic use" and "equitable access". Whereas Art. 44 (2) CS imposes an obligation on ITU member states to use the orbit/spectrum resource efficiently and economically in order to ensure equitable access by all countries,[49] the ITU regulatory regime does not give a definition of any of these terms.
The interpretation of efficient and economic use of the orbit/spectrum resource is left to the discretion of each ITU member. However, member states have impliedly agreed to the objective of "equitable access".[50] Generally, the concept of equity relates to principles of justice and fairness;[51] in the context of Art. 44 (2) CS, the meaning of the term "equitable access" is further clarified when considering two other provisos, i.e. that countries may have equitable access only in conformity with the Radio Regulations, and that the special needs of the developing countries and the geographical situation of particular countries must be taken into account while making use of the orbit/spectrum resource.[52]
Against this background, developing countries have a right to access those orbital positions and use the associated frequencies that have been assigned to them in the allotment plans. Their notifications to the Table of Frequency Allocations of the ITU Radio Regulations are also internationally protected. Any "equitable access", however, depends on the design of the Radio Regulations. Developing countries are thus dependant on further international cooperation in this field.

1.2 Art. I OST

Developing countries might be able to claim access to the GEO and the associated frequencies pursuant to the 1967 Outer Space Treaty (OST). The principles of the OST are generally viewed as part of customary international law, thus binding also states that are not members to the Treaty.[53]
Art. I (2) OST provides for freedom to explore and use outer space, the Moon and other celestial bodies. This includes the use of the GEO, also for commercial purposes.[54] Even though this is not expressly stated in Art. I (2) OST, the US in response to the Bogotá Declaration of eight equatorial states in 1976 emphasised that "commercial satellite communications activities utilizing the geostationary orbit were well in hand and were widely known at the time, and no objection or exception to those activities was made either in the text of the treaty or during its negotiation"[55]. States, including developing countries, are thus entitled to use the GEO and related frequencies in outer space. Such use is not unlimited, however. Rather, Art. I (1) OST provides that "the exploration and use [...] shall be carried out for the benefit and in the interests of all countries, irrespective of their degree of economic or scientific development, and shall be the province of all mankind." Although this provision also limits the space activities of developing countries, it could be understood to grant to them rights in case they are prevented from space activities (i.e. satellite telecommunications) due to the use of specific orbital positions and frequencies by de-

veloped countries. Yet, already at the time of ratification of the OST, the US Senate expressly stated that nothing in Article I, para. 1 "[...] diminishes or alters the right of the United States to determine how it shares the benefits and results of its space activities."[56] This understanding was later confirmed by the 1996 Space Benefits Declaration[57] which, while acknowledging the need for international cooperation, leaves it to the states to determine all aspects of their participation in such international cooperation (para. 2).[58] In the field of satellite telecommunications, international cooperation was concretised by the ITU legal framework.[59] Thus, Art. I (1) OST in any case may not go further in its conferral of rights than does the ITU regulatory framework examined previously.

1.3 Para. 6 WTO Reference Paper

Para. 6 of the WTO Reference Paper[60] acknowledges the right of a WTO Member to exercise spectrum/frequency management, provided it is carried out in an objective, timely, transparent and non-discriminatory manner.[61] States that have accepted the Reference Paper are thus obliged to an objective, timely, transparent and non-discriminatory spectrum/frequency management. However, the Reference Paper reflects a global consensus on key regulatory issues for opening telecommunication markets to competition.[62] It thus aims at liberalising national markets, and does not confer any rights to developing countries regarding access to the frequency/spectrum resource.

1.4 Common Heritage of Mankind

Certain areas that are not subject to state sovereignty have been declared the common heritage of mankind (CHOM). Regarding the Moon and other celestial bodies, this has been stated in Art. 11 (1) of the Moon Agreement of 1979. The Outer Space Treaty only speaks of outer space activities as the province of all mankind, however. If the concept of common heritage of mankind was also applicable to outer space *per se*, it might confer participatory rights regarding satellite telecommunications for developing countries. It is questionable, however, whether a concept exceeding the contents of Art. I (1) OST could exist with the CHOM principle applying to the whole of outer space. In any case, state practice after the Moon Agreement suggests that one-sided, rigid obligations for the attainment of distributive justice is not provided by the CHOM principle.[63]

2. Transfer of (Space) Technologies

With regard to satellite telecommunications, developing countries may have a desire to take an active part in the development and operation of satellite systems, and to participate in the industrial development aspects of such systems.[64] It could thus be asked whether developing countries can claim a right to be transferred technologies by developed countries. However, it should be kept in mind that intellectual property rights (IPRs)[65] in technologies are usually vested with subjects of private law. Against the background of privatisation in the telecommunications sector, and commercialisation of space activities, this will also be true with regard to space technologies. Public international law might have implications in so far as it may influence the specific national laws, or it may even oblige states to a specific administrative conduct. In the latter case, an industrial state might come under a duty to assert the rights to dispose of the respective IPRs so as to be able to directly

transfer these rights to developing countries.[66]
Forms of transfer of intellectual property comprise a transfer of literature, education of local workers, delegation of technicians, engineers and managers, supply of industrial goods and/or industrial plants, patent licences, know-how-licences, technical assistance, and direct investments (industrial cooperation, joint ventures, subsidiaries).[67] Of central importance is the transfer of know-how, which has been defined as "the sum tota of specialist knowledge, operational experience, and the technical production of a manufacturer."[68] Irrespective of the failure of negotiations on an international Code of Conduct on the Transfer of Technology in 1985, technology transfer of developing countries has been a recurrent theme in the multilateral discussions of recent years.[69]

2.1 Art. IX OST

Since the specific interest in the context of this paper is on satellite telecommunications, it may be asked whether space law holds rights of developing countries to be transferred space technologies. According to Art. IX, sentence 1 of the OST, states shall be guided by the principle of cooperation and mutual assistance in the exploration and use of outer space. This wording again is very vague, however, and does not provide detailed obligations for international cooperation.[70] Also the details for mutual assistance are not provided in Art. IX OST. Taking into account para. 2 of the Space Benefits Declaration of 1996,[71] it is doubtful that Art. IX OST confers specific rights to developing countries regarding the transfer of space technology.

2.2 Art. 66 (2) TRIPS

A right of developing countries to be transferred technologies in general, and thus also space technologies, might be founded in Art. 66 (2) of the Agreement on Trade-Related Aspects of Intellectual Property Rights (TRIPS). Art. 66 (2) TRIPS contains a general obligation of developed country Members to promote technology transfer to least-developed countries (LDCs).[72] To this end, they are under a duty to provide incentives to enterprises and institutions in their territory to increasingly engage in transfer of technology to developing countries.[73] Whereas the precise scope of this duty suggests a considerable discretion on the part of the industrial countries, it is clear that the obligation exists and must be discharged.[74] This is emphasised by the general objectives of TRIPS as contained in Articles 7 and 8, which provide that the protection of IPRs have to contribute to the promotion of technical innovation and the transfer and dissemination of technology, in a manner conducive to social and economic welfare, and to the balance of rights and obligations.[75] Moreover, the Doha WTO Ministerial Conference in 2001 agreed that the industrialised countries would give an annual notification of their measures undertaken with respect to their obligation under Art. 66 (2) TRIPS.[76] These notifications[77] show that the obligation contained in Art. 66 (2) TRIPS is taken seriously.[78] The developed countries' discretion is further reduced by the Decision of the WTO Council for TRIPS in 2003 concerning the implementation of Art. 66 (2) TRIPS[79], which lays down an obligation of developed country members to submit reports on actions taken or envisaged to provide incentives for the promotion of technology transfer.[80]

As a result, according to Art. 66 (2) TRIPS, developed countries are thus obliged to promote the transfer of technology to developing countries.[81] However, a specified right of developing countries to be transferred certain technology does not result thereof.

2.3 Art. IV GATS

A treatment parallel to that of Art. 66 (2) TRIPs can be found in Art. IV of the General Agreement on Trade in Services (GATS).[82] According to Art. IV (1) GATS an increasing participation in world trade of developing country members shall be facilitated through negotiated specific commitments. This shall for instance be achieved by the strengthening of their domestic services capacity and its efficiency and competitiveness, *inter alia* through access to technology on a commercial basis. Member states are thus required to negotiate specific commitments in this respect under Part III and IV of the GATS. However, Art. IV (1) GATS has been referred to as "a statement of good intentions"[83] concerning the consideration of the interests of developing countries. Industrialised countries are thus not obliged to make specific concessions for developing countries.[84]

Art. IV (2) GATS obliges developed country Members to establish contact points within two years from the date of entry into force of the WTO Agreement so as to facilitate the access of developing country Members' service suppliers to information, related to their respective markets. Of specific interest to developing countries in this respect is information concerning the improvement of professional qualifications and the availability of service technology.[85] Yet the wording of Art. IV (2) GATS indicates that a right to obtain certain information concerning specific technologies is not included. All in all, Art. IV does not contain any substantial provision favouring the economically weak states.[86] Developing countries can not claim transfer of satellite telecommunications technology from developed countries according to Art. IV GATS.

2.4 Para. 6 of the GATS Annex on Telecommunications

The GATS Annex on Telecommunications[87] expressly acknowledges the telecommunications sector's dual role as a distinct sector of economic activity and as the underlying transport means for other economic activities.[88] Its rationale is to ensure that countries agreeing to trade in various services also offer adequate telecommunications facilities to deliver these services across the border or within their own territory. While the Annex is therefore primarily concerned with the access to markets and the use of infrastructures, it does at the same time recognise the special needs of developing countries. In this respect, it encourages technical cooperation in order to establish an efficient, advanced telecommunications infrastructure to expand their trade in services.[89] To this end, para. 6 (c) of the Annex provides that "[...] Members shall make available, where practicable, to developing countries information with respect to telecommunications services and developments in telecommunications and information technology to assist in strengthening their domestic telecommunications services sector." However, the wording "where practicable" indicates that members retain a wide discretion regarding the provision of such information. Any specific rights of developing countries to obtain such information can thus not be derived from para. 6 (c) of the Annex.

With regard to LDCs, para. 6 (d) of the Annex stipulates that "Members shall give special consideration to opportunities for the least-developed countries to encourage foreign suppliers of telecommunications services to assist in the transfer of technology [...]". Also here, it becomes obvious that, while Members are called upon to promote the transfer of technology to LDCs, no specific rights of developing countries to transfer of technology are contained in the provision. Para. 6 of the Annex thus does not confer rights to developing countries with regard to the transfer of technology.

2.5 Fourth Protocol and Reference Paper

The Fourth Protocol to the GATS[90] in its Annex contains schedules of specific commitments and a list of exemptions from Art. II GATS (national treatment) concerning basic telecommunications services. Whereas the precise meaning of the term "basic telecommunications services" was not clarified, it is clear that it principally includes all sorts of national and international telecommunications services such as e.g. voice telephony, data transmission, fax, facsimile, and also fixed and mobile satellite systems and services;[91] broadcasting of radio and television programmes is not included.[92] The specific commitments undertaken mainly encompass regulations for market access of foreign companies, for foreign investments and for ensuring competition through certain regulatory principles.[93] The schedules annexed to the Fourth Protocol do not provide for transfer of technology, however.

For the same reason, the Reference Paper[94] cannot confer rights to developing countries regarding the transfer of technology. Whereas it may help market access of developing countries to those of developed nations, it does not contain any rights regarding transfer of technology.

3. Provision of continued telecommunications services

Developing countries might be entitled to be provided with continued telecommunications services. This aspect was of great concern to developing countries in the course of INTELSAT's privatisation. Countries qualified as "lifeline countries" were granted to enter into Lifeline Connectivity Obligation (LCO) commitments.[95] Lifeline Connectivity Obligation (LCO) is the obligation assumed by Intelsat Ltd. as set out in the LCO contract to provide continued telecommunications services to the LCO customer.[96] LCO are obligations from an agreement in private law between the private company Intelsat Ltd. and the respective states. ITSO, the remaining international satellite organisation, is not party to these agreements (and does not even have the facilities to provide such services), but instead is responsible for ensuring that the private company fulfils its obligations contained in these contracts.[97] As a result, claims in public international law can only be raised against ITSO to exercise its obligation to ensure Intelsat Ltd.'s conformity with the LCO commitment. Consequently, there is no valid claim against ITSO to provide such services, however.

4. Universal service obligations

Pursuant to para. 3 of the Reference Paper, any member has the right to define the kind of universal service obligation it wishes to maintain in spite of market liberalisation. Such obligations will not be regarded as anti-competitive *per se*, provided they are administered in a transparent, non-discriminatory and competitively neutral manner and are not more burdensome than necessary for the kind of universal service defined by the Member. Universal service obligations are thus in principle accepted, although they may hinder competition.

5. International cooperation

The remaining question, then, is whether there are any participatory rights of developing countries resulting from other sources of public international law. Basically all of the provisions examined above are expressions of some kind of strive towards international cooperation, also in the field of satellite telecommunications. In this respect, they may certainly be seen in the spirit of the purposes of the United Nations as laid down in Art. I of the UN Charter, and the UN Friendly Relations Declaration of 1970[98], which reaffirms that the maintenance of international peace and security and the development of friendly relations and cooperation between nations are among the fundamental purposes of the United Nations. According to Principle (d) of the Declaration, states should *inter alia* co-operate in the economic, social, and science and technology fields, so as to promote economic growth especially of developing countries.

Whereas GA Resolutions are not legally binding, they may reflect a certain degree of *opinio iuris*, which in connection with state practice is a constituent element for the creation of customary international law.[99] It could thus be asked whether customary international law exists that provides for participatory rights of developing countries resulting from an international duty of states to co-operate in the field of science and technology. An *opinio iuris* to this end could be emphasised by the Charter of Economic Rights and Duties of States[100], which in Art. 17 provides that international cooperation for development is the shared goal and common duty of all states.[101] What becomes clear from these documents, however, is that states seem reluctant to commit to specific obligations of cooperation, let alone without consideration. Such understanding is underlined when taking a look at the principle of solidarity in public international law, which may well be regarded as the more general concept underlying these resolutions. In the light of transformation of public international law from a right of co-existence to one of cooperation,[102] it is to be doubted that international solidarity may lead to one-sided obligations. This is especially true when taking into account the principle of reciprocity. Any one-sided rights of developing countries therefore contradict the current understanding of the solidarity principle.

More recent documents regarding ICTs and the digital divide confirm this perception. The Okinawa Charter on Global Information Society, produced by the G8 at its summit in Okinawa in 2000, commits the G8 members to exercise their leadership to, *inter alia*, bridge the digital divide (para. 4). Yet, while providing for concrete actions (that have been implemented, such as the "Digital Opportunity Taskforce" whose report has been endorsed by the G8 Summit Meeting in Genoa in 2001), its language is again very vague ("promote", encourage"). It is thus doubtful that the G8 states meant to express their commitment in terms of corresponding rights for developing countries. Rather, it again remains at the discretion of states to take concrete steps.

Finally, the outcome of the two phases of the World Summit on the Information Society (WSIS) must certainly be taken into account when examining any *opinio iuris* regarding international cooperation to bridge the digital divide. WSIS was set up by the

UN following an ITU initiative,[103] and aimed at building a people-centred, inclusive and development oriented information society by bridging the digital divide.[104] The WSIS Geneva Declaration's 11 Principles set out key issues in this respect and concludes with the commitment of strengthening cooperation in order to tackle these challenges.[105] The Geneva Plan of Action[106] consequently sets out action lines regarding the issues defined in the Declaration. Of particular interest is action line C2.(d)(i), calling for support studies by the ITU so as to broaden access to orbital resources, global frequency harmonization and global systems standardization. Action line C2.(i) encourages the use of unused wireless capacity, including satellite, especially in developing countries. Furthermore, action line D. deals with a "Digital Solidarity Agenda", which aims at putting in place the conditions for mobilizing human, financial and technological resources for inclusion of all in the emerging information society.[107] The Tunis phase of WSIS, then, focussed mainly on financial mechanisms for bridging the digital divide, on internet governance, and on implementation of the Geneva and Tunis decisions.[108] According to para. 31 of the Tunis Commitment, the "representatives of the peoples of the world" commit themselves to work towards the implementation of the Digital Solidarity Agenda (para. 27 of the Geneva Action Plan). The Tunis Agenda for the Information Society consequently deals with implementation and follow-up of the outcomes of Geneva and Tunis. Also here, effective cooperation on all levels is considered essential.[109] While these documents do contain palpable approaches to bridging the digital divide, based on international cooperation, specific corresponding rights can not be derived.

At least with regard to any *opinio iuris* in this respect, there is not a single tangible line that can be drawn from all the resolutions examined previously to the WSIS documents. While the documents may indicate a general consensus that international cooperation is necessary, states seem reluctant to commit to specific obligations, not least of all without consideration. Accordingly, general public international law, i.e. customary international law, does not provide for substantial rights of developing countries regarding certain forms of cooperation with respect to satellite telecommunications.

VI. CONCLUSION

Access to the orbit/spectrum resource is to a certain degree ensured by the ITU regulatory framework within the limits of allotment plans and allocation. There is no specified right to transfer of technology, albeit Art. 66 (2) TRIPS obliges developed countries to promote the transfer of technology to LDCs. Moreover, there is no claim towards ITSO for continued provision of telecommunications services. Developing countries may, however, provide for universal service obligations.

What becomes clear from the above is that it is hard to speak of substantial legal rights with respect to interests regarding satellite telecommunications; commitments to international cooperation do exist, but at the same time contain considerable discretion on the part of the developed nations. In terms of public international law, the outer space legal regime and its concretisation in the ITU regulatory framework suggest that there is some duty to cooperate, the details of which remain unclear and require further cooperation.

[1] *R. S. Jakhu*, Safeguarding the Concept of Public Service in View of Increasing Commercialization and Privatization of Space Activities, with Particular Attention to the Global Public Interest & the Needs of Developing Countries, 5 Sing. J. Int'l & Comp. L. 71, 72.

[2] *P. Malanczuk*, Telecommunications, International Regulation, in: R. Bernhardt (ed.), EPIL IV, 2000, p. 791, 796.

[3] *B. M. Compaine*, The Digital Divide: Facing a Crisis or Creating a Myth?, 2001, p. xi.

[4] *R. S. Jakhu*, Safeguarding the Concept of Public Service, 5 Sing. J. Int'l & Comp. L. 71, 72.

[5] US NTIA Report "Falling through the Net: Defining the Digital Divide", 1999.

[6] *UNESCO*, Many Voices, One World, 1980.

[7] Cf. Res. No. 20 of the Plenipotentiary Conference of the ITU (Nairobi, 1982).

[8] *ITU*, The Missing Link, 1984, p. 13 *et seq.*

[9] Meaning the penetration in terms of one telephone line per 100 inhabitants.

[10] *T. Kelly*, Twenty years of measuring the missing link, in: G. Milward-Oliver (ed.), Maitland+20, 2005, p. 23, 29.

[11] *UNDP*, Human Development Report 2005, 2006, p. 265.

[12] ITU, World Telecommunication/ICT Development Report 2006, 2006, Executive Summary, p. 5.

[13] Cf. also *S. Ospina*, Satellite Service Providers, in: Project 2001, Legal Framework for Commercial Satellite Telecommunications, 2000, p. 140, 157.

[14] *W. v. Kries/B. Schmidt-Tedd/K.-U. Schrogl*, Grundzüge des Raumfahrtrechts, 2002, p. 155; *H. E. Hudson*, From missing links to digital divides, in: G. Milward-Oliver (ed.), Maitland+20, 2005, p. 37, 41.

[15] E.g. still quite high costs both for the telecommunications segment and the terminal equipment/end device compared to terrestrial networks, and the lower transfer rate in comparison to optical fibres, *W. v. Kries/B. Schmidt-Tedd/K.-U. Schrogl*, Grundzüge des Raumfahrtrechts, 2002, p. 155.

[16] *I. Baumann*, Das internationale Recht der Satellitenkommunikation, 2005, p. 548.

[17] *P. Malanczuk*, Telecommunications, in: R. Bernhardt (ed.), EPIL IV, 2000, p. 791, 795.

[18] *I. Baumann*, Das internationale Recht der Satellitenkommunikation, 2005, p. 547.

[19] *R. S. Jakhu*, Safeguarding the Concept of Public Service, 5 Sing. J. Int'l & Comp. L. 71, 84.

[20] *R. S. Jakhu*, Safeguarding the Concept of Public Service, 5 Sing. J. Int'l & Comp. L. 71, 102.

[21] Revised Draft of the ITU Strategic Plan for 2008-2011, Doc. PP-06/28 of 27 June 2006, at para. 2.1.7.

[22] http://www.itu.int/ITU-D/ict/statistics/at_glance/KeyTelecom99.html (date of access: 31.08.2006).

[23] Revised Draft of the ITU Strategic Plan for 2008-2011, PP-06/28 of 27 June 2006, para. 2.1.7.

[24] E.g. Okinawa Charter on Global Information Society of 22 July 2000, para. 15.

[25] *WSIS*, Tunis Commitment, WSIS-05/TUNIS/DOC/7-E of 18 November 2005, and Tunis Agenda for the Information Society, WSIS-05/TUNIS/DOC/6(Rev.1)-E of 18 November 2005.

[26] To the same effect, *D. Gomes De Sousa*, Digital Divide, Proc. 47th IISL Coll., 2005, p. 439.

[27] Art. 38 (1) ICJ-Statute is commonly acknowledged to apply to public international

law in general, *H. Mosler*, General Principles of International Law, in: EPIL II, 1995, p. 511, 515.

[28] *S. Hobe*, Die rechtlichen Rahmenbedingungen der wirtschaftlichen Nutzung des Weltraums, 1992, pp. 36 et seq., 168; *M. L. Smith*, International Regulation of Satellite Communication, 1990, p. 6.

[29] *R. Wolfrum*, Geostationäre Umlaufbahn, in: K. H. Böckstiegel (ed.), Handbuch des Weltraumrechts, 1991, p. 351.

[30] *M. Paterna*, Globalisierung der Telekommunikationsmärkte, 1996, p. 59.

[31] *R. Wolfrum*, Geostationäre Umlaufbahn, in: K. H. Böckstiegel (ed.), Handbuch des Weltraumrechts, 1991, p. 351.

[32] *M. L. Smith*, International Regulation of Satellite Communication, 1990, p. 7.

[33] Currently, the ITU has 190 member states, http://www.itu.int/cgi-bin/htsh/mm/scripts/mm.list?_search=ITUstates&_languageid=1 (date of access: 30.08.2006).

[34] Constitution of the International Telecommunication Union, Done in Geneva on December 1992 as amended in Kyoto, 1994, Minneapolis 1998 and Marrakesh 2002. Hereinafter referred to as CS.

[35] *P. Malanczuk*, Telecommunications, in: R. Bernhardt (ed.), EPIL IV, 2000, p. 791, 792; *R. S. Jakhu/V. R. Serrano*, International Regulation of Radio Frequencies for Space Services, in: Project 2001, Legal Framework for Commercial Satellite Telecommunications, 2000, p. 41, 71.

[36] "assignment of a radio frequency (channel) is the "authorization given by an administration for a radio station to use a radio frequency or radio frequency channel under specified conditions", Art. S.18 of the ITU Radio Regulations.

[37] *I. Baumann*, Das internationale Recht der Satellitenkommunikation, 2005, p. 284 *et seq.*

[38] It has also been described as a universal shared resource. Cf. *D. J. Fleming/E. D. DuCharme/R. S. Jakhu/W. G. Longman*, State Sovereignty and the Effective Management of a Shared Universal Resource: Observations Drawn From Examining Developments in the International Regulation of Radiocommunication, AASL, Vol. X (1985), p. 327, 332.

[39] Cf. *I. Baumann*, Das internationale Recht der Satellitenkommunikation, 2005, p. 276.

[40] *D. J. Fleming/E. D. DuCharme/R. S. Jakhu/W. G. Longman*, State Sovereignty and the Effective Management of a Shared Universal Resource: Observations Drawn From Examining Developments in the International Regulation of Radiocommunication, AASL, Vol. X (1985), p. 327, 332.

[41] "allocation" of a frequency band is the "entry in the Table of Frequency Allocations of a given frequency band for the purpose of its use by one or more terrestrial or space radiocommunications services [...] under specified conditions", Art. S1.16 of the ITU Radio Regulations.

[42] *R. S. Jakhu/V. R. Serrano*, International Regulation of Radio Frequencies for Space Services, in: Project 2001, Legal Framework for Commercial Satellite Telecommunications, 2000, p. 41, 71.

[43] "allotment" is the "entry of a designated frequency channel in an agreed plan, adopted by a competent conference, for use by one or more administrations for a terrestrial or a space radiocommunication service in one or more identified countries or geographical areas and under specified condi-

tions", Art. S1.17 of the ITU Radio Regulations.

[44] *R. S. Jakhu/V. R. Serrano*, International Regulation, in: Project 2001, Legal Framework for Commercial Satellite Telecommunications, 2000, p. 73 *et seq.*

[45] Fixed satellite services (FSS) and mobile satellite services (MSS), Art. S9 and S11 of the Radio Regulations and the respective declarations and recommendations; *I. Baumann*, Das internationale Recht der Satellitenkommunikation, 2005, p. 285. Art. S8.1.

[46] *P. Malanczuk*, Telecommunications, in: R. Bernhardt (ed.), EPIL IV, 2000, p. 791, 793.

[47] *S. Hobe*, Die rechtlichen Rahmenbedingungen der wirtschaftlichen Nutzung des Weltraums, 1992, p. 177.

[48] *I. Baumann*, Das internationale Recht der Satellitenkommunikation, 2005, p. 274.

[49] *R. S. Jakhu*, Legal Issues Relating to the Global Public Interest in Outer Space, October 2005, Paper prepared for Advanced Methods of Cooperative Security Program at the Center for International and Security Studies at Maryland, http://www.cissm.umd.edu/papers/files/jakhu.pdf (date of access: 31.08.2006), p. 38.

[50] *R. S. Jakhu/V. R. Serrano*, International Regulation, in: Project 2001, Legal Framework for Commercial Satellite Telecommunications, 2000, p. 72.

[51] *R. S. Jakhu/V. R. Serrano*, International Regulation, in: Project 2001, Legal Framework for Commercial Satellite Telecommunications, 2000, p. 72.

[52] *R. S. Jakhu/V. R. Serrano*, International Regulation, in: Project 2001, Legal Framework for Commercial Satellite Telecommunications, 2000, p. 72.

[53] *R. S. Jakhu*, Safeguarding the Concept of Public Service, 5 Sing. J. Int'l & Comp. L. 71, 91.

[54] This view is shared by a majority of authors, see e.g. *S. Hobe*, Die rechtlichen Rahmenbedingungen der wirtschaftlichen Nutzung des Weltraums, 1992, p. 66; *K.-H. Böckstiegel*, Legal Implications of Commercial Space Activities, 24th Coll. IISL 1981, p. 1; *O.F. Brital*, Survey from Space of Earth Resources, 13th Coll. IISL 1970, p. 197, 198; *N.M. Matte* (ed.), Space Activities and Emerging International Law, 1984, p. 273.

[55] Press Release USUN-18 (77), April 7, 1977, in: Digest of U.S. Practice in Int'l L., 1977, p. 661.

[56] Senate Comm. On Foreign Relations, Treaty on Outer Space, S. Exec. Rep. No. 8, 90th Cong. 1st Sess. 4 (1967).

[57] Declaration on International Cooperation in the Exploration and Use of Outer Space for the Benefit and in the Interest of all States, Taking into Particular Account the Needs of Developing Countries, UNGA Res. 51/122 of 13 December 1996.

[58] Also see *S. Hobe*, Was bleibt vom gemeinsamen Erbe der Menschheit?, in: K. Dicke *et al.*, Weltinnenrecht, 2005, p. 429, 339.

[59] *S. Hobe*, Die rechtlichen Rahmenbedingungen der wirtschaftlichen Nutzung des Weltraums, 1992, p. 181.

[60] WTO Reference Paper on Basic Telecommunications of 24 April 1996, para. 6: "Any procedures for the allocation and use of scarce resources, including frequencies, numbers and rights of way, will be carried out in an objective, timely, transparent and non-discriminatory manner. The current state of allocated frequency bands will be

made publicly available, but detailed identification of frequencies allocated for specific government uses is not required."

[61] *M. Gonzalez Durantez*, WTO/GATS Negotiations on Basic Telecommunications, Int.T.L.R. 1997, 3(4), 136.

[62] *D. Satola*, Legal and Regulatory Implications of Implementing WTO Telecommunications Commitments in Developing Countries, delivered at London, 28 October 1997, http://siteresources.worldbank.org/INTLAW JUSTICE/Resources/WTO TelecomDevelopmentMarkets.pdf (date of access: 31.08.2006).

[63] See *S. Hobe*, Was bleibt vom gemeinsamen Erbe der Menschheit?, p. 329 *et seq*.

[64] Cf. *N. M. Matte*, Aerospace Law: Telecommunications Satellites, RdC 1980, p. 123, 215.

[65] Legally protected rights resulting from intellectual activity; for a definition of "intellectual property", see Art. 2 (viii) of the Convention Establishing the World Intellectual Property Organization of 14 July 1967, as amended on 28 September 1979.

[66] *R. Schmidt-Diemitz*, Geistiges Eigentum und entwicklungspolitischer Wissenstransfer, GRURInt 1988, p. 287, 291.

[67] *R. Schmidt-Diemitz*, Geistiges Eigentum, GRURInt 1988, p. 287, 290.

[68] *H. Stumpf*, The know-how contract in Germany, Japan and the United States, 1984, p. 10.

[69] *P. Roffe/T. Tesfachew*, Revisting the Technology Transfer Debate: Lessons for the New WTO Working Group, in: Bridges, Vol. V, Issue 2/2002, p. 5.

[70] *K. Focke*, Internationale Zusammenarbeit im Weltraum, in: K.-H. Böckstiegel (ed.), Handbuch des Weltraumrechts, 1991, p. 637, 642.

[71] Cf. supra, at 2.1.2.

[72] Art. 66 (2) TRIPS: „ Developed country Members shall provide incentives to enterprises and institutions in their territories for the purpose of promoting and encouraging technology transfer to least-developed country Members in order to enable them to create a sound and viable technology base."

[73] Art. 66 (2) TRIPS.

[74] *UNCTAD-ICTSD*, Resource Book on TRIPS and Development, 2005, p. 725, 730.

[75] *UNCTAD-ICTSD*, Resource Book on TRIPS, 2005, p. 725, 730.

[76] Para. 11.2 of the Decision on implementation-related issues and concerns of 14 November 2001, WT/MIN/(01)/17.

[77] See, for instance, IP/C/W/431/Add.3 of 7 January 2001, IP/C/W/431/Add.3/Suppl.1 of 14 April 2001, and IP/C/555/Add.6 of 14 December 2005.

[78] To the same effect: *W. Werner*, Grundlagen zum Technologietransfer in der WTO, RIW 2006, p. 187, 188.

[79] Decision of the Council for TRIPS of 19 February 2003, Implementation of Article 66.2 of the TRIPS Agreement, IP/C/28 of 20 February 2003.

[80] *UNCTAD-ICTSD*, Resource Book on TRIPS, 2005, p. 725, 734.

[81] The other provisions of TRIPS are concerned with technical cooperation in order to improve the protection of intellectual property, not with project-oriented transfer of technology, cf. *W. Werner*, Grundlagen zum Technologietransfer in der WTO, RIW 2006, p. 187, 188.

[82] *P. Roffe/T. Tesfachew*, Revisiting the Technology Transfer Debate: Lessons for the New WTO Working Group, in: Bridges, Vol. V, Issue 2/2002, p. 5.

[83] *UNCTAD*, The Outcome of the Uruguay Round: An Assessment, 1994, p. 156.
[84] *M. Koehler*, Das Allgemeine Übereinkommen über den Handel mit Dienstleistungen (GATS), 1999, p. 140.
[85] *M. Koehler*, Das Allgemeine Übereinkommen über den Handel mit Dienstleistungen (GATS), 1999, p. 141.
[86] *R. Senti*, WTO, 2000, marginal note 642.
[87] Hereinafter referred to as the Annex.
[88] Para. 1 of the Annex: "Recognizing the specificities of the telecommunications services sector and, in particular, its dual role as a distinct sector of economic activity and as the underlying transport means for other economic activities [...]".
[89] *P. Malanczuk*, Telecommunications, in: R. Bernhardt (ed.), EPIL IV, 2000, p. 791, 799.
[90] Fourth Protocol to the General Agreement on Trade in Services, entered into force on 1 January 1998.
[91] *I. Baumann*, Das internationale Recht der Satellitenkommunikation, 2005, p. 338.
[92] *M. Gonzalez Durantez*, WTO/GATS Negotiations on Basic Telecommunications, Int.T.L.R. 1997, 3(4), 135, 136.
[93] *I. Baumann*, Das internationale Recht der Satellitenkommunikation, 2005, p. 338.
[94] Reference Paper to the Fourth Protocol to the General Agreement on Trade in Services of 24 April 1996.
[95] *K. Katkin*, Communication Breakdown?, 38 Vand. J. Transnat'l L. 1323, 1361.
[96] See Art. I (h) ITSO-Agreement.
[97] See Art. III ITSO-Agreement.
[98] Declaration on Principles of International Law Concerning Friendly Relations and Co-Operation among States in Accordance with the Charter of the United Nations, of 24 October 1970, UNGA Res. 2625 (XXV).
[99] See *K. Ipsen*, Völkerrecht, 2004, para. 32 marginal note. 47.
[100] UNGA Res. 3281 (XXIX) of 12 December 1974.
[101] Preamble and Art. 17 of the Charter. Art. 17: "International co-operation for development is the shared goal and common duty of all States. Every State should co-operate with the efforts of developing countries to accelerate their economic and social development by providing favourable external conditions and by extending active assistance to them, consistent with their development needs and objectives, with strict respect for the sovereign equality of States and free of any conditions derogating from their sovereignty."
[102] *S. Hobe*, Die Zukunft des Völkerrechts im Zeitalter der Globalisierung, ArchV 37 (1999), p. 253, 278.
[103] Res. 73, ITU Plenipotentiary Conference (Minneapolis, 1998), UN GA Res. 56/183 of 21 December 2001.
[104] Paras. 1, 17 of the Geneva Declaration of Principles of 12 December 2003, WSIS-03/GENEVA/DOC/4.
[105] Para. 65 of the Geneva Declaration of Principles.
[106] Plan of Action of 12 December 2003, WSIS-03/GENEVA/DOC/5.
[107] Para. 27 of the Geneva Declaration of Principles.
[108] Para. 7 of the Tunis Commitment of 18 November 2005, WSIS-05/TUNIS/DOC/7.
[109] Paras. 83 *et seq.* of the Tunis Agenda for the Information Society of 18 November 2005, WSIS-05/TUNIS/DOC/6(Rev.1).

IAC-06-E6.5.8

57th International Astronautical Congress

49th Colloquium on Law of Outer Space (IISL) (E.6.5)

Other Legal Matters, Including the Relationship Between Goverment and Private Sector in Space Activities (5.)

Author: Mr. Otto Gudiño

Ramírez de Arellano y Abogados, S.C., México, otto@rraya.com

MEXICO´S LICENSING PROCESS FOR THE RIGHTS OF TRANSMISSION AND RECEPTION OF SIGNALS RELATED TO BANDS OF FREQUENCIES OF FOREIGN SATELLITE SYSTEMS WHICH COULD OFFER SERVICES IN NATIONAL TERRITORY.

ABSTRACT

In the entire world satellite services are provided by numerous competitors in accordance with international treaties. Even thought regulations vary from country to country making it important for space lawyers and enterprises to know and precise the regulatory and legal frame of each case in the interest of providing global services.

The purpose of this paper is to give a specific study of the regulatory and legal frame as well as the international treaties adopted by Mexico for licensing process for the rights of transmission and reception of signals related to bands of frequencies of foreign satellite systems which could offer services in national territory. Also to be a practical guideline for those enterprises interested in providing commercial services in Mexico´s market by the operation of foreign satellites.

INTRODUCTION

The purpose of this document is to indicate and analyze Mexican regulation and regulation derived from international agreements that form part of Mexican Positive Law, related with the process for the granting of concessions to rights to transmit and receive signals and bands of frequencies associated with foreign satellites which cover and can provide services in Mexican territory, in order to facilitate the entry of new competitors in the satellite communication market under previously established and clear rules.

Unlike the situation in Mexican legislation before 2002, in which there was no real openness to offer these services and the only provider was the company Satélites Mexicanos,

S.A. de C.V. (SATMEX) -**privatized in 1997**-, which had no competitors, today we can see the results in a competitive and well-served market, due to the effective application of the Federal Telecommunications Act [*Ley Federal de Telecomunicaciones*], published on June 7, 1995, largely derived from the signing of bilateral agreements with Argentina, Canada and the USA, and their respective protocols for the transmission and reception of foreign satellite signals to provide satellite services in Mexican territory.

INTERNATIONAL (BILATERAL AND MULTILATERAL) LEGAL CODES.

To aid the understanding of this study, I shall mention the multilateral agreements and bilateral agreements to which Mexico is party and which, as part of Mexican legislation, stem from the Political Constitution of the United Mexican States (Article 133)[1]. In point of fact, under such Article, treaties entered into by the President of the Republic and ratified by the Senate of the Republic are Supreme Law in Mexico. The powers of both the President and the Senate of the Republic are contained in Articles 89 Section X[2] and 76-I[3], of the Federal Constitution, respectively.

RELATED INTERNATIONAL AGREEMENTS AND BODIES:

Below is an overview of the international instruments adopted in forums of an identical kind, to which Mexico is party and which, after ratification by the Senate of the Republic, form part of national law:

- Radiocommunications Regulations adopted at the World Radiocommunications Conferences (WRC) of the International Telecommunications Union (ITU)[4], whose Final Minutes were signed by the Mexican Government and ratified by the Senate of the Republic.

The importance of such international instruments lies, among other things, in the fact that frequencies are awarded to the different telecommunications services; to geostationary satellites, given that the frequencies are associated with them;

[1] Article 133: Agreements which conform to the Constitution, entered into now or hereafter by the President of the Republic, with the approval of the Senate, shall be the Supreme Law of the entire Union.

[2] Article 89 Section I: The powers and obligations of the President are as follows: X. to enter into international agreements, submitting them to the approval of the Senate.

[3] Article 76, Section I: The Senate has exclusive powers to: I. approve international agreements and diplomatic conventions entered into by the Executive of the Union.

[4] WRC held in Istanbul, Turkey in 2000 and in Geneva, Switzerland, in 2003, in which the fundamental amendments to the Radio Regulations were adopted.

as well as the different spatial activities (radioastronomy, exploration of the Earth; teleobservation, etc.)

- Marrakech Agreement, which established the World Trade Organization (WTO) and the General Agreement on Trade in Services, adopted by such Organization, to which Mexico is Party[5].

The instruments adopted by the WTO are part of Mexican law and have been, together with the bilateral or regional (multilateral) agreements signed by Mexico, the guideline for free enterprise and competition.

Regarding satellites, with the opening of the market in satellite services within the WTO (2002), the question arising in relation to the Federal Telecommunications Act is whether it is additionally necessary to sign a Bilateral Agreement to establish reciprocity. My point of view is that the national law must be kept in place to guarantee reciprocity and set the criteria by which providers of satellite capacity shall provide services in the territory of each of the Parties.

Principles which should govern the use by the States of artificial Earth satellites for international direct television broadcasts.[6]

- Such Principles are an important precedent in relation to the rights of individuals to receive information and ideas, which is not incompatible with the sovereign right of the States in applying their national legislation so that satellite operators can provide services in territories of another Party. This question is picked up by Article 30 of the Federal Telecommunications Act is part of the bilateral agreements which Mexico has signed regarding satellites.

<u>BILATERAL AGREEMENTS SIGNED BY MEXICO AND THEIR RESPECTIVE PROTOCOLS, RELATED WITH THE TRANSMISSION AND RECEPTION OF SATELLITE SIGNALS:</u>

<u>Mexico and the United States of America</u>

- Agreement between the Government of the United Mexican States and the Government of the United States of America concerning the transmission and reception of signals from satellites for the provision of satellite services to users in the United Mexican States and the United States of America, signed in Mexico City on April 28, 1996.

- Protocol concerning the transmission and reception of signals from satellites for the provision of Direct-to-Home Satellite services in the United

---

[5] WTO established by Agreement at the meeting held in Marrakech, Morocco, in 1994.

[6] Approved December 13, 1963, by Resolution 1962 (XVII) of the United Nations (UN) General Assembly

Mexican States and the United States of America, signed in the City of Washington, D.C., USA, on November 8, 1996.

- Protocol concerning the transmission and reception of signals from satellites for the provision of fixed services by satellite in the United Mexican States and the United States of America, signed in Mexico City on April 28, 1996.

- Convention for the use of satellites and land stations for the provision of services comprising to, from and within the territories of the United Mexican States and the United States of America, signed in Mexico City on December 21, 1998.

Mexico and Argentina.

- Agreement between the Government of the United Mexican States and the Government of the Republic of Argentina concerning reciprocity in the use of satellites and the transmission and reception of signals from satellites for the provision of satellite services to users in the United Mexican States and the Republic of Argentina, signed in Mexico City on November 26, 1997.

Mexico and Canada.

- Agreement between the Government of the United Mexican States and the Government of Canada concerning the provision of satellite services, signed in Mexico City on April 9, 1999.

- Protocol concerning the transmission and reception of signals from satellites for the provision of mobile-satellite services and associated feeder links in the United Mexican States and Canada, signed in Mexico City on January 16, 2001.

- Protocol concerning the transmission and reception of signals from satellites for the provision of fixed services between the United Mexican States and Canada, signed in Mexico City on January 16, 2001.

It is important to mention that these bilateral agreements and their respective protocols are duly in line with the fundamental principles of reciprocity and non-discriminatory treatment, set forth in the Mexican Constitution and the Federal Telecommunications Act and of course multilateral agreements such as that of the WTO.

In the case of the commitments adopted by the countries within the framework of the WTO, these should provide all the administrative and legal facilities for the granting of licenses and thus avoid obstacles to free enterprise and the services market, as in the case of satellite communication. This is reflected in the Mexican regulatory framework for the granting of concessions. Another of the Mexican laws which apply to the granting of concessions (licenses) in Mexico is the Federal Antitrust Act, whose basic principles are to protect free enterprise and guarantee competition. The bases regarding satellites are fully defined because the competition is open.

The Protocols themselves to the Agreements which I have mentioned indicate as a condition for provided the services that the Party whose satellite will provide services in the territory of the other Party must be duly licensed under the laws of that country. Similarly, the procedures for granting licenses are mutually recognized under the terms of the agreements.

MEXICAN LEGISLATION

Like any activity carried out in Mexico, the regulation of satellite communication stems from the Mexican Constitution, which provides that satellite communications is a **priority area** for national development in the terms of Articles 25 and 28 of the Constitution[7], the "State, by exercising its control over them, shall protect the security and sovereignty of the Nation, and by granting concessions or permits, shall maintain or establish command over the respective means of communications in accordance with the laws applicable thereto."

For its part, Article 27[8], paragraph four, mentions that "The Nation has direct command over all the natural resources... and the space situated in national territory, within the bounds set by international law." To date, no United Nations' Resolution or international instrument that considers it has been issued to demarcate the limits referred to by such Article, however, in this case, Mexico's position in the First Conferences of the Americas on Space, held in Chile, was and is that the jurisdiction or *ius imperium* is exercised by the Mexican Government in connection with the frequencies associated with Mexican satellites, i.e., the Mexican State exercises control over such assets used to propagate the electromagnetic waves which make satellite communication possible.

[7] Article 25 of the Constitution: The Public Sector shall have exclusive charge of the strategic areas set forth in Article 28, fourth paragraph, of the Constitution, with the Federal Government maintaining at all times the ownership and control of any bodies that might be established. It may also participate by itself or with the social and private sectors, in accordance with the law, to foment and organize the priorities areas of development. **Article 28**. The functions exercised exclusively by the State in the following strategic areas shall not constitute monopolies: mail, telegraph and radiotelegraph. Satellite communication and the railroads are priority areas in national development under Article 25 of this Constitution; The State, by exercising its control over them, shall protect the security and sovereignty of the Nation, and by granting concessions or permits, shall maintain or establish command over the respective means of communications in accordance with the laws applicable thereto.

[8] Article 27 of the Constitution. The Nation has direct command over all the natural resources and the space situated in national territory, within the bounds and terms set by international law.

The exercise of control over this national asset corresponds to the State, who may grant concessions to private individuals or entities to work and use it, pursuant to the sixth paragraph of Article 27[9].

In this respect, it is important that the State control referred to by the aforementioned Article 27 is found in the Federal Telecommunications Act in Article 2[10], which refers to Mexico's sovereign right concerning satellite orbits and radioelectric frequencies.

For the creation of laws governing telecommunications and satellite communication in particular, under Article 73, Section XVII, of the Mexican Constitution[11], it is the Mexican Congress which has the authority to issue laws regarding general means of communication. It is worth mentioning that the radioelectric spectrum, telecommunications networks and satellite communication are general means of communication.[12]

The Federal Telecommunications Act regulates satellite communication and, specifically, with regard to the subject matter of this work, Article 30[13] of this Act sets forth the possibility of granting concessions so that foreign satellites **which cover Mexican territory**, may provide services therein, provided **there are agreements signed with the country of origin** in which **reciprocity for Mexican satellites is established**. It should be mentioned that the concessions will only be granted to juridical persons organized under Mexican laws."

This Article 30 set the bases for the issuance of the Satellite Communication Regulations [*Reglamento de Comunicación Vía Satélite*] (RCVS), confirming the following requirements for granting concessions for satellite operators to

[9] Article 27, sixth paragraph: The dominion of the Nation is inalienable and not subject to expiration, and the working, the use or the exploitation of the resources in question, by private individuals or bodies or by companies formed under Mexican laws, may not be done without concessions, granted by the Federal Executive, in accordance with the rules and conditions set forth in the laws.

[10] Article 2 LFT. The State has control over telecommunications, for which purpose it shall protect the security and sovereignty of the Nation. The State shall maintain command over the radioelectric spectrum and the orbital positions assigned to the country.

[11] **Article 73.** Congress has the power: XVII. to enact laws on general means of communication, and on post and mail.

[12] **Article 4.** For purposes of this Act, the radioelectric spectrum, telecommunications networks and satellite communication systems are general means of communication.

[13] **Article 30.** The Secretariat may grant concessions on the rights of transmission and reception of signals and frequency bands associated with foreign satellites which cover and can provide services in Mexican territory, provided there are signed agreements on the matter with the country of origin of the signal and such agreements contemplate reciprocity for Mexican satellites. These concessions shall only be granted to juridical persons organized under Mexican laws.
Furthermore, the international satellites established under the multilateral agreement to which the country is party may operate in Mexican territory.

be able to operate in Mexico: i) they should cover Mexican territory; ii) there should be bilateral agreements in place; and iii) there should be reciprocity for Mexican satellites.

The legal codes regulating satellite communication are:

- Political Constitution of the United Mexican States
- Federal Telecommunications Act [*Ley Federal de Telecomunicaciones*], (LFT)
- Satellite Communication Regulations [*Reglamento de Comunicación Vía Satélite*], (RCVS)
- Foreign Investment Act [*Ley de Inversión Extranjera*], (LIE)
- Federal Antitrust Act [*Ley Federal de Competencia Económica*], (LCE)
- The international agreements already mentioned above.

CONDITIONS FOR USE TO WORK RIGHTS OF TRANSMISSION AND RECEPTION OF FREQUENCIES ASSOCIATED WITH FOREIGN SATELLITES

Mexican regulation concerning the technical conditions for the usage and working of satellite communications are essentially based on the provisions contained in the ITU Radio Regulations (Article V of the Mexico-USA Agreement). Accordingly, satellites have to be properly coordinated with the countries in which the satellite footprint is present, in order to prevent harmful interferences. Similar matters are contemplated in the Bilateral Agreements signed by Mexico. For example, the text of Article IV, Part 2, of the Agreement signed with the United States of America, reads: "The conditions for the transmission and reception of signals from Satellites licensed by each Party or Administration, as the case may be, shall be as agreed in the Protocols, which shall comply with the laws and regulations of each country, and shall be annexed as an integral part of this Agreement..."

Article 9 and 10 of the Satellite Communication Regulations [RCVS] sets forth that in addition to a bilateral agreement signed with the Country and their protocols, there should also be a coordination agreement as set forth in the instruments of the ITU, or at least this should be under negotiation by the administrations of both countries. These provisions are consistent with the Agreements signed by Mexico regarding satellites.

OBLIGATIONS FOR FOREIGN SATELLITE SERVICES PROVIDERS.

The LFT provides that a concession title is required in order to work the rights of transmission and reception of frequency band signals associated with foreign satellites which cover and can provide services in Mexican territory. The obligations can be classified into two kinds: i) to obtain the concession and ii) after obtaining the concession.

To obtain the concession, applicants must submit a satisfactory application to the Secretariat, containing at least:

- The location of the orbital position or satellite orbits and associated frequencies, registered or in process of coordination, as well as the name and documentation of the foreign satellite operator;
- The technical specifications of the foreign satellite system, detailing the characteristics of the coverage over Mexican territory;
- The documentation evidencing the contractual relation between the foreign satellite operator and the applicant who would work the system in Mexican territory;
- The technical specifications of the land transmitter stations which the applicant seeks to install in Mexican territory, for which it shall require a public telecommunications network concession, and the land stations located abroad which, if applicable, shall send signals to Mexican territory, as well as the terminal land stations to be installed in the country;
- The portion and the technical characteristics according to which the concessionary will make its satellite capacity available to third parties, or if applicable, the description of the satellite services which are sought to be provided, as well as the technical specifications of the control center, of the master land stations in Mexican territory and abroad, and of the terminal land stations;
- The business plan, which will include, at least, a coverage, investment and financial program;
- Documentation to demonstrate its legal, technical, financial and administrative capacity;
- The favorable opinion of the Federal Competition Commission;
- Documentation to demonstrate that the applicants will keep control of the services provided in Mexican territory, for which they shall have to evidence:

    1. That they have the necessary technical resources to present the Commission with information concerning the traffic generated in Mexican territory or bound for Mexican territory;

2. That the foreign satellite operator assumes the obligation to comply with the instructions of the concessionaries, in connection with the services provided in Mexican territory;

3. That the foreign satellite operator assumes the obligation to provide the information required of it by the SCT (Secretariat of Communications and Transport) or the Commission, related with the services provided in Mexican territory;

4. That the concessionaries will use a specific numeration to identify the terminal land stations of the users in the country.

- Once the application is received, it is passed on to Federal Telecommunications Board for analysis and evaluation of the respective documentation, who may request further information from the applicants.

- After the aforementioned Commission has issued its opinion and once the Secretariat of Communications and Transport is satisfied the requirements are met, the corresponding concession will be granted.

The term for granting concessions is 120 (one hundred twenty business days).

It should be mentioned that the requirements and the procedure for the granting of the concessions mentioned are set forth in the LFT and in the aforementioned Regulations, which provides the applicant of a concession with legal certainty and this is where the obligations are established in line with the law.

Providers of satellite capacity are subject to obligations of an informative nature, including: statistics, number of users, registration of rates, and in my opinion they do not imply excessive burdens for the concessionary.

The rights of a foreign satellite operate providing services through a Mexican company are the same as those given to domestic operators, i.e., the principle of non-discriminatory treatment is applied.

An important matter with regard to providing satellite services is the satellite capacity provider's obligation to give social access and connectivity. In this respect it should be mentioned that Mexico has developed an important program called E México, whereby access is given to remote areas or those not fundamentally served through authorized domestic or foreign satellites.

In 1998, the Development Sector of the ITU made it one of its objectives to bring telecommunications to the world's most impoverished places, to combat the technological differences that exist between developed and developing countries, known as the "digital divide". They called this UNIVERSAL SERVICE.

Concessionary companies in Mexico such as Panamsat de México, have provided satellite capacity based on which the Mexican Government has developed the first phase of the E México Program.

The obligation to provide satellite capacity is partly free and partly with a differentiated rate.

In Mexico, rates are deregulated, i.e., they are set by the concessionary itself and only have to i) be registered prior to their application; ii) not be discriminatory; iii) not permit cross-subsidies; and iv) guarantee that, with the rate they apply, they will provide a quality service.

As regards requirements under the Federal Antitrust Act, there are established requisites, proceedings and terms, without prejudice to the fact that due to the granting of the first concessions, it could be said that the way ahead has been completely cleared. Furthermore, the writs of amparo filed by SATMEX in 2002 against the granting of the first concessions to allow foreign satellites to operate in Mexico were won by the Mexican Government. Therefore, competition in Mexico is fully guaranteed with clear rules of access to the satellite service market.

Another law we have mentioned as part of the applicable regulation is the one relating to foreign investment, which provides for the possibility of up to a 49% share by direct foreign investment and up to a 90% share by neutral foreign investment (without voting rights but with property rights) may be authorized.

TARIFFS:

Mexican legislation stipulates free tariffs without any type of approval on the part of the authority. That is to say, service providers can freely establish their tariffs, and such tariffs should make it possible to render these services in satisfactory conditions regarding quality, competitiveness and permanence. In order to apply their tariffs, carriers must be bound by the following obligations: i) they must not adopt discriminatory practices; ii) they must not establish cross-subsidies to the services provided in competition by the carriers themselves or through their subsidiaries or affiliates; iii) they must register them before they are applied.

CONCLUTIONS

As I have pointed out in the Introduction to this document, the objective of this study is to establish the following:

1. That applicable Mexican regulations regarding the granting of concessions related to the emission and reception of signals coming from foreign satellites that cover the Mexican territory is established in the Mexican Constitution, the Federal Telecommunications Law and the Satellite Communications Regulations and in the multilateral treaties derived from the WTO, ITU and UN; as well as in the Bilateral Treaties that Mexico has signed with the USA, Canada and Argentina up to this date.

2. That the rules established in Mexican regulations relating to services rendered in the Mexican territory by companies which operate foreign satellites are stated clearly and precisely, a fact which provides certainty to investments in Mexico in this Sector;

3. That due to the fact that competition in this field has been open since the year 2002, when different concessions were granted to Mexican companies in order to operate satellite capacity of foreign satellites, the conditions for accessing the market have been facilitated;

4. In addition to the above-mentioned and in order to provide a greater degree of legal certainty, the pleadings for protection (Amparos) filed by SATMEX, against such opening, were resolved in favor of the Mexican Government.

5. Any foreign satellite carrier which covers the Mexican territory, whose country of origin has signed a treaty with Mexico and provided that reciprocity for Mexican satellites is established, shall be able to participate as partner in Mexican companies and render its services in the national territory, subject to compliance with the requirements stipulated by the Law, without further restrictions.

BIBLIOGRAPHY

INTERNATIONAL UNION TELECOMUNICATIONS CONSTITUTION
1992

FUNDAMENTAL TEXTS OF THE INTERNATIONAL TELECOMUNICATIONS UNION

ADOPTED BY THE PLENIPOTENCIARY CONFERENCE
International Telecommunications Union
1999

WORLD TELECOMUNICATIONS DEVELOPMENT REPORT
International Telecommunications Union
2002

WORLD TELECOMMUNICATIONS/ICT DEVELOPMENT REPORT
International Telecommunications Union
2006

TELECOMMUNICATIONS POLICIES FOR THE AMERICAS
International Telecommunications Union
Interamerican Telecommunications Commission
2000

UNIVERSAL SERVICE SEMINAR
Interamerican Telecommunications Commission
Permanent Consultative Commission
1998

CONSTITUCIÓN POLITICA DE LOS ESTADOS UNIDO MEXICANOS
1917

LEY FEDERAL DE TELECOMUNICACIONES
1995

DERECHO ADMINISTRATIVO I Y II
Serra Rojas
Ed. Porrua, Mex.
1992

LEY FEDERAL DE COMPETENCIA ECONÓMICA
1997

LEY DE INVERSIÓN EXTRANJERA

AGREEMENT BETWEEN THE GOVERNMENT OF THE UNITED MEXICAN STATES AND THE GOVERNMENT OF THE UNITED STATES OF AMERICA CONCERNING THE TRANSMISSION AND RECEPTION OF SIGNALS FROM SATELLITES FOR THE PROVISION OF SATELLITE SERVICES TO USERS IN THE UNITED MEXICAN STATES AND THE UNITED STATES OF AMERICA, SIGNED IN MEXICO CITY ON APRIL 28, 1996.

PROTOCOL CONCERNING THE TRANSMISSION AND RECEPTION OF SIGNALS FROM SATELLITES FOR THE PROVISION OF DIRECT-TO-HOME SATELLITE SERVICES IN THE UNITED MEXICAN STATES AND THE UNITED STATES OF AMERICA, SIGNED IN THE CITY OF WASHINGTON, D.C., USA, ON NOVEMBER 8, 1996.

PROTOCOL CONCERNING THE TRANSMISSION AND RECEPTION OF SIGNALS FROM SATELLITES FOR THE PROVISION OF FIXED SERVICES BY SATELLITE IN THE UNITED MEXICAN STATES AND THE UNITED STATES OF AMERICA, SIGNED IN MEXICO CITY ON APRIL 28, 1996.

CONVENTION FOR THE USE OF SATELLITES AND LAND STATIONS FOR THE PROVISION OF SERVICES COMPRISING TO, FROM AND WITHIN THE TERRITORIES OF THE UNITED MEXICAN STATES AND THE UNITED STATES OF AMERICA, SIGNED IN MEXICO CITY ON DECEMBER 21, 1998.

AGREEMENT BETWEEN THE GOVERNMENT OF THE UNITED MEXICAN STATES AND THE GOVERNMENT OF THE REPUBLIC OF ARGENTINA CONCERNING RECIPROCITY IN THE USE OF SATELLITES AND THE TRANSMISSION AND RECEPTION OF SIGNALS FROM SATELLITES FOR THE PROVISION OF SATELLITE SERVICES TO USERS IN THE UNITED MEXICAN STATES AND THE REPUBLIC OF ARGENTINA, SIGNED IN MEXICO CITY ON NOVEMBER 26, 1997.

AGREEMENT BETWEEN THE GOVERNMENT OF THE UNITED MEXICAN STATES AND THE GOVERNMENT OF CANADA CONCERNING THE PROVISION OF SATELLITE SERVICES, SIGNED IN MEXICO CITY ON APRIL 9, 1999.

PROTOCOL CONCERNING THE TRANSMISSION AND RECEPTION OF SIGNALS FROM SATELLITES FOR THE PROVISION OF MOBILE-SATELLITE SERVICES AND ASSOCIATED FEEDER LINKS IN THE UNITED MEXICAN STATES AND CANADA, SIGNED IN MEXICO CITY ON JANUARY 16, 2001.

PROTOCOL CONCERNING THE TRANSMISSION AND RECEPTION OF SIGNALS FROM SATELLITES FOR THE PROVISION OF FIXED SERVICES BETWEEN THE UNITED MEXICAN STATES AND CANADA, SIGNED IN MEXICO CITY ON JANUARY 16, 2001.

IAC-06-E6.5.9

Reflections on Future Space Legislation in China

Zhao Haifeng
Harbin Institute of Technology, China
zhaohaifeng_c@yahoo.com.cn

Wu Xiaodan
Harbin Institute of Technology, China
wuxiaodan_rain@yahoo.com.cn

ABSTRACT

Since the creation of China's space industry in 1956, the China's space undertaking developed widely and deeply and has been an important part of world space endeavor. In 1981, China became a formal member of CUPUOS and its two subcommittees-the Scientific and Technical Subcommittee as well as the Legal Subcommittee. Thenceforth, China has taken an active part in both technical and legal work under the framework of U.N. Furthermore, China, respectively in 1983 and 1988, acceded to the four main Space Treaties: the Outer Space Treaty, Rescue Agreement, Liability Convention and Registration Convention. In order to fulfill the responsibilities and obligations under the international treaties and strengthen the macro-management on space activities, China National Space Administration (CNSA), as the appropriate authority of China's space activities, has established and enacted some space industry regulations, including: Registration and Management of Space Objects, Management of Launch License of Civil Space, Management Regulation on Special Projects of Civil Space, and Technology Policy for Space Industry. However, as a space-faring country, these national legislations are disproportional to the development of China's space industry. In order to develop its space industry according to the laws and regulations, China is determined to enhance the construction of space legislation. Currently, some regulations, such as Management of Space Activity, Management of Damage Compensation of Launched Space Objects, Management of Space Commercialization and Coordination of International Space Cooperation, are under research and to be promulgated. Moreover, a comprehensive legislation on outer space activities is under preparation. Since we are doing the project on the comparative studies of national legislations, we would give some suggestions for the future Chinese legislation on outer space in the process of the project, the purpose of this paper is to introduce the existing national space legislation in China and contemplate on possible provisions of future outer space regulations.

Since the creation of China's space industry in 1956, China has played a key role internationally in space-related endeavors, having achieved great progress in space technology and in its application. However, as a space-faring country, the status of China's national space legislation is disproportionate to the development of China's space industry. This is due to several reasons. The aim of this paper is to analyze the necessity and feasibility of prospective China space legislation and to provide some suggestions and guidelines related to future space-related legislation.

I. Necessity

The importance of national space legislation has been gradually acknowledged by individual nations and international bodies. The resolution adopted by the UN General Assembly in 2004 explicitly recommended that states conducting space activities, in fulfilling their international obligations under the United Nations treaties on outer space, consider enacting and implementing national laws authorizing and providing for continuing supervision of the activities in outer space of non-governmental entities under their jurisdiction.[1] In China, there is now frequent appeal for strengthening space legislation. The drive for China's space legislation is based on the following:

1. To satisfy the need of increasing space ventures and undertakings. As a space-faring country, Chinese apace activities need be regulated by law, which is the basic requirement of a nation ruled by law. In all space activities--- space technology, space application, or space science---many issues must be regulated and promulgated by uniform laws. Most of the space-faring countries (almost 20 to date) have promulgated space law to govern space activities and affairs. The countries include the following: U.S.A., Argentina, Australia, Belgium, Brazil, Canada, Chile, France, German, Italy, Japan, Norway, Russian, South Africa, Spain, Sweden, Ukraine and United Kingdom. [2] Some other countries are preparing their national space legislation. China is one of the rare space-faring nations without national space law.

2. To fulfill international obligations and responsibilities under international treaties. According to international law, States parities to a treaty are under a duty to implement the terms of that treaty within their national legal system, and national legislation is among the most chosen means to implement international obligations. China acceded to the Outer Space Treaty on December 30, 1983; the Liability Convention and Registration Convention on December 12, 1988; and to the Rescue Agreement on December 14, 1988. Some terms of these international treaties explicitly demand to be implemented by national legislation. Others need to be enacted by clear and detailed national rule because they do not provide detailed rule on implementation. Therefore, there is a necessity to transform international treaties into domestic law in order to implement international engagements.

3. To solve a series of problems arising from the rapid development of space activities in a market economy. The framework of UN space treaties was drafted when States were the only player in outer space and the aims and objects of space activities were limited to politics and military motives. However, the recent trend of space commercialization and privatization has swept across many space-faring nations. China' s space industry, which was founded during a planned economy period is undergoing great changes under a more market-based economy environment. The subjects of space activities are transforming from the unitary state-owned entities under one system to various market economy subjects coming from a different

[1] Paragraph 1 of 59/115 Resolution adopted by the General Assembly in 10th December 2004, Application of the Concept of the "Launching State". A/RES/59/115.

[2] http://www.unoosa.org/oosa/SAP/act2005/nigeria/index.html, last visited on 9the September, 2006.

system;[3] different contractual relations arising from these subjects; the rights and duties relations and legal responsibilities need to be further confirmed between the governmental sectors, governmental sectors and market subjects, market subjects conducting space activities. The commercialization trend comes up in China space industry, especially in the space application field. Therefore, the government must regulate market entrance, commercialization management, space environment protection by legal means and strengthen the macro-management on space activities.

4. To satisfy the need of international cooperation. During the past 30 years, China has made great achievements in international space cooperation. The methods of cooperation are not only bilateral, but also multilateral and even regional cooperation---including commercial launching service. One thing in regional cooperation worthy of mention is the signature of the Asia-Pacific Space Organization Convention and the prompt establishment of Asia-Pacific Space Organization. [4] The numerous problems involved in international cooperation need to be regulated by law, including: intellectual property, the transformation of technologies, the license of importation and exportation, tariff supervision, and foreign exchange management. Some important diplomatic and political issues, including preserving state secrets, maintaining international peace and security, and conforming to international arm control, also need legal regulations. [5]

II. Feasabilility

Conditions are now in place for Chinese space legislation, which are detailed below:

1. The UN space treaties, principles adopted by General Assembly and other national space laws can be used for reference. During a 10-year period following the 1950s, five international space treaties were adopted in the framework of the United Nations and five principles related to space application were adopted by the General Assembly. China has acceded to or approved most of these treaties and principles and has a duty to implement these provisions, among which some rules have become international customs. China should respect these international customs, as they are part of China's legal obligations and framework. The 20 national space laws are significant materials that can be used for reference, which China should seriously consider.

2. China's space policies, space regulations, administrative ordinances, and section rules provide a solid foundation for national space legislation. China has conducted a great deal of space activities and has formed a series of policy, regulations and ordinances.

(1) **Space Policy and management provisions.**

A. Chinese space policies are embodied in the White Paper of China's Space Activities published by the Information Office of the State Council on November 22, 2000.[6] The White Paper expressed the policies, position and viewpoints of the Chinese government in the space field and is the authoritative document of Chinese space undertaking. The White Paper has explicitly put forward that the State will strengthen legislation work and policy management, enact laws and regulations and promulgat industrial policies for the space industry to ensure orderly and standardized development of space activities.

[3] For example, the Harbin Institute of Technology launched a small satellite in 2004.

[4] http://www.npc.gov.cn/zgrdw/common/zw.jsp?label=WXZLK&id=350740&pdmc=rdgb, last visited on 9th September, 2006.

[5] He Qizhi, Huang Huikang, *Outer Space Law*, Qing Dao Press, 2000, p. 250.

[6] Chinese edition see: http://www.china.org.cn/ch-book/hangtian/2000guo.htm , last visited on September 8, 2006.Egnlish edition see : http://www.unoosa.org/oosaddb/showDocument.do?documentUid=360&level2=none&node=CPR1970&level1=countries&cmd=add, last visited on September 8, 2006.

B. From the creation China' s space undertakings in the 1950s through 1996, China has gained valuable experience in space technology management and international commercial launching service and has achieved effective management systems. At present, there are more than 300 rules and standards documents which relate to every respect of space activities. All of the above constitute the basis of China' s space legislation.

(2) Space Legislation.

Space legislation can be divided into two parts: civil space legislation and military space legislation:

A. Civil space legislation. China National Space Administration (CNSA), established in 1998, has attached much importance to the research of space legislation and has gained a series of achievements in promulgating space rules. CNSA and the Ministry of Foreign Affairs (MFA) pronounced the Provisions and Procedures for the Registration of Space Objects on February 8, 2001, which was entered into force on that very day. It is the first administrative regulation on space activities in China, which is in line with the Registration Convention and the practical situation in China and also relatively easy to operate as an institutional regulation.[7] Interim Provisions on License for Civil Space Launching Projects was officially pronounced in the form of a departmental regulation by CNSA on November 21, 2002, and entered into force on December 21, 2002, which established the license management system on the launching non-military spacecraft into outer space from Chinese territory. CNSA and the Ministry of Finance pronounced the Management Provisions on Civil Research Projects concerning National Defense Science and Industry on August 18, 2002, which provided legal rules on the science and research activities on the technology development of civil space activities and military transforming to civil function in the field of national defense science and industry which is financially supported by Ministry of Finance. The other related administrative regulations, such as Provisional Regulation on Liability for Damage Caused by Space Objects,[8] the Management of Space Commercialization and International Space Cooperation and Coordination, are in the process of research and drafting.[9]

B. Military Space Legislation. Military space legislation primarily includes:

a. Regulations of PRC on the Administration of Arms Export promulgated by State Council and Central Military Commission on October 22, 1997, which entered into force on January 1, 1998, and was amended on October 15, 2002. The regulations provide that the arms export should obtain license and was conducted by the arms trading companies designated by the Government. The arms export programs shall be examined and authorized by the authority of China's arms export or together with the related sectors of State Council and Central Military Commission. The Part Eight of The Military Products Export Control List, which promulgated by CNSA and the People's Liberation Army General Armament Department on November 1, 2002 and entered into force on November 15, 2002, is Rockets, Missile, Military Satellite and its Auxiliary Facilities relating to military space products.

b. The State Council pronounced the Regulation of the People's Republic of China on Export Control of Missiles and Missile-related Items and Technologies and

---

[7] See: Liu Xiaohong and Wang Xiaoqing, The first administrative regulation on space activities in China, in Proceedings United Nations/International Institute of Air and Space Law Workshop on Capacity Building in Space Law. ST/SPACE/14. Office for Outer Space Affaires, United Nations Office at Vienna. 2003. p107.

[8] Yin Wenjuan, China's Space Policy, in Proceedings United Nations/Republic of Korea Workshop on Space Law, United Nations Treaties on Outer Space: Actions at the National Level, ST/SPACE/22, Office for Outer Space Affairs United Nations Office at Vienna, New York 2004, p.15.

[9] CNSA, China's Space Activities, 26th April 2004, Bulletin of Space, China Space Law Association, April 2004.

the corresponding Export Control List of the Missile and Missiles-Related Items and Technologies on August 22, 2002, the aim and objects of which is to safeguard the national security and public interests and limit the proliferation of weapons of mass destruction by the means of export control. [10]

In summary, actual Chinese space legislation is limited and in lower layers of the legislation mechanism. Therefore, in a strict sense, there is no real space law.

3. The related research has provided theoretic support for national space legislation. The Chinese Space Law Association and CNSA have made great efforts in space law research for preparing Chinese space legislation. For example, the Chinese Space Law Association has undertaken the project of Research on China's Space Legislation Mechanism and Comparative Studies on the Main National Space Laws.[11] The CNSA has organized the translation of the national space laws and has made plenty of preparation for the national space legislation. Furthermore, some textbooks and papers on space law have been published in international law academic circles. [12] All of these have provided a theoretic basis for China's space legislation.

III. Legislation Path

The hierarchy of the Chinese law is determined by its respective legislative bodies.[13] In first position is the Constitution adopted by the National People's Congress, which has the most authoritative effect. No law or regulation can contradict the Constitution. In second position are the laws formulated by the supreme power organ of authority – the National People's Congress and its Standing Committee. In third position are the administrative laws and regulations promulgated by the State Council (the highest organ of state administration), which must be in accordance to the Constitution and cannot contradict the law. Finally, in fourth position, is the departmental regulation formulated by the Ministries and Commissions of the State Council in accordance with the aforementioned legal norms within the limits of their authorities. The legislative mechanism constitutes a tight hierarchal system. Generally speaking, it is easier to adopt a departmental regulation and more difficult to formulate administrative law and it is more and more difficult to pass law, which takes longer time.

Space legislation, especially a comprehensive law on space activities, is a long-term and difficult task. Although China has a good basis for space legislation, the more reliable method is advancing progress step-by-step according to the degree of need and emergency. In order to push the progress of legislation, the most important element is in realizing the necessity of space legislation. In the field of civil space legislation, we think the appropriate path is to formulate departmental regulations firstly, then the comprehensive administrative regulation. Then, try to put the space legislation on the agenda of national legislation plan and adopt a comprehensive space law and, then finally establish a systematic and comprehensive space law mechanism.

IV. Guideline and Main Content

The guideline of China's space legislation should be as follows: 1) maintain a balance between the national interests and international engagements. China should prepare its space legislation according to the situation of China's space activities and the provisions of the international treaties China has acceded to and should use the other national space law as reference; 2) promote the development of space undertaking,

---

[10] See Gao Guozhu, The Present Situation, Evaluation and Prospect of China Space Legislation, The Proceeding of Seminar on the Present Situation and Prospect of Outer Space Law, August 31st- 1st September, 2006, Harbin, pp.138-139.

[11] See the CNSA Research Report, The Comparative Studies of the Main National Space Laws in the World, July 2003.

[12] Written by Macro Pedrazzi, Zhao Haifeng, translated by Wu Xiaodan, Textbook of International Space Law, Heilongjiang People's Press, August 2006, p. 191.

[13] Zhu Yikun, Concise Chinese Law, Law Press, China, 2003, p. 12.

including space commercialization; 3) promote international cooperation. 4) The content of the legislation should be based on the present system but should also try to establish some new regimes or to reform the actual system, not only taking into account the present situation, but also with foresight to the future.

Regulation on Space Activities under the process of formulating and the future space legislation should firstly incorporate the provisions of the UN and other related international treaties China has acceded. In accordance with the national space legislation throughout the world and China's international engagements and reality, the following aspects are necessary:

1. The aims and objects of space legislation. China's space legislation should promote the development of Chinese space undertaking, explore and use outer space for peaceful purposes, protect China's rights, perform international duties and promote international cooperation according to the related provisions of Constitution and laws.

2. The authority of space activities and its functions. Presently, several state departments supervise space activities and the relationships between them are not so clear. Therefore, it is an important task to define the powers and responsibilities of government organs responsible for the space activities.

3. The entrance systems of space commercialization. Article VI of Outer Space Treaty provides that States Parties to the Treaty shall bear international responsibility for national activities in outer space, whether such activities are carried on by governmental agencies or by non-governmental entities. The activities of non-governmental entities in outer space shall require authorization and continuing supervision by the appropriate State Party to the Treaty. It is becoming increasingly apparent, that the commercialization trend of launching space objects activities in China and the subject of space activities is becoming multiplex, even non-state-owned enterprises are participating in commercial launching activities. Therefore, it is very necessary to adopt a licensing system for space activities by legislation and put into effect the entrance systems for space commercial activities.

4. Industrialization management. China has ascended to the forefront in some important space technology fields, but the legal environment of space activities has lagged far behind. It is an emergent need to adopt laws to regulate the plan and development of space activities, the investment managements, commercial launching service, satellite remote sensing, satellite telecommunication and broadcast, satellite navigation location and promote the rapid development of space activities.

5. Intellectual property. The space laws should explicitly provide protecting intellectual property since it is significant to protect intellectual property in the process of space commercialization.

6. Space objects registration. The Registration Convention to which China has acceded establishes compulsory space objects registration system. According to the provisions, a space object that is launched into Earth orbit or beyond shall be registered. In order to exercise China's jurisdiction and control over the space object both *de facto* and *de juris,* the law should provide the condition and procedure of space objects registration and the legal effects of registration.

7. Rescue of astronauts, the return of astronauts and space objects launched into outer space. China's manned space undertaking has made great strides, which makes this provision more significant. According to the related provisions of Rescue Agreement, it should provide the duties and procedure of search, rescue and return of Chinese astronauts landing out the territory of China by accident or foreign astronauts landing in Chinese territory by accident; or, when the space objects launched by China landing in foreign territory or foreign space objects landing in Chinese territory.

8. National liability and compensation for damages caused by space objects. Under the Outer Space Treaty, the launching state is internationally liable for damage caused by space objects launched by national

government, non-government entities and individual. The Liability Convention articulates the method and procedure of compensation. As the state party to these two international treaties, China should bear the responsibility of damages caused by space objects that China launches or procures launching into outer space. Therefore, the space regulation or law should specify the legal problems of compensation, such as the scope of compensation and the determination of compensation liability, whether there is limit for compensation and the liability division of nation and other liable parties. Meanwhile, compulsory insurance system should be established to protect the national interests.

9. International cooperation. The international cooperation serves a special function in the field of space activities. Outer Space Treaty and related General Assembly resolution all encourage international cooperation. National law should include intellectual property, technology transformation, license of export and import, customs supervision and security system relative to international cooperation. At the same time it should also take into account maintaining international peace and security as well as adherence to the international arms control system.

10. Legal responsibilities. Civil, administrative and criminal responsibilities should be prosecuted according to the situation, whether arising from arbitrarily carrying out space activities or arbitrarily spreading information and causing substantial damages while violating the provisions of space laws.

11. Definition clause. Definitions should be explicit and provide the necessary content for terms, e.g., "space activities," "launching states," etc.

The need for space legislation in China is becoming more and more urgent. China possesses the conditions for adopting space legislation. We firmly believe that Chinese space legislation will be gradually established and become more complete.

Lack Of National Law In Iran, The Main Obstacle For Private Sector In Space Activities

Ali Akbar Golrounia
Faculty Member, Aerospace Research Institute, Iran
ali@ari.ac.ir

Mohsen Bahrami
Director, Aerospace Research Institute, Iran
Professor, Amir Kabir University of Technology, Iran
Mbahrami@ari.ac.ir

Abstract

Space base activities can be considered as a major part of communication infrastructure in any big economy. Furthermore space activities in Iran have been exclusively developed by the public sector in the past few decades. The economy is developing and is becoming more sophisticated. It seems that if Iran can follow its development trend, it would need to develop its space base activities with higher speed. It seems that the government can not afford to keep this sector in public domain any more. Therefore the government must promote the private sector to play a major role in the development of space base activities. Having a National Policy and a National Legislation in each state are essential for development of space base activities for benefit of the society and encouragement of private sector to play a major role in the development of space activities. Same as many other developing countries Iran has no official approved National Policy or National Legislation in respect to the space activities. This study tries to find out what are the main obstacles for development of space base activities in Iran especially by the private sector and shed some light on the area which should be considered by the Iranian government, especially in establishment of its National Policy and National Legislation for space based activities.

Introduction

Space base activities can be considered as a major part of any big economy. The commercial use of outer space has grown sharply in recent years. Many countries especially space fairing nations have the policy of expansion of private sector investment and involvement in civil space related activities. This policy goes beyond the traditional field of space telecommunications and includes commercial space launches as well as remote Sensing and the new field such as space tourism.

Commercialization of space activities is the logical consequences of the progress of space activities. It is well known that such activities contribute to the social welfare of all mankind if the benefits derived there from are used to raise the standard of living.

When the commercial space activities are based on competitiveness, the result will be at reasonable price, and this is one of the reasons which private sector should be involved in space activities.
The size of resources which must be allocated in space base activities especially for developing countries are beyond the government budget limitation and therefore private sector investment is highly important.

Space Activities in Iran

By launching Sinah-1, Iran's first satellite on October-27 2005, Iran became the forty-third country in the world to own a satellite, although Sinah-1 was build by the help of foreign countries and launched by Russian Kosmos-3M space launch vehicle but it had significant role in development of space activities in Iran.

Iran became a founding member of the United Nation's Committee On the Peaceful Uses of Outer Space (UNCOPUOS). The remote sensing techniques and utilization of date acquired by earth resources satellites in the country go back to the launching date of the first of Landsat series satellites. For the time being, the earth resources monitoring and management agencies not only use available data taken by various earth resource satellites, but also are equipped with the most advanced facilities available for data analysis and integration through the use of Geographic Information Systems.

Space remote sensing technologies and their applications are transferred to user communities in governmental and private sectors, by universities and specialized institutes (such as Iranian Remote Sensing Center, National Cartographic Center, Soil Conservation and Watershed Management Research Center, etc). In addition, the space based positioning systems are extensively used by government and private sectors in a wide spectrum of disciplines varying from national mapping projects to local studies as well.
The National Committee on Natural Disaster Reduction within the framework of a joint research projects is also using the space based positioning systems to monitor crust movements along major active quaternary faults.

Satellite meteorological activities are carried out by the Iran's Meteorological Organization (IMO). The systems used for this purpose include Meteosat (PDUS &SDUS) and NOAA (HRPT & APT) receiving stations located at IMO in Tehran. Data taken by these satellites are used by IMO's forecasting center not only for weather purposes but also for atmospheric disaster mitigation objectives.

The Islamic Republic of Iran provides telecommunications services via satellite mainly through INTELSAT and INMARSAT satellite Networks using more than 3500 channels, and via three international gateway earth stations.

Legal framework

Before 2003 space activities in Iran was carried by various independent organization mainly governmental entities. In April 2003, the Iranian Parliament approved a bill to create Iranian Space Agency (ISA) to serve as a policy-formulating organization for space initiatives. The ISA performs research on technology, remote sensing projects, develops national space equipment, and participates in the development of national and international space endeavors. It also coordinates various space-related activities within the country's research institutes, administrative agencies, and universities, these efforts also help the ISA to execute decisions from the Supreme Aerospace Council (SAC). Iranian Parliament created this Council in December 2003 to approve various space-related programs and to promote partnerships among other organizations.
The Council functions with input from senior government official. The ISA' s director serves as the council's secretary, and the President of Islamic Republic functions as chairman. Appointment of the President as the chairman of the Supreme Aerospace Council is the sign of the important of space activities in Iran. Also six Ministers from telecommunications and Information Technology, Science, Research and Technology, Defense, Foreign Affairs, Transportation, Industries and Mining are members of this body.

Among the goals of SAC is to support the private sector and cooperation's activities in outer space. Although this goal has not yet formulated, but an international cooperation is providing Mobil telephone services on the limited scale for some parts of the country.

Main Obstacles

Lack of National Law:

Rules and regulations which private sectors can operate on that bases are not clear and in some parts even do not exist. The area which private sectors can active have not clarified,

Most of the activities are based on negotiation and agreements with officials of related organizations which might be changed in period of time.

According to constitution of ISA this agency is responsible for issuance of all the licenses for space activities in Iran, including, lunching, satellite, operation, ground stations, transmissions of data, etc. however rules and procedures for obtaining such a license is not approved and in some cases even not available.

Lack of Experience

Space activities in Iran are rather new phenomena, especially for private sector which has no experience. Shortages of knowledge in marketing, operation, technology and funds are among the main barrier for private sector in Iran if this sector wants to enter in space activities. Although the Hard Currency Reserve Funds has been established by the government specially to support the private sector for investment and supporting of the economy, but it seems that is essential for private sector to cooperate with international entities to overcome its shortages and gain necessary skills to have successful operation.

International Law and Private Sector Activities in Space

There are two main principles with regard to the private sector activities in outer space, namely the "principle of freedom of Outer space" and the "principle of the common interest".

Article 1 of the Outer Space Treaty stipulates that "Outer Space including the moon and other celestial bodies shall be carried out for the benefit and in the interest of all countries, irrespective of their degree of economic or scientific development".
The same article also stipulates that "there shall be free access to all areas of celestial bodies". The principle of freedom of outer space includes the right of free access, the right of free exploration, and the right of free use. This freedom is granted only to the states.

According to Article 6 of the Outer Space Treaty. "Each State is internationally responsible for its governmental or non-governmental activities and for securing compliance of these activities with the provisions of the Outer Space Treaty ".

The space activities of the non- governmental entities necessitate the authorization and supervision of the appropriate state.
With regard to the principle of "the Common Interest ". Non -governmental entities can carry out space activities although they are not the direct beneficiary of the principle of freedom of outer space. Only it remains the question whether the non-governmental entities can carry out the commercial space activities.

The common interest principle fixes a general goal from which the States must not deviate in their space activities. It does not deal with the concrete sharing of benefits of space exploration and use. Therefore common interest principle is a binding legal rule and that the commercial space activities are in conformity with this principle as long as such activities contribute in a general sense to social welfare through the raising of the standard of living, although its substance is the profit- making transfer of goods and services.

Conclusion

It seems if the private sectors would like to overcome to its problems for activities in outer space, two steps have to be taken; the first step which has to be taken by the Government of Iran is to establish set of rules and regulations with clear policy of space activities by private sector in Iran. The Supreme Aerospace Council (SAC) shall instruct the Iranian Space Agency (ISA) for providing the necessary material for SAC approval. These policies and regulation should clearly address the area which private sectors could be active in outer space. Ways and means which the Iranian Government is going to support the private sector activities in outer space, and the procedures for cooperation's between Iranian private sectors and international companies for doing business in Iran especially in area such as tele- communications, remote sensing, etc.

The second step which mainly has to be taken by the private sectors themselves is to cooperate with international companies to perform joint projects in Iran with regard to outer space activities, this cooperation and partnership will help the Iranian Companies to gain skills and knowledge to overcome the problems such as transfer of technology, operation, marketing and capital investment.

IAC-06-E6.5.11

THE FLIGHT OF BRAZIL'S FIRST ASTRONAUT

Álvaro Fabricio dos Santos
Brazilian Association of Air and Space Law (SBDA)
São José dos Campos, SP, Brazil
alvaro.santos@agu.gov.br

ABSTRACT

On November 12, 1906, at 4:45 pm, a crowd in the Champ Bagatelle, in Paris, witnessed the first motor-driven flight of history. Alberto Santos Dumont, a 33 year-old Brazilian, flew over the French capital moving through a distance of 220 meters (722 feet), 6 meters (20 feet) high, on board of his plane "14-Bis".[1] Nowadays, in the year Brazilians celebrate the centenary of the 14-Bis flight, the first Brazilian astronaut has reached the outer space. After 7 years of training at the NASA's plant, in Houston, Texas, USA, the Brazilian astronaut, Mr. Marcos Pontes, finally accomplished his first flight on board of the Russian spaceship Soyuz to the International Space Station on March 30, 2006. This event definitely has crowned the Brazilian Space Program. On board of the International Space Station, Mr. Pontes tested scientific experiments from Brazilian research institutions and high-schools in a microgravity environment. This paper presents the legal aspects of the binding agreement executed between the Brazilian Space Agency and the Russian Federation Space Agency (Roskosmos) regarding the flight of the Brazilian astronaut, such as insurance premium and criteria for choosing companies. The political decision of contracting the Russian Federation Space Agency for the flight of the Brazilian astronaut and the Brazil's current position regarding its participation in the International Space Station Program are also being pointed out here.

INTRODUCTION

On October 14, 1997 the United States and Brazil established a cooperative program covering the detailed design, development, and operation of on-board equipments and payloads which the Brazilian Space Agency would develop and provide NASA with as part of a North-American contribution to the International Space Station (hereinafter referred to as ISS).

As a bonus for its participation in the ISS Program, NASA offered to Brazil the possibility of having a Brazilian astronaut in one of the North-American space shuttle flights to ISS.

Then, the Brazilian Space Agency selected Mr. Marcos Pontes, aeronautics engineer and jet pilot of the Brazilian Air Force, to be the Brazil's first astronaut. Mr. Pontes clocked up around 2,000 flight hours in twenty-five different aircraft, among them, the F-16 and MIG-29. He has a 16-year experience as well in the area of flight safety procedures. He also got a System Engineering master degree from Naval Postgraduate School,

Monterey, California, USA. He was definitely the best choice.

THE BRAZILIAN PARTICIPATION IN THE ISS PROGRAM

According to the Implementing Arrangement established between the United States and Brazil, the Brazilian contribution to the ISS Program should include the following equipments:

a) The Technology Experiment Facility (TEF), which should provide long-term exposure to the low Earth orbit space environment for active and passive experiments;

b) The Window Observational Research Facility Block 2 (WORF-2), which should provide the ISS capability devoted to observational science and remote sensing development;

c) The Express Pallet, which serves as an interface mechanism that may be utilized to attach small payloads to the U.S. truss segment P3 or S3;

d) The Unpressurized Logistics Carrier (ULC), which is a platform for transportation of unpressurized cargo, and it may be attached to U.S. truss segment;

e) The Cargo Handling Interface Assembly (CHIA), which is the flight support equipment that provides a method of attaching cargo to ULC and allows for orbit a handling of the cargo; and

f) The Attach System Z1-ULC, which provides mounting accommodations for external passive payloads and experiments.[2]

The budget to cover all items Brazil would provide NASA with for its participation in the ISS Program was firstly estimated in US$ 120 million. However, taking into account the projects presented by Boeing Company and the Brazilian Aeronautics Company (Embraer), the Brazilian Space Agency figured out that just one of the items, the Express Pallet alone, would consume the whole estimated budget.

Therefore Brazil has not started the production of those items as previously foreseen, but, instead, a round of discussions was set up between the representatives of NASA and the Brazilian Space Agency. Actually, these discussions are still ongoing, but there is not yet a new official amount to be supported by Brazil for its participation in the ISS Program.

Currently, there are other important space activities to be carried out by Brazil, such as: the new satellites of the Chinese-Brazilian Earth-Observation Satellite Program (CBERS), whose launchings are scheduled for 2007, 2009, and 2011; the commercialization of CBERS data and the implementation of ground stations around the world; the establishment of a Brazilian-Ukrainian company which will commercialize satellite launchings from Alcantara[3]; the re-building of Alcantara Launch Center (CLA) after it suffered the 2004 disaster setback, when twenty-one technicians were killed[4]; and the new project for a Brazilian launch vehicle.

In this context, the ISS Program would become feasible for Brazil only in case of a reduction to its budget.

THE BRAZILIAN ASTRONAUT'S TRAINING

Despite the problems with the ISS Program, as pointed out in the previous item, the Brazilian Astronaut training at the NASA's plant in the Johnson Space Center (Houston, Texas, USA) started on January 12, 1998. The basic trainee program was successfully completed in

December 2000, when Mr. Pontes received the title of "astronaut". Upon conclusion of the first phase, the Brazilian astronaut started the advanced training period in operational maintenance. This phase involved operation revisions and technical qualifications.

Mr. Marcos Pontes trained in Houston by February 12, 2005 and Brazil invested the total amount of US$ 2,631,026.00, according to the following schedule: 1998: US$ 561,738.00 (two payments of US$ 280,869.00); 1999: US$ 290,724.00; 2000: US$ 276,890.00; 2001: US$ 276,890.00; 2002: US$ 276,890.00; 2003: US$ 305,584.00; 2004: US$ 313,636.00; and 2005: US$ 328,674.00.[5]

Since Brazil was not able to fulfill its obligations in the ISS Program as firstly foreseen, the flight of the Brazilian astronaut was postponed *sine die*. However, there was yet another disturbing factor: the Brazilian Astronaut was getting old and there was no reason for Brazil to keep on supporting his expensive training at NASA.

Brazil was taking a serious risk of wasting the whole investment in the traineeships of its astronaut.

Since the new terms for the Brazilian participation in the ISS Program were not defined, the representatives of the Brazilian Space Agency decided to set up discussions with the representatives of the Russian Federation Space Agency (Roskosmos) to become feasible the flight of the Brazilian astronaut on board of the Russian spaceship Soyuz.

It should be emphasized that the relationship between Brazil and the Russian Federation in space area started in 1988 and it is currently getting closer. A Memorandum of Understanding, whose object is the cooperation for developing satellite launching vehicles, was signed in 2004 between both Governments. Beyond that, Russians have been serving as technical consultants for the development of the new project of the Brazilian Satellite Launching Vehicle.

THE AGREEMENT

On October 18, 2005, in Moscow, the President of the Brazilian Space Agency, Mr. Sergio Gaudenzi, and the President of the Russian Federation Space Agency (Roskosmos), Mr. Anatoly Perminov, signed the agreement regarding the flight of Brazil's first astronaut.[6]

The Brazilian Space Agency, in attention to a request from Roskosmos, has not disclosed the official amount paid for the flight. Notwithstanding, the Brazilian media has revealed that it ranges within US$ 10 and US$ 15 million. Both of these values are cheaper than the amount paid by space touring millionaires who have flown on board of the Soyuz, *i.e.,* US$ 20 million.

Mr. Marcos Pontes started his trainee period at Star City, near Moscow, at the Yuri Gagarin Trainee Center, in October 2005, the same month the agreement was signed. Hence, he has became also a "cosmonaut".

At this time, the agreement's price covered the training period of the Brazilian astronaut.

THE INSURANCE PREMIUM

To comply with a requirement pursuant to the agreement, Brazil agreed to contract two insurances regarding the flight of the Brazilian astronaut: the first one to cover complaints from third parties; the second to cover injuries or even the death of the astronaut.

Brazil has contracted the Russian Insurance Center to cover eventual complaints from third parties. The company was indicated by Roskosmos and Brazil paid US$ 214,415.00, covering the amount of US$ 5 million.

The astronaut personal insurance for covering injuries or even his death was provided by Aliança do Brasil, a Brazilian company. Brazil need not pay for this insurance, because the company was interested in joining its name to the flight; the company was sure that it will make a profit from the project. The insurance has covered the amount of US$ 1 million.[7]

THE FLIGHT

On March 30, 2006, at 11:00 pm (Brasília time), from the Launch Center of Baikonur, in Kazakhstan, the Brazil's first astronaut, at age of 43, finally took his flight toward ISS. Beyond the Brazilian, there were two other astronauts on board of Soyuz, the Russian Pavel Vinogradov, and the North-American Jeffrey Williams. The flight was broadcasted by most important Brazilian TV companies, and a lot of Brazilians postponed their bed time in order to watch the flight. It was really a great event for Brazilians. Fortunately, the flight was undertaken as scheduled.

Meanwhile the astronaut was in space, the Legal Subcommittee of the United Nations Committee on the Peaceful Uses of Outer Space started its 45 Session, on April 03, 2006. Many delegations which were attending the Session congratulated Brazil for the successful flight of its astronaut.[8]

On board of Soyuz, Mr. Pontes tested eight scientific experiments: six from research institutions and two from high-schools.

Mr. Pontes stayed in space for ten days, eight of them on board of ISS. On April 8, 2006, at 8:48 pm (Brasília time), the Brazilian astronaut arrived safely near the city of Arkalyk, Kazakhstan, jointly with the Russian cosmonaut Valeri Tokariov, and the North-American astronaut William McArthur.

After few days in Moscow, the Brazilian astronaut returned to Brazil, where he arrived on April 20, 2006. He was received as a hero by Brazilians and welcome by the Brazilian President.

AFTER THE FLIGHT

Since there is not any other space flight planned by Brazil, the question that remained was: what were the plans for the astronaut? He could simply return to its position in the Brazilian Air Force. It was also considered by the Brazilian authorities the possibility of keeping him in NASA to extend his training. However this alternative was discarded due to financial constraints. He could act as a representative of the Brazilian Space Program.

Notwithstanding, he has surprised many people when in May 2006, just one month after his space flight, he applied for his retirement from the Brazilian Air Force.

This attitude has caused a lot of criticism. Many people considered Mr. Pontes a selfish person, because in their opinion his own interest prevailed over the public interest. Since he is no longer a member of the Brazilian Air Force, he is free for making profits from his endeavor.

In his site on the Internet[9], the Brazilian astronaut has stated that he fulfilled his mission; that there was not other flights scheduled for the coming years; that his health was not as good as it used to be; that he hopes to be the first of many others Brazilian astronauts...

Besides these points of view, the fact is that Mr. Pontes had the right of retiring. He fulfilled perfectly the mission for which he was trained. Furthermore, the Brazilian Government has not obliged him to remain as a member of the Brazilian Air Force after the flight.

The most important thing is that Brazil keeps giving its space program the due value it really deserves.

References:

[1] Barros, Henrique Lins de: "Santos Dumont and the Invention of Plane", CBPF, Rio de Janeiro, 2006.

[2] Rolim, Maria Helena Fonseca de Souza: "The USA-Brazil Implementing Arrangement on the International Space Station – Interpretation and Application", Proceedings of the 44th Colloquium on the Law of Outer Space, AIAA, 2002, pp. 87/99.

[3] Monserrat Fº, José: "Brazilian-Ukrainian Agreement on Launching Cyclone-4 From Alcantara – Impact on Brazilian Legislation", presented in the 47th Colloquium on the Law of Outer Space, in Vancouver/Canada, from 4 to 8 October 2004.

[4] Dos Santos, Álvaro Fabricio: "The Brazilian Law #10.821 - Compensation for the Families of the Victims of the Alcantara Disaster", presented in the 47th Colloquium on the Law of Outer Space, in Vancouver/Canada, from 4 to 8 October 2004.

[5] Data kindly provided by Ambassador Carlos José Prazeres Campello, Head of the Department of Space Cooperation of the Brazilian Space Agency.

[6] Data from the site of the Brazilian Space Agency on the Internet: www.aeb.gov.br

[7] Data kindly provided by Ambassador Carlos José Prazeres Campello, Head of the Department of Space Cooperation of the Brazilian Space Agency.

[8] Especially the Russian Federation, Czech Republic, and the members of the Latin-America and Caribbean Group.

[9] www.marcospontes.net

IAC-06-E6.5.12

GNSS THIRD PARTY LIABILITY: THE EUROPEAN EXPERIENCE OF GALILEO

Chiara Lucchini Gilera
Legal Expert
Galileo Joint Undertaking
Brussels, Belgium
chiara.lucchini.gilera@galileoju.com

Abstract

One of the key items discussed at the current stage within the Galileo Project is third party liability. The Public and the Private sector are debating, within the Public Private Partnership nature of the deal, how to best manage the risk of third parties claiming for damages arising from the Galileo System.

Galileo, the European Global Satellite Navigation System (GNSS), is a civil system designed to provide enhanced navigation and timing services to the users. The system's unique features (integrity, authentication, accuracy, precision, availability...) will change the user's perception and expectations towards satellite navigation services. Today GNSS services are exclusively offered by the military systems GPS and GLONASS, which provide only basic navigation and timing information with no guarantee of service or of performance.

Despite the undeniable value of satellite navigation services and despite the advanced features which will be offered by Galileo, GNSS is vulnerable to a number of possible intentional (jamming, spoofing, meaconing...) or unintentional (ionospheric interference, radiofrequency interferences, errors in the operations...) interferences. Such vulnerabilities may affect the ground segment, the space segment or the Signal in Space causing damages. Moreover the uncertainty of the legal regime under which third party claims may be brought, the global dimension of the project and the nature of the Signal in Space (SIS), which is freely broadcasted on air, raises some questions concerning the capacity of an entity to manage the risks arising thereof according to the prudent business test.

Through the analysis of the liability regime of other activities and the compensation mechanisms which are available in certain sectors, some considerations are drawn on the opportunity of establishing a liability regime for GNSS and on the opportunity of setting up an ad hoc compensation structure, which would guarantee trust in the system and adequate compensation to the plaintiffs.

Article

1. INTRODUCTION

A Global Navigation Satellite System (GNSS) is conceived as a core infrastructure, providing time and navigation information to the users. There are at present two GNSS in the world, the American Global Positioning System (GPS) and the Russian GLObal NAvigation Satellite System (GLONASS). Both were developed as military systems. Currently, Europe is developing a civil Global Navigation Satellite System, GALILEO. Based on the information provided by the system, applications will be developed in domains ranging from transport to timing, surveying, science, search and rescue, law enforcement, environment or recreation. In other words, satellite navigation and its applications imply services and downstream activities which carry strong social, safety and economical benefit.

GPS radionavigation signals are today freely broadcasted and received almost worldwide by anyone with a receiver. The signal provider has no control over the users or over the use that is made of the navigation signals. Signal providers have today no technical means to warn the users about abrupt signal degradations or error. Moreover, due to the military nature of the satellite positioning systems signal providers have at present no real political incentive to warn users.

An error in the positioning information, the unavailability of the signal or its misuse may have in some cases only minor effects on the users or may, in other cases, cause damages which may potentially be extremely severe. The global dimension of satellite navigation systems, the broad use of this technology, the different applications and the uncertainty of the legal regime suggest that the risk exposure to claims might be too high and difficult to mitigate.

Since the definition years of Galileo, liability and in particular third party liability in relation to the transmission of the signal in space, has represented an issue of primary concern for lawyers and decision makers.

2. THIRD PARTY LIABILITY

Third party liability is the obligation to repair damages arising by a faulty action or willful misconduct of a person (natural or legal). In other words, third party liability (also referred to as extra-contractual responsibility or tort liability[1]) arises whenever there is the infringement of a right or of an interest (depending on the system of law) safeguarded by legislation or case law. The person claiming for third party liability has to **prove** the **damage, the fault** of the person causing the damage and **the causal relationship between the damage and the action of the faulty person**.

Third party liability becomes a particularly sensitive issue with regard to Galileo. Indeed the system is composed of ground assets distributed throughout different countries, space assets orbiting around the Earth signal in space broadcasted worldwide.

[1] Torts are civil wrongs, other than breaches of contract, recognized by common law as grounds for a lawsuit.

3. THE CASE OF GALILEO

3.1 Program overview

Galileo will be a system of 30 satellites orbiting in Medium Earth Orbit (MEO[2]) and related ground stations to provide timing and positioning information to the users worldwide. The project is developed as a Public Private Partnership (PPP) by the European Commission (EC), the European Space Agency (ESA) and industry. The full constellation will be manufactured, by a private consortium on the basis of the technical design developed under ESA contracts.

The Galileo Joint Undertaking[3] (GJU) is negotiating, on behalf of the EC and ESA, the implementation of the PPP contract, which will be signed by the GNSS Supervisory Authority (GSA)[4] and the Galileo Operating Company (GOC). The contract will establish the terms and conditions under which the system will be operated during the 20 years of the concession period.

Galileo will be the first European infrastructure, as the Community funds allocated to finance its development phase

[2] Medium Earth Orbit MEO is a region of space situated at 20.200 Km altitude between Low Earth Orbit LEO (900/1000 Km) and Geostationary Orbit GEO (35.000 Km)

[3] Council Regulation (EC) No 876/2002 of 21 May 2002 setting up the Galileo Joint Undertaking. *OJ L 138, 28.5.2002, p. 1–8.*

[4] This European Agency was set up by: Council Regulation (EC) No 1321/2004 of 12 July 2004 on the establishment of structures for the management of the European satellite radio-navigation programmes. *OJ L 246, 20.7.2004, p. 1–9.*

were mainly provided by Directorate General Energy and Transport (DG TREN) within the Trans-European Transport Networks. The GSA will be the owner of all the tangible and intangible assets of the project, it will be the entity responsible of ensuring that the interest of the public sector is safeguarded and it will be the regulatory authority for the European radionavigation (Galileo) and augmentation (EGNOS) systems. The GOC will be granted the exclusive right to deploy operate and exploit the system in accordance with the PPP contractual requirements.

3.2 Sources of Third Party Liability

Third party liabilities in the Galileo Project may arise from different sources in respect of the specific phases of the project. In particular a distinction could be made between the period before Full Operational Capacity (FOC) and the period therefrom.

In the pre-FOC phase, third party liability is mostly expected to arise with regard to the assets, while from FOC on the biggest risk exposure is foreseen from the signal transmission.

Signal In Space (SIS) related damages are those presenting the highest uncertainties in terms of risk exposure and required coverage. It is assumed here that the SIS will not fall under the definition of "space object" and therefore will not be disciplined by international space law. Indeed the question whether SIS falls or not under the definition of "space object" is an interesting question, however, it appears rather theoretical. According to the 1972 Liability Convention[5] art 1 a space object includes component parts as well as its launch vehicle and parts thereof. It seams that this concept defines tangible assets and it doesn't seam to extend also to the intangible ones such as the signals in space. Indeed, it is likely that States at the time of ratification of the Treaties didn't have in mind such a wide interpretation of space object.

3.2.1 Assets

Third party liability may arise with regard to the ground segment, the space segment and the Signal In Space.

Ground segment: third party liability for damage to goods or people will fall under the applicable law of the territory in which the damage occurs. The risk in relation to the infrastructure can be mitigated through common third party insurance policies. Special legal regimes might be negotiated with the hosting Country; but it is unlikely that the GSA or the Commission would be able to negotiate, on behalf of the operator, an extraterritoriality regime with special immunities from the national legislation. It would however be recommendable to locate to the best extent possible all elements of the ground segment in territories under EU or ESA member States' jurisdiction.

Space segment: there are mainly two phases of risk concerning the space segment where damages could be caused to third parties: the launch risk and the in orbit risk. Responsibility related to the space segment is regulated by international law and in particular by the 1967 Outer Space Treaty and the 1972 Liability Convention[6].

The Treaties establish a regime of international responsibility of the launching State[7] for activities conducted in outer space. A launching State is held strictly liable for damages caused by elements of the space segment on the surface of the Earth or to aircraft flight. Should the damage occur in outer space, the plaintiff may recover his

[5] Treaty on Principles Governing the Activities of States in the Exploration and Use of Outer Space including the Moon and other Celestial Bodies, 27 January 1967, 610 UNTS 205 entered into force on 10 October 1967. See in particular art VI and VII.

[6] Convention on International Liability for Damage caused by Space Objects, 29 March 1972, 961 UNTS 187. See in particular art II and III.

[7] According to article III of the OST Treaty, the "launching State" can be defined as a "State that launches or procures the launch…and from whose territory or facility an object is launched …".

damage only if he proves the fault of the launching State.
For the launch phase, risk mitigation tools, such as satellite insurance, contingencies, Launch Risk Guarantees (LRG) and spare satellites will be put in place to alleviate the risk exposure. Possible outstanding liabilities will fall under State's responsibility in accordance with international law and specific launching agreements. During the In Orbit phase, liability to third parties shall be covered by the launching State (in the event that his fault is proven) and eventually if provided under particular agreements by insurance or contingencies allocated by the private entities.

In relation to the assets a relevant source of third party liability may be represented by product liability as defined by the EC Directive 85/374[8]. Product liability refers to an area of law ruling the responsibility of manufacturers, distributors, suppliers and retailers according to which, producers are strictly liable ()there is no need to proof the fault) for damages caused by their defective products. Product liability is a risk commonly faced by manufacturers which usually insure the risk through dedicated insurance.

3.2.2 Operations

Signal transmission: is believed to be the most relevant font of third party claims. The Galileo system will provide navigation services with features which will significantly improve the reliance on GNSS. According to the different services, Galileo will provide integrity, authentication, guarantee and continuous availability of service therefore increasing the reliability of the technology and the confidence in its use. However, satellite navigation systems are vulnerable systems which are subject to a number of possible intentional (jamming, spoofing, meaconing...) or unintentional (ionospheric interference, radiofrequency interferences, errors in the operations...) interferences. Such vulnerabilities may cause disruptions or errors in the signals which may easily result in damages suffered by third parties.

In principle there is no difference between services in the nature of third party damages suffered because of SIS malfunctioning. However it may be opportune to briefly recall the different services, which Galileo will provide, to better understand some of the future operator's specific concerns.

Open Service (OS): is basic timing and navigation information freely broadcasted to any user with a capable receiver. No contract is needed for service provision. Any service provider can use the OS and develop applications; the GOC will have no control over such applications. The frequency signal is close to that of GPS and the user of mass market receiver won't be able to tell whether the information received is coming from Galileo or not.
Safety of Life (SoL): is timing and navigation data plus integrity[9] information. Integrity will warn the user on the reliability of the computed position and authentication[10] will prove that the signal received and trusted is truly coming from Galileo. The signal will not be encrypted and it will be mostly used in safety critical domains (aviation, maritime, rail). Certification is also foreseen for specific user's communities and in particular in aviation and in maritime.

---

[8] Council Directive 85/374/EEC of 25 July 1985 on the approximation of the laws, regulations and administrative provisions of the Member States concerning liability for defective products. *OJ L 210, 7.8.1985, p. 29–33.*

[9] Integrity is a measure of the trust which can be placed in the correctness of thc information provided by the total system. The integrity message will worn the user when the system should not be trusted for the intended operation.

[10] Authentication is a process by which a system verifies that the origin of the information is truly the one claimed by the source and that the information has not been modified. It can be achieved in different ways; one of which is electronic signature. In Galileo, Authentication is foreseen by the Mission Requirement Document (MRD) 6 as an encrypted electronic signature proving that the integrity message received is truly coming from a Galileo satellite.

Commercial Service (CS): is timing and navigation data with value added services provided to commercial users against a payment. This service will be provided only to users requesting and paying for the service.
Public Regulated Service (PRS): provides timing and navigation information with encrypted value added services to the EU MS Governments that buy the service. This service will be restricted to selected users under States supervision subject to governmental authorities' decision for defense and civil protection.
Search and Rescue Service (SAR): is not part of the navigation payload, but it will provide positioning information to locate people in distress. SAR will operate within the COSPAS-SARSAT[11] framework according to which States bear no responsibility in relation to SAR services.

Due to the civil nature of the European radionavigation and augmentation system, to its user approach and to the fact that the system is a public infrastructure, it could be argued that the actors involved in Galileo may have towards the users a duty of care[12] of particularly high standards. The proof of the existence of such duty may sensibly increase the chances for a claim by a third party to be recognized valid. Two services in particular may be perceived as particularly critical: the OS and the SoL. Concerning the OS the main concerns address the following considerations: there is no contract for service provision by which special clauses could mitigate the liability exposure, the number of users is unknown, there is no control over the use or misuse of the signal and moreover the OS doesn't generate any revenue which could repay potential liability claims. The Private sector fears to face, in relation to this service, claims of relative small magnitude but very large in number. The Safety of Life is also seen by the operator as a particularly critical service because it will mainly be used in safety critical operation where possible failures may lead to catastrophic scenarios of personal injury or loss of life.

Moreover it is still unclear whether the Signal In Space could be considered (just like electricity, art 2) as a product under the aforementioned product liability Directive. If this was the case, a faulty signal would give raise to the strict liability of the "producer" of the signal. The producer is defined in the Directive as the manufacturer of a finished product, the producer of any raw material or the manufacturer of any component part and any person who by putting his name, trade mark or other feature on the product presents itself as the producer[13]. Thus, the GSA, the GOC and the service providers may possibly

[11] COSPAS-SARSAT is a programme developed through the cooperation of the US, France, Russia and Canada for the search and rescue of people in distress. The USA contributed with the programme SARSAT, France with SARGOS and since 1978 the Soviet Union provided COSPAS, while Canada provided the transponders. On the 1 July 1988 the four Countries have signed the COSPAS-SARSAT intergovernmental agreement to guarantee the continuity of the programme. Today 37 States are part to this agreement.

[12] Duty of care is a requirement that a person acts towards others with the attention, prudence and cautious that a reasonable person in the same circumstances would use.

[13] Council Directive 85/374/EEC of 25 July 1985 Art.3: "1. 'Producer' means the manufacturer of a finished product, the producer of any raw material or the manufacturer of a component part and any person who, by putting his name, trade mark or other distinguishing feature on the product presents himself as its producer.
2. Without prejudice to the liability of the producer, any person who imports into the Community a product for sale, hire, leasing or any form of distribution in the course of his business shall be deemed to be a producer within the meaning of this Directive and shall be responsible as a producer.
3. Where the producer of the product cannot be identified, each supplier of the product shall be treated as its producer unless he informs the injured person, within a reasonable time, of the identity of the producer or of the person who supplied him with the product. The same shall apply, in the case of an imported product, if this product does not indicate the identity of the importer referred to in paragraph 2, even if the name of the producer is indicated".

all be held liable for product liability for faults of the SIS.

3.3 SIS third party liability management

Based on the aforementioned considerations, it is feared that signal malfunctioning might result worldwide in a considerable number of claims. Given the number of domains served, the uncertainties of the legal environment and the absence of internationally agreed financial caps, it is difficult to estimate what would be the magnitude of the risk and therefore the appropriate coverage.

Being Galileo a Public Private Partnership, it is also within the interest of the Public sector to agree with the private counterpart means to operate the system under an adequate coverage which could ensure a sound risk management. Both, the private and the public sector, agree on the need to operate the system under an adequate coverage which a prudent business delivering the signal in space would seek. The assessment of such adequate coverage is particularly difficult in a project like Galileo mainly due to the following circumstances:

- absence of a dedicated legal regime applicable to the signal in space;
- lack of previous experiences;
- non existence of comparable businesses.

4. CHALLENGES FOR GALILEO IN THE ASSESSMENT OF THE ADEQUATE COVERAGE

4.1 The absence of a dedicated legal regime for the SIS

4.1.1 Regulatory initiatives within the aviation domain

For the time being there is no dedicated juridical regime which disciplines the provision of radionavigation signals, however this does not mean that there is no liability regime applicable to the SIS. On the contrary the provision and the use of radionavigation signals falls under a variety of legal frameworks depending on the legislation of the territory in which it is used and according to the specific application domain.

The only attempt to discipline GNSS was made within the aviation domain, but yet no satisfactory solution has been provided, in particular with regard to third party liability. The initiative of the aviation sector was twofold. On one side Member States expressed their concern in relation to the use of GNSS under Article 28 of the Convention on International Civil Aviation[14] (hereinafter referred to as the Chicago Convention). On the other side the civil aviation, which strongly relies on CNS/ATM[15] and in particular on satellite navigation (mainly provided by the Global Positioning System GPS in the absence of any service or performance guarantee), wanted to bring clarity on the responsibilities for signal provision of the different actors. GNSS services are namely provided by primary signal providers, augmentation signal providers, States, Air Traffic Control (ATC), air carriers, aircraft operators and equipment manufacturers. The International Civil Aviation Organization (ICAO) aims to avoid that the variety of national and international

[14] See the Convention on International Civil Aviation of 1944 (Chicago Convention). In particular under article 28, *Air navigation facilities and standard systems*: "Each contracting State undertakes, so far as it may find practicable, to: (a) Provide, in its territory, airports, radio services, meteorological services and other air navigation facilities to facilitate international air navigation, in accordance with the standards and practices recommended or established from time to time, pursuant to this Convention; (b) Adopt and put into operation the appropriate standard systems of communications procedure, codes, markings, signals, lighting and other operational practices and rules which may be recommended or established from time to time, pursuant to this Convention; (c) Collaborate in international measures to secure the publication of aeronautical maps and charts in accordance with standards which may be recommended or established from time to time, pursuant to this Convention".

[15] CNS/ATM, Communications, Navigation, Surveillance/Air Trafic Management.

laws, the different liability regimes and the legal nature of the providers (public, for which special protection might apply or private, which are fully exposed to the risk of claims) limit the determination of liability and reparation of the damage.

According to article 28 of the Chicago Convention, conventional navigation aids are implemented and maintained under States' responsibility. GNSS, as navigation aid, falls under art 28 of the Chicago Convention and consequently States are responsible for the safety of radionavigation services within their jurisdiction[16]. States can delegate to other States the responsibility of air traffic service provision within their territory (Annex 11 to the Chicago Convention), but such delegation is only limited to technical and operational aspects, while safety remains a responsibility of domestic competence.

ICAO concluded that CNS/ATM systems operations and liability issues, in particular, are mostly disciplined by national laws.

According to the Study Group's analysis of various States' national laws, GNSS was likely believed to be governed by the National liability regime of the place where the air traffic control (ATC) agencies[17] are located and that ATC liability is a fault based liability regime based on negligence (proof of fault of action or omission of the ATC in its duty of care) or gross negligence (in case of States).

4.1.2 International Convention

In the attempt to overcome the above mentioned liability related uncertainties, the majority of ICAO contracting States, as reflected by the adoption of Resolution A 32/2018, were in favor of establishing a GNSS International Convention to be applied to all activities employing satellites and ground based equipment, technologies and systems.

A "Draft Convention on the Rights and Obligations of States relating to Global Navigation Satellite Systems for Air Navigation Purposes" was presented at the 10th meeting of ICAO Secretary Group. The document stated some general principles and a description of their objectives addressing the importance of safety, performance requirements and certification. The Convention was seen as the most efficient legal instrument to guarantee worldwide a common approach to liability management. The establishment of a single jurisdiction, or the possibility to recur to arbitration, was proposed in order to ensure certainty of applicable law, procedural effectiveness and equal treatment between Governmental and non-Governmental service providers.

The Convention specifically addressed liability arising from GNSS related damages (system and sub-system technology components or services). Liability was proposed to be strict up to a limit and fault based thereafter (in line with the 1999 Montreal Convention) with joint liability in case of damage being caused by more than one provider. Adequate risk coverage was mandated under the Convention, which also envisaged the possibility of establishing a dedicated compensation fund[19]. No possibility to recur to sovereign immunity protection was envisaged, but it was foreseen the exclusion of fault liability in case of Force Majeure events.

The project of the International Convention was abandoned as consensus on the content of this document was not unanimous, ICAO's

[16] Article 28 of the Chicago Convention disciplines only relations among States and it doesn't give cause of action to private persons to claim compensation for damage.

[17] ICAO AFI Planning and Implementation Regional Group 13th Meeting: *Institutional Aspects of CNS/ATM systems.* Sal, Cape Verde, 25-29 June 2001APIRG/13-WP/25.

[18] 32nd Session of the ICAO Assembly adopted Resolution AS-32/20: *Development and elaboration of an appropriate long term legal framework to govern the implementation of GNSS implementation.* The resolution recognizes the need for a long term legal framework instructs the ICAO Council and Secretariat to ensure the follow up of the recommendations of the World Wide CNS/ATM System Implementation Conference, especially on institutional issues and questions on liability and invites to present proposals for such a framework.

[19] A35-WP/125, LE/11, Appendix C: *Proposal relating to main elements for inclusion in a draft convention.*

Legal and Technical experts[20] recognized the International Convention as being a difficult and long solution to achieve. Moreover the experience in the implementation of CNS/ATM was estimated to be insufficient to allow and the drafting of an international convention was considered premature.

4.1.3 Contractual Framework

A more flexible approach compared to that of the International Convention was presented to the Council at the 33rd ICAO's Assembly by the Study Group. The proposal envisaged to present a Draft Contractual Framework relating to the provision of GNSS Services.
The Contractual Framework contained mandatory elements such as compliance with SARPs and with the 1998 Charter on the Rights and Obligations of States Relating to GNSS Services, the establishment of fault based liability regime, compulsory risk coverage, mandatory recourse to arbitration and recognition of equal treatment between State organizations and private entities.
The Contractual Framework Agreement proposal is twofold as it reflects both public and private law elements. The first addresses obligations between Governments: in particular certification, liability, jurisdiction and the creation of a GNSS Authority addressing the relations between system operators and service providers[21]. The second concerns contractual arrangements among stakeholders, which define responsibilities in the chain of implementation, operation, provision and use of GNSS[22]. In particular these arrangements define the relationship between and the obligations of Air Traffic Service (ATS) providers and GNSS signal providers, augmentation signal providers and potentially other parties.

The Draft Contractual Framework which is today currently under discussion fails to address an issue of paramount importance: third party liability in case of GNSS related damages. However it does address explicitly the issue of contractual liability in the event of loss or damage related to a failure, malfunctioning or improper use[23] of GNSS. Liability would be based on fault and it would apply to each subject to the extent that it has contributed to the occurrence of the damage[24]. Failure to perform obligations shall be governed by the liability regime applicable to the activity for which the signal is utilized and public parties should be subject to the same rules as private parties by submitting themselves to arbitration. The proposed framework

4.2 Lack of previous experiences

A commonly used method to assess what would be reasonable liability coverage for a certain business is that of benchmarking against other similar businesses. However, Galileo is a complex and unique business and no real analogy can be found in the market.
Despite the difference in the philosophy under which the two satellite systems were developed and the resulting consequences, it could, however, be worth exploring how the United States' face the risk of liability claims in relation to the NAVSTAR Global Positioning System (GPS)[25].

---

[20] Resolution A32/20 established a Secretariat Study Group to ensure the follow up of the recommendations of the Rio Conference and a Panel of Legal and Technical experts on GNSS.

[21] The GNSS entity shall be entrusted with the tasks of defining specifications of GNSS signal and services, drafting, negotiating and implementing service level agreements, defining the process for responsibility allocation, managing a compensation GNSS fund and defining the applicable risk coverage requirements.

[22] According to the proposed framework, contracting parties shall ensure that GNSS system operators and service providers provide adequate insurance or other risk coverage to compensate liabilities that might arise out of their non performance and shall establish a compensation fund to compensate shortfalls in the recovery of damages from the liable entity

[23] The meaning of "improper use" is not specified, but it might be interpreted also negligence.

[24] The framework agreement to establish a liability framework based on fault for human errors and strict liability for technical errors.

[25] The following section reflects the content of the article by Brandon E. EHRHART: "A technological dream turned legal nightmare:

The US Government generally enjoys sovereign immunity[26], a doctrine preventing the initiation of suits by private parties against the Federal Government. Despite to its immunity, the US has, in some specific cases, expressly waived this protection. In particular the US can be sued mainly for a tortuous act of a federal employee causing damage or for claims arising out of contracts to which the federal government is a party.

GPS is controlled and operated by the US Federal Government, therefore - in the absence of specific waivers - GPS operations are covered by sovereign immunity.

Under Article 28 of the Chicago Convention, the US Government does not assume any responsibility for the provision of radionavigation signals outside its jurisdiction arguing that decision and authorization to use navigation services pertains to each National State. Therefore, there is no responsibility of the US as signal provider. This might erroneously lead to the assumption that inside its National territory the US would then take responsibility for GPS-related damages, but reality shows to be different.

As previously mentioned, expressed waivers to the US sovereign immunity doctrine allow people suffering damage (also GPS-related) to sue the Government under one of the following Acts, namely: the Foreign Claims Act[27] (FCA) the Suits in Admiralty Act[28] (SAA) and the Federal Tort Claims Act[29] (FTCA). According to the first two Acts a right to compensation is recognized respectively to inhabitants of foreign countries for personal injury, death or property damage caused by non combat activities of US personal overseas (FCA) and for torts committed in navigable waters controlled by the United States (SAA). The Federal Torts Claims Act allows plaintiffs to directly pursue the US before Federal Court for damages arising from negligence resulting from Government employees' acts or contracts to which the Federal Government is a party, therefore most GPS related claims would be brought under the Federal Tort Claims Act.

Specific exceptions such as the discretionary function exception[30] and the foreign country exception[31] limit the scope of the waivers to sovereign immunity and would be the most relevant exceptions as far as GPS related operations are concerned. The question therefore is whether GPS operations could fall within the scope of one of these exceptions.

potential liability of the United States under the Federal Court Claims Act for Operating the Global Positioning System". Vanderbilt Journal of transnational law, Vol. 33, Number 2, March 2000.

[26] Sovereign immunity is a doctrine which precludes law suits against the sovereign without its consent. The doctrine is based on the inherent nature of power and on its spirit of preservation which dates back to the time when it was believed that the King could do no wrong as his sovereignty arose from a divine right. It was therefore believed that no legal right could apply against the authority that makes the law on which the right depends. In earlier days the sovereign immunity doctrine was relaxed through the admission of waivers, as it is believed that nobody is above the rules, not even the State.

[27] Foreign Claims Act, 10 U.S.C.§ 2734-2736. It is a US Federal Law of 1942 providing for compensation to non US citizens for personal injury, death or property damage arising from non combat activities of the US military personnel overseas.

[28] Suits in Admiralty Act, 46 U.S.C. app §§ 741 – 752.

[29] Federal Tort Claim Act, 28 U.S.C. 2680(h).

[30] The United States are immune for any claim based upon an act or omission of an employee of the Government, exercising due care, in the execution of a statute or regulation, whether or not such statute or regulation be valid, or based upon the exercise of or performance or the failure to exercise or perform a discretionary function or duty on the part of the Federal agency or an employee of the Government, whether or not the discretion involved be abused. 28 U.S.C. 2680(a).

[31] The foreign country exception to the FTCA's waiver of sovereign immunity for claims "arising in a foreign country," bars claims based on any injury suffered in a foreign country, regardless of where the tortuous act or omission occurred. 28 U.S.C. § 2680(k).

According to the discretionary function exception, the US - which would be liable under the FTCA - is not liable to compensate claims if the act causing the damage involved an element of judgment or choice by the employee. With regard to GPS, most fixed regulations and procedures rule the operations leaving little room to employee's judgment, which would determine the inapplicability of the exception.

However, the source of the negligent decision is also an element which determinates the applicability of the discretionary function. If the challenged activity results to be a function uniquely undertaken by the Government, the discretionary function would then probably apply. GPS is provided to civilian users, but it is still primary a military system under the Government control, thus it should be considered a unique Government function.

The foreign country exception, immunizes the US - which would be liable under the FTCA - for "any claim arising in a foreign country"; therefore it appears that the US is immune for suits outside its borders.

To determine the applicability of this exception, courts focus on where the damage arises: this is to say the site of the negligent act, rather than where the damage is suffered. As most likely GPS liability would result from an error in the uploading of the ephemeris data from the Colorado Master Control Station (MCS)[32] to the satellites, one could say that the site of negligence is Colorado State in the US territory. The foreign country exception would then not apply, unless the Court would see the damage as being originated in outer space as the Signals in Space are broadcasted by the satellites. From a legal perspective outer space could be seen similar to Antarctica (both regulated by international law and both having no Government) for which the US court recognized the applicability of the foreign country exception in case law Smith vs United States[33].

The US is so far reluctant to waive its sovereign immunity for damage resulting from negligence in GPS operations; therefore GPS does not really provide a benchmark for Galileo. Indeed, for GPS limits of Standard Positioning Service (SPS) performance and limits of condition of use of the receivers are set in the "user manual"; producers don't take responsibility for consequences resulting from the use of their products specifying that radionavigation devices do not substitute traditional navigational methods.

However it should be noted that the applicability of the FTCA exceptions are generally extremely controversial and however always dependent on the courts judgment. Therefore, despite to the opposition of the US and unless the Congress would add another exception to the FTCA for GPS activities and operations, there might be the legal ground for US citizens to sue the Government.

4.3 Non existence of comparable businesses

In the previous section, through the analysis of the sources of third party liability within the Galileo Project, many arguments seemed to confirm that Galileo presents a unique risk profile. The complexity of its organizational structure, the number of actors involved and the technological challenge of the development of a radionavigation system, are all elements which contribute to adding difficulties to the exercise of shaping a defined risk profile.

---

[32] The GPS master control station is located at Falcon Air Force Base in Colorado Springs, Colorado.

[33] Moreover this position was enforced by the famous case law, 507 U.S. 197 (1993), Smith v. United State where no waivers of sovereign immunity were accepted regarding a claim for damage occurred in Antarctica. Antarctica (territory with no government) was considered as a foreign country and the same principle could be considered applicable to GNSS if the negligent act is viewed as arising in "outer space".

Notwithstanding the appreciation of the unique risks of the Galileo Programme, it should be also noted that there are other businesses which are exposed to extremely high and unforeseeable risks, but which anyhow engage in dangerous activities even when they are not in the position to fully undertake their operational risk. It is possible from a comparative analysis of the liability management strategies adopted in other sectors to draw some considerations which could inspire the definition of effective measures for risk management.

5. LIABILITY REGIMES IN OTHER DOMAINS

5.1 Civil aviation

Third party liability in the aviation sector is regulated under an international convention which aims at compensating liability for damages caused by air planes to persons or property on the surface of another contracting State. The Protocol to amend the Convention on damage caused by foreign aircraft to third parties on the surface[34], signed at Montreal in 1978 (Montreal convention) only applies to international flights, while third party damages caused by a national aircraft are ruled by the national legislation.

For damages to goods and/or for loss of life or personal injury caused by an aircraft in flight, by persons or things falling therefrom, liability is limited and channeled to the aircraft owner and operator. The Operator has the obligation to maintain valid insurance or another guarantee up to its liability limits.

Should the total amount of claims exceed the limit of liability, claims are reduced in proportion to their respective amounts. Claims may be brought only in front of the courts of the contracting State where the damage occurred (subject to agreement by the parties also before any other court of contracting States) or it can be submitted to arbitration. Under certain circumstances the operator cannot limit his liability.
No provision foresees a Government step-in for outstanding liabilities.

5.2 Oil Pollution damages

Transportation of oil by sea is a dangerous activity as it may cause very severe environmental damage. This activity is regulated at international level through Conventions The 1992 Protocol on Civil Liability and the 1992 Fund Convention establish a regime and a mechanism to compensate third parties oil pollution damages on the following principles and mechanisms:

- strict and limited liability of the shipowner
- compulsory insurance[35] regime linked to the ship tonnage
- clauses of exclusion of liability
- clauses of exclusion of limitation of liability
- International fund to compensate claims exceeding the shipowners limit
- Funding of the international fund by contributions of any person who has received amounts in excess of 150.000 tonnes of crude oil

The Fund established as an intergovernmental organization (super partes) is recognized in each contracting State as a legal person and provides compensation in case: 1) no liability for damage aroused under the Liability Convention, 2) of financial incapability of the liable owner of the ship to meet its obligations, 3) the damage exceeds the owner's liability.

[34] The Convention on Damage caused by Foreign Aircraft to Third Parties on the Surface was signed at Rome on 7 October 1952.

[35] A major part of the ships has entered Protection and Indemnity Associations, called P&I Clubs which provide insurance on mutual basis. Liability is limited under international conventions or national laws and the insurance cover is limited to the limitation amount applicable to the ship.

Claims are accepted if they are based on real expenses, if there is a link between the expense and the incident and the expense was made for reasonable purposes

The Fund receives two types of contributions: those to the General Fund - which cover both administrative expenses and claims for compensation which do not exceed 4 million SDR per incident - and those to the Major Claims Fund to cover payments for incidents in excess of the amount payable by the General Fund. Should the claims exceed the aggregate amount of compensation, the amount available shall be distributed so that the portion between the claim and the amount of compensation is the same for all claimants.

In 2003 a Supplementary Fund was established to raise the limits available for compensation.

5.3 Nuclear damages

Before 1997, the liability regime for nuclear damage was embodied into two instruments: the IAEA Vienna Convention (which was adopted on 21 may 1963 and entered into force on 12 November 1997) and the OECD Paris Convention on Third Party Liability in the Field of Nuclear Energy of 1960 in force in 1963 and then bolstered by the Brussels Supplementary Convention. In 1992 a Joint Protocol adopted in 1988 entered into force to coordinate the two conventions.

In principle the liability of the operator is supplemented by the international liability of the licensing State and by a third tier of compensation provided by an international fund.
The Conventions foresee compensation for damages caused by nuclear accidents (within the installation or during the carriage or storage) on the territory of any of the contracting States.

The Conventions provide the minimum threshold of the operator's liability. Liability is strict and channeled to the operator of the nuclear installation (or of the carrier under defined circumstances).
Insurance, reinsurance and other financial security is aimed at covering the damages in relation to bodily injury, loss of life, loss of any property (other than the nuclear installation itself) and any property used in connection. States are free through their national legislation to agree on the amount of coverage which they would require from the operators of the installations over their territory. The State throughout which radioactive substances are transported, may request the responsible operator to raise its coverage protection (within the maximum amount).

5.4 Lessons learned

Having briefly presented some of the solutions which were found in other sectors presenting a high risk profile, a strong public interest and an international dimension, some observations can be made. Risks in these sectors are generally secured through different coverage means such as insurances, bank guarantees, internal reserves, industries pooling schemes and compensation funds. States require the private entity uncharged of the operations to maintain compulsory insurance coverage and in some activities additional financial security is provided through international compensation funds. This choice is generally made when there are large numbers of actors which share the same interest on the basis of a risk they all contribute to create.
Funds represent a solid guarantee for compensation, however on the long term they might fail to create a real incentive for the operators for take due care in the course of their activity. The same problem is faced by strict liability regimes coupled with quasi-unrestricted rights to liability limitation. To avoid such risks, international conventions often foresee provisions by which, under certain circumstances, operator's liability limitation is excluded and he is fully exposed to the risks. Where liability regimes are in place, chances of a risk to become uninsurable are usually reduced. Fault-based solutions tend to promote uninsurabillity as the risk is

hardly sizable and it is dependent on a very wide variety of factors. Precedents show that where the insurance market is not in the position to provide coverage, because perhaps the damage is too difficult to size, the contracting parties might prefer regimes of strict liability.

A typical example of this kind of choice is that of the strict and limited liability of the shipowner in case of oil pollution. Oil pollution typically causes environmental damage, which is difficult to define and to fully compensate and in this case States have chosen a regime of strict and limited liability. Damages to be insured may be both tangible and intangible and the intangible risks are those which are often more difficult to size. A solution, in these cases, was found through pool schemes for which a necessary pre-condition is to have a mutual risk which is shared among a large number of parties. If on one hand liability caps can help to promote insurability (as the risk to be insured becomes quantifiable) they may also lead to unfair compensation of the victims and to the violation of the "polluter pays" principle.

It can be observed that generally States don't assume liability for damages arising from activities undertaken by the private sector and even dangerous activities which are of strong public interest are generally no exception.

The nuclear domain represents the only case where public funds are foreseen to cover outstanding liabilities, but liability is channeled to the operator of the nuclear installation that is required to maintain insurance. The State has the obligation to ensure the payment of claims and an international fund is available to further mitigate the risk.

International conventions are very well recognized legal instruments, however the process required to reach an agreement is extremely complex and time consuming. Typically States sit at international negotiation tables in reaction to a catastrophic event (e.g. SOLAS convention in the maritime domain after the Titanic accident), but it is unusual to have an international convention regulating an activity which is still not completely proved. Indeed none of the Conventions analyzed was drafted before the starting of the activity. The establishment of such legal instruments is only achieved after years of experience which showed that there was the need to regulate the activity in order to specifically answer problems that were identified from the experience.

If an international liability regime was to be considered for Galileo and if an international fund was to be established for compensating damages related to the transmission of the signal in space - provided that an agreement could be found - the time frame would not allow the Galileo concession contract to fall under this scheme. Moreover it is difficult to envisage upfront the content and shape of a potential international Convention for Galileo.

An intermediary step could be that of establishing a dedicated compensation fund at European level under an EU Regulation. This would not be a totally new initiative, as the precedent of the European Union Solidarity Fund shows. The Fund, established through Regulation 2012/2002 of 11 November 2002, aimed at providing up to 1 billion euros in case of for Major Natural Disasters. A Regulation at European level may pave the way towards a future wide international liability regime and compensation mechanism.

6. CONCLUSIONS

Satellite navigation provides worldwide undeniable benefits worldwide. The Galileo operator will make available the open signal free of charge and this service will have the advantage to stimulate technological development through numerous applications. Galileo services will assist the mass market users as well as decision makers in the implementation of common policies and will be of key importance for the public sector as well as for the private sector. However GNSS is a vulnerable and complex system which is exposed, under a multitude of juridical regimes, to a great number of risks. As it was done in a number of other sectors, it doesn't seem unreasonable to envisage legislative actions to establish a common legal framework and possibly a compensation mechanism which would recognize to GNSS a fundamental role and would safeguard its continuity over time. The establishment of an international fund for radionavigation could be a way forward for sharing the burden of compensation among all the actors while ensuring better reward to the plaintiffs.

The long timeframe required for International Conventions to be adopted seems to be inappropriate to satisfy the near time needs of the Galileo Project. This constraint could be overcome through the adoption of an EU Regulation establishing a common dedicated liability regime and perhaps a compensation fund. Although geographically very limited for a system that is global, this option may deserve careful consideration as it could represent a good starting point to trigger initiatives with a wider international scope.

REFERENCES

1. Council Regulation (EC) No 876/2002 of 21 May 2002 setting up the Galileo Joint Undertaking. *OJ L 138, 28.5.2002.*

2. Council Regulation (EC) No 1321/2004 of 12 July 2004 on the establishment of structures for the management of the European satellite radio-navigation programmes. *OJ L 246, 20.7.2004.*

3. Treaty on Principles Governing the Activities of States in the Exploration and Use of Outer Space including the Moon and other Celestial Bodies, 27 January 1967, 610 UNTS 205 entered into force on 10 October 1967.

4. Convention on International Liability for Damage caused by Space Objects, 29 March 1972, 961 UNTS 187.

5. Council Directive 85/374/EEC of 25 July 1985 on the approximation of the laws, regulations and administrative provisions of the Member States concerning liability for defective products. *OJ L 210, 7.8.1985.*

6. Convention on International Civil Aviation of 1944 (Chicago Convention).

7. ICAO AFI Planning and Implementation Regional Group 13th Meeting. Agenda item 8: *Institutional Aspects of CNS/ATM systems.* Sal, Cape Verde, 25-29 June 2001APIRG/13-WP/25.

8. ICAO Assembly Resolution A-32/20: *Development and elaboration of an appropriate long term legal framework to govern the implementation of GNSS implementation.*

9. ICAO Assembly, Legal Commission, Resolution A32/20. Agenda Item 36: Report on the establishment of a legal framework with regard to CNS/ATM systems including GNSS development of a contractual framework leading towards a long-term legal framework to govern the implementation of GNSS. A35-WP/125, LE/11, Appendix C: *Proposal relating to main elements for inclusion in a draft convention.*

10. Brandon E. EHRHART: "A technological dream turned legal nightmare: potential liability of the United States under the Federal Court Claims Act for Operating the Global Positioning System". Vanderbilt Journal of transnational law, Vol 33, Number 2, March 2000.

11. Foreign Claims Act, 10 U.S.C.§ 2734-2736.

12. Suits in Admiralty Act, 46 U.S.C. app §§ 741 – 752.

13. Federal Tort Claim Act, 28 U.S.C. 2680(h).

14. Case law, 507 U.S. 197 (1993), Smith v. United State.

15. The Convention on Damage caused by Foreign Aircraft to Third Parties on the Surface was signed at Rome on 7 October 1952.

IAC-06-E6.5.14

TAKING GARBAGE OUTSIDE: THE GEOSTATIONARY ORBIT AND GRAVEYARD ORBITS

Martha Mejía-Kaiser*
(Mexico)

Abstract

The Geostationary Orbit has been recognized as a limited natural resource. Taking into consideration the dynamic development of technology and the finite nature of the geostationary ring, it is not possible to denominate a definitive number of orbital slots. Currently about 350 operational satellites, distributed in an uneven way, use this limited space resource. The particular 'stationary' position of satellites in this orbit makes it a commercially attractive resource, not only for governments and international governmental organizations, but also for the private sector. Geostationary satellites coming to the end-of-life must free their slot in order to leave it to the next satellite. But where are the decommissioned satellites going?

This paper addresses the concept of graveyard orbits and decommissioned geostationary satellites. It also addresses to what extend the graveyard orbit concept is becoming a binding legal regime.

1. INTRODUCTION

1.1. Physical Principles of the Geostationary Orbit.

The Geostationary orbit is a circular orbit, approximately 36,000 km. away from the Earth's surface, positioned exactly above the Earth's equator, with 0° of inclination. Objects positioned in this orbit, complete one revolution in approximately 24 hours. Synchronized with Earth rotation, geostationary objects will appear fixed to a point in the celestial Earth's equator. This particular position enables a large coverage of our planet and satellite owners and operators[1] save the costs of location and tracking antenna systems.

Already the Russian theorist Tsiolkovsky and the Germans Hermann Oberth and Herman Potocnik made reference to the Geostationary Orbit[2]. But in 1945, the British Arthur Clarke was the one who first presented calculations for the placement of a satellite in this part of outer space, addressing the potential utility of the Geostationary Orbit[3].

These theoretic calculations could not be put into practice until 1964, when

* Doctor in Political and Social Sciences, Universidad Nacional Autónoma de México. IISL Member.

the technology was mature enough for placing the first geostationary satellite, the US Syncom III. At the beginning, only governments used this natural space ring. But as the commercial capabilities became more evident, international governmental organizations and private companies started to enter the scene and contracted satellite manufacturers and launching services, to place their own satellites in the Geostationary Orbit.

1.2. The Geostationary Orbit as a Limited Resource.

As the time passed by, the interest in placing satellites in this orbit became more intense and it was clear that it was necessary to set rules. Through the International Telecommunications Union, States started to coordinate their satellite positioning in slots (nominal positions) and the use of electromagnetic frequencies. Interestingly, in the ITU both, slot and frequency coordination, were primarily conceived as a means to avoid harmful interference. Then, the threat of physical satellite collisions was not a priority.

But satellites, as humans, are mortal. As a result of several factors, such as solar radiation pressure and the Earth' gravitation, most satellites in the Geostationary Orbit tend to leave their nominal position. In order to keep them in their slots, satellites have on board fuel tanks which enable them to fire small rockets, from time to time, for correcting their positions. Most geostationary satellites require course corrections for this type of station-keeping once every two weeks.

Long-term geostationary satellites have a fuel capacity sufficient for keeping them 15 years in their nominal position. But once the fuel has been used up, satellites start to drift and leave their slots. These satellites are then considered to be space debris, even if all the instruments on board are still intact.

With the time, the Geostationary Orbit became a crowded place, which is not only used by operational geostationary satellites. Some other functional satellites have orbits that intersect the geostationary ring. Also uncontrolled satellites, as well as rocket stages that delivered satellites to the Geostationary Orbit, are crossing this ring. On top of this, broken satellite parts need also to be considered, which originate from satellite explosions or collisions.

In January 2006, 1089 objects of significant mass have been detected in this orbit[4], of which 344 are operational satellites in their nominal positions.

Space researchers noted that space debris in the geostationary ring was increasing, putting in danger operational satellites. But for several years, their warnings did not move States to take counter-measures.

2. A TECHNICAL PROPOSAL AND A COMMERCIAL WORRY.

2.1. Origin of the Graveyard Orbit Concept.

Some years ago, when a geostationary satellite was approaching its end-of-life, satellite owners and operators typically reserved no or only a small amount of satellite's propellant to free the slot for the follow-on-satellite. In some cases, satellite owners and operators just abandoned dead satellites in their positions. But such abandoned satellites in their nominal position or some km. away from the slot, tend to drift in an orbit "...slightly above the geostationary Orbit",[5] which crosses the Geostationary Orbit constantly, putting in danger operational satellites in the geostationary belt.

At the point, when a geostationary satellite has suffered a malfunctioning and can not be or is not worth to be kept in its slot, some satellite owners and operators make a public statement declaring such as 'decommissioned'. The same declaration may be done, when a healthy satellite reaches its end-of-life, after its fuel is completely used up and it is not longer under control. These declarations are a kind of warning to other satellite operators, which must take into account that decommissioned satellites will drift and may endanger operational satellites in the proximity.

Taking into account that no concept existed for the proper satellite disposal, the Inter-Agency Space Debris Coordination Committee (IADC), which encompasses representatives of governmental space agencies of space fairing countries[6], decided to create some guidelines in this respect. In 1997 the IADC representatives reached a consensus on 'Mitigation Guidelines' to reduce space debris in general[7].

One of these recommendations is about the removal of operational geostationary satellites, approaching their end-of-life, from the geostationary ring to one of the graveyard orbits[8]. Such graveyard orbits should not intercept the geostationary ring and are supposed to be a safe place to keep non-operational satellites far away from useful orbits. The recommendation also requires disposed satellites in a graveyard orbit to be 'passivated', which means fuel remnants are to be depleted, batteries discharged, pressure vessels relieved, etc., in order to avoid satellite explosions that may interact with other disposed satellites.

It seems that, although 'soft law', such recommendations are an easy and logical step to take, but several satellite owners and operators are reluctant to follow them. Why?

2.2. The Value of Fuel.

The economic potential of communication satellites can be measured by their number of transponders. Transponders are devices on board which receive electromagnetic signals (up-link), convert them into another frequency[9], enhances their power and send them back to Earth (down-link). Each transponder may canalize hundreds of telephone calls or several television channels in one electromagnetic signal. Today 'small satellites' have 24 transponders, while 'big' satellites may have around 50. Currently, the annual average profit for one transponder is 2 million US dollars[10].

The amount of fuel required to move a satellite to a graveyard orbit, equals approximately the fuel that a satellite would use to keep its nominal position approximately during 4 months. If an operating satellite comes to its end-of-life four months earlier as calculated by the space owner or operator, this will result in loss of several millions of US dollar in earnings. As in most commercial enterprises, time is valuable, which is the main reason why for-profit satellite owners and operators are reluctant to move a healthy satellite into a graveyard orbit.

Nonetheless, the IADC recommendations are being followed by some satellite owners and operators.

3. CUSTOMARY LAW.

Although the IADC Mitigation Guidelines were meant to be non-binding, this does not mean that satellite disposal into graveyard orbits cannot evolve into a legally binding international custom.

International Custom is being formed by two elements, the exercise of a practice by the members of the international community and their conviction that such exercise is an obligation (*opinio iuris sive necessitatis*)[11].

In respect to the time and intensity of a practice, Verdross and Simma consider that in the current high organized and technical international relations, the particularity of a custom must not be analyzed by the duration of the practice but, as already the International Court of Justice affirmed, under the specific situation that defines if a practice is "extensive and virtually uniform"[12].

In respect to the *opinio iuris*, repetitive practice may create in some cases the conscience among the members of the international community that they are obliged by such behavior and that such behavior is expected from the other members of the international community. In other cases, the wills of the members of the international community may not be based in the conviction of obligation but, as Verdross and Simma affirm, also on the usefulness or fairness of a practice[13] and, in this case, as a preventive measure.

Taking into consideration this two elements, in the case of geostationary satellite disposal, it is necessary to analyze if satellite owners and operators are exercising a repetitive practice in an uniform manner and if the psychological aspect, the *opinio iuris*, is fulfilled.

3.1. Practice.

In the 9 years since the IADC recommendations were issued in 1997, 49 out of 135 satellites that arrived to their end-of-life were reorbited in full accordance with the IADC recommendations. Statistics show that since 2002 there is a steady increase in correct deorbiting practices. From 1997 to 2005, 8 Intelsat, 6 Japanese, 10 US, 3 Russian and 22 satellites from other countries and international organizations, were deorbited in compliance with the IADC recommendations[14].

Statistics show also that a number of decommissioned satellites are deorbited to orbits below the IADC recommendations, i.e. no more than 150 km. from the Geostationary Orbit. Many of these satellites could not reach a IADC graveyard orbit as a result of anomalies or because they were relatively old and not enough fuel was reserved for a higher graveyard orbit. Nonetheless, several of these satellites will not intersect the geostationary belt for at least 200 years or more[15].

Another question is, if the deorbiting practices according to IADC recommendations of private companies or international organizations owning and/or operating geostationary satellites, can be considered as 'State practice' in the formulation of international custom. In this context, art. VI of the Outer Space Treaty[16] provides the link by spelling out that States are responsible for national activities in outer space "...carried by governmental agencies or by non-governmental entities...and international organizations"[17]. Consequently, if a State licenses and supervises space activities of private companies and international organizations, their activities can be attributed to be the practice of the respective State.

3.2. *Opinio Iuris.*

As already indicated, customary law also requires *opinio iuris*, a second element of subjective nature. *Opinio Iuris* is the explanation of the reasons why a subject is exercising certain practice. But, as judge Tanaka expressed[18], in most of the cases the motives that make States to perform certain practice are not explicit. Such motives must be then inferred from facts as the very acts themselves, declarations and national legislations encompassing such practices.

Practices of satellite disposal in graveyard orbits in accordance to IADC recommendations or in lower graveyard orbits, are *per se* an evidence of *opinio iuris*. But there are other indications on the presence of this element, for example national legislation and declarations.

3.2.1. National Legislations in Graveyard Orbits

3.2.1.1. The United States. According to US legislation, satellite owners and operators need an authorization (license) to operate a satellite[19]. Such licenses do not only serve to monitor the space activities of satellite owners and operators, but they serve also to share compensation costs in case of damage provoked by an accident. Thus, licenses are granted if the applicant demonstrates financial backing and a liability insurance.

In order to reduce liability risk, US government recommended satellite owners and operators to move their geostationary satellites in graveyard orbits, before they reached the end-of-life. But such recommendations where not observed as the government wished. From 30 geostationary satellites under US license that reached their end of life between 1997 to 2005, only 10 were correctly disposed in graveyard orbits[20]. Because the United States is one of the major users of the Geostationary Orbit (besides Russia), it became evident that the US was contributing to the pollution in a way that "...could shut down the space industry..."[21].

When the Federal Communications Commission (FCC) drafted legislation on the disposal of satellites in graveyard orbits, satellite owners and operators as PanAmSat Corp. (US), EchoStar Communications Corp. (US) and Americom (US), protested when they learned that such legislation was directed to be applicable in a retroactive manner[22]. They claimed that such legislation would have a strong impact in their financial performance.

In order to reach a compromise with the private sector, in 2004 the FCC agreed to bind only those owners and operators who launched their satellites after the 18th. of March, 2002. Owners and operators who launched their satellites before that date are requested to follow this rule as recommendation.

In respect to satellite disposal, the US regulation mandates that licensed satellite owners and operators submit a statement with substantial information on satellite disposal. Such information must address the amount of fuel reserved for orbit transference, the passivation of satellites[23] and, for geostationary satellites, the targeted graveyard orbit[24].

The legislation is now integrated into the Code of Federal Regulations under Title 47[25]. The Federal Communications Commission is the government body to authorize and supervise satellites life (even before they arrive) to the launching pad until the graveyard orbit. With this regulation, the United States becomes the first country to make the disposal of geostationary satellites in graveyard orbits compulsory.

3.2.1.2. Germany. Under the 'Procedures for the Registration of Satellite Systems before the International Telecommunications Union and the Assignment of German Rights for the Use of Orbits and Frequencies'[26], Germany introduced regulation relating to graveyard orbits.

Paragraph 3.7. stipulates that according to international standards, the use of satellites approaching their end-of-life must be done in such a way that enough reserves of energy, fuel and functionality remain, as to enable the satellite a transfer to a graveyard orbit. Special attention is to be paid to the necessity of changing to a graveyard orbit, for the protection of other satellite systems in the Geostationary Orbit. Authorized users may be given operational orders for the implementation of international standards for avoidance of space debris. The German regulatory authority (*Bundesnetzagentur*) may issue adequate orders to users for the operation at the end-of-life time in order to enforce the international standards in specific situations.

As it can be seen, the German legislation on graveyard orbits does not directly require satellite owners and operators to move their satellites to a graveyard orbit upon exhaustion of the resources. However, the responsible regulatory authority is expressly authorized to issue orders for the enforcement of the (non-binding) international standards. The use of the words 'orders' and 'enforcement' indicates that the compliance with the IADC recommendations is for German owners/operators not just a mere voluntary measure[27].

3.2.1.3. The Effect of National Legislations on *Opinio Iuris*. These two national legislations have a direct (US) or indirect (Germany) binding force for satellite owners and operators. Both national legislations provide evidence about the acceptance of these States to implement at the national level the IADC measures for the protection of the Geostationary Orbit. Such legislations reflect the thoughts that, as Judge Sorensen expressed: "...it is characteristic of our time that new problems and circumstances incessantly arise and imperatively call for legal regulation"[28]. The *opinio iuris* of both States are based on the logic that if today no measures are taken in the proper disposal of geostationary satellites, such commercially valuable celestial belt may become useless.

3.2.2. State Declarations. *Opinio iuris* can also be inferred from the activities of the European Network of Centres on Space Debris that issued an 'European Code of Conduct for Space Debris Mitigation', which contains recommendations for satellite disposal in graveyard orbits. Such code of conduct has been already signed by the *Centre National d'Etudes Spatiales*, the space government agency of France[29]. Also JAXA, the space agency of Japan, has formulated its own code of conduct for space debris mitigation[30] and its current deorbiting practice shows that it is observing the IADC guidelines.

The introduction of compulsory regulations in the US and Germany and the declarations of other States in this respect, clearly reflects that there is an emerging *opinio iuris* in favor of the deorbiting geostationary satellites according to IADC measures. In addition to this emerging *opinio iuris*, the current practice clearly shows that international custom for the deorbiting of dying satellites in graveyard orbits is evolving in what may become a customary norm, of compulsory observance for all members of the international community. In few words, it is clear the *opinio iuris* of this practice is that those States performing such practices agree that the Geostationary Orbit is a precious place, worth to invest resources (fuel and potential earnings) in order to keep it useful.

But before asserting if a new international custom is in the entrance door of the International Public Law, dissenting opinions on the deorbiting of geostationary satellites in graveyard orbits must also be observed.

3.3. Dissenting Positions?

In 1994 the Scientific and Technical Subcommittee of the United Nations Committee on the Peaceful Uses of Outer Space (hereinafter COPUOS) started to devote some attention to space debris, but no rules for the mitigation of space debris evolved. In the following years, IADC representatives developed bonds with COPUOS and information on up-dated space debris situation started to flow to this UN organ.

After the IADC Mitigation Guidelines were issued, a COPUOS Working Group on space debris dedicated its time to draft a text based on the IADC recommendations. Unfortunately, such efforts were degraded by the COPUOS representatives who stressed that if a document is adopted, such would not be legally binding under international law[31]. In 2005, the Working Group presented a report to COPUOS, which states that space debris mitigation practices remain "...voluntary and should be carried out through national mechanisms" and that the Guidelines "...would not be legally binding under international law"[32].

Following the perception in COPUOS that its work products are legally not binding, COPUOS members attempt to counteract the evolving *opinio iuris.* This is a sad aspect of COPUOS, an UN organ that was established for the development of International Space Law. Instead of establishing rules and standards, it tries to dilute emerging customary law.

The contradictory position of States represented in COPUOS and the same adhering to the IADC recommendations, can not be explained. On one hand, States start to create binding regulation at national level and declare at international level to observe the IADC recommendations, but on the other hand such States reject to be legally bound at international level. If States perform a practice but at the same time declare not to be legally bound by it, can we speak of this as an evolving rule of international customary law?

As aforementioned, for the *opinio iuris* of an international custom it is not necessary that States performing a practice only have the conviction of an obligation. They may also consider that such practice is useful, fair or of preventive character, among other considerations.

States taking a contrary position, elevating continuous protests against a practice that looks as if may be transformed into a customary rule, are known as 'persistent objectors'[33]. Such States can not stop the creation of a international customary norm, but may achieve that such norm does not apply to them when the time comes for the recognition as a norm with binding effects. In order to qualify as persistent objectors, States have the burden to present the evidence that they continuously opposed that practice through public declarations. In the present case, on satellite deorbiting practices, States represented at COPUOS that insist that such practices are of no binding nature, so far have not raised protests and many of them even exercise such deorbiting practices. Those States do not qualify as 'persistent objectors'.

Even if in the framework of COPUOS States declare not to be ready for binding regulations on the disposal of geostationary satellites, in some years such declarations will be voided, if the practice of the same States and others increases. In this event, the deorbiting of geostationary satellites according to IADC recommendations will be elevated to a new norm of international customary law with binding effects.

CONCLUSIONS

To solve the problem of the growing congestion of the Geostationary Orbit with operational satellites and space debris, the IADC made technical recommendations for the mitigation of space debris. One of this recommendations deals with the deorbiting of geostationary satellites to graveyard orbits.

The State practice of satellite deorbiting according to these IADC recommendations that started in 1997, is increasing steadily since 2002. This practice demonstrates that the awareness of the protection of the Geostationary Orbit is growing among satellite owners and operators. Such awareness through practice, declarations and implementation of national legislations in some countries, are evidence of the presence of *opinio iuris*. With State practice and the additional *opinio iuris,* a new norm of international custom is in the process of formation.

But in this process, States are captured in a legal contradiction. On one side they perform a practice, implement national legislations and make public declarations to observe such practice, on the other side they declare not to be legally bound by such practice. As the time passes by, and more and more States, international organizations and private companies continue to properly deorbit satellites, a new norm of international custom will crystallize. In this instance, States declarations that the deorbiting of satellites in graveyard orbits according to IADC recommendations are not binding, will have no relevance.

Besides fuel amount considerations for safe arrival of the satellite to the nominal position, for station-keeping and for evasive maneuvers, owners and operators of geostationary satellites will compulsorily have to consider to reserve enough fuel for proper disposal maneuvers.

Once this new international customary rule has solidified, the status of the Geostationary Orbit will rise to a new category of legally protected area.

---

1 Here the words 'owners and operators' are addressing governmental institutions, international organizations and private companies that own a satellite and also entities that are hired to operate a satellite.

2 Kelso T.S., Basics of the Geostationary Orbit, Satellite Times (2004), at www.celestrak.com/columns/v04n07.

3 Clarke Arthur, Extraterrestrial Relays, Wireless World, October (1945).

4 Jehn R. and Klinkrad H., Trends in Reorbiting of Geostationary Satellites, ISTS 2006-r-2-13. (2006).

5 Ib. at p. 4.

6 The Inter-Agency Space Debris Coordination Committee is a non-governmental organization comprising at the present the space agencies of China, France, Germany, India, Italy, Japan, Ukraine, United Kingdom,

4 Jehn R. & Klinkrad H., *Trends in Reorbiting of Geostationary Satellites*, ISTS 2006-r-2-13. (2006).

5 *Id.* at 4.

6 The Inter-Agency Space Debris Coordination Committee is a non-governmental organization comprising at the present the space agencies of China, France, Germany, India, Italy, Japan, Ukraine, United Kingdom, USA, Russian Federation, the European Space Agency and the Scientific and Technical Subcommittee of COPUOS. *Space Debris-Spotlight*, ESA, Mar. 31 (2005), at 3.

7 Jehn R. & Klinkrad H., supra note 4, at 1.

8 IADC guideline 7, directed to diminish the population of non-operational satellites in the Geostationary Orbit, states "spacecraft(s)...that have terminated their operational phases...should be left in orbits (graveyard orbits) that avoid their long-term interference with the Geostationary Region", Perek L., *Current Status of Mitigation Measures on Space Debris*, n. 32 ECSL News, May (2006), at 4.

The parameters of such graveyard orbits are calculated to take into consideration the satellite mass, its average cross-sectional area and the solar radiation pressure. Jehn & Klinkrad, supra note 4, at 1.

Graveyard orbits are between 245 and 435 km. above the geostationary ring. Robotic Geostationary Orbit Restorer, Final Report-Executive Summary, EADS Space Transportation, June 10 (2003), at 1.

9 The frequency has to be converted in order to avoid interference to the same transponder when the signal is sent to a terrestrial station.

10 Robotic Geostationary Orbit Restorer, supra note 8, at 1.

11 VERDROSS A. & SIMMA B., UNIVERSELLES VÖLKERRECHT 346 (3 Auf., 1984).

12 *Id.* at 361.

13 *Id.* at 356.

14 Jehn & Klinkrad, supra note 4, at 4.

15 Jehn & Klinkrad, supra note 4, at 4.

16 Treaty on Principles Governing the Activities of States in the Exploration and Use of Outer Space, Including the Moon and Other Celestial Bodies, Jan. 27, 1967, 18 U.S.T. 2410, T.I.A.S. 6347, 610 U.N.T.S. 205 (effective Oct. 10, 1967).

17 Akehurst considers that State practice can be inferred from "...practice of international organizations and (in theory at least) by the practice of individuals". Akerhurst M., Custom as a Source of International Law (1974-75) BYBIL 53, cited after DIXON M. & MCCORQUODALE R., CASES AND MATERIALS ON INTERNATIONAL LAW 26 (2d. ed., 1995).

18 Judge Tanaka, dissenting opinion on the North Sea Continental Shelf Cases, I.C.J. Reports 1969, at 3, cited after in HARRIS D., CASES AND MATERIALS ON INTERNATIONAL LAW 35-36 (4th. ed., 1991).

19 Code of Federal Regulations, US Government Printing Office, cite 47CFR25.283, Title 47, vol. 2, Chapter I, § 25.102 Station authorization required (2004).

20 Jehn & Klinkrad, supra note 4, at 4.

21 De Selding, P., *FCC Enters Orbital Debris Debate,* Space News, June 28 (2004), *available at* www.space.com/spacenews.

22 *Id.*

23 The applicant shall inform if "...stored energy will be removed at spacecraft's end of life", e.g. releasing residual fuel, leaving fuel valves open, and leaving batteries in a permanent discharge modus. US 47 CFR § 25.114 (14), Applications for space station authorizations.

24 US 47 CFR § 25.114 (14) Applications for space station authorizations.

25 US 47 CFR § 25.283 End-of-life disposal .

26 *Verfahren zur Anmeldung von Satellitensystemen bei der Internationalen Fernmeldunion und Übertragung deutscher Orbit-und Frequenznutzungsrechte, Amtsblatt Reg. TP Nr. 6/2005,* Apr. 6 (2005), S. 239 ff.

27 *3.7. Betrieb am Ende der Lebensdauer: „Der Betrieb von Satelliten bis Ende der Lebensdauer ist so einzurichten, dass für Bahnmanöver zur Auserbetriebnahme (Decommissioning) gemäß internationalen Standards genügend Reserven (an Energie, Treibstoff und Funktionalität) verbleiben". Id.*

"Auf die Notwendigkeit, zum Schutz anderer Satellitensysteme vom geostationären Betriebsorbit auf eine sichere Friedhofsbahn zu wechseln...wird besonders hingewiesen". Id.

„Dem Nutzungsberechtigten können betriebliche Vorgaben zur Umsetzung von internationalen Standards zur Vermeidung von Weltraummüll (Space Debris) gemacht werden. Die Reg. TP kann dem Nutzer zum Betrieb am Ende der Lebensdauer in angemessenem Umfang Weisungen erteilen, um die vorgenannten internationales Standards konkret durchzusetzen".. Id.

28 Sorensen, dissenting Opinion on the North Sea Continental Shelf cases, quoted in. HARRIS, supra note 18, at 38.

IN DEFENSE OF ADVERTISING IN SPACE

J. H. Huebert, J.D.
Columbus, Ohio USA
jhuebert@alumni.uchicago.edu

Walter Block, Ph.D.
Harold E. Wirth Eminent Scholar Endowed Chair in Economics
Loyola University New Orleans
New Orleans, Louisiana USA
walterblock@cba.loyno.edu

ABSTRACT

The prospect of orbiting "space billboards" visible from Earth has disgusted many, and prompted a law against them in the United States along with plans to ban them by international agreement. We, however, disagree with the conventional view, and find legal prohibition of such signs unjustified. This paper examines proposals to put billboards in space, considers the laws affecting such billboards, refutes the aesthetic and astronomical objections to space billboards, and finally concludes that restrictions on space billboards are not justified. Instead, space billboards should be permitted out of respect for private property and free-speech rights.

I. BILLBOARDS IN SPACE

Advertising in space is not new, or particularly controversial in itself. Pizza Hut, for example, paid to place its logo on the side of an unmanned Proton rocket in 2000[1] – and Columbia Pictures advertised the famous Arnold Schwarzenegger flop, *The Last Action Hero*, on the side of a rocket carrying the first private commercial space mission.[2] Such publicity stunts have met with little, if any, negative reaction because, after all, they involve ordinary space vehicles people might not otherwise look at, and the money the sponsors pay presumably goes to fund further space ventures.[3]

Hereafter, when this paper refers to "space advertising" it has in mind something more novel and provocative than those relatively mundane efforts: space billboards. For more than a decade, technology has existed that could put billboards in space. Not merely billboards for the many anticipated space tourists of the near future to see as they pass by,[4] but actual signs in low orbit that would be visible from the Earth's surface.

The first and, to our knowledge, only serious proposal to place billboards in orbit around the Earth came from Michael Lawson, chief executive officer of Space Marketing Concepts, Inc., in April 1993.[5] He proposed "environmental billboards" that would carry – in addition to a marketing message – scientific instruments such as "ozone measuring devices."[6]

According to a report by the International Astronomical Union, the Space Marketing billboards would have been about one square kilometer in dimension and would have been comparable to a full moon in their size and brightness in the sky.[7] Other reports, however, have suggested that space billboards might appear half the size of the moon, perhaps one tenth as bright, and only visible during certain hours, around dusk and dawn.[8]

Lawson's grandest and most specific proposal involved space billboards promoting, or visible during, the 1996 Olympic Games in Atlanta.[9] The City of Atlanta's marketing director even proposed advertising the city itself on a space billboard to then-Mayor Maynard Jackson. He rejected the idea, deeming space billboards "environmental pollution" and noting that – proud as he presumably was of his city – he did not want to see a space billboard promoting it or anything else in the sky.[10]

Lawson's scheme failed for lack of funding – i.e., no one wanted to pay what it would have cost to advertise on one of his proposed billboards.[11] Nonetheless, his plans prompted the United States Congress to ban "obtrusive space advertising" and establish a policy of encouraging other countries to do the same, as discussed in detail in the next section. As a result, no new space-billboard schemes appear imminent, at least in America.

Russian spacecraft designer Alexander Lavrynov, however, purports to have invented a method by which multiple satellites employing sunlight reflectors could create advertising images in the sky visible from Earth.[12] His plan's technological and economic feasibility remain unknown, but Russia has been at the forefront of other space advertising efforts,[13] and also notably launched a failed space mirror intended to light up the night sky in 1999.[14]

II. THE LAW OF SPACE ADVERTISING

A. The United States

As noted above, entrepreneurial efforts to launch space billboards prompted the United States Congress to essentially ban "obtrusive space advertising," defined as "advertising in outer space that is capable of being recognized by a human being on the surface of the Earth without the aid of a telescope or other technological device."[15]

The statute,[16] added October 30, 2000, provides:

> Notwithstanding the provisions of this chapter [49 U.S.C. §§ 70101 et seq.] or any other provision of law, the Secretary [of Transportation] may not, for the launch of a payload containing any material to be used for the purposes of obtrusive space advertising--
>
> (1) issue or transfer a license under this chapter; or
>
> (2) waive the license requirements of this chapter.

The statute further prohibits anyone already holding a license from launching such a payload,[17] and exempts "nonobtrusive commercial space advertising, including advertising on (1) commercial space transportation vehicles; (2) space infrastructure payloads; (3) space launch facilities; and (4) launch support facilities."[18]

Finally, when it passed the above statute, the U.S. Congress also made requests of the U.S. President:[19]

> (1) The President is requested to negotiate with foreign launching nations for the purpose of reaching one or more agreements that prohibit the use of outer space for obtrusive space advertising purposes.
>
> (2) It is the sense of the Congress that the President should take such action as is appropriate and feasible to enforce the terms of any agreement to prohibit the use of

outer space for obtrusive space advertising purposes.

In May 2005, the Federal Aviation Administration proposed new regulations enforcing this statute – essentially seeking to add to the Code of Federal Regulations the same language already in the statue, directing the FAA to review payloads "to determine if the launch of [a] payload would result in obtrusive space advertising."[20] Although the proposed regulations would have added nothing substantive to the already-existing law, they drew strong comments pro and con from the public.[21] Ultimately, the FAA did not adopt the proposed regulations because it concluded that "the statutory prohibitions are sufficient to prevent the launch of a payload containing obtrusive space advertising."[22]

To our knowledge, the United States so far has not had an occasion to enforce its prohibition on obtrusive space advertising.

B. The Rest of the World

The international agreements on space advertising that the United States Congress exhorted the President to enter have yet to materialize. Other major spacefaring nations, notably including Russia, have not enacted similar bans.

Little evidence exists that an international ban is a high priority. Sergei Negoda of the United Nations Office for Outer Space Affairs told NEWSWEEK in 2005 that the issue was "not on the agenda" and likely would not be "unless all member states . . . reach a consensus." He added that the present push for the commercialization of space (also spearheaded by Americans) made such an agenda item unlikely.[23]

To our knowledge, no one has attempted to argue specifically that existing international law bans space advertising. Some, however, have of course maintained that the 1967 Outer Space Treaty – the foremost document in international space law – bans private property or restricts commercial activity in outer space generally. Such views have been widely rejected, however, and seem unlikely to find much support in light of the ever-increasing drive for private entrepreneurial activity in space.[24] Some might also argue that the Outer Space Treaty bars advertising because it requires that outer space be used "for the benefit of all mankind." As we will see below, however, benefits are subjective, and what is a benefit to one person almost certainly will not be viewed as a benefit by another – and conflicts between the two can only be resolved by the arbitrary exercise of violence in the absence of private property rights.

III. AESTHETIC AND ASTRONOMICAL OBJECTIONS TO SPACE ADVERTISING

The primary objections to advertising have been in two categories: aesthetic and astronomical. That is, people have claimed that space advertising should be restricted or banned because of the advertising's supposed aesthetic offensiveness, or because this mode of communication would restrict the supposedly more important activities of astronomers.

In this section, we consider these arguments and offer some ideas on why these objections fail to justify a ban on space advertising. In the next section, we will offer our view that private property rights are the only means of resolving the disputes regarding the appropriateness of space advertising.

A. Aesthetic Concerns

Perhaps the most widespread objection to space advertising is aesthetic.

For example, in exhorting his fellow Congressmen to enact the U.S. ban on space billboards, Representative Edward Markey disparaged such advertising by claiming it would "turn our morning and evening skies, often a source of information and comfort, into the equivalent of the side of a bus."[25] A pamphlet from a gloomily monikered group called the International Dark-Sky Association declares that "worse still" than the alleged astronomical problems space billboards cause is "the destruction of the pristine beauty of humanity's view of the universe."[26] A commenter on the FAA's proposed regulation of obtrusive space advertising argued that such advertising should be prohibited because of its similarity to "ugly billboards along highways."[27] And a legal commentator advocates a treaty banning such advertisements worldwide because of their potential to "interfere with nature in a truly profound way."[28]

These negative views, however, do not tell the whole story.

1. Some People Just Might Like Space Billboards

While it is true that many people dislike the sight or even the thought of billboards or other publicly displayed advertising, it is not true that everyone feels that way. If *everyone* agreed, there would be no controversy.

In fact, some people appreciate terrestrial billboards for the information they convey.[29] Others may appreciate them simply for breaking up what they consider to be the monotony of the natural landscape.[30]

In some cases, people may enjoy billboards aesthetically, independent of the substance of the billboards' message. For example, Sony recently hired graffiti artists to paint the sides of abandoned buildings – without even mentioning its brand names or indicating that it was advertising – to advertise its Playstation Portable video game machine in Philadelphia. Some "anti-blight" advocates were appalled – but others appreciated the graffiti as "art" and considered it an improvement over the status quo.[31]

Further, in holding their apparent view that advertising is everywhere and to everyone unpleasant, anti-advertising advocates seem to forget that advertising is *intended to appeal* to as many people as possible in order to sell them a product.[32] An advertisement that disgusts its viewers is unlikely to serve its purpose well. As economic journalist Virginia Postrel has noted, "Competition pushes commercial artists to create attractive, visually appealing images."[33]

Indeed, given that advertisements are generally designed to be pleasing to people, it seems that those who only wish to see nature unfettered have the more peculiar view. After all, it is merely an accident that the Moon's face has been scarred in the way that it has been over the eons. What if, instead of looking somewhat like a "man in the Moon," the Moon's face coincidentally looked like the Pizza Hut logo? In that case, presumably the anti-advertising advocates would have no problem with the logo's presence and would insist that no one tamper with it. So why is a given image acceptable only because it occurred according to no one's design? It seems to us that anti-advertising advocates bear a heavy burden in attempting to defend the accidental status quo over images actually intended to please and presumably benefit[34] humans.

2. A Sky Full of Spam?

Granted, there is at least one form of advertising that virtually everyone hates: e-mail spam. Indeed, spam has been invoked to scare people into supporting space billboard prohibition.[35] But e-mail spam is fundamentally different from ordinary spam in two critical ways.

First, there are the economics. E-mail spam is almost costless to transmit, so although almost everyone other than its senders hates it, even a tiny handful of favorable responses may make the enterprise worthwhile.[36] Further, spam is not necessarily intended to advertise to or otherwise please the recipient – often it contains nonsense or obscenities serving no apparent purpose. Space billboards, in contrast, would be expensive to create and launch. Indeed, the billboards Lawson proposed in 1993 apparently were so expensive (reportedly $15 to 30 million)[37] that no one was willing to buy space on one. Presumably as technology improves, costs will decrease – but it seems highly unlikely that a spam-like glut will occur, with or without a ban.

Another crucial distinction between spam and space advertising is relevant to our argument in the section that follows. The spammer invades the property rights of the computer owner who does not wish to receive spam,[38] often with impunity because of the ease of hiding one's identity online. Space advertising, however, does not necessarily intrude upon property rights: a person who owns property on Earth does not own the sky above it, nor does anyone else who has not in some way actually possessed the space.[39]

3. Space Advertising is Not Aesthetically Unique

The idea that space advertising presents a novel situation requiring unprecedented legal restrictions fails, because similar forms of advertising already exist.

For example, at present, one can already advertise in the sky by pulling a banner behind an airplane. The Goodyear blimp provides another example of an arguably obtrusive advertising presence overhead – which tends to delight rather than disgust virtually all who catch a glimpse of it.

A case of space-advertising-in-reverse also recently occurred, as men's magazine *Maxim* placed a 75-by-100-foot reproduction of a magazine cover featuring actress Eva Longoria in the Nevada desert.[40] Whether or not this was actually "big enough to be seen from space," as the magazine boasted, it surely was visible to those, say, flying over in an airplane, whether they liked it or not.

Some may distinguish these examples by stating that those advertisements can only be occasionally seen in a relatively limited geographical area, while space billboards could conceivably always be visible.[41] But to date no one except space billboards' opponents has raised the prospect of advertising that would be visible at all times, or in all places. A gigantic space billboard would likely have a limited lifespan in any event because of the large number of collisions with space debris it would face. The Space Marketing project, for example, expected its billboards to be struck by 10,000 pieces of debris per day until its ultimate destruction.[42]

B. Astronomical Concerns

The present authors are not astronomers, and therefore do not question astronomers' claims that space advertising would make ground-based astronomical observation more difficult.[43] We do, however, question their claim that this justifies them in telling the rest of the world what it can and cannot do in the sky.

The common law has never recognized a right to a view – and, though it may have been altered in various cases by legislation, it still does not.[44] That is, for example, if A buys a piece of property and makes observations out of his window with a telescope, then B comes along and puts up a high rise on an adjacent piece of land such that A can no longer make his observations, A has no cause of action against B. Space advertising does not present a situation fundamentally different from this.

There are several serious practical and philosophical objections that can be leveled against the position that people have the rights to own views. First, on the pragmatic front, it would be extremely difficult to establish who owns which view. Merely looking at something is surely less discernable, not to say objective, than "mixing one's labor" with virgin territory, as in the case of homesteading.[45] Then, too, to own something is not merely to be able to (continue) to use it; it is also to be legally able to *prevent* others from so doing. Suppose Jones is the first to see the moon. Thus, under this theory, he owns the view of it. How is he to be able to prevent others from looking at this heavenly body? The problem here is that views are not rivalrous. More than two people, to say the least, can appreciate the sight of the moon. In contrast, cows, cars and candles are rivalrous: if one person uses these things, then others cannot. But the whole point of ownership in the first place is to have a rule determining which person can, and thus which one cannot, access the thing to be owned. If more than one person can look at the moon without interfering with another's view, and if, indeed, millions of people can do so, then what is the point of ownership? There isn't any.[46] Then there are truly anomalous situations; the first person to see a newborn child will in many cases be the obstetrician, not the mother or father. If view ownership is strictly interpreted – and how else are we to interpret it? – this would mean that the medical man, not the parents, is the rightful guardian of the child.

Another rule from the Roman and common law under which astronomers might claim a right to an unrestricted view of the skies has been rejected almost universally: the *ad coelum* doctrine. Under this rule, a party who owned a piece of land also owned everything above it, all the way up through the heavens.[47] This dubious doctrine necessarily died because it would have outlawed aviation and non-advertising satellites.[48]

Thus, rather than invoke a property-rights rule, concerned astronomers seem to want an exception to the rules of property rights. We, however, will advance an argument for strict property rights – with no exceptions for astronomers, astronomer-lovers, or anyone else – in the following section.

For now, we will simply observe that astronomers have failed to make the case that ground-based astronomy is so essential to human well-being that it requires a deviation from the usual rules of property rights. After all, the space-based Hubble telescope has offered unprecedented views of the universe in recent years, free from the so-called light pollution that hampers astronomers' efforts with earthbound telescopes. Undoubtedly, space advertising could reduce the overall level of astronomical observation that occurs – but astronomers have not made the case that an astronomy that tramples on the rights of others results in the economically optimal amount of astronomical research. In the absence of such evidence, the astronomers' efforts appear to be little more than common theft-seeking:[49] that is, seeking government privilege to ensure their continued employment or, at least, advancement of their own special interests.

As with the aesthetic concerns, we again face a situation of conflicting subjective preferences: some favor advertising and less ground-based astronomical observation, while others more highly rank no advertising and more ground-based astronomical research. In Section IV, below, we turn to our proposal to resolve these conflicts: strict private property rights. But first, we address some other pragmatic concerns.

C. Other Pragmatic Concerns

1. Space Advertising May Be Inevitable . . .

Regardless of the merits of the advertising haters, space advertising may be inevitable. The technology exists, and if someone wants to put up the money, he can have his name in lights in space. If the United States will not allow the launch, Russia or another country that cannot afford the luxury of turning down such business will.

If this is the case, then the issue is not whether we should allow space advertising, but whether individuals in a given country, such as the United States, should be allowed to take advantage of it. It seems to us a difficult case to make that one's countrymen should be disadvantaged vis-a-vis foreign competitors simply to make at best a fuzzy moral point.

Further, although we favor no regulation (as discussed below), those who dislike advertising may find the results of a lightly regulated domestic market more pleasing than the products of unfettered launches elsewhere – just as those who hate prostitution might, in a lucid interval, prefer regulated brothels to the crude streetwalking that results from absolute prohibition. Advertisers may find it more economical to obey mild regulations restraining their advertisements at home than to go overseas to avoid them. Thus, those who succeed in achieving absolute prohibition of space advertising in their own country may actually harm their own cause.

2. Or It Might Not Happen at All

It may also be that space advertising will not proliferate regardless of whether it is prohibited or permitted. After all, the Space Marketing venture failed because no one wanted to pay the $15 to 30 million the advertisements are reported to have cost.[50] If that is the case, then the prohibition may appear to be harmless. It is not necessarily harmless in any event, however, because it may discourage otherwise-useful innovation and technology that ultimately unsuccessful space-advertising ventures would have developed, or that those not primarily engaged in advertising do not develop for fear of running afoul of the space-advertising prohibition.

IV. SPACE ADVERTISING, PROPERTY RIGHTS, AND FREE SPEECH

There are no objective criteria for resolving the aesthetic and subjective disputes discussed above. There is, however, a non-arbitrary means for determining whether space advertising should be permitted: private property rights. Several points must be made in this context.

Private property rights are the basis upon which all sorts of potential disputes are solved every day, before they become contentious issues. Who has the right to use a particular piano or canoe? Why, the *owner* of course. If ordinary decisions of this sort had to be settled by courts on a case-by-case basis, we would all die of starvation as litigiousness reached epic proportions and we simply had no time to do anything else. Judges, properly, only rule on the smallest tip of the iceberg in this regard. Virtually all other disputes of this sort are settled by property rights, with no fuss. How does this come about? Initially, virgin territory is turned into the private domain by homesteading; then, it changes hands through any legitimate title transfer[51] such as trade, purchase, gifts, settlement for gambling debts, etc. Should this grocery store carry venison? Should that pizza parlor feature red or blue tablecloths? Should this car be painted orange? Such decisions are commonly made by their *owners*. Why should the decision as to whether or not to allow advertising be made in any other way?

Second, property rights and free speech are inextricably intertwined. There cannot be the one without the other. For, precisely as in the case of all these other "pedestrian" decisions, the determination of what may properly be said in any given place inevitably falls upon the owner of the property in question. May David Duke or Louis Farrakhan speak at the college campus? This depends upon the views on this matter of the owners of the university, the board of trustees. Is it licit that the sonnets of Shakespeare be recited in someone's living room? That crucially depends upon the opinions on this matter of the owner of said living room. The surest enemy of free speech is to allow government to own all pens, paper, ink, printing presses, and the like. For then the issue becomes one of allocation of "society's" scarce resources, and, seemingly, no long a matter of free speech rights, of which there can be none without such implements.

Third, it is entirely possible that advertising in space will not prove economically feasible. Or, if it does, and there is an outcry against it, that anyone whose products are advertised therein will *lose* customers, not gain them. It is entirely possible that advertising might be allowed on Mount Rushmore or in the Grand Canyon, and that it would *backfire* in this regard: a corporate emblem there would be the death knell of sales. But the only way this can be determined is empirically: fashion the law so that this is allowed, and then make a determination post hoc.

Our property-rights view, though it may strike many as radical today, was once the law, not only in space, but also on Earth. In the United States, at least, Courts long recognized that aesthetic issues are inherently subjective[52] and accordingly refused to allow governments to violate property rights solely on aesthetic grounds.[53] As the Ohio Supreme Court put it, "[M]ere aesthetic considerations cannot justify the use of the police power. It is commendable and desirable, but not essential to the public need, that our aesthetic desires be gratified."[54] Similarly, the California Supreme Court struck down a prohibition on terrestrial billboards in 1909, finding that the fact that "appearance of billboards is, or may be, offensive to the sight of persons of refined taste" does not suffice to justify such "a radical restriction of an owner of property to use his property in an ordinary and beneficial way."[55] In recent years, however, the Courts have abandoned this view, essentially giving lawmakers carte blanche in restricting uses of private property because of aesthetic concerns, allowing them to do so either for its own sake or where ostensibly linked to putative "health or safety" concerns.[56]

V. CONCLUSION

Those who would abrogate private-property and free-speech rights face a heavy burden, and here they have failed to meet it.[57] Therefore, space advertising through private property should be presumed legitimate, all laws against it should be repealed, and no treaties restricting it should be established.

Notes

[1] *Living Rooms in Orbit*, AUSTRALIAN, July 13, 2000, at 9.

[2] Don E. Tomlinson & Rob L. Wiley, *People Do Read Large Ads: The Law of Advertising from Outer Space*, 47 FED. COMM. L. J. 535, 541 (1995) (quoting Devera Pine, *Selling America on Orbiting Ads*, OMNI, Feb. 1994, at 27, 27).

[3] Presumably criticism of such advertising efforts would come primarily from those who object to *any* commercial activity in space. On those who object to human activity in space generally, see J.H. Huebert & Walter Block, *Space Environmentalism, Property Rights, and the Law*, 37 U. MEM. L. REV. (forthcoming 2007).

[4] On the booming space tourism business, *see, e.g.,* John Schwartz, *More Enter Race to Offer Space Tours*, N.Y. TIMES, Feb. 18, 2006, at C1.

[5] Tomlinson & Wiley, *supra* note 2, at 539 (citing *Orbiting-Billboard Proposal Gets Astronomers' Attention*, SKY & TELESCOPE, at 10, 10).

[6] *Id.*

[7] United Nations General Assembly Committee on the Peaceful Uses of Outer Space, Background paper by the International Astronomical Union, *Obtrusive space advertising and astronomical research* (2001) (hereafter "International Astronomical Union"), *available at* http://www.unoosa.org/pdf/reports/ac105/AC105_777E.pdf.

[8] Tomlinson & Wiley, *supra* note 2, at 539.

[9] *Id.* at 540.

[10] *Id.* (citing Joseph B. Allen, *New Heights (?) for Advertising*, ASTRONOMY, Sept. 1993 at 13, 15.

[11] International Astronomical Union, *supra* note 7, at 4.

[12] *Billboard in the Sky*, ADVERTISER (Adelaide, Australia), Mar. 12, 2004, at 32.

[13] *See, e.g.,* Todd Halvorson, *Russia Takes the Lead in Space Age Advertising*, SPACE.COM, May 31, 2001, http://www.space.com/news/spaceagencies/russia_market_010531-1.html

[14] *Russian Prototype of Artificial Moon Hits Snag*, ST. LOUIS POST-DISPATCH, Feb. 5, 1999, at A7.

[15] 49 U.S.C. § 70102(9).

[16] 49 U.S.C. § 70109a(a).

[17] 49 U.S.C. § 70109a(b).

[18] 49 U.S.C. § 70109a(c).

[19] U.S. Public Laws 106-391, Title III, § 322(c) (2000).

[20] 70 Fed. Reg. 29,164, 29,168 (May 19, 2005).

[21] These can be read on the FAA docket at http://dms.dot.gov/search/searchResultsSimple.cfm?numberValue=21234&searchType=docket

[22] 71 Fed. Reg. 51968, 51969 (Aug. 31, 2006).

[23] Gersh Kuntzman, *Space Invaders*, NEWSWEEK web-exclusive commentary, June 20, 2005, http://www.msnbc.msn.com/id/8292906/site/newsweek/.

[24] *See, e.g.,* Glenn H. Reynolds, *International Space Law: Into the Twenty-first Century*, 25 VAND. J. TRANSNAT'L L. 225, 230 (1992) (arguing that academic consensus supports private property under the Treaty). And on the view that, regardless of what the Treaty means, it *should* allow for private property, *see, e.g.,* Kurt Anderson Baca, *Property Rights in Outer Space*, 58 J. AIR L. & COM. 1041, 1083-85 (1993); Huebert & Block, *supra* note 3; Wayne N. White, Jr., *Real Property Rights in Outer Space, in* 40 COLLOQUIUM ON THE LAW OF OUTER SPACE 370 (1998).

[25] *No Place in Space for Adverts*, NEW SCIENTIST, July 10, 1993, at 5.

[26] *Grass Root Opposition to Space Billboards*, International Dark Sky Association Information Sheet No. 71 (2000), http://www.darksky.org/resources/information-sheets/is071.html

[27] 71 Fed. Reg. at 51,969.

[28] Tomlinson & Wiley, *supra* note 2, at 563 (Mr. Tomlinson advocates a complete ban; his coauthor, Mr. Wiley, does not).

[29] *See, e.g.,* Lawrence Person, *In Praise of Billboards*, 43 FREEMAN 360 (1993).

[30] *See, e.g.,* Walter Block, *Billboards*, LIBERTARIAN FORUM, Nov.-Dec. 1979, at 8.

[31] *Playstation Ads, Disguised as Graffiti, Spark Controversy*, USA TODAY, Dec. 29, 2005, http://www.usatoday.com/money/advertising/2005-12-29-graffiti-ads_x.htm; on the law and economics of graffiti generally, *see* Daniel J. D'Amico & Walter Block, *A Legal and Economic Analysis of Graffiti* (Ludwig von Mises Institute Working Paper), *available at* http://www.mises.org/journals/scholar/damico.pdf.

[32] *See* ISRAEL M. KIRZNER, COMPETITION AND ENTREPRENEURSHIP (1973).

[33] Virginia Postrel, *The Esthetics Police*, FORBES, Nov. 1, 1999, at 174.

[34] Some, such as John Kenneth Galbraith (THE AFFLUENT SOCIETY (1958)) would disagree with this statement. But see these critiques: Friedrich A. Hayek, *The Non-Sequitur of the "Dependence Effect," in* STUDIES IN PHILOSOPHY, POLITICS, AND ECONOMICS (1967); George Reisman, *Galbraith's Neo-Feudalism*, MISES.ORG, http://www.mises.org/web/2793. For other defenses of advertising, *see* Lee Benham, *The Effect of Advertising on the Price of Eyeglasses*, 15 J. L. & ECON. 337 (1972); WALTER BLOCK, *The Advertiser as Hero, in* DEFENDING THE UNDEFENDABLE 68 (Fox & Wilkes 1991) (1976); Walter Block, *Tobacco Advertising*, INT'L J. OF VALUE BASED MGMT., May 1997, at 221; Walter Block, *Coordination Economies, Advertising and Search Behavior in Retail Markets by Bagwell and Ramey: A Comment*, CROSS CULTURAL MGMT., Vol. 10, No. 1, at 80 (2003); Walter Block, William Barnett II & Stuart Wood, *Austrian Economics, Neoclassical Economics, Marketing and Finance*, Q. J. AUSTRIAN ECON., Summer 2002, at 51; Ronald H. Coase, *Advertising in Free Speech*, 6 J. LEGAL STUD. 1 (1977); ROBERT B. EKELUND & DAVID S. SAUMAN, ADVERTISING AND THE MARKET PROCESS (1985); DAVID OGILVY, OGILVY ON ADVERTISING (1985); MURRAY N. ROTHBARD, MAN, ECONOMY, AND STATE 978-83 (Ludwig von Mises Institute 2004) (1962).

[35] *See, e.g.,* Tom's Astronomy Blog, http://astroblog.captcrash.com/ (May 20, 2005, 06:31 EST).

[36] Christopher Westley, *The Economics of Spam*, IDEAS ON LIBERTY, Nov. 2003, at 8.

[37] Tomlinson & Wiley, *supra* note 2, at 539 (citing *Orbiting-Billboard Proposal Gets Astronomers' Attention,* SKY & TELESCOPE, Nov. 1993, at 10).

[38] *See* Walter Block, Roy Whitehead & N. Stephan Kinsella, *The Duty to Defend Injuries Caused by Junk Faxes: An Analysis of Privacy, Spam, Detection, and Blackmail*, 27 WHITTIER L. REV. 925 (2006).

[39] The precise manner of homesteading that would be necessary to acquire property rights in an orbital path or position above the Earth is beyond the scope of this paper. In any event, under no proper theory does one gain property rights in a space vast distances away simply by looking at it in its present state for a long time.

[40] *Eva Longoria Seen from Space*, MIAMI HERALD, Apr. 7, 2006, at A4.

[41] *See, e.g.,* Tomlinson & Wiley, *supra* note 2, at 563.

[42] *See* International Astronomical Union, supra note 7, at 4.
[43] *See, e.g., id.* at 2-3.
[44] Walter Block, Homesteading, Ad Coelum, Owning Views and Forestalling (2006) (unpublished, on file with the author).
[45] *See* Walter Block, *Earning Happiness Through Homesteading Unowned Land: a comment on 'Buying Misery with Federal Land' by Richard Stroup*, J. SOC., POL. & ECON. STUD., Summer 1990, at 237; HANS-HERMANN HOPPE, THE ECONOMICS AND ETHICS OF PRIVATE PROPERTY: STUDIES IN POLITICAL ECONOMY AND PHILOSOPHY (1993); JOHN LOCKE, SECOND TREATISE OF CIVIL GOVERNMENT (Henry Regnery 1955) (1690); ELLEN FRANKEL PAUL, PROPERTY RIGHTS AND EMINENT DOMAIN (1987); MURRAY N. ROTHBARD, FOR A NEW LIBERTY (1973).
[46] N. Stephan Kinsella makes the same point with regard to patents and copyrights; once the information is widely known, A's use of it detracts from B's use by not one whit. *See* N. Stephan Kinsella, *Against Intellectual Property*, J. LIBERTARIAN STUD., Spring 2001, at 1.
[47] This highly problematic doctrine could be interpreted to cut both ways. That is, according to ad coelum, the owner of a few square miles of earth, and thus the proprietor of an increasing sized conical area extending up into the "heavens," would be justified in placing advertising in "his" area of ownership miles above the earth.
[48] Murray N. Rothbard, *Law, Property Rights, and Air Pollution*, 2 CATO J. 55, 84-86 (1982); *see also* Walter Block & Richard A. Epstein, *Walter Block and Richard Epstein Debate on Eminent Domain*, 1 NYU J. L. & LIBERTY 1144 (2005); Walter Block, Homesteading, Ad Coelum, Owning Views and Forestalling, *supra* note 44.
[49] The term most economists would use in this context is "rent seeking." *See* Gordon Tullock, *Rent Seeking*, *in* 4 THE NEW PALGRAVE: A DICTIONARY OF ECONOMICS 147 (1987). But we see no need to besmirch the ancient and honorable practice of renting by juxtaposing it with such a nefarious practice. For more on this, see Walter Block, *Watch Your Language*, MISES.ORG, Feb. 21, 2000, http://www.mises.org/story/385
[50] International Astronomical Union, *supra* note 7, at 4.
[51] ROBERT NOZICK, ANARCHY, STATE AND UTOPIA (1974).
[52] For economic and philosophical support for this contention see JAMES M. BUCHANAN, *The General Implications of Subjectivism in Economics*, *in* WHAT SHOULD ECONOMISTS DO? 81 (1979); SUBJECTIVISM, INTELLIGIBILITY AND ECONOMIC UNDERSTANDING (Israel M. Kirzner, ed., 1986).
[53] Mark Bobrowski, *Scenic Landscape Protection Under the Police Power*, 22 B.C. ENVTL. AFF. L. REV. 697,703 (1995).
[54] *Id.* (quoting *Youngstown v. Kahn Bros. Bldg. Co.*, 148 N.E. 842 (Ohio 1925)).
[55] Charles F. Floyd, *Billboards, Aesthetics, and the Police Power*, AM. J. ECON. & SOC. (forthcoming), http://www.scenic.org/pdfs/Police_power.pdf (quoting *Varney & Green v. Williams*, 100 P. 867 (Cal. 1909)).
[56] *See* Bobrowski, *supra* note 53, at 708.
[57] We would argue that they fail to meet it in all cases, but that is beyond the scope of this paper. *But see generally* Rothbard, *supra* note 45.

IAC-06-E6.5.16

APPLYING INTERNATIONAL SPACE LAW PRECEDENT TO SPACE TOURISM, SPACE MINING AND SPACE SETTLEMENT

E. E. Weeks, J.D.
Ph.D. Candidate and Lecturer
Northern Arizona University
Political Science Department
Social and Behavioral Sciences, Box 15036
Flagstaff, Arizona 86011, USA
Edythe.Weeks@NAU.EDU
(928) 523-0957

ABSTRACT

A pattern exists whereby U.S. domestic space law has exhibited a tendency of setting commercialization and privatization trends. Over time, commercialization and privatization processes became the norm for satellite telecommunications, remote sensing, space transportation & launch services, space stations and spaceports. This paper provides an overview of space law from its beginning, through its changes, and today's new increased private-sector participation. The position taken herein is that something akin to legal precedent is in the process of being established with respect to private space tourism, private space trips, space exploration and other related space activities. Considering this legal trend - from the formation and purpose of the COMSAT Corporation to the recent political and legal issues surrounding the U.S. Orbit Act - this paper entertains possible emerging legal trends which have begun to spark. This includes possible legal implications of the *New Vision for Space Exploration Policy*, and for space tourism, space mining and space settlements as humankind journeys out to develop the final frontier.

1. A POLITICAL - HISTORICAL ANALYSIS OF SPACE LAW

The evolvement of international space law has largely been ignored by the field of political science/international relations. However, by applying insights from political science, interesting insights are revealed. For example, by understanding outer space politics within the context of three distinct epochs, we are better able to understand and foresee emerging trends. This is part of a formula which will be discussed herein.

1.1 The First Epoch

The first epoch of outer space development began when the Soviet Union launched Sputnik into Earth's orbit on October 4, 1957, and ended around 1979 when détente between the U.S. and the ended. In this historical epoch, political actions were shaped by Cold War fears. Tensions still high after World War I and World War II and the world trembled with concern over preventing a possible World War III. After the Sputnik launch, states immediately held meetings at the United Nations to discuss creating laws to govern the new outer space territory. In political science language, the key political actors were nation states who came together to cooperate through international institutions which they created for the purpose of managing multi-state interests regarding this new territory.

After nearly ten years of extensive negotiations between states working through the United Nations, five international space treaties were enacted to provide the core of space law. These principles (norms) which make up space law were created by three main actors: the United States, the Soviet Union and a group of various states operating through the United Nations.

The U.S. and U.S.S.R. were the two superpowers. As such, they constantly vied for alliances with other states. To this extent, other states had power. Although, the United States has always maintained an interest in a free market direction for space activities, during the first epoch it had to consider the interests of the U.S.S.R. and other states. Early attempts were made by the U.S. in an effort to exercise free market ideology regarding space. For example, as early as 1959, President Eisenhower declared that the U.S. Government . . . "should aggressively encourage private enterprise in the establishment and operation of satellite relays for revenue-producing services" (Jasentuliyana & Lee, 1979-1981, Vol. 1: at 304). However, The U.S. and U.S.S.R. were constantly butting heads. Superpower ideological conflicts created severe impasses during the 1950s and 1960s during space lawmaking negotiations. In addition to focusing on state power, personalities of state leaders mattered too. For example, space law negotiations were constantly halted when President Eisenhower was the leader of the U.S. and Chairman Khrushchev was the leader of the Soviet Union. In comparison, when John F. Kennedy became President, he used a different attitude, as evidenced by various pieces of correspondence to Khrushchev[1]. This change in attitude seems to have alleviated the frequent impasses. This period was the most fruitful period for *international* space lawmaking.

In addition to state power and attitudes of state leaders, the international political environment must also be considered in order to more deeply understand changes in space law. For example, international space lawmaking was most successful during *détente*, when tensions were relaxed and a series of international space treaties were negotiated, drafted and signed by the international community acting through the United Nations. Consistent with this theme, when political détente between the United States and Soviet Union waned in 1979, so did the process of international space lawmaking. This was in spite of all of the successful cooperation within the various international institutions. The Moon Treaty of 1979, the last in a series of five international treaties, was essentially stillborn[2].

1.2 The Second Epoch

Since there was a distinct change in space law in 1979, it makes sense to say that this dramatic shift marked the second epoch of outer space development (1980 to 1991). During the second epoch, a dramatic shift occurred when President Reagan became leader of the United States. The policies regarding space were consistent with the new political mood. Détente had ended and the Cold War had returned right before President Reagan took office. International relations between the two superpowers had "turned sour" (Von Bencke, 1997: 93). President Reagan highlighted this situation and used it as justification for no longer trusting the Soviet Union. As one scholar explains, "upon assuming office, Ronald Reagan immediately began implementing the "get tough" program he had championed during his campaign" (Von Benke, 1997: 93). Another example, in a speech on January 29, 1981, President Reagan asserted that "détente's been a one-way street that the Soviet Union has used to pursue its own aims . . ."[3]. Reagan used this no trust attitude to justify the creation of a myriad of U.S. domestic space laws which were used to privatize and commercialize space activities (Von Bencke, 1997).

With the return of the Cold War, outer space once again was treated as a national security concern, on one hand, yet it became a matter for commercial enterprise o the other. The Reagan Administration issued a large number of National Security Decision Directives[4] regarding national defense, and it consistently procured funds for a Strategic Defense Initiative (SDI). Also, President Reagan increased President Carter's proposed military budget by an additional $6.3 billion even though Carter had already requested a significant increase (Von Bencke, 1997: 93).

Another key aspect of the international political environment during the second epoch involved drastic changes in leadership of the Soviet Union. During the mid-1980s Mikhail Gorbachev had a policy of encouraging some aspects of private economy in the former USSR[5] (Goldman, 1996: 110). After 1985 various events began to change and the relations between the U.S. and Soviet Union improved. For example, in 1987 the U.S. and USSR signed a bilateral agreement regarding cooperation in space[6]. Changes occurring in the Soviet Union included a change in leadership, a decrease in economic and political power, and a decrease in control over the Eastern European bloc countries (Von Bencke, 1997). During Gorbachev's time, "the Soviet Union faced declining world power and general economic collapse" (Von Bencke, 1997: 96). It was during this time and towards the end of the Cold War that Gorbachev began "his policies of liberalization", which "contributed to 1989 revolutions in Bulgaria, Czechoslovakia, East Germany, Romania, Hungary, Poland and March 1990 Declarations of independence from Lithuania and Estonia" (Von Bencke, 1997: 96). As soon as "Gorbachev took power in March 1985, the U.S. and USSR resumed arms negotiations, and from November 19 to 21 of that same year Reagan and Gorbachev met for the first time in Geneva" (Von Bencke, 1997: 97). Once again, nuclear disarmament talks set the tone for outer space cooperation (Von Bencke, 1997: 97). While political issues plagued the other space superpower, the U.S. boldly began to privatize and commercialize space activities. This had been an interest of the U.S. since the beginning of the space age (Krug, 1991; and Von Bencke, 1997).

Although both the first and second epoch occurred during and were influenced by the Cold War era, the second epoch is distinct from the first epoch in two ways. First rapid advances occurred in commercialization of space technology. For example, from 1957 to the mid-1980s global spending on space activities were approximately $300 billion (Dula, 1985: 163). Internationally, space spending during the second epoch had risen to about $100 billion *annually* (Goodrich, 1989: 12). The profit potential of space had been clearly demonstrated and the process of space commercialization had begun. Second, space lawmaking shifted from the international to the domestic arena.

During the second epoch, the United States became the key actor in the growing practice of creating *domestic* space laws rather than to defer to the United Nations. For some, the United Nations international lawmaking machinery had proven to be too slow and too unpredictable to keep pace with the rapid development of commercial applications of space technologies (Goldman, 1996).

During the second epoch, private-sector actors became increasingly relevant and were consistently encouraged to participate in space through various government incentives and domestic legislation (Obermann and Williamson, 1998; d'Angelo, 1994; Brooks, 1991;

Straubel, 1987; and Finch & Moore, 1985). The new domestic laws created to govern newly emerging space industries such as satellite telecommunications, remote sensing, space launch and transportation services and space stations began to thrive and became widely acceptable within the international community. The general public also accepted these commercialization and privatization practices since they were viewed as successful - profitable. These newly emerging industries produced new goods and services with high consumer demand. As the result of these trends the geostationary orbit was divided into territories[7]. Several countries followed the trend of commercializing, privatizing and creating domestic space laws in the second epoch. The agenda for outer space was expanded to include economic interests, which were treated as equally important to national security concerns.

1.3 The Third Epoch

The third epoch is marked by the advent of the Post Cold War era. It is generally understood that after the Cold War, neoliberal policies, deregulation, liberalization, privatization and free market ideas arose as the dominant ideology in the international arena (Mittelman, 2001; Steger, 2001; Gilpin, 2001). With these changes, and the end of the Cold War, neoliberal free market ideology became a dominant belief system (Stiglitz, 2002; Rupert, 2000). This dominance was connected to globalization and privatization processes (Mandelbaum, 2002; Dumenil, Levy & Jeffers, 2004; Moylan & Baccolini, 2003; Yergin & Stanislaw, 2002; Steger, 2001). As Rao & Rao (1998: 1) in *Globalization, Privatization and the Free Market Economy* point out that "three dominant forces shaping societies and economies around the world" are globalization, privatization, and liberalization. The authors describe these three factors as a "multidimensional phenomena" which impact the economic considerations as well as the sociocultural and environmental aspects of societies. Similarly, Cole (1999) provides that privatization has "swept the globe". Furthermore, this dominance was achieved through the process of lawmaking (Aune, 2002; Williams, 2001; Garvey, 2000; Fitzpatrick, 1996). Similarly, Gilpin (2001: 3) sets forth that "since the end of the Cold War, globalization has been the most outstanding characteristic of international economic affairs, and, to a considerable extent, of political affairs as well", and he acknowledges that "globalization has become the defining feature of the international economy at the beginning of the twenty-first century. . .". Linked to this is the tendency to accept free market/free trade principles (Claudon & Wittneben, 1993; Travieso-Diaz, 1996; Roden, 2003; Cafruny & Ryner, 2003). In addition, China and Russia in many ways has joined in this procession towards globalization practices and neoliberal free market hegemony (Molchanov, 2005; Rogachev, 2005; Zhao, 2004; Peng, 2003). After the Cold War, various international conventions and regional trade blocs promoting free market ideology were widely entered into by the international community. These factors point to the dominance of free market ideology in today's Post Cold War environment.

No longer are geo-politics governed by the superpower rivalry between the U.S. and U.S.S.R. U.S. hegemony rose shortly after the fall of the Soviet Union. When considering space law change, it is important to consider these sorts of factors occurring at the international level. These structural changes have impacted, and will continue to impact the outer space development regime in countless ways.

2. IMPACT OF U.S. SPACE LAW ON COMMERCIALIZATION

Space commercialization has become generally accepted by the international space community and by the general publics worldwide. U.S. domestic space law has historically had a dramatic impact on space commercialization. The legal custom during the first epoch was that space lawmaking was regarded as an international affair. The norms and rules of law were debated, negotiated and drafted through the United Nations COPUOS (Jasentuliyana and Lee (1979-1981). During the second epoch, space lawmaking shifted to the domestic arena, partly because of the Reagan Administration's no trust attitude, but also because the international arena took approximately ten years to arrive at an agreement on the Outer Space Treaty of 1967. This is because the process involved approximately 100 nations negotiating, debating and discussing the terms of the international agreements. Meanwhile space technology was being rapidly turned into profitable industries. The U.S. - led custom of creating domestic space laws instead of international space law during the second epoch became acceptable within the international community.

In the Post Cold War era with the dominance of free market ideology and globalization practices, the norm became allowing the market to determine legal principles. Projections of industry success and profitability ratios seem to be increasingly seen as a factor in legal considerations.

The historical record demonstrates the U.S. had an interest in commercializing space technology since the beginning of the space age. However, as stated earlier, during the first and second epochs, the U.S. was not the only superpower. The Soviet Union had reservations about a neoliberal approach to outer space. In spite of this, and notwithstanding Ariane's commercial trailblazing record, the U.S. was a dominant political actor in setting space commercialization trends through the passage of a myriad of domestic space laws. For example, in 1962 the U.S. Congress passed the Communications Satellite Act of for the purpose of commercializing space satellite technologies. President Kennedy had "charged his administration with the need to develop a coherent and cohesive policy with respect to communications satellites" and by July 1961 he called for joint ownership with other nations of a communications satellite system, non-discriminatory access for all countries of the world, and a constructive role for the United Nations in international space communications (Jasentuliyana & Lee, 1979-1981, Vol. 1: at 304). This effort is still seen today as a motion in favor of goodwill to promote space benefits for all people, around the world. This gesture is still remembered, by members of the outer space development community, as an example of one of the great things that the U.S. has done. Shares were offered to the international community when the COMSAT corporation developed into INTELSAT via a U.S. - led international agreement. Many nations participated in space commerce associated with this bourgeoning technology. Around the world today many people use cell phones, the Internet, money transfer systems and enjoy increased GNP due to these space industries. Therefore, beginning with the first epoch and expanding through the second epoch, the U.S. established a pattern of leadership in space commercialization, through U.S. domestic law, which was created and used to facilitate space commercialization. Once industries flourished as the result of these practices, acceptance and adoption by the international community have usually followed.

In the third epoch, U.S. law became more far reaching, often directly calling for changes in the international arena. Examples include, the Land Remote Sensing Policy Act of 1992 increased the level of privatization in remote sensing and the Telecommunications Act of 1996[8], which facilitated the deregulation of the telecommunications industry (Salin, 2002: 212). As a result, U.S. telecommunications policy began to focus on liberalizing international markets. Telecommunications services were included in the General Agreement of Tariffs and Trade (the "GATT"), and the newly created World Trade Organization (WTO) was given the responsibility of "brokering future trade agreements to open up global telecommunications markets" (Wong, 1998: 6)[9]. Another example, in November of 1999 the U.S. Congress passed the Intellectual Property and Communications Omnibus Reform Act[10]. This was a powerful piece of legislation amending Title 17 of the US Code, the Communications Act of 1934, the Satellite Home Viewer Act of 1994, the Trademark Act of 1946 and the Tariff Act of 1930 and several Federal Patent regulations (Salin, 2002: 220). In the spirit of free market protection, it increases the amount of legal protection for inventors from piracy of intellectual properties such as trademark, patent, domain name and publications for services offered by satellite carriers. Perhaps, an even more poignant example is that the two main intergovernmental organizations, INTELSAT and Inmarsat[11], were placed on an agenda to go through the process of privatization. This was mandated through a U.S. domestic law called the U.S. ORBIT Act of 2000. The overall legislative intent was to restructure the two intergovernmental organizations in order to "create a competitive satellite industry in the United States through the restructuring of the ISOs" (Wong, 1998: 2).

3. CUSTOM AND LEGAL PRECEDENT

On October 4, 2004, SpaceShipOne won the 1st annual $10,000,000 Ansari X Prize. A few months earlier, the Federal Aviation Administration Office of Commercial Space Transportation (U.S.) had issued the world's first license for the *private* sub-orbital trip into outer space. This was the first time in history that a privately funded, private spaceship traveled into outer space. This event received wide media coverage and was spoken of as being akin to the historic Charles Lindberg flight. Contrarily, when Sputnik was launched on October 4, 1957 this alerted global panic. State leaders immediately took action calling for meetings and discussions to institute the passage of international space laws (Doyle, 2002; Metcalf, 1999). For example, within days, U.S. President Eisenhower and other leaders contacted the United Nations regarding Sputnik. As Galloway (1997) informs, right after the launch "[t]here was instantaneous reaction by the Senate Armed Services Committee" (Galloway, 1997: 1). During 1958 there were "multiple exchanges of formal correspondence between heads of state of major powers" and "multiple proposals submitted to the United Nations for consideration by the General Assembly" (Doyle, 2002: 83)[12]. Shortly thereafter, debates on space law took place in the United Nations from November 17-24, 1958. During these debates states pressed the United Nations to create a body of law to govern the new territory. In comparison, the SpaceShipOne launch, although the first of its kind in 2004, the SpaceShipOne launch did not arouse global panic or *international* lawmaking activities. No one rushed to the United Nations out of fear or concern. No one requested the COPUOS or its Legal Subcommittee to pass international laws to govern private trips to space. Considering the Post Cold War mood, perhaps no one flinched because privatization and commercialization are increasingly seen as the norm. Can it be that we are witnessing private space travel in the process of becoming a custom - a legal precedent?

Since all pre-SpaceShipOne trips were government operations, the quiet acceptance of this private space trip is an important signifier. It signals that a revolution involving private investment and private spaceships is underway. A shocking number of business moguls, many of whom became billionaires during the Internet revolution, have been testifying before the U.S. Senate Subcommittee on Science, Technology, and Space and the House Subcommittee on Space & Aeronautics, as well as to the President's Commission on Implementation of U.S. Space Exploration, asserting that it is time to expand the role of the private-sector. This includes a mandate to "transform" NASA. Political lobbying activity by new space entrepreneurs is happening concurrently with similar activities by members of the established space industrial base, who have also provided similar testimonies before these tribunals. Exciting? Yes! However, in light of the way international customary law works, legal precedent could be in the process of being established. There should be some concern since these activities may ultimately serve to contradict the express intent of the framers of the international space treaties. Furthermore, since there is a relative silence about this whole proccss, a custom may arise with the affect of being a legal precedent. Reactions to signifying events, such as doing nothing, can cause such acts to become established as custom (Metcalf, 1999: 82-84). After all, this *was* the concern when Sputnik was launched.

4. NEW U.S. POLITICAL ACTIONS

In the U.S., a large number of space entrepreneurs have been busy lobbying Congress to pass legislation to spark increased space privatization, President Bush articulated the New Vision for U.S. Space Exploration Policy in 2004 and created the President's Commission on Moon, Mars and Beyond the same year. The President's Commission published an implementation report which outlines the direction for further outer space development. In addition, several new U.S. domestic laws to foster privatization were passed in December 2004 and December 2005. In addition, the increased reliance on private corporations for space activities has already become main themes for many international space conferences such as International Astronautical Federation Congresses and United Nations Committee on Peaceful Uses of Outer Space workshops.

Considering the new role played by the private-sector and space entrepreneurs, and given the pattern of U.S. trendsetting behavior regarding space commercialization and privatization, recent U.S. legislation and policy may ultimately prove to have an impact which could wind up being disagreeable with various members of the international space lawmaking community. What will happen then? Is the international community on one accord regarding new privatization policy?

Based upon a careful review and analysis of various hearing transcripts of testimonies before the President's Commission on Implementation of U.S. Space Exploration Policy of 2004, similar testimonies before the U.S. House of Representative, Committee on Science, Subcommittee on Space & Aeronautics, and the Senate Subcommittee on Science, Space and Technology, the Commercial Space Launch Amendments Act of 2004, the NASA Authorization Bill of 2005, the President's Commission Report of June 2004, UN Resolution 51/122 (1996), and the IISL Board of Directors Statement of 2004, an incidental legal loophole may have been created which will allow for privatizing space resources. Resources which were once thought to have been deemed "province of mankind" according to the international space law treaties[13]. Since no one can say definitively what the term *province of mankind* really means, there is still a hole in international space law. This is important to address because, as described above, in the third epoch, the dominant ideology gravitates towards free marketization. In addition to all of this, a *new space race* is underway involving private space travel and the newly emerging space tourism industry. This is different from the U.S. – U.S.S.R. Cold War space race, which involved governments in competition for national prestige. The new space race is being run by space entrepreneurs and the legalization of private space travel. At the same time, commercial spaceports are increasingly being commercialized and involved the private-sector. Unique and natural resources such as the platinum group metals are virtually untapped and abundant in outer space, and are fairly easy to get to. The high technology applications for these types of natural resources make them priceless - worth trillions of dollars. Having the means to get to outer space could be in the process of being redefined.

The U.S. has historically set the trend for space commercialization and privatization. Therefore, it seems highly likely that President Bush's New Vision for U.S. Space Exploration Policy could also establish a new trend. For example, Recommendation 5-2 of the Commission report[14] reads:

> The Commission recommends that Congress increase the potential for commercial opportunities related to the national space exploration vision by providing incentives for entrepreneurial investment in space, by creating significant monetary prizes for the accomplishment of space missions and/or technology developments and by assuring appropriate property rights for those who seek to develop space resources and infrastructure.

(President's Commission Report of 2004 at pg. 32)

For years now, the members of the International Institute of Space Law have debated the issue of whether or not private property rights are allowable in accordance with international space law. Now it appears from a reading of the above passage of the President's Commission report that the U.S. may have, arguably, had picked a side in this debate. Only time will tell. Will the private-sector take over outer space exploration and the building of space settlements? Will this be alright with the international space community? Is the U.S. setting another new trend? Will this issue continue to go formally unaddressed by the international space lawmaking community? If so, then a custom will arise, and this new pattern could have the force and affect of legal precedent.

The likelihood of a trend establishing is great if we consider all of the above points coupled with the caveat note appearing at the bottom of the IISL Board of Directors Statement of July 2004 entitled "On Claims to Property Rights Regarding The Moon and Other Celestial Bodies"[15]. The statement itself basically says no to private property rights in outer space. However, the note appearing at the bottom of this statement may arguably be treated as a legal loophole. The note reads:

> Notwithstanding matters covered in the above Statement, the Board of Directors of the IISL recognises that other private activities on the Moon and other celestial bodies are permitted. Article VI of the Outer Space Treaty affirms that non-governmental entities, including private individuals, companies, and organizations, have the right to conduct activities in space in accordance with international space law, and subject to the authorization and continuing supervision of the appropriate State Party. The IISL plans to convene a Workshop to explore

issues regarding the relationship of government and private sector in space.

The phrase "including private individuals, companies, and organizations, have the right to conduct activities . . ." could serve as a legal loophole. In addition, the phrase, "in accordance with international space law" could serve as an addition legal loophole since the issue of whether or not international space law allows or prohibits private property rights is currently stuck in debate status within both the UN COPUOS and the IISL.

CONCLUSION

In addition to these possible legal loopholes, millions of dollars are being offered through various prizes to spur increased privatization of space. This is all linked to space tourism, space mining, and space settlement. In addition to the $10 million dollar Ansari X Prize, many other cash prizes are being offered to spur space entrepreneurship/space privatization, for brave souls willing to take space commercialization to higher heights. Examples include, the NASA Centennial Challenges Prizes ($100,000,000), the America's Space Prize ($50,000,000 million), the Heinlein Prize for Practical Accomplishments in Commercial Space Activities ($500,000) and the NASA Ralph Steckler/Space Grant Space Colonization Research and Technology Opportunity involved awards totaling $1,000,000. At the same time, things are happening at the cultural level to popularize private space travel. For example in a recent article there is a photo of Sir Richard Branson, Chairman of Virgin Galactic and Bill Richardson, Governor of New Mexico. They are both are smiling brightly, as Governor Richardson playfully holds up a small toy-like model of Virgin spacecraft. The article states that Virgin Galactic "will locate the world headquarters and mission control for its personal spaceflight business at the Spaceport in Upham" New Mexico[16]. Another recent article reads: "new rocket development company recently announced plans to build a spaceport in the United Arab Emirates, costly approximately $265 million". It further states that the company's spaceships will be designed by a Russian company. Financiers for this new enterprise, Hamid, Anousheh and Amir Ansari helped to finance the new Ansari X Prize competition"[17]. New commercial spaceports are being constructed at surprising rates. For example Texas has passed new legislation in preparation for creating two new spaceports, and "three telecommunications entrepreneurs from Texas have recently joined Space Adventures, Ltd."[18]. This is in addition to all of the spaceports already recently opened. We are witnessing an emerging new epoch of outer space development. Space tourism has been legalized through U.S. law, and space mining and space settlements have been and currently are being discussed as best suited for private-sector involvement.

ENDNOTES

1 See "Achievements in Space, International Aspects of Exploration and Use of Outer Space, 1954-1962", *Senate Documents, Volume 6*, No. 1, 88th Congress, 1st Session, 1966.

2 Only nine states (Australia, Austria, Chile, Mexico, Morocco, The Netherlands, Pakistan, Philippines and Uruguay) have ratified it and five states (France, Guatemala, India, Peru and Romania) have signed but not ratified. It only took five nations to enter it into force, took five years to get the five requisite signatures. Since the Moon Treaty was adopted by the consensus principle instead of widespread international acceptance, many space law scholars argue that it is not generally accepted as part of international law. Still, the Moon Treaty was enacted and is a UN Treaty.

3 *Public Papers of the Presidents of the United States: Ronald Reagan, 1981* (Washington, D.C. General Printing Office, 1982) at 57.

4 Although Eisenhower, Kennedy, Johnson, Nixon, Ford and Carter all had overseen, in conjunction with the Department of Defense, the "development and deployment

of various types of reconnaissance satellites" (Krug, 1991: 74), President Reagan issued considerably more Presidential Directives and policy statements than any of the former U.S. President.

[5] During Reagan's Presidency there were several leaders of the Soviet Union: Leonid Brezhnev (1964-1982), Yuri Andropov (1983-1984), Konstantin Chernenko (1984-1985) and Mikhail Gorbachev (1985-1991). With the exception of Gorbachev, each played insignificant roles in outer space development.

[6] Bilateral "Agreement Between the United States of America and the Union of Soviet Socialist Republics Concerning Cooperation in the Exploration and Use of Outer Space for Peaceful Purposes" entered into force on April 15, 1987. The 1977 version of this agreement had been allowed to expire in 1982. This agreement committed the two states to "carry out cooperation in such fields of space science as solar system exploration, space astronomy and astrophysics, earth sciences, solar-terrestrial physics and space biology and medicine" and to "encourage international cooperation in the study of legal questions of mutual interest which may arise in the exploration and use of outer space for peaceful purposes".

[7] For more information on the ITU's allocation of orbital slots in the geostationary orbit see Keven V. Cook (Spring, 1999) "The Discovery of Lunar Water: an opportunity to develop a workable moon treaty" *Geo. International Environmental Law Review 11*, 647.

[8] Public Law No. 104, 110 Statute 56; also see H.R. Conference. Rep. No. 104-458, at 1 (1996).

[9] For a detailed critique of the WTO practices and the process of privatization and commercialization of satellite telecommunications see Serrano Virginia Rodriguez (2000) *Trading with Space Resources: The Forces of Privatization and Commercialization Applied to Satellite Telecommunications Through ITU and WTO*, Dissertation, McGill University (Canada).

[10] This Act is also known as the Patent and Trademark Office Efficiency Act as well as the Anticybersquatting Consumer Protection Act; S1948/H.R.1554-H.R.3194, 106th Congress, 1st Session, November 17, 1999.

[11] See Jason Bates (December 27, 2004) "U.S. Government Approves Sale of Intelsat to Private Equity Group" Space News Business Report at http://dev.space.com/spacenews/satellitecomm/intelsat_122704.html.

[12] Refer to U.S. Senate report, *Documents on International Aspects of the Exploration and Use of Outer Space*, 1954-1962, a Staff Report prepared for the Senate Committee on Aeronautical and Space Sciences, May 9, 1963, GPO, Washington, D.C. at pp. 51-52, 55-56, 62-64, and other communications in those pages for examples of letters exchanged between U.S. President Dwight Eisenhower and U.S.S.R. Premier Bulganin. See also C.Q. Christol, *The Modern International Law of Outer Space*, 12-14 (New York: Pergamon Press, 1982); A.G. Haley, *Space Law and Government*, 313-314 (New York: Appleton Century Crofts, 1963) and M.S. McDougal, H.D. Lasswell and I.A. Vlasic, *Law and Public Order in Space*, 205-210 (New Haven: Yale University Press, 1963).

[13] This may later prove to be problematic since the grant of ownership rights to outer space including the Moon or any other celestial bodies, arguably contradicts legal norms established by international law. During the first epoch, international space law treaties and UN declarations agreed upon by an international community of approximately a hundred nations, deemed the outer space territory as a public or commons territory. The international community of nations specifically granted freedom to use outer space to the *province of mankind*, and determined that any such uses would be for the benefit of <u>all</u> mankind. This includes both the resources and the territories.

[14] See the Report of the President's Commission on Implementation of U.S. Space Exploration Policy: *A Journey to Inspire, Innovate and Discover*, ISBN 0-16-073075-9, (U.S. Government Printing Office, Washington, D.C.) (June 16, 2004). In February 2004, President Bush announced a New Vision for U.S. Space Exploration Policy. He also created a commission, the President's Commission on Implementation of United States Space Exploration Policy to advise him on matters of space travel including the Moon, Mars and other celestial bodies, and mandating the holding of a series of public hearings regarding the future of the U.S. space program in addition to creating a new U.S. Space Transportation Policy in January 2005.

[15] http://www.iafastro-iisl.com.

[16] This photo appears on pages 2-3 of the (Spring 2006) *Ad Astra*, explaining that "on December 13, 2005, Sir Richard Branson and Governor Richardson announced a partnership to build the world's first Spaceport in the state".

[17] John Schwartz (February 18, 2006) "More Enter Race to Offer Space Tours" *NYTimes.com*.

[18] Id.

REFERENCES

Aune, James Arnt, *Selling the Free Market: The Rhetoric of Economic Correctness* (Guilford Publications, Inc., 2002).

Brooks, Timothy A., "Comment: Regulating International Trade in Launch Services", *High Technology Law Journal* (1991): 59.

Cole, Daniel H., "From Local to Global Property: Privatizing the Global Environment?: Clearing the Air: Four propositions About Property Rights and Environmental Protection", *Duke Environment Law & Policy, Vol. 10* (Fall 1999) 103.

Claudon, Michael P. and Kathryn Wittneben (eds.), *After the Cold War: Russian-American Defense*

Conversion for Economic Renewal (New York University Press, 1993).
D'Angelo, George V., *Aerospace Business Law* (Westport, CT: Quorum Books, 1994).
Doyle, Stephen E., *Origins of International Space Law and the International Institute of Space Law of the International Astronautical Federation* (Univelt, Incorporated: San Diego, California, 2002).
Dula, Art (1985) "Private Sector Activities in Outer Space" *The International Lawyer Vol. 19*: 159-197.
Dumenil, Gerard, Dominique Levy and Derek Jeffers, Capital Resurgent: *Roots of the Neoliberal Revolution* (Harvard University Press, 2004).
Finch, Edward Ridley Jr. and Amanda Lee Moore in *Astrobusiness: A Guide to the Commerce and Law of Outer Space* (New York: Praeger, 1985).
Fitzpatrick, John P., "The Future of the North American Free Trade Agreement: A Comparative Analysis of the Role of Regional Economic Institutions and the Harmonization of Law in North America and Western Europe", *Houston Journal of International Law* 19 (Fall 1996): 1.
Garvey, Jack I., "A New Evolution for Fast-Tracking Trade Agreements: Managing Environmental and Labor Standards Through Extraterritorial Regulation" *UCLA Journal of International Law and Foreign Affairs* 5 (Spring/Summer 2000): 1.
Gilpin, Robert, *Global Political Economy: Understanding the International Economic Order* (Princeton & Oxford: Princeton University Press, 2001).
Goldman, Nathan C., *American Space Law: International and Domestic 2nd ed.* (San Diego, California: Univelt, 1996).
David Russell Hager (1970) in *Space Law: The United Nations, and the Superpowers: A Study of International legal Development and Codification, 1957-1969,* Dissertation, University of Virginia.
Krug, Linda T. (1991) in *Presidential Perspectives on Space Exploration: Guiding Metaphors from Eisenhower to Bush* (New York Praeger, 1991).
Jacobs, A., "A Private Enterpriser Joins the Space Race", *Industry Week*, November 29, 1982: 52.
Jasentuliyana, Nandasiri and Roy S.K. Lee (1979-1981) *Manual on Space Law, Volumes I, II, III and IV* (Dobbs Ferry, New York: Oceana Publication, Inc., 1979-1981).
Richard M. Obermann and Ray A. Williamson *Space Policy Vol. 14* (February 1998) 17-25.
Mandelbaum, Michael, *The Ideas that Conquered the World: Peace, Democracy, and Free Markets in the Twenty-First Century* (Public Affairs, 2002).
Metcalf, Katrin Nyman *Activities in Space Appropriation of Use?* (Uppsala: Lustus Forlag, 1999).
Mittelman, James H., "Globalization: Captors and Captives pp. 1-16, in James H. Mittelman and Norani Othman (eds.) *Capturing Globalization* (New York: Routledge, 2001).
Moylan, Tom and Raffaella Baccolini (eds.), *Dark Horizons: Science Fiction and the Dystopian Imagination* (Routledge, 2003).
Rao, C.P.P. and C.P. Rao (eds.), *Globalization, Privatization and Free Market Economy* (Greenwood Publishing Group, Incorporated, 1998).
Roden, Mark, "US-China Relations in the Contemporary Era: An International Political Economy Perspective", *Politics* 23(3) (September 2003): 192.
Rupert, Mark, *Ideologies of Globalization: Contending Visions of a New World Order* (2000).
Steger, Manfred B., *Globalism: The New Market Ideology* (Lanham Maryland: Rowman & Littlefield Publishers, Inc., 2002).
Salin, Patrick A., "An Overview of US Commercial Space Legislation and Policies – Present and Future" *Air & Space Law* 27, no. 3 (June 2002): 209-236.
Straubel, Michael S., "The Commercial Space Launch Act: The Regulation of Private Space Transportation, *Journal of Air Law and Commerce* Volume 52 (1987): 941
Stiglitz, Joseph E., *Globalization and Its Discontents* (Norton, W.W. & Company, Inc., 2002).
Travieso-Diaz, Matias F., *The Laws and Legal System of a Free-Market Cuba: A Prospectus for Business* (Greenwood Publishing Group, Incorporated, 1996).
Von Bencke, M. J., *The Politics of Space: A History of U.S. - Soviet/Russian Competition and Cooperation in Space.* Boulder, Colorado: Westview Press, 1997).
Wong, Henry (December 1998) "Comment: 2001: A Space Legislation Odyssey - A Proposed Model For Reforming The Intergovernmental Satellite Organizations" *The American University Law Review*, Vol. 48: 547
Yergin, Daniel and Joseph Stanislaw, *The Commanding Heights: The Battle for the World Economy* (Simon & Schuster Adult Publishing Group, 2002).

SESSION REPORTS

REPORT OF THE IISL SPACE LAW COLLOQUIUM IN VALENCIA, SPAIN, OCTOBER 2006

Contributed by Rapporteurs Petra Vorwig (USA), Sylvia Ospina (Colombia), Martha Mejía-Kaiser (Mexico). Kelly Gable (USA) and Ricky Lee (Australia)
Compiled and edited by Tanja Masson-Zwaan

SESSION 1- LEGAL ASPECTS OF SPACE TRANSPORTATION AND LAUNCHING

Chairmen: Peter van Fenema (Netherlands) and Alvaro Azcarraga (Spain)
Rapporteur: Petra Vorwig (USA)

The first paper presented was "The US 'Vision for Space Exploration', Legal Issues Presented by Innovative Commercial Initiatives" by Mr. Michael Wholley, General Counsel of NASA (USA). Mr. Wholley began his presentation by outlining the elements of the President's 2004 Vision for Space Exploration, which include involvement of international partners and increasing commercial opportunities for space transportation and exploration. In support of the second element, NASA has announced seven prize competitions for a total purse value of US$14 million. Mr. Wholley explained that NASA also has begun investing in cutting edge technology through a venture capital fund. The goal of these and other NASA projects, such as the Commercial Orbital Transportation Services ("COTS") Demonstrations project, according to Mr. Wholley, is to involve commercial entities in the delivery of cargo and crew to outer space, as well as in NASA's vision for the moon, Mars, and beyond. Mr. Wholley expressed hope that commercial transport solutions will reach the demonstration phase in the next 2-4 years. Mr. Wholley noted that the COTS Demonstration agreements between NASA and commercial providers are designed to minimize NASA requirements and oversight of the commercial ventures. For example, NASA waived many of its rights to control IP developed under the agreements, and it has agreed to refrain from using the technology to give the commercial venture an opportunity to commercialize it. Because the US government remains responsible for supervising launches under the Outer Space Treaty, Mr. Wholley noted that the COTS Demonstration launch activities must be licensed by the FAA.

Dr. Frans von der Dunk (Netherlands) presented his paper "Legal Aspects of Private Spaceflight for Tourist Purposes." Given the nature of space tourism, Dr. von der Dunk explained that the bulk of current treaty law would not apply because it focuses on the use of space for political and scientific purposes. He opined that the treaties, particularly the Rescue Agreement, should apply to space tourists so that they would be entitled to some protection in the event of an accident. At the very least, according to Dr. von der Dunk, the Rescue Agreement should apply to the flight crew of a private spacecraft conveying tourists because they should be considered "personnel" under the Agreement. Dr. von der Dunk noted a flaw in this analysis: the crew would be private employees rather than government personnel, and so not clearly covered by the Agreement. Dr. von der Dunk identified a separate problem created by sub-orbital space craft. Under current legal constructs, a sub-orbital craft would not necessarily qualify as a "space object" covered by any of the current outer space law. This could have serious implications with respect to the Registration Convention; however, Dr. von der Dunk noted that sub-orbital vehicles could be registered as aircraft. The author recommended further action to clarify the application of current space law to space tourism activities, but also stressed that national laws need particular attention.

Ms. Axelle Cartier (Netherlands) and Ms. Ioana Cristoiu (Belgium) presented their paper entitled "Space Tourism: Regulatory Framework of the Private Initiatives and Projects with a Special Interest on RLV Regulations." According to Ms. Cartier, the typical customer seeking financing for its space endeavor is a startup with no assets or credit history. Ms. Cartier asserted that reusable launch vehicles (RLVs) may provide an overall lower cost alternative to expendable launch vehicles that will better support the commercialization of space, where the cost of raising capital and developing the transport means are high. Ms. Cartier proceeded to describe the benefits of RLVs, including the lower cost derived for low earth orbit tourist trips and the ability to amortize the cost of the endeavor over numerous launches. She did note that RLVs face serious technical challenges, and the industry's lack of experience with RLVs may mean that the cost has been underestimated. Ms. Cartier explained that the Commercial Space Launch Act of 1984 (CSLA) focused on expendable launch vehicles (ELV), and established the Department of Transportation as the lead agency to coordinate space launch activities. In 2000, the FAA issued final rules defining a licensing process for RLV launch and reentry, but did not address hybrid systems that combined both traditional aircraft technology and operations with spacecraft characteristics and capabilities. Ms. Cartier described the FAA's current experimental licensing process, which has fewer requirements, shorter review periods and involves a different approach to public risk analysis than the process used for conventional launch licenses. The experimental licenses are, however, restricted to certain circumstances, including research.

Ms. Cristoiu discussed the financial challenges that face many private companies attempting to develop private space activities, including market access restrictions, restrictive procurement policies and export controls. Ms. Cristoiu opined that the Space Protocol under development in the International Institute for the Unification of Private Law (UNIDROIT) could support increased funding for smaller space activities.

Mr. Kenneth M. Weidaw's (USA) paper "Commercial Spaceport Development: The Role of Domestic and International Space Law and Regulations" was summarized for the panel. In his paper, Mr. Weidaw predicted that the need for coordinated international space and air traffic management system must become operational to accommodate the growing commercial space launch industry. Mr. Weidaw noted that commercial spaceports are now under development in nine countries, and in the United States alone, six spaceports have been licensed. He noted that government-owned spaceports will also look to the commercial launch industry to fund continued operations, such as transporting cargo and passengers from one spaceport to another or into orbit. Given the state of the commercial space launch industry, Mr. Weidaw recommended that a general convention be convened to devise a space and air traffic management system. In the alternative, the United Nations should take the lead in devising a new international traffic management system.

The paper "Advertising of Private Commercial Space Services in the European Community" was written and presented by Ms. Zeldine O'Brien (Ireland). Ms. O'Brien began her presentation by explaining how European Community (EC) law on advertising may apply to the space tourism/ hospitality industry. Specifically, she posited that space tourism could be considered a "service" under the Treaty of Rome, and therefore subject to Directive 84/450/EC. According to the author, 84/450 protects the economic welfare of potential private space tourists by reducing misleading advertising in a high-risk endeavor. Ms. O'Brien noted that 84/450 establishes a regulatory floor upon which Member States may impose more stringent consumer protection requirements. Ms. O'Brien went on to explain that 84/450 was subsequently amended by Directive 97/55/EC to include restrictions on comparative advertising. Under 97/55, an advertiser generally may provide price comparisons, but if a known brand name exists, it should be included in the comparison. Again, Member States may impose stricter requirements on comparative advertising. Ms. O'Brien explained that misleading advertising may be challenged in national courts, which may order the cessation of the advertising. Advertisers, on the other hand, may challenge strict Member State laws under Articles 28, which protects the free movement of goods between Member States, and 49, which protects the freedom to provide services.

Ms. Rachel Yates (USA) followed with her paper "Minimizing Regulation of Space Tourism to Stimulate Commercial, Private Launch Capabilities." Ms. Yates explained that the primary purpose of the CSLA, as amended, was safety, but it recognized the need for regulatory standards to evolve as the industry matures. In February 2005, the FAA issued draft guidelines for both crew and participants in commercial, suborbital RLVs. It subsequently drafted regulations as required by CSLA and received public comment on them, but the final rules have not been published. The rules were subsequently published on December 15, 2006. Ms. Yates described the various competing interests that must be balanced in the regulations and how that balance was achieved. One competing interest is the tension between the desire to impose specific requirements to improve safety, while allowing for flexibility in design and operation of the spacecraft. The US Congress addressed this conflict by limiting the FAA's authority to regulate design and operations before 2012, with the exception that the FAA may intercede with regulations if serious injury or death results from a spacecraft design. The FAA regulations, in turn, balance the interests by allowing operators to determine the best method for achieving the safety requirements. A second conflict of interest develops between the duty of the government to protect participants and crew and the government's duty to respect an individual's right to choose his/her level of risk. To strike a balance, the regulations focus on making sure the crew and participants are sufficiently trained and that space flight participants receive clear information describing the known hazards, including statistics. Ms. Yates noted that the consent form that must be signed by all space flight participants may not be sufficient to protect the operator from liability, so it may have to obtain a contractual waiver from participants. The regulations also require operators to make their safety records available to participants, but operators are reluctant to do this because the information could benefit competitors. The final competing interests that arise under the FAA's regulatory regime is government regulation versus industry self-regulation. Ms. Yates stated that each company is too focused on survival and every program is too different to assume industry standards can be established. Ms. Yates opined that the FAA's hands-off approach to regulating the industry is appropriate.

The final paper, "US Law Governing Commercial Space Launches," was presented by Prof. Paul Dempsey (Canada). Prof. Dempsey opened his remarks by noting that the market for commercial space travel will continue even as the market for tourism declines because the market for transportation will boom. He explained that the CSLA authorized the FAA to regulate the commercial space transportation industry to the extent necessary to ensure compliance with international law; to protect public safety, property and national security; and to promote space launches and reentries by the private sector. Prof. Dempsey stated that because launches conducted within the US or by US citizens requires FAA authorization, other states with fewer regulations may become states of convenience. The final rules proposed by the FAA established a launch application review process that consists of seven steps: pre-application consultation; policy review and approval; safety review and approval; payload review and determination; financial responsibility determination; environmental review; and compliance monitoring. The author also described the review process for the FAA's experimental permits allowed under the 2004 amendments to the CSLA and used to research and develop operating techniques or for crew training. This process requires the applicant to submit: a program description, a flight test plan, and operational safety documents. Prof. Dempsey opined that space flight passengers may be covered by the Warsaw Convention for aircraft if they are not covered by the Liability Convention. Prof. Dempsey further suggested that the International Civil Aviation Organization may act as an international body capable of harmonizing aviation and space law, particularly for hybrid vehicles that act as both an aircraft and a space craft.

Notes on the discussion:

On the issue of NASA's efforts to encourage commercial development:

- *Mr. Wholley* noted that the COTS Demonstration public announcements indicated that NASA could enter into agreements with commercial participants to share NASA workforce and facilities, including for testing and evaluation purposes.
- *Mr. O'Donnell* noted that waivers issued to NASA contractors may constitute soft law because the Outer Space Treaty holds governments liable for the space activities of their citizens.
- *Prof. Gabrynowycz* responded that waivers are not soft law. They have been a part of the International Space Station Agreement and launch activity since NASA launched the first satellites.

On the issue of regulating comparative advertising in an industry with one participant:

- In response to a question from *Dr. Ospina*, *Ms. O'Brien* noted that such regulation is not possible right now, but after the industry develops, more providers will be available. *Ms. O'Brien* also noted that space companies may attempt to compare the safety of their services to other transportation services.

On the issue of customer consent and company liability under the new US launch regulations:

- *Prof. Christol* noted that if all of the space tourism companies met and agreed on language for an informed consent notice, their actions may be considered anticompetitive.
- *Ms. Yates* responded that companies have asked the FAA to provide language for an informed consent notice, but the FAA has not done so. She opined that each company likely will develop its own consent based on the notices used by extreme sports service providers. She did not perceive a problem with companies getting together to improve safety because such an agreement would not restrain trade.
- *Ms. Yates* was asked if the FAA has established rules to protect commercial ventures from overzealous lawyers. *Ms. Yates* responded that, initially, the FAA appeared to moving toward requiring passengers to submit more medical information, but commercial ventures rejected the proposal under the notion that each new regulatory obligation could lead to increased liability. The companies' concerns led the FAA to back away from requiring increased medical information.
- *Ms. Yates* was asked if providing informed consent notices to foreign citizens would qualify as an export under ITAR. She responded that such disclosure was probably not an export because the notices do not contain

technical information. She noted, however, that providing safety logs to foreign citizens may constitute an export because the logs often describe how a safety problem was fixed.

- In response to a question on liability, *Prof. Dempsey* explained that in 1920 there was a lot of concern over liability in commercial aviation and how such liability would be impacted by conflicts of law. The legal community produced conventions that resolved these issues. In the space tourism context, insurance companies will respond to catastrophe by driving up rates leading to international consensus on liability.

On the issue of public reaction to and simplification of the FAA's regulations:

- In response to a question from *Prof. Jakhu, Ms. Yates* noted that the FAA estimates that five to six companies will join the space tourism industry over the next ten years. During the comment period, the FAA received comments from approximately 25 companies and private citizens.
- *Prof. Dempsey* noted in response to a question that the US has attempted to use more common language in its regulations to ensure operators and consumers can understand them.
-

On the issue of international operations under the FAA's rules:

- *Dr. Azcarraga* noted that many other countries have looked to the FAA's certification rules to create their own launch certification rules. While the US will lead the way in regulating space activities, there is a conflict of interest with other nations that may not impose such strict requirements on operators.
- *Prof. Dempsey* responded that there likely will be states of convenience despite Article 6 of the Outer Space Treaty. He suggested that the next step in space transportation will require EU and FAA rules to apply to all space operators.
- In response to a question regarding how the FAA's decision to certify Virgin Galactic's service as an aircraft intersects with the USA's obligations under Article 6 of the Outer Space Treaty, *Dr. von der Dunk* responded that US legislation on space activities refers to "flight participants," not "passengers" so that the aircraft treaties and space law treaties are not confused.

On the static nature of space law in the face of a developing space tourism industry:

- *Prof. Zhukov* noted that space law is static, and asked about the future of international space law in the space tourism sphere.
- *Dr. van Fenema* argued that when national laws create conflicts between countries, international regulations must be implemented.
- *Prof. Andem* commented that private international law for space activities must be developed.
- *Dr. Azcarraga* noted that international space law was written in a different political climate and the law may need to be adapted.
- *Dr. Dempsey* responded that the space treaties were written with the objective to maintain outer space military-free. The drafters were not looking at commercial development of space. The conventions were not designed to deal with tourism or exploitation.

SESSION 2A - LEGAL ASPECTS OF DISASTER MANAGEMENT
SESSION 2B - PROPERTY RIGHTS ON THE MOON AND LEGAL ISSUES

Chairmen: Prof. Sergio Marchisio (Italy), Prof. Juan Faramiñán (Spain)
Rapporteur: Dr. Sylvia Ospina (Colombia)

This session was divided in two parts: the first one dealt with the legal aspects of disaster management, and the second with property rights on the Moon and Legal

Issues. A total of 10 papers were presented, two of which were summarized.

Dr. S. Ospina's paper dealt with the role of satellites, both remote sensing and telecommunication spacecraft, in times of disaster. The author presented a summary of the Disasters Charter and the Tampere Convention, their differences and similarities. The author highlighted recommendations made by groups involved in disaster and rescue operations, the principal one being the need to relax some of the regulatory and licensing requirements, and / or expedite these procedures; the need to harmonize type approvals for equipment being taken into the territory to provide emergency or relief communications. Lastly, she recommended the need for cooperation between operators of both kinds of satellites, as well as between the different agencies (UN, ITU, and regional organizations, such as CITEL, CTU, etc.) involved in disaster relief efforts, whether prior, during or after the event. More effective assistance could be provided, and greater harmony achieved, by joining the Disasters Charter, and also ratifying the Tampere Convention.

Prof. Hashimoto presented a "case study" of the Asia Satellite Centre, on Tsunami Disaster relief, stressing the importance of information at all levels. He mentioned that after the December 2004 tsunami, the government was essentially wiped out in the Aceh province, and that communications and information are fundamental in disaster relief. He set forth a hierarchy of information systems, based on geography: beginning with regional, then national, and down to the local. The Asia Centre will become a database archive for disaster relief activities, thus playing an essential role even during emergencies.

Dr. O. Ribbelink spoke on the Disasters Charter and GMES, posing a series of important questions, such as: who selects what territory or event is to be monitored by GMES? What to do with all the data that is going to be collected, and who will decide who gets to see and / or use the data? He stated that these are worrisome items, as it is impossible to find out who will be making these decisions. At the European level, several of the space agencies, as well as departments or directorates of the European Commission will be involved, also putting into question the privacy of data and individual privacy. He concluded that there is some responsibility to provide some protection, especially when the State does not react or respond, and where there may be a humanitarian crisis, such as in Darfur.

The second part of the session dealt with property rights on the Moon, and legal issues.

Dr. von der Dunk summarized Prof. G. Gal's paper on the "Interpretation of Article II of the Outer Space Treaty", concluding that Art. II is "self-executing." He also stressed that this Article does not allow for any claims of national sovereign property rights over any part of outer space.

Prof. Pospisil, a physicist from the Czech Republic stated that he would "try to convince" the audience that the Moon is something special, and is a "precious natural resource," with special characteristics which need to be respected. Therefore, the Moon Treaty should be updated, as specified in his paper. In addition to citing several articles of the Moon Treaty to support his arguments, he stated that there is a need for new rules for the Moon, taking into account its special characteristics. Thus, only the near side of the Moon should be exploited or exploited, but for a limited time. The dark side of the Moon (which is never seen from Earth) should be used only for scientific purposes. Even though his paper is entitled "Update of the Lunar [Moon] Treaty".

Ms. C. Jimenez-Monroy spoke on the creation of a legal framework for sustainable development of the Moon, and the need to have "in-situ resource utilization" (ISRU) policies. While observing that there is no life on the Moon, she also stated that any change to the Moon would have some impact on it. As to considering the Moon as part of the "common heritage of mankind", she stated that it was not clear whether appropriation of natural resources would be allowed or not. To conclude, she stressed that the Moon Agreement is not a "dead document". (The author did not provide a hard copy of her paper, making it difficult to follow her arguments at all times.)

Dr. L. Martinez co-authored a paper with Dr. U. Bohlman, "Fly Me to the Moon," which discussed some of the legal and political considerations of long-term space exploration initiatives. The authors are of the opinion that there seems to be more "watching" of space exploration (as in films and TV shows), than actually engaging in it, although different space powers are looking at each other, to see what the other is doing in terms of space exploration. There also seems to be a resurgence of government involvement in the outer space arena, although the USA is still the most commercial, particularly in regard to space tourism.

Prof. P. Larsen's paper, an update on the Status of the UNIDROIT Space Protocol, was summarized by P. Vorwig. While the Aircraft Protocol has come into effect, and ICAO is the Supervising Authority thereof, not much progress has been made on the Space Protocol. The main obstacles have to do with assets and liability, and their meaning under different legal systems. However, the proponents of the Space Protocol consider that working on it should continue, as in the long run it will be beneficial.

Dr. J. Pearce spoke on the "Application of Free Trade Zone Concepts to Space Development." He stated at the outset that he would "discard the Moon Treaty, and look at the Outer Space Treaty instead, what it allows, and what it does not allow. Activities in space are still under State supervision, and responsibility (Art. VI and VII, OST). He suggests using a "Free Trade Zone" concept, particularly in regard to the Moon. The question, however, is whether private parties would be willing to invest under this kind of legal regime.

Dr. Yun Zhao presented good arguments for the creation of a special patent / legal regime for outer space inventions. He noted that there are several key elements to intellectual property, one being the novelty of the invention, and another important factor is the time when the invention was made. In regard to the International Space Station (ISS), only States, not individuals can be owners of the IPRs, but he suggests a special patent regime, that would provide international and national protection to the inventor.
(Dr. Zhao's paper was the winner of the 2006 Diederiks Award.)

SESSION 3 - INTERNATIONAL COOPERATION IN SPACE ACTIVITIES, WITH SPECIAL FOCUS ON REMOTE SENSING

Chairmen: Dr. Joanne I. Gabrynowicz (USA) and Dr. José Monserrat-Filho (Brazil)
Rapporteur: Dr. Martha Mejia-Kaiser (Mexico)

Session 3 started with the presentation of the paper 'European Transformation Countries on their Path to ESA' by Dr. Mahulena Hofmann (Czech Rep.). She commented that some years ago, Hungary, the Czech Republic and Romania participated in various programs of Intercosmos, but without any influence in the decision making. Financial shortages in national space programs at the end of the cold war motivated these States to request for participation in ESA. Dr. Hofmann examined the cooperation agreements with ESA and presented the pros and cons of the different forms of participation forms (full membership, associate membership, participation in ESA programs). The author is of the opinion that by introducing the

Intercosmos know-how into ESA, those States could terminate the anomaly of the cold-war era in space activities.

The second paper presented was 'Eumetsat International Cooperation Activities', authored by Dr. Werner Balogh and P. Valabrega (Germany). This paper outlined the growing and complex data distribution network between Eumetsat, its counterparts and users. The authors were of the opinion that this clear and unproblematic mode of meteorological data distribution should serve as a model for an integral international cooperation in the generation and dissemination of satellite remote sensing data.

Prof. Juan Manuel Faramiñán and Ms. Ma. del Carmen Muñoz authored the paper 'The Cooperation Between ESA and EU Regarding the Earth Observation'. The authors noted that the EU together with ESA are defining a space policy and space programs for Europe, as space activities become an important aspect of European integration. On this basis, the Global Monitoring for Environment and Security (GMES) is supported. Prof. Faramiñán and Ms. Muñoz addressed the legal and institutional instruments to implement the GMES system.

Ms. Masami Onoda (Japan) presented the paper 'Monitoring Greenhouse Gases from Space and the Kyoto Protocol'. Ms. Onoda commented that the Kyoto Protocol obliges State parties to cooperate with self-information about gas emissions in their territory. She was of the opinion that, in addition, other sources of information are required to ensure control and compliance. She raised the possibility of satellite remote sensing serving as a central monitoring tool in order to overcome the sensitiveness of States. But Ms. Onoda underlined that the Kyoto Protocol obligations only address the monitoring of anthropogenic (man-made) emissions. She regretted that it is not possible to perform anthropogenic emissions analysis by satellite remote sensing images only, because the last ones can not be used to distinguish between man-made and natural emissions. The author concluded that, at present, spatial teleobservation for environmental treaty compliance can only play a complementary role in a monitoring system.

The paper 'Global Spatial Data Infrastructure: Issues for Space Law and International Cooperation' was authored by Satya Sagar and Debarupa Banerjee (India). The authors examined several issues arising from the concept of a Global Spatial Data Infrastructure (GSDI), which is the widespread sharing of geographic information on a global level. They commented on the growth of the GSDI and its market orientation. They examined various legal and policy issues of GDSI, such as privacy, copyright and liability. The authors commented on the concern that raw data and other remote sensing products can not be protected under copyright, which is a hurdle for the development of GSDI. As only one of several complex legal questions, the authors identified the legal issues of damages arising from mistakes in the data analysis and presentation. They concluded that there is a need to bring such issues to a single forum for solving the emerging problems of GSDI.

The paper 'The Importance of International Cooperation in Building National Space Data Infrastructure in All Countries' was presented by Prof. José Monserrat Filho (Brazil). With this paper, the author underlined the promotion of economic and social progress, in particular of the developing countries, as a goal stated in several relevant United Nations documents. He commented that this legitimate right could be supported through the access and exploitation of geospatial data by developing countries. Prof. Monserrat referred to the Brazilian delegation, which introduced a corresponding new item to the COPUOS agenda this year. The topic 'International Cooperation in Promoting the Use of Geospatial Data for Sustainable

Development' will be addressed in the next three sessions of COPUOS, with the purpose of fostering international cooperation for remote sensing data gathering, process, analysis and application. He is of the opinion that each country must have the required capacity to work with remote sensing data.

Mr. K. Mukhija and Y. Goyal (India) submitted the paper 'An Analysis of Issues Arising from the Commercialization of Remote Sensing Activities'. The authors of this paper presented an analysis of the copyright and other intellectual property formulas for the legal protection of remote sensing images. They addressed the Indian copyright legislation (as amended in 1994) which requires an 'author' to be the person who creates the work. The authors considered this definition also to apply to remote sensing satellite owners. Nevertheless, Mukhija and Goyal are of the opinion that at present there are no adequate legal international instruments to protect all products. They commented that international cooperation is needed for the creation of proper legal protection. They considered discussions in WIPO about intellectual property rights for space products as a good starting point for the drafting of a convention about remote sensing. Such a convention could provide conditions for "...the exercise of specific copyright" relating to satellite imagery.

The paper 'Remote Sensing Data: Some Critical Comments on the Current State of Regulation and Reflections on Reform' was presented by Dr. Lesley Smith and Ms. C. Doldyrina (Germany). The authors provided an overview of several aspects of the legal protection of satellite remote sensing images. After referring to some national legislations and space policies for remote sensing distribution of spatial systems (US, Russian Fed., Canada, EU, India), the authors addressed the different legal protection formulas used in distribution agreements (copyright, EU Database Protection, classified information, etc.). Dr. Smith and Ms. Doldyrina questioned the applicability of the copyright formula to automatically generated data. In respect to EU Database Protection, the authors referred to several decisions of the European Court of Justice, which held that "...a right cannot be derived from the mere creation of a database". The authors found highly questionable that under those Court decisions such protection applies to remote sensing operators, who only invest in creating a database. They proposed to create precise and clear definitions of remote sensing products, to identify proper legal protection for each of those products and to internationally harmonize the different licensing approaches. For this task, they suggested UNIDROIT as the forum to draft a model law.

The paper by Dr. Maureen Williams (Argentina) on 'The Registration Convention Thirty Years On' was summartised in her absence. Dr. Williams stated that the Registration Convention is insufficient in the current scenario, resulting in the difficulty to determine the link between spacecraft damage and the liable State. She suggested to up-date the Registration Convention through UN Resolutions or other international instruments. She also proposed efforts at national level for appropriate legislation on registration.

Dr. Marianna Morelli (Italy) submitted the paper 'Public and Private Interest in Remote Sensing Activities: the Need for an Effective Legal Environment'. In her presentation, Dr. Morelli identified the balance between public and private interests in remote sensing data as the central political and legal question. She considered that State interests in the protection of data of their own territory have decreased, while the freedom of using remote sensing data from any part of the world has become stronger in recent years. But the tendency to privatize remote sensing activities may produce a distribution problem. She proposed a synergy between public and private interests, in light of the present effort of protecting the world environment.

Mr. Bruce Mann (Canada) presented the paper 'Drafting Legislation to Regulate Commercial Remote Sensing Satellites: A How-to Guide from Canada'. Mr. Mann participated in the drafting of the Canadian Remote Sensing Space Systems Act. The Act was already approved by the Canadian Parliament (Nov. 2005) and soon will enter into force. He provided background information about several important provisions of the Act, like licensing, shutter control, government data priority access, liability, inspections and audits. Under the new Act, non-governmental and governmental institutions (like the Canadian Space Agency) will require a license for the operation of remote sensing systems. Mr. Mann pointed out that UN Principle XII on Remote Sensing will become a mandatory licensing condition in Canada, i.e. it will be compulsory for the licensee to offer raw data to sensed States on a timely base and at reasonable costs.

Dr. Kai-Uwe Schrögl (Germany) presented the position paper of the International Academy of Astronautics named 'Cosmic Study on Space Traffic Management' with contributions of several researchers in the legal and technical field. This study focuses on the growing problems of space debris and launching activities. The authors are of the opinion that space traffic management is necessary for avoiding physical or radio-frequency interference during access, operation in outer space and return to Earth. Although the authors acknowledged that such traffic management will reduce the freedom of space activities, they concluded that legal and technical mechanisms must be explored in order to outline a comprehensive space traffic management with economic benefits for all countries.

SESSION 4 – SPACE LAW AT TIMES OF ARMED CONFLICT

Chairmen: Prof. Jonathan Galloway (USA) and Dr. Ram Jakhu (Canada); *Rapporteur*: Kelly Gable (USA)

Prof. Maurice Andem (Finland) presented his paper "The question of legitimacy of threat or use of force in and from Outer Space: a reflection on the sanctity and legal binding force of the Charter of the United Nations and the 1967 Outer Space Treaty." Prof. Andem recalled the vision of peace among nations held by the founders of outer space law, and discussed the sanctity of outer space. He analogized the UN Charter, the "Bible of International Law," to a contract, and said that the sanctity of contracts is common law in itself. Prof. Andem concluded that states' compliance with the Charter is what will bring peace to the world. Regarding the question whether the use of remote sensing satellites for military purposes is illegal, he argued that it is not right to use force whatsoever, and that there is no equality or morality to using satellite for non-peaceful purposes because developing nations do not have the resources to do so.

The next paper, "Contemporary doctrine of self-fefense in Outer Space" by Prof. S. Bhatt (India) was summarized by Ms. K. Gable. Prof. Bhatt analyzed the contemporary law on individual and collective self-defense. In doing so, he took into consideration the UN Charter, the Chicago Convention of 1944, and the Outer Space Treaty of 1967. Prof. Bhatt then applied the analysis to current international events, including acts of global terrorism such as the September 11, 2001 attack on the United States, and discussed how these events have impacted global security and self-defense.

The third paper, "Military applications and Space Law" by Prof. Gabriella Catalano Sgrosso (Italy), was also summarized by Ms. Gable. In the first part of the paper, the author analyzed the effects of technological process on the relationship between war and space within the context of current national and international regulations, as well as space militarization and the limits put upon it in order to safeguard outer space. In the second part of the paper, the author analyzed the security and defense concepts of individual States, including the Strategic Defense Initiative (SDI), the Russian Defense Initiative (SSDP), SALT I, SALT II, the Limited Test Ban Treaty, the Non-Proliferation Treaty, START I and START II. In the third part of the paper, the author focused on the European Union's concern with the increasing militarization of outer space and the resulting Green Paper and White Paper.

"The Ambit of the Law of Neutrality and Space Security" by Mr. Michel Bourbonniere (Canada), was presented by Mr. Ricky Lee. Mr. Bourbonniere examined the origins and effects of the law of neutrality and its application to the US doctrine of space control, and argued that neutral rights and duties in space are a corollary of the theory of space control promoted by the US doctrine. First, the author argued that the law of neutrality confers on neutral states protection from belligerent acts such as those either expressed or implied by the doctrine of space control. Second, the author argued that the international community is at a diplomatic stalemate on the question of weaponisation of space. The author concluded that the law of neutrality remains a primary normative structure in regulating the practical effects of the doctrine of space control.

Prof. Steven Freeland (Australia) presented his paper "The applicability of the Jus in Bello rules of international humanitarian law to the Use of Outer Space." Prof. Freeland discussed how the development of technology has led to outer space being used more frequently during armed conflict, and that this mandates an understanding of the extent to which international humanitarian law applies to outer space activities. He stated that the existing treaties do not cover every eventuality in outer space and that, therefore, recourse must be made to other sources of applicable legal principles, such as international humanitarian law. Prof. Freeland concluded that: (1) there is an increasing danger that outer space will become a theater of war; (2) the development of more technological uses of outer space heightens that danger; (3) virtually all countries are dependent on space technology, including satellites, that may be considered military targets; (4) some fundamental principles of international humanitarian law would apply to military action in outer space, but the enormity of the consequences of a space war is such that one cannot be sure how these principles would apply; (5) it is necessary to develop specific rules and standards that categorically sanction the weaponization of outer space and the engagement in any form of conflict in outer space and against space assets; and (6) in developing new rules and standards, the "collective humanity" principles of outer space law must be strictly adhered to.

There were a number of questions for Prof. Freeland.

- First, *Prof. Mark Sundahl* (USA) asked whether a state would be able to protect assets from being attacked. Prof. Freeland responded that the right to self-defense, with its attendant principles of necessity and proportionality, would apply to this situation.
- Next, *Mr. Phil Meek* of the US Air Force disagreed with the idea that activities against space assets are illegal and stated that the principles of proportionality and discrimination are not difficult to apply in practice. Prof. Freeland disputed the idea that application is easy and clarified that the point of his paper was that, although international humanitarian law principles do apply in outer space, they are not sufficiently directed to future unknown consequences in outer space.
- Finally, *Mr. William Marte* of the Space Policy Institute in Washington, DC asked whether the International Court of

Justice might give an advisory opinion on the use of space weapons similar to that regarding nuclear weapons, or whether there might be a UN Resolution regarding this issue. Prof. Freeland responded that the UNGA passes a resolution on the prevention of an arms race in outer space every year, and that a treaty on the subject would be difficult to realise.

Prof. Gennady P. Zhukov (Russia) presented his paper entitled "Legal status of dual-uses satellite systems." Prof. Zhukov analysed the legal status of double-use satellite systems and outlined the need to strengthen the immunity of satellite systems due to the threat of international terrorism. He emphasised the need for a multilateral treaty granting immunity to all satellite systems, including purely peaceful satellite systems and dual-use satellite systems. He discussed how bilateral treaties might be turned into multilateral treaties, and described how that would further the goal of granting immunity to these systems.

Next, Prof. Mark Sundahl (USA) presented his paper entitled "Information Warfare: the legal aspects of using satellites and jamming technologies in propaganda battles." Prof. Sundahl addressed the hypothetical question of whether a state may use DBS technology to broadcast a commercial news program into an enemy state in time of war as part of a campaign to win the support of the civilian population. He argued that such commercial news programs do not rise to the level of illegal war propaganda and would not be prohibited by the requirement that outer space be used purely for peaceful purposes, and therefore the prior consent of the receiving state is the only restriction on the broadcasting of such a program. Prof. Sundahl concluded that the prior consent doctrine may be threatened by the United States' recent relaxation of self-defense theory. Finally, the author touched briefly on the right of states to use jamming technology to block illegal satellite transmissions.

There also were a number of questions for Prof. Sundahl.

- First, *Mr. William Marte* asked whether a state being invaded would give consent to such propaganda broadcasts and, therefore, whether the law discussed would be applicable. Prof. Sundahl agreed that a State would probably not give such permission.
- Second, *Prof. Gabrynowicz* stated that she found it curious that Prof. Sundahl put CNN and Voice of America in the same pot, so to speak, as one is a commercial enterprise that could be biased depending on one's viewpoint and the other is straight propaganda. Prof. Sundahl recognized that this was a legitimate concern, but that he had assumed for the sake of discussion that these are content-neutral disseminations - however he acknowledged this may not be so.
- Third, *Dr. Mareni Pichler die Ortega* asked whether, in times of peace, it is necessary to have prior consent. Prof. Sundahl said that yes, prior consent is necessary.
- Finally, *Dr. Frans von der Dunk* said that Prof. Sundahl overlooked *opinio juris* as the other aspect of customary international law and asked whether Prof. Sundahl suggested that states come out in the open about jamming as, if they did so, that might be customary international law. Prof. Sundahl responded that a proper response to this question would require research, but that he believes that states would say it is their right to jam under customary international law.

Ms. Amal Rakibi (France) presented her paper entitled "Galileo's Public Regulated Service: from security to military applications?" Ms. Rakibi described that Galileo is meant for civil purposes and will bring together the European political and space institutions. She argued that nothing prohibits the Public Regulated Service, one of the five service groups of Galileo, from being used for military purposes, but that there are a number of impediments to such use. The chief impediments are the lack of unanimous European will, the overlay of signals, and the access to the encrypted codes and data. Ms. Rakibi concluded that Galileo will not be fully justified without a "dual-use" dimension, and that the barriers to such dual use are more political than legal.

There were several questions for Ms. Rakibi.

- First, *Dr. von der Dunk* asked how the system would deal with the issue that the private operator of the system will want to sell services to anyone who can pay for them. Ms. Rakibi responded that the paper does not analyze commercial issues, but focuses on public international law issues.
- Next, *Mr. Ian Gibson* of the British National Space Center commented that he believes Ms. Rakibi slightly misinterpreted the term "dual use" and suggested looking at Skynet 5 where the civil systems are separate from the military applications. Ms. Rakibi responded that different professions seem to have different definitions of "dual use" and that her definition is to distinguish between civil and military applications because civil applications always have commercial applications.

Prof. Carl Christol (USA) presented his paper entitled "Hurricanes and Remote Sensing." Prof. Christol discussed the applications of the Remote Sensing Principles of 1986 to current environmental issues and described the great effectiveness that satellites have had in capturing environmental data. Prof. Christol discussed the science behind hurricanes in particular, including global warming, and the research and monitoring activities that various national and international governments and organizations, such as the WMO, UNEP and EUMETSAT, have undertaken in studying this and other environmental issues. Prof. Christol stressed that we need to achieve a higher degree of prevention of environmental problems and that satellites can be instrumental in doing so.

In a reaction to this paper, *Mr. Roger Leonard* argued that the connection between carbon dioxide production and global warming is not certain, and that global warming may not be the cause of stronger hurricanes. Prof. Christol responded that the information in his paper comes from regularly conducted scientific polls, and that the science in this area is advancing quickly.

Notes on the discussion:

On the issue of the interpretation of international law:

- *Dr. Ali Akbar Golrounia* (Iran) told about how, when he first started studying outer space law, Prof. Velazquez said that international law is the law of the jungle. This sounded strange to him at the time, but it seems true today, especially in reference to international humanitarian law. The outer space treaties state that outer space is only for peaceful uses, and this does not mean that States may use technology in the way they are now discussing. He argued that the treaties are being interpreted in this way because it is in the interest of those that currently have power to do so.

On whether the Outer Space Treaty is valid during times of armed conflict:

- *Prof. Gabrynowicz* called the session's attention to a paper just published in the Journal of Space Law authored by Latoya Tate, regarding the status of the Outer Space Treaty during war and measures short of war. This paper found that the Outer Space Treaty is a lawmaking treaty, which means that it stays in effect during times of war, and found that, since World War II, the trend in public international law has been to not suspend or terminate treaties in times of war – that is, there is a growing presumption that treaties stay in force during times of war, as this is when the treaties are most needed.

- *Dr. Jakhu* agreed; the consideration that the Outer Space Treaty is valid during armed conflict and the matter of the hierarchy of legal norms, especially contemplating the UN Charter, international humanitarian law, and the outer space treaties are of prime importance
- *Prof. Andem* responded that the real question is "what is international law." He noted that the drafters had to look to other laws, maritime law for example, to make outer space law. He said that we, too, need to look to multiple sources of law in order to interpret outer space law, and that we need to read the laws in context, knowing the whole before we can know a part.
- *Mr. Ricky Lee* responded that, to the extent that the discussion is about international law, we must remember the special status of the UN Charter. Article 103 of the Charter says that if anything conflicts with the Charter, the Charter prevails. Accordingly, states are required to not follow the Outer Space Treaty if an obligation arises under the Charter, such as a General Assembly Resolution. He concluded that the Outer Space Treaty would continue to remain in force during war to the extent that it is not overridden.
- *Prof. Freeland* also agreed that the Outer Space Treaty would continue to apply during time of armed conflict, but that this is not necessarily the entire answer. He said that the Outer Space Treaty has fundamental gaps and is open to multiple interpretations. Accordingly, one must find legal principles to apply, and must recognize that a whole other body of law may also apply.
- *Prof. Yasuaki Hashimoto* (Japan) stated that we must remember that international law includes the law of war.
- *Prof. Gabrynowicz* tied the last few comments together and clarified that no treaty stands in a vacuum, and that part of international law is the law of war, but that these can be tied together. She stated that the neutrality principle (not to harm non-belligerents) and the non-appropriation principle (space is available to all) have in common that they are intended to protect particular persons or things. She stated that what underlies the entire debate is whether to reopen the Outer Space Treaty for amendment, and that in her view it should not be so reopened because not only is it the underpinning of other treaties, but there are parts of it that one could not achieve today given the political administrations of various States.
- *Mr. Lee* agreed that the Outer Space Treaty cannot exist in a vacuum and that one needs to refer to other laws, but stated that one needs to resist the idea of looking too far away from the specifics of treaties that are specific. He said that article 103 of the Charter applies to obligations, not rights, and that article 51 of the Charter involves rights. Therefore, he would not think that the conduct of self-defense would override the Outer Space Treaty. In addition, article 51 applies to territorial sovereignty, and one cannot have territorial sovereignty in outer space, so there cannot be self-defense in outer space.
- *Prof. Andem* stated that the intent of the law must be complied with, and drew an analogy to civil law countries, which have a code that sets forth the law.
- *Prof. Christol* distinguished the two schools of law – the civil law system and the common law system. He recognized that the Charter states that words should be construed in the ordinary sense, but inquired as to what exactly that means. He stated that we

must look at the values underlying the words and that, when one does so, it seems that the literal interpretation of those words may not be the most correct; we must know the purpose and intent behind the words that are drafted.

SESSION 5 - OTHER LEGAL MATTERS, INCLUDING THE RELATIONSHIP BETWEEN GOVERNMENT AND PRIVATE SECTOR IN SPACE ACTIVITIES

Chairmen: Dr. Frans von der Dunk (Netherlands) and Dr. Mª del Carmen Muñoz Rodriguez (Spain)
Rapporteur: Ricky Lee (Australia)

The first paper was entitled "International Space Law in its First Half Century" by Prof. Stephan Hobe (Germany). Prof. Hobe described three phases of space law development: the first being the adoption of the United Nations space treaties, the second being the adoption of General Assembly declarations and the third being the interpretation of the adopted space law instruments. He suggested that there is need to find the motivation to develop new principles and, in particular, the need to revise and reform the Registration Convention and the Moon Agreement.

The second paper was entitled "Small States and Space" by Prof. Francis Lyall (United Kingdom). In his paper, Prof. Lyall reminded us that all States are juridically equal and there is a potential for the use of flags of convenience for spacecrafts. The same problems in maritime law, the competition for location of spaceports and the use of shell companies to avoid legal regulation are all relevant concerns. Prof. Lyall preferred for the International Telecommunication Union to play a more active role in the regulation of private space activities.

The next paper was entitled "The Future of Planetary Protection: Is There Reason for Optimism?" by Dr. Leslie I. Tennen and Dr. Patricia Sterns (United States). In their paper, Dr. Tennen and Dr. Sterns raised significant concerns for forward contamination of other planets in human exploration efforts. They noted that steps are being taken to ensure that the forward contamination of Mars is quarantined and minimised and that this is a source for much optimism.

The fourth paper was entitled "For a Charter on Space as a Common Good" by Ms. Mélanie Vincent (France). In her paper, Ms. Vincent warned that emerging space powers may choose to challenge the existing space powers and become a potential source of conflicts. She suggested that vigilance is need to preserve peace in space for generations to come. She also suggested that attempts to privately appropriate land on celestial bodies must be condemned.

The fifth paper was entitled "Satellite Telecommunications as a Tool for Bridging the Digital Divide – Public International Law Implications" by Ms. Julia Neumann (Germany). In her paper, Ms. Neumann considered the impact of satellite telecommunications on the socio-economic development of a country and the scope and content of space law in relation to such a "right" to benefit from satellite communications.

The sixth paper was entitled "Reflection on Chinese Future Space Legislation" by Prof. Haifeng Zhao (China). Prof. Zhao provided a detailed insight into the space activities presently conducted by China and how such activities may be regulated by future domestic space legislation.

The paper "Lack of National Law in Iran, the Main Obstacle for Private Sector in Space Activities" was presented by Dr. Ali Akbar Golrounia (Iran). In their paper, the authors discussed potential space activities that may be conducted by the private sector, along with a compelling case for the need for domestic legislation to regulate such activities in Iran.

The paper entitled "The Flight of Brazil's First Astronaut" by Dr. Alvaro Fabricio Dos Santos (Brazil) provided us with an in-depth insight into the exploits of the first Brazilian astronaut and the impact of his flight on the development of space law in Brazil.

The paper "GNSS Third Party Liability: The European Experience of Galileo" was written by Ms. Chiara Lucchini Gilera (Italy). She suggested that the main problem with the consideration of liability issues with Galileo is the lack of precedent in the area, even with reference to the NAVSTAR global positioning system. She opined that liability is best limited in order to enable insurance cover or the establishment of an international compensation fund.

The next paper was entitled "Taking Garbage Outside: The Geostationary Orbit and Graveyard Orbits" by Dr. Martha Mejia-Kaiser (Germany). In her insightful paper, Dr. Mejia-Kaiser discussed the problem of congestion in orbits around the Earth, especially the geostationary orbit, and provided some interesting suggestions for the future legal regulation of such orbits with a view to reduce the debris left behind.

The beforelast paper, "In Defence of Advertising in Space", was presented by by Dr. J. H. Hubert and Mr. Walter Block (United States). Dr. Hubert and Mr. Block made a case for the freedom to advertise in outer space, though with reference only to United States domestic legal norms and not to any international law.

The last paper was entitled "Applying International Space Law Precedent to Space Tourism, Mining and Settlement" by Prof. Edythe Weeks (United States). The paper provided an interesting approach to the formulation of the law concerning future human space activities.

Notes on the discussion:

During the discussion that followed, the following comments and points were made:

- *Dr. Lubos Perek* proposed an award for the worst use of space and suggested the billboard in space as a strong contender.
- *Prof. Joanne Gabrynowicz* warned of the dangers of implementing the *Homestead Act* and other US domestic law to outer space. In any event, the *Homestead Act* had significant problems in implementation in the medium to long term.
- *Dr. Sylvia Ospina* reacted to Prof. Hobe's suggestion of amending the Registration Convention and said that it is required to make it more enforceable, such as to deal with insurance aspects.
- *Dr. Roger Bernard* asked about the application of domestic and international space law and the various priorities that may be given by lawyers to them. *Dr. Frans von der Dunk* clarified this by emphasising the delineation between domestic law and international law, such as that of the *Homestead Act*. Dr. Bernard asked why the IISL felt a need to clarify private property rights on the Moon; Dr. von der Dunk stated that the reason was to clarify for those who bought Moon plots that they are worthless as property titles.
- *Dr. Hubert* said that private property rights is the best way of regulating activities in space.
- *Mr. Lee* then pointed out that the issue of billboards in space may have some cover in relation to international law rather than reference only to domestic law and a study along such lines would be better framed.
- *Prof. Gabrynowicz* discussed the legislative development of the domestic law on remote sensing in the US which was done with a view for the commercialisation of the remote sensing industry and, in its failure, ended up to remove Landsat from commercial practice and place it in the public sector and operate it as a public asset.

Enabling the Frontier. Regulatory Challenges for the Utilization of Space

IISL Plenary Session, Valencia, 4 October 2006

Rapporteur : Marie Helen Pichler – Die Ortega, Madrid

PANEL DISCUSSION

Moderator:
Christopher Stott, President & CEP ManSat, COO Excalibur Almaz Ltd, Hon Rep of the Isle of Man Government to the Space Community

Participants:

Art Dula	CEO, Excalibur Ltd
Christian Sallaberger	VP Business Development, MDA
Clayton Mowry	CEO, Arianespace Inc.
John Purvis	General Counsel, SES Global
Frans von der Dunk	Director, IIASL

First topic: 2006 marks the 10th anniversary of the Long March launch vehicle failure that kicked off the changes in 1998 that led to the creation of ITAR, a US agency granting export licences of components to be used in a space craft. The participants discussed the effects of ITAR on the industry and further developments resulting therefrom.

According to Clay Mowry the industry has experienced a deterioration. There has been a significant increase in government monitoring of the industry. Whereas export licences of components to be used in a space craft were previously being processed within a time period of four to five months it takes now seven to ten months to obtain such a licence from ITAR. Both the State and the Defence Department of the US administration are overwhelmed with the number of licences demands. They are dealing now with 60.000 applications per year.

John Purvis echoed the views of C. Mowry. ITAR's procedure is very bureaucratic. A licence applicant is obliged to furnish extensive documentation and the procedure does not deal with the genuine underlying security issues. Since the Technical Assistance Agreements (TAA) have been amended even the so-called expedited procedure still takes four months. The resulting delays are in fact punishing the industry. As a result, non-American industries are looking for other sales opportunities.

Christian Sallaberger agreed with the opinions of the previous speakers and amplifies the negative effects felt by the industry, at least from the view from a Canadian company. The procedure has slowed down business with the US since it results in extra costs for US customers. Thus there is a difficulty of implementing joint programmes. Especially back-end delivery programmes are suffering the implications of the time delaying procedure. Commercially funded deep space venture constitute another example: many US investors would be ready to contribute, however US products are not being used to avoid the ITAR procedure.

The Panel then discussed possible remedies.

Frans Von der Dunk stated that from an international law point of view there were no obstacles for a state to impose a trade control regime. It is within the power of the state sovereignty to impose even tighter control. In the long term, the market outside the US might respond to this demand and develop space components outside of the US.

Art Dula, representing the views of a start up company, firmly stated his opposition to tight trade control regimes. In his view, the US is currently interpreting the term "defence services" too extensively to encompass services that are freely available on the market to impose their licence regime. To obtain a US licence might need six months where in other countries it could be obtained within a day.

Chris Sallaberger replied that from an industry perspective one needs to work with the ITAR regulations. In order to obtain defence contracts in the US it might be a good option for a foreign company to create a US subsidiary – even though the communication between a company within the US and another outside the US, e.g. the non-US mother company of that subsidiary, might be restricted.

Second topic: The effects of Sarbanes Oxley (US Patriot Act 2002) on international investment impacting the space industry: who has been affected by it, clients, customers? If so how?

The panel then discussed briefly the effects of another United States federal law, the Sarbanes–Oxley Act of 2002 (Public Company Accounting Reform and Investor Protection Act of 2002) that was passed in response to a number of major corporate and accounting scandals. The Sarbanes Oxley Act requires companies to comply with extensive reporting obligations.

The panel pointed out that the effects on small companies are 16 times more burdensome than on publicly traded companies. The reporting duties are also strongly felt by the major shareholder of a company. Furthermore, the obligatory responsibility and liability of the senior management of a company has increased significantly.

According to John Purvis companies are encountering major compliance difficulties. To de-register companies from the stock exchange to avoid these reporting duties is however also made difficult.

Art Dula indicated that these rules divert energy from senior management since they are disproportionally concerned with the liability implications of their decisions. There is a move to create non-US companies in order to avoid the implications of the Sarbanes Oxley Act.

Third topic: There is talk of revisiting the Liability Convention. Would this be a good thing to do or better to leave it well enough alone?

Frans van der Dunk expressed his preference for revisiting but not revising the regime established by the 1972 Liability Convention (Convention on international liability for damages caused by space objects). This Convention establishes the principle of state liability regardless of the nationality of the (private) space operator. In his view it is important today to keep this principle of state liability at the same time as differentiating more as regards the application of the Convention' rules, above all concerning the definition of "launching state".

Clay Mowry reported that the US administration, above all the Federal Aviation Authority (FAA), wishes to remove the principle of state liability in favour of the liability of the private space operator. The industry is against such a move which would also affect negatively the young industry of personal space flight operators.

Art Dula disagreed with Clay Mowry as regards the benefits of the Convention. In his view, the obsoleteness of the Convention is demonstrated by the fact that no claim was ever brought under the Liability Convention. He declared that the market offered inexpensive third party liability insurance which would solve the liability problem. He proposed to treat the aircraft and spacecraft industries alike rather than differentiating between them. Therefore the US should implement corresponding legislation to override the rules of the Liability Convention.

Frans van der Dunk pointed out that national law could not supersede international law and that the airlines could not be compared to space flight operators. The FAA should adopt an "hands off" approach to stimulate the industry.

John Purvis recalled that launching satellites is an intensely international activity involving many different states (state of the launching company, of the launching territory, of the operator of the satellite, etc.) requiring international rules.

Art Dula insisted that federal national law might override treaty obligations and proposed to adapt the principles of the Warsaw Convention, limiting liability of air carriers toward passengers, to space flight operations. Such a new "Warsaw-like" convention should replace the Liability Convention.

Frans van der Dunk was against this option: the Warsaw Convention regulates the liability flowing from contracts between contractors and carriers towards private passengers. The Liability Convention on the other side deals with third party liability. Both type of conventions could thus exist alongside each other but could not replace each other. The air law convention corresponding to the Liability Convention would be the Rome Convention that deals with damages caused by an air crash to third parties. Unfortunately it has not been ratified by many States and would thus not be such a good example to follow.

Professor Joanne Gubrynowicz from the University of Mississippi School of Law pointed out the success of the Liability Convention: in her view it is functioning precisely because there has never been brought a claim. Therefore it should not be revised.

A member from the audience, John Crane, a retired US Navy Captain, inquired about an agency to establish traffic management for space. The panel agreed that an international regime, established by the rules of the International Telecommunications Union (ITU), is already in place. The ITU allots orbital slots for satellites and has agreed on rules for frequency co-ordination to protect users against mutual interference.

Fourth topic: New issues in space law – space debris, space property rights

The panel discussed the problem of space debris, i.e. the objects in orbit around Earth created by humans that no longer serve any useful purpose. Space debris has become a growing concern in recent years, since collisions at orbital velocities can be highly damaging to functioning satellites and can also produce even more space debris in the process.

The US, for example, has national rules in place to deal with this problem, the US Government Orbital Debris Mitigation Standard Practices. The declared US policy seeks to minimize the creation of orbital debris by government and non-government operations in space in order to preserve the space environment for future generations.

The panel pointed out that the commercial industry goes to great length to avoid space debris whereas not all governments are keen to comply with the international aim to avoid space debris.

Rachel Gates, a Dutch attorney in the audience, inquired about the emerging challenges for the space industries.

According to John Purvis, every country has its own challenges. Whereas in the US it is only possible to operate satellite services with an up-front licence, the legal situation outside the US is quite different. In Europe, for example, operators are quite free to emit satellite signals without the need for "landing rights" per se, once the ITU frequency co-ordination procedure has taken place. In Africa, on the other hand, satellite signals may only be emitted with "landing rights" and it is necessary to involve domestic operators. Satellite services in third countries may be subject to strict conditions.

Christian Sallaberger: there is a growing interest of private investors to develop space resource industry projects (e.g. mining of minerals on the moon). There exist however legal doubts about the ownership of such resources that have been mined with the financial help of private companies. To ensure the financial interest of investors these doubts have to be cleared to be able to develop such mining projects.

John Purvis pointed out that the Draft UNIDROIT Space Assets Protocol to the Unidroit Convention on International Interests in Mobile Equipment, adopted in November, 2001 in Cape Town, which intends to deal with the issue of securitisation of space investments has encountered serious problems and might never be agreed upon.

Frans van der Dunk stated the need for a regime that it is clear on this issue. He pointed out however that the 1984 Moon Treaty (the Agreement governing the activities of states on the Moon and other celestial bodies) dealing with the activities of states on the moon and other bodies, is very explicit on the principle of non-appropriation of the territory of the Moon by any State.

This principle of non-appropriation is also enshrined in the 1967 Outer Space Treaty (Treaty on Principles Governing the Activities of States in the Exploration and Use of Outer Space, including the Moon and Other Celestial Bodies) which governs the activities of states in space exploration.

Art Dula indicated that the Isle of Man has already a Space Resource Act in place. The ownership of minerals once exploited should be separated from the ownership of the territory from where it is exploited.

Frans Von Der Dunk talked on the suitability of the fishing analogy to the use of resources in Outer Space.

As the time for the event was up, Chris Stott closed the session.

Marie Helen Pichler – Die Ortega
pichler.law@gmx.at

Capitan Haya, 16 - 2A
28020 Madrid
Tel +34 91 555 2960
mobile +34 638 042 178

LATE BREAKING NEWS SESSION: PLANET DEFINITION
VALENCIA, SPAIN

IAC-06-LBN 05

The IAU Resolutions on Planet Definition

Lubos Perek,
Astronomical Institute
Czech Academy of Sciences
Prague, Czech Republic
perek@ig.cas.cz

Recent discoveries of Trans-Neptunian Objects, some larger than Pluto, triggered the IAU to form a working group on "Definition of a Planet" from its Division III members. The Working Group agreed on scientific issues but failed to reach an agreement on social and cultural issues, such as the status of Pluto. In order to include the broader aspects, the IAU formed a new **Planet Definition Committee** whose membership had backgrounds in history, science publishing, writing and education, as well as in planetary science.

Members of the Committee are:

Dr. Richard Binzel, Professor of Earth, Atmosphere, and Planetary Science at MIT and a specialist on asteroids and outer Solar System small bodies. He is a well known and respected educator and science writer.

Dr. André Brahic, Professor at Université Denis Diderot (Paris VII). He is Directeur d'Equipe Astropysique Interactions Multi-echelles He specializes in planetary rings and has co-discovered rings and arcs of Neptune. For the French speaking public, André Brahic is one of the best known popularizers of astronomy.

Dr. Owen Gingerich (Chair), Professor of Astronomy and History of Science. Emeritus at the Harvard-Smithsonian Center of Astrophysics, is an esteemed historian of astronomy with a broad perspective.

Dava Sabel, author of very successful books *Longitude*, *The Planets*, and *Galileo's Daughter*. She has a solid background in, and knowledge of, history of astronomy.

Dr. Junichi Watanabe, Associate Professor and Director of the Outreach Division of the National Astronomical Observatory of Japan. He is a solar system astronomer, highly appreciated in Japan. He has strong connections with amateur astronomers, science editors, schoolteachers and journalists.

Dr. Iwan Williams, Queen Mary, University of London, expert on dynamics and physical properties of Solar System objects. He is President of IAU Division III on Planetary System Science.

Dr. Catherine Cesarsky, Director General of the European Southern Observatory, President of the IAU. She brought to the Committee the perspective of the IAU and of astronomers at large.

The **terms of reference** of the Committee included:

- Discussing broader social implications of any new definition of a planet,
- Recommending a course of action that balances scientific facts with the need for social acceptance of any change,
- Addressing the status of Pluto and of newly discovered TNO's,
- Considering whether the current naming procedures have exacerbated the problem of definition and recommending possible need for revision,
- Attempting to frame resolutions to be put before the Prague General Assembly in August 2006 for possible adoption.

After long discussions at the IAU General Assembly, resolutions 5A, 5B, 6A, and 6B were put before the General Assembly. According to the statutes of the IAU, all present individual members had voting right. Their number was not officially established. It varied slightly around about 400. In the following the resolutions bearing on the definition of a planet are given as adopted or rejected by the vote:

IAU Resolution: Definition of a Planet in the Solar System

Contemporary observations are changing our understanding of planetary systems, and it is important that our nomenclature for objects reflects our current understanding. This applies., in particular, to the designation "planets". The word "planet" originally described "wanderers" that were known only as moving lights in the sky. Recent discoveries lead us to create a new definition, which we can make using currently available scientific information.

Resolution 5A

(adopted by a large majority of votes)

The IAU therefore resolves that planets and other bodies, except satellites, in our Solar System be defined into three distinct categories in the following way:

(1) A planet[1] is a celestial body that (a) is in orbit around the Sun, (b) has sufficient mass for its self-gravity to overcome the rigid body forces so that it assumes a hydrostatic equilibrium (nearly round) shape[2], and (c) has cleared the neighbourhood around its orbit.

(2) A "dwarf planet" is a celestial body that (a) is in orbit around the Sun, (b) has sufficient mass for its self-gravity to overcome the rigid body forces so that it assumes a hydrostatic equilibrium (nearly round) shape[2], and (c) has not cleared the nighbourhood around its orbit, and (d) is not a satellite.

(3) All other objects[3], except satellites, orbiting the Sun shall be referred to collectively as "Small Solar-System Bodies".

Resolution 5B

(rejected)

Insert the word "classical" before the word "planet" in Resolution 5A, Section 1.

---

[1] The eight planets are: Mercury, Venus, Earth, Mars, Jupiter, Saturn, Uranus, and Neptune.

[2] An IAU process will be established to assign borderline objects into either "dwarf planet" and other categories.

[3] These currently include most of the Solar System asteroids, most Trans-Neptunian Objects (TNOs), comets, and other small bodies.

Resolution 6A

(adopted by 237 votes yes, 157 no, 30 abstentions)

The IAU further resolves: Pluto is a "dwarf planet" by the above definition and is recognized as the prototype of a new category of Trans-Neptunian objects.

Resolution 6B

(rejected: 186 no, 183 yes)

The category in resolution 6A is to be called "plutonian objects".

Because of rejection of 6B, the name of the category in 6A will be selected by the standard IAU procedure.

The voting was introduced and managed with high competence and aplomb by Ms Jocelyn Bell Burnell, assisted by the IAU officers and by members of the Planet Definition Committee. All questions raised by the audience were satisfactorily answered. Some questions concerning possible future discoveries, of course, remain. As Ms Bell Burnell said, when we come to it, we shall solve it.

Briefly stated, the changes were necessary. Pluto remains a dwarf planet and becomes a prototype of a new category of objects. Its discovery in 1930 was a glorious achievement because it was made 75 years before its due time.

57TH INTERNATIONAL ASTRONAUTICAL CONGRESS
LATE BREAKING NEWS: PLANET DEFINITION

Legal Implications of the IAU Resolutions on Planet Definition: Some Preliminary Observations

Leslie I. Tennen, Attorney at Law
Law Offices of Sterns and Tennen, Phoenix, Arizona, U.S.A.
Former Commissioner, Arizona Space Commission, Member IISL, IAA

ABSTRACT

This paper will consider the legal aspects of the IAU Resolutions on Planet Definition, paying particular attention to the Outer Space Treaty of 1967 and the Moon Agreement, as well as the COSPAR planetary protection policies. Pertinent terminology within legal texts will be examined, including relevant United Nations General Assembly Resolutions. In addition, the legal significance of the terms "planet," "dwarf planet," and "small solar system bodies" will be explored, together with the binding nature *vel non* of resolutions adopted by scientific bodies.

INTRODUCTION

The International Astronomical Union (IAU) made headlines in August, 2006, when it resolved to remove Pluto from the classification of a "planet." This reclassification was the result of the adoption of new definitions for "planet," "dwarf planet," and "small solar system bodies." This action by the IAU generated substantial public interest, as it changed what had been the prevailing scientific as well as common and popular knowledge for the past 70 years, namely, that there were 9 planets orbiting our sun. But was this a revolutionary development, or has the significance of the IAU resolutions been overestimated? More specifically, what is the legal significance of the scientific definitions of "planet," "dwarf planet," and "small solar system bodies?"

DISCUSSION

The resolutions adopted by the IAU are as follows:

> **Resolution 5A**
>
> The IAU . . . resolves that planets and other bodies, except satellites, in our Solar system be defined into three distinct categories in the following way:
>
> (1) A planet is a celestial body that (a) is in orbit around the Sun, (b) has sufficient mass for its self-gravity to over come rigid body forces so that it assumes a hydrostatic equilibrium (nearly round) shape, and (c) has cleared the neighborhood around its orbit.
>
> (2) A "dwarf planet" is a celestial body that (a) is in orbit around the Sun, (b) has sufficient mass for its self-gravity to overcome rigid body forces so that it assumes a

> hydrostatic equilibrium (nearly round) shape, (c) has not cleared the neighborhood around its orbit, and (d) is not a satellite.
>
> (3) All other objects, except satellites, orbiting the Sun shall be referred to collectively as "Small Solar System Bodies."
>
> **Resolution 6A**
>
> The IAU further resolves: Pluto is a "dwarf planet" by the above definition and is recognized as the prototype of a new class of Trans-Neptunian objects.

The IAU referred to another category of celestial bodies, that of "Trans-Neptunian objects." Although not specifically defined in the resolutions, "Trans-Neptunian objects" appear to include dwarf planets and small solar system bodies with at least part of their orbit beyond the orbit of Neptune. The question is presented, how do these IAU definitions compare and comport with the applicable *corpus juris spatialis*?

The international legal community long has considered natural space objects, but has utilized substantially different terminology than the IAU. In December, 1961, the United Nations General Assembly unanimously adopted Resolution 1721(XVI)A, which provided, in pertinent part

> (a) International law, including the Charter of the United Nations, applies to outer space and celestial bodies;
>
> (b) Outer space and celestial bodies are free for exploration and use by all States in conformity with international law and are not subject to national appropriation

UNGA Resolution 1721 established a precedent for the utilization of the term "celestial bodies" in the legal regulation of outer space. The Outer Space Treaty of 1967 continued this precedent, incorporating the concept into the phraseology of "outer space, including the Moon and other celestial bodies," which appears in the title of the instrument as well as in numerous articles throughout the text.

This formulation of "outer space, including the Moon and other celestial bodies" has been incorporated into subsequent legal texts, including the Moon Agreement of 1979, and UNGA Resolution 51/122 in 1996. Moreover, the phrase has not been revised in the past 40 years, although article 1.2 of the Moon Agreement provides that references to the Moon include orbits around and trajectories to the body.

Conspicuously absent from both the Outer Space Treaty and the Moon Agreement are any references to "planets." Similarly, these international instruments do not mention "dwarf planets," "small solar system bodies," or "Trans-Neptunian objects." The *corpus juris spatialis* expressly applies to the activities of states concerning "celestial bodies," but that term is not specifically defined in the legal texts. Some guidance as to what constitutes a celestial body can be found in the plain language of "the Moon and other celestial bodies," which indicates that the Moon itself is a celestial body.

Fasan has assembled a compilation of efforts by legal authors to define what constitutes a celestial body, with opinions variously including or excluding the sun, and comets, asteroids, and other "planet-like subsidiaries." Nevertheless, there was no dissent noted from the inclusion of planetary bodies and their satellites within the meaning of celestial bodies. Even assuming arguendo that some comets, asteroids or other "planet-like subsidiaries" are not celestial bodies, it seems clear that Pluto, and its satellites, are uniformly considered to be celestial bodies, notwithstanding any scientific definition of "planet" or "dwarf planet." Indeed, the IAU resolutions themselves expressly consider "planets" and "dwarf planets" to be celestial bodies.

To the extent the international scientific community defines terms which are not expressly set forth or unquestionably synonymous with words or phrases contained within treaties and other international agreements, such definitions may not have binding legal effect. However, these definitions may play a crucial role in scientific self-regulation. That is, the actions of scientific governing bodies may be fully applicable to the activities of their constituent members, and compliance may be necessary for the fulfillment of international obligations, both treaty and otherwise. This presupposes, however, that the actions of the governing body were validly adopted in conformity with the laws and regulations of appropriate states, as well as with the internal policies, practices, and governing documents of the adopting organization.

The situation may be quite different if the scientific community was to adopt a resolution which was in direct conflict with an international legal text, for example, by a definition of "celestial body" which excluded Pluto, and thereby removed that body from the protections of the *corpus juris spatialis*. In such a case, from a strictly legal perspective, the treaty or other international agreement would take precedence over scientific self-regulation. Barring such a direct conflict, specific scientific definitions could be considered to be complementary to the more general terminology of the space treaties. Nevertheless, the definitions adopted by one scientific governing body are not necessarily binding on third parties or other scientific organizations.

A case in point concerns the COSPAR planetary protection policy. This scientifically defined policy is intended to protect pristine celestial environments from biological contamination caused by earth-based interplanetary spacecraft, in compliance with international treaty commitments. Pursuant to the current formulation of the COSPAR policy, varying levels of planetary protection are to be implemented, ranging from essentially none, to complete sterilization of spacecraft, depending generally upon the type of mission and target body combination. Significantly, and despite the nomenclature, the planetary protection policy is not restricted to "planets," and the mission type/target body combinations are not differentiated by whether or not the target body is a "planet." Rather, the COSPAR policy extends to both planets and their moons, and is based upon assessments of whether or not the target body is of interest in the search for life. Thus, the applicability of the planetary protection policy to Pluto is not dependent upon its classification as a planet, dwarf planet, or Trans-Neptunian object.

References

IAU Resolutions 5A, 6A, text reproduced in Dissertatio cum Nuntio Sidereo III, August 24, 2006, IAU Congress newspaper, **www.astronomy2006.com/ga-newspaper.php**

UNGA Resolution 1721 (XVI) A, *International Co-operation in the Peaceful Uses of Outer Space,* December 21, 1961

UNGA Resolution 51/122, *Declaration on International Cooperation in the Exploration and Use of Outer Space for the Benefit and in the Interests of All States, Taking into Account the Needs of Developing Countries*, December 13, 1996

Treaty on Principles Governing the Activities of States in the Exploration and Use of Outer Space, Including the Moon and Other Celestial Bodies, *opened for signature* January 27, 1967, 18 U.S.T. 2410, T.I.A.S. No. 6347, 610 U.N.T.S. 205, *text reproduced in* United Nations Treaties and Principles on Outer Space 3 (2002)

Treaty on Principles Governing the Activities of States on the Moon and Other Celestial Bodies, *entered into force* July 11, 1984, *text reprinted in* United Nations Treaties and Principles on Outer Space 27 (2002); *and* 18 I.L.M. 1434 (1979)

COSPAR Planetary Protection Policy, **http://www.cosparhq.org/scistr/PPPolicy.htm**

Fasan, *Asteroids and Other Celestial Bodies - Some Legal Differences*, 26 Journal of Space Law 33 (1998)

Sterns and Tennen, *The Future of Planetary Protection: Is There Reason For Optimism?*, IAF Paper No. IAC-06-E6[1].5 (2006)

IISL-ECSL SPACE LAW SYMPOSIUM 2006 HELD ON THE OCCASION OF THE 45TH SESSION OF THE LEGAL SUBCOMMITTEE OF UNCOPUOS, VIENNA, AUSTRIA

IISL/ECSL Space Law Symposium 2006: "Legal Aspects of Disaster Management and the Contribution of the Law of Outer Space"

Report by Atsuyo Ito

The annual IISL/ECSL space law symposium was held on the occasion of the 45th Session of the Legal Subcommittee of the United Nations Committee on the Peaceful Uses of Outer Space on Monday, 3 April 2006 in Vienna, Austria. **Ambassador Peter Jankowitsch**, Chairman of the Advisory Board of the Austrian Aeronautics and Space Agency and Past Chair of COPUOS, chaired the Symposium. **Sergei Negoda** of the UN Office of Outer Space Affairs served as rapporteur, and IISL Secretary **Tanja Masson-Zwaan** had coordinated the programme.

The 2006 IISL/ECSL symposium concerned Legal Aspects of Disaster Management, a very topical and significant issue, in view of the many disasters happening around the globe each year and the increasing contribution by use of space technology in response to disasters.

The symposium commenced by words of welcome given by Ambassador Peter Jankowitsch followed by four speakers speaking about different topics relating to the legal aspects of disaster management.

Prof. Joanne Gabrynowicz of the National Remote Sensing and Space Law Center of the University of Mississippi, USA spoke about "*Disasters Charter: introduction, initial issues and experiences*". She gave a comprehensive overview of the International Charter on Space and Major Disasters and on the extensive international cooperation to provide satellite data to countries affected by disasters. She first explained the background of the Charter, reviewed its mechanisms and gave definitions of some of the important terms under the Disaster Charter. She then addressed some of the preliminary issues such as cost, type of data provided, and scope of activation. As regards cost, she pointed out that they are considerable, and are higher for some participants than for others. Budget impacts at agency or departmental level, not at national level. It is important to balance agencies' resources and recipients' needs.

She noted that challenges faced by the Charter are on-going and future operational financing, capacity building and evolving relationships and agreements among and between space agencies and other actors. The Disaster Charter is non-binding, however, Prof. Gabrynowicz noted that it might be potentially binding over time if it is confirmed by *opinio juris* and state practice. She observed that new trends would see new forms of international relations, and new institutions could emerge as alternatives to classical legal agreements. As informality becomes more effective, such informal practice will become more and more recognized as authoritative party behaviour. The Disaster Charter serves as a network for the informal exchange of information between different entities dedicated to disaster management. Prof. Gabrynowicz concluded her presentation with the following practical observations:

- Definitional differences exist between the Charter and the UN Remote Sensing Principles but common features do as well and they reinforce one another
- Reality is that decisions of individual lower level government employees and decision-makers impact departmental or agency, not large, national budgets
- The Charter is working.

Prof. Ray Harris of the Department of Geography, University College London, UK, gave an insightful presentation on "*Challenges of Access to Earth Observation for Disaster Management*". He started by showing some satellite images capturing disasters and contended that technology is not the problem but the issue is how we use the information. He mentioned the UN principles on Remote Sensing briefly and then introduced the Data Policy Assessment for GMES (DPAG), an EU project that is a part of Global Monitoring for Environment and Security (GMES), and highlighted the five major concerns with respect to access to data:

- Control over data and information in terms of legal obligation and licenses
- Accessibility of data such as map information and standards and metadata
- European spatial data infrastructure as in INSPIRE progress
- Costs and funding such as pricing of data and whether data is regarded as private or public good
- Archiving issues such as securing long term stewardship beyond a research project life time, who takes responsibility of archiving, lack of legal basis of archiving in Europe

Prof. Harris then showed how map scale of the data in different countries varies to a great extent. Then, he gave recommendations in three main components, namely,

1. control of data and information,
2. quality approval and
3. data dissemination improvements.

- Encryption/ decryption could be used as a technical means of achieving control of data and information
- Decryption keys could be used in terms of humanitarian crisis,
- GMES partnership should use appropriate mechanisms to protect the quality of data and products for instance as a brand rather than as a burden
- Licenses and intellectual property rights are increasingly important.

Lastly, he mentioned some ethical dimensions: questions included who controls the EO data and access to the data, whether society is served by more or less transparency of information as well as privacy laws of individuals. He concluded his presentation by stating that EO data are collected extensively and the key issue is that of access. Access is not just technical but revolves around policies of access.

Prof. Sergio Marchisio, Director of the Institute for International Legal Studies of the National Research Council, Italy, spoke about "*Legal Aspects of Disaster Management; European efforts including the GMES programme*". He gave an overview of the GMES, a joint ESA/EU initiative by talking about the background and legal framework of GMES, with a data policy issue followed by remarks on disaster management from the viewpoint of space law. He noted that Europe has successfully developed and launched advanced observation systems however; the organisations that promote public welfare have been forced to rely on fragmented and poorly presented information. To improve the European capacity in this field, the proposal for GMES emerged in 1998.

A challenge for GMES is to gather relevant data and provide services, which will enable decision-makers to better anticipate or integrate crisis situations relating to the management of the environment, such as natural and human-made disasters.

GMES services can add value by combining different sources, packaging them in a useful way in a fully integrated manner. It is to support implementation of European policy and it is particularly useful for disaster management.

He noted that the diversity of data that the GMES services require and produce will benefit from the development of a data policy. This may vary according to the domains of services provided, but will need to find a balance between "non-discriminatory access", economic viability and the necessary incentives for private service providers to invest in the development of such capacity. An open access to the environmental information for the benefit of citizens should be freely available through GMES.

Then Prof. Marchisio gave some general remarks concerning disaster management from the space law perspective. He mentioned the contribution from the Disaster Charter as a first international instrument to respond to disasters and implementation of Principle XI of the 1986 UN Principles on Remote Sensing, as well as Principle 18 of the UN Declaration on environment and development adopted at Rio de Janeiro in 1992.

Prof. Marchisio concluded that the Indian ocean tsunami has promoted reflection on remote sensing data pricing policy, shifting toward no charge in case of major disasters and that seems to be the most important element to be taken into account, from the legal point of view, in assessing more recent initiatives.

Finally, **Ms. Masami Onoda,** of Kyoto University, Japan, spoke about "*Legal and Policy Aspects of Disaster Management Support from Space in Asia*". She presented the latest Japanese contribution to the Disaster Charter, showing an image from the recently launched ALOS of JAXA following a landslide in Leyte

Island, Philippines. Then, she showed activities for disaster management apart from the Disaster Charter by introducing the disaster management system in the Asia-Pacific Region, "Sentinel Asia". Then, she moved on to speak about the legal aspects of disaster management by pointing out the lack of a comprehensive treaty or legal framework on natural disasters. She expressed the view that international human rights law, humanitarian law and refugee law serve as a basis of the Disaster Charter or the UN Remote Sensing Principles.

Then, she highlighted significant data policy issues, such as to what extent should humanitarian assistance be provided through provision of EO data particularly with respect to balance with cost and technical capability, the balance between open access to data and data protection as well as responsibility arising from data flaws.

She lastly raised the following questions:

- What is the status of international law in relation to natural disasters?
- Are there any general principles or trends?
- What is the relation between disaster monitoring and supervisory techniques at the level of international law?

She concluded her presentation by observing that a first step should be to identify the international obligations with respect to disaster management and to clarify the procedures, in coordination with humanitarian agencies, at the same time addressing the policy issues in order to facilitate the exchange of views between humanitarian agencies and policy makers in order to establish an adequate framework.

Following the presentation of the four speakers, many delegations expressed their views and took part in the discussion.

One delegate mentioned the UN Watercourse Convention, and its relevant provision on disasters.

The issue as to how to distinguish remote sensing data for normal purposes or for disaster management purposes was also mentioned.

Another delegate mentioned the impact of environmental issues, such as climate change and biodiversity loss, on inducing disasters in the mid-long term. Universal mechanisms to protect the planet are needed and space activities can play an important role. As many nations have minimal capacity to respond to disasters, efforts have to be made to include all countries in disaster management.

Some delegates expressed the view that the possible contribution of telecommunications to disaster management should not be forgotten, particularly the Tampere Convention on the Provision of Telecom resources for Disaster Management and Relief Operations and the ITU text setting a concrete example as to how to cope with disasters though international cooperation.

Prof. Vladimír Kopal, Vice-President of IISL, then gave some concluding remarks. He thanked the speakers and gave a summary of the ideas and opinions expressed by the four presenters. He noted that the questions raised by the delegates merit further consideration. **Ambassador Jankowitsch** then closed the symposium and invited all delegates to a reception hosted by IISL and ECSL.

LEGAL AND POLICY ASPECTS OF DISASTER MANGAGEMENT SUPPORT IN ASIA

IISL and ESCL Space Law Symposium 2006
Vienna, April 2006

Masami Onoda
Research Fellow, Japan Society for the Promotion of Science
Graduate School of Global Environmental Studies, Kyoto University
Kyoto, JAPAN

1. Introduction

The International Charter "Space and Major Disasters[1]", initially announced at the 1999 UNISPACE III Conference, has now become a worldwide initiative. Asian countries participate as well, the Indian Space Research Organization (ISRO) joining the Charter in 2001, and the Japan Aerospace Exploration Agency (JAXA) in 2005.

The effort to coordinate space resources is not new in the field of Earth observation. The Committee on Earth Observation Satellites took the challenge up as early as in the 1980s, and a number of attempts have been made in the United Nations, and other multilateral and bilateral forums. Not only within the space community, but also local authorities who actually deal with the disaster management operations need to be involved in developing such a mechanism. Although the space agencies would willingly provide data to demonstrate the usefulness of their space resources, this motivation is not always shared by the user.

This situation is underlined by the fact that, unlike in the field of environmental monitoring, there is no multilateral legal instrument that comprehensively calls for the need of disaster relief nor monitoring, much less for space resources coordination for this purpose[2]. It seems to be that in the field of space-based disaster management support, the activity is still in the stage of voluntary action by space agencies as demonstration efforts.

With such a background, the International Charter can be regarded as an initial attempt of a multilateral framework – taking the form of a voluntary agreement between space agencies – for demonstrating the use of satellite data for disaster management support. At the regional level in Asia, there is also an emerging initiative for utilization of satellite data for Asian countries. In order to consider the present situation of disaster management support from space in Asia, this paper will review the situation in Japan concerning the International Charter, and then introduce an emerging initiative in the Asian region for disaster management, "Sentinel Asia". We will further consider these activities in light of international law, and discuss some data policy issues.

2. Japan and the International Charter

The International Charter, established in 2002, is a framework to promote contributions from space organizations to help areas affected by disasters by providing Earth observation satellite data voluntarily, based on the best efforts of the member organizations. The Parties to the International Charter (space agencies) and "associated bodies"[3] organize the overall cooperation. The activities are coordinated by the Board of representatives from each Party and an Executive Secretariat. No financial exchange takes place among participating organizations.

JAXA joined the International Charter on the occasion of the Third Earth Observation Summit (Brussels, February 16, 2005), with the purpose of promoting contribution to disaster management by Earth observation satellites[4]. It was six years after the initial launch of the International Charter in 1999, a period when Japan did not possess its own satellite in orbit, and there was less incentive to join the Charter until the launch of the "Daichi" (the Advanced Land Observing Satellite (ALOS)) came reasonably in sight. Just after its successful launch in January 2006, Daichi acquired images of the Leyte Island in the Republic of the Philippines, where a huge landslide occurred on February 17. The images were observed and taken by the PALSAR instrument onboard Daichi around 10:50 a.m. February 24 (JST). JAXA provided the images to the International Charter, and to the Asian Disaster Reduction Center (ADRC) – as part of the Asian regional initiative to be described in the next section.

Since this was before the start of operational distribution of ALOS satellite data, the provision of these images was a voluntary act by JAXA, i.e. without official request from the International Charter. This, together with the fact that JAXA joined the Charter a year before ALOS launch, suggests that the International Charter is functioning as an international framework for ALOS data distribution for disaster management support. Such a framework would spare the individual space agencies the work to set up separate systems for this purpose, thus enhancing their capability to work with local authorities worldwide.

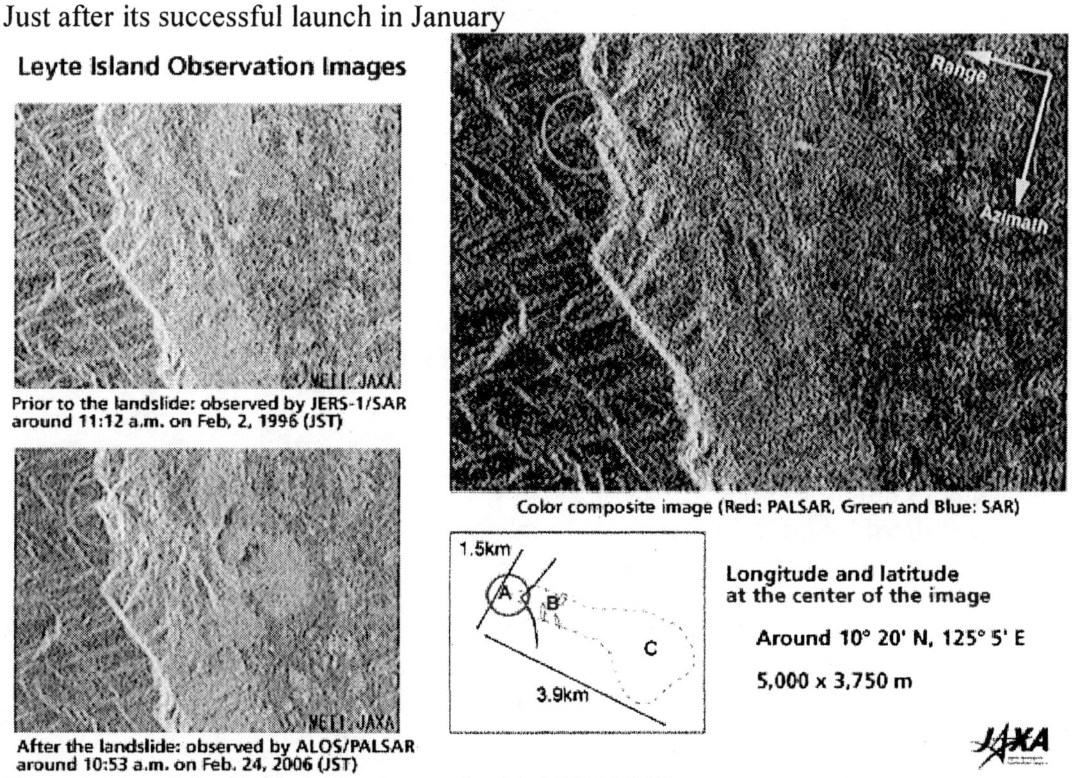

Figure 1: Leyte Island Observation Images by ALOS/PALSAR
Source: JAXA press release *at* http://www.jaxa.jp/press/2006/02/20060225_daichi_e.html

3. "Sentinel Asia"[5]

As the ALOS satellite will become operational in autumn 2006 timeframe, the data is to be utilized for the benefit of Asian countries. For this purpose, there is an ongoing project for developing a disaster management system called "Sentinel-Asia".

"Sentinel Asia" is a project to establish a network using data acquired from satellites (ALOS and MODIS onboard NASA's Terra satellite) for disaster management. The First Joint Project Team Meeting for establishing this system was held in February 2006, in Vietnam. The meeting was organized by JAXA in corporation with the Vietnamese Academy of Science and Technology (VAST), and was supported by the UN-Economic and Social Commission for Asia and the Pacific (UN-ESCAP). 70 participants from 34 agencies of 18 countries, and 4 international organizations attended the meeting to discuss the implementation plan of the "Sentinel-Asia". This was the first step for establishing a "disaster management system in the Asia-Pacific Region", which was agreed upon at the 12th Asia-Pacific Regional Space Agency Forum (APRSAF-12) of October 2005.

In this system, the space agencies, the international community, disaster related organizations, and universities will cooperate in constructing an information-sharing platform to extract and share disaster information. The vision for "Sentinel Asia" is that it will be a fundamental service distributing, in near real-time where possible, disaster-related data products / images in the Asia-Pacific region. An information-sharing platform based on the Internet and Geographic Information System, "Digital Asia", will be utilized for this purpose. Member organizations will also cooperate in capacity building, including disaster status analyses, and training and education. At the first meeting, participants agreed on the concept and basic structure of "Sentinel Asia", which consists of three nodes: Data Provider Node; Research and Training Node; and Local Service Provider Node. To promote Sentinel Asia, a Joint Project Team (JPT) was organized. JPT is open to all the APRSAF member countries, disaster related organizations and regional or international organizations who wish to participate in disaster information sharing activities.

The framework of ALOS data distribution through "Sentinel Asia" project is as follows:

- Once disaster occurs in Asian countries, request of image and data in damaged area is sent to the ADRC (Asian Disaster Reduction Center);
- ADRC accepts such order from Member Countries and notifies JAXA;
- JAXA develops a plan of Action, and JAXA acquires image and data of the damaged area by ALOS and distributes those image and data to the Asian countries through ADRC using communication satellites; and/or JAXA notifies Partner Agencies to support Asian countries.

Compared to the efforts of the International Charter, which is essentially a global initiative of major space agencies, this system is more focused and perhaps manageable, in terms of membership and satellite systems involved. If successful, the realization of such a framework through partnership among regional organizations would facilitate and expand the use of space technology for disaster monitoring in Asian countries[6]. However, the limited space resources at the regional level may imply less time frequency, a crucial factor for disaster monitoring. Thus, the outcomes at both the global and regional levels should be taken into consideration in developing disaster management support systems in the future.

4. International Law and Data Policy Issues

4.1 Obligations under international law

When we look at the international legal basis for such activities, there is a lack of comprehensive treaty or legal framework on natural disasters[7]. For bilateral treaties, there are agreements on specific circumstances or individual disaster response activities, early-warning notification and information sharing, and mutual assistance treaties covering most of central Europe. There are also a limited number of multilateral Treaties, such as the Convention on Assistance in the Case of a Nuclear Accident or Radiological Emergency (1986)[8], and a recent development could be that the Tampere Convention on the Provision of Telecommunication Resources for Disaster Mitigation and Relief Operations (1998) entered into force in 2005[9]. This Convention also contains detailed provisions pertaining to the broader activities of disaster response including offers and requests, privileges and immunities facilities, costs and coordination in the field of emergency telecommunications, including satellite telecommunications. In addition, it also extends some of these provisions to non-governmental organizations and non-state entities, thus extending the cope beyond the States themselves. While remaining in the filed of telecommunications, the Tampere Convention calls for "the sharing of information about natural hazards, health hazards and disasters among the States Parties and with other States, non-State entities and intergovernmental organizations, and the dissemination of such information to the public, particularly to at-risk communities"[10]. This development in the field of multilateral legal instrument for disaster management suggests the need for international coordination of information in the event of disasters.

In general, international human rights law, humanitarian law and refugee law provide the underlying principles for the objectives of the International Charter[11]. Such principles are applicable to space activities under the provisions of Article III of the Outer Space Treaty[12], which states as follows:

> "States Party to the Treaty shall carry on activities in the exploration and use of outer space [...] in accordance with international law, including the Charter of the United Nations, in the interest of maintaining international peace and security and promoting international cooperation and understanding".

This could be understood as establishing the basis for Principle XI of the UN Remote Sensing Principles[13], which states as follows:

> "Remote Sensing shall promote the protection of mankind form natural disasters. To this end, States participating in RS activities that have identified processed data and analysed information in their possession that may be useful to States affected by natural disasters, or likely to be affected by impending natural disasters, shall transmit such data and information to States concerned as promptly as possible."

However, with the ambiguity of the international legal obligations of States in relation to space-based disaster management support, unlike multilateral treaty frameworks on human rights or environmental law, there is a lack of a multilateral international institution for controlling State obligations in this field. The activities through the International Charter, as well as projects such as "Sentinel Asia", remain to be on a best-effort basis cooperation by participating countries. In order to know whether this is a developing process or not, further observation on States' practice and the development of international law is necessary.

4.2 Data policy issues

It should be worthwhile to point out a few data policy issues at this stage. There are three main issues: balance between the space agencies' rendering support and bearing its cost; data rights protection (commercial entities involvement); and responsibility and liability arising from the use of data.

Firstly, to what extent should States provide humanitarian assistance through provision of Earth observation data? In other words, how could the balance between humanitarian assistance and cost be maintained? There is a need to identify the various phases of warning, rescue, refuge, hazard, mitigation, and prevention and the role of Earth observation satellite data, and to agree on setting a line, if necessary, taking into account the financial and technical capabilities.

Secondly, open access to data often conflicts with data rights protection. If any form of commercial distribution of the same satellite data is to be involved, there is a need to carefully determine the terms of conditions of data use. Especially, if the data is to be open to the public, there is a need of government support or compensation to the commercial entity involved. The satellites listed for the International Charter are government-owned and partly commercialized in their data distribution activities in many cases. The same could be said with the case of ALOS data used in Sentinel Asia. While it is generally welcome to space agencies that their data is utilized for public purposes, they should be careful not to deprive the opportunities of the commercial distributor in expanding the role of public purpose data distribution. One solution to this is the government to purchase data from the distributor to provide data to the international framework, and to agree on data rights conditions with the commercial entity. Rather than having the space agency directly provide the data, this would create the incentive for private companies to enhance their capabilities in data applications, which often exceeds the role and capability of space agencies. This is an issue common in any other fields of Earth observation as well. It is crucial for government space agencies to study and determine the optimal policy for public and private relations in satellite data distribution.

Finally, there is the issue of responsibility and liability in case of data flaws, or misuse or misinterpretation in applying satellite data to practical disaster relief implementations. While the members of the International Charter agree to waive any liability under Article 5.4 of the Charter, for Earth observation activities in general, the liability regime applicable to the use of Earth observation data in the data application phase remains unclear. Therefore, members participating in regional frameworks such as "Sentinel Asia" would have to establish a liability regime, and extend it to the participating local authorities as necessary. For the future development of satellite data utilization, particularly in the field of disaster management support, there is a need to establish an unambiguous legal basis for responsibility and liability.

The current situation suggests that much remains to be clarified in the legal and policy domain for Earth observation data use in disaster management support. We may see this as a reflection of the premature status of satellite data utilization in this field. As States and other actors accumulate more practice, and with further studies into these issues, we may well expect that the establishment of agreed policy and legal framework would contribute to the future utilization of space resources in this field.

5. Conclusion

International initiatives for promoting the use of satellite data for disaster management support are developing at the global level through the International Charter, and at the regional level in Asia, a project "Sentinel Asia" has been initiated with the participation of a number of Asian countries. However, the status of international law in relation to natural disasters, the general principles or trends, and relevance to space activities are yet to be established. It seems too early to discuss the role of disaster management support from space in terms of international obligations.

Nevertheless, as these activities develop, various issues regarding the legal status and policy issues arise. It is important to identify the underlying international obligations and to clarify the procedures, in close coordination with humanitarian/disaster related agencies. At the same time, it is essential to address the policy issues in order to establish a working framework. In this way, through accumulation of successful practices, it should be possible to emerge from the space agencies' demonstration phase to constructing a truly effective framework for applying satellite data to the needs of disaster management.

---

[1] Charter On Cooperation To Achieve The Coordinated Use Of Space Facilities In The Event Of Natural Or Technological Disasters, *available at* http://www.disasterscharter.org/charter_e.html (last visited December 22, 2006) [hereinafter International Charter].

[2] On the other hand, in certain areas in environmental law there are obligations of States to cooperate in environmental monitoring: See Masami Onoda, *Satellite Earth Observation As Systematic Observation in Multilateral Environmental Treaties*, 31 Journal of Space Law 339-411 (2005).

[3] International Charter, *supra* note 1, at Art. 1 and 5.2.

[4] Based on a press release by JAXA on February 10, *at* http://www.jaxa.jp/press/2005/02/20050210_disasterscherter_j.html (last visited January 3, 2007) (only in Japanese).

[5] See Sentinel Asia *website at* http://dmss.tksc.jaxa.jp/sentinel/index.php (last visited January 7, 2007).

[6] See JAXA press release *at* http://www.jaxa.jp/press/2006/03/20060301_sac_sentinel_j.html (last visited January 7, 2007) (only in Japanese).

[7] See International Federation of Red Cross and Red Crescent Societies, *International Disaster Response Law: A Preliminary Overview and Analysis of Existing Treaty Law,* Jan. 2003, *available at* http://www.ifrc.org/what/disasters/idrl/research.asp (last visited January 7, 2007).

[8] Convention on Assistance in the Case of a Nuclear Accident or Radiological Emergency, Sept. 26, 1986, 1457 UNTS 133.

[9] Tampere Convention on the Provision of Telecommunication Resources for Disaster Mitigation and Relief Operations, ICET-98, (June, 18, 1998).

[10] Id., Art. 3.2.

[11] See "Humanitarian Charter" Principles *at* www.sphereproject.org/ (last visited January 7, 2007).

The Humanitarian Charter expresses agencies' commitment to these principles, based on agencies' appreciation of their own ethical obligations, and reflects the rights and duties enshrined in international law in respect of which states and other parties have established obligations: The right to life with dignity, the distinction between combatants and non-combatants, the principle of non-refoulement.

[12] Treaty on Principles Governing the Activities of States in the Exploration and Use of Outer Space, including the Moon and Other Celestial Bodies, Jan. 1, 1967, 610 U.N.T.S. 2005 [hereinafter Outer Space Treaty].

[13] Principles Relating to Remote Sensing of the Earth from Space, G.A. Res. 41/65, Annex, U.N. Doc. A/RES/41/65/Annex (Dec. 3, 1986).

Legal Aspects of Disaster Management and the Contribution of the Law of Outer Space
SPACE LAW SYMPOSIUM - Vienna, 3 April 2006

Legal Aspects of Disaster Management: European Efforts Including GMES

Sergio Marchisio

University of Rome La Sapienza
Institute for International Legal Studies – National Research Council - Italy
sergio.marchisio@isgi.cnr.it

1. I have divided my intervention in two parts: the first one deals with the European efforts in disaster management, namely the GMES joint Initiative ESA/EU; the second contains some general remarks concerning disaster management from the space law perspective. Europe has successfully developed and launched advanced Earth observations systems, providing a comprehensive set of operational space missions with permanent and continuous observing capabilities. Unfortunately, organisations that promote public welfare are often forced to rely on fragmented and poorly presented information. To improve the European capacity in this field, the Global Monitoring for Environment and Security (GMES) was foreseen since 1998 with the Baveno Manifest. Following official documents "It represents in simple terms a concerted effort to bring data and information providers together with users, so they can better understand each other and agree on how to make environmental and security-related information available to people who need it". A challenge for GMES is to gather relevant data and provide services which will enable decision-makers to better anticipate or integrate crisis situations relating to the management of the environment, such as natural and human made disasters.

After Galileo, the GMES has became the second European Union's "flagship" in space policy. GMES is an EU-led initiative, in which the European Commission will manage related actions for identifying and developing services and the European Space Agency (ESA) will manage the implementation of the space segment. In this sense, GMES falls within the European model of cooperation in the space field. This model is the result of more than thirty years of joint efforts among European States through the ESA and the European Community (EC). While the ESA, in conformity with the Paris Convention of 1975, has been, and still is responsible for developing a long-term European space policy and carrying out a European space programme, the EC, acting as the first pillar of the EU, has given ground to an "extended" European space policy, as reflected in the European Commission's White Paper of 2003. The latter covers the transitional period (2004-2007) envisaged until the (potential) entry into force of the Treaty establishing a Constitution for Europe. This transitional period is ruled out by the EC/ESA Framework Agreement concluded on November 25, 2003 as a key for the successful implementation of the first phase.

Meanwhile, the draft Constitution for Europe was concluded. The main novelty is that space appears among the EU powers (or competencies) shared with member States, paving the way towards a European space policy (ESP) as a "common" policy governed by the EU legal order. However, this treaty has not yet entered into force.

For this reason, the current stage continues to be characterized by the legal framework for the transitional period. Space is envisaged b the EU as a "relevant technology" to support the implementation of the existing EC policies (transport, trans national networks, industry, research and development) with a multiplicity of legal basis, which enable the EC to call upon to space as a technology to support their implementation.

Accordingly, the ESA-EU relations are currently regulated by the Framework Agreement, which covers all cooperation, relations and interaction of the ESA with the EU and is in course of implementation . The Framework Agreement, which covers a period of cooperation of four years and can be renewed for another period, is seen as a key to the implementation of the first phase referred to in the White Paper. Eight specific fields of cooperation are identified: sciences, technology, earth observation, navigation, communications by satellite, human space flight and microgravity, launchers and spectrum policy related to space.

The Framework Agreement prepared the legal basis for the cooperation between the ESA and the EU, namely in the form of "joint Initiatives", provided for by Article 5. These initiatives have taken different forms, such as Galileo and the GMES.

2. This being the current legal framework of the ESA/EU space related activities, it is worth note to recall that the GMES was endorsed by the ESA and the EU Councils in 2001. In its Communication to the EU Gotheborg Summit, the European Commission called for establishing by 2008 a European capacity for Global Monitoring for Environment and Security (GMES) to gather, interpret and use data and information in support of sustainable development policies. An exploratory initial period, undertaken jointly by the EC and the ESA, took place between 2001 and 2003. It was established that the GMES had to support several EU objectives and policy domains, namely Europe's environmental commitments, within the EU territory and globally, and the Common Foreign and Security Policy, including the European Security and Defence Policy.

Later on, in the Communication of the European Commission to the Council and the European Parliament of 2004, was included a summary of the main actions to be undertaken from 2004 to 2008. This communication – entitled "From concept to Reality"- planned to introduce the first three earth observation services: *emergency management*, land monitoring and marine environment.

The GMES initiative has now reached a stage of maturity where it can progress to its development and implementation phase. This phase coincides with the development of the Galileo satellite-based infrastructure for navigation and positioning, which will be available from 2008 onwards. Compatibility between the two systems will be ensured in order to offer complementary services to users.

The future space components of the GMES need sufficient prior definition, including the incorporation of specific service requirements such as the capability of collecting and distributing large volumes of data at very high speed.

To adequately deploy the GMES services by 2008, substantial improvements will be required in in-situ observing systems both at the EU and global levels. In fact, GMES services add value by combining and linking data from different sources, over extended periods of time, and packaging this information in an accessible and relevant manner.

The diversity of data that the GMES services require and produce will benefit from the development of a data policy. This may vary according to the domains of services provided, but will need to find a balance between "non-discriminatory access", economic viability and the necessary incentives for private services providers to invest in the development of such capacity. From the legal point of view, since the Aahrus Convention of June 1998 on access to environmental information and access to justice requests an open access to the environmental information for the benefit of citizens, a significant part of the GMES information should be freely available.

Finally, considering that some GMES services may include information relating to secure/multiple use purposes, it should be considered that certain added value activities would generate sensitive information requiring controlled access.

The GMES can assist through improved prediction, monitoring and assessment capabilities, in the preparation of strategies to cope with natural hazards and human made disasters, thus contributing to the reduction of the resulting human and economic losses. It is foreseen that the GMES services and observing systems will be instrumental in the development of a European growing role in global environmental monitoring.

The GMES services with their global dimension are a means for international cooperation. The space and in-situ observing systems through the data captured, constitute significant contribution to other international initiatives. It is foreseen that the European Commission will encourage the creation of a GMES partnership that would promote a common approach to the development and deployment of the GMES capacity. Partners will be invited to join the partnership through a GMES Memorandum of understanding.

The operational management of the GMES is still to be fully implemented using the mechanisms provided for by the Framework Agreement between the ESA and the EU. In short terms, the Commission, in partnership with the ESA, has set up a GMES interim structure in the form of a GMES Programme Office, populated in part by seconded experts from member States and relevant international organisations, such as EUMETSAT.

The main functions of this GMES Programme Office are to ensure the coordinated management of on-going GMES related EC and ESA founded projects and to specify more precisely the GMES capacity services and components to be made available by 2008.

Finally, in March 2006, the European Commission has established a new focal point for its GMES-related activities, to be known as the GMES Bureau, the new body responsible for creating an implementation strategy for GMES.

3. All in all, the GMES joint Initiative is to be considered as a positive step. In fact, mainly for disaster management and mitigation, the availability of data is a key point. It means not only to have access to the data needed in a timely manner, but also to obtain data and relevant products and services in an appropriate format for use. There is today a widely availability of remotely sensed images with various spatial, spectral and temporal resolutions and the potential application to disaster prevention and management. Space-based technologies have a real contribution to make in all areas of disaster management and prevention. Measures need to be taken to ensure the deployment of the technologies currently available.

The first tool put in place to cope with disasters prevention and mitigation was the Charter on Cooperation to Achieve the Coördinated Use of Space Facilities in the Event of Natural or Technological Disasters, also known as the "International Charter on Space and Major Disasters". It enable countries in which a natural or technological disaster has occurred to support disaster mitigation activities. Having being concluded among national and international space agencies and institutions of public nature, such as the European Space Agency (ESA), the French CNES, the Canadian Space Agency, the Indian Space Research Organization and the US's NOAA, it is evident that the legal basis of the Charter relies on an international administrative agreement and not, as has been said by some commentators, on a contract of private nature. But what is more important than the legal nature of the Charter, is the fact that, in response to the Indian Ocean tsunami of 26 December 2004, the Charter was activated and, for the first time, raw satellite imagery with a multi-user license was provided for by the space agencies cooperating within this legal framework. The data were hosted by the UNOSAT service and accessible to all entities (UN, governments, NGOs, universities) involved in work related to the international response to the countries affected by the tsunami.

In this sense, the Charter seems to be the first international instrument which gives full implementation to Principle XI of the 1986 UN Principles on remote sensing, as well as to Principle 18 of the UN Declaration on environment and development adopted at Rio de Janeiro in 1992. As a matter of fact, its preamble makes an express reference to the "UN Resolution 41/45 of

1986 on remote sensing of the Earth from space". It seems meaningful to recall these principles: Principle XI establishes that " Remote sensing shall promote the protection of mankind from natural disasters. To this end, States participating in remote sensing activities that have identified processed data and analysed information in their possession that may be useful to States affected by natural disasters, or likely to be affected by impending natural disasters, shall transmit such data and information to States concerned as promptly as possible". Principle 18 of the Rio Declaration provides that: "States shall immediately notify other States of any natural disasters or other emergencies that are likely to produce sudden harmful effects on the environment of other States. Every effort shall be made by the international community to help States so afflicted".

The recent developments and practices – including the Disaster Monitoring Constellation (DMC), an international consortium which comprises a partnership between organizations in Algeria, China, Nigeria, Turkey and the United Kingdom proposed in 1996 to construct a network of five affordable LEO micro satellites which objective is to provide a daily global imaging capability for rapid-response disaster monitoring and mitigation – are of the foremost relevance from the legal perspective. In fact, they indicate that the main UN Principles on remote sensing and sustainable development are beginning to work together in a concrete way in the field of disaster mitigation and prevention.

In this context, it is my understanding that the legal problems related to the use of remote sensing technologies for disaster prevention and management should be assessed in the light of two set of legal principles: on one side, the specific rules governing remote sensing activities in international space law, embodied in UNGA Resolution 41/65 of 3 December 1986 as Principles relating to remote sensing of the Earth from Outer Space; on the other side, the principles of international law on sustainable development codified in the acts adopted at Rio de Janeiro in June 1992, mainly the Rio Declaration on Environment and Development and its subsequent developments, such as the results of the Johannesburg Summit Rio+5 of 2002. Both set of principles, in fact, are already reflected in several treaties, acts of international organisations, declarations of the UN General Assembly, State practice and international commitments of other kind.

A key element of the UN remote sensing legal regime is the emphasis on co-operation, to which Principles V, VIII and XIII are devoted. The first Principle states the obligation of sensing States to promote international co-operation and to make available to other States opportunities for participation on equitable and mutually acceptable terms; the second, affirms the obligation of the United Nations and the relevant agencies of the UN system to promote co-operation, including technical assistance and co-ordination in the area of remote sensing; the third, calls upon sensing States to promote and intensify international co-operation, especially with regard to the needs of developing countries, by the means of consultations, upon request, with the sensed States.

The duty of States to co-operate is indeed a sort of procedural super-principle that would ensure the effective translation of each of the other principles into reality. In this context, the principle of global partnership, following the common but differentiated responsibilities criterion, can be seen as a more recent rephrasing of the obligation to co-operate.

International co-operation and technical assistance are indeed essential to space applications for environmental protection and disaster mitigation and prevention. In the last years, States and international organisations practice in this field has given strong support to the effectiveness of the co-operation principle. Co-operation has become essential not only in expanding the availability of space technology and applications so that all countries may benefit from them, but also, and mainly, in promoting international security in all its forms, including human security against natural and technological disasters.

The full consistency of the remote sensing activities for sustainable development with the applicable international legal regime finds the last, and more conclusive, element of evidence in the principles concerning environmental information and access to data contained in Resolution 41/65. Following Principle X, remote sensing shall promote the protection of the Earth's natural environment, while Principle XI attributes to remote sensing the task of protecting humankind from natural disasters.

The discipline of environmental information set forth in Principles X and XI of the UNGA Resolution, is preceded by a general clause contained in Principle IX, which makes reference to Article IV of the Registration Convention and Article XI of the Outer Space Treaty. Here, the obligation of information concerns not the collected data, but the remote sensing program as a whole that the sensing State is carrying on, and its components. The sensing State must in fact inform not only the UN Secretary general, but also any other State, and particularly the developing ones, which can be affected by the program.

Coming now to the two provisions concerning the disclosure of remote sensing environmental data, it is well known that Principle X deals with ordinary environmental harm, while Principle XI is concerned with *natural disasters*. In the first case, States participating in remote sensing activities that have identified information in their possession capable of adverting any phenomenon harmful to the Earth's natural environment, shall disclose such information to the States concerned. According to Principle XI, the States that have identified processed data and analysed information in their possession that may be useful to States affected by natural disasters or likely to be affected by impending natural disasters, shall transmit such data and information to States concerned as promptly as possible.

While the two dispositions show various differences concerning the kind of information and/or data to be "disclosed" or "transmitted", they appear interlinked, complementary and unified by the fact that no mention is made of conditions, like the non discriminatory basis or the reasonable cost. These conditions are envisaged, on the contrary, in Principle XII for access to remote sensing data by the sensed State. Moreover, Principles X and XI clearly indicate that the States to be informed are not only the sensed States, but, more generally, the States concerned. Information promoting sustainable development is, thereby, given a different status *vis-à-vis* the access to data regime set forth in Principle XII. It is probably more correct to identify the environmental regime on disclosure of data as the general regime, and to regard the Principle XII regime as a special one. It is true indeed that the promotion of the protection of the Earth's natural environment (Principle X) and of the protection of humankind from natural disasters (Principle XI) are typical and general objectives of remote sensing of the Earth's surface from space to improve natural resources management, the protection of the environment and, more in general, the life and security of all human beings.

The two principles just mentioned find corresponding provisions in numerous environmental protection conventions, which provide duties of States to inform each other, particularly in situations of imminent danger.

According to the aforementioned evolution both at level of general principles and conventions in force, it is commonly understood that States should provide prior notification and relevant information to neighbouring and potentially affected States regarding activities that may have a significant adverse environmental effect; they should also provide immediate notification to other States of any natural or technological disaster or similar emergencies that are likely to produce sudden harmful effects on their environment and on their population. Emergency notification allows affected parties the greatest possible opportunities to prepare for, and mitigate, potential damage.

However, it is also evident that some differences must be stressed between the transmission of remote sensing data and information according to Principles X and XI of UN remote sensing principles, and notification of emergencies and natural disasters following Principles 18 and 19 of the Rio Declaration.

The scope of Principles 18 and 19 of the Rio Declaration is to impose an obligation to the State within whose jurisdiction or control the natural disaster or emergency or harmful activities occur, while the Principles on remote sensing require the mere possession by States of information and data on harmful phenomena or natural disasters in order to envisage an obligation of disclosure and transmission, irrespective to the *lieu* of origin of the harm or of the disaster.

Both set of principles, indeed, do not prescribe the obligation of the sensing States to transmit the relevant information to the competent international organisations or to the UN Secretary General. On the contrary, such an obligation should be included as an important provision applicable to environmental information concerning damages and disasters, in order to enhance international co-operation to prevent natural and technological disasters and to minimize their effects. Finally, nor the Rio principles, neither the UN remote sensing principles make explicit reference to information and data concerning imminent threats, natural disasters or serious harms to areas beyond national jurisdictions. Notification and transmission of data in this context is an obligation rooted in customary international law, connected with each State's due diligence obligation to prevent harm not only to another State's environment, but also to areas beyond national jurisdiction.

Another important aspect regards the right of access of sensed States to any primary or processed data "on non-discriminatory basis and on reasonable cost terms", to follow the formulation of Principle XII of the UN set of principles. This provision must not be interpreted in the ambiguous sense that there is a right of access only if this is available on a non discriminatory basis, but rather that the sensing State has an obligation to allow access, and that this access must be non discriminatory and at reasonable cost. State practice confirms that the *opinio iuris* is in favour of this - although not unlimited - right of access.

The tendency towards the privatisation of data retrieval, raw data processing, data analysis and data sales should not impair the principles laid down in the UN code and in sustainable development principles. In order to be consistent with Principle XII of the UN code, commercialization must guarantee the disclosure of data according to Principles XI and XII of the 1986 UN Code. More generally, I believe that the remote sensing environmental information must be free in principle for all users, though at reasonable cost, because of the public aspect of this kind of data. It is also evident that data concerning natural disasters should be allowed for free, due to the extreme constraints and the harmful consequences on the life and security of human beings, as the tsunami case demonstrates.

Even if remote sensing principles maintain their independent *raison-d'être* in the context of the evolution of space law, it is indeed true that international law, in which these principles fall by their legal nature and content, is undergoing a general transformation due to the awareness reached by the international community of the imperative need for global partnership to achieve natural disasters prevention and management.

In conclusion, the tsunami of December 2004 has prompted reflection on remote sensing data pricing policy, shifting toward no charge in case of major disasters. This seems to be really the most important element to be taken into account, from the legal point of view, in assessing the more recent initiatives.

THE EILENE M. GALLOWAY SYMPOSIUM ON CRITICAL ISSUES IN SPACE LAW WASHINGTON D.C., DECEMBER 2006

MAINTAINING SPACE FOR PEACEFUL PURPOSES AND USES THROUGH INTERNATIONAL COOPERATION

Jonathan F. Galloway
Vice President, International Institute of Space Law

"Eilene M. Galloway Symposium on Critical Issues in Space Law"
Cosmos Club, Washington, DC, USA
December 11, 2006

Good Morning. I am very pleased to be here at the Cosmos Club today. My mother and I have spent many decades coming here - the first times being in the 1940s when my father, George Barnes Galloway, was a member and the Club was on Lafayette Square. What I would like to do today is look at some of the abiding concerns and dreams of my mother in the field of space law. She is especially interested in the concepts of "peaceful purposes," "peaceful uses" and "international cooperation," and the positive contributions to be made by the United Nations and its committees such as the Committee on the Peaceful Uses of Outer Space and its functional organizations such as the International Telecommunication Union(ITU). She has also been a fervent advocate of the international cooperative programs of NASA and other Executive Branch agencies. To approach an understanding of these concepts and organizations in the present context, I propose to examine the new U.S. national space policy by comparing it to the previous policy of 1996; to the new Chinese White Paper on Space Activities, and to exisiting international space law, in particular the Outer Space Treaty of 1967(1). Lastly, I will examine the ways in which space law may be developed in the future.

PEACEFUL PURPOSES AND PEACEFUL USES

These two concepts have no agreed upon definitions in international law; yet it is possible to distinguish them thusly. A "peaceful purpose" is an intent to act peacefully, while a "peaceful use" is an act of peace in fact. One may intend to act peacefully but the path to hell is paved with good intentions. For instance, defending the state by putting Anti-Satellite weapons (ASATs) in outer space may be a peaceful defensive purpose, but if the effect is to start an arms race in space and increase international tensions, then there is not a peaceful use or a peaceful consequence. Of course, a peaceful purpose may , in fact, produce peaceful uses or consequences as, for instance, when a state supports disaster managment satellites.

Another distinction is in order. This is between "positive" and "negative" peace. Positive peace is peace with justice, a state of affairs where no one expects war or conflict to result. For instance, one does not expect war to result between most nations in the world. They are at peace. But, in the case of a few relationships, it would not surprise anyone if there were hostilities. These countries are at peace but it is an uneasy peace - a negative peace.

During the Cold War - a negative peace - the two superpowers and space powers agreed to limit conflict in outer space by becoming parties to the Outer Space Treaty and other treaties and agreements associated with detente. In the 1967 OST, one particular Article, Art. II proposed to remove this new frontier from the sphere of great power rivalry. This article states "Outer space, including the moon and other celestial bodies, is not suject to national appropriation by claim of sovereignty, by means of use or occupation, or by any other means." Thus, atavistic colonial antagonisms would be eliminated.

What does the new U.S. National Space Policy of August 31, 2006(2) have to say about these matters? Similar to Section 102(a) of the National Aeronautics and Space Act of 1958(3), the United States commits itself to peaceful purposes and peaceful uses as when it is stated "The United States is committed to the exploration and use of outer space by all nations for peaceful purposes, and for the benefit of all humanity" and when it is stated that "The United States will seek to cooperate with other nations in the peaceful use of outer space to extend the benefits of space,enhance space exploration, and to protect and promote freedom around the world." On the other hand, there is a tone of negative peace as well as positive peace in the policy. Thus, it is posited that "In this new century, those who effectively utilize space will enjoy added prosperity and security and will hold a substantial advantage over those who do not." This is the language of the balance of power and Realism in international relations. In this connection, later in the policy, mention is made of "space control," "force application," "missile defense," and developing "capabilities, plans, and options to ensure freedom of action in space, and, if directed, deny such freedom of action to adversaries. " It is undoubtedly these sorts of goals that have led some commentators to label the policy "jingoistic"(4) and "hubristic."(5) In truth, however, this same language appears in the 1996 National Space Policy(6). The policy is the product of a committee, or , more precislely many committee meetings over many years. Thus, there are continuities but also ambivalences and internal contradictions, as when all humanity is mentioned and, on the other hand, the primacy of the U.S. national interest. Of course, there are three major intervening variables between the policy announcements of 1996 and 2006 - the withdrawal from the ABM Treaty, 9-11 and the Iraq war. These events signal a more unilateralist and preemptive approach to national security policy and perhaps a move from the militarization to the weaponization of space meaning a move from military reconnaissance and communication satellites to the development of weapons which can project force "to, from, in and through" space.

Aspects of this trajectory or tendency are worrisome insofar as the rule of law is concerned. Thus, the March 1, 2005 "National Defense Strategy of the United States" posits that the U.S. is "vulnerable" because other states - "weaker states" - might resort to international law and organization. In characterizing vulnerabilities, the strategy announcement asserts that "our strength as a nation state will continue to be challenged by those who employ a strategy of the weak using international fora, judicial processes, and terrorism."(7) A less forceful version of this same sentiment is found in the new National Space Policy when it is asserted that "The United States will oppose the development of new legal regimes or other restrictions that seek to prohibit or limit U.S. access to or use of space." This formulation probably comes from the Department of Defense and not the Department of State. We must remember that the Executive Branch often does not speak with a unified voice. Bureaucratic politics and rivalries within the Executive can often be noticed and identified. Where one stands on policy often depends on where one sits.

In the current political milieu and given its particular zeitgeist, one cannot expect outer space law to make advances such as in expanding Article IV of the 1967 Outer Space Treaty, something my mother suggested many years ago(8). In fact, it could be a major mistake to open the OST for amendments because this might undermine some of its core principles, in particular Article II. However, one can still highlight peaceful purposes and peaceful uses by identifying what are clearly not peaceful purposes and not peaceful uses in international space law. In Article IV of the OST, we can clearly see that orbiting weapons of mass destruction is a non-peaceful use. In the second paragraph of the same article, we can also see that "the establishment of military bases, installations and fortifications, the testing of any type of weapons and the conduct of military manoeuvres on celestial bodies shall be forbidden." The military has a particular role to play in developing space and that is in scientific research and, more generally in "any other peaceful purposes."(9) Further, the military has a particular interest in mitigating the problem of space debris, and a section of the new space policy is devoted to this issue. This is a worldwide concern to which a voluntary code of conduct following Inter-Agency Space Debris Coordinating Committee (IADC) guidelines can point the way to alleviation (10).

INTERNATIONAL COOPERATION

International cooperation is a salient principle in the National Space Policy. It is stated that "The United States will seek to cooperate with other nations in the peaceful use of outer space to extend the benefits of space, enhance space exploration, and to protect and promote freedom around the world." More specifically, potential cooperation with foreign nations and international organizations is mentioned vis-a-vis "Space exploration; providing space surveillance information consistent with security requirements and U.S. national security and foreign policy interests; (and) developing and operating Earth-observation systems." One might distinguish here between targeted international cooperation with allies in military alliances or in "coalitions of the willing" and general international cooperation in fora such as the United Nations, the International Telecommunication Union and the World Meterological Organization. The former type of cooperation can be associated with the Realist theory of international relations and the later with the Idealistic theory of humankind as a whole. Interestingly enough, no international laws or organizations are referenced in the policy. The 1967 Outer Space Treaty is not mentioned. Neither is the UN Committee on the Peaceful Uses of Outer Space. Nor is there mention of the ITU although there is a section on "Radio Frequency Spectrum and Orbit Management and Interference Protection." On the other hand, the principles of the policy do in certain instances replicate parts of international space law as, for instance, when it is stated that "The United States rejects any claims to sovereignty by any nation over outer space or celestial bodies, or any portion thereof, and rejects any limitations on the fundamental right of the United States to operate in and acquire data from space." Here one naturally thinks of Articles I and II of the Outer Space Treaty.

If we look at cooperative programs which by and large may be said to promote positive peace, we can think of NASA's civil space programs. After the first part of the policy which mainly emphasizes national security, NASA is given prime billing along with the National Oceanic and Atmospheric Administration. My mother is a great fan of NASA's international programs and projects and these have been spelled out in great detail in the NASA History Series "Exploring the Unknown" edited by John M. Logsdon. (There will be eight volumes in this series. Vol. II in particular deals with cooperation between the civilian space program of the United States and those of other countries.) Among the notable projects covered are Apollo-Soyuz, Hubble, SETI, MTPE, and the International Space Station.

If one takes a functional appoach to the evolution of peace between nations, one could say that these programs are where the action is. They go a long way towards fulfilling the mandate in Article I of the Outer Space Treaty - "The exploration and use of outer space, including the moon and other celestial bodies, shall be carried out for the benefit and in the interests of all countries, irrespective of their degree of economic or scientific development, and shall be the province of all mankind." Even if one takes a Realist approach to world politics, one can say, using game theory, that playing national security "games" over time can lead from win-lose outcomes to win-win solutions(11).

CHINA'S SPACE ACTIVITIES IN 2006

For comparative purposes, we should look at China's newly updated space policy of October 12, 2006(12). Similar to the U.S. policy, the Chinese seems to have been written by a committee, or many committees. Reference is made to peaceful purposes and uses and to international cooperation. It is stated that "China is unflinching in taking the road to peaceful development, and always maintains that outer space is the common wealth of mankind." It appears to be a very inclusive document. On the other hand, it is stated "Upholding independence and self-reliance policy, making innovations independently and realizing leapfrogging development. China relied completely on itself when it developed its space industry from scratch." National security is mentioned in the document, but it is not given the prominent place that it has in the U.S. policy. Unlike the U.S. policy, the Chinese version mentions specific international laws such as the Outer Space Treaty and specific UN resolutions such as the 1996 "Declaration on International Cooperation in the Exploration and Use of Outer Space for the Benefit and in the Interest of All States, Taking into Particular Account the Needs of Developing Countries." Further, the document mentions many international organizations and cooperative programs in detail such as those with the World Meterological Organization, the European Space Agency, the ITU, the IAF and COSPAR. In truth, the statement is not so much a policy statement, although it is that; it is also a summary of how the policy is being implemented by specific programs. Still, I think the U.S. document could have had a bit more of this fleshing out and the Chinese a bit less. Specifically, from the perspective of developing space law, one could suggest that the U.S. policy statement reference actual laws. Presumably, if U.S. policy is law, it could state what the law is rather than say "The President authorized a new national space policy of August 31, 2006 that establishes overarching policy that governs the conduct of U.S. space activities." If I were a government lawyer, I would like to be guided by the law rather than policy pronouncements, parts of which are classified.

FUTURE DEVELOPMENTS IN OUTER SPACE LAW

What might be a U.S. approach to developing future space law, for if we stand on our laurels, they may wither or be forgotten? Up the street on Sheridan Circle is the headquarters of the

American Society of International Law. The Society was founded in 1906. For its centennial anniversary, its journal, the American Journal of International Law (AJIL), has been publishing articles some of which examine what is particualarly American about the approach to international law. One by Richard H. Steinberg and Jonathan M. Zasloff identifies four schools of thought in the evolution of the Journal's approach to law(13). In the early years, it was Classicism which maintained that law was a science which could be divorced from every day politics; it could express an essential harmony and evolve and progress over time. Law benefitted everyone and relied on reason. This era came to an end with the rise of fascism during the 1930s. Hans Morgenthau maintained in a 1940 article in the AJIL that law was based on power and could not be understood apart from the international balance of power and the national interest of the great powers Since law and international organization had no independent explanatory significance, the AJIL's corrective to the pure Realist and Machiavellian approach was not long in coming. In the 1950s, Harold Lasswell and Myres McDougal developed a policy-oriented jurispudence called the New Haven School. In this connection, Louis Henkin has pointed out that "almost all nations observe almost all principles of international law and almost all of their obligations almost all of the time."(14)The fourth approach came along in the 1990s; it is called the Constructivist school, which maintains that there is no inherent logic to international relations. What is at its basis is culture and law does not trump culture; it merely reflects it.

If we wish to see international cooperation grow and be directed towards positive peaceful purposes and peaceful uses, I suggest that we use a pragmatic amalgam of the schools of thought outlined above. In the first instance, we should emphasize that law does have an independent explanatory value over time, especially if it becomes customary international law. Second, we should credit Realism with one version of the truth, but iin seeing international relations as a power game, it leaves out the fact that the game is being played over and over and thus the participants might learn the lessons of history and convert the game into a win-win rather than a win-lose one. Thirdly, we should especially credit the New Haven school since Lasswell and McDougal not only wrote theoretical books about law but one in 1963 entitled Law and Public Order in Space. Laslty, we should credit the Constructivists with the insight that ideas and culture matter in making reality of what the rule of law is. If we can act as an invisible college or world epistemic community, we can change reality for the better.

In connection with today's symposium, I am glad that this task is proceeding, especially vis-a-vis celestial bodies and the work of Steve Doyle, interstitial space and the work of George Robinson, policy and law relating to outer space resources and the work of the McGill Workshop on Policy and Law Relating to Outer Space Resources, the Near Earth Orbit protocol work of Russell Schweikart and the Association of Space Explorers and the space traffic management work of Corinne Contant Jorgenson and others at the International Academy of Astronautics.

In closing, let me quote these sentences by Lubos Perek with which my mother would be in total agreement. "Outer Space is unique. Properties of, and conditions in, outer space are quite different from properties and conditions encountered on the ground. Any meaningful regulation has to respect the specific facts of outer space. Consequently, any question has to be considered from points of view of science, technology, and law."(15)

END NOTES

1. Treaty on Principles Governing the Activities of States in the Exploration and Use of Outer Space Including the Moon and Other Celestial Bodies, January 25, 1967; 18 U.S.T.2410, 619 U.N.T.S.2005 (hereinafter OST or Outer Space Treaty).

2. The White House, Office of Science and Technology Policy, "U.S. National Space Policy," August 31, 2006. It should be emphasized that the publicly available policy is the unclassified version. <<US%20National%20Space% 20Policy.pdf>> (released on October 6, 2006).

3. "The Congress hereby declares that it is the policy of the United States that activiities in space should be devoted to peaceful purposes for the benefit of all mankind." National Aeronautics and Space Act, Public Law 85-568, 85th Congress, First Session, July 29, 1958. Section 102(a).

4. "Flexing Our Muscles in Space," Editorial, The New York Times, October 21, 2006, A24.

5. Al Gore's view as reported in Aviation Week & Space Technology. October 30, 2006, 21.

6. The White House, National Science and Technology Council, "Fact Sheet - National Space Policy," September 19, 1996.

7. See note in the American Journal of International Law, vol. 99, no. 3 (July, 2005), 693-694.

8. Eilene Marie Galloway, "Expanding Article IV of the 1957 Space Treaty: A Proposal," Proceedings of the 25th Colloquium on the Law of Outer Space (1982) (American Institute of Aeronautics and Astronautics, 1983), 89-92.

9. Some commentators believe that a peaceful use is a non-military use and not just a non-aggressive use. See, for instance, Bin Cheng, Studies in International Space Law (New York: Oxford, 1997), 521-522.

10. Steven A. Mirmina, "Reducing the Proliferation of Orbital Debris: Alternatives to a Legally Binding Instrument," American Journal of International Law, vol. 99, no.3 (July, 2005), 649-662.

11. Jonathan F. Galloway, "Cooperation, Conflict and Competition in Space Law," Proceedings of the Forty-Sixth Colloquium on the Law of Outer Space (2003) (American Institute of Aeronautics and Astronautics, 2004), 2-8.

12. China's State Council, Information Office, "Full Text: China's Space Activities in 2006," October, 2006. http://english.people.com.cn/200610/12eng20061012_311157.html

13. Richard H. Steinberg and Jonathan M. Zasloff, "Power and International Law," American Journal of International Law, vol. 100, , no. 1 (January, 2006), 64-87.

14. As quoted in ibid., 78.

15. Lubos Perek, "Ex Facto Sequitur Lex: Facts Which Merit Reflection in Space Law in Particular with Regard to Registration and Space Debris Mitigation," in Space Law: Current Problems and Perspectives for Future Regulation, eds. Marietta Benko and Kai-Uwe Schrogl (Utrecht: Eleven International Publishers, 2005), 29-46, 46.

National Center for Remote Sensing, Air, and Space Law
at The University of Mississippi School of Law,
The Journal of Space Law,
and
The International Institute of Space Law
jointly present

The Eilene M. Galloway Symposium on Critical Issues in Space Law

The Cosmos Club
2121 Massachusetts Ave. N. W.,
Washington, D. C.
December 11, 2006

A presentation titled:

Celestial Bodies and Interstitial Space in Current Law,

by Dr. Stephen E. Doyle,
Honorary Director, IISL

Celestial Bodies and Interstitial Space in Current Law

by SE Doyle

Introduction

Following a 3-day International Interdisciplinary Workshop on Policy and Law Relating to Outer Space Resources, held at McGill University in June 2006, the McGill Institute of Air and Space Law published a summary of the Workshop. After reading a draft of that summary, Dr. Eilene Galloway offered four supplemental ideas, which were the stimulus for the convening of this day of discussion and deliberation. Dr. Galloway's ideas were:

1. We ensure that international space law covers outer space, space itself and is not confined to celestial bodies orbiting in space.
2. Do not assume that all agreements on the Moon and Mars are applicable to other celestial bodies. Formulate definitions of "other celestial bodies."
3. Be prepared for the legal effects on sovereignty of machines invented to operate both in air and outer space.
4. Difficulties are created by people who assume that the outer space environment, including planets, etc., are just like the Earth, air, and sea, and can be used in the same ways. Potential economic and legal issues must be evaluated on basic scientific and technological facts.

This paper addresses the question "What is the law currently applicable to outer space, including the Moon and other celestial bodies?" Although a relatively simple question to ask, it elicits an extremely complex answer. We could spend all our allotted time today discussing the questions: "What is outer space, and what are celestial bodies?" Let us agree, for this discussion, that outer space and all in it comprises everything in existence beyond the sentient atmosphere, which scientists tell us ceases totally to have aeronautical support or life support properties somewhere near or beyond 100 kilometers. Let us stipulate that if one is more than 62.5 miles above the Earth, one is in outer space. Following this presentation, Dr. George Robinson will look beyond what law exists today, to describe some of the implications and problems for law in outer space being driven by emerging, accelerating technologies.

Before describing the presently applicable legal framework, I want to say a few words about the environment in which that framework exists. Perhaps the single most ubiquitous aspect of international law during the past century, whether international law applied to the air, the sea, sea beds, telecommunications, technical standards, labor, human rights, or outer space, is the accelerating aspect of change. In all international legal areas in which the community of nations seeks to establish standards of behavior and mutual accommodation, we find significant change not only occurring but accelerating. Dr. Robinson will help explain that observation.

Change in law is brought on by multiple factors including increased population, emerging technologies, expanding world trade, greater international intercourse among nations, political and social responses, as well as the needs of national and international security.

In the four decades from 1961 to 2000, nations of the world established by agreement a substantial body of largely unprecedented laws relating to activities involving spacecraft, spaceflight, and activities in outer space, as distinguished from activities on Earth. Even activities in terracentric applications programs, such as communications, navigation, meteorology, remote sensing, defensive early warning systems, and treaty verification systems, to the extent they involve resources and activity beyond the "atmosphere," are subject to the legal conditions imposed by the law of outer space, or *corpus juris spatialis*, the body of the law of space.

So, what is that body of law? The most widely accepted, signed, and ratified treaty among states relating directly to outer space is the *Treaty on Principles Governing the Activities of States in the Exploration and Use of Outer Space, including the Moon and Other Celestial Bodies*, which entered into force on October 10, 1967. Article III of that 1967 Treaty reads:

> "States Parties to the Treaty shall carry on activities in the exploration and use of outer space, including the moon and other celestial bodies, in accordance with international law, including the Charter of the United Nations, in the interest of maintaining international peace and security and promoting international cooperation and understanding."

Thus we see four major elements of the stated applicable law;

1) international law,
2) the Charter of the United Nations,
3) maintenance of international peace and security, and
4) promotion of international cooperation and understanding.

Let us briefly consider each of these four elements.

1. International Law Generally Considered

When lawyers and diplomats use the term "international law" speaking to each other, they are using shorthand to encompass a broad scope of rules in a simple expression. An appropriate analogy might be to say that we consider all the ways of preparing foods in the various cuisines of the different cultures of our world as encompassed in the phrase "the art of cooking." This term is certainly inclusive, but it doesn't tell us much.

Traditionally, and in current practice, it is fair to say that "international law" includes all of the following subject areas and multiple subdivisions within each area:

- International Conventions (treaties), general or particular,
- International Custom, as evidence of a general practice accepted as law,
- General Principles of Law recognized by civilized nations,
- Agreed use of equitable resolution of disputes,
- Procedures for Arbitration, Accommodation, or Conciliation
- State Sovereignty and Jurisdiction (over persons or territory)
- Recognition of States
- Nationality (of citizens or vessels)
- State Responsibility and Liability (fault-based or absolute)
- International Organizations (public or private)
- Rules of War and Neutrality
- Restraints on Use of Force
- Conventions, Charters and Contracts (public and private)
- Provisions for posts, telecommunications, aviation, other international commerce
- Salvage on the High Seas
- Conflicts of Laws
- Judicial Decisions and Arbitral Findings as "precedents"
- Criminal Law (piracy, slavery, terrorism, etc.)
- Intellectual Property Laws (patents, copyrights, trade marks)
- Property Law (on movable property-chattels, or immovable property-real estate)
- Expropriation or Nationalization
- Customs and Duties on Goods in Commerce
- Embargoes
- Biological Quarantine (plants, animals, persons)

This is a representative, topical survey of international law, in accordance with which States Parties shall carry out activities in outer space, according to Article III of the 1967 Space Treaty. In addition, the specific terms of the Outer Space Treaty apply. We shall consider some of these provisions in a moment.

We need also mention that there are a number of additional particular agreements, which apply among the States which are signatories thereto; and then there are a series of United Nations General Assembly Resolutions containing Declarations of Principles applicable to certain types of activities in outer space. Particular space law agreements include:

- *The Agreement on the Rescue of Astronauts, the Return of Astronauts and the Return of Objects Launched into Outer Space* of 1968;
- *The Convention on International Liability for Damage Caused by Space Objects of 1972;*
- *The Convention on Registration of Objects Launched into Outer Space* of 1976; and
- *The Agreement Governing the Activities of States on the Moon and Other Celestial Bodies* of 1984.

In addition, we have the following series of declarations, adopted by the UN General Assembly:

- The *Declaration of Legal Principles Governing the Activities of States in the Exploration and Use of Outer Space* of 1962;
- The *Principles Governing the Use by States of Artificial Earth Satellites for International Direct Television Broadcasting*, adopted December 10, 1982;
- The *Principles Relating to Remote Sensing of the Earth from Space*, adopted December 3, 1986;
- The *Principles Relevant to the Use of Nuclear Power Sources in Outer Space*, adopted on December 14, 1992; and
- The *Declaration on International Cooperation in Exploration and Use of Outer Space for the Benefit and in the Interest of All States, Taking into Particular Account the Needs of Developing Countries*, adopted on December 13, 1996.

There exist, in addition, a modest but notable list of international treaties, primarily between the United States and the former USSR, now the US ad Russia, directly related to the use of space launch capabilities for potential intercontinental or regional delivery of military warheads. These weapon delivery systems have been dealt with under the following treaties, which entered into force (e.i.f) on the dates indicated:

- 1972 Anti Ballistic Missile Treaty and Interim Agreement e.i.f. 26 May 1972
- 1973 Prevention of Nuclear War Agreement e.i.f. 22 Jun 1973
- 1973 Anti Ballistic Missile Protocol e.i.f. 3 Jul 1974
- 1979 US/USSR Agreement on Limitation of Strategic Offensive Arms e.i.f. 18 Jun 1979
- 1987 US/USSR Treaty on Elimination of Intermediate- and Shorter-range Missiles e.i.f. 8 Dec 1987
- 1988 Ballistic Missile Launch Notification Agreement e.i.f. 31 May 1988

Also related to military activity in space is the 1963 Treaty Banning Nuclear Weapon Tests in outer space and elsewhere e.i.f. 10 Oct 1963

We could list here, but in the interest of time and attention, we will simply reference the substantial number of organizational charters which have been created to establish organizations primarily focused on space activities, usually space technology applications on the Earth. These international institutional conventions and charters also form part of the applicable body of international law relating to activities conducted in outer space.

2. *The Charter of the United Nations*

This often referred to, frequently invoked, usually ignored, and largely ineffectual instrument contains a great deal of information describing the intentions of the founders of the United Nations, and many provisions intended to carry out those intentions. Objectively considered, the Charter of the United Nations may be one of the worst implemented instruments of international law ever devised by the community of nations.

The Charter was formulated by the United Nations Conference on International Organization concluded in San Francisco in June 1945. It entered into force on October 24, 1945. The Charter has 19 chapters and is heavily oriented to the interdiction or neutralization of historic causes of international conflict. It has been amended several times since its adoption for administrative reasons, but its basic provisions have survived essentially as adopted in 1945.

Because this instrument is made expressly applicable to outer space, including the Moon and other celestial bodies, we should consider at least its broadest and most fundamental aspects.

The Preamble to the Charter states, in part:
We the Peoples of the United Nations Determined

- To save succeeding generations from the scourge of war, …
- To reaffirm faith in fundamental human rights, …
- To establish conditions under which justice… can be maintained, and
- To promote social progress and better standards of life in larger freedom,

And for these Ends

- To practice tolerance and live together in peace …
- To unite our strength to maintain international peace and security,
- To ensure … that armed force shall not be used, save in the common interest, and
- To employ international machinery for the promotion of economic and social advancement

Have resolved to combine our efforts to accomplish these aims.

Chapter One of the Charter contains Purposes and Principles, and Article 1 explains means to be employed to: 1) maintain international peace and security, 2) develop friendly relations among nations, 3) achieve international cooperation, and 4) for the UN to be a center for harmonizing the actions of nations. Historically, these principles have been ignored, and actions taken or that fail to be taken, are often inconsistent with these stated purposes. Succeeding chapters of the Charter describe membership (II), organs (III), the General Assembly (IV), the Security Council (V), means for pacific settlement of disputes (VI), actions with respect to threats to the peace, breaches of the peace, and acts of aggression (VII), regional arrangements (VIII), international economic and social cooperation (IX), the Economic and Social Council (X), a declaration regarding non-self-governing territories (XI), the international trustee system (XII), The Trusteeship Council (XIII), the International Court of Justice (XIV), the Secretariat (XV), miscellaneous provisions (XVI), transitional security arrangements (XVII), amendments (XVIII), and provisions for ratification and signature (XIX).

Chapter VII may be considered the heart of the Charter, because it addresses threats to the peace, breaches of the peace, and acts of aggression. The most cursory examination of history for the past sixty years clearly shows that the UN Charter has been far more often breached than employed, and we most assuredly do not have a world at peace, enjoying friendly relations among nations, international cooperation, and harmonization of the actions of nations. To the extent there is any peace or stabilization of relations among States, it can be said that balance or imbalance of power is the most employed means of seeking or maintaining order in our world, and we are not doing that very well. By the terms of Article III of the 1967 Space Treaty, this largely ineffectual Charter is declared applicable to relations among States in outer space. This is not a reassuring situation.

3. The Maintenance of International Peace and Security

The 1967 Outer Space Treaty undertakes to ensure that international peace and security will extend to outer space, and that international cooperation there should be encouraged. We can see by reviewing a few key provisions, how the drafters of the treaty attempted to accomplish the maintenance of international peace and security in space.

Article I provides, among other provisions, that space shall be free for exploration and use by all States, on a basis of equality and in accord with international law. There shall be freedom of scientific investigation and States shall facilitate and encourage international cooperation in such investigation. Article II declares that outer space is not subject to national appropriation by claim of sovereignty, by means of use or occupation, or by any other means. Article III redundantly directs that States shall carry out activities in space in accord with international law, including the UN Charter, in the interest of maintaining international peace and security and promoting international cooperation and understanding.

Article IV, the primary source of constraints on military activities and weapons in space, reads:

> States Parties to the treaty undertake not to place in orbit around the earth any objects carrying nuclear weapons or any other kinds of weapons of mass destruction, install such weapons on celestial bodies, or station such weapons in outer space in any other manner.
>
> The Moon and other celestial bodies shall be used by all States Parties to the Treaty exclusively for peaceful purposes. The establishment of military bases, installations or fortifications, the testing of any type of weapons and the conduct of military maneuvers on celestial bodies shall be forbidden. The use of military personnel for scientific research or for any other peaceful purposes shall not be prohibited. The use any equipment of facility necessary for peaceful exploration of the moon and other celestial bodies shall also not be prohibited.

Article V confers upon astronauts the status of "envoys of mankind." It also provides that any necessary or appropriate assistance shall be provided to astronauts, including to other astronauts, and if forced to land in a foreign territory, they shall be returned promptly to their homeland.

Acknowledging that activities in space may be carried on by non-governmental entities, Article VI provides that States bear international responsibility for their nationals in outer space. States are to authorize and supervise activities of non-governmental entities. Responsibility for activities by international organizations shall be borne by the organization and by the States Parties participating in the organization.

The desire for "demilitarization" of space, underlying the provisions of Article IV, was not successful in precluding the defensive, indirect and monitoring uses of space by States for military purposes, but for the first half century of spaceflight, it appears that the international community has been content to avoid placing of weapons in space or on celestial bodies, and States have avoided conduct of military maneuvers there. Concerning the maintenance of international peace and security, one could say "So far, so good." This appears to be a fragile mutual accommodation. One may hope it will last.

4. Promotion of International Cooperation and Understanding

Provisions of Article VII describing responsibility for damage caused by space objects has been substantially elaborated by the Space Liability Convention of 1972, referred to above.

Article VIII declares the jurisdiction and authority of States Parties over their personnel and objects launched into outer space or on a celestial body. Where objects launched have returned to earth, in their entirety or in pieces, there has been substantial compliance with the provisions relating to return of the national assets to the territory of the State of origin. The one major catastrophic unplanned reentry of a space object on the territory of another states, namely the landing of the USSR's Cosmos 954 spacecraft in Canada, resulted in an amicable resolution of the matter through diplomacy and accommodation, substantially in compliance with the Liability Convention of 1972.

Articles IX and X declare in legal formality that states should seek to be nice to one another and respect one another's rights in space. If there is a perceived problem, consult about it. Each State shall accommodate another's requests for visits or to witness launches. The nature and conditions of observation shall be agreed between the States involved.

The balance of the treaty provides for giving notice of activities to the UN Secretary General and generally keeping the international community informed about what is going on and what discoveries are made. The Treaty concludes with standard "boiler plate provisions," for signature, ratification, entry into force, depositaries, amendment, withdrawal, official languages, and signature. The Treaty emphasizes and repeatedly reiterates the drafters' desires to maintain peace and security in space and to recommend international cooperation, good will, and accommodation among all States active in spaceflight activities. During the first half century of spaceflight it is ostensibly the case that nations have complied with these desires of the drafters.

5. The Relevancies of "International Law"

In the declaration of the applicability of "international law" to activities in space, it is important to keep in mind what this phrase entails. Spaceflight is in many ways dependent upon successful radio communication. Control signals, navigation systems and corrections, data telemetry, information transfer, and vehicle and personnel health monitoring are all important aspects of spaceflight. None of these requisite services can be successfully conducted in an environment devoid of radio control.

The International Telecommunication Union has a body or regulations and a table of international allocations of radio frequencies, which, when complied with, provides the order necessary to ensure successful radio operations in space. Thus, whether an object is in its launch phase, approaching orbital insertion, in orbit around the earth, transferring into translunar space, approaching or orbiting the Moon, or transiting to cislunar space, and outward into the Solar System, the Milky Way Galaxy or beyond, maintenance of radio order is essential to the accomplishment of successful communication and successful near space and deep space missions.

It may appear a small point, but this single aspect of application of and respect for international law in outer space is a fundamentally enabling legal regime, without which chaos would prevail. It is impressive to consider how much we accomplish when we choose to cooperate, and how much we deny ourselves and destroy when we decline to cooperate.

I undertook to present to you a survey of the nature of the law applicable to outer space today, the *corpus jurus spatialis* of our time. I want to repeat my view that it is a delicate fabric existing on the basis of cooperation. But even as we choose to cooperate to maintain the law, the technology overtakes us and causes us to reconsider what we are doing and what we are about to do. Consider the accelerating rates of change in almost every area of interest to activities in outer space. Dr. George Robinson will address some of the anticipated changes ahead, and what those changes may require in our thinking.

Thank you.

National Center for Remote Sensing, Air, and Space Law
at The University of Mississippi School of Law,
The Journal of Space Law,
and
The International Institute of Space Law
jointly present

The Eilene M. Galloway Symposium on Critical Issues in Space Law

The Cosmos Club
2121 Massachusetts Ave. N. W.,
Washington, D. C.
December 11, 2006

A presentation titled:

INTERSTITIAL SPACE: FUTURE INHABITANTS AND EVOLVING *CORPUS JURIS SPATIALIS*

- BY -

DR. GEORGE S. ROBINSON

INTERSTITIAL SPACE: FUTURE INHABITANTS AND EVOLVING *CORPUS JURIS SPATIALIS*

Remarks by <u>Dr. George S. Robinson</u> regarding the current and future "envoys of mankind" on celestial bodies and other components of interstitial space – December 11, 2006, Cosmos Club, Washington, D.C.; *The Eilene M. Galloway Symposium on Critical Issues in Space Law*

I. <u>Defining "Interstitial Space" for *In Situ* Use by Human*kind* and Post Human Inhabitants</u>

For the instant discussion, interstitial space is defined as a component or "property" of matter forming a continuum, whether separating electrons from neutrons and positrons, photons from neutrinos and quarks, asteroids from planets, space dust from human fabricated space habitats, solar systems from galaxies, black holes and 96% of the universe…dark matter, *ad infinitum.* Interstitial space, then, can be viewed both holistically…as in an ocean…and in specific contexts. The operative words for any legal definition of interstitial space might include function, control, intent, use, context…and quantum mechanics at work. Dr. Stephan Hobe provides a good assessment of issues, both settled and unsettled in law, regarding extraction and appropriation of certain space resources…including "celestial bodies", however they may be defined (paper presented at the *International and Interdisciplinary Workshop on Policy and Law Relating to Outer Space Resources: The Example of the Moon, Mars, and Other Celestial Bodies*, held at McGill University last June 28-30, 2006). The focus, here, is on human*kind* or transhuman and post human "envoys of mankind" inhabiting or otherwise existing off-Earth as "*other* celestial bodies", i.e., as components or objects of interstitial space. And "envoy", itself, is defined either as a "representative" or "messenger"' offering a distinctly functional difference between the two words when characterizing the current status of our astronauts and future envoys of mankind in near and deep space.

Before addressing the comparatively fragile nature of humans in an off-Earth environment of interstitial space, it would be helpful to establish a reasonable foundation of expectations for human*kind* and post human alternatives based in part on what is referred to as "Moore's Law." In 1965, Gordon E. Moore was the young director of the Fairchild Research and Development Laboratories, where he made a very interesting discovery, i.e., the complexity of minimum cost semi-conductor components had been doubling once a year, every year, since the first prototype microchip had been produced six years before. He claimed that this doubling would continue every year for the next ten years. In the global computer industry, it is referred to as the power of information technology that doubles every 18 months…again, *ad infinitum.*

Then, in 2002, the twenty-seventh doubling occurred precisely as predicted with a billion transistor chip. If occurring without interruption, technological evolution sustained by the constant of time can and will produce almost unbelievable transformative results when you have a curve that doubles and redoubles consistently. Although the principle and context in which Moore's Law has been applied is occasionally challenged, and in certain instances is without fully supportive empirical data, various computer-related technologies are telescoping dramatically the time it will take for humans to transcend the constraints of their biology, to become transhuman, i.e., human*kind*, and even post human components and/or properties of interstitial space. Both jurisprudence, or legal philosophy, and its positive law practitioners must help prepare, and be prepared for, the changes wrought by this technological transcendence of human biology.

In the context of Moore's Law, we need also be aware of the Singularity Principle, originally conceived by Verner Vinge as the fundamental discontinuity in history created by the technological invention of smarter-than-human intelligence. The Principle has evolved in various ways, but the core concept remains the same, i.e., as noted by Eliezer Yudkowsky, "there is a massive discontinuity approaching, a Singularity, within human history", and it has to do with the "rise of smarter-than-human intelligence, the ability of technology to alter human nature, the final conquest of material reality through nanotech, or some other fundamental change in rules."

Now, returning to the defining of interstitial space and its component parts, it should be noted that scientists have not really defined "celestial body" in scientific terms, other than to say what one is, e.g., a planet...a natural object of certain mass, density, volume, location, and the like. But humans and human*kind* in outer space, as well as on Earth, are natural objects...every bit as much, for example, as a planet and even the International Space Station and artificially intelligent robotics and biorobotics used as extensions of human senses and the unenhanced or enhanced central nervous system. Not to accept this means we tend to raise ourselves all too frequently much too far above our biological origins in trying to understand what and who our species is...and *how* the principles inherent in Natural Law Theory might apply in an endless variety of circumstances.

Now, how does "the law" apply to these entities occupying interstitial space? One tangible definition of "interstitial space" is that it is *not* simply a vacuum without properties of its own. ***Query***: If space exists between, and as a part of, the properties of matter, is there really such a thing as interstitial space...a non-existent entity? Perhaps, but only when expressed as a *space-time* continuum, i.e., a relatively short time between quantum matter, between "things", as scientists might define it. And measurable space-time depends in large part on the density and mass of a given "thing."

II. The Limits to Unenhanced *Homo sapiens sapiens* in, and as a Part of, Interstitial Space

Among many other scientists, Robert Park, of the American Physical Society, asserted that "[s]ending people into space is very old-fashioned, sort of a hangover from the Cold War era. Robots can do just about everything in space better and cheaper." What may be a statement of the obvious to some, may be difficult to accept by others. And that statement asserts unaltered human biology in its pristine form is too fragile, cumbersome, and "expensive" to rely on long-term and permanently as our envoys, explorers, resource exploiters, and permanent settlers of deep space...or as permanent inhabitants of interstitial space even in near-Earth orbit. For unaltered humans in space, highly advanced external life-support technology, or internal biotechnological integrations that do away with periodic homeostasis and other systemic re-acclimations on Earth's surface, are necessary.

The most significant potential for the consequences of internally unenhanced human fragility in space (other than failure of external life support technology) may well be referred to as the "enemy within." The human body under normal circumstances is host in symbiotic relationships to myriad types of viruses, bacteria, fungi, and the like, all held in a constant state of balanced tension by the host immune system. When that system is disrupted, say, by unusual amounts and types of irradiation deriving, for example, from a solar flare, the T-cells of the immune system are the most vulnerable to the resulting irradiation and may diminish within 24 hours sufficient to cause death of the host body within three days after exposure. Stress, alone, may cause chronic infections and accelerated death through overburdening and disruption of the immune system.

Additionally, irradiation can precipitate mutation of cells that results in accelerated forms of cancer. The effects of radiation on the central nervous system, on cataract formation, and the immune system create high risks to human space flight at present, simply because they are not known…the number of relevant experiments and resulting usable data are unacceptably *de minimus*. The relative unknown factor is true also for the loss of calcium, muscle mass, homeostasis, and occurrence of chronic space adaptation syndrome (failure or compromise of inner ear functions and consequent loss of balance and orientation with resulting nausea, etc., resulting primarily from a gravity-free or low gravity environment). These are but a small handful of the known components and obstacles that mark or evidence human vulnerability and fragility in a space environment…natural or synthetic.

The active or passive space "tourism" of human biology (other than of short duration or the extremely long-term reliance on cryogenics, embryo freezing and "hatching" at the ultimate destination in space, advanced human hibernation, postponement of aging through genetic intervention, i.e., reprogramming the genetic coding relating to organic death, and space born second, *et seq.*, generations), is nonsensical in terms of the hostility *in extremis* of space to unaltered/unenhanced human biology. It also is unnecessary if the real philosophical and theological constructs influencing or directing human*kind* movement off Earth are to ensure the ultimate survival of the cognitive, sentient, and sapient essence(s) of *Homo sapiens sapiens, Homo sapiens alterios, Homo alterios spatialis,* etc.

Humans and human*kind* will be relied on to convey or represent these messages of human/human*kind* "essences" to and in space. For purposes of the instant discussion, however, the term "soul" is not addressed as a part of, or synonymous with, the "essence" of humans or of human "nature." Here, the discussion is limited to biologically empirical data, leaving the definition of "soul" in a theological context to the humanists and the "Chief Judge of the Most Supreme Court." Nevertheless, the door remains open to empirically-based biological definitions of what constitutes a human or human*kind* soul.

Human "essence" or "nature" is assessed in the context of distinguishing taxonomic criteria (e.g., relying in part on genome/genetics and biological systemics, such as the reproductive system, skeletal system, endocrine system, vascular system, integumentary system, digestive and alimentary systems, and even morphology and ethology, etc.). These distinguishing factors may well help reduce to manageable portions for cyberspace (are cyberspace *personas* separate and distinct from their creators for purposes of separate accountability under cyberlaw?) and outer space lawyers the concept of an intelligent and independently accountable telepresence under some future regime of law. Focusing on the biologically based expressions of human "essence" and "nature" will demand a greater spectrum of criteria in astronaut or "envoy" selection than has heretofor been thought necessary. They, in effect, will become a very small number of "elitist" envoys or representatives of the entire species, or, ultimately, human*kind*/transhumans. Even for comparatively short- duration manned space objectives, such as missions to Earth's moon and Mars, and long- term or permanent habitation of that sister planet, it is less difficult to change what is human and what are human*kind* cognitive, sentient, and sapient essences than it is to terraform the planet and "*other* celestial bodies", or otherwise create technologically artificial, long-term life support habitats for *Homo sapiens sapiens*; particularly in deep space.

It should be noted briefly here that incipient research into the human epigenome, the array of chemical markers and switches sitting on top of the DNA that tells the genes what to do, as well as when and where to do it, indicates the long-debunked theory of Jean-Baptiste Lamarck was inherently correct, to a degree, i.e., that external environmental changes to the genome/genes could in fact be passed along to succeeding generations (e.g., diet, smoking, synthetic vitamins, etc.). Although these "acquired" changes...more often than not "defects"...seem to result for the most part in abnormal and frequently harmful characteristics, the possibility of adaptation to abnormal environments by directed changes to the epigenome may allow humans or human*kind* in future generations to adapt "naturally" to Earth-alien environments.

Epigenetics illuminates some of the subtle nuances that bring "nature" and "nurture" together in a fashion that may help us shape the societies in which we hope to live in the future...perhaps on "other" celestial bodies. "If environment has a role to play in changing your genome," says Moshe Szyf, a research pharmacologist at McGill University in Montreal, "then we've bridged the gap between social processes and biological processes."

III. Evolution versus Devolution?

For purposes of defining "the law" as it might apply to future intelligent component inhabitants of interstitial space serving as "envoys of mankind/human*kind*", it might be expressed as the "neurophysiological interpretation reflecting the survival dictates of an evolving sentient species." This definition can apply to humans and human*kind* regardless of physical location.

On Earth, we rely on the genesis of our controlling jurisprudence deriving from the secular-humanist principles of Natural Law Theory. But is that Theory adequate to serve as the foundation of intellectually articulated bio-ecological dictates for humans (and humans in biotechnologically integrated transition, i.e., human*kind* or transhumans)? Can it serve effectively as the foundation of a pseudo-human presence in space: For example, an independently interactive "telepresence", the latter being defined as the projection of a user's sensory, cognitive, and motor capabilities to a distant environment? Alternatively, the distant environment can be recreated virtually at the location of the user or operator. In the former case, the user's sensory channels can be linked to remote sensors. For example, a user's vision can be linked to remote cameras, providing an exocentric or egocentric frame of reference. The user's actions in the proximal locality drive the movements of the remote actuators. In this case the task environment is digitalized and recreated as a virtual interactive environment surrounding the operator in which local actions are transformed into distant actions…all in and through interstitial space.

Mars, for example, can be explored by sending to its surface small robots and sensors, and, with virtual reality, people can have a *virtual* presence on Mars or anywhere else in interstitial space, perhaps even creating electronic virtual presence communities. Now, suppose those robots are bio-technological integrations with humanlike characteristics that allow self-replication (as in the case of current nanotechnology self-replication capabilities) and metabolic activities. Add advanced artificial intelligence capabilities, or expanded anthropocentric intelligence, or sentient capabilities in human biotechnologically integrated form…are we really looking at a robotic entity, or are we seeing the incipient stages of a species alteration invoking a reassessment of the applicability of Linnaean taxonomic principles? Are we in fact looking at the next steps in human and human*kind* evolution, i.e., transhumans leading to post humans, beyond the biologist's and taxonomist's definition of "evolution" as a change in the gene pool of a population over time?"

Now, very briefly, a "transhuman" may be said quite simply to be a transitioning form between *Homo sapiens sapiens*, i.e., being human, and becoming "post human." In many ways, given the current and near-term state of invasive medicine and biotechnological integration capabilities, a good many humans in the industrialized world…including our current "Envoys of Mankind"…might be considered as in the first phases of being "transhuman." Perhaps it is both correct and safe to say that it is still a bit too early to attempt a determinative and, therefore, fully useful definition of "transhuman." Nevertheless, at the very basis of transhumanism and the "creation" of transhumans are the incipient steps in the re-interpretation of what it means to be human.

In the realm of evolved and evolving biorobotics, we are addressing those characteristics of emerging beings with intellectualizing capabilities that outperform, or function differently in a totally unique fashion, those characteristics of humans and even certain enhanced human*kind* with basic biological properties of the human species still intact. These are entities for which there is no ambiguity regarding their differentiation from *Homo sapiens sapiens*. "Post" humans are "in addition to", and not necessarily a replacement of, humans. And post humans may be differentiated by the environments in which they will be designed to function; in the current circumstances, long-duration and permanently off Earth, primarily in *outer* interstitial space. In fact, as mused by Nick Bostrom, a highly noted and respected member of the faculty of philosophy at Oxford University,

> "Posthumans could be completely synthetic artificial intelligences, or they could be enhanced uploads…or they could be the result of making many smaller but cumulatively profound augmentations to a biological human. The latter alternative would probably require either the redesign of the human organism using advanced nanotechnology or its radical enhancement using some combination of technologies such as genetic engineering, psychopharmacology, anti-aging

therapies, neural interfaces, advanced information management tools, memory enhancing drugs, wearable computers, and cognitive techniques."

There are broad basic principles of biology shared by all carbon-based life forms. One is "grow or die" and another is "seed dispersal", or pursuit of new ecotones and other forms of survival adaptation. Human and/or human*kind* migration off Earth is not only necessary, it is critical to the survival of the human species, or its very essence or nature...and it has been taking place since carbon-based life occurred and evolved in its simplest form. With increasing complexification of earthly biota, reflecting both the Singularity Principle...at least in part...and Moore's Law, life must continue to evolve and migrate into new ecotones, niches of nature, where it can compete and survive.

Evolution of *Homo sapiens sapiens* has followed the same path, and the essence or nature of the species, in one form or another...collectively and individually...must continue its migration into space to help assure its survival through the biological (and now biotechnological) principle of seed dispersal. That *essence* or *nature* must be defined with sufficient empirical data to have it reflected in the next step of human evolution; a biotechnological evolution with a short time span available, given the evolving and telescoping nature of technology consistent with Moore's Law and, perhaps, the Singularity Principle itself. Evolve...or devolve.

IV. Humans, Human*kind*, and Post Humans: Early Distinguishing Characteristic(s)

So, it may well be that the parameters or characteristics that define exactly what it means to be "conscious" is the determinative factor of differentiation once reproduction by sexual and asexual means, parthenogenesis, biological *ex vitro* manipulation/fertilization, etc., are eliminated as a necessity for entity or species continuum. In this respect, the most likely *in situ* architects, e.g., construction workers, explorers, miners/managers/engineers/scientists/resource control, capture, and commercial exploiters of resources found both on celestial and "other" celestial bodies...however those terms are defined in specific contexts...will be transhumans and, ultimately, post humans, i.e., humans altered *in extremis* (both in terms of morphology and significant portions...if not all...of the central nervous system and supporting systemics).

Defining the distinction between transhumans and posthumans may likely rest upon determining empirically the essence, or nature, of *Homo sapiens sapiens* by, in turn, grasping the quantifiability of "consciousness." Interestingly, the traditional, but rather archaic definitions of "consciousness" offered by Webster's include "the quality or state of being aware...of something within oneself." The word "conscious" is defined as "sharing another's knowledge or awareness of an inward state or outward fact." Now, the definition of "awareness" are endless, and also not empirically helpful. Nevertheless, for purposes of the instant discussion, the long struggle that preceded the current secular understanding of "consciousness", and what it means, will be set aside.

From the melding and interaction of Rene Descartes' theory of *res extensa* (material substance) and thinking substance (*res cogitans*) in the 17th century, through John Watson's and Ivan Pavlov's observable results of consciousness found in resultant behavior; the "siren song of Sigmund Freud's theory of the unconscious mind"; Francis

Crick's 1976 move from Cambridge University to the Salk Institute to pursue his self-absorbing research on the biological basis of consciousness that would lead to the causes, as well as the correlates, of consciousness; and Crick's protégé Cristophe Koch's ensuing research based on the belief that here are "very specific neurons that subserve consciousness", and his belief that the "real challenge will be …to develop genetic techniques to selectively activate specific groups of neurons to see how they are related to different conscious states"; to the currently intense and broad-scale research into consciousness that has even led to the fledgling field of "neurotheology" attempting to manage in a reductionist fashion something we call the human "soul." Imagine, once this element of consciousness that defines *Homo sapiens sapiens* approaches an understanding based in large part on underlying empirical data…we change it to create something we call a true transhuman and post human.

Most importantly, however, is having a strong grasp of the empirical underpinnings of "consciousness" and "conscious awareness." From a taxonomic perspective, if the distinction between genus (Homo) and species (sapiens) is "consciousness" and level or quality of sentient and abstract reasoning, then we must ask whether biotechnologically integrated robots (biobots) with better indicators of consciousness and conscious awareness with abstract reasoning will be a new species or subspecies of *Homo sapiens sapiens*. Or will such an entity be characterized as no more than a biotechnological extension of human reasoning used to "assist" humans in a critical space-time and human biologically threatening off-Earth environment? At this point, consciousness seems to be an integral component in the defining of the human species.

But just what is "consciousness" or "conscious awareness?" In terms of biological evolution, is it possible that consciousness and abstract reasoning is an unnecessary "add-on", not essential to survival of the species, let alone the individual representative? Does a *coma* qualify for consciousness, or is it the "potential" for consciousness and abstract reasoning that determines what constitutes humanity or humanness…human essence or human nature? Does a coma with a "subconscious" awareness qualify as "conscious" awareness? Does a foetus born without the ability to be conscious (e.g., severe hydrocephalism) fail to qualify for possessing human "essence" or human "nature" under the "conscious awareness" test? At what point in, or part of, a coma can it be determined that an individual is no longer possessive of a "self", the basis of the Terri Schiavo issue that came before the Florida courts and the U.S. Supreme Court? Does telepresence either in cyberspace or outer space, or on "other celestial bodies" incorporate "consciousness", or is it simply a *reflection* of the consciousness of the programmer/user, etc.? Is the existence of a genome, alone, determinative of a species that exhibits "consciousness" and abstract reasoning? Is it, perhaps, a simple percentage of gene sequencing, *ad infinitum*? And what about "avatar" consciousness…?

Recent research at the Salk Computational Neurobiology Laboratory indicates that our "consciousness" is less a factor in decision making than we have assumed to date. As for "*un*conscious" decision making, the research suggests the factors normally associated with evolutionary and survival requirements of the individual representative of the species are the directive factors, i.e., obtain necessary nutrition sources, replicate, avoid predators, protection from natural elements, etc. Consciousness, then, would be a form of explaining and rationalizing what the unconscious already has done. True or not, the issue has been joined by neuroscientists, cognitive psychologists, artificial intelligence specialists, philosophers, and theologians.

As noted, above, we assume *conscious awareness* is becoming increasingly biologically/biochemically/biophysically measurable through ongoing research. The human "soul" is God's. What is being addressed, here, is whether conscious *awareness* is becoming sufficiently identifiable empirically that, in a transhuman or post human, intelligent biobot or other form of advanced artificial or enhanced intelligence, it can be considered independently accountable under some form of law. The next issue for research and assessment, then, is whether such "artificial" conscious *awareness* must also be responsive to involuntary deprivation as a means of enforcement in order to be treated as independently accountable under law. That issue, however, is for a separate undertaking.

Nevertheless, for the moment it is reasonably safe to assume that the human mind, that three pound blob of gray matter, is more than the sum of all the body parts that support it, i.e., not just a carbon based biological "technology" that responds to external and internal stimuli. At a minimum, there is something very troubling about this empirically based reductionist approach to defining what makes a species, a subspecies, and a representative specimen, unique, i.e., the approach lurks somewhere in the causative factors for the hard-core humanist on one side and the equally as hard-core secularist on the other. This mystery of "consciousness" and abstract reasoning approached by scientist-reductionists have certainly complicated the long path of the secularists to reduce the essence of "humanity" to the consequences of material causes.

Now, the issue becomes whether these evolving biotechnological entities existing in interstitial space as "envoys of mankind" can be reasonably considered "*other* celestial bodies" that have been referred to by Mrs. Eilene Galloway. Will our Natural Law Theory be looked to for defining legal principles, or will these other non-anthropocentric intelligent and significantly or fully autonomous entities exist with some unique and independent accountability under some yet-to-be-defined theory and dependent legal regimes? More importantly, perhaps, is the question whether this is *really* a problem for practitioners of *corpus juris spatialis*. Is it a relatively imminent issue? The fact remains that the issue *is* critical since the basic research and development have been and are being conducted...is happening now within the first phases of astronaut transhumanism occurring, and telepresence situated in interstitial space, as well as on celestial bodies, in its rudimentary, but tangible, stages.

V. Natural Law Theory and Outer Space: Is No Legal Theory Safe Anymore?

Can Natural Law Theory serve as the genesis of a unique *corpus juris spatialis*? Many variations of Natural Law Theory have evolved over the centuries, and in its most classical form at the outset, the Theory espoused views that opposed, or were the opposite of, traditional moral skepticism. The Thomist vision of Natural Law viewed it as the rational nature of humans given by God, emphasizing the nexus between why there was a Creation and God's purpose for human beings in that Creation. This, in turn, defined how humans "ought" to lead there lives, i.e., Thomism asserts that a primary principle of Natural Law Theory is that all humans must do what is "good" and abstain from acts of "evil." In a fashion, it was an early attempt at Einstein's *Theory of Everything*, that is, an attempt to "read the mind of God."

Later, in ancient Greece, moral laws deriving from Natural Law Theory were seen to be reflections of positive law since they varied from nation to nation, or culture to culture, according to their expressions in legislation and implementing rules. Since these laws were transitory, they were not really considered binding in the sense that they were Devine Dictates. This was a kind of early cultural relativism that was opposed by the likes of Plato, Aristotle, and Cicero, who believed that morality was not relative, but rather inherent in the nature of humans, i.e., it must be obeyed regardless of whether it is reduced to legislation and implementing positive rules. Currently, we call this "moral objectivism", and it forms the basis of classical Natural Law Theory. All that is needed to qualify as Natural Law Theory is that it embraces the view that moral law is independent of legislative acts; but that there also is nothing that dictates moral laws as immutable.

So, what is the necessity for any connection between Natural Law Theory and the view that morality is immutable, i.e., non-transferrable through biotechnological evolution to transhumans, particularly post humans? Here, of course, the pragmatic or empirically quantifiable characteristics of the "essence" or "nature" of being *Homo sapiens sapiens* are being examined.

Whether the Thomist view, the view of Natural Law Theory and moral dictates associated with Thomas Aquinas, or the more secularist view premised on evolving empirical data underlying the bioecological nature of *Homo sapiens sapiens*, it is a traditional weakness in the many variations of Natural Law Theory that they are unclear, at best, in their applications. The basic conclusion in determining the relationship between the amorphous and transitory characteristics of morality and the alledgedly abiding principles of human rights embraced by Natural Law Theory (i.e., each human has certain rights simply by virtue of being born or even simply being conceived) is that we must act in accordance with our human nature. And, again, we are back to researching and assessing what constitutes human "nature."

What is *natural* for us *to do*, individually and collectively, particularly as significantly *enhanced* human*kind* and post humans? Do we know everything there is to know about Natural Law? Answer: No. Is Natural Law a continuously unfolding event requiring legal philosophers to analyze constantly evolving scientific data and technology that may add, amend, or otherwise compromise existing human and human*kind*/post human rights deriving from Natural Law Theory? Answer: Yes. Our knowledge of Natural Law precepts and principles will always be incomplete as humans and transhumans evolve. Although Dr. Ernst Fasan seems to believe these higher forms of intelligent life flowing from the loins and minds of human*kind* "will still be human", and referred to perhaps as *Homines sapientes sapientes* (personal letter to the author, 11/02/06), a new BioTechoNatural Law Theory may well have to be formulated and implemented once two or more post humans have been created, self-replication, and independent metabolic capabilities have been accomplished…and *artificial* consciousness has been achieved in the context of advanced artificial intelligence.

We also have to look at what indicia are used by taxonomists to distinguish between two species/subspecies of the same genus. Is it the genome? The number of genes? Gene sequencing, etc.? Is it the simple existence of a specific genome that determines a genus, species, or subspecies? Or is it a percentage of the gene sequencing expressions that is determinative? Just how subtle can the genetic transition be between one species to another under current taxonomic criteria? And then, what will the unfolding research in epigentics do to the commonly accepted view that your deoxyribonucleic acid (DNA) is who you are...and the belief, say, of Prof. Szyf at McGill University, that "unlike genetic mutations, epigenetic changes are potentially reversible?" Further, epigentics offers the perspective that "free will" has an impact on our understanding of genetic dictates. In all, however, we may just have to formulate an entirely new taxonomic Kingdom, in addition to the Animal and Plant Kingdoms.

Then, again, we may well be at the point in human and human*kind* evolution where the "bush" of evolution splits yet again...and an entirely different entity is created that is not anticipated or encompassed in the Linnaean system of taxonomy; that is, not only is it not human or human*kind*, it "thinks" and communicates in a fashion totally outside an organic, (regardless of whether carbon-based), non-anthropocentric form of intelligence, but capable of cross communication with varying forms of traditional carbon-based biology. We are beginning to find these cross-communications capabilities between humans and other orders of animals, such as the cetaceans (whales, porpoises, etc.).

VI. A Passing Conclusion

***Unsettled Issues*:**
Will the U.S. National Aeronautics and Space Administration continue its belief and related policies that robotic and biorobotic autonomy will be the future of space exploration...and settlement? At what point will Homo sapiens sapiens *have evolved itself into a new species or subspecies through biotechnological integration and/or the creation of a highly advanced form of autonomous artificial intelligence exhibiting some recognizable form of conscious awareness and personal deprivation for purposes of enforcement sanctions? And at what point will these entities be of sufficiently independent and autonomous "personhood" to invoke a unique theory of jurisprudence resulting in positive laws to which they would be individually accountable for their decisions and actions?*

****

And that is where we seem to be from one perspective in determining whether the human creation of self-replicating entities with an artificial "consciousness" and metabolic capabilities can be individually and separately accountable to a regime of positive law deriving from existing Natural Law Theory...or whether a new Non-Natural Law Theory must be allowed to develop for altered/enhanced biotechnologically integrated individuals functioning solely in *outer,* non-Earth, interstitial space as an "other" celestial body; perhaps as *Homo alterios spatialis* in accordance with Linnaean taxonomic principles.

Again, as noted by Eilene Galloway, potential legal issues must be evaluated on basic scientific and technological facts. Legal philosophers and practicing space lawyers must be prepared to pluck a petal and disturb the fabric of the universe in an empirically knowledgeable fashion. Clearly, space jurisprudents and practicing lawyers with a broad spectrum of expertise must keep up with, and stay ahead of, the anticipated technological and biotechnological users of interstitial space, commercial or military. All the more important, perhaps, if the "users" are actually a part of interstitial space and involve highly advanced artificial intelligence, advanced forms of human intelligence, sophisticated forms of telepresence (and perhaps even teleportation), cyberspace among the "celestial bodies" and "...other celestial bodies" composing interstitial space, and, finally, fully post human "Envoys of Mankind."

At some point, sooner rather than later, humans, human*kind*/transhumans, and post humans, will have to communicate and otherwise interact effectively in interstitial space. To accomplish this task, a formal framework of rather unique values and principles will have to be formulated. With an eye to Moore's Law, this, too, may have to be accomplished much sooner rather than later. Additionally, it may well become one of the most critical issues for consideration by multidisciplinary experts, including space jurisprudents and practicing space lawyers who currently are defining and assessing that body of law frequently referred to as *corpus juris spatialis*...or, perhaps, even *corpus juris spatialis interstitialis*.

The not-so-simple question remains, however; i.e., are we creating autonomous entities who or which can be held individually accountable under a regime of positive law based on principles of existing Natural Law Theory...or will we be faced with interacting with entities having principles and values deriving from some unique legal theory of interspecies interaction as yet unknown to us? As noted previously, an infrastructure of laws based on empirical data is needed to guide relations between and among humans, human*kind*/transhumans, and post humans. The time to start formulating this infrastructure is well at hand, if not of critical moment, for space lawyers.

SUGGESTED READING

-Francis Crick, *The Astonishing Hypothesis: The Scientific Search for the Soul* (1994).

-Ray Kurzweil, *The Age of Spiritual Machines: When Computers Exceed Human Intelligence* (1999).

-Joel Garreau, *Radical Evolution: The Promise and Peril of Enhancing our Minds, Our Bodies – And What it Means to be Human* (Doubleday, New York – 2004).

-Leonard Susskind, *The Cosmic Landscape: String Theory and the Illusion of Intelligent Design* (Little, Brown and Co., 2005).

-G.S.Robinson, "No Space Colonies: Creating a Space Civilization and the Need for a Defining Constitution (30 Journal of Space Law No.1, pp. 169-179; 2004). Also by Robinson, "Transcending to a Space Civilization: The Next Three Steps Toward a Defining Constitution" (31 Journal of Space Law No. 1, pp.147-175; 2006), and G.S.Robinson and Lauria, R., "Legal Rights and Accountability of Cyberpresence: A Void in Space Law/Astrolaw Jurisprudence" (Annals of Air and Space Law Vol. XXVIII, pp. 311-326 (2003).

-E.S. Yudkowsky, "Staring into the Singularity" (http://sysopmind.com/singularity.html 5/227/01).

-S. Hobe, "Adequacy of the Current Legal Regulatory Framework Relating to the Extraction and Appropriation of Natural Resources"; paper presented at the June 28-30,

2006 *International and Interdisciplinary Workshop on Policy and Law Related to Outer Space Resources: The Example of Moon, Mars, and Other Celestial Resources*, McGill University, Institute of Air and Space Law, Montreal, Canada.
- D. O'Neil, "Classification of Living Things: An Introduction to the Principles of Taxonomy with a Focus on Human Classification Categories", (http://www.anthro.palomar.edu/animal/ -July 21, 2006).
-*Epigentics*-Wikipedia,The Free Encyclopedia (http://en.wikipedia.org/wiki/Main_Page.).
-J. Kesan – Learning Cyberlaw in Cyberspace, "Personal Jurisdiction in Cyberspace: Brief Summary of Personal Jurisdiction Law, at (http://www.cyberspacelaw.org/kesan/kesan1.html).
- E.S. Yudkowsky, "The Singularitarian Principles", 1999-2000; rev. 4/19/ 2001 (http://sysopmind.com/sing/principles.ext.html).

Eilene M. Galloway Symposium on Critical Issues in Space Law
The Near-Earth Object (NEO) Protocol

Russell L. Schweickart
Chairman, Association of Space Explorers Committee on Near-Earth Objects, 125 Red Hill Circle, Tiburon, CA 94920

Abstract: Near-Earth objects (NEOs) are being discovered at an accelerating rate in response to a Congressional directive in 1998 that NASA should discover 90% of all such object greater than 1 kilometer in diameter by 2008. The discovery rate is about to increase even more since Congress revised the goal in December 2005 calling for the discovery of 90% of all NEOs greater than 140 meters in diameter by 2020. This program is popularly known as the Spaceguard Survey. The discovery of over 4600 NEOs in the past eight years, 713 of which are greater than 1 km in diameter has been very impressive. Nonetheless these numbers will be dwarfed by the anticipated discovery of over 400,000 NEOs, of which approximately 40,000 will exceed the 140 meter diameter goal at the completion of the revised program.

Based on this very large anticipated database of NEOs and on the experience of the current program, it is certain that thousands of these NEOs will have at least a small probability of impacting Earth within the next 100 years. Of these thousands, perhaps dozens will have predicted impact probabilities high enough to warrant attention and potentially action. These specifics, in combination with the extant capability, with adequate advanced warning, to launch robotic space missions to deflect threatening NEOs will create a worldwide call for action to protect the public from the potential devastation of an unimpeded impact.

Given the inherent international nature of the NEO threat and the inevitable shifting of risk between nations in the process of deflection, the United Nations will have to be prepared to make, in a time constrained environment, a series of complex and vital decisions to assure that the world public is protected from a potentially devastating but preventable natural disaster.

Background:

The knowledge that the Earth has been subjected to impacts by asteroids and comets throughout its history has been known by astronomers and geologists for centuries. Public awareness of this reality became widespread during the last two decades of the 20th century due primarily to the claim by Alvarez, et al, in 1984 that the end-cretaceous mass extinction which eliminated the dinosaurs and approximately 75% of all species living at the time (65 million years ago) was caused by the impact of an asteroid or comet. Their claim was strongly reinforced with the discovery of the Chicxulub impact crater in the Yucatan Peninsula of Mexico in the mid 1980s.

In 1993, while conducting one of the first dedicated astronomical searches for Earth approaching asteroids, the team of Shoemaker, Shoemaker and Levy discovered a disrupted comet which subsequently, as predicted, crashed into Jupiter. This event, the impact of the Shoemaker-Levy 9 comet was watched in real time by dozens of major telescopes both on Earth and in space and made clear to the world that major impacts between asteroids and comets continue to occur.

Early Warning

In response to these and other developments the US Congress established what has come to be called the Spaceguard Survey, directing NASA to discover 90% of the NEO population greater than 1 kilometer in diameter by 2008. While this program has been making steady progress since its 1998 inception, the destructive power of the much larger population of objects down to diameters of 140 meters and below was called to the attention of Congress by many sources resulting in a revision of the Spaceguard Survey goal in December, 2005. In the FY2006 NASA Authorization Congress directed NASA to discover 90% of all NEOs with diameters of 140 meters and greater by 2020.

The challenge of meeting this far more ambitious goal is currently being addressed by NASA and the Congress and a plan to achieve it is under development. Regardless of the specific implementation details the NEO discovery rate will increase dramatically over the next decade effectively increasing the known population of NEOs from approximately 4,600 today to well over 400,000. This fact becomes a powerful driving force in the consideration of future public policy for protecting life and property from this cosmic natural hazard.

Whenever a NEO is discovered by the search telescopes it is intensively observed to determine its orbit as accurately as possible. Once an orbit is calculated it is projected forward in time for 100 years to determine whether or not, within the uncertainty of the observations, there exists an intersection (i.e. a collision possibility) with the Earth. Generally this is not the case; however of the 4600 NEOs discovered to date there are approximately 135 which do have some small probability of Earth impact. Of these one or two have been tracked over enough time that they bear watching.

When the revised search program reaches a comparable level of completion these numbers will rise dramatically with the "risk table" (i.e. those with some non-zero probability of impact) growing to the thousands of potential impactors. Of these there are likely to be as many as 100 which fall into the watchful category. Indeed some few may exhibit probabilities of impact that cause general concern.

It is this rapid increase in the anticipated discovery rate which recommends preparation today for the potential of finding one on which action may need to be taken. The essence of the search program is to make such a discovery decades prior to the projected date of impact.

Deflection/Mitigation

At the same time that NASA has been discovering, tracking and cataloging NEOs others have been concerned with and addressing the question of what can be done when one is discovered posing an unacceptable level of impact threat. While NASA and the University of Pisa (Italy) have regularly analyzed and reported the probability of impact (if any) for each discovered NEO over the next 100 years, they have not gone beyond this early warning analysis to address mitigation options should a potential impact rise to a significant level of concern. In large measure NASA's inaction in this regard is due to the lack of assigned responsibility for NEO impact mitigation and the consequent absence of budgetary authority.

In light of this deficiency in public policy several non-governmental organizations have addressed both the technical and policy aspects of NEO impact mitigation. Suffice to say here that the current assessment of the deflection challenge is that, using existing technology all but the most improbable fraction of the total threat (much less than 1%) can be diverted from impact.

The deflection technologies break several ways; impulsive vs. slow and nuclear vs. non-nuclear, being the primary descriptors.

Impulsive methodologies are those which provide a sudden, virtually instantaneous shove to the asteroid. The most obvious scheme is to simply run a spacecraft into the NEO, albeit in the correct direction. This capability was conceptually demonstrated in the July 4, 2005 Deep Impact mission where a US spacecraft impacted comet Tempel 1. While most NEOs of concern are considerably smaller than comet Tempel 1 the mission nevertheless demonstrated the intercept and impact capability.

Another impulsive technique employs a nuclear weapon or explosion on or nearby the asteroid to be deflected. The "favored" technique according to most proponents is a so-called stand-off blast wherein a neutron enhanced nuclear device explodes in the immediate proximity and proper direction from the NEO causing an instantaneous vaporization and explosion of the exposed surface off the asteroid. This departing high velocity surface material shoves the asteroid in the opposite direction as it flys off the asteroid surface.

A fascinating slow deflection technique employs the mutual gravitational attraction between an asteroid and a nearby spacecraft as a towrope. In this application a robotic spacecraft rendezvous with and positions itself immediately in front of (or behind) the asteroid and "hovers" there using very low thrust ion engines. Since the gravity tractor maintains its position in front of the asteroid the weak gravitational attraction between them effectively pulls the asteroid toward the spacecraft. While this technique is relatively weak it has the advantages of not having to touch the asteroid (which is presumably rotating or tumbling) and the spacecraft, with its radio transponder, provides to the Earth a continuous and precise current orbit for both itself and the asteroid.

This last characteristic points to a critical distinction between the impulsive and slow push techniques. While the impulsive methods have greater power (i.e. total impulse) than the gravity tractor (or slow techniques in general) both the kinetic impact and nuclear explosion produce highly uncertain results due to their unknown interaction with the asteroid and the variability of individual asteroids. Conversely the gravity tractor is relatively weak (although some deflections fall within its capability) but the deflection is precise and fully controlled. What appears to be of growing interest is the combination of a kinetic impact for the main push followed by the gravity tractor to precisely determine the result and "trim" the maneuver if required.

International Decision Making

While we can know that a NEO is probably headed for an impact and we have existing technology that can be used to deflect it from an impact, nothing will in fact happen unless a decision to act is made. Who will or should make such a decision?

One of the challenging characteristics of a NEO impact threat is that its probability of occurrence evolves over time and is never known perfectly. The orbit determination for a NEO is dependent (primarily) on optical tracking and as anyone with a technical background knows there is no such thing as a perfect measurement. Since all measurements have some small degree of error there is always an uncertainty in the precise position and velocity of an asteroid. This inherent uncertainty decreases as more measurements are made over time. Conversely even small uncertainties in our current knowledge of the position and velocity of the NEO propagate into much larger uncertainties as the position of the asteroid is projected forward to the time of potential impact.

It is therefore not unusual for an asteroid to require tracking for several years before the uncertainty in precisely where it will be at the time of anticipated impact is smaller than the dimensions of the Earth. In many cases what this will translate into is that a decision of whether or not to deflect a specific threatening NEO will have to be made while the uncertainty is still larger than the Earth. In other words, at the latest time a specific asteroid can be successfully deflected it may not be known whether or not it will actually impact Earth. Waiting for such certainty is not an option and a deflection mission may have to be mounted while the probability of impact is (for example) only 1 in 10, or less.

In such cases it will be unknown where on Earth the NEO will impact, or indeed if it will impact. In general the path of risk, the narrow corridor within which the asteroid will hit, if it is going to hit, extends fully across the entire planet. Therefore, at the latest time a decision to deflect must be made, there will be many nations across whose territory this path of risk traverses. For this, and many additional technical reasons, a NEO deflection decision is an international challenge and not that of any one nation.

Furthermore liability considerations will play a major role in any decision to divert an asteroid. The deflection of a threatening asteroid must either cause it to pass in front of the Earth at the time of impact or behind it rather than hitting it. As a consequence of this any deflection, if only partially successful, may have a new impact point on Earth somewhere along the path of risk in the direction toward which the deflection was targeted. Since by touching (i.e. changing the orbit of) the asteroid an act of God has been converted into an act of humankind the deflecting agent may be very seriously exposed to legal action by the impacted state. It is therefore highly unlikely that a nation state would assume such responsibility absent indemnification having been prearranged.

Since every nation on Earth is at risk of a NEO impact it is clear that international agreements with broad national inputs will have to be developed. However it is also clear in considering the timing requirements which may prevail at the time a threat matures that there is no time available for debate if a deflection is to be successfully executed.

In considering this very challenging international decision process the Association of Space Explorers (ASE) concluded that the international community would need to have in place a boilerplate agreement with specific decision thresholds and criteria such that when a threat materializes the specifics of the situation can be applied and an immediate (or timely) decision emerge.

An analog to the decision process the UN will confront in considering the NEO threat exists in the form of "Mission Rules" which have been developed prior to every human mission in the US space program. Mission rules are a set of codified procedures developed in the months and years before every mission which emerge from a process of considering each possible failure that can occur during that mission. The best response to many such failures is complex and highly debatable. Discussion and debate on these rules may go on for many months and require considerable research and simulation. However, once agreed to and documented they are available for immediate action if and when such failures occur during the mission. Many failures in a space mission demand rapid if not immediate response and month-long debates cannot be tolerated in real-time without jeopardizing the safety of the crew and success of the mission.

The development of an agreed set of thresholds, criteria, and obligations, as well as an agreement on indemnification and other legal instruments will be challenging to develop. Yet if a generalized decision-system is not developed prior to a specific threat arising, it is highly likely that a debate between the subset of nations threatened in a specific instance will be prolonged and acrimonious and perhaps not resolved at all.

The ASE has therefore assumed the challenge of bringing this issue to the attention of the United Nations, specifically COPUOS, with the intention of developing an agreed international NEO deflection decision process prior to any specific threat arising. Such an agreement (or set of instruments) would contain within it the criteria by which equitable and timely decisions can be made when an actual threat develops. Such criteria and guidelines would be developed and agreed upon independent of national borders and boundaries but rather on general principles of common human interest. Should such a decision system not exist at the time a specific threat arises the debate will then revert to power politics and competing national self interest. While the inputs of nations will be essential in the development of a pre-determined decision process, the time for those inputs is nevertheless prior to the emergence of a specific threat.

In order to facilitate the development of such a decision system the ASE is bringing together, in a set of workshops, a pre-eminent group of international experts in diplomacy, international law, space policy and technology, disaster management , etc. Over a period of two years this group of Principals will develop and confront the multitude of challenging decisions facing the international community and generate, as a work product, a draft UN instrument (treaty, guidelines, convention, TBD) codifying a coordinated process for reaching a timely decision on NEO deflection. The output of this series of workshops will be submitted to the Scientific and Technical Subcommittee (STSC) of COPUOS in February 2009 for consideration and deliberation.

ASE has worked with COPUOS (where it enjoys formal observer status) for the past several years making formal technical presentations in STSC on the NEO challenge in 2006 and 2007. ASE also has formal membership on Action Team 14 (NEO) of STSC and will enter the draft NEO agreement into the UN process via the AT-14 adopted workplan.

THE EILENE M. GALLOWAY SYMPOSIUM
ON CRITICAL ISSUES IN SPACE LAW
WASHINGTON D.C., DECEMBER 2006

SPACE TRAFFIC MANAGEMENT
IAA COSMIC STUDY

Corinne Contant Jorgenson
Advancing Space Consulting Group, United States
cmj@advancingspace.com

Kai-Uwe Schrogl
European Space Policy Institute, Austria
kai-uwe.schrogl@espi.or.at

Petr Lala
Czech Republic
petr@lala-web.cz

I. Scope of the Study

Space traffic already takes place. It seems, however, minuscule with regard to the dimension of near-Earth outer space. Around 13.000 man-made objects larger than about 10 cm are currently tracked out of which only 650 are operational spacecraft. On the surface, the management of space traffic does not appear to be a pressing problem. Investigated further, this judgement has to be challenged. A high level or even growing number of launches from more and more launch sites and space ports, the entering of non-governmental entities, the positioning of satellite constellations, an increase in space debris and the advent of reusable launch vehicles supports this judgement. Considering this scenario, conceptualizing space traffic management will turn out to become a relevant task during the next two decades. Space traffic management will, however, limit the freedom of use of outer space. Therefore an international consensus on internationally binding regulations will only be achieved, if States identify a certain urgency and expect a specific as well as collective benefit from this.

II. Definition of Space Traffic Management

The dimension of this task can be assessed, when the following definition of space traffic management is taken as a starting point:

> Space traffic management
> means the set of technical

and regulatory provisions for promoting safe access into outer space, operations in outer space and return from outer space to Earth free from physical or radio-frequency interference.

Since an authoritative definition of space traffic management does not yet exist, this definition has been set up for the purpose of this study. Through this definition, the purpose of space traffic management becomes clear: it is to provide appropriate means so that space activities can be conducted without harmful interference. By that it supports the universal freedom to use outer space as laid down in the Outer Space Treaty of 1967. It should also be clear that for this purpose of achieving a common good, actors have to follow specific rules, which is also in their self-interest.

III. Dimensions and Phases of Space Traffic

Space traffic touches two dimensions: the scientific and technical area, and the regulatory field that are analyzed in this study. Then, those two dimensions of space traffic are applied to analyzing the three phases of space traffic: the launch phase, the in-orbit operation phase, and the re-entry phase. Below are the findings.

IV. Findings

Space Traffic: Current Status and Prospects for 2010 and 2020

- The motion of space objects is influenced by different forces, which cannot be accounted for precisely. Errors in predictions of space object motion are primarily caused by variations of atmospheric density, and the error in predicted position in orbit increases with the square of elapsed time. For this reason, positions of all objects should be monitored systematically and precisely.
- The large majority of active satellites have no maneuver capability and most others have only a limited capacity to change their trajectory.
- There is a slow but steady decline of launch activities since 1980.
- There is a rise in the number of launch vehicles (today 18). There is also a rise in the number of launch centers (today 11).
- The prospects for the introduction of full/partly RLV are still open. In any case, by 2020 they would probably still be limited to supporting missions below 1000 km.
- Human spaceflight has been accounting for 13% of launches during the past 20 years. It might rise with the emergence of new actors in this field but dramatically only beyond 2020.
- Technologies like tethers, stratospheric platforms or space elevators, which might be introduced in the future, will have to be taken into account when rules in particular for the launch and re-entry phase are developed.
- The population of space debris is continuously growing in number (today around 100,000 objects larger than 1 cm, most of them not catalogued).

- The number of catalogued objects is steadily rising (today 13,000 objects larger than approximately 10 cm).
- The number of active satellites remains at 6-7% of total catalogued objects.
- Capabilities for space surveillance rest with the US (and to a smaller extent to Russia and some singular capabilities in Europe); the US provides data and processed information on a voluntary basis.
- The capacity and accuracy of current space monitoring systems is not sufficient to cover small objects and provide for orbital avoidance service for all space assets.
- There are two major catalogues of space population, which is a far cry from the needed unified system of monitoring space traffic.
- Information on space weather is still limited but important for the operation of space objects as well as the prediction of the debris environment.
- The constant monitoring and information of space weather would be a useful tool for implementing a space traffic management system.

<u>The Current Legal and Regulatory Framework</u>

- The general principles of space law provide for a basis and rationale to establish a space traffic management regime.
- There exist some singular rules in international space law as well as in international telecommunication law, which constitute elements for a space traffic management system (especially for the GEO through the ITU). They are, however neither complete nor are they harmonized. ITU rules, aiming at the avoidance of radio-frequency interference are far more advanced than rules, aiming at the avoidance of physical interference.
- In this context, the IADC space debris mitigation guidelines of 2002 (non-binding soft law) encompass elements of space traffic management (use of disposal orbits, notification in case of controlled re-entry; but so far no provisions on the environment, i.e. avoidance of polluting the atmosphere/troposphere).
- Space law is, however, lacking numerous provisions, which are essential for a comprehensive traffic management regime (i.e. pre-launch notification). Of particular importance is a legal recognition of a difference between space objects considered as valuable assets by their owners, and space debris which have no value at all.
- A space traffic management regime has to touch also the question of harmonizing national space legislation (mostly to be established) and its consequential licensing standards and procedures, since they provide the building blocks for assuring technical safety.
- In the context of arms control/disarmament negotiations notification practices (prior to launch) are currently discussed, thus surpassing the status of civilian space law and negotiations in UNCOPUOS.
- The implementation of a comprehensive space traffic management regime would require additional regulation (with regard to information and the execution of

space missions), which would further limit the freedom of use of outer space; in order to achieve a consensus on this, States have to perceive a certain urgency and have to expect a specific as well as collective benefit (as they receive from existing regulation).

- There are interfering factors, in particular military doctrines, which might hinder the establishment and working of a space traffic management regime.

Comparable Traffic Regimes

In international spaces such as high sea—and outer space—no territorial jurisdiction applies. Only personal jurisdiction does. When rules such as traffic management are concerned, this system is far from being efficient. It is the reason why in the high sea, the exclusivity of the flag State is due to be overruled by an extension of the territorial jurisdiction of one or some States. This solution is not acceptable for space activities as there is no territorial jurisdiction involved. The solution of the port State is not usable as, for the time being a satellite does not fly back to Earth, the solution of extension of "coastal" jurisdiction is also impossible for obvious technical reasons. These difficulties should be taken into consideration if and when Space Traffic Management will be set in force.

The Launch Phase

- There is a rise in the number of launch vehicles (today 18).
- There is also a rise in the number of launch centers (today 11).
- The prospects for the inauguration of full/partly RLV are still open. In any case, by 2020 they would still be limited to supporting missions below 1000 km.
- Human space flight might only change dramatically beyond 2020.
- Safety certifications should be introduced.
- A clarification of the term "space object" is needed.
- The question of delimitation of air space and outer space should be revisited.
- The concept of the "launching State" has to be clarified.
- A pre-launch notification is necessary.
- Obligatory information in cases of damage is relevant.
- An international level playing field for transport services should be aimed for with a balance of public and private/economic interest.

The In-Orbit Operation Phase

- Maneuvering and in-orbit collision avoidance (with regard to other operational space objects as well as with regard to space debris) is growing in number and importance.
- Maneuvering in the GEO is intensely applied but with little consideration of possible collisions.
- Reliable collision probabilities can be estimated only when reliable information exists, which currently is not guaranteed.
- There is no prioritization with regard to maneuvers.
- There is no prioritization of certain space activities, no “right-of-way-rules”, nor is any kind of utilization

of space ruled out (except it is against the peaceful uses).

- There is no traffic separation ("one-way-traffic").
- There are no "zoning" rules (restriction of certain activities in certain areas).
- There are no communication rules (advance notification and communication if orbits of other operators are passed).
- The ITU system of nominal orbital positions finds application only to satellites in the GEO.
- Private/commercial actors have started (i.e. through SUIRG and ITU) coordinating against radio-frequency interference.

The Re-Entry Phase

- Intentional (RLVs as well as active debris mitigation) and un-intentional de-orbiting (natural debris mitigation through decay) is now more frequent but care should be taken that large debris structures will be de-orbited in fragments.
- Responsibilities and liabilities for damages caused by space objects or its components ensue not only from international space law but also from the general provisions of national (tort) civil and administrative law.
- The generally shared wish to reduce space debris raises the question, whether regulation should also set a standard under which conditions a re-entry activity is in general legitimate and under which conditions it is not.
- Notification of, and coordination with, local and downrange air traffic, maritime authorities, and local government officials are already considered a best practice in coordinating launch activities.
- Space Law and Air Law have to solve the open issue of passage of space objects through airspace (the Chicago Convention does not apply to space objects in air space).
- The question is posed to introduce certain internationally recognized descent corridors and possibly even impact areas which are not frequently used by other traffic and which might be dedicated to space traffic.

IV. Conclusions

Framework

In the following, a model is provided on how a comprehensive space traffic management regime for 2020 could look like. There could be drafting of an international inter-governmental agreement building on and not replacing the existing treaties. It would include provisions for liability and the basic principle that States are the primary actors but that provisions of the agreement are applicable for private activities as well through national licensing regimes (certain issues will be clarified in the agreement).
This international inter-governmental agreement would:
- Comprise a legal text, which cannot be changed easily and technical annexes, which can be adapted more easily (modeled from ICAO or IMO)
- Contain three parts:

1. Securing the Information Needs

- Defines necessary data (on trajectories as well as radio frequencies)

- Sets provision for the data (sources, governmental as well as private, including financing)
- Establishes a database and distribution mechanisms for data (format of the database, access to data on request, collision warning as a service)
- Establishes an information service on space weather

2. Notification System

- Sets pre-launch notification with better parameters than Registration Convention as well as other provisions (e.g. ITU and proposed UNIDROIT Protocol)
- Provides information on the end of active/operational lifetime of space objects
- Provides pre-notification of orbital maneuvers and active de-orbiting (communication rules and cooperation provisions)

3. Traffic Management

- Clarifies "space objects", including legal distinction between valuable objects and valueless space debris
- Clarifies "fault" in case of damage caused in outer space
- Sets delimitation for the launch phase and clarifying the concept of the "launching State"
- Provides traffic management rules based on the use of the database for the purpose of collision avoidance, including:
  - Safety provisions for launches
  - Zoning (selection of orbits)
  - Right of way rules for in-orbit phase
  - Prioritization with regard to maneuver
  - Specific provisions for GEO (in harmonization with ITU rules)
  - Specific rules for LEO satellite constellations
  - Debris mitigation mechanisms
  - Safety provisions for re-entries
  - Environment provisions (pollution of the atmosphere/troposphere, etc.)
- Clarifies "space objects", including legal distinction between valuable objects and valueless space debris
- Gives a framework and main features for national licensing regimes, which implement the provisions of the agreement
- Sets out an enforcement mechanism (e.g. renouncement of access to information) and dispute settlement
- Clarifies institutionalized interlinks with ICAO and ITU

4. Organization

- The provisions of the three agreements are in a first step monitored by UNCOPUOS and handled by UNOOSA
- In a second step, post 2020:
  - The new agreement may be (together with the existing space treaties) replaced by a comprehensive Outer Space Convention;
  - ICAO's mandate may be enlarged to cover both the aviation and space traffic management legal frameworks;
  - UNCOPUOS as well as UNOOSA functions could be integrated into new ICAO;
  - Space activities by private actors will develop into the same legal status as in air traffic.

<u>Possible first steps in improving the situation in space traffic</u>

• Space debris guidelines

Currently developed Inter-Agency Space Debris Coordinating Committee (IADC) guidelines for mitigating space debris are an important, positive step toward space traffic management. They should be endorsed by the UNCOPUOS as a UN legal document with a view to make their acceptance and implementation universal.

• Collision avoidance

Cataloguing activities (U.S. Strategic Command, European Space Agency, Russian Space Agency, and private companies) should be improved and coordinated. Improvements could include development and deploying new sensors, improving analytical techniques, and incorporating data from sensors not primarily intended for tracking orbiting space objects. Improvements to the GSO catalogue would be considered a priority and should be treated as such by the IADC Subgroup on Measurement.

• Enforcement and checking mechanisms

Neither the UN nor the ITU has any enforcement or checking mechanisms. These are within the power of sovereign states. The ITU list of radio space stations as well as the UN Register of objects launched into outer space reflect governmental announcements only. This situation should be changed, resulting in obligatory registration and provision of unified sets of relevant data.

• Distinction between valuable spacecraft and worthless space debris

The UNCOPUOS or its Subcommittees should start discussing whether or not space debris are space objects in the sense used in space law treaties. If it is decided that space debris are space objects, an additional protocol should be elaborated stating what provisions of the treaties apply to valuable spacecraft and which provisions apply to space debris. If it is decided that space debris are not space objects, the protocol should determine under what conditions space debris can be removed or re-orbited in order to prevent collisions or close encounters with valuable spacecraft.

ADDENDA

15th Manfred Lachs Space Law Moot Court Competition 2006

CASE CONCERNING THE SALE AND OPERATION OF CERTAIN COMMERCIAL REMOTE SENSING SATELLITES

(GALATEA V THALASSA: PROTEUS INTERVENING)

PART A: INTRODUCTION

The 15th Manfred Lachs Space Law Moot Court Competition was held during the Valencia IISL Colloquium. The *Case concerning the Sale and Operation of Certain Commercial Remote Sensing Satellites (Galatea v Thalassa: Proteus Intervening)* was written by Ricky Lee. Preliminaries were held at regional level in Europe, North America and in the Asia Pacific region. The Finals were judged by three Judges of the International Court of Justice.

The final was hosted by the Supreme Court of Valencia. The local organising committee managed to obtain a lot of support; the local sponsors were:

- Generalitat Valenciana - Conselleria de Justicia, Interior y Administraciones Públicas
- Facultad de Derecho, Universitat de València
- Universidad Nacional de Educación a Distancia (UNED) in Valencia
- University CEU-Cardenal Herrera, and
- Colegio Notarial de Valencia.

In addition, McGill IASL, ESA/ ECSL and JAXA sponsored the winners of the regional rounds, and DLR published the Brochure of the moot court.

Results of the world finals:

- **Winner**: University of Auckland, New Zealand (James Townshend and Jonathan Orpin; Coach: Mr. Isaac Hikaka).

- **Runner-up:** Institute of Air and Space Law, McGill University (IASL), Montreal, Canada (Michael Taylor, Susan Trepczynski and Andrew Williams; Coach: Prof. Ram Jakhu).

- 2nd **Runner-up**: Catholic University, Leuven, Belgium (Emmanuel De Groof, Gareth Price and Batist Paklons; Coach: Dr. Walter Thiebaut).

- **Eilene M. Galloway Award** for Best Written Brief: Institute of Air and Space Law, McGill University.

- **Sterns and Tennen Award** for Best Oralist: Mr Andrew Williams (Institute of Air and Space Law, McGill University).

Participants in the regional rounds

In North America:

- William and Mary School of Law (WMS)
- Golden Gate University School of Law (GGU)
- George Washington University School of Law (GWU)
- University of North Dakota - Department of Space Studies(UND)
- Georgetown University Law Center (GU)
- University of North Carolina School of Law (UNC)
- Santa Clara University School of Law (SCU)
- American University, Washington College of Law (AU)
- Institute of Air and Space Law, McGill University (IASL)
- Western New England College School of Law (WNE)

In Europe:

- Warsaw UniversityDepartment, Institute of International Relations, Poland
- Katholieke Universiteit, Leuven, Belgium
- Leiden University, International Institute of Air and Space Law, Leiden, Netherlands
- Universidad de Jaén, Derecho y Administración y Dirección de Empresas, Jaén, Spain
- Université libre de Bruxelles, Belgium
- University of Bremen, Germany

In the Asia Pacific:

- University of Queensland, Brisbane
- Flinders University of South Australia, Adelaide
- University of Sydney, Sydney
- University of Technology, Sydney
- University of New South Wales, Sydney
- University of Melbourne, Melbourne
- China University of Political Science and Law, Beijing
- National Law School of India University, Bangalore
- University Law College, Bangalore
- M S Ramaiah College of Law, Bangalore
- University of Lucknow, Lucknow
- Gujarat National Law University, Gandhinagar
- Tamil Nadu Dr Ambedkar Law University, Chennai
- Hidayatullah National Law University, Raipur
- Mahatma Gandhi University, Ernakulam
- National Academy of Legal Studies and Research, Hyderabad
- Amity Law School, New Delhi

- West Bengal National University of Juridical Sciences, Kolkata
- Balaji Law College, Pune
- Indian Law Society Law College, Pune
- University College of Law, Dharwad
- Bangalore Institute of Legal Studies, Bangalore
- University of Delhi, Delhi
- National Law University, Jodhpur
- Guru Nanak Dev University, Jalandhar
- University of Mysore, Mysore
- Karnatak Lingayat Education Society Law College, Bangalore
- University of Mumbai, Mumbai
- Kerala Law Academy Law College, Thiruvananthapuram
- Dr Ambedkar Government Law College, Chennai
- Padjadjaran University, Bandung
- Parahyangan Catholic University, Bandung
- Aoyama Gakuin University, Tokyo
- Sophia University, Tokyo
- University of Kyoto, Kyoto
- University of Tokyo, Tokyo
- Waseda University, Tokyo
- University of Auckland, Auckland
- National University of Singapore, Singapore
- Chulalongkorn University, Bangkok

Contact details regional rounds:

- *North America:* Milton (Skip) Smith SSMITH@sah.com
- *Europe:* Nawel Faye (new contact!) Nawel.Faye@esa.int
- *Asia Pacific:* Ricky Lee asiapacific@spacemoot.org

Judges for written briefs:

- Dr. Peter van Fenema, Adj. Professor, McGill Institute of Air and Space Law, Montreal / Consultant, The Netherlands
- Prof. Joanne Gabrynowicz, Director, National Remote Sensing and Space Law Center, University of Mississippi School of Law USA
- Prof. VS Mani, Director, Gujarat National Law University, India
- Dr. Martha Mejia-Kaiser, Independent researcher, Mexico
- Prof. Masami Onoda, Kyoto Univ. Graduate School of Global Environmental Studies, Japan
- Dr. Leslie Tennen, Law Offices of Sterns and Tennen,, Phoenix, AZ, USA

Judges for semi finals:

- Ms. Marcia Smith, Director, Space Studies Board, The National Academies, USA
- Dr. Olivier Ribbelink, Head, Research Department Public International Law, TMC Asser Institute, The Netherlands
- Prof. Steven Freeland, School of Law, University of Western Sydney, Australia

Judges for finals:

- H.E. Judge Abdul Koroma, ICJ
- H.E. Judge Peter Tomka, ICJ
- H.E. Judge Bernardo Sepúlveda, ICJ

PART B: THE PROBLEM

CASE CONCERNING THE SALE AND OPERATION OF CERTAIN COMMERCIAL REMOTE SENSING SATELLITES

Galatea v Thalassa: Proteus Intervening

STATEMENT OF FACTS

1. The Republic of Galatea and the neighbouring Kingdom of Thalassa are both industrialised States with a long history of competition, rivalry and even warfare. They are both coastal States on the western shores of the Nereid Ocean. However, relations between them have improved in recent years and many commercial ties exist between the governmental and private entities of the two States.

2. SpaceSense Corp. is a company incorporated in Galatea that is 51% owned by the Government of Galatea. The remaining 49% is owned by private investors in Galatea. SpaceSense operates a fleet of remote sensing satellites and provide images of the 19 States bordering the Nereid Ocean on a commercial basis to commercial interests in Galatea, Thalassa and most of the States covered by the SpaceSense satellite fleet. Two of the satellites, SRS-1 and SRS-3, were both launched by the government-owned Galatean Space Agency into low Earth orbit in 1993 from a facility located in Galatea that is owned and operated by the Galatean Space Agency.

3. NeoImage, Inc. is a company incorporated in Thalassa that is 100% owned by Thalassian private interests. NeoImage developed a new image processing technology, providing images of remarkable detail. Its original business plan was to purchase raw (or primary) imaging data from third-party satellite data providers. The data would then be processed using NeoImage's proprietary technology, and then resold to its commercial customers.

4. In 2000, SpaceSense had scheduled the launch of SRS-17 and SRS-18, which are intended to replace four satellites that are classified as obsolete, including SRS-1 and SRS-3. However, it was estimated that a further six years of operational lifespan existed in both of the retiring satellites. After four months of difficult negotiations, NeoImage agreed to buy both SRS-1 and SRS-3 from SpaceSense for an undisclosed amount. Both companies were at the time in the process of being listed on their respective domestic stock exchanges and, consequently, were keen to finalise the sale as quickly as possible. It was agreed verbally between the presidents of the two companies that the ownership and operation of both satellites were to be transferred at midnight on 1 April 2001. In their haste, no written arrangements were in place prior to 1 April 2001 and none have been concluded since then, between SpaceSense and NeoImage and between Galatea and Thalassa concerning the sale of the satellites. However, during a visit by the foreign minister of Thalassa to Galatea in March 2001, the two foreign ministers issued a joint communiqué that provided, among other statements: The Governments of Galatea and Thalassa both welcome the sale and purchase of SRS-1 and SRS-3, acknowledge that the two Governments have international legal obligations concerning those satellites and agree to consult and indemnify each other to the extent that any loss arises from such international obligations.

5. On 1 April 2001, NeoImage took over the control and operation of the satellites SRS-1 and SRS-3 from its new custom-built ground control facility in Thalassa. As the communication protocols and frequencies were unchanged, SpaceSense continued to retain the ability to control and operate the two satellites from its control facility in Galatea. Two months later, NeoImage began selling processed images of all 19 coastal States from both satellites on the commercial market.

6. The Democratic People's Republic of Proteus is a militaristic State on the northern coast of the Nereid Ocean. Proteus, along with the neighbouring Commonwealth of Larissa, gained independence in 1971 from Galatea after a violent armed struggle. Ever since then, a state of war had existed between Proteus and Larissa, resulting in three major wars and numerous skirmishes. The Governments of both States have long been customers of both SpaceSense and NeoImage for domestic civilian applications.

7. In May 2002, the Government of Larissa ordered high resolution processed images of various locations in Proteus from NeoImage. Using the SRS-1 and SRS-3 satellites, NeoImage obtained the image data of those locations, processed them and sold them to Larissa on its usual terms of trade. The locations in question included several army barracks, air bases, naval installations and nuclear facilities. In the subsequent months, Larissa ordered and obtained more high resolution images of the same and other locations, most of which were military

installations of Proteus. These sales were kept confidential by both NeoImage and the Government of Larissa, although NeoImage suspected at the time that the images might be used for military purposes.

8. In September 2002, fierce fighting broke out again in what became known as the Fourth North Nereid War between Proteus and Larissa. The Larissan Air Force destroyed all the military installations and army concentrations of Proteus with a degree of accuracy that surprised the Government of Proteus. After intensive mediation by the Secretary-General of the United Nations and several resolutions of its Security Council, a ceasefire was declared and the guns fell silent. By then, around 40% of the army, 72% of the air force and all the nuclear facilities of Proteus had been destroyed.

9. During the Fourth North Nereid War, NeoImage quickly came to the conclusion that Larissa had used the images provided by NeoImage for targeting purposes. This conclusion was reached by studying television news and other media reports as to the locations of the air strikes by Larissa, which revealed that they were the same locations as the images provided by NeoImage. Through private channels, NeoImage protested to the Government of Larissa and obtained assurances that Larissa would no longer use images provided by NeoImage for military purposes.

10. The intelligence organisations of Proteus were instructed by the President of Proteus to investigate the causes of the accurate destruction of its forces by Larissa. In January 2003, a highly placed source in the Government of Larissa revealed to Proteus the transactions between NeoImage and Larissa. In the interest of protecting the source from exposure at the time, the Government of Proteus refrained from taking any action against NeoImage and kept this information secret within only the highest levels of its Government. However, it did embark on a secret program to conceal its military facilities and installations from remote sensing satellites.

11. In March 2003, civilian agencies within the Government of Proteus had sought from various commercial providers, including SpaceSense and NeoImage, high resolution images of coastal and rural areas for agricultural and water conservation purposes. NeoImage feared that Proteus would discover its contribution to the military activities of Larissa during the previous war and, consequently, refused the orders. Sadly, the images obtained from SpaceSense and other providers were of an insufficient resolution.

12. After a successful covert operation by Proteus to extract its highly placed secret source in Larissa in October 2003, Proteus publicly revealed its evidence that images were supplied by NeoImage to the Government of Larissa for military purposes. Proteus brought proceedings in the domestic courts of Thalassa against NeoImage for its role in the damage sustained by Proteus during the last war.

13. On 1 January 2004, during New Year celebrations, SpaceSense technical staff at its ground control facility had inadvertently resumed control of both SRS-1 and SRS-3 and, in the process, failed to notice or correct a malfunction in the altitude control of both SRS-1 and SRS-3 that independently and coincidentally occurred at the time. The malfunction caused the computers onboard both spacecraft to perceive erroneously that their altitudes were higher than they actually were, causing the onboard engines on both spacecraft to begin an automatic descent until both spacecraft had entered the atmosphere of the Earth. While SRS-1 was completely destroyed during its descent through the atmosphere, most parts of SRS-3 survived re-entry and landed in a munitions factory in the capital of Proteus. The explosions caused by the impact resulted in heavy casualties and serious property damage.

14. Subsequent independent investigations reveal that the malfunction in the altitude control systems of both spacecraft would have occurred even if SpaceSense had not resumed control of the spacecraft. The cause of the malfunction is unknown. It is also unclear whether the NeoImage control staff would have been able to correct the malfunction if they had been in control of the spacecraft at the time.

15. After the destruction of the two satellites, NeoImage lost most of its customers in the resulting wave of international indignation and was declared bankrupt in August 2004 before it could commence legal action against SpaceSense for the return of both satellites. The legal action brought by the Government of Proteus against it remained unresolved at the time.

16. In September 2004, Proteus began negotiations with both Galatea and Thalassa, seeking compensation for the damage caused by the in-orbit operations and re-entry of the SRS-1 and SRS-3 satellites. After protracted negotiations, the three States agreed that Proteus was entitled to a specified amount of compensation, which was not hitherto disclosed.

However, since there was no agreement as to who, Galatea or Thalassa, or both, was liable to pay such compensation, the three states agreed to jointly refer this issue to the International Court of Justice.

17. On 1 November 2005, Galatea and Thalassa jointly referred the issues of their respective liability for decision by the Court. Proteus was joined as an intervener with the consent of both Galatea and Thalassa, but it was agreed by all three States that Proteus was not to assume an active role in the proceedings.

18. Galatea seeks declarations that:

(i) Galatea has been fully compliant with its obligations under international law as far as the supply of high resolution remote sensing data over the military installations and facilities of Proteus for military purposes is concerned, and under the March 2001 joint communiqué Thalassa bears any international responsibility for those activities;

(ii) In the absence of any specified arrangement on dealing with third-party claims for unlawfulness of activities involving SRS-1 and SRS-3, Thalassa is fully and exclusively responsible in any case where activities involving SRS-1 and SRS-3 would be considered to violate rights of Proteus under international law for the refusal by NeoImage to supply to Proteus remote sensing data over Protean territory;

(iii) In the absence of any specified arrangement on dealing with third-party claims for liability involving SRS-1 and SRS-3, Thalassa is fully and exclusively liable for any claim addressed to Galatea and Thalassa jointly or severally under international law for damage caused to Proteus by the reentry of SRS-3 into the atmosphere of the Earth;

(iv) Galatea is not liable under international law for the economic loss suffered by Thalassa by the loss of both SRS-1 and SRS-3; and

(v) all other relief sought by Galatea in its memorials and oral submissions should be granted and all relief sought by Thalassa should be denied.

19. Thalassa seeks declarations that:

(i) Thalassa has been fully compliant with its obligations under international law as far as the supply of high resolution remote sensing data over the military installations and facilities of Proteus for military purposes is concerned, and under the March 2001 joint communiqué Galatea bears any international responsibility for those activities;

(ii) In the absence of any specified arrangement on dealing with third-party claims for unlawfulness of activities involving SRS-1 and SRS-3, Galatea is fully and exclusively responsible in any case where activities involving SRS-1 and SRS-3 would be considered to violate rights of Proteus under international law for the refusal by NeoImage to supply to Proteus remote sensing data over Protean territory;

(iii) In the absence of any specified arrangement on dealing with third-party claims for liability involving SRS-1 and SRS-3, Galatea is fully and exclusively liable for any claim addressed to Galatea and Thalassa jointly or severally under international law for damage caused to Proteus by the reentry of SRS-3 into the atmosphere of the Earth;

(iv) Galatea is liable under international law for the economic loss suffered by Thalassa by the loss of both SRS-1 and SRS-3; and

(v) all other relief sought by Thalassa in its memorials and oral submissions should be granted and all relief sought by Galatea should be denied.

20. Both SRS-1 and SRS-3 were registered with the Secretary-General of the United Nations in accordance with the 1975 Registration Convention, with Galatea listed as the "launching State" and the "State of registry". No notification of any change of status of SRS-1 and SRS-3 was lodged subsequent to the sale of the spacecraft.

21. Galatea, Proteus and Thalassa are parties to the 1967 Outer Space Treaty, the 1972 Liability Convention, the 1968 Rescue Agreement and the 1975 Registration Convention. All three States were founding members of the United Nations in 1945. Galatea has signed and ratified the 1979 Moon Agreement but Proteus and Thalassa have never signed it nor recognised it as being part of international law.

22. Galatea and Thalassa are both members of the International Telecommunication Union and the World Trade Organisation, while Proteus is a member of the International Telecommunication Union but not the World Trade Organisation.

23. Larissa is a member of the United Nations but is not party to the Outer Space Treaty, the Liability Convention, the Rescue Agreement, the Registration Convention or the Moon Agreement. It is a member of the World Trade

Organisation but is not a member of the International Telecommunication Union.

ADDITIONAL FACTS

1. The March 2001 joint communiqué was in writing and issued to the press.

2. When SpaceSense technical staff resumed control, they were unaware that they had resumed control of SRS-1 and SRS-3, nor was the NeoImage technical staff aware that they had lost control of the satellites. Only one ground control facility can control a satellite at any given time.

3. It is unknown whether the altitude malfunction occurred before, concurrently or after SpaceSense had resumed control of the satellites. It is also unknown what steps, if any, were taken by SpaceSense technical staff that caused the resumption of control.

4. Proteus actually became a member of the United Nations in 1972 and is considered a "developing country" by the United Nations Development Programme. None of the relevant States have signed nor ratified the Vienna Convention on the Law of Treaties.

PART C: FINALISTS BRIEFS

A. WRITTEN BRIEF FOR GALATEA

AGENTS:

Michael Taylor, Susan Trepczynski, Andrew Williams (Institute of Air and Space Law, McGill University Montreal, Canada)

ARGUMENT:

I. Thalassa is liable for NeoImage's covert sale of remote sensing data to Larissa

Thalassa is liable to Proteus for NeoImage's sale of remote sensing data of Protean military installations to Larissa. Galatea had no part in, or knowledge of, NeoImage's remote sensing of Protean military facilities or the sale of this data to Larissa. Thalassa, on the other hand, should have known about these activities.

A. Thalassa had a heightened duty to ensure its territory would not be used to harm Proteus.

Under international law, every State has an obligation "not to allow knowingly its territory to be used for acts contrary to the rights of other States."[1] This obligation extends to persons and private entities under the State's effective jurisdiction.[2] States are not only responsible for their own acts and the acts of their agents;[3] they also have a duty to use due diligence in "preventing, suppressing, and repressing injurious acts."[4] Due diligence is measured by international standards.[5] If a State fails to use due diligence to protect a foreign State, the State will be directly responsible for this failure "since failures by its officials will be imputed to the State as its own acts."[6] States are liable for failing to prevent or suppress acts they could have prevented if they should have known about

[1] *Corfu Channel* (merits) (U.K. v. Alb.), 1949 I.C.J. 4, 22 (9 Apr.); *see also Trail Smelter* (U.S. v. Can.), 3 R.I.A.A. 1911 (1941), *reprinted in* 35 AM. J. INT'L L. 684, 713 (1941) ("A State owes at all times a duty to protect other States against injurious acts by individuals from within its jurisdiction.").

[2] BIN CHENG, STUDIES IN INTERNATIONAL SPACE LAW 616 (1997).

[3] IAN BROWNLIE, PRINCIPLES OF PUBLIC INTERNATIONAL LAW 431-439 (2003); CHENG, *supra* note 2, at 605.

[4] CHENG, *supra* note 2, at 604.

[5] *Id.* at 605.

[6] *Id.* at 604, 616.

them.[7] Moreover, the duty to protect foreign States can be heightened by treaty.

The 1967 Treaty on Principles Governing the Activities of States in the Exploration and Use of Outer Space, Including the Moon and Other Celestial Bodies (OST),[8] establishes basic rights and duties of States carrying on activities in outer space. In particular, Article VI declares that States "shall bear international responsibility for national activities in outer space".[9] Article VI clarifies that direct State responsibility for national activities extends to activities "carried on . . . by *non-governmental* entities" for the express purpose of "assuring that national activities are carried out in conformity with the provisions" of the OST.[10] In this regard, Article VI mandates that the "activities of non-governmental entities in outer space . . . shall require authorization and continuing supervision by the appropriate State".[11] The effect of Article VI on Thalassa is two-fold. Thalassa is directly responsible for NeoImage's outer space activities as if they were its own, and Thalassa has assumed a heightened duty to protect foreign States.

1. Thalassa was the appropriate State to supervise NeoImage's outer space activities.

On 1 April 2001, SpaceSense transferred ownership and operational control of SRS-1 and SRS-3 to NeoImage.[12] NeoImage is incorporated in Thalassa, fully owned by Thalassean private interests, and controlled from a Thalassean facility.[13] NeoImage thus possesses a genuine connection[14] to Thalassa, making it indisputable that NeoImage has a Thalassean *nationality*.

Since NeoImage is a Thalassean company, Thalassa can effectively exercise jurisdiction and control over it. It follows that "every State Party should be directly responsible for any space activity that is within its legal power or competence to control, whether by governmental agencies or by non-governmental entities."[15] Thalassa has the legal authority to monitor and control the space activities of its nationals within its territory, and it is in the best position to do so. As a State Party to the OST, Thalassa has agreed to do all of these things. Thalassa is therefore internationally responsible for NeoImage's space activities.

2. NeoImage aided Larissa in its war against Proteus.

This Court has declared that "the principle of neutrality . . . is of a fundamental character . . . [and] is applicable . . . to all international armed conflict".[16] Hence, "[t]he supply, in any manner, directly or indirectly, by a neutral Power to a belligerent Power, of . . . war material of any kind whatever, is forbidden."[17] War material includes any item whose character makes it obvious it is destined for use in armed conflict.[18] The strategic importance of remote sensing data as war material is evinced by the domestic legislation of two leading space-faring States—the United States and Canada—restricting the sale of remote sensing data to protect foreign States.[19]

Larissa was a belligerent when it ordered high resolution imagery from NeoImage in May 2002; Larissa and Proteus have been in a perpetual state of war for 35 years.[20] Thalassa was therefore prohibited from supplying Larissa with war material for use against Proteus, and it should have prevented NeoImage's sales to Larissa. The military benefit to Larissa of remote sensing imagery of Protean military facilities cannot be disputed. Larissa used this imagery to destroy Protean military installations and army concentrations with a high degree of accuracy.[21] Larissa waged this war with NeoImage's assistance. Hence, NeoImage's sales of remote

[7] *Corfu Channel*, *supra* note 1, at 23-24 (holding Albania liable for permitting the mining of its territorial waters).

[8] 27 Jan. 1967, 610 U.N.T.S. 205.

[9] *Id.* art VI.

[10] *Id.* (emphasis added).

[11] *Id.*

[12] *Compromis*, ¶ 4.

[13] *Compromis*, ¶¶ 3, 5.

[14] The need for a genuine connection or "effective link" to establish nationality is a requirement of customary international law. BROWNLIE, *supra* note 3, at 395-406; *see also* discussion on the need for genuine links *infra* Part 0.

[15] Bin Cheng, *Article VI of the Space Treaty Revisited: "International Responsibility," "National Activities," and "The Appropriate State,"* 26 J. SPACE L. 7, 23 (1998).

[16] *Legality of the Threat or Use of Nuclear Weapons* (advisory opinion) 1996 I.C.J. 1 (8 July) at ¶ 89.

[17] Convention (XIII) on the Rights of and Duties of Neutral Powers in Naval War, 18 Oct. 1907, art. 6, *reprinted in* 2 SUPP. AM. J. INT'L L. 202 (1908).

[18] *See, e.g.*, Declaration Concerning the Laws of Naval War, 26 Feb. 1909, arts. 22-44 (defining contraband of war for purposes of the establishment of an international prize court), *reprinted in* 3 SUPP. AM. J. INT'L L. 179, 196-207 (1909).

[19] Land Remote Sensing Policy Act, 15 U.S.C. §§ 5622(b)(2), 5651(a) (U.S.); Remote Sensing Space Systems Act, R.S.C. 2005, ch. 45, § 4(3)(a) (Can.).

[20] *Compromis*, ¶ 6.

[21] *Id.* ¶ 8.

sensing imagery to Larissa were contrary to Thalassa's legal obligation to remain neutral in the armed conflict between Larissa and Proteus.

3. NeoImage chose to remain ignorant of Larissa's use of its imagery.

A State that assists another in the commission of a wrongful act is also internationally responsible for that wrongful act.[22] The responsible State need not positively know that it is assisting the other State in the commission of a wrongful act; it must only do so "with knowledge *of the circumstances* of the internationally wrongful act".[23]

In assessing NeoImage's "knowledge of the circumstances," this Court should apply "general principles of law recognized by civilized nations".[24] One such principle is the British doctrine of "wilful blindness"[25] or, as it is known in the United States, the "deliberate ignorance" doctrine.[26] This doctrine has been specifically applied in the United States to corporations when their agents suspect a criminal violation but deliberately choose not to investigate further.[27]

Larissa repeatedly requested imagery of Protean military facilities over a four-month period, and NeoImage suspected Larissa would use the imagery for military purposes.[28] Because Larissa and Proteus were in a state of war,[29] NeoImage should have sought assurances from Larissa about how the data would be used. Instead, NeoImage kept its sales confidential.[30] NeoImage deliberately chose to remain ignorant of Larissa's intentions in spite of its well-founded suspicions.

This Court has previously made liberal inferences of fact from circumstantial evidence. In *Corfu Channel*, this Court found that Albania knew about acts committed in its territorial waters despite its denials and the unavailability of direct proof of knowledge.[31] In finding for the United Kingdom, this Court stated, "indirect evidence is admitted in all systems of law, and its use is recognized by international decisions."[32] This Court should therefore find that NeoImage remained wilfully blind.

4. NeoImage's knowledge and corresponding acts are imputable to Thalassa.

Thalassa is directly responsible for NeoImage's outer space activities and had a heightened duty to continuously supervise those activities. If Thalassa had known about NeoImage's remote sensing of Proteus over the four-month period, it would have had a duty to prevent the sales of imagery to Larissa. Thalassa is internationally responsible for NeoImage's outer space activities and it is liable for NeoImage's breaches of international law relating to those outer space activities. Because Thalassa allowed its territory and private entities to be used for acts contrary to Protean rights, Thalassa is internationally responsible to Proteus for these acts. This responsibility includes the corresponding duty to pay for damage caused by breaches of international law.[33]

5. Thalassa acknowledged its international responsibility for the satellites.

In March 2001, a month before the satellites were transferred to NeoImage, the foreign ministers of Galatea and Thalassa released a written joint communiqué welcoming the sale.[34] In this communiqué, both governments expressly "acknowledge [they] have international legal obligations concerning those satellites."[35] The two governments also agreed to "indemnify each other to the extent that any loss arises from such international obligations."[36] The communiqué

[22] Draft Articles on the Responsibility of States for Internationally Wrongful Acts, G.A. Res. 56/83, Annex, art. 16, U.N. GAOR, 56th Sess., U.N. Doc. A/RES/56/83 (2001) [hereinafter Draft Articles].

[23] *Id.* (emphasis added).

[24] Statute of the International Court of Justice, 3 Bevans 1179, 59 Stat. 1031, art. 38(1)(c).

[25] *See, e.g., United States v. Jewell*, 532 F.2d 697, 701 (9th Cir. 1976) (discussing what "British commentators have denominated 'willful blindness' or 'connivance' [i.e.,] the case of the actor who is aware of the probable existence of a material fact but does not satisfy himself that it does not in fact exist"); *see also* Matthew E. Beck & Matthew E. O'Brien, *Corporate Criminal Liability*, 37 AM. CRIM. L. REV. 261, 270 (2002) (discussing cases applying the deliberate ignorance doctrine to corporations).

[26] *Jewell*, 532 F.2d at 700-703.

[27] *United States v. Bank of New England, N.A.*, 821 F.2d 844 (1st Cir. 1987) (teller suspected a customer's deposits and withdrawals violated federal reporting requirements, but chose not to investigate the transactions).

[28] *Compromis*, ¶ 7.

[29] *Id.* ¶ 6.

[30] *Id.* ¶ 7.

[31] *Corfu Channel*, *supra* note 1, at 18.

[32] *Id.*

[33] *See, e.g., Alabama Claims* Arbitration (1872), *in* 1 MOORE, ARBITRATIONS 653 (ordering the United Kingdom to pay compensation to the United States for damage caused by the ship *Alabama* when the United Kingdom, as a neutral, allowed the *Alabama* to be constructed in its territory, knowing that it would enter into service with the Confederacy).

[34] Additional Facts, ¶ 1.

[35] *Compromis*, ¶ 4; Additional Facts, ¶ 1.

[36] *Compromis*, ¶ 4

thus publicly evinces Thalassa's intent to accept its international obligations.

The communiqué not only acknowledges both States' international obligations, it also is a binding treaty between Galatea and Thalassa. It meets all requirements for a treaty under the Vienna Convention on the Law of Treaties.[37] Though none of the Parties to this proceeding have ratified the Vienna Convention, its articles are either existing principles of customary international law or "presumptive evidence of emergent rules of general international law."[38] In this case, the communiqué was in writing,[39] and was issued by foreign ministers, persons with full authority to bind their respective States.[40]

While the communiqué does not list Thalassa's international obligations, under customary international law it is appropriate to consider any other agreement made in connection with the conclusion of the treaty,[41] as well as "any relevant rules of international law applicable in the relations between the parties."[42] In this case, the communiqué specifically refers to the transfer agreement between SpaceSense and NeoImage, welcoming "the sale and purchase of SRS-1 and SRS-3."[43] The transfer of ownership and control is thus an important consideration.

Additionally, the relevant rules of international law include the space treaties ratified by both Galatea and Thalassa: the OST,[44] the Convention on International Liability for Damage Caused by Space Objects[45] and the Convention on Registration of Objects Launched into Outer Space.[46] These treaties mostly address the duties and responsibilities of the launching State. Since Thalassa is not the launching State of SRS-1 and SRS-3, its international obligations arise under Article VI of the OST, which imposes direct State responsibility for national activities in outer space and a heightened duty to continuously supervise them. Because of this provision, Thalassa bears international responsibility for NeoImage's space activities.

B. Galatea is not internationally responsible for NeoImage's outer space activities.

Article VI of the OST limits international responsibility to *national activities*.[47] Because NeoImage is a Thalassean company operating solely in Thalassa, Galatea could not effectively supervise NeoImage. To do so, Galatea would have had to violate Thalassa's sovereignty by repeatedly intervening in its internal affairs. A State may not violate the principle of non-intervention in the domestic or territorial jurisdiction of another State to exercise jurisdiction over extra-territorial activities.[48] Moreover, international law does not require States to do the impossible, or, as it is said, *ad impossible nemo tenetur*.[49] Galatea was therefore not an appropriate State to supervise NeoImage's activities.

1. Galatea was the State of registry only because it was the launching State.

Article VIII of the OST provides that the State on whose register an object is listed "shall retain jurisdiction and control"[50] over it. When the OST was adopted, the drafters did not foresee significant private activity taking place in space.[51] The drafters never considered the possibility of on-orbit satellite transfers between private parties located in different States. In light of the growth of outer space activities carried on by private enterprises, the U.N. General Assembly recently called upon States to provide information on their "current practices regarding on-orbit transfer of ownership of space objects,"[52] reflecting a concern that literal application of Article VIII to on-orbit transfers may be unworkable in certain circumstances. This case is such a circumstance.

In interpreting Article VIII of the OST, this Court should consider the Registration Convention, which limits registration to launching States.[53] Since Thalassa did not launch SRS-1 and SRS-3, it could not register them

[37] 22 May 1969, 1155 U.N.T.S. 331 [hereinafter Vienna Convention].

[38] BROWNLIE, *supra* note 3, at 580; *see, e.g., Territorial Dispute* (Libya v. Chad), 1994 I.C.J. 6 (3 Feb.) (confirming that Article 31 represents customary international law of treaty interpretation).

[39] Additional Facts, ¶ 1; Vienna Convention, *supra* note 37, art. 2(1)a.

[40] Vienna Convention, *supra* note 37, art. 7(2)(a).

[41] *Id.* art. 31(2).

[42] *Id.* art. 31(3)c.

[43] *Compromis*, ¶ 4.

[44] OST, *supra* note 8.

[45] 29 Mar. 1972, 961 U.N.T.S. 187 [hereinafter Liability Convention].

[46] 14 Jan. 1975, 1023 U.N.T.S. 15 [hereinafter Registration Convention].

[47] OST, *supra* note 8, art. VI.

[48] BROWNLIE, *supra* note 3, at 309

[49] Cheng, *supra* note 15, at 25.

[50] OST, *supra* note 8, art. VIII.

[51] *See* CHENG, *supra* note 2, at 607 (noting "in 1967 . . . non-governmental space activities were regarded still as most exceptional").

[52] G.A. Res. 59/115, ¶ 3, U.N. GAOR, 59th Sess., U.N. Doc. A/RES/59/115 (2005).

[53] *See* Vienna Convention, *supra* note 37, art. 31(3)(a); Registration Convention, *supra* note 46, arts. I.c, II.1.

under the Registration Convention. In only one instance has a satellite registration been changed from one State to another—when the United Kingdom transferred AsiaSat and Apstar registrations to the People's Republic of China.[54] In that case, however, the transfer was possible because the United Kingdom and China were both launching States.[55] As the only launching State, Galatea had no choice but to retain its status as the "State of registry".

2. The State of registry cannot always effectively exert jurisdiction and control.

The Registration Convention does not anticipate the situation presented here, in which one State—in this case, Thalassa—was not a launching State. The Convention only discusses the possibility of multiple launching States, allowing them to "jointly determine which one of them shall register the object . . . bearing in mind the provisions of Article VIII" of the OST.[56] This registration would be "without prejudice to appropriate agreements concluded *or to be concluded* among the launching States on jurisdiction and control over the space object".[57] States can therefore "make more or less what arrangement they want, separating, if they so wish, registration from jurisdiction and control, without even having to record such arrangements in the register."[58] Agreements between launching States, current and future, only affect their *inter se* relations. They cannot prejudice third States.[59] In this respect, the requirement of linking jurisdiction and control to registration "cannot be said to have been taken too seriously either [in 1967] or subsequently".[60]

Though Thalassa was not a joint launching State, it implicitly entered into an arrangement separating registration from jurisdiction and control. In deciding whether Article VIII of the OST should literally apply to the sale of SRS-1 and SRS-3, this Court may look to "any subsequent practice . . . which establishes the agreement . . . regarding its interpretation".[61] Galatea and Thalassa had to separate registration from jurisdiction and control as a practical necessity. NeoImage contracted for ownership and operation of the satellites. After SpaceSense transferred control of the satellites to NeoImage, Thalassa became the "appropriate State"[62]—and the only State—that could authorize and continuously supervise NeoImage's activities. In effect, Thalassa assumed Galatea's duties under Article VIII of the OST without becoming the State of registry.

3. Jurisdiction and control must be based on genuine links.

This Court has stressed the need for genuine links with respect to a State's jurisdiction and control. In *Military and Paramilitary Activities in and Against Nicaragua*, this Court stated that, "to give rise to legal responsibility . . . it would in principle have to be proved that that State had effective control . . . in the course of which the alleged violations were committed."[63] In *Nottebohm*, this Court did not allow Liechtenstein to assert a claim against Guatemala on behalf of a German national after hastily giving him citizenship.[64] Finding no genuine connection between Liechtenstein and the German national, this Court declared that "nationality must correspond with the factual situation."[65] In *Barcelona Traction, Light and Power Company, Limited* this Court dismissed Belgium's attempt to assert claims against Spain on behalf of Belgian shareholders in a Canadian company.[66] Only Canada—the company's State of nationality—could seek redress for its losses.[67]

International law favours a functional analysis with respect to ships and aircraft because registration is merely evidence of nationality, while "*bona fide* national ownership, rather than registration or authority to fly the flag, provides the appropriate basis for protection of ships."[68] Satellites are like ships and aircraft in that they are high value, mobile assets requiring registration. The requirement for genuine links was explicitly included into the 1982 Convention on the Law of the Sea[69] and in 1958 Convention

---

[54] U.N. Doc. ST/SG/SER.E/333 (3 Apr. 1998); U.N. Doc. ST/SG/SER.E/334 (3 Apr. 1998).

[55] *Id.*

[56] Registration Convention, *supra* note 46, art. II.2.

[57] *Id.* (emphasis added).

[58] Bin Cheng, *Space Objects and Their Various Connecting Factors, in* OUTLOOK ON SPACE LAW OVER THE NEXT 30 YEARS 214 (Gabriel Lafferranderie & Daphné Crowther eds., 1997).

[59] Liability Convention, *supra* note 45, art. IV(2).

[60] Cheng, *supra* note 58, at 214.

[61] Vienna Convention, *supra* note 37, art. 31(3)(b).

[62] OST, *supra* note 8, art. VI.

[63] *Military and Paramilitary Activities in and Against Nicaragua* (Nicar. v. U.S.), 1986 I.C.J. 4, 64 at ¶ 115 (27 June) [hereinafter *Military and Paramilitary Activities*].

[64] *Nottebohm*, Second Phase (Liech. v. Guat.), 1955 I.C.J. 4 (6 Apr.).

[65] *Id.* at 22.

[66] *Barcelona Traction, Light and Power Company, Limited*, Second Phase, (Belg. v. Spain) 1970 I.C.J. 3 (5 Feb.) [hereinafter *Barcelona Traction*].

[67] *Id.* at 48-51.

[68] BROWNLIE, *supra* note 3, at 398 n.167, 410, 472.

[69] 10 Dec. 1982, 1833 U.N.T.S. 3 [hereinafter CLOS].

on the High Seas.[70] In discussing the need for registration, both Conventions mandated that there be "a genuine link between the State and the ship,"[71] requiring the State to "*effectively exercise its jurisdiction and control* in administrative, technical and social matters over ships flying its flag."[72]

Yet "international law has a reserve power to guard against giving effect to ephemeral, abusive, and simulated creations."[73] Suppose that NeoImage's satellites had been damaged by satellites owned by France. It is doubtful that Galatea could claim damages on NeoImage's behalf because NeoImage is a Thalassean company. If Galatea cannot make a claim on NeoImage's behalf, it should not have to answer for NeoImage's outer space activities. In light of the rapid increase of non-governmental activities in space, the real link to jurisdiction and control is "the traditional connecting factor of nationality."[74] States with "effective jurisdiction" are the most appropriate States to exercise it.[75] Effective jurisdiction exists when a State's legal ability to physically exercise its State functions cannot be overridden by that of any other State.[76] Thalassa's legal power and competence to continuously supervise NeoImage was superior to that of any other State. This Court should therefore acknowledge the *de facto*, if not *de jure*, arrangement between Thalassa and Galatea separating registration from jurisdiction and control.

4. Separating registration from jurisdiction and control has not prejudiced Proteus.

It is undisputed that Proteus is entitled to compensation for the damage it suffered, and it will receive this compensation; the amount has already been determined.[77] This Court is simply being asked to apportion the burden of compensation based on the respective fault and responsibility of Thalassa and Galatea. Galatea acknowledges it is both the State of registry and the launching State. These two facts, however, are not reliable factors for apportioning the burden of compensation.

The drafters of the space treaties were most concerned that injured States be promptly compensated in full.[78] In this respect, registration only assists injured States in identifying the launching State.[79] But the launching State is not necessarily the most culpable State, just as registration is not necessarily an accurate reflection of jurisdiction and control.

5. Galatea is not liable as a launching State for NeoImage's activities.

Article VII of the OST makes each State that launches an object into space internationally liable for damage "by such object or its component parts".[80] Similarly, the Liability Convention makes each launching State "absolutely liable to pay compensation for damage caused by its space object".[81] Both provisions impose liability only when damage is *physically caused* by a space object in a crash, explosion, or some other direct harm.[82] Neither provision makes Galatea liable for NeoImage's sale or refusal to sell remote sensing data. Even if Galatea is liable under the Liability Convention, its provisions are intended to promptly and fully compensate injured States, but do not address the apportionment of liability between States sharing international responsibility, which is the real issue before this Court.

The Liability Convention imposes joint and several liability on all launching States, granting injured States the right to seek full compensation from any or all of them.[83] In apportioning liability between States, the Liability Convention

[70] 29 Apr. 1958, 450 U.N.T.S. 82 [hereinafter High Seas Convention].

[71] CLOS, *supra* note 69, art. 91; High Seas Convention, *supra* note 70, art. 5(1).

[72] CLOS, *supra* note 69, art. 94(1) (emphasis added); High Seas Convention, *supra* note 70, art. 5(1) (emphasis added).

[73] BROWNLIE, *supra* note 3, at 467.

[74] Cheng, *supra* note 58, at 214-15.

[75] Cheng, *supra* note 15, at 24.

[76] *Id.*

[77] *Compromis*, ¶ 16.

[78] *See, e.g.*, Liability Convention, *supra* note 44, pmbl. ("ensur[ing], in particular, the prompt payment under . . . this Convention of a full and equitable measure of compensation").

[79] *See* Registration Convention, *supra* note 46, pmbl. ("Recalling further . . . the liability of launching States").

[80] OST, *supra* note 8, art. VII.

[81] Liability Convention, *supra* note 45, art. II.

[82] *See* CARL Q. CHRISTOL, SPACE LAW: PAST, PRESENT, AND FUTURE 219-20 (1991) (explaining "a claimant would be required to show that the harm flowed directly or immediately from, and as the probable or natural result of, the malfunctioning of the space object"); BRUCE A. HURWITZ, STATE LIABILITY FOR OUTER SPACE ACTIVITIES IN ACCORDANCE WITH THE 1972 CONVENTION ON INTERNATIONAL LIABILITY FOR DAMAGE CAUSED BY SPACE OBJECTS 12-20 (1992) (discussing the Liability Convention's applicability to various types of damage); W. F. Foster, *The Convention on International Liability for Damage Caused by Space Objects*, 10 CAN. Y.B. INT'L L. 137, 155-60 (1972) (same).

[83] Liability Convention, *supra* note 45, art. IV(2).

provides that the burden of compensation will be apportioned between the States to the extent each was at fault; if the extent of the fault for each State cannot be established, the burden of compensation will be apportioned equally between them.[84] The Liability Convention is silent when it comes to assigning fault to a non-launching State with international responsibility. Thalassa was not a launching State, so the Liability Convention does not technically apply, but the burden-sharing provisions are compelling as a matter of logic. For this and other reasons that will soon be apparent, Thalassa should bear the entire cost of all damages to Proteus.

II. Thalassa is responsible for NeoImage's refusal to supply Proteus with data.

Only Thalassa is liable for NeoImage's refusal to supply Proteus with remote sensing data of its territory. Just as Galatea lacked the legal power and competence to effectively monitor NeoImage's supply of remote sensing data to Larissa, Galatea lacked the authority to compel NeoImage to share remote sensing data with Proteus. Only Thalassa could effectively exercise jurisdiction over NeoImage in this respect.[85] Thalassa should therefore be liable for NeoImage's refusal to share data with Proteus, a refusal resulting in yet another violation of international law.

A. The Principles declare norms of customary international law.

In 1986, the U.N. General Assembly, by resolution, adopted the Principles Relating to Remote Sensing of the Earth from Outer Space (Principles).[86] When a U.N. General Assembly resolution declares principles of customary international law, the resolution is binding *erga omnes*.[87] Even if it is not binding, the resolution can have normative value by providing "evidence important for establishing the existence of a rule or the emergence of an *opinio juris*."[88] In this light, the Principles have the hallmarks of a declaration of customary international law for three reasons.

First, the Principles reaffirm (often repeating verbatim) provisions from treaties or pre-existing rules of international law.[89] They reaffirm respect for international law and treaties such as the U.N. Charter, the OST, and the Registration Convention.[90] They reaffirm the principles of freedom of outer space,[91] international responsibility for space activities,[92] respect for State sovereignty,[93] the right to request consultations,[94] and the need to keep the U.N. Secretary-General informed about outer space activities.[95] Most importantly, they reaffirm that *all* outer space activities, including remote sensing, "shall be carried out for the benefit and in the interests of all countries, irrespective of their degree of economic, social or scientific and technological development, and taking into particular consideration the needs of the developing countries."[96] This last provision contains language almost identical to Article I of the OST.[97] The requirement to share remote sensing data, whether upon request or to avert harm, was thus already implicit, if not explicit, in the OST. In all their essentials, the Principles merely reaffirm provisions of the existing treaties and norms of general international law.

Second, the U.N. General Assembly adopted the Principles by consensus and without objection.[98] For a State to oppose a rule of customary international law, it must clearly show opposition from the time of the rule's inception;[99] it is too late to oppose the rule after it is established.[100] Even if a State opposed the rule from its inception, the dissension only prevents the rule from binding the dissenting State; it does not affect the rule's application to other States.[101] In any event, Thalassa did not object to the Principles when they were adopted by consensus

[84] *Id.*

[85] *See supra* Part 0 (discussing the need for genuine links).

[86] G.A. Res. 41/65, Annex, U.N. GAOR, 41st Sess., U.N. Doc. A/RES/41/65 (1986).

[87] *See, e.g., Military and Paramilitary Activities, supra* note 63, ¶¶ 188, 191 (holding that a U.N. General Assembly resolution on friendly relations among States reflected customary international law); *Armed Activities on the Territory of the Congo* (Congo v. Uganda) (merits), 2005 I.C.J. 1, 56 at ¶162 (19 Dec.) (reaffirming that this same resolution on friendly relations among States is "declaratory of customary international law").

[88] *Legality of the Threat or Use of Nuclear Weapons, supra* note 16, ¶ 70.

[89] CHENG, *supra* note 2, at 590; CHRISTOL, *supra* note 82, at 91.

[90] Principles, *supra* note 86, princs. III, IX.

[91] *Id.* princ. IV.

[92] *Id.* princ. XIV.

[93] *Id.* princ. IV.

[94] *Id.* princ. XIII.

[95] *Id.* princ. IX.

[96] *Id.* princ. II; *see also id.* princs. IV, XII.

[97] OST, *supra* note 8, art. I.

[98] CHENG, *supra* note 2, at 589; CHRISTOL, *supra* note 82, at 73.

[99] REBECCA M.M. WALLACE, INTERNATIONAL LAW: A STUDENT INTRODUCTION 12 (1997); *see also* BROWNLIE, *supra* note 3, at 11 (discussing the persistent objector and the subsequent objector).

[100] WALLACE, *supra* note 99, at 11.

[101] *Id.*

and it has apparently not objected to them until now.

Third, the compromise struck by the Principles ended controversy. The Principles "achieved a balance"[102] and represented "equitable legal relations"[103] between the States. Meanwhile, the sensed States' fears of being exploited by the remote sensing activities of sensing States did not materialize during the 18-year period from 1968 to 1986 when the Principles were negotiated.[104] Quite the opposite, the sharing of remote sensing data convinced sensed States that important benefits could be derived from this new technology.[105] The Principles were therefore grounded in existing State practice before being adopted by consensus.[106] Because the Principles conformed to both existing practices and treaties, it was felt that "nothing of substance would be gained by going the treaty route."[107] The Principles ended controversy precisely because of what they purported to reflect: the "valid and constructive marriage between treaty law and customary international law."[108]

B. Proteus had a right to remote sensing data of its territory.

NeoImage's refusal to supply Proteus with remote sensing data was contrary to the Principles. Principle XII specifically grants a sensed State an internationally recognized right of access to remote sensing data of its territory. The Principle states:

As soon as the primary and the processed data concerning the territory under its jurisdiction are produced, the sensed State *shall* have access to them on a non-discriminatory basis and on reasonable cost terms. The sensed State *shall* also have access to the available analysed information . . . on the same basis and terms, *taking particularly into account the needs and interests of the developing countries.*[109]

NeoImage acted contrary to this Principle by refusing to supply Proteus with remote sensing data of its territory *on any terms*. NeoImage's action is especially egregious for ignoring Proteus's needs as a developing country.[110] Thalassa should therefore bear international responsibility for NeoImage's failure to conform to Principle XII.

C. Proteus suffered harm from NeoImage's refusal to supply it with remote sensing data.

Although Proteus obtained remote sensing data from other suppliers, this data was inferior to that of NeoImage.[111] Proteus suffered harm from NeoImage's refusal to supply it with remote sensing data because it was denied access to data it had a right to obtain under customary international law. This Court should therefore hold Thalassa internationally responsible—fully and exclusively—for NeoImage's violations of the Principles.

III. Thalassa is solely liable for damage caused to Proteus by the crash of SRS-3.

Thalassa is liable for damage caused by the crash of SRS-3. NeoImage owned SRS-3 at the time of its crash, and Thalassa is internationally responsible for NeoImage's outer space activities. Thalassa is therefore internationally responsible for damage caused by the crash of SRS-3.

A. Galatea's international obligations merely guarantee Proteus will be compensated.

Galatea concedes Proteus may seek full compensation from Galatea for damage caused by SRS-3. Galatea is liable to Proteus under the Liability Convention because it was the launching State,[112] a fact established at the time of the launch that cannot be changed. But Thalassa, not Galatea, should ultimately be responsible for the damage caused by SRS-3. The real purpose of the liability provisions in the OST and the Liability Convention is to guarantee injured States will be fully and promptly compensated.[113] The need to apportion fault or assign ultimate responsibility among responsible States is altogether different.

The Liability Convention recognizes this difference. Although it creates joint and several liability among multiple launching States,[114] the Convention permits them to conclude agreements regarding how they intend to apportion among themselves financial obligations for which they are liable.[115] In permitting apportionment agreements, the Convention declares such

[102] U.N. Doc. A/AC.105/C.2/SR.439, 5, (3 Apr. 1986) (Brazil's view), *cited in* CHRISTOL, *supra* note 82, at 74.

[103] U.N. Doc. A/AC.105/C.2/SR.440, 5, (8 Apr. 1986) (Mexico's view), *cited in* CHRISTOL, *supra* note 82, at 74.

[104] CHRISTOL, *supra* note 82, at 74.

[105] *Id.*

[106] *Id.* at 93.

[107] *Id.*

[108] *Id.* at 94.

[109] Principles, *supra* note 86, princ. XII (emphasis added).

[110] Additional Facts, ¶ 5.

[111] *Compromis*, ¶ 11.

[112] *Id.* ¶ 2.

[113] *See, supra* note 78.

[114] *Id.* art. V.1.

[115] *Id.* art. V.2.

agreements cannot prejudice the right of injured States to seek the entire compensation from any one of them.[116] Though the Liability Convention does not apply to non-launching States, an injured State can always seek compensation from a responsible State under Article VI of the OST.[117] A State with international responsibility for national activities in outer space is also liable for those activities.[118] As this Court declared in *Corfu Channel*: "it follows from the establishment of responsibility that compensation is due".[119] A responsible State cannot escape liability because it was not a launching State.

If an injured State can seek compensation from a responsible State under Article VI of the OST, there is no reason why a launching State cannot also seek indemnity from a non-launching State, especially when it has an indemnity agreement with that State. The responsible State is accountable to the international community as a whole. Thalassa is therefore internationally responsible to both Proteus and Galatea. Though Galatea is internationally liable to Proteus as a launching State, ultimate responsibility rests with Thalassa.

B. Thalassa is internationally responsible for damage caused by SRS-3.

As has been repeatedly emphasized, Thalassa bears international responsibility for NeoImage's outer space activities. These activities are national activities, which include the activities of non-governmental entities. Consequently, any space activity undertaken by a corporation is imputable to its State of incorporation, "as if it were [the State's] own act, for which it bears direct responsibility."[120]

In apportioning fault between Galatea and Thalassa, this Court should apply internationally recognized principles of law and equity. The OST expressly refers to *international law*,[121] thereby incorporating it into the Treaty. Likewise, the Liability Convention refers to *international law* and to principles of *law* and *equity*.[122] While the Liability Convention does not apply to a non-launching State, it does apply to Galatea and its logic in apportioning fault is compelling. In *North Sea Continental Shelf*, this Court declared:

Whatever the legal reasoning of a court of justice, its decisions must by definition be just, and therefore in that sense equitable. Nevertheless, when mention is made of a court dispensing justice or declaring the law, what is meant is that the decision finds its objective justification in considerations lying not outside but within the rules, and in this field it is precisely a rule of law that calls for the application of *equitable principles*.[123]

Similarly, in this proceeding it is a rule of law within the Liability Convention that calls for the application of equity. NeoImage is ultimately at fault for four indisputable reasons based on equity. First, NeoImage must have assumed the risk its satellites might cause damage when it took control of them. Otherwise, NeoImage could avail itself of the benefits of operating satellites without any of the associated risks. Galatea, on the other hand, would be burdened by risks with no attendant benefits, a manifestly unjust and inequitable result.

Second, NeoImage failed to change the satellites' communication protocols, which would have prevented SpaceSense from inadvertently resuming control. Furthermore, as a member of the International Telecommunication Union (ITU),[124] Thalassa had a duty to notify the ITU about its new use of satellite communication frequencies.[125] Had Thalassa done so, Galatea would have had sufficient notice to avoid resuming control.

Third, because NeoImage failed to continuously monitor the satellites, the loss of control went unnoticed.[126] This failure to monitor is the primary reason for the satellites' loss. If NeoImage had properly monitored them, NeoImage might have been able to regain control and correct the altitude malfunction. NeoImage may have also been able to assure a controlled re-entry into the earth's atmosphere, thereby mitigating the damage to Proteus.[127] NeoImage's

[116] *Id.*

[117] OST, *supra* note 8, art. VI.

[118] Frans G. von der Dunk, *Liability Versus Responsibility in Space Law: Misconception or Misconstruction?*, *in* PROCEEDINGS OF THE THIRTY-FOURTH COLLOQUIUM ON THE LAW OF OUTER SPACE 367 (1991).

[119] *Corfu Channel*, *supra* note 1, at 23-24; see also Cheng, *supra* note 15, at 10 (commenting that "responsibility is a broader concept than liability").

[120] Cheng, *supra* note 15, at 15.

[121] OST, *supra* note 8, art. III.

[122] Liability Convention, *supra* note 45, art. XII.

[123] (F.R.G v. Den/F.R.G. v. Neth.), 1969 I.C.J. 3, 49 at ¶ 88 (20 Feb.) (emphasis added).

[124] *Compromis*, ¶ 22.

[125] INTERNATIONAL TELECOMMUNICATION UNION RADIO REGULATIONS (2004), art. 11.1 (discussing new frequency assignments) and art. 11.2 (discussing duty of State to notify ITU).

[126] Additional Facts, ¶ 2.

[127] INTER-AGENCY DEBRIS COORDINATION COMMITTEE, IADC SPACE DEBRIS MITIGATION GUIDELINES, ¶¶ 3.4.2, 5.3.2 (2002), *at* http://www.iadc-online.org/docs_pub/IADC-

failure to monitor the satellites is imputable to Thalassa under Article VI of the OST. Therefore, only Thalassa is liable for the damage to Proteus.

Finally, Thalassa should have warned Proteus of the re-entry of SRS-3 into the earth's atmosphere. Such a warning might have permitted Proteus to mitigate damage to its territory. With advance warning, Proteus could have evacuated the probable crash site or taken other appropriate measures, thus reducing the number of causalities. Under international law, a State has a duty to warn others if its activities may harm them.[128] This duty is implicit in Article IX of the OST, imposing an obligation on States to conduct their outer space activities "with due regard to the corresponding interests of all other States Parties".[129]

One of the "governing principles" that emerged following the crash of Soviet satellite Cosmos 954 over Canada in 1978—the only international precedent for the type of damage at issue here[130]—was the "duty to forewarn."[131] In 1992, the U.N. General Assembly included this duty in the Principles Relevant to the Use of Nuclear Power Sources in Outer Space.[132] Principle 5 imposes a duty to forewarn when the "space object is malfunctioning with a risk of re-entry . . . to the Earth."[133]

A minimum of regard by Thalassa for the interests of Proteus would have included a warning that space objects were likely to crash into its territory. Thalassa's failure to provide any sort of warning violated its duties to the international community and likely contributed to the severity of the damage suffered by Proteus. As a result, this breach should be taken into account in the apportionment of damages.

C. Thalassa agreed to indemnify Galatea.

The communiqué offers an additional reason for finding Thalassa exclusively liable for the damage caused by SRS-3; Thalassa agreed to indemnify Galatea. It should do so.[134] In the communiqué, the foreign ministers of Galatea and Thalassa agreed that both governments had "international obligations concerning those satellites"[135] and that they would "indemnify each other to the extent that any loss arises from such international obligations."[136]

If the communiqué has any meaning, Thalassa must have accepted international responsibility for NeoImage's outer space activities, the only international obligation it could have assumed without being a launching State.[137] Direct State responsibility for NeoImage's satellites includes liability for any damage they caused.[138] The communiqué does not limit the scope of Thalassa's international obligations with respect to the satellites. Because Thalassa agreed to indemnify Galatea, Thalassa is solely liable for the damage caused by SRS-3.

D. SpaceSense's resumption of control over SRS-3 is irrelevant.

Although SpaceSense resumed control of SRS-3 prior to the crash,[139] this fact is irrelevant for three reasons. First, the resumption of control was inadvertent.[140] SpaceSense did not intentionally take control of SRS-3, and may not have done anything at all to resume control of the satellites.[141] The Parties have stipulated that "[i]t is unknown what steps, *if any*, were taken by SpaceSense technical staff that caused the resumption of control."[142] In any case, SpaceSense was unaware it had resumed control of SRS-3.[143] The resumption of control was unintended and unwanted.

Second, the altitude malfunction would have occurred even if SpaceSense had not resumed control of the satellites.[144] More than one independent investigation confirmed that the malfunction's cause and timing are unknown.[145] The malfunction may have occurred "before,

101502.Mit.Guidelines.pdf (declaring that controlled re-entry is preferable).

[128] *Corfu Channel*, *supra* note 1, at 23-23 (holding that the obligation of a State to warn of "imminent danger" is a well-recognized principle of international law).

[129] OST, *supra* note 8, art. IX.

[130] Steven Freeland, *There's a Satellite in My Backyard – Mir and the Convention on International Liability for Damage Caused by Space Objects*, 24 U. NEW SOUTH WALES L.J. 462, 473 (2001).

[131] Alexander F. Cohen, *Cosmos 954 and the International Law of Satellite Accidents*, 10 YALE J. INT'L. L. 78, 79 (1985); HURWITZ, *supra* note 82, at 128.

[132] G.A. Res. 47/68, U.N. GAOR, 85th Sess., U.N. Doc. A/RES/47/68 (1992).

[133] *Id.* princ. 5.

[134] Vienna Convention, *supra* note 37, art. 26 ("*Pacta sunt servanda*"); *see also* Cheng, *supra* note 15, at 16 (stating that "compliance with treaty obligations is a fundamental principle of international law").

[135] *Compromis*, ¶ 4.

[136] *Id.*

[137] *See supra* Part 0.

[138] See *Corfu Channel*, *supra* note 1, at 23-24 ("[I]t follows from the establishment of responsibility that compensation is due".).

[139] *Compromis*, ¶ 13; Additional Facts, ¶¶ 2, 3.

[140] *Compromis*, ¶ 13.

[141] Additional Facts, ¶ 3.

[142] *Id.* (emphasis added).

[143] *Id.* ¶ 2.

[144] *Compromis*, ¶ 14.

[145] *Id.*; Additional Facts, ¶ 3.

concurrently or after" SpaceSense resumed control of the satellites.[146] The resumption of control had nothing to do with the malfunction.

Third, NeoImage likely would not have been able to correct the malfunction, since it was unaware of the loss of control.[147] In addition, independent investigations revealed that NeoImage may not have been able to correct the malfunction had it been in control of the spacecraft at the time.[148] The combination of the failure to notice the loss of control *and* the uncertainty over whether the malfunction could have been corrected if the loss of control was noticed makes it unlikely that SpaceSense's resumption of control had any impact on the situation. It is therefore irrelevant that SpaceSense inadvertently resumed control of the satellites.

E. Thalassa should make full reparations to Proteus for damage caused by SRS-3.

The obligation of a responsible State to make full reparations is well settled.[149] In *The Factory at Chorzów*, the Permanent Court declared:

> The essential principle . . . is that reparation must, as far as possible, wipe out all the consequences of the illegal act and re-establish the situation which would, in all probability, have existed if that act had not been committed. . . . [S]uch are the principles which should serve to determine the amount of compensation due for an act contrary to international law.[150]

This passage has been cited and applied on many occasions,[151] and is codified in Article 31 of the Draft Articles on State Responsibility for International Wrongful Acts, which provides that reparation for injury "includes any damage, material or moral, caused by the internationally wrongful act of a State."[152] Because Thalassa is internationally responsible for all of NeoImage's activities, it should fully compensate Proteus.

IV. Galatea is not liable for Thalassa's economic loss.

Galatea should not have to compensate Thalassa for economic losses caused by the loss of SRS-1 and SRS-3 or the resulting wave of international indignation directed at NeoImage.

A. Thalassa has failed to exhaust its local remedies.

Thalassa seeks compensation for economic damages allegedly caused to a private Thalassian company, creating a claim of diplomatic protection. Before Thalassa can assert a claim under general international law against Galatea, Thalassa must exhaust its local remedies. As this Court noted in *Interhandel*:

> The rule that local remedies must be exhausted before international proceedings may be instituted is a well-established rule of customary international law; the rule has been generally observed in cases in which a State has adopted the cause of its national. . . . Before resort may be had to an international court in such a situation, it has been considered necessary that the State where the violation occurred should have an opportunity to redress it by its own means, within the framework of its own domestic legal system.[153]

Moreover, the Draft Articles also acknowledge the rule.[154] NeoImage has failed to bring proceedings in the domestic courts of Galatea; therefore Thalassa's claim is barred.

B. The transfer of SRS-1 and SRS-3 was not an outer space activity.

No rule of general international law makes a State directly answerable to another for purely commercial transactions of its nationals.[155] Moreover, the OST and the Liability Convention also do not contain such a rule.[156] Article VI of the OST creates international responsibility only for certain kinds of national activities—outer space activities. Direct State responsibility is thus limited to activities occurring *in outer space*. Galatea respectfully submits that, if the activity does not occur *in outer space*, then it is not an

---

[146] Additional Facts, ¶ 3.

[147] *Id.* ¶ 2.

[148] *Compromis*, ¶ 14.

[149] *See, e.g., The Factory at Chorzów* (Ger. v. Pol.) 1928 P.C.I.J. (ser. A) No. 17, at 47.

[150] *Id.*

[151] *See, e.g., Avena and Other Mexican Nationals* (Mex. v. U.S.) (merits), 2004 I.C.J. 11, 105 at ¶ 119 (31 Mar.); *Arrest Warrant of 11 April 2000* (Congo v. Belg.) (merits), 2002 I.C.J. 5, 67 at ¶ 76 (14 Feb.).

[152] Draft Articles, *supra* note 22, art. 31(2).

[153] *Interhandel* (Switz. v. U.S.) (preliminary objections), 1959 I.C.J. 6, 27 (21 Mar.). See also *Electtronica Sicula S.p.A. (ELSI)* (U.S. v. Ital.) (merits), 1989 I.C.J. 15 (20 Jul.).

[154] Draft Articles, *supra* note 22, art. 44(b).

[155] *Barcelona Traction*, *supra* note 66, ¶¶ 56-58. The official commentaries to the Draft Articles also note "international law acknowledges the general separateness of corporate entities [and the State] at the national level". International Law Commission, *Commentaries to the Draft Articles on Responsibility of States for Internationally Wrongful Acts,* 53rd Sess., Supp. No. 10, 107, U.N. Doc. A/56/10.

[156] CHENG, *supra* note 2, at 487 (stating the OST's drafters probably did not intend direct State responsibility "in respect of breaches of rules and obligations under domestic and private law, such as contracts").

outer space activity under Article VI.[157] In this respect, the legal transfer of a satellite from one owner to another is not an outer space activity, even if the satellite is already in orbit when the transfer occurs.

SpaceSense sold SRS-1 and SRS-3 on 1 April 2001 when the satellites were already in orbit. The location at the time of sale is immaterial because all negotiations and the final agreement between SpaceSense and NeoImage occurred on the earth.[158] If a satellite is sold before its launch and the sale is not part of a launch contract, the sale itself is not an outer space activity. As between Galatea and Thalassa, it should not matter that the sale was concluded after the satellites were in orbit. The launching is relevant only to third States that suffer damage; it does not alter Galatea and Thalassa's relations *inter se*. Any other view of Article VI would lead to manifestly absurd or unreasonable results, an outcome that international law specifically seeks to avoid.[159]

An overly broad reading of Article VI of the OST would "internationalize" every transaction tangentially or remotely related to an outer space activity. For example, virtually every telecommunications dispute could involve direct State responsibility because it involved the use of a satellite. Moreover, a State like Thalassa could find itself internationally liable for a domestic matter such as a labor dispute involving NeoImage and a foreign citizen employed at NeoImage's ground control facility. The drafters of the OST could not have intended such a broad reading of Article VI. Because the sale and purchase of the satellites was not itself an outer space activity, Galatea is not internationally liable for it.

C. Thalassa cannot recover damages from Galatea based upon the Liability Convention.

The Liability Convention precludes recovery for damage caused to "foreign nationals during such time as they are participating in the operation of that space object from the time of its launching *or at any stage thereafter*".[160] Following the sale of SRS-1 and SRS-3, NeoImage was a foreign national (from the perspective of Galatea as the launching State), and, as the sole owner and operator of the satellites, NeoImage was undisputedly participating in their operation. Accordingly, Article VII bars Thalassa from recovering damages under the Liability Convention.

D. SpaceSense sold the satellites without a warranty.

Assuming *arguendo* that Galatea was directly responsible for SpaceSense's sale of SRS-1 and SRS-3, SpaceSense sold the "used" satellites to NeoImage without a warranty. No rule of international law gives rise to an implied warranty for satellites. Moreover, the Convention on Contracts for the International Sale of Goods (CISG)[161] does not apply in this case. The CISG does not apply to sales "of ships, vessels, hovercraft or aircraft".[162] Though space objects or spacecraft are not expressly mentioned, space assets have the same characteristics as the listed objects. All of these items—ships, vessels, hovercraft, and aircraft—are high value assets requiring registration. Satellites, like aircraft, are "mobile equipment of high value or particular economic significance,"[163] requiring registration.[164] The CISG therefore does not apply to the sale of satellites.

Moreover, SpaceSense did not guarantee that the satellites would remain functional for a specific period of time. SpaceSense classified the satellites as "obsolete" and replaced them, though it was "estimated" that the satellites had an operational lifespan of six more years,[165] a claim that NeoImage was free to independently evaluate. Estimates are inherently imprecise and can be incorrect. SpaceSense sold the satellites essentially "as is." In buying used satellites, NeoImage bore the risk the estimate was incorrect; it also would reap the benefit of an understated estimate. The satellites functioned properly for nearly three years. Because SpaceSense sold the satellites without any warranty, Galatea is not directly responsible to Thalassa for them.

---

[157] The on-orbit sale of a satellite had not likely been considered by the drafters of the OST. *Id.* at 607.

[158] *Compromis*, ¶ 4.

[159] Vienna Convention, *supra* note 37, art 32(b).

[160] Liability Convention, *supra* note 45, art. VII (emphasis added).

[161] 10 Apr. 1980, 1489 U.N.T.S. 3.

[162] *Id.*, art. 2(e).

[163] *See, e.g.*, Convention on International Interests in Mobile Equipment, 16 Nov. 2001, art. 2(3) *available at* http://www.unidroit.org/english/conventions/mobile-equipment/mobile-equipment.pdf (entered into force 1 Mar. 2006). This Convention will eventually apply to spacecraft. It currently applies only to aircraft because the protocol on space assets is still being negotiated. Committee on the Peaceful Uses of Outer Space, Legal Subcommittee, *Report of the Legal Subcommittee on its forty-fifth session,* ¶ 108 U.N. Doc. A/AC.105/871 (2006).

[164] OST, *supra* note 8, art. VIII; Registration Convention, *supra* note 46.

[165] *Compromis*, ¶ 4.

Even if SpaceSense had guaranteed that the satellites would work for six years, no conclusion can be drawn as to the cause of the altitude malfunction. The malfunction may have occurred for reasons unrelated to any defect. The malfunction could have occurred because of how NeoImage operated the satellites. Thalassa has the burden of proving the cause of the malfunction. In the absence of evidence, Galatea should not be responsible for the malfunction.

Despite the loss of SRS-1 and SRS-3, NeoImage could have returned to its original business plan of purchasing raw imaging data from other providers and processing it for resale to commercial customers.[166] It failed to do so, however, because it lost most of its customers—the real cause of its economic losses.

E. Thalassa's economic losses resulted primarily from NeoImage's use of the satellites.

Much of Thalassa's economic loss can be attributed to NeoImage losing "most of its customers in the resulting wave of international indignation".[167] The wave of international indignation[168] was due in large part to NeoImage's secretive supply of remote sensing data to Larissa, which Larissa used to attack Proteus and which formed the basis of Proteus's suit against NeoImage in Thalassean courts.[169] The indignation may have also been due in part to NeoImage's refusal to provide image data to Proteus, a blatant violation of customary international law, especially in light of Proteus's status as a developing nation. The indignation was certainly due to the damage caused by the crash of SRS-3.[170] In any case, the wave of international indignation was specifically directed at NeoImage,[171] not SpaceSense. The American statesman, James Madison, noting the value of world public opinion, explained why the new American republic would do well to pay attention to the judgment of other nations: "in doubtful cases . . . the presumed or known opinion of the impartial world may be the best guide that can be followed."[172] In a case like this one, there can be no doubt. The international community could not be totally wrong. Thalassa alone should bear its economic losses.

SUBMISSIONS TO THE COURT

For the foregoing reasons, the Republic of Galatea, Applicant, respectfully requests the Court to adjudge and declare that:

1. Thalassa is liable to Proteus for permitting NeoImage to sell Larissa remote sensing data of Protean military installations.
2. Thalassa is liable to Proteus for NeoImage's refusal to sell Proteus remote sensing data of Protean territory for agricultural and water conservation purposes.
3. Thalassa is liable to Proteus and must indemnify Galatea for the crash of SRS-3 onto Protean territory under the indemnity agreement.
4. Galatea is not liable to Thalassa for economic damages caused by the international community's indignation at NeoImage and the loss of SRS-1 and SRS-3.

[166] *Compromis*, ¶ 3.
[167] *Id.* ¶ 15.
[168] *See, e.g.*, Theodor Meron, *The Martens Clause, Principles of Humanity, and Dictates of Public Conscience*, 94 AM. J. INT'L L. 78 (2000) (describing "the dictates of public conscience" as a key factor in determining the legality of conduct during an armed conflict).
[169] *Compromis*, ¶¶ 12, 15.
[170] *Id.*
[171] *Id.*

[172] THE FEDERALIST PAPERS NO. 63 (James Madison), *reprinted in* THE COMPLETE MADISON: HIS BASIC WRITINGS 245 (Saul K. Padover ed.) (1973).

B. WRITTEN BRIEF FOR THALASSA

AGENTS:

James Townshend and Jonathan Orpin
(University of Auckland, New Zealand)

ARGUMENT:

1. Thalassa has fully complied with its obligations under international law as far as the supply of high resolution remote sensing data of the military installations and facilities of Proteus for military purposes is concerned, and under the March 2001 joint communiqué Galatea bears any international responsibility for those activities

Thalassa submits that it has fully complied with its obligations under international law as far as the supply of high resolution remote sensing data of Protean military facilities is concerned because:

(a) NeoImage Inc's (hereinafter "**NeoImage**") actions were legal under international law;
(b) Should this Court find NeoImage's actions were illegal, Galatea bears international responsibility for them; and
(c) No injustice is created by holding Galatea responsible.

A. *NeoImage's activities were legal under international law*

Thalassa submits that NeoImage's activities were legal under international law. In this regard Thalassa makes two submissions. First, remote sensing of military installations and facilities is a peaceful use of space. Secondly, State responsibility does not extend to ground activities.

(i) Remote sensing of military installations and facilities is a peaceful use of space

Space must be used for peaceful purposes. Article III of the Treaty on Principles Governing the Activities of States in the Exploration and Use of Outer Space, including the Moon and Other Celestial Bodes (hereinafter "**Outer Space Treaty**") provides that:

> State parties to the Treaty shall carry on activities in the exploration and use of outer space, including the Moon and other celestial bodies, in accordance with international law, including the Charter of the United Nations, in the interest of maintaining international peace and security and promoting international cooperation and understanding.

Article IV provides:

> States Parties to the Treaty undertake not to place in orbit around the Earth any objects carrying nuclear weapons or any other kinds of weapons of mass destruction, install such weapons on celestial bodies, or station such weapons in outer space in any other manner.
>
> The Moon and other celestial bodies shall be used by all States Parties to the Treaty exclusively for peaceful purposes. The establishment of military bases, installations and fortifications, the testing of any type of weapons and the conduct of military manoeuvres on celestial bodies shall be forbidden. The use of military personnel for scientific research or for any other peaceful purposes shall not be prohibited. The use of any equipment or facility necessary for peaceful exploration of the Moon and other celestial bodies shall also not be prohibited.

Thalassa submits that NeoImage's activities were not in breach of international law on an ordinary interpretation of the words used in the Outer Space Treaty.[1]

Article III simply provides that space is to be used for peaceful purposes and affirms that the principles of international law apply in space. NeoImage's conduct was peaceful and in conformity with international law. It merely supplied remote sensing imagery to other States. That simply involved capturing images and selling them on the open market. The fact that the images were ultimately used, by a third party government, for a military purpose does not

[1] Article 31(1) of the Vienna Convention on the Interpretation of Treaties provides that a "treaty shall be interpreted in good faith in accordance with the ordinary meaning to be given to the terms of the treaty in their context and in light of its object and purpose." Although neither State is a party to the Vienna Convention on the Law of Treaties reliance may be placed on it as in many respects it is a codification of existing customary law: Presence of South Africa in Namibia, 1971 I.C.J. 54, at 47 (June 21).

affect the peaceful nature of NeoImage's conduct.[2]

Article IV only prohibits *certain specified* military uses of space. The first paragraph of Article IV prohibits the placement of nuclear weapons or weapons of mass destruction "in orbit around the Earth." The second paragraph of Article IV prohibits using "the Moon and other celestial bodies" for certain military purposes.[3] Neither paragraph is applicable here. NeoImage has not placed any weapons in space and nor has it made any use, military or otherwise, of the Moon or any other celestial bodies.

That ordinary interpretation of the words of Articles III and IV is supported by an examination of State practice in the area.[4] Military use of remote sensing data is widespread and common place. A short list of examples of State practice illustrates the point:

(a) Detailed Satellite Pour L'observation de la Terre (hereinafter "**SPOT**") imagery of Soviet military installations, including photographs of Soviet nuclear weapon storage facilities, was widely available and published in the 1980s;[5]
(b) SPOT acknowledges that remote sensing data and photographs are sold to military customers worldwide,[6] reportedly selling 80 per cent of its material to military buyers;[7]
(c) SPOT promotes military uses of its images. Its company brochure previously detailed the intelligence gathering uses of its data;[8]
(d) During the First Gulf War the Pentagon confirmed buying remote sensing images to supplement the photographs taken by its own spy satellites;[9]
(e) During the Iran/Iraq war both countries purchased remote sensing imagery that was used for attack planning;[10] and
(f) Pakistani and Israeli nuclear facilities have been repeatedly sensed and imaged.[11]

Indeed, as Professor Bin Cheng has observed:[12]

> Military reconnaissance satellites have not only become simply a fact of international life that States just have to learn to live with, but also a vital instrument in the process of arms control and the preservation of international peace.

Feder has similarly observed that:[13]

> Satellite reconnaissance, however, is not expressly prohibited by the Treaty, despite its military applications. Under the Treaty, space is to be used solely for peaceful purposes; therefore the issue is whether the use of spy satellites falls within that realm. [Most commentators view military reconnaissance as legal within the peaceful purposes provision of the Outer Space Treaty.] The use of satellite reconnaissance does not violate international law, which grants every nation the right to conduct espionage.[14]

---

[2] That is not to say that the attack on Proteus itself was legal. Larissa, a member of the United Nations, breached Art 2(4) of the Charter of the United Nationals by attacking Proteus.

[3] The two paragraphs of Article IV should, in Thalassa's submission, be read as separate prohibitions: the first paragraph dealing with the use of outer space; and the second paragraph the use of the Moon and other celestial bodies. See Bin Cheng, *Definitional Issues in Space Law: the 'Peaceful Use' of Outer Space, Including the Moon and Other Celestial Bodies, in* STUDIES IN INTERNATIONAL SPACE LAW, 513 (Bin Cheng ed. Clarendon Press 1997), 516 – 519.

[4] Article 31(3)(b) of the Vienna Convention on the Law of Treaties provides that the interpretation of treaties is to be informed by "any subsequent practice in the application of the treaty which establishes the agreement of the parties regarding its interpretation".

[5] *French Spot Satellite Shows Soviet Northern Fleet Facilities,* AVIATION WEEK & SPACE TECH., Mar. 2, 1987, at 44.

[6] *Satellite Photography Receives Boost as SPOT 2 is Launched*, DEFENSE ELECTRONICS, Mar. 1990, at 78.

[7] Swahn, *International Surveillance Satellites – Open Skies for All?*, 25 J. PEACE RESEARCH 229, (No. 3) (1988) at 232.

[8] Harry Feder, *The Sky's the Limit? Evaluating the International Law of Remote Sensing*, 23 NYU J INT'L L & POL 599, 604 (1990-1991), at 624-625.

[9] *Id*, 625.

[10] Barber, *French Sold Spy Photos to Saddam*, FIN. TIMES (London), Jan. 11, 1991, 1.

[11] Zimmerman, *Evidence of Spying*, BULL. ATOM. SCIENTISTS , Sept. 1989, at 24.

[12] Bing Cheng, *Legal and Commercial Aspects of Gathering Data by Remote Sensing, in* STUDIES IN INTERNATIONAL SPACE LAW (Bin Cheng ed. Clarendon Press 1997) 572, 586.

[13] Feder, *supra* note 8, 605-606. The text quoted in square brackets is footnoted in the original article. Citations from that footnote are omitted.

[14] This Court may have regard to the writings of commentators as Article 38(1)(d) of the Statute of the International Court of Justice allows the Court to apply "the teachings of the most highly qualify publicists of the various nations, as a subsidiary means for the determination of rules of law."

Finally, reference to the *travaux préparatoires* of the Outer Space Treaty supports this interpretation. The United States' representative to the First Committee of the United Nations said, "Outer space should only be used for peaceful – that is, non-aggressive and beneficial – purposes. The test of any space activities must not be whether it is military or non-military, but whether or not it is consistent with the United Nations Charter and other obligations of law."[15]

Accordingly Thalassa submits that NeoImage's actions were not in breach of international law and that it is entitled to a declaration accordingly.

(ii) State responsibility does not extend to ground activities

In addition Thalassa submits that State responsibility does not extend to ground activities.

Under Article VI of the Outer Space Treaty "State Parties to the Treaty … bear international responsibility for national activities in outer space". As is apparent from the plain meaning of those words States only bear responsibility for "activities in outer space". As one commentator has noted "the Outer Space Treaty provision used by Principle XIV does not apply international responsibility to what are in essence ground activities."[16] That is also the view of the British National Space Centre.[17] Thalassa submits that this interpretation is correct.

Accordingly, NeoImage was entitled to take satellite imagery of the earth from outer space. The only part of its conduct that might potentially be in breach of the Outer Space Treaty was the supply of that imagery to Proteus. That activity, however, took place on the surface of the earth, not in outer space. Accordingly, Thalassa submits that NeoImage's actions were not "activities in outer space" and that it is entitled to a declaration that it has fully complied with its international obligations.

B. *Galatea bears international responsibility for NeoImage's activities*

If this Court finds that NeoImage's activities were in breach of international law, Thalassa submits that it is Galatea, the launching State, that is legally responsible for NeoImage's actions.

At international law States are not, as a general rule, responsible for the acts of private citizens and corporations.[18] Space law, however, provides a rare exception to this principle in the Outer Space Treaty.[19] The regime of responsibility and liability in outer space is contained in Articles VI and VII of the Outer Space Treaty. Article VI provides:

> State Parties to the Treaty shall bear international responsibility for national activities in outer space, including the Moon and other celestial bodies, whether such activities are carried on by governmental agencies or by non-governmental entities, and for assuring that national activities are carried out in conformity with the provisions set forth in the present Treaty. The activities of non-governmental entities in outer space, including the Moon and other celestial bodies, shall require authorization and continuing supervision by the appropriate State Party to the Treaty. …

The effect of that article is that States are responsible for activities that would not as a matter of customary international law be imputed to States. Article VI ascribes to States "international responsibility for national activities in outer space". The issue before this Court is whether Galatea or Thalassa is responsible for the activities of NeoImage.

The Outer Space Treaty, however, contains no definition of the term "national activities". In determining the meaning of that phrase Thalassa submits that it is helpful to have regard to the surrounding provisions of the Outer Space Treaty, particularly Article VII, which in conjunction with Article VI sets out the regime of State responsibility and liability for non-

[15] Travaux Préparatoires of the Treaty on the Principles Governing the Activities of States in the Exploration and Use of Outer Space, including the Moon and Other Celestial Bodies A/C.1/PV.1289; 3 Dec.1962, at 13.

[16] Feder, *supra* note 8, 638.

[17] Review of the Concept of the "Launching State" – Report of the Secretariat, A/AC.105/768 21 Jan. 2002.

[18] Peter Lovett 3 Int. Arb. 2990 (1892), at 2991.

[19] The exception is particularly striking if it is born in mind, as Professor Kerrest points out, that not even in ultra hazardous industries like the nuclear industry are States responsible for the activities of private interest. See Armel Kerrest's paper *International Legal Regime for Outer Space: The Liability Convention* (last visited July 19, 2006) < http://fraise.univ-brest.fr/~kerrest/IDEI/Kerrest-liab-the-hague.pdf>.

governmental entities in outer space. Such an approach to interpretation was taken by the Permanent Court of International Justice in *Competence of the International Labour Organisation*[20] and is mandated by Article 31(1) of the Vienna Convention on the Law of Treaties.[21]

Article VII provides:

> Each State Party to the Treaty that launches or procures the launching of an object into outer space, including the Moon and other celestial bodies, and each State Party from whose territory or facility an object is launched, is internationally liable for damage to another State Party to the Treaty or to its natural or juridical persons by such object or its component parts on the Earth, in air space or in outer space, including the Moon and other celestial bodies.[22]

The combined effect of Articles VI and VII is that the State bears "international responsibility" for "national activities" in outer space, while the launching State is "internationally liable" for any damage caused. Although responsibility is dealt with in Article VI and liability in Article VII, Thalassa submits that international responsibility and liability for damage caused by space objects is to be borne by the same State and is not severable. Thalassa makes two arguments in support of this submission.

First, liability cannot logically be separated from responsibility. The two represent different sides of the same coin. In *Chorzów Factory* the Permanent Court of International Justice established that legal responsibility entails a legal obligation to make reparations.[23] That is to say that a State is liable as a result of its responsibility.[24] It follows there where there is no State responsibility there cannot be liability, as breaches of international law will not be attributed to the State.

Secondly, the fact that the different terms 'liability' and 'responsibility' are used is merely a peculiarity of the English language which is not reflected in other versions of the text, which are equally authoritative.[25] The French version uses the same word 'responsabilité' in both Articles VI and VII, the Spanish version the same phrase 'responsables internacionalmente' and the Russian version repeats the phrase 'международную ответственность'. The Chinese text likewise employs the phrase '国际责任' in both articles.

Thalassa submits that read as a whole and taking account of the peculiarities of the English language the Outer Space Treaty imposes both liability and responsibility on the same State. The State that is responsible for particular space activities will also be liable for them, and conversely that State that is liable for particular space activities will be responsible for them.

It is clear from Article VII of the Outer Space Treaty that the launching State is liable for damage caused by its space object. Articles II and III of the Liability Convention are to the same effect.

Accordingly, Thalassa submits that on a proper interpretation of Articles VI and VII of the Outer Space Treaty the nationality of space activities under Article VI is determined by reference to the launching state. Moreover Thalassa submits that in the instant case Galatea was the launching State of SRS-1 and SRS-3 and is accordingly responsible for NeoImage's activities.

The term "launching State" is defined in Article 1(c) of the Liability Convention:

The term "launching State" means:

(i) A State which launches or procures the launching of a space object;

---

[20] Competence of the International Labour Organisation, 1922 P.C.I.J (ser. B) Nos. 2 and 3 (Aug. 12). At page 23 the Court held that "it is obvious that the Treaty must be read as a whole, and that its meaning is not to be determined merely upon particular phrases which, if detached from the context, may be interpreted in more than one sense."

[21] Article 31(1) of the Vienna Convention on the Law of Treaties, *supra* note 1.

[22] Articles II and II of the Convention on International Liability for Damage Caused by Space Objects (hereinafter "**Liability Convention**") similarly make the launching State liable for damage caused by its space object.

[23] Chorzów Factory (Merits), 1928 P.C.I.J. (ser. A) No. 17 (Sept.13), at 29. See also Reparation of Injuries Suffered in the Service of the United Nations, 1949 I.C.J. 174, (April 11) at 184.

[24] Bin Cheng, *International Responsibility and Liability for Launch Activities*, 20 AIR AND SPACE LAW 297 (1995), at 300.

[25] Article XVII of the Outer Space Treaty provides that "the Chinese, English, French, Russian and Spanish texts are equally authentic".

(ii) A State from whose territory or facility a space object is launched.

It is evident that there are four ways a State may be considered the launching State:[26]

(a) If it launches a space object;
(b) If it procures the launch of a space object;
(c) If a space object is launched from its territory; and
(d) If a space object is launched from its facility.

Galatea is the launching State on all four tests:

(a) SRS-1 and SRS-3 were launched by the government-owned Galatean Space Agency;
(b) The launch was procured the Galatean Space Agency;
(c) SRS-1 and SRS-3 were launched from a ground control facility in Galatea; and
(d) The facility used was owned and operated by the Galatean Space Agency.

In addition, Galatea has acknowledged that it is the launching State. Article II(1) of the Convention on Registration of Objects Launched into Outer Space (hereinafter "**Registration Convention**") provides that "[w]hen a space object is launched" it shall be registered on an appropriate national registry. Article IV(1) provides that each "State of registry" shall furnish certain information, including the name of the launching State, a designator or registration number, and basic orbital parameters, to the Secretary-General of the United Nations. Article IV(2) allows the "State of registry" to provide "additional information concerning a space object on its registry". "State of registry" is defined by Article I(c) as "a launching State on whose registry a space object is carried in accordance with article II." Galatea is listed on the Secretary-General's register as being the "launching State" and "State of registry" of SRS-1 and SRS-3. No notification of any change of status has been lodged subsequent to the sale of the spacecraft.

Accordingly, Thalassa submits that Galatea is the "launching State" of both SRS-1 and SRS-3 and that it is responsible for the activities of NeoImage.

C. *No injustice is created by holding Galatea responsible*

Finally, Thalassa notes that no injustice is created by holding Galatea responsible for the activities of NeoImage for two reasons.

First, Article IV(2) of the Registration Convention allows the "State of registry" to provide "additional information concerning a space object on its registry". Galatea could have used this provision to remove itself as the launching State and State of registry on the Sectary-General's register. There is an established State practice of States doing exactly this:

(a) Satellites AsiaSat-1, AsiaSat-2, APSTAR-1 and APSTAR-IA were launched from China and registered by the United Kingdom.[27] On 1 January 1997, the State of registry of these satellites was changed from the United Kingdom to the Hong Kong Special Administrative Region of China when Hong Kong returned to Chinese control. In this instance both China and the United Kingdom informed the United Nations of this change in the State of registry.[28]
(b) The satellite BSB-1A was originally registered with the United Nations by the United Kingdom.[29] It was subsequently listed as Sirius 1 on the Swedish register of objects launched into outer space, which was conveyed to the United Nations following the purchase of the satellite in orbit in 1996.[30]

Secondly, the parties could have reached an explicit agreement as to who was to be responsible and liable for the activities of NeoImage. Article V of the Liability Convention allows such agreements in the case of joint

---

[26] It is also clear from Article V(1) of the Liability Convention that two or more States may the launching States of the same space object.

[27] *Information Furnished in Conformity with the Convention on Registration of Objects Launched Into Outer Space*, U.K. Notes Verbale to the Secretary-General., ST/SG/SER.E/222 (1990); ST/SG/SER.E/300 (1996); ST/SG/SER.E/300/Corr.1 (1996); and ST/SG/SER.E/316 (1996).

[28] *Information Furnished in Conformity with the Convention on Registration of Objects Launched Into Outer Space*, U.K. Note Verbale to the Secretary-General ST/SG/SER.E/333 (1998); *Information Furnished in Conformity with the Convention on Registration of Objects Launched Into Outer Space*, P.R.C. Note Verbale to the Secretary-General, ST/SG/SER.E/334 (1998).

[29] *Information Furnished in Conformity with the Convention on Registration of Objects Launched Into Outer Space*, U.K. Note Verbale to the Secretary-General ST/SG/SER.E/219 (1990).

[30] *Information Furnished in Conformity with the Convention on Registration of Objects Launched Into Outer Space*, Swed. Note Verbale to the Secretary-General, ST/SG/SER.E/352 (1999).

launches. Article XXIII(2) of the Liability Convention specifically provides that States may conclude international agreements to supplement the provisions of the Liability Convention, as does Article XIII of the Outer Space Treaty.

In the instant case Galatea failed to notify the Secretary-General of any change in the state of registry or launching State of SRS-1 and SRS-3. In fact it continues to be listed as both. Moreover, Galatea entered into no explicit agreement concerning State liability and responsibility for SRS-1 and SRS-3. It merely issued an ambiguous joint communiqué with Thalassa prior to the sale which, rather than disclaiming its obligations acknowledged that it had existing "international legal obligations concerning [the] satellites".

Accordingly, Thalassa submits that no injustice is created by holding Galatea liable for the activities of NeoImage has Galatea could have taken steps to end or amend its liability but failed to do so.

2. In the absence of any specified agreement on dealing with third-party claims for unlawfulness of activities involving SRS-1 and SRS-3, Galatea is fully and exclusively responsible in any case where activities involving SRS-1 and SRS-3 would be considered to violate rights of Proteus under international law for the refusal of NeoImage to supply to Proteus remote sensing data over Protean territory

Thalassa submits that it has fully complied with its international obligations under international law with respect to the refusal by NeoImage to supply Proteus with remote sensing data of the Protean territory because:

(a) NeoImage's refusal to supply remote sensing date was legal under international law;
(b) If this Court finds that NeoImage's actions were illegal, Galatea bears international responsibility for them; and
(c) No injustice is created by holding Galatea responsible.

A. *NeoImage's refusal to supply remote sensing data was legal under international law*

Principle XII of the Principles Relating to Remote Sensing of the Earth from Outer Space (hereinafter "**Remote Sensing Principles**") provides that remote sensing data is to be made available to States on a non-discriminatory basis:

As soon as the primary data and the processed data concerning the territory under its jurisdiction are produced, the sensed State shall have access to them on a non-discriminatory basis and on reasonable cost terms. The sensed State shall also have access to the available analysed information concerning the territory under its jurisdiction in the possession of any State participating in remote sensing activities on the same basis and terms, taking particularly into account the needs and interests of developing countries.

Notwithstanding that Principle Thalassa submits that NeoImage's refusal to supply remote sensing data was not a breach of international law for two reasons. First, Principle XII does not represent customary international law. Secondly, State responsibility does not extend to ground activities.

(i) Principle XII does not represent customary international law

The Remote Sensing Principles take the form of a General Assembly Resolution. As such while they may be evidence of the opinions of State governments,[31] the Principles are not binding on States in their own right, although they could, of course, represent customary international law.[32] It is Thalassa's submission, however, that Principle XII has not attained the status of customary international law for the following reasons.

First, a number of countries including the Federal Republic of Germany, the Netherlands, Japan, and the United States have indicated that they do not consider the Remote Sensing Principles to be a binding source of international law.[33]

Secondly, the following review of domestic legislation establishes that Principle XII is not indicative of State practice:

(a) Australia: The Space Activities Act 1998 contains no provision requiring information to be made available on a non-discriminatory basis.

[31] Military and Paramilitary Activities in and against Nicaragua (Nicar. v U.S.) (Merits), 1986 I.C.J. 4 (June 27), paras. 187-195 and 203-205; Legality of Nuclear Weapons Advisory Opinion (GA) (1996) 35 ILM 814.
[32] Under Article 13 of the United Nations Charter the General Assembly can only make "recommendations".
[33] M COUSTON, DROIT SPATIAL ECONOMIQUE 86 (Sides, 1994).

(b) South Africa: The Space Affairs Act 1993 contains no provision requiring information to be made available on a non-discriminatory basis.

(c) Sweden: Neither the Swedish Act on Space Activities[34] nor the Swedish Decree on Space Activities[35] requires information to be made available on a non-discriminatory basis.

(d) United Kingdom: The Outer Space Act 1986 contains no provision requiring information to be made available on a non-discriminatory basis.

(e) United States: Section 103(b) of the Land Remote-Sensing Commercialization Act 1984 sets out that it is "the policy of the United States that civilian unenhanced remote-sensing data be made available to all potential users on a nondiscriminatory basis". The non discrimination policy does not extent to enhanced or analysed data. Similarly section 501 of the Land Remote Sensing Policy Act 1992 provides that only "unenhanced data generated by the Landsat system or any other land remote sensing system funded and owned by the United States Government shall be made available to all users" on a non-discriminatory basis.

(f) Ukraine: The Ordinance of the Supreme Soviet of Ukraine on Space Activity[36] contains no provision requiring information to be made available on a non-discriminatory basis.

Thirdly, to the extent that there is a practice of making information available on a non-discriminatory basis, such a practice does not extend to the type of information Proteus was denied access to. The Remote Sensing Principles draw a distinction between "primary data", "processed data", and "analysed information". Primary data is essentially "raw data ... acquired by remote sensors", processed data the "products resulting from the processing of the primary data", and analysed information "information resulting from the interpretation of processed data, inputs of data and knowledge from other sources".[37] The major domestic regime that mentions non-discrimination (the United States legislation) only applies to "unenhanced" data which is defined as "unprocessed or minimally processed signals or film products collected from civil remote sensing space systems".[38] Analysed information would not come within that definition. Proteus requested high resolution images of coastal and rural areas. NeoImage's business was to take raw data and process the images to provide greater detail. The product being sold by NeoImage was therefore analysed information, and to the extent that there is a State practice of making information available on a non-discriminatory basis, it does not extend to the provision of analysed information.

In addition Thalassa submits that to apply Principle XII would be an unjust fetter on freedom of contract as Principle XII requires that both primary and processed data be made available to the sensed State at "reasonable cost-terms" as soon as the data are produced. It is submitted that this would prevent private companies from being able to set their own price for the product of their enterprise.

In regard to analysed information, there is a further obstacle. Analysed information is to be made available on reasonable cost-terms, "taking particularly into account the needs and interests of the developing countries". The requirement of the particular consideration of the needs and interests of developing countries may in fact result in companies having to provide the analysed information at below-cost prices, providing a disincentive for their activities. Further, it would place an undue burden on private companies, requiring them to act as a global conscience.

Furthermore, Thalassa submits that the distinction drawn between data gathered "for the purpose of improving natural resources management, land use and the protection of the environment"[39] and data gathered for military purposes is ultimately illusory. An image of a dam or river could as easily be used for military purposes as environmental purposes. The ultimate use or purpose of the data is dependent upon the end user, rather than the provider. As such, there is no compelling reason why a State should be able to discriminate in the provision of "military images" but not "environmental images".

For the forgoing reasons, Thalassa submits that NeoImage's refusal to provide high resolution

[34] Swedish Act on Space Activities, 1982, 963 (Swed.)

[35] Swedish Decree on Space Activities, 1982, 1069 (Swed.).

[36] Ordinance of the Supreme Soviet of Ukraine on Space Activity (Law No 503/96-VR of 15 November 1996) (Ukr.).

[37] Remote Sensing Principles, Principle 1(b), (c), and (d).

[38] Land Remote-Sensing Commercialization Act 1984, §104(4) (U.S.).

[39] Principle I(a), Remote Sensing Principles.

images to Proteus was not a breach of international law.

(ii) State responsibility does not extend to ground activities

In addition Thalassa submits that State responsibility does not extend to ground activities. In this regard Thalassa repeats its earlier submissions. As the refusal to provide information took place on the earth it was not an activity in outer space and Thalassa is not responsible for NeoImage's refusal.

B. *Galatea bears international responsibility for NeoImage's non-supply*

In the alternative if this Court finds that NeoImage's non-supply of remote sensing data was in breach of international law, Thalassa submits that Galatea as the launching State bears international responsibility for NeoImage's conduct. In this regard Thalassa repeats its earlier submissions.

C. *No injustice is created by holding Galatea responsible*

Finally, Thalassa repeats its earlier observation that no injustice is created by holding Galatea responsible for NeoImage's conduct.

3. In the absence of any specified arrangement on dealing with third-party claims for liability involving SRS-1 and SRS-3, Galatea is fully and exclusively liable for any claim addressed to Galatea and Thalassa jointly or severally under international law for damages caused to Proteus by the re-entry of SRS-3 into the atmosphere of the Earth

A. *The Liability Convention applies.*

The Outer Space Treaty makes provision for liability for damage caused by space objects. Article VII of the Outer Space Treaty provides that:

Each State Party to the Treaty that launches or procures the launching of an object into outer space, including the Moon and other celestial bodies, and each State Party from whose territory or facility an object is launched, is internationally liable for damage to another State Party to the Treaty or to its natural or juridical persons by such object or its component parts on the Earth, in air space or in outer space, including the Moon and other celestial bodies.

Article VII does not specify whether liability is absolute or fault-based, nor does it draw distinction between damage caused on the surface of the Earth and damage caused in space. It also makes no provision for the apportionment of liability between States that may, in relation to a single space object, jointly fall under the Article. The Article makes no provision for a mechanism for delivery or determination of compensation.[40] Finally, the provision only assigns liability for damage "to another State Party to the Treaty".

Thalassa submits that the Liability Convention affirms and elaborates Article VII of the Outer Space Treaty and that the Court should apply the Liability Convention: a convention that deals specifically with liability for damage caused by space objects. The Liability Convention is a victim-oriented treaty as is clear from the Preamble which states:

Recognising the need to elaborate effective international rules and procedures concerning liability for damage caused by space objects and to ensure, in particular, the prompt payment under the terms of this Convention of a full and equitable measure of compensation to victims of such damage.

The Liability Convention is clear in its terms precisely so that victims of damage caused by space objects can easily identify a source of compensation and obtain prompt payment. As such, Thalassa asks the Court to give effect to the purpose and clear words of the Liability Convention and grant a declaration that Galatea is liable for the damage suffered by Proteus as a result of the crash of SRS-3.

Galatea is a party to the Liability Convention, and the Convention is therefore binding on Galatea. The Liability Convention establishes a regime for determining liability for damage caused by space objects. Article II of the Liability Convention provides:

A launching State shall be absolutely liable to pay compensation for damage caused by its space object on the surface of the Earth or to aircraft in flight.

[40] Bin Cheng, *The 1972 Convention on International Liability for Damage Caused by Space Objects, in* STUDIES IN INTERNATIONAL SPACE LAW, (Bin Cheng ed. Clarendon Press 1997), at 291-292.

The notion of a "launching State" is defined in Article I of the Liability Convention, at paragraph (c):

The term "launching State" means:
i. A State which launches or procures the launching of a space object;
ii. A State from whose territory or facility a space object is launched

On an ordinary interpretation of Article II of the Liability Convention,[41] the present situation is clearly covered. As the respondent has previously submitted, Galatea is plainly the launching State. Moreover, the damage caused by SRS-3 occurred "on the surface of the Earth", as when SRS-3 lost altitude, it crashed into the Earth's surface, landing in a Protean munitions factory causing heavy casualties and serious property damage.

On that basis it is submitted that Galatea is liable for the loss suffered by Proteus as a result of the crash. Moreover, Galatea is absolutely liable; there are no defences to liability and it does not matter how the damage suffered is caused.[42]

B. *Liability is unaffected by the sale of the satellites SRS-1 and SRS-3.*

Thalassa further submits that liability was unaffected by the sale of SRS-1 and SRS-3. The Liability Convention clearly contemplates a situation where more than one State is involved in launching and/or operating a satellite. However, even in such a situation, liability is assigned by the notion of the "launching state". Article V(1) provides that:

Whenever two or more States jointly launch a space object, they shall be jointly and severally liable for any damage caused.

Article V has no application to the present case as Thalassa does not satisfy any of the definitions of "launching state" in Article I(c). As such, Galatea is exclusively and fully liable for the damage caused to Proteus.

Article VII further provides that:

> The provisions of this convention shall not apply to damage caused by a space object of a launching State to:
>
> a. Nationals of that launching State;
> b. Foreign nationals during such time as they are participating in the operation of that space object from the time of its launching or at any stage thereafter until its descent, or during such time as they are in the immediate vicinity of a planned launching or recovery area as the result of an invitation by that launching state.

Again, Article VII has no application as Proteus at no material time participated in the operation of the space object. As such, Galatea has no defence to its liability.

Thalassa further submits that liability was unaffected by the March 2001 communiqué as the terms of the communiqué are too vague and too broad to transfer Galatea's liability to Thalassa. Consequently, Thalassa submits that Galatea remains liable to Proteus under the Liability Convention.

C. *Galatean liability is consistent with general international law*

Even if the application of Article II of the Liability Convention were in doubt, Thalassa submits that there exists a principle of general international law that provides that a "State shall be absolutely liable to pay compensation for damage caused by its space object on the surface of the Earth".[43] This is reflected in the repetition of this principle in both the Liability Convention and Article VII of the Outer Space Treaty. It is also consistent with the rule extracted from the *Trail Smelter Arbitration* that:[44]

A State owes at all times a duty to protect other States against injurious acts by individuals from within its jurisdiction.

Galatean responsibility is consistent with Article VI of the Outer Space Treaty which provides that States bear international responsibility for national activities in outer space, whether those activities are carried out by governmental agencies or non-governmental entities.[45] Thalassa submits that Galatea was responsible for the activities of SpaceSense Corp. (hereinafter

[41] Vienna Convention on the Interpretation of Treaties, *supra* note 1, Article 31(1).
[42] IAN BROWNLIE, SYSTEM OF THE LAW OF NATIONS: STATE RESPONSIBILITY (PART I) (1983), at 42.

[43] Bin Cheng, *International Responsibility and Liability for Launch Activities*, 20 AIR AND SPACE LAW 297 (1995), AT 306.
[44] Trail Smelter Arbitration (U.S. v. Can.), 3 R.I.I.A. 1905, 1963. See also Corfu Channel (U.K v. Albania) (Merits), 1949 I.C.J. 4 at 22.
[45] See paras. 1.3 above.

"**SpaceSense**"), which was in control of the satellites at the material time. Applying the test enunciated by the International Court of Justice in *Barcelona Traction, Light and Power Company*, that the nationality of a corporation must be derived either from the place of incorporation, the territory in which the company has its offices or from national links including the centre of administration (*siège social*), SpaceSense is a Galatean national.[46] It is a company incorporated in Galatea, 100% owned by Galatean interests (including a 51% holding by the government of Galatea) and operating out of Galatea. As such, at general international law, Galatea was responsible for SpaceSense and owed an obligation to prevent harm caused by their nationals to other States, even where the harmful activity is itself lawful.[47]

Liability is merely an incident of responsibility. In the *Chorzów Factory Case* the Permanent Court of International Justice said that:[48]

It is a principle of international law, and even a general conception of law, that any breach of an engagement involves an obligation to make reparation.

In the *Chorzów* case the Court was speaking of treaty and contractual engagements. The principle, however, is equally applicable to any obligation arising from law. This was confirmed by the International Court of Justice in its advisory opinion on *Reparation for Injuries Suffered in the Service of the United Nations* where the principle was reiterated and applied to the breach of any engagement capable of giving rise to international responsibility.[49]

Once SpaceSense had assumed control of the satellites, even presuming such an assumption of control was lawful, Galatea assumed liability for any damage caused in breach of its obligation under *Trail Smelter*. Galatea is therefore liable to Proteus at general international law for the damage caused by the crash of SRS-3.

4. Galatea is liable under international law for the economic loss suffered by Thalassa by the loss of both SRS-1 and SRS-3

[46] Barcelona Traction, Light and Power Company Ltd (Belg. v. Spain), 1970 I.C.J. 3 (Feb. 5).

[47] Trail Smelter Arbitration (U.S. v. Can.), 3 R.I.I.A. 1905, 1963.

[48] Chorzów Factory (Merits), 1928 P.C.I.J. (ser. A) No. 17 (Sept.13), at 47.

[49] Reparation of Injuries Suffered in the Service of the United Nations, 1949 I.C.J. 174 (April 11), at 184.

A. *The Liability Convention applies and such a claim under is not barred by Article VII*

Article VII of the Liability Convention provides:

> The provisions of this Convention shall not apply to damage caused by a space object of a launching State to:
> [...]
> (b) Foreign nationals during such time as they are participating in the operation of that space object from the time of its launching or at any stage thereafter until its descent, or during such time as they are in the immediate vicinity of a planned launching or recovery area as the result of an invitation by that launching State.

Thalassa submits that the Article VII does not apply and that accordingly a claim under the Liability Convention is not barred.

(i) The damage was not caused "during such time as [NeoImage] was participating in the operation of" SRS-1 and SRS-3

Article VII provides that the Liability Convention "shall not apply to damage caused by a space object of a launching State to ... [f]oreign nationals *during* such time as they are participating in the operation of that space object".[50] That is NeoImage must have been participating in the operation of SRS-1 and SRS-3 when the damage was caused. Thalassa claims two different types of damages: the loss of its satellites; and the subsequent economic loss NeoImage suffered. It suffered the loss of SRS-1 when it descended into the atmosphere, the loss of SRS-3 when it crashed, and the economic loss following those events. At none of those times was NeoImage operating either satellite. SpaceSense had resumed control of both satellites. As only one ground control facility can control a satellite at any given time, NeoImage was not involved in the operation of either satellite at the time the damage was caused.

Accordingly, Thalassa submits that the present claim does not come within the Article VII exception to the Liability Convention, so a claim under the Convention is not barred.

B. *The Liability Convention allows recovery for economic loss*

[50] Emphasis added.

Thalassa submits that the claim for the economic loss it suffered as a result of the loss of SRS-1 and SRS-3 is a recoverable head of damage, as economic loss falls within the scope of the term "damage" under the Liability Convention. Article I of the Convention defines "damage" in the following terms at paragraph (a):

The term "damage" means loss of life, personal injury or other impairment of health; or loss of or damage to property of States or of persons, natural or juridical, or property of international intergovernmental organizations.

First, Thalassa submits that the words of the Convention must be given their ordinary meaning without a fetter on recovery being implied into either Article I or II.[51] Moreover, the interpretation of the Convention is informed by reference to its context.[52] Context is provided by the Preamble which recognised "the need to elaborate effective international rules and procedures concerning liability for damage ... and to ensure, in particular, the prompt payment ... of a *full and equitable* measure of compensation to victims".[53] Furthermore, Article XII of the Liability Convention itself provides:

The compensation which the launching State shall be liable to pay for damage under this Convention shall be determined in accordance with international law and the principles of justice and equity, in order to provide such reparation in respect of the damage as will restore the person, natural or juridical, State or international organisation on whose behalf the claim is presented to the condition which would have existed if the damage had not occurred.[54]

Secondly, reference to the *travaux préparatoires* supports Thalassa's submission. Due to a consensus that the Liability Convention should be victim-oriented, no fetters on what constituted valid heads of damage were inserted. The State parties also rejected a proposal by the USSR to exclude radiation damage.[55]

Thirdly, the interpretation of the Convention is informed by reference to wider principles of international law.[56] With respect to damages the general position is that "reparation must, as far as possible, wipe out all the consequences of the illegal act."[57] This was affirmed in *LAFICO and Burundi* in which the Court held that the following principles applied in determining the scope of damages:[58]

They must compensate for the loss suffered. The victim must be put back into the state in which he would have been if no unlawful act had taken place. In other words, reparation must as far as possible be neither inferior nor superior to the loss suffered and must cover both the damage incurred (*damnum emergens*) and the loss of anticipated profits (*lucrum cessans*).

This is further affirmed by Article 36(2) of the International Law Commission Draft Articles on State Responsibility, which provides that compensation "shall cover any financially assessable damage including loss of profits insofar as it is established".[59]

As a matter of international law it is therefore submitted that loss of profits and relational economic loss are recoverable heads of damage subject to limitations such as "causation, remoteness, evidentiary requirements and accounting principles."[60] As a background principle of international law, this informs the interpretation of the Convention. Clearer language would have been expected if the drafters of the Liability Convention wanted to displace this rule.

Thalassa submits that read in conjunction with background international law principles and the concerns expressed during drafting, as well as the clear words of the Convention itself, the Liability

[51] Vienna Convention on the Law of Treaties, *supra* note 1, Article 31(1).

[52] *Id.*

[53] Emphasis added.

[54] Emphasis added.

[55] Travaux Préparatoires of the Convention on International Liability for Damage Caused by Space Objects A/AC.105/C.2/L.4; 4 June 1962.

[56] Article 31(3)(c) of the Vienna Convention provides that in interpreting treaties "[t]here shall be taken into account, together with the context ... any relevant rules of international law applicable in relations between the parties."

[57] Chorzów Factory (Merits), 1928 P.C.I.J. (ser. A) No. 17 (Sept.13), at 47.

[58] LAFICO and the Republic of Burundi, 96 I.L.R. 279 (1994), at 323

[59] JAMES CRAWFORD, THE INTERNATIONAL LAW COMMISSION'S ARTICLES ON STATE RESPONSIBILITY: INTRODUCTION, TEXT AND COMMENTARIES, 230 (Cambridge University Press, 2002). The Draft Articles were commended to the General Assembly for possible future adoption; see Responsibility of States for Internationally Wrongful Acts, A/RES/56/83 (12 Dec 2001).

[60] LAFICO and the Republic of Burundi, *supra* note 58.

Convention allows recovery for economic loss. Accordingly, it is submitted that the economic loss suffered by Thalassa is recoverable under the Liability Convention.

C. *The economic loss is not too remote*

As the respondent noted above, although the Liability Convention allows for recovery of damages, recovery is still limited by the usual principle of remoteness. In *Angola* it was said that:[61]

> [E]veryone agrees that ... it is none the less necessary to exclude losses unconnected with the initial act, save by an unexpected concatenation of exceptional circumstances which could only have occurred with the help of causes which are independent of the author of the act and which he could in no way have foreseen.

The question of remoteness is therefore a question of foreseeability. Thalassa submits that the loss it has suffered was clearly foreseeable. It is plainly obvious that a satellite crash may result in serious damage, such as SRS-3 caused when it crashed in the Protean capital. That such a crash would cause outrage resulting in a loss of custom, is also foreseeable. The link between the crash and the loss Thalassa has suffered cannot be regarded as "unexpected" or "exceptional". It required no independent acts; it merely followed as a natural and probable result of the crash. As such, the economic loss is recoverable from Galatea.

C. *In any event, Thalassa can recover for economic loss under the Outer Space Treaty or under general principles of international law*

Even if this Court rejects the foregoing submission that Thalassa can recover from Galatea under the Liability Convention, Galatea is still liable for the economic loss Thalassa suffered under the Outer Space Treaty or at general international law.

(i) Thalassa has exhausted its domestic remedies

As a preliminary point to claims both under the Outer Space Treaty and at general international law, there is a general principle of international law, affirmed in *Interhandel*, that a State must exhaust its domestic remedies before international proceedings may be instituted.[62] In the *Interhandel* case the International Court of Justice held that:[63]

> The rule that local remedies must be exhausted before international proceedings may be instituted is a well-established rule of customary international law; the rule has been generally observed in cases in which a State has adopted the cause of its national whose rights are claimed to have been disregarded in another State in violation of international law. Before resort may be had to an international court in such a situation, it has been considered necessary that the State where the violation occurred should have an opportunity to redress it by its own means, within the framework of its own domestic legal system.

First, Thalassa submits that by submitting the matter to the International Court of Justice, Galatea has submitted to the jurisdiction of the Court under Article 36(2) of the Statute to the International Court of Justice which provides that States "may at any time declare that they recognise as compulsory ... the jurisdiction of the Court". Thalassa and Galatea jointly submitted the matter to the Court and formulated the issues to present to the Court. No issues of jurisdiction were raised. Accordingly, Thalassa submits that Galatea has accepted this Court's jurisdiction.

Secondly, Thalassa submits that the bankruptcy exhausted NeoImage's domestic remedies. In both common and civil law systems bankruptcy prevents the bankrupt party taking or defending any causes of action, although that right may be exercised by the administrator of the bankrupt estate.[64] In the present case Thalassa is bringing

---

[61] Angola (Portugo-German Arbitral Tribunal), 2 R.I.A.A. 1011 (1928), at 1031. Translation taken from Bin Cheng, General Principles of Law as Applied by International Courts and Tribunals 250 (Stevens & Sons Ltd, 1953).

[62] This issue is not raised if the Liability Convention applies as Article XI provides that: "Presentation of a claim to a launching State for compensation for damage under this Convention shall not require the prior exhaustion of any local remedies which may be available to a claimant State or to natural or juridical persons it represents."

[63] Interhandel (Switz. v. U.S.) 1959 I.C.J. 6 (March 21), at 27.

[64] For example in the United States the right passes to the trustee in bankruptcy (11 U.S.C.A. ß704 (2000) (U.S.)); in England and Wales the bankrupt's causes of action vest in the trustee in bankruptcy (*Re Byrne*

the case on behalf of NeoImage.[65] The question then is whether NeoImage had remedies still available to it in Galatea. The test appears to be whether there is an effective remedy available "as a matter of reasonable possibility".[66] In the circumstances Thalassa submits that there is not. A bankrupt party cannot bring an action on its own accord, so Thalassa (claiming on behalf of NeoImage) could not either.

(ii) The Outer Space Treaty

Thalassa submits that Galatea is liable for the damage caused by the satellites under Article VII of the Outer Space Treaty:

Each State Party to the Treaty that launches or procures the launching of an object into outer space, including the Moon and other celestial bodies, and each State party from whose territory or facility an object is launched, is internationally liable for damage to another State Party to the Treaty or to its natural or juridical persons by such object or its component parts on the Earth, in air space or in outer space, including the Moon and other celestial bodies.

Thalassa repeats its earlier submission, that Galatea is the sole launching State. Accordingly, under Article VII Galatea is liable for the damage caused to Thalassa on the face of the Earth. Unlike the Liability Convention the Outer Space Treaty contains no definition of damage. Accordingly, the question of the recoverability of economic loss must be assessed against the backdrop of the general principles of international law. As Thalassa has already argued, international law ordinarily allows a party to recover economic loss. Thalassa repeats its earlier submissions. Furthermore, Thalassa repeats its earlier submissions, that the claimed damages are foreseeable and can accordingly be recovered.

(iii) General International Law

Thalassa repeats its earlier submission that economic loss is recoverable at general international law so long as it is foreseeable. It now submits that Galatea is liable for that economic loss at general international law.

States owe an obligation to prevent harm caused by their nationals to other States, even where the harmful activity is itself lawful.[67] States must take appropriate steps to prevent harm being caused to other nations.

Thalassa repeats its submission that SpaceSense is a Galatean national and so Galatea is responsible and so liable for any damage caused. SpaceSense assumed control of the satellites SRS-1 and SRS-3, an action which in and of itself may constitute a breach of the sale and purchase agreement. However, once SpaceSense had assumed control of the satellites, even presuming such an assumption of control was lawful, Galatea assumed liability for any damage caused, and therefore Galatea is liable to Thalassa at general international law for the economic loss suffered.

SUBMISSIONS TO THE COURT

For the foregoing reasons, the Government of Thalassa, Respondent respectfully requests the Court to adjudge and declare that:

1. Thalassa has been compliant with its obligations under international law concerning the supply of high resolution remote sensing data over the military installations and facilities of Proteus.
2. Galatea is fully and exclusively liable for the unlawfulness of activities involving SRS-1 and SRS-3 that would be considered to violate the rights of Proteus by NeoImage refusing to supply remote sensing data of Protean territory to Proteus.
3. Galatea is fully and exclusively liable for any claim for damage caused to Proteus by the re-entry of SRS-3 into the atmosphere.
4. Galatea is liable under international law or the economic loss suffered by Thalassa by the loss of both SRS-1 and SRS-3.
5. All other relief sought by Thalassa in its memorials and oral submissions should be granted and all relief sought by Galatea should be denied.

(1892) 9 Morr. 213); in Australia only the trustee in bankruptcy may institute any proceedings relating to he estate (s134(1)(j) of the Bankruptcy Act, 1966, (Austl.)). Similar provisions apply in civil law countries, for example, in France the right to initiate and appear in proceedings passes from the bankrupt party to the syndic (C. Com. Art 443 (Fr.)).

[65] Barcelona Traction, Light and Power Company, Ltd (Belg. v. Spain), 1970 I.C.J. 3 (Feb. 5)

[66] Norwegian Loans (Fr. v. Nor.), 1957 I.C.J. 144-5 (6 July).

[67] Trail Smelter Arbitration (U.S. v. Can.), 3 R.I.I.A. 1905 (1941), 1963.

INTERNATIONAL INSTITUTE OF SPACE LAW
of the
INTERNATIONAL ASTRONAUTICAL FEDERATION

Standing Committee on the Status of International Agreements Relating to Activities in Outer Space

Chairman:
Andrei D. Terekhov
Deputy Director
General Legal Division
Office of Legal Affairs
United Nations

ANNUAL REPORT – 2006

Background

At the meeting of the IISL Board of Directors held at Brighton, United Kingdom, in October 1987, the Board decided to create a standing committee of the Institute to prepare and submit at each annual Colloquium a report on the status of agreements relating to activities in outer space.

Institute members who can contribute substantively to the work of the committee are invited to serve on it. Membership is open to any interested IISL member. The committee members help collect, review and verify data concerning selected space agreements. Agreements of general global applicability or regional applicability are selected for reporting. Bilateral agreements are not included in the report. In general, the agreements included in the present report, and their status, are believed to be valid as of 1 January 2006.

Coded entries are used in the table as follows:

R = ratification, accession or succession
S = signature only
D = declaration of acceptance of rights and obligations

When no entry is made in a column opposite a state's name, that state has not signed that agreement, or is not a party to it, or that state has withdrawn from the agreement. Changes from last year are highlighted by "**".

At the meeting of the IISL Board of Directors held at Paris, France, in April 1998, the Board decided that the report should also contain basic data concerning Declarations of Principles Relating to Activities in Outer Space adopted by the General Assembly of the United Nations.

COMMITTEE MEMBERSHIP

Prof. Dr. K.-H. Böckstiegel
Institut für Luft- und Weltraumrecht
University of Cologne
Albertus-Magnus-Platz 5000
Cologne, 41 GERMANY

Prof. Carl Q. Christol
1041 Anoka Place
Pacific Palisades, CA 90272
USA

Prof. Dr. Aldo Armando Cocca
Lavalle 1527, piso 10
1048 Buenos Aires
ARGENTINA

Prof. Dr. Isabella Diederiks-Verschoor
President Emeritus, IISL
Leestraat 43, 3743 EH Baarn
NETHERLANDS

Dr. Stephen E. Doyle
3431 Bridget Brae
Shingle Springs
CA 95682
USA

Dr. Eilene Galloway
4612 29th Place, NW
Washington, D.C. 20008
USA

Prof. Dr. Vladimir Kopal
IAF General Counsel
Vidlicová 2200
16000 Prague 6 - Dejvice
CZECH REPUBLIC

Mr. G. Lafferranderie
ESA Staff Member
Chairman of the European Centre for Space Law (ECSL)
8-10, rue Mario Nikis
Paris 75738 FRANCE

Prof. Francis Lyall
Department of Public Law
University of Aberdeen
Aberdeen, AB243UB
SCOTLAND

Mrs. Tanja L. Masson-Zwaan
Van der Oudermeulenlaan 11A
2243 CR Wassenaar
NETHERLANDS

Mr. David Sagar
Flat 4, 51 Cadogan Gardens
London SW3 2 TH
UNITED KINGDOM

Dr. A. D. Terekhov (Chairman)
Office of Legal Affairs
Room 3430P, UN Secretariat
New York, NY 10017 USA

Mr. Leo A. Webb
4041 Valley Oaks Drive
Clinton, IA 52732-9467
USA

AGREEMENTS INCLUDED

1. **1963 NTBT** - **Treaty Banning Nuclear Weapon Tests in the Atmosphere, in Outer Space and Under Water; done at Moscow on 5 August 1963; entered into force on 10 October 1963. (14 UST 1313; TIAS 5433; 480 UNTS 43)**
http://fletcher.tufts.edu/multi/texts/BH454.txt

2. **1967 OST** - **Treaty on Principles Governing the Activities of States in the Exploration and Use of Outer Space, including the Moon and Other Celestial Bodies; done at Washington, London and Moscow on 27 January 1967; entered into force on 10 October 1967. (18 UST 2410; TIAS 6347; 610 UNTS 205)**
http://www.unoosa.org/oosa/en/SpaceLaw/outerspt.html

3. **1968 ARRA** - **Agreement on the Rescue of Astronauts, the Return of Astronauts and the Return of Objects Launched into Outer Space; done at Washington, London and Moscow on 22 April 1968; entered into force on 3 December 1968. (19 UST 7570; TIAS 6599; 672 UNTS 119)**
http://www.unoosa.org/oosa/en/SpaceLaw/rescue.html

4. **1972 LIAB** - **Convention on International Liability for Damage Caused by Space Objects; done at Washington, London and Moscow on 29 March 1972; entered into force on 1 September 1972. (24 UST 2389; TIAS 7762; 961 UNTS 187)**
http://www.unoosa.org/oosa/en/SpaceLaw/liability.html

5. **1975 REG** - **Convention on Registration of Objects Launched into Outer Space; done at New York on 14 January 1975; entered into force on 15 September 1976. (28 UST 695; TIAS 8480; 1023 UNTS 15)**
http://www.unoosa.org/oosa/en/SORegister/regist.html

6. **1979 MOON** - **Agreement Governing the Activities of States on the Moon and Other Celestial Bodies; done at New York on 18 December 1979; entered into force on 11 July 1984. (18 ILM 1434; UN doc. A/RES/34/68 of 14 December 1979, Annex)**
http://www.unoosa.org/oosa/en/SpaceLaw/moon.html

7. **1971 ITSO** - **Agreement Relating to the International Telecommunications Satellite Organization (ITSO) with annexes; done at Washington on 20 August 1971; entered into force on 12 February 1973. (23 UST 3813, 4091; TIAS 7532)**
The current agreement is believed to have entered into force on 18 July 2001; it may be found at–
http://www.itso.int/php_docs/tpl1_itso.php?dc=agreement
The 1971 agreement, with annexes and Operating Agreement, may be found at–
http://fletcher.tufts.edu/multi/texts/BH585.txt

8. **1976 IMSO** - **Convention on the International Mobile Satellite Organization (IMSO) with annex; done at London on 3 September 1976; entered into force on 16 July 1979. (31 UST 1, 135; TIAS 9605)**
The current agreement entered into force on 31 July 2001; it may be found at–
http://www.imso.org/public/convclean1.pdf
The 1976 agreement, as amended 1985, with Protocol (1981), may be found at–
http://fletcher.tufts.edu/multi/texts/BH688.txt

9. **1971 INTR** - **Agreement on the Establishment of the "Intersputnik" International System and Organization of Space Communications; done at Moscow on 15 November 1971; entered into force on 12 July 1972. (862 UNTS 3)**
The Protocol on Amendments to the Agreement (4 November 2002), and the current Operating Agreement (4 February 2003) may be found at–
http://www.intersputnik.com/archive/Protocol_on_amendments_eng.pdf
http://www.intersputnik.com/archive/Operating_agreement_eng.pdf [Note: *Not all the Parties to the 1971 Agreement have yet ratified the new Intersputnik Agreements.*]
The 1971 agreement, with annexes, may be found at–
http://www.intersputnik.com/archive/Agreement_1971_eng.pdf

10. **1976 INTC** - **Agreement on Cooperation in the Exploration and Use of Outer Space for Peaceful Purposes (INTERCOSMOS); done at Moscow on 13 July 1976; entered into force on 25 March 1977. (16 ILM 1)**
http://www.jaxa.jp/jda/library/space-law/chapter_2/2-2-2-7_e.html [Note: *The document served from this website omits the words "and Use" in the title and is incorrectly dated "1973" instead of "1976" in the note following the title.*]

11. **1976 ARBS** - **The Agreement of the Arab Corporation for Space Communications (ARABSAT); done at Cairo on Wednesday, 14 Rabi Al Akhar 1396 H., corresponding to April 14, 1976; entered into force on July 16, 1976. (Space Law and Related Documents, U.S. Senate, 101st Congress, 2nd Session, 395 (1990))**
http://www.jaxa.jp/jda/library/space-law/chapter_2/2-2-2-15/index_e.html

12. **1975 ESA** - **Convention for the Establishment of a European Space Agency (ESA) with annexes; done at Paris on 30 May 1975; entered into force on 30 October 1980. (14 ILM 864)**
http://www.esa.int/convention/

13. **1982 EUTL** - **Convention Establishing the European Telecommunications Satellite Organization (EUTELSAT); done at Paris on 15 July 1982; entered into force on 1 September 1985. (XI Annals of Air and Space Law 416 (1986); UK Misc. No. 4, Cmnd. 9154 (1984))**
The current agreement entered into force 28 November 2002; it may be found at–
http://www.assemblee-nationale.fr/11/pdf/projets/pl2173.pdf
The 1982 agreement, with annexes, may be found at–
http://www.jaxa.jp/jda/library/space-law/chapter_3/3-2-2-2/index_e.html

14. **1983 EUMT** - **Convention for the Establishment of a European Organization for the Exploitation of Meteorological Satellites (EUMETSAT); done at Geneva on 24 May 1983; entered into force on 19 June 1986. (Federal Republic of Germany Bundesgesetzblatt, Jahrgang 1987, Teil 11, p. 256 (1987). This Convention has been published in the national bulletins of the ratifying States)**
http://www.jaxa.jp/jda/library/space-law/chapter_3/3-2-2-6/index_e.html

15. **1974 BRUS** - **Convention Relating to the Distribution of Programme-carrying Signals Transmitted by Satellite; done at Brussels on 21 May 1974; entered into force on 25 August 1979. (1144 UNTS 3)**
http://www.jaxa.jp/jda/library/space-law/chapter_2/2-2-2-11_e.html

The texts of all the above agreements, except 1974 BRUS, 1982 EUTL and 1983 EUMT, were published in Space Law and Related Documents, U.S. Senate, 101st Congress, 2nd Session, June 1990.

Treaty Status Table as of January 1, 2006

TREATY ---- STATE	(1) 1963 NTBT	(2) 1967 OST	(3) 1968 ARRA	(4) 1972 LIAB	(5) 1975 REG	(6) 1979 MOON	(7) 1971 ITSO	(8) 1976 IMSO	(9) 1971 INTR	(10) 1976 INTC	(11) 1976 ARBS	(12) 1975 ESA	(13) 1982 EUTL	(14) 1983 EUMT	(15) 1974 BRUS
Afghanistan	R	R					R		R						
Albania													R		
Algeria	S	R		S			R	R			R				
Andorra													R		
Angola							R								
Antigua and Barbuda	R	R	R	R	R										
Argentina	R	R	R	R	R		R	R							S
Armenia	R						R						R		R
Australia	R	R	R	R	R	R	R	R							R
Austria	R	R	R	R	R	R	R					R	R	R	R
Azerbaijan							R		R				R		
Bahamas	R	R	R				R	R							
Bahrain							R	R			R				
Bangladesh	R	R					R	R							
Barbados		R	R				R								
Belarus	R	R	R	R	R			R	R				R		
Belgium	R	R	R	R	R	R	R	R				R	R	R	S
Benin	R	R		R			R								
Bhutan	R						R								
Bolivia	R	S	S				R								
Bosnia and Herzegovina	R		R	R			R	R					R		R
Botswana	R	S	R	R			R								
Brazil	R	R	R	R	*R*		R	R							S
Brunei Darussalam							R	R							
Bulgaria	R	R	R	R	R		R	R	R	R			R		
Burkina Faso	S	R					R								
Burundi	S	S		S	S		S								
Cambodia				S											
Cameroon	S	S	R				R	R							
Canada	R	R	R	R	R		R	R				(1)			
Cape Verde	R						R								
Central African Republic	R	S		S			R								
Chad	R						R								
Chile	R	R	R	R	R	R	R	R							
China		R	R	R	R		R	R							
Colombia	R	S	S	S			R	R							
Comoros							R	R							
Congo			S				R								
Costa Rica	R		S	S			R	R							R
Cote d'Ivoire	R						R								S
Croatia	R						R	R					R		R
Cuba		R	R	R	R		R	R	R	R					
Cyprus	R	R	R	R	R		R	R					R		S

Note: (1) Canada has a Cooperation Agreement with ESA, but is not a Member.

Treaty Status Table as of January 1, 2006

TREATY ---- STATE	(1) 1963 NTBT	(2) 1967 OST	(3) 1968 ARRA	(4) 1972 LIAB	(5) 1975 REG	(6) 1979 MOON	(7) 1971 ITSO	(8) 1976 IMSO	(9) 1971 INTR	(10) 1976 INTC	(11) 1976 ARBS	(12) 1975 ESA	(13) 1982 EUTL	(14) 1983 EUMT	(15) 1974 BRUS
Czech Republic	R	R	R	R	R		R	R	R	R			R		
Dem. People's Rep. of Korea							R		R						
Dem. Rep. of the Congo (formerly - Zaire)	R	S	S	S			R								
Denmark	R	R	R	R	R		R	R				R	R	R	
Djibouti											R				
Dominican Republic	R	R	S	R			R								
Ecuador	R	R	R	R			R								
Egypt	R	R	R	S			R	R			R				
El Salvador	R	R	R	S			R								
Equatorial Guinea	R	R					R								
Estonia													R		
Ethiopia	S	S					R								
Fiji	R	R	R	R			R								
Finland	R	R	R	R			R	R				R	R	R	
France		R	R	R	R	S	R	R				R	R	R	S
Gabon	R		R	R			R	R							
Gambia	R	S	R	S			R								
Georgia							R		R				R		
Germany	R	R	R	R	R		R	R	R			R	R	R	R
Ghana	R	S	S	S			R	R							
Greece	R	R	R	R	R		R	R				R	R	R	R
Guatemala	R			S		S	R								
Guinea							R								
Guinea-Bissau	R	R	R				R								
Guyana		S	R												
Haiti	S	S	S	S			R								
Holy See		S					R						R		
Honduras	R	S		S			R								
Hungary	R	R	R	R	R		R	R	R	R			R		
Iceland	R	R	R	S			R	R					R		
India	R	R	R	R	R	S	R	R	R						
Indonesia	R	*R*	R	R	R		R	R							
Iran (Islamic Republic of)	R	S	R	R	S		R	R							
Iraq	R	R	R	R			R	R			R				
Ireland	R	R	R	R			R					R	R	R	
Israel	R	R	R	R			R	R							S
Italy	R	R	R	R	*R*		R	R				R	R	R	R
Jamaica	R	R	S				R								R
Japan	R	R	R	R	R		R	R							
Jordan	R	S	S	S			R				R				
Kazakhstan		R	R	R	R	R	R		R				R		
Kenya	R	R		R			R	R							R
Kuwait	R	R	R	R			R	R			R				
Kyrgyzstan							R		R						
Lao People's Dem. Republic	R	R	R	R					R						

Treaty Status Table as of January 1, 2006

TREATY ---- STATE	(1) 1963 NTBT	(2) 1967 OST	(3) 1968 ARRA	(4) 1972 LIAB	(5) 1975 REG	(6) 1979 MOON	(7) 1971 ITSO	(8) 1976 IMSO	(9) 1971 INTR	(10) 1976 INTC	(11) 1976 ARBS	(12) 1975 ESA	(13) 1982 EUTL	(14) 1983 EUMT	(15) 1974 BRUS
Latvia								R					R		
Lebanon	R	R	R	S			R	R			R				S
Lesotho		S	S												
Liberia	R							R							
Libyan Arab Jamahiriya	R	R					R	R			R				
Liechtenstein				R	R		R						R		
Lithuania													R		
Luxembourg	R	S	S	R			R					R	R	R	
Madagascar	R	R	R				R								
Malawi	R						R								
Malaysia	R	S	S				R	R							
Maldives			R												
Mali	S	R		R			R								
Malta	R		S	R			R	R					R		
Marshall Islands								R							
Mauritania	R						R				R				
Mauritius	R	R	R				R	R							
Mexico	R	R	R	R	R	R	R	R							R
Micronesia (Fed. States of)							R								
Monaco			S				R	R					R		
Mongolia	R	R	R	R	R		R		R	R					
Morocco	R	R	R	R		R	R	R			R				R
Mozambique							R	R							
Myanmar	R	R	S												
Nepal	R	R	R	S			R								
Netherlands	R	R	R	R	R	R	R	R				R	R	R	
New Zealand	R	R	R	R			R	R							
Nicaragua	R	S	S	S	S		R		R						R
Niger	R	R	R	R	R		R								
Nigeria	R	R	R	*R*			R	R							
Norway	R	R	R	R	R		R	R				R	R	R	
Oman				S			R	R			R				
Pakistan	R	R	R	R	R	R	R	R							
Panama	R	S		R			R	R							R
Papua New Guinea	R	R	R	R			R								
Paraguay	S						R								
Peru	R	R	R	R	R	*R*	R	R							R
Philippines	R	S	S	S		R	R	R							
Poland	R	R	R	R	R		R	R	R	R			R		
Portugal	S	R	R				R	R				R	R	R	R
Qatar				R			R	R			R				
Republic of Korea	R	R	R	R	R		R	R							
Republic of Moldova													R		
Romania	R	R	R	R		S	R	R	R	R			R		
Russian Federation	R	R	R	R	R		R	R	R	R			R		R

Treaty Status Table as of January 1, 2006

TREATY ---- STATE	(1) 1963 NTBT	(2) 1967 OST	(3) 1968 ARRA	(4) 1972 LIAB	(5) 1975 REG	(6) 1979 MOON	(7) 1971 ITSO	(8) 1976 IMSO	(9) 1971 INTR	(10) 1976 INTC	(11) 1976 ARBS	(12) 1975 ESA	(13) 1982 EUTL	(14) 1983 EUMT	(15) 1974 BRUS
Rwanda	R	S	S	S			R								R
Samoa	R														
San Marino	R	R	R										R		
Saudi Arabia		R		R			R	R			R				
Senegal	R		S	R			R	R							S
Serbia and Montenegro	R	S	R	R	R		R	R					R		R
Seychelles	R	R	R	R	R										
Sierra Leone	R	R	S	S											
Singapore	R	R	R	R	S		R	R							R
Slovakia	R	R	R	R	R			R		R			R		
Slovenia	R		R	R									R		R
Somalia	S	S	S				R				R				
South Africa	R	R	R	S			R	R							
Spain	R	R	R	R	R		R	R				R	R	R	S
Sri Lanka	R	R		R			R	R							
St. Vincent and Grenadines		R	R	R	R										
Sudan	R						R				R				
Suriname	R														
Swaziland	R		R				R								
Sweden	R	R	R	R	R		R	R				R	R	R	
Switzerland	R	R	R	R	R		R	R				R	R	R	R
Syrian Arab Republic	R	R	R	R			R		R		R				
Tajikistan							R		R						
Tanzania							R	R							
Thailand	R	R	R				R								
The former Yugoslav Republic of Macedonia													R		R
Togo	R	R		R			R								R
Tonga	R	R	R					R							
Trinidad and Tobago	R	S		R			R								R
Tunisia	R	R	R	R			R	R			R				
Turkey	R	R	S				R	R					R	R	
Turkmenistan									R						
Uganda	R	R					R								
Ukraine	R	R	R	R	R			R	R				R		
United Arab Emirates		R		R	R		R	R			R				
United Kingdom	R	R	R	R	R		R	R				R	R	R	
United Rep. of Tanzania	R			S			R								
United States of America	R	R	R	R	R		R	R							R
Uruguay	R	R	R	R	R	R	R								
Uzbekistan							R								
Venezuela	R	R	S	R			R								
Viet Nam		R					R	R	R	R					
Yemen	R	R	R				R		R		R				
Zambia	R	R	R	R			R								
Zimbabwe							R								

Treaty Status Table as of January 1, 2006
~ Totals for 178 States ~

TREATY ---- STATE	(1) 1963 NTBT	(2) 1967 OST	(3) 1968 ARRA	(4) 1972 LIAB	(5) 1975 REG	(6) 1979 MOON	(7) 1971 ITSO	(8) 1976 IMSO	(9) 1971 INTR	(10) 1976 INTC	(11) 1976 ARBS	(12) 1975 ESA	(13) 1982 EUTL	(14) 1983 EUMT	(15) 1974 BRUS
"Old" Ratifications	124	97	88	82	45	11	148	88	25	10	20	17	49	18	27
"New" Ratifications		1		1	2	1									
Total Ratifications	**124**	**98**	**88**	**83**	**47**	**12**	**148**	**88**	**25**	**10**	**20**	**17**	**49**	**18**	**27**
"Old" Signatures	10	26	24	25	4	4	1								10
"New" Signatures															
Total Signatures	**10**	**26**	**24**	**25**	**4**	**4**	**1**								**10**
~ Changes in status since the 2005 Report ~															
Agreements for which status has changed:		(2) 1967 OST		(4) 1972 LIAB	(5) 1975 REG	(6) 1979 MOON									
Brazil	R	R	R	R	*R*		R	R							S
Indonesia	R	*R*	R	R	R		R	R							
Italy	R	R	R	R	*R*		R	R				R	R	R	R
Nigeria	R	R	R	*R*			R	R							
Peru	R	R	R	R	R	*R*	R	R							R

Treaty Status Table as of January 1, 2006, for certain IGOs

TREATY *(See Note below.)* ---- ORGANIZATION	(3) 1968 ARRA	(4) 1972 LIAB	(5) 1975 REG	(6) 1979 MOON
European Space Agency (ESA)	D	D	D	
European Org. for the Exploitation of Meteorological Satellites (EUMETSAT)	*D*	*D*	D	
European Telecommunications Satellite Org. (EUTELSAT)		D		
Totals for 3 Organizations:	**2**	**3**	**2**	

Note: The Committee believes that only four of the agreements covered in the report (1968 ARRA, 1972 LIAB, 1975 REG and 1979 MOON) provide for a declaration of acceptance of rights and obligations ("D") by IGOs.

Declarations of Principles Relating to Activities in Outer Space adopted by the General Assembly of the United Nations

1. **Declaration of Legal Principles Governing the Activities of States in the Exploration and Use of Outer Space (General Assembly resolution 1962 (XVIII)). Adopted without vote on 13 December 1963. http://www.unoosa.org/oosa/SpaceLaw/gares/html/gares_18_1962.html**

2. **Principles Governing the Use by States of Artificial Earth Satellites for International Direct Television Broadcasting (General Assembly resolution 37/92). http://www.un.org/documents/ga/res/37/a37r092.htm Adopted by 107 votes to 13, with 13 abstentions, on 10 December 1982 as follows (voting results are reproduced from UN document A/37/PV.100 of 17 December 1982):**

 In favour: Afghanistan, Algeria, Argentina, Bahrain, Bangladesh, Barbados, Benin, Bhutan, Bolivia, Botswana, Brazil, Bulgaria, Burma, Botswana, Burundi, Byelorussian Soviet Socialist Republic, Central African Republic, Chad, Chili, China, Colombia, Comoros, Congo, Cuba, Cyprus, Czechoslovakia, Democratic Kampuchea, Democratic Yemen, Djibouti, Dominican Republic, Ecuador, Egypt, El Salvador, Ethiopia, Fiji, Gabon, Gambia, German Democratic Republic, Ghana, Guyana, Haiti, Honduras, Hungary, India, Indonesia, Iran (Islamic Republic of), Iraq, Jamaica, Jordan, Kenya, Kuwait, Lao People's Democratic Republic, Liberia, Libyan Arab Jamahiriya, Madagascar, Malaysia, Maldives, Mali, Malta, Mauritania, Mauritius, Mexico, Mongolia, Mozambique, Nepal, Nicaragua, Niger, Nigeria, Oman, Pakistan, Panama, Papua New Guinea, Peru, Philippines, Poland, Qatar, Romania, Rwanda, Sao Tome and Principe, Saudi Arabia, Senegal, Sierra Leone, Singapore, Solomon Islands, Somalia, Sri Lanka, Sudan, Suriname, Syrian Arab Republic, Thailand, Togo, Trinidad and Tobago, Tunisia, Turkey, Uganda, Ukrainian Soviet Socialist Republic, Union of Soviet Socialist Republics, United Arab Emirates, United Republic of Cameroon, United Republic of Tanzania, Upper Volta, Uruguay, Venezuela, Viet Nam, Yemen, Yugoslavia, Zaire, Zambia.

 Against: Belgium, Denmark, Germany, Federal Republic of, Iceland, Israel, Italy, Japan, Luxembourg, Netherlands, Norway, Spain, United Kingdom of Great Britain and Northern Ireland, United States of America.

 Abstaining: Australia, Austria, Canada, Finland, France, Greece, Ireland, Lebanon, Malawi, Morocco, New Zealand, Portugal, Sweden.

3. **Principles Relating to Remote Sensing of the Earth from Outer Space (General Assembly resolution 41/65). Adopted without vote on 3 December 1986. http://www.un.org/documents/ga/res/41/a41r065.htm**
[Note: *The document served from this website omits the word "Outer" in the title.*]

4. **Principles Relevant to the Use of Nuclear Power Sources in Outer Space (General Assembly resolution 47/68). Adopted without vote on 14 December 1992. http://www.un.org/documents/ga/res/47/a47r068.htm**

5. **Declaration on International Cooperation in the Exploration and Use of Outer Space for the Benefit and in the Interests of All States, Taking into Particular Account the Needs of Developing Countries (General Assembly resolution 51/122). Adopted without vote on 13 December 1996. http://www.un.org/documents/ga/res/51/a51r122.htm**

Note: A copy of this report can be downloaded from the Institute's web site– http://www.iafastro-iisl.com/main%20pages/committee_8.htm

INTERNATIONAL INSTITUTE OF SPACE LAW

INSTITUT INTERNATIONAL DE DROIT SPATIAL

3-5, RUE MARIO NIKIS
75015 PARIS - FRANCE

Tél. 33-1-45.67.42.60
Telefax 33-1-42.73.21.20

STATUTES

ARTICLE I

The name of the Institute shall be the International Institute of Space Law.

ARTICLE II

The purposes and objectives of the Institute shall include:

(a) The providing of advice to the President of the International Astronautical Federation when requested;
(b) Cooperation with appropriate international organizations and national institutions in the field of space law;
(c) The holding of meetings, colloquia and competitions on juridical and social science aspects of space activities, thereby providing forums for individuals from different legal systems and regions of the world to engage in the free expression and exchange of ideas relevant to space law and policy;
(d) The preparation or commissioning of studies and reports;
(e) The publication of books, proceedings, reports and other papers;
(f) The granting and presentation of awards and certificates;
(g) The conduct of such other activities as may be considered desirable in fostering the development of space law and studies of legal and social science aspects of the exploration and use of outer space.

ARTICLE III

Section 1

Individuals distinguished by their contributions to or of proven interest in the field of space law or other social science aspects related to space activities, may be elected as members of the Institute by the Board of Directors upon an application recommended in each case by a Director, or by three members of the Institute.

Section 2

Corporate bodies and other institutions actively engaged or otherwise interested in the field of space law or other social science aspects related to space activities, may be elected by the Board of Directors as institutional members of the Institute upon an application recommended in each case by a Director, or by three members of the Institute. Corporate bodies and other institutions that are members of the International Astronautical Federation (IAF) may be elected as institutional members of the Institute so long as no prejudice to the IAF is thereby incurred.

Section 3

Election to membership of the Institute shall be by a majority vote of the voting members of the Board of Directors in attendance at an annual or special meeting of the Board, or by a majority of affirmative answers of the voting members of the Board if the vote is held by mail.

ARTICLE IV

Section 1

All members of the Institute shall pay annual membership dues in accordance with the Bye-laws. These dues are expressed in terms of units.

Section 2

The Board of Directors shall establish the value of the unit in which membership dues are expressed. Alterations in the value of the unit shall take effect for each member or institutional member at the end of the period for which the relevant membership dues have been paid.

Section 3

Members of the Institute who are in default of their membership dues shall lose the right to vote in an annual or other meetings. Members of the Institute may be removed from the membership of the Institute by decision of the Board of Directors, if they are in arrears of membership dues for more than two years.

Section 4

On cause shown, the Board of Directors may reduce or remit the membership fee for a particular member.

Section 5

The Board of Directors may remove from membership of the Institute any member whom they judge to have violated the principles of the Statutes. Such decisions shall be taken by a two thirds majority vote of the voting members of the Board present at the meeting at which the decision is taken.

ARTICLE V

Section 1

An annual meeting of the Institute shall be held each year, and special meetings may also be held, at such times and places as the Board of Directors may determine.

Section 2

The Board of Directors shall submit to each annual meeting a report on the activities of the Institute. The report shall outline the events and accomplishments of the preceding year and put forward the policy and projects of the Institute for the future.

Section 3

The annual meeting shall elect from among the members of the Institute, by a majority vote of the members present, the officers and other Directors of the Board, with due regard to the provisions of Article VI, Sections 2 and 3.

ARTICLE VI

Section 1

The governing body of the Institute is the Board of Directors. The officers of the Institute are the President, two Vice-Presidents, the Secretary and the Treasurer. The President, Presidents Emeriti, the two Vice-Presidents, the Secretary, the Treasurer and fourteen other Directors shall be the voting members of the Board. Any Honorary Directors of the Institute and the Presidents of the International Astronautical Federation and of the International Academy of Astronautics ex officio shall be non-voting members of the Board of Directors.

Section 2

The Institute will seek that the membership of the Board of Directors shall reflect and represent the different regions of the world and different legal systems, due regard being paid especially to those countries in which significant space programmes or considerable efforts to develop space law have been made.

Section 3

The officers and other Directors shall be elected for a period of three years, and may be re-elected. Members of the Nomination Committee acting in accordance with the Bye-laws, and members of the Institute when electing officers and other members of the Board, shall take account of the desirability of ensuring both a continuity and an adequate rotation of membership within the Board. The election of the officers and other Directors shall be effected on the basis of the principle of progressive rotation. Each year, about one third of them shall be elected.

Section 4

In the case of a vacancy occurring in the Board of Directors between two annual meetings, the Board may appoint an acting officer or other Director to fill the vacancy until the expiry of the relevant term, subject to the approval of that appointment by the next annual meeting.

If a Director is appointed as an acting officer, the Board may make a similar appointment of a new Director to fill the vacancy so caused.

Section 5

An outgoing President, who has served in that capacity over several years and has contributed substantially to the development and the activities of the Institute, may be elected for life as a President Emeritus by a majority vote of the members of the Institute present at its meeting.

Section 6

On the recommendation of the Board of Directors, persons who have made outstanding contributions to international cooperation in the peaceful uses of outer space, or to the development of space law, as well as officers and other Directors of the Institute, who have served for several succeeding terms and have contributed substantially to the work of the Institute, may be elected as Honorary Directors. They may attend meetings of the Board of Directors in a consultative capacity.

ARTICLE VII

Section 1

The President of the Institute shall guide and supervise the activities of the Institute pursuant to its Statutes and in accordance with its Bye-laws. The President shall represent the Institute in its external relations, including those with the International Astronautical Federation.

Section 2

The Board of Directors shall:

(a) Carry out the purposes and objectives of the Institute as set forth in Article II of these Statutes;
(b) Implement the resolutions and directives adopted at the annual meetings of the Institute;
(c) Create standing committees with appropriate terms of reference and powers for their functions;
(d) Create ad hoc committees and working groups for specific purposes and functions;
(e) Appoint members of the Institute to fill vacancies occurring in the membership of the Board of Directors in accordance with Art. VI (4) of these Statutes;
(f) Supervise the correspondence of the Institute and provide for the safekeeping of the archives thereof;
(g) Establish a secretariat as appropriate, designate its duties and supervise all its activities;
(h) Arrange for meetings and colloquia;
(i) Arrange for the publication of books, proceedings, reports and other papers;
(j) Make recommendations concerning the awarding of medals, certificates and prizes;
(k) Approve budgets and supervise accounts;
(l) Accept donations and legacies, and funds from private sources, and contributions from national and international organizations, governments and agencies;

(m) Approve the annual reports of the President and the Treasurer to be presented at the annual meetings of the Institute, and the annual report of the President to be presented at the plenary meeting of the General Assembly of the Federation.

Section 3

At least ten of the voting members of the Board of Directors present at its meeting, including the President or Acting President shall constitute a quorum. Where in exceptional cases a matter must be decided by mail, the same number of answers shall be required for a valid decision of the Board if a vote is held by mail.

Section 4

Decisions of the Board of Directors shall be taken, so far as possible, by consensus. Where a decision is taken by vote, Directors may cast their votes by mail or other written means on any action proposed to be taken by the Board. Except where these Statutes and relative Bye-laws provide otherwise, decisions by vote of the Board shall be valid when taken by a majority of the voting members present, or indicating their view in writing. In the case of a tie, the President shall have a casting as well as a deliberative vote.

Section 5

The ordinary affairs of the Board of Directors and of the Institute shall be conducted in accordance with the Bye-laws of the Institute. These Bye-laws shall be adopted by the Institute at an annual or special meeting by a majority vote of its members present upon a recommendation of the Board of Directors.

Section 6

The membership of standing committees, of ad hoc committees and of working groups, shall be determined by the President in consultation with the Board of Directors.

Section 7

The President, in consultation with the Board shall, by the end of April of each year, appoint the Chairman and members of the Nomination Committee responsible for nominating candidates for election as officers or other Board members whose terms of office are to begin after each annual meeting. The Committee shall be composed of not less than three, but not more than five members. The Report of the Nomination Committee shall be submitted to the President not later than one month before the annual meeting.

ARTICLE VIII

Section 1

These Statutes and Bye-laws shall be adopted at a meeting of the Board of Directors by a two-thirds majority vote of the voting members of the Board, subject to confirmation of this adoption at the next annual meeting of the Institute by a simple majority of members of the Institute present at that meeting.

Section 2

These Statutes and Bye-laws may be amended at any meeting of the Board of Directors by a two-thirds majority vote of the voting members of the Board, subject to confirmation of the amendment at the next annual meeting of the Institute by a simple majority of members of the Institute present at that meeting. All members of the Institute shall be informed of the intention to present such an amendment for confirmation at least six weeks prior to the next annual meeting.

Section 3

The Institute shall not enact Statutes or Bye-laws or amendments to either which are inconsistent with the provisions of the Constitution of the International Astronautical Federation, or its resolutions pertaining to the Institute.

BYE-LAWS

1. The President of the Institute shall preside at meetings of the Institute and of the Board of Directors. If unable to do so, the President may appoint one of the Vice-Presidents, and, if either of them is unable to do so, another Director to preside at a particular meeting. If the President is unable so to appoint or has not done so in time, a Vice-President, or if necessary another Director, appointed by a majority of the members of the Board present, shall preside and have the powers of the President for the purpose.

2. The Board of Directors shall endeavour to take decisions by consensus, but, if necessary, voting in the Board of Directors shall be by a show of hands, the President or Secretary informing the meeting of the views of those not present who have notified their view in writing on a matter. Such written views shall, wherever possible, be treated as votes on the matter under discussion.

3. The Board of Directors shall cause minutes to be kept of its meetings and of all actions taken by the Board. Such minutes shall be deposited with the Secretariat of the International Astronautical Federation and any member of the Institute in good standing may inspect them at any reasonable time.

4. A Nomination Committee, itself appointed by the President in consultation with the Board, shall make recommendations to the annual meeting as to elections of the officers and other Directors of the Board. A person may be elected to the Board of Directors even though his or her name is not included in the list of recommendations made by the Nomination Committee. The Board and members attending shall be informed of the recommendations of the Nomination Committee which shall be made available at the latest by forty-eight hours prior to the annual meeting. In making its recommendations the Nomination Committee shall have regard to the distinction of the contribution made to space law by potential nominees, as well as to the provisions of Article VI Sections 2 and 3 of the Statutes of the Institute.

5. The responsibilities of the Secretary of the Institute include:

(a) Maintaining the list of members of the Institute;
(b) Maintaining all necessary records, including financial records;
(c) Making arrangements for meetings of the Board;
(d) Taking the minutes of the meetings of the Board, and the annual and other meetings of the Institute;
(e) Depositing copies of the minutes of the Board with the International Astronautical Federation, and with the approval of the Board, making suitable arrangements for, the custody of the records of the Institute;
(f) In consultation with the Board and with the Secretariat of the International Astronautical Federation, making arrangements for the annual and other meetings of the Institute;
(g) Coordinating the Institute's involvement in the preparation of and making arrangements for any moot court or other competition involving or run by the Institute;
(h) Conducting the routine correspondence of the Institute;
(i) Communicating with members of the Institute, including preparing and seeing to the circulation of the Newsletter.

6. The responsibilities of the Treasurer of the Institute include:

(a) Ingathering membership dues and receiving donations and other monies received for or arising from the work of the Institute;
(b) Operating appropriate bank accounts on behalf of the Institute;
(c) Preparing appropriate budgets for approval by the Board;
(d) Paying bills incurred by the Institute or its officers in the carrying out of the purposes of the Institute from monies held by the Institute.

6. The President of the Institute shall refer an application for membership of the Institute to a membership committee, which he shall appoint, and the Board shall be informed of the report of that committee before it decides on the election of the applicant.

7. The Secretary of the Institute shall be informed in writing of any proposals for the amendment of the Statutes or Bye-laws of the Institute, other than those made by the Board, at least twelve weeks prior to the annual meeting, and any such proposal must be supported in writing by at least twenty individual fully paid-up members of the Institute.

8. The annual membership dues payable by an individual member of the Institute shall be one unit of contribution dues. Honorary Directors, if not otherwise members of the Institute, are exempt from the requirement to pay annual membership dues. Corporate or institutional members of the Institute shall pay three or more units of contribution dues of membership dues a year, the level of contribution being selected by the Institutional member in agreement with the Board of Directors.

9. A corporate or institutional member paying three contribution units per year has the right to nominate up to three representatives to vote in the annual meeting. Each additional contribution unit allows the institutional member to nominate one additional such representative.

10. A member of the Institute remains in good standing in the Institute provided that membership dues are not in arrear, and that a current mailing address has been received by the Secretary.

AUTHOR INDEX

PROCEEDINGS OF THE FORTY-NINTH COLLOQUIUM ON THE LAW OF OUTER SPACE

SUPPLEMENT

INTERNATIONAL INSTITUTE OF SPACE LAW

2–6 OCTOBER 2006
VALENCIA, SPAIN

The World's Forum for Aerospace Leadership

Published and Distributed by
AMERICAN INSTITUTE OF AERONAUTICS AND ASTRONAUTICS

Editor:
Corinne M. Contant Jorgenson
Washington, D.C., USA

INTRODUCTION

BY

N. JASENTULIYANA

PRESIDENT

Once again, this year was a busy year for the members of the Institute. Considering the multidisciplinary nature of issues arising from the exploration and use of outer space, the Institute's programs must afford opportunities to analyze national and international legal matters in the total context of space science, technology as well as social sciences by rallying the specialists in various disciplines relating to space activities.

With this in view, multiple events were organized, during the year under review, to provide such interdisciplinary interaction among scholars and practitioners. The Plenary Session organized by the Institute in Valencia on the subject of 'Enabling the Frontier: Regulatory Challenges to the Utilization of Space', with a panel consisting of scientists, managers and lawyers, attracted a large number of scientists and engineers attending the International Astronautical Congress and was a resounding success.

Similarly, the Institute had the honor to co-organize with the Institute of Air and Space Law at McGill University, an 'International Interdisciplinary Workshop on Policy and Law Relating to Outer Space Resources: The Example of the Moon, Mars and Other Celestial Bodies', in honor of our Honorary Director Dr. Eilene Galloway to commemorate her one hundredth birthday. It was held in Montreal in June, and a group of leading space scientists, engineers, managers, lawyers and academics examined every facet of the subject and produced an extensive report. Later, on 11th December, the Institute co-organized with the National Center for Remote Sensing, Air & Space Law at the University of Mississippi School of Law, a one day interdisciplinary meeting, the Eilene M. Galloway Symposium on Critical Issues in Space Law, at the Cosmos Club in Washington DC and attended by a group of invited high level space scientists, lawyers and astronauts.

Two other opportunities for a broad-scale discussion of space issues were provided by the fourth in the Institute's series of regional conferences held in Bangkok in August on the subject of 'Asian cooperation in space activities: a common approach to legal matters'. The other was the IISL/ECSL Symposium organized in Vienna for the benefit of members of the Legal Sub-Committee of the United Nations COPUOS on the subject of 'Legal Aspects of Disaster Management and the Contribution of the Law of Outer Space'.

As for other significant aspects of the Institute's work, it is gratifying that younger members are taking an active part in the work of the Institute as evinced by the large number of papers presented by young authors in Valencia as was the case in other recent Colloquia. The Institute encouraged this trend with the award of the Diederiks-Verschoor Medal and Prize for the best paper presented by a young author at the annual Colloquia.

Another manifestation of the interest of the young is the enthusiastic participation of large number of university students in the Manfred Lachs Space Law Moot Court Competition. This year, the number of universities participating in the competition at regional level increased significantly.

In recognition of the desirability of strengthening the important role played by the younger members of the Institute and students, proposals are being considered for enhancing the presentation of papers and discussion by young authors at the annual Colloquia, including the possibility of arranging for a special session for the presentation and discussion of such papers. This proposal is also considered in the context of enabling at the same time to raise the level of papers and discussions at the other sessions of the Colloquia. Thus, the Institute continues to explore innovative ways of increasing its effectiveness. Specific proposals are being formulated and will be considered soon.

In the mean time, continuing activities of the Institute have proceeded in a most satisfactory manner. The annual Colloquium held in Valencia attracted a good number of scholars who presented papers and conducted a spirited discussion of current and important space law issues. The Manfred Lachs Space Law Moot Court Regional Competitions in North America, Europe and Asia Pacific regions continued to be successfully conducted, as was the finals of the competition held in Valencia judged by three judges of the International Court of Justice. The Institute is grateful to the judges for their generous support, which makes the competition uniquely prestigious. The annual IISL dinner in Valencia was held at an elegant location with an historic ambiance and with the judges of the World Court and other high ranking IAC and local officials in attendance.

Cooperation with the United Nations continued with the holding of the annual symposium organized by IISL with ECSL during the Legal Sub-Committee of COPUOS and the preparation of two reports (one, on the work of the Institute and the other, comprising part of the "Highlights in Space" publication of the UN). Several IISL members attended the annual meetings of COPUOS and its subsidiary bodies as well as the workshops conducted by the United Nations for the benefit of participants from developing countries.

The Institute continued close cooperation with IAA particularly in the work of the IAA/IISL joint legal/scientific Roundtable on Nuclear Power Systems in Space. held in Valencia. The Institute also continued its close collaboration with IAF.

Finally, I wish to place on record my grateful appreciation of the support given by members of the Institute without which a voluntary organization such as the Institute cannot thrive. Foremost among them, is of course, our dedicated and highly competent Secretary, Ms. Tanja Masson-Zwaan, who spared no effort in seeing that multifaceted tasks are carried out in due time. Her continuing friendly and efficient cooperation with the Board and members at large, is vital to the success of the work of the Institute. Our Treasurer Dr. Frans von der Dunk has carried out his tasks in a very professional manner and this year, he undertook the additional burden of carrying out the arduous task of establishing the Institute as an association in the Netherlands, a task that he successfully completed, for all of which, the Institute is most grateful to him.

The Local Organizing Committee members overseeing the arrangements for IISL activities in Valencia led by Ms. Esther Enjuto should be congratulated and thanked for the outstanding arrangements they made for the Valencia Colloquium, the Moot Court and the Annual Dinner.

I am grateful to Dr. Sylvia Ospina and Dr. Ingo Baumann for assisting the Institute in preparing the Institute's contribution to the report on Highlights in Space that were submitted to the United Nations; to Dr. Andrei Terekhov, Chairman of the committee which prepared the report on the Status of International Space Treaties; to Dr. Corinne Contant-Jorgenson and AIAA staff who assisted in the preparation of the manuscript of the Institute's annual Proceedings published by AIAA; to Prof. Ram Jakhu for organizing the Workshop in Montreal and Prof. Paul Dempsey for his strong support for the meeting; to Dr. Stephen Doyle for preparing the final report of the Montreal Workshop and conducting the task force charged to help in its preparation; Prof. Joanne Gabrynowicz for organizing the one day meeting held in Washington DC and Ms. Marcia Smith for her support for this event; to Prof. Nipant Chitasombat for organizing the IISL Regional Conference in Bangkok, Thailand; to Mr. Chris Stott for organizing the IISL Plenary in Valencia; to Mr. Ricky Lee, Dr. Skip Smith and Mr. Alberto Marchini for organizing the regional rounds of the Moot Court; the judges of the semifinals and the written briefs of the Moot Court and the team that prepared the case; to the members of the nominating committee and members of the jury which selected the best paper presented at the Valencia Colloquium; as well as to the other members of the Institute who assisted its work in numerous other ways. Without their commitment the work of the Institute would not be carried out with success and therefore their support is gratefully acknowledged.

I look forward to another successful year in which new orientations and activities that are already under consideration would be introduced to enhance the continuing work of the Institute.

GENERAL INFORMATION

I. Background

The International Institute of Space Law (IISL) was founded by the International Astronautical Federation (IAF) in 1960. The IISL replaced the Permanent Committee on Space Law which the IAF had created in 1958 under the chairmanship of Andrew G. Haley. Since 1958, the IISL has held annual colloquia on space law in many nations. The IISL presently has elected individual and institutional members from over 40 countries, who are distinguished for their contributions to space law development. While a component of the IAF, the IISL is authorized to function autonomously in accordance with its Statutes.

The purposes and objectives of the Institute include the cooperation with appropriate international organizations and national institutions in the field of space law, the carrying out of tasks for fostering the social science aspects of astronautics, space travel and exploration, the organization of meetings and colloquia on juridical and sociological aspects of the space sciences, and the publication of proceedings, reports and other publications. Each year, the Institute publishes a report of the Standing Committee on the Status of International Agreements Relating to Activities in Outer Space, headed by Dr. A. Terekhov.

The financial resources of the Institute are derived from membership dues, research grants, remuneration received from the sale of its publications, and donations received from individuals, associations, institutions, foundations, and other organizations with interests in the development of law governing space activities.

II. IISL and the United Nations

IISL members have been appointed by the International Astronautical Federation as Official Observers to annual sessions of the United Nations (UN) Committee on the Peaceful Uses of Outer Space and its Legal Subcommittee. In addition, the IISL has, like in past years, prepared a report on legal developments under contract with the UN, to be published in the annual Highlights in Space Report, and provides yearly reports on its activities to the Legal Subcommittee.
On 26 and 27 March 2007 the IISL and ECSL will again co-organize a symposium for the delegates and staff of the Legal Subcommittee session. The symposium, which for the first time will cover two half days, will deal with *Space Law Capacity Building*.

III. 49th IISL Colloquium

The 49th IISL Colloquium was held from 2-6 October 2006 in Valencia, Spain. Around 70 papers had been accepted for 5 sessions. About 15 papers were withdrawn, and 6 were summarized by others. The colloquium was well attended and discussion was good. Most papers and presentations had been uploaded to the central system. The following sessions were held:

1. Legal aspects of space transportation and launching;
2. Legal aspects of disaster management;
3. International cooperation in space activities, with special focus on remote sensing;
4. Space law at times of armed conflict;
5. Other legal matters, including the relationship between government and private sector in space activities.

A Scientific/Legal Roundtable was held in Valencia on "Nuclear Power Systems in space – the new reality".
IISL also organised a Plenary Session on the topic 'Enabling the Frontier: Regulatory Challenges to the Utilization of Space'. Finally. Lastly, a late breaking news (LBN) event on the new definition of planets was initiated by IISL.

Manfred Lachs Space Law Moot Court Competition

The 15th Manfred Lachs Space Law Moot Court Competition was held during the Valencia IISL Colloquium. The *Case concerning the Sale and Operation of Certain Commercial Remote Sensing Satellites* (*Galatea v Thalassa: Proteus Intervening)* was written by Ricky Lee.

Preliminaries were held at regional level in Europe (6 teams), North America (10 teams) and in the Asia Pacific region (40 teams). The Finals were judged by three Judges of the International Court of Justice, Judge Abdul Koroma, Judge Peter Tomka and Judge Bernardo Sepúlveda.

The local organising committee, the Generalitat Valenciana - Conselleria de Justicia, Interior y Administraciones Públicas, the Facultad de Derecho, Universitat de València, the Universidad Nacional de Educación a Distancia (UNED) in Valencia, the University CEU-Cardenal Herrera, and Colegio Notarial de Valencia kindly sponsored the 2006 World Finals and IISL Dinner. In addition, McGill IASL, ESA/ ECSL and JAXA sponsored the winners of the regional rounds, and DLR published the Brochure of the moot court.

The results of the world finals were as follows:

- **Winner**: University of Auckland, New Zealand (James Townshend and Jonathan Orpin; Coach: Mr. Isaac Hikaka)
- **Runner-up:** Institute of Air and Space Law, McGill University (IASL), Montreal, Canada (Michael Taylor, Susan Trepczynski and Andrew Williams; Coach: Prof. Ram Jakhu)
- **2nd Runner-up**: Catholic University, Leuven, Belgium (Emmanuel De Groof, Gareth Price and Batist Paklons; Coach: Dr. Walter Thiebaut)
- **Eilene M. Galloway Award** for Best Written Brief: Institute of Air and Space Law, McGill University
- **Sterns and Tennen Award** for Best Oralist: Mr Andrew Williams (Institute of Air and Space Law, McGill University)

A report on the competition, the case and the finalists' briefs are published in this volume. The competition will be held for the 16th time in Hyderabad, India, in September 2007.

IV. Awards

A Lifetime Achievement Award was presented to Dr. Lubos Perek (Czech Republic), and a Distinguished Service Award was presented to Mr. Leslie Tennen (USA).

The Dr. I.H.Ph. Diederiks-Verschoor Award and Prize were given for the 6th time in Valencia, to Dr. Yun Zhao from City University in Hong Kong, for his paper "Protection of Intellectual Property Rights in Outer Space", published in these Proceedings. This Award honours the best paper presented at an IISL Colloquium by an author not older than 40 years and who has not published more than five papers in the Proceedings of IISL Colloquia. A total of 4 papers had been submitted. The Award consists of a medal and a money prize of 500 Euros.

V. Publications

• *Proceedings IISL Colloqiuia*: The Fukuoka Proceedings have been published by the AIAA. The publication contract with AIAA has been renewed up to and including the publication of the proceedings of the 2010 Colloquium.

• *Proceedings India Conference:* ISRO has published the Proceedings of the conference held in Bangalore in June 2005.

• *Summary Report of the McGill Workshop:* The McGill Institute of Air and Space Law has published a summary report of the "IASL-IISL International and Interdisciplinary Workshop on Policy and Law Relating to Outer Space Resources: the Example of the Moon, Mars and Other Celestial Bodies", held in June 2006 in Montreal. McGill will also publish the proceedings of the Workshop.

• *Proceedings of the Bangkok regional space law conference*: The McGill Institute of Air and Space Law will publish the proceedings of this IISL regional conference, held in August 2006 in Bangkok, Thailand.

• *History of the IISL:* the book "Origins of International Space Law and the International Institute of Space Law of the International Astronautical Federation" (Univelt, 2002, see http://univelt.com/univeltpubs/index.html for details) can be purchased at the special price of USD 25. Contact the Secretary.

• *Standing Committee on the Status of International Agreements Relating to Activities in Outer Space*, Dr. Terekhov's report is as usual included in these Proceedings.

• *UN Contract for IISL contribution to Highlights in Space Report:* the report has been prepared by Dr. Sylvia Ospina and Dr. Ingo Baumann.

VI. Registering the IISL

The General Assembly in Valencia adopted by consensus a proposal for amendment of the Statutes, necessary to comply with Dutch law in order to register the Institute in the Netherlands. After registration, a new committee will look at the Bye-Laws and other issues that may need updating.

VII. The Eilene Galloway Symposium on Critical Issues in Space Law

On December 11, 2006, this event was organised by the National Center for Remote Sensing, Air, and Space Law at the University of Mississippi School of Law, the Journal of Space Law, and the IISL, at the Cosmos Club in Washington DC.

Speakers were Dr. Jonathan F. Galloway, Dr. Stephen Doyle, Dr. George Robinson, Dr. Rusty Schweickart and Ms. Corinne Jorgenson, and a Panel Discussion was moderated by Prof. Joanne Irene Gabrynowicz. Mrs Galloway was unable to attend in pertson, but a special video message by her was broadcast for the participants.

The Center will host "The 2nd Eilene M. Galloway Symposium on Critical Issues in Space Law" on December 10, 2007 at the Cosmos Club.

VIII. 50th IISL Colloquium

The 50th IISL Colloquium on the Law of Outer Space will be held from 24 to 28 September 2007 in Hyderabad, India. The theme is: Touching Humanity: Space for Improving Quality of Life. The Colloquium will have the following session-topics:

1. *The Impact of Outer Space Law on Regional Policies*

This session will focus on outer space policy and the legal implication on national law in Europe, Asia and America. Particularly, it will look into regional coordination as well as current and future programs and legislations.

2. *Legal Issues of Private Spaceflight and Space Tourism*

Since the X-Prize was won in October 2004, plans for private spaceflight bringing tourists into outer space have rapidly grown. The session solicits papers addressing the many legal aspects of these developments, as well as the broader contexts of private spaceflight in the service of public manned missions.

3. *New Legal Developments in the Protection of the Space Environment*

This session will combine views on space debris and planetary protection. In the field of space debris mitigation, the UN is in the course of adopting guidelines and national space legislation and licensing regimes provide new means for establishing innovative regulation. In the field of planetary protection, the recent plans for space exploration have to be checked with existing and to-be-developed regulations. The session aims at providing new ideas for legal but also ethical approaches.

4. *Legal Aspects of Satellite Navigation*

Legal aspects of satellite navigation including air traffic services applications, are becoming ever more important with

GALILEO shortly coming online, GPS being planned for modernization and Russia's efforts to bring GLONASS back to full operational status. Moreover, these developments take place in a broader context such as satellite communications and remote sensing (including geographical information systems). This session intends to address the legal issues involved both at the global and national levels.

5. *40th Anniversary of the Outer Space Treaty, and other legal matters*

In this session, authors are invited to write papers focusing on the 40th Anniversary of the Outer Space Treaty, not only looking back but also discussing its values for the future of space activity. They may also address any other matters relating to the law of outer space, with special emphasis on recent developments.

In Hyderabad, the IISL will celebrate its 50th Colloquium, as well as the 40th anniversary of the Outer Space Treaty and the 50th of the International Geophysical Year (IGY). IISL may organise a one day event prior to the IAC. Ideas are to be finalised.

A *Scientific/Legal Roundtable* will be held in Hyderabad on "Google Earth et al. – Pros and cons of easier access to satellite images".

IISL has also proposed a *Plenary Session* which has been accepted. It will address "New Space Industry Actors in the Global Market Place; Policy and Regulatory Aspects".

Manfred Lachs Space Law Moot Court Competition

The world finals of the 16th Manfred Lachs Space Law Moot Court Competition will be held during the 2007 Colloquium in Hyderabad. The *Case Concerning International Liability (Emeralda v Mazonia)* was written by Jean-François Mayence and David Sagar. Three Judges of the International Court of Justice will be invited to judge the Finals. Regional rounds will be held in the Asia Pacific, Europe, and North America, and details about each round and the case are on www.spacemoot.org

IX. 51st IISL Colloquium

The 51st Colloquium on the law of outer space will be held during the IAF Congress in Glasgow, Scotland, from 29 September – 3 October 2008. The session topics for this colloquium will be decided in Spring 2007.

X. Elections 2006

Board of Directors:

Dr. von der Dunk, Prof. Galloway, Prof. Kopal, Prof. Kosuge, Ms. Masson-Zwaan, Prof. Monserrat, Mr. Murthi, Dr. Ospina, Prof. Gabrynowicz, and Prof. Kapustin were (re-)elected. Prof. Kopal and Prof. Galloway were (re-) elected Vice-President. Ms. Masson-Zwaan was re-elected Secretary, and Dr. von der Dunk was re-elected Treasurer. Ms. Marcia Smith and Dr. Terekhov had announced that they would not stand for re-election.

Members: The following 2 institutional and 22 individual members were elected throughout 2006:

INSTITUTIONAL:

MacDonald, Dettwiler and Associates, Ltd
Ms. Indra Heed
13800 Commerce Parkway
Richmond, BC,
V6V 2J3 CANADA
T 1-604 278 3411
F 1-604 231 2759
E iheed@mdacorporation.com

Devas Multimedia America, Inc.
Mr. Ramachandran Viswanathan
CEO & President
One Metro Center,
700 12th Street, NW, Suite 700
Washington, DC 20005. USA
T 1-202-536-3240
E rv@devasmedia.com

INDIVIDUAL:

Dr. iur. Ingo BAUMANN
Contract Management
German Aerospace Centre DLR
Linder Höhe
51147 Cologne, GERMANY
T 49-2203 601 2908
F 49-2203 601 2893
E ingo.baumann@dlr.de

Prof. Dr. Christian BRÜNNER
University of Graz, Institute for Austrian, European & Comparative Public Law, Political Sciences & Public Administration
Universitätsstrasse 15 C/3, A-8010 Graz, AUSTRIA
T 43 316 380 3388
F 43 316 380 9450/
E christian.bruenner@uni-graz.at

Dr. Maria BUZDUGAN
McGill University, IASL
3661 Peel street
Montreal Quebec H3A 1X1 CANADA
T 1-514 3985093
F 1-514 398 8197
E Maria.Buzdugan@mcgill.ca

Ms Macha EJOVA
Analyst Space & Communications
Euroconsult
163, Bld Lefebvre 75015 Paris, FRANCE
ejova@euroconsult-ec.com/ ejovama@voila.fr

Dr. Annette FROEHLICH
Angerstrasse 14
D86179 Augsburg, GERMANY
T 49 221 470 2988
E annette.froehlich@web.de

Mr. Isaac HIKAKA
PO Box 2026, Shortland Street
Auckland, NEW ZEALAND
T 64 9912 7116 / 64 2121 69532
F 64-9912 7109
E isaac.hikaka@lsl.co.nz

Mr William N. HULSEY
Principal, Hulsey Intellectual Property Lawyers P.C.
1250 S. Capital of Texas Highway, Bldg 3, S. 610
Austin, Texas 78746, USA
T 1-512 795 1295
F 1-512 795 1295
E bill.hulsey@hulseyiplaw.com

Corinne JORGENSON
President , Advancing Space Consulting Group
10509 Center Street, Suite 100
Fairfax, VA 22030, USA
T 1-703-655-3813
F 1-703-352-2998
E cmj@advancingspace.com

Ms Yukiko KODACHI
3-15-7 Kamitakada Nakano-ku
Tokyo, 164-0002 JAPAN
T 3-3386 8459
F 3-3386 8459
E kodachov@nifty.com

Ms. Donna LAWLER
Corporate Counsel
SingTel Optus Pty Limited
Level 29 101 Miller Street,
North Sydney NSW 2022, AUSTRALIA
T (612) 9342 9361
F (612) 9342 7667
E Donna.Lawler@optus.com.au

Mr. Philip MEEK
Associate General Counsel, USAF
6319 Falling Brook Drive
Burke, Virginia 22015, USA
T 1-703 697 4370
F 1-703 695 0889
E philip.meek@pentagon.af.mil

Mr Muhamed MUSTAQUE
M.K. Associates
Power House Extension road, Cochin-18
Kerala , PIN 682018 INDIA
T 91-9447197815
F 91-4842397815
E mushiamm@hotmail.com /
mushiamm@yahoo.com

Ms Julia NEUMANN
Schaafenstrasse 27-29
D50676 Cologne, GERMANY
T 49 221 5800668
E jneuman4@uni-koeln.de

Ms. Zeldine O'BRIEN
134 Broadmeadows
Swords, County Dublin, IRELAND
T 44-1-840 3514
E zeldineobrien@gmail.com

Ms. Isabel PESSOA-LOPES
Consultant, Space Risks
Flat 3, "Redholme", The Hermitage
Richmond, Surrey TW10 6SH, UNITED KINGDOM
T 44-20 894 84 862
E ipl@spacerisks.com

Mr. Ray PURDY
Faculty of Laws, University College London
Bentham House, Endsleigh Gardens
London WC1H 0EG, UNITED KINGDOM
T 44-207 679 4554
F 44-207 679 1440
E raymond.purdy@ucl.ac.uk

Prof. Sang-Myon RHEE
Professor of Law, College of Law,
Seoul National University
Gwanag-gu, Seoul 151-743, SOUTH KOREA
T 82-2 880 7561
F 82-2 871 7408
E smrhee@snu.ac.kr

Prof. Eligar SADEH
Professor of Space Studies
Department of Space Studies, Univ. of North Dakota
Clifford Hall Room 532
4149 University Ave. Stop 9008
Grand Forks, ND 58202-9008 USA
T 1-701-777-3462
F 1-701-777-3711
E sadeh@space.edu

Ms Amanda SHAFER
Associate
Shearman & Sterling LLP
801 Pennsylvania Ave., N.W.
Washington, D.C. 20004, USA
T 1-202 508 8105
amanda.shafer@shearman.com

Ms. Justine WHITE
University of Witswatersrand
PO Box 1044
Gallo Manor, 2052, SOUTH AFRICA
T 27-11 656 9122
F 27-11 656 9106
E whitej@law.wits.ac.za

Prof.. Haifeng ZHAO
Professor and Dean,
Harbin Institute of Technology, School of Law
92 West Dazhi Street
P.O. Box 235, Harbin, 150001, P.R. CHINA
T 86- 451 86402419
F 86- 451 86402419
E zhaohaifeng-c@yahoo.com.cn

Ms. Ilaria ZILIOLI
Contracts Officer
ESA, 8-10, rue Mario Nikis
75015 Paris, FRANCE
T +33.1.53697179
E ilaria.zilioli@esa.int

TRIBUTE TO DR. EILENE MARIE GALLOWAY-SLACK

Dr. Eilene Marie Galloway-Slack was born in Kansas City, Missouri, on May 4, 1906. She married George Galloway in 1924 and has two sons, David and Jonathan, six grandchildren, and five great-grandchildren.

Dr. Galloway graduated from Swarthmore College in 1928 and holds honorary doctorates from Swarthmore and Lake Forest College.

She was working as a senior specialist in international relations of what is now known as the Congressional Research Service at the Library of Congress. Among her many functions, she worked with Senate Majority Leader Lyndon B. Johnson and Chairman Richard Russell of the Senate Armed Services Committee. She also took part in drafting the National Aeronautics and Space Act of 1958, which established NASA and has remained an enduring framework for U.S. civil space policy. Dr. Galloway acted as a consultant to NASA and the State Department on policy and law, regarding the exploration and utilization of outer space.

At the occasion of her 100th birthday, Hon. Bart Cordon mentioned rightly during a session of the House of Representatives that, throughout her professional career, Dr. Galloway has been an influential force in the development and analysis of domestic and international space policy and law.

She is an Honorary Fellow of the American Institute of Aeronautics and Astronautics. Also, she received the Lifetime Achievement Award from the International Academy of Astronautics and the International Institute of Space Law and numerous other awards.

The International Institute of Space Law was very happy to have Eilene Galloway as Vice President from 1967 to1979. After that she was elected Honorary Director. Even now, the Institute continues to consult her for advice. She has lived her life of distinguished service to the United States and to the space community and she has been an inspiration to us all—and above all, a reliable friend.

INTERNATIONAL INSTITUTE OF SPACE LAW FORTY-NINTH COLLOQUIUM ON THE LAW OF OUTER SPACE

Valencia, Spain, 2–6 October 2006

The futuristic Palacio de Congresos, where the meetings were held.

Judges P. Tomka, A. Koroma, and B. Sepúlveda of the International Court of Justice with the finalists from McGill University (Canada) and the University of Auckland (New Zealand); the latter won the Manfred Lachs Trophy, while the former won the awards for Best Brief and Best Oralist.

First session, with Chairmen Dr. Peter van Fenema (Netherlands) and Dr. Alvaro Azcárraga (Sener, Spain), Rapporteur Petra Vorwig (USA), and Speaker Gen. Michael Wholley (NASA General Counsel, USA).

Dr. Leslie Tennen (USA) with the IISL Distinguished Services Award, and Dr. Lubos Perek (Czech Republic) with the IISL Lifetime Achievement Award.

Dr. Zhao Yun (Hong Kong) won the Isabella H.Ph. Diederiks-Verschoor Award for best paper by a young author; the award consists of a medal and a prize.

Semifinals between the regional winners from Europe (University of Leuven, Belgium) and Asia Pacific [University of Auckland (New Zealand)], with the judges, Dr. Olivier Ribbelink (Netherlands), Prof. Steven Freeland (Australia), and Ms. Marcia Smith (USA).

Dr. Rosa Maria Ramirez de Arrellano (Mexico), Prof. Elisabeth Back Impallomeni (Italy), and Mr. and Mrs. Casal (Switzerland).

Guests at the IISL Annual Dinner at the Masia del Siglo XIX, outside Valencia.

IASL - IISL INTERNATIONAL AND INTERDISCIPLINARY WORKSHOP ON POLICY AND LAW RELATING TO OUTER SPACE RESOURCES: THE EXAMPLE OF THE MOON, MARS & OTHER CELESTIAL BODIES

McGill Institute of Air and Space Law, Montreal, Canada, 28–30 June 2006

Mr. Howard Baker, Dr. Leslie Tennen, IISL Honorary Director Dr. Steven Doyle, IISL Board Member Dr. Patricia Sterns, IISL President Nandasiri Jasentuliyana, Secretary Tanja Masson-Zwaan, and Treasurer Dr. Frans von der Dunk.

IISL Board Member Prof. Ram Jakhu with Dr. Leslie Tennen and Board Member Dr. Patricia Sterns.

Former classmates at McGill IASL, Prof. Paul Larsen, Dr. Jasentuliyana, and Dr. Steven Doyle, with their professor, Prof. Ivan Vlasic (2nd from left).

IISL SPACE LAW CONFERENCE 2006 ASIAN COOPERATION IN SPACE ACTIVITIES: A COMMON APPROACH TO LEGAL MATTERS

Bangkok, Thailand, 1–4 August 2006

Left to right: Speaker Dr. Visoot Tuvayanond (Thailand); Session Chairs Prof. V. Kopal (Czech Republic) and Prof. Elisabeth Back Impallomeni (Italy); Commentators Prof. Robert C. Beckman (Singapore) and Prof. Cheng Cia-jui (Taiwan ROC); and Rapporteur Dr. Maria Buzdugan (McGill IASL).

HRH Princess Maha Chakri Sirindhorn of Thailand, who opened the conference, welcomed by Prof. Nipant Chitasombat (Thailand), Tanja Masson-Zwaan (IISL Secretary), Prof. V. Kopal (IISL Vice-President), and Prof. Sompong Sucharitkul (Thailand).

Dr. I.B.R. Supancana (Indonesia) and Mr. K.R.S. Murthi (India).

Prof. V.S. Mani (India) and Prof. S.M. Rhee (Rep. of Korea).

Group photo of speakers and participants.

Prof. Sergio Marchisio (Italy), IISL Secretary Tanja Masson-Zwaan, and Ms. Debarupa Banerjee (India).

THE EILENE M. GALLOWAY SYMPOSIUM ON CRITICAL ISSUES IN SPACE LAW

Washington, D.C., December 2006

(Photos courtesy of The National Center for Remote Sensing, Air, and Space Law of the University of Mississippi School of Law.)

Mrs. Eilene Galloway receiving a visit from Prof. Joanne Gabrynowicz, her son Prof. Jonathan Galloway, and Tanja Masson-Zwaan on the occasion of the event held at the Cosmos Club.

Dr. George Robinson, Dr. Rusty Schweickart, Prof. Joanne Gabrynowicz, Prof. Jonathan Galloway, and Dr. Maria Buzdugan.

Dr. Amanda L Moore, Ms. Corinne Jorgenson, and Mr. Jason Steptoe, NASA HQ.

Dr. Stephen Doyle with the Summary Report of the Montreal Workshop held in June 2006, which was at the basis of the Cosmos Club event. In the background, a video is playing containing a message from Dr. Eilene Galloway, who had initiated the Montreal Workshop.

Galloway Symposium participants.

ISBN-13: 978-1-56347-877-2
ISBN-10: 1-56347-877-3

Printed in the U.S.A.